For Reference

Not to be taken from this room

GREAT
AMERICAN
COURT CASES

GREAT AMERICAN COURT CASES

Volume IV:
Business and
Government

FIRST EDITION

Mark Mikula and
L. Mpho Mabunda,
Editors

Allison McClintic Marion,
Associate Editor

The Gale Group

DETROIT • SAN FRANCISCO • LONDON • BOSTON • WOODBRIDGE, CT

Staff

Mark F. Mikula, L. Mpho Mabunda, Editors

Allison McClintic Marion, Dawn R. Barry, Rebecca Parks, Dave Oblender, Associate Editors
Elizabeth Shaw, Brian J. Koski, Gloria Lam, Catherine Donaldson, Assistant Editors
Linda S. Hubbard, Managing Editor, Multicultural Team

Susan Trosky, Permissions Manager
Margaret A. Chamberlain, Permissions Specialist

Victoria B. Cariappa, Research Manager
Barbara McNeil, Research Specialist

Evi Seoud, Assistant Production Manager

Cynthia Baldwin, Product Design Manager
Eric Johnson, Art Director

Barbara Yarrow, Graphic Services Manager
Randy A. Bassett, Image Database Supervisor
Robert Duncan, Imaging Specialist

Theresa Rocklin, Manager, Technical Support Services
Jeffrey Muhr, Technical Support

Library of Congress Cataloging-in-Publication Data

Great American court cases / Mark F. Mikula and L. Mpho Mabunda, editors;
Allison McClintic Marion, associate editor. -- 1st ed.
     p. cm.
   Includes bibliographical references and index.
    Contents: v. 1. Individual liberties -- v. 2. Criminal justice -- v. 3. Equal protection and family law
-- v. 4. Business and government.
   ISBN 078762947-0 (set).
    1. Law--United States.--Cases. 2. Civil rights--United States-Cases. I. Mikula, Mark F. II. Mabunda,
L. Mpho., 1967-. III. Marion, Allison McClintic.
KF385.A4g68 1999
349.73--dc2

                                                               99-11419
                                                                 CIP

Copyright © 1999
The Gale Group
27500 Drake Road
Farmington Hills, MI 48331-3535
http://www.galegroup.com
800-877-4253
248-699-4253

ISBN 0-7876-2947-2 (set) Vol 1 ISBN 0-7876-2948-0; Vol 2 ISBN 0-7876-2949-9;
Vol 3 ISBN 0-7876-2950-2; Vol 4 ISBN 0-7876-2951-0

10 9 8 7 6 5 4 3 2 1

CONTENTS

Volume IV

CONTENTS

Volume I, II, III

This abbreviated view shows just the issues covered in the other volumes. Consult the Cumulative Index that appears in each volume for all the cases, people, events, and subjects in all four volumes.

Volume I: Individual Liberties

Volume II: Criminal Justice

Volume III: Equal Protection and Family Law

PREFACE

U.S. citizens take comfort and pride in living under the rule of law. Our elected representatives write and enforce the laws that govern everything from familial relationships to the dealings of multi-billion-dollar corporations, from the quality of the air to the content of the programs broadcast through it. But it is the judicial system that interprets the meaning of the law and makes it tangible to the average citizen through the drama of trials and the force of court orders and judicial opinions.

The four volumes of *Great American Court Cases* profile nearly 800 judicial proceedings. The editors consulted textbooks, curriculum guides, and authoritative Internet sites to identify cases studied for their influence on the development of key aspects of law in the United States. Although the majority of the cases resulted in decisions by the U.S. Supreme Court, nearly 60 cases from state courts or lower-level federal jurisdictions are included because of their impact or their role in an emerging point of law. Comprehensiveness requires that fundamental cases from the nineteenth century and earlier, such as *Marbury v. Madison* (1803) and *Swift v. Tyson* (1842), are included. This is especially true in Volume IV, which covers how laws have shaped the government. Nevertheless, to serve the information needs of today's users, most of the cases are from the twentieth century, with emphasis on the last three decades.

Scope and Arrangement

The case profiles are grouped according to the legal principle on which they reflect, with each volume covering one or two broad areas of the law as follows:

- *Volume I: Individual Liberties* includes cases that have influenced such First and Second Amendment issues as freedom of the press, privacy, the right to bear arms, and the legal concerns emerging from the growth of the Internet. Libel, the Establishment Clause, and other important facets of freedom of speech and freedom of religion are treated in separate essays with their own cases.

- *Volume II: Criminal Justice* covers cases that establish the rights of the accused before, during, and after trial, or address criminal law and procedure, search and seizure, drug laws, the jury, damages, and capital punishment.

- *Volume III: Equal Protection and Family Law* includes cases related to two broad areas of law. Equal protection issues covered in this volume include the broad range of civil rights related issues, from affirmative action, segregation, and voting rights to the special concerns of immigrants, juveniles, the disabled, and gay and lesbian citizens. Family issues covered include child support and custody and reproductive rights. Sexual harassment and the right to die are also represented in this volume.

- *Volume IV: Business and Government* also encompasses two major spheres of the law. Consumer protection, antitrust, and labor-related cases supplement the business fundamentals of contracts and corporate law. The government cases document the legal evolution of the branches of the federal government as well as the federal government's relation to state power. Separate topics address environmental law, military issues, national security, taxation, and the legal history of Native American issues. Appendixes in this volume also present the full text of the U.S. Constitution and its amendments and a chronological table of Supreme Court justices.

Coverage

Issue overviews, averaging 2,000 words in length, provide the context for the case profiles that follow. Case discussions range from 750 to 2,000 words according to their complexity and importance. Each provides the background of the case and issues involved, the main arguments presented by each side, and an explanation of the court's decision, as well as the legal, political, and social impact of the decision. Excerpts from the majority, concurring, and dissenting opinions are often included. Cross-references lead the user to related cases, while suggestions for further reading launch in-depth

Deciphering Legal Citations

Great American Court Cases includes citations for the cases covered in the profiles. Three sources, *United States Reports* (U.S.), the *Supreme Court Reporter* (S.Ct.), and the *Lawyers' Edition* (L.Ed.), all cite Supreme Court cases in separate series, resulting in three distinct citation numbers for each case. The citations for *Great American Court Cases*, in most cases, are drawn from *United States Reports*. On rare occasions, because there is a lag between the time that a case is heard and the time that its companion volume is published, the citation has been drawn from another reporter, usually the *Supreme Court Reporter*. In all cases, the structure of the citation is as follows: the volume number precedes the abbreviation for the reporter and is followed by the page number. For instance, *Davis v. Bandemer*, 478 U.S. 109, is included in volume 478 of *United States Reports*, beginning on page 109. Citations for cases tried below the level of the Supreme Court follow a similar structure with an abbreviation for the reporter associated with the lower court falling between the volume and page number. The case *In re Quinlan*, 355 A.2d 647, is covered in volume 355 of the *Atlantic Reporter*, second series (cases for states in the East), beginning on page 355.

research. Within each issue section, the cases are arranged from earliest to most recent to indicate the evolution of precedent.

The editors have had to make hard choices when a single case has bearing on more than one issue, as often occurs. The landmark reproductive rights decision in *Roe v. Wade*, for example, is based upon an assertion of privacy rights, so the case could have been placed with either issue. Also, the case of *Marbury v. Madison*, while establishing the concept of judicial review, dealt foremost with a separation of powers issue at the time that it was decided, meriting its inclusion in the separation of powers section of Volume IV. Users should consult the cumulative index that appears in each volume to find cases throughout the set that apply to a particular topic.

A small percentage (under 10 percent) of cases were previously covered in *Women's Rights on Trial* or *Great American Trials*, both Gale products. Selection criteria for each publication were different, but the *Great American Court Cases* editors preferred this slight overlap to omission of landmark cases. Entry elements particular to *Great American Court Cases*, such as the Supreme Court justices' votes, have been added to the material, along with updating as appropriate.

The editors determined that with the focus on constitutional law, sensationalistic cases, such as the O. J. Simpson trial and the trial of Ted Kaczynski, were more appropriately covered in the sidebars that complement the main text rather than receiving full treatment in the main body of the text. Also, at the time of publication, the impeachment trial of Bill Clinton had not reached its conclusion. It, therefore, does not receive coverage in this series.

Additional Features

Great American Court Cases has several features to enhance its usefulness to students and non-professional researchers:

The **legal citation** appears at the head of each case profile, enabling researchers to access the authoritative records of the court action. The "Deciphering Legal Citations" sidebar that is part of this preface explains the elements that make up the citations and remarks on the abbreviations for the various series, called "reporters," where records are published.

Each case opens with a **factbox** so the user can quickly scan (when available): the names of litigants; the initiating litigant's claim; the names of chief lawyers on each side; the name of the judge or justice who wrote the majority opinion or decision, as well as names of those who concurred or dissented; the date and location of the decision; the summary of the decision and comments on the decision's significance.

Sidebars in the case profiles highlight interesting aspects of the legal process or arguments, key participants, or related facts and incidents. Some outline the arguments for and against a particular issue or line of reasoning, which will promote critical thinking as well as fuel debates or mock-trials. Some also discuss related cases that did not warrant their inclusion as a main case in the text.

Approximately **300 photographs and graphics** depict individuals and events related to the cases.

A broad overview of the court system and the disciplines of law is presented in a general essay regarding the structure of the legal system.

Contributors have tried to present the issues and proceedings in language accessible to high school, college, and public library users. Legal terms must sometimes be used for precision, however, so a **glossary** of more than 600 words and phrases appears in each volume.

Users interested in a particular case can locate it by name (e.g., *Brown v. Board of Education*) in the **Alphabetical Listing of Cases** in the back of each volume. Those who wish to trace the changing focus of legal interest and opinion over time will find the **Chronological Listing of Cases** in the back of each volume helpful.

A **Cumulative Index** to cases, people, events, and subjects appears in each volume. The Cumulative Index is repeated in each volume to ensure that multiple users of the set have simultaneous access to its complete contents.

Audience for Great American Court Cases

The four volumes of *Great American Court Cases* cover more U.S. Supreme Court and state or lower federal court cases in greater depth than other works for a non-professional user. The selection of issues and cases, the consistent treatment, and the minimal use of legal jargon were designed with the student user in mind. Court cases bring important issues into focus in a dramatic way. They are increasingly used in curricula for studies of U.S. government, civics, history, and journalism. Law magnet school and pre-law courses can use *Great American Court Cases* to introduce important content in an accessible manner, while mock court programs will find a wide range of source material here. Students with interdisciplinary writing assignments and exercises in critical thinking will also find inspiration. Beyond the classroom, a broad range of people from activists to history buffs and Court TV watchers, will find the set compelling and useful.

Acknowledgments

Leah Knight, Meggin Condino, and Linda Irvin conceptualized *Great American Court Cases* and solicited feedback from potential users. A number of public and school librarians as well as teachers contributed to the development of the set. While several provided early input, Hilda Weisburg of Morristown High School in New Jersey continued to answer questions to help shape the product through its development. Kathy Nemeh and Diane Carter reviewed selected material for legal accuracy.

Two websites, which are freely available to the public, proved indispensible as resources for fact gathering and checking. These websites are the Findlaw site located at http://www.findlaw.com and the Oyez Oyez Oyez site located at http://court.it-services.nwu.edu.oyez.

Suggestions Are Welcome

The editors welcome suggestions on any aspect of this work. Please send comments to: Editors, *Great American Court Cases*, Gale Group, 27500 Drake Rd., Farmington Hills, MI 48331.

THE AMERICAN LEGAL SYSTEM

The most basic function of the American legal system is to maintain peace by resolving disputes. Federal and state courts, tribunals, and administrative bodies do this by applying laws to cases between specific individuals or organizations.

The primary sources of applicable law are federal and state constitutions, statutes, and administrative regulations. Constitutions establish the structure of government, define and limit its power, and seek to protect individuals from unreasonable or unlawful exercises of that power. Legislatures enact statutes—criminal laws, for example—that govern a wide variety of conduct. Administrative bodies promulgate regulations to govern specific areas of business, such as telecommunications and securities.

In theory, courts apply these existing laws rather than creating new law. The legislatures and administrative bodies, however, cannot always anticipate every possible set of circumstances, and the laws do not clearly dictate a result in every case. Frequently, too, the law is intentionally vague to give the courts flexibility to interpret it in ways which serve general public policies rather than to accomplish specific results. There are, however, constitutional limits on how vague a law may be. In general, it must fairly apprise individuals of behavior that it prohibits or compels.

In practice, then, American courts often make law when they decide cases. Under the doctrine of *stare decisis,* courts at the same or lower level in the judicial hierarchy must follow the first court's interpretation of the law in subsequent cases with similar facts. Higher courts in the judicial hierarchy may either accept the lower court's interpretation or reverse it by interpreting the law differently. Courts in other states may rely on the first court's interpretation as persuasive authority concerning the application of similar laws in their states. This tradition of binding and persuasive authority is a by-product of the American judicial system's origins in the common law system of England.

Origins of the American Judicial System: State Judicial Systems

When America declared its independence in 1776, the 13 original colonies had largely informal judicial systems based loosely on the English system of common law. Common law is the body of law that developed in English courts on a case-by-case basis. Under the common law, judges placed great reliance on decisions in prior cases with similar facts. Although state courts today apply laws enacted by legislatures and administrative bodies, they continue the common law tradition of case-by-case interpretation of these laws and reliance on prior judicial decisions.

As the United States expanded southward and westward, it acquired Mexican, Spanish, and French territories, which had legal systems based on the European civil law tradition. Under that tradition, courts in Europe applied detailed civil codes that the legislatures had designed to resolve all potential disputes. Civil codes reflected the natural law concept that there are unchanging, God-made laws that govern human behavior. Unlike in common law systems, civil law courts were not supposed to interpret the law beyond what was provided in the civil codes—they simply resolved disputes by applying the appropriate portion of the code. While the English common law tradition dominated the formation of American state legal systems, remnants of the civil law tradition exist even today, most notably in Louisiana, which based its legal system on the civil law of France.

Origins of the American Judicial System: Federal Judiciary

The federal judiciary was born in 1789 upon adoption of the U.S. Constitution, which vested the judicial power of the United States in "one supreme Court, and in such inferior Courts as the Congress may from time to time ordain and establish." The Constitution created a judicial system that contains elements of both the common and civil law traditions. The latter is evident in one of the purposes expressed in the Constitution's preamble—to "secure the Blessings of Liberty." The

Constitution, however, is subject to case-by-case interpretation by the U.S. Supreme Court, which usually limits itself by the principle of *stare decisis*.

Origins of the American Judicial System: Federalism

The existence of separate federal and state judicial systems in the United States is a hallmark of federalism, which means these systems share authority to resolve legal disputes in their geographic boundaries. Federal and state courts sometimes have concurrent jurisdiction to resolve disputes arising from the same set of circumstances. For instance, federal and state authorities both took judicial action following the bombing of the Alfred P. Murrah Federal Building in Oklahoma City in 1995. Federal and state courts occasionally have exclusive jurisdiction over certain areas of the law. State courts, for instance, typically have exclusive jurisdiction to handle child custody disputes, while federal courts exclusively handle bankruptcy cases. The U.S. Constitution determines whether state and federal courts have concurrent or exclusive jurisdiction over a particular issue.

Structure and Operation of the Courts: Judicial Hierarchy

American state court systems are hierarchical. Most states have trial courts of general jurisdiction where the judges preside over all types of cases, both civil and criminal. Most states also have special courts of limited jurisdiction that hear only certain kinds of cases—domestic relations and family court, juvenile court, and courts for the administration of wills are typical examples. There also are state courts of inferior jurisdiction, such as justices of the peace, small claims court, and traffic court, that handle petty matters. Appeals from all lower courts usually go first to an intermediate appellate court, often called the court of appeals, and then to the state's highest court, often called the supreme court. When a case involves application of the U.S. Constitution or federal law, the parties sometimes may appeal from the state's highest court to the U.S. Supreme Court.

The federal judiciary is similarly hierarchical. Federal district courts handle trials in civil and criminal cases, and appeals from some federal administrative agencies. The federal judiciary also has special courts of limited jurisdiction, such as the Court of Federal Claims, the Court of International Trade, and the Tax Court. Appeals from federal district courts go to one of 11 numbered circuit courts of appeals covering different geographical regions, or to the District of Columbia Court of Appeals. Appeals from the Court of Federal Claims and the Court of International Trade go to the Federal Court of Appeals. Parties may appeal a case from the appellate courts to the U.S. Supreme Court.

Structure and Operation of the Courts: Criminal and Civil Procedure

The progress of a case through the court system is governed by rules of procedure. There are separate rules of civil and criminal procedure because criminal cases require special constitutional safeguards for the accused. The following illustration explains the procedure in a civil case, which generally is a dispute between private individuals. Some of the notable differences between civil and criminal procedures are noted in this discussion.

Rules of civil procedure define and limit the roles of the various persons in a case. The party who brings a case is called the plaintiff, and the person being sued is the defendant. (In criminal cases there is a prosecutor instead of a plaintiff.) As the American legal system is adversarial, the parties are represented by lawyers who must zealously protect their clients' interests. A jury typically hears the evidence and determines the outcome under the substantive law as instructed by the judge. The judge acts as a referee to enforce the rules and explain the applicable law.

While the federal and state courts each have their own rules of civil procedure, the federal process is fairly representative. A federal case begins when a plaintiff files a complaint and summons in a federal district court. The complaint explains the nature of the plaintiff's claim against the defendant. The summons notifies the defendant to appear and to answer the complaint by either admitting or denying the plaintiff's allegations. If the defendant fails to appear and answer, the court may enter a default judgment against the defendant and order the relief sought by the plaintiff. If the defendant appears, he typically files an answer that denies the plaintiff's allegations. The plaintiff's complaint, the defendant's answer, and any reply by the plaintiff are called the pleadings.

The defendant next may file a motion to dismiss, which argues that even if the plaintiff proves everything in his pleadings, the law does not provide any relief. If the judge grants this motion, she dismisses the case. If not, the parties proceed to the discovery phase.

The purpose of discovery is to help the parties identify and narrow the issues for trial, and to require the parties to disclose all of their evidence. The parties begin discovery by making mandatory disclosures containing basic information, such as the identity of persons and documents with evidence related to the pleadings. The parties then answer interrogatories and take depositions. Interrogatories are written questions that a party must answer in writing under an oath that acknowledges a penalty for perjury. Depositions are oral, transcribed proceedings by which a prospective witness, who also is under oath, answers verbal questions posed by the lawyers. Interrogatory answers and deposition transcripts may be used at trial as evidence or to impeach a witness's testimony if she contradicts what she said during discovery.

After discovery, the defendant may make a motion for summary judgment, which argues that even with everything that discovery has revealed, the plaintiff is unable to prove a violation of law warranting relief. If the judge grants this motion, she dismisses the case. Otherwise the case proceeds to trial.

The trial begins when the judge and parties pick a jury. (In civil cases for which there was no right to a jury trial upon adoption of the U.S. Constitution, or when the parties do not want a jury trial, the parties have a bench trial before a judge without a jury.) In some cases a grand jury, consisting usually of 23 members, is called to determine whether grounds exist for a criminal proceeding to be initiated by the state. To pick the jury, the judge or lawyers pose questions to prospective jurors. After hearing the answers, the parties may dismiss a set number of prospective jurors for any reason, although they may not discriminate unlawfully. The parties further may dismiss an unlimited number of jurors for good cause, such as bias in the prospective juror's responses.

Once they have selected 12 jurors, the lawyers present opening statements, which give the jury a roadmap of what the evidence will prove. The plaintiff then presents his case by the testimony of witnesses and the admission of documents into the record of evidence. The presentation is governed by rules of evidence, which the judge enforces to determine what the jury can and cannot hear. The rules of evidence are supposed to give the jury only the most reliable evidence. The defendant is allowed to cross-examine the plaintiff's witnesses to challenge their accuracy, truthfulness, and bias. The defendant presents his evidence after the plaintiff, who then may cross-examine the defendant's witnesses.

At the close of the evidence, each party may ask the judge to enter judgment in his favor on the ground that a reasonable jury could only reach one verdict under the evidence presented. If the judge denies this motion, she instructs the jury about the applicable substantive law, the lawyers make closing arguments to explain the result their clients seek, and the jury retires to deliberate and reach a verdict. After the jury (or the judge in a bench trial) delivers its verdict, each party may ask the judge to reverse the verdict or order a new trial based upon errors the judge made applying the rules of procedure, rules of evidence, or substantive law. If these motions are denied, the parties may file a notice of appeal to the proper circuit court of appeals. Notably, if a person is found not guilty in a criminal proceeding that is not declared a mistrial, that person cannot be tried again for the same crime. This concept of dou-

ble jeopardy has its origin in the Fifth Amendment, which prevents people from being placed at risk of conviction more than once for a single offense.

Cases in the courts of appeals are heard by a panel of three judges. The parties file briefs that explain the errors they think the trial judge made under the rules of procedure, rules of evidence, or substantive law. The court of appeals does not hear the evidence anew, but relies on the record—the trial testimony and documents entered into evidence before the district court. The court also might hear oral argument, during which the parties' lawyers may respond to questions posed by the judges on the panel. The judges then study the record, briefs, and oral argument, discuss the case among themselves, vote on the result, and issue a decision based on the majority vote.

Dissatisfied parties may appeal to the U.S. Supreme Court, which is composed of nine justices. The procedure is similar to that in the courts of appeal, with one major exception: a party first must file a petition for a writ of *certiorari* to convince the Supreme Court that the case is important enough to warrant consideration. The Supreme Court grants the writ—by a vote of four or more justices—for only approximately five percent of the thousands of petitions it receives each year. These lucky few file briefs and engage in oral argument as they did before the court of appeals. After the justices vote, one of the justices voting in the majority writes an opinion explaining the Court's decision. Dissatisfied parties have no further avenue of appeal from this court of last resort.

Structure and Operation of the Courts: Alternative Dispute Resolution

The procedure for pursuing a case, especially a civil case, from trial through appeal is time-consuming. It can take one or more years to get a verdict in the trial court, and five or more years for an appeal to the court of appeals and the Supreme Court. The legal fees and other costs can amount to hundreds of thousands or millions of dollars. The vast majority of civil cases thus settle before going to trial, which means the parties resolve their dispute by agreement. Most criminal cases also settle, a process called plea-bargaining.

Efforts to reduce costs in civil cases have popularized an area of legal procedure called alternative dispute resolution, or ADR. Arbitration, the best known form of ADR, is an informal, abbreviated trial where one or more neutral arbitrators hears and decides the case like a judge and jury. Conciliation, a less common form of ADR, involves submission of the dispute to a neutral third party for her investigation and recommendation. With mediation the parties try to negotiate a resolution with the assistance and guidance of a neutral mediator.

Today many contracts include a clause that requires parties to use ADR to resolve their disagreements. Whether or not they have a contract, many parties voluntarily pursue ADR before going to court. State courts increasingly require parties in certain types of cases to try arbitration or mediation before proceeding to trial. The American Arbitration Association and other organizations support these efforts by designing ADR systems and procedures.

Types of Law

In the United States, where most courts hear cases concerning all areas of law, categorizing the laws is largely arbitrary. In *An Introduction to the Legal System of the United States,* Professor E. Allan Farnsworth suggested a useful distinction between public and private law. Public law generally concerns disputes between the government and individuals. Private law concerns disputes between private individuals.

Types of Law: Public Law

Public law, as described by Professor Farnsworth, includes constitutional, criminal, trade regulation, labor, and tax law. Constitutional law is embodied in the decisions of the U.S. Supreme Court that interpret the federal Constitution. Many of these cases concern whether conduct by the legislative or executive branches of the federal government violate constitutional definitions or limitations on their powers. Under the "political question" doctrine, however, the Supreme Court will decline to decide such a case if the Constitution reserves the issue for the legislative or executive branch without judicial interference.

A large majority of constitutional law cases concern the protection of individual rights from unlawful federal conduct. The Bill of Rights, which comprises the first ten amendments to the Constitution, is the primary source of these rights. For example, the First Amendment protects the freedom of speech, while the Fourth Amendment protects the right to be free from unreasonable search and seizure. The Constitution also protects individual rights from unlawful state conduct. The most important source of this protection is the Fourteenth Amendment, which contains the Due Process and Equal Protection Clauses. By interpretation of these clauses, the U.S. Supreme Court has applied the rights and protections found in the Bill of Rights to state conduct.

Criminal law mostly appears in state penal codes. These codes, while largely based on the common law of England, reflect an effort to arrive at uniform, reliable definitions of crimes. The codes define everything from felonies, such as murder and rape, to misdemeanors and petty offenses. There also are federal sources of criminal law, most notably relating to interstate conduct, such as drug trafficking and fraudulent

use of the mails. Another important source of federal criminal law is the statute that protects civil rights, such as the right to be free from discrimination on the basis of race, color, or creed. Criminal law cases also can involve issues of constitutional law, such as the rights of the accused to remain silent and to be represented by an attorney.

Trade regulation includes antitrust law, which seeks to prevent monopolies and other restraints of trade under America's system of free enterprise. It also includes laws designed to prevent unfair competition among businesses. Labor law protects the well-being of employees and the rights and duties of labor unions. Tax law primarily concerns the federal income tax.

Types of Law: Private Law

Private law, often referred to as civil law, includes tort, contract, family, commercial, and property law. States are the primary source of private law. Tort law is a system of providing compensation between individuals for private wrongs, such as battery and defamation. The enforcement of promises or obligations between individuals is the subject of contract law. Family law deals with the relationships between husband and wife or parent and child: marriage and divorce; spousal abuse and support; and child custody, abuse, support, and adoption. Commercial law, derived primarily from the Uniform Commercial Code, governs the sale and lease of goods. Property law governs transactions in real estate.

The Appointment of Judges

The process for appointing state judges varies from state to state. Most state trial judges are elected by popular vote or by the state legislature. The supreme court judges in most states are appointed for a fixed term by the governor, and then periodically stand unopposed for reelection based on their records. In some states the judges of the highest court are elected by popular vote. State judges usually serve for a fixed term of years or for life, and can be removed only for gross misconduct by formal proceedings.

Federal judges are appointed by the president with the advice and consent of the Senate. This process typically results in the appointment of judges who are members of the president's political party. If the Senate judiciary committee is controlled by the president's opposition party, the confirmation process can be hotly contested. Federal judges are appointed for life, and can be removed only by impeachment and conviction by Congress.

The Role of Judges

State and federal judges perform various important roles in the American legal system. Trial judges referee cases under the rules of procedure and evidence. The trial judge also instructs the jury concerning the substantive law that is applicable to the case. In bench trials, the judge determines the facts, law, and result without a jury. The role of appellate judges is to review the record of evidence before the trial court, decide the applicable substantive law, and either affirm or reverse the result below. In doing so, the appellate judge may announce principles of law for application by trial judges in future cases.

Limitations on Judicial Power

In *Marbury v. Madison* (1803), the Supreme Court said "[i]t is emphatically the province and duty of the judicial department to say what the law is." Judicial power, however, is not unlimited. The U.S. Constitution is the primary source for limitations on federal judicial power. The Constitution constrains federal courts to hear only "cases and controversies," which means actual cases rather than hypothetical situations or stale disputes. Under the political question doctrine, federal courts will not address issues reserved to the legislative or executive branches of the federal government. Congressional authority under the Constitution also limits judicial power. Congress may impeach and convict federal judges for "Treason, Bribery, or other high Crimes and Misdemeanors." If Congress is dissatisfied with a court's interpretation of a statute, it may pass legislation to correct the interpretation, as long as it acts within the constitutional limitations on its own power.

Similarly, state judicial power is restricted by state constitutions, the process for selection and removal of state judges, and the ultimate supremacy of the U.S. Constitution over both state and federal statutes and case law.

Bibliography and Further Reading

Calvi, James V., and Susan Coleman. *American Law and Legal Systems,* 3d ed. Upper Saddle River: Prentice Hall, 1997.

Farnsworth, E. Allan. *An Introduction to the Legal System of the United States,* 3d ed. New York: Oceana Publications, Inc., 1996.

Fowler, Michael Ross. *With Justice for All? The Nature of the American Legal System.* Upper Saddle River: Prentice Hall, 1998.

Van Dervort, Thomas R. *Equal Justice Under the Law.* Minneapolis/Saint Paul: West Publishing Company, 1994.

CONTRIBUTORS

Shannon Armitage

Beth Babini

Holly Barton

Daniel Brannen

Carol Brennan

Michael Broyles

ByLine Communications

Holly Caldwell

Jo-Ann Canning

Diane Carter

Richard Chapman

Chapterhouse

Linda Clemmons

Amy Cooper

Richard Cretan

Julie Davis

Michael Eggert

Grant Eldridge

Robert Gluck

Joel Golden

Carrie Golus

Nancy Gordon

Connor Gorry

Bridget Hall

Richard Clay Hanes

Lauri Harding

James Heiberg

Karl Heil

Robert Jacobson

Constance Johnson

Lois Kallunki

John Kane

Christine Kelley

Edward Knappman

Judson Knight

Paul Kobel

Jacqueline Maurice

Olivia Miller

Nancy Moore

Melynda Neal

New England Publishing Associates

Helene Northway

Carol Page

Akomea Poku-Kankam

Debra Reilly

Mary Scarbrough

Robert Schnakenberg

Bryan Schneider

Maria Sheler-Edwards

Elizabeth Shostak

Ginger Strand

Karen Troshynski-Thomas

Katherine Wagner

Linda Walton

Michael Watkins

Daniel Wisher

Susan Wood

Lisa Wroble

BUSINESS AND CORPORATE LAW

Historical Development

By far the most universal and resilient of business structures, both on the national and international level, is the corporation. Most state, federal and international regulatory control is directed at corporate business. Therefore, more emphasis is placed on corporations than on other business forms in the discussions that follow.

Corporate business structures date back to at least the sixteenth century, when merchants of England faced not only the perils of dangerous sea voyages, but also the prospect that they and their descendants could be liable for cargo losses due to bad weather or pirates. Some early well known corporations include the East India Company and the Hudson's Bay Company, and many American colonies were themselves chartered as corporations. Early corporate charters consisted of a grant from the crown that limited investors' liability for losses of the corporate assets equal to the amount of their investments. The early corporations were also granted monopoly powers over territories and industries that were considered critical to the interests of the English state.

As the U.S. Constitution makes no specific reference to corporations, the individual states retained the power to regulate them. By 1800, about 200 corporate charters had been granted by the states. In 1886, the U.S. Supreme Court ruled, in *Santa Clara County v. Southern Pacific Railroad,* that a private corporation is a "natural person" under the U.S. Constitution, and therefore protected under the Bill of Rights, including the right to free speech and other constitutional protections (excepting those of the privileges and immunities clause). Big business expanded rapidly across America and the world. In 1901, J.P. Morgan and John D. Rockefeller joined forces to control 112 corporate directorates, combining $22.2 billion in assets under the entity of the Northern Securities Corporation of New Jersey. In today's terms, that massive sum of monies would be the equivalent of the total assessed value of thirteen to fifteen of the southern states of America.

Today, the corporate charter is a grant of privilege extended by a state to one or more investors to serve a public purpose. Most states have standardized their requirements for the formation, continuation and dissolution of corporations by adoption of the Model Business Corporation Act (MBCA). Corporations remain the most popular form of business structure because of their limited liability, their perpetual life, the ease with which they can raise capital, the transferability of their shares or interest, and the limitations placed on the powers of the shareholders that bind the corporation.

Corporations Distinguished

A "proprietorship" is a declaration to operate as a business, such as an entrepreneurship. It requires no special documentation to be created, but local regulation may require the filing of "DBA" ("doing business as . . .") documents in the county clerk's office. The business itself is usually not taxed on its earnings; rather, the earnings (or losses) are passed on to the proprietor as personal income or loss. Taxes are generally lower than that of a comparably-sized corporation, which would also pay taxes on income paid out as nondeductible dividends. This often creates more "up-front" operating funds for the business. However, an important disadvantage of proprietary business is that personal liability attaches to any debts incurred by the business. This means that if a proprietorship defaults on payment for business equipment, the individual proprietor's personal assets are at risk. Civil suits, including those for personal injury, would name both the business and the owner as defendants, or combine them, e.g., "John Doe, individually, and John Doe and Associates, Defendants." Additionally, the assets and liabilities of the proprietorship can only be voluntarily transferred by sale, gift or testamentary disposition, along with the relinquishment of managerial authority.

General partnerships are voluntary associations of two or more individuals who work together for a common business purpose. Profits and losses are shared equally, and principles of agency apply. This means that each partner is an agent of the partnership, is liable for all partnership debts, and can bind the partnership and other partners through his/her actions or conduct. No formal state requirements are necessary to form or maintain a partnership, but partners commonly enter into written agreements to specify their understanding of the allocation of profits or responsibilities. Like a proprietorship, a partnership does not pay income tax, and profits pass directly to the partners as personal income. In addition to the disadvantage of potential personal liability for each partner, partnerships also lack business continuity. A partnership is deemed dissolved as a matter of law, without formal or documentary action, whenever a partner dies, retires, or otherwise violates the terms of the partnership. Bringing in new partners creates a new partnership, often accompanied by the shuffling of responsibilities and new allocations of shared interest according to the respective contributions of time, money or skill to the partnership. Again, the law presumes equal sharing of profits, irrespective of individual contribution, unless there is a contractual agreement between parties to the contrary.

A subspecies of partnership is that of the "limited partnership, " which, as the name implies, limits the liability of the limited partners to the extent of their investment in the partnership. No personal liability can attach beyond that. However, mostly out of concern for an unknowing public which may deal with the limited partnership, its creation is contingent upon the filing of a certificate of limited partnership with a designated state agency, typically the secretary of state. (Most states have adopted the Uniform Partnership Act to standardize the requirements of both general and limited partnerships in the eyes of the law.) Associated with the limited liability of a partner is the restriction of limited management in the affairs of the partnership, and a limited partner who participates in partnership business may be stripped of limited liability in any subsequently-litigated dispute. A limited partnership, therefore, must have at least one general partner who assumes responsibility for the management of the partnership.

Corporations, by contrast, are entities created solely by the state. Upon the filing of requisite forms for incorporation with appropriate state offices, a certificate of incorporation is then granted. The corporation is presumed to exist perpetually unless affirmatively dissolved. Corporations differ from other business forms in that the corporation itself owns corporate property; investors only own shares of interest in the corporation. Thus, a corporation's creditors normally cannot reach a shareholder, and a creditor of a shareholder cannot reach the corporation. An exception to this is the theory of "piercing the corporate veil," where the corporation is used to achieve criminal or personal objectives which serve to defeat public policy or interest.

Management of corporate business is accomplished through a board of directors elected by shareholders having voting rights commensurate with the class of stock they own. Most for-profit corporations are "publicly held" and sell shares of stock on the open market, following the publication of a "prospectus" to potential investors which is intended to advise them of the corporation's financial health, stock performance, anticipated growth, and associated risk. Despite constant changing of shareholders and their respective controls of interest, corporations continue to exist, merge, split into parent and subsidiary companies, and otherwise restructure without interruption of the corporate status in the eyes of the law.

Nonprofit businesses or associations (including trusts) have the added advantage of tax exemption and limited immunity or indemnification of trustees, officers or directors from personal liability. However, in most states, nonprofit corporations can be sued in the same manner as can for-profit corporations.

State Regulation of Business

States apply the provisions of the Uniform Commercial Code (UCC) to all businesses involved with commercial transactions (sales of goods, some services, commercial paper, bank deposits and collections, letters of credit, bulk transfers, warehouse receipts, bills of lading, investment securities, and secured transactions). A wide array of state laws also protect individuals from business misconduct through various regulatory provisions, including licensing requirements regulating minimum standards for the providing of goods or services to consumers. Examples include the requirement for building permits and licensing of certain skilled trades and professions. Surprising, however, is the fact that many states do not require a business to maintain liability insurance, and judgments against those businesses may require forced dissolution or liquidation of business assets to satisfy such debts. Most states also have "long-arm" statutes to facilitate jurisdiction of state courts over out-of-state businesses whose products or services have caused harm within a state. Most states also recognize a "products liability" cause of action for defective products manufactured or sold by businesses.

Federal Regulation

On a national level, several federal agencies and entities have regulatory and enforcement powers over business concerns. Penalties include the imposition of fines, the revocation of licenses or charters, and the restriction of business transactions. Entities such as the Federal Wage and Labor Board insure protection of business employees from unfair work requirements. The Environmental Protection Agency (EPA) and Occupational Safety and Health Administration (OSHA) protect both the environment and the workforce from harmful business practices and workplaces. The Securities and Exchange Commission (SEC) protects the public from illegal stock deals, "insider trading" to manipulate stock value, and fraudulent representation of corporate assets or status for the purpose of inducing private investment. The Food and Drug Administration (FDA) regulates the sale and distribution of controlled substances and food or drug additives or products not tested or approved by it. The U.S. Department of Agriculture regulates minimum standards for the quality of food products, and imposes strict liability for defective products. Antitrust acts protect the public from corporate monopolies and "price fixing." Bankruptcy laws ensure that creditors and investors of businesses have their interests protected against illegal or fraudulent claims or defenses. Federal laws may also regulate and restrict the involvement of citizens with foreign businesses to protect national interests. Examples include prohibitions on transactions with certain countries which may compromise national security interests, or certain transactions with those countries, such as arms sales or the importation of toxic or dangerous products. The above represents just a few examples of federal control over business interests.

International Business

After World War II, the push for a global economy led to the creation and development of three important transnational organizations: the International Bank for Reconstruction and Development (commonly known as the World Bank), the International Monetary Fund (IMF) and the General Agreement on Tariffs and Trade (GATT). The three agencies together, although formally designated as special agencies of the United Nations (UN), are commonly referred to as the "Bretton Woods" institutions, after a meeting of 44 nations in Bretton Woods, New Hampshire in July of 1944, to reach agreement on the future of global economy. Together and separately, they intended to address such global issues as growth rates of independent countries, expansion of exports, increased value of exports, attraction of new foreign investment, and the ability to repay debt.

However, in reality, to attract foreign investors, governments often suppressed union organizing to hold down wages, benefits and labor standards. They have given tax breaks and subsidies to foreign corporations and slackened environmental regulations. Falling prices for export commodities, increased demand for manufactured imports resulting from reduced tariff barriers, and profit repatriation by foreign investors have resulted in continuing trade deficits for most countries. In 1992, low-income countries' excess of imports over exports increased from $6.5 billion to almost $35 billion. In 1993, the United States executed the controversial North American Free Trade Agreement (NAFTA) addressing the sharing of labor and resources between the U.S., Canada and Mexico. Most treaties and compacts also contain language incorporating "the most favored nation" clause guaranteeing reciprocal commercial concessions between covenanting nations. Behind the scenes of all this international economic reform and redress are transnational corporations.

On 1 January 1995, a new global entity, the World Trade Organization (WTO) was created by the GATT. The WTO essentially represents the world's highest judicial and legislative body for the adjudication and enforcement of substantive agreements relating to international trade and commerce.

Although the GATT-WTO is an agreement among countries, in truth, corporate membership on its private panels far exceeds that of private interests. A 1991 study released by the Public Citizen's Congress Watch found that of 111 members of the three main trade advisory committees, only two represented labor unions. There was one unfilled seat for an environmental advocacy organization, and there were no consumer representatives. In sharp contrast, corporate interests were well represented, filling some 90-plus seats with representatives from such giants as IBM, General Motors, Dow Chemical, AT&T, Bethlehem Steel, Time-Warner, 3M, Bank America, Corning, American Express, Mobil, Amoco and Hewlett-Packard. Of the 92 corporate representatives on the three advisory panels, roughly one-third of them had been assessed more than $12 million in fines by the U.S. Environmental Protection Agency (EPA). These same corporations had collectively contributed nearly one million dollars in a failed attempt to defeat California's Safe Drinking Water and Toxics Enforcement Act, and put out another two million dollars to successfully defeat another California initiative called Big Green, which, among other things, would have imposed tighter standards for the discharge of toxic chemicals. Another example is in the tobacco industry. When Taiwan was working on a law to restrict cigarette sales, advertising and public smoking areas, the U.S. trade representative responded by threatening to call for trade sanctions against Taiwan.

When such a concern is brought before the WTO, the contending parties present their case in a secret hearing before a panel of three experts whose identities remain confidential. There is no provision for the presentation of alternative views, such as *amicus* (friend of the court) briefs, from nongovernmental organizations, unless the panel chooses to solicit them. The WTO has the authority to recommend trade sanctions, penalties, or both, which are voted upon by the membership. The downside to this is that it must be remembered that the WTO is a *trade* organization, and its mandate is to eliminate barriers to international trade and investment, a shot in the arm for transnational corporations.

Going into the twenty-first century, transnational corporations and business conflicts of interest remain global priorities. To be sure, the creation of business profit is necessarily predicated upon the creation of correlative debt. The interrelationship and interdependency between world trade and corporate profit all but wholly controls the global economy. International manipulation of trade barriers, tariffs, bans, treaties and other regulatory red tape continues to warrant review and control. Of continued concern is the ability of corporations to use their economic power to drive out competitors from the market, to absorb competitors by merger and acquisition, or to form alliances with competitors to control pricing and market territory. Federal anti-trust laws have limited power on the international front.

One area requiring increased attention is that of intellectual property rights—copyrights, patents and trademarks. U.S. companies have successfully pursued extended patent protection for all genetically-engineered organisms, from microorganisms and seeds, up to plant and animals (excluding only genetically-engineered humans). By patenting the processes by which genes are inserted into a species of seeds, a few corporations have obtained monopoly rights over genetic research. Proponents argue that such control will aggressively promote agricultural genetic research and improve global food security. Critics argue that it will prevent private research among farmers and businesses not working for the patent-holder, effectively preventing the growth of independent seed stocks without the payment of royalties.

The electronic transmission of information transnationally raises numerous concerns too complex for discussion at this time. It is sufficient to say that the future of a global economy is dependent upon the communication of information from forum to forum, most of it through private business venture. Continued global effort toward uniformity of regulation, in combination with the establishment of enforcement powers, is key to the future of business around the world.

Bibliography and Further Reading

Barber, Hoyt L. *How to Incorporate Your Business*. Blue Ridge Summit: Liberty House, 1989.

Clawson, Dan, with Alan Neustadtl and Denise Scott. *Money Talks*. New York: Basic Books, 1992.

Friedman, Scott. *Forming Your Own Limited Liability Company*. Chicago: Upstart Publishing, 1996.

Hopkins, Bruce R. *A Legal Guide to Starting and Managing a Nonprofit Organization*. New York: John Wiley & Sons, Inc., 1993.

Korten, David C. *When Corporations Rule the World*. West Hartford and San Francisco: Kumarian Press, Inc. and Berret-Koehler Publishers, Inc., co-publishers, 1995.

SOUTH CAROLINA STATE HIGHWAY DEPARTMENT V. BARNWELL BROS., INC.

Legal Citation: 303 U.S. 177 (1938)

Appellants
South Carolina State Highway Department, et al.

Appellees
Barnwell Bros., Inc. et al.

Appellants' Claim
That South Carolina restrictions on the weight and width of trucks did not violate the Commerce Clause of the Constitution.

Chief Lawyers for Appellants
Steve C. Griffith, Thomas W. Davis, and Eugene S. Blease

Chief Lawyers for Appellees
S. King Funkhouser and Frank Coleman

Justices for the Court
Hugo Lafayette Black, Louis D. Brandeis, Pierce Butler, Charles Evans Hughes, James Clark McReynolds, Owen Josephus Roberts, Harlan Fiske Stone (writing for the Court)

Justices Dissenting
None (Benjamin N. Cardozo and Stanley Forman Reed did not participate)

Place
Washington, D.C.

Date of Decision
14 February 1938

Decision
Found for the appellants, reversing the lower court's order to enjoin enforcement of the state regulations.

Significance
The Court reaffirmed that if Congress had not specifically regulated an issue relating to interstate commerce, the states could do so, as long as their regulations did not give their own states' businesses an unfair advantage over out-of-state firms. The Court also found that a state could pass laws affecting interstate commerce, if local safety concerns outweighed any burden on that commerce.

Giving Congress the ability to regulate commerce was a top priority for the framers of the Constitution. Under the old Articles of Confederacy, the states operated almost as mini-nations, imposing tariffs on each other and issuing their own money. "Most of our political evils," wrote James Madison, "may be traced to our commercial ones." Article I, section 8 of the Constitution gives Congress the power to regulate interstate commerce, and the legislature has used the Commerce Clause broadly to achieve national goals. But that power is not absolute; the Supreme Court has found instances in which the states can still pass laws affecting interstate commerce, as in *South Carolina State Highway Department v. Barnwell Bros., Inc.*

In 1933, South Carolina passed a law that limited the width of trucks on its highways to 90 inches. The weight of the loads carried was also restricted, to no more than 20,000 pounds. Various truckers and shippers, including Barnwell Bros., Inc., brought suit to prevent the state from enforcing the law. The restrictions were much tougher than the ones in neighboring states and would have affected up to 90 percent of the trucks that passed through South Carolina. The district court found that the restrictions were unreasonable and a burden on interstate commerce. The court ordered South Carolina not to enforce the law.

The defendants in that trial, which included the state of South Carolina and some railway companies, then appealed to the Supreme Court. The Court, with three members absent, voted unanimously to reverse the lower court and uphold the South Carolina regulations.

Intrastate and Interstate Interests Treated the Same

Writing for the Court, Justice Stone noted that "few subjects of state regulation are so peculiarly of local concern as is the issue of state highways . . . The state has a primary and immediate concern in their safe and economical administration." Despite that, South Carolina's restrictions may have been unconstitutional if they had contradicted congressional guidelines on the weight and width of trucks. However, the Motor Carrier Act, passed by Congress in 1935, did not set national standards for trucks, so the states were free to

Big Rig Road Hazards

- Fatigue and lack of sleep are the number one causes of collisions involving big trucks.

- A National Transportation Safety Board survey found that fatigue was a factor in 30 to 40 percent of truck accidents.

- In more than 30 percent of crashes in which a truck driver died, fatigue was the most likely cause.

- In one survey, at least 19 percent of truck drivers admitted to falling asleep at the wheel within the past month.

- A survey of long-haul truckers driving from Washington to Minnesota demonstrated that nearly 60 percent of those trucks drove longer than they were supposed to.

- Logging false hours is so common that many drivers call them "comic books" or "joke books."

- Truckers attribute their willingness to break hours of service rules to financial pressures.

- One out of eight traffic fatalities in 1997 resulted from an accident involving a big rig.

- 98 percent of the people killed in two-vehicle accidents involving a passenger vehicle and a large truck in 1997 were occupants of the passenger vehicle.

- In 1997, 717 large truck occupants died, a 16 percent increase over 1996.

Source(s): National Highway Traffic Safety Administration.

set their own. In addition, the state established those guidelines to ensure safety on the highways, and in this case that safety issue outweighed any burden on interstate commerce.

Another key point was whether the South Carolina regulations discriminated against interstate businesses, thereby giving state firms an unfair competitive advantage. All trucks, however, were subject to the restrictions. Stone commented, "The fact that [the regulations] affect alike shippers in interstate and intrastate commerce in large number within as well as without the state is a safeguard against their abuse."

Underlying that sentiment was the assumption that if the regulations were grossly unfair, South Carolina truckers could use their political influence in the state legislature to have the laws changed. The Court, however, should not be involved in determining if the details of the statute were reasonable, once it had established that the state did have the right to pass them. Stone wrote:

> When the action of a Legislature is within the scope of its power, fairly debatable questions as to its reasonableness, wisdom, and propriety are not for the determination of courts, but for the legislative body . . . It is not any the less a legislative power committed to the states because it affects interstate commerce, and courts are not any more entitled, because interstate commerce is affected, to substitute their own for the legislative judgment.

After losing their case in the Supreme Court, the appellees and other South Carolina truckers did just as Stone implied: they went to the state legislature. Three months after the Supreme Court decision, the South Carolina legislature expanded its width and weight regulations for trucks.

Future Restrictions on the States

After *South Carolina State Highway Department*, the Supreme Court was not always so sympathetic to the states regarding the Commerce Clause. In general, the Court gave the states less leeway in regulating railways versus highways. In *Southern Pacific Co. v. Arizona* (1945) the Court struck down a state law limiting the number of cars on trains traveling through Arizona. In that case, the Court said the safety issue involved did not outweigh the burden on interstate commerce.

Gradually, the Court also limited the states' power over regulating highways. It struck down an Illinois law that required a specific type of mud flap for trucks using state highways. In *Bibb v. Navajo Freight Lines* (1959), the Court said the state law was not discriminatory, but its safety intent did place an unreasonable burden on interstate commerce. Later decisions struck down state laws prohibiting double-trailer trucks and other oversized trucks on state highways.

Related Cases

Village of Euclid v. Ambler Realty Co., 272 U.S. 365 (1926).
Baldwin v. G. A. F. Seelig, Inc., 294 U.S. 511 (1935).
Southern Pacific Co. v. Arizona, 325 U.S. 761 (1945).
Bibb v. Navajo Freight Lines, 359 U.S. 520 (1959).

Bibliography and Further Reading

Biskupic, Joan, and Elder Witt. *Guide to the U.S. Supreme Court.* Washington, DC: Congressional Quarterly, Inc., 1997.

Bowen, Catherine Drinker. *Miracle at Philadelphia.* Boston: Little, Brown and Company, 1966.

Elliott, Stephen P., ed. *A Reference Guide to the U.S. Supreme Court.* New York: Facts on File Publications, 1986.

Hall, Kermit L., ed. *The Oxford Companion to the Supreme Court of the United States.* New York: Oxford Press, 1992.

New York Times, 15 February 1938.

Nowak, John E., Ronald D. Rotunda, and J. Nelson Young. *Constitutional Law,* 2nd ed. St. Paul: West Publishing Company, 1984.

WICKARD V. FILBURN

Legal Citation: 317 U.S. 111 (1942)

Appellant
Claude R. Wickard, U.S. Secretary of Agriculture

Appellee
Roscoe C. Filburn

Appellant's Claim
That the practice of producing surplus wheat and keeping it on a farm should be fined by the federal government.

Chief Lawyers for Appellant
Francis Biddle, U.S Attorney General; Charles Fahy, U.S. Solicitor General

Chief Lawyer for Appellee
Webb R. Clark

Justices for the Court
Hugo Lafayette Black, William O. Douglas, Felix Frankfurter, Robert H. Jackson (writing for the Court), Frank Murphy, Stanley Forman Reed, Owen Josephus Roberts, Harlan Fiske Stone

Justices Dissenting
None (James Francis Byrnes did not participate)

Place
Washington, D.C.

Date of Decision
9 November 1942

Decision
The Supreme Court upheld the Agricultural Adjustment Act of 1938 and the fine imposed under it on Filburn.

Significance
Wickard was the highwater mark of the Court's extension of federal regulatory power under the Commerce Clause.

Franklin D. Roosevelt was elected to the presidency in 1932 and immediately set about attempting to lift the nation out of the Great Depression. The first set of economic and social reforms constituting what was called the "New Deal" was passed almost immediately after Roosevelt took office the next year. Almost as quickly, most of the reform legislation was declared unconstitutional by the ultra-conservative majority that controlled the Supreme Court. Roosevelt responded in 1935 by introducing a second set of programs, essentially amounting to a second New Deal. When the justices disapproved of some of these measures too, Roosevelt developed a plan to "pack" the Court with justices of his own choosing who would approve his legislative package. The court-packing plan failed in Congress, but Roosevelt still got his wish. In 1937, the justices who opposed the New Deal began to retire, while other swing votes on the Court began to rule the president's way.

The Second Agricultural Act (1938), the legislation at issue in *Wickard v. Filburn,* had already passed constitutional muster in *Mulford v. Smith,* in which the Court had approved tobacco-growing quotas. The issue in *Wickard* was somewhat different, for this case concerned excess production of a crop, wheat, which was never taken to market. Also, by the time *Wickard* worked its way up to the Supreme Court, only one of the eight justices who decided the case was a holdover from the pre-Roosevelt era. That justice, Owen Roberts, was the crucial swing vote—the "switch in time that saved nine [justices]"—who began to reorient the Court in 1937. *Wickard* marked the Court's greatest expansion of federal regulatory power under the Commerce Clause of the Constitution.

Roscoe C. Filburn worked a small farm in Ohio, where in additional to raising poultry and producing dairy products for the market, he planted a small crop of wheat. The wheat was intended for use by his family and for animal feed. In 1941, he sowed twelve more acres of wheat than were permitted under the Second Agricultural Act. The extra planting yielded 249 bushels of wheat on which he was obliged to pay a fine of 49 cents per bushel. Filburn responded by filing suit in federal court against the secretary of agriculture and oth-

President Franklin D. Roosevelt and members of his cabinet, including Secretary of Agriculture Claude R. Wickard, 1941. © AP/Wide World Photos.

ers, asking the court to declare that the quota requirements of the act violated his right to due process under law. After the district court ruled that the federal government could not fine Filburn, the secretary of agriculture appealed this decision to the U.S. Supreme Court.

Supreme Court Extends Commerce Power to Production

Writing for a unanimous Court, Justice Jackson held that even unmarketed excess production has an effect on interstate commerce. As such, it could be regulated under the federal government's commerce power, granted in Article I, section 8 of the Constitution, which permits Congress to "regulate Commerce . . . among the several States." Filburn's excess production, of itself, was insignificant, but when combined with other unmarketed excess wheat production, it had a clear impact on interstate commerce:

> The maintenance by government regulation of a price for wheat undoubtedly can be accomplished as effectively by sustaining or

increasing the demand as by limiting the supply . . . That appellee's own contribution to the demand for wheat may be trivial by itself is not enough to remove him from the scope of federal regulation where, as here, taken together with that of many others similarly situated, is far from trivial . . . Congress may properly have considered that wheat consumed on the farm where grown if wholly outside the scheme of regulation would have a substantial effect in defeating and obstructing [the Second Agricultural Act's] purpose to stimulate trade therein at increased prices.

The Court had long debated whether the commerce power authorized federal control only of goods moving through interstate commerce, or of production itself. *Wickard* put to rest this long argument about whether "indirect" or only "direct" effects on interstate commerce could be regulated. After this case, which originated during the hard times of the 1930s and 1940s, economic realities would determine the extent of federal regulation.

Justice Robert H. Jackson. © Photograph by Harris and Ewing. Collection of the Supreme Court of the United States.

Related Cases

United States v. E. C. Knight, 156 U.S. 1 (1895).
Shreveport Rate Cases, 234 U.S. 342 (1895).
Mulford v. Smith, 307 U.S. 38 (1939).

Bibliography and Further Reading

Albertson, Dean. *Roosevelt's Farmer: Claude R. Wickard in the New Deal.* New York, NY: Columbia University Press, 1961.

Hamilton, David E. *From New Day to New Deal: American Farm Policy from Hoover to Roosevelt, 1928-1933.* Chapel Hill: University of North Carolina Press, 1991.

Johnson, John W., ed. *Historic U.S. Court Cases, 1690–1990: An Encyclopedia.* New York: Garland Publishing, 1992.

Romasco, Albert U. *The Politics of Recovery: Roosevelt's New Deal.* New York, NY: Oxford University Press, 1983.

BIBB V. NAVAJO FREIGHT LINES

Legal Citation: 359 U.S. 761 (1959)

Appellant
State of Illinois

Appellee
Navajo Freight Lines and other interstate trucking companies

Appellant's Claim
Illinois should be allowed to require contoured mudguards on the rear fenders of trucks and trailers.

Chief Lawyer for Appellant
Latham Castle

Chief Lawyer for Appellee
David Axelrod

Justices for the Court
Hugo Lafayette Black, William J. Brennan, Jr., Tom C. Clark, William O. Douglas (writing for the Court), Felix Frankfurter, John Marshall Harlan II, Potter Stewart, Earl Warren, Charles Evans Whittaker

Justices Dissenting
None

Place
Washington, D.C.

Date of Decision
25 May 1959

Decision
Illinois may not require contoured rear mudguards.

Significance
The Court normally upheld state safety regulations. However, the safety advantages of contoured mudguards were too inconclusive to justify the "great burden" they imposed on interstate motor carriers. Hence the Illinois law was unconstitutional under the "commerce clause."

Under an Illinois law effective 8 July 1957, all trucks and trailers operating in that state had to be equipped with contoured rear-fender mudguards. Navajo Freight Lines and other interstate trucking companies challenged the law's constitutionality. When it was overturned by the district court, Illinois appealed to the Supreme Court. (Bibb lent his name to the case as state director of public safety.)

When May a State Regulate Interstate Commerce?

Article I, section 8 of the Constitution grants Congress power "to regulate Commerce with foreign Nations, and among the several states, and with the Indian Tribes." However, the Constitution is silent as to whether the states (in addition to Congress) may or may not pass laws that affect interstate commerce.

The Supreme Court has recognized a state "police power" to regulate business and industry in order to protect public health and safety. Often state regulations significantly affect the movement of goods and service between the states. Nevertheless, the Court has upheld state laws that pass three tests. First, a state law can not conflict with a valid federal law. Second, the regulation has to be rationally related to a legitimate state end. Finally, the burdens (financial and otherwise) the regulation imposes have to be outweighed by the state's interest in enforcing the regulation.

When *Bibb* reached the Supreme Court, the justices unanimously affirmed the district court decision, with Justice Douglas delivering the Court's opinion. Justice Douglas began by affirming the principle that state "safety measures carry a strong presumption of validity." Citing *Southern Pacific Co. v. Arizona* (1945), Douglas declared that the Court overruled state safety laws only when their benefits in reducing accidents and causalities were "slight or problematical." In these cases, the small benefits do not "outweigh the national interest in keeping interstate commerce free from interferences which seriously impede it."

Illinois' Peculiar Mudguards

By requiring unusual mudguards, the Illinois law placed a heavy burden on interstate commerce. Only Illinois

---

Interstate Commerce Act of 1887

At one point railroads were regulated by states, but those efforts were unsuccessful because the laws were too rigid. Then the Granger Laws were implemented, which arose out of specific complaints that farmers had against the railroads. Farmers believed that the rates charged to transport their goods by the railroads were too high. Yet, the Grangers Laws were also unsuccessful because they lacked uniformity.

Then in 1886, the Supreme Court ruled in *Wabash, St. Louis & Pacific Ry. Co. v. Illinois* that the Commerce Clause of the Constitution allowed only for federal regulation of interstate commerce, which resulted in the Interstate Commerce Act of 1887.

The Interstate Commerce Act outlawed unfair discrimination against shippers with the use of rebates, pools, drawbacks and long-short haul discrepancies. It required that railroad rates be reasonable and published and could not be changed without adequate public notices. Later, the Interstate Commerce Commission was created to enforce compliance.

Source(s): *West's Encyclopedia of American Law.* Volume 1. Minneapolis, MN: West Publishing, 1998.

---

mandated contoured mudguards. Straight mudguards were required in Arkansas and permitted in at least 45 other states.

Substantial and repeated costs would be incurred to install, maintain, and replace the contoured mudguards. Since the two states required different types of mudguards, the cost would be especially high for vehicles operating in both Illinois and Arkansas. These trailers would have to stop to change mudguards every time they crossed the state border.

In addition, the law would seriously interfere with the trucking companies' "interline operations." Using this procedure, two carriers interchanged entire trailers rather than unloading and reloading the cargo. Interlining was particularly important in shipping perishable goods and explosives carried under seal. A firm not operating in Illinois would not equip its trailers with contoured mudguards. Thus its trailers could not be used by Illinois companies under the "interlining" procedure.

Small Benefits Do Not Justify Great Costs

The attorneys for Illinois did not attempt to rebut claims that the law burdened interstate commerce. Instead they argued that contoured mudguards increased safety. Specifically contoured mudguards "prevented the throwing of debris into the faces of drivers of passing cars and into the windshields of a following vehicle." However, Justice Douglas noted, these safety advantages had not been proved. Moreover, contoured

mudguards created new safety hazards not found when straight mudguards were used.

Justice Douglas concluded that this was one of the rare cases where a state safety measure was unconstitutional even though it did not discriminate against persons from other states.

> We deal not with absolutes but with questions of degree. The state legislatures plainly have great leeway in providing safety regulations for all vehicles—interstate as well as local . . . Yet the heavy burden which the Illinois mudguard law places on the interstate movement of trucks and trailers . . . [goes beyond] the permissible limits even for safety regulations.

Related Cases

Southern Pacific Co. v. Arizona, 325 U.S. 761 (1945).
Raymond Motor Transp., Inc. v. Rice, 417 F.Supp. 1352 (1976).

Bibliography and Further Reading

Biskupic, Joan, and Elder Witt, eds. *Congressional Quarterly's Guide to the U.S. Supreme Court,* 3rd ed. Washington, DC: Congressional Quarterly, Inc., 1996.

Gavit, Bernard. *The Commerce Clause of the United States Constitution.* New York: AMS Press, 1970.

Tribe, Laurence. *American Constitutional Law,* 2nd ed. Mineola, NY: Foundation, 1978.

WARDS COVE PACKING V. ATONIO

Legal Citation: 490 U.S. 642 (1989)

Petitioner
Wards Cove Packing Company, Inc., et al.

Respondent
Frank Atonio, et al.

Petitioner's Claim
That an earlier court judgment showing discrimination though "disparate impact" was incorrect.

Chief Lawyer for Petitioner
Douglas M. Fryer

Chief Lawyer for Respondent
Abraham A. Arditi

Justices for the Court
Anthony M. Kennedy, Sandra Day O'Connor, William H. Rehnquist, Antonin Scalia, Byron R. White (writing for the Court)

Justices Dissenting
Harry A. Blackmun, William J. Brennan, Jr., Thurgood Marshall, John Paul Stevens

Place
Washington, D.C.

Date of Decision
5 June 1989

Decision
A racially segregated workforce does not show discrimination on the part of the employer if that workforce is a reflection of the pool of applicants, and thus is not in violation of the Civil Rights Act of 1964. Furthermore, in such cases the plaintiff, not the employer, must show proof that a specific hiring or personnel policy is responsible for an unfairly segregated workforce.

Significance
The decision was seen as pro-business—favoring a deregulated corporate climate by making it harder for employees to bring suit against their employers—and also marked a new era for the Court, now with a block of conservative justices on the bench.

In the late 1960s, Frank Atonio filed suit, along with several other co-workers at an Alaskan fish cannery, charging that the practices of their employer, Wards Cove Packing Company, hindered their ability to obtain promotions and better-paying jobs within the company. Atonio, a Samoan, and the others—also non-whites—held the more arduous unskilled canning factory jobs, while at the company's offices most of the skilled positions were filled by whites. A majority of the cannery workers were Native Alaskan or Filipino, and they ate and bunked separately from the office workers; jobs were even described with derogatory racial epithets. Almost all of the office positions offered better pay, and more pleasant working conditions. An aptitude test for all job candidates, a common practice, was one hiring practice that Wards Cove used in personnel decisions, and Atonio and the others charged that these kinds of tests served to segregate the workforce along color lines.

Title VII

Since the passage of the United States Civil Rights Act of 1964, many employment discrimination suits have achieved legal victory under Title VII of the act, which barred discrimination in employment on the basis of race, sex, religion, or national origin. A liberal Supreme Court, weighing similar employment-discrimination suits, had ruled throughout the 1960s and 1970s that even though employers may not have *intent* to discriminate, the presence of such barriers as aptitude tests or educational requirements nevertheless constitute a violation of the act. In legal terms, this was known as the "disparate impact" theory—even though a company may not intend to bar protected groups from certain jobs, there may be tests or practices that prevent minorities from enjoying a full range of social and economic opportunities.

Throughout the liberal years of the Court, one cornerstone of this legal issue had remained constant: employers charged with violation of the Title VII statute were obliged to prove in court that tests or other practices were necessary to the functioning of the business. This forced companies under fire to hire consultants (often at great expense) to conduct statistical studies

---

What Is White Collar Crime?

The term white collar crime was first introduced by sociologist Edwin H. Sutherland, during a speech before the American Sociological Association in 1939. He defined white-collar crime as "a crime committed by a person of respectability and high social status in the course of his occupation." That means that the crime must be related to the job or occupation, and is committed by someone in a position of status within the company. Typically, murder manslaughter and robbery would not be considered white-collar crimes since they are not apart of routine work procedures.

The U.S. Attorney General's Office defined white collar crime in a annual report as "illegal acts that use deceit and concealment—rather than application or threat of physical force or violence—to obtain money, property, or service; to avoid the payment or loss of money; or to secure a business or personal advantage."

Source(s): *Criminal Law.* Fourth Edition. Boston, MA: McGraw-Hill, 1998.

---

and prove that weeding out applicants via aptitude tests, for instance, was integral to the demands of the job. One significant decision had come in 1971 with *Griggs v. Duke Power Company,* in which a unanimous ruling, written by Chief Justice Warren Burger, declared that the standardized employment tests had no relevance to the job in question.

New Era

Griggs was considered a precedent-setting ruling, in part because it broadly interpreted the Title VII statute and placed the burden of proving the absence of discriminatory policy on the employer, not the employee or the protected group filing suit. Many companies, fearful of becoming defendants in such suits, reviewed the stratification of their workforce (a higher percentage of minorities in entry-level, low-wage jobs, for instance) and began to revise hiring and promotion practices to provide more opportunities for protected groups—in effect, implementing their own affirmative-action policies.

In the case of the Wards Cove employees, which dated back to 1974, a district court had rejected the plaintiff's claims, contending that a union hiring agreement was responsible for the predominance of non-white workers in cannery jobs. A higher court, the Ninth Circuit Court of Appeals, overturned that decision in 1987, saying that the plaintiffs had indeed shown that "disparate impact" had occurred through Wards Cove hiring practices and that the company and another cannery named in the suit were indeed obligated to prove through statistical evidence that employment tests were relevant to the jobs in question. The companies appealed the decision, and the case came before the Supreme Court during the 1988-89 term.

New Majority

It was a conservative Court that ruled on *Wards Cove.* President Ronald Reagan, taking office in 1980 and re-

elected for a second term in 1984, had achieved one of the goals of his "Reagan Revolution": to finalize the turn to the right that the Court had taken in the early 1970s. Reagan had unusual presidential fortune in the opportunity to appoint several Supreme Court justices upon the retirements of senior members, and he did so with conservative judges who sometimes faced heated questioning in Senate confirmation hearings. The Reagan appointments were Sandra Day O'Connor in 1981, Antonin Scalia in 1986, and Anthony M. Kennedy in 1988; in 1986 the president elevated Justice William H. Rehnquist, an appointee of Richard Nixon and a staunch conservative, to Chief Justice. With Byron H. White, on the Court since 1962, the justices now wielded a majority over their more liberal-leaning colleagues like William J. Brennan, Jr., and Thurgood Marshall.

In June of 1989, the Court announced their 5-4 vote on *Wards Cove.* The majority opinion, written by White, stated that the mere presence of racial imbalance within a workforce does not show a violation of Title VII. Instead, in order to prove that "disparate impact" discrimination had occurred, White stated, plaintiff employees must compare the racial makeup of the company with the demographics of the qualified applicants in the area. Furthermore, the opinion of the Court declared, employees have to show that a *specific* company policy keeps the workforce unfairly segregated. The justices reversed the ninth court decision, and sent it back for further trial at the district court level.

Pro-Business Climate

Legal analysts asserted that the decision was a flexing of conservative muscle that negated an array of significant civil-rights decisions that favored plaintiffs in the area of discrimination litigation over the last two decades. In effect, it seemed to repudiate *Griggs* and place a large and deliberate obstacle to employee suits against employers. To many, it appeared to invalidate the necessity of affirmative-action quotas in the workplace, whether court-imposed or voluntary. On the other hand, White's opinion pointed out that there had been "misunderstanding" in the Court's previous interpretations of the Civil Rights Act in past decisions. The *Wards Cove* decision was also consistent with the Republican tone of American politics during the 1980s, through which a thriving, unregulated business climate was given preference.

The *Wards Cove* case incensed Democratic lawmakers. With the 1991 Civil Rights Act, signed by President George Bush, the *Griggs* precedent, forcing much of the burden of proof onto the employer, became law. However, it did uphold one part of the *Wards Cove* decision in requiring that the plaintiff employee had to identify a specific company practice in their challenge.

Related Cases

Griggs v. Duke Power Co., 401 U.S. 424 (1971).
Washington v. Davis, 426 U.S. 229 (1976).

Bibliography and Further Reading

Allen, Billie Morgan, Robert K. Robinson, and Bobby C, Vaught. "*Wards Cove Packing Co. v. Atonio:* Implications for Disparate Impact." *Labor Law Journal*, February 1990, pp. 102-107.

Biddle, Richard E. "*Wards Cove Packing vs. Atonio* Redefines EEO Analyses." *Personnel Journal*, June 1990, pp. 56-65.

Greenhouse, Linda. "Court, Ruling 5 to 4, Eases Burden on Employers in Some Bias Suits." *New York Times,* 6 June 1989, p. A1.

———. "Job Ruling Makes It Clear: Court Has Shifted Right." *New York Times,* 7 June 1989.

Greenlaw, Paul S. "Proving Title VII Discrimination." *Labor Law Journal,* July 1991, pp. 407-417.

Gullett, C. Ray, and Michael Styles. "*Wards Cove* on Remand: Implications for Equal Employment Opportunity." *Labor Law Journal,* September 1991, pp. 635-639.

———. "The Civil Rights Act of 1991: Did It Really Overturn *Wards Cove?*" *Labor Law Journal,* July 1992, pp. 462-465.

Hogler, Raymond L., and Jeanette N. Cleveland. "*Wards Cove* and the Theory of Disparate Impact: From Bad Law to Worse Policy." *Labor Law Journal,* March 1990, pp. 138-151.

Jacoby, Tamar. "A Question of Statistics." *Newsweek,* 19 June 1989.

Kammeyer, W. Randall. "Disparate Impact Cases under the Civil Rights Act of 1991." *Labor Law Journal,* October 1992, pp. 639-651.

Myers, Donald W., and Carol D. Rasnic. "Did *Wards Cove* Overrule *Griggs*? A Contrary View." *Labor Law Journal,* June 1990, pp. 370-375.

"Supreme Court Redefines Scope of Civil Rights Acts." *Personnel Journal,* August 1989, pp. 22-26.

CONSUMER PROTECTION

History

Consumer protection and product safety include the efforts made by government, nonprofit organizations, businesses, and individuals to create, protect, and enforce the rights of consumers who buy products or services. While the idea of consumer protection is not new—there have been laws regarding uniform weights and measures since the fledging days of the United States—interest in consumer rights legislation has flourished in tandem with society's technological and economical advances. For instance, the mass commercialization of products during the industrial revolution spawned laws in the late 1890s and early 1900s regarding food purity. And the rise in consumer credit as well as product safety awareness, spurred much consumer protection legislation during the 1960s and 1970s.

The passage of the pure food and drug legislation, in 1906, came in response to efforts led by crusaders who were concerned about unsanitary conditions and high prices. One such crusader was Upton Sinclair, author of the novel *The Jungle*. Sinclair was considered a muckraker because his book depicted the harsh and filthy environment inside the Chicago stockyards. Public reaction to Sinclair's exposition led to an investigation by the federal government and subsequent meat-inspection legislation.

In 1938 Congress added to the 1906 legislation by enacting the Food, Drug and Cosmetic Act, which required manufacturers to prove the safety of new drugs before being allowed to put them on the market. The Food and Drug Adminsitration (FDA) of the Department of Health and Human Services is responsible for administering the pure food and drugs acts. These acts were created to ensure that food, drugs, vaccines, devices, and cosmetics are safe, properly labelled, and pure. Over the years, the acts have been strengthened with additional amendments, such as a 1962 requirement that manufacturers prove the effectiveness, as well as the safety, of drugs before they are marketed to consumers.

In a 1962 message to the Congress, President John F. Kennedy outlined the basic tenents of consumer rights, which he described as: the right to safety, the right to be informed, the right to choose, and the right

to be heard. These principles form the foundation for the consumer-rights movement. President Lyndon B. Johnson advanced consumer rights in 1964 by creating the post of Special Assistant for Consumer Affairs, and in 1967 formed the Consumer Federation of America, which served as the national organization of consumer, cooperative, and labor groups.

At the forefront of the consumer-rights movement since the 1960s has been Ralph Nader, a lawyer and consumer advocate. Nader's 1965 muckraking book, *Unsafe at Any Speed,* exposed questionable manufacturing and design practices of automobile manufacturers. The book spurred the passage of the National Traffic and Motor Vehicle Safety Act of 1966. Nader has organized a network of young people, called Nader's Raiders, who conduct researching, writing, and lobbying efforts in a variety of areas related to consumer protection.

Consumer Protection Laws

Consumers enter into transactions to purchase goods or services every day. These transactions are considered legally binding contracts because consideration (motive to enter into a contract) is being given on both sides; the merchant is providing the product and the consumer is agreeing to pay, whether the payment be in the form of cash or credit.

The Uniform Commercial Code

The Uniform Commercial Code (UCC), which has been adopted in most states, is a comprehensive body of laws governing uniformity and fair dealing with transactions. It provides remedies and rights for both the buyer and seller. The UCC includes provisions for the sale of goods, commercial paper, bank deposits and collections, bulk transfers, investments securities, and secured transactions.

Additionally, the UCC contains provisions for several types of warranties. Warranties are the assurances, or promises, made by the seller, to the buyer, concerning the quality or condition of the merchandise. If there is a breach of the warranty, a consumer may cancel a contract or sue for damages. Warranties can either be express or implied. Express warranties are clear promises made, either orally or in writing, by the seller to the buyer, and often are included in a written contract. These promises must be factual, not subjective, such as, "this car drives like a dream." This statement is an example of sales hyperbole that is not to be taken literally. However, if a catalog has a picture of a pin and states that the pin is 22-karat gold, then the pin must be 22-karat gold. Implied warranties, however, are created by law and exist without the seller having actually made them.

The UCC covers two such implied warranties. The warranty of merchantability covers transactions over $500. Under this warranty, the seller is extending a guarantee to the buyer that the merchandise is fit for the purpose for which it was designed. The warranty of fitness for a particular purpose states that if a seller knows that merchandise is to be used for a special purpose and if the buyer is relying on the seller's judgment when purchasing the product for that purpose, then the seller has warranted that the merchandise will be acceptable for the buyer's intended use. Sellers can disclaim either of these two implied warranties, by putting into writing, at the time of the sale, statements such as, "merchandise sold as is" or "merchandise sold with faults."

The Magnuson-Moss Act is a federal law covering consumer products that cost more than $15. Under Magnuson-Moss, if a seller or manufacturer provides a written contract, the contract must be clearly visible and the terms and conditions must be expressed in clear language. The Magnuson-Moss Act requires that a written warranty contain certain information including the effective date of the warranty and who is entitled to protection under the warranty.

Both federal and state regulations provide relief to consumers who may have made a hasty purchase. Generally, consumers have a 72-hour cooling-off period in which they may cancel any contract they have made from a door-to-door solicitation. The reason for these laws is that presumably sellers will make high-pressured sales presentations in the buyer's home. If the cancellation is made within the three-day period, buyers do not have to give a reason but they may lose their downpayment or have to pay a cancellation fee.

Federal regulations also assist consumers who have problems with their credit. The Fair Credit Reporting Act allows consumers to view and correct erroneous information that is being reported on their credit history. The Fair Credit Billing Act of 1975 has procedures for billing dispute settlements and makes credit card companies liable for the quality of the merchandise that consumers pay for with their credit cards.

There are several organizations to help buyers who believe they have purchased a defective product. Consumers may contact their local Better Business Bureau (BBB). The BBB keeps track of such complaints against businesses and make this information available to the public. Small claim courts, for cases involving amounts less than several thousand dollars, are another possible venue to resolve a buyer-purchaser dispute.

Many states have also enacted "lemon laws," which provide protection to automobile owners who experience repeated problems with their vehicles. These laws were created because automobiles are expensive and are quite often a necessity for most consumers. Additionally, a defective automobile may be a safety hazard. If a consumer can prove that a car is defective and a manufacturer cannot correct the problem, the automobile maker may be liable for furnishing the consumer with a new vehicle or refunding the purchase price.

Product Safety

The Consumer Product Safety Commission (CPSC) was created in 1973 and is the U.S. federal government agency responsible for guaranteeing that more than 10,000 consumer products are safe for use. The CPSC creates safety standards and can ban or recall items from the marketplace that are hazardous. The commission enforces regulations such as the Flammable Fabrics Act of 1953, which governs the fire-resistance requirements for fabrics. Other acts that the CPSC regulates include the Hazardous Substances Act of 1960 (with later amendments), which requires that product labels contain warning and safety information.

The FDA regulates processed foods, drugs, medical devices, and cosmetics. The agency ensures that these items are safe and that their labels are correct. The FDA also makes certain that food is wholesome and that drugs are effective. If products are unsafe, the FDA has the authority to take the merchandise off store shelves. Radition-emitting products, including microwave ovens, also fall under the charge of the FDA.

The National Highway Traffic Safety Administration (NHTSA) oversees motor-vehicle safety. The NHTSA has the power to recall defective automobiles. The agency sets safety standards for the nation's highways and investigates automobile defects that impact the vehicle's safety.

Truthful Advertising

In order to make informed purchases, consumers need to have accurate information regarding the product or service they are considering buying. Several federal laws require manufacturers to disclose information that potential buyers need to make purchasing decisions. For example, the Fair Packaging and Labeling Act of 1966 is responsible for ensuring that labels carry information such as the product's quantity and ingredients. The Truth in Lending Act of 1968 mandates that applicants for credit loans be given accurate and clear information regarding the cost and terms of the loan they have applied for. Individual states have enacted consumer packaging laws as well. For instance, in order for consumers to compare the costs of products, many states have regulations that require supermarkets to show item cost based on unit measurements, such as weight or count.

The Federal Trade Commission (FTC) is the federal agency responsible for ensuring that advertising is not false or misleading. In addition, the FTC regulates interstate business and enforces consumer protection laws. The FTC has the authority to make companies withdraw any false advertising and may require the company to correct the misleading ads.

Private organization also provide services to aid consumers in making sound purchasing decisions. One of the most well known of these organizations is the nonprofit Consumers Union of United States, Inc. Consumers Union was established in 1936 and conducts impartial private tests on a wide range of goods and services. It then disseminates the test results in a variety of formats, including the periodical *Consumers Reports*. On a worldwide basis, the International Organization of Consumers Union (IOCU) is a network of over 125 organizations in more than 50 countries that provides an international platform for consumer protection and product testing.

Bibliography and Further Reading

Johnson, Daniel. *The Consumer's Guide to Understanding and Using the Law*. Cincinnati, OH: Betterway Books, 1981.

Reader's Digest Family Legal Guide. Pleasantville, NY: Reader's Digest Association, Inc., 1981.

TYSON & BROTHER V. BANTON

Legal Citation: 273 U.S. 418 (1927)

Appellant
Tyson & Brother Co.

Appellees
Joab H. Banton, Vincent B. Murphy

Appellant's Claim
That a U.S. district court erred in upholding the constitutionality of New York's ticket resale law.

Chief Lawyer for Appellant
Louis Marshall

Chief Lawyers for Appellees
Felix Benvenga, Robert P. Beyer

Justices for the Court
Pierce Butler, James Clark McReynolds, Harlan Fiske Stone, George Sutherland (writing for the Court), William Howard Taft, Willis Van Devanter

Justices Dissenting
Louis D. Brandeis, Oliver Wendell Holmes, Edward Terry Sanford

Place
Washington, D.C.

Date of Decision
28 February 1927

Decision
The district court opinion was reversed, thus invalidating the New York law.

Significance
The case was a significant battle in the evolving balance between the rights of private business and state regulation in the name of public welfare.

"A Public Interest"

During the 1920s, New York city and state officials grew concerned about complaints that ticket resale agencies and "scalpers" were charging the public exorbitant prices for theatre tickets. In 1922, the New York State legislature acted by passing a law limiting the resale price of any ticket to a theatre or other place of amusement to 50 cents above the original price printed on the ticket. The law was clearly designed as a public service, but it was eventually ruled unconstitutional by a sharply divided Supreme Court.

Even though unlicensed ticket scalpers were major targets of the resale rule, New York's licensed Theatre Ticket Brokers Association decided to contest the new law. One agency, Tyson & Brother, filed suit against the enforcers of the statute, New York County District Attorney Joab Banton and New York State Comptroller Vincent Murphy. An initial challenge failed in the U.S. District Court for the Southern District of New York, which found nothing unconstitutional in the law. Tyson & Brother appealed the decision. They claimed that the threat of severe resale law penalties prevented the agents from testing the law in court by selling even one ticket, depriving them of their liberty and property without the due process of law guaranteed by the Fourteenth Amendment. By making their claim a constitutional issue, Tyson & Brother succeeded in having their appeal heard by the Supreme Court on 6 and 7 October 1927.

District Attorney Banton's lawyer, Felix Benvenga, argued that widespread abuses by ticket price gougers provided a need for regulation. Comptroller Murphy's attorney, Robert Beyer, defended the state's legislation on broader grounds. Theatres and other places of public amusement were "affected by a public interest," which justified the state's rightful exercise of police power. Since reselling tickets was an integral part of the theatre business, it should also be subject to state regulation.

Nevertheless, five of the nine Supreme Court justices voted to reverse the district court's decision, rendering New York's law invalid. In Justice Sutherland's written opinion delivered on 28 February 1927, the state's

---

Scalping

Touting or "ticket scalping" has been around sporting events as long as the theory of supply and demand. "Scalpers" range from street venders trying to make an extra buck to national brokers catering to the elite class of entertainment seekers. Some national brokers make millions of dollars off of the resale of tickets to sporting events at inflated prices using fax machines and web sites. Ticket scalping is legal in ten states, illegal in nine, and regulated in 32 others under certain restrictions. Some argue that ticket scalping is a regrettable aspect of organized sports while others suggest it is merely a function of supply and demand like any other business.

The ticket scalping business soared in the 1990s and with its success came abuses. The most profitable events for brokers are: the Final Four, the Masters, and the Superbowl. In some cases brokers took advanced payments without providing tickets. To prevent such abuses a group of brokers got together to form the National Association of Ticket Brokers (NATB). Members of the NATB encourage ticket buyers to check up on brokers to make sure they belong to the organization before purchasing from them.

Source(s): *Sports Illustrated,* 7 April 1997 Vol. 86, no. 14, p. 102.
The Economist, 25 May 1991, Vol. 319, no. 7708, p. 21.

---

defense of the law failed on a wide range of points. The Court rejected the notion that theatres were "affected with a public interest." Unlike utility companies or corporations whose conduct affected the lives of millions of people, theatres were not exclusively devoted to public use. It was true that theatres were required to be licensed and inspected as public places, yet such licenses did not put a theatre owner under the same sort of obligation to provide entertainment that required a public utility licensee, for example, to provide acceptable telephone service.

The majority also agreed with the appellant's contention that the tickets were private property, with which the agents could do as they pleased. Unlike the lower court, Sutherland and the other concurring justices agreed that the Fifth and Fourteenth Amendment protections of property did apply to tickets which the agents had acquired for resale.

A Round of Dissents

The Court's decision was far from unanimous. While a five-vote majority found nothing in the Fourteenth Amendment to suggest that tickets were not to be protected as property, four dissenting judges could find nothing in the same amendment prohibiting regulation in the public interest. Justice Holmes saw nothing in the entire Constitution that prevented the people of New York from enacting protective regulations like the resale law, if widespread agreement existed that such a law should be passed. Justice Holmes was less concerned with the merits of the New York case in particular than with what he considered to be the Court's repudiation of the public's will, properly expressed through their legislature. "We fear to grant power," wrote Holmes, "and are unwilling to recognize it when it exists."

Holmes was joined in his opinion by Justice Brandeis, both of whom added their signatures to a separate dissent by Justice Stone. Noting that the resale law did not attempt to set the price of tickets—the law merely required each ticket to have its price printed on its face and limited resale profit to 50 cents per ticket, a sum even most licensed agents agreed was the norm—Stone found no constitutional basis for forbidding regulation.

A third separate dissent was filed by Justice Sanford, who noted that some agents were in collusion with theatre owners willing to sell advance tickets in large numbers. While this premature exchange of money benefited owners worried about unsuccessful shows and agents who wanted to monopolize access to the best theatre seats, the arrangement left the public with no protection against extortionate resale rates. Justice Sanford reminded the Court of its decision in *Munn v. Illinois* (1876). In that decision, the Court found that the price of grain could not be regulated, but because grain elevators controlled public access to the product, they were found to be subject to regulation. Justice Sanford cast the ticket resale agents in a similar intermediary role and believed that the public should not be at their mercy.

The Court's controversial decision was met with predictable approval by the Theatre Ticket Brokers Association, whose members promised not to use the Court's decision as an excuse to inflate the resale price of tickets unfairly. The *New York Times* was less optimistic about the results of the law's invalidation, responding with an editorial entitled "Ticket Scalpers Win." The Supreme Court's decision doomed the resale law, but the vigor of New York State investigators remained undiminished, filling the papers with tales of Broadway ticket frauds.

Related Cases

Munn v. Illinois, 94 U.S. 113 (1876).

Nebbia v. People of New York, 291 U.S. 502 (1934).

Olsen v. State of Nebraska ex rel. Western Reference and Bond Association, 313 U.S. 236 (1941).

New Jersey Association of Ticket Brokers v. Ticketron, 543 A.2d 997 (1998).

Bibliography and Further Reading

"Agencies Keep Ticket Price Level." *New York Times,* 1 March 1927, p. 12.

"Anti-Gouging Law On Theatre Tickets Declared Invalid." *New York Times,* 1 March 1927, pp. 1, 12.

Hall, Kermit. L., ed. *The Oxford Companion To The Supreme Court Of The United States.* New York: Oxford University Press, 1992.

"Ticket Scalpers Win." *New York Times,* 2 March 1927, p. 24.

PENNELL V. SAN JOSE

Legal Citation: 485 U.S. 1 (1988)

Appellants
Richard Pennell and Tri-County Apartment House Owners Association

Appellees
City of San Jose and City Council of San Jose

Appellants' Claim
That the provisions of the San Jose City rent control ordinance violated the Takings Clause of the Fifth and Fourteenth Amendments and the Due Process and Equal Protection Clauses of the Fourteenth Amendment.

Chief Lawyer for Appellants
Harry D. Miller

Chief Lawyer for Appellees
Joan R. Gallo

Justices for the Court
Harry A. Blackmun, William J. Brennan, Jr., Thurgood Marshall, William H. Rehnquist (writing for the Court), John Paul Stevens, Byron R. White

Justices Dissenting
Sandra Day O'Connor, Antonin Scalia (Anthony M. Kennedy did not participate)

Place
Washington, D.C.

Date of Decision
24 February 1988

Decision
The U.S. Supreme Court held that the appellants' claim was premature. There was no evidence that the tenant hardship provision of the San Jose City rent control ordinance was ever applied. Nor did the provision violate the Due Process Clause or the Equal Protection Clause because the ordinance was related to a legitimate interest of protecting tenants.

Significance
San Jose's rent control ordinance was crafted to protect the interests of both landlords and their tenants. Many San Jose landlords feared the possibility of having to operate at a loss of income if, because a tenant might not be able to afford a rent increase, city hearing officers judged that the increase was inappropriate. The Court found that tenant hardship provisions were not unconstitutional providing that they consistently served a state's legitimate interest in protecting tenants and were not arbitrary or discriminatory. Thus, the U.S. Supreme Court not only found that tenant hardship was as relevant a consideration as the interests of landlords, but that government had a legitimate interest in protecting the interests of consumers.

The city of San Jose, California, enacted a rent control ordinance in 1979 in order to solve problems raised by the growing shortage of, and the increasing demand for, housing. The ordinance sought to prevent excessive and unreasonable rent increases, alleviate undue hardship on individual tenants, and assure that landlords had fair and reasonable return on their property. A landlord was only entitled to raise the annual rent of a tenant by no more than eight percent. If a tenant was subject to a greater increase, the ordinance dictated that a hearing before a Meditating Hearing Officer would determine whether the proposed increase was "reasonable under the circumstances." The ordinance established seven acceptable circumstances. Six related to the landlord's cost of providing adequate rental units or to the condition of the rental market, and the seventh was "Hardship to Tenants," which considered the economic and financial hardship imposed on a tenant by a proposed increase. This last provision was aimed at protecting poor tenants from unjustified rent increases.

Richard Pennell, an individual landlord, and the Tri-County Apartment House Owners' Association, which represented owners and lessors of real property located in San Jose, filed suit in a state court seeking a declaration that the rent control ordinance, and in particular the tenant hardship provision, was "facially unconstitutional and therefore . . . illegal and void." They argued that the first six factors were objective, and the tenant hardship provision amounted to a transfer of the landlord's property to individual "hardship" tenants. The trial court sustained their claim that the tenant hardship provision violated the Takings Clause of the Fifth and Fourteenth Amendments by obligating private landlords to assume public burdens (possible poverty of their tenants) without just compensation. (The Fifth Amendment dictates that no person's private property shall be taken for public use without just compensation. This provision was designed to bar government from forcing some people alone to bear public burdens which, in all fairness and justice, should be borne by the public as a whole.) The California Court of Appeal affirmed the ruling, adding that the tenant hardship provision also violated the Equal Protection Clause of the Fourteenth Amendment. (The Equal Pro-

Rent Control

Rent control is a controversial system by which the federal, state, and local governments regulate rent rates by placing ceilings on the amount that private individuals can be charged for rent. It was initiated during World War II as part of a broader effort to control increasing prices. Rent control policies usually target urban areas and are designed to help the economically disadvantaged during an inflationary economy (increases in the cost of living such as occurred during World War II and the early 1970s). Four states currently permit rent control: New York, New Jersey, California, and Massachusetts.

In recent years, rent control has been abused by tenants in sound financial standing. In response to abuses of the system, which is costing property owners, property owners have organized to end the practice. One side effect of rent control is the increase of rent prices in non-controlled regions imposed by property owners to offset the losses incurred by rent control. The Alliance of Small Property Owners is a grassroots campaign to end rent control representing a group of small property owners in NY, NJ, CA, and MA. Boston and New York have made efforts to eliminate rent control in recent years.

Source(s): *USA Today Magazine,* July 1998, Vol. 127, no. 2638, p. 20.

---

tection Clause protects citizens from varying treatment by a state's statute, unless the difference in treatment is rationally related to a legitimate state interest.)

Dissatisfied with the decision of the court of appeal, the city of San Jose appealed and won a reversal from the Supreme Court of California. At the hearing, the landlords added another argument, stating that the tenant hardship provision violated the Due Process Clause of the Fourteenth Amendment. Under the Due Process Clause, a state price regulation is unconstitutional if arbitrary, discriminatory, or demonstrably irrelevant to the policy the legislature is free to adopt. The majority of the California Supreme Court judged that the tenant hardship provision did not arbitrarily select those landlords with hardship tenants to bear a burden that ought to be borne by all of society. The disparate treatment between landlords with and landlords without hardship tenants was justified by the state legislature's policy of protecting tenants. Pennell and the Tri-County Apartment House Owners Association then appealed to the U.S. Supreme Court.

"Hardship Tenants" a Landlord's Hardship?

Having heard oral arguments, the U.S. Supreme Court affirmed the decision of the Supreme Court of California. Before turning to the merits of the landlords' contentions, Justice Rehnquist considered the claim of the appellees (the city of San Jose and the City Council of San Jose) that the landlords lacked standing to challenge the constitutionality of the ordinance. Article III of the Federal Constitution requires that a litigant who challenges a statute must demonstrate a realistic danger of sustaining a direct injury as a result of the statute's operation or enforcement. The complaint of the landlords stated relevant facts, but did not allege that Pennell or any other member of the Tri-County

Association had "hardship tenants" who might trigger the ordinance's hearing process, or that they had been or would be aggrieved by the determination of a hearing officer that a certain proposed rent increase was unreasonable on the basis of tenant hardship. Rehnquist noted that when standing was challenged on the basis of the pleadings, the Supreme Court accepted as true all material allegations of the complaint, and construed the complaint in favor of the complaining party. Thus, the mere likelihood that the ordinance might be enforced against members of the association and the probability that a landlord's rent would be lower than in the absence of the ordinance evidenced sufficient possibility of actual injury. The landlords had standing to challenge the ordinance.

They first argued the tenant hardship provision of the ordinance violated the Fifth and Fourteenth Amendments' prohibition against taking of private property for public use without just compensation (the Takings Clause). They conceded the first six factors of the ordinance (relating to landlord's costs and to the condition of the rental market) were reasonable. They protected the only legitimate purpose of rent control: the elimination of "excessive" rents caused by San Jose's housing shortage. The landlords, however, challenged the seventh provision, "hardship to a tenant," because it did not serve the purpose of eliminating excessive rents. Rather, by providing assistance to hardship tenants, landlords feared that the possibility of operating at a loss was tantamount to delivering ownership of their property to their tenants. Thus, the ordinance forced individual landlords to shoulder the "public" burden of subsidizing their poor tenants' housing without just compensation.

Justice Rehnquist found that this argument was premature. There was no evidence that the tenant hardship provision had ever been applied by a hearing officer to reduce a rent below the figure set after considering the other six specified factors. In fact, the ordinance did not require that a hearing officer reduce a proposed rent increase on the grounds of tenant hardship, but only made it mandatory that tenant hardship be considered. The takings analysis, Rehnquist wrote, requires "essentially ad hoc, factual inquiry" because the constitutionality of statutes ought not be decided except in an actual factual setting that made such a decision necessary. In this case there was no instance of application of the tenant hardship provision. The mere fact that a hearing officer was enjoined to consider hardship to the tenant in fixing a landlord's rent did not present a sufficiently concrete factual setting for the adjudication of the takings claim.

Rehnquist also rejected the landlords' argument that the Ordinance was facially invalid under the Due Process Clause of the Fourteenth Amendment. The standard for determining whether a state price-control regulation was constitutional under the Due Process Clause was well established—price control was unconstitutional if arbitrary, discriminatory, or demonstrably irrelevant to the adopted policy of a (state) legislature. Nobody disputed that the ordinance's purpose of preventing unreasonable rent increases caused by the city's housing shortage was a legitimate exercise of the city's police powers. But the attorney for Pennell and the Tri-County Association claimed that it was arbitrary, discriminatory, and demonstrably irrelevant for the city of San Jose to attempt to accomplish the additional goal of reducing the burden of housing costs for low-income tenants. They thought the objective of alleviating individual tenant hardship was not a policy the legislature was free to adopt. The Supreme Court, however, held the protection of consumer welfare as a legitimate and rational goal of price or rate regulation. The Court noted that only in the context of the six other factors did the ordinance allow tenant hardship to be considered. Rehnquist thus concluded that the ordinance carefully protected both the legitimate interests of the landlord and the tenant and did not violate the Fourteenth Amendment's Due Process Clause.

The Supreme Court disagreed with the landlords that the ordinance violated the Equal Protection Clause of the Fourteenth Amendment. Rehnquist explained that the city of San Jose and its Council needed only show that the classification scheme embodied in the ordinance was "rationally related to a legitimate state interest." The ordinance's tenant hardship provision was designed to serve the legitimate purpose of protecting tenants. It was not irrational, therefore, for the ordinance to treat landlords differently on the basis of whether or not they had hardship tenants. The Court concluded that it was premature to consider the landlords' claim under the Takings Clause and rejected their facial challenge to the ordinance under the Due Process

and Equal Protection Clauses of the Fourteenth Amendment.

In writing the dissenting opinion, Justice Scalia agreed that the tenant hardship provision of San Jose's rent control ordinance did not, on its face, violate either the Due Process Clause or the Equal Protection Clause of the Fourteenth Amendment. However, he disagreed with the Court's opinion that the landlords had filed suit prematurely. He felt it was inappropriate for landlords to suffer loss by having to wait until they could show loss from a particular case due "to the consequences of [the hardship factor] in the ultimate determination of the rent." Further, it was unreasonable to thus shield alleged injustice from judicial scrutiny. Scalia also emphasized the unfairness of making one citizen pay to remedy a social problem that was not of her or his creation. His view was that San Jose had not merely regulated rents, but used rent regulation to establish a welfare program privately funded by landlords who happened to have "hardship" tenants.

Impact

San Jose's rent control ordinance was carefully crafted to protect both landlords and tenants. The U.S. Supreme Court found no evidence that any landlord in San Jose was or would ever be aggrieved by the application of the tenant hardship provision of the ordinance. The majority judged that a city's ordinance which sought to ensure fair and equitable rent control did not violate clauses of either the Fifth or Fourteenth Amendments if its provisions were not arbitrary, discriminatory, or irrelevant to state policy. Further, the Court found that when the provisions of an ordinance such as those of San Jose served a legitimate state interest (in this case, rent control that specifically protected low-income tenants), it was not inconceivable that some landlords would be subject to different treatment depending on whether or not they had "hardship tenants." The Court reasoned that tenants' hardship was as equally relevant as landlords' interests when a city ordinance served a legitimate purpose. Thus, in rendering their decision, the Court emphasized that cities (and states) had a legitimate interest in protecting consumer welfare.

Related Cases

Armstrong v. United States, 364 U.S. 40 (1960).
Hodel v. Virginia Surface Mining & Reclamation Assn., 452 U.S. 264 (1979).
Vance v. Bradley, 440 U.S. 93 (1979).
Kaiser Aetna v. United States, 444 U.S. 164 (1979).
FCC v. Florida Power Corp., 480 U.S. 245 (1987).
First English Evangelical Lutheran Church of Glendale v. County of Los Angeles, 482 U.S. 304 (1987).

Bibliography and Further Reading

Porter, Philip K. "Taking Property and Just Compensation." *Southern Economic Journal,* October 1994, p. 555.

DENVER AREA EDUCATIONAL CONSORTIUM V. FEDERAL COMMUNICATIONS COMMISSION

Legal Citation: 518 U.S. 727 (1996)

Petitioner
Denver Area Educational Consortium, et al.

Respondent
Federal Communications Commission, et al.

Petitioner's Claim
That various regulations implementing the Cable Television Consumer Protection and Competition Act, which regulated indecent and obscene programming on cable television, violated the free speech rights of cable access programmers and cable television viewers under the First Amendment.

Chief Lawyer for Petitioner
I. Michael Greenberger

Chief Lawyer for Respondent
Lawrence G. Wallace

Justices for the Court
Stephen Breyer (writing for the Court), Ruth Bader Ginsburg, Anthony M. Kennedy, Sandra Day O'Connor, David H. Souter, John Paul Stevens

Justices Dissenting
William H. Rehnquist, Antonin Scalia, Clarence Thomas

Place
Washington, D.C.

Date of Decision
28 June 1996

Decision
That the portion of the regulations which permitted cable operators to restrict offensive or indecent programming on leased cable channels was constitutional. However, those portions of the regulations which allowed the operator to restrict such programming on public access channels, and which required cable operators to put patently offensive programming on separate channels which cannot be received unless a viewer requests to have the channel "unblocked," were unconstitutional restrictions on free speech.

Significance
The plurality opinion suggests a sweeping change in how First Amendment claims are analyzed by the Supreme Court. The opinion, if adopted in other contexts, has the potential to revolutionize how the Court views First Amendment problems arising in areas of new technology. However, for the short-term, the Court's decision seems to be limited to regulations of cable television, and is significant in that it allows somewhat greater restrictions on speech in the cable television context than in other types of media.

In the 1949 case *Kovacs v. Cooper*, Justice Thomas Jackson noted the difficulties in analyzing First Amendment free speech issues in technologically new areas of communication: "The moving picture screen, the radio, the newspaper, the handbill, the sound truck and the street corner orator have differing natures, values, abuses, and dangers. Each . . . is a law unto itself." Justice Jackson's oft-quoted observation gained increasing importance in the 1980s and 1990s, as the Court struggled to apply the First Amendment rules to new technological areas, such as the Internet, cellular phones, and cable television.

One of the most troubling areas for the Supreme Court over the years has been the area of broadcast media. While the Court has consistently extended broad protection to free speech rights of print and other media, it has struggled to define the proper scope of First Amendment protections in the case of radio and television broadcasts. Although the Court unanimously struck down a law regulating indecent and pornographic speech on the Internet in the case of *Reno v. American Civil Liberties Union,* less than a year later in *Denver Area Consortium,* the Court was sharply divided over how to apply the First Amendment's prohibition on laws restricting free speech to certain portions of the Cable Television Consumer Protection Act containing similar regulations of indecent speech on cable television.

Denver Area Consortium involved a challenge to three sections of the act brought by several cable television programmers and viewers. Specifically, the petitioners challenged sections 10(a), 10(b), and 10(c) of the act, which were enacted in 1992, and the Federal Communication Commission's regulations implementing those sections. All three sections related to offensive or indecent programming on cable television. Section 10(a) allowed cable operators to prohibit offensive or indecent programming on "leased access channels," that is, channels leased to private programmers. If the cable operator permitted programming defined as indecent by the Federal Communications Commission regulations on leased access channels, section 10(b) required the cable operator to "segregate and block" such programming, by putting such programming on a single channel and blocking access to the channel, unless the cable subscriber requested access to the channel in writing. Finally, section 10(c) applied the rule of section 10(a), allowing a cable operator to prohibit offensive or indecent programming on public access channels, which are channels left open to public, educational, and government programming.

By simple vote counting, the Court found that section 10(a) was constitutional by a 7-2 vote, that section 10(b) was unconstitutional by a 6-3 vote, and section 10(c) was unconstitutional by a 5-4 vote. More importantly, however, the justices were sharply divided over the approach to be used in analyzing the regulations, issuing six separate opinions in the case. In general terms, the justices' opinions can be broken down into three separate approaches.

Justice Breyer's Contextual Balancing Approach

Justice Breyer, who was joined in his approach by Justices Stevens, Souter, and O'Connor, refused to apply any test previously formulated in other areas of the media under the First Amendment. Breyer's approach rejected the attempt of the other justices to create categories of media for First Amendment cases. He reasoned that such a categorical approach "import[s] law developed in very different contexts into a new and changing environment, and . . . lack[s] the flexibility necessary to allow government to respond to very serious problems without sacrificing the free exchange of ideas the First Amendment is designed to protect." Thus, Justice Breyer favored a "contextual assessment" of the law, in which a regulation on speech is upheld if it "properly addresses an extremely important problem, without imposing, in light of the relevant interests, an unnecessarily great restriction on speech."

Applying this contextual approach, Justice Breyer, joined by Justices Stevens and Souter, found that section 10(a) was constitutional, but that both sections 10(b) and 10(c) were unconstitutional. With respect to section 10(a), Justice Breyer concluded that the statute was designed for an important purpose, the need to protect children from pornographic and patently offensive material. He also reasoned that, in allowing cable operators to block offensive programming, Congress appropriately balanced this interest against the interests of adults wishing to view such programming, because there were alternative avenues for adults to receive this programming, such as home video, theatres, and direct broadcast satellite television. Thus, Justice Breyer concluded that section 10(a) was constitutional.

However, Justice Breyer also found that the "segregate and block" provision of section 10(b) was unconstitutional, because the provision was overly restrictive. He noted that the provision required significant

advanced planning on the part of a cable subscriber who wanted to view a particular offensive program, and would have been better served by a less restrictive means of blocking such programming to subscribers who did not want to receive it. For example, rather than automatically blocking such programming and requiring a written request by a subscriber for it, a cable operator could simply allow a subscriber to request to have the channel blocked. Thus, he concluded that the "segregate and block" provision was not a reasonable balance of the government's interest in protecting children and the free speech rights of cable television programmers and viewers.

Finally, Justice Breyer also found section 10(c), allowing cable operators to ban offensive programming on public access channels, unconstitutional. He again concluded that the balance struck by Congress between the need to protect children and the free speech rights of cable programmers and viewers was unreasonable. He reasoned that there was significantly less evidence of offensive programming on public access channels and that, because programming on such channels is usually controlled by supervising boards composed of people affiliated with nonprofit or local government organizations, there was already an effective way of limiting such programming on public access channels. Although she agreed with Justice Breyer on the other two sections, Justice O'Connor disagreed with respect to section 10(c). She found no reason to distinguish this section from section 10(a), as they were essentially the same provision, only directed at two different types of channels.

Justice Kennedy's Categorical Approach

In contrast to the approach taken by Justice Breyer, Justice Kennedy, who wrote an opinion for himself and Justice Ginsburg, favored a "categorical" approach. He reasoned that "[w]hen confronted with a threat to free speech in an emerging technology, [the Court] ought to have the discipline to analyze the case by reference to existing First Amendment principles." In Justice Kennedy's view, cable television falls into the same category as speech in a "public forum," such as a speaker standing on a street corner. This is so, Justice Kennedy concluded, because cable television operators have access to cable through a government franchise. As Justice Kennedy analogized, cable programming (particular public access programming), is "the video equivalent of the speaker's soapbox or the electronic parallel to the printed leaflet."

Thus, Justice Kennedy applied the same test used in other "public forum" cases, namely, the strict scrutiny test. Under the strict scrutiny test, a regulation on speech is valid only if it is narrowly tailored to achieve a compelling government interest. Although agreeing that Congress's purpose of protecting children from viewing indecent programming was compelling, Justice Kennedy concluded that neither section 10(a) nor section 10(c) was narrowly tailored to achieving that purpose. First, he reasoned, the sections merely permit a cable operator to ban offensive programming; thus, cable operators remain free to allow such programming, and such programming will inevitably reach children in certain areas. Second, sections 10(a) and 10(c) deprives adults of access to indecent programming, not just children. Thus, Justice Kennedy concluded: "Sections 10(a) and (c) present a classic case of discrimination against speech based on its content. There are legitimate reasons why the government might wish to regulate or even restrict the speech at issue here, but [sections] 10(a) and 10(c) are not drawn to address those reasons with the precision the First Amendment requires."

Justice Thomas's Categorical Approach

Justice Thomas, who was joined by Chief Justice Rehnquist and Justice Scalia, also favored a categorical approach similar to that of Justice Kennedy. Criticizing Justice Breyer's "assiduous attempts to avoid addressing" the issue of "how and to what extent the First Amendment protects cable operators, programmers, and viewers from state and federal regulation," Justice Thomas concluded that cable television should be afforded protections similar to those of the print media. However, Justice Thomas concluded that the restrictions in the act affected the free speech rights of the cable operators, not the cable programmers and viewers who were challenging the regulations. He concluded that the regulations actually increased the free speech rights of cable operators, by allowing them to exercise editorial control over the programs run by the cable programmers. He reasoned that cable programmers have no constitutional right of access to cable television; rather, programmers have a right of access only because Congress had mandated that cable operators set aside a certain number of channels for leased and public access programming. He concluded that, "[v]iewing the federal access requirements as a whole, it is the cable operator, not the access programmer, whose speech rights have been infringed." Thus, because the act merely restored free speech rights to the cable operators, without infringing on any constitutional right of access to cable for programmers, Justice Thomas concluded that the act was constitutional.

Impact

The Court's decision in *Denver Area Consortium* will likely have little impact outside the area of cable tele-

vision regulation. About one year after the Court's decision the Court unanimously found similar restrictions on indecent material on the Internet to violate the First Amendment in *Reno v. American Civil Liberties Union* (1997). In *Reno,* the Court unanimously applied the strict scrutiny test, not mentioning Justice Breyer's contextual approach and barely even citing its decision in *Denver Area Consortium.* Although lower federal courts have attempted to apply the various approaches taken in the case to other cable television regulations, it appears that outside this limited area the Court's decision will have little, if any, impact.

Related Cases

Kovacs v. Cooper, 336 U.S. 77 (1949).
Federal Communications Commission v. Pacifica Foundation, 438 U.S. 726 (1978).
Sable Communications of California, Inc. v. Federal Communications Commission, 492 U.S. 115 (1989).
Turner Broadcasting Systems, Inc. v. Federal Communications Commission, 512 U.S. 622 (1994).
Reno v. American Civil Liberties Union, 512 U.S. 844 (1997).

Bibliography and Further Reading

Caristi, Dom. *Expanding Free Expression in the Marketplace: Broadcasting and the Public Forum.* New York: Quorum Books, 1992.

"Clueless." *Detroit News,* July 4, 1996, A10.

Emord, Jonathan W. *Freedom, Technology, and the First Amendment.* San Francisco: Pacific Research Institute for Public Policy, 1991.

Fein, Bruce. "Sowing Seeds of Dubiosity." *Washington Times,* July 9, 1996, p. A14.

Gewirtz, Paul. "Constitutional Law and New Technology." *Social Research,* fall 1997, p. 1191.

Hearn, Ted. "Adult Nets Urge Court to Stay Scramble Law." *Multichannel News,* July 22, 1996, p. 40.

Powledge, Fred. *An ACLU Guide to Cable Television.* New York: American Civil Liberties Union, 1972.

Schroeder, Theodore. *"Obscene" Literature and Constitutional Law: A Forensic Defense of Freedom of the Press.* New York: Da Capo Press, 1972.

Simon, Glenn E. "Cyberporn and Censorship: Constitutional Barriers to Preventing Access to Internet Pornography by Minors." *Journal of Criminal Law and Criminology,* spring 1998, p. 1015.

CONTRACT LAW

What Is a Contract?

A contract is a promise between two or more persons involving the exchange of some good or service. Some of the basic elements of a contract include: an offer and an acceptance; "capacity," or being of legal age and sound competence; "mutual assent," or agreement on the terms of a contract; and "consideration," or compensation for goods or services rendered. The element that distinguishes a contract from an informal agreements is that it is legally binding: the law provides a remedy in the event that the promise is not fulfilled. By law, certain types of contracts must be in writing, but oral contracts are valid in many situations. An oral contract may be held to exist even in the absence of agreement as to all its terms.

Sources of Contract Law: The Statute of Frauds

The Statute of Frauds was enacted in England in 1677, and it has been adopted in one form or another by all 50 states. In order to prevent fraud on the part of either party in the exchange of goods, the statute requires a written contract for: one, the sale of land; two, the assumption of the obligations of another party, such as the co-signing of a loan; three, transactions that take more than one year to complete; and four, sale of personal property for more than $5,000 (under the Uniform Commercial Code, discussed below, the threshold is $500).

The Uniform Commercial Code

The Uniform Commercial Code (UCC) is the main body of law that governs transactions involving goods. It was developed by the National Conference of Commissioners on Uniform State Laws and the American Law Institute, a nonprofit legal research organization. Since its completion in 1952 it has been adopted by all 50 states (Louisiana, however, did not adopt all of the code). The purpose of the code is to facilitate commerce by simplifying and clarifying the law regarding commercial transactions and to create a uniform set of rules nationwide. The UCC is largely based on common law, which means that it usually adheres to legal guidelines established in court cases. However, in many cases the

UCC is forced to establish codes outside of traditional legal precedent in order to conform to the rapid pace of modern business practices.

In the United States, the UCC governs the sale of tangible, movable goods, property leases such as business equipment, and financial transactions such as bank deposits and letters of credit. The sale of services and real property are not covered by the UCC. International transactions are governed by the United Nations International Sale of Goods Convention, adopted by the United States in 1988, provided the foreign country involved is party to that agreement. Various state and federal statutes regulate contracts for services, consumer credit, the sale of land, and other specialized areas such as employment. Where no relevant statute exists, contracts are evaluated using common law principles. *The Restatement of Contracts,* created and published by the American Law Institute, summarizes and "restates" common law principles of contract. Although it does not have the force of law, it is heavily relied upon by legal professionals, including judges, who often quote it in written opinions.

Classification of Contracts

For purposes of analysis, legal scholars have classified contracts in many different ways. The most common classifications of contracts include: "express" and "implied" contracts; "void" and "voidable" contracts; and "enforceable" and "unenforceable" contracts.

Express and Implied Contracts

Express contracts, which may be written or oral, are contracts in which the terms of the agreement made are explicitly stated: when a valid offer is accepted, an express contract has been created. Implied contracts, usually referred to as "implied in fact," are contracts that are formed by the behavior of the parties in the absence of directly negotiating the specifics of the transaction. Making an appointment with a repairman to have a broken washing machine fixed is an implied contract—the repairman may reasonably expect to be paid for making the repairs. The term "implied in fact" is used to distinguish this type of implicit arrangement from an "implied in law" contract, or "quasi-contract."

A quasi-contract is not an actual contract; it is a non-binding legal mechanism used in special circumstances to prevent one party from being severely harmed or unjustly enriched by an implicit arrangement.

Void and Voidable Contracts

The term "void contract" is an oxymoron—a contract held to be void does not exist under law. In other words, although two parties may have come to an agreement, it is not recognized as a legal contract. Perhaps the simplest example of a void contract is a contract formed in which one party agrees to perform an illegal act. A contract that is illegal in part may be void in that respect, however, it is still a valid contract if the deletion of the illegal portion of the contract does not defeat the purpose of the broader agreement. Agreements in which an essential feature of a valid contract is lacking, are void contracts as well. Voidable contracts are contracts that may be canceled by one of the two parties involved. A contract may be voidable for various reasons, but in most cases a voidable contract provides for one of the parties to withdraw from the agreement without penalty.

Enforceable and Unenforceable Contracts

A contract may be enforceable or unenforceable. An enforceable contract is one for which a legal remedy is offered in the event that the contract is not fulfilled. A contract may be unenforceable when certain statutory requirements have not been met. For example, an oral contract to buy land would not be enforceable because the Statute of Frauds requires such an agreement to be in writing. Similarly, statutes of limitations, which limit the length of time available for legal action, may apply to contracts of certain types and render them unenforceable after a certain period of time.

Validity of Contracts

Several requirements must be met for a contract to be valid and legally binding. The agreement must specifically define the terms under which the promise can be considered fulfilled by both parties. In addition, the agreement must prescribe remedies for conditions unfulfilled by one of the parties involved. The essential feature defining these requirements are: "capacity," "mutual assent," and "consideration."

Capacity

Fundamentally, two or more parties enter into a contract. A "party" may be an individual, a group of people, or even an "artificial person" such as a corporation. The parties to a contract must have the legal capacity to enter into that contract. Persons who are deemed incompetent due to physical or mental illness lack capacity to enter into contracts. Minors, which in most states refers to persons under the age of 18, may enter into contracts. However, any contract involving a minor is voidable. When a contract involving a minor goes unfulfilled it may be affirmed or disaffirmed when the minor reaches maturity, or legally becomes an adult. Parties to a contract also must have the legal right to do what the contract promises; for example, one cannot sell what one does not own.

Mutual Assent

Traditionally, mutual assent has been described as a "meeting of the minds." This means that the parties involved in a contract must come to an agreement about the particulars of the transaction. Mutual assent is demonstrated by "offer" and "acceptance."

An offer is made when someone proposes an exchange of some sort. "I will sell you my guitar for $400" is an example of an offer. (Advertisements are usually not offers because they lack specific parties.) When the offer is accepted, the parties have mutually assented to enter into a contract.

Both offers and acceptances must be explicit in a contract. The statement "I might sell you my guitar for $400" would be considered an intent to negotiate rather than an actual offer. "Sure, I'll give you $300 for it" or "Yes, if you include the case and some strings" would not be an acceptance because the terms "accepted" are not the terms originally offered; such a statement would be deemed a counter-offer.

Consideration

Consideration must also be present for a legal contract to be formed. The essence of consideration is that a party receives some kind of benefit in return for his promise. Consideration may consist of money, goods, or a promise to do or not do something. The statement "I'll give you my guitar" is not a contract because the giver would receive no specified consideration in return.

When the mutual assent of legally capable parties—which includes an offer and an acceptance, accompanied by consideration—to a specific exchange or set of promises occur, a valid contract has been formed.

Interpretation of Contracts

When interpreting contracts courts tend to avoid questions regarding the intent of the parties involved in the contract and rely on the contract itself, particularly when the contract is in written form. Under the "plain meaning" rule, the words of a contract are to be read according to their plain, everyday meanings, with the exception of terms that have been specifically defined in the contract. To discourage the drafting of deliberately ambiguous language, any ambiguous terms in a contract is interpreted in a way that penalizes the party that drafts the document. In other words, if "party X" deceptively drafts a contract with ambiguous language such that the terms of the contract benefit the interests of "party X" over "party Y," the ambiguous language of the contract will deliberately be interpreted to benefit "party Y."

Contracts are frequently modified to reflect a change in preference by one of the parties or because unforeseen circumstances arise. For instance, a person may contract with a builder to have a house constructed but during the course of construction he or she may desire that more rooms be included, or the builder may be forced to change the agreed-upon completion date due to problems with the weather. Both the initial contract and the subsequent modifications may be in written or oral form. Contracts can be designed to accommodate future complications by including provisions that leave matters open. For example, a contract may leave certain matters to be resolved at a later date to reflect future conditions such as changes in prices or availability of goods. Such modifications may be in writing but are more often simple oral agreements.

Interpreting contracts is often difficult because of the complexity and subjectivity of the agreement. To simplify the process a set of standard procedures for interpretation are usually followed. First, the latest and most final agreement of the parties is considered to be the valid contract. Second, written agreements are given much more weight than oral agreements. In fact, in cases involving written contracts, oral evidence that either contradicts or supplements a written agreement, may not be introduced if the written contract is deemed final and complete. Oral evidence may be considered when a contract is final but incomplete, but only as an addition to the contract; oral evidence in contradiction of the basic terms of the contract is not allowed.

Enforcement of Contracts

When a party does not fulfill the promise made in a valid, enforceable contract at the time such fulfillment, or "performance," is due, the contract has been "breached." At this point legal remedy may be sought. (Legal remedy may be sought even before this time, if a party has indicated it will not honor its previously agreed upon promise.) Most commonly, some form of monetary compensation is sought for a breach of contract. In some cases, the contract may have stipulated the maximum amount of money recoverable in the event of breach. Specialized laws regulate damages for many types of contracts, such as sales of goods, real estate transactions, and employment contracts.

The most common form of compensation sought for a breach of contract is "compensatory damages," which is an estimation of the loss incurred or the gain prevented, by the other party's failure to honor the contract. Thus compensatory damages may include the

projected loss of profits by a business due to a breach of contract even if such a stipulation was not included in the original contract. "Punitive damages," which are intended to punish the party who has breached the contract rather than merely to compensate the aggrieved party, traditionally are not considered part of contract law. Punitive damages are usually awarded in situations involving illegal conduct. In some cases "specific performance" may be sought, which means that the specific promise of the contract must be fulfilled. This usually occurs in the instance of a contract for the sale of some unique commodity or service, rather than a replaceable item. The most common example of a "specific performance" case is land. Land is considered unique for obvious reasons, but other items such as rare or unusual antiques or artwork, might also be sought in a specific performance suit.

There are a number of valid defenses to a claim of breach of contract. As mentioned above, contracts involving minors are open to subsequent invalidation. "Mutual mistake" occurs when both parties to a contract have made an erroneous assumption about something material to the contract such as the condition of a piece of equipment or the size of a parcel of land. Contracts made under "duress," that is, under threat of force or some other consequence, may be subsequently voided. A contract may also be voided if a party has entered it under "undue influence." For example, if someone is given alcohol until his or her judgment is impaired, then enters into a contract, the contract may be justifiably voided.

A party may cite "unconscionability" to defend a breach of contract if the contract in question is so unjust that no reasonable person would have agreed to its conditions had he or she clearly understood its provisions. (This often occurs in contracts containing fine print or contracts that are laden with unintelligible jargon). "Misrepresentation" is also grounds for justifiable breach of contract. For example, when a certain material provision of a contract misleads one of the parties, such as claiming an automobile is in good condition when it is not, is a valid defense for breach of contract. However, a person who enters a contract is responsible for reading all of its terms and raising questions before signing it. Lastly, a party may cite "impossibility" to justify a breach of contract if intervening events have made it impossible to fulfill the contract.

Bibliography and Further Reading

Burnham, William. *Introduction to the Law and Legal System of the United States.* St. Paul, MN: West, 1995.

Calamari, John D. and Joseph M. Perillo. *The Law of Contracts.* 3rd ed. St. Paul, MN: West, 1987.

Murray, John Edward. *Murray on Contracts.* 3rd ed. Charlottesville, VA: Michie Co., 1990.

FLETCHER V. PECK

Legal Citation: 10 U.S. 87 (1810)

Appellant
Robert Fletcher

Appellee
John Peck

Appellant's Claim
Peck had purchased some land from the state of Georgia, which he later sold to Fletcher. Subsequently, the Georgia state legislature rescinded the original sale to Peck. Fletcher's claim was that he had bought the land in good faith and that Peck was guilty of breach of contract.

Chief Lawyers for Appellant
Luther Martin

Chief Lawyer for Appellee
John Quincy Adams, Robert Goodloe Harper, Joseph Story

Justices for the Court
Samuel Chase, William Cushing, William Johnson, Henry Brockholst Livingston, John Marshall (writing for the Court), Thomas Todd, Bushrod Washington

Justices Dissenting
None

Place
Washington, D.C.

Date of Decision
16 March 1810

Decision
That a legislature could repeal or modify the acts of a preceding legislature, but it could not invalidate a previously made contract.

Significance
This was the first time a state law was found invalid because it conflicted with the U.S. Constitution.

The story of *Fletcher v. Peck* is the story of bribery, corruption, and the sanctity of contracts. From one of the most scandalous episodes in Georgia state history came a major legal decision that ratified the importance both of contracts and of the federal government.

The story began in 1795, when the Georgia state legislature sold huge portions of its western lands, known as the Yazoo lands. Eventually, this area became the states of Alabama and Mississippi. Meanwhile, the 30 million acres were sold by the state of Georgia for the bargain price of $500,000, or only one-and-a-half cents per acre. Even in 1810, that price was ridiculously low.

Land Grabs and Corrupt Legislators

Virtually every member of the state legislature had been bribed by the land companies to whom the land was sold. As a result, all but one member of the legislature voted in favor of the sale. Moreover, many legislators were financially involved in the project, so when the lands were resold to third parties, they got a share of the profits.

Not surprisingly, the public was outraged at this massive example of corruption. The Act of 1795, which the legislature had passed to ratify the sale, was publicly burned and all evidence of its passage was supposedly erased from public records. Voters threw out the old legislators and elected new ones. The new legislature tried to regain the lands, offering to refund the purchase price to the land companies involved. Not surprisingly, the companies wanted to hold on to their bargains and refused to return the land.

Innocent Third Parties

Meanwhile, the land companies were re-selling the bargain lands to people and companies who had not been involved in the original scandal. New legal questions arose regarding the status of these new owners and whether or not they were entitled to hold on to the lands which they had bought in good faith. It was a question of whether the sale of the land was tainted to the extent that these new owners were not actually owners at all.

Ex Post Facto Law

Ex post facto law literally means "law from after the fact." Ex post facto law refers to a law that would include, as a criminal act, all violations of a law committed before the law was established. In other words, an ex post facto law would apply retroactively to citizens who committed an act before it was considered a crime. Ex post facto laws are considered unfair in most societies and are prohibited in the United States under Article I, Section 10 of the Constitution. Ex post facto laws should not be confused with retroactive laws which apply to civil law.

Only criminal legislation, not civil legislation, is affected by the constitutional prohibition of ex post facto laws.

In order for a law to be considered a violation of the prohibition, it must damage the offender in some way. For example, a law that makes parole requirements more restrictive for a certain crime cannot be applied to individuals who committed the crime before the law was enacted. The use of ex post facto laws to prosecute former Nazis for war crimes, in particular the crime of "aggressive war," generated considerable debate over whether retroactive law could be applied to criminal behavior.

Source(s): *Baltimore Law Review*, Vol. 21, 1992.

One of these new owners was Robert Fletcher, a citizen of New Hampshire. He had bought some 15,000 acres of Yazoo land for $3,000. The man who sold it to him, Massachusetts citizen John Peck, had put a covenant in the deed, assuring Fletcher that:

> [T]he title to the premises as conveyed by the state of Georgia, and finally vested in the said Peck, has been in no way constitutionally or legally impaired by virtue of any subsequent act of any subsequent legislature of the . . . state of Georgia.

In other words, Peck had promised Fletcher that even though the Georgia state legislature had rescinded the terms of the original sale, Peck still had the right to sell the land to Fletcher.

Fletcher was not entirely comfortable with this arrangement. It seemed to him that the Georgia legislature was likely to demand the return of the land. He was angry that Peck had taken money from him for land that he might have to return. As a result, he sued Peck for breach of contract in an attempt to recover the money that he had paid.

Contracts and the Constitution

When the case made it to the Supreme Court 25 years later, the United States was torn between two competing political philosophies. One was known as federalism, which maintained that the federal government was more important than any state government and that one of the most important functions of any gov-

---

Marvin Mandel Trial

Maryland Governor Marvin Mandel's trial was a national scandal, exposing massive political corruption at the highest level of state government. The reversal of Mandel's conviction signaled a limit on the ability to attack state crimes through federal statutes.

When a group of businessmen and investors purchased the Marlboro Race Track in Prince George's County, Maryland, in December of 1971, they approached Mandel for help. They wanted to increase the number of racing days that the track could operate in one year and acquire interests in other Maryland race tracks. In exchange for his assistance Mandel received cash, valuables, and interest in a waterfront development from the investors.

On 21 August 1977, the jury found Mandel guilty of federal mail fraud and racketeering. Mandel went to prison and served 19 months before his sentenced was commuted.

On 12 November 1987, Judge Frederic N. Smalkin of the U.S. District Court of Maryland, overturned Mandel's conviction. Smalkin did not deny the strong evidence of bribery and dishonesty presented at Mandel's trial. However, he insisted that the prosecutors had stretched their interpretation of federal mail fraud and racketeering laws in order to prosecute Mandel for what were, in effect, state crimes.

Source(s): Knappman, Edward W., ed. *Great American Trials*. Detroit, MI: Visible Ink Press, 1994.

---

ernment was to protect the sanctity of property. The other major philosophy of the time was known as republicanism. This philosophy focused on democracy—the rights of every individual—rather than on property, and on states' rights rather than federal sovereignty.

When *Fletcher v. Peck* was heard by the Court, it was embodied in the crux of this controversy. The question of which aspect of the case should be given primacy became a pivotal issue: the state legislature's wish to rescind the land deal, or the property rights of the people who had bought the land.

The Supreme Court decision was a major step in establishing the sanctity of both contracts and the U.S. Constitution. In an apparently unanimous decision written by Chief Justice Marshall, the Court made three major points:

(1) The original land grant made by the Georgia state legislature was, in effect, a contract.

(2) The U.S. Constitution protects the sanctity of contracts. Indeed, Article I, Section 10, Clause 3 of the Constitution provides that "No State shall . . . pass any . . . law impairing the obligation of contracts . . ."

(3) Therefore, the state of Georgia was not legally able to rescind the contract it had entered into when it had granted the Yazoo lands to the original companies—even if bribery and corruption had gone into the making of the contract.

Thus, the Court's decision upheld the two basic tenets of federalism: the supremacy of the federal government over the state governments, and the sanctity of private property. After all, wrote Chief Justice Marshall, there must be some limit to what government could do. And, "where are [these limits] to be found, if the property of an individual, fairly and honestly acquired, may be seized without compensation?"

Related Cases

Dartmouth College v. Woodward, 4 Wheat. 519 (1819).
Sturges v. Crowninshield, 4 Wheat. 122 (1819).
Charles River Bridge v. Warren Bridge, 11 Pet. 420 (1837).
Dodge v. Woolsey, 18 How. 331 (1856).

Bibliography and Further Reading

Epstein, Lee, and Thomas G. Walker. *Constitutional Law for a Changing America: Institutional Powers and Constraints,* 3rd ed. Washington DC: Congressional Quarterly, 1998.

Johnson, John W. *Historic U.S. Court Cases, 1690-1990: An Encyclopedia.* New York: Garland Publishing, 1992.

Kauper, Paul G. *Constitutional Law: Cases and Materials.* Boston: Little, Brown, 1972.

McClellan, James. *Joseph Story and the American Constitution.* Norman, OK: University of Oklahoma Press, 1971.

Mitchell, Broadus, and Louise Pearson Mitchell. *A Biography of the Constitution of the United States,* 2nd edition. New York: Oxford University Press, 1964, 1975.

Saye, Albert B. *American Constitutional Law.* St. Paul, MN: West, 1979.

TRUSTEES OF DARTMOUTH COLLEGE v. WOODWARD

Legal Citation: 17 U.S. 518 (1819)

Appellant
Dartmouth College

Appellee
State of New Hampshire

Appellant's Claim
That the action of the state of New Hampshire reconstituting the charter of Dartmouth College as Dartmouth University and appointing a new board of trustees was a violation of the constitutional protection against actions impairing contracts.

Chief Lawyer for Appellant
Daniel Webster

Chief Lawyers for Appellee
Joseph Hopkinson for old trustees; John Holmes and William Wirt, for State of New Hampshire

Justices for the Court
William Johnson, Henry Brockholst Livingston, John Marshall (writing for the Court), Joseph Story, Bushrod Washington

Justices Dissenting
Gabriel Duvall (Thomas Todd did not participate)

Place
Washington, D.C.

Date of Decision
12 March 1818

Decision
That the state could not alter the charter of a private educational institution as it was a contract.

Significance
The decision helped establish the principle that corporations, such as Dartmouth College, were protected from alteration by states for public reasons.

In 1769, Dartmouth College had received a charter from the King of England, establishing it as a college. Over the years, the state of New Hampshire had granted lands to the college, and the college had taken on the function of providing higher education in the state. On 27 June 1816, New Hampshire amended the charter of Dartmouth College, reconstituting it as Dartmouth University, with a new board of trustees, incorporating some of the older board, and establishing the power of the state to name future board members. William Woodward, the secretary-treasurer of the College, was reappointed as secretary-treasurer of the newly-chartered university.

In five separate lawsuits that were later combined into one, trustees of the original college sued the state of New Hampshire, claiming that under the U.S. Constitution the state had no authority to pass laws impairing the obligations of contracts. The original charter, they claimed, was such a contract.

Daniel Webster, arguing for the appellant, pointed out that to take property away from an institution is an act of forfeiture, and should be the action of the judiciary, not of the legislature. The charter which the King had issued was such that not even Parliament could have annulled it, and it was thus improper for the state of New Hampshire to believe that it could. The corporation established was a lay corporation, not a civil corporation, and therefore it did not belong to the public. Rather, it belonged to the trustees and to those they appointed to succeed them.

John Holmes, arguing for the state of New Hampshire, pointed out that the charter was not to a private institution, but was a grant of a public nature.

Chief Justice Marshall, who wrote the opinion of the court, noted that states did have the power to change contracts. No one doubted that states had the power, for example, to allow for divorce, which is the breaking of marriage contracts. However, in the case of corporate charters, Chief Justice Marshall suggested that if a charter was to a public corporation, the state would have the power to alter such a charter. But if a charter was to a private corporation, then the federal government had an obligation under the Constitution to pro-

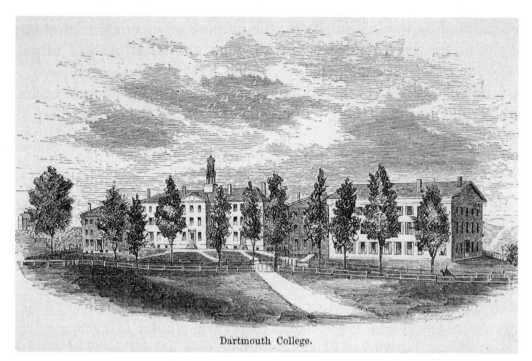

Dartmouth College.

An engraving of Dartmouth College. © Archive Photos.

tect the corporation from the state. A corporation, Chief Justice Marshall pointed out, is an artificial being—immortal, but it may act as an individual. However, it does not have a political character, in that it cannot vote or run for office. Ultimately, he held that the charter to the college was a contract in the letter and spirit of the Constitution and it could not be violated or impaired without violation of the Constitution. The ruling of the state court was reversed.

One of the consequences of the case was that in the future, when states chartered colleges or other institutions of a semi-public nature, the states reserved in the chartering legislation the right to amend the charter in later years. In later years, the distinction between a civil institution employed in the administration of the government and a teaching institution became increasingly blurred, and the sharp distinction once made by Chief Justice Marshall has become increasingly hard to apply.

Related Cases
Allen v. McKean, 1 F.Cas. 489 (C.C.D.Me 1833).
Charles River Bridge v. Warren Bridge, 36 U.S. 420 (1837).

Bibliography and Further Reading
Epstein, Lee, and Thomas G. Walker. *Constitutional Law for a Changing America: Institutional Powers and Constraints,* 3rd ed. Washington DC: Congressional Quarterly, 1998.

Friendly, Henry J. *The Dartmouth College Case and the Public-Private Penumbra.* Austin: The University of Texas at Austin, 1971.

Johnson, John W. *Historic U.S. Court Cases, 1690–1990: An Encyclopedia.* New York: Garland Publishing, 1992.

Shirley, John M. *The Dartmouth College Case and the Supreme Court of the United States.* New York: Da Capo Press, 1971.

PROPRIETORS OF THE CHARLES RIVER BRIDGE V. THE PROPRIETORS OF THE WARREN BRIDGE

Legal Citation: 36 U.S. 420 (1837)

Appellant
The proprietors of the Charles River Bridge

Appellee
The proprietors of the Warren Bridge

Appellant's Claim
That it held an exclusive charter to operate a toll bridge, and the state of Massachusetts violated the Contract Clause of the Constitution by granting a charter to another bridge company.

Chief Lawyers for Appellant
Warren Dutton, Daniel Webster

Chief Lawyers for Appellee
Simon Greenleaf, John Davis

Justices for the Court
Henry Baldwin, Philip Pendleton Barbour, Roger Brooke Taney (writing for the Court), James Moore Wayne

Justices Dissenting
John McLean, Joseph Story, Smith Thomson (John Catron and John McKinley not yet appointed)

Place
Washington, D.C.

Date of Decision
12 February 1837

Decision
Denied appellant's claim.

Significance
In the past, the Court had usually defined the Contract Clause broadly, defending the interests of corporations. In *Charles River Bridge*, however, the Court ruled that a state charter did not grant a company any implicit rights; the exact terms of the contract had to be stated. In a larger sense, the Court also recognized that at times a state's power to promote the public welfare outweighed the rights of a corporation.

Article I, section 10 of the Constitution says, in part, that no state shall pass any law "impairing the obligations of contracts." Although perhaps not one of the best-known constitutional passages among most Americans, the Contract Clause entered into more Supreme Court decisions during the nineteenth century than any other part of the Constitution.

Economic arrangements bound by contract and then altered or revoked by the states frequently found their way to the High Court. During the tenure of Chief Justice Marshall, the Court tended to side with the interest of corporations over the states. Marshall defined the Contract Clause broadly, and he wrote a series of important decisions reflecting that interpretation. In *Fletcher v. Peck* (1810), Marshall ruled a state could not revoke a land grant—even if there was fraud involved. Later, Marshall said a charter given to a corporation was the same as a contract and received protection under the Contract Clause, so the state of New Hampshire could not alter a charter granted to Dartmouth College (*Dartmouth College v. Woodward* [1819]).

By 1837, however, Chief Justice Marshall had passed away, and a new man held his position. Roger Taney had been appointed by Andrew Jackson in 1835, and he shared some of Jackson's Democratic politics, including an affinity for states' rights. In one of the first decisions written by Taney, he showed the Court would now take a different approach to the Contract Clause and the economic assumptions that guided Marshall's interpretation of it.

Two Bridges in Boston

The case of *Proprietors of the Charles River Bridge v. the Proprietors of the Warren Bridge* pitted two Boston companies in a clash over tolls. Each firm owned a bridge spanning Boston's Charles River into Charlestown. The Charles River Bridge Company had received a charter in 1785 to operate its toll bridge. Over the years, the bridge had proved lucrative for its owners, which included, at different times, John Hancock and Harvard University. But by the 1820s, many Bostonians resented paying the toll, and they convinced the state to erect a free bridge over the Charles River. In 1828, Massachusetts granted a charter for this bridge, the Warren

Bridge. Its operators would collect a toll for six years, to pay off building expenses, then open the bridge for free crossings.

The proprietors of the Charles River Bridge were understandably upset. Without its bridge monopoly, the company would lose revenue from the tolls. The company sued the proprietors of the Warren Bridge, seeking an injunction to stop construction of the new bridge. The Charles River Bridge Company argued that the state had violated the charter and thus the Contract Clause of the Constitution. The Massachusetts courts denied the injunction, and in 1831, the Supreme Court took up the case.

At that time, Chief Justice Marshall, with his sympathy toward the Contract Clause, was still on the bench. The Charles River Bridge Company hired Daniel Webster, who had successfully argued and won the *Dartmouth* case before Marshall a dozen years earlier. Now a U.S. senator from Massachusetts, Webster was one of the most prominent lawyers in the country. Fate, however, took away any advantage the appellants might have had entering their appeal. As various justices—including Marshall—fell ill or died, the case was continually postponed. It took six years before *Charles River* was finally decided.

Taney's Defense of "Happiness and Well Being"

Charles River was reargued 19-26 January 1837, with just seven justices seated. By then, the Warren Bridge was open for free, and the Charles River Bridge was out of business. But the issues raised by the case were still important. Webster argued that the original charter had implied an exclusive right for his client to control the bridge traffic between Boston and Charlestown. The Court voted 4-3 to reject this claim.

Chief Justice Taney dismissed Webster's argument of any implied powers granted by the 1785 charter, and wrote that the government had a legitimate interest in guaranteeing the public had convenient means of transportation. The people, through its elected officials, granted the charter, and "in grants by the public, nothing passes by implication." The state was obliged to uphold the terms outlined in the charter, but the company could not infer any privileges not specifically granted. The charter said nothing about competing bridges.

Taney's decision reflected his belief in states' rights and the need, at times, to limit property rights or business interests. He wrote:

. . . the object and end of all government is to promote the happiness and prosperity of the community by which it is established, and it can never be assumed that the government intended to diminish its power of accomplishing the end for which it was created . . . While the rights of private property are sacredly guarded, we must not forget the that the community also have rights, and that the happiness and well being of every citizen depends on their faithful preservation.

The three dissenting justices—McLean, Story, and Thompson—each wrote separate opinions. Story's is the most often cited. He did see in the grant an exclusive right for the Charles River Company to collect tolls over the river. He also thought courts should, in general, broadly interpret a company's rights as granted by a public contract. Story said the majority's decision would send a frightening signal to the grantee of a public charter; once the company was successful, the state could "overthrow its rights and . . . take away its profits."

Today, most legal scholars accept Taney's decision, and many of his later opinions supporting property and business interests. But in *Charles River,* says legal historian James Ely, Taney saw that "existing property rights could sometimes be destroyed to make room for innovations and improvements."

Related Cases
Fletcher v. Peck, 10 U.S. 87 (1810).
Dartmouth College v. Woodward, 17 U.S. 518 (1819).

Bibliography and Further Reading
Elliott, Stephen P., ed. *A Reference Guide to the U.S. Supreme Court.* New York: Facts on File Publications, 1986.

Epstein, Lee, and Thomas G. Walker. *Constitutional Law for a Changing America: Institutional Powers and Constraints,* 3rd ed. Washington DC: Congressional Quarterly, 1998.

Hall, Kermit L., ed. *The Oxford Companion to the Supreme Court of the United States.* New York: Oxford Press, 1992.

Johnson, John W. *Historic U.S. Court Cases, 1690–1990: An Encyclopedia.* New York: Garland Publishing, 1992.

Witt, Elder, ed. *The Supreme Court A to Z.* Washington, DC: Congressional Quarterly, Inc., 1993.

Young, James V. *Landmark Constitutional Law Decisions.* Lanham, Maryland: University Press of America, 1993.

TEXAS V. WHITE

Legal Citation: 74 U.S. 700 (1869)

Appellant
State of Texas

Appellees
George W. White, John Chiles, et al.

Appellant's Claim
That securities sold to the appellees by a Confederate military board were the property of the state of Texas and should be returned.

Chief Lawyers for Appellant
R. T. Merrick, George W. Pascal

Chief Lawyers for Appellees
P. Phillips, J. M. Carlisle, S. S. Cox, J. W. Moore

Justices for the Court
Salmon Portland Chase (writing for the Court), Nathan Clifford, David Davis, Stephen Johnson Field, Samuel Nelson

Justices Dissenting
Robert Cooper Grier, Samuel Freeman Miller, Noah Haynes Swayne (James M. Wayne had died in office and had not been replaced)

Place
Washington, D.C.

Date of Decision
12 April 1869

Decision
In favor of the state of Texas.

Significance
By declaring that the Confederate states had never legally been severed from the United States, the Court provided a legal basis for Reconstruction to proceed.

The Missing Bonds

In the years immediately following the Civil War, debate was furious over what rights the states of the former Confederacy would retain or be forced to forfeit before they were reintegrated into the Union. The U.S. Supreme Court settled a fundamental part of this issue based on the result of a lawsuit over the unlikely matter of a bond transfer.

On 1 January 1851, the U.S. government paid the state of Texas $5,000,000 in federal bonds to settle boundary claims. Most of the bonds, which were redeemable in 15 years, were sold by the Texas state government to investors. However, some of the securities were channeled into the state treasury as a school fund. These bonds were still in the treasury when Texas seceded from the Union on 4 March 1861 and joined the Confederacy.

After the members of the sitting state government of Texas either resigned or were ejected from office, the new Confederate Texas legislature passed a bill requiring any securities in the treasury to be sold to pay for munitions. A military board entrusted with this duty sold and delivered 135 bonds to the investment firm of White & Chiles on 15 March 1865. Seventy-six more bonds were transferred to English bankers in return for a delivery of cotton cards and medical supplies to be handled by White & Chiles.

At the outbreak of the Civil War, the U.S. Treasury had been warned that the Texas military board might sell the securities. The bonds were easily identifiable, since each bore a number and was to be endorsed by the governor of Texas. Ultimately, the U.S. Treasury did not have to decide whether or not to honor most of the bonds sold by the rebel military board. In October of 1865, four months after the Civil War ended, an agent of the state of Texas, G. W. Paschal, told the *New York Herald* that the bond transfer was a conspiracy between the Confederate Texas government and White & Chiles. Judge Paschal, who had remained faithful to the Union, warned the public that he considered the transaction to be illegal and would ask the U.S. Treasury to refrain from making any payments on the bonds. Paschal announced through the press that the bonds were still the property of the state of Texas.

Justice Salmon Portland Chase. © The Library of Congress.

By that time, a re-formed non-Confederate Texas government had passed a law authorizing the state's governor to recover the sold securities. The new Texas government filed suit for recovery of the bonds, claiming that they had been seized by persons hostile to the United States, who had acted in concert with White & Chiles with the aim of overthrowing the federal government. The suit also noted that the bonds were overdue at the time of transfer and had never been endorsed by any governor of Texas. The suit asked for an injunction preventing White & Chiles and the other purchasers from receiving any payment from the U.S. government so that the bonds might be returned to Texas.

The Texas claim presented a problem that was both legal and political, because secession had left the state's relation to the Union without a clear definition. In the Reconstruction Acts passed by the U.S. Congress in March of 1867, Texas was no longer considered to be a state. Responding to the lawsuit, George White and John Chiles—who had already sold the bonds—argued that Texas had forfeited its statehood and was in no legal position to sue anyone. They believed that the bonds were negotiable on their face value. So did the purchasers named in the suit, who claimed under oath that they had no idea Texas had a claim against the bonds when they were purchased.

Political Fact or Legal Fiction?

The case was brought before the U.S. Supreme Court on 5 February 1869 and was sufficiently complicated to take three days to argue. Nevertheless, the Court returned its decision relatively quickly on 12 April. By a 5-3 vote, the Court returned jurisdiction over the bonds to the state of Texas.

The decision hinged on the nature of American statehood. Chief Justice Chase noted that a state was comprised of a combination of people, territory, and government. Of these, the people or "political community" were the primary component, not a government. By the logic of the Court's majority, Texas had "entered into an indissoluble relation" upon assuming statehood in 1845. "The act which consummated her admission into the Union was something more than a compact; it was the incorporation of a new member into the political body," wrote Justice Chase. "And it was final. The union between Texas and the other States was as complete, as perpetual, and as indissoluble as the union between the original States."

The Court considered the state's secession from the Union to be inconsistent with the constitutional concept of "a perpetual Union," which had been agreed to by Texans upon assuming their statehood. All acts of the Confederate Texas legislature—including the disputed bond sale—were "utterly without operation in law." Despite the Civil War, the Court found that Texans had never ceased being American citizens. To decide otherwise, Chase wrote, would be to conclude that the war had not been fought to save the Union, but had been instead a war of conquest, waged against "foreigners."

The majority's conclusion that Texas had continued to be a state, in spite of the war, brought a pointed dissent from Justices Grier, Swayne, and Freeman. Justice Grier's written opinion noted that the Supreme Court had jurisdiction only in cases involving actual states and rejected the idea that Texas had remained a part of the Union. During its eight years as a "rebel state," Grier noted, Texas was not represented in the U.S. Congress, had not participated in the national presidential election, and was presently under the military rule of the federal government. "Politically, Texas is not a State in this Union," wrote Grier, insisting that the case should be decided on the basis of "political fact," not upon "a legal fiction."

The Court's decision that the Constitution created "an indestructible Union, composed of indestructible States" was not received well by Northern Radical politicians intent on punishing the defeated Confederate states. The decision was equally unwelcome among Southern Democrats, who hoped that the defeated states would be reintegrated into the Union with their prewar governmental powers intact. While the Court's decision affirmed the compact between states and the federal government, it also acknowledged the right of the U.S. Congress to control how Reconstruction would proceed. In this sense, the decision strengthened the hand of Republican Reconstructionists, who presided over the healing of a troubled but indivisible nation which, in theory at least, had never been torn asunder.

Related Cases
Luther v. Borden, 48 U.S. 1 (1849).
National League of Cities v. Usery, 426 U.S. 833 (1976).

Bibliography and Further Reading
Hall, Kermit. L., ed. *The Oxford Companion To The Supreme Court of the United States.* New York: Oxford University Press, 1992.

Johnson, John W., ed. *Historic U.S. Court Cases, 1690-1990: An Encyclopedia.* New York: Garland Publishing, 1992.

Keller, Morton. *Affairs of State: Public Life In Nineteenth Century America.* Cambridge: Belknap Press, 1977.

Kurland, Phillip B., and Gerhard Casper, eds. *Landmark Briefs and Arguments of the Supreme Court of the United States,* Vol. 5. Arlington: University Publications of America, 1975.

Warren, Charles. *The Supreme Court in United States History.* Boston: Little, Brown & Co., 1926.

ALLGEYER V. LOUISIANA

Legal Citation: 165 U.S. 578 (1897)

Petitioner
E. Allgeyer & Co.

Respondent
State of Louisiana

Petitioner's Claim
That states do not have the right to pass legislation that deprives citizens of their Fourteenth Amendment rights to due process and equal protection.

Chief Lawyer for Petitioner
Branch K. Miller

Chief Lawyer for Respondent
M. J. Cunningham

Justices for the Court
David Josiah Brewer, Henry Billings Brown, William Rufus Day, Melville Weston Fuller, Horace Gray, John Marshall Harlan I, Rufus Wheeler Peckham (writing for the Court), George Shiras, Jr., Edward Douglass White

Justices Dissenting
None

Place
Washington, D.C

Date of Decision
1 March 1897

Decision
Found in favor of Allgeyer and reversed a lower court ruling by finding that due process guarantees protect Allgeyer's right to purchase insurance from Atlantic Mutual of New York.

Significance
The ruling established that states cannot enact laws depriving citizens of their Fourteenth Amendment due process and equal protection rights. Expanding the interpretation of "liberty," the Court held that the term includes the right to enter into any contracts considered proper, necessary, and essential among other rights not identified before. The decision greatly expanded the concept of substantive due process and restricted state powers to regulate business activities for the next 40 years.

Ratification of the Fourteenth Amendment in 1868 guaranteed due process protection from state laws. The amendment reads in part that no state "shall . . . deprive any person of life, liberty, or property without due process of law." The meaning of "liberty" and "property" in the Due Process Clause became the subject of later Supreme Court rulings. Under due process, the Court generally assessed whether procedures required by state laws were reasonable and not arbitrary. This line of inquiry focused solely on the way laws were applied, not so much the subject of the laws themselves. However, the intent of state laws began to attract attention as well, as demonstrated in *Butchers' Union Co. v. Crescent City Co.* (1884). In that case, the Court ruled that a person had liberty to freely choose an occupation.

The Regulation of Business

Regarding business activities, before the latter part of the nineteenth century the Supreme Court commonly used the Constitution's Commerce Clause or Contracts Clause to overrule what it determined arbitrary and unreasonable interference with the freedom to establish business contracts. However, usually the federal government allowed states to rather freely regulate commerce within their borders. In the 1890s, as trade greatly expanded nationally and internationally, states increasingly passed laws designed to protect their citizens and businesses. The Louisiana legislature passed Act No. 66 of 1894 prohibiting individuals and corporations from contracting with marine insurance companies who did not conform with Louisiana law. The penalty for disobeying the law was a fine of $1000 for each offense paid to charity.

E. Allgeyer & Co., located in New Orleans, was a cotton exporter who sold to companies in Great Britain and greater Europe. They shipped the sold cotton from the port of New Orleans to foreign ports. On 27 October 1894, Allgeyer mailed an insurance certificate in New Orleans to Atlantic Mutual Insurance Company of New York for the purchase of $200,000 of insurance. The Atlantic Marine had no agent or place of business in the state of Louisiana at the time. The letter notified Atlantic Mutual that 100 bales of cotton

Rufus Wheeler Peckham

Rufus Wheeler Peckham (1838-1909) served on New York's supreme court and court of appeals before being nominated to the Supreme Court by Grover Cleveland in 1895. Peckham is considered to be one of most level-headed justices to have served on the Supreme Court, often handing down opinions contrary to his own political persuasion. Many of his opinions contributed to the development of the political principles that are the foundation for American government. Some of the cases in which Peckham handed down influential opinions include: *United States v. Trans-Missouri Freight Association; Hopkins v. United States; Addyston Pipe and Steel Company v. United States;* and *Maxwell v. Dow.*

Ironically, Peckham is best known for an opinion he handed down which, in retrospect, was widely consid-

ered a misinterpretation of the Fourteenth Amendment. Peckham wrote the majority opinion for *Lochner v. New York* (1905), a case which challenged the ten-hour work day for laborers. Peckham's decision allowed individuals to make arrangements to work beyond the ten hours per day permitted by law. Justice Oliver Wendell Holmes took issue with the decision, in a now famous dissenting opinion, arguing that the Fourteenth Amendment was not designed to promote radical individualism at the expense of social and economic justice.

Source(s): *Webster's American Biographies,* Springfield, MA: G. & C. Merriam Co., 1974.

had been shipped to foreign ports. In reaction, the state of Louisiana filed suit against Allgeyer in December of 1894 claiming that they violated Act No. 66. The state sought a $3000 fine for three alleged violations of the act.

Consistent with previous case law on the subject, Allgeyer responded that Act No. 66 was unconstitutional by depriving them of property without due process of law. In addition, they were not given equal protection of the laws in violation of the constitutions of both Louisiana and the United States. Allgeyer asserted that since its business partner, Atlantic Mutual, was a New York corporation with an office in the state of New York, the insurance contract was in the state of New York, not Louisiana. In fact, the initial open contract was signed in New York City. Allgeyer further argued that the U.S. Constitution protected the general right to execute contracts in other states.

The district court held that a state can impose conditions on companies operating businesses within its borders. Companies must comply with those conditions or violate the law. In addition, Article 236 of the Louisiana Constitution prohibited out-of-state insurance companies from conducting business in the state unless they have a place of business and an authorized agent in the state. Because the Allgeyer contract was considered legal in New York, it was in Louisiana as well. The moment the letter was mailed while still in New Orleans the cotton was legally insured. In addition, the court observed that at the time of mailing the contract, the 100 bales of cotton were in the state of Louisiana. To not have violated the law, New York citizens conducting business in another state must pay a license and employ an authorized agent

in that state. However, the court asserted the case was not really about the contract itself, but the constitutional rights of Louisiana's citizens. Therefore, the trial court rejected Louisiana's argument, found Act No. 66 an unconstitutional restriction, and ruled in favor of Allgeyer.

Louisiana appealed the case to the state supreme court, which reversed the decision and ruled in favor of the state. The court based its opinion on the fact that Allgeyer, while in the state of Louisiana, insured cotton located in the state with an out-of-state insurance company. Since the cotton was insured the instant Allgeyer mailed the letter, Act No. 66 applied.

The Louisiana Supreme Court, in addressing the broader issue of liberty, wrote,

> There is in the statute an apparent interference with the liberty of defendants in restricting their rights to place insurance on property of their own whenever and in what company they desired, but in exercising this liberty they would interfere with the policy of the state that forbids insurance companies which have not complied with the laws of the state from doing business within its limits. Individual liberty of action must give way to the greater right of the collective people in the assertion of well-defined policy, designed and intended for the general welfare.

The state supreme court found Allgeyer guilty of one violation of Act No. 66 and assessed a fine of $1,000. Allgeyer appealed to the U.S. Supreme Court, who agreed to hear its case.

Liberty to Contract

By a unanimous decision, the Court reversed the Louisiana Supreme Court's decision and ruled Act No. 66 unconstitutional. With various rulings already addressing the Fourteenth Amendment's meaning of liberty, Justice Peckham, writing for the Court, extended the meaning of liberty to include

> the right of the citizen to be free in the enjoyment of all his faculties; to be free to use them in all lawful ways; to live and work where he will; to earn his livelihood by any lawful calling; to pursue any livelihood or avocation; and for that purpose to enter into all contracts which may be proper, necessary, and essential.

Peckham relied on a precedent recently set in *Hooper v. State of California* (1895). *Hooper* recognized that states had legal authority to prohibit out-of-state insurance companies from doing business within their borders. It also held that citizens had rights under the Fourteenth Amendment to contract with anyone they chose for insurance. States could not deprive a citizen that right to contract. The key difference between *Hooper* and Allgeyer's situation was that a contract had been signed in the state of California with a company not licensed to do business in that state. Peckham found that Allgeyer had only sent a notification in the mail to Atlantic Mutual. The actual business transaction of signing a open contract had occurred earlier in New York. As written, Peckham observed that Allgeyer did violate Louisiana's Act No. 66. However, the Louisiana law inappropriately interfered with Allgeyer's liberty by restricting their right to purchase insurance for property with whom they chose. Neither Allgeyer nor Atlantic Mutual were in violation of the Louisiana constitution since Atlantic Mutual was not conducting business in the state.

Peckham, in discussing the Fourteenth Amendment, explained,

> The 'liberty' mentioned in that amendment means, not only the right of the citizen to be free from the mere physical restraint of his person, as by incarceration, but the term is deemed to embrace the right of the citizen to be free in the enjoyment of all his faculties; to be free to use them in all lawful ways; to live and work where he will; to earn his livelihood by any lawful calling; to pursue any livelihood or avocation; and for that purpose to enter into all contracts which may be proper, necessary, and essential to his carrying out to a successful conclusion the purposes above mentioned.

Peckham struck down Act No. 66 as unconstitutional and concluded Allgeyer was free to contract with Atlantic Mutual.

Impact

The *Allgeyer* decision marked a decrease in state powers and increased federal oversight over state activities. For the first time, the Court expanded the view of "liberty" by extending the Due Process Clause to protect businesses against state regulation. The clause, originally intended following the Civil War to protect personal rights, replaced the Commerce Clause as key in protecting commercial activity. Specifically, *Allgeyer* recognized the right to make contracts free of state regulation. Such an application of substantive due process concepts protected businesses from governmental intrusion into certain economic and property interests. The decision was further reinforced in *Lochner v. New York* (1905), striking down a New York state law setting maximum hours for bakers.

Allgeyer began a 40-year period noted for striking down as "arbitrary" various forms of state economic legislation. This trend continued until the New Deal era of the 1930s when the Court changed course again and more freely recognized reforms and regulations passed by states during the economic recovery from the Great Depression of 1929. Substantive due process later became applied to personal civil rights freedoms in the 1960s. By the 1990s, rights to privacy, marriage, and to bear children, though not mentioned in the first ten amendments to the Constitution, were identified by the courts as fundamental freedoms. The period of more limited state powers continued until the 1990s, when a swing back to strengthening states' rights occurred.

Related Cases

Butchers' Union Co. v. Crescent City Co., 111 U.S. 746 (1884).
Hooper v. State of California, 155 U.S. 648 (1895).
Lochner v. New York, 198 U.S. 45 (1905).

Bibliography and Further Reading

Butler, Henry N., and Larry E. Ribstein. *The Corporation and the Constitution.* Washington, DC: AEI Press, 1994.

Gillman, Howard. *The Constitution Besieged: The Rise and Demise of Lochner Era Police Powers Jurisprudence.* Durham, NC: Duke University Press, 1993.

Keynes, Edward. *Liberty, Property, and Privacy: Toward a Jurisprudence of Substantive Due Process.* University Park, PA: Pennsylvania State University Press, 1996.

Paul, Ellen F., and Howard Dickman, eds. *Liberty, Property, and the Future of Constitutional Development.* Albany: State University of New York Press, 1990.

ADAIR V. UNITED STATES

Legal Citation: 208 U.S. 161 (1908)

In 1894, a violent strike broke out at the Pullman railroad yards in Chicago. When unrest spread to 27 other states, President Grover Cleveland used the army to crush the strike. In direct response to the Pullman strike, Congress passed the 1898 Erdman Act to help secure labor peace.

Erdman applied solely to railroads engaged in interstate commerce. The first sections provided for mediation, conciliation, and bidding arbitration in industrial disputes. The tenth section, the one challenged in *Adair*, prohibited certain antiunion activities. Specifically, railroads could not make employees promise not to join a union (the so-called "yellow dog" contract). This same section also prohibited railroads from firing employees because of their union activity.

In October of 1906, William Adair, an official of the Louisville and Nashville Railroad Company, fired O. B. Coppage solely because he belonged to the Order of Locomotive Firemen. When Adair was prosecuted and convicted, his attorneys appealed to the Supreme Court.

New Laws to Protect Workers' Rights

The Erdman Act was only one of numerous labor laws brought before the High Court from the 1880s. As the United States became more industrialized, both Congress and individual states passed laws regulating the conditions of workers. These laws limited hours of work, prohibited child labor, and improved the conditions of working women. They promoted safety and legalized worker's compensation for workplace injuries. They also outlawed "yellow dog" contracts and required employers to pay wages in cash rather than in company script.

Taken together, these labor laws greatly increased the power of governments in new ways. Were they a legitimate expression of congressional and state authority? There were few precedents in the traditions of American (and British) common law.

Gradually, the Supreme Court developed guidelines which overturned some federal and state labor laws. Liberty of contract was protected as part of due process under the Fifth Amendment, which states that "No

Petitioner
William Adair

Respondent
United States

Petitioner's Claim
That Adair's conviction under the Erdman Act, which made it a crime to fire an employee for belonging to a labor union, should be reversed.

Chief Lawyers for Petitioner
Benjamin D. Warfield, Henry L. Stone

Chief Lawyers for Respondent
Charles Bonaparte, William R. Harr

Justices for the Court
David Josiah Brewer, William Rufus Day, Melville Weston Fuller, John Marshall Harlan I (writing for the Court), Rufus Wheeler Peckham, Edward Douglass White

Justices Dissenting
Oliver Wendell Holmes, Joseph McKenna (William Henry Moody did not participate)

Place
Washington, D.C.

Date of Decision
17 January 1908

Decision
The Court reversed the petitioner's conviction by the lower court; the Erdman Act was unconstitutional when it forbade firing an employee for belonging to a labor union.

Significance
The *Adair* decision strengthened the legal doctrines of liberty of contract and substantive due process, and it therefore limited the scope of federal and state regulation of working conditions.

person shall be . . . deprived of life, liberty, or property without due process of law." The Fourteenth Amendment incorporated the Fifth and protected due process rights against state laws.

State governments could abridge these rights, but only under specific conditions. Article I of the Constitution empowers Congress to "regulate commerce . . . among the several states." As for the states, they have a police power to protect public safety, health, and morals. However, for a law to be constitutional, it had to be directly connected to one of these legitimate goals: safety, health, or the regulation of interstate commerce. Governments could not act solely to redistribute power from business to organized labor.

The classic statement of freedom of contract came in *Lochner v. New York* (1905). In this case, the Court invalidated a state law limiting bakers to ten hours of work a day. There was no direct connection, the Court ruled, between safety and fewer hours of work. Thus, "[s]tatutes of the nature of that under review, limiting the hours in which grown and intelligent men may labor and earn their living, are mere meddlesome interferences with the rights of the individual."

The Right to Fire Is Absolute

Oral arguments in *Adair* were presented in October of 1907, and the Court issued its decision on 27 January 1908. Writing for the majority, Justice Harlan reversed Adair's conviction. Justices McKenna and Holmes issued separate dissents. Justice Moody, recently appointed and a former attorney general, disqualified himself.

Harlan's decision declared that the relevant section of the Erdman Act was unconstitutional. The law took away defendant Adair's liberty and property and thus was contrary to the Fifth Amendment. Throughout his decision, it should be noted, Harlan personalized the argument by focusing on Adair and not the railroad which employed him. Harlan did this deliberately to avoid having to consider whether a corporation is a "person" protected by the Due Process Clause.

Harlan directly related *Adair* to the 1905 *Lochner* decision. As in the earlier case, the Erdman law interfered with freedom of contract. An employer had the right to fire for any reason, just as an employee had the right to quit for any reason (which is the legal right justifying strikes). The law gives equal protection to the employer's liberty to fire and the employee's liberty to quit. The Fifth Amendment protects these rights

against actions by the federal government. The Fourteenth Amendment protects them against state governments.

Harlan did not turn liberty of contract into an absolute right. Under the Commerce Clause, Congress has broad authority to regulate and restrain contracts.

> Congress has a large discretion in the selection or choice of the means to be employed in the regulation of interstate commerce, and such discretion is not to be interfered with except where that which is done is in plain violation of the Constitution.

There is, however, simply no connection between membership in labor unions and the carrying on of interstate commerce. Labor unions seek to improve their members' conditions. This is "an object entirely legitimate and to be commended rather than condemned." However, a person:

> . . . will faithfully perform his duty, whether he be a member or not a member of a labor organization . . . It is the employee as a man and not as a member of a labor organization who labors in the service of an interstate carrier.

Harlan's opinion in *Adair* united and spoke for the Court. For the next 30 years, the justices used the legal doctrines of liberty of contract and substantive due process to overturn a variety of regulatory laws. The Court did not fully and finally abandon these doctrines until the 1930s in response to the Great Depression and President Franklin D. Roosevelt's New Deal.

Related Cases

Lochner v. New York, 198 U.S. 45 (1905).
Phelps Dodge Corp. v. N.L.R.B., 313 U.S. 177 (1941)
Hotel and Restaurant Employees and Bartenders Intern. Union Local 54 v. Danziger, 709 F.2d 815 (1983).

Bibliography and Further Reading

Fiss, Owen. *History of the Supreme Court of the United States. Volume VIII: Troubled Beginnings of the Modern State.* New York: Macmillan, 1993.

Kens, Paul. *Judicial Power and Reform Politics: The Anatomy of Lochner v. New York.* Lawrence: University Press of Kansas, 1990.

Semonche, John E. *Charting the Future: The Supreme Court Responds to a Changing Society, 1890-1920.* Westport, CT: Greenwood, 1978.

BAILEY V. ALABAMA

Legal Citation: 219 U.S. 219 (1911)
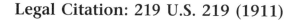

Plaintiff
Alonzo Bailey

Defendant
State of Alabama

Plaintiff Claim
Alabama's peonage law was unconstitutional because the Thirteenth Amendment provided protection against involuntary servitude. To compel servitude in liquidation of a debt restricted personal rights; involuntary servitude applied in situations other than slavery.

Chief Lawyers for Plaintiff
Edward S. Watts, Fred S. Ball, Daniel W. Troy

Chief Defense Lawyers
Alexander M. Garber, Thomas W. Martin

Justices for the Court
William Rufus Day, John Marshall Harlan I, Charles Evans Hughes (writing for the Court), Joseph McKenna, William Henry Moody, Edward Douglass White

Justices Dissenting
Oliver Wendell Holmes, Horace Harmon Lurton (Willis Van Devanter not yet appointed)

Place
Washington, D.C.

Date of Decision
3 January 1911

Decision
Alabama's conviction and sentencing of the plaintiff to hard labor for refusal to perform service and refund advanced money was criminal and incompatible with the Thirteenth Amendment.

Significance
Statutory provisions of Alabama law held that failure to fulfill a contractual obligation to work was tantamount to an intent to defraud an employer. However, the U.S. Supreme Court concluded that Alabama's peonage law (compulsory service in payment of a debt) provisions were improper according to constitutional safeguards under the Thirteenth Amendment. The conviction of the lower court was thus overturned and states were given clear guidance that the provisions of the Thirteenth Amendment applied not merely to slavery but also whenever statutory provisions infringed on the personal freedom of workers.

Alonzo Bailey, the plaintiff, contracted to work for the Riverside Company for one year. He agreed to provisions of a written contract and consented to a salary of $12 per month. He received payment in advance and agreed to perform the duties of farm hand in Montgomery County. After one month, Bailey left the job and did not return his $15 advance to the company. He was consequently accused with planning to deceive his employer and subsequently convicted for fraud under Alabama's peonage law.

Under the Alabama State Code of 1896,

> any person who, with intent to injure or defraud his employer, entered into a written contract for service, and thereby obtained from his employer money or other personal property, and with intent and without just cause, and without refunding the money or paying for the property, refused to perform the service, should be punished as if he had stolen it.

Two amendments in 1903 and 1907 resulted in expanding the scope of statutory provisions and resulted in language that stipulated that "refusal or failure to perform service contracted for, or to refund the money obtained, without just cause, should be *prima facie* evidence of the intent to injure." In essence, if an individual entered into a contract of employment and quit without offering "just cause," he was charged with intent to defraud and harm the employer and held criminally liable.

When his case was adjudicated in the lower court, Bailey asked that instructions to the jury explain that provisions of the Alabama's statute were invalid because "refusal or failure . . . to perform the service alleged" or refund his advance did not "of itself make out a *prima facie* case" which proved "intent to injure or defraud" his employer. However, in the lower court, the presiding judge saw no relevance in his assertion. The jury thus concluded that terms of the statute clearly characterized Bailey's actions as criminal failure to perform service in accordance with his contract, to return advanced money, and to show any warranted reason to cease work for the Riverside Company. Explaining that circumstances demonstrated "*prima facie* evidence"

Involuntary Servitude

Although the Thirteenth Amendment to the Constitution abolished slavery it was not until *United States v. Kozminski* (1988) that slavery, in its derivative form, involuntary servitude, was formally outlawed. For roughly a 50 year period beginning with the *Slaughterhouse Cases* (1872), the courts failed to make a meaningful distinction between involuntary servitude and slavery; the practice of involuntary servitude therefore continued well into the twentieth century. In *Bailey v. Alabama* (1920) and subsequent cases the distinction was made that involuntary servitude applies to any situation where one man is coerced, or has no alternative but to work for another man's profit.

In *United States v. Shackney* (1964) for example a Mexican family was psychologically coerced (by the threat of deportation) to work on a chicken farm. This practice met the definition of involuntary servitude and was prohibited. The concept of holding an individual in involuntary servitude was broadened in *United States v. Kozminski* (1988) to include forcing labor upon the mentally incompetent.

Source(s): *Toledo Law Review*, Volume 20, summer 1989.

(Latin meaning "on the face of it") with intent to injure and defraud the employer, the jury found Bailey guilty. Alonzo Bailey took exception to the court's instructions to the jury and the verdict which ensued and later and brought suit under a writ of *habeas corpus*. The Supreme Court of Alabama sustained his conviction and held that no constitutional defectiveness existed under the Alabama's statute.

When the plaintiff's case came before the U.S. Supreme Court, the justices first made clear their intention to adjudicate without regard to race (Bailey was black). Justice Hughes pointed out that "the statute, on its face, makes no racial discrimination;" neither did the record of proceedings indicate discrimination based on race. Moreover, because "citizens of all the states are interested in the maintenance of the constitutional guaranties," the Court's reason for choosing to render a decision was to address coercive, oppressive statutory limitations by the state of Alabama.

The majority opinion held that violation of Bailey's contract was not a crime itself. Nothing indicated that the plaintiff had not planned to honor his contract nor had intended to defraud his employer when the contract was joined. Justice Hughes believed that for such a conviction to be justified, "intent should be established by competent evidence, aided only by such inferences as might logically be derived from the facts proved, and should not be the subject of mere surmise or arbitrary assumption." Only provable, concrete evidence indicated criminal behavior. The Court found no supportable evidence, only "conjecture" and "speculation" about circumstances that might prove the plaintiff had intent to injure or defraud. The Court held that it was inappropriate to convict only on the belief that the plaintiff's behavior (refusal to continue service without offering just cause), the breached contract, and the failure to repay the money established viable *prima*

facie evidence. Without proving fraudulent intent, such acts could be characterized solely as a debt. Accordingly, the U.S. Supreme Court faulted amendments made to the Alabama statute (in 1903 and 1907) that a breach of contract and failure to pay a debt indicated *prima facie* evidence of a criminal act. Further, the majority opinion ruled that the jury should not have been instructed to merely consider statutory presumptions without considering specific, concrete evidence. Statutory provisions that authorized a jury to convict on the basis of the violation of contract and the failure to pay a debt should have not been accepted alone as "evidence" that gave sufficient cause to convict. Further, the Court questioned the legitimacy of the statutory presumptions wherein a defendant "stood, stripped by the statute of the presumption of innocence, and exposed to conviction for fraud upon evidence only of breach of contract and failure to pay."

The Court found that the jury which considered Bailey's case plainly followed instructions of the Alabama statute without giving sufficient attention to ascertain if there were actually indicators of fraudulent intent. Thus, the Court overturned the findings of the lower courts. Under Alabama's peonage statute, workers were, *de facto,* constrained by its provisions and burdened by serial sanctions and criminal charges if they breached an employer's contract. Disputing the validity of the statute, the majority found it inappropriate to hold individuals criminally liable for refusal to perform a contract or pay a debt. Retaining workers under such statutory sanctions, in effect, served as a "means of compulsion" by which employees were forced into work.

The justices emphasized that the Thirteenth Amendment provided protection from slavery and involuntary servitude; statutory presumptions like Alabama's thus violated constitutional rights. The majority opinion stressed that peonage servitude (forcible work in order to pay debt) in this case appeared unavoidable through the way the state enforced contract law. Accordingly, workers contracted to perform labor in Alabama by way of contract, with no opportunity to breach the agreement voluntarily, operated on no other premise but that of peonage servitude. Considering that the Thirteenth Amendment prohibits involuntary servitude (except as punishment for crime), the justices explained that existence of such a statutory exception did not entitle states to enforce penal laws only because an individual refused to continue service or failed to pay a debt. Involuntary bondage could only be authorized if meted out as punishment for a crime.

The Supreme Court found that lower court decisions were inappropriately influenced by unconstitutional statutory provisions. Bailey's actions were characterized as criminal solely because he ceased working. Moreover, designating his indebtedness as fraud was not consistent with constitutional provisions of the Thirteenth Amendment. Concluding that Alabama's statute was deficient, the justices found no evidence to impose criminal liability on the plaintiff "under the name of fraud." Neither could the majority discover the appropriateness in the definition of *prima facie* evidence under Alabama statute; instead, the Court named it a "convenient instrument for coercion." Not only was compulsory service prohibited if the payment of debt was in question, but "refusal or failure to perform the act or service, without refunding the money" was incompatible with the Thirteenth Amendment. The Court majority overruled the judgment of Alabama's Supreme Court.

Minority Opinion

The two dissenting justices reasoned that since contracts for labor were not prohibited under the Thirteenth Amendment, it was not unreasonable for the state of Alabama to enforce legal constraints if a laborer was in breach of contract. The minority opinion rationalized that a laborer was not a slave simply because the exercise of state power imposed criminal liability for wrongful conduct. They pointed out that if failure to pay a debt could not, as a consequence, impose imprisonment then compulsory work by prisoners could be considered as peonage as well. Further they felt that there was nothing improper in considering violation of a contract as criminal and, as such, failure to return an advance on wages clearly evidenced dishonest intent. Thus, the minority opinion reasoned that statutory provisions of the Alabama code were legal and

valid in prosecuting the plaintiff for his "fraudulent intent." In summarizing the minority opinion, Justice Holmes explained that "if there is an excuse for breaking the contract, it would be found in external circumstances, and can be proved." It was the conclusion of the minority justices that Alabama correctly directed that money obtained by fraud should be regarded the same as murder or theft and, consequently, punished as a criminal offense. Therefore, the minority justices believed the ruling of lower courts was correct and that their adherence to Alabama's statutory provisions did not infringe on the Thirteenth Amendment.

Impact

The U.S. Supreme Court resolved to hear *Bailey v. Alabama* because their decision would impact the authorization of "peonage laws." Finding that simple nonpayment of debt or refusal to work did not evidence nor prove intent to defraud an employer, the majority reasoned that the plaintiff's behavior could not be regarded as criminal and treated for penalties of hard labor. Consistent with the abolition of peonage in 1867 and the prohibition of any system that could force servitude for debt, the Court found that Alabama's statute was unconstitutional. This ruling expanded protection of laborers by finding that the plaintiff's breach of a labor contract could not be subjected to criminal penalty. The Court's ruling also provided significant instruction to state legislators and jurists regarding the applicability of the Thirteenth Amendment to safeguard individual rights and provide protection from forced labor.

Related Cases

Henderson v. New York, 92 U.S. 547 (1875).
Clyatt v. United States, 197 U.S. 207 (1905).
Ex parte Riley, 94 Ala. 82, 10 So. 528 (1907).
Keller v. United States, 213 U.S. 138 (1909).

Bibliography and Further Reading

Carrier, Michael A. "Justice Oliver Wendell Holmes: Law and the Inner Self." *Michigan Law Review*, May 1995, p. 1894.

Hall, Kermit L., ed. *The Oxford Companion to the Supreme Court of the United States*. New York, Oxford University Press, 1992.

Pope, James Gray. "Labor's Constitution of Freedom." *Yale Law Journal*, January 1997, p. 941.

BLOCK V. HIRSH

Legal Citation: 256 U.S. 135 (1921)

Appellant
Block

Appellee
Hirsh

Appellant's Claim
That the appellant should be allowed to remain in his apartment by reversing a lower court decision invalidating a rent control law as unconstitutional.

Chief Lawyer for Appellant
Jesse C. Adkins

Chief Lawyer for Appellee
William G. Johnson

Justices for the Court
Louis D. Brandeis, John Hessin Clarke, William Rufus Day, Oliver Wendell Holmes (writing for the Court), Mahlon Pitney

Justices Dissenting
Joseph McKenna, James Clark McReynolds, Willis Van Devanter, Edward Douglass White

Place
Washington, D.C.

Date of Decision
18 April 1921

Decision
The Court reversed the earlier decision. The rent control law was constitutionally valid, and Block could remain in his apartment at the old rent.

Significance
The Court held that the federal government's power to wage war justifies otherwise illegal actions taken by local governments during wartime emergencies.

Congress normally bases regulatory measures on one of the powers given in Article I, section 8, of the Constitution—usually either the power to raise taxes or the power to regulate interstate commerce. During the early years of the twentieth century, the Supreme Court scrutinized federal and state regulations to ensure that these did not destroy an individual's rights to due process of law and liberty of contract. The Court sometimes invalidated laws because these did not directly relate to the taxation or commerce clauses.

The Supreme Court has been much less scrupulous about the constitutionality of regulations under congressional war powers. The Constitution gives Congress the power to declare war and to raise and support armies. Agreeing that Congress may do whatever is necessary to win a war, the Court has upheld new and drastic forms of regulation during wartime.

In October of 1919, Congress imposed rent control on the District of Columbia, under a law expiring in two years. If a tenant continued to pay the former rent, he could not be evicted when his lease ran out. An appointed commission could raise rents to provide landlords a "reasonable" return on their investment. By giving 30 days notice in writing, a landlord could regain an apartment needed for his own use.

Congress based the rent control law on its police powers as the local government in the district. The war, it declared, had created an emergency situation. Rental conditions in the district endangered public health, burdened public officials, and embarrassed the federal government.

Hirsh Needs a Home

A certain Hirsh (the records do not mention his or his tenant's first name) purchased an apartment building on F Street in Washington, where Block occupied the cellar and ground floor. Hirsh claimed that he wanted Block's apartment for his own use; however, he did not give Block 30 days notice as the law provided.

Instead, Hirsh challenged the constitutionality of the entire rent control law. The act was unconstitutional because it took away Hirsh's property and put it under Block's control. Thus the law took private prop-

Congressional Police Power

Congressional police power refers to the federal government's constitutionally defined jurisdiction in maintaining domestic order. Under the Constitution the federal government is limited in their ability to police the states. The power to regulate interstate commerce is the only provision that permits the federal government to intervene in matters of domestic order outside of federally defined crimes such as treason, kidnapping, and crimes involving drugs. Under the Tenth Amendment, the states are reserved the right to construct and enforce criminal law. However, the federal government has stretched the power to regulate interstate commerce to expand their police power.

The alleged mishandling of the Waco and Ruby Ridge incidents by federal law enforcement agents, which were highly publicized, have stimulated debate over the jurisdiction of congressional police power. In *United States v. Lopez* (1995) the Supreme Court ruled that the federal government does not have a police power to define or enforce a state criminal code.

Source(s): *CATO Institute for Policy Analysis*, no. 216, 10 October 1994.

erty for public and not for private use. By taking private property without compensation, it deprived its owner of due process of law, guaranteed by the Fifth Amendment.

The District of Columbia Court of Appeals invalidated the rent control law and held that Hirsh was entitled to occupancy. Block appealed to the Supreme Court, where the United States appeared as *amicus curiae* to defend the rent control law.

The Supreme Court reversed the appeals court and upheld the law by 5-4. Justice Holmes wrote the majority decision supported by Justices Day, Pitney, Brandeis, and Clarke. Justice McKenna wrote a scathing dissent, supported by Chief Justice White and Justices Van Devanter, and McReynolds.

War Justifies Unlimited Governmental Powers

For the majority, Justice Holmes asserted that the congressional declaration of a housing emergency simply stated "a publicly notorious and almost world-wide fact." The only question was whether Congress could "meet [this emergency] in the way in which it has been met by most of the civilized countries of the world."

Under wartime circumstances, matters of purely private concern may become matters of public interest, thereby giving government regulatory powers it would not possess in peace time. These police powers can apply to real property and rents. Both eminent domain and zoning regulations show that tangible property is not "exempt from the legislative modification required from time to time in civilized life." If governments can limit the height of buildings, they can limit the amount of rent.

> Housing is a necessary of life. All the elements of a public interest justifying some degree of

public control are present. The only matter that seems to us open to debate is whether the statute goes too far.

And that was a matter which the courts would determine as cases arose.

The law provided for a "reasonable" rent, Holmes noted. Therefore, Holmes ruled, the law does no more than deprive the landlord of unjust profits from crowded conditions. In this, it goes no further than "the more debatable usury laws." The end justified the means used, and rent controls have been adopted for the same purpose all over the world.

Even in Wartime, Any Violation of the Constitution Is Evil

Justice McKenna's dissent responded both to this decision and to Holmes' decision in the companion case *Marcus Brown Co. v. Feldman* (1921), approving rent control in New York City. McKenna's dissent presented an impassioned defense of the traditional and constitutional limits on arbitrary government power. Under the Fifth and Fourteenth Amendments, states cannot take property without due process of law. And Article I, section 10, specifically states that "No State shall . . . pass any . . . law impairing the obligation of contracts."

The grounds of dissent, said McKenna, are these "explicit provisions of the Constitution of the United States." Their application is so plain that no further argument is needed. Whatever the excuse, including the supposed demands of war, a violation of the Constitution "is an evil—an evil in the circumstance of violation, of greater evil because of its example and malign instruction."

These violations of the Constitution will, moreover, do nothing to advance public health or the operations of the federal government. He sought to answer the question of why these provisions were needed.

The answer is, to supply homes to the homeless . . . If the statute keeps a tenant in, it keeps a tenant out . . . Its only basis is that tenants are more numerous than landlords.

Housing is scarce, it was said, and therefore it could be taken from those who had it.

If such an exercise of government be legal, what exercise of government is illegal? Houses are a necessary of life, but other things are as necessary. May they too be taken from the direction of their owners and disposed of by the Government?

In controlling rents, the majority had argued that Congress simply imitated the laws of other countries. Have conditions in the United States and in the rest of the world, come to the point that they

are not amenable to passing palliatives, so that socialism, or some form of socialism, is the only permanent corrective or accommodation? It is indeed strange that this court, in effect, is called to make way for it and, through the instrument of a Constitution based on personal rights . . . to declare legal a power exerted for their destruction.

McKenna's dissent was eloquent, but Holmes's decision for the majority set lasting precedents. The Court, in fact, held invalid an attempt to continue rent control in the District until *Chasleton Corp. v. Sinclair* (1924). In this case, Justice Holmes declared that the emergency that had justified the 1919 law no longer existed. When war returned, however, Congress in 1942 set up an office to fix the prices of all residential rents and most other goods. Once again the Supreme Court placed no limits on governmental power in wartime.

Related Cases
Marcus Brown Co. v. Feldman, 256 U.S. 170 (1921).
Chasleton Corp. v. Sinclair, 264 U.S. 543 (1924).
Berman v. Parker, 348 U.S. 26 (1954).

Bibliography and Further Reading
Bickel, Alexander, and Benno Schmidt. *History of the Supreme Court of the United States. Volume IX: The Judiciary and Responsible Government, 1910-1921.* New York: Macmillan, 1984.

Paul, Ellen, and Howard Dickman. *Liberty, Property, and Government: Constitutional Interpretation Before the New Deal.* Albany: State University of New York Press, 1989.

Semonche, John E. *Charting the Future: The Supreme Court Responds to a Changing Society, 1890-1920.* Westport, CT: Greenwood, 1978.

HOME BUILDING & LOAN ASSOCIATION V. BLAISDELL

Legal Citation: 290 U.S. 398 (1934)

Appellant
Home Building & Loan Association

Appellee
John H. Blaisdell

Appellant's Claim
That the 1933 Minnesota Mortgage Moratorium Law, intended to avert mortgage foreclosures during the Great Depression, violated the Contract Clause of Article I of the Constitution, which bars state impairment of the obligations of contracts.

Chief Lawyers for Appellant
Karl H. Covell, Alfred W. Bowen

Chief Lawyers for Appellee
Harry H. Peterson, William S. Ervin

Justices for the Court
Louis D. Brandeis, Benjamin N. Cardozo, Charles Evans Hughes (writing for the Court), Owen Josephus Roberts, Harlan Fiske Stone

Justices Dissenting
Pierce Butler, James Clark McReynolds, George Sutherland, Willis Van Devanter

Place
Washington, D.C.

Date of Decision
8 January 1934

Decision
By a vote of 5-4, the Supreme Court upheld the Minnesota statute.

Significance
Blaisdell is important not just because it upheld a significant Depression-era law modeled on the New Deal, but because the close vote in the case illustrates the deep schism between those who endorsed a radically progressive approach to the nation's woes and those who wanted to perpetuate the Court's *laissez-faire* attitude towards economic matters.

In 1933, in the midst of the Great Depression, Minnesota passed the Mortgage Moratorium Law. The law was modeled on President Franklin D. Roosevelt's New Deal program for national economic relief and attempted to provide protection to farmers and other property owners against mortgage foreclosure "during the continuance of the emergency and in no event beyond 1 May 1935." It authorized the Minnesota state courts to consider exempting troubled mortgagors from foreclosure if the mortgagors requested such judicial consideration.

Mr. and Mrs. John H. Blaisdell owned a house and a parcel of land in Hennepin County, Minnesota, for which the Home Building & Loan Association held the mortgage. When the Blaisdells defaulted on their loan payments, the mortgage lender prepared to foreclose on their home. Unable to obtain a new loan, the Blaisdells applied in state district court for an extension of the mortgage redemption period to enable them to find another lender or otherwise raise the needed money.

The court decided in the Blaisdells' favor, and the decision was upheld by the Supreme Court of Minnesota. The lender then appealed this decision to the U.S. Supreme Court, claiming that the Minnesota Mortgage Moratorium Law violated the Contract Clause of Article I of the Constitution, which provides that "No State shall enter into any . . . law impairing the Obligation of Contracts."

Supreme Court Finds That the Contract Clause Is Not Absolute

Chief Justice Hughes and swing vote Justice Roberts joined the more liberal members of the Court to create a one-vote majority favoring the Blaisdells and upholding the Minnesota statute. Writing for the Court, Hughes noted that, "While emergency does not create power, emergency may furnish the occasion for exercise of power." The state, he said, had always held the power to protect its citizens. While under normal conditions the Contract Clause would preempt the exercise of this power, owing to the dire economic circumstances that gave rise to the Great Depression, other considerations must prevail:

Justice Charles Evans Hughes. © Photograph by Harris and Ewing. Collection of the Supreme Court of the United States.

[T]he question is no longer merely that of one party to a contract as against another, but of the use of reasonable means to safeguard the economic structure upon which the good of all depends.

Writing for the four dissenting justices, Justice Sutherland refused to concede that the Contract Clause could be overridden. Instead, he insisted, it must be read literally. If state legislatures were allowed to create laws that interfered with existing contracts between individuals—even during a national economic emergency—soon other excuses would be found for violating contractual relationships. Sutherland was addressing what had for decades been the Supreme Court's most pronounced characteristic: its belief in the sanctity of contracts and laissez-faire attitude towards nearly all economic matters that came before it.

Justice Sutherland and the three other dissenting justices—Butler, McReynolds, and Van Devanter—made up the so-called "Four Horsemen" (after the biblical Four Horsemen of the Apocalypse who wreaked havoc on the land) who consistently voted against Roosevelt's attempts to pull the country out of its economic doldrums. In 1937, frustrated by these rebuffs, Roosevelt developed a plan to "pack" the Court with additional justices who shared his views. Although this plan was ultimately defeated, Roosevelt succeeded in breaking up the conservative voting block on the Court and instituting New Deal reforms.

Related Cases

Railroad Commission Cases, 116 U.S. 307 (1886).
Block v. Hirsch, 256 U.S. 135 (1921).
Marcus Brown Holding Co. v. Feldman, 256 U.S. 170 (1921).
Edgar A. Levy Leasing Co. v. Siegel, 258 U.S. 242 (1922).
Stephenson v. Binford, 287 U.S. 251 (1932).

Bibliography and Further Reading

Butler, Henry N. *The Corporation and the Constitution.* Washington, DC: AEI Press, 1995.

Size of the Supreme Court

There are currently nine justices serving on the Supreme Court: one chief justice and eight associate justices. The number was established in 1869 and has not been altered since. According to Article III, Section 1 of the Constitution, Congress has the power to determine the structure and jurisdiction of the federal judicial system. Congress has changed the size of the Supreme Court on seven different accessions throughout American history, often as a result of westward expansion, but occasionally driven by an underlying political motive. For example, when Andrew Johnson nominated Henry Stanbey to replace Justice John Catron in 1865, Congress changed the number of justices from ten to seven in an attempt to stack the deck against Johnson's Reconstruction initiatives.

The most radical, and blatantly political, attempt to change the size of the Supreme Court came from Franklin D. Roosevelt who, in 1937, moved to increase the number of justices to 15 in an effort to pack the Court with justices sympathetic to his New Deal legislation. Roosevelt's efforts were not in vain, however, as the Court, fearing legislative and executive encroachment on its powers, began upholding some of Roosevelt's policies.

The Great Depression

The Great Depression was a period of U.S. and worldwide economic depression during the 1930s, characterized by failing businesses, rampant unemployment, and decreased prices for agricultural products. The Great Depression began with the stock market crash of 1929 and lasted for roughly a decade—the longest depression experienced by industrialized nations. Due to decreasing value of assets caused by the stock market crash, many banks failed. In 1933 11,000 out of 25,000 of the banks in the United States went out of business.

Prior to the Great Depression it was uncommon for governments to intervene in free market economies because of the widely held belief that a capitalist economy had the inherent ability to stabilize itself. President Roosevelt introduced a series of legislative proposals know as New Deal including public works programs, the Emergency Banking Act, and the FDIC legislation to counteract the effects of the Depression. This radically changed the complexion of the U.S. economy. As a result of the Depression the federal government began intervening in economic affairs to previously unheard of proportions. Ironically, it was not until the outbreak of World War II, which caused an increase in demand for production and new jobs, that the U.S. and world economies began to stabilize.

Source(s): *World Book Encyclopedia,* 1993, p. 364.

Lash, Joseph P. *Dealers and Dreamers: A New Look at the New Deal.* New York: Doubleday, 1988.

Leuchtenburg, William Edward. *The Supreme Court Reborn: The Constitutional Revolution in the Age of Revolution.* New York: Oxford University Press, 1995.

ASHWANDER V. TENNESSEE VALLEY AUTHORITY

Legal Citation: 297 U.S. 288 (1936)

Petitioner
George Ashwander

Respondent
Tennessee Valley Authority

Petitioner's Claim
That the Tennessee Valley Authority (TVA) was not a legitimate federal agency, and that it did not have the authority to sell the electrical power that was a by-product of its dam construction.

Chief Lawyers for Petitioner
Forney Johnston, James M. Beck

Chief Lawyers for Respondent
John Lord O'Brian, Stanley F. Reed

Justices for the Court
Pierce Butler, Charles Evans Hughes (writing for the Court), James Clark McReynolds, Owen Josephus Roberts, Harlan Fiske Stone, George Sutherland, Willis Van Devanter

Justices Dissenting
Louis D. Brandeis, Benjamin N. Cardozo

Place
Washington, D.C.

Date of Decision
17 February 1936

Decision
Legislation establishing the TVA was upheld by a 8-1 vote, as was its right to sell electrical power.

Significance
Today Ashwander is remembered primarily for Justice Brandeis's "Ashwander rules," which provide guidelines for avoiding overly broad constitutional interpretation.

The Tennessee Valley Authority, a program to promote rural electrification, was created in 1933 as part of President Franklin Roosevelt's "first" New Deal. The *Ashwander* case came about when minority shareholders of the Alabama Power Company objected to the company's proposal to purchase some of the surplus energy generated by one of the TVA's dams. Claiming that the TVA lacked the authority to sell its energy, the shareholders also challenged the constitutionality of the statute that created the federal agency. In the name of one of their members, George Ashwander, a group of shareholders filed suit against the TVA in federal district court.

After the district court annulled the contract between the TVA and the power company, the TVA appealed to the United States Fifth Circuit Court of Appeals, which then reversed the ruling of the lower court. Ashwander petitioned the U.S. Supreme Court for review.

Ashwander marked one of the only times that the Supreme Court upheld the legitimacy of New Deal agencies prior to Roosevelt's 1937 court-packing plan. (The plan ultimately failed to receive congressional approval, but four conservative justices who opposed Roosevelt's progressive economic and social agenda soon left the Court anyway). Surprisingly, the Court dismissed the shareholder's suit, by implication upholding the statute that created the TVA by a vote of 8-1. Chief Justice Hughes, writing for the Court, added that the Constitution grants the federal government the right to sell property (in this case, energy) that properly belongs to it. Justice Brandeis, in a concurring opinion, added that the Court should never have heard the case in the first place, as it was chiefly a shareholders' internal dispute that did not actually involve any constitutional questions.

Brandeis Proposes "Ashwander Rules"

It is primarily for Justice Brandies's concurrence, in fact, that *Ashwander* is remembered. To buttress his assertion that the Supreme Court should sidestep judging the constitutionality of legislation wherever possible, and to help the Court determine what to avoid, Brandeis proposed the following rules:

Louis Brandeis

Louis Brandeis was an associate justice of the Supreme Court (1916-1939) and social reformer best know for work done on behalf of the labor movement, including a campaign to overturn *Lochner v. New York*, which permitted an unlimited work day for laborers. He was often referred to the "peoples' attorney" for his efforts in defense of the common man against big business. Brandeis, along with partner Samuel Warren, developed the notion of the "Right to Privacy" with an article written for the Harvard Law Review in 1890. Because of his uncompromising support of individual liberties, minority rights, and social justice he is considered one of the greatest justices to have served on the Supreme Court.

Brandeis wrote a brief for a case involving the institution of a ten hour work day for women. The "Brandeis brief," as it became know, was so influential that the Supreme Court upheld the ten hour work day making reference to the brief in its written opinion. The brief also significantly changed the way legal cases were argued by legitimizing social science data in argumentation. Brandeis was also instrumental in establishing the Federal Reserve System (1913) and the Federal Trade Commission (1939).

Source(s): Edward Frank Magill. *Great Lives From History.* Salem Press, 1987.

1. The Court will not pass upon the constitutionality of legislation in a friendly, nonadversary, proceeding . . . 2. The Court will not "anticipate a question of constitutional law in advance of the necessity of deciding it . . ." 3. The Court will not "formulate a rule of constitutional law broader than is required by the precise facts to which it is to be applied . . ." 4. The Court will not pass upon a constitutional question although properly presented by the record, if there is also present some other ground upon which the case may be disposed . . . 5. The Court will not pass upon the validity of a statute upon complaint of one who fails to show that he is injured by its operation . . . 6. The Court will not pass upon the constitutionality of a statute at the instance of one who has availed himself of its benefits . . . 7. "When the validity of an act of the Congress is drawn in question, and even if a serious doubt of constitutionality is raised, it is a cardinal principle that this Court first ascer-

tain whether a construction of the statute is fairly possible by which the question may be avoided."

Related Cases

Pollock v. Farmers' Loan & Trust Company, 157 U.S. 429 (1895).
Gall v. Exxon Corp., 418 F.Supp. 508 (1976).
LaShawn A. v. Barry, 69 F.3d 556 (1995).

Bibliography and Further Reading

Hall, Kermit L. *The Supreme Court and Judicial Review in American History.* Washington, DC: American Historical Association, 1985.

Maidment, R. A. *The Judicial Response to the New Deal: The U.S. Supreme Court and Economic Regulation, 1934–1936.* Manchester, NY: Manchester University Press, 1991.

Murphy, Walter, William Harris, and James Fleming. *Constitutional Interpretation.* Mineola, NY: Foundation Press, 1986.

EL PASO V. SIMMONS

Legal Citation: 379 U.S. 497 (1965)

Appellant
City of El Paso

Appellee
Greenberry Simmons

Appellant's Claim
That the property in question was rightfully returned to the state of Texas after its forfeiture by Greenberry Simmons.

Chief Lawyer for Appellant
William J. Mounce

Chief Lawyer for Appellee
Greenberry Simmons

Justices for the Court
William J. Brennan, Jr., Tom C. Clark, William O. Douglas, Arthur Goldberg, John Marshall Harlan II, Potter Stewart, Earl Warren, Byron R. White (writing for the Court)

Justices Dissenting
Hugo Lafayette Black

Place
Washington, D.C.

Date of Decision
18 January 1965

Decision
The U.S. Supreme Court reversed the decision of the U.S. Court of Appeals for the Fifth Circuit.

Significance
The case of *El Paso v. Simmons* dealt with important constitutional issues concerning the Contract Clause of the Constitution, raising questions involving impairment of contracts, legislation affecting contracts, motives for modifying the obligation of a contract by a state, and the limit or extent of a state's power to do so.

Case Background

The land in question was originally sold by the state of Texas in 1910, under a State Land Board program that sold public land for one-fortieth of the principal and annual interest and principal payments. The purpose of the public land sale was to encourage the settlement of Texas and to provide funds for the Permanent Free School Fund. If the interest was not paid according to the contract, the statute caused the land to be forfeited back to the state for resale. A provision of the statute allowed the purchasers to reclaim their land if they paid the full amount of interest due, as long as no third party had intervened. In 1941, the state amended some of the provisions, including the one mentioned, so that it now limited the right of reinstatement to only "five years from the date of forfeiture." Then, in 1951, the right was further limited to only the "last purchaser from the State and his vendees or their heirs." On 21 July 1947, the land in question was forfeited and returned to the state for resale as the interest remained unpaid. A notice about the forfeiture and an explanation of the 1941 act was sent to the last purchaser of the property, but it was returned. On 23 July 1952, Greenberry Simmons filed an application for reinstatement, including all of the interest due, which was denied because it was over the five year limit by two days. The land was sold in 1955 to the city of El Paso. Simmons filed suit against the city, but lost. The court of appeals reversed that decision "on the ground that the constitutional prohibition against impairment of contracts forbade application of the 1941 statute to the contract in question." The case went on to be heard by the U.S. Supreme Court to consider the possibility that the 1941 amendment may violate the Contract Clause of the Constitution.

A Violation of the Contract Clause or a Lawful Remedy?

First, the Court addressed the matter of jurisdiction and dismissed the improper appeal, but granted a writ of *certiorari* in its place. With this matter now in order, Justice White, writing for the Court, noted that the appellant, the city of El Paso, cited three Supreme Court cases including *Wilson v. Standefer* (1902), *Waggoner v.*

Flack (1903), and *Aikins v. Kingsbury* (1918) where the Court found that

> the state statutes existing when the contracts were made were not to be considered the exclusive remedies available in the event of the purchaser's default since there was no promise, express or implied, on the part of the State not to enlarge the remedy or grant another in case of breach.

The court of appeals had rejected this argument, finding that the 1941 statute constituted "a change in the obligation of a contract" which violated the Contract Clause of the Constitution. The Supreme Court, however, did not address the correctness of the court of appeals, but "assuming the provision for reinstatement after default to be part of the State's obligation, we do not think its modification by a five-year statute of repose contravenes the Contract Clause." While "the power of a State to modify or affect the obligation of a contract is not without limit," the majority opinion found that "the objects of the Texas Statute make abundantly clear that it impairs no protected right under the Contract Clause."

Justice White continued in the opinion to summarize the history and purpose of the sale of public land in Texas. He also discussed the amendments that Texas sought to halt the abuse of the land laws by some purchasers. The 1941 amendment, requiring that the right of reinstatement be limited to five years after forfeiture, was enacted "to restore confidence in the stability and integrity of land titles and to enable the State to protect and administer its property in a businesslike manner." Thus, the opinion of the majority reversed the decision of the court of appeals.

The only dissenting justice was Justice Black, who objected to the majority opinion, saying that it was a "balancing away" of the Fifth Amendment, through the Fourteenth, which says that private property may not be taken away from a person for public use without just compensation (*Lynch v. United States* [1934], *Griggs v. Allegheny County, Contributors to the Pennsylvania Hospital v. City of Philadelphia* [1917]). He maintained that the Court attempted to justify changing the terms of the contract because, overall, the land sale had become a "bad bargain," losing millions of dollars for the state of Texas. According to Justice Black,

> if the hope and realization of profit to a contract breaker are hereafter to be given either partial or sufficient weight to cancel out the unequivocal constitutional command against impairing the obligations of contracts, that command will be nullified by what is the most common cause for breaking contracts. I cannot subscribe to such a devitalizing constitutional doctrine.

Impact

The opinions of the case of *El Paso v. Simmons* have been cited in at least 15 U.S. Supreme Court cases, and three circuit Court cases; many involving the basic constitutional rights according to the Contract Clause of the Constitution. Contractual obligations affect the lives of almost every American, regardless of age or wealth.

Related Cases

Waggoner v. Flack, 188 U.S. 595 (1903).
Contributors to the Pennsylvania Hospital v. City of Philadelphia, 245 U.S. 20 (1917).
Aikins v. Kingsbury, 247 U.S. 484 (1918).
Home Building and Loan Assn. v. Blaisdell, 290 U.S. 398 (1934).
Lynch v. United States, 292 U.S. 571 (1934).
Ferguson v. Skrupa, 372 U.S. 726 (1963).

Bibliography and Further Reading

Cushman, Robert F. *Cases in Constitutional Law,* 7th ed. Englewood Cliffs, NJ: Prentice-Hall, Inc., 1989.

FUENTES V. SHEVIN

Legal Citation: 407 U.S. 67 (1972)

Appellant
Margarita Fuentes

Appellee
Robert L. Shevin

Appellant's Claim
Denying debtors a hearing before merchandise is reposed by private creditors violates the Fourteenth Amendment's guarantee that no state shall deprive any person of property without due process of law.

Chief Lawyer for Appellant
Michael Abbott

Chief Lawyer for Appellee
Herbert T. Schwartz

Justices for the Court
William J. Brennan, Jr., William O. Douglas, Thurgood Marshall, Potter Stewart (writing for the Court)

Justices Dissenting
Harry A. Blackmun, Warren E. Burger, Byron R. White (Lewis F. Powell, Jr., and William H. Rehnquist did not participate)

Place
Washington, D.C.

Date of Decision
12 June 1972

Decision
The Court set aside two three-judge federal district court decisions that upheld the constitutionality of laws in Florida and Pennsylvania, which allowed private creditors to repossess merchandise under a writ of replevin, without proper notice or a hearing. Derived from common law, replevin allows for the return of specific merchandise that was taken improperly or wrongfully.

Significance
Fuentes v. Shevin established that even if debtors failed to make payments and had signed a contract agreeing to do so, they were, nonetheless, entitled to proper notice and a hearing before private creditors could repossess merchandise or chattel.

Debtors' Rights and Contractual Agreements

Margarita Fuentes, a Florida resident, purchased a gas stove and service policy from Firestone Tire and Rubber Co. under a sales contract, which required monthly payments over a specified period of time. Fuentes later purchased a stereophonic phonograph under a similar agreement. The stove and stereo cost $500. The contract entitled Fuentes to keep the merchandise, unless she failed to make the payments and Firestone kept the titles to the merchandise. Fuentes made the payments for more than a year, but with roughly $200 remaining on her bill a dispute developed over servicing of the stove. Firestone filed suit in small-claims court for repossession of both the stove and stereo. At that same time, even before Fuentes received a summons to answer the complaint, the company also got a writ of replevin ordering a sheriff to seize the stove and stereo immediately.

Under Florida law, Firestone, only had to fill out the proper forms and submit them to the clerk of the small claims court. The clerk approved the documents and issued a writ of replevin. That same day, a deputy sheriff accompanied by a Firestone representative, went to Fuentes's home and repossessed the stove and stereo. Later, Fuentes filed suit in a federal district court under the grounds that the state's replevin procedures violated the Due Process Clause of the Fourteenth Amendment.

In a separate action in Pennsylvania, several people filed a similar claimed that also challenged the constitutionality of that state's replevin process. Three of the claimants had purchased a bed, a table and other household goods under a sales contract similar to the one signed by Fuentes. The creditors filed writs of replevin, claiming that the debtors had failed to make their installment payments as required under the contracts. One of the appellants in the Pennsylvania case was divorced from a local deputy sheriff and was in custody battle for their son. The ex-husband filed a writ of replevin that ordered seizure of the child's clothes, furniture and toys.

In both the Florida and Pennsylvania cases, a three-judge district court upheld the constitutionality of the

Writ of Replevin

Replevin, also known as clan and delivery, Detinue, Revindication, and Sequestration refers to legal action taken by the owner of some item (usually of personal value) in an effort to reclaim possession of an item that has been wrongfully taken. It is one of the oldest forms of legal action originating in the fourteenth century as a means of protecting tenants from landlords. Landlords used to take possession of personal valuables to compensate for past due rent—items which often exceeded the value of rent owed.

Replevin, most often referred to as claim and delivery, is considered a "possessory" action because the main objective of the suit is to regain possession of a particular good, however, compensation beyond the repossessed item is often sought. Replevin can only be used to recover tangible personal property which must be adequately described by the plaintiff, for example in the case of a stolen family heirloom. Stock certificates and valuable intellectual property such as mathematical formulas can be recovered in replevin suites but not undocumented ideas.

Source(s): Black, Henry Campbell. *Black's Law Dictionary.* St. Paul, MN: West Publishing Co, 1990.

states' statutes. The Florida law did not require the applicant to prove before the seizure that the claimant was entitled to the merchandise. Instead, one merely had to assert that he was entitled to the property and file a complaint. Just as the debtor received the complaint for repossession of the property, the property was repossessed. The merchandise was seized without any prior notice or opportunity to dispute the writ of replevin. After the property was repossessed, the debtor eventually had an opportunity for a hearing. In addition, the Florida statute required the law enforcement officer, who seizes the property, to hold it for three days, during which the debtor could reclaim the merchandise by posting a security bond for double the value of the merchandise. If the debtor failed to post the bond in that three-day period the property reverted back to the creditor or whoever filed the writ of replevin. The Pennsylvania statute, varied only slightly from the Florida law, but presented no opportunity for a hearing. In order for the debtor to receive a hearing, that individual must have filed a lawsuit.

In writing for the majority, Justice Stewart first addressed whether the statutes were "constitutionally defective" for not providing hearings at a "meaningful time." The Florida statute allowed for a hearing after the merchandise was seized, but the Pennsylvania statute only allowed a hearing if the debtor initiated a lawsuit. Neither required a hearing before the property was repossessed. Justice Stewart wrote:

The constitutional right to be heard is a basic aspect of the duty of government to follow a fair process of decision making when it acts to deprive a person of his possessions. The purpose of this requirement is not only to ensure abstract fair play to the individual. Its purpose, more particularly, is to protect his use and possession of property from arbitrary encroachment—to minimize substantively unfair or

mistaken deprivation of property, a danger that is especially great when the State seizes goods simply upon the application of and for the benefit of a private party. So viewed, the prohibition against the deprivation of property without due process of law reflects the high value, embedded in our constitutional and political history, that we place on a person's right to enjoy what is his, free of governmental interference.

Having an opportunity to contest or dispute the repossession of property was the only way to prevent the process from being unfair, he reasoned. "The Fourteenth Amendment draws no bright lines around three-day, 10-day, or 50-day deprivations of property. Any significant taking of property by the State is within the purview of the Due Process Clause." Even if the debtors were still paying for the merchandise, they were still entitled to due process. In fact, Justice Stewart reasoned that even if the debtors failed to obey their contracts and defaulted on their payments that they were still entitled to a hearing before property in their possession was seized. "The right to be heard does not depend upon an advance showing that one will surely prevail at the hearing," he wrote.

The lower courts reasoned that the debtors were not entitled to due process protection because the materials seized did not merit it because they were not "absolute necessities of life." Justice Stewart believed that conclusion was reached by reading *Snaidich v. Family Finance Corp.* (1969) and *Goldberg v. Kelly* (1970) too narrowly. In both those cases, the Court ruled the Constitution requires a hearing before wages were garnished and before certain welfare benefits were terminated. "Both decisions were in the mainstream of past cases, having little or noting to do with the absolute 'necessities' of life but establishing that due process requires an opportunity for a hearing before deprivation of property takes effect," Justice Stewart wrote. He added: "It is not the business of a court adjudication of due process rights to make its own critical evaluation of those choices and protect only the ones that, by its own lights, are 'necessary.'"

The majority recognized that in some circumstances, such as meeting the needs of a war effort or to protect against the economic disaster or a bank failure warrant, delaying a hearing or proper notice was warranted. However, the replevin laws in Florida and Pennsylvania allowed

> summary seizure of a person's possessions when no more than private gain is directly at stake. The replevin chattels, as in the present cases, may satisfy a debt or settle a score. But state intervention in a private dispute hardly compares to state action furthering a war effort or protecting the public health.

Finally, Justice Stewart addressed the contractual obligations of the debtors. He reasoned, that while the contracts stated the property could be reposed for failure to make payments it made no mentioned of waiving a right to a prior hearing.

> The appellees do not suggest that these provisions waived the appellants' right to a full post-seizure hearing to determine whether those events had, in fact, occurred and to consider any other available defenses. By the same token, the language of the purported waiver provisions did not waive the appellants' constitutional right to a pre-seizure hearing of some kind.

In a dissenting opinion, Justice White argued that in light of *Younger v. Harris,* which was announced after the district court's ruling, those rulings should be vacated and the cases reconsidered. *Younger v. Harris* established that the federal courts would not supercede the state courts unless the case resulted from bad faith or harassment. Justice White also reasoned that if the debtor has indeed defaulted on payments that the creditor should be allowed to repossess the property. "Dollar-and-cents considerations weigh heavily against false claims of default as well as against precipitate action that would allow no opportunity for mistakes to surface and be corrected." He further argued that creditors could maneuver around the majority's ruling by simply making it clear in the contractual language that they can repossess the merchandise. He concluded: "None of this seems worth the candle to me. The procedure that the Court strikes down is not some barbaric hangover from bygone days. The respective rights of the parties secured transactions have undergone the most intensive analysis in recent years."

Impact

Fuentes v. Shevin followed several other cases that established due process for procedures where they had not been viewed as required under the Due Process Clause of the U.S. Constitution. In *Goldberg v. Kelly* (1970) the Court ruled that before welfare benefits could be terminated that the recipient was entitled to a hearing. In *Bell v. Burson* (1971) the Court ruled that a driver could not lose his license unless a hearing was held. Yet, the most important aspect of *Fuentes* was in consumer rights because it afforded consumers protections and rights that were unavailable before.

Related Cases

Snaidach v. Family Finance Corp, 395 U.S. 337 (1969).
Goldberg v. Kelly, 397 U.S. 254 (1970).
Bell v. Burson, 402 U.S. 535 (1971).
Arnett v. Kennedy, 416 U.S. 134 (1974).
Cleveland Board of Education v. Loudermill, 470 U.S. 532 (1985).

Bibliography and Further Reading

Biskupic, Joan, and Elder Witt. *Guide to the U.S. Supreme Court,* 3rd ed. Washington, DC: Congressional Quarterly Inc., 1997

Gunther, Gerald, and Kathleen Sullivan. *Constitutional Law,* 13th ed. New York: The Foundation Press Inc., 1997.

Hall, Kermit L., ed. *The Oxford Companion to the Supreme Court of the United States.* New York: Oxford University Press, 1992.

ALLIED STRUCTURAL STEEL CO. V. SPANNAUS

Legal Citation: 438 U.S. 234 (1978)

Petitioner
Allied Structural Steel Company, an Illinois corporation

Respondent
Warren Spannaus, Attorney General of Minnesota

Petitioner's Claim
That a Minnesota statute governing pensions and benefits protection violated the Contract Clause in Article I, Section 10 of the Constitution.

Chief Lawyer for Petitioner
George B. Christensen

Chief Lawyer for Respondent
Byron E. Starns, Chief Deputy Attorney General of Minnesota

Justices for the Court
Warren E. Burger, Lewis F. Powell, Jr., William H. Rehnquist, John Paul Stevens, Potter Stewart (writing for the Court)

Justices Dissenting
William J. Brennan, Jr., Thurgood Marshall, Byron R. White (Harry A. Blackmun did not participate)

Place
Washington, D.C.

Date of Decision
28 June 1978

Decision
That the Minnesota Private Pension Benefits Protection Act violated the Contract Clause, which limits powers of the state to abridge existing contractual obligations, by imposing restrictions on the petitioner which created a "substantial and severe" impact. The Court ruled that the act could not be justified under the terms whereby other statutes had survived similar attacks, because it had not been enacted "to deal with a broad, generalized economic, or social problem."

Significance
Until *United States Trust Co. v. New Jersey* (1977), there had been no significant Contract Clause challenges before the Court since the 1930s. *Allied Structural Steel Co. v. Spannaus*, the next Contract Clause case of note after *United States Trust*, strengthened the impact of the clause and proved that it was not, in Justice Stewart's words, "a dead letter."

Allied Is Finished with Minnesota—But Not Vice Versa

Allied Structural Steel, a company chartered in Illinois, had a Minnesota office in which it employed 30 persons. In 1963, the company adopted a general pension plan whereby a salaried employee who reached the age of 65 would be entitled to receive a monthly pension. The amount was computed by multiplying one percent of his or her average monthly earnings by the total number of years he or she had been employed; so if someone had worked for the company 20 years, earning an average of $2,000 a month in salary, the employee's pension would be $20 multiplied by 20 years, or $400 a month. There was no minimum length of service required by the company before employees were entitled to receive the pension. The size of the pension would, however, depend on the number of years worked. The plan further stipulated that an employee would receive the pension if he or she (1) had worked 15 years for the company and reached the age of 60; or (2) was at least 55 years of age, and the sum of his or her age and years of service with the company was at least 75; or (3) was less than 55 years of age, but the sum of the age and years of service was at least 80. (For example, a 50 year-old employee who had worked 30 years for the company would qualify under the third option.)

Each year the company made contributions to the fund, according to the predictions its accountants made regarding eventual payout needs. Just as the company had voluntarily chosen to inaugurate the plan, it reserved the right to change the plan in whole or in part, or to terminate it at any time and for any reason. If it did terminate the plan, however, Allied promised to distribute the funds, first to meet obligations it had made to employees who were already retired, and then to those eligible for retirement. Any remaining balance would be distributed to the employees under the plan who had not yet retired. The plan further stated, "No employee shall have any right to, or interest in, any part of the Trust's assets upon termination of his employment or otherwise, except as provided from time to time under this Plan, and then only to the extent of the benefits payable to such employee out of the assets of the Trust." Furthermore, the plan noted that the company could dismiss employees at any time and for any reason, and that the plan itself served as no guarantee that it would not do so. By most standards, it was a fair and equitable plan, given the fact that the company had entered into it voluntarily and that the funds came from the company, not from the employees. As Justice Stewart later observed, "In sum, an employee who did not die, did not quit, and was not discharged before meeting one of the requirements of the plan would receive a fixed pension at age 65 if the company remained in business and elected to continue the pension plan in essentially its existing form."

In 1974, two events occurred which would ultimately lead to the Supreme Court's review of *Allied Structural Steel Co. v. Spannaus*. On April 9, the State of Minnesota passed its Private Pension Benefits Protection Act. The act imposed a "pension funding charge" on any private company that (1) employed 100 or more people, at least one of whom was a Minnesota resident; (2) maintained a pension plan; (3) terminated the plan or closed a Minnesota office; and (4) did not have pension funds sufficient to cover full pensions for all employees who had worked for the company for at least ten years. Under the act, the employer would have to purchase deferred annuities, payable to the employees at normal retirement age, to satisfy the deficiency.

This was clearly at odds with Allied's plan, and the situation came to a head that summer, when the company set in motion a plan to close its Minnesota office—a plan which it had made before Minnesota passed its act. On 31 July, Allied dismissed 11 of its 30 Minnesota employees, and in August it notified the Minnesota Commissioner of Labor and Industry, in accordance with Minnesota law, that it was closing its Minnesota office. As it turned out, at least nine of the discharged employees had at least ten years' worth of service each. Though they did not yet qualify for the company's pension plan, they qualified for pensions under the Minnesota Act, and on August 18, the state presented Allied with a pension funding charge of some $185,000.

Allied brought a suit in federal district court asking for injunctive and declaratory relief. The Minnesota Act was unconstitutional, according to the company's legal counsel, because it impaired the company's contractual obligations under the pension agreement. At issue was the Contract Clause of the Constitution: "No State shall . . . pass any . . . Law impairing the Obligation of Contracts." The three-judge panel ruled that the Minnesota statute was constitutional as applied to Allied Structural Steel's pension plan. Allied appealed to the Supreme Court, and the Chamber of Commerce of the United States filed a brief of *amicus curiae* urging reversal.

Not a "Dead Letter"

The Court voted 5-3 for reversal. Justice Stewart, writing for the majority, held that the Contract Clause imposed limits on the power of a state to interfere in existing contractual relationships, and although the clause did not "obliterate" the state's police power, it did create limits "even in the exercise of [a state's] otherwise legitimate police power." The level of interference by the state in this situation, and the impact thereof, "was both substantial and severe." The act required Allied to retroactively change a plan it had had in place for the 11 years preceding the passing of Minnesota's statute, and furthermore, the retroactivity aspect of the act was applied selectively. It was directed "only to those employers who terminated their pension plans or who, like the appellant, closed their Minnesota offices, thus forcing the employer to make all the retroactive changes in its contractual obligations at one time." Finally, the act had not been created to deal with a "broad, generalized economic or social problem," which constituted an emergency over a limited period of time. Such had been the case in 1934, when the Court reviewed *Home Building & Loan Association v. Blaisdell;* and it was not, in the view of the Court, the case now.

The Contract Clause, as Stewart explained, had once been "the strongest single constitutional check on state legislation." The passage of the Fourteenth Amendment in 1868, however, had diminished the power of the clause; thenceforth the Due Process Clause of that amendment had sufficed to protect individuals or corporations from interference by states. "Nonetheless," Stewart said, "the Contract Clause remains part of the Constitution. It is not a dead letter. And its basic contours are brought into focus by several of the Court's 20th-century decisions."

Most important among the latter was *Home Building & Loan Association v. Blaisdell* (1934). In that case, which ironically also involved Minnesota, the state had passed a law placing a moratorium on the requirements of individuals to make regular mortgage payments. The moratorium was a response to the Depression, and to the fact that many people were unable to come up with the money to pay their mortgages. It extended the grace period to 1 May 1935. When a mortgage company challenged the law, the Court upheld it for five reasons: the statute dealt with an emergency situation; it "was enacted to a protect a basic societal interest, not a favored group;" the relief was "appropriately tailored" to the emergency situation; the conditions it imposed were reasonable; and the legislation imposed a time limit on the emergency measures.

Three other cases reinforced the Court's decision in *Home Building & Loan Association*: *W. B. Worthen Co. v. Thomas* (1934), *W. B. Worthen Co. v. Kavanaugh* (1935), and *Treigle v. Acme Homestead Assn.* (1936). The first two dealt with Arkansas' laws, the third with a Louisiana statute; and in each case the Court found the laws invalid under the Contract Clause. The first of the *Worthen* cases involved an Arkansas' statute preventing creditors of a deceased person from making claims on the proceeds from that person's life insurance policy. Here the Court found that the provision "was not precisely and reasonably designed to meet a grave temporary emergency in the interest of the general welfare."

Just the year before *Spannaus*, the Court had considered *United States Trust Co. v. New Jersey* and again ruled against a state because its legislation "was neither necessary nor reasonable." In examining the Minnesota law, the only evidence of its original intent that the Court could find was a statement made by the district court, not the Minnesota legislature. The lower court had opined that the plant-closure problem had come to Minnesota's attention after the White Motor Corporation had closed a Minnesota plant. In all respects, "the Minnesota law simply does not possess the attributes of those state laws that in the past have survived challenge under the Contract Clause of the Constitution." In the narrowness of its aim, Stewart concluded, it "was leveled, not at every Minnesota employer . . . but only at those who had in the past been sufficiently enlightened as voluntarily to agree to establish pension plans for their employees."

The Dissenters Take the Fourteenth

Justice Brennan filed a dissenting opinion in which he was joined by Justices Marshall and White. Brennan, too, offered a look into the Court's historical record with regard to states and contracts, but he viewed this not in light of the Contract Clause, but from the perspective of the Fourteenth Amendment's Due Process Clause. Since he found nothing in the act which violated the latter, he voted to affirm the lower court's judgment.

The Contract Clause, Brennan wrote, had not been "intended to embody a broad constitutional policy of protecting all reliance interests grounded in private contracts." Rather, it had arisen from "widespread dissatisfaction" over debtor-creditor contracts in force when the United States was created. "Thus, the several provisions of Article I, 10 . . . were targeted directly at this wide variety of debt relief measures." With its use of the Contract Clause, rather than the Fourteenth Amendment, as a means of interpreting contracts, the Court "threaten[ed] to undermine the jurisprudence of

property rights developed over the last 40 years," Brennan wrote.

When he addressed the present case from the perspective of the Due Process Clause, making reference to the Court's decision in *Usery v. Turner Elkhorn Mining Co.* (1976), Brennan found that Minnesota's act passed constitutional muster. In his view, the act did indeed "remedy a serious social problem: the utter frustration of an employee's expectations that can occur when he is terminated because his employer closes down his place of work." Furthermore, the act was "not wholly retrospective in its operation" since it only imposed the fine on companies who closed their plants after the enactment of the statute.

Impact

Expectations that *Spannaus* would inaugurate a new era for the Contract Clause proved to be short-lived. In *Exxon Corp. v. Eagerton* (1983), the Court restricted the application of its *Spannaus* ruling to statutes whose "sole effect" was "to alter contractual duties." Four years later, in *Keystone Bituminous Coal Association v. DeBeni* (1987), the Court rejected a Contract Clause challenge to a Pennsylvania law.

Related Cases

Euclid v. Ambler Realty Co., 272 U.S. 365 (1926).
Home Building & Loan Association v. Blaisdell, 290 U.S. 398 (1934).
W. B. Worthen Co. v. Thomas, 292 U.S. 426 (1934).
W. B. Worthen Co. v. Kavanaugh, 295 U.S. 56 (1935).

Bibliography and Further Reading

Biskupic, Joan, and Elder Witt. *Guide to the U.S. Supreme Court,* third ed. Washington, DC: Congressional Quarterly Inc., 1997.

Graham, Robert A. "The Constitution, the Legislature, and Unfair Surprise." *Michigan Law Review,* November 1993, p. 398.

Hall, Kermit L., ed. *The Oxford Companion to the Supreme Court of the United States.* New York: Oxford University Press, 1992.

Levy, Leonard W., ed. *Encyclopedia of the American Constitution.* New York: Macmillan, 1986.

Witt, Elder. *Congressional Quarterly's Guide to the Supreme Court,* 2nd ed. Washington, DC: Congressional Quarterly Inc., 1990.

NOLLAN V. CALIFORNIA COASTAL COMMISSION

Legal Citation: 483 U.S. 825 (1987)

Appellant
James and Marilyn Nollan

Appellee
California Coastal Commission

Appellant's Claim
That a stipulation by the California Coastal Commission, whereby the appellant was required to grant the public an easement to pass across their beachfront property, constituted a violation of the Takings Clause in the Fifth and Fourteenth Amendments.

Chief Lawyer for Appellant
Robert K. Best

Chief Lawyer for Appellee
Andrea Sheridan Ordin, Chief Assistant Attorney General of California

Justices for the Court
Sandra Day O'Connor, Lewis F. Powell, Jr., William H. Rehnquist, Antonin Scalia (writing for the Court), Byron R. White

Justices Dissenting
Harry A. Blackmun, William J. Brennan, Jr., Thurgood Marshall, John Paul Stevens

Place
Washington, D.C.

Date of Decision
26 June 1987

Decision
The Court ruled that although the commission's conditioning of appellant's rebuilding permit on the granting of a public easement might have been lawful if it had "substantially furthered governmental purposes," the measure in question did not. Rather, it constituted a violation of the Takings Clause in the Fifth Amendment, and was therefore struck down by the Court.

Significance
Thomas Jefferson expressed in the Declaration of Independence that no man should be stripped of "life, liberty, and the pursuit of happiness." In its original formulation, however, by the British philosopher John Locke, the last of these had been "the pursuit of property." Constitutional protection of these rights is embodied in the Fifth Amendment to the Constitution, which continues in part that ". . . nor shall private property be taken for public use, without just compensation."

Mr. and Mrs. Nollan Build Their Dream Home

For years, James and Marilyn Nollan had leased a parcel of beachfront property in Ventura County, California. The site near Santa Barbara, perhaps two hours' drive north of Los Angeles, was popular for swimming and sunbathing: a quarter mile to the north lay the Faria County Park, a public beach, and 1,800 feet to the south was another public area known as "The Cove." The property's oceanside boundary had been determined in conjunction with mean high tide. Between the shoreline and the main portion of the property stood an eight-foot-high concrete sea wall. Hence between the sea wall and the water, even at high tide, there was a strip of sand which constituted a private beach belonging to the property leased by the Nollans.

The land contained a bungalow, which the Nollans regularly subleased to others, but after years of use as a rental property, the 504-square-foot house needed replacing. Meanwhile, the Nollans had decided to purchase the lot, which the owners said they could do on condition that they demolish the bungalow and build a new home there. In accordance with this desire and with state law, the couple went to the California Coastal Commission to request a coastal development permit. They submitted an application on 25 February 1982 in which they proposed demolition of the bungalow and its replacement with a three-bedroom house comparable to those in the neighborhood.

The Nollans were told that the commission would grant their application—if they agreed to allow the public an easement, or a right to pass through their property. According to this easement, pedestrians could use the portion of the Nollans' property between the high-tide line and the seawall as a walkway to move between the public beaches on either side. The Nollans protested, and the commission overruled their objections. On 3 June 1982, the couple filed a petition for writ of administrative *mandamus*, an injunction ordering a public official to undertake a specific action, with the Ventura County Superior Court. The court agreed with their claim that the commission's restriction on their development could not be imposed in the absence of proof that building their house would actually have

Takings Clause of the Fifth and Sixth Amendments

The Taking Clause or "just compensation" principle is a provision of the Constitution that suggests that the government must compensate individuals for the confiscation of private property. In a 1922 opinion Justice Oliver Wendell Holmes extended the Takings Clause to include situations where government regulation causes a significant decrease in the value of an individual's property.

Despite early efforts to define a general formula to determine when or if an individual should be compensated for a taking, they are now dealt with on a case by case basis. There is some debate over the original intent of the Takings Clause. Some argue that only the seizure of property by the government warrants compensation while others contend that government regulation limiting the use and hence value of a piece of private property should also be compensated. The government weighs factors of public benefit against private loss to determine whether an individual is due compensation for takings. For example, if an individual owns a building which happens to be defined as an historic building, that individual would not be compensated if the government prohibited a potentially profitable venture (e.g. selling it to a chain department store); the individual could still profit from renting the building out.

Source(s): www.plannersweb.com

a clear and negative impact on public access to the beach. The court remanded the case to the commission for a full hearing.

At the hearing, officials for the commission announced that the new house would add to "a 'wall' of residential structures" that would "psychologically" prevent the public "from realizing [that] a stretch of coastline exists nearby that they have every right to visit." This "burden" on public access could only be offset by providing the public with an easement across the Nollans' property. The Nollans then filed a supplemental petition with the superior court, this time arguing that the commission violated the Takings Clause of the Fifth Amendment, which had been applied to the states in the Fourteenth. Again the superior court ruled for the petitioners, and ordered the Commission to strike the permit condition.

The Commission appealed to the California Court of Appeals; meanwhile the Nollans, without notifying the Commission, satisfied the condition of their purchase option by tearing down the bungalow. According to the later record of the U.S. Supreme Court, they built their house and bought the property, all in fulfillment of the plan they apparently had with the property's earlier owners—but without the approval of the commission. The court of appeals reversed the ruling of the superior court, and ruled in favor of the commission. Its opinion on the Coastal Act was based on its reading of the California Public Residence Code Annotated. The precedent for its ruling on the constitutional question came from an earlier California case involving similar issues.

When the Nollans appealed to the Supreme Court of the United States, they raised only the constitutional issue. Briefs of *amici curiae* (friends of the court) urging affirmance of the court of appeals's ruling were filed by officials representing the states of Alabama, Arkansas, Connecticut, Delaware, Florida, Hawaii, Illinois, Iowa, Kansas, Louisiana, Maine, Maryland, Massachusetts, Minnesota, Missouri, Nebraska, New Hampshire, New Jersey, New York, North Carolina, North Dakota, Oregon, Rhode Island, Tennessee, Texas, Vermont, Washington, West Virginia, and Wisconsin—29 states in all—as well as the Council of State Government, Designated California Cities and Counties, and the Natural Resources Defense Council. Solicitor General Fried of the United States filed a brief urging reversal. The California Association of Realtors and the National Association of Home Builders also filed briefs.

Limits on the State's Power to Take

The Court voted, 5-4, to reverse. Justice Scalia, delivering the opinion for the majority, began by pointing out that

> Although the outright taking of an uncompensated, permanent, public-access easement would violate the Takings Clause, conditioning appellants' rebuilding permit on their granting such an easement would be lawful land-use regulation if it substantially furthered governmental purposes that would justify denial of the permit.

In other words, if the government had some good reason to effectively lay claim on the land—and if it compensated the landowner for taking the property—then an action such as that of the commission with regard to the Nollans would be constitutional. But such was not the case in the present situation "since the condition does not serve public purposes related to the permit requirement." Among the reasons for the commission's demand had been that the public could not see the beach, and therefore would not be fully aware of their right to walk on it. How, Scalia asked by implication, would an easement across the beach side of the property make it easier to see the beach from the road, on the other side of the house? He further dismissed the commission's claim that the access requirement was part of a "comprehensive program" by the state to increase public access to the beach. If this was so, Scalia indicated, the state would have to pay the cost for this, and not "compel coastal residents alone to contribute to the realization of that goal."

Scalia devoted considerable attention to refuting the dissent of Justice Brennan, and early in his opinion, he wrote: "To say that the appropriation of a public easement does not constitute the taking of a property interest but rather (as Justice Brennan contends) 'a mere restriction on its use,' is to use words in a manner that deprives them of their ordinary meaning." The Court had held in *Loretto v. Teleprompter Manhattan CATV Corp.* (1982) quoting *Kaiser Aetna v. United States* (1979) that "the right to exclude [others is] 'one of the most essential sticks in the bundle of rights that are commonly characterized as property.'" In the present situation, although the commission had not proposed to take the Nollans' property per se, Scalia wrote that the rule nonetheless imposed a "permanent physical occupation" by creating a situation in which "individuals are given a permanent and continuous right to pass to and fro, so that the real property may continuously be traversed, even though no particular individual is permitted to station himself permanently upon the premises."

Scalia then addressed the question of whether the condition of an easement constituted taking, and he used as his standard the relationship between the condition and its purported aim. The "lack of nexus" between the easement and its ostensible purpose "converts that purpose to something other than what it was." If the commission had truly been interested in whether people could see the beach from the road, Scalia suggested, it might have issued limitations on the height of the house—which would have been perfectly lawful. But in the present situation the purpose was "quite simply, the obtaining of an easement to serve some valid government purpose, but without payment of compensation." This, Scalia held, was "an out-and-out plan of extortion."

Dissent: "It Is Private Landowners Who Are the Interlopers"

Justices Blackmun, Brennan, Stevens, and Marshall all dissented. Of the dissenting opinions, the one filed by Brennan, with which Marshall joined, was by far the longest and most forceful. Brennan urged greater flexibility for states to make rules affecting private property, and criticized the Court's "cramped standard" of interpreting restrictions on state authority. As for

Scalia's claim that the easement was invalid because it had nothing to do with the condition it was supposed to address, Brennan held that the state was responsible for all aspects of public access to the public tidewaters. This included "visual access" (in the commission's words) from the road, as well as "lateral access" from beach to beach. To Brennan, this wide-ranging authority constituted "flexibility" on the state's part, and "The Court's insistence on a precise fit between the forms of burden and condition on each individual parcel along the California coast would penalize the commission for its flexibility, hampering the ability to fulfill its public trust mandate."

Instead of expecting so much from the states, Brennan suggested, the Court should turn its attentions to another quarter: "The Court's demand for this precise fit," he wrote,

> is based on the assumption that private landowners in this case possess a reasonable expectation regarding the use of their land that the public has attempted to disrupt. In fact, the situation is precisely the reverse: it is private landowners who are the interlopers.

In any case, "[t]he physical intrusion permitted by the deed restriction is minimal," and the Court had declared in *Pruneyard Shopping Center v. Robins* (1980) that physical access to private property could be permitted as long as it did not "unreasonably impair the value or use of [the] property."

In Brennan's view, California had done at least as much for the Nollans as the Nollans had done for California. It had allowed them to replace their tiny one-story bungalow home with a two-story house three times its size. Thus they had enjoyed an increase in their property values even with the easement—an increase that, in Brennan's eyes, the state had given the Nollans by allowing them to spend their money on building the house. Furthermore, by imposing deed restrictions on other landowners along the beach, the commission had made it possible for the Nollans to walk wherever they chose. If California had allegedly deprived the Nollans of the full value of their development, the problem was that the Nollans had flawed expectations, since the commission "was under no obligation to approve" the couple's proposal for the development of their property. In any case, Brennan wrote, quoting *Andrus v. Allard* (1979), "the interest in anticipated gains has traditionally been viewed as less compelling than other property-related interests."

Justices Blackmun and Stevens also issued dissenting opinions, though theirs were less clearly critical of the Nollans' claim that they had full rights to their property. Blackmun took issue chiefly with the Court's concern for a "necessary correlation between the burden created by a development and a condition imposed pursuant to the State's police power to mitigate that burden," which he described as "an 'eye for an eye' mentality."

Stevens, with whom Blackmun joined, made note of the Court's "remarkable ruling" in *First English Evangelical Lutheran Church of Glendale v. County of Los Angeles* (1987), when it held that "local governments and officials must pay the price for the necessarily vague standards" of zoning and development laws. As Stevens noted, in *San Diego Gas & Electric Co. v. San Diego* (1981), Justice Brennan had proposed then that officials who made mistakes which hurt citizens—mistakes such as the Coastal Commission had apparently made—they should be liable for "temporary taking" of property and should be punished severely. (Given the fact that Brennan was one of the dissenters in that case, however, it is likely that he meant this to be taken in some way other than literally—perhaps simply to make a point about a ruling with which he disagreed.) Stevens, observing that "I like the hat that Justice Brennan has donned today better than the one he wore in San Diego," concluded that he agreed with Brennan in the present case.

Impact

Nollan belonged to a trend in favor of property rights, a reaction to the statist movement that had begun in the era of Roosevelt and the New Deal. (The latter was in turn a reaction to abuses by big business in the name of private property during the late nineteenth and early twentieth centuries.) After *Nollan*, landowners gained more victories in *Lucas v. South Carolina Coastal Council* (1992) and *Dolan v. City of Tigard* (1994). In the first of these, the Court upheld a landowner's right to receive compensation for a government coastal protection plan which rendered his land virtually unusable; in the second, the Court held that local governments

must show "rough proportionality" between the conditions they imposed on people developing their land, and the alleged evils these conditions were intended to address. The issues raised in *Nollan* continue to be volatile ones, particularly in an era fraught with environmental concerns which encourage governments to place severe restrictions on land use—or even, in some disputed cases, to entirely deprive individuals of their land in the interests of protecting an endangered species.

Related Cases

Euclid v. Ambler Realty Co., 272 U.S. 365 (1926).
Williamson v. Lee Optical of Oklahoma, Inc., 348 U.S. 483 (1955).
Penn Central Transportation Co. v. New York City, 438 U.S. 104 (1978).
Pruneyard Shopping Center v. Robins, 447 U.S. 74 (1980).
Loretto v. Teleprompter Manhattan CATV Corp., 458 U.S. 419 (1982).
First English Evangelical Lutheran Church v. County of Los Angeles, 482 U.S. 304 (1987).
Lucas v. South Carolina Coastal Council, 505 U.S. 1003 (1992).
Dolan v. City of Tigard, 114 S. Ct. 2481 (1994).

Bibliography and Further Reading

Hall, Kermit L., ed. *The Oxford Companion to the Supreme Court of the United States.* New York: Oxford University Press, 1992.

Witt, Elder. *Congressional Quarterly's Guide to the U.S. Supreme Court,* 2nd ed. Washington, DC: Congressional Quarterly, Inc., 1990.

Witt, Elder. *The Supreme Court A to Z. CQ's Encyclopedia of American Government,* rev. ed. Washington, DC: Congressional Quarterly, Inc., 1994.

ENVIRONMENTAL LAW

Overview

Up until the 1960s, environmental regulation in the United States was mostly left to state and local governments. There was very little, if any, national control. Since most regulation occurred at the city and state government level, it was difficult for authorities to enforce laws beyond their own territories, especially if the source of the pollution emanated from another region or state. Business and industries that caused large amounts of pollution could affect vast areas around them with little concern of either discovery or the payment of legal reparations.

The climate during the 1960s was ripe for the federal government to adopt a national strategy on environmental regulation. The country was becoming more aware that complete freedom for business and industry resulted in large scale environmental damage and that safety limits needed to be instituted to protect waterways, air, natural resources, and scenic areas.

Several elements influenced the national movement toward greater control over polluters. First, the 1960s was a decade of incredible commercial growth. There was greater production on the part of manufacturing and industry and that consequently resulted in greater consumption. More waste was produced, national cancer rates soared, and the public enjoyed an unbridled economic growth that brought with it a high price tag. Second, in 1962, Rachel Carson published *Silent Spring*. In her book, she questioned the use of chemical pesticides and demonstrated how they could penetrate the food chain through reproductive dysfunctions, thereby posing significant health risks to animals and humans. National suspicion grew over the use of pesticides, prompting research and eventually contributing to the ban of the pesticide DDT in the United States in 1973. Third, on 22 April 1970, the first Earth Day was held. This educated hundreds of thousands of Americans to the need for sound environmental health. Fourth, the occurrence of several environmental catastrophes throughout the last two decades gradually made the country conscious of the destructive power of pollution and the contamination of the environment. Events that contributed to increased attention on the environment included: the nuclear accident at Three Mile island in Harrisburg, Pennsylvania, in 1979; a devastating emission of poisonous gas at a Union Carbide plant in Bhopal, India, in 1984; the discharge of radiation at the Chernobyl nuclear power plant in the Soviet Union in 1986; the dumping of 11 million gallons of oil into Prince William Sound, Alaska, in 1989; and the burning of hundreds of oil wells in Kuwait during the Persian Gulf war in 1991.

As more evidence of environmental degradation appeared, the United States federal government was forced to delegate a greater focus on regulation. State and local governments played a major role in the battle against pollution, but it was the U.S. Congress that passed the most comprehensive laws, requiring the states to shape their pollution control programs to fit federal standards. States are free to set tougher standards within their own jurisdictions, but they must adhere to the federal minimums.

The first significant federal legislation came with the passage of the National Environmental Policy Act (NEPA) in 1969. It required that all federal government agencies follow certain rules when considering a proposed project. These rules include requiring federal agencies to use a systematic procedure in environmental decision making. Detailed reporting, commonly called impact studies, regarding the effects of proposed projects must be completed. The report for a proposed project must include the expected environmental impacts, any unavoidable negative impacts, short and long-term benefits and consultation with other involved agencies.

In 1970, the Environmental Protection Agency (EPA) was created in response to mounting environmental concern in the United States. The main responsibility of the EPA is the management of many complex and highly technical programs that regulate such broad and diverse problems as air and water pollution, waste disposal and toxic contamination. The EPA's primary duty is to require compliance with several major environmental statutes, including the Clean Air Act of 1963, the Clean Water Act of 1977, the Resource Conservation and Recovery Act of 1976, the Toxic Substances Control Act of 1976, and the Comprehensive Environmental Response, Compensation, and Liability Act of 1980, also known as Superfund.

Industrial, recreational, agricultural, and commercial activities that degrade the environment must be restricted through laws which balance the benefits and risks between the economic costs and the desired environmental outcomes. Setting limits on economic activity is a difficult task, especially when lawmakers and scientists are involved. The following statutes reflect the effort involved in trying to balance between these benefits and risks.

Clean Air Act

In 1963, the first Clean Air Act was passed. While it was amended and strengthened in 1965 and 1967, much of the enforcement for controlling air pollution continued to rest with the individual states. A more comprehensive Clean Air Act was passed in 1970, and it was further fortified in 1977 and 1990. One of the longest and most complicated of the environmental laws, the Clean Air Act withholds federal highway funding to states that do not meet air quality standards.

Motor vehicles are the main source of air pollution. With the introduction of catalytic converters in 1975, auto emissions of hydrocarbons and carbon monoxide have been reduced by 90 percent and nitrogen oxides by 75 percent. State and federal environmental agencies can penalize, fine, and imprison those who violate the Clean Air Act. However, it is difficult to police polluters, and as a result, many who disobey the law go unpunished.

Clean Water Act

The Clean Water Act (CWA) was enacted in 1977 in response to nationwide water pollution issues. The CWA established national programs for the prevention, reduction, and elimination of pollution in national navigable waters and groundwater. The CWA functions primarily by requiring persons or businesses engaging in polluting activities to obtain a permit from the EPA. This permit details the amount, type, and manner in which the substance may be discharged into the water. If permit conditions are violated, the permit holder is subject to civil or criminal penalties. The CWA authorizes each state to implement and enforce its provisions.

There are three categories of water pollution sources: point sources, non-point sources and dredge and fill operations. Point sources refer to any discernable, confined conveyance from which a pollutant may be discharged, such as a pipe or ditch. Non-point source pollution is spread by rainwater and melting snow runoff into, over, and through soils to surface water or through soils to underground reservoirs. The EPA considers non-point source pollution the largest cause of water contamination in the nation. Agricultural activ-

ities are the biggest contributor to this type of water pollution via the use of pesticides, herbicides, and fertilizers. Logging and mining operations, waste disposal sites and landfills, urban areas and roads, and atmospheric deposition are secondary sources of non-point source pollution. Finally, dredge and fill operations include sludge disposal, dredging operations, and in-water construction.

Safe Drinking Water Act

The Safe Drinking Water Act (SDWA) was designed to correct flaws in the Clean Water Act. The SDWA requires that the EPA set primary drinking water regulations for any pollutants that may have an adverse effect on human health. It focuses on groundwater contamination whereas the CWA focuses on surface water contamination. The primary objectives of the SDWA are: to protect the nation's sources of drinking water; and to protect public health to the maximum extent possible, using proper water treatment techniques. The EPA has set primary drinking water standards entitled "maximum contaminant levels" (MCL) for 27 pollutants, and secondary MCLs for nearly 82 additional contaminants that can be found in tap water. The National Wildlife Federation estimates that 100,000 violations of the SDWA occur every year nationally.

In August of 1996 the SDWA was updated to overhaul the act's standard-setting process and to establish a funding mechanism to help states improve their drinking systems. The major innovations to the SDWA include the greater responsibility of individual states as well as a revolving fund system which allows states more latitude in monitoring contaminants. States are permitted to have partnerships with public water systems, local governments and private companies to achieve their goal of water contaminant reduction.

Resource Conservation and Recovery Act

The Resource Conservation and Recovery Act (RCRA) was passed in 1976 to address management of the country's huge volume of solid waste. The law requires that the EPA regulate the management of hazardous waste, which includes waste solvents, batteries, and many other substances considered potentially harmful to human health and to the environment. RCRA controls all aspects of hazardous wastes from the point of generation, to treatment, storage, and disposal. Those states that meet the EPA specifications are eligible for monetary assistance and technical support. The RCRA was further amended in 1984 to include recycling as part of the state requirement for a solid waste disposal plan.

Comprehensive Environmental Response, Compensation, and Liability Act

The Comprehensive Environmental Response, Compensation, and Liability Act (CERCLA) of 1980, popularly known as Superfund, is an act that provides for liability, compensation, cleanup, and emergency response for hazardous substances released into the environment. It was created in response to the Love Canal tragedy and includes cleanup of inactive hazardous waste disposal sites, such as abandoned warehouses, manufacturing facilities, processing plants, and landfills.

The Superfund program is administered by the EPA through the Office of Solid Waste and Emergency Response in cooperation with individual states. Once Superfund locates a hazardous site anywhere in the United States, it investigates and then cleans up the site. When those responsible for the damage cannot be located, Superfund passes the cost of the cleanup on to the taxpayer. Over 30,000 toxic waste disposal sites have been targeted for cleanup.

In 1986 when Congress amended the Superfund law, it added the Emergency Planning and Community Right-to-Know Act (EPCRA). This came as a result of public fears over the Union Carbide chemical release in Bhopal, India. The EPCRA is designed to help communities prepare for and respond to emergencies involving hazardous substances. It also requires facilities to report hazardous chemical inventories and comply with toxic chemical reporting. Any facility that releases more than a predetermined amount of certain hazardous substances into the environment must notify the appropriate state and local emergency planning entities immediately.

Toxic Substances Control Act

The Toxic Substances Control Act (TSCA) of 1976 governs the manufacturing, importing, distributing, and processing of all toxic chemicals. TSCA requires that all such chemicals be inspected and approved by the EPA before they enter the market. The EPA has the option of restricting the chemical run tests and gathering data during its preapproval judgment of whether the chemical represents a threat to health or the environment. The TSCA has never been strictly enforced because of deficient funding and the large volume of chemicals constantly being developed and manufactured.

Federal Insecticide, Fungicide, and Rodenticide Act

The Federal Insecticide, Fungicide, and Rodenticide Act (FIFRA) of 1972, regulates the manufacture, storage and application of EPA registered pesticide products. The impetus for the passage of this legislation was national concern about the beneficial effects of pesticides used to control insects, rodents and fungi in comparison to the environmental harm caused by the use of pesticide products. Congress required the EPA through FIFRA to obtain toxicological, health, and environmental effects data on all pesticides in use.

Endangered Species Act

In 1973, the Endangered Species Act (ESA) was enacted to stop the extinction of many species of wild animals and plants in the United States, other nations, and at sea. It provided mechanisms for the conservation of ecosystems on which endangered species depend. It also discouraged the exploitation of endangered species in other countries by banning the importation and trade of any product made from such species. Of critical concern was the loss of biodiversity through species extinction. This is an irreversible process and a fundamental environmental problem. The Secretaries of the Interior and Commerce administer the ESA. The National Marine Fisheries Service is responsible for marine species while the U.S. Fish and Wildlife Service is responsible for freshwater and terrestrial species.

The ESA provides two levels of protection for listed species. Those that are considered to be in immediate danger of extinction are listed as endangered and are provided with stringent protection regulations. If a plant or animal is in danger of extinction throughout all or a significant portion of its range (the region in which it lives), then it is considered endangered. Species that are likely to become endangered in the future are listed as threatened and protected with less restrictive regulations. A candidate species is a species under review for listing. The ESA prohibits the using, taking, possessing, selling, or marketing for sale or trade those species registered on the endangered list. Any international species may be recorded on the endangered species list.

Once a species is confirmed for the listing, a critical habitat must be specified. The critical habitat is the area which is required for the species to essentially thrive. Through this special protection the conservancy of the species is instituted. A species may be listed as endangered or threatened for one or more of the following reasons: alteration or reduction of habitat or range; overuse for business, recreational, scientific, or educational purposes; futile protection regulations; disease, predatory effects or poaching, and any other natural forces or human activities affecting the survival possibilities. Generally, the economic impact as well as other factors are taken into consideration when designating critical habitat.

The ESA requires that the Secretary of Interior institute a recovery plan for listed species. A recovery team sets down parameters and management plans specific to the endangered species' critical habitat. By May of 1997 only slightly more than half of the listed U.S. species had recovery plans. More than 1,200 species worldwide, including more than 600 in the U.S. alone, are listed as threatened or endangered. Additionally, over 3,500 species are under consideration for listing.

A similar act to the ESA is the Marine Mammal Protection Act (MMPA) of 1972, which was enacted as a result of the large number of dolphins that were being killed by tuna fishing operations in the early 1970s. The MMPA protects all species of whales, dolphins, sea lions, seals, polar bears, walrus, manatees, and sea otters from the impact of human activities. In the United States, 30 percent of endangered species are aquatic.

Sanctions

Administrative, civil, and even criminal sanctions may be used to enforce environmental laws. The possible types of restrictions may include denial or revocation of operational permits, the closing of operations, poor publicity, economic sanctions, fines, or even imprisonment. These sanctions occur at various levels of environmental enforcement—national, regional, and local.

The United States has had much experience in enforcing environmental requirements against public authorities. With only a few exceptions, the U.S. federal government has waived its exemption from fines and financial penalties. It has given both state governments and citizens the right to take the federal government and its agencies to court if the government authorities do not comply with federal, state, or local environmental requirements. However, it is easier for environmental associations such as Greenpeace and Sierra Club, and not individuals, to seek legal action as they have greater resources and expertise for advancing public interests in court. Based on the U.S. Constitution's Article III "case or controversy" requirement, a plaintiff's alleged injury must show fact, causation, and redressability. Proving these three requirements can be difficult for a single citizen.

Despite the comprehensive scope of diverse environmental laws, many corporate and individual polluters go undetected. General principles or guidelines are necessary to interpret and implement a flexible environmental law. These principles must include precautions in regulating pollution, cooperation between the regulating bodies and industry, maintenance of biodiversity, non-degradation of natural resources, the idea of polluter-pays, access to information and participation, and the theory of burden of proof. As stated by Sevine Ercmann in *Environmental Law,* "These principles should orient the decision-makers when they take decisions interpreting or enforcing certain issues under different circumstances. National and global environmental deterioration has gone too far, and confidence and patience in experimenting with new tools of enforcement are diminishing." As international environmental destruction escalates at a greater rate than in the United States, it is important to remember that everyone is made vulnerable by environmental problems wherever they occur. The destruction of the tropical rainforest, the widespread damage done by acid rain, global warming, ocean dumping, and ozone depletion are but a few of the international concerns for countries throughout the world. Strict comprehensive, enforceable treaties dealing with these issues will require nations to relinquish some autonomy in their economic activities. However, without these measures in place, the future of the environment is in jeopardy.

Bibliography and Further Reading

Bureau of National Affairs Editorial Staff. *U.S. Environmental Laws.* Washington DC: Library of Congress, 1986.

Ercmann, Sevine. "Enforcement of Environmental Law in United States and European Law: realities and expectations." *Environmental Law,* 1996, Vol. 26, no. 4 p. 1213-1239.

Firestone, David B. and Frank C. Reed. *Environmental Law for Non-Lawyers.* Woburn, MA: Butterworth, 1983.

Government Institutes, Inc. *Environmental Statutes 1993 Edition.* Rockville, MD: Government Institutes, 1993.

Newton, David E. *Taking a Stand Against Environmental Pollution.* New York: Franklin Watts, 1990.

Rosenbaum, Walter A. *Environmental Politics and Policy.* 2nd ed. Washington DC: CQ Press, 1991.

Schwartz, Meryl. *The Environment and the Law.* New York: Chelsea House Publishers, 1993.

Vig, Norman J., and Michael E. Kraft. *Environmental Policy in the 90's.* Washington DC: Congressional Quarterly, 1990

EUCLID V. AMBLER REALTY CO.

Legal Citation: 272 U.S. 365 (1926)

Appellant
Village of Euclid, Ohio

Appellee
Ambler Realty Co.

Appellant's Claim
That a decree of the U.S. District Court for Northern District of Ohio enjoining enforcement of village zoning regulations should be reversed.

Chief Lawyer for Appellant
James Metzenbaum

Chief Lawyer for Appellee
Newton D. Baker

Justices for the Court
Louis D. Brandeis, Oliver Wendell Holmes, Edward Terry Sanford, Harlan Fiske Stone, George Sutherland (writing for the Court), William Howard Taft

Justices Dissenting
Pierce Butler, James Clark McReynolds, Willis Van Devanter

Place
Washington, D.C.

Date of Decision
22 November 1926

Decision
The Court upheld the village's right to enact zoning, reversing the Ohio court's decision.

Significance
The decision established the right of local governments to control land use through zoning laws.

Public Welfare Versus Private Ownership

Euclid, Ohio lies a few miles inland from the shore of Lake Erie, northeast of the city of Cleveland. In 1926, the village of Euclid won a case in the U.S. Supreme Court which affirmed the right of local governments to control the use of land through zoning.

To avoid being engulfed by the approaching growth of the nearby city, on 13 November 1922 Euclid's Village Council passed zoning ordinances governing the use of local land. Six distinct zones were created within Euclid's boundaries, each with its own rules stipulating what the town considered to be acceptable types of development. The first zone, for example, was to be reserved for single family dwellings, with industry completely prohibited. At the other end of the scale, the sixth zone allowed usage for manufacturing, fuel storage, penal institutions, or whatever else land owners might desire to build. Four intermediate district classifications set rules over what balance of business and residential development would be allowed in each.

The Ambler Realty Company had bought 68 acres of vacant land in Euclid prior to the village council's action. Most of the realty company's holdings lay within the U-6 or "industrial" zone defined by the town. Some of the land, however, lay within the more restrictive zones, disallowing Ambler's plans to sell the real estate for industrial development. Ambler Realty took the village to federal court over the new local law, claiming that zoning rules diminished the value of their investment property to only a quarter of what the land was worth as industrial real estate.

Because courts generally deferred to the constitutional rights of private property owners, Ambler Realty had good reason to hope that their suit would succeed. Instead of attacking the specifics of Euclid's regulations, however, the suit assaulted the concept of zoning itself, attempting to push such regulation out of the way. As land owners, Ambler Realty claimed that the village council's rule-making infringed upon the company's rights to due process and equal protection under the law, as guaranteed by the Fourteenth Amendment. From a legal standpoint, this strategy was a fatal mistake.

Ambler Realty was initially successful. The Federal Court for the Northern District of Ohio granted the company an injunction in January of 1924, enjoining Euclid's building inspector from enforcing the zoning laws. The decision found that preventing the realtors from reselling their property for its maximum potential value amounted to depriving the company of "property" (i.e. resale profit) without due compensation. Euclid's law was declared unconstitutional.

Court Rules for "A Changing World"

By presenting their case as a constitutional issue, Ambler Realty left the door open for the village of Euclid to appeal the federal court's decision before the U.S. Supreme Court. The case was argued in Washington, D.C., on 27 January 1926 and reargued on 12 October 1926. On 22 November, the Court reversed the federal court injunction by a 6-3 vote. Justices Van Devanter, McReynolds, and Butler dissented without producing a written comment on the case.

Ambler Realty claimed that zoning diminished the value of their property, thus depriving them of both the liberty to use the land according to their own wishes and a substantial amount of potential resale value. The Court reaffirmed the importance of protecting the rights of private property ownership. Yet the Court also approved of zoning in broad terms, justifying regulation only in cases where it was designed to protect public welfare.

Justice Sutherland's written opinion noted the similarities between Euclid's statutes and the so-called "nuisance laws," with which municipalities had previously governed land use. Nuisance laws were usually written and invoked to contain problems like pollution, vice, or possible disease. The Court found that Euclid's zoning laws were similarly defensible as a means of promoting public welfare. While a few state courts opposed zoning, the Court pointed to a majority of states whose laws supported a growing societal consensus that zoning helped reduce or control residential overcrowding, traffic congestion, crime, noise, disease, and pollution.

The Court did not declare zoning to be an omnipotent principle. It was generally appropriate in Euclid's case, but the Court proposed that some laws governing use of specific parcels of land might be found to be unconstitutional. Since Ambler Realty had sought relief from Euclid's statutes only in broad terms, the Court was not required to rule on any particular instances in which the zoning regulations might have been unfair. Only the potential use of Ambler Realty's land had been at issue in their suit, but the Court found zoning rules regarding building height and breadth to be equally constitutional. Justice Sutherland noted that zoning laws could have been oppressive if applied in past eras. Now, however, the Court approved of zoning as an idea whose time had come, reflecting the increasing urbanization of American life, the arrival of automobiles, and safety concerns relating to public transit.

The Supreme Court's decision legitimized the fundamental idea of zoning in the eyes of the law. Zoning disputes were usually fought in state courts prior to the *Euclid v. Ambler Realty Co.* decision. Ironically, this did not change. State courts had no rule by which to guide their decisions before the *Euclid* conflict. The Supreme Court's ruling disposed of the debate over zoning as a concept, allowing the lower courts to more uniformly address specific issues in future individual land use cases.

Related Cases

Washington ex rel. Seattle Trust Co. v. Roberge, 278 U.S. 116 (1928).
Village of Belle Terre v. Boraas, 416 U.S. 1 (1974).
Young v. American Mini Theatres Inc., 427 U.S. 50 (1976).
Moore v. City of East Cleveland, 431 U.S. 494 (1977).
City of Renton v. Playtime Theatres, 485 U.S. 41 (1986).

Bibliography and Further Reading

"Euclid Case Hailed as Zoning Victory." *New York Times,* 28 November 1926, sec. 11, p. 9.

Hall, Kermit. L. ed. *The Oxford Companion To The Supreme Court Of The United States.* New York: Oxford University Press, 1992.

"Important Decision Expected On Zoning." *New York Times,* 14 November 1926, sec. 11, p. 1.

Kurland, Phillip B., and Casper, Gerhard, ed. *Landmark Briefs and Arguments of the Supreme Court of the United States,* Volume 24. Arlington: University Publications of America, 1975.

Nelson, Robert H. *Zoning and Property Rights.* Cambridge: MIT Press, 1977.

"Zoning Is Upheld By Supreme Court." *New York Times,* 23 November 1926, p. 17.

HURON PORTLAND CEMENT CO. V. CITY OF DETROIT

Legal Citation: 362 U.S. 440 (1960)

Appellant
Huron Portland Cement Co.

Appellee
City of Detroit

Appellant's Claim
That the city of Detroit had no right to enforce a local anti-pollution ordinance against ships owned by the Huron Portland Cement Company, given that those ships had been "inspected, approved and licensed" by the Federal Government for interstate commerce; moreover, even if Detroit's law was not in conflict with federal law, enforcement of the statute was an unreasonable restraint of interstate commerce.

Chief Lawyer for Appellant
John F. Hathaway

Chief Lawyer for Appellee
Alfred E. Lindbloom

Justices for the Court
Hugo Lafayette Black, William J. Brennan, Jr., Tom C. Clark, John Marshall Harlan II, Potter Stewart (writing for the Court), Earl Warren, Charles Evans Whittaker

Justices Dissenting
William O. Douglas, Felix Frankfurter

Place
Washington, D.C.

Date of Decision
25 April 1960

Decision
That the Detroit anti-smoke ordinance was constitutional, even when applied to ships licensed by the federal government, and that the criminal provisions of the Detroit law did not impose "an undue burden" on interstate commerce.

Significance
This case was an important step forward in establishing cities' right to institute environmental legislation, even if such laws caused difficulties for business. It was also another step in the ongoing effort to determine the balance of power between federal and local government.

In the 1960s, concerns about the environment were far less common than they are today. The word "pollution" was still a new term, while the idea that an industrial plant might release toxic fumes or dangerous by-products was a relatively rare notion. In this context, *Huron Portland Cement Co. v. City of Detroit, et al.* stands as an early example of the Supreme Court upholding environmental legislation.

Hand-Fired Boilers and Coal Smoke

The Huron Portland Cement Co. was a Michigan company engaged in the manufacture and sale of cement. Its fleet of five vessels traveled across the Great Lakes, carrying cement to various customers from its mill in Alpena, Michigan. Huron Portland Cement Co. had made certain to have all its ships inspected, approved, and licensed by the U.S. Coast Guard. However, two of its vessels, the S.S. *S.T. Crapo* and the S.S. *John W. Boardman* were equipped with hand-fired Scotch marine boilers. When these boilers were operating, they burned fuel coal in such a way as to emit huge quantities of dense, black smoke.

The City of Detroit, mindful of the enormous amount of industry it then contained, had passed the Smoke Abatement Code, which limited the amount of smoke any combustion equipment could emit. If an owner's device emitted more than the legal amount of smoke, he or she might be liable for a fine of $100 and a 30-day jail sentence, so the Huron Portland Cement Company found itself in violation of the Detroit law.

Criminal charges were brought against the company. The company responded by taking the city to court. The company argued that its ships had been licensed by the federal government and approved for interstate trade. In order to get licensed, the ships had even been inspected by the Coast Guard.

Regulating Interstate Commerce

The company argued that the Detroit laws were clearly unreasonable. They imposed an unfair burden on interstate commerce, and on those grounds alone, they should be found unconstitutional. The Supreme Court did not agree.

Early Pollution Regulations

Major pollution regulation is administered by the federal government in cooperation with the states. Efforts to regulate pollution began before World War II. Early pollution regulation focused on preserving clean air and drinking water. The rapid increase of industrial output in the United States brought on greater challenges for the environment in such areas as hazardous waste disposal, ozone depletion, climate change, chemical plant accidents, and medical waste.

In the 1970s the federal government began to take a lead role in environmental law. Earth Day of 1970 was the symbolic starting point of federal involvement pollution regulation, though regulation began in the 1940s. There have been roughly nine major laws enacted to regulate pollution, beginning with the Federal Insecticide, Fungicide, and Rodenticide Act (1947). Other major legislation enacted to regulate pollution includes: the Water Pollution Control Act (1948); Air Pollution Control Act (1955); National Environmental Policy Act (1970); the Safe Drinking Water Act (1974); Toxic Substances Control Act (1976); and the Pollution Prevention Act (1990). There have also been hundreds of minor regulatory laws adopted to control pollution.

Source(s): Davies, J. Clarence, and Jan Mazurek. *Pollution Control in the United States: Evaluating the System.* Resources for the Future, 1998.

When it finally heard the case on appeal, the Court found that the Detroit laws were completely justified. Writing for the majority, Justice Stewart explained:

> The ordinance was enacted for the manifest purpose of promoting the health and welfare of the city's inhabitants. Legislation designed to free from pollution the very air that people breathe clearly falls within the exercise of even the most traditional concept of what is . . . known as the police power.

The Court went further. In addition to affirming Detroit's right to regulate its air quality, Stewart asserted the government's general right to make laws protecting its citizens, even if such laws might adversely affect interstate commerce. This was true even though only the federal government could actually regulate the commerce between states:

> . . . it must be borne in mind that the Constitution when "conferring upon Congress the regulation of commerce . . . never intended to cut the States off from legislating on all subjects relating to the health, life, and safety of their citizens, though the legislation might indirectly affect the commerce of the country. Legislation, in a great variety of ways, may affect commerce and persons engaged in it without constituting a regulation of it, within the meaning of the Constitution."

"At War With the Federal License"

Justices Douglas and Frankfurter strongly disagreed with the majority opinion. They argued that, "[t]he requirements of the Detroit smoke ordinance are squarely in conflict with the federal statute." The dissenters agreed that there were many areas in which local regulations might be added to federal ones. Speed limits, traffic regulations, or rules for using a dock might all exist alongside of federal laws for inspecting and licensing boats. But, wrote Douglas, in those cases:

> . . . we would have local laws not at war with the federal license, but complementary to it . . . This case [on the other hand] . . . involves the collision between a local law and a federal law . . .

Local vs. Federal Control

In a sense, both the majority and the minority of the Court were trying to balance two competing interests in *Huron Cement Co.* On the one hand, local units of government had the right to use "police power" to protect their citizens. On the other hand, companies engaged in interstate commerce had the right to expect a uniform standard that would apply in all fifty states, so that once they were licensed by the federal government, they could feel sure that they would be allowed to operate anywhere in the country.

Related Cases

South Carolina State Highway Department v. Barnwell, 303 U.S. 177 (1938).
Southern Pacific Co. v. Arizona ex rel. Sullivan, 325 U.S. 761 (1945).
Bibb v. Navajo Freight Lines Inc., 359 U.S. 520 (1959).
Hunt v. Washington State Apple Ad. Comm., 432 U.S. 333 (1977).
Kassell v. Consolidated Freightways Corp., 450 U.S. 662 (1981).

Bibliography and Further Reading

Toh, Kevin G. "Are Credit-Card Late Fees 'Interest'?" *Michigan Law Review,* March 1996, p. 1294.

TRAIN V. CITY OF NEW YORK

Legal Citation: 420 U.S. 35 (1975)

Appellant
Russell E. Train, Administrator, Environmental Protection Agency

Appellee
City of New York

Appellant's Claim
That the Environmental Protection Agency (EPA) did not have to allot federal funds in their entirety to states according to the Federal Water Pollution Control Act Amendments of 1972.

Chief Lawyer for Appellant
Robert H. Bork, U.S. Solicitor General

Chief Lawyer for Appellee
John R. Thompson

Justices for the Court
Harry A. Blackmun, William J. Brennan, Jr., Warren E. Burger, William O. Douglas, Thurgood Marshall, Lewis F. Powell, Jr., William H. Rehnquist, Potter Stewart, Byron R. White (writing for the Court)

Justices Dissenting
None

Place
Washington D.C.

Date of Decision
18 February 1975

Decision
The EPA had to disburse funds in their entirety to states seeking financial assistance under the Federal Water Pollution Control Act; Court of Appeals for the District of Columbia Circuit decision affirmed.

Significance
That despite a presidential veto of the sum of moneys to be disbursed to states, the EPA was required to disburse the maximum allotments set forth in the Congressional Amendments to the Water Pollution Control Act.

The Federal Water Pollution Control Act was designed to help mitigate water pollution around the country. In 1972 the act was amended to provide financial assistance to states for improvements made to their sewers and sewage treatment plants. For this purpose, section 207 of the amendments designated maximum amounts of 5 million dollars and 6 million dollars to be allocated for fiscal years 1973 and 1974 respectively. The administrator for the Environmental Protection Agency was responsible for disbursing these funds according to a schedule set forth in section 205 (a) of the amendments. Congress passed the Amendments on 4 October 1972 and President Richard Nixon vetoed them on 17 October 1972. Even though Congress overrode the veto, President Nixon wrote a letter to the EPA administrator directing him to disburse only 2 million dollars and 3 million dollars for fiscal years 1973 and 1974 respectively.

When the administrator abided by the president's directive, the city of New York filed a class action suit seeking the 5 million dollar and 6 million dollar maximums due the municipality according to the Congressional Amendments. The city of New York brought their case before the District Court of the District of Columbia. A motion by the EPA to dismiss the suit was denied in May of 1973. After the district court granted the city of New York a summary judgment, the court of appeals found that the Water Pollution Control Act "requires the Administrator to allot the full sums authorized to be appropriated" according to section 207 of the amendments. Administrator Train promptly asked the U.S. Supreme Court to review the decision.

Petition for a Writ of *Certiorari*

The Supreme Court granted Train's request for a review, a process called a petition for a writ of *certiorari*. Train maintained that the language of section 205 (a) setting forth the disbursement duties of the administrator provides for a maximum dollar amount, not a minimum to be provided to the states. As evidence, he quoted the original legislation, which stated that: "all sums authorized to be appropriated pursuant to [section 207] . . . shall be allotted by the Administrator." In the legislation actually enacted into law as the 1972 amend-

---

The Environmental Protection Agency

The Environmental Protection Agency is an independent agency within the U.S. government established in 1970. At that time the EPA's budget was roughly $1 billion; the EPA's current budget is nearly $8 billion. The current administrator of the EPA is Carol M. Browner. The EPA sets standards for environmental protection and monitors businesses to see that these standards are maintained. The EPA conducts research, offers grants, and monitors the activity of environmentally suspect industries, and oversees the impact of other federal agencies on the environment. Among its accomplishments the EPA has curbed pollution of the air and water, regulated hazardous waste disposal sites, cooperated in a world wide effort to limit the substances that deplete the ozone layer, and fined companies for violations of standards established by the EPA.

In recent years one of the central functions of the EPA has been administering the Comprehensive Environmental Response, Compensation and Liability Act of 1980, commonly known as Superfund. Congress initially approved $1.6 billion for the fund which was designed to clean up hazardous waste sites. In the early 1980s the agency was investigated by Congress for allegations of the misuse of funds in the Superfund project.

Source(s): www.epa.gov

---

ments, the word "all" was deleted. Train argued that the omission of the word all meant that he need not allot the maximum amounts. During the Supreme Court review, Justice White wrote in the opinion of the Court:

> The Administrator's arguments based on the statutory language and its legislative history are unpersuasive . . . It appears to us that the word 'sums' has no different meaning and can be ascribed no different function in the context of [section] 205 than would the words 'all sums.'

In affirming the court of appeals decision, the Supreme Court also found that the legislative text did not provide for executive intervention. Although the wording of the amendments was altered slightly from first draft to enactment, this was not sufficient justification for President Nixon's directive concerning diminished financial assistance. Justice White opined, "we cannot accept the . . . deletion of the one word from [section] 205 (a) as altering the entire complexion and thrust of the Act." Thus, Train was responsible for disbursing the maximum amounts described in the 1972 amendments of the Water Pollution Control Act to the city of New York.

Related Cases
Huron Portland Cement Co. v. City of Detroit, 362 U.S. 440 (1960).
Philadelphia v. New Jersey, 430 U.S. 141 (1977).

Bibliography and Further Reading
Biskupic, Joan, and Elder Witt, eds. *Congressional Quarterly's Guide to the U.S. Supreme Court*, 3rd ed. Washington, DC: Congressional Quarterly, Inc., 1996.

PHILADELPHIA V. NEW JERSEY

Legal Citation: 430 U.S. 141 (1977)

Appellant
City of Philadelphia

Appellee
State of New Jersey

Appellant's Claim
That a New Jersey law prohibiting disposal of liquid or solid waste within its borders, which "originated or was collected outside the state," violated the Commerce Clause of the Constitution.

Chief Lawyer for Appellant
Herbert F. Moore

Chief Lawyer for Appellee
Steven Skillman

Justices for the Court
Harry A. Blackmun, William J. Brennan, Jr., Thurgood Marshall, John Paul Stevens, Potter Stewart (writing for the Court), Byron R. White

Justices Dissenting
Warren E. Burger, Lewis F. Powell, Jr., William H. Rehnquist

Place
Washington, D.C.

Date of Decision
27 January 1978

Decision
The New Jersey legislature discriminated against other states under the Commerce Clause by banning disposal of waste from Philadelphia in the Garden State.

Significance
Under *Philadelphia v. New Jersey* environmental protectionism was found to be just as unconstitutionally "illegitimate" as any other barrier "isolating the state from the national economy." The decision effectively barred state legislatures from giving inhabitants of its own state "preferred rights," even to protect the natural ecology or as a safeguard against fears of possible "contagion."

The *per curium* decision in *Philadelphia v. New Jersey* meant "the court was ruling that the great compact drawn up in Philadelphia in 1787 implied a common undertaking that no state would try to solve its problems primarily at the expense of the people of other states." So argued famed Watergate prosecutor Archibald Cox in his book, *The Court and the Constitution*. New Jersey could not protect its environment "by discriminating against the waste of other states," Cox concluded.

Mounting public concern about environmental degradation in the late 1960s and early 1970s led to the passage of many state and federal laws. Perhaps the most notable state law was a 1974 New Jersey law prohibiting the dumping of out-of-state solid and liquid wastes in the Garden State other than garbage fed to pigs. New York and Philadelphia, which had been finding it "expedient or necessary," to use New Jersey as a dump for decades, protested. The New Jersey Supreme Court, however, agreed with the state legislature that any economic burden that New York and Philadelphia suffered as a consequence was "slight." The state court also found the need to protect New Jersey's health, resources, and environment against a "cascade of rubbish."

The city of Philadelphia sued New Jersey, citing the 1851 Supreme Court decision *Cooley v. The Board of Wardens*. That decision said prescribed state regulations, in the absence of federal statutes, "require uniformity" while "admitting of diversity." Under that formula, the Supreme Court had overturned many state laws designed to protect jobs, industries, and financial resources. Quarantines of diseased animals were notable exceptions. Such quarantines had been upheld, Justice Stewart wrote in *Philadelphia v. New Jersey* because:

> [D]iseased livestock required destruction as soon as possible because their very movement risked contagion. The New Jersey law is not such a quarantine law. There has been no claim here that the very movement of waste into or through New Jersey endangers health, or that waste must be disposed of as

Landfills

Landfills are the most commonly used methods of disposing of hazardous waste. However, landfills are considered to be an inefficient and dangerous means of waste disposal. There are over six thousand hazardous waste landfills in the United States. Some of these landfills are owned by companies designed to deal exclusively with waste disposal, while others are run by companies who generate large amounts of hazardous waste by-product in the production of goods.

When hazardous waste businesses fail, the government is left to clean up the abandoned sites. The Compre-

hensive Environment Response Compensation and Liability Act of 1980 (or Superfund) was established, in large part, to deal with such eventualities. Due to federal regulations established in the late 1980s and early 1990s, which tightened restrictions on where landfills could be established, there has been a shortage of landfill space in the U.S.

Source(s): *American City and County*, Vol. 109, no. 8, July, 1992, p. 38.

---

soon and as close to its point of generation as possible.

The justice continued:

> The harms caused by the waste are said to arise after its disposal in landfill sites, and, at that point, as New Jersey concedes, there is no basis to distinguish out-of-state waste from domestic waste. If one is inherently harmful, so is the other. Yet New Jersey has banned the former while leaving its landfill sites open to the other.

New Jersey was engaged in "an obvious effort," Justice Stewart concluded, "to saddle those outside the state with the entire burden of slowing the flow of refuse into New York's remaining landfill sites. That legislative effort is clearly impermissible under the Commerce Clause of the Constitution."

Justice Rehnquist dissented on behalf of himself and Chief Justice Burger:

> New Jersey should be free . . . to prohibit the importation of solid waste because of the health and safety problems that such wastes poses to its citizens . . . I do not see why a state may not ban the importation of items whose importation risks contagion, but cannot ban the importation of items which, although they may be transported . . . without undue hazard, will then simply pile up in an ever increasing danger to the public's health and safety. The Commerce Clause was not drawn with a view to having the validity of state laws turn on such pointless distinctions.

Justice Rehnquist then drew a distinction of his own, differing from Justice Stewart's, between the refuse of

New Jersey and that of other states. New Jersey's own dumping of wastes in landfills, Rehnquist argued:

> . . . does not mean that solid waste is not innately harmful. New Jersey out of sheer necessity must treat and dispose of its solid waste in some fashion, just as it must treat New Jersey cattle suffering from hoof-and-mouth disease. It does not follow that New Jersey must, under the Commerce Clause, accept solid waste or diseased cattle from outside its borders and thereby exacerbate its problems.

Solid waste, however, is not the equivalent of contaminated cattle, nor can anyone, including future chief justices, logically prove a negative. Without some positive proof to the contrary, the fact that solid waste may not be "innately harmful" is not proof that it is, in fact, "innately harmful." The conclusion in *Philadelphia v. New Jersey* is still a standing law.

Related Cases

Cooley v. The Board of Wardens, 53 U.S. 299 (1891).
Dutchess Sanitation, Inc. v. Town of Plattekill, 433 F.Supp. 580 (1977).

Bibliography and Further Reading

Bickel, Alexander, and Benno Schmidt. *History of the Supreme Court of the United States*. New York: Macmillan, 1984.

Cox, Archibald. *The Court and the Constitution*. Boston: Houghton-Mifflin, 1987.

Rehnquist, William H. *The Supreme Court, How It Was, How It Is*. New York: William Morrow & Co., Inc., 1987.

PACIFIC GAS & ELECTRIC CO. v. ENERGY RESOURCES COMMISSION

Legal Citation: 461 U.S. 190 (1983)

Petitioner
Pacific Gas & Electric Company

Respondent
State Energy Resources Conservation and Development Committee of California

Petitioner's Claim
That two California statutes governing development of nuclear power plants were preempted by the federal Atomic Energy Act of 1954 and were thus invalid under the Supremacy Clause of the Constitution.

Chief Lawyer for Petitioner
John R. McDonough

Chief Lawyer for Respondent
Laurence H. Tribe

Justices for the Court
Harry A. Blackmun, William J. Brennan, Jr., Warren E. Burger, Thurgood Marshall, Lewis F. Powell, Jr., William H. Rehnquist, Sandra Day O'Connor, John Paul Stevens, Byron R. White (writing for the Court)

Justices Dissenting
None

Place
Washington, D.C.

Date of Decision
20 April 1983

Decision
The Court having judged that one of the two statutes was not ripe for review, held that the remaining California law did not conflict with the authority of the federal government because it addressed issues of economics, not nuclear safety.

Significance
Pacific Gas & Electric Co. v. Energy Resources Commission provides a judicial framework for evaluating the limits of state and federal law with regard to specific areas of authority. In its review of the case, the Court applied a test—assessing the conflict, if any, between state and federal policies—that promised to offer guidelines for other cases involving preemption of federal authority.

"Swords into Plowshares"

In the years that followed World War II, the federal government redirected the uses of nuclear energy which had powered the bombs dropped over Japan at the end of the war. Justice White of the Supreme Court, using a phrase drawn from the Bible, referred to "[t]he turning of swords into plowshares"—that is, "the transformation of atomic power into a source of energy in American society." To this end, Congress in 1946 authorized the civilian application of atomic power, and in that year it passed the Atomic Energy Act, which created the Atomic Energy Commission (AEC). For the next eight years, the federal government maintained full control over the use of nuclear technology. Then came the Atomic Energy Act of 1954, which, as Justice White later noted, "grew out of Congress' determination that the national interest would be best served if the Government encouraged the private sector to become involved in the development of atomic energy for peaceful purposes."

Nuclear energy, of course, has not been without its attendant controversies over the potential dangers involved, including questions over disposal of nuclear waste—a key issue in *Pacific Gas & Electric Co. v. Energy Resources Commission*. A nuclear reactor must periodically have its fuel rods replaced, meaning that the radioactive waste fuel must be removed to a place where it will not be able to seep into the water table or otherwise contaminate natural resources and endanger human lives. Because nuclear power plant operators originally assumed that the fuel would be reprocessed, storage pools made to hold it were relatively limited in capacity and design. Over time, however, it became clear that, for whatever reason, the fuel would not be reprocessed. This resulted in large stores of radioactive waste—8,000 metric tons of it, according to the Court's record in 1983, a number expected to grow by a factor of nine in the years leading up to 2000. Over time, a variety of schemes had evolved for disposing of these wastes, including proposals to place it beneath permanently frozen ice sheets in Greenland and Antarctica, or even to shoot it into space via rockets. The most likely of these proposals involved placing it in subsurface salt deposits.

Thus it was evident, as Justice White noted, that "problems of how and where to store nuclear wastes [have] engendered considerable scientific, political, and public debate." The disposal of nuclear wastes involved not only safety considerations but also economic concerns. The lack of any viable option for long-term disposal would render nuclear energy an unpredictable resource, and therefore an economically inefficient form of energy as well. The dual safety and economic concerns springing from the issue of nuclear-waste disposal set the stage for the issues debated in *Pacific Gas*.

Pacific Gas Takes on the Energy Commission

Responding to these concerns, in 1974 the State of California passed the Warren-Alquist State Energy Resources Conservation and Development Act. Under the act, which was amended in 1976 to add new regulations, operators of nuclear power plants and other power-generating plants had to apply for certification by the State Energy Resources Conservation and Development Commission, or "Energy Commission" for short. Out of the myriad statutes covered in the act, sections 25524.1(b) and 25524.2 became the subject of debate in the case before the Court. Section 25524.1(b) provided that the Energy Commission had the authority to determine, prior to the building of a new nuclear power plant, that there would be adequate storage space for the spent fuel rods "at the time such nuclear facility requires such storage." Section 25524.2 addressed long-term concerns arising from nuclear wastes by placing a moratorium, or stoppage, on the certification of new plants until the Energy Commission "finds that there has been developed and that the United States through its authorized agency has approved and there exists a demonstrated technology or means for the disposal of high-level nuclear waste."

In 1978, Pacific Gas & Electric Company, along with another utility, Southern California Edison Company, filed an action against the Energy Commission in federal district court. They requested a declaration that several provisions in the Warren-Alquist Act—including the two mentioned above—were invalid under the Supremacy Clause of the Constitution, which establishes the importance of the federal government's power over that of the states. Since Washington already had the Atomic Energy Act in place, the petitioners charged, Warren-Alquist had to be unconstitutional. The district court agreed.

The Court of Appeals for the Ninth Circuit held that the petitioners had standing to challenge the statute, but that 25524.1(b) was not "ripe for review"—i.e., the law had not been allowed sufficient tests in practice before its judicial review. The reason given for this was that "we cannot know whether the Energy Commission will ever find a nuclear plant's storage capacity to be inadequate." As for the challenge to 25524.2, the court judged that the nuclear moratorium provisions were not preempted by federal law because sections 271 and 274(k) of the Atomic Energy Act provided authorization for the states to regulate nuclear power plants "for purposes other than protection against radiation hazards."

As the case came before the Supreme Court, a number of parties filed briefs of *amici curiae* (friends of the court) on either side. Deputy Solicitor General Claiborne argued for the United States as *amicus curiae* urging reversal, and the following entities filed briefs on the side of the petitioner: the Atomic Industrial Forum, Hans A. Bethe et al., the Edison Electric Institute, the Fusion Energy Foundation, the Legal Foundation of America, and the Pacific Legal Foundation et al. A number of states, through their attorneys general or other officials, filed briefs of *amici curiae* urging affirmance: Alaska, Arizona, Arkansas, Connecticut, Hawaii, Illinois, Iowa, Kansas, Kentucky, Louisiana, Maine, Massachusetts, Minnesota, Mississippi, Missouri, Montana, Nevada, New Hampshire, New Mexico, New York, North Carolina, Ohio, Oklahoma, Oregon, Pennsylvania, South Carolina, Vermont, Washington, West Virginia, Wisconsin, and Wyoming. In all, 31 states weighed in on the side of California, as did that state's Public Utilities Commission and the New England Legal Foundation.

An Economic Issue, Not a Safety Issue

The Court affirmed the court of appeals' ruling in a unanimous decision. Justice White, writing for the Court, first addressed the question of whether the statutes were ripe for judicial review. Section 25524.1(b), he held, was not ripe for review. With regard to that statute, White wrote that "a court should not stretch to reach an early, and perhaps a premature, decision regarding [it]." Section 25524.2 was ripe, for if power plants went ahead with their operations without knowing whether the moratorium imposed by the statute was valid, this "would impose a palpable and considerable hardship on the utilities, and may ultimately work harm on the citizens of California."

Given, then, that 25524.2 was ripe for review, White next turned to the question of preemption and found that the statute was not preempted by the Atomic Energy Act. From the time the federal act was passed in 1954 until the present, White explained, Congress had maintained a system of dual regulation over nuclear plants: the federal government held control over safety issues, whereas the states exercised "their traditional authority over economic questions such as the need for additional generating capacity, the type of generating facilities to be licensed, land use, and ratemaking." The Court held that 25524.2 was directed toward economics, rather than safety, in its purpose and thus was fully within California's authority.

In no way, the Court further held, did 25524.2 conflict with national policy, even with a decision by the Nuclear Regulatory Commission (NRC) to allow continued licensing of reactors despite concerns regarding waste disposal. Again, the NRC's authority, as that of a federal nuclear regulatory agency, was in the realm of safety, leaving states to make economic determinations regarding nuclear power. "And as there is no attempt on California's part," White wrote,

> to enter the field of developing and licensing nuclear waste disposal technology, a field occupied by the Federal Government, 25524.2 is not preempted any more by the NRC's obligations in the waste disposal field than by its licensing power over the plants themselves.

Furthermore, the Nuclear Waste Policy Act, enacted into law by Congress in 1982, did not appear to have been passed with the intention of superseding states' decision-making power with regard to waste disposal and the opening of new plants.

Finally, section 25524.2 did not in any way operate at cross-purposes to the aim embodied in the Atomic Energy Act of developing commercial uses for nuclear power. As the court of appeals had observed, Justice White wrote, "Promotion of nuclear power is not to be accomplished 'at all costs.'" Instead, Congress had given the states authority to decide whether to build a nuclear plant or one using traditional fuel sources. "California's decision to exercise that authority," White held, "does not, in itself, constitute a basis for preemption."

Blackmun Upholds the Principle of a Safety Moratorium

Justice Blackmun, in an opinion joined by Justice Stevens, concurred in part and concurred in the judgment. He took issue, however, with the idea implicit in the Court's argument that a state motivated solely by safety concerns, rather than economic ones, lacked the authority to prohibit the construction of nuclear plants. He then addressed the three reasons why the Court held that a safety-motivated decision to prohibit construction would be preempted: (1) "the Federal Government has occupied the entire field of nuclear safety"; (2) a state judgment on safety would place a state in conflict with the NRC; and (3) a moratorium on further plant construction would, in the Court's words, "be in the teeth of the Atomic Energy Act's objective to insure that nuclear technology be safe enough for widespread development and use."

With regard to the first argument, Justice Blackmun held that Congress had not attempted to control the wide field of "nuclear safety concerns," only the smaller realm of safe plant construction and operation.

Thus if the federal government attempted to preempt the states, given the fact that its area of authority was not large enough to cover all contingencies, this would create a "regulatory vacuum." As for the second argument, the issue of conflict with the NRC, Blackmun held that while the NRC had authority to determine whether it was safe for construction of a plant to proceed, it was not in a position to order that such construction take place. Finally, with regard to the state's possible obstruction of federal goals regarding nuclear development, Blackmun maintained that the federal government's policy of encouraging nuclear development should not be interpreted as an attempt to prevent states from developing alternative sources of energy.

Impact

Pacific Gas did not serve to change the course of federal regulations over nuclear power. Indeed, it weighed far less on nuclear power and the political issues involved than did *Metropolitan Edison v. People Against Nuclear Energy* (1983), decided the same year, or the famous *Silkwood v. Kerr-McGee* (1984) case. The significance of *Pacific Gas* lay in its illustration of concurrent powers, the operation of federal and state authority in harmony. Its result was an affirmation of the power of federalist principles in the American political framework.

Related Cases

Power Reactor Development Co. v. Electrical Workers, 367 U.S. 396 (1961).
Metropolitan Edison v. People Against Nuclear Energy, 460 U.S. 766 (1983).
Silkwood v. Kerr-McGee Corp., 464 U.S. 238 (1984).
New York v. United States, 505 U.S. 144 (1992).

Bibliography and Further Reading

Biskupic, Joan, and Elder Witt, eds. *Guide to the U.S. Supreme Court*, 3rd ed. Washington, DC: Congressional Quarterly, Inc., 1997.

Chandler, Ralph C., Richard A. Enslen, and Peter G. Renstrom. *The Constitutional Law Dictionary*. Santa Barbara, CA: ABC-Clio, 1991.

Chiappetta, Vincent F. "United States Nuclear Energy Policy After *Pacific Gas* and *Silkwood*." *Arizona State Law Journal*, 1985.

"Constitutional Law—The Supremacy Clause—The California Nuclear Moratorium— *Pacific Gas & Electric Co. v. Energy Resources Commission*." *New York Law School Law Review*, Vol. 30, 1985.

Levy, Leonard W., ed. *Encyclopedia of the American Constitution*. New York: Macmillan, 1986.

NEW YORK V. UNITED STATES

Legal Citation: 505 U.S. 144 (1992)

Petitioners
State of New York; County of Allegany, New York; County of Cortland, New York

Respondent
United States et al.

Petitioners' Claim
That the Low-Level Radioactive Waste Act Amendments of 1985, which regulated states' management of nuclear waste, violated the Tenth Amendment's reservation of powers for the states, as well as the Guarantee Clause of the Constitution.

Chief Lawyer for Petitioners
Peter H. Schiff, Deputy Solicitor General of New York

Chief Lawyer for Respondent
Wallace, U.S. Deputy Solicitor General

Justices for the Court
Anthony M. Kennedy, Sandra Day O'Connor (writing for the Court), William H. Rehnquist, Antonin Scalia, David H. Souter, Clarence Thomas

Justices Dissenting
Harry A. Blackmun, John Paul Stevens, Byron R. White

Place
Washington, D.C.

Date of Decision
19 June 1992

Decision
That two of the act's three incentives to encourage compliance with federal waste-management laws were constitutional under the Commerce Clause; but that a third provision punishing non-compliance was unconstitutional, because it violated the Tenth Amendment.

Significance
This case addressed the constitutional principles of sovereignty and severability. The Tenth Amendment reserves for the states all powers not delegated to the federal government, but in the century preceding the *New York* decision, the Court had tended to favor the federal government in Tenth-Amendment cases. The *New York* ruling placed limitations on both federal and state power. Less obvious was the relevance of the case to severability or separability, which is the idea that the Court can invalidate certain portions of a statute but leave others intact.

Radioactive Waste

"We live in a world full of low level radioactive waste," Justice O'Connor wrote in the Supreme Court's *New York v. United States* ruling. As she observed, such waste comes from "luminous watch dials, smoke alarms, measurement devices, medical fluids, research materials, and the protective gear and construction materials used by workers at nuclear power plants." Industry produces such waste, as do hospitals, research institutions, and governments. That waste is most often buried in the ground at specific dumping sites. Few people choose to have such a site near them, since the waste is harmful to the environment and to human health.

In 1962, Congress established the first dumping site for low-level radioactive waste in Beatty, Nevada. During the next decade, it set up five more sites, in Maxey Flats, Kentucky; West Valley, New York; Hanford, Washington; Sheffield, Illinois; and Barnwell, South Carolina. Between 1975 and 1978, three of the sites—in Illinois, Kentucky, and New York permanently closed. This left only the Nevada, Washington, and South Carolina dumps, to which the rest of the country shipped its waste. The two western sites shut down temporarily in 1979, and the governors of Nevada and Washington announced plans for permanent shutdowns. Thus, South Carolina was to be left to bear the burden for the entire nation. In response to the situation, that state's governor ordered the Barnwell site to accept half of the waste it had previously received.

Congress was compelled to act, so in 1980, following a set of recommendations submitted to it by the National Governors' Association (NGA), it passed the Low-Level Radioactive Waste Policy Act. The act held each state responsible for dealing with its own radioactive waste, which could be done "most safely and efficiently . . . on a regional basis." Therefore it authorized states to make regional compacts for waste disposal, but it did not penalize states who failed to participate in such compacts. By 1985, only three compacts had been approved—and these had been formed around the existing "sited states" of South Carolina, Nevada, and Washington. Not surprisingly, other states had been reluctant to create sites, and 31 states not covered by regional compacts would have no available place to dump their wastes.

Based on a proposal submitted by the NGA, the 1985 act proposed a compromise: the three sited states would continue to accept the rest of the nation's waste for seven more years, until 1992, by which time the states not covered by regional compacts would be expected to make other arrangements for their waste disposal. "The mechanics of this compromise," Justice O'Connor wrote, "are intricate," and involved a graduated surcharge system whereby the cost of dumping by non-sited states would increase with time: $10 per cubit foot in 1986-87; $20 in 1988-89; and $40 in 1990-92. Under the act, states had three forms of incentive to comply with the statute's requirement that they develop their own arrangements for waste disposal. The first of these was monetary: the U.S. secretary of energy would collect one-quarter of the surcharges collected by the sited states in an escrow account, from which the states who complied would receive payments. The second incentive involved access—specifically, the denial of access to waste-disposal sites for non-sited states (i.e., states without any compact agreement), and graduated surcharges for each period in which they failed to make the necessary steps for compliance. Then there was the third incentive, the "take-title provision," which the Court would later deem "the most severe." If a state failed to provide for disposal, either within its borders or through a regional compact, by 1 January 1996, it would be required to "take title to the waste." The act further provided that the state would "be obligated to take possession of the waste, and shall be liable for all damages directly or indirectly incurred . . . as a consequence of the failure of the State to take possession of the waste . . ." This could potentially cost states large sums of money, not only for the waste disposal itself, but from claims against states by entities wishing to dispose of such waste.

In the years from 1985 to 1992, Congress approved nine regional compacts, covering 42 of the states. In a brief to the U.S. Supreme Court, the federal government explained that New York was a state that generated "a relatively large share of the Nation's low level radioactive waste," but had not joined a regional compact. Instead, it had identified five potential dumping sites, three in Allegany County and two in Cortland County. Residents of those counties opposed the state's plan, so New York and the two counties filed suit against the United States in 1990. The states of Washington, Nevada, and South Carolina also included themselves as defendants. The district court dismissed the complaint, and the petitioners appealed. They had originally raised a number of constitutional challenges to the act, but by the time the case reached the Supreme Court, their opposition rested on the Tenth Amendment and the Guarantee Clause, which holds in part that "The United States shall guarantee to every State of this Union a Republican Form of Government, and shall protect each of them against invasion . . ."

Briefs of *amici curiae* urging reversal of the lower court's ruling were filed by officials representing the states of Arizona, Arkansas, California, Illinois, Indiana, Kentucky, Maine, Massachusetts, Nebraska, New Jersey, Ohio, Pennsylvania, Rhode Island, South Dakota, Texas, West Virginia, and Wisconsin; for the territory of Guam; and for the Council of State Government. Briefs urging affirmance were filed by the American College of Nuclear Physicians et al., the American Federation of Labor and Congress of Industrial Organizations (AFL/CIO), and the Rocky Mountain Low-Level Radioactive Waste Compact. Briefs were also filed by the states of Connecticut and Michigan, and US Ecology, Inc.

"Take-Title" Provision

The Court voted unanimously to uphold the first two forms of incentive, and by a vote of 6-3 it ruled that the "take-title" incentive was unconstitutional. Justice O'Connor, writing for the Court, noted that it had used as its standards the affirmative grants to Congress contained in the Commerce and Spending Clauses of Article I, as well as the principle of state sovereignty embodied in the Tenth Amendment.

The constitutionality of congressional authority over interstate disposal of low-level radioactive waste had been established in *Philadelphia v. New Jersey* (1978). But a review of other Court decisions such as *Hodel v. Virginia Surface Mining & Reclamation Assn., Inc.* (1981)— not to mention an examination of the concerns raised by the Framers at the Constitutional Convention— offered a counterbalancing claim. Specifically, as Justice O'Connor wrote, Congress lacked the power to "commandeer the States' legislative processes by directly compelling them to enact and enforce a federal regulatory program"; rather, it was incumbent on Congress to "exercise legislative authority directly upon individuals." In spite of that, methods existed whereby Congress could "urge" a state, without coercion, to comply with a federal program. It could use its spending power to influence a state's actions by attaching conditions on the dispensing of federal funds, a principle upheld in *South Dakota v. Dole* (1987). Also, in a situation where Congress had regulatory authority over private activity under the Commerce Clause, it could offer to the states the choice of either regulating their activities according to federal standards, or of having their laws pre-empted by the federal government.

The petitioners had put forth an argument regarding the portion of the act which required states to deal with their own radioactive waste problems, an idea which Justice O'Connor rejected. That provision, the petitioners claimed, was a direct order from Congress to the states, and could be viewed as such by separating it from the rest of the act. Justice O'Connor held, however, that the clause in question was not a "separable mandate." Viewed on its own, the clause would clearly constitute a violation of the balance between federal and state powers, and would thus raise another issue; but Justice O'Connor held that it could not be viewed on its own. Rather, the act should be construed "as a whole to comprise three sets of incentives to the States."

The Court next dealt with the first of these incentives. In establishing the monetary incentive, the Court ruled, Congress acted "well within" its authority under the Commerce and Spending Clauses, and thus the Tenth Amendment had not been violated in that particular instance. By authorizing sited states to place surcharges on radioactive waste, Congress was simply enabling interstate commerce, and the collection of a percentage of that charge by the Secretary of Energy was "no more than a federal tax on interstate commerce, which petitioners do not claim to be an invalid exercise of either Congress' commerce or taxing power." Furthermore, the monetary incentive met the four requirements established in *Dole*. As for the claim by the petitioners that the escrow account arrangement was "nonfederal" because it collected funds separately from various states, rather than doing so in a blanket fashion, the Court responded that nothing in the Spending Clause prevented this. In any case, by choosing to comply or not, states were free to control whether or not they paid into the account or received a refund for compliance.

The access incentives were constitutional as well, as they were "a conditional exercise of Congress' commerce power along the lines of that approved in *Hodel*," and thus did not violate the Tenth Amendment either. Once again, states had a choice: they could either comply with regulations, or they could be denied access to disposal sites. In no way did Congress force them to regulate their waste disposal, make any expenditures, or participate in any federal program.

The third incentive, the one labeled "take-title," was more problematic. The "choice" it offered—of either taking title to the waste and the resulting liabilities, or of complying with the federal program, was coercive and hence forbidden under the Tenth Amendment. By forcing waste-generators (e.g. industry) to transfer their waste to the state, and by requiring states to become liable for the waste, Congress was attempting to "commandeer" the states into compliance with a federal program. Likewise the requirement that states had to regulate waste in accordance with federal direction was unconstitutional as well. The "choice" offered in the take-title provision, Justice O'Connor wrote, "is no choice at all." Hence, the Court ruled this provision invalid.

Justice O'Connor dealt with several arguments raised by the respondents. The federal government had claimed that there were limited situations in which it was permissible for Congress to coerce states, but the Court rejected this and similar propositions. Likewise the Court rejected the sited states' contention that the act could not be ruled an unconstitutional infringement on New York's sovereignty because officials of that state had been given the opportunity to challenge the act's passage and had not; in fact, they had supported it. Consent of state officials, Justice O'Connor suggested, was irrelevant, "since the Constitution protects state sovereignty for the benefit of individuals, not States or their governments, and since the officials' interests may not coincide with the Constitution's allocation."

The Court held that the act did not violate the Guarantee Clause because nothing in it "c[ould] be reasonably said to deny New York a republican form of government." Up to this point, the ruling had concerned itself with sovereignty, but the Court concluded by establishing the severability of the act, whereby the "take-title" clause could be removed in order to preserve the constitutionality of the rest of the statute. The guideline for severability was that if a part of a law could be removed from the rest without defeating the purpose of the larger statute, then it was severable. (To make an analogy, a printer or audio speakers would be considered "severable" portions of a computer system; the processing unit and monitor would not, because to remove them would impair the system's entire function.) Because the act still contained two incentives powerful enough to encourage compliance, and since removal of the take-title clause would not place a burden on other states' citizens as no regional compacts were required to accept New York's waste after the final transition period, the act would remain effective with or without the take-title provision.

Dissent: Upsetting a "Delicate Compromise"

Justices Blackmun, Stevens, and White dissented from the Court's ruling on the "take-title" incentive, and two filed dissenting opinions. White's, in which Blackmun and Stevens joined, was by far the longer. He began it by tracing the history of the act from his perspective, as a "delicate compromise" between the states and the federal government—a balance which in his view the Court would upset by its ruling. "I am unmoved," Justice White wrote, "by the Court's vehemence in taking away Congress' authority to sanction a recalcitrant unsited State now that New York has reaped the benefits of the sited States' concessions." By no means did the provision place undue penalties on New York; in order to be effective, the act had to offer some sort of punitive measures to discourage noncompliance.

Justice White also offered a reading of *Hodel* and *FERC v. Mississippi* (1982), another case that the Court had cited in its ruling, which differed sharply from the Court's view of those cases. Indeed, White questioned the very basis of the distinction that the Court had made between federal statutes that regulated both states and private parties, as opposed to those which placed a regulation solely on states. While conceding the value of the system of checks and balances between the powers of the federal government and those of the states, White held that in the present case, that concept had been wielded for no good purpose. The act did not pose a genuine threat to state sovereignty, he held, whereas the situation it was made to address—nuclear waste—was a "crisis of national proportions." The Court's ruling on the act, a judgment which White viewed as defeating the flexibility offered by the "delicate compromise," did nothing to further the solution of that crisis.

Justice Stevens also concurred in part and dissented in part, holding that "The notion that Congress does not have the power to issue a simple command to state governments to implement legislation enacted by Congress . . . is incorrect and unsound." After all, the Court had power to resolve controversies between the states, and if one state took action against another over an issue arising from a regional compact, the Court had authority to adjudicate it. If the Court had such power to decide issues between states, Justice Stevens asked, why did Congress not have similar authority to order the states to comply with federal law?

Impact

New York v. United States continued the Tenth-Amendment roller-coaster ride whose highs and lows had been marked by *Usery* and *Garcia*. Despite the fact that the Court had only invalidated one of three provisions, some considered the ruling a victory for state sovereignty. To others, it seemed that the alleged movement in favor of the Tenth Amendment, first heralded after *Usery,* was a revolution that consistently refused to take place. The severability principle implement in *New York,* however, did help reinforce a notion of flexibility on the Court's part in ruling on disputes between the state and federal governments.

Related Cases

National League of Cities v. Usery, 426 U.S. 833 (1976).
Philadelphia v. New Jersey, 437 U.S. 617 (1978).
Hodel v. Virginia Surface Mining & Reclamation Assn., Inc., 452 U.S. 264 (1981).
FERC v. Mississippi, 456 U.S. 742 (1982).
Pacific Gas & Electric Co. v. Energy Resources Commission, 461 U.S. 190 (1983).
South Dakota v. Dole, 483 U.S. 203 (1987).
Seminole Nation of Florida v. Florida, 517 U.S. 44 (1996).

Bibliography and Further Reading

"Constitutional Structure." *Harvard Law Review,* November 1992, pp. 173-83.

Du Pont, Pete. "Pleading the Tenth: With the Demise of Liberalism, Can Federalism be Brought Back to Life?" *National Review,* November 27, 1995, p. 50.

Handman, Christopher T. "The Doctrine of Political Accountability and Supreme Court Jurisdiction." *Yale Law Journal,* October 1996, p. 197.

Jensen, Erik M., and Jonathan L. Entin. "Commandeering, the Tenth Amendment, and the Federal Requisition Power." *Constitutional Commentary,* summer 1998, p. 355.

Johnson, John W., ed. *Historic U.S. Court Cases, 1690–1990: An Encyclopedia.* New York: Garland Publishing, 1992.

Rivkin, David B., Jr., and Lee A. Casey. "Federalism (cont'd)." *Commentary,* December 1996, p. 47.

Rosenbloom, David H., and Bernard H. Ross. "Toward a New Jurisprudence of Constitutional Federalism." *American Review of Public Administration,* June 1998, p. 107.

Weiner, Richard D. "Federalism and the Disposal of Low-Level Radioactive Waste." *Natural Resources Journal,* winter 1994, pp. 197-223.

Wilson, Jerome L. "States Need a Simple Guarantee of Rights." *The National Law Journal,* February 13, 1995, p. A21.

Wise, Charles. "Judicial Federalism: The Resurgence of the Supreme Court's Role in the Protection of State Sovereignty." *Public Administration Review,* March-April 1998, p. 95.

Wise, Charles, and Rosemary O'Leary. "Intergovernmental Relations and Federalism in Environmental Management and Policy." *Public Administration Review,* March-April 1997, p. 150.

Witt, Elder. *Congressional Quarterly's Guide to the Supreme Court,* 2nd ed. Washington, DC: Congressional Quarterly Inc., 1990.

———. *The Supreme Court A to Z. CQ's Encyclopedia of American Government,* Rev. ed. Washington, DC: Congressional Quarterly, Inc., 1994.

C & A Carbone v. Town of Clarkstown, New York

Legal Citation: 511 U.S. 383 (1994)

Petitioner
C & A Carbone, Inc.

Respondent
Town of Clarkstown, New York

Petitioner's Claim
That a Clarkstown ordinance requiring all haulers to deposit waste at a private transfer station in return for deeding over the station to the city in five years violated the Commerce Clause of the Constitution.

Chief Lawyer for Petitioner
Betty Jo Christian

Chief Lawyer for Respondent
William C. Brashares

Justices for the Court
Ruth Bader Ginsburg, Anthony M. Kennedy (writing for the Court), Sandra Day O'Connor, Antonin Scalia, John Paul Stevens, Clarence Thomas

Justices Dissenting
Harry A. Blackmun, William H. Rehnquist, David H. Souter

Place
Washington, D.C.

Date of Decision
16 May 1994

Decision
An ordinance enabling Clarkstown, New York to obtain title to a waste station in return for requiring all waste haulers to use the station under private ownership for five years discriminated in interstate commerce.

Significance
The regulatory powers of state and local governments cannot be used to favor local firms by generating business for them or obstructing the business activities of outside companies.

Officials of Clarkstown, New York near the New Jersey border thought they had come up with a foolproof way of obtaining a $1.4 million waste recycling and transfer station for only $1, until a tractor-trailer ran into an overpass on the Palisades Interstate Highway. When police discovered the truck was hauling 23 bales of solid waste from C & A Carbone's Clarkstown plant to a land fill in Indiana, the plant was placed under surveillance.

Over the next six days, Clarkstown police seized six other Carbone tractor trailers loaded with waste destined for disposal sites in Illinois, Florida and West Virginia, as well as Indiana. The town asked the New York Supreme Court for an injunction requiring Carbone to ship all its waste to a transfer station on Route 303 in Clarkstown at a cost of $81 a ton. Local waste haulers were mandated to do so under a Clarkstown "flow control" ordinance that guaranteed the private owners of the station 120,000 tons annually at the $81 rate over five years in return for the deed.

The Clarkstown injunction was granted and New York courts upheld the town ordinance as constitutional, but the U.S. District Court differed. The Supreme Court granted a writ of *certiorari*, and in the majority decision that followed, found that "the flow control ordinance does regulate interstate commerce, despite the town's position to the contrary."

The town argued before the Supreme Court that the ordinance was "in practical effect a quarantine" preventing "garbage from entering the mainstream of interstate commerce until it was made safe." However, the majority disagreed and the decision, written by Justice Kennedy, concluded that the ordinance:

> . . . drives up the cost of out-of-state interests . . . and prevents everyone except the favored local operator from performing the initial processing step . . . These effects are more than enough to bring the Clarkstown ordinance within the purview of the Commerce Clause.

Consequently, Justice Kennedy concluded, the ordinance "in practical effect" was a "hoarding" rather than a quarantine measure. It was designed to favor "a single local processor" rather than promote public health. As a precedent, an earlier decision striking down a "local processing requirement that at least (milk) pasteurizers within five miles of the city" was cited.

Justice O'Connor agreed the ordinance was unconstitutional, but not because of "discrimination in interstate commerce" but rather by placing an "undue burden" on commerce. Furthermore, Clarkstown had erred in giving "a waste processing monopoly to the transfer station," noted Justice O'Connor. However, she was more concerned that the decision could also overturn similar laws in 20 other states allowing "flow control." The result could be the "type of balkanization the clause is primarily intended to prevent," she wrote. The Court was interfering unnecessarily in traditional local government concerns, according to O'Connor.

The three dissenting justices worried that the majority was unnecessarily creating new law. The majority had alluded to "well settled principles" in its decision, Justice Souter wrote in the dissent joined by Chief Justice Rehnquist and Justice Blackmun. The majority did ". . . strike down an ordinance unlike anything this Court has ever invalidated," adding that previous decisions had only struck down laws which discriminated against all out-of-town providers of service. Clarkstown, however, had only differentiated "between the one entity responsible for getting the job done and all other enterprises (local as well as out-of-town), regardless of their location." That entity, he further noted, was "directly aiding the government in satisfying a traditional government responsibility."

The ordinance had been passed as part of the town's efforts to comply with a 1989 consent decree with the state Department of Environmental Conservation. The decree required Clarkstown to close the town landfill, clean up the damage caused by years of dumping, and build the transfer station. Consequently, Justice Souter argued that the transfer station operator was:

> essentially an agent of the municipal government . . . a municipal facility, built and operated under a contract with the municipality and soon to revert entirely to municipal ownership.

The majority's equation of the ordinance's effect with "hoarding" ignored "this distinction between public and private enterprise."

When legislation does not come into "conflict with the Commerce Clause's overriding requirement of a national 'common market,'" Souter concluded, the court is faced with "a balancing test . . . an accommodation of conflicting national and local interests." The Clarkstown ordinance met that accommodation test, Souter declared. The ordinance:

confers a privilege on the municipal government alone . . . that does not discriminate between local and out-of-town participants in the private market . . . and that is not protectionist in its purpose or effects.

Related Cases

Philadelphia v. New Jersey, 437 U.S. 617 (1978).

Chemical Waste Management, Inc. v. Hunt, 504 U.S. 334 (1992).

Fort Gratiot Sanitary Landfill, Inc. v. Michigan Dept. of Natural Resources, 504 U.S. 353 (1992).

Bibliography and Further Reading

Barnett, Paul, and Jeff Bailey. "Garbage Haulers Win Big Victory on High Court." *Wall Street Journal*, May 17, 1994.

"Clarkstown Court Loss May Bring Trash Woes." *New York Times*, May 20, 1994.

"Courts Might Settle Flow Control Issue Before Congress Can Pass Oxley Bill." *Solid Waste Report*, November 2, 1995.

Diederich, Michael D., Jr. "Can Municipalities Manage Their Own Solid Waste?" *Environment*, May 1995, p. 3.

"Federal Policy: Flow Control SWANA Backs Chaffee Bill on Flow Control." *Solid Waste Report*, June 26, 1997.

Greenhouse, Linda. "Justices Strike Down Local Laws Restricting Waste Shipments." *New York Times*, May 17, 1994.

Lerg, Leslie Juddis. "Will *Carbone* Spark Solid Waste Crisis?" *New Jersey Law Journal*, June 27, 1994.

Markoe, Jeannine. "1996 Legislative Wrap-Up: Dismal Start, Strong Finish." *Government Finance Review*, December 1996, p. 58.

Phalon, Richard. "Bargains in Garbage." *Forbes*, August 15, 1994, p. 104.

"Slants & Trends." *Solid Waste Report*, June 4, 1998.

Tabin, Barrie, and Carol Kocheisen. "Cities Take Hit on Flow Control." *Nation's Cities Weekly*, May 23, 1994, p. 11.

Terrazas, Michael. "Going With the Flow of Flow Control." *American City and County*, October 1995, p. 62.

Ward, Janet. "Supreme Court Rulings Affect Waste Industry." *The American City and County*, July 1994.

Wilt, Catherine A., and Gary A. Davis. "Local Control Wasting Away: Will Congress Level the Solid Waste Playing Field?" *Policy Studies Journal*, spring 1996, p. 123.

UNITED STATES V. BESTFOODS

Legal Citation: 118 S.Ct. 1876 (1998)

Petitioner
United States

Respondent
CPC International Inc. (later renamed Bestfoods), Aerojet-General Corporation, Cordova Chemical Company, Cordova Chemical Company of Michigan

Petitioner's Claim
That CPC International was liable, under Section 107(a)(2) of the Comprehensive Environmental Response, Compensation, and Liability Act of 1980 (CERCLA) for costs of cleaning up industrial waste at a former subsidiary's chemical plant.

Justices for the Court
Stephen Breyer, Ruth Bader Ginsburg, Anthony M. Kennedy, Sandra Day O'Connor, William H. Rehnquist, Antonin Scalia, David H. Souter (writing for the Court), John Paul Stevens, Clarence Thomas

Justices Dissenting
None

Place
Washington, D.C.

Date of Decision
8 June 1998

Decision
That the petitioner had failed to establish CPC/Bestfoods's parental responsibility, either in a direct or derivative sense, for the environmental damage in question.

Significance
The Court's unanimous decision in *United States v. Bestfoods* provided a framework for establishing the limits of responsibility on the part of a corporate parent—parenthood being defined by the ownership of a controlling interest in another corporation's stock—for damages incurred by a polluting subsidiary. On the one hand, the Court held that derivative liability can be established only when the "corporate veil" has been "pierced"—that is, when it is established that the subsidiary is acting only as a proxy for the parent. On the other hand, the Court found that parental responsibility does not follow from simple ownership of a subsidiary; rather, it must be shown that the parent acted as an operator in the subsidiary's facility. The decision relied on the Court's distinction between subsidiaries and facilities, which invalidated a lower court's tests regarding actual control as opposed to capacity to control.

Don't Drink the Water

In 1957, Ott Chemical Company, which manufactured products for the pharmaceutical, veterinary, and agricultural industries, began operation of a plant in a rural area near Muskegon, in western Michigan. Founder Arnold Ott served as president and principal shareholder. Eight years later, in 1965, CPC International incorporated the Ott Chemical Company as a subsidiary. Thus, there were three entities named "Ott": the original company, its founder, and the later subsidiary. To avoid confusion when the case came before it in 1998, the Supreme Court designated the first Ott Chemical Company as Ott I, and the CPC subsidiary as Ott II. Likewise when CPC changed its name to Bestfoods not long before the Court reviewed the case, this too added confusion. Hence, the named defendant is designated by its later name, but in the review of the case it is referred to by its old name, which it held at the time of the actions in question.

Soon after its incorporation, Ott II purchased Ott I's assets in exchange for CPC stock. Ott I ceased to function as such, but the new owners retained Ott I's personnel, including its managers and Arnold Ott himself. In fact Mr. Ott, along with other executives and board members, took paid positions not with Ott II, but with CPC, the parent company. In 1972, Ott II again changed hands when CPC sold it to Story Chemical Company, which retained it for five years, until it went bankrupt in 1977. Soon after Story Chemical disappeared from the scene, the Muskegon site received a visit from a Michigan Department of Natural Resources (MDNR) team, and thus began a barrage of litigation that would include the liability dispute reviewed in *United States v. Bestfoods.*

Regardless of owner, the purpose of the Muskegon plant remained the same: the manufacture of chemicals, which produced a hazardous by-product in the form of chemical waste. The dumping of hazardous substances, both "intentional and unintentional," in the Court's words, "significantly polluted the soil and ground water at the site." Specifically, the plant had discharged waste into on-site lagoons, which were not properly lined to prevent seepage into the water table, a practice which continued at least until 1968. In addition, through 1972, Ott II workers had buried hundreds of drums containing hazardous waste, and had scattered literally thousands of drums in the surrounding woods. This was all clearly "intentional," but in addition, there were numerous "unintentional" spills from railroad cars, and from a cement-lined basin that repeatedly overflowed.

Thus, as the Court reported, when MDNR "examined the site for environmental damage, it found the land littered with thousands of leaking and even exploding drums of waste, and the soil and water saturated with noxious chemicals." The MDNR report indicated that "Groundwater pumped to the surface contained foam and a brownish color like root beer," and the soil was "purplish" from all the hazardous waste in it. Not only was the groundwater contaminated with pollutants such as phosgene gas, benzene, phenol, methyl chloride, and methyl isocyanate, but with its introduction to the water table, the contamination was seeping ever further. As water seeks its own level, the hazardous waste moved ever onward toward two nearby creeks, from where it entered the nearby community's water supply. This situation could not continue, and MDNR proposed a solution which promised to address the environmental problem—but created a host of legal ones.

Shifting the Burden to the Responsible Parties

Attempting to remedy the situation at the Muskegon factory, MDNR began looking for a corporation that would purchase the site and help pay for its cleanup. Naturally, given the situation, the state was not inundated with offers, but finally in late 1977, it found Aerojet-General Corporation, which agreed to buy the Muskegon plant from Story Chemical's bankruptcy trustee. In order to do so, Aerojet created Cordova Chemical Company (which the Court designated as Cordova/California) as a wholly owned subsidiary to purchase the property, and Cordova/California in turn established its own wholly owned subsidiary, Cordova Chemical Company of Michigan (Cordova/Michigan). The latter operated as a chemical manufacturer at the site until 1986.

But in the intervening years, the federal government began to take an increasing interest in cleaning up the Muskegon plant and sites like it. Congress in 1980 passed CERCLA, the Comprehensive Environmental Response, Compensation, and Liability Act, to respond to situations such as the one that occurred at the Muskegon plant. The act, the Court noted in *Exxon Corp. v. Hunt,* was, "As its name implies, . . . a comprehensive statute that grants the President broad power to command government agencies and private parties to clean up hazardous waste sites." In the following year, 1981, the federal Environmental Protec-

tion Agency (EPA) assessed the Muskegon site in particular, and called for a clean-up plan that would cost tens of millions of dollars. However, rather than merely shift the burden of this cleanup to the taxpayers—many of whom were themselves victims of environmental irresponsibility on the part of corporations—the federal government in 1989 took legal action against CPC, Aerojet, Cordova/California, Cordova/Michigan, and Arnold Ott himself.

The basis for the legal action was a provision in CERCLA for a "Hazardous Substance Superfund," which would pay for environmental cleanups. Money for this Superfund would come in part from lawsuits against those responsible for the hazardous substances in the first place, including "any person who at the time of disposal of any hazardous substance owned or operated any facility." The act defined "person" as a corporate entity, and similarly delineated the terms of "facility" in a common-sense fashion. With regard to "owner or operator," however, it was more vague, defining these as "any person owning or operating" a facility. This, the Court noted, was a tautology, or a redundant, information-free statement. As it pointed out in *Exxon,* CERCLA "unfortunately, is not a model of legislative draftsmanship." It was a fact that would be highlighted by the legal actions surrounding the cleanup.

Ott I and Ott II, both defunct by the time of the 1989 suit, were not included among the named defendants in the EPA case, and Arnold Ott himself would end up settling out of court just before the case actually came to trial. As for CPC, Aerojet, and the latter's two Cordova subsidiaries, in the Court's words these entities, along with MDNR, "launched a flurry of contribution claims, counterclaims, and cross-claims." The district court therefore opted to consolidate all the cases into liability, remedy, and insurance coverage phases. As of 1991, the case had not gone beyond the first of the three phases, liability.

A Question of Parenthood

In 1991, a fifteen-day bench trial on the question of liability focused on issues of corporate parenthood. Specifically, the district court sought to determine whether CPC, as the parent company of Ott II, and Aerojet, parent to the Cordova companies, had "owned or operated" the Muskegon facility within the definition established under Section 107(a)(2) of CERCLA. In so doing, the court noted that a corporate parent may be liable either directly, inasmuch as it operates a facility, or indirectly, when "the corporate veil can be pierced under state law." Thus, if either CPC or Aerojet could be found to have operated the facility by "exert[ing] power or influence over its subsidiary by actively participating in and exercising control over the subsidiary's business during a period of disposal of hazardous waste," liability could be established. Whereas "mere oversight" does not make a corporate parent an "operator"—and thus liable—actual participation in operations does. In evaluating CPC's liability, the district court noted that the parent had selected the board of directors for Ott II, and had installed CPC officials in the subsidiary's executive ranks. Particularly telling, in the district court's view, was the fact that one G. R. D. Williams, a CPC employee, "played a significant role in shaping Ott II's environmental compliance policy." CPC was consequently held liable, as was Aerojet, which the court found subject both to direct and derivative liability due to the fact that it "totally dominated Cordova/Michigan, creating a complete identity of interests between the parent and its wholly owned subsidiary"—a situation that, under Michigan law, justified piercing the corporate veil.

The case next came before the Court of Appeals for the Sixth Circuit, which in a divided decision reversed in part. That court ended up vacating its decision, granting a hearing *en banc* (that is, with full judicial authority) to a thirteen-judge Court of Appeals panel. By a 7-6 decision, this court reversed the district court, noting that a parent corporation might conceivably supplant the functions of its subsidiary entirely, but otherwise rejecting the lower court's analysis. "[W]hether the parent will be liable as an operator," the Sixth Circuit court observed, "depends upon whether the degree to which it controls its subsidiary and the extent and manner of its involvement with the facility, amount to the abuse of the corporate form that will warrant piercing the corporate veil and disregarding the separate corporate entities of the parent and subsidiary." According to this analysis, neither CPC nor Aerojet had directly operated the Muskegon facility, because both had "maintained separate personalities, and the parents did not utilize the subsidiary corporate form to perpetrate fraud or subvert justice."

"A Relaxed, CERCLA-Specific Rule of Derivative Liability"

The subsequent Supreme Court case involved only CPC/Bestfoods, as the Aerojet action touched on questions unrelated to the issue of corporate veil-piercing. The Court, which reviewed the case in June of 1998—some forty years after Ott I first began operating at, and presumably polluting, the Muskegon site—handed down a unanimous ruling that upheld the Sixth Circuit's decision. Nonetheless, the Court's opinion, delivered by Justice Souter, noted aspects of the appeals court's reasoning which it deemed faulty.

In the first part of its ruling, the Court observed that it is an accepted principle of corporate law—one which CERCLA did not purport to invalidate—that corporate parents are not automatically liable for the actions of their subsidiaries. An exception to this principle, of course, would occur when (and only when) the corporate veil could be pierced. One example of an instance in which veil-piercing would be justified is when "the corporate form would otherwise be misused to accomplish certain wrongful purposes, most notably fraud, on the shareholders' [i.e., parent's] behalf." In the absence of clearly defined stipulations in CERCLA regarding the definition of corporate parenthood, the Court found, the wisest course would be to refer to common law, or in this case to the "general principle of corporate law that a parent corporation (so-called because of control through ownership of another corporation's stock) is not liable for the acts of its subsidiaries."

The Court held that only "a corporate parent that actively participated in, and exercised control over, the operations of its subsidiary's facility may be held directly liable [as an operator] in its own right" under Section 107 of CERCLA. Addressing questions of direct, rather than derivative, liability, the Court sought to clarify CERCLA's definition of "operator," and found that in the present context of an environmental cleanup, "an operator must manage, direct, or conduct operations specifically related to the leakage or disposal of hazardous waste, or decisions about compliance with environmental regulations." The Sixth Circuit had been correct to reject the district court's analysis of direct liability, which had rested merely on the fact of CPC's ownership of the subsidiary. Instead of this parent-subsidiary focus, the Court found, the district court should have based its analysis on the question of whether CPC actually "operated"—i.e., directly participated in the operations of—the facility. Inasmuch as an officer or director of Ott II had a role in CPC as well, in accordance with common-law principles, their actions should be attributed to Ott II rather than to the parent. By failing to focus on the more significant parent-facility relationship, and by mistakenly attributing the actions of Ott II officers to CPC, the district court had overstepped commonly accepted standards of limited liability. Hence it would have created "what is in essence a relaxed, CERCLA-specific rule of derivative liability" that neither justified in the common law nor in CERCLA's (and Congress's) silence on the subject.

But the Court also faulted aspects of the Sixth Circuit's ruling, inasmuch as it "limit[ed] direct liability under CERCLA to a parent's sole or joint venture operation, so as to eliminate any possible finding that CPC is liable as an operator on the facts of the case." Thus it had ignored the possibility of a joint officer or director who claims to operate on behalf of the subsidiary, or both the subsidiary and the parent, but in fact operates solely on behalf of the parent. To make this determination, the appeals court needed only to observe "norms of corporate behavior (undisturbed by any CERCLA provision)." Such a route offered promise, the Court noted, due to "evidence that an agent of CPC alone [G. R. D. Williams] engaged in activities at Ott II's plant that were eccentric under accepted norms of parental oversight at a subsidiary's facility." The fact that Williams had been instrumental in shaping the environmental compliance policy of the subsidiary, in the Court's view, suggested a possibility not so much that CPC fully controlled Ott II (as the district court had held), but that it actually was operating the Muskegon plant directly. Had this been shown, the results of *United States v. Bestfoods* might have been quite different. But this was beyond the Court's directive in the present case, as Justice Souter noted: "The findings [with regard to Williams's role] are enough to raise an issue of CPC's operation of the facility, though this Court draws no ultimate conclusion, leaving the issue for the lower courts to reevaluate and resolve in the first instance."

Impact

Stephen L. Kass and Jean M. McCarroll, who published several pieces in the *New York Law Journal* regarding the liability of corporate parents under CERCLA, wrote that the Court's decision in *Bestfoods* had "brought some precision and balance to the task of determining under what circumstances a corporate parent may be charged with liability as an operator of its subsidiary's polluting facility." But to Peter M. Gillon, who presented a critique of the case in *Toxics Law Reporter*, the ruling "represents a valiant, although not altogether successful, attempt to provide . . . clarity" regarding questions of liability. In Gillon's view, the Court's inability to draw bright lines regarding corporate liability leaves corporations in a position of unnecessary uncertainty. Even Kass and McCarroll, while taking a more positive view of the ruling in terms of the direction it provides

for future decisions, concluded that "some murky areas remain." Nonetheless, they hailed the *Bestfoods* decision for offering a distinction between the tests of direct and derivative liability, and for "its sensible and proper deference to the fact-finding role of the trial court." Kass and McCarroll on the one hand, and Gillon on the other, do seem to agree on one general principle: that the *Bestfoods* decision can be best understood as an attempt to define, rather than to conclude, questions regarding the corporate parent's liability in hazardous waste cleanups or other situations.

Related Cases

Chicago, M. & St. P. R. Co. v. Minneapolis Civic and Commerce Assn., 247 U.S. 490 (1918).
Edmonds v. Compagnie Generale Transatlantique, 443 U.S. 256 (1979).
Exxon Corp. v. Hunt, 475 U.S. 355 (1986).
Pennsylvania v. Union Gas Co., 491 U.S. 1 (1989).
United States v. Texas, 507 U.S. 529 (1993).

Bibliography and Further Reading

Falk, Donald M. "Justices Forestall Business Liabilities." *The National Law Journal*, 10 August 1998, p. B11.

Gillon, Peter M. "The Liability of Parent Companies under CERCLA: 'United States v. Bestfoods.'" *Toxics Law Reporter*, 29 June 1998, p. 3.

Kass, Stephen L., and Jean M. McCarroll. "Corporate Parent Liability under CERCLA." *New York Law Journal*, 26 June 1998, p. 3.

Shanoff, Barry. "Are Parents Liable for Subsidiary Sin?" *World Wastes*, August 1998, pp. 82-83.

FEDERAL POWERS AND SEPARATION OF POWERS

Preamble

Best known for the inspiration of its Preamble, the Constitution of the United States is the official document that formed the structure and operation of the federal government. The framers who drafted the Constitution presented it on 17 September 1787, over eleven years after the U.S. had declared its independence from Great Britain. With it they sought "to form a more perfect union, establish justice, insure domestic tranquility, provide for the common defense, promote the general welfare, and secure the blessings of liberty" for the people of the new United States. These objectives were the product of much debate concerning the necessary elements of a fair system of government, a debate that grew out of America's experience under the monarchy of Great Britain.

The Tyranny of the Monarchy

Great Britain had operated the American colonies under an economic concept called mercantilism. Under mercantilism, Great Britain expected the colonies to export raw materials such as food, timber, and furs at low prices while importing finished products at higher prices. Mercantilism worked best for Great Britain if the colonies were prohibited from trading with other countries. The colonies, however, often failed to remit taxes, and tended to trade with other countries in a manner favorable to their own economic development.

After the French and Indian Wars ended in 1763, leaving Great Britain in heavy debt, the British Parliament embarked on a mission to bring the colonies under strict financial control. The result was a series of legislation that became known as the Intolerable Acts. This legislation included the Stamp Act of 1765 and led to the American rallying cry "No taxation without representation." The colonists ultimately reacted to Britain's financial campaign with revolt, and the Revolutionary War ensued.

The Articles of Confederation

Prior to the war, the colonists formed the First Continental Congress in September of 1774 to send a message to Great Britain that they would not tolerate deprivation of their life, liberty, and property. There was no real effort, however, to form a central government until the Second Continental Congress approved the Articles of Confederation in 1777. While the Articles established a national legislature with a one vote per state system, it only succeeded in forming a loose collection of states, not a strong national government. The latter did not occur until after Britain agreed to recognize colonial independence in the Treaty of Paris in 1783.

Constitution of the United States

The Constitutional Convention met in Philadelphia on 25 May 1787 with the intention to revise the Articles of Confederation. After much debate and compromise, the framers decided to create a stronger central government with three branches—legislative, executive, and judicial. The framers based this structure on the separation of powers, a concept developed by the eighteenth century philosopher Montesquieu. Montesquieu's theory was that tyranny usually results when power is concentrated in a single government body. After their experience with Great Britain, the framers intended to balance power among various bodies, resulting in a fairer government.

The details led to conflict over the power to be divided. Virginia submitted a plan for a bicameral (two-house) legislature whose representatives would be elected by the states based on their population. This proposal favored heavily populated states. New Jersey countered with a plan for a unicameral (one-house) legislature based on equal representation for all states. The New Jersey plan gave less populated states an equal voice in federal government. The resolution of this conflict became known as the Connecticut Compromise. The framers agreed to a bicameral legislature with a Senate based on equal representation for the states and a House of Representatives based on the population of each state.

Legislative Department

Article I of the Constitution created the legislative department, also known as Congress, comprised of the Senate and the House of Representatives. The Senate contains 100 members, two from each of the 50 states.

While originally elected by their state legislatures, senators today are elected by the people and serve six year terms, with one third of the Senate up for reelection every two years. Through legislation in 1929, Congress set the total number of representatives in the House at 435. The people elect their representatives every two years, with the national census determining the number of representatives for each state.

Congress' enumerated powers and restrictions are more detailed than for any other branch, probably because the framers were most concerned with abuse of legislative power. Under the Taxing and Spending Clause, Congress may "lay and collect taxes, duties, imports, and excises, to pay the debts and provide for the common defense and general welfare of the United States." Domestically, the Commerce Clause gives Congress exclusive authority to regulate anything that has the slightest effect on, or connection with, commerce that crosses state boundaries. Internationally, Congress may regulate foreign affairs through its power to raise and finance an army and navy, declare war, and regulate foreign commerce. Congress also may enact any law "necessary and proper" for carrying out its enumerated powers. This has been called the "elastic clause" because it allows Congress to enact any law for which it has a plausible justification under its specified powers.

Influenced by the Intolerable Acts, however, the framers carefully formulated restrictions on Congress' power. Except in the cases of rebellion or invasion, Congress cannot eliminate the right to a writ of *habeas corpus,* which is a court order requiring an explanation of why a prisoner is being held. Congress also may not pass a bill of attainder, which is a law imposing punishment without trial on a specific individual. Finally, Congress may not pass an *ex post facto* law, which retroactively declares an act to be criminal. Other major restrictions appeared later in the First Amendment to the Constitution, contained within the Bill of Rights and adopted in 1791. Under the First Amendment, Congress may not pass legislation establishing, forbidding, or governing religion. Congress also may not abridge the freedom of speech, freedom of the press, the right of peaceful assembly, and the right to petition government for a redress of grievances.

Executive Department

Article II of the Constitution vests the executive power, the power to enforce the law, in the President of the United States. The only legal requirement for the position is that one must be a natural born citizen over 35 years of age who has resided in the U.S. for at least 14 years. The president serves a four year term and is limited by law to two such terms. Although the nation votes on election day, the Electoral College technically selects the president. Each state appoints Electors to the College equal to the state's total representatives and senators in Congress. The Electors may select any person to be president, but traditionally vote in accordance with the majority of the popular vote in their state.

The Constitution says surprisingly little about the specific powers and duties of the president. Perhaps this reflects the framer's reluctance to concentrate federal power in one person. Only through constitutional interpretation, custom, and necessity has the position developed into one of considerable power. As the commander-in-chief, the president has ultimate control over the army and navy. This curious role for a non-military person was a reaction to Britain's tendency to "render the Military independent of, and superior to, the Civil power." Presidents traditionally have used this power to effect considerable influence over foreign affairs, such as with President Bush's deployment of troops during the Persian Gulf War. The president also has the power to make treaties (with the advice and consent of the Senate).

Domestically, the president has the duty to "take care that the laws be faithfully executed." The president delegates many of these duties to the executive agencies, such as the Department of Justice, which are headed by the members of the president's cabinet. Finally, the president has the duty to "give to the Congress information of the state of the Union, and recommend to their consideration such measures as he shall judge necessary and expedient." The president thus becomes actively involved in proposing and shaping national legislation, including the national budget.

If the president becomes unable to fulfill his duties, the vice-president takes his place. Until then, the vice-president has only one constitutional duty—he serves as president of the Senate and votes if the Senate is equally divided. Otherwise the vice-president typically chairs various commissions and represents the U.S. at domestic and foreign ceremonies and occasions. Significantly, however, the vice-presidency has become a stepping stone to the presidency. In the twentieth century, seven vice-presidents eventually have become president—Theodore Roosevelt, Calvin Coolidge, Harry Truman, Lyndon Johnson, Richard Nixon, Gerald Ford, and George Bush.

Judicial Department

The Articles of Confederation had not created a national judiciary. Instead, state courts heard cases involving federal law, resulting in inconsistency and confusion. The framers rectified this by vesting federal judicial power in the Supreme Court and "such inferior courts as the Congress may from time to time ordain and establish." By statute Congress has created a three-tiered judicial system with district courts at the bottom, courts of appeal in the middle, and the Supreme Court at the top. There are eleven courts of appeal corresponding to eleven geographical regions, each of which contains a number of judicial districts. Cases generally are tried in the district courts, appealed to the courts of appeal, and then appealed to the Supreme Court as a last resort. Only cases involving ambassadors, other public ministers and consuls, and those in which a state is a party may be brought directly before the Supreme Court without going through a district court or court of appeals.

The Constitution specifically enumerates the types of cases that may come before the federal courts. First and foremost are cases arising under the Constitution, the laws of the United States, and treaties. The federal courts also may hear cases of maritime and admiralty jurisdiction, which means cases arising on the navigable waters of the United States. Federal judicial power also extends to cases in which the United States is a party and cases between two or more states, between a state and citizens of a different state, and between citizens of different states.

Federal courts generally determine guilt or innocence in criminal or civil cases. Criminal cases involve enforcement of the criminal laws. Civil cases involve disputes between private parties. In addition, the courts have authority to issue writs of *habeas corpus,* a power the Constitution specifically prohibits Congress from taking away. The courts also may issue writs of *mandamus,* which force government officials to carry out their public duty. The courts also issue arrest and search warrants in accordance with the Fourth Amendment. An important constitutional limitation on all of these powers is that the federal courts may act only in actual cases or controversies. This means they may not issue opinions in the absence of an actual legal dispute.

The Fourth Branch?

Although not created by the Constitution, independent executive agencies sometimes are called the fourth branch of the federal government. They arose in the wake of the Industrial Revolution and typically are charged with regulating areas of big business. Congress creates independent agencies with legislation, and the president selects the agency head with the advice and consent of the Senate. Unlike cabinet members, who serve at the president's whim, independent agency heads can be removed from office only for cause and serve for a fixed number of years.

Curiously, the independent executive agencies usually have powers that resemble all three branches of federal government. They serve as legislative bodies when they enact their own regulations. The Environmental Protection Agency, for example, enacts regulations limiting pollution emissions by industry. Independent agencies also have executive functions, such as when the Interstate Commerce Commission checks to ensure that trucks have proper safety features.

Finally, the independent agencies act like courts when they hold hearings and issue fines for violations of their regulations. Their powers, however, are not unlimited. Congress may alter, amend, or appeal legislation delegating authority to an agency. The president may remove the head of an agency for cause. The courts may declare agency action to be unconstitutional or outside the grant of authority from Congress.

Checks and Balances

Separation of powers is not the only defining concept in the Constitution. The framers also were concerned with the potential for abuse of the power they divided. To limit such abuse, they built checks and balances into the system. Each branch thus serves as a watchdog over the others.

The president checks Congress in many informal ways, such as refusing to use power delegated to the executive branch by Congress. His primary tool, however, is the power to veto legislation. Congress, in turn, may override a presidential veto with a vote by two thirds of both houses. Congress further checks the president by determining the executive budget. Congress has the authority to confirm various presidential appointees, such as cabinet members, judges, and ambassadors. Finally, Congress has the power to impeach all nonmilitary members of the executive branch, including the president.

The president checks the courts by appointing all federal judges, including the Supreme Court justices. Because judges are appointed for life, the president thus may influence the federal judiciary for years after his term expires. With the power of judicial review, the judiciary checks the president by reviewing executive orders and agency actions for their constitutionality. If a court finds an action unconstitutional, it is void.

The judiciary similarly checks Congress by reviewing legislation in particular cases for its constitutionality. Congress checks the judiciary with the theoretical power to eliminate all federal courts except the Supreme Court. Congress also influences the judiciary by confirming or rejecting the president's judicial nominees. Recent battles over nominees such as Robert Bork and Clarence Thomas are examples of this power.

The Tenth Amendment

Soon after the creation of a strong central government, Congress decided to clarify that the framers never intended to eliminate entirely the authority of the states. In the Bill of Rights, proposed by Congress in 1789, the Tenth Amendment provides that "the powers not delegated to the United States by the Constitution, nor prohibited by it to the States, are reserved to the States respectively, or to the people." This provision is the cornerstone of an ongoing battle between federal and state authority. If the framers improved on the monarchy of Great Britain, they certainly did not eliminate the power struggles inherent in national government.

See also: **Federalism and State Powers, Judicial Powers, Judicial Review, Legislative Powers, Taxation, Voting Rights**

Bibliography and Further Reading

Bishop, Hillman M., and Samuel Hendel, eds. *Basic Issues of American Democracy.* New York: Meredith Corporation, 1970.

Casper, Gerhard. *Separating Powers: Essays on the Founding Period.* Cambridge: Harvard University Press, 1997.

Ferguson, John H., and Dean E. McHenry. *The American Federal Government.* New York: McGraw-Hill Book Company, 1977.

Sanford, William R., and Carl R. Green. *Basic Principles of American Government.* New York: Amsco School Publications, Inc., 1983.

Sargent, Lyman Tower, ed. *Political Thought in the United States: A Documentary History.* New York: New York University Press, 1997.

Shelley, Fred M., J. Clark Archer, Fiona M. Davidson, and Stanley D. Brunn. *Political Geography of the United States.* New York: The Guilford Press, 1996.

Weissberg, Robert. *Understanding American Government.* New York: Holt, Rinehart and Winston, 1980.

CHISHOLM V. GEORGIA

Legal Citation: 2 U.S. 419 (1793)

Plaintiff
The heirs of Alexander Chisholm

Defendant
State of Georgia

Plaintiff's Claim
That the state of Georgia allow the heirs of Alexander Chisholm, all of who reside in South Carolina, to inherit his properties in Georgia.

Chief Lawyer for Plaintiff
Edmund Randolph

Chief Defense Lawyer
Thomas P. Carnes

Justices for the Court
John Blair, William Cushing, John Jay, Thomas Johnson, James Wilson

Justices Dissenting
James Iredell

Place
New York, New York

Date of Decision
18 February 1793

Decision
That Chisholm's heirs could sue the state of Georgia for their property.

Significance
Confirmed interpretation of Article III, section 2 of the U.S. Constitution as allowing citizens of one state to bring suit against the government of another state. Overturned by adoption of the Eleventh Amendment to the Constitution in 1798.

Among the more pressing questions facing the United States in the years following its independence was the relationship of the federal government to the state and of the states to each other. Many issues remained unclear, although the scrapping of the Articles of Confederation pointed to increased centralization of authority at the expense of autonomy for the states. Considerable difference of opinion existed regarding the correct interpretation of Article III, Section 2 of the U.S. Constitution, which delineated the relationship between state and federal statutes as follows:

> The judicial power shall extend to all cases, in law and equity, arising under this constitution, the laws of the United States, and treaties made, or which shall be made under their authority . . . to controversies between two or more states, between a state and citizens of another state, between citizens of different states, between citizens of the same state claiming lands under grants of different states, and between a state, or the citizens thereof, and foreign states, citizens, or subjects.

In 1792, the state of Georgia confiscated the properties of Alexander Chisholm upon his death because none of his heirs currently resided in the state. Chisholm's heirs resolved to sue Georgia to recover their inheritance. The case came before the U.S. Supreme Court on 11 July 1792. The primary issue to be decided concerned the jurisdiction of federal courts in a dispute between a citizen and a state.

When the state of Georgia failed to appear at the Court, Edmund Randolph, counsel for the plaintiffs and a signer of the Constitution, moved that if the state failed to appear, or to show cause preventing an appearance within four days, that the Court enter a judgement in favor of the plaintiffs. The state of Georgia's failure to contest the case was based on its belief that the Court would subscribe to an interpretation of Article III, Section 2 of the U.S. Constitution that barred citizens of one state from suing the government of another state. Many individuals felt that to allow such suits would prove too great an abridgement of the autonomy of the states. Randolph countered the pos-

Justice John Jay. © Painting by Stuart Gilbert. National Archives and Records Administration.

sibility of the Court's adopting this opinion by advancing two arguments. He maintained that the state could be considered a "party defendant" before the Supreme Court due to a suit brought by a citizen from another state, asserting that the Constitution ". . . derives its origin immediately from the people; and the people individually are, under certain limitations, subject to the legislative, executive, and judicial authorities thereby established. The states are in fact assemblages of these individuals who are liable to process." Randolph also argued that the Judiciary Act of 1789 validated an interpretation of Article III, Section 2 allowing individual citizens to sue states in which they did not reside.

The Court ruled in favor of the plaintiffs on 18 February 1792, and served notice to the governor and attorney general of Georgia that judgement by default would be made against the state for failure to appear in court. Justices Blair, Cushing, Jay, and Wilson entered consenting opinions, with Jay's in particular upholding Randolph's view of ultimate sovereignty residing in individuals, with the states merely representing, for

Edmund Randolph, U.S. Attorney General. © Engraving by Currier and Ives. The Library of Congress/Corbis.

legal purposes, aggregations of individuals. Georgia ignored the Court's order, however, and judgement was finally entered against the state in February of 1794.

Public sentiment in favor of state's rights soon became a factor in the case, however, and a constitutional amendment was proposed in December of 1793 that stated:

> . . . the judicial power of the United States shall not be construed to extend to any suit in law of equity commenced or prosecuted against one of the United States by citizens of another state, or by citizens or subjects of any foreign state . . .

The writ against the state of Georgia was never served, and the proposed amendment was ratified as the Eleventh Amendment to the U.S. Constitution in 1798.

Related Cases

Fletcher v. Peck, 10 U.S. 87 (1810).
Cohens v. Virginia, 19 U.S. 264 (1821).

Bibliography and Further Reading

Biskupic, Joan, and Elder Witt, eds. *Congressional Quarterly's Guide to the U.S. Supreme Court,* 3rd ed. Washington, DC: Congressional Quarterly, Inc., 1996.

Cushman, Robert F. *Leading Constitutional Decisions.* Englewood Cliffs, NJ: Prentice-Hall, Inc., 1982.

Hall, Kermit L., ed. *The Oxford Companion to the Supreme Court of the United States.* New York: Oxford University Press, 1992.

Johnson, John W. *Historic U.S. Court Cases, 1690–1990: An Encyclopedia.* New York: Garland Publishing, 1992.

Reardon, John J. *Edmund Randolph.* New York: Macmillan Publishing, 1974.

MARBURY V. MADISON

Legal Citation: 5 U.S. 137 (1803)

Plaintiffs
William Marbury, William Harper, Robert R. Hooe, Dennis Ramsay

Defendant
James Madison, U.S. Secretary of State

Plaintiffs' Claim
That Madison had illegally refused to deliver judicial commissions to their rightful recipients.

Chief Lawyer for Plaintiffs
Charles Lee

Chief Defense Lawyer
Levi Lincoln, U.S. Attorney General

Justices for the Court
Samuel Chase, William Cushing, John Marshall (writing for the Court), William Paterson, Bushrod Washington

Justices Dissenting
None (Alfred Moore did not participate)

Place
Washington, D.C.

Date of Decision
24 February 1803

Decision
Plaintiffs could not force Madison to deliver the commissions because the Judiciary Act of 1789 was unconstitutional.

Significance
Marbury v. Madison may be the most important case in American history, because it established the principle of judicial review.

In the late eighteenth century and the early nineteenth century, the two parties dominating the American political scene were the Federalists and the Democratic-Republicans. In the presidential election of 1800, the Electoral College had a tie vote, and it fell to the House of Representatives to decide the outcome. After a bitter battle and 36 ballots, on 17 February 1801 the House voted for the Democratic-Republican candidate, Thomas Jefferson.

The outgoing president, the Federalist John Adams, had as his secretary of state the distinguished lawyer John Marshall. In January of 1801, Adams secured Marshall's nomination as chief justice of the Supreme Court. Marshall was sworn in on 4 February, but continued to serve as Adams's secretary of state until 3 March, when Adams's term ended. Meanwhile, Adams and the Federalists in Congress had been moving to pack the federal judiciary with as many new Federalist judges as possible before the Jefferson administration took power.

As part of the Federalists' effort to preserve their control over the judicial arm of government, on 27 February 1801 Congress gave Adams the power to appoint justices of the peace for the District of Columbia. On 2 March, one day before the end of his term, Adams appointed 42 justices of the peace, and Congress approved their appointments the next day. As secretary of state, Marshall signed and sealed the necessary judicial commissions, but the commissions were not delivered by the end of 3 March. Jefferson's term began on 4 March, and he ordered his new secretary of state, James Madison, not to deliver the commissions. Jefferson decided to view the commissions as invalid unless delivered.

Marbury Goes to Court

Having demonstrated his power, Jefferson ultimately allowed most of the Adams appointees to take their offices. One of the appointees that Jefferson did not allow to take office, William Marbury, filed a petition with the Supreme Court on 16 December 1801 requesting that the Supreme Court order Madison to deliver Marbury's commission. Marbury was joined by three other disappointed appointees, William Harper, Robert R. Hooe, and Dennis Ramsay. Of course, by now Mar-

Justice Alfred Moore

Although he was a member of the Supreme Court at the time of *Marbury v. Madison,* Associate Justice Alfred Moore (1755-1810) did not take part in that historic decision. His five years on the Court (1799-1804) were unremarkable, and he wrote only one recorded opinion.

The son of a colonial judge in North Carolina, Moore studied law and was admitted to the bar at age 20. He fought in the Revolutionary War as a soldier and saboteur. He served on the North Carolina legislature in 1782 and 1792, and he held the position of attorney general for his home state. He argued the case of *Bayard v. Singleton* (1787), a state case that, as *Marbury v. Madison* would do, touched on the then-controversial issue of judicial review.

Moore led his state in ratifying the U.S. Constitution in 1788. He stepped down from his position as attorney general to protest the creation of a state solicitor general position. He lost a race for the senate in 1795 by a margin of just one vote.

In 1799, President John Adams nominated him to the U.S. Supreme Court, but Moore's poor health caused him to miss the judicial review debates that included *Marbury v. Madison.* His sole opinion was in *Bas v. Tingy* (1800), on an undeclared naval conflict between the United States and France. In 1804 Moore retired from the Court and died six years later in North Carolina. Among his other achievements was the establishment of the University of North Carolina.

Source(s): *West's Encyclopedia of American Law* St. Paul, MN: West Group, 1998.

---

shall had been the chief justice for over nine months. Under the Judiciary Act of 1789, the Supreme Court had the power to issue the order Marbury requested, called a writ of *mandamus.*

On 18 December 1801 Marshall ordered a hearing on Marbury's petition, to take place at the Court's next session. The Court's next session did not occur until the Court's February Term of 1803. The hearing began on 10 February 1803. Charles Lee, a Federalist and former attorney general, represented Marbury and the others. Jefferson's attorney general, Levi Lincoln, represented Secretary of State Madison.

Charles Lee argued that Madison, as secretary of state, was not only an official of the executive branch, bound to obey the president, but a public servant obligated to perform his duty and deliver Marbury's lawful commission. Therefore, the Court must exercise its authority under the Judiciary Act to issue a writ of *mandamus* against Madison. Lincoln said practically nothing, except that the issue of the commissions was purely political and thus not subject to the judiciary.

Marshall Proclaims the Doctrine of Judicial Review

On 24 February 1803 Marshall issued the Court's opinion. Marshall proceeded in three steps. First, he reviewed the facts of the case. Marshall stated that Marbury had the right to receive his commission:

> To withhold his commission, therefore, is an act deemed by the court not warranted by law, but violative of a vested right.

Second, Marshall analyzed Marbury's legal remedies. He concluded that the Judiciary Act clearly entitled Marbury to the writ of *mandamus* he requested. Marshall's third and final question, therefore, was whether the writ of *mandamus* could be issued by the Supreme Court. Although the Judiciary Act would allow the Court to issue the writ, Marshall was concerned about the Court's authority under Article III, Section 2, Paragraph 2 of the Constitution, which states:

> In all cases affecting ambassadors, other public ministers and consuls, and those in which a State shall be a Party, the Supreme Court shall have original jurisdiction. In all other cases . . . the Supreme Court shall have appellate jurisdiction . . .

If the Court did not have original jurisdiction, then under the Constitution Marbury could not go directly to it to get his requested writ of *mandamus.* He would have to go to a federal district court, and only if he lost there could he then appeal to the Supreme Court under its appellate jurisdiction. As Marshall stated:

> To enable this court, then, to issue a *mandamus,* it must be shown to be an exercise of appellate jurisdiction . . .

Marshall now addressed the critical question of whether the Court would use the authority that the Judiciary Act granted it, but that the Constitution denied it, to issue Marbury's writ of *mandamus.* Marshall said no, it would not. No act of Congress, including the Judiciary Act, could do something forbidden by the Constitution:

James Madison, U.S. Secretary of State. © AP/Wide World Photos.

Certainly all those who have framed written constitutions contemplate them as forming the fundamental and paramount law of the nation, and consequently, the theory of every such government must be, that an act of the legislature, repugnant to the constitution, is void.

Therefore, because the Judiciary Act violated the Constitution, it was unenforceable. Marbury and the others could not get their writ of *mandamus* from the Court because their petition had been sent to the Court directly, not on appeal. In declaring the Judiciary Act unconstitutional, Marshall set forth for the first time the doctrine of judicial review. Judicial review means that the federal courts, above all the Supreme Court, have the power to declare laws unenforceable if they violate the Constitution:

> It is emphatically the province and duty of the judicial department to say what the law is. Those who apply the rule to particular cases, must of necessity expound and interpret the rule. If two laws conflict with each other, the courts must decide on the operation of each.

Marshall's decision meant that the Court would not give his fellow Federalist Marbury the writ of *mandamus*. Nevertheless, it was a brilliant move. In refusing to confront Jefferson, Marshall had asserted a new and potent power for the judiciary, namely the doctrine of judicial review. Despite various issues, such as whether Marshall should have removed himself from the case because of his role as Adams's secretary of state, *Marbury v. Madison* permanently established the principle of judicial review. This power to overturn unconstitutional laws is the basis for the courts' power today to prevent such evils as civil rights violations.

Related Cases

Martin v. Hunter's Lessee, 14 U.S. 304 (1816).
Cohens v. Virginia, 19 U.S. 264 (1821).
Baker v. Carr, 369 U.S. 186 (1962).
Michigan v. Long, 463 U.S. 1032 (1983).
Honda v. Oberg, 512 U.S. 415 (1994).

Bibliography and Further Reading

Baker, Leonard. *John Marshall: A Life in Law.* New York: Macmillan, 1974.

Berger, Raoul. *Congress v. the Supreme Court.* Cambridge: Harvard University Press, 1969.

Beveridge, Albert J. *The Life of John Marshall.* Atlanta: Cherokee Pub., 1990.

Bickel, Alexander M. *The Least Dangerous Branch: the Supreme Court at the Bar of Politics.* New Haven: Yale University Press, 1986.

Cusack, Michael. "America's Greatest Justice?" *Scholastic Update,* January 1990, p. 11.

Ellis, Richard E. *The Jeffersonian Crisis: Courts and Politics in the Young Republic.* New York: Oxford University Press, 1971.

Johnson, John W., ed. *Historic U.S. Court Cases, 1690–1990: An Encyclopedia.* New York: Garland Publishing, 1992.

Levy, Leonard Williams. *Judicial Review and the Supreme Court.* New York: Harper & Row, 1967.

McHugh, Clare. "The Story of the Constitution: Conflict and Promise." *Scholastic Update,* September 1987, pp. 8–11.

Warren, Charles. *The Supreme Court in United States History.* Littleton: F. B. Rothman, 1987.

SAMUEL CHASE IMPEACHMENT

Senate Document #876, 62nd Congress, 2nd Session (1805)

Prosecution
United States

Defendant
Samuel Chase, U.S. Associate Supreme Court Justice

Plaintiff's Claim
That Chase should be removed from his post for committing "High Crimes and Misdemeanors" within the meaning of Article II, Section 4 of the Constitution.

Prosecutors
"Trial managers" John Randolph, Caesar Rodney

Chief Defense Lawyers
Robert Goodloe Harper, Joseph Hopkinson, Luther Martin

Judges
The U.S. Senate, with Vice-President Aaron Burr presiding

Place
Washington, D.C.

Date of Decision
1 March 1805

Decision
Chase was found not guilty and was allowed to remain in his post.

Significance
Congress for the first and only time exercised its constitutional prerogative to try a justice of the U.S. Supreme Court.

Samuel Chase was born in Somerset County, Maryland, in April of 1741. During the next 70 years, until his death in 1811, he would become one of America's most famous and controversial founding fathers.

Chase was active in politics from an early age, and was elected to colonial Maryland's Assembly on the strength of his anti-British platform. Chase was Maryland's delegate to the Continental Congress of 1774 in Philadelphia and was one of the signers of the 1776 Declaration of Independence. After fighting in the Revolutionary War, during which he became friends with George Washington, Chase returned to Maryland. Chase used his influence in the Federalist party to further his judicial career, and he swiftly rose through a succession of ever more prestigious posts. Chase was appointed presiding justice of Baltimore's Criminal Court. Then in 1791 he was appointed Chief Justice of the Maryland Court of Appeals. Finally in 1796 he was appointed to the U.S. Supreme Court. Chase's Supreme Court nomination had George Washington's personal backing.

From the Maryland courts to the Supreme Court, Chase was an openly Federalist judge and he never hid his political loyalties. He zealously enforced the Federalist-sponsored Alien and Sedition Acts, and supported the strict prosecution of persons involved in anti-government demonstrations and allegedly treasonous activities. Chase presided at several trials involving supporters of his fellow founding father and presidential contender Thomas Jefferson. Jefferson was the candidate of the opposing Democratic-Republican Party, and won the hotly contested election of 1800.

Congress Impeaches Chase

Jefferson had a series of political struggles with the Federalists, whose supporters such as Chase and Supreme Court Chief Justice John Marshall dominated the federal judiciary. The decision of the Court in *Marbury v. Madison* (1803), which established the principle of judicial review, was not revered by Jefferson.

In an attempt to change the makeup of the Supreme Court, Jefferson played a part in orchestrating impeachment proceedings against Chase. Jefferson tried to ex-

---

Samuel Chase

Associate Justice Samuel Chase (1741-1811) was the only member of the Supreme Court against whom impeachment proceedings have been brought in more than 200 years. In addition to being an outspoken leader in the American Revolution and a signer of the Declaration of Independence, he sat on the Supreme Court for 15 years, from 1796 to his death in 1811.

Involvement with questionable business schemes forced his removal from the Continental Congress, but in the 1780s Chase managed to revive his political career. He became involved in further scandal as a Baltimore judge later in the decade, and was very nearly removed by the state general assembly. Through the intercession of a friend, however, President George Washington was persuaded in 1796 to appoint Chase to the Supreme Court.

The impeachment proceedings brought against him, orchestrated by Thomas Jefferson in conjunction with the Congress, were unsuccessful, but Chase's career as an effective judge was over. He suffered increasing attacks of gout and died on 19 June 1811.

Source(s): *The National Cyclopedia of American Biography* New York: James T. White, 1895

---

ploit his party's domination of the Senate, where 25 of the 34 Senators were Democratic-Republicans and only nine were Federalists. Under Article II, Section 4 of the Constitution, federal judges can be impeached for "High Crimes and Misdemeanors," and under Article I, Section 3 the trial must be conducted before the Senate. Jefferson's allies in the House of Representatives passed Articles of Impeachment against Chase, which were duly received by the Senate.

The Senate's High Court of Impeachment, presided over by Vice-President Aaron Burr, opened on 4 February 1805. The "trial managers," or prosecutors, were John Randolph and Caesar Rodney. Chase's lawyers were Robert Goodloe Harper, Joseph Hopkinson and Luther Martin. There were eight articles, which named a variety of Democratic-Republican grievances against Chase concerning the trials he had presided over. The charges ranged from allegedly giving a false legal definition of treason during the trial of one John Fries in Article One to allegedly making very political comments to a Baltimore grand jury in Article Eight.

There was certainly plenty of evidence that Chase was a highly opinionated Federalist judge, who had perhaps acted with little regard for courtroom niceties, but there was very little proof that his actions were serious enough to be deemed constitutional violations.

Even the Democratic-Republican senators felt uncomfortable. Trial manager Rodney in his closing argument lamely begged the Senate:

> Remember, if this honorable court acquit the defendant, they declare in the most solemn manner, . . . that he has . . . behaved himself well, in a manner becoming the character of a judge worthy of his situation.

On 1 March 1805 the Senate voted on Chase's impeachment. On each of the eight articles, enough Democratic-Republican senators joined the Federalists in voting "not guilty" so that Chase was acquitted of all the charges against him. Chase continued to serve on the Supreme Court until he died in June of 1811.

Chase's acquittal was a defeat for Jefferson, who may have planned to impeach Chief Justice Marshall if Chase was found guilty. The Samuel Chase impeach-

Justice Samuel Chase. © Corbis-Bettmann.

ment was the first and only time Congress impeached a justice of the U.S. Supreme Court.

Related Cases

Aaron Burr Trial, 25 Fed. Cas. 187 (1807).
President Andrew Johnson Impeachment Trial.
United States v. Nixon, 418 U.S. 683 (1974).

Bibliography and Further Reading

Elsmere, Jane Shaffer. *Justice Samuel Chase.* Muncie, IN: Janevar Publishing, 1980.

Haw, James. *Stormy Patriot: the Life of Samuel Chase.* Baltimore: Maryland Historical Society, 1980.

Johnson, John W., ed. *Historic U.S. Court Cases, 1690–1990: An Encyclopedia.* New York: Garland Publishing, 1992.

Rehnquist, William H. *Grand Inquests: the Historic Impeachments of Justice Samuel Chase and President Andrew Johnson.* New York: Morrow, 1992.

McCULLOCH v. MARYLAND

Legal Citation: 17 U.S. 316 (1819)

Appellant
James William McCulloch

Appellee
State of Maryland

Appellant's Claim
That a fine imposed by the State of Maryland for operating the Bank of the United States in Baltimore was an improper interference with federal government operations.

Chief Lawyer for Appellant
Daniel Webster

Chief Lawyer for Appellee
Joseph Hopkinson

Justices for the Court
Gabriel Duvall, William Johnson, Henry Brockholst Livingston, John Marshall (writing for the Court), Joseph Story, Bushrod Washington

Justices Dissenting
None (Thomas Todd did not participate)

Place
Washington, D.C.

Date of Decision
7 March 1819

Decision
That the power to operate a bank was an implied power of the federal government under the Constitution.

Significance
The Court established the principle of implied powers, paving the way for the expansion of the role of the federal government.

The Bank Issue

In 1816, the federal government had established the second bank of the United States, operating in Philadelphia. In order to facilitate its operations, the bank set up a branch in Baltimore in 1818 and appointed James W. McCulloch as cashier in that branch. In February of 1818, the state of Maryland passed a law requiring all banks operating in the state to obtain a license from the state and to use a state stamp on all papers issued. The federal bank under McCulloch began operations in Baltimore in May of 1818; however, McCulloch did not obtain a license or use the state stamps. Accordingly, the state brought action against McCulloch, and fined him $2500. He appealed the fine to the Supreme Court.

The counsel for the state of Maryland pointed out that the Constitution did not specifically grant power to the federal government to establish a bank. When the first bank of the U.S. had been established in 1791, it might have been justified as an implied power of the federal government in collecting taxes and providing for a single currency. However, since the 1790s, many state banks had grown and could now perform those functions. Furthermore, when Congress set up the Second Bank in 1816, it did not grant power to the directors of that bank to establish branches. When such a branch was established, it could not claim to be exempt from the power of the states to tax, as that would be an invasion of state sovereignty.

McCulloch's counsel argued that the federal government had the right to charter a bank as part of its regular financial operations. He further pointed out that a state could not tax a federal activity. If that were allowed, it would allow the separate states to control the federal government and would weaken the federal government to the point that it resembled the government under the Articles of Confederation. He pointed out, in addition, that if a bank were constitutional, branches of the bank were constitutional.

John Marshall wrote the opinion of the Court, accepting McCulloch's arguments but going further. Marshall noted that in Article 10 of the Constitution, the founding fathers had left out the phrase "expressly" in referring to powers granted to the federal government. He noted that the government must have ample means to achieve defense and the regulation of commerce. National defense requires that federal bills be paid in distant and remote parts of the country. The powers granted to the government implied ordinary and ample means of implementing those powers. Defense required means of moving funds from place to place, and the bank was necessary to the ends. It was convenient and useful to the government to operate a bank, and establishing branches was an ordinary and necessary aspect of the operation. He agreed with Webster that a state could not tax the ordinary and useful operations of the federal government, and so the Court unanimously ruled in favor of James McCulloch.

The *McCulloch* decision established that the federal government had to rely on implied powers in the Constitution if it was to operate. The doctrine of implied powers justified many actions of the federal government as it expanded its role in the growing nation. It continued to be cited during New Deal legislation in the 1930s and federal civil rights legislation in the 1960s.

Related Cases
Thurlow v. Commonwealth of Massachusetts, 46 U.S. 504 (1847).
First Agricultural National Bank of Berkshire County v. State Tax Commission, 392 U.S. 339 (1968).

Bibliography and Further Reading
Beveridge, Albert J. *The Life of John Marshall*. Boston: Houghton Mifflin, 1919.

Epstein, Lee, and Thomas G. Walker. *Constitutional Law for a Changing America: Institutional Powers and Constraints*, 3rd ed. Washington DC: Congressional Quarterly, 1998.

Gunter, Gerald, ed. *John Marshall's Defense of McCulloch v. Maryland*. Stanford, CA: Stanford University Press, 1969.

Johnson, John W., ed. *Historic U.S. Court Cases, 1690–1990: An Encyclopedia*. New York: Garland Publishing, 1992.

Daniel Webster. © Photograph by Matthew Brady. The National Archives/Corbis.

FOSTER V. NEILSON

Legal Citation: 27 U.S. 253 (1829)

Petitioners
James Foster, Pleasants Elam

Respondent
David Neilson

Petitioners' Claim
That a grant of land in Spanish West Florida in 1804 was valid under the terms of an 1818 treaty, even though the U.S. government had previously claimed its rights to the land.

Chief Lawyers for Petitioners
Coxe, Webster

Chief Lawyer for Respondent
Jones

Justices for the Court
Gabriel Duvall, William Johnson, John Marshall (writing for the Court), Joseph Story, Smith Thomson, Bushrod Washington

Justices Dissenting
None (John McLean was not yet appointed)

Place
Washington, D.C.

Date of Decision
January 1829

Decision
That the interpretation of treaties respecting national boundaries is a political matter committed to the Congress and the president, and not the courts. Accordingly, the courts are bound by the determination of Congress and the president that the land at issue was part of the United States in 1804, and the grant to the petitioners was invalid.

Significance
By deferring to the will of Congress and the president, the Court established what has come to be known as the "political question" doctrine. Under this doctrine, still relied upon today, the Court will not decide matters which raise purely political, rather than legal matters, particularly in the field of foreign relations.

At the conclusion of the 1700s, Spain controlled the entire Florida peninsula, known as East Florida, and a strip of land extending from the Florida panhandle through southern Alabama, Mississippi, and Louisiana, ending at the Mississippi River. However, as Spain's power in both Europe and North America weakened, Spain found it increasingly difficult to control the inhabitants of the Floridas and to keep France (in Louisiana) and the United States from asserting claims to the Floridas. In 1800, Spain and France signed the Treaty of St. Ildefonso. According to Spain's interpretation of the treaty, Spain agreed to transfer only its land in Louisiana to France. The land owned by France in Louisiana was then transferred to the United States in 1803 by the Louisiana Purchase.

The United States, however, disagreed with Spain's interpretation of the Treaty of St. Ildefonso. In 1810, President James Monroe issued a proclamation declaring that all of Spanish West Florida was given to France, and thus to the United States in the Louisiana Purchase. President Monroe ordered U.S. troops to occupy the lands. Congress supported President Monroe's interpretation of the Treaty of St. Ildefonso by passing a number of laws relating to the disputed territory, including several acts establishing the boundaries of Louisiana and the Mississippi Territory, and permitting Alabama to become a state. The conflicting claims were resolved by the 1818 Treaty of Amity between the United States and Spain. This treaty confirmed the U.S. control over the entire region of both East and West Florida. However, the treaty also provided that any grants of land made by the Spanish government in the region prior to the signing of the treaty were valid.

Against this historical backdrop, in March of 1826, James Foster and Pleasants Elam brought a suit in the U.S. district court to recover land in Louisiana, about 30 miles east of the Mississippi River. The plaintiffs claimed "title," or ownership, to the land through a grant made by the Spanish government in 1804. The defendant, David Neilson, who was in possession of the land, claimed that the grant by the Spanish government was invalid because the land was transferred to France in 1800 and then to the United States in 1803. Therefore, because Spain did not control the land in

1804, the Spanish government did not have any authority to grant title to the land. The plaintiffs countered that the Treaty of Amity, signed in 1818, confirmed Spain's interpretation of the earlier treaty because it specifically provided that all grants made prior to 1818 by the Spanish government would be considered valid. The district court concluded that the land belonged to the United States through the Louisiana Purchase, and therefore the Spanish government had no authority to transfer the land to the plaintiffs. The plaintiffs then appealed the decision to the U.S. Supreme Court.

The Court declined to adopt its own interpretation of the various treaties at issue, concluding that the issue was decided more properly by the president and Congress as the political branches of the government. The Court reasoned that because President Monroe had declared the land to be part of the land acquired by the United States through the Louisiana Purchase, and Congress had subsequently passed laws asserting control over these areas, the political branches of the government had taken the position that the land belonged to the United States. The Court then concluded:

> After these acts of sovereign power over the territory in dispute, asserting the American construction of the treaty by which the government claims it, to maintain the opposite construction in its own courts would certainly be an anomaly in the history and practice of nations. If those departments which are entrusted with the foreign intercourse of the nation, which assert and maintain its interests against foreign powers, have unequivocally asserted . . . rights of dominion over a country of which it is in possession, and which it claims under a treaty; if the legislature has acted on the construction thus asserted, it is not in its own courts that this construction is to be denied. A question like this respecting the boundaries of nations, is, as has been truly said, more a political than a legal question; and in its discussion, the courts of every country must respect the pronounced will of the legislature.

The Court also held that the Treaty of Amity signed in 1818 did not make the previous Spanish grants valid. Although this portion of the Court's decision was overruled a few years later in the 1833 case of *United States v. Percheman*, the Court's decision in *Foster* continues to have significance. The decision helped establish what has come to be known as the "political question" doctrine. Under this doctrine, which was first suggested in the famous case of *Marbury v. Madison* (1803), courts will not decide cases inherently political in nature, because such decisions are made more properly by the president and Congress as the political branches of the government. Since *Foster* was decided, the Supreme Court has declined to rule on political questions relating to foreign affairs, qualifications of members of Congress, and procedures used by the Senate for impeaching the president.

Related Cases

Marbury v. Madison, 5 U.S. 137 (1803).
United States v. Percheman, 32 U.S. 51 (1833).

Bibliography and Further Reading

Corwin, Edward S. *The President: Office and Powers 1787-1957.* New York: New York University Press, 1957.

Schubert, Glendon A. *The Presidency in the Courts.* Minneapolis: University of Minnesota Press, 1957.

Tebeau, Charlton W. *A History of Florida.* Coral Gables, Fla.: University of Miami Press, 1971.

BARRON V. BALTIMORE

Legal Citation: 32 U.S. 243 (1833)

Appellant
John Barron

Appellee
The mayor and city council of Baltimore, Maryland

Appellant's Claim
The Fifth Amendment to the U.S. Constitution required Baltimore to compensate Barron for having "taken" his property by significantly compromising the usefulness of his wharf.

Chief Lawyer for Appellant
Charles Mayer

Chief Lawyer for Appellee
Roger Brooke Taney

Justices for the Court
Gabriel Duvall, William Johnson, John Marshall (writing for the Court), John McLean, Joseph Story, Smith Thompson

Justices Dissenting
None (Henry Baldwin did not participate)

Place
Washington, D.C.

Date of Decision
16 February 1833

Decision
The Supreme Court had no jurisdiction in this case because the Fifth Amendment applied only to the federal government and not to the states.

Significance
Barron established the principle that the rights enumerated in the first ten amendments (the "Bill of Rights") do not limit the powers of the states. This legal doctrine was not reversed until the twentieth century, when the Supreme Court gradually incorporated the Bill of Rights into the Fourteenth Amendment.

Early in the nineteenth century, John Barron and John Craig owned a large and profitable wharf at Baltimore, Maryland. The older sections of Baltimore's harbor often became filled with stagnant water, garbage, and debris. Trying to end this health hazard, the city council carried out an extensive public works program between 1815 and 1821. Contractors regraded and paved streets, built embankments, and diverted streams toward the wharf.

The City Makes Barron's Wharf Useless

During storms, these streams carried sand and silt down to the harbor and deposited it in front of Barron's wharf. The water grew steadily shallower until no sizable vessel could use the wharf. In 1822, Barron sued the city in the Baltimore County Court, asking for money to compensate him for the loss of his business. (John Craig was deceased by then, and Barron represented his former partner's interests as well as his own.)

Barron argued that Baltimore had violated his property rights under state law, but the city's attorneys denied any liability. The Maryland legislature had granted the city power to pave streets and regulate the flow of water. The inadvertent silting up of the harbor was a general nuisance affecting all the city's inhabitants and not directed toward Barron in particular.

Barron won his case in the Baltimore County Court, which awarded him $4,500 in damages. The city appealed to the Maryland Court of Appeals, the state's highest court. When it ruled against Barron on all points, his lawyers carried the case to the U.S. Supreme Court on a writ of error. The records do not explain why the Supreme Court did not hear Barron's appeal until 1833, some ten years after the original suit in the state courts.

Charles Mayer, Barron's attorney, went to Washington, D.C. prepared to present two separate arguments. The city derived its powers from the state, and its acts had wronged Barron under state law. Alternatively, Barron was a citizen of the United States. As such, he was owed protection under the Constitution's Fifth Amendment, which forbids the taking of private property for public use "without just compensation." The Supreme

Court had jurisdiction because this constitutional question was involved.

To defend its interests, Maryland sent one of its legal giants, Roger Brooke Taney, the state's attorney general. Shortly afterwards, President Andrew Jackson raised Taney to U.S. attorney general. He eventually succeeded Marshall as chief justice of the Supreme Court.

When the day came for oral arguments, the Court told Attorney Mayer to discuss only whether the Supreme Court had jurisdiction under the Fifth Amendment. When Mayer finished, it then was Taney's turn to speak for Maryland. But Chief Justice Marshall stopped him short before he could address the Court.

The Bill of Rights Does Not Apply to the States

When the decision was given, Marshall spoke for a unanimous Court. Marshall dismissed Barron's suit because the Supreme Court had no jurisdiction in the matter. Barron had appealed from a state court. Thus the Supreme Court could act only if it were true that the Fifth Amendment restrained the state of Maryland. But none of the provisions of the Bill of Rights applied to the states.

"The question thus presented is," Marshall began, "of great importance, but not of much difficulty." He then advanced three arguments in support of his conclusion—one based on the nature of the Constitution, one on its language, and one on its history.

In his first argument, Marshall repeated his often expressed union theory of popular sovereignty. Through state constitutions, the people of each state united and directly created a state government. Through the U.S. Constitution, the people of the United States came together and created a general government. The constitution the people had given each level of government determined that level's powers.

> The Constitution was ordained and established by the people of the United States for themselves, for their own government, and not for the government of the individual states. Each state established a constitution for itself, and . . . provided such limitations and restitutions on the powers of its particular government as its judgment dictated. The people of the United States formed such a government for the United States as they supposed . . . best calculated to promote their interests.

The U.S. Constitution created a federal government, and the people did the creating. Thus, the powers and limitations they conferred through that Constitution were "naturally" and "necessarily" applicable only to the federal government the Constitution created.

The concept of sovereignty with the people helped explain the Constitution's language. The Constitution contains three kinds of statements limiting power, Marshall declared. Some statements directly mention the federal government, while others mention the states. Yet a third type, which includes the Fifth Amendment, places limits on power framed in general terms, without specifically mentioning either the federal or the state government.

These general limitations, Marshall argued, must be read as applying only to the federal government. As proof he quoted Article I, Section 9: "No bill of attainder or ex post facto law shall be passed." This is immediately followed by Article I, Section 10: "No state shall . . . pass any bill of attainder . . ." Obviously, the general limit in Section 9 applied only to the federal government. If it also affected the states, Section 10 simply would not be needed.

To further explain his interpretation, Marshall presented a third argument, one based on the history of the Bill of Rights. Had the people, he noted, wanted to limit state governments, they would have called state constitutional conventions. Such conventions provided a much simpler procedure than the "unwieldy and cumbrous machinery" of amending the U.S. Constitution. Moreover, when the Constitution was ratified, the Bill of Rights was added precisely because the people feared the federal government and not because they dreaded abuses of power by state governments. This reason for opposing ratification of the Constitution was "universally understood" and "part of the history of the day."

Barron was John Marshall's last constitutional opinion, written when he was already in failing health and profoundly worried about the state of the union. Federal-state relations were in a crisis. In 1832, a convention in South Carolina had nullified a congressional tariff law. The same year, Georgia had refused to enforce a Supreme Court decision (*Worcester v. Georgia*) affecting Native American rights.

While Marshall was sensitive to these political conflicts, his decision was historically accurate. The surviving records of the conventions ratifying the Constitution supported his statements. So did a significant body of previous decisions by state courts.

As Marshall stated, *Barron* was of enormous significance. Later courts accepted the decision and expanded it to all of the Bill of Rights. Thus they prevented the federal government from interfering when a state allegedly violated an individual's civil rights.

After the Civil War, the Fourteenth Amendment (ratified in 1868) required the states to provide "due process" ("nor shall any State deprive any person of life, liberty, or property, without due process of law.") to its citizens. Since the 1920s, the courts have incorporated various rights into the Fourteenth Amendment by defining them as essential to "due process." But the process has been slow, inconsistent, and controversial.

American law and American society might have evolved in entirely different ways had Marshall ruled otherwise in *Barron*. Yet his decision was totally consistent with the beliefs of the Constitution's authors. Firmly convinced that local officials posed little threat to individual rights, the nation's founders primarily feared the distant and oppressive federal government.

Related Cases

Worcester v. Georgia, 31 U.S. 515 (1832).
Watkins v. United States, 354 U.S. 178 (1957).

Bibliography and Further Reading

Currie, David. *The Constitution in the Supreme Court: The First Hundred Years, 1789-1888.* Chicago: University of Chicago Press, 1985.

Johnson, John W. *Historic U.S. Court Cases, 1690–1990: An Encyclopedia.* New York: Garland Publishing, 1992.

White, George. *History of the Supreme Court of the United States. Vols. III-IV: The Marshall Court and Cultural Change, 1815-1835.* New York: Macmillan, 1988.

PRIGG V. PENNSYLVANIA

Legal Citation: 41 U.S. 539 (1842)

Appellant
Edward Prigg

Appellee
State of Pennsylvania

Appellant's Claim
That laws passed by the U.S. Congress regulating interstate retrieval of fugitive slaves take precedence over state laws on the same subject.

Chief Lawyers for Appellant
Meredith, Nelson

Chief Lawyer for Appellee
Johnson, Attorney General of Pennsylvania

Justices for the Court
Henry Baldwin, John Catron, Peter Vivian Daniel, John McKinley, Joseph Story (writing for the Court), Roger Brooke Taney, Smith Thompson, James Moore Wayne

Justices Dissenting
John McLean

Place
Washington, D.C.

Date of Decision
1 March 1842

Decision
Upheld Prigg's claim and overturned two lower courts' decisions convicting Prigg of kidnapping under an 1826 Pennsylvania law.

Significance
The ruling upheld the Supremacy Clause of the Constitution in which federal laws take precedence over state laws when regulating the same activity. The Commerce Clause of the Constitution is one major avenue for the national government to exercise its authority over states. From the 1930s New Deal era through the 1970s the federal government significantly grew by increasingly regulating many facets of life. By the 1980s states' rights proponents began to reverse the trend. Debates over federal controls continued into the late 1990s focused on proposed national health care reforms.

At the center of issues intensively debated by the founders of the United States was federalism, the distribution of power between the federal and state governments. Dispute over the degree of centralization of political power in the United States highlighted by debates between Alexander Hamilton and James Madison led to formation of the first political parties in the nation. As a result, the Supremacy Clause was written into Article IV of the Constitution providing the primary basis for the federal government's power over states. The article states the "acts of the Federal Government are operational as supreme law throughout the Union . . . enforceable in all courts of the land. The states have no power to impede, burden, or in any manner control the operation of" federal law.

With slavery another major issue, the founders also reached compromise in which the Southern states could continue slavery while Congress received broad powers to regulate commerce. Article I of the Constitution states that "Congress shall have Power . . . to regulate commerce with foreign Nations, and among the several States." The Constitution also contained a Fugitive Clause in that states had rights to retrieve fugitives, including fugitive slaves, from other states to which they had fled. However, the Constitution did not describe the responsibility of the state receiving the request or how the request should be made.

Problems soon arose. In 1791, Pennsylvania requested the return of a fugitive from Virginia, but Virginia chose not to comply. Two years later Congress responded with passage of an act more fully addressing apprehension of fugitives from justice and slaves escaping the service of their masters. The 1793 fugitive slave law allowed for their arrest without a warrant, relying only on the oath of the owner or their agent regarding their claim. In 1826, Pennsylvania passed a law in direct conflict by requiring a warrant and testimony of "indifferent witnesses." The federal law protected slave owners "from all unnecessary delay and expense" while state law allowed for the alleged fugitive to ask for a delay while a court heard their case. The owner could be charged with court expenses. Whereas the federal law provided penalties for the hindering owners, the Pennsylvania law only gave the owner a right to seek damages.

Justice John McLean. © Archive Photos.

Owing Service

Margaret Morgan was a black slave in the state of Maryland "owing service" to Margaret Ashmore. In 1832, Morgan fled from Maryland to Pennsylvania. Over a year after arriving in Pennsylvania, Morgan gave birth to a child. Several years later, in February of 1837, Ashmore hired attorney Edward Prigg "to seize and arrest the said negro woman." Prigg proceeded to obtain an arrest warrant from a justice of the peace in York County, Pennsylvania for Morgan and her children. A constable for the county promptly apprehended them, but upon delivery to the court the justice of the peace refused to take further action for their return. Prigg then took action on his own and brought Morgan and the children back to Ashmore in Maryland. As a result, Prigg was arrested and charged with kidnapping under the 1826 Pennsylvania law.

In 1839, a jury in a lower court found Prigg guilty of violating the Pennsylvania law. Prigg appealed to the Supreme Court of Pennsylvania arguing the Pennsylvania state law violated the U.S. Constitution by creating procedures that obstructed the retrieval of fugitive slaves and therefore was invalid. The Pennsylvania Supreme Court, however, affirmed the lower court's ruling. Prigg next took his case to the U.S. Supreme Court where the state of Maryland also argued on his behalf that the 1826 Pennsylvania law was constitutionally invalid.

Federal Supremacy

Justice Story, writing for the Court, noted, "Few questions which have ever come before this Court involve more delicate and important considerations." In describing the Fugitive Clause of the Constitution, Story wrote "that the object of this clause was to secure to the citizens of the slave-holding states the complete right and title of ownership in their slaves, as property, in every state in the Union into which they might escape." Story added that without the clause, each non-slave state could "have declared free all runaway slaves coming within its limits . . . and . . . created the most bitter animosities." Story found the "clause manifestly contemplates the existence of a positive, unqualified right on the part of the owner of the slave, which no state law or regulation can in any way qualify, regulate, control or restrain." Regarding the supremacy of the 1793 federal fugitive law, Story found that Congress had acted "within the scope of the constitutional authority" and that if state laws on the same subject, particularly those contrary to the intent of the federal law, were allowed to stand "confusion . . . would be endless." Story found that since the right of owners to retrieve fugitive slaves was provided in the Constitution, it was "an absolute, positive right and duty, pervading the whole Union with an equal and supreme force, uncontrolled and uncontrollable by

Given the association of slavery with commerce in the nation's early years, slavery cases were considered by the Supreme Court as commerce issues focused on property rights rather than human rights. In 1825 in the first slave case before the Court, *The Antelope,* Chief Justice John Marshall wrote that in "claims in which the sacred rights of liberty and of property come in conflict with each other . . . this Court must not yield to feelings which might seduce it from the path of duty, but must obey the mandates of the law." The property rights of slave owners prevailed in the courts.

Regarding division of power between the federal government and states, a number of cases prior to 1840 were decided favoring states' rights to govern their own jurisdictions with minimal influence from the federal government. However, beginning in 1840 the supremacy of the federal government began to be defined. In *Holmes v. Jennison,* the Court ruled states did not have power to engage in foreign affairs. Next, the Court ruled that federal courts could overrule state court interpretations of state law. Increasingly, questions of states' authority were tied to questions of slavery. In *Groves v. Slaughter* in 1841 the Court ruled states had the right to exclude slavery.

state sovereignty or state legislation." Therefore, Story repeated the words of Chief Justice John Marshall in a previous case by stating "the subject is as completely taken from the state legislatures, as if they had been forbidden to act."

In conclusion, Story wrote that "the inherent and sovereign power of a state, to protect its jurisdiction and the peace of its citizens . . . shall not conflict with a defined power of the federal government." The federal law was clearly constitutionally valid and the Pennsylvania law was unconstitutional and void as argued by Prigg and Maryland. Edward Prigg was found not guilty and the case remanded back to the Pennsylvania Supreme Court.

Impact

The *Prigg* ruling maintained that federal law held supremacy over state laws regarding fugitive slaves. It also served to weaken the ability of states to protect peoples within their boundaries and led to greater sectional conflict over slavery. Over the next 15 years it became clear the slavery question could not be resolved in the courts. In both *Jones v. Van Zandt* (1848) and *Ableman v. Booth* (1859), the Court reaffirmed the 1793 federal fugitive slave law and the property rights of slave owners. The Court maintained its role was to uphold the laws and that the moral question of slavery was "a political question, settled by each state for itself . . . and which we possess no authority as a judicial body to modify or overrule."

The primary legal question addressed by *Prigg* was the separate rights of states and Congress to regulate certain activities. Though the Court affirmed the supremacy of federal law in several cases in the early 1840s, an era of limited federal government, however, continued until 1932 with the beginnings of New Deal programs during the depression. The judicial doctrine of "preemption" in which Congress could enact laws that took precedence over existing state laws on the same subject was soon established further clarifying the supremacy of federal government. In the *Hines v. Davidowitz* (1941) case, the Court ruled that federal law regulating the registration of aliens preempted state law. By the 1960s regulatory laws were increasingly passed by both Congress and the states making preemption legal cases more frequent. An example was the Voting Rights Act of 1965 in which a federal law preempted state laws by imposing consistent national anti-discrimination standards.

After decades of increasing centralized power held by the federal government, in the mid-1980s the Court began to roll back federal supremacy. This trend towards states' rights was further fueled by the 1994 election of a Republican-controlled Congress that campaigned against centralized government. A key target was the Commerce Clause of the Constitution giving Congress power to regulate matters involving the national economy. In *United States v. Lopez* (1995) the Court ruled that the Commerce Clause did not give Congress power to ban guns near schools as the government argued. The ruling was the first in six decades to hold that Congress could not regulate a private activity under the Commerce Clause. Despite this increased support for states' rights in the 1990s, several factors led to increased efforts at federal preemptions including the explosion in telecommunications technology. Increased electronic commerce, including Internet shopping and banking, posed major threats to state sales tax schemes and traditional state regulation of banks. Again, the debate over states' rights versus centralized federal government control erupted as it had over two centuries ago with the Hamilton-Madison debates.

Related Cases

The Antelope, 10 Wheat. 66 (1825).
Jones v. Van Zandt, 5 How. 215 (1848).
Ableman v. Booth, 62 U.S. 506 (1859).
Hines v. Davidowitz, 312 U.S. 52 (1941).
United States v. Lopez, 514 U.S. 549 (1995).

Bibliography and Further Reading

Finkelman, P. "*Prigg v. Pennsylvania* and Northern States Courts." *Civil War History*, Vol. 25, March 1979, pp. 5–35.

Johnson, John W., ed. *Historic U.S. Court Cases, 1690–1990: An Encyclopedia.* New York: Garland Publishing, 1992.

Nogee, J. "The Prigg Case and Fugitive Slavery, 1842–50." *Journal of Negro History*, Vol. 39, January 1954, pp. 27–42.

Walker, David B. *The Rebirth of Federalism: Slouching Toward Washington.* Chatham, NJ: Chatham House Publishers, 1995.

PRIZE CASES

Legal Citation: 67 U.S. 635 (1863)

Petitioners
Owners of four ships as claimants: *Hiawatha, Crenshaw, Amy Warwick,* and *Brilliante*

Respondent
United States

Petitioners' Claim
That the seizure of these ships for violation of blockade was illegal, because the war was a civil war, not an international war.

Chief Lawyer for Petitioners
Charles Edwards

Chief Lawyer for Respondent
Richard Henry Dana, Jr.

Justices for the Court
David Davis, Robert Cooper Grier (writing for the Court), Samuel Freeman Miller, Noah Haynes Swayne, James Moore Wayne

Justices Dissenting
John Catron, Nathan Clifford, Samuel Nelson, Roger Brooke Taney

Place
Washington, D.C.

Date of Decision
10 March 1863

Decision
The Court ruled the president could insitute a wartime blockade without congressional approval.

Significance
The case determined that the Union government could pursue the naval war against the Confederacy as if it were an international war, using the rules of blockade.

The Issue of Belligerency

The *Prize Cases* referred to the adjudication during the American Civil War of four captures of ships which had violated the blockade of the South by the Union Navy. The cases raised questions which could have worked against the Union war effort. The Supreme Court's ruling supported the Union position, establishing the right of a government to set up a blockade of its own ports during an insurrection, and establishing the right of the president to set up the blockade without a declaration of war by Congress. The issue in international law was complicated by the fact that the Union did not want to treat the Confederacy as an international belligerent or give it belligerent status, while at the same time the Union sought to close the ports of the South by blockade. Since blockades can only be used against belligerents, the Union appeared to want to have it both ways.

In the *Prize Cases*, if the courts ruled that a blockade existed, foreign powers might regard that as recognition of the status of the Confederacy as a belligerent state. However, if the courts ruled that the blockade was not legal, then the power of the president to conduct the war through seizure of merchant ships carrying arms and other contraband to the Confederacy would be impaired.

The Captured Ships

The four ships, *Hiawatha, Crenshaw, Amy Warwick,* and *Brilliante* had all been condemned in lower courts after having been seized by the Union Navy. *Hiawatha* was a British barque captured in Hampton Roads in May of 1861. While the ship was loading a cargo of cotton for export, the captain had received word that the blockade was in effect. Lower courts sustained the seizure and forwarded the case to the Supreme Court for ruling on the constitutional issues.

Amy Warwick had been taken off Cape Henry in July of 1861 by the U.S. gunboat *Quaker City*. A court in Boston upheld the seizure of property aboard the vessel belonging to residents of Virginia, arguing that property belonging to persons resident in enemy territories was subject to condemnation if taken at sea. The schooner *Crenshaw* was owned by two partners, one Southern and one Northern, and the ship was carrying a cargo of tobacco from Richmond, Virginia to Liverpool, England when it was seized in May of 1861. Lower courts ruled that property aboard the ship belonging to Englishmen was exempt from seizure, but condemned all the rest of the cargo. *Brilliante* was a schooner owned by an American and a Mexican citizen, carrying cargo that belonged to the owners of the vessel and to two other Mexicans. Captured in June of 1861 while anchored off Biloxi, Mississippi, it was found to be carrying cargo it had picked up in New Orleans, Louisiana, after the beginning of the blockade. In a local court in Key West, Florida, the seizure was upheld, and the owners appealed to the Supreme Court.

While these four cases were being heard in the Supreme Court, other cases which had arisen from the blockade were postponed, pending a decision in Washington, D.C. Even so, the *Prize Cases* were not heard until June of 1863, after Abraham Lincoln had appointed new members to the Supreme Court. Even with his own appointees in the Court, however, the decision was close.

The case for the government was argued by Richard Henry Dana, Jr., famous for his factual novel, *Two Years Before the Mast* (1840). Dana argued that the government's right to capture property had no relationship to the status of the owners. Rather, if the owners were under the jurisdiction of the enemy, the government could seize the property, because that control gave the enemy an interest in the property. Further, he argued that the state of war existed, even if it had not been declared by Congress. The president could exercise war powers without such a declaration. The state of war gave the U.S. government belligerent rights, but no such rights were to be assumed for the Confederacy, because an area in rebellion did not have the same rights as a sovereign nation.

Each of the groups of claimants were represented by different attorneys, but Charles Edwards handled the petitioners in the cases of the *Crenshaw* and the *Hiawatha*. The attorneys for the claimants argued that the rebels could not be considered enemies, and the conflict could not be considered war. However, Justice Grier, in writing the majority opinion of the Court, accepted Dana's argument that the war was a fact and that Lincoln was empowered to pursue the war without waiting for Congress to recognize it. Justice Nelson wrote the minority opinion, holding that no war could exist before Congress acted to recognize it in July of 1861. Since the president had no power to set up a blockade or to conduct war before that date, the minority held, the decrees of condemnation of property should be set aside.

The most far-reaching effect of the *Prize Cases* was to uphold the president's claim to extensive emergency

Attorney Richard Henry Dana, Jr. © Photograph by J. W. Black & Company. The Library of Congress/Corbis.

powers. The precedent set in the *Prize Cases* may have discouraged legal challenges to other acts of President Lincoln during the war, including suspension of free speech and press, the Conscription Act, and the Emancipation Proclamation. The *Prize Cases* established the theory that the president had extraordinary powers to preserve the nation and that he could exercise them legally. Furthermore, the Court had ruled that the Union had full powers as a belligerent but that the Confederacy could claim no such powers. The Court accepted the paradox that the Union could exercise all power which would come with an international war, but that it could also exercise sovereign power over the area in rebellion.

Related Cases
Keppel v. Petersburg R. Co., 14 F.Cas. 357 (C.C.D.Va. 1868).
Holiday Inns, Inc. v. Aetna Ins. Co., 571 F.Supp. 1460 (S.D.N.Y. 1983).

Bibliography and Further Reading
Bernath, Stuart L. *Squall Across the Atlantic: American Civil War Prize Cases and Diplomacy.* Berkeley: University of California Press, 1970.

Epstein, Lee, and Thomas G. Walker. *Constitutional Law for a Changing America: Institutional Powers and Constraints,* 3rd ed. Washington DC: Congressional Quarterly, 1998.

Johnson, John W., ed. *Historic U.S. Court Cases, 1690–1990: An Encyclopedia.* New York: Garland Publishing, 1992.

Randall, J. G. *Constitutional Problems Under Lincoln.* New York: D. Appleton, 1926.

Robinton, Madeline. *An Introduction to the Papers of the New York Prize Court, 1861-1865.* New York: Columbia University Press, 1945.

ANDREW JOHNSON TRIAL

Prosecution
United States Senate

Defendant
President Andrew Johnson

Crime Charged
"High Crimes and Misdemeanors" within the meaning of Article II, Section 4 of the Constitution.

Chief Prosecutors
Seven "trial managers" from the House of Representatives

Chief Defense Lawyers
William Maxwell Evarts, Benjamin R. Curtis

Judges
The United States Senate, with Chief Justice Salmon Portland Chase presiding

Place
Washington, D.C.

Date of Decision
26 May 1868

Decision
Not to impeach.

Significance
The U.S. Congress for the first time exercised its constitutional prerogative to try a president of the United States for impeachable offenses. Johnson survived the Senate impeachment trial by one vote, but his hopes for re-election in 1868 were destroyed. Johnson was succeeded by the corrupt administration of Ulysses S. Grant.

After five years of bloody civil war, the Union emerged victorious. President Abraham Lincoln and his Republican administration were vindicated. On 14 April 1865, to the shock and horror of the Union, while attending a performance at Ford's Theatre, Lincoln was assassinated by John Wilkes Booth. The next day Vice-President Andrew Johnson was sworn in as president of the United States. Ironically, the man who would lead the United States into the Reconstruction era was a Southerner.

Born in North Carolina and raised in Tennessee, Johnson entered into politics and had enjoyed a successful career with the Democratic Party. He was chosen to represent Tennessee in the United States Senate. When the Southern states left the Union to form the Confederacy, Johnson was widely admired in the North for being the only Southern senator to remain loyal while his state seceded.

Johnson's loyalty and newfound fame caught the attention of President Lincoln. First, Lincoln appointed Johnson the Union's military governor of Tennessee. When Lincoln was up for re-election in 1864 against General George McClellan, Lincoln chose Johnson as his running mate. As a Southern Democrat and loyalist, Johnson would attract moderate voters in addition to the abolitionist and radical Republican forces already in Lincoln's camp.

Lincoln won the election of 1864. Although his assassination makes it impossible to know for certain how his Reconstruction administration would have proceeded, he had chosen Johnson as vice-president and had used the phrase "with malice toward none, with charity for all" in advocating leniency toward the South. Thus, many historians have concluded that Lincoln would have pursued a moderate and conciliatory approach toward the reunited Confederate states.

Johnson Becomes an Unpopular President

Johnson lacked the stature that Lincoln had enjoyed as the president who held the Union together. Although Lincoln would probably have approved of Johnson's moderate policies toward Reconstruction, Johnson did not have the prestige necessary to convince Congress

The Emancipation Proclamation

Although Abraham Lincoln was opposed to slavery before he became president in 1861, he did not initially believe that the federal government should become involved in the issue. Events forced the transformation that led to Lincoln's issuance of the Emancipation Proclamation on 1 January 1863. When Lincoln became president, 11 slaveholding states seceded, launching the Civil War. Lincoln began to perceive the war as not simply over preserving the Union, but over freedom. He drafted the Emancipation Proclamation in July of 1862.

He waited for a Union victory before announcing the proclamation to the nation, after the Battle of Antietam on 17 September 1862, the bloodiest day in American history. On 22 September Lincoln issued the preliminary Emancipation Proclamation, which freed slaves only in the Confederate states, but not in the slaveholding Union states of Missouri, Kentucky, Maryland, and Delaware. (Lincoln needed those states to remain in the Union in order to win the war.) The proclamation would not go into full effect until 1 January giving the Confederate states an opportunity to surrender before losing their slaves. The Confederacy continued to fight, the war ended two years later, and all slaves throughout the United States were freed.

Source(s): Prokopowicz, Gerald J. "The Emancipation Proclamation: A History for Teachers," Lincoln Museum, http://www.thelincolnmuseum.org.

---

or the American people that he was suited to the job. The electorate of the victorious Union, having undergone the bloodiest war in American history, sent mostly Republicans to Congress because the Republicans had been Lincoln's party. Within Congress, the Republican majority became Johnson's enemy.

The political antagonism between Johnson and Congress was further aggravated by Johnson's opposition to the Fourteenth Amendment, which expanded constitutional protection of basic civil liberties, and such congressional initiatives as establishment of the Freedmen's Bureau to assist freed slaves. Johnson went on a nationwide speaking tour, known as the "Swing Around the Circle," in which he made a series of abrasive and blunt speeches full of accusations against his political enemies in Congress. The Swing Around the Circle only served to further erode Johnson's public support.

Sensing vulnerability, Congress moved against Johnson by passing the Tenure of Office Act, which limited Johnson's ability to remove cabinet officials without congressional approval. Predictably, Johnson fought the act, particularly because he wished to rid his cabinet of Secretary of War Edwin M. Stanton, who was now allied with the opposition. When Johnson attempted to fire Stanton, Congress retaliated. Thaddeus Stevens, a representative from Pennsylvania who spoke for radical Republicans in favor of harsh treatment for the South as "conquered territory," led the House of Representatives to a 126-47 vote in favor of a short but historic resolution:

"Resolved,

that Andrew Johnson, President of the United States, be impeached of high crimes and misdemeanors in office."

The Senate Tries President Johnson

Although the House of Representatives had adopted the resolution to impeach Johnson, Article I, Section 3 of the Constitution mandates that the Senate must conduct the impeachment trial. This provision further states that at least two-thirds of the Senate must vote in favor of impeachment and, because a presidential impeachment was at issue, that Chief Justice Salmon P. Chase of the Supreme Court must preside.

Therefore, the House appointed seven congressmen as "trial managers" or prosecutors for the impeachment. These congressmen were John A. Bingham, George Boutwell, Benjamin F. Butler, John A. Logan, Thaddeus Stevens, Thomas Williams and James F. Wilson. Although Stevens had been the House leader, illness forced him to relinquish most of his authority to Butler.

Butler was a colorful character. A general in the Union Army during the Civil War, he was the military governor of New Orleans after the city was taken. During his governorship, he tolerated no pro-Southern dissent. One day when Butler perceived that he had been slighted by a group of New Orleans women, he issued an order that any woman showing "contempt for a United States officer" should be considered a "woman of the town plying her avocation" and thus implicitly subject to prosecution for prostitution. After the war, Butler returned to Massachusetts and was elected to the House.

Butler lost no time in launching the House's case against Johnson. From the beginning, however, it was clear that the proceedings would be dominated by the political struggle between Johnson and Butler. Legal niceties were secondary.

Impeachment

Impeachment is a formal indictment of an official of the executive or judicial branch of the federal government. The indicted individual then goes on trial. If convicted, he or she is removed from office. Only the highest figures in the executive and judicial branches of government—the president, the vice president, cabinet members, the chief justice of the Supreme Court, associate justices of the court, and federal judges—are subject to impeachment, which is carried out by the legislative branch.

The Constitution discusses impeachment in six clauses. Under constitutional provisions, the House of Representatives—the body of government thought to be the most closely tied to the people of the United States—votes on articles of impeachment, which are presented by the House Judiciary Committee. If the House approves the articles, the Senate tries the impeachment.

As of 1995, only 14 individuals had ever had articles of impeachment voted against them, and the two most famous of these—President Andrew Johnson and Supreme Court Associate Justice Samuel Chase—were not impeached. In 1998, President Bill Clinton became the first U.S. President to be impeached and the second to have impeachment proceedings brought against him.

Source(s): Bacon, Donald C., et al., eds. *The Encyclopedia of the United States Congress.* New York: Simon & Schuster, 1995.

Under Butler's direction, the trial managers presented the House's articles of impeachment. These eleven articles consisted of various non-specific charges of "high crimes and misdemeanors" against Johnson. For example, Johnson was accused of making "intemperate, inflammatory, and scandalous harangues" against Congress during the Swing Around the Circle. Johnson's response to these vague charges was quick and furious:

Impeach me for violating the Constitution! Damn them! I have been struggling and working ever since I have been in this chair to uphold the Constitution they trample underfoot! I don't care what becomes of me, but I'll fight them until they rot! I shall not allow the Constitution of the United States to be destroyed by evil men who are trying to ruin this government and this nation!

The trial began on 30 March 1868. After initial confusion, the trial managers decided to pursue a two-pronged attack. They would attempt to prove that Johnson's opposition to the Tenure of Office Act was unconstitutional and that Johnson had flagrantly abused his office with his comments about Congress. The testimony of the witnesses the trial managers produced was not limited to these issues, however. There was testimony on practically any matter that could

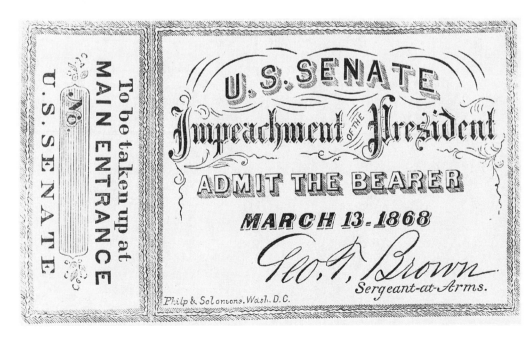

A ticket for admission to the impeachment trial of President Johnson. © AP/Wide World Photos.

serve to discredit Johnson, such as Johnson's alleged excessive drinking habits.

Johnson's defense rested with William Maxwell Evarts, a New York attorney highly regarded throughout the North, and Benjamin R. Curtis, a former Supreme Court justice. Other lawyers, such as former Attorney General Henry Stanbery, assisted with the defense. All of Johnson's counsel felt strongly enough about the importance of the case that they worked free of charge.

Senate Republicans Thwart Johnson's Defense

Johnson's lawyers attempted to introduce evidence showing that Johnson's opposition to the Tenure of Office Act was no more than a legitimate desire to test the constitutional validity of the act in the federal courts. The defense offered to produce witnesses who could testify that Johnson's opposition to the act on constitutional grounds had long preceded his quarrel with Secretary of War Stanton. Chief Justice Chase ruled that this evidence was admissible. Although a two-thirds vote of the Senate was necessary for a conviction of impeachment, it took only a simple majority vote to decide procedural matters. Therefore, despite Chase's rulings, the Senate repeatedly voted to prevent the defense from producing its witnesses concerning Johnson's legitimate opposition to the act.

The second prong of the trial managers' attack concerned Johnson's public statements. But the defense argued that the Senate could hardly impeach Johnson for exercising the right of freedom of speech that the Constitution gave to every American. Butler's retort made little legal sense but was good rhetoric and played well with the anti-Johnson public of the North:

> Is it, indeed, to be seriously argued here that there is a constitutional right in the President of the United States, who, during his official life, can never lay aside his official life, can never lay aside his official character, to denounce, malign, abuse, ridicule, and condemn, openly and publicly, the Congress of the United States: a coordinate branch of the government?

The Consciences of Seven Republicans Save Johnson

Throughout the two-month-long trial, Johnson's defense lawyers repeatedly saw their sound legal argu-

ments thwarted by purely political forces. However, seven Republican senators were disturbed by how the proceedings had been manipulated in order to give a one-sided presentation of the evidence. Senators William Pitt Fessenden, Joseph S. Fowler, James W. Grimes, John B. Henderson, Edmund G. Ross, Lyman Trumbull, and Peter G. Van Winkle defied their party and public opinion and voted against impeachment.

The Senate met on 26 May 1868, for the final vote. The shift by the seven Republicans proved critical: the tally was 35-19 in favor of impeachment, one vote short of the two-thirds majority necessary to impeach Johnson. Johnson was acquitted. But his political career never recovered. Later in 1868 the war hero General Ulysses S. Grant was elected the next president of the United States.

Related Cases

Samuel Chase Impeachment, Senate Document #876, 62nd Congress, 2nd Session (1805).
United States v. Nixon, 418 U.S. 683 (1974).

Bibliography and Further Reading

Aymar, Brandt, and Edward Sagarin. *Laws and Trials That Created History.* New York: Crown Publishers, 1974.

Dorris, Jonathan Truman. *Pardon and Amnesty Under Lincoln and Johnson.* Chapel Hill: The University of North Carolina Press, 1953.

Gerson, Noel B. *The Trial of Andrew Johnson.* Nashville and New York: Thomas Nelson Inc., 1977.

Paul, M. "Was Andrew Johnson Right?" *Senior Scholastic,* (Teachers' Edition), November 1982, p. 26.

Simpson, Brooks D., Leroy F. Graf, and John Muldowny. *Advice After Appomattox: Letters to Andrew Johnson.* Knoxville: The University of Tennessee Press, 1987.

Smith, Gene. *High Crimes and Misdemeanors: the Impeachment and Trial of Andrew Johnson.* New York: William Morrow and Company, 1977.

Strong, George Templeton. *Diary.* New York: Macmillan Co., 1952.

Trefousse, Hans L. *Andrew Johnson, a Biography.* New York and London: W. W. Norton & Company, 1989.

SELECTIVE DRAFT LAW CASES

Legal Citation: 245 U.S. 366 (1918)

Appellants
Joseph F. Arver, et al.

Appellee
United States of America

Appellants' Claim
That the Selective Draft Act of 1917 violated Article I, Section 8 and the First and Thirteenth Amendments, among other provisions of the Constitution.

Chief Lawyers for Appellants
T. E. Latimer, Edwin T. Taliferro, Harry Weinberger

Chief Lawyer for Appellee
John W. Davis, Solicitor General

Justices for the Court
Louis D. Brandeis, John Hessin Clarke, William Rufus Day, Oliver Wendell Holmes, Joseph McKenna, James Clark McReynolds, Mahlon Pitney, Willis Van Devanter, Edward Douglass White (writing for the Court)

Justices Dissenting
None

Place
Washington, D.C.

Date of Decision
7 January 1918

Decision
Denied the appellants' claim.

Significance
The case marked the Supreme Court's first hearing of a legal challenge to the federal government's power to draft men into the military. The Court's decision upheld that power.

For most of its early history, the United States relied on volunteers to fight its wars. The first national draft, or conscription, occurred during the Civil War. Relative to the North, the Confederacy had a small population, and it needed a draft to ensure that it had enough soldiers. The Union followed with its own draft in 1863. Not all the potential northern soldiers, however, willingly embraced the draft.

The Union's 1863 Conscription Act let wealthier Americans hire other people to fulfill their military obligations. This provision stirred anger among the poor, who felt that the burden of war was falling on their shoulders. Riots broke out in cities across the North, including a particularly bloody one in New York. The Conscription Act, however, was never tested in the Supreme Court, so the legality of a national draft was left unchallenged until World War I, when Congress instituted another draft.

The Selective Service Act of 1917 did not allow substitutes, as the 1863 law had, and it did allow for conscientious objector status: men who opposed war for religious reasons could avoid combat. Still, many people opposed the draft law. Although almost 24 million men did register for the draft, another two to three million did not. Hundreds of thousands more did register, but then failed to report when drafted or deserted soon after. The U.S. government arrested many of these men who tried to avoid military service, and some of them challenged the draft law.

A "Supreme and Noble Duty"

Joseph Arver was one of the many Americans who did not register for the draft. After his arrest, Arver, along with a number of other draft resisters from his home state of Minnesota, brought suit against the federal government. The Supreme Court heard the cases of the draft resisters together. Arver and the others argued that Congress had no explicit constitutional right to impose a draft, and even if it did, the particulars of the 1917 act were unconstitutional, as they tried to give legislative powers to the president and state officials. Furthermore, forced military service was a form of involuntary servitude, which was forbidden by the Thirteenth Amendment. Lastly, the provisions for conscientious objector status violated the First Amendment's prohibition against the establishment of religion.

A unanimous Court rejected all of the appellants' arguments and upheld the Selective Service Act. Chief Justice White began his decision by examining Article l, Section 8 of the Constitution, which gives Congress the power to raise and support armies, using all laws "necessary and proper" to execute that power. To White, those words were clear: "As the mind cannot conceive an army without the men to compose it, on the face of the Constitution the objection that it does not give power to provide for such men would seem to be too frivolous for further notice."

White went on to say that just governments have a duty to their citizens, and the citizens have a "reciprocal obligation" to provide military service in times of need, when the state compels that service. On almost all the other points raised by Arver and the others, White quickly dismissed their merit, especially the argument referring to the Thirteenth Amendment. White saw no comparison between involuntary servitude and ". . . the exaction by government from the citizen of the performance of his supreme and noble duty of contributing to the defense of the rights and honor of the nation . . ."

After the *Selective Draft Law Cases,* the government had a clear right to conscript soldiers; however, arguments arose over specific provisions of subsequent draft laws. Most of the cases that reached the Court dealt with conscientious objector status. The Court has upheld the government's right to make an objector perform alternative service, rather than face combat. In *Clay v. United States* (1971), with former heavyweight boxing champion Muhammad Ali as the appellant, the Court cited a three-part test for determining if someone had legitimate claim to conscientious objector status: the claim is based on religious beliefs, the claimant opposes war in any form, and the belief is sincere.

America's last draft ended in 1973, as the Vietnam War was drawing to a close. Draft registration ended two years later, but President Jimmy Carter reintroduced it in 1980. The next year, in *Rostker v. Goldberg,* the Court denied a claim that the draft registration was unconstitutional because it did not include women. Another draft case, in 1984, gave Congress the power to withhold federal student aid to men who refused to register for the draft.

Related Cases

United States v. O'Brien, 391 U.S. 367 (1968).
Clay v. United States, 403 U.S. 698 (1971).
Rostker v. Goldberg, 453 U.S. 57 (1981).
Selective Service System v. Minnesota Public Interest Research Group, 468 U.S. 841 (1984).

Bibliography and Further Reading

Biskupic, Joan, and Elder Witt. *Guide to the U.S. Supreme Court,* 3rd edition. Washington, DC: Congressional Quarterly, Inc., 1997.

Foner, Eric, and John Garraty, editors. *The Reader's Companion to American History.* Boston: Houghton Mifflin, 1991.

Hall, Kermit L., editor. *The Oxford Companion to the Supreme Court of the United States.* New York: Oxford Press, 1992.

New York Times, 8 January 1918.

Witt, Elder, ed. *The Supreme Court A to Z.* CQ's Encyclopedia of American Government. Washington, DC: Congressional Quarterly, Inc., 1993.

EX PARTE GROSSMAN

Legal Citation: 267 U.S. 87 (1925)

Petitioner
Philip Grossman

Respondent
District of Illinois

Petitioner's Claim
That the president's pardon covers all offenses in the case of the petitioner, and the courts may not convict the appellant of crimes that have been pardoned.

Chief Lawyer for Petitioner
Louis J. Behan

Chief Lawyers for Respondent
Amos C. Miller, F. Bruce Johnstone

Justices for the Court
Louis D. Brandeis, Pierce Butler, Oliver Wendell Holmes, Joseph McKenna, James Clark McReynolds, Edward Terry Sanford, George Sutherland, William Howard Taft (writing for the Court), Willis Van Devanter

Justices Dissenting
None

Place
Washington, D.C.

Date of Decision
2 March 1925

Decision
The Supreme Court ruled that the president could pardon all offenses except in cases of impeachment.

Significance
The Supreme Court affirmed the president's power to grant reprieves and pardons for all offenses.

The term "Prohibition" refers to the era from 1919 to 1933, when the manufacture, sale, and consumption of alcohol was forbidden by law throughout the United States. The idea of prohibition predates the Prohibition Era, which was the culmination of efforts begun as early as the 1830s. Throughout the nineteenth century, the anti-alcohol temperance movement was tied with a strain of reform-minded progressivism. The Women's Christian Temperance Movement (WCTU), for instance, is considered an early feminist organization.

Temperance forces took advantage of the shortage of grain after World War I and pushed through the Eighteenth Amendment in 1919, establishing Prohibition. The Volstead Act, passed the same year, defined an intoxicating beverage as one containing at least 0.5 percent alcohol.

Philip Grossman was found guilty by the district court of having disobeyed a temporary injunction, issued under the National Prohibition Enforcement Act, forbidding illicit trafficking in liquors on certain premises. He was sentenced by the district court to pay a fine and to imprisonment for one year in the Chicago House of Corrections—a judgment which was affirmed by the circuit court of appeals.

The president issued a pardon commuting the sentence to the fine, with the condition that the fine be paid, which Grossman did. Having been thereupon released from custody, Grossman was again committed by district court, upon the grounds that the pardon was ineffectual. He then sought a writ of *habeas corpus*, directed to Graham, the Superintendent of the House of Corrections.

Chief Justice Taft delivered the opinion of the Court, rebutting the respondent's argument that stated that the president's power extended only to offenses against the United States and that contempt of court was not such an offense. Criminal contempt, on the contrary, in relation to the prohibition law is an "offense against the United States," and pardonable by the president. "Offenses against the United States," in the pardon clause, include criminal contempts, and accord with ordinary meanings of the words and are not inconsistent with other parts of the Constitution where the term "offense" and the narrower terms "crimes" and "criminal prosecutions" appear. The contention that to admit the power of the president to pardon criminal contempts would erode the independence of the judiciary and would violate the principle of separation of the three departments of the government was considered and rejected.

Soon after Franklin D. Roosevelt became president in 1933, Prohibition ended when the Eighteenth Amendment was repealed by the Twenty-first, the only instance of a constitutional amendment directly nullifying a previous one.

Related Cases

Ex parte Garland, 71 U.S. 333 (1866).
United States v. Woodley, 726 F.2d 1328 (1983).

Bibliography and Further Reading

Berkman, Harvey. "Will the President Pardon His Friends." *National Law Journal,* Vol. 19, no. 10, November 4, 1996.

Hurwitz, Howard L. *An Encyclopedic Dictionary of American History.* New York: Washington Square Press, 1974.

Robbins, James S. "Pardon Me, Mr. President." *Washington Times,* January 2, 1997.

MYERS V. UNITED STATES

Legal Citation: 272 U.S. 52 (1926)

Appellant
Lois P. Myers, administrator of the estate of Frank S. Myers

Appellee
United States

Appellant's Claim
That President Woodrow Wilson illegally dismissed Frank Myers from his job as postmaster, and Myers was owed back pay.

Chief Lawyers for Appellant
Will R. King, Martin L. Pipes

Chief Lawyer for Appellee
James M. Beck, U.S. Solicitor General

Justices for the Court
Pierce Butler, Edward Terry Sanford, Harlan Fiske Stone, George Sutherland, William Howard Taft (writing for the Court), Willis Van Devanter

Justices Dissenting
Louis D. Brandeis, Oliver Wendell Holmes, James Clark McReynolds

Place
Washington, D.C.

Date of Decision
25 October 1926

Decision
The Court held that the executive branch had the right to remove federal employees and it affirmed the decision by the U.S. Court of Claims to deny Myers any back pay.

Significance
Myers was the first major case that addressed a president's constitutional right to remove executive officials without the consent of Congress. In its decision, the Supreme Court gave the president broad removal powers.

In 1876, Congress passed a law giving the Senate the authority to approve the president's appointment and removal of postmasters. In 1917, President Woodrow Wilson named Frank Myers a postmaster in Portland, Oregon. Under the terms of the 1876 law, Myers should have served a four-year term as postmaster. But three years later, Wilson dismissed Myers from the job without obtaining the Senate's consent. Myers petitioned the U.S. Court of Claims, saying his dismissal was illegal, and he asked for more than $8,000 in back pay, the money he would have earned his last year as postmaster. The court denied his petition, saying Myers had waited too long to file his suit.

Myers appealed the decision to the Supreme Court, but he died before the case was decided. His wife Lois, as administrator of his estate, took his place as the appellant. The Supreme Court ruled 6-3 that Myers was not owed the money. The Court disagreed that Myers had taken too long to file his claim; instead, it ruled on the constitutionality of the 1876 law.

History of Appointment and Removal Powers

The Constitution spells out the appointment process, giving the president the power to name ambassadors, judges, and other public officials, with the Senate's approval. But except for impeachment, the Constitution does not address removing appointed officials. In 1789, the first Congress wrestled with this situation as it tried to establish the practical operation of the new federal government. James Madison proposed setting up an executive office to handle foreign affairs; the secretary of this office would be confirmed by the Senate, but the president would have the authority to remove the secretary without the Senate's consent. The so-called "Decision of 1789" said that the president had an inherent power of removal—one not specifically granted in the Constitution, but implied. For more than 70 years, Congress did not challenge this right in any meaningful way.

During the Reconstruction Era, however, Congress was eager to assert its power at the expense of President Andrew Johnson. The president opposed the plans of the "Radical Republicans" who controlled Congress.

William Howard Taft

William Howard Taft (1857-1930) was the only American to hold the offices of president of the United States (1909-13) and chief justice of the Supreme Court (1921-30.) As president, he appointed more Supreme Court justices, proportionately, than anyone before or since: six in a single four-year term. As chief justice of the Supreme Court, he was not noted for his opinions, but he introduced several significant changes in how the Court operated.

Taft graduated from Yale in 1878 as salutatorian and earned top honors at Cincinnati Law School in 1880. In 1890, President Benjamin Harrison appointed him solicitor general of the United States, and, in 1892, he became a federal judge. President William McKinley appointed Taft chairman of a special commission to the Philippines in 1900, and, in 1904, he became secretary of war under Roosevelt. In 1908, he won election as president over Democrat William Jennings Bryan.

In 1921, Taft was appointed Chief Justice of the Supreme Court by President Warren G. Harding. Although his was the era of Prohibition and other weighty legal concerns, his primary successes as chief justice were administrative. In February of 1930, Taft retired from the Court at age 73. He died a month later.

Source(s): *The National Cyclopedia of American Biography* Volume XXIII. New York: James T. White, 1933.

One of Johnson's own cabinet members, Edwin M. Stanton, was a vocal supporter of the laws Johnson fought. To thwart any attempt by Johnson to fire Stanton, Congress passed the Tenure of Office Act in 1867. The law forced a president to seek Senate approval before removing a cabinet member. Johnson thought the law was unconstitutional and defied it, removing Stanton and naming a replacement. Stanton, meanwhile, refused to step down from his position. He barricaded himself in his office, cooking meals there and conferring with his congressional allies.

Johnson's defiance of the Tenure of Office Act led to his impeachment in the House of Representatives. At Johnson's trial in the Senate, he was acquitted by just one vote. The constitutionality of the Tenure of Office Act was never tested, and the law was repealed in 1887. But before that repeal, Congress passed the act regulating the removal of postmasters, and that law brought the removal issue in front of the Supreme Court.

A Former President Defends Presidential Powers

Chief Justice Taft wrote the Court's decision in *Myers*. Taft, when he had served as president from 1909-1913, had generally accepted constitutional limits on a president's power. But his decision in this case asserted broad removal powers for the chief executive.

Taft used the Decision of 1789 as the foundation for his opinion. He remarked that many of the members of that first Congress had been at the Constitutional Convention and so understood the framers' intent. Congress had set a precedent with its interpretation of the president's removal powers, and although the Court

was not bound to accept it, Taft did. He said that the 1867 Tenure of Office Act had been unconstitutional, and so was the 1876 law regarding postmasters.

Taft wrote that the president, as chief executive, had to carry out the nation's laws. Though the Constitution did not explicitly say so, the president had an inherent power to appoint subordinates who would help him in his executive duty. Taft also saw another inherent power:

> The further implication must be, in the absence of any express limitation respecting removals, that as his selection of administrative officers is essential to the execution of the laws by him, so must be his power for removing those for whom he cannot continue to be responsible . . . A veto by the Senate—a part of the legislative branch of the government—upon removals is a much greater limitation upon the executive branch, and a much more serious blending of the legislative with the executive, than a rejection of a proposed appointment. It is not to be implied.

Without the ability to remove an appointee on his own, the president lacked a tool for enforcing discipline among his subordinates. Removal powers gave the president an effective, immediate level of control as he performed his duty of executing the nation's laws. Congressional limits on that power violated the notion of separation of powers between the three branches of the federal government.

Three Strong Dissents

Each of the three justices who opposed the *Myers* decision had separate, but similar concerns. Justice

McReynolds feared the Court went too far by giving the executive branch independent power to remove federal employees. Congress has constitutional authority to appoint and remove "inferior officers" without the president's input. McReynolds said if Congress could appoint lesser officials, it should also be able to limit their removal.

Justice Holmes argued that the position of postmaster was created by Congress and should be dissolved by Congress. The Court's ruling defined the president's executive powers too broadly. "The duty of the president to see that the laws be executed is a duty that does not go beyond the laws or require him to achieve more than Congress sees fit to leave within his power."

Finally, Justice Brandeis distinguished between the president's removal powers regarding higher and lower offices. Removing an inferior officer—such as a postmaster—was not "an essential of government." Congress also had an obligation to protect the rights of federal employees. While Taft stressed separation of powers, Brandeis looked more to the idea of checks and balances; Congress should "preclude the exercise of arbitrary power. The purpose [of separation of powers] was, not to avoid friction, but by means of the inevitable friction incident to the distribution of the governmental powers among the three departments, to save the people from autocracy."

Nine years later, the Court did take back some of the broad presidential removal powers granted in *Myers*. In *Humphrey's Executor v. United States* the Court said Congress had the right to approve the removal of government officials whose jobs were not purely related to executive duties.

Related Cases

Ex parte Grossman, 267 U.S. 87 (1925).
Humphrey's Executor v. United States, 295 U.S. 602 (1935).
Youngstown Sheet and Tube Co. v. Sawyer, 343 U.S. 579 (1952).
Wiener v. United States, 357 U.S. 349 (1958).
Schick v. Reed, 419 U.S. 256 (1974).

Bibliography and Further Reading

Blum, John M., et al. *The National Experience,* 4th ed. New York: Harcourt Brace Jovanovich, 1977.

Hall, Kermit L., ed. *The Oxford Companion to the Supreme Court of the United States.* New York: Oxford Press, 1992.

Norton, Mary Beth, et al. *A People and a Nation: A History of the United States,* Vol. 2. Boston: Houghton Mifflin Company, 1982.

Nowak, John E., Ronald D. Rotunda, and J. Nelson Young. *Constitutional Law,* 2nd ed. St. Paul: West Publishing Company, 1984.

Stone, Geoffrey R., et al. *Constitutional Law.* Boston: Little, Brown and Company, 1986.

Witt, Elder, ed. *The Supreme Court A to Z.* CQ's Encyclopedia of American Government. Washington, DC: Congressional Quarterly, Inc., 1993.

POCKET VETO CASE

Legal Citation: 279 U.S. 655 (1929)

Petitioners
Okanogan, Methow, San Poelis, Nespelem, Colville, and Lake Indian Tribes or Bands of Washington State

Respondent
United States

Petitioners' Claim
That the U.S. Court of Claims erred in finding a suit by the Okanogan Indians, et al. to be without legal foundation.

Chief Lawyer for Petitioners
William S. Lewis

Chief Lawyer for Respondent
William D. Mitchell, U.S. Attorney General

Justices for the Court
Louis D. Brandeis, Pierce Butler, Oliver Wendell Holmes, James Clark McReynolds, Edward Terry Sanford (writing for the Court), Harlan Fiske Stone, George Sutherland, William Howard Taft, Willis Van Devanter

Justices Dissenting
None

Place
Washington, D.C.

Date of Decision
27 May 1929

Decision
The court of claims decision was affirmed.

Significance
The Court's decision legitimized presidential rejection of legislation by use of the "pocket veto."

President Coolidge's Pocket Veto and the Washington Tribes

Whenever a new law is passed by both houses of the U.S. Congress, the proposed statute is passed to the president, who has the option of approving the law by signing it or rejecting it with a veto. A vetoed bill is normally returned to Congress with the president's objections noted so that Congress can reconsider the bill. If the president neither signs nor vetoes the bill within ten days, not counting Sundays, the measure automatically becomes law.

If Congress passes the measure and then adjourns, however, leaving the president less than the required ten days to consider the bill, the president may ignore the bill. Under such circumstances, the lack of a presidential signature prevents the bill from becoming law. This is called a pocket veto.

Presidents, beginning with James Madison, used the pocket veto to reject legislation handed to them at the close of congressional terms. Yet the constitutionality of the pocket veto was not tested in the Supreme Court until 1929, in a case which pitted the legislative and executive branches of the government against each other.

In 1926, Congress passed a bill allowing a group of American Indian tribes from the state of Washington to present a bill to the court of claims for the loss of tribal lands. The bill was signed by the 69th Congress and presented to President Calvin Coolidge on 24 June 1926. When Congress adjourned on 3 July, President Coolidge had still not signed the bill. If Congress had not gone home for the summer, it could have expected the bill back by 6 July, a date which passed with no word from the White House.

When the Okanogan Indians and other tribes presented their suit to the court of claims, they assumed that ten working days of Congress had passed, automatically making their bill law even without Coolidge's signature. The court of claims, however, dismissed the Indians suit, ruling that the congressional bill upon which their claims were based had been "pocket-vetoed" and was therefore invalid.

The Washington tribes were not the only ones outraged. A 1925 congressional resolution providing for a

The Pocket Veto

The Constitution mandates that the president has ten days to veto a bill; if he does not return it with a veto during that time, the bill will automatically become a law. But if Congress is adjourned when those ten days are up, he may "pocket" the bill, thus vetoing it by default. This is the pocket veto, which has been used in two-fifths of all presidential vetoes. Supporters of a strong executive have favored the pocket veto, whereas adherents of a strong parliamentary government have tended to be opposed to it. Advocates stress that, though the pocket veto is not spelled out in the Constitution, it is a safety valve left there by the framers as a way of making government less rigid by allowing greater input from the executive branch in certain situations. Furthermore, Congress puts itself in the situation of being stymied by a pocket veto. Detractors argue that the pocket veto gives the president too much power and that the veto itself is a mere constitutional loophole.

Source(s): Nelson, Michael, ed. *The Presidency A to Z: A Ready Reference Encyclopedia.* Washington: Congressional Quarterly, 1994.

federal takeover of the Muscle Shoals power station in Alabama had also been placed on the president's desk. It too lacked a presidential signature. Congressional supporters of the Indian relief bill—along with those who had voted for the Muscle Shoals resolution—were pitted against the White House. The Washington tribes appealed the court of claims' decision to the Supreme Court, which accepted the case to rule on the collision between the legislative and executive branches of the government.

When the case was heard on 11 March 1929, U.S. Attorney General William D. Mitchell argued the case for the executive branch, proposing that the court of claims' judgment should stand. Mitchell noted that 119 important cases had been decided by pocket vetoes in the past century. To suddenly declare that the practice was invalid would create havoc within the legislative process, opening the way for retroactive legal challenges. The so-called pocket vetoes, Mitchell argued, were an accepted method of disposing of legislation a president might otherwise formally veto.

The Indians' attorney, William S. Lewis, responded that the bill had been properly forwarded to President Coolidge for his signature. Lewis argued that Congress had merely gone home for the summer recess and had not adjourned. When the required ten days passed without the president signing the bill or returning it with a veto and enumerating his objections, the bill had automatically become law. To this, Attorney General Mitchell replied that there was no way to return a bill to a body that was not in session. Ten days, by Mitchell's definition, meant ten calendar days.

Attorney Lewis was joined by Texas Representative Hatton W. Sumners, the senior member of the House of Representatives Judiciary Committee. Sumners appeared before the Supreme Court with an *amicus curiae* or "friend of the court" brief supporting the Okanogan position. Congressman Sumners argued that the pocket veto gave presidents powers not granted by the Constitution. These included an absolute veto, eliminating any opportunity to overcome presidential rejection of legislation with a vote by two-thirds of Congress. A pocket veto also sidestepped a president's responsibility to explain executive objections to a bill.

Justice Edward Terry Sanford. © Collection of the Supreme Court of the United States.

A Definition of Adjournment

On 27 May, the Supreme Court unanimously affirmed the court of claims' decision not to hear the Okanogan claims. In the written opinion, Justice Sanford emphasized that Congress had no power to shorten or lengthen the amount of time a president was allowed to consider a bill. The Court placed responsibility for providing the ten-day consideration period on Congress, which had adjourned without giving the president the required time to sign the bill or apply a normal veto.

Even under this interpretation, the case centered upon what the Constitution meant by the word "adjournment." The Court agreed with Attorney General Mitchell's contention that an adjournment as referred to in the ten-day rule meant any cessation of congressional activity. The Constitution did not qualify its definition with the word "final." Since there was no mention of "legislative days" or any other descriptive adjective in the Constitution, the Court declared that the rule simply applied to ten calendar days.

Past Congresses and presidents had accepted the use of pocket vetoes for over a century. In judging constitutional issues, the Court concluded, such a "long settled and well established practice" could not be ignored.

Ironically, President Coolidge, whose missing signature brought about the suit, left office before the Court finally and officially legitimized the use of pocket vetoes. In 1938, in its *Wright v. United States* decision, the Court declared that a clerk or other representative of Congress could receive a presidential veto during a short recess and deliver it upon Congress's return. While this had the practical effect of providing a ten-day period for executive perusal of new legislation even when Congress was not in its chambers, later presidents continued to employ pocket vetoes, often with controversial results.

Related Cases

Myers v. United States, 272 U.S. 52 (1926).
Wright v. United States, 302 U.S. 583 (1938).

Bibliography and Further Reading

Hall, Kermit L., ed. *The Oxford Companion to the Supreme Court of the United States.* New York: Oxford University Press, 1992.

Kurland, Phillip B., and Gerhard Casper, eds. *Landmark Briefs and Arguments of the Supreme Court of the United States,* Vol. 26. Arlington: University Publications of America, 1975.

"Mitchell Files Brief To Pocket Veto." *New York Times,* March 9, 1929, p. 7.

New York Times, March 12, 1929, p. 16.

Witt, Elder. *Congressional Quarterly's Guide to the U.S. Supreme Court,* 2nd ed. Washington DC: Congressional Quarterly, 1990.

NEBBIA V. NEW YORK

Legal Citation: 291 U.S. 502 (1934)

Appellant
Leo Nebbia

Appellee
People of the State of New York

Appellant's Claim
That the government had no power to regulate retail prices for milk sales.

Chief Lawyer for Appellant
Arthur E. Sutherland

Chief Lawyer for Appellee
Henry S. Manley

Justices for the Court
Louis D. Brandeis, Benjamin N. Cardozo, Charles Evans Hughes, Owen Josephus Roberts (writing for the Court), Harlan Fiske Stone

Justices Dissenting
Pierce Butler, James Clark McReynolds, George Sutherland, Willis Van Devanter

Place
Washington, D.C.

Date of Decision
5 March 1934

Decision
The Supreme Court upheld the New York Milk Control Act of 1933.

Significance
Ever since the *Munn v. Illinois* decision in 1877, the Court had distinguished between public enterprise, which the state may regulate, and private enterprise, which it may not. With *Nebbia*, the Court did away with this distinction once and for all.

In 1933, in the midst of the Great Depression, New York State created a Milk Board, whose job it was to set minimum and maximum retail prices for milk prices. The board fixed nine cents as the price to be charged for a quart of milk. The purpose of this price fixing was to ease the economic hardship being experienced both by retailers and their customers.

Leo Nebbia was the proprietor of a small grocery store in Rochester, New York. He sold two quarts of milk and a 5-cent loaf of bread for 18 cents, as a result of which he was charged with violating the Milk Control Act. After successive appeals to the county court and the New York Court of Appeals failed, Nebbia appealed to the U.S. Supreme Court.

Supreme Court Declares that the State Can Regulate Any Business

In 1877, the Court decided *Munn v. Illinois* that although there are certain businesses which are immune from state control, those "in which the public has an interest"—in that case, it was grain elevators—are subject to regulation by state governments. One argument advanced against this ruling was that state regulatory power was in conflict with the Commerce Clause of Article I, section 8 of the Constitution, which gives Congress the power "To Regulate Commerce . . . among the several States." The other was that state regulation of business was unconstitutional because of the Due Process Clause of the Fourteenth Amendment, which provides: "No state shall . . . deprive any person of life, liberty, or property without due process of law."

This second argument was adopted in an important dissenting opinion written by Justice Stephen J. Field. Field elaborated the argument into a legal theory that came to be known as "substantive due process," which holds that the Constitution protects certain rights—most notably, property—from all legislative interference. Field's theory proved to be highly influential for the remainder of the nineteenth century and lasted well into the next century. It determined the outcome of most economic issues that came before the Court during that period, causing a majority of the justices to vote consistently in support of business interests. In

Public Enterprise and Private Enterprise

Private enterprise is any type of economic activity that is undertaken with privately owned capital and with the aim of earning an income for private interests. The capital may be owned by an individual, a partnership, or a corporation. A company which has issued shares of stock is referred to as a "public" company, but it is public only in the sense that anyone can buy shares. For the purposes of this discussion, a "public" company is another example of private enterprise.

By contrast, the public sector, though it too takes part in economic undertakings, seldom does so for profit-making purposes. A government typically funds its activities through taxation or defrays costs by means of a user's toll, as is the case on many highways. There is a considerable gray area between public and private enterprise in joint-venture operations such as airports.

Source(s): Scruton, Roger. *A Dictionary of Political Thought,* second edition. London: Macmillan, 1996.

1885, for instance, the Court denied that the Sherman Anti-Trust Act applied to manufacturing monopolies in *United States v. E. C. Knight,* and ruled that the Sherman Act could be used as a weapon against labor unions in *In re Debs.*

With the onset of the Great Depression, however, it became harder for the justices to support substantive

Justice Josephus O. Roberts, c. 1930. © Photograph by Harris and Ewing. Collection of the Supreme Court of the United States.

due process, which in effect gave business free rein. The American people were suffering and while the federal government adopted President Franklin Roosevelt's New Deal program of economic reforms, states shaped legislation along the same lines. One such piece of New Deal-inspired state legislation was the New York Milk Control Act of 1934 at issue in *Nebbia.*

Writing for the Court, Justice Roberts now declared that the state could regulate not just businesses "affected with the public interest," but any economic activity it saw fit to control:

> [I]n the absence of other constitutional restriction, a state is free to adopt whatever economic policy may reasonably be deemed to promote public welfare, and to enforce that policy by legislation adapted to its purpose. The courts are without authority either to declare such policy, or when it is declared by the legislature, to override it.

The old substantive due process argument was laid out for the dissent by Justice McReynolds, who maintained that the Due Process Clause of the Fourteenth Amendment gave the Supreme Court the authority to uphold any economic legislation it found reasonable and to override any it found unreasonable. McReynolds's dissent was joined by three other justices: Van Devanter, Sutherland, and Butler. These four justices tended to vote together as a bloc—particularly on economic issues. The consistency of their conservative stance caused them to be popularly known as the Four Horsemen, after the Four Horsemen of the Apocalypse, who brought ruin to the land in the last book of the Bible. Often they were joined by one or more of the "swing votes" on the Court to defeat New Deal legislation. Although they lost the debate in *Nebbia,* it was not until Roosevelt announced his plan to "pack" the Court with justices of his own choosing that the Four Horsemen permanently lost their clout.

Related Cases

Munn v. Illinois, 94 U.S. 113 (1877).

In Re Debs, 158 U.S. 564 (1895).

Northern Securities Co. v. United States, 193 U.S. 197 (1904).

Buchanan v. Warley, 245 U.S. 60 (1917).

Block v. Hirsh, 256 U.S. 135 (1921).

Adkins v. Children's Hospital, 261 U.S. 525 (1923).

Meyer v. Nebraska, 262 U.S. 399 (1923).

Near v. Minnesota, 283 U.S. 697 (1931).

Bibliography and Further Reading

Johnson, John W., ed. *Historic U.S. Court Cases, 1690–1990: An Encyclopedia.* New York: Garland Publishing, 1992.

Leuchtenburg. William E. *The FDR Years: On Roosevelt and His Legacy.* New York, NY: Cornell University Press, 1995.

Parrish, Michael E. *Anxious Decades: America in Prosperity and Depression, 1920-1941.* New York: W. W. Norton, 1992.

Rosenof, Theodore. *Economics in the Long Run: New Deal Theorists and Their Legacies, 1933-1993.* Chapel Hill: University of North Carolina Press, 1997.

HUMPHREY'S EXECUTOR V. UNITED STATES

Legal Citation: 295 U.S. 602 (1935)

Appellant
Samuel F. Rathbun, as Executor of the Estate of William E. Humphrey, deceased

Appellee
United States

Appellant's Claim
That the president cannot remove an appointed commissioner without just cause.

Chief Lawyer for Appellant
William J. Donovan

Chief Lawyers for Appellee
Attorney General Homer S. Cummings, Solicitor General Stanley F. Reed

Justices for the Court
Louis D. Brandeis, Pierce Butler, Benjamin N. Cardozo, Charles Evans Hughes, James Clark McReynolds, Owen Josephus Roberts, Harlan Fiske Stone, George Sutherland (writing for the Court), Willis Van Devanter

Justices Dissenting
None

Place
Washington, D.C.

Date of Decision
27 May 1935

Decision
The Court ruled that the president did not have the power to remove an appointed official without consent from Congress.

Significance
President Franklin Roosevelt was so angered by Supreme Court challenges to his authority—and by *Humphrey's Executor* in particular—that he developed a plan to "pack" the Court with his own appointees as part of his effort to institute New Deal economic reforms.

In 1931, Herbert Hoover nominated William E. Humphrey to succeed him as a commissioner at the Federal Trade Commission after Hoover was elected president. Humphrey was duly confirmed by the Senate. He was to serve a term of seven years. However, on 25 July 1933, Hoover's successor as chief executive, Franklin Roosevelt, sent Humphrey a letter requesting his resignation. The letter did not find fault with Humphrey's performance, and it was widely believed that Roosevelt simply wanted to replace the commissioner with someone more in tune with his program of economic reform. When Humphrey refused to resign, Roosevelt exercised the power granted him by Article II of the Constitution and removed him from office.

Humphrey did not acquiesce in this decision but continued to insist that he was still a member of the commission, entitled to perform the duties and to receive the salary of a commissioner. He brought suit in the court of claims, a court created to hear claims against the federal government, seeking back wages. After he died, the executor of his estate carried on his suit, which the court of claims referred to the Supreme Court for adjudication.

Separation of Powers Requires That the President's Removal Power Be Limited

Writing for a unanimous Court, Justice Sutherland noted that the Federal Trade Commission was a creation of Congress, and that although the commissioners were appointed by the president, they performed duties which were both legislative and judicial. Therefore, Sutherland concluded, the commissioners must be beyond the control of the executive branch, otherwise, the doctrine of the separation of powers, which divides government into three coequal but separate branches, would be violated. Roosevelt had, in the Court's view, clearly violated this separation in discharging Humphrey without good cause:

> We think it plain under the Constitution that illimitable power of removal is not possessed by the President in respect of officers of . . . quasi legislative or quasi judicial agencies . . . For it is quite evident that one who holds his

office only during the pleasure of another cannot be depended upon to maintain an attitude of independence against the latter's will.

Roosevelt believed that in removing Humphrey from office, he was acting according to legal precedent set by the Court itself. In *Myers v. United States* (1926), the Court had ruled that it was within the president's power to remove a postmaster—an executive branch appointee—from office for almost any reason. Now, however, the Court distinguished a postmaster from a trade commissioner, saying that *Myers* had concerned a political appointee whose responsibilities were solely executive in nature.

Roosevelt was irate. To his way of thinking, the majority of justices then sitting on the Court were splitting hairs in an effort to thwart him and his New Deal agenda of economic reforms, with which he intended to lift the country out of the Great Depression. Not long after *Humphrey's Executor* was handed down, Roosevelt developed a plan to "pack" the Court with additional justices whom he would appoint. Although Congress defeated this plan to increase the size of the Court in 1937, by then Roosevelt had exerted enough pressure on the Court to compel some of its more conservative members to resign. Over the next few years, he was able to appoint a total of eight justices. After mid-1937, the Court upheld every major piece of New Deal legislation it was asked to consider. Roosevelt paid a price for his victory, however, losing the faith of many Democratic supporters who believed that Roosevelt himself had violated the separation of powers doctrine by playing politics with the Supreme Court.

Related Cases

Myers v. United States, 272 U.S. 52 (1926).

A.L.A. Schechter Poultry Corp. v. United States, 295 U.S. 495 (1935).

United States v. Curtiss-Wright Export Corp., 299 U.S. 304 (1936).

Wiener v. United States, 357 U.S. 349 (1958).

Bibliography and Further Reading

Corwin, Edward Samuel. *Corwin on the Constitution.* Vol 1. *The Foundations of American Constitutional and Political Thought, the Powers of Congress, and the President's Power of Removal.* Ithaca, NY: Cornell University Press, 1981.

Evans, Diana, et al. *Who Makes Policy? The Struggle for Control Between Congress and the Executive.* Chatham, NJ: Chatham House Publishers, 1994.

Schroedel, Jean Reith. *Congress, the President, and Policymaking: A Historical Analysis.* Armonk, NY: M. E. Sharpe, 1994.

UNITED STATES V. CURTISS-WRIGHT EXPORT CORP.

Legal Citation: 299 U.S. 304 (1936)

Appellant
United States

Appellee
Curtiss-Wright Export Corporation

Appellant's Claim
That the president has the power to prohibit arms sales to warring nations.

Chief Lawyers for Appellant
Homer S. Cummings, U.S. Attorney General; Martin Conboy

Chief Lawyer for Appellee
William Wallace

Justices for the Court
Louis D. Brandeis, Pierce Butler, Benjamin N. Cardozo, Charles Evans Hughes, Owen Josephus Roberts, George Sutherland (writing for the Court), Willis Van Devanter

Justices Dissenting
James Clark McReynolds (Harlan Fiske Stone did not participate)

Place
Washington, D.C.

Date of Decision
21 December 1936

Decision
The Supreme Court upheld the presidential resolution prohibiting the arms sales.

Significance
Using broad language to describe executive power in the area of foreign affairs, the Court provided a justification not only for the exercise of presidential authority under immediate consideration, but for many future presidential decisions concerning U.S. activity abroad.

In the mid-1930s, Bolivia and Paraguay went to war over the Chaco region of South America after oil was found there. The House of Representatives and the Senate together passed legislation authorizing the president to place an embargo on shipments of arms to warring countries. President Franklin Roosevelt then proclaimed the embargo, prohibiting arms sales to Bolivia and Paraguay.

Curtiss-Wright Export Corporation was later indicted for violating the embargo. Claiming that the embargo was an illegitimate exercise because Congress had delegated legislative power to the executive branch, Curtiss-Wright prevailed in federal district court. The government then asked the Supreme Court to review this decision.

Court Upholds Broad Presidential Powers in Foreign Affairs

Most conflicts between the legislative and executive branches involve political questions which the Supreme Court lacks the power to resolve. In *Curtiss-Wright,* however, the dispute did not concern domestic governance but foreign affairs. Writing for the Court, Justice Sutherland stressed that this was not an area governed by express grants of power by the Constitution:

> [T]he investment of the federal government with the powers of external sovereignty did not depend upon the affirmative grants of the Constitution. The powers to declare and wage war, to conclude peace, to make treaties, to maintain diplomatic relations with other sovereignties, if they had never been mentioned in the Constitution, would have vested in the federal government as necessary concomitants of nationality . . .

Sutherland went on to say that if sovereignty—the power of an independent nation—rested in the federal government, then the executive branch must control relations with foreign sovereigns. Therefore, he reasoned, no express grant in the Constitution of a "foreign affairs" power was necessary to enable the president to act in these matters. In the case of the South

American arms embargo, wrote Sutherland, "[W]e are . . . dealing not alone with an authority vested in the President by an exertion of legislative power, but with such an authority plus the very delicate, plenary and exclusive power of the President as the sole organ of the federal government in the field of international relations."

The breadth of the Court's holding in *Curtiss-Wright* has been used countless times to justify presidential initiatives in foreign affairs that are presented to Congress only for rubber stamp approval. President Lyndon Johnson, for example, sent half a million American soldiers to fight in Vietnam without Congress having exercised its constitutional power to declare war. This action in part accounted for the passage in 1973 of the War Powers Act over President Richard Nixon's veto. The War Powers Act—which also cited *Curtiss-Wright* as authority—was intended to curb presidential war making by requiring that the legislative and executive branches reach a collective agreement before committing American troops abroad.

The growth of the power of the presidency in modern times owes much to this landmark decision. Ironically, perhaps, the Court's refusal to cross the boundary into matters of foreign policy itself grows out of the doctrine of separation of powers. Political questions which can be resolved by the political branches of government—Congress and the presidency—have traditionally been considered off limits to judicial intervention.

Related Cases
Carter v. Carter Coal Co., 298 U.S. 238 (1936).
Massieu v. Reno, 915 F.Supp. 681 (1996).
Velasquez v. Frapwell, 160 F.3d 389 (1998).

Bibliography and Further Reading

Barber, Sotirios A. *The Constitution and the Delegation of Congressional Power.* Chicago, IL: University of Chicago Press, 1975.

Briggs, Philip J. *Making American Foreign Policy: President-Congress Relations from the Second World War to Vietnam.* Lanham, MD: University Press of America, 1991.

FitzGerald, John L. *Congress and the Separation of Powers.* New York, NY: Praeger, 1986.

Johnson, John W., ed. *Historic U.S. Court Cases, 1690–1990: An Encyclopedia.* New York: Garland Publishing, 1992.

NATIONAL LABOR RELATIONS BOARD V. JONES & LAUGHLIN STEEL CORP.

Legal Citation: 301 U.S. 1 (1937)

Appellant
National Labor Relations Board

Appellee
Jones & Laughlin Steel Corporation

Appellant's Claim
That Congress has the power to pass legislation that regulates the economy by protecting the rights of organized labor.

Chief Lawyers for Appellant
Attorney General Homer S. Cummings, Solicitor General Stanley F. Reed, and J. Warren Madden

Chief Lawyer for Appellee
Earl F. Reed

Justices for the Court
Louis D. Brandeis, Benjamin N. Cardozo, Charles Evans Hughes (writing for the Court), Owen Josephus Roberts, Harlan Fiske Stone

Justices Dissenting
Pierce Butler, James Clark McReynolds, George Sutherland, Willis Van Devanter

Place
Washington, D.C.

Date of Decision
12 April 1937

Decision
The Supreme Court upheld the National Labor Relations Act, signaling its willingness to uphold legislation regulating the relationship between business and labor.

Significance
The National Labor Relations Act was generally regarded as the most radical of Franklin Roosevelt's New Deal proposals. In upholding it, the Supreme Court gave a clear signal that it was abandoning its previous allegiance to the concept of freedom of contract, empowering organized labor.

The National Labor Relations Act of 1935 (NLRA) was the most daring part of President Franklin Roosevelt's attempt to combat the severe economic woes of the Great Depression with a loose collection of legislation he called the New Deal. The New Deal, which gave Congress unprecedented control of the economy, was based on the power given Congress in Article I, section 8 of the Constitution to "regulate Commerce . . . among the several states." For decades, the Supreme Court had curtailed Congress's power under the Commerce Clause, emphasizing instead a *laissez faire* approach to economic matters—that is, letting the market take care of itself, free from government intervention. The cornerstone of this philosophy was freedom of contract, which the Court said was protected by the Due Process Clause of the Fifth Amendment, which says that "No person shall be . . . deprived of life, liberty, or property, without due process of law." Nothing would seem to be more opposed to the Court's exalted conception of the right of employers and employees to bargain free of government interference than legislation designed to protect labor unions.

In the mid-1930s, relations between Jones & Laughlin Steel Corporation and the employees at its Aliquippa, Pennsylvania, plant were disintegrating. Alleging that Jones & Laughlin was engaging in unfair labor practices such as discriminating against union members in hiring and firing, Local 200 of the Amalgamated Association of Iron, Steel, and Tin Workers of America filed a complaint with the National Labor Relations Board (NLRB), the agency charged with enforcing the NLRA. The NLRB upheld the complaint and ordered the corporation to cease its unfair practices. When Jones & Laughlin refused to comply, the NLRB petitioned the Fifth Circuit Court of Appeals to enforce the order. The circuit court, however, claimed that the order exceeded the bounds of federal power, and declined to enforce it. The NLRB then looked to the U.S. Supreme Court.

Prior to 1937, Roosevelt and the Supreme Court had done battle over the New Deal, with the Court striking down virtually every important piece of legislation designed to alleviate the Great Depression by regulating the economy. In 1937, however, Roosevelt

The New Deal

As a candidate for president, Franklin D. Roosevelt had promised "a new deal for the American people." Following his inauguration in 1933, he introduced policies that would be called the New Deal—economic and judicial initiatives aimed at helping the nation recover from the Great Depression. During the fabled first "Hundred Days" of his administration, Roosevelt ushered through Congress more legislation than had been passed in a comparable period of time at any point in American history. Among these was the creation of the Federal Emergency Relief Administration, which distributed a half-billion dollars in federal aid to the states. It was followed by initiatives to put out-of-work Americans back to work in what Roosevelt's critics called "alphabet agencies": the CCC (Civilian Conservation Corps), the Agricultural Adjustment Administration (AAA), the Works Progress Administration (WPA), and the National Recovery Administration (NRA). A protracted battle with the Senate in 1937 over Roosevelt's attempt to load the Supreme Court with justices loyal to him effectively ended the New Deal era, though Roosevelt continued to be a popular president.

Source(s): *West's Encyclopedia of American Law.* St. Paul, MN: West Group, 1998.

brought about a constitutional crisis by developing a plan to "pack" the Court with enough justices of his own choosing to override what had been the majority's opposition to the New Deal. The court-packing plan ultimately failed to pass in Congress, but it did succeed in persuading at least two members of the Court, Chief Justice Hughes and Roberts, to reorient their attitudes towards Roosevelt's program. On 12 April 1937, less than a week after Roosevelt announced his court-packing plan, the Supreme Court handed down five decisions sustaining the constitutionality of the NLRA.

Employees of Jones & Laughlin Corporation vote whether or not the Steel Organizing Committee is to be recognized as the sole bargaining agency.
© UPI/Corbis-Bettmann.

Court Recognizes Collective Bargaining as a "Fundamental Right"

Chief Justice Hughes wrote the opinion for the five-member Court majority upholding the NLRA in *Jones & Laughlin.*

> The congressional authority to protect interstate commerce from burdens and obstructions is not limited to transactions which can be deemed to be an essential part of a "flow" of interstate or foreign commerce. Burdens and obstructions may be due to injurious action springing from other sources . . . That power may be exerted to protect interstate commerce "no matter what the source of the dangers which threaten it." [Quoting *Second Employers' Liability Cases*(1912)]

In other words, a strike could interfere with interstate commerce. To prevent labor unrest in a time of economic crisis, the Supreme Court was more than willing to support the NLRA, which imposed a duty on employers to negotiate with their workers. But Hughes's opinion went even further, recognizing workers' "fundamental right" to organize. As a result of *Jones & Laughlin,* the power of unions would expand to fill the void left by the death of *laissez faire.*

Related Cases

United States v. E. C. Knight, 156 U.S. 1 (1895).
Adair v. United States, 208 U.S. 161 (1908).
Loewe v. Lawlor, 208 U.S. 274 (1908).
A.L.A. Schechter Poultry v. United States, 295 U.S. 495 (1935).
Carter v. Carter Coal Co., 298 U.S. 238 (1936).

Bibliography and Further Reading

Gordon, Colin. *New Deals: Business, Labor, and Politics in America, 1920-1935.* New York, NY: Cambridge University Press, 1994.

Johnson, John W., ed. *Historic U.S. Court Cases, 1690–1990: An Encyclopedia.* New York: Garland Publishing, 1992.

Maidment, R. A. *The Judicial Response to the New Deal: The U.S. Supreme Court and Economic Regulation, 1934-1936.* New York, NY: Manchester University Press, 1991.

Vittoz, Stanley. *New Deal Labor Policy and the American Industrial Economy.* Chapel Hill: University of North Carolina Press, 1987.

UNITED STATES V. BELMONT

Legal Citation: 301 U.S. 324 (1937)

Petitioner
United States

Respondent
Morgan and Eleanor R. Belmont, executors of the last will and testament of August Belmont, deceased

Petitioner's Claim
That a U.S. district court erred in dismissing the U.S. government's claims against the August Belmont Company.

Chief Lawyer for Petitioner
Stanley Reed, U.S. Solicitor General

Chief Lawyer for Respondent
Cornelius Wickersham

Justices for the Court
Louis D. Brandeis, Pierce Butler, Benjamin N. Cardozo, Charles Evans Hughes, James Clark McReynolds, Owen Josephus Roberts, Harlan Fiske Stone, George Sutherland (writing for the Court), Willis Van Devanter

Justices Dissenting
None

Place
Washington, D.C.

Date of Decision
3 May 1937

Decision
Diplomatic relations between the United States and the Soviet Union dictated that the bank must release the funds.

Significance
The decision affirmed the power of presidential executive orders. The Court reasoned that some types of treaties do not require Senate approval to be implemented.

Millions In Limbo

When the Soviet Union nationalized the Petrograd Metal Works in 1918, not all of the business's assets were within easy reach of the new Soviet government. Earlier that same year, the metal works had deposited $24,438 with a New York City private banking firm, August Belmont & Company. The money remained in New York for nearly 20 years before a U.S. Supreme Court decision made its release possible.

During the first tumultuous years of the Soviet regime, hundreds of millions of dollars in claims were filed by Americans whose business with Russian firms was disrupted by the Soviet takeover of private enterprise. Likewise, huge sums aimed by Soviet claimants against American interests remained uncollected because no formal diplomatic relations existed between the United States and the Soviet governments.

This legal standoff lasted until 1933, when President Franklin D. Roosevelt recognized the Soviet Union by executive order. In some quarters, Roosevelt's decision to recognize the Soviet government was controversial. Because the president established diplomatic relations by issuing an executive order, debate or approval by Congress was not required.

Financial claims were among the issues discussed by the Roosevelt administration and Soviet People's Commissar of Foreign Relations Maxime Maximovitch Litvinoff. In a reciprocal agreement signed on 16 November 1933, each side agreed to release and transfer the job of weighing and collecting claims to the government on whose soil the claim was being made. In the Petrograd Metal Works case, this meant that the United States agreed to pursue the claim of the Soviet government on the money withheld by the Belmont firm, in return for Soviet action on claims by Americans against Russian nationals.

The August Belmont Company, however, refused to release the disputed money. The U.S. government responded with a lawsuit. After August Belmont died in 1924, the federal suit named the executors of his estate, Belmont's widow Eleanor and Morgan Belmont. At first, the federal government's claim was dismissed by the U.S. District Court for the Southern District of

August Belmont. © Photograph by Oscar White. Corbis Corporation.

New York. The court agreed that the Belmont case was within the scope of the Roosevelt-Litvinoff accord. Since the deposit was made in New York and not on Soviet territory, however, the court decided that appropriating the money would amount to confiscation, an act which was against the public policy of both the state of New York and the United States. Dismissal of the case amounted to a decision that the U.S. government was not entitled to sue the Belmont company.

The Power of International Compacts

With dozens of similar claims involving millions of dollars pending in other courts, the federal government persisted, appealing the New York court's decision before the U.S. Supreme Court on 4 March 1937. This time, the Belmont firm was found to be liable to legal action. On 3 May 1937, the Supreme Court reversed the New York court's decision, paving the way for the federal claim to proceed.

In an opinion written by Justice Sutherland, six of the nine justices agreed that President Roosevelt had acted within his power to recognize the Soviet Union as a sovereign state. Consequently, any diplomatic agreements arrived at through executive action, such as the Litvinoff accord, were legitimate. Justice Sutherland noted that binding treaties between the U.S. and foreign nations required approval by the Congress. The Litvinoff agreement, however, was an "international compact" made by executive order and was legal as an exercise of presidential power.

The Court would not consider the idea that appropriating the Petrograd account might violate any New York State policies. Under no circumstances, the Court ruled, could a state policy be found to legally supersede an agreement between the national government and a sovereign foreign power. The external powers of the U.S. government could be exercised without regard to state laws.

Furthermore, the Court did not accept the argument that U.S. government claims on the Petrograd account were in violation of the Fifth Amendment's clause prohibiting the confiscation of private property. Justice Sutherland's written opinion noted that the money in question was not the private property of the Belmont firm, which was only a custodian of the disputed sum. The money had been the property of the Petrograd Metal Works, which had been dissolved by the Soviet government. As a matter of general principle, the Supreme Court was not in the business of judging the acts of foreign governments on their own soil.

Three justices agreed with the result of Justice Sutherland's opinion, but for a different reason. Justices Stone, Brandeis, and Cardozo were uneasy about the majority's theory that the state of New York had no right to refuse to transfer funds. Still, the justices agreed that the federal government had the right to pursue a legal claim to the Petrograd account, just as long as it was understood that the government had no more or less legal standing in the suit than the Soviets as a claimant.

Ultimately, the Court's decision in the *Belmont* case would be of less significance to the parties involved in the lawsuit over the Petrograd Metal Works account than as a precedent establishing that presidential executive power was not to be subjected to the rules of individual states.

Related Cases

Moscow Fire Insurance Co., v. Bank of New York and Trust Co., 20 N.E.2d 758 (1930).
United States v. Pink, 315 U.S. 203 (1942).
American International Group, Inc. v. Islamic Republic of Iran, 657 F.2d 430 (1981).

Bibliography and Further Reading

Biskupic, Joan, and Elder Witt, eds. *Congressional Quarterly's Guide to the U.S. Supreme Court,* 3rd ed. Washington, DC: Congressional Quarterly, Inc., 1996.

Cushman, Robert F. *Cases in Constitutional Law,* 7th ed. Englewood Cliffs, NJ: Prentice-Hall, Inc., 1989.

Cushman, Robert F. *Leading Constitutional Decisions.* Englewood Cliffs, NJ: Prentice-Hall, Inc., 1982.

Kurland, Phillip B. and Gerhard Casper, eds. *Landmark Briefs and Arguments of the Supreme Court of the United States,* Vol. 33. Arlington: University Publications of America, 1975.

YOUNGSTOWN SHEET & TUBE CO. V. SAWYER

Legal Citation: 343 U.S. 937 (1952)

Petitioner
Youngstown Sheet & Tube Co.

Respondent
Charles Sawyer, Secretary of Commerce

Petitioner's Claim
That in seizing control of steel production during the Korean War in order to prevent a labor strike, the executive branch exceeded its constitutional authority.

Chief Lawyer for Petitioner
John W. Davis

Chief Lawyer for Respondent
Philip B. Perlman, Solicitor General

Justices for the Court
Hugo Lafayette Black (writing for the Court), Tom C. Clark, William O. Douglas, Robert H. Jackson, Sherman Minton, Stanley Forman Reed, Fred Moore Vinson

Justices Dissenting
Harold Burton, Felix Frankfurter

Place
Washington, D.C.

Date of Decision
2 June 1952

Decision
The Supreme Court ruled against the executive branch steel seizure.

Significance
Also known as the *Steel Seizure Case, Youngstown* is of lasting importance because it upheld the balance of power between the executive and legislative branches.

In 1952, United States troops were still engaged in hostilities on the Korean peninsula while the United Nations attempted to negotiate an armistice. On 20 March of that year, after the steel industry refused to abide by a Wage Mediation Board award, steel workers threatened to go out on strike. Because of the threat to production in an industry so vital to U.S. military action, President Harry S. Truman issued an executive order commanding Secretary of Commerce Charles Sawyer to seize control of the nation's steel mills. Sawyer directed the steel companies to operate according to government regulations.

The president immediately gave Congress formal notice of his action, and Congress took no action in response. Truman based his actions on the executive power vested in him by Article II of the Constitution and by his powers as commander-in-chief, as well as the many historical precedents of executive branch seizure of industry without congressional approval. Steel industry executives, however, argued that the controlling law was the Taft-Hartley Labor-Management Relations Act of 1947, which permitted Congress to become involved—and that it could be employed only after collective bargaining broke down. The history of the act showed that during debate over Taft-Hartley, Congress had specifically rejected a provision authorizing executive branch seizure of industries experiencing labor strife.

On 30 April 1952, the U.S. District Court for the District of Columbia granted Youngstown Sheet & Tube and other steel industry plaintiffs a preliminary injunction barring the executive branch from controlling the steel mills. This injunction was stayed the same day by the District of Columbia Circuit Court of Appeals. On 3 May, the Supreme Court agreed to review this case, the outcome of which was vital not just to the war effort but to the U.S. economy.

Supreme Court Rebuffs Presidential Claims of Inherent Authority

On 2 June 1952, the Court handed down its opinion. Writing for the Court, Justice Black declared that the president had no power to intervene in labor disputes without express consent of the Congress. To do so was to exercise a legislative function and therefore violate the doctrine of separation of powers. Four of the five justices who joined his opinion— Jackson, Clark, Douglas, and Frankfurter—also wrote concurring opinions of their own. Of these, Jackson's was the most salient regarding the most contentious issue in the case: Congress's silence in the face of Truman's actions. For Jackson, this silence did not indicate acquiescence but a refusal to authorize the seizure:

> When the President takes measures incompatible with the expressed or implied will of Congress, his power is at its lowest ebb, for then he can only rely upon his own constitutional powers minus any constitutional powers of Congress over the matter . . . the current seizure . . . can be supported only by any remainder of executive power after subtraction of such powers as Congress may have over the subject. In short, we can sustain the President only by holding that seizure of such strike-bound industries is within his domain and beyond control by Congress . . . I am not persuaded, that history leaves open to question . . . that the executive branch, like the Federal Government as a whole, possesses only delegated powers. The purpose of the Constitution was not only to grant power, but to keep it from getting out of hand.

There was, in short, no inherent executive power to seize private industry. After the Court ruled the steel seizure unconstitutional, the United Steel Workers called for another strike, but this was promptly settled on 24 June when the industry agreed to wage increases. The long term effect of the *Steel Seizure Case* decision was to restrain presidential claims of implied authority in such areas as executive privilege and national security. In practice, however, the Court itself has shown great deference to the president's claims of implied powers. It has upheld inherent presidential authority in the area of foreign affairs, which has traditionally separated legislative control over domestic affairs from executive authority over external matters. In *Dames & Moore v. Regan* (1981), for example, the Court condoned President Jimmy Carter's resolution of the hostage crisis with Iran despite the fact that his actions went beyond the powers granted him by law. In other areas, the Court has declined to recognize implied executive powers. But even in *United States v. Nixon* (1974), in which the Court rejected President Richard Nixon's attempts to hang on to his tape recordings of conversations about the Watergate break-in and cover up, the Court stressed that the executive branch is entitled to great deference in protecting the confidentiality of presidential affairs, both foreign and domestic.

Related Cases
Dalton v. Specter, 511 U.S. 462 (1994).

Bibliography and Further Reading
Gilmour, Robert S., and Alexis A. Halley, eds. *Who Makes Public Policy? The Struggle for Control Between Congress and the Executive.* Chatham, NJ: Chatham House Publishers, 1994.

Marcus, Maeva. *Truman and the Steel Seizure Case: The Limits of Presidential Power.* New York, NY: Columbia University Press, 1977.

Westin, Alan F. *The Anatomy of a Constitutional Law Case: Youngstown Sheet and Tube Co. v. Sawyer; The Steel Seizure Decision.* New York, NY: Macmillan, 1958.

REID V. COVERT

Legal Citation: 351 U.S. 487 (1957)

Appellant
Curtis Reid, Superintendent of the District of Columbia Jail

Appellee
Clarice B. Covert

Appellant's Claim
That a district court wrongfully issued a writ of *habeas corpus* for Covert, who was awaiting retrial on murder charges.

Chief Lawyer for Appellant
Marvin E. Frankel

Chief Lawyer for Appellee
Frederick Bernays Weiner

Justices for the Court
Tom C. Clark (writing for the Court), Harold Burton, John Marshall Harlan II, Sherman Minton, Charles Evans Whittaker

Justices Dissenting
Hugo Lafayette Black, William O. Douglas, Earl Warren, (Felix Frankfurter did not participate)

Place
Washington, D.C.

Date of Decision
11 June 1956

Decision
Reserved the lower court's issuance of the writ.

Significance
The Court ruled that a section of the Uniform Code of Military Justice, regarding trials for civilians who commit crimes abroad, was constitutional. The issue, however was not definitively settled here, as the Court reheard the case the following year.

After World War II, America took on new responsibilities as a world power. By the mid-1950s, U.S. armed forces were stationed in more than 60 countries, and spouses and children often accompanied military personnel on their foreign assignments. By executive order, the United States had agreements with some countries, such as England and Japan, that if these civilian relatives committed a crime, they would be tried in American court-martials, not the native courts.

The military's authority to try civilians abroad rested in the Uniform Code of Military Justice. The UCMJ, enacted in 1950, codified the judicial system for all branches of the military. Article 2 (11) of the code stated relatives accompanying armed forces personnel abroad were subject to trial in a court-martial for any crimes they committed outside the continental United States. This section of the UCMJ was at the heart of *Reid v. Covert*.

Clarice Covert was married to Edward Covert, a sergeant in the U.S. Air Force stationed in England. Mrs. Covert murdered her husband on the air base and was tried by a court-martial, found guilty, and sentenced to life in prison. Covert was flown to the United States and confined in a federal prison in West Virginia. She appealed her verdict, and on a legal technicality, the U.S. Court of Military Appeals set aside her conviction. The court ordered that she receive a new trial at an air base in Washington, D.C. Covert was transferred to a Washington jail to await this second trial.

During her stay in Washington, Covert sought a writ of *habeas corpus* in district court. The district court issued the writ, and the government appealed to the Supreme Court.

Two Cases, One Outcome

At the same time the Court agreed to hear *Reid,* it took on a similar case, *Kinsella v. Krueger.* Like Clarice Covert, Dorothy Kinsella Smith had lived abroad with her husband, a U.S. Army colonel. Like Covert, Kinsella Smith murdered her husband and was sentenced by a court-martial to life imprisonment. Kinsella Smith, however, had been denied a writ of *habeas corpus* by a different district court. Now, the Supreme Court issued different decisions, but with the same outcome.

In a 5-3 vote, with Justice Frankfurter reserving judgment, the Court reversed the lower court's granting of a writ to Covert and affirmed the denial of a writ for Kinsella Smith. Both women had claimed Article 2 (11) of the UCMJ was unconstitutional; Covert, in addition, argued she was no longer under the jurisdiction of the court-martial once she left England and returned to America.

Justice Clark wrote the decision for both cases, and he addressed the constitutional issue in *Kinsella*. The Court, Clark said, has long held that Congress can set up courts outside of the United States, and "the procedure in such tribunals need not comply with the standards prescribed by the Constitution for Article 3 Courts." (Article 3 outlines the federal court system.) Congress thus had authority to include in the UCMJ court-martials for civilians living abroad.

In his *Reid* decision, Clark also dismissed the claim that the court-martial no longer had jurisdiction for Covert's case. He wrote:

> An entirely different case might be presented if Mrs. Covert had terminated her status as a person "accompanying the armed forces without the continental limits of the United States" by returning to this country voluntarily. But this is not the case. The issue here is whether we should create an exception to the general rule that jurisdiction of a tribunal, once acquired, continues until final disposition . . . It would be unreasonable to hold that the services retained jurisdiction of military prisoners that they kept in foreign countries but lost jurisdiction of prisoners confined in penal institutions in the United States.

Time On Covert's Side?

The Supreme Court had acted with unusual speed on *Reid* and *Kinsella*. It agreed to hear the cases in March 1956 and decided the cases less than three months later, on the last day of the Court's term. That quickness led to Justice Frankfurter's reservation of a judgment. "Reflection is a slow process," he wrote. "Wisdom, like good wine, requires maturing."

Haste was also on the minds of the three dissenters, Chief Justice Warren and Justices Black and Douglas. They issued this brief statement:

> The decisions just announced have far-reaching importance. They subject to military court-martial, even in time of peace, the wives, mothers and children of members of the Armed Forces serving abroad even though these dependents have no connection whatever with the Armed Forces except their kinship to military personnel and their presence abroad. The questions raised are complex, the remedy drastic, and the consequences far-reaching upon the lives of civilians. The military is given new powers not hitherto thought consistent with our scheme of government. For these reasons, we need more time than is available in these closing days of the Term in which to write our dissenting views.

The complexity and seriousness of *Reid,* perhaps coupled with the concerns over the speed of the deliberations, worked in Covert's favor. She asked for a rehearing of the case, and on 5 November 1956, six justices agreed. The rehearing in 1957 resulted in the Court's deciding that military courts had no jurisdiction over a civilian.

Related Cases

McCulloch v. Maryland, 17 U.S. 316 (1819).
Missouri v. Holland, 525 U.S. 416 (1920).
Toth v. Quarles, 350 U.S. 11 (1955).
Reid v. Covert, 354 U.S. 1 (1957).

Bibliography and Further Reading

Hall, Kermit L., ed. *The Oxford Companion to the Supreme Court of the United States.* New York: Oxford University Press, 1992.

New York Times, June 12, 1956; November 6, 1956.

Nowak, John E., Ronald D. Rotunda, and J. Nelson Young. *Constitutional Law,* 2nd ed. St. Paul: West Publishing Company, 1984.

MUSKOPF V. CORNING HOSPITAL DISTRICT

Legal Citation: 11 Ca. Rptr. 89 (1961)

Appellant
Louisa C. Muskopf, et al.

Appellee
Corning Hospital District

Appellant's Claim
That the hospital district was liable for negligence in the appellant's injury, and not immune from tort liability on the grounds of its government status.

Chief Lawyers for Appellant
P. M. Barceloux, Burton J. Goldstein

Chief Lawyers for Appellee
Glenn D. Newton, William W. Coshow

Justices for the Court
Maurice P. Dooling, Jr., Phil S. Gibson, Raymond E. Peters, Roger J. Traynor (writing for the court), Thomas P. White

Justices Dissenting
Marshall F. McComb, B. Rey Schauer

Place
Bank, California

Date of Decision
27 January 1961

Decision
That the doctrine of government immunity from tort liability was mistaken, and the hospital district could be held liable.

Significance
The case broadened the scope for individuals bringing suit against municipal and state governments for personal injuries.

Torts and Liability

When Louisa C. Muskopf, a patient with a broken hip, fell in Corning Memorial Hospital and further injured her hip, she and her husband sued the hospital district for negligence. Counsel for the defendant argued— without contending the facts of the case—that grounds for a suit had not been established. The argument, which was sustained by the superior court of Tehama County, held that hospital district was "a state agency exercising a governmental function and as such was immune from tort liability." A tort is an injury or harmful wrong resulting from something other than a breach of contract for which a citizen can demand restitution. The Supreme Court of California reversed the Tehama County court's judgment on 27 January 1961, firmly rejecting the rule of governmental immunity from tort liability.

Sovereign Immunity

The concept that the government is immune from tort liability is sometimes said to stem from the ancient English maxim "The king can do no wrong." One reading of this maxim interprets it as the basis for the common law concept of "sovereign immunity," which precludes a suit against the sovereign without the sovereign's consent. The purpose of sovereign immunity, however, was not to deny the injured restitution, but rather to indicate that the king's courts could not have jurisdiction over the king.

Justice Traynor, noting the concept of sovereign immunity, in his majority opinion went on to provide a history of the court's erosion of the rule of governmental immunity. He acknowledged that the rule is "riddled with exceptions." First, municipal corporations were "held subject to the court's equitable distribution," then they were "held liable for their proprietary acts." Proprietary acts are those the state undertakes for the benefit of its citizens—such as building a park—rather than those fundamental to it as a government—such as passing laws. According to the Federal Tort Claims Act of 1946, which was meant to give citizens harmed by the government a means of obtaining relief, there is no governmental immunity for proprietary acts. Although some forms of immunity

---

Tort Liability

A tort is an act of wrongdoing which violates the laws as they apply to all persons—as opposed to the rules that govern the signers of a contract—and for which damages may be claimed. Torts are identified either as intentional, or as arising from negligence. When someone seeks damages from another party on the basis of a tort, this is called a tort action, and tort liability relates to the exposure of a given party to a tort action.

As the frequency of tort actions has risen, beginning in the 1970s, so has the prevalence of concern over tort liability. This has had effects both beneficial and detrimental to the health of American society. On the one hand, individuals and corporations are much more circumspect regarding the kind of careless behavior that could lead to a tort action on the basis of negligence. Thus for instance a manager of a fast-food restaurant might tell an employee to mop up a spill before any customers slip on the floor, because the wet floor is "a lawsuit waiting to happen." On the other hand, people have been prone to take advantage of the comfortable financial positions of corporations by taking them to court for any wrongdoing.

Source(s): "Tort Liability." Fort Hays State University, http://bigcat.fhsu.edu.

---

have been consistently upheld by the courts, such as immunity from citizens suing the government for injuries incurred while serving in the military during an act of war, Traynor wrote that "for years the process of erosion of governmental immunity has gone on unabated." Traynor noted that this erosion was not necessarily negative, though. Although suits against municipalities, states, or the federal government imposed a burden on the public, the court held that "[p]ublic convenience does not outweigh individual compensation."

The Narrowing of Immunity

An additional issue was raised by the fact that much of that erosion had occurred legislatively. The dissenting judges in *Muskopf v. Corning Hospital District* held that waiving governmental immunity was the prerogative of the legislature, not the courts, since a series of statutes had removed immunity in specific areas. Traynor's opinion asserted that "a series of sporadic statutes, each operating in a separate area of governmental immunity" did not prevent the court from accepting or rejecting immunity in other areas.

Overall, the decision reached was representative of the ongoing move away from the idea of sovereign immunity. Although citizens always had the ability to sue particular individuals for the redress of injuries, public opinion throughout the twentieth century increasingly favored the idea that the government should be held accountable if they inflict wrongs. The narrowing of immunities available to state and local government agencies was partly the result of the Civil Rights movement, which saw more and more individuals taking action against official harrassment and intimidation, and more and more demands for accountability on the part of government.

Related Cases

Doe v. McMillan, 412 U.S. 306 (1979).
Nixon v. Fitzgerald 457 U.S. 731 (1982).
Crawford-El v. Britton, 118 S.Ct. 1584 (1998).

Bibliography and Further Reading

Schuck, Peter H. *Suing Government: Judicial Remedies for Official Wrongs.* New Haven: Yale University Press, 1983.

UNITED STATES V. NIXON

Legal Citation: 418 U.S. 683 (1974)

Appellant
United States

Appellee
Richard M. Nixon, President of the United States

Appellant's Claim
That the president had to obey a subpoena ordering him to turn over tape recordings and documents relating to his conversations with aides and advisers concerning the Watergate break-in.

Chief Lawyers for Appellant
Leon Jaworski, Philip A. Lacovara

Chief Lawyer for Appellee
James D. St. Clair

Justices for the Court
Harry A. Blackmun, William J. Brennan, Jr., Warren E. Burger (writing for the Court), William O. Douglas, Thurgood Marshall, Lewis F. Powell, Jr., Potter Stewart, Byron R. White

Justices Dissenting
None (William H. Rehnquist did not participate)

Place
Washington, D.C.

Date of Decision
24 July 1974

Decision
President was ordered to turn over the tapes and other documents to the prosecutors.

Significance
The president is not immune from judicial process, and must turn over evidence subpoenaed by the courts. The doctrine of executive privilege entitles the president to a high degree of confidentiality from the courts if the evidence involves matters of national security or other sensitive information, but the president cannot withhold evidence.

By the spring of 1974, the government investigation into the Watergate break-in and the subsequent coverup was moving full-steam ahead. Despite President Richard M. Nixon's repeated denials, it was becoming increasingly clear to Congress and the public that senior Nixon administration officials, and probably Nixon himself, had been actively involved in the coverup. On 1 March 1974, a 19-person federal grand jury indicted U.S. Attorney General John N. Mitchell for conspiracy to obstruct justice in the proceeding in *United States v. Mitchell*. Six other persons, all senior Nixon administration officials employed in the White House or the Committee to Re-Elect the President (CREEP), were indicted as co-conspirators: Charles W. Colson, John D. Ehrlichman, H.R. Haldeman, Robert C. Mardian, Kenneth W. Parkinson, and Gordon Strachan. Nixon also was included, but as an unindicted co-conspirator.

On 18 April 1974, Special Prosecutor Leon Jaworski, charged with the responsibility of conducting the Watergate investigation for the government, went to Judge John Sirica of the U.S District Court for the District of Columbia. In response to Jaworski's request, Sirica issued a subpoena ordering Nixon to produce "certain tapes, memoranda, papers, transcripts, or other writings" related to the specific meetings and conversations detailed in the subpoena. The material was to be turned over by 2 May 1974, for use in the trial, scheduled for 9 September 1974. Jaworski was able to identify the time, place, and persons present at these discussions because he already possessed the White House daily logs and appointment records.

Nixon Fights the Subpoena

Nixon turned over edited transcripts of 43 conversations, which included portions of 20 conversations named in the subpoena, on 30 April 1974. On 1 May, however, Nixon's attorney, James D. St. Clair, went to Sirica and asked that the subpoena be quashed. Nixon had hoped that the transcripts, which had been publicly released, would satisfy the court's and the public's demand for information without turning over the tapes. Nixon was wrong: Sirica denied St. Clair's motion on 20 May 1974. Sirica ordered "the President or any subordinate officer, official, or employee with custody

Presidential Succession

After the assassination of President John F. Kennedy and the succession of Vice President Lyndon B. Johnson to the presidency, Americans became concerned about the issue of presidential succession. For the next 14 months the vice-presidency remained vacant. Most Americans were shocked to learn that if Johnson, who had suffered a heart attack in 1955, died during 1964, John McCormack, the 73-year-old Speaker of the House of Representatives, would become president. Next in line was Carl Hayden, the 87-year-old president *pro tempore* of the Senate.

This situation was rectified on 10 February 1967 when the Twenty-fifth Amendment was ratified. This amend-

ment allowed the president to nominate a new vice-president, who would take office after approval by a majority vote in each house of Congress. It also added provisions governing temporary presidential disability, specifying the circumstances and provisions by which a vice-president would become acting president.

The provisions for naming a new vice-president have only been invoked twice. In 1973 when President Richard M. Nixon selected Rep. Gerald Ford to replace Spiro T. Agnew; and in 1974 after Nixon resigned the presidency, Ford became president and Nelson A. Rockefeller of New York was chosen as the new vice president.

---

or control of the documents or objects subpoenaed" to turn them over to the court by 31 May 1974.

On 24 May 1974, a week before Sirica's deadline, St. Clair filed an appeal to the U.S. Court of Appeals for the District of Columbia Circuit. Both sides realized, however, that the critical legal issue of whether the courts could subject the president to subpoenas and other forms of judicial process would ultimately have to be decided by the U.S. Supreme Court. Further, both sides were acutely aware of the political stakes and were anxious to avoid lengthy litigation. Therefore, on 24 May 1974 Jaworski took the highly unusual step of asking the Supreme Court to grant *"certiorari* before judgment," namely to take the case without waiting for the court of appeals to make a decision. The effect of bypassing the court of appeals would be to get a fast and final decision from the Supreme Court, and on 6 June 1974, St. Clair also requested *certiorari* before judgment.

On 15 June 1974 the Supreme Court granted Jaworski's and St. Clair's requests and decided to take the case from the court of appeals. St. Clair represented Nixon, and Jaworski was assisted by Philip A. Lacovara for the government. Justice Rehnquist, a Nixon appointee to the Court, excused himself from the case.

There is a popular notion that the judicial system, especially the Supreme Court, is above politics. This would seem to be a myth. When Jaworski and Lacovara went into the Supreme Court building on 8 July, there were hundreds of cheering spectators on the steps. The justices themselves were obviously involved as well, and grilled both sides during the oral argument. Justice Powell questioned Nixon's claim that the tapes had to be kept secret to protect the public interest:

Mr. St. Clair, what public interest is there in preserving secrecy with respect to a criminal conspiracy?

St. Clair responded lamely:

The answer, sir, is that a criminal conspiracy is criminal only after it's proven to be criminal.

The government's attorneys were questioned thoroughly as well, particularly on the issue of whether the grand jury set a dangerous precedent by naming the president as a co-conspirator when the prosecutors had not even requested an indictment. In response to Justice Powell's concerns, Lacovara stated:

Grand Juries usually are not malicious. Even prosecutors cannot be assumed to be malicious . . . I submit to you, sir, that just as in this case a Grand Jury would not lightly accuse the President of a crime, so, too, the fear that, perhaps without basis, some Grand Jury somewhere might maliciously accuse a President of a crime is not necessarily a reason for saying that a Grand Jury has no power to do that.

The Supreme Court issued its decision on 24 July 1974, less than three weeks later. During the intervening time, the justices struggled to write an opinion on which all eight of them could agree. Although Supreme Court justices are free to dissent as they see fit, they wanted a unanimous decision in this case because of the important issues at stake concerning the relationship between the executive and the judiciary. A split decision would weaken the impact of the Court's decision. Although Burger was the chief justice and nominally in charge of writing the opinion, in fact, all eight justices wrote or contributed to portions of the decision.

Nixon Order to Release

After dispensing with some initial procedural issues, the Court went to the main issue, namely whether the president was cloaked with immunity from judicial

President Richard Nixon leaves the White House after resigning.
© AP/Wide World Photos.

process under the doctrine called "executive privilege." First, the Court restated the principle of *Marbury v. Madison* (1803) that "it is emphatically the province and duty of the judicial department to say what the law is:"

> [Notwithstanding] the deference each branch must accord the others, the judicial power of the United States vested in the federal courts by Article III, section 1, of the Constitution can no more be shared with the Executive Branch than the Chief executive, for example, can share with the Judiciary the veto power, or the Congress share with the Judiciary the power to override a Presidential veto. Any other conclusions would be contrary to the basic concept of separation of powers and the checks and balances that flow from the scheme of a tripartite government. We therefore reaffirm that it is the province and the duty of this Court to say what the law is with respect to the claim of privilege presented in this case.

Next, the Court addressed Nixon's two principal arguments in favor of executive privilege. First, St. Clair argued that for the presidency to function, conversations and other communications between high government officials and their advisors had to be kept confidential. Otherwise, if every statement could be made public, advisors would be reluctant to speak freely, and the decision-making process would suffer. Second, St. Clair argued that the very nature of the doctrine of separation of powers gave the president judicial immunity. In rejecting both arguments, the Court stated that while confidentiality was important, it could be maintained

by letting a judge review evidence *in camera*, namely alone in his or her chambers:

> The President's need for complete candor and objectivity from advisers calls for great deference from the courts. However, when the privilege depends solely on the broad, undifferentiated claim of public interest in the confidentiality of such conversations, a confrontation with other values arises. Absent a claim of need to protect military, diplomatic, or sensitive national security secrets, we find it difficult to accept the argument that even the very important interest in confidentiality of Presidential communications is significantly diminished by production of such material for *in camera* inspection with all the protection that a District Court will be obliged to provide.

Further, the Court stressed that recognizing Nixon's broad claim of executive privilege could seriously compromise the judicial system's obligation to assure the dispensation of justice in criminal trials:

> The impediment that an absolute, unqualified privilege would place in the way of the primary constitutional duty of the Judicial Branch to do justice in criminal prosecutions would plainly conflict with the function of the courts under Article III [of the Constitution] . . . In this case the President challenges a subpoena served on him as a third party requiring the production of materials for use in a criminal prosecution; he does so on the claim that he has a privilege against disclosure of confiden-

tial communications. He does not place his claim of privilege on the ground they are military or diplomatic secrets.

Given that Nixon had not asserted any specific reason why the courts should not have the tapes in the *United States v. Mitchell* trial, the justices ordered Nixon to turn them over to Judge Sirica for *in camera* inspection.

Ordering a president to do something is one thing; enforcing that order is another. The judicial branch is a co-equal branch of government, but as one of the framers of the Constitution commented, it "possesses neither sword nor purse," meaning that it is without the military power of the executive branch or the taxing power of the legislative branch. The judiciary depends ultimately on its stature and public respect for the democratic system for enforcement of its orders. During oral argument, St. Clair had hinted darkly that Nixon "had his obligations under the Constitution," leaving it unclear whether Nixon would obey the Court's order to turn over the tapes to Sirica.

Nixon was in San Clemente, California, when he received word of the Supreme Court's unanimous decision from his aide, Alexander Haig. Within a day, however, Nixon issued a public statement that he would comply with the Court's order. The relevant part of Nixon's statement was:

> While I am, of course, disappointed in the result, I respect and accept the court's decision, and I have instructed Mr. St. Clair to take whatever measures are necessary to comply with that decision in all respects.

Nixon turned over 64 tapes to Sirica, some of which included highly incriminating conversations between Nixon and his aides shortly after the Watergate break-in. Congress was ready to impeach him, and Nixon realized that his presidency was doomed. On 8 August 1974, Nixon announced his resignation and Vice President Gerald Ford became president at noon on 9 August, the effective date of the resignation. Because Ford exercised his power to pardon Nixon, Nixon never stood trial. Nevertheless, the case established an important precedent, namely that if there is any executive privilege, it does not permit the president to withhold evidence needed by the courts. Finally, the case sounded the death knell for the political career of Richard Nixon, who had formerly been one of America's most popular and successful presidents.

Related Cases

Marbury v. Madison, 5 U.S. 137 (1803).
Ashwander v. Tennessee Valley Authority, 297 U.S. 288 (1936).
Baker v. Carr, 369 U.S. 186 (1962).
United States v. Mitchell, 386 U.S. 972 (1967).

United States v. United Stated District Court, 407 U.S. 297 (1972).
Clinton v. Jones, 520 U.S. 681 (1997).

Bibliography and Further Reading

Biskupic, Joan, and Elder Witt, eds. *Congressional Quarterly's Guide to the U.S. Supreme Court,* 3rd ed. Washington, DC: Congressional Quarterly, Inc., 1996.

Cushman, Robert F. *Cases in Constitutional Law,* 7th ed. Englewood Cliffs, NJ: Prentice-Hall, Inc., 1989.

———. *Leading Constitutional Decisions.* Englewood Cliffs, NJ: Prentice-Hall, Inc., 1982.

Epstein, Lee, and Thomas G. Walker. *Constitutional Law for a Changing America: Institutional Powers and Constraints,* 3rd ed. Washington DC: Congressional Quarterly, 1998.

Hall, Kermit L., ed. *The Oxford Companion to the Supreme Court of the United States.* New York: Oxford University Press, 1992.

Johnson, John W., ed. *Historic U.S. Court Cases, 1690–1990: An Encyclopedia.* New York: Garland Publishing, 1992.

Leon Jaworski. © AP/Wide World Photos.

SCHICK V. REED

Legal Citation: 419 U.S. 256 (1974)

Petitioner
Maurice Schick

Respondent
George J. Reed

Petitioner's Claim
That President Eisenhower's decision to commute Schick's death sentence on the condition that he never be granted parole was unconstitutional.

Chief Lawyer for Peititoner
Homer E. Moyer, Jr.

Chief Lawyer for Respondent
Louis F. Claiborne

Justices for the Court
Harry A. Blackmun, Warren E. Burger (writing for the Court), Lewis F. Powell, Jr., William H. Rehnquist, Potter Stewart, Byron R. White

Justices Dissenting
William J. Brennan, Jr., William O. Douglas, Thurgood Marshall

Place
Washington, D.C.

Date of Decision
23 December 1974

Decision
Eisenhower's no-parole condition did not violate the Constitution.

Significance
In *Schick v. Reed*, the Supreme Court ruled that limits to the president's power to pardon can be set only by constitutional amendment.

In 1954, Maurice Schick, a master sergeant in the United States Army stationed in Japan, was tried before a court-martial for the murder of an eight-year-old girl. He admitted to the killing, but contended that he was insane at the time that he committed it. After a board of psychiatrists concluded that Schick was suffering from a nonpsychotic behavioral disorder and was mentally aware of and able to control his actions, the court-martial rejected Schick's defense and he was sentenced to death on 27 March 1954. In 1960, President Dwight D. Eisenhower, acting under authority granted by the Constitution, commuted Schick's sentence from death to life imprisonment, on the condition that he would never be eligible for parole.

Had Schick originally received a sentence of life imprisonment, he would have been eligible for parole consideration in March of 1969. Two years after that date, having served 17 years of his sentence, Schick filed suit in the U.S. District Court for the District of Columbia to require the United States Board of Parole to consider him for parole. The chairman of the United States Board of Parole, George J. Reed, asked the U.S. District Court for a summary judgment in the government's favor.

The Lower Court Rulings

The U.S. District Court for the District of Columbia granted Reed's motion for a summary judgment. The Court of Appeals for the District of Columbia affirmed this decision. In doing so, the courts upheld the power of a president to grant commutations and pardons with conditions attached. The court of appeals also rejected Schick's argument that the 1972 *Furman v. Georgia* decision—which commuted all pending death sentences to life in prison—meant he should have been eligible for parole.

The Supreme Court Ruling

On 23 December 1974 the Supreme Court issued its decision. By a vote of 6-3, it affirmed the ruling of the court of appeals. Chief Justice Burger wrote the majority opinion, in which he was joined by Justices White, Stewart, Blackmun, Powell, and Rehnquist. Justice Marshall wrote a dissenting opinion, in which he was joined by Justices Douglas and Brennan. The majority's decision rested on three points.

Presidential Pardoning Power

One month after Gerald Ford became president following the resignation of his successor, Richard Nixon in August of 1974, he pardoned Nixon of any wrongdoing associated with the Watergate scandal. Many criticized Ford's actions, and some have blamed his defeat by Democratic candidate Jimmy Carter in the 1976 elections on widespread antipathy regarding his pardon of Nixon.

Should the president even be allowed to make pardons? Viewed from one angle, the idea smacks of autocracy. On the other hand, the presidential pardon makes sense in instances where prejudice or other factors have interfered with the handing down of a just verdict. Many intellectuals in the 1920s believed that Nicola Sacco and Bartolomeo Vanzetti had been falsely accused of murder on the basis of their anarchist beliefs rather than the evidence, and called for a presidential pardon. The pardon for Sacco and Vanzetti never came, however. As for Nixon's pardon, the nation had already been through a prolonged series of investigations and hearings related to Watergate, and the American people were ready to move on.

The President Can Commute With Conditions

In his majority opinion, Chief Justice Burger held that the president has the power to attach conditions when he commutes the sentence of a convicted person. He based this determination on previous cases that had been before the Court, and on his understanding of the history of an executive's power to pardon:

> [T]his Court has long read the Constitution as authorizing the President to deal with individual cases by granting conditional pardons. The very essence of the pardoning power is to treat each case individually . . . Presidents throughout our history as a Nation have exercised the power to pardon or commute sentences upon conditions that are not specifically authorized by statute . . . We therefore hold that the pardoning power is an enumerated power of the Constitution and that its limitations, if any, must be found in the Constitution itself.

No Parole Condition Held To Be Constitutional

Schick had argued that a condition denying him parole was itself unconstitutional. Chief Justice Burger dismissed this argument out of hand:

> The no-parole condition attached to the commutation of his death sentence is similar to sanctions imposed by legislatures such as mandatory minimum sentences or statutes otherwise precluding parole; it does not offend the Constitution.

Furman v. Georgia Did Not Apply

Schick's most inventive argument concerned *Furman v. Georgia,* the 1972 Supreme Court decision that struck down 39 state capital punishment laws as unconstitutional. Following that decision, all pending death sentences were automatically commuted to simple life imprisonment—with parole eligibility. Schick claimed that his "death sentence"—as commuted by President Eisenhower—should have reverted to this sentence as well. Chief Justice Burger was not persuaded:

> It is correct that pending death sentences not carried out prior to *Furman* were thereby set aside without conditions such as were attached to petitioner's commutation. However, petitioner's death sentence was not pending in 1972 because it had long since been commuted.

The dissenters, led by Justice Marshall, did not disagree with Chief Justice Burger's determination that the president had the right to grant a conditional commutation of sentence. However, they strongly disagreed on the other two points, claiming that the *Furman* decision required the substitution of a simple life sentence, and that the no-parole condition was "extra legal" and thus not within the scope of the president's powers.

Related Cases

Ex parte Grossman, 267 U.S. 87 (1925).
Grosjean v. American Press Co., 297 U.S. 233 (1936).
Trop v. Dulles, 356 U.S. 86 (1958).
Furman v. Georgia, 408 U.S. 238 (1972).

Bibliography and Further Reading

Biskupic, Joan, and Elder Witt, eds. *Congressional Quarterly's Guide to the U.S. Supreme Court,* 3rd ed. Washington, DC: Congressional Quarterly, Inc., 1996.

Encyclopedia of the American Constitution. New York, NY: Macmillan Publishing Company, 1986.

IMMIGRATION AND NATURALIZATION SERVICE V. CHADHA

Legal Citation: 462 U.S. 919 (1983)

Petitioner
Immigration and Naturalization Service

Respondent
Jagdish Rai Chadha

Petitioner's Claim
The court of appeals ruling that the legislative veto was an unconstitutional violation of the separation of powers was incorrect.

Chief Lawyer for Petitioner
Rex E. Lee, U.S. Solicitor General

Chief Lawyer for Respondent
Alan B. Morrison

Justices for the Court
Harry A. Blackmun, William J. Brennan, Jr., Warren E. Burger (writing for the Court), Thurgood Marshall, Sandra Day O'Connor, Lewis F. Powell, Jr., John Paul Stevens

Justices Dissenting
William H. Rehnquist, Byron R. White

Place
Washington, D.C.

Date of Decision
23 June 1983

Decision
The legislative veto provision found in the Immigration and Nationality Act, which permitted either branch of Congress to veto a deportation suspension authorized by the attorney general, was unconstitutional.

Significance
The typical one-house legislative veto is unconstitutional because it violates both the president's veto power and the bicameral structure of Congress.

Jagdish Rai Chadha was an East Indian native who, in 1966, was admitted into the United States on a nonimmigrant student visa. Although his visa expired in 1972, he remained in the United States. In 1974, he was ordered by the Director of the Immigration and Naturalization Service to appear in court and show cause why he should not be deported out of the United States. Pursuant to the Immigration and Nationality Act, a deportation hearing was held to determine if Chadha should be forced to leave the country. During the hearing, Chadha admitted that he overstayed his visa, but requested that his deportation be suspended. Section 244(a)(1) of the Immigration and Nationality Act permitted the attorney general, at his discretion, to order such a suspension. The suspension was ordered because, among other things, "it would be difficult if not impossible for Chadha to return to Kenya or Great Britain due to his East Indian derivation." As mandated by the Immigration and Nationality Act, Congress was given notice of the suspension. The suspension remained in effect for a year and a half, but in December of 1975, the House of Representatives, acting under the permitted authority of the Immigration and Nationality Act Section 244(c)(2), vetoed the suspension and reopened the case. Although Chadha objected to the reopening of the case, claiming section 244(c)(2) was unconstitutional, the immigration judge determined that it had no authority to rule on Chadha's objection and ordered his deportation. Chadha appealed the deportation determination to the Board of Immigration Appeals, but it affirmed the lower court ruling.

Under Section 106(a) of the act, Chadha filed a petition with the U.S. Court of Appeals to review his deportation. The Immigration and Naturalization Service joined Chadha in arguing that the veto provision, allowed by section 244(c) of the act, was unconstitutional. The court of appeals agreed that the legislative veto provision of the Immigration and Nationality Act was an unconstitutional violation of the separation of powers doctrine. The court ruled that the House, which represents the legislative branch of government, was taking the veto power out of the hands of the president, who represents the executive branch. The act permitting one house of the legislative branch to veto the decision of the attorney general consequently allowed the legislature to retain an executive function. Circuit Court Judge Kennedy then directed the attorney general to stop any actions in furtherance of Chadha's deportation based on the House of Representatives resolution.

The Immigration and Naturalization Service appealed the decision to the Supreme Court, through a petition for a writ for *certiorari*. *Certiorari* was granted and the case was argued before the Supreme Court on 22 February 1982 and reargued on 7 October 1982. In a 7-2 decision, the Supreme Court held the legislative veto to be unconstitutional. However, unlike the lower court, the Supreme Court did not base its reasoning on the separation of powers doctrine, but rather on bicameralism and the Presentment Clause. Thus, although the Supreme Court affirmed the lower courts ruling, the rationale behind the reaffirmation was entirely different. Further, the Court ruled that Section 244(c)(2) was severable from the remainder of the act and the act remained a valid law. In other words, the Court did not deem the entire act to violate the Constitution, but rather, the legislative veto could be struck down without tampering with the validity of the rest of the act.

The key decision of the Supreme Court was the determination of whether the legislative veto exercised by the House of Representatives constituted an act of legislative power. If it was not an act of legislative power, then the Court might have used the same rationale of the lower court, specifically the violation of the separation of powers. However, the Court ruled that the legislative veto before them constituted legislative power. To determine if an act is an exercise of such power, the court must consider whether the act had the "purpose and effect of altering the legal rights, duties and relations of persons . . . outside the legislative branch." Since the legislative veto overruled the attorney general's determination not to deport Chadha, it affected the duties of an individual outside the legislative branch. Thus, the veto was a legislative power. Consequently, the Court ruled that the legislative veto was an act of legislative power and could, therefore, not use the rationale that it was a violation of the separation of powers, as the lower court did. However, congressional acts which have the purpose and effect of legislative power are acts which require bicamerality and presentment.

Article I, Sections 1 and 7 of the United States Constitution require both houses to pass a bill before it becomes a law. In the Immigration and Nationality Act, either house can veto the attorney general's suspension of deportation. The single house veto provision clearly violated the bicameral requirement of the Constitution.

Furthermore, the Court found that the act's legislative veto violated the Presentment Clause of the U.S. Constitution. Article I, Section 7, Clause 2 of the Constitution states that the Presentment Clause is found in

the United States Constitution, Article I, Section 7, Clause 3. It states that, in order for a bill to become a law, the bill must be presented to the president of the United States and be either signed or vetoed, with the acknowledgement that Congress can override a veto. If the president signs the bill or Congress overrides the presidential veto, then it becomes a law. In the case before the courts, one house vetoed Chadha's deportation suspension and ordered him deported. The congressional decision was never presented to the president and since the Court determined the veto to be a legislative power, the Constitution demands such a presentment. Therefore, the Court ruled that this type of legislative veto was unconstitutional because it violated bicameralism and presentment.

The framers of the Constitution developed this finely tuned and exhaustive procedure in order to ensure that laws were well thought out and legislative power only exercised after an "opportunity for full study and debate in seperate settings." Furthermore, the Court noted that the one-house veto may be a faster way of achieving authority over aliens.

> The veto authorized by Section 244(c)(2) doubtless has been, in many respects, a convenient shortcut; the "sharing" with the Executive by Congress of its authority over aliens in this manner is, on its face, an appealing compromise. In purely practical terms, it is obviously easier for action to be taken by one House without submission to the president; but it is crystal clear from the records of the Convention, contemporaneous writings and debates, that the Framers ranked other values higher than efficiency.

Thus, the Court ruled that efficiency is not a reason for bypassing the procedures outlined in the Constitution. Furthermore, where the framers intended one House to bypass the procedures of bicameralism and presentment, they specifically and narrowly defined those exceptions. Areas where one House can act outside the scope of presentment and bicameralism include: Article I, Section 2, Clause 6, allowing the House of Representatives alone the power to initiate impeachment; Article II, Section 2, Clause 2, allowing the Senate alone the power to approve or disapprove presidential appointments; and Article II, Section 2, Clause 2, granting the Senate the power to ratify treaties. The Court noted that nowhere does the legislative veto found in the act fit into any exceptions to the normal procedures. Thus, the veto was unconstitutional and Chadha was allowed to have his deportation suspended.

The decision in this case showed that the only way Congress could reverse the attorney general's decision on suspending deportation was to pass a law under the normal rules of bicameralism and presentment. Thus, the Supreme Court protected both Chadha's and the attorney general's constitutional rights. Additionally, the decision protected the framers' intentions, written almost one hundred years earlier.

Related Cases
Myers v. United States, 272 U.S. 52 (1926).
The Pocket Veto Case, 279 U.S. 655 (1929).
Ashwander v. Tennessee Valley Authority, 297 U.S. 288 (1936).
United States v. Lovett, 328 U.S. 303 (1946).

Bibliography and Further Reading
Auld, L. Patrick. "Justice Byron White and Separation of Powers." *Presidential Studies Quarterly,* spring 1998, p. 337.

Grinberg, Michele "Immigration and Naturalization Service v Chadha: The Legislative Veto Declared Unconstitutional." *West Virginia Law Review,* Vol. 86, 1984, p. 461.

Gunther, Gerald. *Constitutional Law,* 12th ed. New York: Foundation Press, 1991.

Hill, Larry B. "Is American Bureaucracy an Immobilized Gulliver or a Regenerative Phoenix?" *Administration & Society,* November 1995, p. 322.

Hurley, Patricia A. "Weapons of Influence: The Legislative Veto, American Foreign Policy, and the Irony of Reform." *American Political Science Review,* July 1993, p. 490.

Ides, Allan. "The Jurisprudence of Justice Byron White." *Yale Law Journal,* November 1993, p. 419.

Johnson, John W., ed. *Historic U.S. Court Cases, 1690–1990: An Encyclopedia.* New York: Garland Publishing, 1992.

Tribe, Lawrence. *American Constitutional Law.* New York: Foundation Press, 1988.

BOWSHER V. SYNAR

Legal Citation: 478 U.S. 714 (1986)

Appellant
Charles A. Bowsher, Comptroller General of the United States

Appellee
Mike Synar, Member of Congress

Appellant's Claim
That a provision of the Balanced Budget and Emergency Deficit Reduction Program of 1985, giving budget-cutting authority—an executive function—to the comptroller general—a legislative branch employee—did not violate the principle of separation of powers.

Chief Lawyer for Appellant
Lloyd M. Cutler

Chief Lawyer for Appellee
Alan B. Morrison

Justices for the Court
William J. Brennan, Jr., Warren E. Burger (writing for the Court), Thurgood Marshall, Sandra Day O'Connor, Lewis F. Powell, Jr., William H. Rehnquist, John Paul Stevens

Justices Dissenting
Harry A. Blackmun, Byron R. White

Place
Washington, D.C.

Date of Decision
7 July 1986

Decision
By a vote of 7-2, the Supreme Court struck down the contested provision.

Significance
Bowsher v. Synar, with its fine distinctions between the functions of different branches of the government, helped redefine the doctrine of separation of powers for the modern age.

In 1985, Congress passed the Balanced Budget and Emergency Deficit Reduction Act, also known as the Gramm-Rudman-Hollings Act, which set a cap on the amount of deficit spending Congress could undertake between the years 1986 and 1991. Any resulting cuts were to be implemented by the comptroller general, a legislative branch employee who can be removed from the job only by joint resolution of both houses of Congress.

Immediately after the act was signed into law, Representative Mike Synar and 11 other members of Congress filed a complaint in the U.S. District Court for the District of Columbia asking the court to declare the new law unconstitutional. A three-judge panel of the district court struck down the reporting provisions of the law, citing the role of the comptroller general in implementing the cuts as a violation of the constitutionally imposed separation of powers. The comptroller general then appealed this decision directly to the U.S. Supreme Court.

By a vote of 7–2, a majority of the justices agreed with the district court's decision. The act assigned responsibilities to the comptroller general that were executive in nature. But because the comptroller general was subject to removal by Congress, Congress had essentially retained these responsibilities for itself, thus assuming a duty that properly belonged to the executive branch of government.

The Court Refines the Meaning of Separation of Powers

After the Articles of Confederation had created the United States of America in 1777, they were found to be unworkable—in part because they concentrated all federal power in a single governmental body. This prototype Congress was not subject to the checks and balances of either an executive or a judiciary, and the founders feared that it might come to resemble the monarchy that they had so recently fought with for their independence. Consequently, when the Confederation Congress called for a Constitutional Convention to draft a new foundation document, the framers of the Constitution based their plan on a three-party (tripartite) government. While the people had the power to elect representatives (originally only to the

The Balanced Budget and Emergency Deficit Control Act

The Balanced Budget and Emergency Deficit Control Act, signed into law by President Ronald Reagan on 12 December 1985, is better know as the Gramm-Rudman-Hollings Act, so named for its Senate cosponsors Phil Gramm, Warren Rudman, and Ernest "Fritz" Hollings. For years both political parties, but particularly Republicans, had expressed concern over the growing federal budget deficit. The act, whose purpose was to eliminate the deficit, represented a compromise agreement between the two parties.

Accordingly, the act established a "maximum deficit amount" for federal spending. Starting in 1986 and continuing to 1991, the size of that maximum would gradually taper down to zero. If the deficit exceeded its maximum as established for a given year, the act called for across-the-board cuts in spending, half of which would come from defense programs, the other half from non-defense programs. The determination of those budget reductions would be made separately by the Office of Management and Budget (OMB), a unit of the executive branch, and the Congressional Budget Office (CBO), a part of the legislative branch. Each of these agencies would present their findings to the comptroller general, who would make recommendations to the president.

House; state legislatures elected Senators), all legislation passed by Congress could be vetoed by the president. With the development of the doctrine of judicial review, it became clear that the judiciary would have the final authority in determining the constitutionality of legislative and executive branch actions.

Mike Synar. © AP/Wide World Photos.

The separation of powers was never meant to be absolute. As James Madison wrote in No. 47 of *The Federalist Papers* in 1788, although the control of the whole of one branch would not be vested in the same entities which controlled the whole of another branch, the three departments would inevitably share some power. The "blending" that Madison wrote about became more and more pronounced as federal government evolved, but in *Bowsher,* the Court was called upon to redraw boundaries which had become blurred. Writing for the Court, Chief Justice Burger did so:

> Appellants suggest that the duties assigned to the Comptroller in the Act are essentially ministerial and mechanical so that their performance does not constitute "execution of the law" in a meaningful sense. On the contrary, we view these functions as plainly entailing execution of the law in constitutional terms. Interpreting a law enacted by Congress to implement the legislative mandate is the very essence of "execution" of the law . . . Congress of course initially determined the content of the Balanced Budget and Emergency Deficit Control Act; and undoubtedly the content of the Act determines the nature of the executive duty. However . . . once Congress makes its choice in enacting legislation, its participation ends. Congress can thereafter control the execution of its enactment only indirectly—by passing new legislation.

Fortunately, the Gramm-Rudman-Hollings Act contained a fallback provision—one which conformed to the job description outlined in the Court's opinion. In the event that the comptroller general could not carry out his reporting duties under the act, deficit reduction proposals would be submitted to the president by means of a joint resolution of both houses of Congress. Rather than invalidating the statutory provisions giving Congress the power to remove the comptroller general, the Court recommended that Congress merely adhere to the alternative it had provided for itself.

Related Cases

Myers v. United States, 272 U.S. 52 (1926).
Humphrey's Executor v. United States, 295 U.S. 602 (1935).
Wiener v. United States, 357 U.S. 349 (1958).

Bibliography and Further Reading

Divided Democracy: Cooperation and Conflict Between the President and Congress. Washington, DC: CQ Press, 1991.

Ginsberg, Benjamin. *Politics By Other Means: The Declining Importance of Elections in America.* New York: Basic Books, 1990.

The Invention of the Modern Republic. New York: Cambridge University Press, 1994.

Seto, Theodore P. "Drafting a Federal Balanced Budget Amendment That Does What It is Supposed to Do (and No More)." *Yale Law Journal,* March 1997, p. 1449.

Stover, Carl P. "The Old Public Administration is the New Jurispurdence." *Administration & Society,* May 1995, p. 82.

DELLUMS V. BUSH

Legal Citation: 752 F. Supp. 1141 (1990)

Plaintiff
Ronald V. Dellums, et al.

Defendant
George Bush, President of the United States

Plaintiff's Claim
That the president of the United States violated Article I of the U.S. Constitution and the 1973 War Powers Resolution by neither providing Congress with notice nor obtaining a congressional declaration of war before initiating a military offensive against Iraq.

Judge
Harold H. Greene

Place
Washington, D.C.

Date of Decision
13 December 1990

Decision
Denied Dellums' request for an injunction against presidential military action by ruling that the dispute over massive U.S. troop build-up in the Persian Gulf region was not ready for judicial attention.

Significance
The ruling perpetuated the courts' position in avoiding disputes between members of Congress and the president over commitment of U.S. military forces abroad. The district court held that it would not assume Congress' role in resolving political questions involving foreign policy. In a string of undeclared wars through the last half of the twentieth century from Korea to Bosnia, debate raged over the war powers of the president and Congress, and the role, if any, of the courts. Many congressional members contended that only Congress, through the declaration of war, could commit forces. Others insisted that the president, as commander-in-chief, was the logical initiator, with Congress serving as a check primarily through funding controls.

The framers of the Constitution, not trusting a president to hold sole power to commit the nation to war, divided war powers between the executive and legislative branches. Article II names the president commander-in-chief of the armed forces, giving him power to conduct war. Article I gives Congress the power to "raise and support armies" including funding support, and to "declare war." The Constitution does not address what happens if Congress votes not to declare war, but hostilities proceed. During the early period of the nation, the Court strongly restricted presidential war powers. In *Ex parte Milligan* (1866) the Court limited President Andrew Johnson's efforts to try civilians in military courts. Congress declared war on five occasions: the War of 1812, the Mexican War, the Spanish-American War, World War I, and World War II.

With the beginning of the Cold War in 1946, a common perception took hold that the constitutional separation of war powers established in the eighteenth century no longer applied in a world of imminent nuclear war danger. The president, many argued, needed greater leeway to act quickly and decisively in deterring threats arising from the world-wide spread of Communism. Beginning with the Korean War, the presidents increasingly sent military forces abroad despite lacking clear congressional support. When hearing cases involving foreign policy issues, particularly on war, the Court often relied on the "political question doctrine." As provided in *Baker v. Carr* (1962), the doctrine stated that such issues are often purely political in nature and must be resolved by the two political branches of government.

The emergence of the Vietnam War in the 1960s created particularly antagonistic relations between the president and members of Congress. The federal courts either refused to hear cases involving constitutional challenges to the wars or readily ruled in favor of the president. By the early 1970s, congressional support for the war faded further and funding was greatly diminished. A federal appeals court ruled in *Mitchell v. Laird* (1973) that hostilities in Indochina constituted a war without congressional declaration. It also concluded that President Richard Nixon had no recourse but "to bring the war to an end." In an attempt to avoid future legal conflicts between Congress and the president over war powers, Congress passed the War Powers Resolution late in 1973 over Nixon's veto. The law stated that in the absence of a declaration of war the president must report to Congress within 48 hours of introducing military forces into hostilities and must withdraw the troops within 60 days unless Congress approves an extension or demands faster withdrawal.

The resolution brought little relief, as Congress and presidents continued to battle over a variety of foreign policy issues. Importantly, the U.S. Supreme Court ruled in *Goldwater v. Carter* (1979) that "a dispute between Congress and the president is not ready for judicial review unless and until each branch has taken action asserting its constitutional authority." Justice Powell wrote that the

> Judicial Branch should not decide issues affecting the allocation of power between the President and Congress until the political branches reach a constitutional impasse. Otherwise we would encourage small groups or even individual Members of Congress to seek judicial resolution of issues before the normal political process has the opportunity to resolve the conflict . . . If the Congress chooses not to confront the President, it is not our task to do so.

Therefore, the Court could not rule on that case because Congress had not voted on the matter. In *Lowery v. Reagan* (1987) a federal court held that it could not rule on a dispute between 110 members of Congress and the president concerning use of U.S. military ships in the Persian Gulf to escort Kuwaiti oil tankers during the Iran-Iraq war. The Court considered the dispute a political fight within Congress itself regarding application of the War Powers Resolution.

Iraqi-U.S. Relations

Following a bloody war with Iran in the early 1980s, Iraq turned to the United States for food and trade to revive its devastated economy. Iraqi trade grew significantly throughout the 1980s despite some congressional opposition. Meanwhile disputes increased between Iraq and Kuwait over war debts, oil policies, and, most importantly, location of a shared boundary. On 2 August 1990, Iraq abruptly invaded Kuwait, leading President George Bush to quickly send U.S. military forces to the Persian Gulf region to stabilize the situation. Over 230,000 U.S. troops were in the region by November. Bush then unexpectedly announced a substantial increase in military presence for the purpose of having an "offensive military option" to force Iraqi's retreat from Kuwait. He received support from the United Nations Security Council to use force if necessary. Though Congress had expressed support for presidential actions in the Persian Gulf earlier in the fall, Bush did not ask Congress for a declaration of war prior

to the substantial build-up that was destined to reach 380,000 troops. In reaction, on 19 November, 53 members of the House of Representatives, including congressman Ronald V. Dellums and one U.S. Senator, filed suit in U.S. District Court for the District of Columbia requesting an injunction against further use of military force until Congress could take action.

Dellums argued Bush had violated the War Powers Resolution and also denied Congress their constitutional right under the War Declaration Clause to debate and vote on the imminent military action. In response, the government argued the "harmonization" of war powers between the two branches was a political, not legal, issue for which the courts had no authority to become involved. Given the "political question doctrine" and lack of established standards, the courts possessed little means to decide if the "offensive military attack" was an act of war. The government also argued the threat of military action was not imminent, only a possibility, and that Bush might still ask for a declaration yet. Lastly, the government contended a congressional member could not challenge the constitutionality of an action simply "because he failed to persuade a majority of his colleagues of the wisdom of his views."

A Congressional Duty

U.S. District Judge Harold H. Greene disagreed with most of the government's arguments. As to whether he could judge what constituted a war, Greene in this instance found the military build-up too vast to pose anything less than war requiring "congressional approval . . . if Congress desires to become involved." Disagreeing with the argument that courts could not rule on issues relating to foreign affairs, Greene found that many court decisions touch on foreign affairs to varying degrees. Greene also found Dellums had standing as an "injured" party due to the obvious "imminent danger of hostilities" and his interest in protecting his constitutional right to vote. Greene found Dellums had no other practical means available, such as a "joint resolution counselling the President to refrain from attacking Iraq," due to the lack of time available and little effect a resolution would likely have.

The critical issue identified by Greene was whether or not everything had been done beforehand to make this case ready for a final resolution. In this instance, Greene pointed out, "No one knows the position of the Legislative Branch on the issue of war or peace with Iraq." Therefore, action by the court "would be both premature and presumptuous" to offer a decision, particularly when involving "such sensitive issues as . . . military and foreign affairs." Congress, as a body, had not even indicated it wanted to debate or consider a declaration of war. Consequently, as the U.S. Supreme Court had ruled in *Goldwater*, "there must be an actual conflict between the parties." That is, it must be at least the majority of the legislative branch challenging the president, not just "about ten percent of its membership." In conclusion, Greene ruled the case was not yet ready for judicial action and declined to issue an injunction.

Impact

In a companion case before the same district court, a National Guard officer challenged the president's constitutional authority to assign him to the Persian Gulf without Congress declaring war. A different judge more forcefully applied the political question doctrine in *Ange v. Bush* (1990) by ruling the court had no legal authority to settle the dispute.

Following the two district court decisions, Bush requested a resolution from Congress supporting any action necessary to push Iraq out of Kuwait. Bush insisted he was not constitutionally compelled to seek it. On 12 January 1991, Congress passed such a resolution. Several days later a missile and air assault began against targets in Iraq and on 24 February a massive ground offensive began, chasing Iraqi forces into Iraq. Four days later, Iraq announced it would comply with U.N. demands and Bush declared a cease-fire. However, hostilities and threats persisted with Iraq through the 1990s. Following an assassination attempt on Bush while visiting the Middle East in spring of 1993, President Bill Clinton launched a missile assault on Iraq. Dellums again was an opponent to the presidential action.

Later, Clinton dispatched a U.S. military force to war-torn Bosnia and Hercegovina with eventual deployment of 20,000 troops by 1996. Like Bush in 1990, Clinton did not seek a declaration of war from Congress, relying instead on his constitutional powers as commander-in-chief and authority to conduct foreign relations. Clinton, like Bush, did ask for an expression of congressional support but did not consider it necessary. Congress responded with funding, but did not pass a support resolution.

The decision in *Dellums* continued the trend established shortly after inception of the Cold War, with courts yielding to presidential actions in cases of foreign hostile actions. The presidents have consistently considered the 1973 War Powers Resolution unconstitutional as no president had given Congress the required notice. The courts have similarly declined to require the president to conform. The three branches fell into a behavior pattern. The president determined when and where to wage war, Congress approved such decisions through resolutions and funding bills, and the judicial branch generally stayed out of war powers disputes.

The constitutional delegation of war powers has long been debated. Some, like Dellums, insisted that the War Declaration Clause gave exclusive authority to Congress to commit troops to foreign soil. Others believed that war declaration was more to satisfy international law standards and enact wartime measures on the home front. Congress could most effectively stop hostilities by simply withholding funds, or even impeaching the president. Some believed that the framers of the Constitution intended to guard against having war decisions made by a single person who well might gain personally from engaging in war. Presidents Nixon, Reagan, Bush, and Clinton were accused of using foreign wars to gain political popularity.

History has shown that cooperation between the branches is necessary to wage a successful war. The Constitution permits sufficient flexibility in the decision-making process to allow for many different ways to fight a war.

Related Cases

Mitchell v. Laird, 488 F.2d 611 (1973).
Goldwater v. Carter, 444 U.S. 996 (1979).
Lowry v. Reagan, 676 F. Supp. 333 (1987).
Ange v. Bush, 752 F. Supp. 510 (1990).

Bibliography and Further Reading

"Anguished, Senators Vote to Support Bosnia Mission; Clinton Off to Paris Signing." *New York Times,* December 14, 1995.

Sweet, Barry N. "Legal Challenges to Presidential Policies on the Use of Military Force." *Policy Studies Journal,* spring 1996, p. 27.

Treanor, William M. "Fame, the Founding, and the Power to Declare War." *Cornell Law Review,* Vol. 82, 1997, pp. 695-772.

Whicker, Marcia Lynn, James P. Pfiffner, and Raymond A. Moore, eds. *The Presidency and the Persian Gulf War.* Westport, CN: Praeger Publishers, 1993.

NIXON V. UNITED STATES

Legal Citation: 506 U.S. 224 (1993)

Petitioner
Walter Nixon, U.S. District Judge

Respondent
United States, et al.

Petitioner's Claim
That Senate Rule XI, which allowed a Senate committee to hear evidence against an impeached official and present a report to the full Senate, violated the Constitution's Impeachment Trial Clause.

Chief Lawyer for Petitioner
David Overlock Stewart

Chief Lawyer for Respondent
Kenneth Starr, U.S. Solicitor General

Justices for the Court
Harry A. Blackmun, Anthony M. Kennedy, Sandra Day O'Connor, William H. Rehnquist (writing for the Court), Antonin Scalia, David H. Souter, John Paul Stevens, Clarence Thomas, Byron R. White

Justices Dissenting
None

Place
Washington, D.C.

Date of Decision
13 January 1993

Decision
That Nixon's claim regarding Senate Rule XI was nonjusticiable—that is, it was outside the Court's control, since the Constitution provided that the "Senate shall have sole Power to try any impeachments."

Significance
Nixon v. United States was one of those rare cases in which the Court's decision was not to decide. In calling upon the Court to overrule the Senate in an area of authority granted to that body by the Constitution, the petitioner was asking the Court to do something forbidden to it. In this sense the ruling was in the spirit of *Marbury v. Madison* (1803), the Court's first significant decision, in which it refused to order that an appointed judge be allowed to take his office because to do so would be to overstep its powers.

Another Nixon, a Different Impeachment

Usually when the name "Nixon" is used in the context of impeachment, people think of President Richard M. Nixon, against whom the House of Representatives initiated impeachment proceedings for his role in the coverup of the Watergate scandal. President Nixon was never impeached, however, because he chose to resign his office. The Nixon in *Nixon v. United States* was Walter Nixon, Chief Judge of the U.S. District Court of the Southern District of Mississippi. Following reports that Nixon had accepted a bribe from a businessman in exchange for intervening on behalf of the businessman's son, who was under by prosecution by a local district attorney, a grand jury conducted an investigation of his activities. He was convicted on two counts of making false statements before a grand jury, and sentenced to prison. Unlike his namesake, Nixon never resigned, and therefore he continued to collect his judicial salary while in prison.

On 10 May 1989, the House of Representatives adopted three articles of impeachment against Nixon for high crimes and misdemeanors. The first two of these charged him with giving false testimony before the grand jury, the third with bringing disrepute on the federal judiciary. The House duly presented the articles to the Senate, which voted to invoke its own impeachment rule. Under Senate Rule XI, a presiding officer appoints a committee of senators to "receive evidence and take testimony;" upon appointment, the committee held four days of hearings during which ten witnesses, including Nixon himself, testified. The committee then presented to the full Senate a complete transcript of its proceedings, along with a report summarizing the evidence it had gathered. Nixon, along with the House impeachment manager, presented a brief to the Senate, and together the two sides argued on the Senate floor for the full three hours allotted for that purpose. Nixon gave a personal appeal, then he, as well as the House impeachment manager, answered questions from senators. By a vote greater than the two-thirds majority required, the Senate elected to convict Nixon on the first two articles. The presiding officer then entered a judgment ordering the impeached judge to step down from his office.

Nixon filed suit in district court, seeking a declaratory judgment and the reinstatement of his salary on the grounds that Senate Rule XI violated Article I, section 3, clause 6 of the Constitution. The latter grants the Senate authority to "try"—the word would become significant—all impeachments, and Nixon held that because the evidentiary hearings did not take place before the full Senate, the impeachment proceedings were not a trial *per se*. The district court, however, held that his claim was nonjusticiable: because it involved the power expressly given to the Senate to "try any impeachments," it was out of the court's hands. When Nixon took the case to the Supreme Court, the Washington Legal Foundation filed an *amici curiae* brief urging affirmance, and the advocacy group Public Citizen filed one urging reversal. The chief lawyer for the United States was Solicitor General Kenneth Starr, whose name would soon become a household word when he was appointed independent counsel in investigations involving President Bill Clinton.

Simple Words: "Try" and "Sole"

The Supreme Court voted to affirm. Chief Justice Rehnquist, writing for a unanimous Court, cited the Court's statement in *Baker v. Carr* (1962) that a controversy was nonjusticiable in any situation where there was "a textually demonstrated constitutional commitment of the issue to a coordinate political department; or a lack of judicially discoverable and manageable standards for resolving it . . ." This meant that if the Constitution had already given another department, in this case the Senate, the power to decide a case, or if the Court lacked any power to make a ruling, then a case was nonjusti-

ciable. These two ideas could not be entirely separated, of course, as the chief justice pointed out: if there were no "judicially . . . manageable standards" for deciding a question, that usually indicated that it was already committed by the Constitution to another "political department."

The Impeachment Trial Clause in Article I, section 3 of the Constitution embodied in its language a "textual commitment" of impeachment proceedings to the Senate, Rehnquist held. The Court rejected Nixon's claim that the word "try" referred to a "judicial-style trial by the full Senate:" the word was not sufficiently precise, either as it was understood at the time the Constitution was written or in the present day, to make such a determination. What could be determined, however, was that the clause went on to provide "three very specific requirements" for impeachment proceedings: Senators had to be under oath, convictions had to be by a vote of two-thirds or greater, and in a case where the president himself was under trial, the chief justice would preside. As for the word "sole" in the provision "the Senate shall have the sole Power to try all Impeachments," this too had a common-sense meaning—"that this authority is reposed in the Senate alone." Nixon had tried to construe "sole" to mean that the full Senate had to conduct the entire impeachment, including the testimony and evidence-gathering; this reading, however, would "impose on the Senate additional procedural requirements that would be inconsistent with the three express limitations that the Clause sets out." If there was any further doubt as to whether the judicial branch had power to intervene in these proceedings, a review of the Constitutional Con-

U.S. District Judge Walter Nixon (left) listens to his attorney, David Stewart, during an impeachment hearing before a House judiciary subcommittee, 1988. © AP/Wide World Photos.

vention and the subsequent applications of the clause would dispel it.

Justice Rehnquist offered two other reasons why the case was nonjusticiable. First of all, if the Court had to review Senate impeachment proceedings, this would result in "exposing the country's political life—particularly if the President were impeached—to months, perhaps years, of chaos during judicial review of Senate impeachment proceedings." A second reason was that if the Court did find fault with some aspect of the Senate proceedings, it would face a "difficulty of fashioning judicial relief" other from simply dismissing the judgement of conviction.

Finally, the Court's holding of nonjusticiability was consistent with its ruling in *Powell v. McCormack* (1969). Unlike in *Powell,* if the Court allowed the Senate full authority to interpret the word "try," this would not result in any unintended violation of some other constitutional provision. Courts could review legislative action that "transgresses identifiable textual limits"— the Supreme Court itself does so all the time—but that simple three-letter word "try" did not give the judicial branch power to place limits on the Senate's authority in this instance.

White Questions the Justiciability Ruling

Three justices filed concurring opinions. Justice Stevens wrote that there was no need to haggle over the words "try" and "sole;" all the Court needed to settle the case was to recognize "the central fact that the Framers decided to assign the impeachment power to the Legislative Branch." Justices White and Souter in their concurring opinions, Stevens wrote, were also looking too deeply into the question, raising "improbable hypotheticals."

Justice White, joined by Justice Blackmun, wrote an opinion concurring in the judgment. He considered the case to be justiciable, he said, but since the Senate had fulfilled its constitutional obligation, he was able to concur. To Justice White, "the issue is whether the Constitution has given one of the political branches final responsibility for interpreting the scope and nature of such a power" as that indicated in the Senate's authority to try impeachments. Despite the Court's ruling in *Baker,* White wrote, there were few instances where this "final responsibility" was so clearcut. It was not that the framers of the Constitution specifically wanted to keep the judiciary out of impeachment proceedings; rather, the issue of impeachment "vexed" them. Quoting *The Federalist,* White observed that the framers were more afraid of placing in one branch "the awful discretion, which a court of impeachments must necessarily have." Hence White questioned the Court's understanding of the word "try" as not offering a judicially manageable stan-

dard—that is, as a term that excluded the judiciary from impeachment proceedings.

Justice Souter concurred in the judgment, but he disagreed with the Court's unwillingness to consider the possibility that Senate impeachment proceedings might be justiciable in certain circumstances. Referring to a hypothetical situation raised by Justice White, in which the Senate might choose to impeach an official simply because he was "a bad guy," Souter wrote that in such a situation, "judicial interference might well be appropriate."

Impact

To some, the Court's decision in *Nixon* seemed, quite literally, judicious because it kept the Court out of an area constitutionally mandated to the Senate. Others took issue with the ruling. Rebecca L. Brown in *Supreme Court Review,* for instance, held that officials subjected to impeachment should have the same protection of the judicial branch given to any individual under the Constitution. Thomas D. Amrine in *Harvard Journal of Law & Public Policy* also faulted the decision as a retreat from *Baker* and *Powell.* Those two cases had seemed to indicate a willingness on the Court's part to offer judicial review of impeachments. In Amrine's view, the present ruling suggested that in the future the Court might decline to put limits on the powers of other branches.

Related Cases

Baker v. Carr, 369 U.S. 186 (1962).
Powell v. McCormack, 395 U.S. 486 (1969).
Associated General Contractors v. City of Jacksonville, 508 U.S. 656 (1993).
Reno v. Catholic Social Services, 509 U.S. 43 (1993).

Bibliography and Further Reading

Amrine, Thomas D. "Judicial Review of Impeachment Proceedings." *Harvard Journal of Law and Public Policy,* autumn 1993, pp. 809–820.

Biskupic, Joan, and Elder Witt. *Congressional Quarterly's Guide to the U.S. Supreme Court,* 3rd ed. Washington, DC: Congressional Quarterly, Inc., 1996.

Brown, Rebecca. "When Political Questions Affect Individual Rights: The Other Nixon v. United States." *Supreme Court Review,* 1993, pp. 125–155.

Epstein, Lee, and Thomas G. Walker. *Constitutional Law for a Changing America: Institutional Powers and Constraints,* 3rd ed. Washington DC: Congressional Quarterly, 1998.

Hall, Kermit L., ed. *The Oxford Companion to the Supreme Court of the United States.* New York: Oxford University Press, 1992.

"Justiciability." *Harvard Law Review,* November 1993, pp. 293–312.

Pious, Richard M. "The Constitutional and Popular Law of Presidential Impeachment." *Presidential Studies Quarterly,* fall 1998, p. 806.

Tushnet, Mark V. "Policy Distortion and Democratic Debilitation." *Michigan Law Review,* November 1995, p. 245.

Witt, Elder. *Congressional Quarterly's Guide to the Supreme Court,* 2nd ed. Washington, DC: Congressional Quarterly Inc., 1990.

CLINTON V. JONES

Legal Citation: 520 U.S. 681 (1997)

Petitioner
William Jefferson Clinton, President of the United States

Respondent
Paula Corbin Jones

Petitioner's Claim
That the president of the United States is immune from a lawsuit challenging his actions prior to his taking office during the term of his presidency.

Chief Lawyer for Petitioner
Robert S. Bennett

Chief Lawyer for Respondent
Gilbert K. Davis

Justices for the Court
Stephen Breyer, Ruth Bader Ginsburg, Anthony M. Kennedy, Sandra Day O'Connor, William H. Rehnquist, Antonin Scalia, David H. Souter, John Paul Stevens (writing for the Court), Clarence Thomas

Justices Dissenting
None

Place
Washington, D.C.

Date of Decision
27 May 1997

Decision
That the president does not enjoy immunity from a civil lawsuit for conduct not related to his official acts.

Significance
The Court's decision reemphasizes that although the president may not be sued for acts relating to his official duties, the president is subject to the same laws regulating purely private conduct to which the general population is subject.

Bill Clinton was elected president of the United States in 1992, and was re-elected in 1996. In May of 1994, Paula Corbin Jones, a former employee of the state of Arkansas, filed a civil lawsuit against Clinton in the U.S. District Court for the Eastern District of Arkansas. Jones claimed that in 1991, while Clinton was still governor of Arkansas, Clinton made unwanted sexual advances toward her and that when she rejected these advances, she was retaliated against by her superiors at work. Clinton immediately filed a motion in the district court seeking to dismiss the lawsuit on the basis of presidential immunity. The dismissal would allow Jones to refile the lawsuit after President Clinton left office. The district court denied the motion to dismiss, but ruled that any trial should be postponed until after Clinton's presidency. Both parties appealed the decision of the district court to the U.S. Court of Appeals for the Eighth Circuit. The court of appeals agreed with the district court that Clinton did not have immunity from the lawsuit, but disagreed that the trial should be postponed until after Clinton's term was over. President Clinton then appealed the decision to the U.S. Supreme Court.

Court Rejects Immunity Claim

On appeal, President Clinton argued that the Constitution provides the president with a temporary immunity, during his term of office, from a civil lawsuit concerning events that occurred before he took office. President Clinton first argued that other Supreme Court cases granting immunity to executive officials applied to his case. In particular, President Clinton relied on the Supreme Court's earlier decision in *Nixon v. Fitzgerald*. In *Fitzgerald*, the Court held that a president is entitled to absolute immunity from any lawsuit seeking monetary damages which challenge his official acts. In other words, the president cannot be sued for conduct which relates to his duties as the president. However, the Court rejected President Clinton's argument that the *Fitzgerald* case provided immunity for actions not related to the president's official duties. The Court reasoned that *Fitzgerald* emphasized that presidential immunity was based on the functions of the presidency, and thus the *Fitzgerald* decision was inapplica-

Should Civil Suits against the President Be Stalled Until He Is Out of Office?

The administration of President Bill Clinton, with its many attendant scandals, raised a number of issues concerning the presidency, ethics, and the law. Among these issues was the question, "Should civil suits against the president be stalled until he is out of office?" Given Clinton's enormous popularity, it is likely that the majority of Americans would have said "yes."

But as various Supreme Court justices have observed in different situations, America's is a government "of laws, not of men." Should Bill Clinton be exempt from the law because he is popular, or because he is president? Should a president be subject to civil suits? Many

Americans considered Jones's suit something less than a grave matter.

To look specifically at Clinton, Jones, or the suit, however, is to miss the point. In answering the question regarding presidents and civil suits, Americans should evaluate it without regard to personalities. Then they would be left with two issues: on the one hand, there was the fact that the president should not be above the law; on the other hand, responding to personal lawsuits brought against him would distract him from the important business of being president.

ble to a lawsuit challenging conduct which occurred before Clinton become president.

President Clinton also argued that he could not be subject to suit during the term of his presidency based on the doctrine of separation of powers. The separation of powers doctrine deals with the allocation of power among the three branches of government: executive, legislative, and judicial. President Clinton argued that separation of powers principles were implicated because subjecting him to a lawsuit during his presidency would impose burdens on the performance of his official duties. The Court noted that in other contexts, the judicial branch has reviewed the official actions of the president and other executive officials. Also, various presidents have been subpoenaed by federal courts or have provided videotaped testimony in court proceedings. The Court then reasoned:

> If the Judiciary may severely burden the Executive Branch by reviewing the legality of the President's official conduct, and if it may direct appropriate process to the President himself, it must follow that the federal courts have the power to determine the legality of his unofficial conduct. The burden on the President's time and energy that is a mere by-product of such review surely cannot be considered as onerous as the direct burden imposed by judicial review and the occasional invalidation of his official actions. We therefore hold that the doctrine of separation of powers does not require federal courts to stay all private actions against the President until he leaves office.

The Supreme Court's decision was an important reminder of the principle that dates back to the adoption of the Magna Carta in the thirteenth century: in a democratic nation no person, including the president, is above the law. Thus, under the Supreme Court's deci-

sion, a sitting president may not avoid a civil lawsuit merely because he or she happens to be president. Rather, the president will enjoy immunity only where the actions relate to the official acts and duties of the presidency.

Related Cases
Nixon v. Fitzgerald, 457 U.S. 731 (1982).

Bibliography and Further Reading
Berger, Raoul. *Executive Privilege: A Constitutional Myth.* Cambridge: Harvard University Press, 1974.

"Bill, Paula, Ken & You." *The Nation,* March 16, 1998, p. 6.

Corwin, Edward S. *Presidential Power and the Constitution: Essays,* edited by Richard Loss. Ithaca: Cornell University Press, 1976.

Grossman, Joel B., and David A. Yalof. "The 'Public' Versus the 'Private' President." *Presidential Studies Quarterly,* fall 1998, p. 821.

Kelly, Michael. "Class." *The New Republic,* June 16, 1997, p. 6.

Klaidman, Daniel, and Stuart Taylor, Jr. "A Troubling Legal Legacy." *Newsweek,* August 24, 1998, p. 25.

Lane, Charles. "Unprotected." *The New Republic,* August 10, 1998, p. 6.

Mitchell, John B. "Another Chat with the Lady in the Grocery Line: *Clinton v. Jones.*" *Constitutional Commentary,* fall 1998, p. 441.

Rosen, Jeffrey. "One Bite at the Apple: Why Paula Jones Has No Case." *The New Republic,* February 3, 1997, p. 14.

————". Exposed: Paula Jones and the Enfeebled Presidency." *The New Republic,* June 16, 1997, p. 14.

Rotunda, Ronald D., and John E. Nowak. *Treatise on Constitutional Law: Substance and Procedure,* 2nd ed. 4 vols. St. Paul: West Publishing Co., 1992.

"Sex, Lies, and Audiotape." *The New Republic,* February 9, 1998, p. 7.

Tribe, Laurence H. *American Constitutional Law,* 2nd ed. Mineola, NY: Foundation Press, Inc., 1988.

Troy, Daniel E. "The Indictment Option." *National Review,* April 6, 1998, p. 26.

RAINES V. BYRD

Legal Citation: 521 U.S. 811 (1997)

Appellant
Frederick D. Raines, Director, U.S. Office of Management and Budget, et al.

Appellee
Senator Robert Byrd, et al.

Appellant's Claim
That appellees lacked standing to challenge the recently passed Line Item Veto Act.

Chief Lawyer for Appellant
Walter E. Dellinger, U.S. Solicitor General

Chief Lawyer for Appellee
Alan Morrison

Justices for the Court
Ruth Bader Ginsburg, Anthony M. Kennedy, Sandra Day O'Connor, William H. Rehnquist (writing for the Court), Antonin Scalia, David H. Souter, Clarence Thomas

Justices Dissenting
Stephen Breyer, John Paul Stevens

Place
Washington, D.C.

Date of Decision
26 June 1997

Decision
That the appellees lacked standing for their case under Article III, section II, of the Constitution, which authorizes the judicial branch to review only "cases" and "controversies." Since appellees could not "allege a personal injury that is particularized, concrete, and otherwise judicially cognizable," the case had to be vacated.

Significance
By the time *Raines v. Byrd* came before the Supreme Court, President Bill Clinton had used the line item veto to strike $2 billion from the annual budget. Many have hoped that the Line Item Veto would prove an effective weapon against "pork barrel spending," appropriations of money by legislators with the purpose of benefiting their districts, states, or favorite interest groups. The actual presidential authority granted by the act, however, was not as large as it seemed on first glance. By not ruling on the constitutionality of the act itself, the Court left that question open for another case.

Political Ironies

The line-item veto case involved political ironies. Usually Republicans and conservatives have been associated with spending cuts in general, and line-item veto proposals in particular, and indeed a Republican, Senator Dan Coats of Indiana, authored the legislation that would become the Line Item Veto Act. Yet President Bill Clinton, as a member of the executive branch if not as a Democrat, favored the veto as well. Thus the legal action in *Raines v. Byrd* pitted five Democrats— Senators Robert Byrd, Carl Levin, and Daniel Patrick Moynihan, and Representatives David Skaggs and Henry Waxman—along with liberal Republican Mark Hatfield, against a Democratic administration. President Clinton, in spite of differences with Republicans in the legislative branch, found that he had their support to veto spending proposals emanating from either House of (the Republican-dominated) Congress.

When the Republicans, for the first time in 40 years, regained a majority in both Houses during the 1994 elections, they did so with a promise of sweeping reforms embodied in a set of proposals called the "Contract with America." Of these, the line-item veto was the only one that enjoyed the president's support. On 27 March 1996, the Senate approved the Line Item Veto Bill by a 69-31 vote, in which four of the appellee Senators in *Raines* voted "nay". The following day, the House voted on its own Line Item Bill, which it passed by a vote of 232-177—again without the support of the two representatives who later became involved in the *Raines* legal action. On 29 March, the six appellees filed a complaint with the District Court for the District of Columbia, naming in their suit the secretary of the treasury and the director of the Office of Management and Budget (OMB).

A later *USA Today* article suggested why those two officers, particularly the OMB director, would be named in the suit: his staff had the job of scouring legislation to find suspected pork-barrel projects for the president's veto. "We have numbers of projects in bills where the only thing we know about them is the title," OMB Director Franklin Raines told the paper. "There's nothing in the record, nothing in the report, nothing in the bill that tells you what it is." The reason for such mystery is that if the purpose of a measure is unknown, it is not likely to be challenged—at least, such was the case until the passage of the Line Item Veto Act. "Some powerful lawmakers bury their projects deep in the legislation in hopes of avoiding scrutiny," Susan Page reported; therefore, "budget officials end up calling staffers on congressional subcommittees for clues or tracking down aides to the members of Congress suspected of being the likely sponsors. The last weapon is the threat that a mystery item may be vetoed if it can't be explained."

The legislators who brought the legal action known as *Raines v. Byrd*—designated as "appellees" by the Supreme Court because they were by the time the case reached the nation's highest bench—charged that the veto "unconstitutionally expands the President's power." They further charged that the act "violates the requirements of bicameral passage [i.e., by both houses] . . . by granting to the President, acting alone, the authority to 'cancel' and thus repeal provisions of federal law." The act provided that members of Congress "or any individual adversely affected by [this act] may bring an action, in the U.S. District Court for the District of Columbia, for declaratory judgment and injunctive relief on the ground that any provision of this part violates the Constitution." Therefore, the legislators did just that. In their suit, they held that the act "directly and concretely" affected them in three ways: by altering "the legal and practical effect of all votes they may cast on bills containing such separately vetoable items"; by taking from them their "constitutional role in the repeal of legislation"; and by changing the constitutionally fixed balance of power between the executive and legislative branches.

The OMB Director and other appellants moved to have the case dismissed, holding that the appellees lacked standing to sue, and further charging that their case was not "ripe" because sufficient time had not passed since the act's introduction into law. On 10 April 1997, the district court denied this motion, ruling that the legislators had standing, and that their claim was ripe. The court further granted the appellees' summary judgment motion, holding that the act diluted their voting power as members of the legislative branch under Article I of the Constitution, and further holding that the case had standing under Article III.

Embodied in the act was a direct appeal to the Supreme Court to adjudicate any suit challenging its constitutionality. Therefore on 18 April, eight days after the district court's ruling, the appellants filed a statement with the High Court asking it to note probable jurisdiction. On 21 April, the appellees filed a memorandum in response, agreeing with the appellants' jurisdiction request. The Court duly noted probable jurisdiction, and in effect "moved the case to the top of the pile" on the basis of the constitutional questions involved.

Not a "Case" or "Controversy"

By a 7-2 majority, the Court ruled that the appellees lacked standing to sue. Chief Justice Rehnquist, who delivered the Court's opinion, noted that Article III, section 2 of the Constitution enumerates the types of "cases and controversies" which federal courts have power to decide. These include disagreements between citizens, a citizen and a state, a state and the federal government, and so on. In order to be judged as "having standing," the appellees would have to show, in the chief justice's words, "a personal injury that is particularized, concrete, and otherwise judicially cognizable." In other words, a person bringing a suit has to point to a specific law that the accused has violated, and to show how that action has affected the plaintiff. The Court had always been strict on issues of judicial standing, the chief justice noted, particularly in instances where the dispute involved two branches of the federal government.

As for the question of legislative standing—that is, the standing of appellees to sue as members of Congress—this was a question on which "This Court has never had occasion to rule . . ." The appellees had tried to cite *Powell v. McCormack* (1969), which involved the exclusion of Representative Adam Clayton Powell from his congressional seat due to allegations of financial wrongdoing, but the Court found that *Powell* was no guide. The appellees could not claim, as Powell had, that they had been "singled out for specially unfavorable treatment as opposed to other members of their respective bodies." Rather, they were claiming that the act caused "a type of institutional injury which damages all Members of Congress equally." Furthermore, that injury was really a loss of political power in their offices, as opposed to the loss of something to which they were personally entitled.

Nor did the appellees find much help in *Coleman v. Miller* (1939), the only case in which the Court had upheld standing for legislators who claimed an institutional injury—i.e., something that affected an entire legislative body. In that instance, a state legislature had been locked in a tie vote on ratification of an amendment to the federal Constitution, and the state's lieutenant governor had broken the tie by casting the deciding vote. The legislators in *Coleman* had "a plain, direct and adequate interest in maintaining the effectiveness of their votes," whereas the appellees in the present case could not point to a single bill that had been defeated because of the Line Item Veto. They had been given a chance to vote against the act when it was under debate, had done so—and had lost, fair and square. "To uphold standing here would require a drastic extension of *Coleman*," the chief justice wrote, ". . . for there is a vast difference between the level of vote nullification at issue in *Coleman* and the abstract dilution of institutional power appellees allege." The legislators in *Coleman* could point to a specific measure that had failed because of the lieutenant governor's intervention; those in the present case, however, could only make vague references to possible violations of constitutional principle.

Throughout the nation's history, there had been numerous situations in which one member or another of the executive or legislative branches had cause to challenge a measure on the basis of "claimed injury to official authority or power." The Court cited, for instance, the Tenure of Office Act of 1867, The Pocket Veto case of 1929, and the Federal Election Campaign Act struck down in *Buckley v. Valeo* (1976). Again and again, there had been such instances, in which the parties involved had at least as much standing as those in the present case, but they had not initiated legal action. This was a fortunate thing, because the Constitution provided a limited role for courts, which the framers never intended as arenas in which to decide every possible disagreement.

The proper place to decide the present disagreement, the Court concluded, was where it had begun: in Congress. Whereas the appellees had not been authorized by their respective Houses to take the present legal action—"indeed, both Houses actively oppose their suit"—they did have voting power as members of the legislative branch. As such, they possessed the potential to either repeal the act or at least to exempt bills from its reach (as they could do simply by adding such a proviso in the bill itself, as the *Post* had observed.) Finally, the Court's ruling did not prevent someone with genuine standing to challenge the act—a statement which paved the way for a later line-item veto challenge.

Counter-Arguments in the Constitution and Coleman

Justice Souter, joined by Justice Ginsburg, concurred in the judgment. He took issue merely with the Court's ruling that the injury claimed was not appropriately "personal" and "concrete" to fulfill Article III requirements. First of all, there were problems with the requirement than an injury was to be deemed "personal" and not official in nature, and Justice Souter held that "the official nature of the harm here does not preclude standing." Second, he did not hold that the injuries claimed were so general that they could be deemed as lacking the sufficient degree of concreteness. Nonetheless, "a suit challenging the constitutionality of this Act brought by a party from outside the Federal government . . . would expose the Judicial Branch to a lesser risk" than would the present one, which required it to judge between two other branches of the federal government. "The virtue of waiting for a private suit," Justice Souter wrote, "is only confirmed by the certainty that another suit can come to us." Again, a member of the Court helped pave the way for a challenge.

Justice Stevens, in a dissenting opinion, held that the Line Item Veto was indeed unconstitutional because it forced members of the legislative branch to vote on "truncated" or abbreviated bills. Furthermore, senators and representatives would have no power to vote against the abbreviated bill "that survives the President's cancellation authority." Under Article I, section 7 of the Constitution, members of the legislative branch are granted the power to vote on "Every bill . . . before it become a law," whereas under the Line Item Veto Act, they would be deprived of such a right. "In my judgment," Justice Stevens wrote, "the deprivation of this right—essential to the legislator's office—constitutes a sufficient injury to provide every Member of Congress with standing to challenge the constitutionality of the statute."

Justice Breyer also dissented, holding that the issue at hand was "a case or controversy." Justice Felix Frankfurter in *Coleman* had held that the courts traditionally "leave intra-parliamentary controversies to parliaments and outside the scrutiny of law courts," but the present case presented different circumstances. (And, Justice Breyer noted, Justice Frankfurter's opinion was a dissenting one.) The present case, Justice Breyer held, was at least as strong as *Coleman,* and he noted that the Constitution "does not draw an absolute line between disputes involving a 'personal' harm and those involving an 'official' harm." Taking further issue with the Court's reading of *Coleman,* Justice Breyer observed that like the legislators in the earlier case, the members of Congress in the present one "will likely vote in the majority for at least some appropriations bills that are then subject to presidential cancellation . . ." Therefore their votes "are threatened with nullification too," and on the basis of *Coleman,* Justice Breyer ruled that the appellees did indeed have standing.

Impact

In the aftermath of *Raines,* responses were drawn on predictable lines. Coats, the act's author, called the ruling "a victory for common sense and fiscal integrity." Moynihan, one of the appellees, suggested that a future case would result in the act being ruled unconstitutional. On 31 October 1997, several months after the decision, Susan Page of *USA Today* assessed its impact in an article entitled "Line-Item Veto Alters Political Landscape." The veto, Page wrote, "has changed the budgetary balance of power, giving the president the final say over small projects that legislators often see as essential to their districts' livelihood or their own political future." The predicted challenge to the act soon came, with *Clinton v. City of New York* (1998). This time the litigants were a diverse group including several New York hospitals and a group of potato-growers' from Idaho, and the case named the president himself. U.S. District Judge Thomas F. Hogan struck down the line-item veto in February of 1998, and the Supreme Court declared the act unconstitutional on 27 April.

Related Cases

The Pocket Veto Case, 279 U.S. 655 (1929).
Coleman v. Miller, 307 U.S. 433 (1939).
Powell v. McCormack, 395 U.S. 486 (1969).
Allen v. Wright, 468 U.S. 737 (1984).
Clinton v. City of New York, 188 S.Ct. 2091 (1998).

Bibliography and Further Reading

Biskupic, Joan. "High Court to Decide Legality of Line-Item Veto." *Washington Post,* February 28, 1998, p. A-2.

Carelli, Richard. "Court Gives Clinton Line Item Veto." *Washington Post,* June 26, 1997.

Dewar, Helen. "Line-Item Veto Case Is Heard by High Court." *Washington Post,* May 28, 1997, p. A-8.

Page, Susan. "Line-Item Veto Alters Political Landscape," *USA Today,* October 31, 1997, p. 6-A.

Reischauer, Robert D. "Line Item Veto: Little Beef and Mostly Bun," *Washington Post,* April 10, 1996, p. A-19.

Tsilas, Vicky. "Lawmakers Lack Standing to Challenge Line-Item Veto Law." *Tax Notes,* June 30, 1997, pp. 1810-11.

CLINTON V. CITY OF NEW YORK

Legal Citation: 118 S.Ct. 2091 (1998)

Appellants
President William J. Clinton and other government officials

Appellees
City of New York, Snake River Potato Growers, Inc., et al.

Appellants' Claim
That the Line Item Veto Act of 1996 delegating increased law making powers to the president by Congress was constitutional.

Chief Lawyer for Appellants
Seth P. Waxman, U.S. Solicitor General

Chief Lawyers for Appellees
Charles Cooper, Louis Cohen

Justices for the Court
Ruth Bader Ginsburg, Anthony M. Kennedy, William H. Rehnquist, David H. Souter, John Paul Stevens (writing for the Court), Clarence Thomas

Justices Dissenting
Stephen Breyer, Sandra Day O'Connor, Antonin Scalia

Place
Washington, D.C.

Date of Decision
25 June 1998

Decision
Ruled in favor of New York and affirmed a lower court decision by finding that the line-item veto law violated constitutional procedures for making laws.

Significance
The decision recognized the limits of Congress in delegating its legislative powers to the president and maintained a traditional separation of power between the two branches of government. The Court asserted that Congress could alter the president's role in determining the final text of a law only by constitutional amendment. No constitutional provisions otherwise exist for presidents to enact, repeal, or amend laws. Having witnessed the application of the veto for 18 months and given the strong Court ruling, support diminished for further efforts at instituting a line-item veto power.

In defining the legislative process for making laws, the framers assigned the president veto power in section 7 of Article 1 of the Constitution, later known as the Presentment Clause. The section reads that a bill passed by Congress "shall, before it becomes a law, be presented to the President of the United States: If he approve he shall sign it, but if not he shall return it." Congress could still pass the law as written over the president's veto with two thirds vote of each house. The veto was seen as a barrier against hastily enacting "improper" laws.

Since the 1870s, presidents have often sought line a item veto option, vetoing portions of bills while the remainder became law. In the early 1970s, President Richard M. Nixon liberally applied an impounded strategy, a constitutionally questionable process of not spending funds Congress had obtained. In reaction, Congress passed the Budget and Impoundment Control Act of 1974 requiring congressional approval of impoundment "cuts."

The Line Item Veto

The line-item veto issue came to the political forefront during the 1980s as the national deficit dramatically rose. President Ronald Reagan's administration contended the problem was not due to his tax cuts or defense buildup, but rather Congress' large domestic spending programs under Democratic leadership. The Republicans identified the line-item veto as a key issue in their 1994 "Contract With America" during the 1994 national elections. Upon victoriously assuming control of Congress after the elections, the Republicans were suddenly faced with enacting the law while having a Democrat president. As an amendment to the 1974 Impoundment Act, Congress passed the Line Item Veto Act and President Bill Clinton signed it into law in April of 1996. But the Republican leaders delayed its effective date to January of 1997 in hopes they might recapture the presidency in the previous November elections.

The Line Item Veto Act granted the president power to cancel three kinds of provisions signed into law: (1) all discretionary spending not required by law; (2) any new direct spending; and, (3) limited tax benefits. Under the new law, Congress would, as usual, approve tax and funding bills and send them to the president

The Line-Item Veto

For years, American leaders in the executive and legislative branches of government have bandied about the idea of a line-item veto. The president possesses veto power over legislation. The line-item veto would give him even greater power by allowing him to strike certain provisions ("line items") within appropriations bills. Supporters of the line-item veto have suggested that it allows him to "hold the pork"—as in pork-barrel spending, which occurs when a legislator works a costly government project (but one which benefits his or her constituents) into an appropriations bill. Oppo-

nents of the line-item veto have argued that it would upset the traditional balance of power between the branches of government, and would require the enumeration of all budgetary details in appropriations bills. It would also mean that the primary negotiation of a bill would take place not on the legislative floor but at the veto stage, largely removed from the public eye.

Source(s): Bacon, Donald C., et al., eds. *The Encyclopedia of the United States Congress.* New York: Simon & Schuster, 1995.

for his signature. However, after signing the legislation, the president had five days to eliminate specific lines of spending and notify Congress of his deletions. Congress could resurrect the lined out items within 30 days by a single majority vote. Also, any spending deleted had to be applied to reducing the deficit, not for some other purpose. Rather than being an actual veto, in an effort to avoid violating the Constitution, the deletion was more an enhanced recision power, since it occurred after passage of the law.

Some Senate opponents, led by Senator Robert C. Byrd (D-WV), contested the bill's validity. However, the Supreme Court ruled in *Raines v. Byrd* (1997) they lacked legal standing to pursue the claim since they had suffered no actual injury or loss.

In total, Clinton used his new, historic power to veto 82 legislative items with Congress overriding only one, a military construction bill providing $287 million for 38 projects. The line-item vetoes that stood reversed $869 million in spending and tax breaks. Among those items canceled was one affecting New York State and another affecting Idaho potato farmers.

The Social Security Act had authorized the federal government to provide substantial funding to states to help finance indigent medical care. However, Congress passed legislation in 1991 directing that these federal subsidies would be reduced by the amount of certain taxes assessed by the states on health care providers. As a result, in 1994 Congress required New York to return improper excess Medicaid payments to the United States. The state lobbied Congress for relief. In August of 1997, Congress responded by resolving the matter in New York's favor, saving the state some $2.6 billion for the five year period. Six days later, President Bill Clinton sent notices to the Senate and House of Representatives canceling that part of the law claiming it improperly gave preferential treatment to one state.

Another specific spending item also caught Clinton's attention. A company profiting from the sale of prop-

erty is generally subject to a capital gains tax. However, a business could sell to another through a merger or stock transaction without being taxed. Excluded from such tax relief were farmer's cooperatives. The Taxpayer Relief Act of 1997 offered such tax breaks to businesses selling processing plants to farmers cooperatives. Clinton canceled this limited tax benefit as well.

In reaction to the cancellations, two separate lawsuits were filed in U.S. district court against Clinton and other federal officials. The New York case involved New York City, two hospital associations, a hospital, and two unions representing health care employees. The second action involved a farmer's cooperative, Snake River Potato Growers Inc., representing of about 30 potato growers in Idaho, and an individual officer of the cooperative. The court combined the cases and determined that legal standing existed in each.

In February of 1998, the district court found the line-item vetoes unconstitutional. The very nature of the laws after the presidential cancellations was different from that agreed upon by both houses of Congress. Therefore, the court found that Clinton violated Article I of the Constitution when he "vetoed" only parts of the laws. The court concluded the Line Item Veto Act significantly disrupted the carefully designed balance of powers among the three branches of government. Clinton appealed the decision directly to the Supreme Court.

Presentment Clause Violated

None of the parties disputed before the Court that the New York spending item was not an "item of new direct spending" or the other not a "limited tax benefit." Both qualified for potential elimination under the Line Item Veto Act. The issue was clearly the new presidential authority itself. By a 6-3 vote the Court affirmed the district court's decision. Justice Stevens, writing for the majority, wrote that the Presentment Clause provided the president only two choices upon receipt of a bill from Congress, approval or veto.

Senator Daniel Patrick Moynihan of New York speaks during a press conference, 1997. © Photograph by Ed Bailey. AP/Wide World Photos.

Stevens underscored important differences between a president vetoing a bill in its entirety and the Line Item Veto Act. The veto of an entire bill takes place before it becomes law, the partial cancellation occurs afterwards. Stevens found that Clinton essentially amended two acts of Congress by repealing a portion of each. The Constitution contained no provision authorizing the president to amend or repeal statutes. Although Articles I and II of the Constitution both assigned important responsibilities to the president directly related to the lawmaking process, neither provided for piece-meal revision of existing laws.

Consequently, the Line Item Veto Act clearly authorized the president to amend laws for his own policy reasons outside the procedures established in Article I of the Constitution. Stevens was not swayed by Clinton's contention that the president's new authority to cancel new direct spending and tax benefit items was like his traditional authority not to spend appropriated funds. The critical difference was that previous laws allowing presidential spending discretion had very specific congressional guidance. Stevens summarized,

We do not lightly conclude that their action was unauthorized by the Constitution . . . Our

decision rests on the narrow ground that the procedures authorized by the Line Item Veto Act are not authorized by the Constitution. If there is to be a new procedure in which the President will play a different role in determining the final text of what may become a law, such change must come not by legislation but through the amendment procedures set forth in Article V of the Constitution.

Old Power Under New Name?

Justice Breyer, joined in dissent by Justice O'Connor and Justice Scalia, wrote, "In my view the Line Item Veto Act does not violate any specific textual constitutional command, nor does it violate any implicit Separation of Powers principle. Consequently, I believe that the Act is constitutional." Breyer, acknowledging that the functioning of the three branches of government with one another is always evolving, summarized his dissent,

I recognize that the Act before us is novel. In a sense, it skirts a constitutional edge. But that edge has to do with means, not ends. The means chosen do not amount literally to the enactment, repeal, or amendment of a law. Nor, for that matter, do they amount literally to the "line item veto" that the Act's title announces . . . They do not improperly shift the constitutionally foreseen balance of power from Congress to the President. Nor, since they comply with Separation of Powers principles, do they threaten the liberties of individual citizens. They represent an experiment that may, or may not, help representative government work better. The Constitution, in my view, authorizes Congress and the President to try novel methods in this way. Consequently, with respect, I dissent.

Scalia contended that the president's discretion under the Line Item Veto Act was no broader than the discretion traditionally granted the president in his execution of spending laws. Scalia wrote,

The title of the Line Item Veto Act, which was perhaps designed to simplify for public comprehension, or perhaps merely to comply with the terms of a campaign pledge, has succeeded in faking out the Supreme Court. The President's action it authorizes in fact is not a line-item veto . . . and insofar as the substance of that action is concerned, it is no different from what Congress has permitted the President to do since the formation of the Union.

Impact

The Court ruled that a president holds no constitutional power to sign into law a bill different from the one sent to him by Congress. Though some supporters of the line-item veto vowed to pursue its acceptance, many became disillusioned after seeing how ineffective it appeared to be in practice. Sparingly using the new authority, Clinton reduced the 1997 budget less than one-tenth of one percent. Clinton largely sought to minimize conflict with Republican leadership who controlled Congress because of legislation he wished to see passed. The brief experiment demonstrated that effects on the legislative process were more political than fiscal. The president's role to bargain with Congress and influence laws was greatly increased, even changing how Washington lobbyists operated.

Governors of 43 states held line item veto power with few issues raised over their authority. But many asserted, the role of the president was far different than a state governor. Still, proponents claimed such a "veto" power served as a symbolic reminder to legislators to maintain some fiscal responsibility by minimizing expensive pet projects for their constituents back home.

Related Cases

Bryant v. Yellen, 447 U.S. 352 (1980).
Immigration and Naturalization Service v. Chadha, 462 U.S. 919 (1983).
Raines v. Byrd, 521 U.S. 811 (1997).

Bibliography and Further Reading

Fisher, Louis. *Constitutional Conflicts Between Congress and the President.* 4th ed. Lawrence: University Press of Kansas, 1997.

Fisher, Louis. *The Politics of Shared Power: Congress and the Executive.* 4th ed. College Station, TX: Texas A & M University Press, 1998.

Krehbiel, Keith. *Pivotal Politics: A Theory of U.S. Lawmaking.* Chicago: University of Chicago Press, 1998.

Spitzer, Robert J. *The Presidential Veto: Touchstone of the American Presidency.* Albany, NY: State University of New York Press, 1988.

Spitzer, Robert J. "The Item Veto Dispute and the Secular Crisis of the Presidency." *Presidential Studies Quarterly,* fall 1998.

United States House Committee on Rules. *The Use and Application of the Line Item Veto.* Washington, DC: U.S. Government Printing Office, 1997.

FEDERALISM AND STATE POWERS

Definition of Federalism

Federalism may be characterized as a system of government under which power is divided between the national government and various state governments. An important feature of federalism is that the national and state governments are each supreme, or sovereign, within their own sphere of power. However, the national government may enact legislation which directly effects the states' citizens without seeking the states' consent.

Under this dual system of sovereignty, the national government is granted those powers which facilitate the efficient operation of a central authority, as well as compel the respect of other countries. By way of example, it is empowered to regulate commerce between the states, lay and collect taxes, and declare war. Through representation in Congress, the citizens of each state are assured of participation in the national government and are provided with an avenue by which to protect and promote local interests.

History of Federalism in America

During the early years of this nation, many regarded the concept of a strong central government with suspicion and scorn. According to popular political thought, a republican form of government could survive only in a relatively small country. As a result, the Articles of Confederation, the Constitution's predecessor, conferred few powers on the national government. Ratified in 1781, the Articles of Confederation expressly retained the states' "sovereignty, freedom and independence." The states kept all power which was not expressly granted to Congress. Under this scheme, Congress had been deprived of the essential powers to tax and regulate commerce. A financial nightmare arose when the states failed to provide the central government with revenue. Moreover, the Articles of Confederation failed to establish a federal judiciary. Instead, Congress had been authorized to resolve certain types of disputes.

In 1787, a Constitutional Convention was convened for the purpose of remedying the inherent weaknesses under the Articles of Confederation. The delegates debated competing plans: (1) the Virginia Plan, which proposed a strong national government with authority to define its own power, as well as that of the states; and (2) the New Jersey Plan, which favored strong state governments. The New Jersey Plan received little support since it was too similar to the Articles of Confederation.

A heated dispute arose between large and small states over the proper means of determining representation in both chambers of the national legislature. While the large states advocated representation according to population, the small states called for equal representation. They finally settled on a solution known as the Great Compromise, which allowed equal voting power for each state in the Senate and representation by population in the House of Representatives. Many viewed the recognition of state equality as a concession to state sovereignty. In the end, however, the delegates voted in favor of a strengthened central government, with executive, legislative, and judicial branches. Article VI of the Constitution provided that "[t]his constitution, and the laws of the United States which shall be made in pursuance thereof; and all treaties made, or which shall be made under the authority of the United States, shall be the supreme law of the land." Such language would have been unthinkable under the Articles of Confederation, which was so protective of state sovereignty that it referred to the union between the states merely as "a firm league of friendship."

The Constitution was the subject of intense political debate after it was submitted to state conventions for ratification in accordance with Article VII, which required ratification by nine states. Anti-federalists greatly feared that the proposed central government would ultimately obliterate state sovereignty. They also argued that, unlike some state constitutions, the Constitution lacked a bill of rights. In support of the Constitution, Alexander Hamilton, James Madison, and John Jay authored a series of articles known collectively as the *Federalist*. It is regarded as one of the most significant political documents in this country's history because it sets forth explanations as to the various provisions under the Constitution.

Shortly after the Constitution was ratified in 1788, the Bill of Rights (the first ten amendments) was proposed by Congress and ratified in 1791 by three-fourths of the states, as required under Article V. The Bill of Rights placed limitations on the federal government's ability to infringe upon the personal liberties and fundamental rights of the citizenry. For example, the First Amendment prohibited Congress from enacting laws which abridged the freedom of speech, while the Fourth Amendment forbade unreasonable searches and seizures. However, these limitations were not yet applicable to the states. At that time, the states were constitutionally forbidden only from passing bills of attainder, *ex post facto* laws, and laws impairing the obligation of contracts, all of which were specifically mentioned under Article I, in the main body of the Constitution.

During the Civil War, the issue of state sovereignty was crucial inasmuch as the Southern states insisted that, as independent entities, they had the right to secede from the Union. The outcome of the Civil War settled once and for all that the ultimate sovereign power of this country was vested in the national government.

Following the Civil War, the Fourteenth Amendment was added to the Constitution. Section 1 provided that "[a]ll persons born or naturalized in the United States, and subject to the jurisdiction thereof, are citizens of the United States and of the State wherein they reside. No State shall make or enforce any law which shall abridge the privileges or immunities of citizens of the United States; nor shall any State deprive any person of life, liberty, or property without due process of law; nor deny to any person within its jurisdiction the equal protection of the laws." The Fourteenth Amendment clearly rendered state citizenship secondary to national citizenship. Moreover, the Fourteenth Amendment made the Bill of Rights applicable to the states, which meant that the states were legally bound to honor and protect their citizens' federally-conferred rights. During subsequent years, Congress has used its constitutionally-granted powers, especially its authority to regulate interstate commerce, to further encroach upon state autonomy.

Present-Day Relationship Between National Government & States

Congress has certain enumerated powers pursuant to Article I, Section 8 of the Constitution. By way of example, Congress is authorized to coin money, regulate commerce between the states and with Indian tribes and foreign countries, lay and collect taxes, declare war, raise and support armies, and provide and maintain a navy. Other congressional powers include, but are not limited to, establishing a post office, fixing the standard for weights and measures, establishing a uniform rule for naturalization, and creating inferior federal courts. (Article III, Section 1 established only the Supreme Court). Furthermore, the Necessary and Proper

Clause under Article I, Section 8 gives Congress the authority "[t]o make all laws which shall be necessary and proper for carrying into execution the foregoing powers, and all other powers vested by this constitution in the government of the United States, or in any department or officer thereof." However, the Constitution sets forth several restrictions as to the exercise of congressional power. For example, Article I, Section 9 forbids Congress from suspending the writ of *habeas corpus,* except when the public safety may require it. Article I, Section 9 also bars Congress from passing bills of attainder and *ex post facto* laws, as well as from bestowing titles of nobility.

Moreover, Congress is required to fulfill several constitutionally-imposed mandates. Under Article IV, Section 4, Congress is obligated to guarantee each state a republican form of government and to protect the states against invasion and, upon proper application, against domestic violence. With respect to the states, the Tenth Amendment provides that "[t]he powers not delegated to the United States by the Constitution, nor prohibited by it to the States, are reserved to the States respectively, or to the people." In other words, the states retain their "police power" to enact laws for the health, safety, and welfare of their citizens. Similar to Congress, state legislatures are faced with constitutional limitations on their powers. For instance, Article I, Section 10 forbids states from entering into treaties, coining money, or emitting bills of credit, all of which would interfere with Congress' ability to govern.

As to the states' exercise of authority over their citizens, Article I, Section 10 precludes the states from passing bills of attainder, *ex post facto* laws, and laws impairing contracts. Furthermore, the restrictions placed on the federal government under the Bill of Rights are applicable to the states via the Fourteenth Amendment.

It is not uncommon for both Congress and state governments to enact legislation with respect to a particular matter. Under the doctrine of preemption, a state statute must be invalidated if Congress has "occupied the field," which means that Congress has intended to the be the sole regulator of the matter in question. For instance, Congress has clearly preempted the right to coin money. Not only is Congress empowered to coin money, but states are specifically forbidden from coining money. On the other hand, Congress and state governments may have concurrent, or shared, power with respect to certain matters. Although Congress is authorized to fix the standard of weights and measures, courts have upheld local regulations in this area.

While Congress preempts the right to regulate interstate commerce (commerce between states), states have the authority to regulate intrastate commerce (commerce within a state) pursuant to their reserved power under the Tenth Amendment. However, a state statute will be invalidated if it substantially or unreasonably places a burden on interstate commerce. All aspects of interstate commerce—from the actual transportation of a product to the wage regulation of employees involved in interstate commerce—have been subjected to congressional authority. In reality, Congress has aggressively used the Commerce Clause as a means of exercising a federal "police power" to legislate over the health, safety, and welfare of the national citizenry, at the expense of state power. For example, in *Champion v. Ames* (1903), the Supreme Court upheld a federal statute which prohibited the transportation of lottery tickets across state lines. Of course, Congress' underlying motive had been to control gambling, rather than oversee interstate commerce.

Modern Relationship Between States

Article IV, Section 1 provides that "[f]ull faith and credit shall be given in each state to the public acts, records, and judicial proceedings of every other state . . ." Furthermore, Article IV, Section 2 provides that "[t]he citizens of each state shall be entitled to all privileges and immunities of citizens in the several states." Taken together, the above language means that states should honor valid judgments rendered in sister states and should not discriminate against another state's citizens. As a practical matter, however, a state may balk at recognizing a claim which is valid in another state if it regards such a claim to be against its own public policy.

See also: **Federal Powers and the Separation of Powers, Judicial Powers, Judicial Review, Legislative Powers**

Bibliography and Further Reading

Dudley, William, ed. *The Creation of the Constitution.* San Diego, CA: Greenhaven Press, Inc., 1995

Levy, Leonard W., ed. *The Framing and Ratification of the Constitution.* New York, NY: Macmillan Publishing Company, 1971

Livingston, John C. *The Consent of the Governed.* New York, NY: Macmillan Publishing Company, 1971

Wood, Gordon S. *The Creation of the American Republic 1776-1787.* New York, NY: W. W. Norton & Company, 1969

EAKIN V. RAUB

Legal Citation: 12 S & R Penn. Rep. 330 Pa. (1825)

Plaintiffs
James Eakin, et al.

Defendants
Daniel Raub, et al.

Plaintiffs' Claim
That a state statute imposing a new period of limitations in which to bring a claim, as applied to bar plaintiff's claim, violated the state constitution, and that the Pennsylvania Supreme Court had the power to declare the statute void.

Chief Lawyer for Plaintiffs
B. Tilghman

Chief Defense Lawyer
Joseph Hemphill

Justices for the Court
Tilghman, Duncan

Justices Dissenting
John B. Gibson

Place
Philadelphia, Pennsylvania

Date of Decision
16 April 1825

Decision
That the state supreme court has the power to review legislative acts and, if contrary to the state constitution, declare such acts void.

Significance
As an historical matter, the actual decision of the Pennsylvania Supreme Court in *Eakin v. Raub* is of little importance. Although the case involved a major issue—the power of the court to declare acts contrary to the state constitution void—the two justices in the majority gave this issue short shrift. However, Justice Gibson's dissenting opinion is widely regarded as being the most effective refutation of the theory of judicial review, and it is this dissenting opinion which makes *Eakin* noteworthy.

In 1803, the U.S. Supreme Court decided the case of *Marbury v. Madison,* almost universally regarded as the most important court decision in American history. In *Marbury,* Chief Justice John Marshall established the theory of judicial review as a matter of federal law, concluding that the Supreme Court has the power to review laws enacted by Congress and declare legislative acts which violate the U.S. Constitution void, even though the judiciary is granted no such express power in the Constitution. While today the power of judicial review is accepted unquestioningly, such was not always the case. Indeed, after the Court's decision in *Marbury* such eminent leaders as Thomas Jefferson, Andrew Jackson, and Abraham Lincoln all expressed doubt about the validity of judicial review and the power of the courts to declare legislative acts void. In 1825, the Pennsylvania Supreme Court, in *Eakin v. Raub,* accepted Justice Marshall's position in *Marbury* as applied to the power of the state courts to declare legislative acts transgressing the state constitution void.

The facts of *Eakin,* and the ultimate issue in that case from the parties' perspectives, are relatively uninteresting and of little import. Furthermore, the opinion of Chief Justice Tilghman, accepting Chief Justice Marshall's view of judicial review, adds little to the historical support for the power of judicial review. Much more important, however, was the dissenting opinion of Justice John Gibson, which is widely regarded as the most effective attack on Chief Justice Marshall's *Marbury* opinion and his theory of judicial review ever authored. In an opinion often cited by opponents of the theory of judicial review, Justice Gibson attempted, and in many respects succeeded, to offer a point-by-point refutation of Marshall's decision.

Marshall v. Gibson: Head to Head

Justice Marshall offered a number of justifications for the conclusion that the judiciary has the power to declare void legislative acts which are contrary to the Constitution, despite the fact that the Constitution provides no such explicit power. Justice Marshall first supported the theory of judicial review by reasoning that the power of judicial review is necessary to preserve a written constitution as the law which is superior to all other legislative acts. In Marshall's view, if a court cannot strike down a law which violates the Constitution, then the legislature may, in effect, amend or repeal the Constitution by simply passing laws, rather than formerly amending the Constitution. Justice Gibson countered that a constitution may be better preserved by the citizens of the state, and not the courts. He reasoned that "it rests with the people, in whom full and sovereign power resides to correct abuses in legislation, by instructing their representatives to repeal the obnoxious act." He reasoned that any powers not expressly granted in a constitution are reserved to the people, who are the ultimate sovereigns in a democratic regime. Thus, he concluded, while it may be wise to allow the courts to exercise this power, the people, in forming the constitution, did not do so, and the courts may not do so on their own.

Justice Marshall next justified his theory of judicial review on the argument that the legislature only has authority granted to it by the Constitution, and thus because the legislature has no authority to pass a law which is prohibited by the Constitution, the law is simply void of itself, even without a court declaring it so. Again, Justice Gibson countered this reasoning. In Justice Gibson's view, this merely elevated the judiciary above the legislature, although it does not necessarily follow that a court's opinion on the matter is more correct than the legislature's: "But it will not be pretended that the legislature has not at least an equal right with the judiciary to put a construction on the constitution; nor that either of them is infallible; nor that either ought to be required to surrender its judgment to the other." Yet, in Justice Gibson's view, judicial review requires just that; the legislature must surrender its judgment to the judiciary.

Justice Marshall, in his *Marbury* opinion, also justified the power of judicial review on the ground that, if a court enforces an unconstitutional law, then the court itself is committing its own act in violation of the Constitution. Justice Gibson, in his *Eakin* dissent, concluded that this was merely a reformulation of Marshall's previous argument. Justice Gibson concluded that Marshall's argument follows only if it is assumed that the judiciary has authority over the legislature to declare laws unconstitutional. If it does not, as Gibson thought, then a court is making no affirmative act when it does not strike down an unconstitutional law.

Justice Marshall's fourth asserted reason for concluding that a court has the power to strike down unconstitutional laws was that judges are required by the constitution to take an oath supporting the Constitution. Justice Gibson, however, found this reasoning to be circular. In his view, this oath required a judge to uphold the Constitution in the exercise of his ordinary judicial powers. Only if it is assumed that the ordinary judicial power includes the power of judicial review does the oath to uphold the Constitution require a judge to declare an unconstitutional law void. However, as Justice Gibson noted, the foundation of this argument is nothing more than "an assumption of the whole ground in dispute," that is, the argument assumed its own conclusion.

Justice Gibson concluded by reasoning that the Constitution grants to the courts only the "judicial power," but does not define what is meant by that phrase. However, he disagreed with the assumption that the judicial power includes the power to declare unconstitutional laws void. Rather, in his view, based on the common law development of the courts, "[i]t is the business of the judiciary to interpret the laws, not scan the authority of the lawgiver." Thus, he concluded, "it rests with the people, in whom full and absolute sovereign power resides, to correct abuses in legislation, by instructing their representatives to repeal the obnoxious act." Ultimately, Chief Justice Marshall's view as expressed in *Marbury* carried the day, and it is virtually unquestioned that the courts have the power to declare laws contrary to the Constitution void. Yet, Justice Gibson's opinion remains a stark reminder of the somewhat tenuous foundation upon which this power is based, and reveals some of the political and judicial philosophies underlying Marshall's decision in *Marbury*, not the least of which was to "flex the Court's muscle." Thus, as Charles Haines observed on page 284 of his work on judicial supremacy, "[a]ny one who considers the opinion [of Judge Gibson] can readily perceive that reason and logic had comparatively little weight with those who resolutely set about to make judicial review a part of the American political system."

Related Cases
Marbury v. Madison, 5 U.S. 137 (1803).

Bibliography and Further Reading
Bickel, Alexander M. *The Least Dangerous Branch: The Supreme Court at the Bar of Politics*. Indianapolis: Bobbs-Merrill, 1962.

Clinton, Robert L. *Marbury v. Madison and Judicial Review*. Wichita, KS: University of Kansas Press, 1989.

Dewey, Donald O. *Marshall v. Jefferson: The Political Background of Marbury v. Madison*. New York: Knopf, 1970.

Epstein, Lee, and Thomas G. Walker. *Constitutional Law for a Changing America: Institutional Powers and Constraints*, 3rd ed. Washington DC: Congressional Quarterly, 1998.

Haines, Charles G. *The American Doctrine of Judicial Supremacy*. New York: Russell & Russell, Inc., 1952.

Hamilton, Alexander. "The Federalist No. 78." *The Federalist Papers*. Clinton Rossiter, ed. New York: Mentor Books, 1961.

Warren, Charles. *The Supreme Court in United States History*. Boston: Little Brown & Co., 1926.

MUNN V. ILLINOIS

Legal Citation: 94 U.S. 113 (1877)

Appellant
Munn & Scott

Appellee
State of Illinois

Appellant's Claim
That the state law of Illinois requiring that a warehouse operate under a state license and that it conform to state-set rates violated the due process guarantee of the Fourteenth Amendment.

Chief Lawyers for Appellant
W. C. Goudy, John N.Jewett

Chief Lawyer for Appellee
Attorney General of Illinois

Justices for the Court
Joseph P. Bradley, Nathan Clifford, David Davis, Ward Hunt, Samuel Freeman Miller, Noah Haynes Swayne, Morrison Remick Waite (writing for the Court)

Justices Dissenting
Stephen Johnson Field, William Strong

Place
Washington, D.C.

Date of Decision
1 March 1877

Decision
That it was appropriate for the state to regulate a state activity; that even though grain elevators operated as part of an interstate network of commerce, it was legitimate for the state to regulate them as long as Congress had not legislated in the area; that the act of Illinois setting up state regulation was not repugnant to the Constitution.

Significance
The decision demarcated between strictly state regulation of domestic commerce within a state and interstate commerce which should be regulated by Congress; it further indicated that business activities were protected by the Fourteenth Amendment of the Constitution, even though that amendment had been passed to protect former slaves.

Setting the Boundary Between State and Federal Regulation

The state of Illinois had passed a law on 25 April 1871, requiring that warehouses take out a license and that they charge rates for storage of grain that did not exceed a state-established rate. The next year, on 29 June 1872, the state filed an action against the firm of Munn & Scott for operating a warehouse without a license and for charging rates higher than permitted under the state regulation. The Illinois Supreme Court ruled in favor of the state, and Munn & Scott appealed the case to the U.S. Supreme Court.

Attorneys for the appellant argued that the state had deprived Munn & Scott of their property rights by requiring a license and by setting maximum rates. They pointed out that rights to property were not worth anything except to the extent that the property could be put to a use. The free use of the property had been regulated by the state, thus depriving the owners of rights in the property. The Fourteenth Amendment expressly prohibited states from depriving individuals of property without due process of law.

In his opinion, Chief Justice Waite pointed out that the state had not infringed on the area of federal jurisdiction, in that Congress had not sought to regulate grain warehouses under the interstate commerce clause. In this case, Waite appeared to be warning the states that legislation in areas involving major railroad commerce, such as grain, could readily impinge on a federal jurisdiction, although it had not done so in this case. Waite recognized that state and federal jurisdictions in interstate commerce could easily interfere with each other. In keeping with a modest view of the federal role, and in keeping with a high regard for state and local interests that was typical of the era of the 1870s, Waite ruled that the grain elevators, even though connected to a national network, were essentially local operations. A state could regulate business which was entirely within a state, and the grain elevators fit that category.

As to the right of the state to regulate business, under the Fourteenth Amendment, Waite argued that private property exposed to the public for public use is also exposed to public regulation in the public interest. If an owner did not want his property to be used in any way by the public, then the public had little reason to regulate it, but once it was used for public purposes, the owner had to expect regulation. Waite based this principle on a long tradition of British and American common law which gave the government power to set fees for ferries and bridges, for inns and other places of public convenience, and to require licenses for many categories of business.

Two justices, Field and Strong, dissented from Waite's opinion, indicating that they believed that the mere act of regulating, requiring a license, and setting prices consisted of "depriving" property rights under the Fourteenth Amendment. Even though a minority opinion, the fact that members of the Court regarded the Fourteenth Amendment as applicable to commerce and not simply to civil rights, suggested that the principles addressed in such cases as *Munn* and the *Slaughterhouse Cases*, would have implications for business activities in the future.

Related Cases

Slaughterhouse Cases, 16 Wallace 36 (1873).
American Sugar Refining Co. v. Louisiana, 217 U.S. 563 (1900).
Nebbia v. New York, 291 U.S. 502 (1934).

Bibliography and Further Reading

Biskupic, Joan, and Elder Witt. *Congressional Quarterly's Guide to the U.S. Supreme Court,* 3rd ed. Washington, DC: Congressional Quarterly, Inc., 1996.

Cushman, Robert F. *Leading Constitutional Decisions.* Englewood Cliffs, NJ: Prentice-Hall, Inc., 1982.

Epstein, Lee, and Thomas G. Walker. *Constitutional Law for a Changing America: Institutional Powers and Constraints,* 3rd ed. Washington DC: Congressional Quarterly, 1998.

Frankfurter, Felix. *The Commerce Clause under Marshall, Taney, and Waite.* Gloucester, MA: Peter Smith, 1978.

Hall, Kermit L., ed. *The Oxford Companion to the Supreme Court of the United States.* New York: Oxford University Press, 1992.

Johnson, John W., ed. *Historic U.S. Court Cases, 1690–1990: An Encyclopedia.* New York: Garland Publishing, 1992.

COYLE V. SMITH

Legal Citation: 221 U.S. 559 (1911)

Appellant
W.H. Coyle

Appellee
Thomas P. Smith, Secretary of State of Oklahoma, et al.

Appellant's Claim
The state of Oklahoma was denied equal status among the states by being required to locate its capital in the town of Guthrie under the Congressional Enabling Act admitting the territory to the Union.

Chief Lawyers for Appellant
Frank Dale, G. G. Hepner, John Burford

Chief Lawyers for Appellee
Charles West, B. C. Barwell, Joseph W. Bailey

Justices for the Court
William Rufus Day, John Marshall Harlan I, Charles Evans Hughes, Joseph Rucker Lamar, Horace Harmon Lurton (writing for the Court), Willis Van Devanter, Edward Douglass White

Justices Dissenting
Oliver Wendell Holmes, Joseph McKenna

Place
Washington, D.C.

Date of Decision
29 May 1911

Decision
Let stand a 1910 popular initiative establishing the capital of Oklahoma in Oklahoma City rather than Guthrie, thereby revoking the 1906 "irrevocable" agreement admitting the state to the Union.

Significance
Coyle v. Oklahoma made it clear the states were politically equal by denying Congress the power, in granting statehood to territories, to withhold any of the powers and functions that belong to states.

All states are equal, but those that formed "a more perfect Union" first have sometimes tried to withhold powers that properly belong to states from territories seeking admission or seceding states wanting readmission.

The Supreme Court put a stop to the practice in a case in which the territory of Oklahoma had "irrevocably" agreed in 1906 to locate its capital in the town of Guthrie. In 1910, however, the people of Oklahoma, through a popular initiative, decided the capital should be moved forthwith from Guthrie to Oklahoma City and allocated $600,000 for public buildings there.

Congress apparently had not learned from previous cases involving Texas and Alabama, in which the Supreme Court had overturned conditions set by Congress in return for statehood status. Indeed, more substantive concerns were at issue in those cases which had been decided in favor of the states. In the 1845 case of Alabama, Congress had demanded the new state cede ownership of the submerged lands under its navigable waters to the federal government. Congress wanted to keep the waters open as public highways, but the Court found the intention could not override common-law title all states shared in submerged lands. Alabama was entitled to the same "sovereignty and jurisdiction," the Court ruled:

> To maintain any other doctrine is to deny Alabama has been admitted to the Union on an equal footing with the other states.

In 1865, Texas, still "unreconstructed" after the Civil War, claimed payment of $5 million in bonds pledged in 1850 by the United States to Texas, redeemable on 31 December 1864. Texas no longer had legal standing, however, federal attorneys argued, because the state, after seceding, was no longer a "state" within the meaning of the Constitution. The Court disagreed, saying secession was constitutionally impossible:

> The Constitution, in all of its provisions, looks to an indestructible union, composed of indestructible states.

Consequently, when *Coyle v. Oklahoma* came before the bench, Justice Lurton ruled the only question was whether the "restriction was a valid limitation upon the power of the state." Although Lurton produced relatively few opinions as a Supreme Court justice, he was respected as common law authority:

> "This Union" was and is a union of states, equal in power, dignity and authority . . . That one of the original thirteen states could now be shorn of such powers by an act of Congress would not now for a moment be entertained.

The constitutional equality of the states, Lurton concluded "is essential to the harmonious operation of the scheme upon which the Republic was organized. When that equality disappears we may remain a free people, but the Union will not be the Union of the Constitution."

Related Cases
South Carolina v. Katzenbach, 383 U.S. 301 (1966).

Bibliography and Further Reading

Bickel, Alexander M., and Benno C. Schmidt. *History of the Supreme Court of the United States.* New York, Macmillan, 1984.

Biskupic, Joan, and Elder Witt, eds. *Congressional Quarterly's Guide to the U.S. Supreme Court,* 3rd ed. Washington, DC: Congressional Quarterly, Inc., 1996.

Cushman, Robert F. *Cases in Constitutional Law,* 7th ed. Englewood Cliffs, NJ: Prentice-Hall, Inc., 1989.

———. *Leading Constitutional Decisions.* Englewood Cliffs, NJ: Prentice-Hall, Inc., 1982.

Hall, Kermit L., ed. *The Oxford Companion to the Supreme Court of the United States.* New York: Oxford University Press, 1992.

Morgan, H. Wayne, and Anne Hodges. *Oklahoma, A History.* New York, Norton, 1984.

PACIFIC STATES TELEPHONE & TELEGRAPH COMPANY V. OREGON

Legal Citation: 223 U.S. 118 (1912)

Appellant
Pacific States Telephone & Telegraph Company

Appellee
State of Oregon

Appellant's Claim
That the state of Oregon was no longer a republican form of government, since it gave citizens the right to pass laws by initiative and referendum.

Chief Lawyer for Appellant
E. S. Pillsbury

Chief Lawyers for Appellee
A. M. Crawford, Jackson H. Ralston

Justices for the Court
William Rufus Day, John Marshall Harlan I, Oliver Wendell Holmes, Charles Evans Hughes, Joseph Rucker Lamar, Horace Harmon Lurton, Joseph McKenna, Willis Van Devanter, Edward Douglass White (writing for the Court)

Justices Dissenting
None

Place
Washington, D.C.

Date of Decision
2 February 1912

Decision
The Court denied it had jurisdiction and dismissed the case.

Significance
Citing a clear precedent, the Court reaffirmed that it had no constitutional authority to decide a political issue, such as the validity of a state government. The Court's dismissal of *Pacific States* upheld a state's right to introduce initiative and referendum reforms.

In *Democracy in America,* the French aristocrat Alexis de Tocqueville observed, "Scarcely any political question arises in the United States that is not resolved, sooner or later, into a judicial question." De Tocqueville's assertion, however, was too sweeping; the Supreme Court has found political questions it will not address. To preserve the separation of powers between the judicial and legislative branches, the Court developed the "political question doctrine," which it has invoked in cases that are purely political.

The doctrine first clearly arose in *Luther v. Borden* (1848), a case concerning Article IV, section 4 of the Constitution. In the "Guarantee Clause," the federal government guarantees that each state will have a republican form of government. In *Luther,* two political factions in Rhode Island claimed to be the legitimate government of the state. The case asked the Court to decide which one should be in power. The Court, however, denied it had jurisdiction. Deciding if a state had a republican government was a political question, one that had to be resolved by Congress. That reasoning was at the heart of the Court's decision in *Pacific States* as well.

Progressive Politics On Trial

In the early twentieth century, political and social reform was sweeping across America. The reformers, called Progressives, tried to ease the plight of immigrants and the poor, improve conditions in the workplace, and reduce the influence of large corporations on state and local politics. Progressive tools for political reform stressed direct democracy—giving more political powers to the voters—and included the initiative and the referendum. With the initiative, voters of a state could introduce new laws, bypassing the legislature. A referendum allowed citizens to accept or reject laws passed by the government. The use of the initiative and the referendum was popular in the Great Plains and Far West, and in 1902, Oregon amended its constitution to include these reform measures.

The reforms, however, were not popular with some companies, which were often the target of laws passed through initiative and referendum. In Oregon, the

Pacific States Telephone and Telegraph Company disliked a law that levied a two percent tax on the profits of telegraph and telephone companies doing business in the state. Oregon voters had initiated the law in 1906; it went into effect the following year. Pacific States refused to pay the tax, and Oregon sued for its money. In court, the company cited Article IV, Section 4 of the Constitution for its defense. By introducing the initiative and referendum, Pacific States claimed, Oregon ceased to have a republican government, which relies on elected representative to make laws. Oregon's courts upheld the state's tax, and Pacific States took its claim to the U.S. Supreme Court.

In a unanimous decision, the Court dismissed Pacific States' case. In his decision, Chief Justice White referred heavily to the Court's decision in *Luther*. Deciding if a state government was republican was strictly a political issue that only Congress could determine. Pacific States would have had a better chance, White said, if it had attacked the tax itself on constitutional grounds. But the suit had an "essentially political nature . . . [that] . . . is at once made manifest by the understanding that the assault which the contention here advanced makes is not on the tax as a tax, but on the state as a state. It is addressed to the framework and political character of the government by which the statute levying the tax was passed."

White noted the irony of using the Guarantee Clause as grounds for the case. By asking the Court to hear such a blatantly political question, the appellant was trying to blur the separation of judicial and legislative powers spelled out in the Constitution. Pacific States' case "rests upon the assumption that the states are to be guaranteed a government republican by destroying the very existence of a government republican in form in the nation."

The Political Question Doctrine Since *Pacific States*

By strongly reaffirming the precedent set in *Luther*, the Court clearly showed it would not get involved in Guarantee Clause cases. But if cases involving a political question had other grounds, the Court would consider it. That happened in 1962, in *Baker v. Carr*. The case addressed political reapportionment—the redrawing of voting district boundaries—in Tennessee. *Baker* relied on both the Guarantee and Equal Establishment Clauses. Based on the Equal Establishment grounds, the Court decided the case.

Since *Baker*, the Court has decided other cases with political question issues. Indeed, some legal scholars argue that many Supreme Court cases have significant political overtones, and the Court elects to hear them. The political question doctrine becomes a subjective way of avoiding political issues the Court finds too controversial or that might infringe on the constitutional responsibilities of the other branches of the government.

Related Cases
Luther v. Borden, 48 U.S. 1 (1848).
Baker v. Carr, 369 U.S. 186 (1962).

Bibliography and Further Reading

Hall, Kermit L., ed. *The Oxford Companion to the Supreme Court of the United States*. New York: Oxford University Press, 1992.

Norton, Mary Beth, et al. *A People & A Nation: A History of the United States*, Vol. 2. Boston: Houghton Mifflin Company, 1982.

Stone, Geoffrey R., et al. *Constitutional Law*. Boston: Little, Brown and Company, 1986.

Tocqueville, Alexis de. *Democracy in America*, Vol. 1. New York: Vintage Books, 1945.

STATE OF MISSOURI V. HOLLAND

Legal Citation: 525 U.S. 416 (1920)

Appellant
Frank W. McAllister, Attorney General of Missouri

Appellee
Ray P. Holland

Appellant's Claim
That federal laws pursuant to the Migratory Bird Act and enforcement thereof were an invasion of sovereign states rights as set forth in the Tenth Amendment.

Chief Lawyers for Appellant
Alexander C. King, Solicitor General; William L. Frierson, Assistant Attorney General

Chief Lawyers for Appellee
John T. Gose, J. Harvey

Justices for the Court
Louis D. Brandeis, John Hessin Clarke, William Rufus Day, Oliver Wendell Holmes (writing for the Court), Joseph McKenna, James Clark McReynolds, Edward Douglass White

Justices Dissenting
Mahlon Pitney, Willis Van Devanter

Place
Washington, D.C.

Date of Decision
19 April 1920

Decision
The Court ruled in favor of Holland, upholding the U.S. government's treaty and its relevant statutes.

Significance
By affirming Congress' right to make treaties whose terms might supercede state laws, the Court established one of the first wildlife protection laws.

Bird Protection and Treaty-Making

Legislative controls for the protection of wildlife were rare during the 1800s. The few existing laws were state laws, not federal regulations. By the beginning of the twentieth century, however, the decimation of bird species through careless hunting practices and wholesale slaughter for items like feathers used in the feminine millinery industry produced growing pressure for some kind of control.

On 16 August 1916, the United States and Great Britain (acting on behalf of its colony, Canada) signed a treaty recognizing migratory birds as an international food resource and as ecologically important consumers of vegetation-destroying insects. When the U.S. Congress ratified the treaty by passing the Migratory Bird Act on 3 July 1918, it became a federal offense to capture, kill, or sell migratory bird species named in the treaty. Regulations formulated by the secretary of agriculture prohibited spring shooting, set bag limits on ducks and geese, and permanently forbade the hunting of certain nongame species. The act was backed by politically influential hunters, who were generally comfortable with the modest new controls.

Yet the government of the state of Missouri, which lies on the bird migration route between Canada and the United States, challenged the new law. The state, whose hunting season was four months longer than the new federal law allowed, saw the treaty as an invasion of its sovereign rights. When U.S. game warden Ray P. Holland arrested Missouri Attorney General Frank McAllister for shooting ducks out of season, the legal confrontation between the two men's bosses began. The state sued Holland to prevent him from enforcing the Migratory Bird Act and its regulations, implicitly challenging his employer, the federal government.

Rather than challenge specific regulations, the state attempted to scrap all of the new laws by declaring the entire treaty unconstitutional. The Tenth Amendment states that "powers not delegated to the United States by the Constitution, nor prohibited by it to the States, are reserved to the States respectively, or to the people." Missouri argued that all birds found within its borders were essentially the property of the state and thus sub-

The Migratory Bird Treaty

The National Wildlife Refuge System of the United States is an outgrowth of environmental concerns elicited by the rapid disappearance of bird species such as the tern, the egret, and the heron during the late nineteenth century. The Committee for the Protection of North American Birds of the American Ornithologists' Union urged President Theodore Roosevelt to take action. In 1903, he established the nation's first bird refuge at Pelican Island Reservation in Florida. Under Roosevelt's administration, the refuge system for wildlife expanded. In 1908, Congress initiated the purchase of a bison range in Montana, and by 1930 the federal government owned some 5 million acres of wildlife-refuge land, on which it operated 86 refuges.

As part of this push toward environmental awareness, the United States in 1916 signed the Migratory Bird Treaty with Canada. The treaty established the importance of protecting species flying back and forth between countries and set up a foundation whereby the federal government would manage and maintain migratory wildlife. This was followed by the Migratory Bird Conservation Act of 1929 and the Migratory Bird Hunting Stamp Act of 1934.

Source(s): Eblen, Ruth A. and William R. Eblen, eds. *The Encyclopedia of the Environment* Boston: Houghton Mifflin, 1994.

ject to state, not federal, control. By this rationale, the treaty and its enforcement provisions were an unconstitutional interference with Missouri's rights as a state.

This argument proved to be unsuccessful. A U.S. district court in Missouri ruled that while the enforcement provisions of the act would have been unconstitutional if the treaty did not exist, passage of the treaty validated federal control. The state appealed this decision before the Supreme Court on 2 March 1920.

The Ownership of Nature

The U.S. government's position included a list of 23 bird species threatened with extinction by the contemporary habits of sport hunters, some of whom boasted of killing as many as 10,000 birds in one night. Yet the case heard by the Court had become less about bird life than about states rights and the power of the U.S. government to make treaties. The state of Kansas filed a brief, supporting Missouri's position. Only six weeks after hearing arguments, however, on 19 April 1920, the Court ruled in favor of the federal government.

The majority opinion written by Justice Holmes reflected that the Court had focused on the Tenth Amendment in reaching a decision. Holmes noted that earlier congressional attempts to protect bird life by passing laws had been found unconstitutional. Congress had no right to displace state statutes, including those based on the assumption that migratory birds were the property of the individual sovereign states and their citizens. State law, however, could not supercede international agreements made by Congress in important matters of national interest. With Holmes citing a long-established tradition of treaties whose terms were observed by both the states and the nation as a whole, the Court affirmed Congress' right to enact legislation by implementing treaties.

Holmes stated that migratory birds were in fact "owned" by no one, much less by states whose territory the birds crossed while in transit. Without the protections offered by the treaty, Holmes noted, there might not be any birds for either the states or the U.S. government to regulate. "We see nothing in the Constitution that compels the Government to sit by while a food supply is cut off and the protectors of our forests and our crops are destroyed," Holmes wrote. If the states could have been relied upon to protect the wildlife, he added, the case would never have come to court.

Justices Van Devanter and Pitney dissented from the majority opinion, but through the Court's affirmation of Congress' power to enact legislation through treaties, the Migratory Bird Act survived. Proponents of states' rights continued to cite the *State of Missouri v. Holland* decision as an abuse of federal power, through which the will of state governments was unjustly bypassed. The successful defense of the Migratory Bird Act, however, remains a historical landmark among laws which protect wildlife in the national interest.

Related Cases

Baldwin v. Franks, 120 U.S. 678 (1887).
Baldwin v. Montana Fish and Game Commission, 430 U.S. 371 (1978).

Bibliography and Further Reading

Gibbons, Felton, and Deborah Strom. *Neighbors To The Birds: A History of Birdwatching In America.* New York: W. W. Norton, 1988.

Kurland, Phillip B., and Gerhard Casper, eds. *Landmark Briefs and Arguments of the Supreme Court of the United States.* Arlington: University Publications of America, 1975.

Phillips, John C. *Migratory Bird Protection in North America.* Cambridge: International Wild Life Protection American Committee, 1934.

Swain, Donald C. *Federal Conservation Policy 1921-1933.* Berkeley: University of California Press, 1963.

ERIE R. CO. V. TOMPKINS

Legal Citation: 304 U.S. 64 (1938)

Petitioner
Erie Railroad Company

Respondent
Tompkins

Petitioner's Claim
That state law, rather than federal court decisions, should determine whether the railroad was liable for injuries Tompkins suffered when walking along the railroad's right-of-way.

Chief Lawyer for Petitioner
Theodore Kiendl

Chief Lawyer for Respondent
Fred H. Rees

Justices for the Court
Hugo Lafayette Black, Louis D. Brandeis (writing for the Court), Charles Evans Hughes, Owen Josephus Roberts, Harlan Fiske Stone, Stanley Forman Reed

Justices Dissenting
Pierce Butler, James Clark McReynolds (Benjamin N. Cardozo did not participate)

Place
Washington, D.C.

Date of Decision
25 April 1938

Decision
The U.S. Supreme Court upheld the petitioner's claim and reversed the circuit court of appeal's validation of the trial jury's award of damages.

Significance
Erie R. Co. v. Tompkins profoundly changed the allocation of judicial power between state and federal courts. The majority opinion settled a long-standing controversy about the validity of states' common (judge-made) law in "diversity of citizenship" cases in which the citizen of one state sues the citizen of another in federal court. The Court rejected the doctrine established in *Swift v. Tyson* (1842) that federal judges could ignore law made by state judges because the Judiciary Act of 1789 did not consider judges' decisions to be law. By allowing federal courts to create general law which superseded state law, the Swift doctrine represented "an unconstitutional assumption of power by the Courts of the United States." This case elevated states' judge-made law to the status of laws made by state legislatures, and was a victory for states' rights, in the literal sense of the term.

Erie R. Co. v. Tompkins is a multi-layered case. On the surface, it is a claim for damages against a railroad by a plaintiff in Pennsylvania who was hit by a moving train's open boxcar door. At another level, the case involves widespread and growing confusion about the power federal judges have when dealing in federal courts with "diversity of citizenship" cases, in which a citizen of one state sues a citizen of another. The Supreme Court used this case as an occasion to clarify the situation by holding unconstitutional a 96-year-old doctrine of a case presented before a former Court, *Swift v. Tyson*.

Tompkins was a citizen of Pennsylvania. Erie Railroad Company was a corporation chartered in New York, and therefore a New York "citizen." Tompkins's suit against Erie was tried in federal district court in New York; the jury found that the railroad was negligent and awarded Tompkins $30,000 in damages. The railroad appealed to a federal court of appeals, and lost again. The railroad then asked the U.S. Supreme Court for a writ of *certiorari* an order to a lower court to send up the record of a case, usually issued when the higher court decides that the case involves "a substantial federal question."

Erie Railroad's request posed two questions. First, should its liability toward Tompkins have been determined by Pennsylvania law, even thought the law had been made by judges rather than by the state legislature? Second, did the evidence not show conclusively that Tompkins had contributed to the accident by failing to heed the moving train's warnings, consisting of the locomotives headlight and horn? Tompkins argued that the long-standing rules of the Supreme Court held that issues involving negligence were to be determined by federal judges reading of general law, which was higher than local law.

The notion that general law existed had been the Supreme Court's guide since it was invoked by Justice Joseph Story in the 1842 case *Swift v. Tyson*. In interpreting Section 34 of the Judiciary Act of 1789, Justice Story said, "In the ordinary use of language, it will hardly be contended, that the decisions of courts constitute laws. They are, at most, only evidence of what the laws are, and are not, of themselves laws . . . The laws of a state are more usually understood to mean the rules and enactments promulgated by the legislative authority thereof, . . ." He added, "The interpretation and effect of contracts and other instruments of a commercial nature are to be sought . . . in the general principles and doctrines of commercial jurisprudence."

In its review of the original case, the Circuit Court of Appeals held that it need not deal with the question of whether the judge-made law in Pennsylvania was valid, since questions involving liability are questions of "general law."

The Court Changes Course

On a 6-2 vote, the U.S. Supreme Court held that the Circuit Court of Appeals was in error in its view that there was such a thing as "general law", and sent the case back for further review. More significantly, it held that the doctrine of *Swift v. Tyson* was "an unconstitutional assumption of powers" by federal courts, and said, in a strikingly clear sentence, "There is no federal general common law."

Writing for the majority, Justice Brandeis began by announcing that the question was, should the "oft-challenged" doctrine of *Swift v. Tyson* be "disapproved"? The answer was yes, for three reasons.

First, because of *Swift v. Tyson*'s interpretation of section 34 of the Judiciary Act of 1789, federal courts had assumed a power that even Congress could not have given them. Brandeis cited eight law review articles written between 1873 and 1917 questioning that interpretation, and then accepted as authoritative a law professor's 1923 research finding in the *Harvard Law Review* that the original intent of section 34 was to ensure that federal courts followed the laws of the state, "unwritten as well as written."

Citing nine law review articles written between 1928 and 1935, Brandeis then noted that criticism of the doctrine had increased after the 1928 so-called Taxicab cases, in which a Kentucky cab company reincorporated in Tennessee in order to win a case in federal court that it could not have won as a Kentucky citizen in a Kentucky state court.

Second, *Swift v. Tyson* had created much confusion. Instead of increasing uniformity in the development of common law, state courts were decreasing it by continuing to issue their own opinions on questions of common law. Further, there was no clear line between cases that belonged to "general law" and to state law. Brandeis observed that as of 1937, there had already been nearly 1,000 lower court decisions trying to find the distinction between the two kinds of law.

Worse, *Swift v. Tyson* created injustices. It effectively nullified equal protection of the law, since citizens could win in federal courts cases they could not win in state courts, merely by moving from one state to another, or, in the case of corporations, by reincorporating in a different state, without even moving. In this way, "noncitizens" had more power than "citizens" in diversity of citizenship cases. Further, federal courts kept expanding the list of legal topics included under "general law," which meant that the effects of "grave discrimination" by noncitizens against citizens was now far-reaching.

Justice Brandeis's third reason for concluding that the doctrine of *Swift v. Tyson* was unconstitutional was that it "is an invasion of the authority of the state, and, to that extent, a denial of its independence." Interestingly, Brandeis was quoting from an 1892 dissent by Justice Field. Brandeis said clearly that the law to be applied in diversity of citizenship cases is the law of the state, and that whether the law is made by the state's legislature or by its judges "is not a matter of federal concern." He stated flatly that "[t]here is no federal general common law." Congress has no power to declare substantive rules of common law in states and nowhere does the Constitution give such power to the federal courts. He then cited Justice Oliver Wendell Holmes dissenting opinion in the 1928 Taxicab cases to the effect that "[t]he authority and only authority is the State, and . . . the voice adopted by the State as its own . . . should utter the last word." Curiously, in rejecting the concept of "federal general common law," he did not mention Justice Holmes's famous characterization of that concept in *Southern Pacific Co. v. Jensen* (1917) as a "brooding omnipresence in the sky."

With this ruling, the Court invalidated the doctrine of *Swift v. Tyson*; it did not reverse the case, as such. Nor, as Brandeis pointed out, did his opinion hold unconstitutional section 34 of the Federal Judiciary Act of 1789. "We merely declare," he concluded, that the doctrine's use by the Supreme Court and lower federal courts has "invaded rights which are . . . reserved by the Constitution to the several states."

A "Radical Change"

In his dissent, Justice Butler, joined by Justice McReynolds, argued that the majority has held unconstitutional the Judiciary Act of 1789, "and especially section 34." He also argued that federal courts now have to adhere to state court decisions, and that Congress is now powerless to remedy the situation. "It is," he said, "hard to foresee the consequences of the radical change so made."

He also argued that it was not necessary for the Court to consider "any" constitutional question in this case, but since, as he understood the majority opinion, it had invalidated the Judiciary Act of 1789, then the Court was required by law to allow the U.S. attorney general to present arguments on behalf of the act's constitutionality. For that matter, he added, Congress would have to be consulted as well.

Butler agreed that the lower court's judgment should be reversed, not for the constitutional reasons given by the majority but because Tompkins's own negligence contributed to his injuries.

Justice Reed concurred with the majority opinion but would have preferred the Court to say "the course pursued" by federal courts based on the doctrine of *Swift v. Tyson* was "merely erroneous," rather than "unconstitutional."

Impact

By dismissing the concept of federal general common law and by putting law made by state judges on equal footing with law made by state legislatures, *Erie R. Co. v. Tompkins* reduced the power of federal courts in diversity of citizenship cases and greatly enhanced the power of state courts. In later diversity of citizenship decisions, the "policy" established by the *Erie* case came to stand for two things: it discouraged "forum-shopping" and discouraged unequal administration of the laws. Diversity of citizenship cases continue, but federal courts hearing them are now, "in effect, only another court

of the State" whose law determines the outcome, according to *Guaranty Trust Co. v. York* (1945). The practice of "forum-shopping" has not ceased choosing a federal court over a state court but "law-shopping" has; that was one of *Erie R. Co. v. Tompkins* main points.

Twenty-five years after *Erie,* Justice Harlan in *Hanna v. Plumer* (1965) said that *Erie* and the cases following it have not stated "a workable doctrine." One question raised by the decision regards whether *Erie* meant that congressionally established federal rules of procedure had to give way to state law? The answer to this question has not been provided in a way that satisfies all members of the judiciary.

Related Cases

Swift v. Tyson, 41 U.S. 1 (1842).
Southern Pacific Co. v Jensen, 244 U.S. 205 (1917).
Ragan v. Merchants Transfer & Warehouse Co., 337 U.S. 530 (1949).
Hanna v. Plumer, 380 U.S. 460 (1965).

Bibliography and Further Reading

Warren, Charles. "New Light on the History of the Federal Judiciary Act of 1789," *Harvard Law Review,* Vol. 37, no. 49, 1923.

SOUTHERN PACIFIC CO. V. ARIZONA

Legal Citation: 325 U.S. 761 (1945)

Appellant
Southern Pacific Company

Appellee
State of Arizona

Appellant's Claim
That the Arizona Supreme Court erred in its ruling that the state's Train Limit Law was constitutional.

Chief Lawyer for Appellant
Burton Mason

Chief Lawyer for Appellee
Harold N. McLaughlin

Justices for the Court
Felix Frankfurter, Robert H. Jackson, Frank Murphy, Stanley Forman Reed, Owen Josephus Roberts, Wiley Blount Rutledge, Harlan Fiske Stone (writing for the Court)

Justices Dissenting
Hugo Lafayette Black, William O. Douglas

Place
Washington, D.C.

Date of Decision
18 June 1945

Decision
In favor of appellant, invalidating the Train Limit Law.

Significance
The Court ruled that state regulations which burden interstate commerce are unconstitutional.

The Arizona Train Limit Law

By the time the Southern Pacific Company and the state of Arizona squared off before the U.S. Supreme Court, the two sides had been battling before courts for 15 years. The germ of the controversy lay within a 1912 Arizona law prohibiting operation of railroad trains of more than 14 passenger cars or 70 freight cars within the state. At the time it was passed, the law was uncontroversial because it reflected a relatively standard train length. As track systems were modernized and stronger locomotives appeared, the Arizona limit became a nuisance to the Southern Pacific Company. The railroad found that it had to stop and shorten its freight trains at terminals near the New Mexico and California borders in order to pass through Arizona without being heavily fined. It was only a matter of time before the issue landed in court.

In 1939, after ten years of unsuccessful preliminary legal skirmishes, the Southern Pacific Company filed suit against Arizona Attorney General Joe Conway, asking a federal court to declare that the Train Limit Law was unconstitutional. In an unusual legal maneuver, Conway ignored the suit. The court dismissed the case, since no controversy appeared to exist for it to adjudicate. When Southern Pacific began to run long trains through the state, however, the railroad forced Conway's hand. He filed suit against Southern Pacific in April of 1940 for violating the Train Limit Law. In its defense, the railroad responded by attacking the constitutionality of the law.

After months of exhaustive hearings, the railroad convinced the Pima County Court that longer trains were safer and less financially burdensome than those operating under the limit law. Conway quickly appealed the case to the Arizona Supreme Court. This time, the state law was interpreted to be valid. On 23 December 1943, the Arizona Supreme Court reversed the county court's judgment and found the railroad liable for fines due to violation of the Train Limit Law.

Appeal to the U.S. Supreme Court

The railroad appealed the Arizona court's decision before the U.S. Supreme Court on 27 and 28 March

The Commerce Clause

Congress is authorized, under Article 1, Section 8, Clause 3, of the Constitution, "to regulate Commerce with foreign Nations, and among several States, and with the Indian Tribes." This is the Commerce Clause, the basis for a number of Supreme Court challenges involving alleged attempts by individuals, companies, or—in the case of Southern Pacific Co. v. Arizona—states to impede the flow of interstate commerce.

"Commerce," as defined by the Constitution, has a very broad meaning. The term encompasses any sort of business or commercial exchange and all interstate communication via telephone, telegraph, radio, or other electronic means. In addition, it refers to all interstate travel, whether for business or for personal reasons.

States have control over their intrastate commerce, but interstate commerce is completely under federal control. This provision was designed to prevent competition between states with seaports and those without and to help to preserve the doctrine of federalism in the operation of the country's internal affairs.

Source(s): West's Encyclopedia of American Law. St. Paul, MN: West Group, 1998.

1945. The state of Arizona continued to insist that the limit law was a public safety regulation. While the "commerce clause" of section 8 of the U.S. Constitution gives Congress the power to regulate commerce between the states, neither Congress nor the Interstate Commerce Commission (I.C.C.) had the right to pass laws over-riding local safety statutes. Only when local laws were in conflict with some national policy could congressional legislation supersede the local statute. Even if this were the case in the Southern Pacific dispute, attorneys for the state of Arizona argued, such a conflict should be debated and corrected by Congress, not by the Court.

The U.S. Supreme Court justices agreed that federal regulation alone should not displace local laws based upon safety considerations. In the Court's decision of 18 June 1945, however, the majority found the railroad's safety statistics more compelling than those offered by Arizona. In the written opinion, Chief Justice Stone noted that the accident rate on Arizona's limited railway lines was higher, not lower, than in other states with comparable rail systems.

Yet the Court's decision centered on the effect of the limit law on interstate commerce. Shortening the length of trains passing through Arizona resulted in the railroads having to assemble hundreds more trains annually, which slowed the pace of transportation well beyond the state's borders. By obstructing the I.C.C.'s mandate to promote adequate, economical, and efficient national transportation service, the limit law placed an unacceptable burden on interstate commerce. The Arizona Supreme Court's decision was reversed.

Justices Black and Douglas dissented in separate opinions. Both agreed that federal regulations should only intrude on state transportation laws if local discrimination against interstate commerce existed. Neither judge was convinced that this was the case in the Southern Pacific suit, nor did they accept that longer trains were safer. Both agreed that the Arizona law should be allowed to stand as a safety measure.

Justice Black accused the majority of making life more dangerous for railway workers in the name of economic expediency. By his logic, this was not even a decision the Court should make. Justice Black felt that the train limit case was a public policy issue which should be settled by elected officials, not by a court.

Despite the dissents, the Court asserted its right to settle the dispute between Arizona and the Southern Pacific Company. "The commerce clause," wrote Justice Stone, "even without the aid of congressional legislation, protects against state legislation which is inimicable to the national commerce, and in such cases, where Congress has not acted, this Court, and not the state legislature, is the final arbiter of the competing demands of state and national interests."

Related Cases

Leisy v. Hardin, 135 U.S. 100 (1890).
Baldwin v. G. A. F. Seelig, Inc., 294 U.S. 511 (1935).
South Carolina State Highway Dept. v. Barnwell Brothers, Inc., 303 U.S. 177 (1938).

Bibliography and Further Reading

Biskupic, Joan, and Elder Witt. *Congressional Quarterly's Guide to the U.S. Supreme Court,* 3rd ed. Washington, DC: Congressional Quarterly, Inc., 1996.

Cortner, Richard C. *The Arizona Train Limit Case.* Tucson, AZ: University of Arizona Press, 1970.

Kurland, Phillip B. and Casper, Gerhard, ed. *Landmark Briefs and Arguments of the Supreme Court of the United States.* Vol. 43. Arlington: University Publications of America, 1975.

INTERNATIONAL SHOE CO. V. STATE OF WASHINGTON

Legal Citation: 326 U.S. 310 (1945)

Appellant
International Shoe Company

Appellee
State of Washington

Appellant's Claim
As a Delaware-based corporation whose factory was located in Missouri, International Shoe was not liable to pay into the state unemployment compensation fund in the state of Washington.

Chief Lawyer for Appellant
Henry C. Lowenhaupt

Chief Lawyer for Appellee
George W. Wilkins, Assistant Attorney General of the State of Washington

Justices for the Court
Hugo Lafayette Black, William O. Douglas, Felix Frankfurter, Frank Murphy, Stanley Forman Reed, Owen Josephus Roberts, Wiley Blount Rutledge, Harlan Fiske Stone (writing for the Court)

Justices Dissenting
None (Robert H. Jackson did not participate)

Place
Washington, D.C.

Date of Decision
3 December 1945

Decision
That International Shoe was liable to pay state unemployment tax in Washington State because it had had "minimum contacts" with that state.

Significance
The *International Shoe* decision has been used for the past 50 years to help establish the circumstances under which a person or corporation comes under the jurisdiction of a state that is not a state of primary residence.

If a person who lived in the state of Colorado was taking a road trip through the Midwest and was the cause of a minor traffic accident in Minnesota, the Minnesota resident involved in the accident could sue the Colorado driver under the laws of Minnesota. The out-of-state driver could not claim that, as a Colorado resident, he was only bound by decisions made in Colorado state court. In legal terms, this kind of problem is known as one of personal jurisdiction. Because the Colorado driver committed an act within Minnesota that led to the suit, he is bound by Minnesota state law.

Now suppose that a large shoe company has several sales agents working in Washington state. The shoes that the company sells are all made in St. Louis, Missouri. The company's legal headquarters are in Delaware. The only thing the company does in Washington is to have its salespeople sell shoes there. The salespeople live and work in Washington, but the corporation is not located there. The question is raised as to whether the company is liable to pay unemployment tax—a percentage of the salespeople's salaries—to the state of Washington.

This was the problem faced by the Supreme Court in the case of *International Shoe Co. v. State of Washington* The decision made by the Court still carries enormous influence in settling problems of personal jurisdiction today.

Corporations, People, and Legal Fictions
Legally, a corporation is considered a person under U.S. law. That is why corporations are covered by laws that govern personal jurisdiction. As Chief Justice Stone recalled in his majority decision for *International Shoe*, ". . . the corporate personality is a fiction, although a fiction intended to be acted upon as though it were a fact." Under our federal system, the Constitution treats each state as its own sovereignty. Therefore, when talking about International Shoe—a U.S. company—the Court nevertheless referred to it as "a foreign corporation," meaning "foreign" to the state of Washington.

Minimum Contacts and Personal Jurisdiction
The *International Shoe* case began when the state of Washington sent a notice by registered mail to the com-

pany's home office, calling on the company to pay its back taxes to the Washington unemployment compensation system. The state also personally delivered a notice to one of the company's salespeople in Washington. Unemployment tax was levied on companies as a percentage of each employee's earnings, and International Shoe had several sales agents based in Washington earning commissions totaling more than $31,000—a considerable sum in 1945. Washington State wanted the tax due on those earnings.

International Shoe argued that even though its salespeople solicited orders in Washington, it did not really have a "presence" in that state. And because it was not present, it did not come under the jurisdiction of the state. Therefore, Washington could not require it to pay unemployment tax.

In such a situation the idea of a corporation as a person becomes relevant. If a person is in Colorado, he cannot be expected to show up in a Minnesota court just because someone in Minnesota decides to sue him. If the person gets a Minnesota subpoena, he could argue that, in fact, he is not present in Minnesota, and that, therefore, Minnesota does not have any personal jurisdiction over him. Likewise, if the Colorado resident gets a bill for Minnesota state income tax, and he did not earn any of his income in Minnesota, he could claim that the state had no jurisdiction.

However, as in our previous example, suppose a person had a traffic accident in Minnesota and then drove home to Colorado. It could be said that he had had certain "minimum contacts" with Minnesota—he had a traffic accident there. This contact would in fact make him liable to the jurisdiction of a Minnesota state court.

Likewise, if a person had lived and worked in Minnesota half the year and then moved to Colorado, that would constitute enough contact with the state to make him liable for Minnesota state income tax—even if he happened to be living in Colorado the day the tax bill became due. These are examples of times when a state has jurisdiction over a person even when the person is not physically present in the state.

An Important Precedent

By the same token, the Court reasoned that the International Shoe Company had had "certain minimum

contacts" with the state of Washington. The Court held that if these "minimum contacts" were enough to satisfy "traditional notions of fair play and substantial justice," the company was liable to Washington State's jurisdiction. Given that International Shoe did sell shoes and maintain a sales staff in Washington State, the Court ruled that it did have these minimum contacts and was therefore liable for the tax.

The Court's reasoning was based on two major points: (1) To the extent that a corporation enjoys the privilege of conducting business within a state, it should also expect to meet the obligations of doing business within that state; (2) To the extent that a corporation wants to employ labor, it may expect to be taxed.

International Shoe set a major precedent for laws about personal jurisdiction. Unfortunately, for future lawyers, plaintiffs, and defendants, the decision was not far-reaching enough to specify exactly what constituted "minimum contact."

Related Cases

International Harvester Co. v. Kentucky, 234 U.S. 579 (1914).
People's Tobacco Co. v. American Tobacco Co., 246 U.S. 79 (1918).
Southern Pacific Co. v. Arizona, 325 U.S. 761 (1945).
Burger King Corp, v. Rudzewicz, 471 U.S. 462 (1985).
Asahi Metal Industry Co. v. Superior Court of California, 480 U.S. 102 (1987).

Bibliography and Further Reading

Dessem, R. Lawrence. "Personal Jurisdiction after Asahi: The Other (International) Shoe Drops." *Tennessee Law Review,* Vol. 55, no. 1, fall, 1987, pp. 41-93.

Lee, Mona A. "Burger King's Bifurcated Test for Personal Jurisdiction: The Reasonableness Inquiry Impedes Judicial Economy and Threatens a Defendant's Due Process Rights." *Temple Law Review,* Vol. 66, no. 3, fall, 1993, pp. 945-968.

Louis, Martin B. "Jurisdiction over Those Who Breach Their Contracts: The Lessons of Burger King." *North Carolina Law Review,* Vol. 72, no. 1, November, 1993, pp. 55-89.

FERGUSON V. SKRUPA DBA CREDIT ADVISORS

Legal Citation: 372 U.S. 726 (1963)

Petitioner
William M. Ferguson

Respondent
Skrupa DBA Credit Advisors

Petitioner's Claim
That Kansas legislation regulating the business of "debt adjusting" did not constitute a violation of constitutional due process.

Chief Lawyer for Petitioner
William M. Ferguson

Chief Lawyer for Respondent
Lawrence Weigand

Justices for the Court
Hugo Lafayette Black (writing for the Court), William J. Brennan, Jr., Tom C. Clark, Arthur Goldberg, John Marshall Harlan II, William O. Douglas, Potter Stewart, Earl Warren, Byron R. White

Justices Dissenting
None

Place
Washington, D.C.

Date of Decision
22 April 1963

Decision
Kansas legislation regulating debt adjusting was held not to be a violation of the Due Process Clause.

Significance
With its decision in *Ferguson v. Skrupa DBA Credit Advisors* the Supreme Court expressly disavowed its previous practice of assessing the wisdom of state legislation regulating economic activity.

The Facts of the Case

Skrupa, a citizen of the state of Kansas, was in business as a "debt adjuster" making payments to a client's creditors for a monthly fee. Concerned that this activity would lend itself "to grave abuses against distressed debtors, particularly in the lower income brackets," the state passed a law restricting the practice of debt adjustment to lawyers only. Skrupa filed a suit challenging this regulation. He claimed that his business was a "useful and desirable" one, that his activities were not "inherently immoral or dangerous," and that therefore the business could not be "absolutely prohibited" by the state.

Skrupa scored a victory in district court. A three-judge panel heard all the evidence and ruled that, while Skrupa's business did fall within the scope of the law, the act constituted an unreasonable regulation of a lawful business, in violation of the Due Process Clause of the Fourteenth Amendment. The court ordered Kansas to cease enforcing the statute. The state then appealed this decision to the U.S. Supreme Court.

High Court Rules

On 22 April 1963, the Supreme Court issued its decision. A unanimous majority voted to overturn the district court's decision. Justice Black penned the opinion of the Court, while Justice Harlan issued a short statement concurring in the judgment. The Court's decision left Kansas "free to decide for itself" whether or not to regulate the debt adjustment business.

In presenting his argument, Justice Black first reviewed the High Court's history with regard to cases involving state regulation of economic activity. "There was a time when the Due Process Clause was used by this Court to strike down laws which were thought unreasonable," Black wrote, "that is, unwise or incompatible with some particular economic or social philosophy." He concluded that it was time to re-evaluate the Court's policy with regard to judicial review of legislation. "Under the system of government created by our Constitution," he opined, "it is up to legislatures, not courts, to decide on the wisdom and utility of legislation." For Black, the long-standing Supreme Court belief "that due process autho-

Justice Hugo Lafayette Black. © Photograph by Peter Ehrenhaft. Collection of the Supreme Court of the United States.

rizes courts to hold laws unconstitutional when they believe the legislature has acted unwisely has long since been discarded. We have returned to the original constitutional proposition that courts do not substitute their social and economic beliefs for the judgment of legislative bodies, who are elected to pass laws."

Broad Scope for State Legislatures

In deciding this case, Black and his fellow justices explicitly disavowed the Court's historical role in evaluating "the wisdom, need, or appropriateness" of legislation. While conceding that debt adjustment may in fact have some social utility, Black argued that state legislatures should be given "broad scope to experiment with economic problems." "We conclude that the Kansas Legislature was free to decide for itself that legislation was needed to deal with the business of debt adjusting," Black concluded. "If the State of Kansas wants to limit debt adjusting to lawyers, the Equal Protection Clause does not forbid it." Justice Harlan concurred in the Court's judgment "on the ground that this state measure bears a rational relation to a constitutionally permissible objective."

Impact

The Supreme Court's decision in *Ferguson v. Skrupa* was about more than just the legality of debt adjusting in the state of Kansas. It put the Court on record as affording states wide latitude to regulate economic activity within their borders. This important shift in direction would affect many subsequent cases.

Related Cases

Levy v. Louisiana, 391 U.S. 68 (1968).
Kahn v. Shevin, 416 U.S. 351 (1974).

Bibliography and Further Reading

Chandler, Ralph C. *The Constitutional Law Dictionary.* Santa Barbara, CA: ABC-Clio, 1987.

Cushman, Robert, with Susan P. Koniak. *Leading Constitutional Decisions.* Englewood Cliffs, NJ: Prentice-Hall, Inc., 1992.

Menez, Joseph Francis. *Summaries of Leading Cases of the Constitution.* Savage, MD: Littlefield, Adams, 1990.

BALDWIN V. MONTANA FISH AND GAME COMMISSION

Legal Citation: 436 U.S. 371 (1978)

Appellant
Lester Baldwin, et al.

Appellee
Fish and Game Commission of Montana

Appellant's Claim
That Montana's state game regulations violated Article IV, Section 2 of the U.S. Constitution and the Equal Protection Clause of the Fourteenth Amendment.

Chief Lawyer for Appellant
James H. Goetz

Chief Lawyer for Appellee
Paul A. Lenzini

Justices for the Court
Harry A. Blackmun (writing for the Court), Warren E. Burger, Lewis F. Powell, Jr., William H. Rehnquist, John Paul Stevens, Potter Stewart

Justices Dissenting
William J. Brennan, Jr., Thurgood Marshall, Byron R. White

Place
Washington, D.C.

Date of Decision
23 May 1978

Decision
Montana's state fish and game laws were constitutional, and the appellant was not entitled to any relief from them.

Significance
The ability of states to regulate hunting, fishing, and environmental protection was upheld, even if such regulation discriminated against nonresidents of the state in question.

The state of Montana has long been renowned for its hunting and fishing, and maintains a thriving industry based on the outfitting and guiding of hunting and fishing parties. In the early 1970s, Lester Baldwin, a resident of Montana, was a state-licensed hunting guide specializing in the pursuit of elk. The majority of Baldwin's clients were from other states and traveled to Montana for the express purpose of elk hunting. In 1975, Montana's hunting regulations that required state residents pay $4 for an elk-hunting license, while nonresidents were required to purchase a combination hunting license, entitling them to shoot two deer and one elk, for $151.

Four of Baldwin's clients, who traveled from Minnesota to Montana each year to hunt elk, balked at the discrepancy between license fees for residents and nonresidents and, along with Baldwin, filed suit against the state in the U.S. District Court for the District of Montana. The plaintiffs sought relief from Montana licensing requirements, claiming that the state game laws violated their rights as set forth in Article IV, Section 2 of the U.S. Constitution and reiterated in the Equal Protection Clause of the Fourteenth Amendment. The district court ruled against Baldwin, et al., and the group appealed their case to the U.S. Supreme Court, which heard arguments on 5 October 1977.

Attorneys for the appellants argued that Montana's game laws, by discriminating against nonresidents in their fee structures, violated Article IV, Section 2 of the Constitution, which states in part that "citizens of each state shall be entitled to all privileges and immunities of citizens in the several states," as well as the Equal Protection Clause of the Fourteenth Amendment, which states in part that "no state shall make or enforce any law which shall abridge the privileges or immunities of citizens of the United States."

The respondents countered that Montana residents already paid for game conservation and regulation programs through their state taxes, and that the state itself, by emphasizing wildlife conservation, had sacrificed economic development for the benefit of all and was due compensation from residents of more economically developed and environmentally degraded areas. Finally, the appellees presented evidence that nonresident hunters, by virtue of their general lack of experience, were a more difficult enforcement problem for state game wardens than resident hunters.

On 23 May 1978, the Court upheld the decision of the district court. In rejecting the appellants' claim that the Montana game laws violated Article IV, Section 2 of the Constitution, the Court noted that this passage had "been interpreted to prevent a state from imposing unreasonable burdens on citizens of other states in pursuit of their common callings within the state," and that the game laws as they existed posed no threat to the right to hunt elk. The Court also found that the state game laws did not violate the Equal Protection Clause of the Fourteenth Amendment, since the laws' primary intent was the maintenance and improvement of the hunting conditions that drew the appellants to Montana in the first place. Chief Justice Burger, in a concurring opinion, noted that the right of states to regulate and preserve wildlife for the common good had long been recognized in U.S. law.

Justices Brennan, Marshall, and White dissented, noting that states should only be allowed to discriminate against nonresidents if "the presence or activity of nonresidents was the source or cause of the problem or effect with which the state sought to deal." They added that, "the discrimination practiced against nonresidents bore a substantial relation to the problem they presented." They did not feel that the presence of nonresident hunters had caused any extraordinary elk conservation problems for Montana.

Baldwin v. Montana Fish and Game Commission confirmed the ability of states to regulate hunting and fishing and environmental quality within their borders, even if such regulation is applied unequally to state residents and nonresidents. Environmental and wildlife management legislation was judged to be both a substantial state regulatory interest and a means of preserving finite resources for the public good, and as such, is beyond the purview of the Equal Protection Clause of the Fourteenth Amendment.

Related Cases

Hicklin v. Orbeck, 437 U.S. 518 (1978).
Supreme Court of New Hampshire v. Piper, 470 U.S. 274 (1985).
Supreme Court of Virginia v. Friedman, 487 U.S. 59 (1988).

Bibliography and Further Reading

Biskupic, Joan, and Elder Witt, eds. *Congressional Quarterly's Guide to the U.S. Supreme Court,* 3rd ed. Washington, DC: Congressional Quarterly, Inc., 1996.

Lund, Thomas Alan. *American Wildlife Law.* Berkeley: University of California Press, 1980.

PENN CENTRAL TRANSPORTATION COMPANY V. CITY OF NEW YORK

Legal Citation: 438 U.S. 104 (1978)

Appellant
Penn Central Transportation Company

Appellee
City of New York

Appellant's Claim
That New York City had taken its private property in violation of the Fifth and Fourteenth Amendments when designating the Grand Central Terminal as an historic landmark.

Chief Lawyer for Appellant
Daniel M. Gribbon

Chief Lawyer for Appellee
Leonard J. Koerner

Justices for the Court
Harry A. Blackmun, William J. Brennan, Jr. (writing for the Court), Thurgood Marshall, Lewis F. Powell, Jr., Potter Stewart, Byron R. White

Justices Dissenting
Warren E. Burger, William H. Rehnquist, John Paul Stevens

Place
Washington, D.C.

Date of Decision
26 June 1978

Decision
That the city of New York's designation of the Grand Central Terminal as a historic landmark, and the limitations on the use of the property inherent in that designation, did not constitute a taking of Penn Central's property.

Significance
Governments at all levels may impose limitations on land use without abridging the property rights of individuals and corporations as set forth in the Fifth and Fourteenth Amendments to the Constitution.

Many cities in the United States underwent extensive urban renewal programs in the early and mid-1960s. With construction of new commercial properties proceeding at a rapid pace, municipalities became concerned about losing historically or aesthetically outstanding buildings to the wrecking ball. As such, many cities, including New York City, passed ordinances allowing the city government to designate specific buildings and sites as protected landmarks. New York City's version was the Landmarks Preservation Law of 1965 (LPL), which created a Landmarks Preservation Commission (LPC) empowered to designate buildings, sites, and districts as being of historic interest. Such designation would allow the city to demand that a building's owner keep its exterior in "good repair," and forced building owners to secure LPC approval before making any alterations to their properties. Owners of designated buildings were allowed under the LPL to seek judicial review of the LPC's designation.

On 2 August 1967, the LPC declared the Grand Central Terminal, a building designed in the French beaux-arts style and opened in 1913, a designated historic building and the surrounding block a historic area. The building's owner, Penn Central Transportation Company, opposed the designation but failed to seek judicial review of the decision as it was entitled to do under the law. The LPC's designation was confirmed by the Board of Estimate on 21 September 1967.

Despite the designation of the Terminal and its surroundings as historically important, Penn Central entered into an agreement with UGP Properties, Inc., wherein UGP would construct a multistory office building above the existing terminal. Two plans for construction were presented to the LPC, one calling for the new building to be cantilevered over the terminal, and one calling for a partial demolition of the terminal to allow new construction. The LPC rejected both plans, ruling that in each case the original building would be so overshadowed by the new construction that its historical character would be lost. To compensate the companies, the city of New York offered to transfer the air rights to eight nearby parcels which could serve as alternative sites for the proposed building. The companies did not find these alternative sites suitable, however,

Grand Central Station,
New York City.
© Archive Photos.

and filed suit against the city of New York in the New York Supreme Court, claiming that the LPC could not prevent them from building lawfully on the site, and that the city's designation of the terminal as historical had constituted a "taking" of their property, for which compensation should be forthcoming. The state supreme court ruled in favor of the companies by affirming that the LPL was unconstitutional as applied to the terminal but refused to rule on the takings issue. The companies took their case to the U.S. Supreme Court, which agreed to hear the case. Arguments were presented on 17 April 1978.

Attorneys for Penn Central repeated their argument that the city of New York, in designating their terminal a historic landmark, had deprived the company of the gainful use of the air rights above the terminal, which would have accommodated the construction of the proposed UPC office building. They also held that the City's landmarks law effected a taking by reducing the value of their property and inhibiting its use. Furthermore, they stated that the city's landmarks law did not impose identical restrictions on all structures of a similar character, and therefore could not be fairly or consistently applied. Finally, they maintained that the city appropriated their property for a strictly governmental purpose that impaired the revenue potential of the property.

The Supreme Court affirmed the decision of the New York Court of Appeals and held that the designation of the terminal as a historic site did not constitute a "taking." The Court noted that the LPC did not prohibit any and all new construction to enhance the terminal, but rather would allow construction that would "harmonize in scale, material and character with the terminal." It was also clear that the terminal could continue to be used as it always had been following its designation as a historic landmark. Furthermore, the Court observed that the city's transferable development rights program should have enabled Penn Central and UPC to receive compensation for whatever losses they incurred through the designation of the terminal as a historic landmark. Finally, the Court stated categorically that the LPL did not effect a "taking" of the appellants' property, and that such a law was constitutional when applied for the general welfare and enforced so as to allow for compensation for loss of revenue of owners of historic properties.

This decision opened the way for more effective protection of historically, culturally, and environmentally important areas for the common good.

Related Cases

Barron v. Baltimore, 32 U.S. 243 (1833).
Village of Euclid v. Ambler Realty Co., 272 U.S. 365 (1926).
United States v. Causby, 328 U.S. 256 (1946).
Berman v. Parker, 348 U.S. 26 (1954).
Young v. American Mini Theaters, 427 U.S. 50 (1976).

Bibliography and Further Reading

Biskupic, Joan, and Elder Witt, eds. *Congressional Quarterly's Guide to the U.S. Supreme Court,* 3rd ed. Washington, DC: Congressional Quarterly, Inc., 1996.

Hall, Kermit L., ed. *The Oxford Companion to the Supreme Court of the United States.* New York: Oxford University Press, 1992.

Holmes, Barnham. *The Fifth Amendment.* Englewood Cliffs, NJ: Silver Burdett Press, 1991.

REEVES, INC. V. STAKE

Legal Citation: 447 U.S. 429 (1980)

Petitioner
Reeves, Inc., a Wyoming concrete distributor

Respondent
Stake, et al., members of the South Dakota Cement Commission

Petitioner's Claim
That South Dakota's refusal to sell cement to an out-of-state buyer, due to a "cement shortage" which compelled it to prefer purchasers from within the state, constituted "hoarding" and was a preferential system forbidden by the Commerce Clause of the Constitution.

Chief Lawyer for Respondent
William J. Janklow

Chief Lawyer for Petitioner
Dennis M. Kirven

Justices for the Court
Harry A. Blackmun (writing for the Court), Warren E. Burger, Thurgood Marshall, William H. Rehnquist, Potter Stewart

Justices Dissenting
William J. Brennan, Jr., Lewis F. Powell, Jr., John Paul Stevens, Byron R. White

Place
Washington, D.C.

Date of Decision
19 June 1980

Decision
In a ruling that relied heavily on the Court's earlier decision in *Hughes v. Alexandria Scrap Corporation* (1976), the Court held that South Dakota was acting as a "participant," rather than as a "regulator," in the interstate market. Hence, its withdrawal of its product for sale to out-of-state purchasers did not constitute a violation of the Commerce Clause.

Significance
Reeves, Inc. v. Stake developed the "participant-regulator" distinction which first appeared in *Hughes v. Alexandria Scrap Corporation* four years earlier. It helped solidify the understanding that a state, when it operated as a "participant" in interstate commerce, could undertake actions that, were it operating as a "regulator," would constitute protectionist practices forbidden under the Commerce Clause.

Cementing Commerce Between South Dakota and Wyoming

In the early 1900s, according to a report by the South Dakota State Cement Commission, South Dakota had only one cement plant. That one plant, which "had been operating successfully for years," was "bought by the so-called trust [a monopoly] and closed down." At the recommendation of the commission, South Dakota established its own state-run cement plant. This was in line with the sentiments of the Progressive Era, symbolized first by President Theodore Roosevelt and later by Wisconsin's Governor Robert La Follette. In reaction to the abuses of big business during the late nineteenth and early twentieth centuries, the Progressives increasingly came to rely on government rather than private enterprise to meet the needs of the people. Hence, the Cement Commission noted in its recommendation that "capitalists" would not consider it to their "advantage to build a new plant within the state." Therefore, South Dakota needed its own plant.

The need for cement was particularly great because of a regional shortage in that product, a shortage which "interfered with and delayed both public and private enterprise." This was not, however, because cement was a natural resource that had to be retrieved from the environment—a key point in *Reeves, Inc. v. Stake*. Rather, as the Supreme Court would later note in a comment drawn from a 1978 report by the Portland Cement Association,

> [C]ement is a finely ground manufactured mineral product, usually gray in color. It is mixed with water and sand, gravel, crushed stone, or other aggregates to form concrete, the rock-like substance that is the most widely used construction material in the world.

With the cement shortage "threatening the people of this state," in the words of the Cement Commission (which the Court simply referred to as "the Commission"), "there would be a ready market for the entire output of the plant within the state."

The state began building a plant in Rapid City in 1919, and the plant soon began producing more cement than builders in South Dakota could use. Even-

---

Hughes v. Alexandria Scrap Corporation

The Supreme Court's *Reeves, Inc. v. Stake* opinion relied heavily on its judgment in *Hughes v. Alexandria Scrap Corporation*, (1976). The earlier case involved a Maryland statute whereby the state paid a bounty to scrap processors who presented an inoperable automobile more than eight years old to the state. In 1974, Maryland amended its provisions regarding these junk cars, or "hulks," establishing a requirement that out-of-state scrap processors must present a certificate of title or police documentation to show that the hulk was obtained legally. Alexan-

dria Scrap Corp., a Virginia company, brought a lawsuit charging that the statute was a violation of the Constitution's Commerce Clause, infringing on the company's right to equal protection under the law. After a district court granted a summary judgement in favor of the company, the case was appealed to the Supreme Court, which reversed the ruling by a 6-3 majority, holding that Maryland was acting as a participant in the scrap-metal market, not a regulator. Thus, its laws did not interfere with the flow of interstate commerce.

---

tually, its clientele spread to nine nearby states, many of which were (like South Dakota) sparsely populated and lacking in the abundant commercial facilities to which most residents of the East and West Coasts were accustomed. During the period from 1970 to 1977, some forty percent of the plant's output was sold to buyers outside the state of South Dakota, one of whom was Reeves, Inc. The latter, a ready-mix concrete distributor based in the even more sparsely populated state of Wyoming, had begun operations in 1958, and had facilities in the Wyoming towns of Buffalo, Gillette, and Sheridan. As the supplier of more than half of the ready-mix concrete for three northwestern Wyoming counties, Reeves brought a great deal of business to the South Dakota plant. Over the course of a twenty-year relationship, Reeves's purchases from the commission grew to $1,172,000 in 1977, and by 1978, it was buying 95 percent of its cement from that one source.

This dependency proved unfortunate when the plant's production slowed down in 1978 due to difficulties at the Rapid City facility. Such problems were compounded when a sudden building boom in the region and the nation resulted in a "serious cement shortage" of the type that had influenced the establishment of the plant nearly 60 years before. In response to this situation, the commission "reaffirmed" its policy of supplying South Dakota customers first, then of honoring any contracts with outside buyers on a first-come, first-served basis. Reeves, however, lacked even a supply contract, and since it was definitely an out-of-state buyer, it "was hit hard and quickly by this development," in the words of the Supreme Court. On 30 June 1978, the plant sent word to Reeves that it could not continue filling the company's orders. Less than a week later, on 5 July, it turned away a Reeves truck that had arrived to pick up an order. Faced with a crisis, Reeves suddenly had to cut production by a staggering 76 percent in mid-July—the height of the building season.

On 19 July 1978, Reeves brought a suit against the commission in district court, challenging the plant's

policy of giving preference to South Dakotans, and seeking injunctive relief. The district court ruled that the "hoarding" of cement practiced by South Dakota went against the spirit of the Constitution's Commerce Clause. The U.S. Court of Appeals for the Eight Circuit, however, reversed this decision. Citing *Hughes v. Alexandria Scrap Corporation,* it held that South Dakota had "simply acted in a proprietary capacity," the permissibility of which had been established in that case.

States As Participators: "Good Sense and Sound Law"

The Supreme Court held, 5-4, that "South Dakota's resident-preference program for the sale of cement does not violate the Commerce Clause." Writing for the majority, Justice Blackmun held that there was nothing in the clause to stop any state—assuming Congress did not expressly prohibit it—"from participating in the market and exercising the right to favor its own citizens over others." The Commerce Clause, according to the Court, was established primarily to respond to issues relating to state taxes and "regulatory measures impeding free private trade in the national market-place," and the Court found no evidence that South Dakota had attempted to impose such impediments to interstate trade. Given the touchy matter of state sovereignty, the Court held that any minor adjustments necessary in this area should be left up to Congress rather than the judicial branch. As for Reeves's arguments for invalidating South Dakota's program of preferring state residents, the Court found them "weak at best."

Much of the Court's ruling in *Reeves* went back to its opinion in *Alexandria Scrap,* and Blackmun began his reasoning with a brief review of the earlier case. The state of Maryland had a program in place to encourage the removal of abandoned automobiles from its roadways and junkyards by offering a financial incentive for each wrecked car turned recovered. The original legislation, passed in 1969, provided that anyone presenting a wrecked car should be able to provide documentation proving ownership. That stipulation did not apply to "hulks," or inoperable cars more than eight years old. In 1974, however, the state legislature amended the statute to require documentation for hulks as well, and specifically required "more exacting documentation" (in the Court's words) from out-of-state persons presenting such vehicles. According to the suit filed by Alexandria Scrap, a Virginia processor of hulks, "the practical effect was substantially the same" as if Maryland had simply stopped paying any money for hulks brought by unlicensed suppliers to licensed non-Maryland processors such as Alexandria Scrap.

The district court struck down Maryland's legislation, but the Supreme Court reversed on the grounds that the statute questioned in *Alexandria Scrap* was not "the kind of action with which the Commerce Clause is concerned." Maryland, the Court reasoned, had not "sought to prohibit the flow of hulks, or to regulate the conditions under which it may occur. Instead, it ha[d] entered into the market itself to bid up their price." Thus, it characterized the state of Maryland as a market participant rather than a market regulator. Addressing the case before the Court in *Reeves,* Justice Blackmun wrote that "the basic distinction drawn in *Alexandria Scrap* between States as market participants and States as market regulators makes good sense and sound law."

Just as the Court in *Alexandria Scrap* had written that "nothing in the purposes animating the Commerce Clause prohibits a state, in the absence of congressional action, from participating in the market and exercising the right to favor its own citizens over others," so Justice Blackmun wrote now that there was "no indication of a constitutional plan to limit the ability of the States themselves to operate freely in the free market." The issue of state sovereignty further counseled judicial restraint in an area which the Court judged to be the province of Congress.

As for the question of whether South Dakota had operated as a regulator or a participant, the Court held it to be the latter. In making the claim that South Dakota had "exploited" the interstate market, Blackmun wrote, the petitioner had used "self-serving" language: "An equally fair characterization is that neighboring States long have benefited from South Dakota's foresight and industry."

The remainder of the Court's opinion was devoted to addressing four specific arguments offered by Reeves's council. First, the petitioner had charged that South Dakota was practicing economic "protectionism" by favoring its own citizens over others. The Court "[found] the label 'protectionism' of little help in this context." Usually the term refers to a national policy of placing heavy duties on imports to encourage the sale of goods produced at home, but here it was used to describe a state policy of "[limiting] benefits gener-

ated by a state program to those who fund the state treasury and whom the State was created to serve." Second was the petitioner's charge of "hoarding." In the Court's view, that term only made sense when describing a policy of preventing the interstate flow of natural resources such as coal, timber, or wild game, not something like cement. Cement is "the end product of a complex process whereby a costly physical plant and human labor act on raw materials." Third, Reeves's counsel had charged that the commission program impeded commerce by creating a situation in which South Dakota suppliers of ready-mix concrete had a competitive advantage in the out-of-state market. This argument the Court found without merit, because it seemed to imply that South Dakota should be barred from selling its cement elsewhere—"even a greater measure of protectionism and stifling of interstate commerce than the present system allows." Finally, the petitioner argued that South Dakota, having replaced free-market or private suppliers, should be forced to operate as a free-market supplier—i.e., supplying goods entirely on a first-come, first-served basis, without state preference. The Court held this argument "simplistic and speculative," since there was no guarantee that a free-market supplier would even be operating in South Dakota at that point if the commission had not established its plant six decades earlier. "Indeed," Justice Blackmun wrote, "it is quite possible that petitioner would never have existed—far less operated successfully for 20 years—had it not been for South Dakota cement."

A Warning Against "Balkanization"

Justice Powell, in a dissenting opinion joined by Justices Brennan, White, and Stevens, wrote that in fact the South Dakota policy "represents precisely the kind of economic protectionism that the Commerce Clause was intended to prevent." Justice Powell agreed with the Court. He said, that South Dakota could sell cement without violating the clause—but it could not "withhold its cement from interstate commerce in order to benefit private citizens and businesses within the State" and still remain within the scope of the Commerce Clause.

After a brief review of the meaning of interstate commerce, both in the Constitution and in the Court's interpretation, Justice Powell made what he held was a key distinction. If a public entity undertook an enterprise integral to the functioning of traditional government—e.g., police or fire protection—then, as the Court had ruled in *National League of Cities v. Usery* (1976), the Clause should not apply to it. But if the state entered the private market in order to operate a commercial enterprise that benefited its own citizens, it was within the scope of the clause, which had been placed in the Constitution to prevent "economic

Balkanization." His implication was that without the proper flow of interstate commerce as governed by the clause, the states of the Union would become fragmented like the nations of Europe's Balkan Peninsula, which at that time—more than a decade before the conflicts in Bosnia, Croatia, and elsewhere—were already known for their many ethnic, cultural, and national divisions.

Justice Powell then addressed what he saw as the differences between the present case and *Alexandria Scrap*, and thus arrived at a different answer to the question of whether South Dakota had acted as a participant or a regulator. Whereas Maryland's policy had done nothing to cut off interstate trade, South Dakota's clearly had. Thus, though he "share[d] the Court's desire to preserve state sovereignty," Powell wrote that he had to stand by the Commerce Clause "as a limitation on that sovereignty." In its decision, "the Court today approves protectionist policies," and its decision could not be reconciled with the purpose of a free national economy.

Impact

Reeves solidified the "participant-regulator" distinction first established in *Alexandria Scrap*. Three years later, with *White v. Massachusetts Council of Construction Employers, Inc.* (1983), the Court reinforced its holding in the two earlier cases by upholding a mayor's executive order that set aside a fixed number of jobs on city projects for local residents.

Related Cases

Hughes v. Alexandria Scrap Corporation, 426 U.S. 794 (1976).
National League of Cities v. Usery, 426 U.S. 833 (1976).
White v. Massachusetts Council of Construction Employers, 460 U.S. 204 (1983).

Bibliography and Further Reading

Carvajal, Alejandr. "State and Local 'Free Burma' Laws: The Case for Sub-National Trade Sanctions." *Law and Policy in International Business,* winter 1998, p. 257.

Chandler, Ralph C., Richard A. Enslen, and Peter G. Renstrom. *The Constitutional Law Dictionary.* Santa Barbara, CA: ABC-Clio, 1991.

Levy, Leonard W., ed. *Encyclopedia of the American Constitution.* New York: Macmillan, 1986.

"Limiting Interstate Commerce Clause Scrutiny—*Reeves, Inc. v. Stake.*" *DePaul Law Review,* Vol. 30, spring 1981, pp. 685-704.

Phillips, Greer L. "Commerce Clause Immunity for State Proprietary Activities: *Reeves, Inc. v. Stake.*" *Harvard Journal of Law and Public Policy,* Vol. 4, summer 1981, pp. 365-80.

PENNHURST STATE SCHOOL & HOSPITAL V. HALDERMAN

Legal Citation: 451 U.S. 1 (1981)

Petitioner
Pennhurst State School & Hospital

Respondent
Terri Lee Halderman

Petitioner's Claim
That the federal court cannot award injunctive relief against state officials where the relief is justified through state law.

Chief Lawyer for Petitioner
H. Bartow Farr III

Chief Lawyer for Respondent
Thomas K. Gilhool

Justices for the Court
Warren E. Burger, Sandra Day O'Connor, Lewis F. Powell, Jr. (writing for the Court), William H. Rehnquist, Byron R. White

Justices Dissenting
Harry A. Blackmun, William J. Brennan, Jr., Thurgood Marshall, John Paul Stevens

Place
Washington, D.C.

Date of Decision
23 January 1984

Decision
The Eleventh Amendment of the Constitution bars federal courts from granting an injunction ordering state officials to conform their conduct to state law.

Significance
In accordance with the Eleventh Amendment, if a legal claim is brought against a state official for violating a state law, then the federal court has no jurisdiction to grant relief unless the state actions are also violative of federal law.

Terri Lee Halderman was a resident of Pennhurst State School and Hospital, which is a state institution in Pennsylvania that was established for the care of the mentally retarded. In 1974, Halderman brought a class action suit on behalf of the present and any future residents of Pennhurst against the hospital, its officials, and other state and county officers, including the Pennsylvania Department of Public Welfare. The suit alleged that the hospital violated the plaintiffs' rights under the Eighth and Fourteenth Amendments, the Developmentally Disabled Assistance and Bill of Rights Act, as well as the Pennsylvania Mental Health and Retardation Act of 1966 (MH/MR).

In 1977, the district court ruled in favor of the plaintiffs, stating:

> Conditions at Pennhurst are not only dangerous, with the residents often physically abused or drugged by staff members, but also inadequate for the habilitation of the retarded. Indeed, the court found that the physical, intellectual, and emotional skills of some residents have deteriorated at Pennhurst.

The district court held that the conditions at Pennhurst violated: (1) the Due Process Clause and the MH/MR Act, both of which provide for "minimally adequate habilitation," (2) The Eight Amendment's "freedom from harm" provision, applied to the states through the Fourteenth Amendment, and (3) the Equal Protection Clause and the Rehabilitation Act, both forbidding "discriminatory habilitation." Additionally, the district court held that "due process [requires] that if a state undertakes the habilitation of a retarded person, it must do so in the least restrictive setting [for] that individual's needs." The court ordered the retarded residents be removed and Pennhurst provide other living arrangements for the patients. A special master was appointed to oversee and implement these changes. The court ordered the hospital to be closed.

Pennhurst appealed this decision to the court of appeals. They based their appeal on the Eleventh Amendment of the U.S. Constitution, arguing that the amendment stated that the federal court did not have jurisdiction to rule on a state claim. The Federal Court

The Developmentally Disabled Assistance and Bill of Rights Act

Passed by Congress in 1975, the Developmentally Disabled Assistance and Bill of Rights Act set up a joint federal and state program under which the federal government offered financial assistance to states establishing and maintaining programs for the developmentally disabled or mentally retarded. State participation in the act was voluntary, and states could either comply with the act's provisions or miss out on federal funding. Under the "bill of rights" section of the act, developmentally disabled persons "have a right to appropriate treatment, services, and habilitation" in "the setting that is least restrictive of . . . personal liberty."

Like the Americans with Disabilities Act (ADA) of 1990, the Developmentally Disabled Assistance and Bill of Rights Act was an outgrowth of the Rehabilitation Act of 1973. The latter prohibited discrimination on the basis of disability in any activities with federal funding. The ADA would extend this prohibition to the state and local governments and to the private sector.

Source(s): Bradley, David, and Shelley Fisher Fishkin, eds. *The Encyclopedia of Civil Rights in America.* Armonk, NY: Sharpe, 1998.

of Appeals held that the Eleventh Amendment did not bar it from granting this type of injunctive relief against state officials because the same result would have been obtained with respect to the state-law claim. Thus, the court argued that it had pendant jurisdiction over the state portion. (Pendant jurisdiction exists when state and federal claims derive from a common nucleus of operative fact and the disposition of the nonfederal claims is deemed necessary to rule on the federal claim. In such cases, jurisdiction is said to extend to the entire claim, not just the federal parts.) Although the appellate court affirmed the lower court's decision and adopted the least restrictive means standard, it did not rely on the constitutional grounds, and only on the MH/MR Act. The court of appeals did not order the hospital to close, however, but rather stated that it was within the discretion of the district court and/or its court-appointed special master to determine on a case-by-case basis, which patients should be removed.

The Supreme Court noted three arguments presented to them by the hospital: (1) the Eleventh Amendment forbids federal courts from ordering state officials to conform their conduct to state law, (2) comity (the recognition of one court by another) prohibits the district court from issuing the injunction, and (3) the district court erred when it appointed the special master and others to supervise decisions on state law issues. In a 5-4 decision, the Supreme Court reversed the lower courts holding as to the first issue, and thus, never needed to address the final two claims.

The Eleventh Amendment bars suits against state officials where the state is a party, regardless of whether the injunctive relief is sought. However, in *Ex parte Young* (1908), the Court derived an exception to this rule. They determined that a suit challenging the actions of a state official, on federal constitutional claims, is not an action against the state, and thus, not violative of the Eleventh

Amendment. This was an attempt at balancing the notion that federal law is supreme to state while still giving the states the sovereign immunity that is granted them in the Constitution.

The majority reasoned that *Young* does not and cannot apply to this case. Here, the lower federal courts were granting injunctive relief ordering state officials to act in conformity with state law. The Court found this to be the determining factor in the case. *Young* held that a state official's actions cannot violate federal law, but here the lower courts were stating that a state officials actions could not violate their own state's law. Here, the issue before the federal court was wholly a state issue.

Lawyers, judges, and other persons involved in the application of the law agree that this decision established an interesting precedent. Before this case, federal courts were inclined to avoid the constitutional issues if relief could be granted on non-constitutional grounds. However, in light of this holding, state law violation could no longer serve as the basis for an injunction, so the Court would have no choice but to rule on the federal constitutional claims. Before this case, if a court found a violation of state law, the state officials could change its laws if they were unhappy with the federal court's conclusion. However, after this case, if the court now determines that the state law violates the federal constitution, the state cannot undo or otherwise undermine the ruling. In any event, this case placed a much tighter restraint on the powers of the federal courts over the states.

Related Cases

Ex Parte Young, 209 U.S. 123 (1908).

Ashwander v. Tennessee Valley Authority, 297 U.S. 288 (1936).

Hutto v. Finney, 437 U.S. 678 (1978).

Bibliography and Further Reading

Althouse, Ann. "How to Build a Separate Sphere: Federal Courts and State Power." *Harvard Law Review,* Vol. 1485, 1987.

Berman, Michael N. "Removal and the Eleventh Amendment: The Case for District Court Remand Discretion to Avoid a Bifurcated Suit." *Michigan Law Review,* December 1993, p. 683.

Gearhart, Camille. "Confronting the Fictions of the Eleventh Amendment." *Washington Law Review,* Vol. 407, 1985.

Randall, Jane S. " *Pennhurst v. Halderman:* A Bill of Rights in Name Only." *University of Toledo Law Review,* Vol. 214, no. 1.

SUPREME COURT OF NEW HAMPSHIRE V. PIPER

Legal Citation: 470 U.S. 274 (1985)

Appellant
Supreme Court of New Hampshire

Appellee
Kathryn A. Piper

Appellant's Claim
That the New Hampshire state law limiting admission to the bar to residents did not violate the Constitution's Privileges and Immunities Clause.

Chief Lawyer for Appellant
Martin L. Gross

Chief Lawyer for Appellee
Jon Meyer

Justices for the Court
Harry A. Blackmun, William J. Brennan, Jr., Warren E. Burger, Thurgood Marshall, Sandra Day O'Connor, Lewis F. Powell, Jr. (writing for the Court), John Paul Stevens, Byron R. White

Justices Dissenting
William H. Rehnquist

Place
Washington, D.C.

Date of Decision
4 March 1985

Decision
The Supreme Court affirmed the judgment of the Court of Appeals for the First Circuit that New Hampshire's limiting of bar admission to state residents violated the Privileges and Immunities Clause.

Significance
The practice of law was held to be a business like any other, protected by the federal guarantee against state-to-state discrimination.

Rights of Non-residents

The *Supreme Court of New Hampshire v. Piper* was an important states' rights case. At issue were the individual states' abilities to grant privileges to residents that were denied to non-residents. The Supreme Court upheld its ruling that a state must show substantial reason for any difference in treatment between residents and non-residents. Although the New Hampshire Supreme Court argued that such reasons were present in the case of the practice of law, the U.S. Supreme Court disagreed.

New Hampshire rules excluded non-residents from its bar. Kathryn Piper, a resident of Vermont who lived about four hundred yards from the New Hampshire border, received permission to take the New Hampshire bar exam by filing a statement of her intent to become a New Hampshire resident. After passing the bar, Piper was not allowed to swear in, and filed an application for an exception from the residency requirement. The New Hampshire Supreme Court denied her request, and she then filed an action in federal district court, claiming that the residency requirement violated Article 4, Section 2 of the United States Constitution.

The Privileges and Immunities of United States Citizens

Article 4, Section 2 includes a section known as the Privileges and Immunities Clause. One of several items intended at the nation's formation to create a national economic union, the Privileges and Immunities Clause gave citizens of one state the right to conduct business in another state on equal terms with that state's citizens. The clause was not used as commonly as the Commerce Clause, which protects interstate commerce. Although Alexander Hamilton, in *The Federalist,* called the idea that no state could discriminate against the citizens of another state "the basis of the Union," the Supreme Court had largely interpreted the Privileges and Immunities Clause as meaning that states needed to show good reason in order to discriminate against non-residents. Nonetheless, the district court and the court of appeals both affirmed that the residency requirement denied Piper her rights under the Privileges and Immunities Clause, finding that the opportunity to practice law was a "fundamental right" that was being denied her.

The New Hampshire Supreme Court argued that there were substantive reasons for the residency requirement. Nonresidents, it argued, would have fewer reasons than residents to familiarize themselves with local rules and procedures, and would be less likely "to behave ethically, to be available for court proceedings, and to do *pro bono* and other volunteer work in the State." The U.S. Supreme Court, like the two courts preceding it, determined that these were not substantial enough reasons for discrimination. The practice of law, wrote Justice Powell in the Court opinion, was not an exercise of state power that justified a residency requirement. Furthermore, his opinion suggested that there were positive benefits to having out-of-state residents practice law in a state. For instance, they might be more likely to represent people raising unpopular federal claims.

Variety of Opinions

The decision was not unanimous. Justice White, while concurring in the result, filed an opinion in which he argued that the residency requirement should be excepted in Piper's particular case, since she lived so near New Hampshire and "would be indistinguishable from other New Hampshire lawyers." But he also expressed his opinion that the case should be decided on those grounds alone. The Court need not, according to White, "decide the facial validity of the New Hampshire residency requirement." He thus agreed with the result of the decision, but not every aspect of Powell's opinion.

Justice Rehnquist filed a dissenting opinion, arguing that the practice of law was different from the practice of other professions. The practice of law, he asserted, was "non-national," since laws themselves were created locally and intended to respond to local interests. Rehnquist summarized:

> Put simply, the State has a substantial interest in creating its own set of laws responsive to its own local interests, and it is reasonable for a State to decide that those people who have been trained to analyze law and policy are better equipped to write those state laws and adjudicate cases arising under them. The State therefore may decide that it has an interest in maximizing the number of resident lawyers, so as to increase the quality of the pool from which its lawmakers can be drawn.

Related Cases

Baldwin v. Montana Fish and Game Commission, 436 U.S. 371 (1978).
Hicklin v. Orbeck, 437 U.S. 518 (1978).

Bibliography and Further Reading

Biskupic, Joan, and Elder Witt, eds. *Congressional Quarterly's Guide to the U.S. Supreme Court*, 3rd ed. Washington, DC: Congressional Quarterly, Inc., 1996.

LAMBERT V. BLACKWELL

Legal Citation: 134 F.3d 506 (1997)

Appellant
Lisa Michelle Lambert

Appellee
Charlotte Blackwell and the State of Pennsylvania

Appellant's Claim
That she should be granted *habeas corpus* and should be allowed to claim innocence from having committed the murder for which she was convicted.

Chief Lawyer for Appellant
Peter S. Greenberg

Chief Lawyer for Appellee
Richard A. Sprague

Justices for the Court
Arthur L. Alarcon, Morton Greenberg, Carol Mansmann (writing for the court)

Justices Dissenting
None

Place
Lancaster, Pennsylvania

Date of Decision
29 December 1997

Decision
Ruled against Lambert, returning her to prison.

Significance
By denying a petition for federal writ of *habeas corpus*, the ruling spotlights the late twentieth century role of federalism in constitutional criminal law. Federal courts increasingly deferred to state court systems in criminal justice cases. Actions by the Supreme Court and Congress in the 1990s significantly narrowed the ability of state prisoners to obtain federal writs of *habeas corpus*. Federal courts would not accept petitions if any unresolved aspects to the case existed in state courts. Claims simply of innocence, even based on new evidence, were not enough. Advocates for the protection of individual constitutional rights were concerned with the treatment that individuals would receive from states given fewer federal checks.

Writ means court order and *habeas corpus* comes from Latin meaning "you have the body." A writ of *habeas corpus* is therefore a court order directing someone, such as a prison warden, to produce a prisoner at a specific place and time. The court may then determine the legality of the detainment. The *habeas corpus* writ provides a powerful means to correct legal errors by releasing prisoners after convictions even where all procedural safeguards and appeals had been applied. The prisoner holds responsibility to initiate the writ process by submitting to the court a petition explaining how their imprisonment violates a constitutional right.

Such writs have a long history in English common law, first used by English courts to question detentions by feudal lords. The writ of *habeas corpus* is addressed briefly in Article I of the U.S. Constitution recognizing its important role except "in Cases of Rebellion or Invasion" for purposes of "public Safety." As such, President Abraham Lincoln suspended *habeas corpus* writs during the Civil War.

Use of the *habeas corpus* writ began expanding in the latter 19th century. The Habeas Corpus Act of 1867 extended authority of federal courts to issue writs for any person detained, including state prisoners. Beginning with *Brown v. Allen* (1953), a series of Court rulings further expanded *habeas corpus* law into the realm of civil rights protection. In 1963 the Court ruled in *Fay v. Noia* that prisoner access to federal review was itself a fundamental right, and in *Townsend v. Sain* the Court ruled that federal judges should not defer to state judge's findings but apply federal law independently.

Comity and Exhaustion

A critical feature of federal courts overseeing state court decisions in criminal cases is the requirement of "exhaustion." The requirement means a person must have pursued all claims related to a case in one court before pursuing them in another. The interests of "comity" and federalism play significant roles in requiring exhaustion of all potential state remedies before federal involvement. Comity means one court should not act within its jurisdiction until another court with similar powers and already involved in the case has an opportunity to fully rule on the matter. This means state courts should also have the opportunity to respond to allegations they erred before federal courts become involved. Federalism essentially refers to the division of powers between federal and state governments, and the degree of freedom that states have from federal control. That degree has varied through time based on prevailing theories. The Court held in *Frisbie v. Collins* (1952) that only in cases of "special circumstances" should a federal court accept a case with unexhausted claims. However, the Court did not offer examples of such circumstances, leaving much uncertainty.

Given these principles, federal courts only issued writs for petitions alleging substantial constitutional violations. The Due Process Clause of the Fifth and Fourteenth Amendments were commonly the basis for petitions, including claims of prosecutorial misconduct and ineffective assistance of legal counsel. Often, in such situations the prisoner was allowed an evidentiary hearing to review their evidence.

Public pressure from victims' rights advocates and others seeking swifter criminal proceedings mounted through the 1970s. A transformation of the Supreme Court toward dramatically decreasing the amount of federal court involvement in state judicial proceedings began with *Wainwright v. Sykes* (1977). Central to related debates were arguments about the appropriate role of federal court jurisdiction in a system based on federalism. Eventually, use of federal *habeas corpus* writs was substantially narrowed by the 1990s. In *Herrera v. Collins* (1993) the Court held that claims of "actual innocence" were insufficient to justify writs. Newly discovered evidence was no longer enough by itself.

In the mid-1990s the ruling in *Schlup v. Delo* (1995) and the passage of the Anti-Terrorism and Effective Death Penalty Act (AEDPA) of 1996 brought even tougher standards to the *habeas corpus* appeals process. Prisoners challenging their convictions were required to show "clear and convincing" evidence for courts to accept their petitions, a considerably more difficult standard. The act more clearly required exhaustion of all claims at the state level before a federal judge could consider issuing a writ. All claims in a federal *habeas corpus* petition must have been previously presented to state courts for action. Such a requirement avoided "piecemeal" litigation by forcing all claims to be decided in a single proceeding. The exhaustion requirement could be waived if no actual state process existed for a particular case, or if it was proven that the state could not effectively protect a petitioner's rights.

A Teenage Love Triangle

In June of 1991, 15-year-old Laurie Show had a brief romantic involvement with Lawrence "Butch" Yunkin, the boyfriend of Lisa Lambert. Lambert, an 18-year-old resident of rural Pennsylvania, accosted Show on

several occasions regarding the relationship. On 20 December 1991, Show was brutally murdered at her home, her throat slashed. Authorities arrested Lambert, six months pregnant with Yunkin's child, and her friend Tabitha Buck on homicide charges. Buck was convicted of second degree murder and sentenced to life in prison. Yunkin pled guilty to hindering apprehension by assisting the two after the murder and received 10 to 20 years in prison. In July of 1992 the Court of Common Pleas of Lancaster County, Pennsylvania, convicted Lambert of first-degree murder and sentenced her to life in prison.

Following conviction, Lambert raised various allegations of trial error and misconduct by the state prosecutor but the court denied her motions. Lambert next filed a motion for a retrial based on new evidence from Yunkin's later testimony in other court proceedings. She also claimed ineffective lawyer assistance in her original trial for failure to present various forms of crucial evidence. In March of 1995 a Pennsylvania state court denied Lambert's motion. The Superior Court of Pennsylvania also denied her later appeal in January of 1996 as did the Pennsylvania Supreme Court in July of 1996.

Lambert next filed a federal *habeas corpus* petition in September of 1996 with the U.S. District Court of the Eastern District of Pennsylvania. Not only did she carry her previous claims forward, but also added new ones including "actual innocence" of the murder and police misconduct. Lambert alleged a massive effort by police and prosecutors to frame her for the murder. The state responded that Lambert's case was not entitled to federal review because she had not exhausted state court remedies for the newer claims. Despite state arguments, the court decided to conduct an evidentiary hearing on the claims of innocence and prosecutorial misconduct because of the case's "highly unusual circumstances." After two weeks of hearings, the district court found in April of 1997 that a recent amendment to Pennsylvania criminal law had effectively eliminated any means for Lambert to contest her conviction in state courts. Therefore, all possible state remedies were exhausted. The court issued the writ, released Lambert from custody, and prohibited Pennsylvania from holding a retrial since the state could not be trusted in this case. The federal judge found that the case was filled with police perjury, witness tampering, fabricated evidence, and suppression of evidence by the state prosecutor leading to "a manifestly unjust incarceration." The judge sent his opinion to the U.S. Attorney General for possible legal action against state prosecutors and police. Pennsylvania immediately appealed to the federal court of appeals.

Back to Prison

Both Lambert and Blackwell agreed that Lambert was raising new issues not addressed in the state courts.

However, Lambert contended a federal court could issue writs when "extraordinary circumstances are present." Federal Circuit Judge Mansmann, writing the decision, found such circumstances were not adequately defined in case law and, thus, not a valid defense. Consequently, Mansmann wrote that unlike the district court the appeals court could not so quickly pass over Lambert's claims of exhaustion and "must consider whether Lambert is required to present her unexhausted claims to the Pennsylvania courts." Mansmann found Lambert's extensive claims "present unresolved questions of fact and of state law and, thus, the interests of comity and justice are better served by requiring complete exhaustion" by Pennsylvania courts. Mansmann found no authority for the district court to waive the exhaustion requirement since Pennsylvania had not requested such a waiver as required in the revised AEDPA.

Mansmann wrote the assessment of Lambert's "actual innocence" claim was unnecessary. Such an examination, also prohibited under AEDPA, would "deprive the state courts of an opportunity to correct their own errors, if any." Mansmann reversed the district court's not guilty verdict and reinstated her life sentence. Lambert's ten months of freedom came to an end. Mansmann ordered the district court to dismiss the writ petition and allow Lambert to pursue her unexhausted claims in the appropriate Pennsylvania state court.

Impact

Following the decision, Lambert appealed to the U.S. Supreme Court and requested an emergency release pending the Court's action. In early August of 1998, Justice David H. Souter denied her request for release. Later in August, a Pennsylvania court rejected Lambert's appeal. The judge wrote that Lambert "was the only person with the level of emotion [needed] . . . to have performed that dreadful act."

Lambert revealed how extreme an "actual innocence" claim must be to obtain a writ of habeas corpus under the AEDPA. The case also marked a rare occasion in which a person convicted of murder was ordered released by a federal judge without returning the case to state courts. Some asserted the writ standard had become too tough for petitioners to prove errors—that

if actually proven, such extensive misconduct might warrant prosecution as attempted murder by wrongfully seeking death penalties for the accused.

Lambert also highlighted the larger debate over federalism in the U.S. legal system. During the Warren Court era, a doctrine of national supremacy prevailed in which the federal courts held expansive powers over review of state actions, including state court decisions. By the 1990s the alternate theory of federalism, dual sovereignty, again prevailed where states held a high degree of independence over such issues as health, education, and criminal justice. By the late 1990s, many were concerned over how fair and consistent state judges, less susceptible to federal oversight, would apply review procedures. The Court and Congress had substantially limited the ability of state prisoners to seek review of alleged civil rights violations outside the state court systems that originally convicted them. The role of federal courts under the changing habeas corpus system was still being defined as the twentieth century drew to a close.

Related Cases

Frisbie v. Collins, 342 U.S. 519 (1952).
Brown v. Allen, 344 U.S. 443 (1953).
Townsend v. Sain, 372 U.S. 293 (1963).
Fay v. Noia, 372 U.S. 391 (1963).
Wainwright v. Sykes, 433 U.S. 72 (1977).
Herrera v. Collins, 113 S. Ct. 853 (1993).
Schlup v. Delo, 513 U.S. 298 (1995).

Bibliography and Further Reading

"'The Great Writ' Hit: A New Law Will Curb Death-Row Appeals." Newsweek, May 6, 1996.

Harriger, Katy J. "The Federalism Debate in the Transformation of the Federal Habeas Corpus Law." Publius, Vol. 27, no. 3, 1996, pp. 1-22.

Liebman, James S., and Randy Hertz. Federal Habeas Corpus Practice and Procedure, 2nd Ed. Charlottesville, VA: Michie Co., 1994.

"Rewriting the Great Writ: Standards of Review for Habeas Corpus Under the New 28 U.S.C. Sec. 2254." Harvard Law Review, Vol. 110, 1997, p. 1869-1885.

JUDICIAL POWERS

The Judicial Branch

The judicial system, along with the executive and legislative systems, comprise the three branches of the U.S. government. The judicial branch is composed of federal and state courts and the judges who preside in these courts. The purpose of the judiciary is to interpret laws and make rulings on legal questions. Additionally, it determines if laws passed by legislatures, on a national, state, or local level, violate the U.S. Constitution. The courts also consider the constitutionality of the actions taken by the executive branch. This process, called judicial review, allows the judiciary to void or nullify any laws or actions that they decide are unconstitutional. In response, the legislative branch may ratify a Constitutional amendment in order to make the legislation lawful. In this way, the judicial branch plays a crucial role in the government's system of checks and balances.

The authority of the federal court system is granted by Article III, Section 1, of the Constitution, which states: "The judicial power of the United States, shall be vested in one supreme court, and in such inferior courts as the Congress may from time to time ordain and establish." Article III, Section 2, of the Constitution extends the jurisdiction of the federal courts to cases, in law and equity, that arise under the Constitution and federal legislation, including: controversies to which the United States is a party; such as those originating from treaties with other countries; controversies between states; and controversies between the citizens of one state and citizens of another state. State court systems operate under the laws and constitution of the individual states.

The U.S. Supreme Court is the highest court in the country and the court of last resort for the appeal process. It is the final decision-making body regarding constitutionality. The Court is located in Washington, D.C., and starts its term on the first Monday in October.

While the Court is constitutionally mandated to hear the entirety of certain cases, such as those that involve foreign ambassadors or lawsuits between states, the justices have leeway to determine whether or not they will hear other cases that have been brought before them. As a rule, the nine justices usually select cases that they believe address important constitutional questions or involve contradictory rulings on federal statutory laws by lower courts. They may uphold or overturn the prior ruling. If the Court declines to review an appeal, however, the lower court's ruling is binding.

Powers of the Courts

The power of the various other federal courts has been established by statutes passed by Congress. The courts hear cases from all 50 states and the U.S. territories. The courts are divided into 12 judicial circuits and from there, subdivided into more than 90 judicial districts. The rulings from the federal district courts may be reviewed by one of the 12 judicial circuits of the U.S. court of appeals, called the circuit courts of appeals before 1948. These courts are limited to hearing matters that are brought before them on appeal and usually consist of at least three judges. The only court higher than the court of appeals is the Supreme Court. The purpose of the court of appeals is to lighten the burden of the Supreme Court and thus make the judicial process move more quickly for litigants. In 1982 the U.S. Court of Appeals for the Federal Circuit was established. This specialized court handles appeals in which the U.S. government is a party. It reviews cases involving copyright, tax, patent, federal employment law, and claims against the United States for money damages.

There is at least one U.S. district court in each state and the District of Columbia. Each district court has one or more district judges, the exact number is determined by the population of the area that the court serves and is authorized by Congress. In addition, a District Court has a clerk, a U.S. attorney, a U.S. marshall, U.S. magistrates, bankruptcy judges, probation officers, court reporters, and support staff. These federal trial courts try both criminal and civil cases and are the court of origination for cases that arise under the Constitution or U.S. laws and treaties and involve more than $10,000 in damages. They also may review federal administrative decisions and rulings made by the bankruptcy courts.

Article I, Section 8, of the Constitution grants Congress the power to "establish . . . uniform laws on the subject of bankruptcies throughout the United States." The Bankruptcy Reform Act of 1978, amended in 1984 and 1986, serves as the federal government's bankruptcy legislation. Over ninety percent of bankruptcies are voluntary, meaning that the debtor was not forced to file a bankruptcy petition by creditors. The federal bankruptcy law ensures that there is equality among creditors and that the debtor's assets are distributed fairly and that the debtor's obligations are discharged as expediently as possible. The law also allows debtors to try a financial reorganization plan in an effort to avoid complete liquidation of assets. The bankruptcy courts are part of the U.S. district courts and try bankruptcy cases with jurisdiction over a debtor's property, regardless of the property's location. Bankruptcy judges are appointed by the president and serve a 14-year term.

While most federal courts are constitutional in nature, some courts have been authorized through legislation and are considered legislative courts. The specialized jurisdiction of these courts has been defined by Congress because the courts were not provided for in the original Constitution. Examples of legislative courts include the U.S. Claims Court, the U.S. Court of International Trade, and the U.S. Court of Customs and Patent Appeals.

The Federal System of Courts

An appeal is a request to a higher court for a reversal of a lower court's decision. The U.S. Supreme Court is the ultimate appellate court and may review the decisions of lower courts, such as the U.S. Court of Appeals, the Court of Appeals for the Federal Circuit, and individual state supreme courts. A judgment by the U.S. Supreme Court cannot be appealed. Usually, an appellate court will review the application of law in a trial court. It does not attempt to rule on the lower court's finding of facts. For instance, an appellate court may rule as to whether or not there was an error in the instructions given to the jury and whether or not this error might have been prejudicial to the defendant's case. The court would not, however, attempt to determine the guilt or innocence of the defendant.

In order for a court to hear a case, it must have jurisdiction, or authority, over the subject matter. For instance, the U.S. bankruptcy courts do not hear divorce actions. Generally, the federal courts handle matters that involve a federal question. A federal question is a legal issue that relates to either the U.S. Constitution, federal laws, or treaties between the United States and other countries. However, there are times when federal courts have jurisdiction in state-related cases, such as when the parties are from different states or when the parties in the dispute are a state government and a citizen of another state.

Federal judges are appointed by the president with the advice and consent of the Senate. These appointments are for life terms and the judges can only be removed from their positions for misconduct. There are no stated requirements in the U.S. Constitutions for any specific qualifications necessary to become a U.S. Supreme Court justice. However, as a rule, most justices have been lawyers and have, in fact, been judges in other court systems. U.S. Supreme Court justices may only be removed from their office by impeachment.

The State System of Courts

The process to become a state judge varies by each state. In many, the governor appoints judges, who may then run for retention every few years. In some states, judges are elected political officers.

The trial courts on the state level are composed of courts that have general jurisdiction and those with limited jurisdiction. State courts hear cases regarding federal law if the amount in the controversy is less than $10,000. General jurisdiction, or unlimited jurisdiction, trial courts hear cases involving civil and criminal cases. Limited jurisdiction courts are defined by state statutes and their specific purposes vary from state to state. For example, depending on the state, the Justice of the Peace Courts may try misdemeanors, preside over minor civil and criminal cases, or commit offenders. Justices of the peace may have their authority limited to a city or extended to include an entire state. A justice of the peace also performs administrative duties, such as marriage ceremonies.

Special Courts

Family courts are special courts that deal with legal problems involving family relations. Family courts may handle cases, as defined by statutes, that involve guardianship, child neglect, and juvenile delinquency. Because of the nature of the family courts, the proceedings are sometimes more informal than in civil or criminal courts. A probate court, or surrogate's court, is another special type of court. It hears cases involving wills and inheritance but also sometimes handles adoptions and competency hearings. Limited jurisdiction courts operating on a local level deal with cases where the law violations are less severe than those handled by the general jurisdiction courts. Limited jurisdiction courts include traffic, police, and municipal courts. Small claims courts, or people's courts, are courts where people can go for disputes that involve lesser monetary amounts, usually under a few thousand dollars. The court procedures and rules of evidence in small claims disputes are less formal and claimants are quite often not allowed to have an attorney represent their case.

Some states offer intermediate appellate courts, which review the decisions of the general jurisdiction courts and the limited jurisdiction courts. From there, an appeal can be brought to the state supreme court.

If there is no appellate court, the state supreme court hears appeal cases from the both the general and the limited jurisdiction courts. The state supreme court's decision can be appealed to the U.S. Supreme Court but only if there is a constitutional question. State supreme courts also regulate the practice of law and often serve as the state's final authority on professional discipline or responsibility. The state supreme courts go by several names, including Supreme Court of Errors, Supreme Judicial Court, or Court of Appeals.

See also: **Federal Powers and the Separation of Powers, Federalism and State Powers, Judicial Review, Legislative Powers**

Bibliography and Further Reading

Johnson, Daniel. *The Consumer's Guide to Understanding and Using the Law.* Cincinnati, OH: Betterway Books, 1981.

Reader's Digest Family Legal Guide. Pleasantville, NY: Reader's Digest Association, Inc., 1981.

MARTIN V. HUNTER'S LESSEE

Legal Citation: 14 U.S. 304 (1816)

Plaintiff
Thomas Bryan Martin

Defendant
David Hunter

Plaintiff's Claim
That he, not Hunter, was the rightful owner of a grant of land in Virginia, known as the Northern Neck, left to him by Thomas, Lord Fairfax, a British subject whose title to the land derived from charters from the English kings Charles II and James II.

Chief Lawyer for Plaintiff
Jones

Chief Defense Lawyer
Tucker

Justices for the Court
Gabriel Duvall, William Johnson, Henry Brockholst Livingston, Joseph Story (writing for the Court), Thomas Todd, Bushrod Washington

Justices Dissenting
None (John Marshall did not participate)

Place
Washington, D.C.

Date of Decision
20 March 1816

Decision
That Martin was indeed the rightful owner of the land—and that the Commonwealth of Virginia must recognize the validity of his claim.

Significance
Because the Commonwealth of Virginia had refused to recognize an earlier decision of the Supreme Court awarding the land to Martin, the case was a testing ground for whether state or federal power would prevail. *Martin v. Hunter's Lessee* was one of the major cases establishing the supremacy of federal over state courts.

In the early days of the United States, many aspects of the country's new government were constantly being tested. Because the United States had originated as 13 separate colonies, one of the major conflicts in the new country was the tension between state and federal power. Many key court cases in the nation's early decades established the supremacy of the federal government over the states.

The state-federal issue was so central that it helped create the names of the nation's first two political parties. The Federalists, led by John Adams and Alexander Hamilton, believed in a strong central government. Part of their agenda was to insure that a strong elite—almost an aristocracy—would have charge of national affairs, for they tended to mistrust "the common people."

The Democratic-Republicans, on the other hand, led by Thomas Jefferson and James Madison, believed in decentralized power and tended to have faith in the ordinary citizen. They saw federal power as less democratic and preferred to support the sovereignty of individual states.

The President vs. the Supreme Court

When Jefferson was president, his Democratic-Republican administration had frequently clashed with the Supreme Court, which was dominated by Federalists. Jefferson had even planned to impeach all the justices, in order to replace them with Democratic-Republicans. He actually did impeach Samuel Chase, but when the Senate acquitted Chase, Jefferson's plan was foiled.

Jefferson was succeeded by President James Madison, who was able to appoint the Court's first Democratic-Republican justice, Joseph Story. The Democratic-Republicans hoped that the brilliant Story would be a fitting match for the powerful Federalist chief justice, John Marshall. Instead, Story and Marshall became allies.

Rightful Owner or Alien Enemy?

The roots of the *Martin* case go all the way back to the American Revolution, when Virginia passed laws to confiscate the property of the Loyalists (people still loyal to the King of England). Thomas Lord Fairfax was such a Loyalist, and he chose not to recognize Virginia's action. He simply left the property—known as Northern Neck—to Denny Fairfax (previously Denny Martin), a British subject. To confuse matters further, Lord Fairfax, although a Loyalist, was a citizen and resident of Virginia until his death in 1781. His heir, Denny Fairfax, was a native-born British subject who lived in England until his death, sometime between 1796 and 1803.

Meanwhile, the Commonwealth of Virginia had confiscated the Fairfax property, which passed into the hands of David Hunter. Thus, by virtue of the "seal of the commonwealth of Virginia," David Hunter owned the land. But by virtue of the Treaty of Paris (1783) and Jay's Treaty (1794), national treaties that protected Loyalist holdings, the Fairfax heir—Thomas Bryan Martin—owned the land.

In 1813, Thomas Bryan Martin brought suit to establish his claim to the land. The case, known as *Fairfax's Devisee v. Hunter's Lessee,* reached the Supreme Court, which found in favor of Martin and the Fairfax family. Marshall, who had a family connection to the Fairfax family, recused himself (took himself off the case). So the author of the decision was the man whom the Democratic-Republicans had trusted to defend states' rights against the federal government, the man they had expected to uphold the rights of the people against the British aristocracy, Justice Story.

Not surprisingly, Story's decision infuriated advocates of states' rights, who claimed that his ruling had reduced the states to mere administrative units without any real power to make important decisions. Virginia, too, was not pleased. The state courts actually refused to do the legal work necessary to pass the land over to Martin. They said they were under no obligation to obey the Supreme Court.

Once again, Martin brought suit, this time in the case known as *Martin v. Hunter's Lessee.* Once again, Marshall recused himself while playing an important role behind the scenes. Story again wrote the decision.

"The Supreme Law of the Land"

In a unanimous decision for the Court, Story rebuked the state courts of Virginia for not abiding by the ruling of the Supreme Court. Although state judges are called upon to decide cases, their authority rested not in the laws and constitution of their own states, Story argued, but rather in the "supreme law of the land"—the U.S. Constitution.

Thus, Story explained, if state courts did not recognize the authority of the appellate court (the court to which cases are appealed), then there is no uniform, national power that applies equally to the entire United States. Each state court would then be able to interpret the Constitution as it pleased, which would have the same effect as not having a single constitution to unite the country.

By the same token, federal laws and treaties must also be open to final interpretation by a single, supreme court. Therefore, Story said, if the Supreme Court interpreted U.S. law and U.S. treaties to mean that Martin and not Hunter was the rightful owner of the Virginia property, the Virginia courts must agree—or face the spectre of a truly divided nation. To quote Story's own words:

> The constitution of the United States was ordained and established, not by the states in their sovereign capacities, but emphatically, as the preamble of the constitution declares, by "the people of the United States" . . . The constitution was not, therefore, necessarily carved out of existing state sovereignties, nor a surrender of powers already existing in state institutions . . . [T]he judicial power of the United States [is established as] . . . one great department which [is] . . . in many respects, national, and in all, supreme. It is a part of the very same instrument which was to act not merely upon individuals, but upon states; and to deprive them altogether of the exercise of some powers of sovereignty, and to restrain and regulate them in the exercise of others.

Story's opinion in *Martin v. Hunter's Lessee* is considered the most important in his 34 years on the Court. It stands as a landmark in the history of "federal judicial supremacy"—the notion that the federal courts are supreme. The story of conflict between states' rights and federal standards has continued throughout the decades, most notably over the issues of slavery and civil rights. Ironically, the perception of which side was "liberal" and which "conservative" has changed over the years, but the issue remains an important one in American politics.

Related Cases
Marbury v. Madison, 5 U.S. 137 (1803).
Fairfax's Devisee v. Hunter's Lessee, 7 Cr. 602 (1813).
Cohens v. Virginia, 19 U.S. 264 (1821).

Bibliography and Further Reading

Epstein, Lee, and Thomas G. Walker. *Constitutional Law for a Changing America: Institutional Powers and Constraints,* 3rd ed. Washington DC: Congressional Quarterly, 1998.

Hall, Kermit L., ed. *Oxford Companion to the Supreme Court of the United States.* New York: Oxford University Press, 1992.

Johnson, John W., ed. *Historic U.S. Court Cases, 1690–1990: An Encyclopedia.* New York: Garland Publishing, 1992.

Williams, Jerre S. *The Supreme Court Speaks.* Freeport, NY: Books for Libraries Press, 1956, 1970.

ABLEMAN V. BOOTH AND UNITED STATES V. BOOTH

Legal Citation: 62 U.S. 506 (1858)

Petitioners
Jeremiah S. Black, U.S. Attorney General; Stephen Ableman

Respondent
Sherman Booth

Petitioners' Claim
Booth, who had been freed by the Wisconsin State Supreme Court, should serve the sentence imposed by a federal court.

Chief Lawyer for Petitioner
Jeremiah S. Black

Chief Lawyer for Respondent
No counsel appeared for the respondent.

Justices for the Court
John Archibald Campbell, John Catron, Nathan Clifford, Peter Vivian Daniel, Robert Cooper Grier, John McLean, Samuel Nelson, Roger Brooke Taney (writing for the Court), James Moore Wayne

Justices Dissenting
None

Place
Washington, D.C.

Date of Decision
7 March 1859

Decision
A state court cannot grant a writ of *habeas corpus* to a prisoner arrested under the authority of the United States and in federal custody.

Significance
The *Ableman* decision emphasized our dual form of government and the independence of state and federal courts from one another. It is illegal for state officials to interfere with United States officers acting under federal laws. Ironically, while *Ableman* arose from arguments over the proslavery Fugitive Slave Law, this same principle of federal judicial supremacy was used to override state efforts to preserve racial segregation during the 1960s.

The *Ableman* cases reflected the dramatic events and fiery controversies that immediately preceded and led to the U.S. Civil War. Benammi S. Garland owned a slave, Joshua Glover, who worked as the foreman on Garland's farm near St. Louis, Missouri. In 1852, Glover escaped and fled to Wisconsin.

Joshua Glover Is Saved from the Slave Catchers

Glover found work at a sawmill near Racine, Wisconsin, where Garland discovered him. On 10 March 1854, Glover and two black friends were playing cards in a cabin on the outskirts of Racine. Garland appeared at the cabin with two U.S. deputy Marshalls and four other men. Struggling with his attackers, Glover was badly hurt. He was handcuffed and taken to a jail in Milwaukee. (At this time, the federal government had no jails of its own and borrowed prison facilities from state and local governments.)

Abolitionists in Milwaukee soon learned of Glover's arrest. Among their leaders was Sherman M. Booth, the fiery editor of an abolitionist newspaper. Booth rode throughout the city, stopping at each street corner to rise in his saddle and shout, "Freemen! To the rescue! Slave catchers are in our midst! Be at the court-house at two o'clock!"

On the evening of 11 March, a large crowd gathered outside the Milwaukee courthouse. Booth gave a passionate speech attacking the return of fugitive slaves. The mob then broke down the door, took Glover out, and put him a ship leaving for Canada. Throughout Wisconsin and other northern states, abolitionists cheered his release.

On 15 March, U.S. Marshall Stephen V. R. Ableman arrested Booth under a warrant issued by a federal court commissioner. Booth was charged under the Fugitive Slave Law with having aided a slave's escape. Because he refused to provide bail money, the commissioner ordered him held for trial before the U.S. District Court of Wisconsin.

Wisconsin Nullifies Federal Laws

On 27 May, while the state supreme court was on vacation, Booth applied to Associate Justice Abram Smith

Belva Ann Lockwood (1830-1917)

At the time of the *Ableman* cases, very few woman were involved in the practice of law. But in 1879, Belva Ann Lockwood drafted a law, which was later passed by Congress, that admitted women to practice before the Supreme Court. She then became the first woman to put the law into action as the first woman lawyer to practice before the Court.

Lockwood was originally a teacher when she moved to Washington, D.C. to pursue a legal career. She had already had a full life, though she was only 30. Lockwood did not pursue a higher education for herself when young. In fact, it was not until the death of her husband left her in need of supporting her young daughter that she decided she needed further schooling to make ends meet. She graduated school with honors as a teacher, and started work at the prestigious Lockport Union School. It was in her time as a teacher that she first became known as a feminist, as she encouraged the girls to polish their public speaking skills. At this time Lockwood discovered and fostered her interest in the law and the political activism of women such as Susan B. Anthony. It was these interests that drew her to Washington, D.C. in the first place.

Lockwood gained entry to the newly founded National University Law School, where she quickly realized her dream of becoming a lawyer. The work was hard, and the treatment in the male-dominated field was harsh, but Lockwood made it through the course, ultimately being the only student (of the 14 women she started with) to receive her diploma in the end. This unequal treatment only served to strengthen Lockwood's feminist determination, and led her hand in many of her legal battles. She worked tirelessly during her life for women's suffrage, equal rights, and Native American rights.

Source(s): http://www.stanford.edu/group/WLHP/papers/lockwood.htm

http://www.netsrq.com/~dbois/lockwood.html

Belva Ann Lockwood © The Library of Congress/Corbis.

for a writ of *habeas corpus*. Booth asked to be released because he was being held under an unconstitutional law. Justice Smith ordered Booth's release on 7 June. Smith asserted the state's right to intervene, and declared the Fugitive Slave Law unconstitutional because it denied trial by jury to fugitive slaves, thus taking their liberty without due process of law. In July, at Marshall Ableman's request, the Wisconsin Supreme Court reviewed Justice Smith's decision and upheld it. Ableman appealed this decision to the U.S. Supreme Court.

In January 1855, while this appeal was pending, Booth was rearrested on a new warrant from the U.S. District Court for Wisconsin. He was tried by jury, convicted, sentenced to one month in jail, and fined $1,000. Once more Booth appealed to the Wisconsin Supreme Court. On 3 February, the court freed him for a second time, again ruling that he was illegally con-

fined under an unconstitutional law. It declared that the state, as sovereign, had the power to protect its citizens against a wrongful federal law.

Without using the word, the Wisconsin court had advanced an extreme statement of the "nullification" doctrine—the theory that a state could render congressional laws null and void within its territory. John Calhoun of South Carolina had originally advanced this nullification doctrine in 1828. Four years later, a state convention had declared the tariffs of 1828 and 1832 null and void in South Carolina. Thus nullification is sometimes considered a Southern state's right. In this case, however, it was the northerners of Wisconsin that nullified a federal law (the Fugitive Slave Law) because of their anti-slavery convictions.

The U.S. attorney for Wisconsin appealed regarding Booth's second release, and the Supreme Court com-

An editorial cartoon, c. 1866. © The Library of Congress/Corbis.

bined the two Booth cases into one. Although the defiant Wisconsin court refused to send its records to Washington, the U.S. Supreme Court obtained a copy by subterfuge.

Stung by the criticism over its *Dred Scott* decision, the Court delayed hearings on the *Booth* cases until January 1859. U.S. Attorney General Jeremiah S. Black appeared for the United States and, nominally, also for Ableman, who had long since retired from the office of federal marshal. No one appeared for Booth and the state of Wisconsin, who did not recognize the Supreme Court's authority in this case.

Federal Courts Are Supreme over State Courts

Writing for a unanimous Court, Chief Justice Taney presented his decision in March 1859. Taney forcefully

upheld the supremacy of the federal government and the federal courts. By using the device of *habeas corpus,* Taney declared, the Wisconsin Supreme Court had nullified the judgment and sentence of a U.S. district court. In so doing, it had asserted that state courts were supreme over federal courts. If state courts could nullify the Fugitive Slave Law, they also could nullify any other federal law. This inevitably, Taney reasoned, would lead to chaos through conflicting decisions in various states.

Trying to prevent local interests, passions, and prejudices from dominating, Taney continued, the founders had made the federal government supreme within the sphere of action assigned to it. This supremacy could be maintained only if federal judicial power were supreme over state courts. State governments should not be jealous of this federal supremacy, for it was given by the Constitution, created by the people of all the states.

Taney admitted that a state court could use the process of *habeas corpus* to inquire into any and all imprisonments. But, as soon as a state judge or court is told "that the party is in custody under the authority of the United States, they can proceed no further." This was the heart of the matter. A federal prisoner is "within the dominion and exclusive jurisdiction of the United States."

Even if a federal court ruled wrongly regarding federal laws, only a higher federal court could correct it. A state court had no authority to correct proceedings in a national court. However, for the record, Taney stated that the Fugitive Slave Law of 1859 was fully authorized by the U.S. Constitution.

The Wisconsin Supreme Court refused even to acknowledge Taney's decision. Booth finally was arrested in March 1860 and imprisoned in the customs house in Milwaukee. Because he would not pay his fine, he remained in jail until early in 1861. A state court commissioner issued a writ of *habeas corpus,* but the Marshall ignored it.

Although jurisdictional law sometimes may seem arcane, Justice Taney's *Ableman* decision was of profound significance in affirming national sovereignty and the supremacy of federal law. But no Supreme Court decision could compel the abolitionists to obey laws they considered unjust. Despite Taney's efforts, only a war could resolve the deep moral divisions of slavery.

Related Cases
Dred Scott v. Sandford, 60 U.S. 393 (1856).

Bibliography and Further Reading
Campbell, Stanley. *The Slave Catchers: Enforcement of the Fugitive Slave Law, 1850-1860.* Chapel Hill: University of North Carolina Press, 1970.

Currie, David. *The Constitution in the Supreme Court: The First Hundred Years 1789-1888.* Chicago: University of Chicago Press, 1985.

Johnson, John W. *Historic U.S. Court Cases, 1690–1990: An Encyclopedia,* Vol. 2. New York: Garland Publishing, 1992.

Hyman, H. H., and William M. Wiecek. *Equal Justice Under Law: Constitutional Development, 1835-1875.* New York: Harper and Row, 1982.

Swisher, Carl. B. *History of the Supreme Court of the United States.* Volume V: *The Taney Period, 1836-64.* New York: Macmillan, 1974.

Ex Parte McCardle

Legal Citation: 74 U.S. 506 (1869)

Petitioner
United States

Respondent
William H. McCardle

Petitioner's Claim
That McCardle had incited insurrection and impeded post-Civil War Reconstruction.

Chief Lawyers for Petitioner
Matthew H. Carpenter, Lyman Trumbull

Chief Lawyers for Respondent
Jeremiah S. Black, David Dudley Field, Charles O'Conor, W. L. Sharkey, Robert J. Walker

Justices for the Court
Salmon Portland Chase (writing for the Court), Nathan Clifford, David Davis, Robert Cooper Grier, Stephen Johnson Field, Samuel Freeman Miller, Samuel Nelson, Noah Haynes Swayne

Justices Dissenting
None

Place
Washington, D.C.

Date of Decision
12 April 1869

Decision
That the Supreme Court was without jurisdiction to render a decision, because Congress had repealed certain appeals legislation.

Significance
For the first and only time in American history, Congress exercised its authority to prevent the Supreme Court from hearing certain types of politically sensitive cases.

After the Civil War, the victorious Union Army occupied the defeated Confederacy and the period known as Reconstruction began. On 2 March 1867, Congress passed a law entitled "An Act to Provide for the More Efficient Government of the Rebel States," which officially provided for the military administration of the South. The act abolished the legal existence of the Southern states, and divided the Confederacy into a series of military districts, each commanded by a general who possessed extensive powers to suppress any act of defiance.

In the city of Vicksburg, Mississippi, public resentment against the Union was particularly high. The city was strategically located on the Mississippi River and had fallen to the Union after a long and bloody battle siege by General Ulysses S. Grant. After the Civil War, the Fourth of July was not celebrated in Vicksburg for 75 years.

William H. McCardle was the editor of a local newspaper, the *Vicksburg Times*. McCardle published various articles criticizing Reconstruction in general and Major General Edward O. C. Ord in particular. Ord was the Commanding General of the Fourth Military District, which included Vicksburg. General Ord was not amused. He had McCardle arrested in November of 1867 for various offenses relating to inciting insurrection and impeding Reconstruction. On 11 November 1867, McCardle sent a petition to the Circuit Court of the U.S. for the Southern District of Mississippi, asking for a writ of *habeas corpus,* meaning a court order to free McCardle from illegal imprisonment. The circuit court refused McCardle's request, and McCardle appealed to the Supreme Court.

Congress Denies McCardle Access to Supreme Court

The Supreme Court is the only federal court specifically provided for by the Constitution. Under Article III, section 2, the Supreme Court has original jurisdiction, meaning sole authority, only in "Cases affecting Ambassadors, other public Ministers and Consuls, and those in which a State shall be Party." In all other cases, the Supreme Court has jurisdiction only on

Reconstruction

The Reconstruction was the period between 1865 and 1877, directly following the Civil War, in which the federal government attempted to redress imbalances in the former Confederate states through a series of Draconian measures. President Lincoln had planned to offer the South a relatively liberal peace, and his successor, Andrew Johnson, approached the situation similarly. Johnson stipulated that Southern states accept the Thirteenth Amendment, which guaranteed civil rights for freed slaves.

With Johnson's effectiveness ended by the commencement of impeachment proceedings against him, the radical Republicans in Congress assumed *de facto* control over the defeated states, and proceeded to impose a harsh peace. Congress made it difficult for the South-

ern states, now under martial law, to reenter the Union, and though each had gained readmission by 1870, it was with much acrimony. Likewise the federal government, while disenfranchising many Southerners, supported government by a coalition of freed slaves and "carpetbaggers."

Southerners reacted through the Ku Klux Klan and other extralegal means. The old leadership began to resume control, sometimes by proxy. By 1877, the federal government had removed its troops, and the South entered a period of reaction against the abortive attempt at modernization.

Source(s): Hurwitz, Howard L. *An Encyclopedic Dictionary of American History.* New York: Washington Square Press, 1974.

appeal from such federal courts as Congress may decide to create and from such state supreme courts. This appellate jurisdiction is expressly subject to "such Exceptions, and under such Regulations as the Congress shall make."

On 24 September 1789, Congress passed the Judiciary Act, which was the basis for the federal court system and gave the Supreme Court various appellate powers. On 5 February 1867, Congress amended the Judiciary Act to enable the Supreme Court to hear appeals in *habeas corpus* cases. It was precisely this amendment, called the Habeas Corpus Act of 1867, that enabled the Court to hear the *McCardle* case.

The Radical Republicans who controlled Congress feared that the *McCardle* case would give the Court an excuse to overturn Reconstruction legislation and end martial law in the South. Therefore, on 27 March 1868, Congress passed a law repealing the appeal provisions of the Habeas Corpus Act of 1867:

And be it further enacted, That so much of the act approved February 5, 1867, entitled, 'An act to amend an act to establish the judicial courts of the United States, approved September 24, 1789,' as authorized an appeal from the judgment of the Circuit Court to the Supreme Court of the United States, or the exercise of any such jurisdiction by said Supreme Court, on appeals which have been, or may hereafter be taken, be, and the same is hereby repealed.

The case came before the Supreme Court during the 1868 December term. The hearing focused on the effect of Congress' repeal of the Court's jurisdiction. If the Court did not have jurisdiction, the validity or inva-

lidity of McCardle's imprisonment was irrelevant. Sharkey argued that Congress' action was unconstitutional because it was designed solely to affect the *McCardle* case:

Its language is general, but, as was universally known, its purpose was specific. If Congress had specifically enacted 'that the Supreme Court of the United States shall never publicly give judgment in the case of McCardle, already argued, and on which we anticipate that it will soon deliver judgment, contrary to the views of the majority in Congress, of what it ought to decide,' its purpose to interfere specifically with and prevent the judgment in this very case would not have been more real or, as a fact, more universally known.

Congress Could Not Be Denied

Carpenter and Trumbull responded by citing the plain language of Article III, section 2 of the Constitution, under which Congress' authority to restrict the Court's appellate jurisdiction could not be denied. Further, Carpenter and Trumbull pointed out that the language of Congress' repeal of the Court's authority "embraces all cases in all time." Although Sharkey was certainly accurate in describing Congress' real motivations, Carpenter and Trumbull correctly pointed out that legally, any assumption that the repeal was aimed specifically at McCardle could not be proven and therefore was "gratuitous and unwarrantable."

By the end of the 1868 December Term, Chief Justice Chase announced the Court's unanimous decision. Chase held that McCardle's appeal was dismissed for lack of jurisdiction, because of Congress' repeal of the

Court's authority. Chase stated in blunt terms that Congress had undeniably exercised its power to create exceptions to the Court's authority:

> The provision of the act of 1867 affirming the appellate jurisdiction of this court in cases of *habeas corpus* is expressly repealed. It is hardly possible to imagine a plainer instance of positive exception.

The *McCardle* case was the only time in American history that Congress used its power under the Constitution to prevent the Supreme Court from hearing certain types of politically sensitive cases. There have been periodic movements in Congress to restrict the Court's authority to hear school desegregation cases, school prayer cases, abortion cases and other politically sensitive cases, but nothing has ever happened. However the Court did not completely surrender to Congress' actions. Only one year later, in 1869, the Court agreed to hear a case very similar to McCardle's called *Ex Parte Yerger,* and side-stepped Congress' repeal of the Court's authority. Yerger was released from custody before the Court could hear the case and get into any

confrontation with Congress. As more than one legal commentator has opined, given the need for the different branches of government to work peacefully with each other, it may be politically healthy that the limits of congressional power under the Constitution have never been completely clarified.

Related Cases
Toth v. Quarles, 350 U.S. 11 (1955).
Westmoreland v. CBS, 770 F. 2d 1168 (1984).

Bibliography and Further Reading

Franklin, John Hope. *Reconstruction: After the Civil War.* Chicago: University of Chicago Press, 1961.

Morris, Richard B. *Encyclopedia of American History.* New York: Harper & Row, 1982.

Tortora, Anthony. "Ex parte McCardle." *National Review,* September 19, 1980, pp. 1140–1141, 1157.

Trefousse, Hans L. *Historical Dictionary of Reconstruction.* Westport, CT: Greenwood Press, 1991.

MANTON V. UNITED STATES

107 F.2d 834 (1939)

In 1939, Martin T. Manton was the senior circuit judge of the U.S. Circuit Court of Appeals for the Second Circuit, a position second only to the nine members of the U.S. Supreme Court. As a lawyer, Manton had made more than a million dollars before his appointment to the bench in 1916. His fortune, invested in real estate and business, had been severely depleted by the Depression.

With his friend William J. Fallon and several other men, Manton was indicted in April of 1939 for conspiring to influence, obstruct, and impede justice and to "defraud the United States of its right to have its legal functions exercised free from unlawful impairment."

"Without Regard to the Merits"

The indictment noted that Manton was a stockholder in, or "wholly or substantially owned or controlled" a number of corporations that had cases pending in his court between 1930 and 1939. It charged that Fallon actively proposed to those litigants that his close friendship with Manton could get them favorable action, and that such parties actively sought Fallon's help "in virtue of Manton's office, position, power and influence." Finally, the indictment charged that Manton would accept and receive sums of money as gifts, loans, and purported loans in return for such action, and would corruptly act in each of these cases without regard to the merits.

Manton moved to quash the indictment, claiming it charged not one conspiracy but several separate conspiracies on one count, that it did not state an offense, and that more than one crime was charged in the indictment. The motion was overruled.

The trial soon produced evidence that Manton's downfall resulted from continuing his business activities after appointment to the bench. Many suits that reached his court involved patent-infringement disputes, with the loser doomed to heavy losses. Evidence showed that Manton owned stock in companies that were litigants and in whose favor he decided.

In one case, a patent infringement suit brought by Schick Industries against Dictograph Products Company, one Archie Andrews, the principal stockholder in Dictograph, provided Fallon with $10,000 in cash

Appellants
Martin T. Manton, George M. Spector

Appellee
United States

Appellants' Claim
Reversal of conviction for conspiracy to obstruct the administration of justice and to defraud the United States, and dismissal of sentence.

Chief Lawyers for Appellants
William J. Hughes, Harry E. Rat

Chief Lawyer for Appellee
John T. Cahill

Judges
George Sutherland, Harlan F. Stone, Charles E. Clark

Place
New York, New York

Date of Decision
4 December 1939

Decision
Manton's conviction was upheld. He was sentenced to two years imprisonment and $10,000 fine.

Significance
This unique appeal brought the senior judge of the country's most prominent federal appeals court before his own colleagues. With all but one of the court's judges disqualified because of their previous association with the appellant, a special federal court had to be constituted to hear the appeal. The case, involving a scandal unique in federal court history, established a landmark in the delineation of conspiracy to obstruct justice.

through an intermediary, who gave a receipt for the money for the purchase of Dictograph stock. Fallon went off to see Manton and returned within the hour to say, "Everything is O.K. You can go and tell Archie Andrews that he is going to get the decision in his favor." The decision was against Schick.

The district court jury found Manton guilty. He received the maximum sentence: two years in federal prison and a $10,000 fine. He appealed. Paradoxically, the appeal had to land in his own court, where all his fellow judges except one disqualified themselves as his close associates. Only Judge Charles E. Clark, who had been appointed to the bench after Manton resigned while under investigation, could hear the appeal. Therefore, a special federal court was constituted. Its judges were former Supreme Court Justice George Sutherland, Supreme Court Justice Harlan F. Stone, and Judge Clark.

"Conspiracy Constitutes the Offense"

Considering Manton's claim that the indictment wrongly set forth a number of distinct conspiracies in a single count, the special court found that the conspiracy constitutes the offense irrespective of the number or variety of objects which the conspiracy seeks to attain, or whether any of the ultimate objects be attained or not.

Manton's contention, it said, "confuses the conspiracy, which was one, with its aims, which were many." The offense was the single continuing agreement among Manton and his cronies to sell judicial action to all willing to pay the price.

Altogether, the court's review found, Fallon had procured some $186,146 for Manton in 28 "distinct overt acts in pursuance of the conspiracy." In conclusion, the court noted that a mass of canceled checks, promissory notes, and other accounts was "so plainly at variance with the claim of Manton's innocence as to make the verdict of the jury unassailable."

Manton requested review by the U.S. Supreme Court. It denied his petition, and he went to federal prison at Lewisburg, Pennsylvania, on 7 March 1940. While eligible for parole after eight months, he served 19 months before he was released on 13 October 1941. He died in 1946.

Bibliography and Further Reading

"Ex-Judge Manton of U.S. Bench Here." *The New York Times,* November 18, 1946, p. 23

"Manton Conviction in Sale of Justice Upheld on Appeal." *New York Times,* December 5, 1939, p. 1.

YOUNGER V. HARRIS

Legal Citation: 401 U.S. 37 (1971)

Appellant
Evelle J. Younger

Appellee
John Harris, Jr.

Appellant's Claim
That the respondent's indictment for violation of California's criminal syndicalism law should stand, and that he should face trial for his offense.

Chief Lawyer for Appellant
Clifford K. Thompson, Jr.

Chief Lawyer for Appellee
A. L. Wirin

Justices for the Court
Hugo Lafayette Black (writing for the Court), Harry A. Blackmun, William J. Brennan, Jr., Warren E. Burger, John Marshall Harlan II, Thurgood Marshall, Potter Stewart, Byron R. White

Justices Dissenting
William O. Douglas

Place
Washington, D.C.

Date of Decision
23 February 1971

Decision
That the California criminal syndicalism statute could be enforced in good faith regardless of its constitutional validity, and that the respondent's indictment would stand.

Significance
The decision upheld the long-standing policy of the Supreme Court's enjoining state criminal prosecutions only in situations where the enforcement of unconstitutional statutes would cause irreparable harm to the accused.

John Harris, Jr., was arrested for distributing written materials advocating radical social and economic change through political action and was indicted under the state of California's criminal syndicalism statute. This law defined a criminal syndicalist as:

> Any person who: 1. By spoken or written words or personal conduct advocates, teaches or aids and abets criminal syndicalism or the duty, necessity or propriety of committing crime, sabotage, violence, or any unlawful method of terrorism as a means of accomplishing a change in industrial ownership or control, or effecting any political change; or 2. Willfully and deliberately by spoken or written words justifies or attempts to justify criminal syndicalism or the commission or attempt to commit crime, sabotage, violence or unlawful methods of terrorism with intent to approve, advocate, or further the doctrine of criminal syndicalism; or 3. Prints, publishes, edits, issues or circulates or publicly displays any book, paper, pamphlet, document, poster or written or printed matter in any form, containing or carrying written or printed advocacy, teaching, or aid and abetment of, or advising, criminal syndicalism . . .

The penalty for a conviction as a criminal syndicalist was one to fourteen years in prison.

Following his indictment in California State Court, Harris filed a complaint with the federal district court asking that his indictment be revoked and claiming that the existence of the criminal syndicalism statute infringed upon his First and Fourteenth Amendment rights. Other plaintiffs joined Harris's suit. Jim Dan and Diane Hirsch, members of the Progressive Labor Party, claimed that the statute would hinder their party in the lawful pursuit of its political aims; and Farrell Broslawsky, a teacher of history at Los Angeles Valley College, claimed that the prosecution of Harris made him doubt that he could legally teach his students about Communism. The federal district court sided with the complaints and compelled District Attorney Evelle J. Younger to abandon his prosecution of Harris.

The district court also declared the state criminal syndicalism statute void for "vagueness and overbreadth in violation of the First and Fourteenth Amendments." Younger then appealed the district court's decision to the U.S. Supreme Court, which heard arguments in the case on 16 November 1970.

The Court first dealt with the claims of Harris's corespondents, agreeing with the state of California that they had no standing in the case. Broslawsky, Dan, and Hirsch could participate in the case only if they could demonstrate that a prosecution of them for their beliefs or affiliations was imminent, a claim they had not made. By their own admission, the three had only joined the case because they "felt inhibited" by Harris's prosecution.

The Court also ruled against Harris without deciding the constitutionality of the California criminal syndicalism statute, citing a 1793 act of Congress prohibiting federal writs of injunction to stay state criminal prosecutions.

> During all this lapse of years from 1793 to 1970 the statutory exceptions to the 1793 congressional enactment have been only three: (1) "except as expressly authorized by Act of Congress"; (2) "where necessary in aid of its jurisdiction"; and (3) "to protect or effectuate its judgements".

The Court interpreted these exceptions as allowing a federal enjoinment of a state criminal prosecution only when "absolutely necessary for protection of constitutional rights" or "where the danger of irreparable loss (to the accused) is both great and immediate."

Although it found against Harris, the Court implied that California's criminal syndicalism statute might well be unconstitutional. It also implied that Harris might have been more successful had his attorneys used different tactics. "The accused should first set up and rely upon his defense in the state courts, even though this involves a challenge of the validity of some statute, unless it plainly appears that this course would not afford adequate protection." Harris may have been better off seeing his case through in state court and then appealing the verdict if he was convicted.

This decision did not break new legal ground, but rather upheld a long-standing reluctance to interrupt state criminal prosecutions while they are in progress.

Related Cases
Whitney v. California, 274 U.S. 357 (1927).
Brandenburg v. Ohio, 395 U.S. 444 (1969).

Bibliography and Further Reading
Biskupic, Joan, and Elder Witt. *Congressional Quarterly's Guide to the U.S. Supreme Court,* 3rd ed. Washington, DC: Congressional Quarterly, Inc., 1996.

The Federal Role in Criminal Law. Thousand Oaks, CA: Sage Periodicals Press, 1996.

Hall, Kermit L., ed. *The Oxford Companion to the Supreme Court of the United States.* New York: Oxford University Press, 1992.

Israel, Jerold H. *Criminal Procedure and the Constitution.* St. Paul, MN: West Publishing Company, 1993.

SCHLESINGER V. HOLTZMAN

Legal Citation: 414 U.S. 1321 (1973)

Petitioner
James Schlesinger, Secretary of Defense

Respondent
Rep. Elizabeth Holtzman (D-NY) and several Air Force officers

Petitioner's Claim
That without decisive opposition by Congress the president has constitutional authority to conduct air combat over Cambodia.

Justices for the Court
Harry A. Blackmun, William J. Brennan, Jr., Warren E. Burger (writing for the Court), Thurgood Marshall, Lewis F. Powell, Jr., William H. Rehnquist, Potter Stewart, Byron R. White

Justices Dissenting
William O. Douglas

Place
Washington, D.C.

Date of Decision
4 August 1973

Decision
Upheld the U.S. claim and affirmed a court of appeals decision by reversing Justice Douglas's decision to temporarily halt U.S. bombing in Cambodia.

Significance
The ruling established that the president can commit U.S. forces to combat when not decisively challenged by Congress. The Court has consistently avoided foreign policy disputes between the president and Congress and also resisted making adverse decisions against presidential action during times of war. By invoking the "political decision doctrine," the Court has held that legal challenges by members of Congress against the president are more political questions than legal and should not be left to the courts to resolve.

Consistent with the separation of powers in the federal government, the Constitution splits the power of waging war between the legislative and executive branches. Congress in Article I has power to declare war and raise and maintain armies. The president, acting as commander in chief, conducts war as allowed by Article II. The Supreme Court's role in the process has historically been minor. The "political question doctrine" evolved through Court history in which the Court established that certain issues, often involving foreign policy, can only be resolved by the "political" branches of government and are not subject to judicial resolution.

A key Court decision regarding presidential powers was delivered in the opinion associated with *United States v. Curtiss-Wright Export Corp.* in 1936. The Court found that the power to wage war did not primarily derive from the Constitution, but was a natural part of being a sovereign nation. Others, though, still insisted the Constitution played a greater role in the decision to wage war than the Court acknowledged and therefore the act of declaring war was subject to judicial review. Rarely has the Court actually issued a decision on a challenge during the actual course of a war. Often, decisions followed the conclusion of war activities, thus avoiding the disruption of ongoing efforts.

Following united efforts between Congress and the White House in World War II, the role of the president in conducting wars gradually become more expansive. The president's ability to act with greater swiftness, secrecy, and decisiveness posed a distinct advantage in a world of nuclear deterrence and Cold War. Congress' inaction in setting foreign policy essentially gave the president much greater leeway in committing U.S. forces to places such as Korea in 1950. During the Korean conflict, Congress did not issue formal declarations of war.

Recognizing the difficult task of passing bills on controversial foreign policy issues, Congress began to allow resolutions, called "legislative vetoes," into various forms of legislation when opposing certain presidential actions. By the 1970s with the increasing rift between the executive branch and Congress over the Vietnam War, the practice of issuing legislative vetoes became a popular means of expressing congressional foreign policy preferences.

The Court ruled on several occasions that Congress' appropriation of funds to support an undeclared war constituted congressional approval. The Vietnam War was such a case. In addition to approving funds, Congress passed the Gulf of Tonkin Resolution in 1964 which gave President Lyndon Johnson essentially unlimited war powers to commit U.S. forces in Southeast Asia. The undeclared nature of the Vietnam War was challenged on several occasions in the lower courts, but the Supreme Court consistently refused to hear appeals of lower court decisions. By late April of 1970 President Richard Nixon publicly acknowledged U.S. military involvement in Cambodia where the United States was launching a series of major attacks. Following withdrawal of ground troops from Cambodia later that June, Congress prohibited further use of funds for military operations in Cambodia. But the bombing in Cambodia continued, focusing on supposed Communist troop sanctuaries. Congress revised its position by stating funds could be spent, but only for purposes of ensuring the safety of U.S. troop withdrawal or to aid in the release of American prisoners of war.

In January of 1973 the Paris cease-fire agreement with North Vietnam was signed. By early April the last American troops left Vietnam and all known prisoners of war were released. However, the bombing of Cambodia continued. Responding to outrage in the United States and other countries, Congress intensified its efforts through early 1973 to end American air combat over Cambodia by refusing to authorize increased funding requested by the executive branch. Finally, by late June Congress took actions to discontinue funding of all combat activities in North and South Vietnam, Laos, and Cambodia as of mid-August. The use of a congressional defense appropriations bill to ban ongoing military combat operations and limit presidential options was unprecedented.

A Unique Series of Events

In July of 1973 shortly after Congress' action to cut off funding, Congressional Representative Elizabeth Holtzman, a Democrat from New York, and several U.S. Air Force officers serving in Asia filed suit in U.S. district court challenging the constitutional basis for continued bombing. Holtzman argued the military action was not authorized by Congress and consequently violated the Constitution.

The United States argued before the court that congressional action in setting the mid-August ending date represented approval of the bombing prior to that date. However, the district court disagreed by finding no real congressional authority for the United States combat in Cambodia. The court issued a permanent injunction halting all military operations in that country after 27 July.

The United States appealed the district court decision to the U.S. Court of Appeals for the Second Circuit seeking a delay of the district court's injunction. On 27 July the appeals court issued a temporary delay of the injunction in order to hear the government's argument. With the Supreme Court out of session, Holtzman immediately appealed the court action directly to the Supreme Court's Justice Marshall. Holtzman was taking advantage of a Court rule that allows a justice to individually issue a "stay," a suspension of a previous judicial decision, to temporarily stop action so that the entire Court may hear it when next convened as a group. In *Holtzman v. Schlesinger*, Marshall wrote on 1 August that there were "questions of standing, judicial competence, and substantive constitutional law which go to the roots of the division of power in a constitutional democracy." Because of the near unprecedented role of the Court in such disputes over the constitutionality of waging undeclared war on foreign soil, the issue clearly deserved the full Court's deliberation. Marshall denied Holtzman's appeal of the delay on the injunction.

The following day Holtzman's attorney traveled to the home town of Justice Douglas in the state of Washington. On 3 August Justice Douglas concurred with Holtzman and reinstated the bombing injunction. The Solicitor General of the United States on 4 August requested Chief Justice Burger bring the full Court into session to act on Douglas's decision. The request was instead directed back to Justice Marshall.

The Court Defers Action Again

In issuing his decision, Justice Marshall wrote on behalf of the other seven concurring justices with whom he communicated that day. Marshall, noting that the court of appeals had scheduled a hearing on the case for 8 August, wished to not insert the Court in the dispute at that time and reversed Douglas's order. Marshall reissued the stay against the district court's original injunction stopping the bombing.

Douglas, being the lone dissenter, wrote that though he disagreed with the Court's action regarding the bombing issue, his concern was even greater over the manner in which the Court overruled his decision. Douglas pointed out that a single justice has legal authority to issue stays during a recess, but another justice does not have legal authority to reverse that stay once granted. Douglas also noted the Court did not have legal authority to decide cases unless at least six justices were present. He asserted telephone calls did not legally serve the same purpose as the justices being in a single location to study briefs and exchange views. Douglas wrote, "A Gallup Poll type of inquiry of widely scattered Justices" was contrary not only to law that requires a quorum of six justices to be present, but to the principles of the Court as "a deliberative body that acts only on reasoned bases after full consideration." In *Rosenburg v. United States,* the Court had determined that it was "necessary and proper to meet together in Special Term before stays granted by an individual Justice out of Term could be overturned."

Impact

On 8 August, the court of appeals did hear the case. The court permanently reversed the district court's injunction on the bombing, allowing military action to proceed. The U.S. bombing missions had continued throughout this time period, even through the several hours that Douglas's reinstatement of the injunction was in effect. Eventually, the bombing did stop by mid-August as Congress had directed, and before the case could reach the full Supreme Court. The district court's earlier injunction against the bombing on behalf of a member of Congress was unique in U.S. legal history.

The doctrine also arose in non-war foreign policy issues such as *Goldwater v. Carter* in 1979 in which President Jimmy Carter sought to terminate a defense treaty with Taiwan in order to normalize relations with China. Due to the lack of congressional action to stop Carter, the Court dismissed the case. The Court found Carter's actions were inherently political and could not be judged in a court of law.

The Cambodian bombing issue also led to passage of the Wars Powers Act over Nixon's veto in November of 1973. In an effort to reclaim war powers from the presidency, the act empowered Congress to order troop withdrawals through joint house resolutions in cases where Congress had not declared war or given any other form of authorization. The War Powers Act, however, did not fare well in Supreme Court decisions, with the Court continuing to defer to the president in foreign policy. In responding to cases filed by members of Congress challenging use of U.S. forces in the Middle East in the late 1980s, the Court dismissed the cases by invoking the political question doctrine. Congressional attempts to reform the War Powers Act continued into the 1990s.

The Court also found congressional use of legislative vetoes unconstitutional in the 1983 *Immigration and Naturalization Service v. Chadha* ruling. The Court held the use of such legal tools was counter to the constitutional principles of shared powers by circumventing presidential authority. Congress has continued to use them, however, with few legal challenges.

The *Schlesinger* case dramatized the Supreme Court's reluctance to be involved in disputes between the presidency and Congress over foreign policy in general, and issues of war in particular. The Court has consistently held that a true confrontation between Congress as a whole and the president must first occur before the Court should be brought into the dispute. In essence, the Court has chosen not to perform the work of Congress in contesting presidential actions. Congress has been very reluctant to appear not to back the president in foreign crises, especially where the safety of American forces are at risk. The political question doctrine has meanwhile served the purpose of not leaving federal courts open to undercutting national unity in times of crises.

Related Cases

United States v. Curtiss-Wright Corp., 299 U.S. 304 (1936).
Rosenburg v. United States, 346 U.S. 273 (1953).
Holtzman v. Schlesinger, 414 U.S. 1304 (1973).
Goldwater v. Carter, 444 U.S. 996 (1979).
Immigration and Naturalization Service v. Chadha, 462 U.S. 919 (1983).

Bibliography and Further Reading

Biskupic, Joan, and Elder Witt. *Guide to the U.S. Supreme Court.* Washington, DC: Congressional Quarterly, 1997.

Lindsay, James M. *Congress and the Politics of U.S. Foreign Policy.* Baltimore: The Johns Hopkins University Press, 1994.

Peterson, Paul E., ed. *The President, The Congress, and the Making of Foreign Policy.* Norman, OK: University of Oklahoma Press, 1994.

MORRISON V. OLSON

Legal Citation: 487 U.S. 654 (1988)

Appellant
Alexia Morrison

Appellee
Theodore B. Olson, et al.

Appellant's Claim
That Title VI the Ethics in Government Act of 1978, which established a special court and authorized the attorney general of the United States to recommend that the court appoint an independent counsel to investigate wrongdoing by federal officials, was not in violation of the Appointments Clause, or the principle of separation of powers, in the Constitution.

Chief Lawyer for Appellant
Alexia Morrison (*pro se*)

Chief Lawyer for Appellee
Thomas S. Martin

Justices for the Court
Harry A. Blackmun, William J. Brennan, Jr., Thurgood Marshall, Sandra Day O'Connor, William H. Rehnquist (writing for the Court), John Paul Stevens, Byron R. White

Justices Dissenting
Antonin Scalia (Anthony M. Kennedy did not participate)

Place
Washington, D.C.

Date of Decision
27 June 1988

Decision
That the Ethics in Government Act did not violate the Appointments Clause in Article II, the limitations on judicial duties in Article III, or the principle of separation of powers; accordingly, the judgment of the lower court was reversed.

Significance
The independent counsel statute had been a volatile issue in government ever since its passage in the wake of the Watergate scandal. In that instance, prominent officials in the administration of President Richard M. Nixon were charged with wrongdoing connected with a break-in at Democratic party offices prior to the 1972 presidential election. Title VI of the Ethics in Government Act, providing for a special counsel to be appointed by the attorney general of the United States in order to investigate such matters that arose in the future, was adopted in 1978. In the eyes of many, its passage violated the principle of separation of powers embodied in the Constitution by creating a judicial office with wide authority in the sector of government normally reserved for the executive branch. *Morrison v. Olson* tested this contention.

The Creation of the Independent Counsel

The Watergate scandal began with a break-in at offices belonging to the Democratic party in Washington's Watergate Hotel during the summer of 1972. By the time it ended with the resignation of President Richard M. Nixon in August of 1974, the foundations of the federal government had been shaken by a series of cover-ups, investigations, and controversies that pitted the executive, legislative, and judicial branches against one another. One particularly thorny conflict had been the antagonistic relationship between the executive branch and the special counsel appointed to investigate the president and others. In 1978, Congress passed the Ethics in Government Act, Title VI of which provided for the appointment of an "independent counsel" whose job it would be to prosecute high-level officials for violation of federal criminal laws. Legislators hoped that the creation of the independent counsel would remedy the problems experienced by the special prosecutor, because the new office would have greater powers and independence.

Under Title VI, if the attorney general received information he considered "sufficient to constitute grounds to investigate whether any person [covered by the Act] may have violated any Federal criminal law," he was authorized to conduct a preliminary investigation. Upon completion of this investigation, or at the end of 90 days, the attorney general would then report to a court called the Special Division, which had also been created by the act. If the attorney general had determined that there were "reasonable grounds to believe the further investigation or prosecution [was] warranted," he would ask the Special Division to appoint an independent counsel.

Under the act, the counsel had "full power and independent authority to exercise all investigative and prosecutorial functions and powers of the Department of Justice, the Attorney General, and any other officer or employee of the Department of Justice." The counsel's duties would include conducting investigations and grand jury proceedings, participating in the proceedings and litigation of civil and criminal courts, and appealing decisions by those courts. His or her powers would include "initiating and conducting prosecutions

The Ethics in Government Act

In the wake of Watergate and other scandals that plagued the legislative and executive branches of government in the 1970s, Congress passed the Ethics in Government Act in October of 1978. Among the act's many provisions was a requirement that federal officials provide detailed disclosure regarding their financial dealings. The act further circumscribed the activities of former federal officials lobbying with agencies for whom they had worked. In addition, that act established an Office of Government Ethics to implement provisions regarding financial disclosure and potential conflicts of interest on the part of the executive branch. The most notable of the act's provisions was its establishment of a special prosecutor, renamed an independent counsel in 1983, to investigate the activities of high officials within the executive branch. It was this force that was brought to bear against the Reagan and Bush administrations in the person of Lawrence Walsh, Iran-Contra independent counsel, and later against the Clinton administration with Whitewater independent counsel Kenneth Starr. Detractors of the independent counsel provision have argued that it is being used as a political weapon.

Source(s): Bacon, Donald C., et al., eds. *The Encyclopedia of the United States Congress* New York: Simon & Schuster, 1995.

in any court of competent jurisdiction, framing and signing indictments, filing information, and handling all aspects of any case, in the name of the United States." In addition, the counsel could appoint employees, request and receive assistance from the Department of Justice, accept referrals from the attorney general, and dismiss matters if he or she deemed them unworthy of investigation.

These were broad powers, resulting in an office which combined functions of an investigator with that of a prosecutor, and the term "independent" in the title seemed to suggest an even wider range of authority. The counsel could only be removed under two situations: if the attorney general requested such removal, and then "only for good cause"; or if the office itself was terminated, either because the counsel said his or her work was finished, or because the Special Division deemed the investigation concluded. Congress provided additional oversight, since the act required the counsel to report to it from time to time. Congress could also ask the attorney general to appoint an independent counsel to investigate a situation it considered worthy of attention, and though the attorney general was not compelled to do so, he or she was required to at least respond to the request.

"How the Act Works in Practice"

The situation which occasioned *Morrison v. Olson*, Chief Justice Rehnquist would later write in his majority opinion for the Supreme Court, "provide[s] an example of how the Act works in practice." In 1982, two House subcommittees issued subpoenas requiring the Environmental Protection Agency (EPA) to hand over documents relating to the enforcement of the so-called "Superfund Law," the Comprehensive Environmental Response, Compensation, and Liability Act of 1980. President Ronald Reagan, acting on the advice of U.S.

Attorney General William French Smith, directed the EPA Administrator to invoke executive privilege—that is, to inform Congress that the EPA would not surrender the documents because to do so would impair its functioning as an office of the executive branch charged to deal with specific and sensitive matters. The administrator did so, and the House voted to hold him in contempt. The administrator then filed a lawsuit against the House; but when the Reagan administration agreed to give the House subcommittees limited access to the documents in March of 1983, the matter seemed to be concluded.

In 1984, however, the House Judiciary Committee began an investigation into the Justice Department's handling of the situation. Among those called to testify was Theodore Olson, who had been assistant attorney general for the Office of Legal Counsel (OLC) at the time of the executive privilege order. During the Judiciary Committee investigation, the Justice Department withheld certain documents from Congress. When the committee published its report in 1985, it suggested that Olson had given false testimony on 10 March 1983, and further charged that Deputy Attorney General Edward Schmults and Carol E. Dinkins, assistant attorney general for the Land and Natural Resources Division, had obstructed the committee's investigation by withholding documents. At that time, the Judiciary Committee chairman requested that the attorney general appoint an independent counsel to investigate Olson, Schmults, and Dinkins.

After going through the procedure outlined in the act, the Special Division appointed James McKay as independent counsel to investigate Olson only, but McKay later resigned, and in his place the Special Division appointed Alexia Morrison on 29 May 1986. The following January, Morrison asked the attorney general

(Edwin Meese III had been appointed in 1985) for authority to investigate Schmults and Dinkins as well, and was denied. She then asked the Special Division for such permission, but after consideration of the matter, the Special Division ruled that the attorney general's refusal was final. Nonetheless, Morrison was given authority to investigate whether Olson had conspired with others—including Schmults and Dinkins—to obstruct the investigation.

When, under Morrison's direction, a grand jury in May and June of 1987 issued subpoenas to Olson, Schmults, and Dinkins, the three moved to have the subpoenas quashed on the grounds that the act's creation of the independent counsel office was unconstitutional. A district court denied the motion on 20 July 1987, and upheld the constitutionality of the act. It also ordered that the appellees be held in contempt for refusing to comply with the subpoenas, but stayed the contempt orders pending expedited appeal.

On appeal, the lower court's ruling was reversed, as the court of appeals' majority held that the independent counsel was not an "inferior officer." The latter was a reference to the Appointments Clause in Article I, Section 2, Clause 2 of the Constitution, which states that "the Congress may by law vest the appointments of such inferior Officers, as they think proper . . . in the Heads of Departments." In this case, of course, the department head would be the attorney general; but the court held that the independent counsel was a "principal officer," who under the Appointments Clause must be appointed by the president and confirmed by the Senate—as is the case, for instance, with a Cabinet official. Also, the court found in the act violations of a number of other constitutional principles, including limitations placed on the judiciary in Article III, and the principle of separation of powers.

When the case came before the U.S. Supreme Court, Morrison argued it herself, with Michael Davidson for the Senate arguing as *amicus curiae*. Other entities filed briefs of *amici curiae* urging reversal, including the American Bar Association, Common Cause (represented by Archibald Cox, special prosecutor in Watergate), the Center for Constitutional Rights, Public Citizen, and Burton D. Linne et al. Noted attorney Laurence H. Tribe also filed a brief on behalf of Lawrence E. Walsh, independent counsel in the investigation of the Iran-Contra scandal involving illegal arms sales by the Reagan administration. Briefs, presumably urging reversal, were also filed by the Speaker and Leadership Group of the House of Representatives and the American Federation of Labor and Congress of Industrial Organizations (AFL/CIO). For Whitney North Seymour, Jr., U.S. Solicitor General Fried argued the case as *amicus curiae* in support of the appellees, and briefs of *amici curiae* urging affirmance were filed

by Michael Deaver of the Reagan administration and Edward H. Levi, attorney general under the Ford administration.

An "Inferior" Officer

The Court voted 7-1 (newly appointed Justice Anthony M. Kennedy took no part in the decision) to reverse the ruling of the court of appeals. Chief Justice Rehnquist, writing for the Court, first dismissed a question concerning whether the constitutional issues could be addressed under the specific circumstances of the case, then turned to the heart of the matter. He addressed in turn the three principal constitutional concerns raised by the court of appeals relating to the Appointments Clause, the limitations of powers under Article III, and the separation of powers principle.

The power of the Special Division to appoint the independent counsel, the Court held, did not violate the Appointments Clause. The Court judged the counsel an "inferior" officer (which, in accordance with the clause, may be appointed by Congress) because even though her role made her by definition "independent" from the attorney general, the latter still had power to remove her from office. This, the Chief Justice wrote, "indicates that she is to some degree 'inferior' in rank and authority." The act only empowered her to perform specific duties, and then only when the Special Division had commissioned her to do so at the request of the attorney general. Furthermore, her office was temporary in its functioning, another sign of its apparently "inferior" power.

The appellees had argued, however, that even if she was an "inferior" officer, the clause did not give Congress the power to make "interbranch" appointments—that is, to appoint such an officer outside the executive branch. But the Court held that the clause gave Congress "significant discretion" to make the appointment within the judicial branch. This was particularly so, the Chief Justice added, because an investigation of the executive branch by a member of that branch might create a conflict of interest—i.e., an appointee of the president might feel certain loyalties to him, and might thus be hindered in prosecuting him effectively.

As for Article III, which prevents the judiciary branch from undertaking executive or administrative duties of a non-judicial nature, Rehnquist held that

> There can be no Article III objection to the Special Division's exercise of the power . . . to appoint independent counsel, since the power itself derives from the Appointments Clause, a source of authority for judicial action that is independent of Article III.

Congress had created the temporary office of the counsel, and it was constitutional for it to allow the Special Division power to define the scope of the counsel's duties—as long as those were "demonstrably related to the factual circumstances" that caused the investigation in the first place. The Special Division's "miscellaneous" powers, such as its authorization to "'receive' (but not to act on or specifically approve)" reports from the counsel or the attorney general, did not constitute an invasion of the executive branch's authority. The Special Division's power to terminate the independent counsel's office was not "administrative" to the extent that it would constitute an Article III violation because the act did not give the Special Division "anything approaching" the termination power vested in the attorney general. Nor was the Special Division authorized to approve or disapprove actions either by the counsel or the attorney general.

Lastly, the Court addressed the issue of separation of powers, the principle whereby none of the three branches of government may encroach on the authority vested in another branch. Rather than permitting Congress to remove officials from the executive branch outside of "its established powers of impeachment and conviction," the act "puts the removal power squarely in the hands of the Executive Branch" by giving the attorney general full oversight of the counsel. Simply because the removal could only be for a "good cause" did not mean that Congress intended to use that language to exercise undue authority over the attorney general; rather, that phrase helped to ensure that the independent counsel could and would remain independent. Nor, the Court held, did the case "involve an attempt by Congress to increase its powers at the expense of the Executive Branch." Though the attorney general was required to respond to a request by Congress for the appointment of an independent counsel, he was not required to then make that appointment. "Other than that," the Chief Justice wrote, "Congress' role under the Act is limited to receiving reports or other information and to oversight of the independent counsel's activities . . ." In conclusion, the Court held that the act gave the executive branch a sufficient degree of authority over the independent counsel "to ensure that the President is able to perform his constitutionally assigned duties."

Dissent: A Suit About Power

Justice Scalia, the Court's lone dissenter, began his dissenting opinion by referring to the oft-quoted phrase "a government of laws and not of men," which originated from the Massachusetts Constitution of 1780—in a clause delineating the separation of powers doctrine. The framers of the Constitution knew what they were doing, Scalia indicated, when they incorporated the separation principle into their own document, and it was designed to address situations such as the one presently before the Court. "This is what this suit is about," Scalia wrote. "Power." Sometimes attempts to circumvent the separation of powers came to the Court

"clad, so to speak, in sheep's clothing," with their intent hidden; "[b]ut this wolf comes as a wolf."

Scalia then proceeded to trace the history of the case, portraying it as a battle of wills principally between the president and Congress—a situation, that is, of men and not of laws. The present case addressed two questions: "Is the conduct of a criminal prosecution . . . the exercise of purely executive power?" and "Does the statute deprive the President of the United States of exclusive control over the exercise of that power?" The Court had "[s]urprisingly" answered in the affirmative to both questions, but had skirted what Scalia held was "the inevitable conclusion that since the statute vests some purely executive power in a person who is not the President of the United States it is void." It did not matter whether the statute in question reduced the president's power only slightly; that it did so at all meant that it violated the separations doctrine. As for the Court's claim that a member of the executive branch could not investigate that branch, Scalia asked,

> Is it unthinkable that the President should have such exclusive power, even when alleged crimes by him or his close associates are at issue? No more so than that Congress should have the exclusive power of legislation, even when what is at issue is its own exemption from the burdens of certain laws.

He referred to the Civil Rights Act of 1964, which forbids discrimination in employment—but exempts Congress, which passed the act, from its provisions.

Scalia addressed the Court's holding that the independent counsel was an "inferior officer," and observed, "The Ambassador to Luxembourg is not anything less than a principal officer, simply because Luxembourg is small." In other words, an ambassador is an ambassador, whether he is appointed to the embassy of a superpower or a tiny nation such as Luxembourg; similarly, an independent counsel is not necessarily an "inferior officer" simply because the scope of her oversight is "small (though far from unimportant)."

Scalia then discussed the limitations of Article III, and noted that the Court's decision in the present case invalidated *Humphrey's Executor v. United States* (1935). The latter ruling, Scalia observed, had been made by a Court "bent on reducing the power of President Franklin Roosevelt." Given its overtly political purpose, "One can hardly grieve the shoddy treatment given today to *Humphrey's Executor* . . . But one must grieve for the Constitution." The present ruling would allow too much leeway to an independent counsel, Scalia held, and while he pointed out that he cast no aspersions on the character of Morrison or the other individuals involved, he was concerned about the broad powers accorded to them by the act. Most of all, however, he was concerned that the act—and the Court's ruling—removed executive power from the place where such power belonged: in the executive branch.

Impact

Morrison v. Olson was seen as a victory for Congress. One of the immediate effects of the decision was that it upheld the conviction by independent counsel of two of President Reagan's former White House aides. It gave strength to the investigation then being conducted by independent counsel Walsh regarding the Iran-Contra scandal, which extended past Reagan's term and throughout that of his successor, George Bush. Though the Court approached its ruling from the viewpoint of law and not politics—indeed, the man appointed by Reagan to sit in the Chief Justice's seat delivered the opinion—the political implications of the case could not be ignored. In Watergate and Iran-Contra, the special counsel, and later the independent counsel provisions, had been used by a Democratic Congress against a Republican president. Later, with the appointment of independent counsel Kenneth Starr to investigate alleged wrongdoing by President Bill Clinton in the Whitewater land deal and the Lewinsky sex scandal, it would be seen as a tool wielded by a Republican Congress against a Democratic president. To some, the independent counsel provision seemed a necessary if unpleasant provision to maintain the balance of power in the federal government; to others it appeared that, like Dr. Frankenstein in Mary Shelley's famous horror story, Congress had created a monster.

Related Cases

Myers v. United States, 272 U.S. 52 (1926).
Wiener v. United States, 357 U.S. 349 (1958).
United States v. Nixon, 418 U.S. 683 (1974).
Buckley v. Valeo, 424 U.S. 1 (1976).
Mistretta v. United States, 488 U.S. 361 (1989).
Clinton v. Jones, 520 U.S. 681 (1997).

Bibliography and Further Reading

Bartholomew, Paul C., and Joseph F. Menez. *Summaries of Leading Cases on the Constitution,* 13th ed. Savage, MD: Littlefield Adams, 1990.

Bork, Robert H. "Against the Independent Counsel." *Commentary,* February 1993, p. 21.

Clayton, Cornell W. "Separate Branches—Separate Politics: Judicial Enforcement of Congressional Intent." *Political Science Quarterly,* winter 1994, p. 843.

Godes, Niles L., and Ty E. Howard. "Independent Counsel Investigations." *American Criminal Law Review,* spring 1998, p. 875.

Hall, Kermit L., ed. *The Oxford Companion to the Supreme Court of the United States.* New York: Oxford University Press, 1992.

Harriger, Katy J. "Separation of Powers and the Politics of Independent Counsels." *Political Science Quarterly,* summer 1994, p. 261.

Johnson, John W., ed. *Historic U.S. Court Cases, 1690–1990: An Encyclopedia.* New York: Garland Publishing, 1992.

Kalir, Erez. "Superior Logic: Reno is Right on Special Prosecutors." *The New Republic,* September 14, 1998, p. 14.

O'Sullivan, Julie. "The Independent Counsel Statute: Bad Law, Bad Policy." *American Criminal Law Review,* spring 1996, p. 463.

Witt, Elder. *Congressional Quarterly's Guide to the Supreme Court,* 2nd ed. Washington, DC: Congressional Quarterly Inc., 1990.

Witt, Elder, ed. *The Supreme Court A to Z. CQ's Encyclopedia of American Government,* rev. ed. Washington, DC: Congressional Quarterly, Inc., 1994.

JUDICIAL REVIEW

Definition

The term judicial review refers to a court's review of a decision of a lower court in order to determine whether an error was made. When speaking of the Supreme Court, the term also refers to the Court's power to pass judgment on the constitutionality of actions of state and federal legislatures and courts. The most common form of judicial review is the review of a lower court decision by a higher court, whether it be state or federal. Courts usually review these decisions in the appeals process, when a losing party in a case claims an error was made and appeals to the higher court to examine the decision.

The Functions of Judicial Review

Judicial review has three functions. First, it allows justice to be served by striking down erroneous decisions by lower courts. Second, appellate courts monitor the performance of lower courts; lower courts have an incentive to apply the law correctly if the possibility exists that their decisions may be overturned. Third, important controversies regarding the law are examined and resolved for the future guidance of courts and individuals. This third function is the primary concern of the highest courts, which in most cases agree to hear appeals only at their discretion.

There is no right to appeal guaranteed by the U.S. Constitution. The right to appeal is created by state constitution or by federal or state statute. How a case may be brought through a state court system on appeal depends on both the court system structure and statute. In most instances, after a case is first tried there is a right of appeal to the next higher court. Typically, after one appeal further appeal is allowed only at the discretion of the higher court. Defendants in certain types of cases may have the right of automatic appeal to the state supreme court, however. For example, in some states defendants in death penalty cases have the right of appeal from the trial court directly to the state supreme court.

Appeals are not new trials. No jury is assembled; instead a panel of several judges, usually at least three, review the case for error. The facts of the case as found by the jury (or the judge in a non-jury trial) are accepted

by the appellate court, and the appellant may not introduce new facts that could have been presented at the trial. This is because the credibility of witnesses and other matters of fact are best determined by the jury at the time of the controversy; the appellate court has only a cold record and is not able to directly examine the demeanor of witnesses.

What the appellate court does examine is the application of law and rules of procedure to determine their validity. Depending on the contentions of the appeal, they typically examine the proper application of the rules of evidence as to the admission of evidence by both parties; the proper instruction of the jury as to the questions of law involved; whether the evidence supports the verdict; and whether applicable rules or guidelines for sentencing were followed. In most cases only the contentions or error made in the appeal are considered, and the claim must have been raised at the time of trial. Only the most extreme cases of plain error are considered if issues are not made part of the trial record when they occur.

If error is found, it must be substantial enough to have significantly affected the outcome of the trial. Harmless error in procedural details or other error that would make no difference to the outcome is insufficient to alter the judgment of the lower court.

Appellate Procedure

The structure of state court systems varies widely. Some states have separate civil and criminal trial courts, and some have more than one level of appellate review. Typically, however, aside from special courts of limited jurisdiction, a three-tier structure can be discerned: the trial court level, the appellate level, and the state supreme court, which mirrors that of the federal system of district courts, courts of appeals, and the Supreme Court.

The appeals procedure is similar for both the state and federal courts of appeals as well as with the state supreme courts and the U.S. Supreme Court. With some exceptions, appeal is allowed only after final judgment in a case. After the final judgment in a case is rendered, the losing party may believe he or she lost the case because the law was not properly applied or that procedural rules were not properly followed. The person may then file for an appeal. Appeals must be commenced within a specified time from the delivery of final judgment.

The appealing party, now called the appellant or sometimes the plaintiff in error, now must file a brief in support of the claim of error, which will state the applicable facts of the case and of law and an argument supporting the contention of error. Specific rules, which may vary depending on the court and jurisdiction, must be followed as to the form and length of the brief. A complete record of the case must be sent to the appellate court, which will include a complete transcript of the trial, the verdict, and the final judgment entered. The opposing party in the case, now called the appellee, is notified of the intent to appeal and also files a brief in response. At this point the case is scheduled for oral argument.

After the court has reviewed the record and the briefs and heard oral argument, it makes its ruling in the form of a written opinion setting forth its decision and the legal reasoning behind it. Most lower court decisions are unanimously affirmed by appellate courts. If error is found, the appellate court may reverse the decision, modify it, or remand (return) it to the lower court for further proceedings. If the judgment is affirmed, the appellant may seek an appeal in a higher court. If there is no higher court except the state or federal court of last resort, any appeal is only at the discretion of that court.

Appeals to the U.S. Supreme Court

The jurisdiction of the Court to hear cases is of two types: original and appellate. Cases of original jurisdiction are those for which the Supreme Court is the court of first rather than last resort, such as suits between states; that is, the Court is the trial court for these cases. Other examples of original jurisdiction are certain limited appeals from cases involving the reapportionment of legislative districts and the disposition of questions of law from lower courts. Most cases the Court hears, however, are cases of appellate jurisdiction, appeals after a judgment in a lower court.

The Court hears appellate cases only at its own discretion. To seek a review of one's case by the Court, a party must file a petition for a writ of *certiorari,* which is a command to the lower court to send the record of the case to the Supreme Court for review. The justices vote on each petition, and if four of them want to hear the case, *certiorari* is granted. If *certiorari* is denied, no further litigation is possible and the matter is closed.

For *certiorari* to be granted, appeal from a decision of a lower federal court must involve a constitutional question or a question of federal law. If the case arose in a state court, all state appeals must have been exhausted. The Court denies *certiorari* in the great majority of cases; the controversy of individual parties is of less concern to the Court than unresolved questions of constitutional interpretation and federal law.

If *certiorari* is granted, the record of the case is delivered to the Court, along with briefs by the appellant and appellee (sometimes called petitioner and respondent), and the procedure from there follows the outline given above. The Court then reviews the record, and oral argument is heard by the Court. The appellant and appellee are each allowed a brief time in which to argue their positions. A party may not have time to discuss all the issues; thus the party's brief must contain the argument as well, in all its particulars. The justices may question the appellant and appellee when they present their oral arguments, even interrupting them to do so if they desire.

After oral argument is heard, the justices meet in private and discuss the case, and later vote on its disposition, with the majority vote determining the outcome. A opinion is then written and issued; the chief justice assigns the writing of the opinion, unless he is in the minority, in which case the senior justice in the majority assigns the writing. Drafts of the opinion may be discussed and revised before the final version is issued. A justice or justices may write a concurring opinion if they have reached the same conclusion for other or additional reasons or they wish to stress some point not mentioned in the majority opinion. A minority member or members may issue a dissenting opinion explaining their reasons for disagreeing with the majority.

If the judgment of the lower court is affirmed, the matter is concluded. If error is found, the Court may modify the judgment, reverse it, or remand it to the lower court for further proceedings.

See also: Judicial Powers

Bibliography and Further Reading

The Guide to American Law: Everyone's Legal Encyclopedia. St. Paul, MN: West, 1983.

Hornstein, Alan D. *Appellate Advocacy in a Nutshell.* St. Paul, MN: West, 1984

Hazard, Geoffrey C. Jr., and Michele Taruffo. *American Civil Procedure: An Introduction.* New Haven, CT: Yale University Press, 1993.

James, Fleming, and Geoffrey C. Hazard Jr. Civil Procedure. Boston: Little, Brown, 1985.

CALDER V. BULL

Legal Citation: 3 U.S. 386 (1798)

Petitioners
Mr. and Mrs. Calder

Respondents
Mr. and Mrs. Caleb Bull

Petitioners' Claim
That Connecticut legislation granting a rehearing of a probate dispute violated the Constitution's prohibition of *ex post facto* laws.

Justices for the Court
Samuel Chase (writing for the Court), William Cushing, James Iredell, William Paterson

Justices Dissenting
None (Oliver Ellsworth and James Wilson did not participate)

Place
Washington, D.C.

Date of Decision
8 August 1798

Decision
Connecticut's legislation was not a constitutional violation because the *ex post facto* provision applies only to criminal cases.

Significance
The Supreme Court's decision in *Calder v. Bull* changed the course of American jurisprudence by eliminating consideration of *ex post facto* violations in civil cases.

The Facts of the Case

Article 1, section 10 of the U.S. Constitution prohibits the enactment of *ex post facto* laws, laws drafted "after the fact." The specific meaning and application of this provision was not clarified by the Supreme Court until it ruled in the case of *Calder v. Bull*.

This case arose out of a dispute between two married couples, the Calders and Bulls, over the estate left behind by Normand Morrison, a physician who died in 1793. Although the Bulls were the express beneficiaries of Morrison's estate, the Calders secured the property rights to some of the deceased's possessions. The Bulls then took the Calders to Connecticut probate court, which ruled in the Calders' favor. By law, the Bulls then had 18 months to appeal this ruling. When that time period expired, they entreated the state legislature to pass a law changing the time limit on appeals. Upon rehearing the case, the probate court then ruled in favor of the Bulls. Unwilling to accept this reversal, Calder took the case to the U.S. Supreme Court. He claimed that the Connecticut legislation was a violation of Article 1, section 10.

High Court Rules

On 8 August 1798, the Supreme Court ruled on the case. Two of the six justices did not weigh in on the dispute, while each of the other four issued his own opinion. All of them agreed on the outcome, however. Connecticut's legislation granting the Bulls a new hearing in probate court was found not to be an *ex post facto* law. The Court went even further in limiting the *ex post facto* provision to the realm of criminal law. The Calders' claim to Morrison's property was negated and the rights of possession were conferred upon the Bulls.

Justice Chase wrote the lead opinion in the case. In rendering his judgement, he relied upon the insight that, while all *ex post facto* laws are by definition retroactive, not all retroactive laws are *ex post facto* laws—and only the latter are unconstitutional. Chase limited his definition of an *ex post facto* law to four important types, all in the criminal rather than civil realm:

> 1st. Every law that makes an action, done before the passing of the law, and which was

innocent when done, criminal; and punishes such action. 2nd. Every law that aggravates a crime, or makes it greater than it was, when committed. 3rd. Every law that changes the punishment, and inflicts a greater punishment, than the law annexed to the crime, when committed. 4th. Every law that alters the legal rules of evidence, and receives less, or different, testimony, than the law required at the time of the commission of the offence, in order to convict the offender.

Prohibitions against *ex post facto* laws, Chase concluded, were designed to protect citizens against unscrupulous prosecution, not to safeguard their private property rights. As Chase wrote: "The restraint against making any *ex post facto* laws was not considered, by the framers of the Constitution, as extending to prohibit the depriving a citizen even of a vested right to property."

To further buttress his argument, Chase pointed out constitutional language that expressly barred the passage of laws which impaired the obligations of private contracts. This, in his view, was an attempt by the framers to provide protections of property rights which were left unprotected by the *ex post facto* clause. If the framers had intended for the *ex post facto* clause to cover property disputes, these passages would have been redundant.

Chase's fellow justices largely agreed. Justice Paterson echoed his view that the ban on impairment of contracts suggested that the framers of the Constitution intended the prohibition of *ex post facto* laws to include "crimes, pains, and penalties, and no further." And Justice Iredell expressed the view that the purpose of the *ex post facto* clause did not extend to "civil cases, to cases that merely affect the private property of citizens."

Impact

The Supreme Court's decision in *Calder v. Bull* had a substantial impact on legal history. As a consequence of this decision, individuals deprived of vested property rights could no longer cite the *ex post facto* prohibition in their argument for relief. Instead they relied on constitutional protections on the sanctity of contracts to protect themselves against legislative action that threatened their property rights.

Related Cases

Pigeon v. Buck, 237 U.S. 386 (1915).
Fred T. Ley Co. v. United States, 273 U.S. 386 (1927).
Adamos v. New York Life Insurance Company, 293 U.S. 386 (1935).
Bowen v. Kizer, 485 U.S. 386 (1988).

Bibliography and Further Reading

Chandler, Ralph C. *The Constitutional Law Dictionary.* Santa Barbara, CA: ABC-Clio, Inc., 1987.

Cushman, Robert Fairchild with Susan P. Koniak. *Leading Constitutional Decisions.* Englewood Cliffs, NJ: Prentice-Hall, Inc., 1992.

Menez, Joseph Francis. *Summaries of Leading Cases of the Constitution.* Savage, MD: Littlefield, Adams, 1990.

UNITED STATES V. PETERS

Legal Citation: 9 U.S. 115 (1809)

Appellant
United States

Appellee
Richard Peters

Appellant's Claim
That Judge Peters should be obliged to act upon a *mandamus* or writ enforcing the judgement of a federal appeals court in favor of Gideon Olmstead, et al, despite a conflicting decision by Pennsylvania's Court of Admiralty.

Justices for the Court
Samuel Chase, William Cushing, William Johnson, Henry Brockholst Livingston, John Marshall (writing for the Court), Thomas Todd, Bushrod Washington

Justices Dissenting
None

Place
Washington, D.C.

Date of Decision
1809

Decision
Judge Peters was directed to execute the *mandamus*.

Significance
The decision established that a state cannot annul the judgements nor determine the jurisdiction of U.S. federal courts.

The Fate of the *Active*

This early decision bolstering the power of federal courts stemmed from an act of lawlessness on the high seas. During the Revolutionary War, a Connecticut sea captain named Gideon Olmstead was captured by the British Navy. Olmstead, who was no stranger to privateering, was sent to Jamaica and pressed into service along with his shipmates Artimus White, Aquilla Rumsdale, and David Rumsdale. The Connecticut sailors were forced to work aboard the sloop *Active,* which set sail for New York with a load of supplies for the British forces. On 6 September 1778, however, Olmstead and his compatriots overcame the British crew and headed for New Jersey.

Before the sloop could reach its new destination, it was intercepted by an armed brig belonging to the state of Pennsylvania, the *Convention*. Along with the *Le Gerard,* a privateer sailing nearby, the *Convention* escorted the *Active* into the port of Philadelphia. The captains of the two American warships quickly claimed any profit from the sale of the captured sloop and its cargo as their own. This was unwelcome news to the Connecticut sailors who had actually seized the vessel. Nevertheless, after a jury hearing, Pennsylvania's Court of Admiralty decided that any proceeds from the sale of the *Active* would be divided between the Commonwealth of Pennsylvania, which owned the *Convention,* and the officers and men of the three vessels involved. Under this arrangement, Olmstead and his shipmates would receive only one quarter of the total value of the sloop.

Olmstead and his fellows filed an appeal with the Court of Commissioners of Appeals in Prize Causes for the United States. On 15 December 1778, this U.S. appeals court reversed the Pennsylvania court's ruling and directed that the proceeds from the ship's sale should be directed to Olmstead, White, Rumsdale, and Clark. Here the squabbling over the fate of the *Active* and its cargo began in earnest.

Court of Admiralty Judge George Ross, who was entrusted with the disposition of the captured ship, would not honor the appeal court's verdict. While Judge Ross agreed that the U.S. court had the power to overturn the court of admiralty's verdict, he also pointed out that the case had been decided appropriately by a jury, whose opinion he was bound to honor under Pennsylvania's laws. Judge Ross ordered the *Active* to be sold. Olmstead quickly got an injunction ordering the marshall in charge of the sale to deliver the proceeds to the appeals court. The marshall ignored the order and delivered the money to Judge Ross, against whom Olmstead and the others filed suit.

Judge Ross had the sale proceeds transformed into U.S. loan certificates. Rather than hold the state of Pennsylvania's share of 11,496 pounds, Ross turned the certificates over to David Rittenhouse, a prominent Philadelphian who was the state's treasurer. Rittenhouse in turn gave Judge Ross a certificate of indemnity against any future claims upon the sum.

Rittenhouse was willing to hand the loan certificates over to the state of Pennsylvania at any time, yet the state did not act. The certificates sat in Rittenhouse's personal account accruing interest.

The *Gideon Olmstead and others v. Rittenhouse's Executrixes* Case

After Rittenhouse died, Olmstead and the other claimants brought suit against Elizabeth Serjeant and Esther Waters, the executrixes of the Rittenhouse estate,

Justice Henry Brockholst Livingston. © The Library of Congress/Corbis.

demanding that the money be turned over in accordance with the court of appeals decision. Pennsylvania's General Assembly finally became interested in the money and passed an act in 1801 demanding that Rittenhouse's estate deliver the certificates to the state treasury. With the state of Pennsylvania and Olmstead both claiming the certificates, the executrixes refused to give them to anyone.

This paralysis lasted until 1808, when Olmstead and the others attempted to get Philadelphia U.S. District Court Judge Richard Peters to grant an attachment against the Rittenhouse estate. When Peters refused, Olmstead succeeded in obtaining a writ of *mandamus,* an order to carry out the higher federal court's decision. Yet Peters stated that he would decline to order the certificates to change hands as long as the state of Pennsylvania was still involved as a claimant. Judge Peters cited the Eleventh Amendment to the Constitution, which prevents the judicial power of the United States from extending to any lawsuit prosecuted against any of the individual states. Since Rittenhouse had been Pennsylvania's treasurer, Peters ruled, the state could claim jurisdiction over the case.

A more pressing concern to Judge Peters was that the state of Pennsylvania was threatening to use armed force to prevent the appeals court sentence from being carried out. Faced with the state militia on one side and a federal writ on the other, Judge Peters returned the *mandamus* to the U.S. Supreme Court and waited for a decision.

To Prevent "A Solemn Mockery"

The Court's 1809 decision commanded Judge Peters to act on the *mandamus.* Chief Justice Marshall pointed out that the disputed certificates had never been the actual property of the state of Pennsylvania. They had always been in the possession of David Rittenhouse or his estate. Since Rittenhouse had always acted as a private citizen in the affair, the Eleventh Amendment prohibition against making a state a party in a lawsuit was not an issue.

In a broader sense, the Court also repudiated the contention that the Pennsylvania legislature's 1801 act demanding the money was legally superior to the federal appeals court decision.

"If the legislatures of the several States may, at will, annul the judgements of the courts of the United States, and destroy the rights acquired under those judgements," wrote Justice Marshall, "the Constitution itself becomes a solemn mockery, and the nation is deprived of the means of enforcing its laws by the instrumentality of its own tribunals."

The Supreme Court declared that states could neither annul the judgements nor determine the jurisdiction of federal courts. Since the court of appeals in the

Active case had been formed by the Continental Congress, its decision superceded Pennsylvania's Court of Admiralty. Judge Peters was ordered to act on the *mandamus,* while making sure that the executrixes of the Rittenhouse estate were protected from any possible legal repercussions. Rittenhouse's papers left no doubt that he had been willing to be rid of the disputed money as soon as its rightful owners were determined.

The Court's decision was extremely unpopular in Pennsylvania. As a matter of national law, however, the decision strengthened the power of federal courts in an era when the struggle over the relative rights of states and the U.S. government was still young.

Bibliography and Further Reading

Middlebrook, Louis F. *Maritime Connecticut During the American Revolution.* Salem: Essex Institute, 1925.

Warren, Charles. *The Supreme Court In United States History.* Boston: Little, Brown & Co., 1926.

COHENS V. VIRGINIA

Legal Citation: 19 U.S. 264 (1821)

Appellants
Philip and Mendes Cohen

Appellee
State of Virginia

Appellants' Claim
A $100 fine under Virginia state law for selling tickets in Virginia for a national lottery authorized by Congress in the District of Columbia flouted congressional authority.

Chief Lawyers for Appellants
David B. Ogden, William Pickney

Chief Lawyers for Appellees
James Barbor, Daniel Webster

Justices for the Court
Gabriel Duvall, William Johnson, Henry Brockholst Livingston, John Marshall (writing for the Court), Joseph Story, Thomas Todd, Bushrod Washington

Justices Dissenting
None

Place
Washington, D.C.

Date of Decision
3 March 1821

Decision
The justices, on the facts, upheld a fine imposed by a state court, while asserting the Supreme Court's authority, under the Constitution, to review state court decisions.

Significance
Cohens v. Virginia crowned a series of decisions asserting the Supreme Court's authority to, in the words of Marshall, "decide all cases of every description under the laws of the United States." In this 1821 decision, Marshall legally demolished the claims of states' rights which would politically plunge the nation into Civil War in 1861: "The Constitution and laws of a state, insofar as they are repugnant to the Constitution and laws of the United States are absolutely void."

It was a cynical appeal, brought by two highly paid lawyers, on behalf of two speculators hoping to reap a multi-state harvest from a District of Columbia lottery. But it provided Chief Justice Marshall with grounds to assert the supremacy of the Union over the states.

In words that anticipated those of Abraham Lincoln in defending the Union 40 years later, Marshall unequivocally asserted the "We, the People" with which the Constitution began meant the Union, Congress and the Supreme Court created by that Constitution reigned over the states:

> The United States form . . . a single nation . . . In war, we are one people. In all commercial regulations, we are one and the same people. In many other respects, the American people are one; and the government which is alone capable of controlling and managing their interests in all these respects is the government of the Union.

"It is their government, and in that character they have no other," Marshall declared in perhaps his most important decision—and in some of his most ringing words: "America has chosen to be a . . . nation; and for all these purposes, her government is complete . . . it is competent . . . it is supreme."

Albert Beveridge, Marshall's biographer, wrote that *Cohens v. Virginia* was one of the most famous cases in American jurisprudence, but, "on the merits, it amounted to nothing." But, as Beveridge added, although the "practical result of the appeal was nothing, it afforded John Marshall the opportunity to tell the Nation its duty."

Philip and Mendes Cohen, owners of a lottery authorized by Congress to operate in the District of Columbia, hoped to gleen the spare cash of people in other states. But officials in Norfolk, Virginia, zealously guarding the coffers of that state's lottery, fined the Cohens $100 for siphoning off the cash of Virginia citizens.

Marshall agreed with the constitutional claims of the Cohens' lawyers. David B. Ogden of New York, argued that Virginia had no authority to impose such fines since a "sovereign state, independent of the Union," does not exist. If federal courts did not review the deci-

Lotteries in America

The lottery in America dates to 1612, when the Virginia Company introduced a lottery with the authorization of the British sovereign. The practice caught on in the colonies, and lotteries served as a significant means of raising money to fund the American Revolution. Among the supporters of the lottery concept were Thomas Jefferson and Benjamin Franklin.

Lotteries continued to be popular throughout the late eighteenth century and most of the nineteenth. By the mid-nineteenth century, the eastern states were raising some $66 million in annual funds by means of lotteries, and the practice expanded to the West. By the late 1800s, a variety of factors, including corruption in the operation of lotteries, served to virtually extinguish them in all states except Louisiana. In 1890, Congress passed the Anti-Lottery Act.

Since their reintroduction in New Hampshire in 1964, however, lotteries have proven more popular than ever, and with congressional authorization of new lottery standards in 1974, more states have started lotteries. Lotteries, however, continue to be a controversial means of raising funds: according to detractors, they disproportionately drain the finances of the poor.

Source(s): *West's Encyclopedia of American Law.* St. Paul, MN: West Group, 1998.

sions of state tribunals, federal authority would be surrendered, leaving "the Union a mere league or confederacy," argued William Pinckney, another Cohens' attorney and the nation's highest paid lawyer.

"On the merits," however, Marshall concurred with Virginia's attorneys, agreeing that the state had the power to regulate lottery sales within its borders. The District of Columbia lottery allowed by Congress was "only co-extensive with the city," Marshall ruled.

States' rights advocates were enraged—and suspicious—claiming the appeal had been "arranged . . . feigned" just to give Marshall an opportunity to assert national over states' interests. Even if the appeal was, "never was such contrivance so justified," Beveridge concluded.

Related Cases

Martin v. Hunter's Lessee, 14 U.S. 304 (1816).
McCullouch v. Maryland, 17 U.S. 316 (1819).
Michigan v. Long, 463 U.S. 1032 (1983).

Bibliography and Further Reading

Beveridge, Albert J. *Life of John Marshall.* Boston, Houghton-Mifflin, 1916.

Bickel, Alexander M., and Benno C. Schmidt. *History of the Supreme Court of the United States.* New York, Macmillan, 1984.

Johnson, John W., ed. *Historic U.S. Court Cases 1690–1990.* New York: Garland Publishing, 1992.

Schwartz, Bernard. *A History of the Supreme Court.* New York, Oxford University Press, 1993.

MISSISSIPPI V. JOHNSON

Legal Citation: 71 U.S. 475 (1866)

Plaintiff
State of Mississippi

Defendants
Andrew Johnson, General Edward O. C. Ord

Plaintiff's Claim
That the Supreme Court should prevent President Andrew Johnson from carrying out the provisions of the Reconstruction Act of 1867.

Chief Lawyers for Plaintiff
W. L. Sharkey, R. J. Walker

Chief Defense Lawyer
Henry Stanberry, U.S. Attorney General

Justices for the Court
Salmon Portland Chase (writing for the Court), Nathan Clifford, David Davis, Stephen Johnson Field, Robert Cooper Grier, Samuel Freeman Miller, Samuel Nelson, Noah Haynes Swayne, James Moore Wayne

Justices Dissenting
None

Place
Washington, D.C.

Date of Decision
15 April 1867

Decision
Denied plaintiff's claim.

Significance
The Court refused to limit a president's power to carry out the laws passed by Congress, keeping the separation of powers intact. By not ruling on the Reconstruction Act, the Court let stand the voting rights given to newly freed slaves. The ruling also helped define the executive's immunity from lawsuits designed to limit its political duties.

Before *Mississippi v. Johnson,* an acting president had never been named as an individual defendant in a case heard before the Supreme Court. But the case arose during a uniquely difficult time in American history. In the aftermath of the Civil War, the country was trying to heal itself and address the issues raised by the end of slavery. Collectively, the political programs implemented to restore order and rebuild the country were called Reconstruction.

In some ways, Reconstruction still pitted North against South, though now the battle was fought with words and laws, not cannons, and the victorious North held the clear advantage. Following the lead of Abraham Lincoln, President Andrew Johnson tried to make Reconstruction a conciliatory process. But by 1867, a faction in Congress known as the Radical Republicans had taken control of Reconstruction. Many of these Republicans had been strong abolitionists before the war. Now, their primary concern was asserting control over the beaten Confederacy and establishing the rights of the South's newly freed slaves.

The Reconstruction Act of 1867 was one of the Radical Republicans first major legislative programs. The act divided the old Confederacy into five regions, each ruled by a military governor, with military courts to hear civil matters. As a condition for reentering the Union, the Southern states were also required under the act to draft new constitutions that gave African Americans the right to vote. (The law, however, did not extend that right to Northern blacks.)

The Reconstruction Act threw the South into an uproar. Within a month of the bill's passage, the state of Mississippi charged the act was blatantly unconstitutional. The state asked the Supreme Court to impose a permanent injunction preventing President Johnson and the area's military governor, Edward O. C. Ord, from executing the law.

The Case Against Johnson and the Reconstruction Act

In their motion to the Court, attorneys W. L Sharkey and R. J. Walker attacked the bill's intent. "It annuls and abrogates the state government and state consti-

---

Salmon Portland Chase

Salmon Portland Chase (1808-73), sixth chief justice of the Supreme Court, served on the Court at the height of the Reconstruction Era, from 1864 to 1873. He presided over pivotal cases such as *Mississippi v. Johnson* (1866), *Ex Parte Milligan* (1866), the *Test-Oath* Cases (1867), and the *Slaughterhouse* Cases (1873).

An opponent of slavery, Chase gained a reputation as a defender of runaway slaves in his Cincinnati law practice. He ran for the Senate with the Free-Soil Party in 1848 and became known as a leading anti-slavery senator, outspoken in his opposition to the 1854 Kansas-Nebraska Act. In 1855 Chase, who helped form the Republican Party, became governor of Ohio. In 1860

Chase, then back in the Senate, sought the presidency. But when Abraham Lincoln emerged as the party favorite, he accepted a position as secretary of the treasury. Chase ran against Lincoln in the 1864 elections, months after he resigned his Cabinet post. Lincoln nominated Chase as chief justice in 1864. Initially opposing the radical Republicans and advocating a moderate approach toward the former Confederacy, Chase upheld the powers of Congress and the principles of the Reconstruction in cases such as *Texas v. White* (1868).

Source(s): *West's Encyclopedia of American Law*. St. Paul, MN: West Group, 1998.

---

tutions, and substitutes a mere military power." The federal government had already gotten into constitutional trouble using military authority in civil matters. In 1866, the Court ruled in *Ex Parte Milligan* that the government could not declare martial law in areas outside a war zone that had existing civil governments and courts. Mississippi was no longer at war with the federal government, and the state did have its own civil government in place.

Sharkey and Walker also asserted that the Supreme Court did have jurisdiction in this matter. "The Constitution is supreme; all officers are subordinate to the supreme law, and consequently subordinate to the command of the department [the Supreme Court] whose duty it is to enforce subordination by declaring the meaning, the extent, and the limitations of the Constitution."

Without mentioning it by name, the plaintiffs also brought up the precedent of *Marbury v. Madison*. In that famous 1803 decision, Chief Justice John Marshall had distinguished between a president's "ministerial" and "political" duties. The Court could compel the president to carry out a ministerial duty ordered by Congress. In this case, the plaintiffs argued, carrying out the Reconstruction Act was ministerial, and so fell under the Court's jurisdiction.

The Court Says No

The Supreme Court denied the motion to consider the permanent injunction against the Reconstruction Act. The Court noted that bringing suit against a sitting president was unprecedented, and that was held against the plaintiffs. But the Court also relied on specific points of law in its decision.

Writing for the Court, Chief Justice Chase first looked at the issue of ministerial versus political duties.

Executing the Reconstruction Act, he argued, was a political duty.

> A ministerial duty . . . is one in respect to which nothing is open to discretion. It is a simple, definite duty, arising under conditions admitted or proved to exist, and imposed by law . . . Very different is the duty of the President in the exercise of power to see that the laws are faithfully executed, and among these laws the acts named in the bill . . . he is required to assign generals to command in the several military districts, and to detail sufficient military force to enable such officers to discharge their duties under the law . . . The duty thus imposed on the President is in no sense just ministerial. It is purely executive and political.

The Court did not examine the constitutionality of the Reconstruction Act, remarking that even if it were unconstitutional, the Court could not prevent the president from executing it. The Constitution, the Court reasoned, requires Congress to pass the laws, the president to execute them, and the Court to review them once they have been put into place. But the Court has no power to review a law before it is executed. The Court kept the separation of powers intact.

After the decision in *Mississippi,* President Johnson did carry out the Reconstruction Act. The Court again examined the law's constitutionality in 1868, when the state of Georgia filed a similar suit. The Court let the Radical Republicans carry out their brand of Reconstruction.

In a judicial sense, *Mississippi* helped shape the notion of executive immunity. The president was now immune from suits that tried to prevent him from carrying out a law—if it fell under his political duties. Eventually, presidential immunity was expanded, in

Nixon v. Fitzgerald (1982). In that case, the Court ruled the president was immune from personal liability lawsuits for acts he performed while in office.

Related Cases

Marbury v. Madison, 5 U.S. 137 (1803).
Ex parte Milligan, 71 U.S. 2 (1866).
Nixon v. Fitzgerald, 457 U.S. 731 (1982).

Bibliography and Further Reading

Elliott, Stephen P., ed. *A Reference Guide to the U.S. Supreme Court.* New York: Facts on File Publications, 1986.

Epstein, Lee, and Thomas G. Walker. *Constitutional Law for a Changing America: Institutional Powers and Constraints,* 3rd ed. Washington DC: Congressional Quarterly, 1998.

Foner, Eric. *Reconstruction 1863–1877.* New York: Harper and Row, 1988.

Hall, Kermit L., ed. *The Oxford Companion to the Supreme Court of the United States.* New York: Oxford University Press, 1992.

Witt, Elder, ed. *The Supreme Court A to Z. CQ's Encyclopedia of American Government.* Washington, DC: Congressional Quarterly, Inc., 1993.

Young, James V. *Landmark Constitutional Law Decisions.* Lanham, MD: University Press of America, 1993.

KILBOURN V. THOMPSON

Legal Citation: 103 U.S. 168 (1881)

Plaintiff
Hallett Kilbourn

Defendant
John G. Thompson, Michael C. Kerr, John M. Glover, Jeptha
D. New, Burwell P. Lewis, A. Herr Smith

Plaintiff's Claim
Kilbourn objected to the fact that he had been called before
a committee of Congress, and, refusing to answer questions, had been jailed for contempt of Congress. He
brought suit against Thompson, the sergeant-at-arms, as
well as against the five members of the congressional committee that had called him.

Chief Lawyers for Plaintiff
Charles A. Eldredge, Enoch Totten, Noah L. Jeffries

Chief Defense Lawyers
Walter H. Smith, Frank H. Hurd

Justices for the Court
Salmon Portland Chase, Nathan Clifford, Stephen Johnson
Field, John Marshall Harlan I, Ward Hunt, Stanley Matthews,
Samuel Freeman Miller (writing for the Court), Morrison
Remick Waite, William Burnham Woods

Justices Dissenting
None

Place
Washington, D.C.

Date of Decision
28 February 1881

Decision
That Congress had exceeded its powers in subpoenaing and
imprisoning Kilbourn, because the congressional investigation for which he had been called did not actually concern
legislation; however, because of congressional immunity,
only Thompson could be punished for the improper action.

Significance
This case was the first time the Supreme Court had reviewed
a congressional investigation, and the decision constituted
a significant limitation on congressional powers.

On 6 December 1875, a new House of Representatives
convened with the Democratic Party in the majority
after the 36th through the 43rd Congresses had been
dominated by the Republican Party. The newly elected
politicians were eager to take decisive action.

On 24 January 1876, the House moved into a new
type of activity: investigation. The huge corporation of
Jay Cooke & Co. had gone into bankruptcy, amidst
rumors of corruption and financial scandal. Indeed, the
bankruptcy was pending before the District Court for
Eastern Pennsylvania. Cooke's company actually owed
the U.S. government money. Moreover, a trustee of
Cooke's estate had recently made a settlement that was
alleged to be disadvantageous to Cooke's creditors—
including the government. This the House proposed to
investigate.

Although Congress had never before engaged in
such activities, the House passed a resolution directing
the Speaker to appoint a five-member committee, with
the power to subpoena witnesses and related documents. The committee sent for Hallett Kilbourn.

An Uncooperative Witness

Kilbourn has the distinction of being the first uncooper-
ative witness before a congressional committee. Although
he did obey the subpoena by appearing before Congress,
he refused to produce the papers he was asked for,
and he likewise refused to answer any questions put to
him by Congress. Therefore, on 14 March 1876, the
Speaker of the House sent John S. Thompson, House
Sergeant-at-Arms, to find Kilbourn and bring him into
custody.

Kilbourn continued to refuse to cooperate, even to
the extent of telling the committee the names and
addresses of the five members of the real-estate pool.
Since this was information that the committee surely
already had, Kilbourn's refusal was more symbolic than
an actual hindrance to the committee's work, but the
committee was incensed at this affront to their authority. They decided to find Kilbourn in contempt, and he
was taken by the sergeant-at-arms to "the common jail
of the District of Columbia."

Samuel R. Lowery, African American Lawyer

At the time that *Kilbourn* was argued, very few African Americans practiced law. Samuel Lowery was a notable exception. Lowery (1832-1900) was raised by his father and schooled (along with his father) in the ways of being a Christian pastor by the Reverend Talbot Fanning at Franklin College in Nashville, where his father worked as a farmer, livery stable operator and janitor. This education led him to his first position as a minister in 1848, but his good fortune was short-lived. As debates over slavery raged in the South, free African Americans were finding themselves the target of great hatred and violence. In 1856 Samuel had to leave his church as he and his father moved North to find a better life for themselves. Although Samuel found himself in the pulpit once again by 1859, at the Harrison Street Christian Church in Cincinnati, Ohio, he longed to return to his southern home.

It was five years before the Union Army occupation of Nashville allowed for the African American community in the southern city to thrive again. When Lowery returned to his home town it was with a mission.

He became a Christian Church missionary and worked to found the Tennessee Manual Labor University, making his father the president. Like the school that his father had worked for so many years before, their university taught agriculture, mechanical arts and Christian ethics. Unfortunately, the school fell under hard times when a fundraising venture ended in Samuel Lowrey's being excommunicated from the white Christian Church. Without their funding, the university was forced to close.

It was also during this time that Lowery had started to study and practice law. After moving to Huntsville, Alabama in 1875, and establishing another school (Lowery's Industrial Academy), his continued practice of the law earned him admittance to the bar of the U.S. Supreme Court on 2 February 1880. He was the first African American to receive this honor.

Source(s): http://www.tnstate.edu/library/digital/lowery.htm

There Kilbourn languished for 45 days. Eventually, Kilbourn managed to enter a writ of *habeas corpus* with the Supreme Court of the District of Columbia. The District of Columbia court found in Kilbourn's favor, and Kilbourn promptly sued the men who had caused him to be imprisoned: John S. Thompson plus the five members of the committee. The case eventually made it to the Supreme Court.

Preserving the Separation of Powers

One of the cornerstones of the American system is the notion of the separation of powers. The legislative branch is charged with making the laws; the executive branch is required to enforce the laws; and the judicial branch is expected to interpret the laws. If a person is believed to have broken a law, the proper place to investigate the matter and to determine a response is supposed to be in court.

This doctrine was further defined when the Supreme Court ruled in *Kilbourn v. Thompson,* for the Court held that Congress had exceeded its powers by investigating Cooke & Co. in the first place. In an apparently unanimous opinion written by Justice Miller, the Court pointed out that British Parliamentary tradition—the foundation for the American system—holds no precedent for the punishment of a private citizen for refusing to testify before a legislative body. True, the House had the power to punish its own members. The House also had the power to do a great deal that might be

necessary to fulfill its legislative mission. However, Justice Miller wondered what could possibly be the legislative intent behind conducting this investigation.

> To inquire into the nature and history of the real-estate pool. How indefinite! What was the real-estate pool? Is it charged with any crime or offence? If so, the courts alone can punish the members of it. Is it charged with a fraud against the government? Here, again, the courts, and they alone, can afford a remedy . . . Can the rights of the pool, or of its members, and the rights of the debtor, and of the creditor of the debtor, be determined by the report of a committee or by an act of Congress? If they cannot, what authority has the House to enter upon this investigation into the private affairs of individuals who hold no office under the government.

Since the House had no authority to investigate the matter in the first place, the Court said, it certainly had no power to hold Kilbourn in contempt. Kilbourn's suit was upheld.

Congressional Immunity

However, the Court was not willing to go so far as to say that the members of Congress who had improperly conducted their investigation should be punished.

The Constitution holds that members of Congress "shall not be questioned in any other place" for any speech or debate that takes place in Congress. The framers of the Constitution believed such a provision was necessary if members of Congress were to feel free to make laws that might sometimes be unpopular or controversial. Therefore, no one who had been elected to Congress could be punished for what happened to Kilbourn.

Thompson, however, was not a member of Congress, and he could be punished. The question of what his punishment should be was remanded to a lower court. Meanwhile, however, the Supreme Court had established an important principle: Congress had no right to investigate the affairs of a private citizen, nor to punish private citizens for refusing to answer questions in improper investigations. Although later Court decisions gave Congress somewhat more latitude to investigate and interrogate, *Kilbourn v. Thompson* was an important step in defining the scope of congressional powers.

Related Cases

Calder v. Bull, 3 U.S. 386 (1798).
Ex parte Milligan, 71 U.S. 2 (1866).
Loan Association v. Topeka, 87 U.S. 655 (1875).
United States v. Cruikshank, 92 U.S. 542 (1876).

Bibliography and Further Reading

Biskupic, Joan, and Elder Witt, eds. *Congressional Quarterly's Guide to the U.S. Supreme Court,* 3rd ed. Washington, DC: Congressional Quarterly, Inc., 1996.

Fairman, Charles, *History of the Supreme Court of the United States,* Vol. VII, *Reconstruction and Reunion, 1864–1888.* New York: Macmillan, 1987.

Hall, Kermit L., ed. *The Oxford Companion to the Supreme Court of the United States.* New York: Oxford University Press, 1992.

CHICAGO, MILWAUKEE, AND ST. PAUL RAILWAY COMPANY V. THE STATE OF MINNESOTA

Legal Citation: 134 U.S. 418 (1890)

Plaintiff
The Chicago, Milwaukee, and St. Paul Railway Company

Defendant
State of Minnesota ex rel. the Railroad and Warehouse Commission of the State of Minnesota

Plaintiff's Claim
The state of Minnesota wrongly granted power to the Warehouse and Railroad Commission to limit charges on behalf of freight carriers in the state.

Chief Lawyers for Plaintiff
John W. Cary, W. C. Goudy, J. H. Howe, W. H. Norris

Chief Defense Lawyers
Moses E. Clapp, H. W. Childs

Justices for the Court
Samuel Blatchford (writing for the Court), David Josiah Brewer, Stephen Johnson Field, Melville Weston Fuller, John Marshall Harlan I, Samuel Freeman Miller

Justices Dissenting
Joseph P. Bradley, Horace Gray, Lucius Quintus C. Lamar

Place
Washington, D.C.

Date of Decision
24 March 1890

Decision
The U.S Supreme Court reversed the writ of *mandamus* issued by the Supreme Court of Minnesota, and remanded the case back to the lower court for further proceedings because the lower court denied the Chicago, Milwaukee, and St. Paul Railway Company due process of law.

Significance
The U.S. Supreme Court confirmed that the state of Minnesota, hence all states, have the legislative power to craft laws regulating rates of transport. However, the manner in which the state of Minnesota executed their authority via the Railroad and Warehouse Commission—not allowing the Chicago, Milwaukee, and St. Paul Railway Company representation before the commission rate hearings—breached the Fourteenth Amendment of the U.S. Constitution. Thus, while states could legally regulate service rates, rate hearings and decisions had to be conducted in a manner which permitted participation and input by all affected parties.

In March of 1887, the state of Minnesota established a Railroad and Warehouse Commission. The duties of this commission were defined in a legislative act of Minnesota (General Laws of 1887, chapter 10). The first section of this act proclaimed that any common carrier "engaged in the transportation of passengers or property . . . from one place or station to another, both being within the State of Minnesota" would be liable to its provisions. Thus, the commission was authorized to force any common carrier to change its tariffs if it found such charges "unreasonable" and "unequal." The commission, however, was obliged to notify carriers, in writing, and explain why such charges were unlawful. If a common carrier overlooked such notification and refused to follow or adopt recommended charges it was subject to a writ of *mandamus* (a written order to undertake a certain legal procedure; subject to the *mandamus* are individuals, public officials, companies, and courts). In essence, the Railroad and Warehouse Commission had total authority and autonomy in determining what constituted lawful rate charges.

The commission, joined by the Board of Trade Unions of Farmington, Northfield, Faribault and Owatonna, petitioned the Chicago, Milwaukee, and St. Paul Railway Company (C M & St. P Railway) complaining that their charge for transport of milk was unjust. The petition stated that the company charged four cents per gallon of milk for shipment from Owatonna to St. Paul and Minneapolis, but from Faribault, Dundas, Northfield and Farmington to St. Paul and Minneapolis, the price was three cents per gallon. The commission requested that charges should be replaced with ones determined fair by the commission. Officials from C M & St. P Railway refused to change rates arguing that their charges were even lower than in some parts of the country. In response, the commission and the Board of Trade Unions met at the office of the commission in St. Paul. They concluded that transport charges of three cents per gallon of milk was high and that two-and-one-half cents was fair.

The commission reported their findings to C M & St. P Railway. The report protested that the company overcharged for its service and announced that the sum of two and one-half cents was just compensation. The

"Our Overworked Supreme Court"

Cartoonist Joseph Keppler depicted "Our Overworked Supreme Court" in a cartoon with that caption published in the humor magazine *Puck* on 9 December 1885. The scene showed the Supreme Court justices awash amidst a pile of paper. It symbolized the extraordinary caseload in which the court was regularly mired at the time.

In the Supreme Court of John Jay, the first chief justice (1789-95), the caseload was light, and justices often spent time on administrative matters. By the time of the Civil War, the size of the docket had grown to some 300 cases. By the time of Keppler's cartoon, the Court was swamped with more than 1,300 cases.

In 1891, Congress gave the Court some relief with the passage of the Circuit Court of Appeals Act, which established the appellate court system as a buffer between the lower courts and the High Court.

Source(s): "Federal Judiciary (Library of Congress Manuscripts: An Illustrated Guide)." http://lcweb.loc.gov.

Commission ruled that the new, set rate should be charged regardless of the transport distance in the state. When the Railway Company refused to comply, the state attorney general applied for a writ of *mandamus* from the Minnesota Supreme Court. Consequently, the court issued an "alternative" writ of *mandamus*. (Although the court's deadline for the response to be filled and returned was 14 December 1887, C M & St. P Railway responded on 23 of December, 1887.)

The heart of the company's response debated whether the state had a legal ground to establish a regulatory commission with such vast authority. The brief pointed out that C M & St. P Railway succeeded all franchises granted by the Congress of the United States in 1857 to the Cedar Valley Railroad Company and that under the ninth section of the charter, the directors of the company were granted exclusive right to regulate the rates of transport. The only clause in the charter was that the company had to "assure a reasonable rate."

C M & St. P Railway applied twice for a peremptory writ of *mandamus*, but the Minnesota Supreme Court denied their application both times. The court affirmed the writ and issued an order that the railroad must obey the decision of the Railroad and Warehouse Commission. To counter this decision, the company submitted a writ of error (written order, usually, from a superior court to a lower one to send a record of the case for review) to the U.S. Supreme Court.

States' Rights Versus Commercial Rights

John W. Cary argued the case for the plaintiff. He claimed the ruling of the state court had no legal ground for the state to limit transport rates, and that such a move was incompatible with the charter the federal government had granted to public railroads, as in *Stone v. Farmers L. & T. Co.* (1886). The company had been deprived of its property and its use without the due process of law (*Allnutt v. Inglis*) and, in another unrelated case involving the railway, *Chicago, Milwaukee and St. Paul Railway Co. v. Ackley* (1876). Cary maintained the court was mistaken in its opinion that rates set by the commission were final, lawful, and that C M & St. P Railway should not have to abide by the commission's rulings. The state court was also mistaken in issuing a writ of *mandamus*.

W. C. Goudy argued for the plaintiff as well. In presenting his arguments, Goudy suggested that the decision of the Railroad and Warehouse Commission should be subjected to judicial investigation. He believed the sections of the statute of Minnesota which authorized regulatory action by the railroad commission final were repugnant to the Fifth and Fourteenth Amendments. As precedent, Goudy cited *Munn v. Illinois* (1877), and *Gibbons v. Ogden* (1824). Moreover, he claimed the state court disregarded its own previous ruling in *Brown v. Maryland* (1827).

Counsel for the state of Minnesota argued that the state's supreme court did not exceed its jurisdiction and the writ of *mandamus* was a legitimate use of available leverage to force a common carrier to comply with the commission's ruling. Moreover, according to a prior ruling made in *Chicago, Burlington and Quincy Railroad Company v. Chicago* (1876), the judgment of the state court was obligatory before the U.S. Supreme Court. The attorney for the defendant reasoned that if not protected by their charters, railroad companies and, subsequently, their transport rates are subject to state control. He concluded that the general statute regulating common carriers or their transport charges did not inevitably deprive railroads of their property without due process of law if a ruling was not in collision with a railroad's charter as stated in *Richmond, F. & P. R. Co. v. Richmond* (1877).

On a 6-3 vote, the U.S. Supreme Court reversed the decision of the lower court. In writing their decision, the Court was careful to state that the legislature of the state of Minnesota had a right to form such a commission and that the decision of the Railroad and Warehouse Commission was indeed obligatory. The Supreme Court was also careful to acknowledge that their authority did not extend to making a determination whether the state's set rate was just. The charter that gave competence to the directors of the company to regulate the transport charges did not mean that the state abandoned its right to intervene when there existed a compelling need for the state to set rates. Furthermore, a federal charter protected a company and excluded it from legal liability only if its (federal) grant clearly stated so, which was clearly not within the charter of the C M & St. P Railway. However, the Court also found that the company was denied due process in the Minnesota Railroad and Warehouse Commission hearings because it had no opportunity to appear and justify the basis for their transport rates. The Supreme Court thus found the writ of *mandamus* issued by the Minnesota Court to be "repugnant to the U.S. Constitution" and remanded the case back to the lower court for further adjudication.

Justice Bradley, writing the dissenting opinion, felt the Court neglected precedence set in *Munn v. Illinois;* interestingly, his main objection to the majority opinion was that the case presented a legislative rather than judicial issue. However, he agreed with the majority opinion that states retained the authority to craft laws (within the limits of the U.S. Constitution) and so the state of Minnesota did not surpass its power by founding the Railroad and Warehouse Commission. Bradley went on to posit that "due process of law does not always require the court. It merely requires such

tribunals and proceedings as are proper to the subject in hand." Moreover, he also agreed that while the U.S Constitution tacitly granted state governments the ability to make their own regulatory bodies and code, states were obliged to conduct fair hearings.

Impact

At the time *Chicago, Milwaukee, and St. Paul Railway Company v. the State of Minnesota* was adjudicated, cases dealing with regulation of private corporations and monopolies were increasingly presented to the Supreme Court. In fact, another case was argued concurrently before the Court, *Minneapolis Eastern Railway Co. v. the State of Minnesota.* Interestingly, the railroads accepted the decision of the Minnesota Railroad and Warehouse Commission. No official record exists that positively identifies the reason for the company's decision to accept the state's rate, however, it is quite likely that in a legal atmosphere which was perceived as actively pursuing the extent of state and federal regulatory capabilities, the railroads capitulated in their own best interest. In upholding states' rights to found commissions and regulatory bodies to monitor common carriers, the U.S. Supreme Court showed its firm support to limit the potential for monopoly by railroads. Yet, even though the Court only indirectly mitigated unreasonable transport charges set by railroads, this and similar rulings ensured an economic climate which promoted free and fair market competition in the United States.

Related Cases

Gibbons v. Ogden, 22 U.S. 9 (1824).
Brown v. Maryland, 25 U.S. 419 (1827).

A political cartoon depicting the overworked Supreme Court. © Drawing by J. Keppler. The Library of Congress.

Chicago, Burlington and Quincy Railroad Company v. Ackley, 94 U.S. 155 (1876).

Chicago, Milwaukee and St. Paul Railway Co. v. the State of Minnesota, 94 U.S. 179 (1876).

Winona R. Co. v. Blake, 94 U.S. 180 (1876).

Munn v. Illinois, 94 U.S. 113 (1877).

Richmond, F. & P. R. Co. v. Richmond, 96 U.S. 521 (1877).

Stone v. Farmers L. & T. Co., 116 U.S. 326 (1886).

Bibliography and Further Reading

Biskupic, Joan, and Elder Witt, eds. *Congressional Quarterly's Guide to the U.S. Supreme Court,* 3rd ed. Washington, DC: Congressional Quarterly, Inc., 1996.

Hall, Kermit L., ed. *The Oxford Companion to the Supreme Court of the United States.* New York: Oxford University Press, 1992.

RAILROAD COMMISSION OF TEXAS V. PULLMAN COMPANY

Legal Citation: 312 U.S. 496 (1941)

Appellant
Railroad Commission of Texas, et al.

Appellee
Pullman Company, et al.

Appellant's Claim
That under Texas law it had authority to regulate Pullman sleepers, and that a federal district court erred in preventing enforcement of this regulation.

Chief Lawyers for Appellant
Cecil A. Morgan, Cecil C. Rotsch

Chief Lawyer for Appellee
Ireland Graves

Justices for the Court
Hugo Lafayette Black, William O. Douglas, Felix Frankfurter (writing for the Court), Charles Evans Hughes, James Clark McReynolds, Frank Murphy, Stanley Forman Reed, Harlan Fiske Stone

Justices Dissenting
None (Owen Josephus Roberts did not participate)

Place
Washington, D.C.

Date of Decision
3 March 1941

Decision
Reversed the lower court's order to enjoin enforcement of the regulation and directed the case be heard in the state courts.

Significance
The *Pullman* decision clearly articulated for the first time the Supreme Court's "abstention doctrine." This doctrine defines when a federal court may choose not to exercise its jurisdiction, even though a constitutional issue exists, to first let a state court try to resolve the question. As used in *Pullman*, the abstention doctrine frees the states from having the federal government unnecessarily involved in their affairs.

The Supreme Court has often limited the cases it hears, based on its interpretation of Article III of the Constitution, which established the Court. At times, acts of Congress, such as the Judiciary Acts of 1789 and 1875, have also limited or expanded the Court's jurisdiction. For many years, however, the Court seemed to follow the words of Chief Justice John Marshall: "It is most true, that this Court will not take jurisdiction if it should not: but it is equally true, that it must take jurisdiction if it should . . . We have no more right to decline the exercise of jurisdiction which is given, than to usurp that which is not given."

But Marshall's view was not absolute. In the 1930s, the Court heard a number of cases in which it could have ruled, but chose not to, or ordered other federal courts to defer to the state courts. This idea of abstaining from jurisdiction was first clearly stated in *Railroad Commission of Texas v. Pullman Company*, and is sometimes called the *Pullman* abstention doctrine.

After the Civil War, George Pullman invented the luxury railroad sleeping car and helped revolutionize transcontinental travel in America. In the 1940s, the Pullman Company was still a major force in train travel. When the Texas Railroad Commission issued an order that affected staffing on Pullman sleepers, the company, along with the railroad lines, took the matter to court.

Race, Economics, and State Law

On the less populated stretches of Texas, railroads usually equipped their trains with just one Pullman car. When a train had just one Pullman, the car was under the control of a porter, who reported to the train conductor. Trains with more than one Pullman had their own Pullman conductor. At the time, the porters were all African American; the Pullman conductors were all white. The Texas Railroad Commission issued an order requiring all trains traveling through Texas to have a Pullman conductor in charge of all sleeping cars.

The order was generally interpreted as racially based, as it would provide jobs for more white conductors in Texas. The order may have also been an attempt to deprive the black porters of any authority on the trains.

A porter on a Pullman car in Chicago, Illinois, c. 1943. © Photograph by Jack Delano. The Library of Congress/Corbis.

In any event, the Pullman Company and the railroads filed suit in federal district court, seeking to enjoin the order. The companies argued that the order was not authorized under Texas law and violated their due process and equal protection rights, as defined in the Fourteenth Amendment. The Pullman porters also joined the suit, claiming the commission's order violated the Fourteenth Amendment by discriminating against blacks.

The district court found it had jurisdiction on the matter and said Texas law did not give the commission authority to issue the order. The court forbade the order from taking effect. The Texas Railroad Commission then appealed to the Supreme Court. In a 7-0 ruling, the Court said the district court should have abstained from deciding this case and let the state courts decide the issue. The Court reversed the lower court's ruling and, while acknowledging the district court's jurisdiction, ordered the matter to be heard in the state courts.

In his decision, Justice Frankfurter admitted the case brought up meaningful constitutional issues. But the constitutional controversies might have been addressed and resolved by state courts examining state law, making the federal courts' involvement unnecessary. Jus-

tice Frankfurter also said that the state courts were better equipped to examine ambiguities in the state law:

> What practices of the railroads may be deemed to be 'abuses' subject to the Commission correction is . . . doubtful. Reading the Texas statutes and the Texas decisions as outsiders without special competence in Texas law, we would have little confidence in our independent judgement regarding the application of that law to the present situation . . . The last word on the statutory authority of the Railroad Commission in this case belongs neither to us nor to the district court but to the Supreme Court of Texas.

Frankfurter thus spelled out when the abstention doctrine applied. A federal court should not hear a case when a state statute, ambiguous and not yet definitively interpreted by a state court, is challenged at the federal level on constitutional grounds. By abstaining, the federal courts gave the state courts a chance to resolve the ambiguity and perhaps the constitutional issue. Frankfurter said abstention had been exercised before, if not so clearly defined, and the doctrine was ". . . appropriate to our federal system whereby the federal court, 'exercising a wise discretion,' restrain their authority because of 'scrupulous regard for the rightful independence of the state governments' and for the smooth working of the federal judiciary."

The Abstention Doctrine Since *Pullman*

Justice Frankfurter remained a strong proponent of the abstention doctrine, believing the federal courts should only decide constitutional issues when there was no other way to resolve them. The doctrine was eventually used in a variety of cases, and in 1959 it was extended to civil rights cases (*Harrison v. National Association for the Advancement of Colored People*).

The doctrine seemed to lose prominence after Frankfurter's retirement in 1962. Some justices expressed displeasure with the doctrine's effects on the litigants. By abstaining, the federal courts forced the parties to begin the legal process again in the state courts, which often took years and created hefty legal expenses.

By the 1970s, the Court tended to find that using the abstention doctrine was the exception, not the rule, even when the grounds for exercising it were present. Judges have leeway to hear a case that might qualify for abstention, if a statute violates basic freedoms.

Related Cases

Harrison v. National Association for the Advancement of Colored People, 360 U.S. 167 (1959).

Stuart Circle Parish v. Board of Zoning Appeals of City of Richmond, 946 F.Supp. 1225 (1996).

Roe v. City of Milwaukee, WL 790728 (E.D.Wis. 1998).

Bibliography and Further Reading

Biskupic, Joan, and Elder Witt. *Guide to the U.S. Supreme Court.* Washington, DC: Congressional Quarterly, Inc., 1997.

Hall, Kermit L., ed. *The Oxford Companion to the Supreme Court of the United States.* New York: Oxford University Press, 1992.

Nowak, John E., Ronald D. Rotunda, and J. Nelson Young. *Constitutional Law,* 2nd ed. St. Paul: West Publishing Company, 1984.

BOND V. FLOYD

Legal Citation: 385 U.S. 116 (1966)

Petitioner
Julian Bond

Respondent
State of Georgia

Petitioner's Claim
That the Georgia House of Representatives, to which the petitioner had been elected, could not refuse to seat him because of his statements criticizing the Vietnam War.

Chief Lawyers for Petitioner
Howard Moore, Jr., Leonard B. Boudin, Victor Rabinowitz

Chief Lawyers for Respondent
Arthur K. Bolton, William L. Harper, Alfred L. Evans, Jr., Paul L. Hanes

Justices for the Court
Hugo Lafayette Black, William J. Brennan, Jr., Tom C. Clark, William O. Douglas, Abe Fortas, John Marshall Harlan II, Potter Stewart, Earl Warren (writing for the Court), Byron R. White

Justices Dissenting
None

Place
Washington, D.C.

Date of Decision
5 December 1966

Decision
The Georgia House could not refuse to seat Bond, whose statements were protected by the free speech provisions of the First Amendment.

Significance
State legislators enjoy the same absolute right to free speech as other citizens.

Julian Bond was the communications director of the Student Nonviolent Coordinating Committee (SNCC), a black lobbying and direct action group. In June of 1965, Bond was elected to the Georgia House of Representatives by a large majority. Just before the House was to meet in January of 1966, SNCC issued a controversial statement regarding the war in Vietnam.

The SNCC declaration said that the U.S. government was responsible for the murder of southern Blacks, that the United States was the aggressor in Vietnam, and that young men should break the law by refusing to be drafted.

> We are in sympathy with, and support, the men in this country who are unwilling to respond to a military draft which would compel them to contribute their lives to United States aggression in Vietnam in the name of the "freedom" we find so false in this country.

A radio reporter interviewed Julian Bond by telephone right after the SNCC statement was released. Bond endorsed the statement's contents.

By 10 January, when the Georgia House convened, 75 House members had challenged Bond's right to be seated, and the clerk refused to admit him. When interviewed by a special committee of the House, Bond stuck by his earlier statements. Nevertheless, he asked to take the oath to support the constitutions of his state and the United States required of all legislators by those same documents. (Article Six of the U.S. Constitution requires that legislators in every state take this oath.)

The House voted 184-12 not to seat Bond. His statements, the House said, made it clear that he could not in good faith take the constitutional oaths. Bond's assertions gave aid and comfort to America's enemies, and they violated the Selective Service law. They "are reprehensible and are such as tend to bring discredit to and disrespect of the House."

Bond sued before the Federal District Court, asserting that by refusing his seat to him, the legislature had violated his First Amendment right to free speech. By a 2-1 decision, the District Court rejected his claim. Bond appealed to the Supreme Court.

Qualifications to Run for Congress

The Constitution presents few restrictions regarding who may run for a seat in the Senate or the House of Representatives. The Qualifications Clause, in Article I, sections 2 and 3, makes stipulations in only three areas: age, citizenship, and residency. To run for the House, one must be at least 25 years of age, a U.S. citizen for at least seven years, and a resident of the state from which one intends to run. As for senators, they must be 30 years of age or older, citizens for nine years or more, and residents of their respective states.

Congress has upheld these as the requirements for service in the Senate or House. The Supreme Court, with its ruling in *Powell v. McCormack* (1969), affirmed the constitutional criteria as the only guidelines. Nonetheless, the two houses of Congress have often acted as judges of their members' qualifications, and both chambers have the authority to expel members. Expulsions in the House have occurred only four times: three of them in the Civil War era and the fourth in connection with the ABSCAM bribery scandal in 1981.

Source(s): Bacon, Donald C., et al., eds. *The Encyclopedia of the United States Congress.* New York: Simon & Schuster, 1995.

Can States Require That Legislators Meet Ethical Standards?

In their arguments before the Court, Georgia's attorneys held that the legislature had exclusive jurisdiction to determine whether an elected representative was qualified to take office. Thus, it could decide whether a specific representative could, without hypocrisy, take the constitutionally mandated oaths.

Bond, the state further argued, had counseled young men to violate the Selective Service laws. Obviously, "advocating violation of federal law demonstrates a lack of support for the Constitution." The state questioned how Bond could take the oath the U.S. Constitution requires.

The key question, in effect, was whether Georgia could impose a stricter standard on legislators than on other citizens.

The State declines to argue that Bond's statements would violate any law if made by a private citizen, but it does argue that even though such a citizen might be protected by his First Amendment rights, the State may nonetheless apply a stricter standard to its legislators.

Writing for a unanimous Court, Chief Justice Warren reversed the decision of the district court and ruled that the Georgia House could not refuse to seat Bond. Warren held that the Supreme Court had the jurisdic-

Julian Bond, 1966.
© *UPI/Corbis-Bettmann.*

ABSCAM Trials

In 1980 and 1981 a series of trials, known as the ABSCAM trials, were heard in New York on the government sting operation that had resulted in the discovery of many highly placed corrupt political figures. Most notably brought under scrutiny were: U.S. Congressman Michael J. Myers; Mayor Angelo J. Errichetti of Camden, New Jersey; Louis C. Johanson, a Philadelphia councilman; Howard L. Criden, Johanson's former law partner; Senator Harrison A. Williams, Jr.; and attorney Alexander Feinberg, an associate of Williams. Other public officials were caught and either expelled from office or turned out by voters at the next election.

In the first ABSCAM trial Myers, Errichetti, Johanson, and Criden were all found guilty on 30 August 1980.

Their attempts to have the convictions overturned were rejected by Judge George C. Pratt on 24 July 1981. In a 136-page decision, he said of the accused: "Their major defense has been that they were tricked into committing the crime on videotape. The government's need to unmask such conduct more than justifies the investigative techniques employed in these cases. Without question these convictions were reliable, and no constitutional right of any defendant has been infringed."

Williams and Feinberg were found guilty in a separate trial on 1 May 1981.

Source(s): Knappman, Edward W., ed. *Great American Trials.* Detroit, MI: Visible Ink Press, 1994.

tion to review the case. Bond had claimed that the Georgia House had deprived him of his free speech rights under the First Amendment. The courts had imposed these rights on the states by "incorporating" them into the Fourteenth Amendment.

Maximum Freedom to Say Anything, Anywhere, at Any Time

Warren also rejected Georgia's claim that a state can apply a stricter standard of conduct to legislators than to other citizens. Warren first argued that Bond's statements did not violate the law. He then rejected the claim that a legislator's freedom of speech can, under the U. S. Constitution, be any less than that of everyone else.

Warren asserted that a legislator's very function requires maximum freedom of speech. "The manifest function of the Amendment in a representative government requires that legislators be given the widest latitude to express their views on issues of policy." Warren referred to *New York Times v. Sullivan*, (1964). In that decision, the Court had stated that "debate on public issues should be uninhibited, robust, and wide-open." Surely, legislators have as much First Amendment protection as other citizens.

Legislators have an obligation to take positions on controversial political questions so that their constituents can be fully informed by them, and be better able to assess their quali-

fications for office; also so they may be represented in governmental debates by the person they have elected to represent them.

In its decisions during the 1960s, the Supreme Court made freedom of speech an absolute right. Chief Justice Warren did not explicitly overrule earlier Supreme Court decisions. Nevertheless, *Bond* affirmed free speech claims in circumstances in which the Court previously had denied such claims. It is striking that the Court protected Bond's expressions of sympathy for draft resisters while the nation was engaged in military conflict. In 1919, Justice Oliver Wendell Holmes had upheld Eugene Debs's imprisonment (*Debs v. United States*) for statements almost identical to those Bond made nearly 50 years later.

Related Cases
Debs v. United States, 249 U.S. 211 (1919).
New York Times v. Sullivan, 376 U.S. 254 (1964).

Bibliography and Further Reading
Emerson, Thomas I. *The System of Freedom of Expression.* New York: Random House, 1970.

Graber, Mark A. *Transforming Free Speech: The Ambiguous Legacy of Civil Libertarianism.* Berkeley: University of California Press, 1991.

Kalvern, Harry. *A Worthy Tradition: Freedom of Speech in America.* New York: Harper & Row, 1988.

AMCHEM PRODUCTS V. WINDSOR

Legal Citation: 521 U.S. 591 (1997)

Petitioners
Amchem Products and 19 other companies

Respondents
George Windsor and other individuals

Petitioners' Claim
Appellants desired to settle a large class-action suit with a number of individuals and families; respondents in this case were a group of persons involved in the suit who objected to the settlement under Rule 23 of the Federal Rules of Civil Procedure.

Justices for the Court
Ruth Bader Ginsburg (writing for the Court), Anthony M. Kennedy, William H. Rehnquist, Antonin Scalia, David H. Souter, Clarence Thomas

Justices Dissenting
Stephen Breyer, John Paul Stevens, (Sandra Day O'Connor did not participate)

Place
Washington, D.C.

Date of Decision
25 June 1997

Decision
That the "sprawling class" represented in the large class-action settlement did not constitute a class at all under Rule 23.

Significance
On the level of events current to the Court's ruling in *Amchem Products*, the decision was significant in that it helped further define the framework for a number of large class-action suits that were due to become an increasingly prominent part of legal life in the following years. Examples of such cases include not only those involving asbestos manufacturers, but also cases relating to silicone breast implants and, perhaps most important of all, tobacco companies. But in a larger sense, *Amchem* signalled the Court's determination to stand by the constitutional separation of powers, thus leaving the resolution of certain matters involving asbestos litigation to Congress—even though it might "speed things up" for the courts to take matters into their own hands.

Beginning in the 1970s, there was a series of lawsuits in the United States involving asbestos, a product used widely from the 1930s through the 1950s because of its fire-resistant qualities. Exposure to asbestos was found to cause cancer and other fatal diseases, such as asbestosis, and since these diseases sometimes had a latency period of several decades before they made themselves known, litigation over asbestos continued long after the product ceased to be used.

By the 1980s and 1990s, a glut of asbestos litigation had begun to form within the courts, slowing down the pace of operations of the American legal system, according to the finding of the United States Judicial Conference Ad Hoc Committee on Asbestos Litigation, which was appointed by the Supreme Court chief justice in September of 1990. The committee recommended that Congress form its own agency to resolve disputes over asbestos claims, but by the mid-1990s, Congress had taken no such action. Instead, the federal courts had put all asbestos complaints into a single judicial district, the U.S. District Court for the Eastern District of Pennsylvania.

Once the cases were consolidated, the lines were drawn. On the one side was a consortium of 20 companies, including Amchem Products, called the Counsel for the Center for Claims Resolution (CCR.) On the other were the individuals, and families of individuals, who had claims against such companies, represented by attorneys Ronald L. Motley, Gene Locks, and Joseph F. Rice. Starting in November of 1991, CCR attempted to get agreement from the plaintiffs for an omnibus offer which would settle a large proportion, if not all, of the present and future asbestos-related cases. After some negotiation, the settlement offer was narrowed down to focus solely on claims that had not yet entered litigation. In the negotiations, attorneys for persons with cases pending also endeavored to represent those with future cases, which would later be judged a conflict of interest.

Once CCR had settled, for some $200 million, the claims of those with cases pending (so-called "inventory claimants"), it instituted the settlement in question in *Amchem Products*. On 15 January 1993, CCR and the attorneys for the plaintiff presented the Pennsylvania district court judge with the complaint, answer, proposed settlement agreement, and joint motion for conditional class certification. Thus there would be no litigation, and the aim was to settle the matter as quickly as possible. Nine lead plaintiffs were identified in the complaint, which stated that these represented all persons in the plaintiff class, which had no subclasses. Under the terms of the settlement, all claims not filed before 15 January 1993 would be settled in terms that did not adjust future payments for inflation, and which capped the number of claims payable annually.

Clearly such an offer was in CCR's best interests, but many of the plaintiffs were eager to take it as well. A number of plaintiffs, however, opted out of the settlement, and so informed Judge Reed, who had been appointed by the head trial judge, Judge Weiner, to review the fairness of the proceedings. Nonetheless, the district court found that the case met the requirements of Rule 23 of the Federal Rules of Civil Procedure, which makes stipulations regarding the number of persons involved in a class-action suit, the commonality of their claims, and the preponderance of such claims within the class.

The objectors, however, took the case—which up to this point had the name *Georgine v. Amchem Products, Inc.* to the U.S. Court of Appeals for the Third Circuit. The latter vacated the lower court's certification, holding that the requirements of Rule 23 had not been satisfied.

The Proper Question of Class Certification

When CCR took the case to the Supreme Court, its claim was that the objectors had no case. But the Court, which upheld the appeals court's ruling, found that it was the settlement offer itself which lacked proper legal standing. Justice Ginsburg gave the opinion for the Court, in which Chief Justice Rehnquist and Justices Scalia, Kennedy, Souter, and Thomas joined. In it she outlined the elements of Rule 23, which had taken shape with a 1966 revision which delineated conditions to be met before a class could be certified for a class action suit.

Principal among the concerns outlined in parts (a) and (b) of Rule 23, Ginsburg noted, are questions as to whether the proposed group has sufficient unity of claims to constitute a class. The importance of these questions remains even when settlement, rather than trial, is proposed. A "common interest" alone would not satisfy the predominance requirement of Rule 23(b)(3), she said, since that amounts to a virtual redundancy. In fact, "No settlement class called to the Court's attention is as sprawling as the one certified here."

Turning to the adequate representation clause of Rule 23, in section (a)(4), Ginsburg again found the

class wanting, as there were conflicts of interest, as noted above. "Representatives must be part of the class and possess the same interest and suffer the same injury as the class members," she said; otherwise, by definition, they are not representative. In the case of "the currently injured, the goal is generous immediate payments." But this is clearly not in the interest of those not currently injured, who may find in another decade or so that they are suffering serious—and expensive—injuries.

Given that the class referred to in the so-called class action suit was not a class at all as defined in Rule 23, the Court saw no need to rule on the adequacy of the notice given within the suit itself, which was the original basis for the case being brought to the Court's attention. As to the need suggested earlier by the investigating committee, that Congress take action by appointing a "nationwide claims processing regime," the Court noted that this was up to the legislative body, which had so far taken no action. But Rule 23 simply "cannot carry the large load the settling parties and the District Court heaped upon it."

Breyer Urges Action

Justice Breyer, in an opinion with which Justice Stevens joined, concurred in part and dissented in part. He agreed with the Court's basic stance that the settlement offer itself was a relevant factor to use in considering whether a group constituted a class; however, as he said, he found "several problems with the approach which lead me to a different conclusion."

In Breyer's view, the need for a settlement in the case made it extremely important for the Court to go ahead and allow such a settlement to take place. Furthermore, in looking at the settlement offer itself, he saw more commonality in the claimants than the rest of the Court did. As for the question of conflict of interest in representation, to Breyer it appeared that the Court was trying to "second-guess" the court of appeals, without allowing that court to consider that particular question. Generally, Breyer viewed the settlement as fair, and therefore, "in the absence of further review by the Court of Appeals, I cannot accept the majority's suggestions that 'notice' is inadequate."

Related Cases

Huron Portland Cement Co. v. City of Detroit, 362 U.S. 440 (1960).
Georgine v. Amchem Products, Inc. 83 F. 34d 610 (1996).
Walker v. Liggett Group, Inc. 175 F.R.D. 226 (1997).
In re Prudential Insurance Co. of America Sales Practices Litigation, 148 F.3d 283 (1998).

Bibliography and Further Reading

"Court Overview: High-Stakes Asbestos Cases Reach Supreme Court." *Detroit News,* November 2, 1996.

"Legal Group Urges Court to Disregard Asbestos Suit Minus Physical Ailment." *Occupational Health & Safety Letter,* January 6, 1997.

Seiberg, Jaret. "Court Ruling May Shield Banks From Class Actions." *American Banker,* July 2, 1997, p. 3.

Shoop, Julie Gannon. "High Court Upholds Dismissal of Asbestos Class Action." *Trial,* August 1997, p. 69.

Sloan, Clifford M. "Supreme Court to Decide Major Class Action Settlement Case." *Corporate Legal Times,* January 1997.

Stranahan, Susan Q., and Donna Shaw. "Georgine Ruling Raises Questions About the Tobacco Deal and Other Broad Accords." *Philadelphia Inquirer,* June 26, 1997.

LABOR AND LABOR PRACTICES

Introduction

The story of organized labor in America is one of struggle. Labor unions were viewed by many, especially employers and capitalists, as unlawful organizations. The law was almost always favorable to employers over employees: even the Sherman Anti-Trust Act, which was passed in order to curb corporate concentration, was used as a weapon—it furnished the rationale for injunctions against many types of union activity, from organizing to picketing to striking, as illegal restraints of trade. Federal troops were called in to stop strikes at times, and illegal and violent behavior by unions was punished while authorities looked the other way when employers engaged in similar behavior. Only the First Amendment guarantee of free association prevented the outlawing of unions altogether.

Not only law but social theory held that unions were socialistic, un-American organizations. In the latter part of the nineteenth century the theory of Social Darwinism—the survival of the fittest—was popular: those who did not prosper were morally deficient, and aiding them only weakened the human race. Economic outcomes were best left to nature and a *laissez-faire* economic system.

Workers were supposed to take what the market offered, and it usually was not much. Twelve-hour workdays and six-day workweeks for wages barely at the subsistence level were common. Working conditions were often extremely dangerous, and many workers were killed or maimed in industrial accidents. As immigration and urbanization increased, large populations of unskilled laborers lived in slums in appalling conditions of poverty. Many were casual workers, day laborers with no permanent employment.

The success of workers' attempts to organize largely depended on the level of skill needed to perform their jobs. It was harder to replace skilled labor than unskilled labor, and such workers often possessed knowledge of manufacturing or other procedures that their employers did not. Thus tradesmen such as typesetters unionized earlier than other less skilled workers. Railroads became unionized in the mid-nineteenth century due to their skilled workers and also because of their capacity to disrupt the economy on a large scale.

As the American economy became more and more industrialized, labor unrest grew. Numerous large, violent strikes occurred, and literal battles were fought between workers and agents of the employers. Unions were still hampered by a hostile legal climate and by internal differences over methods, as well as by their own hostility toward immigrants and African Americans, who during strikes had little compunction about replacing those who excluded them.

By the late nineteenth century, labor unrest seemed nearly constant, but it was not until the 1900s that the tide began to turn for labor. Bit by bit, legislation was passed that slowly began to construct a set of rights and procedures by which workers could organize and bargain collectively with government sanction.

During the Great Depression of the 1930s, labor conditions worsened for many as employers tried to take advantage of high unemployment (as high as 25 percent of the labor force) to force down their costs. Public opinion began to turn in favor of organized labor, and for workers seeking to organize, the high point of legislative action came with the passage of the National Labor Relations Act (NLRA) in 1935.

After passage of the NLRA, union membership grew rapidly, and by the late 1940s about one in three workers was a union member. By the late 1950s, however, union membership began to decrease, and today only about 16 percent of the workforce is unionized.

Federal Labor Legislation

The two most important federal acts relating to organized labor are the Wagner Act and the Taft-Hartley Act. The following describes both acts and lists their major provisions.

The Wagner Act

The National Labor Relations Act (NLRA), also called the Wagner Act after its sponsor, Democratic Senator Robert F. Wagner from New York, was enacted in 1935. With the passage of the NLRA Congress moved for the first time to lay out a legal framework for dealing with labor unrest. The act applies to all employers and employees involved in interstate commerce. Among the groups not covered by the NLRA, however, are domestic servants working in their employers' homes, children and spouses of employers, and independent contractors. (Managerial employees are also not covered, nor are railroad and airline employees, who come under the jurisdiction of the Railway Labor Act of 1926).

The National Labor Relations Act legitimized and codified the rights of workers to organize and bargain collectively and to strike. It prohibits domination of, interference with, or financing of unions by employers; interference with the rights of employees to organize and bargain collectively; the placing of conditions on employment to discourage workers from organizing; and firing of, or discrimination against, employees who testify or file charges under the act. And most importantly, it requires employers to bargain collectively with unions that it has certified. Violation of any of these rules is deemed an unfair labor practice.

In order to enforce these rules, the National Labor Relations Board (NLRB) was established as an independent federal agency. An important part of its jurisdiction is the supervision of union elections and the enforcement of laws prohibiting unfair labor practices by either labor or management. The NLRB has the power to order employers to cease unfair labor practices and to order the reinstatement of workers with back pay when necessary. The five members of the board, as well as the general counsel are appointed by the president with the consent of the Senate, the general members for five years and the general counsel for four years. The general counsel is responsible for prosecuting unfair labor practice cases.

The Taft-Hartley Act

Public opinion turned against organized labor in the postwar period, and over the veto of President Harry S. Truman Congress passed the Labor-Management Relations Act of 1947, called the Taft-Hartley Act after its sponsors, Sen. Robert J. Taft, and Rep. Fred A. Hartley. The act amended the NLRA and was a response to what many felt were the coercive actions of too-powerful unions. It defined and prohibited unfair labor practices by unions, removed foremen from coverage under the NLRA, and banned the closed shop. Unions were barred from refusing to bargain collectively as well. A further restraint on large unions was the act's provision authorizing the president to declare a potentially large, disruptive strike (such as by railroad or steel workers) a national emergency strike and postpone it for 80 days.

The Taft-Hartley Act also authorized lawsuits against unions for contract violations; established a 60-day no-strike, no-lockout period in situations in which either party wished to cancel an existing labor agreement; barred coercion of non-union employees by unions; prohibited secondary boycotts (boycotts by striking employees against third parties that the firm being struck does business with); and required unions to file reports on financial and other matters in order to receive NLRB protection. In 1959 the act was amended by the Landrum-Griffin Act (Labor-Management Reporting and Disclosure Act), which dealt with the relations between unions and their members.

An Overview of Labor Law

Labor law is complicated and sometimes contradictory and is practiced largely by specialist attorneys. The NLRB has great discretion in determining facts that are often subjective (such as a party's intent), and for the many rules there are also many exceptions, often hinging on subjective judgments by the NLRB. The goal for the NLRB is to attempt to balance the rights of workers with those of employers. What follows is a rudimentary overview of law regulating the conduct of labor unions and employers.

Union Organizing Campaigns

Employers may not prohibit organizing efforts of workers on company property during nonworking time such as lunch periods, rest breaks, and before and after shifts, but generally they may ban non-employee organizers from company property. Employers may give captive speeches discouraging union formation to employees during work hours, and they are not required to give the union an opportunity to reply, but captive speeches are prohibited in the 24-hour period directly preceding an election. Employers are also barred from threatening to cut the pay of employees if they vote to form a union or discriminating against those who support a union. Employers may not poll employees regarding their views on a pending union election unless union supporters have asked to be recognized without holding an election, and then polling must be by secret ballot. In cases of repeated unfair labor practices by an employer, the NLRB may order the employer to recognize the union.

Union organizers and employees wishing to organize may not threaten or intimidate employees into supporting the formation of a union.

Elections

Elections can take place for three possible reasons: to vote on joining a union, to vote on switching membership from one union to another, and to vote on decertifying a union. When 30 percent of an employer's workforce desire an election, it usually must be held, with some major exceptions. No election may be held within twelve months of any prior election or within twelve months of the creation of a union. Elections are also barred during the first three years of any labor agreement except during a period directly before the expiration of that agreement. Elections may also be overturned and held again if the NLRB finds evidence of irregularities in the conduct of the election.

All full-time employees are eligible to vote; in some cases part-timers may vote as well. Salts, union organizers who become employees of firms in order to organize them, are usually permitted to vote. If the union wins a majority, it is now certified by the NLRB as the bargaining agent of the employees.

Collective Bargaining Agreements

The NLRB oversees the regulation of labor negotiations. Typical subjects of negotiation are wages and benefits, methods and timing of payment, pensions, safety, work rules, employee grievance procedures, seniority, and layoffs. The NLRB classifies subjects of bargaining as mandatory, permissible, or illegal. The subjects just mentioned are classified as mandatory; this means that one side may not refuse to negotiate them if the other side wishes to do so. Refusal to negotiate a mandatory subject is an unfair labor practice. One form of "refusal to negotiate" is one party's changing the terms of employment without bargaining. This is allowed only when an agreement has expired and an impasse in negotiations has been reached. The NLRB may order a party to cease its refusal to negotiate and may order reinstatement of employees and pay adjustments as it sees fit.

Permissible subjects are those that lay outside the direct terms of the employment of the workers, such as the opening of another plant by the employer or community activities by the union or the employer. Either side may refuse to negotiate these items if it wishes to do so. Illegal subjects are those which involve activity illegal under labor law, such as the closed shop, or activities illegal under other laws, such as age or race discrimination in hiring.

Both sides must bargain in good faith. This means that unreasonable demands may not be made, that no prior conditions to bargaining may be set, and that unresolvable issues may be shelved while less intractable problems are dealt with. Further, each side may ask the other to provide certain types of information.

The Closed Shop, the Union Shop, the Agency Shop, and the Open Shop

In a closed shop prospective employees must already be union members before they can be hired. The Taft-Hartley Act banned the closed shop—it is an illegal subject of bargaining, which unions may not bring to the negotiating table.

In a union shop new employees must join the union within thirty days or be fired. The NLRA is ambiguous regarding the union shop, with one section seemingly permitting the union shop while another seems to forbid it. Labor contracts often include union shop clauses,

but both unions and employers usually act as if the contract mandates an agency shop, which is legal.

Employees in an agency shop are not required to join the union, but they must pay union initiation fees and dues, and they can be fired if they refuse. The union is the bargaining agent for all employees in an agency shop, whether or not they join the union, although unions may not discipline nonmembers for violation of union rules, such as fining them for crossing a picket line and returning to work during a strike.

Twenty-one states have right-to-work laws, which bar unions from requiring nonmembers to pay any dues at all; federal law does not prohibit such legislation by states. A union workplace in a right-to-work state is called an open shop.

Union Monies

Unions spend money raised through member dues for a variety of purposes, not all of which are directly related to bargaining, such as legislative lobbying, organizing new shops, and donations to charitable causes. These expenditures are not illegal, but the union is explicitly authorized by law to spend dues money only on collective bargaining. Members (and nonmembers in agency shops) who object to union expenditures on political activity or other activities not directly related to collective bargaining are entitled to make their objection known to the union and to receive a refund of the portion of their dues spent for such purposes, on free speech grounds.

Arbitration and Mediation

Employee grievances may be subject to arbitration, depending on the specifics of the labor agreement in force. Arbitrators or panels of arbitrators will hear both sides of the dispute and come to a decision, which is usually binding on the parties. Mediators, however, enter into negotiations with the parties in order to facilitate resolution of the dispute. Two private agencies often used are the Federal Mediation and Conciliation Service and the American Arbitration Association.

Strikes

Strikes are divided into two categories: economic strikes and unfair labor practice strikes. Economic strikes are those that take place over issues such as wages and benefits. An unfair labor practice strike occurs when workers strike over an employer's unfair labor practice, particularly the refusal to negotiate. The main difference between the two types lies in the rules regarding an employer's hiring of workers to replace those who are on strike. An employer may hire replacement workers in either case, but only temporary replacements may be hired during an unfair labor practice strike; during an economic strike an employer may hire permanent replacements.

An election held during a strike is usually a decertification election, in which workers may choose to no longer be represented by the union. In such cases permanent replacement workers may vote, but temporary replacements may not vote. Any worker who has not been replaced may vote, and workers who have been permanently replaced may vote in any election for one year after the start of the strike.

A striker who abandons the strike and wants to return to work must be accepted by the employer, if the job is still there and no permanent replacement has been hired. Employers may not discriminate against leaders of the strike in such situations, but they may refuse to accept strikers who have engaged in misconduct during the strike, such as vandalism of company property or intimidation of replacement workers.

Lockouts

A lockout occurs when employees are prevented from working by the employer. When a contract has expired and the employer wants concessions on mandatory subjects of bargaining from the union, he may legally lock them out. Lockouts for the intimidation of workers, such as before a union election, are illegal, as are lockouts over permissible subjects of bargaining.

Child Labor

The perception of child labor as a social evil to be eradicated began with industrialization and wage labor. In earlier times children had always worked, and for them to do so was regarded not as a necessary evil but as a positive good. Religious proscriptions against idleness and the acquisition of work skills weighed heavily in favor of child labor. Children who worked also did not become dependent on public welfare. Work in the preindustrial age, however, did not put children into a hazardous, impersonal environment. Children typically worked as apprentices in tradesmen's shops and in the homes and on the farms of their families. Apprentice work usually included some rudimentary general education as well as specific occupational training; children who worked on family farms were not separated from their parents, and they performed jobs assigned with their youth taken into account.

As organized manufacturing came into being, it was natural for factory owners to use children as laborers. In 1790 the workforce at Samuel Slater's first mill in Rhode Island consisted mostly of children ages seven to 12. Soon large numbers of children worked in factories under harsh conditions in unhealthy, dangerous environments. In most cases their parents needed their children's contribution to family income, so there was little resistance to the factory child labor system.

Opposition slowly grew to child labor as its deleterious effects spread through the population. Many children grew up malformed from constant physical labor,

became sick, or died in accidents. A further impetus to opposing child labor was the growing recognition of the need for education; as various impediments to suffrage grew, literacy as a requisite for citizenship became apparent. Slowly, states began to enact child labor laws, setting minimum age requirements for work. Standards were not strict, however; for example, in the 1850s minimum work ages were ten in New Jersey, twelve in Rhode Island, and nine in Connecticut. Children often fared worse in the South, where children as young as six and seven worked in textile mills.

By 1913 most states required a minimum age of 14 for factory work, but agricultural and domestic work was not regulated. Further, the laws that did exist were poorly enforced. Additionally, competition from firms in other less-regulated states kept pressure on employers to keep costs down.

The Struggle for Federal Child Labor Legislation

While state laws remained lax, poorly enforced, and in some cases nonexistent, action on a federal level did not really begin until the twentieth century. A group of social reformers created the National Child Labor Committee in 1904, which was instrumental in pressing for national child labor regulation.

The first Congressional bill to regulate child labor was introduced in 1906 by Sen. Albert J. Beveridge of Indiana, but the bill did not pass. After the release of a Congressional study of child labor in 1912, the Federal Children's Bureau was created as a fact-gathering agency and clearinghouse for information on child labor. Although the agency had no power to regulate, its investigations into labor conditions nationwide aided reformers greatly by providing them with information they would otherwise have had to gather themselves, thus freeing more of their time for political efforts.

Reformers were elated two years later when Congress passed the Keating-Owen Federal Child Labor Act. The act established a minimum working age of 14 and regulated hours of work for children from 14 to 16 years old in certain establishments, including mines, factories, and mills, and banned the interstate shipment of goods produced in violation of these standards.

Backed by the Executive Committee of Southern Cotton Manufacturers, Roland Dagenhart, father of two children who worked in a North Carolina cotton mill contested the validity of the law. In 1918 the case went to the Supreme Court, which struck down the act as an unconstitutional regulation of matters purely local (*Hammer v. Dagenhart.*)

In February 1919, less than a year later, Congress enacted the same standards codified by Keating-Owen in a revenue bill. This time, violation of the law subjected producers to a 10 percent tax on their net profits. The Supreme Court struck down the law in *Bailey v. Drexel Furniture Co.* The case before us cannot be distinguished from that of *Hammer v. Dagenhart.*

Child labor opponents now decided that a constitutional amendment would be necessary to effect national regulations that could not be invalidated by the Court. In 1924 Congress adopted a proposal for a constitutional amendment that would not by itself regulate child labor but would enable Congress to do so legally. The amendment was vigorously opposed by the National Association of Manufacturers, the Southern Textiles Association, and other industry groups: according to its opponents, the subversive amendment was favored by Bolshevists and Communists. Catholic groups such as the National Council of Catholic Women worked with the National Child Labor Committee in support of the bill, but much of the Catholic hierarchy, particularly in Massachusetts and New York, opposed the bill as a possible threat to parochial education and the authority of parents.

After each attempt to eradicate child labor failed, conditions grew worse. Finally the onset of the Great Depression began to change people's thinking: Why worry about employers' rights to hire children when one out of four adults was without a job? By 1932 only six states had ratified the amendment, but in 1933 alone fourteen more endorsed it.

The next legislation affecting child labor was the National Industrial Recovery Act of 1933, the purpose of which was to coordinate business practices in order to deal with the worsening depression generally, rather than to solve the child labor problem alone. It prescribed codes for fair competition and fixed wages and hours, and also established minimum age rules. In 1935 the act was declared unconstitutional in *A.L.A. Schecter Poultry Corporation v. United States.*

Congress passed two laws that were not invalidated by the Court, since they dealt expressly with federal action. The Jones-Costigan Act of 1934 regulated child labor on farms receiving federal assistance, and the Walsh-Healey Public Contracts Act of 1936 forbade boys under 16 and girls under 18 from employment in work under federal contracts worth more than $10,000.

Twenty-eight states had ratified the child-labor amendment by 1938, but it became largely moot and action on it lapsed when Congress passed the Fair Labor Standards Act. Perhaps convinced it was necessary to change its view in light of Roosevelt's 1937 attempt to add six more justices to the Supreme Court in order to create a Court more amenable to the New Deal and by widespread social upheaval, including the increasing popularity of socialism as a cure for the country's troubles, the Court performed its famous switch in time that saved nine and began supporting Roosevelt's New Deal programs. Three years later the Court upheld the legality of the act in *United States v. Darby.*

The Fair Labor Standards Act (FSLA) covered all firms producing goods for interstate commerce. It established minimum wages, maximum hours, and overtime pay for covered employees. It established age requirements for children, particularly for hazardous jobs. The act was later strengthened in 1949 to ban oppressive child labor in interstate commerce, and coverage was broadened to include all firms engaged in interstate commerce, not merely those producing goods for interstate commerce, which brought more industries under the act. The Fair Labor Standards Act remains the primary law regulating child labor today.

Regulation of Child Labor Today

Today all states have child labor laws, but when both the FSLA and state law apply, the more restrictive rule must be followed. Federal child labor law is enforced by the U.S. Department of Labor.

Nonfarm jobs

Children from 16 to 17 years old may work in any non-hazardous job; there is no limitation on the number of hours they may work. Jobs classified as hazardous include work with explosives or radioactive materials, work using various types of machinery, and operation of motor vehicles. Most jobs in certain industries such as logging and meat packing are also deemed hazardous.

Children aged 14 to 15 may work in certain non-hazardous jobs, but limitations are more stringent than for 16- and 17-year-old youth; e.g., they may not work in construction jobs. The hours they may work are regulated during the school year to no more than three hours on a school day and no more than 18 hours during a school week; when school is not in session they may work up to 40 hours per week. They may not work before 7:00 a.m. or after 7:00 p.m. during most of the year; the evening limit is extended to 9:00 p.m. from June 1 to Labor Day.

Children younger than 14 may work only in businesses owned by their parents (with hazardous jobs not permitted) and certain exempt jobs such as acting and delivery of newspapers.

Farm Jobs

Farm labor is considerably less restricted. Children of any age may perform any job without restriction on farms owned or operated by their parents. Youths age 16 or older may work in any farm job without limitation on hours or type of job. Youths age 14 and 15 may work in non-hazardous jobs outside of school hours. Farm jobs classified as hazardous include handling explosives or pesticides, working on ladders or scaffolding more than 20 feet high, and operating most farm machinery, such as harvesting and earth-moving machinery.

Children 12 and 13 years old may work outside school hours in non-hazardous jobs, provided they have parental consent. Children younger than twelve may not work on farms covered by the FSLA's minimum wage provisions. With parental consent they may work in non-hazardous jobs on other farms. Children age 10 and 11 may work harvesting crops for up to eight weeks between June 1 and October 15; their employers must obtain special exemption from the Department of Labor for this.

Bibliography and Further Reading

American Social History Project. *Who Built America? Working People and the Nation's Economy, Politics, Culture, and Society.* 2 vols. New York: Pantheon, 1989, 1992.

Dawley, Alan. *Struggles for Justice: Social Responsibility and the Liberal State.* Cambridge, MA: Harvard University Press, Belknap Press, 1991.

Federal Child Labor Laws in Farm Jobs. Fact Sheet No. ESA 91-2. Washington, DC: Employment Standards Division, U.S. Department of Labor. (http://www.lect-law.com)

Federal Labor Laws. *Congressional Digest,* June-July 1993. http://www.lectlaw.com

Gold, Michael Evan. *An Introduction to Labor Law.* 2nd ed. Ithaca, New York: Cornell Univ. Press, ILR Press, 1998.

Growth of Labor Law in the United States. Washington, DC: U.S. Department of Labor, 1967.

Handy Reference Guide to the Fair Labor Standards Act. WH Publication 1282. Washington, DC: Employment and Standards Administration Wage and Hour Division, U.S. Department of Labor. http://www.lectlaw.com

Trattner, Walter, L. *Crusade for the Children: A History of the National Child Labor Committee and Child Labor Reform in America.* Chicago: Quadrangle Books, 1970.

IN RE DEBS

Legal Citation: 158 U.S. 564 (1895)

Defendant
Eugene V. Debs

Crimes Charged
Contempt of court and conspiracy.

Chief Prosecutors
John C. Black, T. M. Milchrist, Edwin Walker

Chief Defense Lawyers
Clarence Darrow, S. Gregory, Lyman Trumbull

Judges
Peter Grosscup, William A. Woods

Place
Chicago, Illinois

Date of Decision
12 February 1895

Decision
Guilty of contempt, no verdict on conspiracy.

Significance
In one of the most egregious cases of the courts siding with industry against labor, a federal judge issued an injunction ordering the American Railway Union to stop a strike against the Pullman Company and sentenced the strike's leader, Eugene Debs, to six months in jail for violating the injunction. The government then put Debs on trial for conspiracy but dropped the case in mid-trial. The Supreme Court upheld Debs's sentence for contempt of court in a major confirmation of federal judges' power to enforce their orders.

In the late nineteenth century, as heavy industry grew and railroads spread across the country, commercial centers like Chicago and other cities mushroomed. With this industrial growth, however, came growing abuses. Ownership of industry was concentrated in a handful of wealthy men, while the factory workers and others who made industrialization possible were not protected by the government. Companies were able to get away with paying workers low wages for long hours. Furthermore, most companies did not give workers benefits such as sick leave or disability pay. To make matters worse, there were many "company towns" where workers rented their houses and bought food from stores—all owned by the very company that employed them.

The city of Chicago, where the famous Haymarket Riot occurred, was home to one of the most flagrant abusers of industrial power. George M. Pullman's Pullman Palace Car Company manufactured world-famous railroad cars. The company operated its own company town just outside of Chicago. Not surprisingly, it was named Pullman, Illinois.

The company charged workers higher than average rent to live in company-owned housing while paying substandard hourly wages. Furthermore, in 1893 the company responded to an economic depression by cutting wages 25 percent. In the winter of 1893, conditions were grim in Pullman, Illinois.

The "Debs Rebellion"

Eugene Debs was born in 1855 to a blue-collar Midwestern family. He began his career as a lowly railroad worker. However, he soon discovered that his real gift was in politics, and he rose quickly in the budding union movement. By 1893 Debs was president of the American Railway Union. Although the ARU was primarily a railroad-track workers union, in the spring of 1894 many Pullman employees joined. On 11 May 1894, the smoldering discontent in Pullman ignited and all 3,300 workers went on strike. Although it is likely that the strike was a spontaneous local event not called by the ARU, Debs quickly went to Pullman and assumed leadership of the strike. Because the ARU represented workers in nearly every railroad

---

Contempt of Court

Conduct that defies or undermines the authority and justice of a court is considered contempt of court and is punishable by jail, fines, and other forms of retribution. A court can charge plaintiffs, defendants, lawyers, court personnel, jurors, witnesses, and observers with contempt of court for inappropriate behavior. In addition, a court generally has considerable latitude in making contempt charges. Contempt of court charges also can be categorized as civil or criminal and direct or indirect. Contempt of court charges intend to discourage behavior that undermines the court's authority and prevents the court from administering justice.

However, because courts have ample latitude for determining what amounts to contempt of court and how to punish it, some legal scholars argue that the courts have too much power and leeway for determining and punishing contempt of court. Because judges who make criminal contempt charges sometimes hear these cases, they may issue punishments that are too severe, especially when they are the offended party. Critics point to cases where judges imposed excessive fines and jail sentences relative to the offenses committed. In some cases people who have refused to give courts requested evidence have been incarcerated for several years as a result.

Source(s): *West's Encyclopedia of American Law.* Minneapolis, Minnesota: West Publishing, 1998.

---

system in the United States, and the railroads threw their support behind Pullman, the strike soon became a nationwide railway work stoppage. The resulting paralysis of the American rail network was dubbed the "Debs Rebellion."

President Grover Cleveland was alarmed by the strike and sided with Pullman and the railroads. His attorney general, Richard Olney, went to federal judges Peter Grosscup and William A. Woods to ask for a court order stopping the strike. Ironically, one of Olney's arguments in asking for the injunction was that the ARU strike violated the Sherman Anti-Trust Act of 1890. The Sherman Anti-Trust Act was intended to break up large corporate monopolies and gave federal judges broad powers to issue orders stopping actions they deemed harmful to interstate commerce. At Olney's suggestion, Grosscup and Woods twisted the act's meaning and, on 2 July 1894, used their power to order Debs and the other ARU leaders to abandon the strike. The order even made answering a telegram from the strikers a violation of the terms of the injunction.

Furious, Debs and the ARU leadership resolved to ignore the injunction. Because violating a court order constituted contempt of court, Judge Woods had Debs hauled into court and sentenced him to six months in jail. Contempt of court is the traditional means by which judges enforce their authority, requiring no trial or jury. The government also charged Debs with conspiracy to block the federal mail: the ARU's nationwide railroad work stoppage had halted a Rock Island Railroad train carrying mail for the post office. In the meantime, the federal government's actions were not limited to legal arenas. President Cleveland sent federal troops to Chicago to crush the strike.

Debs Tried for Conspiracy

Unlike with the contempt charge, the government had to try Debs before a jury on the conspiracy charge. The ARU retained the famous lawyer Clarence Darrow, who was assisted by S. Gregory and former Illinois Supreme Court Judge Lyman Trumbull. The prosecutors were John C. Black, T. M. Milchrist, and Edwin Walker.

When the trial opened 26 January 1895, Darrow made it clear to the jury that the issue at trial was not Debs's guilt but the government's desire to crush the union movement. Referring to an executive committee of the railroads called the General Managers' Association, Darrow said:

> This is an historic case which will count much for liberty or against liberty . . . Conspiracy, from the days of tyranny in England down to the day the General Managers' Association used it as a club, has been the favorite weapon of every tyrant. It is an effort to punish the crime of thought.

Darrow cleverly decided to subpoena George Pullman and the members of the General Managers' Association to testify at the trial. While the real opposition to the "Debs Rebellion" was being served with legal process, the prosecutors grilled Debs. They hoped to provoke him into a socialist tirade against American industry and thus alienate the jury. Prosecutor Walker asked Debs how he defined the word "strike." Debs, however, merely responded in a detached manner:

> A strike is a stoppage of work at a given time by men acting in concert in order to redress some real or imaginary grievance.

> Walker: Mr. Debs, will you define the meaning of the word "scab"?

A scab in labor unions means the same as a traitor to his country. It means a man who betrays his fellow men by taking their places when they go on strike for a principle. It does not apply to non-union men who refuse to quit work.

After Debs's testimony, events took a surprising turn. Judge Grosscup, probably influenced by George Pullman and the General Managers' Association, who were reluctant to testify in open court, stated on the day after Debs's testimony that:

Owing to the sickness of a juror and the certificate of his physician that he will not be able to get out for two or three days, I think it will be necessary to adjourn the further taking of testimony in this case.

Grosscup then adjourned the case. In a remarkable turn of events, the trial never reconvened. In effect, the government dropped the conspiracy charge. It has never been conclusively determined whether this decision was the result of Pullman's influence or the weakness of the government's case.

Darrow and Debs's other lawyers appealed the still-valid contempt conviction. However, on 27 May 1895, the U.S. Supreme Court rejected their pleas and refused to overturn Woods's decision. (Legal citation reflects the Supreme Court case.) Debs served his six-month sentence in Illinois's Woodstock Prison with other ARU leaders jailed for contempt. *In Re Debs* has been cited many times since to demonstrate the sweeping powers of federal judges to punish those who violate court orders.

Debs' Political Career Continued

Although his strike was crushed, Debs left prison with his political reputation intact. He became the leading spokesman for the American left, and was the presidential candidate for the American Socialist Party in every election (except 1916) from 1900 to 1920. He lost every election.

When the United States entered World War I, Debs was outraged. He criticized President Woodrow Wilson in the harshest terms, and in *United States v. Debs* was charged with treason. For the most part, the charges against Debs were the result of his support of the International Workers of the World, known as the "Wobblies." This time, however, a court found Debs guilty. Debs's appeals to the Supreme Court were unsuccessful. While in prison, Debs ran for the fifth and final time as the Socialist Party's candidate for president. Again, he was unsuccessful in his bid to become the nation's chief executive.

Stung by Debs's criticism, President Wilson refused to pardon him. Among Debs's choice comments about Wilson were such gems as:

Eugene Debs. © AP/Wide World Photos.

No man in public life in American history ever retired so thoroughly discredited, so scathingly rebuked, so overwhelmingly impeached and repudiated as Woodrow Wilson.

Warren G. Harding, who won the 1920 presidential election, was more charitable. Harding pardoned Debs in December of 1921 and even invited him to the White House on Christmas Day. But Debs found that the Socialist Party had lost its political force. He spent his final years with his wife in quiet retirement and died in 1926.

Related Cases

Northern Securities Co. v. United States, 193 U.S. 197 (1904).
Patton v. United States, 281 U.S. 276 (1930).
Nebbia v. New York, 291 U.S. 502 (1934).
Ex Parte Quirin, 317 U.S. 1 (1942).

Bibliography and Further Reading

Coleman, McAlister. *Eugene V. Debs, a Man Unafraid.* New York: Greenberg, 1930.

Ginger, Ray. *The Bending Cross.* New Brunswick, NJ: Rutgers University Press, 1949.

Johnson, John W., ed. *Historic U.S. Court Cases, 1690–1990: An Encyclopedia.* New York: Garland Publishing, 1992.

Noble, Iris. *Labor's Advocate.* New York: Julian Messner, 1966.

Selvin, David F. *Eugene Debs.* New York: Lothrop, Lee & Shepard, 1966.

HOLDEN V. HARDY

Legal Citation: 169 U.S. 366 (1898)

Plaintiff
Holden

Defendant
Hardy

Plaintiff's Claim
That a Utah state law limiting mine and smelter workers to an eight-hour day was unconstitutional under the Fourteenth Amendment, because it deprived both employers and their workers of their right to make contracts and so denies them the equal protection of the law.

Chief Lawyer for Plaintiff
Jeremiah M. Wilson

Chief Defense Lawyer
Charles J. Pearce

Justices for the Court
Henry Billings Brown (writing for the Court), Melville Weston Fuller, Horace Gray, John Marshall Harlan I, Joseph McKenna, George Shiras, Jr., Edward Douglass White

Justices Dissenting
David Josiah Brewer, Rufus Wheeler Peckham

Place
Washington, D.C.

Date of Decision
28 February 1898

Decision
That the Utah law was not unconstitutional, but rather was a valid use of the state's "police power" since the federal government has the right to preserve the public health, and since working long hours in a mine or smelter is patently unhealthy, the law is valid.

Significance
The case was an important step in establishing the federal government's right to regulate business.

The second half of the nineteenth century in America was the age of "robber barons," industrial giants whose power to shape the nation's economy and political life seemed virtually unlimited. Big business was opposed by working people who were trying to unionize, as well as by middle-class people who were trying to pass state and federal reforms. However, these efforts to limit the power of business were often seen by the courts as going beyond the legitimate power of government.

One way to understand the climate of the time is to think of a person's right to enter into a contract as one of the greatest liberties known to humanity. The freedom to make one's own contract was viewed as so precious that only very grave circumstances could justify the government, or anyone else, interfering with it.

Many people at the time saw things differently. They argued that individual workers could not possibly make free and fair contracts with huge corporations. The corporations had enough power and wealth to force workers to agree to virtually any wages and working conditions, unless either a union contract or a government law intervened. Indeed, many people at the time thought the government's role should be to intervene on the side of the weak and powerless.

The justices of the Supreme Court, however, tended not to support this activist view of the government's role. They saw federal legislation as doubly problematic because it interfered with individual liberty to make contracts, and it usurped power that rightly belonged to the states. In order to justify most types of social legislation, the Court believed that one of four issues had to be at stake: morals, general welfare, safety, or health.

Utah Limits the Miner's Workday

At the turn of the century, Utah was a major mining area. The Utah state legislature had passed a law limiting the workday in mines and smelters (places where metal is melted down) to eight hours, except in the event of an emergency. As a result, a mine and smelter owner named Holden was charged with unlawfully employing John Anderson for ten-hour days in his Old Jordan mine in Bingham canyon and with unlawfully employing William Hooley to work twelve-hour days in his smelter.

In the first case, Holden was found guilty and ordered to pay a fine of fifty dollars plus costs, a substantial sum in those days. If Holden refused to pay, he would be sent to the county jail for 57 days. Holden was also found guilty and similarly punished in the second case.

Holden appealed to the Supreme Court, basing his case on three arguments.

1) The Utah law deprived people of their right to make contracts.

2) The Utah law was "class" legislation; that is, it did not treat all citizens equally. Only mining and smelter employees were forbidden to work more than eight hours a day; only mining and smelter owners were forbidden to require their workers to work more than eight hours. Workers and employers in other industries were given more freedom.

3) The Utah law deprived some people, including Holden, of equal protection under the law, and deprived him, his workers, and others in his industry of liberty without due process of law.

"A Progressive Science"

In preparing to rule on this case, the Supreme Court realized that it was dealing with a new situation. Usually, the Court tried to rely solely on the Constitution when deciding a case. It also tried to guide itself by "common law," the customs inherited from centuries of legal tradition in England. In his majority opinion, Justice Brown explained that the law was "a progressive science." In other words, law was a discipline that changed with the times.

Justice Brown wrote that "certain . . . classes of persons, particularly those engaged in dangerous or unhealthful employments, have been found to be in need of additional protection," protection that was not explicitly provided by the Constitution.

When asked whether miners and smelters were in need of additional protection, Justice Brown answered in the affirmative. He pointed out that the nature of mining and smelting had changed a great deal since the Constitution was ratified, and that

> in the vast proportions which these industries have since assumed, it has been found that they can no longer be carried on with due regard to the safety and health of those engaged in them, without special protection against the dangers necessarily incident to these employments.

In short, Justice Brown, speaking for the majority, affirmed that the Utah law was valid and that Holden's prosecution under the law was justified. The principle that the government could regulate the working conditions of at least some workers had been established.

Miners and Bakers

If labor activists and reformers thought that *Holden v. Hardy* meant that the Supreme Court was now firmly on the side of labor, they were sadly mistaken. Only a few years later, in 1905, the Court ruled in *Lochner v. New York* that a New York state law setting a maximum 60-hour week for bakers was unconstitutional. The two judges who had dissented in *Holden v. Hardy* were joined by three other colleagues, for a narrow 5-4 margin. The majority opinion, written by Justice Peckham, held that bakers should be free to enter into any contract, including one that required them to work more than 60 hours a week. Justice Peckham argued that bakers were fully competent adults who were not in need of special protection.

The reasons for the Court's vastly different rulings in two cases that, on the surface, appear so similar are uncertain. Some scholars believe that the Court had simply changed with the times, becoming more conservative in response to the increasing agitation for social reform. Other scholars believe that the two cases are perfectly consistent. In both cases, the Court was unwilling to interfere with the right of contract except to protect "health," "safety," "morals," or "welfare." These scholars believe that the Court saw mining as unhealthy, dangerous work, while baking was seen as relatively safe. Therefore, unless working longer hours could be shown to endanger the baker, the federal government had no right to interfere.

During the next several decades, the Court would prove extremely reluctant to approve of labor legislation. Despite the landmark nature of *Holden v. Hardy*, it would be many years before true workplace reform was accepted by the courts.

Related Cases
Lochner v. New York, 198 U.S. 45 (1905).
Muller v. Oregon, 208 U.S. 412 (1908).
Bunting v. Oregon, 243 U.S. 426 (1917).
Adkins v. Children's Hospital, 261 U.S. 525 (1923).
Morehead v. New York, 298 U.S. 587 (1936).
West Coast Hotel v. Parrish, 300 U.S. 379 (1937).

Bibliography and Further Reading
Bartholomew, Paul C. *Summaries of Leading Cases on the Constitution,* 9th ed. Towota: NJ: Littlefield, Adams & Co., 1954, 1976.

Biskupic, Joan, and Elder Witt. *Congressional Quarterly's Guide to the U.S. Supreme Court,* 3rd ed. Washington, DC: Congressional Quarterly, Inc., 1996.

Fiss, Owen M. *History of the Supreme Court of the United States, the Troubled Beginnings of the Modern State,* Vol. VIII. New York: Macmillan, 1993.

Hall, Kermit L., ed. *The Oxford Companion to the Supreme Court of the United States.* New York: Oxford University Press, 1992.

LOCHNER V. NEW YORK

Legal Citation: 198 U.S. 45 (1905)

Appellant
Joseph Lochner

Appellee
People of the State of New York

Appellant's Claim
That Lochner had not violated the New York Bakeshop Act because the law was an unreasonable exercise of police power.

Chief Lawyers for Appellant
Frank Harvey Field, Henry Weismann

Chief Lawyer for Appellee
Julius M. Mayer, attorney general of New York

Justices for the Court
David Josiah Brewer, Henry Billings Brown, Melville Weston Fuller, Oliver Wendell Holmes, Joseph McKenna, Rufus Wheeler Peckham (writing for the Court)

Justices Dissenting
William Rufus Day, John Marshall Harlan I, Edward Douglass White

Place
Washington, D.C.

Date of Decision
17 April 1905

Decision
In protecting the right to contract for labor, the Court overruled New York's Bakeshop Act, which regulated sanitary conditions and the number of hours that employees could work.

Significance
Lochner v. New York postponed protective legislation for women for decades, becoming one of the most controversial decisions in the history of the Supreme Court.

Lochner v. New York began in the Guilded Age and ended in the Progressive Era when *laissez-faire* capitalism began to clash with a new reforming impulse in America. The conflict embroiled Joseph Lochner, owner of a tiny bakery in Utica, New York, that made biscuits, breads, and cakes for early-morning customers. Lochner's employees worked late, sometimes sleeping overnight on the premises. In April 1901, baker Aman Schmitter labored more than sixty hours a week.

Receiving a complaint, police arrested Lochner, charging him with violating New York's Bakeshop Act. The law set minimum standards for sanitation and fixed the number of hours that the mostly male bakers could work—at no more than ten hours a day or sixty hours a week.

Approximately ten months after his arrest, Lochner's case went to trial in the county court. Lochner refused to plead either guilty or innocent and offered no defense, intending to appeal. This tactic left Judge W. T. Dunmore only two choices: to sentence the defendant to a fifty-dollar fine or fifty days in jail. On the same day of the conviction, Lochner's attorney, William S. Mackie, filed an appeal to the Appellate Division of the Supreme Court of New York.

He argued that the Bakeshop regulations interfered with Lochner's right to earn a living, a liberty protected under the U.S. Constitution. Three of five judges disagreed, believing that the statute was a valid exercise of the state's power. Again Mackie appealed and lost.

A Baker's Lawyer

Finally, Lochner changed attorneys. His new lawyer, Henry Weismann, was an unlikely advocate. Ten years earlier he had been a lobbyist for the Journeyman Bakers Union and editor of the union's newsletter, the *Bakers' Journal*. He had urged his comrades to agitate for the eight-hour bakeshop law.

Resigning from the *Bakers' Journal* in 1897, Weismann opened two bakeries of his own. He joined forces with the Retail Bakers' Association to dilute the impact of the Bakeshop Act. As he told the *New York Times,* "The truth . . . is that I have never been in sympathy with the radicals in the labor movement."

Lochner's Home Bakery in Utica, New York, c. 1900. © Oneida County Historical District.

Weissman, who had not passed the bar, asked attorney Frank Harvey Field to join him. The key argument of the new team was that the Bakeshop law violated a doctrine called "liberty of contract"—meaning the right to operate a business, or contract one's labor, so long as this did not interfere with the equal rights of others. State courts embraced this doctrine during the late nineteenth century. (One example was an 1886 Pennsylvania Supreme Court decision to overrule a law that required coal miners to be paid in cash, not goods.)

However, critics argued that the state already placed restrictions on contracts, such as prohibiting the practice of medicine without a license. They claimed the "liberty of contract" doctrine protected the exploitation of workers, who were the weaker parties in labor contracts.

At the time, the U.S. Supreme Court had only once used "liberty of contract" to overrule a state law (in *Allgeyer v. Louisiana* [1897]). Mostly, the Court preferred to leave state laws intact. So Field and Weismann faced an uphill battle when they argued that the Bakeshop Act had violated the liberty of contract of the workers and employers of New York State. Baking was not a dangerous profession, they said, and the Bakeshop Act, as it concerned hours, was never intended to protect the health of employees. Instead it was a prohibitive labor law, an illegitimate use of the police power of the state, because it deprived bakers of their due process rights.

Due Process and Daniel Webster

In 1819, Daniel Webster had argued that in nullifying the charter of a private college, New Hampshire had performed a semi-judicial act that had, in effect, deprived Dartmouth of its "substantive due process" rights under the Fifth Amendment of the Constitution.

The Weissman-Field team—elaborating on this theory that a state may not invade the rights of persons or property—posed a series of questions to test whether legislators truly had the health and safety of the public in mind when they passed a law:

> Does a danger exist? Is it of sufficient magnitude? Does it concern the public? Does the proposed measure tend to remove it? Is the restraint or requirement in proportion to the danger? Is it possible to secure the object sought without impairing essential rights and principles? Does the choice of a particular measure show that some other interest than safety or health was the actual motive of legislation?

Julius M. Mayer, the newly appointed attorney general, made a surprisingly brief 18-page response. He said baking required heavy lifting and carrying; because of the flour dust and germs in the air, lung diseases sickened workers. Tuberculosis killed many of them. Therefore, the state could regulate work hours for the public good.

A Surprise Verdict

By a 5-4 vote the Supreme Court preferred elevated liberty of contract over the rights of employees to a safe workplace and reasonable hours. Speaking for the Court, Justice Rufus Peckham said:

> There is no reasonable ground for interfering with the liberty of person or right of free contract, by determining the hours of labor, in the occupation of a baker . . . A law like the one before us involves neither the safety, the morals, nor the welfare of the public . . .

Justice Harlan, six-feet-two-inches tall—who, according to his wife, "walked as if the whole world belonged to him"—joined White and Day in dissenting. Harlan quoted professors and writers who felt baking was a hard occupation, and pointed out that Congress and nearly all the states had passed laws concerning "particular occupations involving the physical strength and safety of workmen . . . Many, if not most, of those enactments fix eight hours as the proper basis of a day's labor." He was referring to hazardous jobs, such as mining.

Oliver Wendell Holmes, on the Court less than two years, also dissented in a separate opinion that people quoted for years to come. He put his finger on the unspoken assumption of the majority:

> The liberty of the citizen to do as he likes so long as he does not interfere with the liberty of others to do the same, which has been a shibboleth for some well-known writers, is interfered with by school laws, by the Post Office, by every state or municipal institution which takes his money for purposes thought desirable, whether he likes it or not.

Rufus Wheeler Peckham. © The Library of Congress/Corbis.

Effect on Women

For years the economic rights upheld in *Lochner v. New York* were used to invalidate laws regulating the hours, wages, and work conditions of women (for instance, *Adkins v. Children's Hospital* in 1923). During the 1930s, the Court relied on *Lochner* to frustrate the New Deal legislation of President Franklin D. Roosevelt, making it a symbol of unfairness. In 1940, the Court formally disavowed the Lochner philosophy in *United States v. Darby*. By this time, most states had already enacted laws protecting women in the workplace. In the climate of reform, few imagined the disastrous effects that the laws—despite their immediate relief—would have on women's employment opportunities.

Protective legislation for women may have harmed as well as helped female workers. Because women were "protected" from performing equally with men in lifting, working night shifts, selling spirits, and working while pregnant—to give a few examples—they suffered disastrous economic discrimination. Since they could not compete equally with men, they did not earn equal wages, obtain the same jobs, win promotions, or receive equal benefits. In 1964, the Civil Rights Act, Title VII, brought the promise of relief. Seven years later, the Supreme Court for the first time sued a company under the act for sex-discrimination. The case was *United States v. Libbey-Owens-Ford,* and it marked an historic turning point in the equal treatment of women in the workplace.

Related Cases

Allgeyer v. Louisiana, 165 U.S. 578 (1897).
Wilson v. New, 243 U.S. 332 (1917).
Adkins v. Children's Hospital, 261 U.S. 525 (1923).
West Coast Hotel v. Parrish, 300 U.S. 379 (1937).

Bibliography and Further Reading

Cushman, Robert E. *Leading Constitutional Decisions.* New York: Appleton-Century-Crofts, 1958.

Goldstein. Leslie. *The Constitutional Rights of Women: Cases in Law and Social Change.* Madison: University of Wisconsin Press, 1989.

Johnson, John W., ed. *Historic U.S. Court Cases, 1690–1990: An Encyclopedia.* New York: Garland Publishing, 1992.

Kanowitz, Leo. *Women and the Law: The Unfinished Revolution.* Albuquerque: University of New Mexico Press, 1969.

Kens, Paul. *Judicial Power and Reform Politics. The Anatomy of Lochner v. New York.* Lawrence: University Press of Kansas, 1990.

Otten, Laura A. *Women's Rights and the Law.* Westport, CT: Praeger, 1993.

Tribe, Laurence H. *American Constitutional Law,* 2d ed. Mineola, NY: The Foundation Press, 1988.

LOEWE V. LAWLOR

Legal Citation: 208 U.S. 274 (1908)

Appellant
D. E. Loewe

Appellee
Martin Lawlor

Appellant's Claim
That the union of which Martin Lawlor was the business agent, the United Hatters Union of North America, was acting against the Sherman Anti-Trust Act in unlawful restraint of trade by attempting to organize a boycott of Loewe's company, the Danbury Hatters, in order to force Loewe to permit his company to be unionized.

Chief Lawyers for Appellant
James M. Beck, Daniel Davenport

Chief Lawyers for Appellee
John Kimberly Beach, John H. Light

Justices for the Court
David Josiah Brewer, William Rufus Day, Melville Weston Fuller (writing for the Court), John Marshall Harlan I, Oliver Wendell Holmes, Joseph McKenna, William Henry Moody, Rufus Wheeler Peckham, Edward Douglass White

Justices Dissenting
None

Place
Washington, D.C.

Date of Decision
3 February 1908

Decision
That the United Hatters Union was indeed acting in restraint of interstate commerce, even though its activities had actually been limited to a single state, and that union members were personally liable to be sued or fined for the activities of their union.

Significance
Loewe v. Lawlor was the first major application of the anti-trust laws to a labor union.

The end of the nineteenth century and the beginning of the twentieth century was a time of great transition in the United States. Huge corporations, known as trusts, had formed, often creating monopolies that controlled the prices of key products. At the same time, working people had begun to form unions, organizations that enabled them to demand better wages and working conditions from their employers.

In 1890, concerned about the growing power of the trusts, Congress passed the Sherman Anti-Trust Act. This act held, in part:

1. Every contract, combination in the form of trust or otherwise, or conspiracy, in restraint of trade or commerce among the several states, or with foreign nations, is hereby declared to be illegal. Every person who shall make any such contract or engage in any such combination or conspiracy, shall be deemed guilty of a misdemeanor, and, on conviction therefore, shall be punished by fine not exceeding five thousand dollars, or by imprisonment not exceeding one year, or by both said punishments, in the discretion of the court.

2. Every person who shall monopolize, or attempt to monopolize, or combine or conspire with any other person or persons, to monopolize any part of the trade or commerce among the several states, or with foreign nations, shall be deemed guilty of a misdemeanor, and on conviction therefore, shall be punished by fine not exceeding five thousand dollars, or by imprisonment not exceeding one year, or by both said punishments, in the discretion of the court . . .

3. Any person who shall be injured in his business or property by any other person or corporation by reason of anything forbidden or declared to be unlawful by this act, may sue therefore in any circuit court of the United States . . . and shall recover three fold the damages by him sustained, and the costs of suit, including a reasonable attorney's fee.

The Congress that passed the Sherman Anti-Trust Act clearly intended it to combat the "restraint of trade" practiced by the big corporations that fixed prices, controlled distribution, and often drove smaller companies out of business. But on 3 February 1908, the Supreme Court made history by applying the antitrust law to the United Hatters of North America Union.

"Look for the Union Label"

The background to *Loewe v. Lawlor* is a classic story of early labor history. The United Hatters were a union of some 9,000 members, primarily in the Northeast and Midwest, with some members in California and in Ontario, Canada. Six of the union's locals, with about 3,000 members, were located in Connecticut.

Following the union principles of "unity" and "strength in numbers," the United Hatters had affiliated with the American Federation of Labor (AFL), a group of unions that is the predecessor of today's AFL-CIO. In 1908, the AFL had over 1.4 million members in the United States and Canada—a small fraction of America's working people.

In those days, there was virtually no legislation that protected union activity, and union members were frequently fired or harassed in order to discourage them and their fellow workers from joining the union. Despite the adverse conditions, the United Hatters had managed to organize some 70 of the nation's 82 hat factories. That left only 12 unorganized shops, one of which was the Danbury Connecticut company, D. E. Loewe & Co., known as Danbury Hatters.

According to the union, Danbury Hatters had:

> . . . discriminated against the union men in their employ, had thrown them out of employment because they refused to give up their union cards and teach boys, who were intended to take their places after seven months' instruction, and had driven their employes [sic] to extreme measures by their persistent, unfair and un-American policy of antagonizing union labor, forcing wages to a starvation scale and given boys and cheap, unskilled foreign labor preference over experienced and capable union workmen . . .

The union needed to decide how to respond to this apparent harassment. One approach might have been a strike. In those days, however, there was no law to prevent an employer from replacing striking workers with non-union labor. And while workers were on strike, they did not get paid.

So the United Hatters tried another tactic: they called a boycott. With the help of the AFL, they called on union members and sympathizers across the nation to refuse to buy hats that were made by Danbury Hatters, or indeed, any hat that did not have a union label.

"Lawful Combination" or Restraint of Trade?

Danbury Hatters was not happy about this threat to its business. The company owner, D. E. Loewe, brought suit against individual members of the United Hatters, including the union's business agent, Martin Lawlor.

Loewe referred to the provisions of the Sherman Anti-Trust Act cited above, which he claimed entitled him to "three fold" the amount he had lost through the boycott, plus court costs for the suit itself. Altogether, Loewe wanted $80,000.

Loewe's argument was straightforward: by combining with unions across the country to boycott his goods, United Hatters was unlawfully restraining his trade. From Loewe's point of view, the working men and women that were refusing to buy his hats were no different from a huge corporation that tried to drive a little company out of business.

Of course, the union saw it differently. They pointed out that the Sherman Anti-Trust Act was a federal law, which applied only to trade between states. But, they said, the United Hatters local that was trying to organize Danbury Hatters existed only in Connecticut, within the boundaries of a single state. Only thirteen years before, in an 1895 case called *United States v. E. C. Knight,* the Court had ruled that the local activities of a nationwide Sugar Trust did not come under the provisions of the Anti-Trust Act. The union probably expected that its own local activities would find similar toleration. After all, the union's lawyer pointed out, the United Hatters was not an illegal trust but a "lawful combination."

Seeking a Political Solution

In a unanimous ruling, all nine justices found that the secondary boycott organized by the United Hatters was illegal under the Sherman Anti-Trust Act, which, said the Court, "prohibits any combination which essentially obstructs the free flow of commerce between the States . . ." Moreover, the Court added:

> A combination may be in restraint of interstate trade and within the meaning of the Anti-Trust Act although the persons exercising the restraint may not themselves be engaged in interstate trade . . . The Anti-Trust Act of July 2, 1890 makes no distinctions between classes. Organizations of farmers and laborers were not exempted from its operation . . .

Therefore, said the Court, Martin Lawlor did indeed owe $80,000 in damages to D. E. Loewe.

Unions across the country were furious with the decision in *Loewe v. Lawlor.* They were also scared. If manufacturers could sue them for such enormous sums every time they tried to organize, they would soon be unable to take any action at all.

Since the judicial system seemed so unsympathetic to labor, unions tried the legislative route. They helped pass the Clayton Antitrust Act of 1914, which specifically exempted labor unions from suits brought under the antitrust laws. Real legal relief for labor, however, was not to come until the 1930s, when heightened labor militancy and an increased number of strikes created a whole new set of laws recognizing workers' right to organize.

Related Cases

Adair v. United States, 208 U.S. 161 (1908).
Standard Oil Co. v. United States, 221 U.S. 1 (1911).
Duplex Printing Press Co. v. Deering, 254 U.S. 443 (1921).
National Labor Relations Board v. Jones and Laughlin Steel Corp., 301 U.S. 1 (1937).

Bibliography and Further Reading

Bartholomew, Paul C. *Summaries of Leading Cases on the Constitution.* Totowa, NJ: Littlefield, Adams & Co., 1976.

Furer, Howard. *The Supreme Court in American Life, The Fuller Court, 1888–1910,* Vol. V. Millwood, NY: Associated Faculty Press, Inc., 1986.

Hall, Kermit L., ed. *The Oxford Companion to the Supreme Court of the United States.* New York: Oxford University Press, 1992.

MULLER V. OREGON

Legal Citation: 208 U.S. 412 (1908)

Appellant
Curt Muller

Appellee
State of Oregon

Appellant's Claim
That Oregon's 1903 maximum hours law for women is unconstitutional.

Chief Lawyers for Appellant
William D. Fenton, Henry H. Gilfry

Chief Lawyers for Appellee
H. B. Adams, Louis Brandeis

Justices for the Court
David Josiah Brewer (writing for the Court), William Rufus Day, Melville Weston Fuller, John Marshall Harlan I, Oliver Wendell Holmes, Joseph McKenna, William Henry Moody, Rufus Wheeler Peckham, Edward Douglass White

Justices Dissenting
None

Place
Washington, D.C.

Date of Decision
24 February 1908

Decision
That Oregon's maximum hour law for women was constitutional because females are a "special class" in need of protection.

Significance
Pigeonholing women as a special (weaker) class sex in need of minimum wages and maximum hours won the battle but lost the war, perpetuating sex-segregation in the work place.

On 18 September 1905, an Oregon launderer, Mrs. Elmer Gotcher, brought a complaint against her boss at the Portland Grand Laundry. She claimed Curt Muller had let his overseer, Joe Hazelbock, make her work more than ten hours on 4 September. This violated Oregon's "hour law" for women, which read "no female (shall) be employed in any mechanical establishment, or factory, or laundry in this state more than ten hours during any one day."

The county court agreed, sentencing Muller to pay a $10 fine. He appealed, but the state supreme court affirmed the decision. Believing the state law to be unconstitutional, Muller appealed to the U.S. Supreme Court.

However, he underestimated the forces arrayed against him. When Florence Kelley, executive secretary of the National Consumers' League, and Josephine Goldmark, a Barnard tutor, heard of his appeal, they seized an opportunity. They believed that working long hours was harmful to females workers, especially mothers and pregnant women. With hours laws under legal attack in several states, Kelley and Goldmark decided to test Muller's appeal.

The women faced opposition from two sources. The first was from other feminists. Alice Paul and members of her National Woman Party passionately opposed singling out women as needing special protection, believing that all women needed to compete with men on an equal playing field. If women could end discriminatory laws, especially those denying them the vote, they would achieve equality.

The second was from jurists who honored the idea of "liberty of contract," which included the freedom to contract labor. The courts viewed this doctrine as sacrosanct. They believed that Article I, Section 10, of the Constitution prohibited states from passing any law "impairing the Obligation of Contracts." The Due Process Clauses of the Fifth and Fourteenth Amendments also protected liberty of contract ("nor shall any state deprive any person of life, liberty or property, without due process of law"). Progressives such as Kelley and Goldmark argued that the state had a "special interest" in helping workers who labored in dangerous jobs (mining) or in sweat shops that flourished during America's post-Civil War industrial expansion.

A Clash of Ideas

These two ideas—the state's "special interest" in regulating business and the Constitution's protection of "liberty of contract"—clashed dramatically during the Progressive Era (1900 to World War I). In 1905, the Supreme Court upheld "liberty of contract" in *Lochner v. New York* by overturning a state law setting sixty hours a week as the maximum hours that (mostly male) bakers could work. The *Lochner* decision effectively blocked protective legislation for women. Kelley and Goldmark attempted to circumvent it.

They turned to 51-year-old Louis Brandeis, the husband of Goldmark's sister, Alice. Known as "the people's attorney," Brandeis had made a career of expanding the law to address the social needs of people. He had represented several states whose wages and hours laws were under attack.

Brandeis agreed to help on two conditions: first, Oregon had to hire him as its attorney, and second, the National Consumers' League had to provide him with a massive amount of statistical information on working women within two weeks. Goldmark and Kelley, laboring around the clock, gave him a 113-page document. It marshaled facts and figures showing that working long hours affected the health and morality of females. For the first time the Supreme Court would hear an argument based on human welfare instead of legal reasoning. The new argument became known as the "Brandeis brief."

Before the Supreme Court, Muller's side argued that to deny women the right to work more than ten hours a day interfered with their liberty to make contracts and diminished their power to support themselves. Since Oregon law gave married women equal contractual and personal rights to men, the state could not use its police power to infringe on these rights.

With modern reasoning, Muller's attorney pointed out that the Oregon law was unconstitutional because "the statute does not apply equally to all persons similarly situated, and is class legislation."

With Friends Like These . . .

Brandeis, however, claimed that women *as a group* needed special protection, using the widespread assumption that women were the "weaker sex." He said it was "common knowledge" that to permit women to work more than ten hours a day in factories, laundries, and the like "[was] dangerous to public health, safety, morals [and] welfare."

This argument forced the Court to reconsider *Lochner v. New York*. The Court had ruled that New York's law was not a legitimate exercise of the police power of the

Lace House Laundry with proprietor Curt Muller standing center, 1903. © Mrs. Fran Whisnant, Portland, Oregon.

state and interfered with the right of male bakers to contract their labor. The question was whether women were any different?

Nineteen state legislatures, under pressure from suffragists and some union leaders, had placed women in a special class, regulating their hours of work. Justice Brewer, speaking for the majority, noted that the laws were "significant of a widespread belief that woman's physical structure, and the functions she performs in consequence thereof, justify special legislation restricting or qualifying the conditions under which she should be permitted to toil."

In a view that seemed progressive for its time but now appears paternalistic, Brewer said:

> That woman's physical structure . . . place her at a disadvantage in the struggle for subsistence is obvious. This is especially true when the burdens of motherhood are upon her. Even when they are not . . . continuance for a long time on her feet at work, repeating this from day to day, tends to injurious effects upon the body, and, as healthy mothers are essential to vigorous offspring, the physical well-being of woman becomes an object of public interest and care in order to preserve the strength and vigor of the race.

For these reasons, Brewer decided that a woman "is properly placed in a class by herself, and legislation designed for her protection may be sustained." The Court unanimously affirmed the lower court's decision requiring Muller to pay the fine and court costs. The Brandeis brief had been a success.

The Aftermath

After Muller, many states passed wages and hours laws and other statutes regulating the conditions of work. However, in 1923, the Supreme Court ruled this legislation was unconstitutional in *Adkins v. Children's Hospital*. Then the Great Depression of the 1930s forced the Court to reverse its decision. In the 1937 case *West Coast Hotel v. Parrish*, the Court—drawing on *Muller v. Oregon*—overruled its 1923 decision in *Adkins v. Children's Hospital* to uphold Washington State's minimum wage law for women and minors. The justices had nudged the liberty of contract doctrine off its pedestal.

West Coast Hotel v. Parrish paved the way for the Fair Labor Standards Act of 1938, which extended to men the wages and hours laws women had won. In *United States v. Darby* (1941), the Court ruled that minimum wage laws for men were constitutional.

Over time protective legislation—although it brought relief to millions—kept women in low paying, temporary, unskilled jobs. The laws barred women from working overtime and holding good (male) jobs. For instance, females could not sell spirits, deliver the mail, work in foundries and mines, or run elevators. The American Federation of Labor in 1914 turned its back on its earlier support for protective legislation and used the "weaker sex" argument to keep poorly paid women from working with men. It stopped women from working as printers or streetcar conductors and endorsed unequal pay for the same work.

On 28 February 1908, the *New York Times* wrote of the *Muller* decision, "We leave to the advocates of women suffrage to say whether this decision makes for, or against, the success of their cause." *Muller* gave relief to women and children and opened the door to more humane working conditions for men. However, it further segregated the workplace and provided an excuse for unions and employers alike to keep the wages of women low—trends that remain to this day.

Related Cases
Lochner v. New York, 198 U.S. 45 (1905).
Adkins v. Children's Hospital, 261 U.S. 525 (1923).
West Coast Hotel v. Parrish, 300 U.S. 379 (1937).
United States v. Darby, 312 U.S. 100 (1941).

Bibliography and Further Reading
Goldstein, Leslie Friedman. *The Constitutional Rights of Women*. Madison: The University of Wisconsin Press, 1989.

Hoff, Joan. *Law, Gender, and Injustice*. New York: New York University Press, 1991.

Johnson, John W., ed. *Historic U.S. Court Cases, 1690–1990: An Encyclopedia*. New York: Garland Publishing, 1992.

Kanowitz, Leo. *Women and the Law: The Unfinished Revolution*. Albuquerque: University of New Mexico Press, 1969.

Mezey, Susan Gluck. *In Pursuit of Equality: Women, Public Policy, and the Federal Courts*. New York: St. Martin's Press, 1992.

COPPAGE V. KANSAS

Legal Citation: 236 U.S. 1 (1915)

Appellant
T. B. Coppage

Appellee
State of Kansas

Appellant's Claim
Kansas statute prohibiting "yellow dog contracts" did not violate the Due Process Clause of the Fourteenth Amendment.

Chief Lawyers for Appellant
R. R. Vermilon, W. F. Evans

Chief Lawyers for Appellee
John S. Dawson, Attorney General of Kansas; J. I. Sheppard

Justices for the Court
Joseph Rucker Lamar, Joseph McKenna, James Clark McReynolds, Mahlon Pitney (writing for the Court), Willis Van Devanter, Edward Douglass White

Justices Dissenting
William Rufus Day, Oliver Wendell Holmes, Charles Evans Hughes

Place
Washington, D.C.

Date of Decision
25 January 1915

Decision
The Kansas statute, which outlawed yellow dog contracts, was an invalid and repressive infringement of an employer's right to engage in "freedom of contract" under the Fourteenth Amendment.

Significance
This decision of the U.S. Supreme Court enjoined the state of Kansas from enforcing an act banning "yellow dog contracts." The U.S. Supreme Court reasoned that existence of such laws were inconsistent with "freedom of contract" provisions guaranteed under the Due Process Clause of the Fourteenth Amendment. In overruling the lower court's decision to sustain the appellant's conviction, the justices expressed that inequalities between employers and employees were not sufficient to allow statutory provisions to restrict the right of an employer to enter into a free and binding contract. This ruling reflected the last breath of an American industrial revolution which tended to privilege employer's rights over those of labor.

The state of Kansas passed an act in 1903 which prevented employers from stopping employees from joining labor unions as a condition of employment. The main provisions of the Kansas statute were in two parts. The first specifically prohibited companies from any action that would "coerce, require, demand, or influence any person or persons to enter into any agreement, either written or verbal, not to join or become or remain a member of any labor organization or association, as a condition of such person or persons securing employment, or continuing in the employment." The second part stipulated that any member of a firm who violated the statutory provisions of the first provision of the statute would be guilty of a misdemeanor and fined by an amount not less than $50 or imprisoned no less than 30 days.

In the summer of 1911, Hedges, an employee of the St. Louis & San Francisco Railway Company (Frisco Lines), was required to sign a written agreement presented to him by T. B. Coppage (superintendent of Frisco Lines), wherein he agreed to relinquish membership in his labor union if he wanted to retain his job. Hedges, however, did not want to withdraw from the union so he was discharged. Coppage, was charged in a Kansas court and found guilty of preventing his employee from membership in a union. He was ordered to pay a fine or go to a jail. Coppage appealed his conviction to the Kansas State Supreme Court. Nevertheless, the judgment of the lower court was affirmed; the Kansas State Supreme Court concluded that Kansas law prohibiting yellow dog contracts was constitutional.

Employers' Rights Upheld

The U.S. Supreme Court overruled the judgment of the lower courts. The majority did not find any element of pressure or duress in the appellant's actions. The justices considered Coppage's act an appropriate exercise of employer rights under Fourteenth Amendment provisions regarding "freedom of contract." They found that Hedges was not coerced when he was asked to sign a contract containing provisions to which he was not willing to accede. The Court believed he had opportunity to decide and choose whether to withdraw from membership in his union or remain in the service of

---

Yellow-Dog Contracts

With the growth of labor unions in the nineteenth century and the early twentieth century, employers looked for ways to hire lower-wage workers. One of the more successful methods employers used was having potential employees sign contracts declaring that they were not presently union members and that they would not become union members, or what became known as yellow-dog contracts.

Although some states had laws that prohibited employers from forcing employees to sign yellow dog contracts, in 1915 the U.S. Supreme Court struck down

such state laws as unconstitutional, arguing that they obstructed the freedom of contract of both employers and employees. However, Congress passed the Norris-LaGuardia Act of 1932 that prohibited yellow-dog contracts. The Norris-LaGuardia Act strengthened the position of labor unions and its policies became the standard means for resolving labor disputes in following years.

Source(s): *West's Encyclopedia of American Law.* Minneapolis, Minnesota: West Publishing, 1998.

---

his employer. The Court reasoned that requirements presented to Hedges by the representative of the railway company (Coppage) were not unconstitutional and that no coercion was evident because Hedges had opportunity to "exercise a voluntary choice."

In a comparable, related case, *Adair v. United States* (1908), a yellow dog contract was held as being constitutionally legal under what the justices viewed as being an issue of "freedom of contract" despite legislation passed by Congress which were aimed at prohibition of such practices. Justice Pitney, in writing for the majority, maintained that

> under constitutional freedom of contract, whatever either party has the right to treat as sufficient ground for terminating the employment, where there is no stipulation on the subject, he has the right to provide against by insisting that a stipulation respecting it shall be a sine qua non of the inception of the employment, or of its continuance if it be terminable at will.

The Court reasoned that, as in *Adair,* there had to be an equal balance between employer and employee rights. As in *Adair,* justices chose to privilege an employer's property rights and due process rights under the Fifth Amendment. The Court rationalized that if it was unconstitutional for the government "to deprive an employer of liberty and property for threatening an employee with loss of employment, or discriminating him (the employee) because of his membership in a labor organization," then it was equally illegal for states to "similarly punish an employer for requiring his employee, as a condition of securing or retaining employment, to agree not to become or remain a member of such an organization while so employed." (Clearly, the 1915 Court, under Chief Justice White, was at odds with the slow, eventual movement of legislators towards legislation which would eventually proscribe yellow dog contracts.)

Concluding that the notion of an employer's right to "freedom of contract" was sufficient to justify Coppage's actions (on behalf of his company), the majority felt that Kansas's yellow dog legislation was "arbitrary" and infringed on the equal rights of companies. The law was an inappropriate "exercise of the police power of the state." The justices did not feel that the appellant had exercised compulsory influence and thus, his actions did not represent a violation of law. The justices for the majority did not deny that states were granted the right to exercise police power to prohibit potential coercive requirements in contracts between employers and employees. But they could not accept the findings of lower courts that (as an authorized representative of his company) Coppage's action should be treated as criminal and punishable when he offered Hedges, without "undue influence," an option to remain in the employ of Frisco Lines or leave, and Coppage left Hedges free to make a decision.

The Court reasoned that the Kansas statute prohibiting yellow dog contracts represented an unfair requirement on employers when negotiating a contract with employees. Due process provisions of the Fourteenth Amendment safeguarded "liberty," "property", and "freedom of contracting." Justices reasoned that "inequalities of fortune" were legal and recognizable as a natural process of negotiating and making contracts. Thus, the Court viewed Kansas law as an indirect attempt to overthrow such inherent inequities without recognizing the existence of an employer's constitutional guarantees that safeguarded company interests.

The majority justices posited that the Kansas law was not properly legislated because it infringed on an employer's right to make contracts favoring the interests of the employer's company. The Court believed Kansas statute outlawed the "exercise of personal liberty and property rights" and represented an inappropriate application of the state's police power. Further, under the Fourteenth Amendment, an employer's contracting rights were abridged because the statute denied an employer the opportunity to decide whether membership in a labor organization was an acceptable condition of employment. Characterizing the relationship between employer and employee as a "voluntary relationship," the Court found inappropriate legislation that characterized as criminal conduct an employer's prescription of terms under which an employee could continue relations with his employee.

The justices pointed out that freedom of choice was equal for both parties (for the employer to employ a laborer who met its needs, and for the laborer to choose whether to relinquish union membership in order to remain employed.) Offering an employee such an option could not be characterized as deprivation of any constitutional freedom. Both parties were free to "say no" if not satisfied with terms of employment; thus, as a part of the process of equal bargaining, conditions of employment did not have to be regarded as unlawful or coercive if an employer's requirements legitimately exercised his right to "freedom of contract." The majority justices were persistent and clear that no "legislative restrictions" were legitimate if they obstructed the exercise of rights under "freedom of contract," therefore the Kansas statute was illogical. Consequently, the jailing of Coppage was improper when his conduct did not exceed legal limits.

Dissent Over "Freedom Of Contract"

Dissenting justices acceded that the concept of "freedom of contract" was under constitutional protection, but in certain circumstances was subject to restriction and control by a state, especially "in the interests of the public health, safety, and welfare." In *Frisbie v. United States*, the Court had ruled there was no absolute, unrestricted right to freedom of contract, therefore, contracts were subject to limitations to accommodate a public interest.

The dissenting justices did not believe that the Kansas law was so arbitrary as to be unconstitutional. Its statutory provisions did not prevent an employer from exercising the right to dismiss an employee. However, the justices believed non-union membership was an unacceptable reason to refuse continued employment or to be precondition for employment. Unlike the majority, the minority justices reasoned that the *Adair* case "dealt solely with the right of an employer to terminate relations of employment with an employee, and involved constitutional protection of his right to do so, but did not deal with the conditions which he might exact or impose upon another as a condition for employment."

The minority opinion viewed the Kansas statute as a legitimate effort to proscribe compulsive and coercive contracting requirements by preventing employers from making non-union membership a term of employment. The justices did not feel both parties maintained contractual parity if an employer discharged an employee for reasons which only the employer found satisfactory. The justices found difficulty in believing that the options Coppage presented to Hedges did not imply elements of coercion. Thus, Kansas law did not surpass the "legitimate exercise of police power" because the state enacted statutory provisions which "put limitations upon the sacrifice of rights which one man may exact from another as a condition of employment."

Impact

The U.S. Supreme Court's ruling in *Coppage v. Kansas* was later invalidated by reforms in the New Deal era and subsequent legislative reorganization of modern labor law by the National Labor Relations Act in 1935. As one of the final vestiges of unregulated employment practices during the industrial revolution, the Court majority held that Kansas inappropriately provided "penalty for coercing or influencing or making demands upon or requirements of employees, laborers." In essence, the Court ruled that employees could not belong to any organization which advocated on their behalf working conditions without approval of an employer. However, within two decades, political and social pressures were brought on by social disillusionment with corporate America after the economic trauma of the stock market crash in 1929, and the pervasive depression which followed. Reasoning that unregulated exploitation could no longer be justified by false economic prosperity, the government was forced to reconsider the meaning of appropriate employer/employee relations.

Related Cases

Frisbie v. United States, 157 U.S. 160 (1895).
Holden v. Hardy, 169 U.S. 366 (1898).
Adair v. United States, 208 U.S. 161 (1908).
Chicago, B. & Q. R. Co. v. McGuire, 219 U.S. 549 (1911).

Bibliography and Further Reading

Brauneis, Robert. "'The Foundation of Our "Regulatory Takings" Jurisprudence.'" *Yale Law Journal*, December 1996, p. 613.

Hall, Kermit L., ed. *The Oxford Companion to the Supreme Court of the United States*. New York: Oxford University Press, 1992.

May, James. "Competition Policy in America: 1888–1992, History, Rhetoric, Law." *Antitrust Bulletin*, summer 1997, p. 239.

Pope, James Gray. "Labor's Constitution of Freedom." *Yale Law Journal*, January 1997, p. 941.

WILSON V. NEW

Legal Citation: 243 U.S. 332 (1917)

Appellant
Francis M. Wilson, U.S. Attorney for the Western District of Missouri

Appellees
Alexander New and Henry C. Ferris, as Receivers of the Missouri, Oklahoma, & Gulf Railway Company

Appellant's Claim
The act of 3 September 1916 entitled "An Act to establish an eight-hour day for employees of carriers engaged in interstate and foreign commerce, and for other purposes" is constitutional and is aimed at establishing an eight-hour standard for work and wages and establishing a minimum wage.

Chief Lawyers for Appellant
John William Davis, U.S. Solicitor General; Frank Hagerman; E. Marvin Underwood; Thomas W. Gregory, U.S. Attorney General

Chief Lawyers for Appellees
Walker D. Hines, John G. Johnson, Arthur Miller

Justices for the Court
Louis D. Brandeis, John Hessin Clarke, Oliver Wendell Holmes, Joseph McKenna, Edward Douglass White (writing for the Court)

Justices Dissenting
William Rufus Day, James Clark McReynolds, Mahlon Pitney, Willis Van Devanter

Place
Washington, D.C.

Date of Decision
19 March 1917

Decision
Appeal from the District Court of the United States for the Western District of Missouri to review a decree which enjoined the enforcement of a statute fixing an eight-hour workday for, and temporally regulating the ages of, railway employees engaged in the operation of trains upon interstate railway carriers. Reversed and remanded, with directions to dismiss the bill.

Significance
Established the power of Congress to fix a maximum work day and to fix a minimum wage within the public sector of work.

Before March of 1916, two systems controlled wages of railroad employees. One was an eight-hour standard of work and wages with additional pay for overtime, governing about 15 percent of the railroads. The other was a stated mileage task of 100 miles to be performed during ten hours, with extra pay for any excess, in force on about 85 percent of the roads. In March, however, the organizations representing the employees of the railroads made a formal demand on railroad employers that, except for passenger trains, the 100-mile task be fixed for eight hours. They also made various demands on salary and wage adjustments. The employers refused the demands, and the employees, through their organizations, by concert of action, took the steps to call a general strike of all railroad employees throughout the country.

President Woodrow Wilson invited a conference between the parties. He proposed arbitration. The employers agreed, but the employees rejected it. The president then suggested the eight-hour standard of work and wages. The employers rejected it, but the employees accepted it. With no agreement in sight, the employees called a general strike. The president, trying to avert a commercial disaster and grave personal suffering if the strike was not prevented, asked Congress to fix, by law, the eight-hour standard of work and wages, and to create an official body for observing the operation of the legislation. Congress responded by enacting the statute, the validity of which is considered here.

The effect of the Act of 3 and 5 September 1916 is not only to establish a permanent eight-hour standard for work and wages as between the carriers and employees affected, but also to fix a scale of minimum wages for the eight-hour day and proportionally for overtime, to be in force only during the limited period defined by the act.

The Court ruled that in an emergency arising from a nationwide dispute over wages between railroad companies and their train employees, in which a general strike with dire consequences overhangs the country, Congress had power to prescribe a standard of minimum wages, not confiscatory in its effects but obligatory on both parties, in order to avert calamity and offer opportunity to both parties to substitute a standard on

The Eight-Hour Workday

With the growth of industrialization in the United States in the mid- to late-nineteenth century, workers began to demand shorter work hours to reduce incidence of injury from performing repetitive tasks. Advocates of shorter hours also argued that shorter hours coupled with higher wages would increase consumption and therefore help businesses and the economy expand, and that shorter hours would increase worker productivity. In the 1920s, Henry Ford became one of the first industrialists to adopt the eight-hour workday. In the 1930s, the National Industrial Recovery Act instituted a 40-hour work week, which essentially made the eight-hour workday law until overturned by the U.S. Supreme Court in 1935. However, most businesses had accepted the economic and productivity arguments for the shorter workday by then.

During the second half of the twentieth century, the workday remained around eight hours. Consequently, critics of the eight-hour workday point out that since World War II, the eight-hour workday has remained the norm and that even with the rise of technology the workday has not decreased for most jobs. Arguments in favor of shorter work days range from ones asserting that shorter work days will bring about a greater quality of life to ones contending that shorter work days will prevent layoffs and unemployment.

Source(s): Levitan, Sara A., and Richard S. Belous. *Shorter Hours, Shorter Weeks.* Baltimore: The Johns Hopkins University Press, 1977.

their own. The business of common carriers by rail was one aspect of public business, and this public interest gives right of regulation to the full extent necessary to secure and protect it. Although emergency may not create power, it may afford reason for exerting a power already enjoyed.

The Court ruled that, viewed as an act fixing wages, the statute merely illustrated the character of regulation essential, and hence permissible, for the protection of the public right. The act did not invade the private rights of carriers, since all their business and property must be redeemed subject to the regulatory power to insure fit relief by appropriate means.

The Court also said that the act did not invade private rights of employees, since their rights to demand wages according to their desire and to leave employment if the demand is reused, were not such as they might be if the employment were in private business, but are necessarily subject to limitation by Congress, the employment accepted being in a business charged with a public interest which Congress may regulate under the commerce power.

Bibliography and Further Reading

Biskupic, Joan, and Elder Witt, eds. *Congressional Quarterly's Guide to the U.S. Supreme Court,* 3rd ed. Washington, DC: Congressional Quarterly, Inc., 1996.

Hall, Kermit L., ed. *The Oxford Companion to the Supreme Court.* New York: Oxford University Press, p. 636.

BUNTING V. OREGON

Legal Citation: 243 U.S. 426 (1917)

Appellant
Franklin O. Bunting

Appellee
State of Oregon

Appellant's Claim
A 1910 Oregon labor law, limiting the number of hours an employee may work in a day and invoking an overtime wage of one-and-half times the regular wage, was unconstitutional.

Chief Lawyers for Appellant
W. Lair Thompson, C. W. Fulton

Chief Lawyers for Appellee
Felix Frankfurter, George M. Brown, J. O. Bailey

Justices for the Court
John Hessin Clarke, William Rufus Day, Oliver Wendell Holmes, Joseph McKenna (writing for the Court), Mahlon Pitney

Justices Dissenting
James Clark McReynolds, Willis Van Devanter, Edward Douglass White (Louis D. Brandeis did not participate)

Place
Washington, D.C.

Date of Decision
9 April 1917

Decision
The Supreme Court held that the Oregon labor law did not violate the Fourteenth Amendment. The labor law, while limiting the number of hours a laborer could work in specific occupations, did not bar an employer from negotiating wages with employees. The Court also held that the Oregon state labor law did not exceed its constitutional limits. It upheld the Due Process Clause of the Constitution by allowing employers the freedom of contract to negotiate wages.

Significance
Bunting v. Oregon affirmed the state's authority in enacting labor laws that regulated the number of hours a laborer in selected occupations could work in order to protect the health and well-being of the employee. This authority was granted by the Due Process Clause of the Fourteenth Amendment of the U.S. Constitution. While substantive due process does not grant the state unlimited power to enact legislation arbitrarily, it does provide a mechanism whereby the state has the ability to protect "the health, peace, morals, and general welfare."

Proper Exercise of Police Power

In 1910 the state of Oregon enacted a statute that limited the number of hours a laborer could work in specific occupations. The statute provided a maximum of ten hours per day of work service in manufacturing plants, mills, and factories. A laborer could work an additional maximum of three hours of overtime per day provided he was paid a rate of time-and-a-half of his regular wages. The violation of this statute was a misdemeanor charge carrying a $50 fine.

Franklin O. Bunting was cited with a violation of the Oregon labor statute. He had an employee working in Lake View Flouring Mill who was working a 13-hour day and who was not compensated for the three hours overtime at the time-and-a-half rate. Bunting pleaded "not guilty" and the case went to trial. The district court found Bunting guilty. Because of the constitutional question, the case was remanded to the state supreme court where the lower court's ruling was affirmed.

Bunting claimed that the Oregon law violated both the U.S. Constitution and the Oregon State Constitution. He believed that he was denied due process of the law as guaranteed by the Constitution because the law was not a regulation of work hours, but, rather, a regulation of wages. Bunting claimed that the law forced employers to pay employees for a 13-hour-day at a rate that was higher than the fair market value of the services provided. This, he concluded, took profits property from the employer and gave it to the employees.

The U.S. Supreme Court first heard the case on 18 April 1916. It was reargued on 19 January 1917 with a decision delivered the following April. The Court was required to answer two questions in deciding the case. First, was the Oregon State labor law a wage law or was it hours of service law? They, then, had to address whether the law itself violated the Constitution of the United States and the Oregon State Constitution. Did the legislation provide an excessive amount of police power to the state in enacting and enforcing laws that benefited the governmental majority and caused harm to the citizens of Oregon?

Justice McKenna entered the opinion for the Court. In reviewing the state statute and Bunting's claim, the

Court affirmed that the labor law placed limits only on the number of hours a laborer could work in order to protect his health. They concurred that the Due Process Clause permitted states to enact maximum-hour laws for workers in specific occupations that were deemed physically demanding or performed under special conditions. The opinion of the Court supported the Oregon State Supreme Court's decision that the purpose of the law was to limit hours in particular industries. Justice McKenna wrote that the labor law made no attempt to fix the minimum or maximum standard of wage. There is no wage specified in the law. Wages were left to the determination of the negotiating parties: employer and employee. The rate of time-and-a-half of the regular wage was deemed a mild penalty for causing the laborer to work beyond the ten hour limit.

The overriding issue in *Bunting v. Oregon* was whether the enactment of the Oregon maximum hour labor law exceeded the appropriate exercise of police power by the state. In previous cases the Supreme Court held that a state had the authority to enforce legislation that protected workers from conditions that were physically demanding and which were concerned with the health and physical well-being of the worker. In *Mugler v. Kansas* (1887) the Supreme Court stated that police power of the state was "no more than the power to promote public health, morals, and safety." It was the opinion of the concurring justices that the Oregon labor law did not prevent an employer from negotiating the best wage standards possible for the benefit of his business, but that it did protect the laborer's health and general welfare.

Impact

Bunting v. Oregon was a significant step in establishing the basic elements of the Fair Labor Standards Act of 1938. It affirmed the state's authority in enacting legislation that would protect workers in hazardous occupations. If the statute merely limited the number of hours of service in specific industries in an effort to oversee the health and general welfare of workers and did not set a minimum or maximum standard of wages, the state was within its appropriate level of power to enact the law. Laws regulating the maximum number of hours of labor did not violate the Fourteenth Amendment of the Constitution of the United States.

The establishment of the Fair Labor Standards Act of 1938 relied upon cases such as this one to provide equitable power to both the employer and employee to negotiate wages and contracts, and to protect both parties from any unfair advantages. Laws regulating the hours of labor or service still come under review today, including discussions of overtime and compensation hours instead of overtime wages (Working Families Flexibility Act, 1997).

Related Cases

The Slaughterhouse Cases, 83 U.S. 36 (1873).
Allgeyer v. Louisiana, 165 U.S. 578 (1897).
Holden v. Hardy, 169 U.S. 366 (1898)
Lochner v. New York, 198 U.S. 45 (1905).
Muller v. Oregon, 208 U.S. 412 (1908).
Coppage v. Kansas, 236 U.S. 1 (1915).
Adkins v. Children's Hospital, 261 U.S. 525 (1923).
Morehead v. New York, 298 U.S. 587 (1936).
West Coast Hotel v. Parrish, 300 U.S. 379 (1937).

Bibliography and Further Reading

National Association of Quick Printers. "Congress Turns Its Attention Toward Comp Time." *Washington Wire,* May 1997.

Phillips, Michael J. "How Many Times Was *Lochner*-Era Substantive Due Process Effective?" *Mercer Law Review,* http://review.law.mercer.edu/48313.thm#text133

HAMMER V. DAGENHART

Legal Citation: 247 U.S. 251 (1918)

Appellant
W. C. Hammer, U.S. Attorney for the Western District of North Carolina

Appellee
Roland Dagenhart

Appellant's Claim
That Roland Dagenhart, by allowing his two teenaged sons to work in a North Carolina cotton mill, was in violation of the Keating-Owen Act, which limited child labor.

Chief Lawyers for Appellant
John William Davis, U.S. Solicitor General; Roscoe Pound, Dean of Harvard Law School

Chief Lawyer for Appellee
Junius Parker

Justices for the Court
William Rufus Day (writing for the Court), Joseph McKenna, Mahlon Pitney, Willis Van Devanter, Edward Douglass White

Justices Dissenting
Louis D. Brandeis, John Hessin Clarke, Oliver Wendell Holmes, James Clark McReynolds

Place
Washington, D.C.

Date of Decision
3 June 1918

Decision
That Congress did not have the right to exclude from interstate commerce all goods manufactured by child labor, as the Keating-Owen Act had tried to do.

Significance
The case established the Supreme Court of the 1920s as highly conservative and a powerful opponent to those in Congress, and in state legislatures, who were trying to en-act social-welfare legislature limiting the work day, insuring health and safety in the workplace, and abolishing child labor.

By the time the Supreme Court decided *Hammer v. Dagenhart* in 1918, many generations of U.S. children had worked long hours at difficult and dangerous jobs—on farms, in mines, in factories. At the turn of the century, one-sixth of all children between the ages of 10 and 15 years was working for money, often at jobs that paid a few cents an hour for work that lasted ten or even 12 hours a day. Children were particularly in demand as workers in the South's growing textile industry, which relied on cheap labor.

Slowly but surely, a child-labor reform movement began to gain ground. In 1907, Senator Albert Beveridge tried to get the Senate to pass anti-child labor legislation. Although he did not succeed, he did draw national attention to the issue.

Opponents of child labor faced two difficult obstacles. The first was the widespread belief that labor contracts were individual matters that ought not be interfered with by the government. For the government to say that children should not work more than 10 hours, or that children under the age of 14 should not work at all, was considered an infringement of a parent's and an employer's liberty to enter into a contract.

To complicate matters further, labor legislation was believed to be the province of state government, not federal. Since using child labor was cheaper than hiring adult workers, many people argued that their state could not afford to pass anti-child-labor legislation. Otherwise, they claimed, states that could use child labor could sell their goods more cheaply, putting those that could not at a disadvantage.

The Keating-Owen Act

The people who wanted to pass child labor laws thought they saw a way around this problem. They wanted to pass federal legislation outlawing child labor so that no state would be at a particular disadvantage, since it would not face competition from any other state.

The problem was that, under the Tenth Amendment, states are supposed to have all power that the Constitution does not specifically give to the federal government. Making a national law to regulate labor condi-

---

Child Labor Law in the United States Today

Although children were exploited as a source of cheap labor at the beginning of the century when they worked long hours and received low wages, today federal and state laws protect children or minors under 18 years old among others from such "sweat shop" conditions. In addition, these laws keep children safe from exposure to hazardous substances and conditions and children are barred from holding certain jobs even if they have parental consent.

Various state and federal regulations such as the Fair Labor Standards Act of 1938 and the Child Labor Act of 1916 prohibit or restrict the employment of children

in various occupations, especially those with potentially dangerous conditions including ones involving toxic substances and heavy machinery. One state, for example, considers the operation of a log-loading machine too dangerous for minors. Furthermore, other regulations cover the employment of children in certain occupations, under certain conditions, after specific hours, and when school is in session.

Source(s): *West's Encyclopedia of American Law* Minneapolis, Minnesota: West Publishing, 1998.

---

tions would seem to be in violation of the Tenth Amendment.

Representative Edward Keating and Senator Robert L. Owen thought they saw a way around this problem. Their Keating-Owen Act attacked child labor on a federal level through a kind of back door. Rather than dealing directly with contracts or working conditions, the Keating-Owen Act dealt with interstate commerce, which everyone agreed was the province of the federal government. The Keating-Owen Act prohibited the shipment of any products that both were shipped from state to state and were made in factories or mines that employed children under age 14, or that allowed children between ages 14 and 16 to work more than eight hours a day. This also included employers that required children to work six days a week, after 7 p.m., or before 6 a.m. The act also said that no products could be shipped from an establishment where those labor conditions had occurred within 30 days prior to the goods being shipped.

The Act Is Challenged

No sooner was the Keating-Owen Act passed than David Clark started to organize against it. Clark was the publisher of a trade journal in Charlotte, North Carolina, a major textile center. He was also a member of the Executive Committee of Southern Cotton Manufacturers.

Clark knew he needed a test case. He went out and found Roland Dagenhart, who worked with his two teenaged sons at the Fidelity Manufacturing Company, a small cotton mill in Charlotte. Dagenhart's older son, Reuben, was 15, and if the Keating-Owen Act were enforced, he would have to work far fewer hours per week. Dagenhart's younger son was only 13, so he would not be allowed to work at all. When Fidelity Manufacturing said it would observe the new law, Clark provided the lawyers to sue both the company and W. C. Hammer, the U.S. Attorney for the Western District of North Carolina, who would presumably be the one to enforce the law. Clark sought an injunction—a

---

Child Labor Act

In part of the federal government's efforts to restrict and eliminate worker exploitation—especially the exploitation of children—in the early part of the twentieth century, Congress passed the Keating-Owen Act of 1916, commonly called the Child Labor Act. This act sought to stop children from working long hours for low wages in hazardous conditions by outlawing interstate commerce of goods manufactured by children. The Child Labor Act's legal foundation stemmed from the Constitution's Commerce Clause, which empowered Congress to regulate interstate commerce.

In *Hammer v. Dagenhart* the U.S. Supreme Court struck down the Child Labor Act, arguing that harmless manufactured goods were not part of the commerce regulated by the federal government and that Congress had overstepped its boundary. The Court felt that regulating commerce was up to states and that the Child Labor Act undermined the system of government set forth in the Constitution.

Source(s): *West's Encyclopedia of American Law* Minneapolis, Minnesota: West Publishing, 1998.

---

court ruling that would prevent the company from obeying the act and that would keep the federal government from enforcing it.

To Regulate or To Destroy?

The government made its case by showing how destructive child labor was, both to children and to their families. Moreover, the government attorney said that if the federal government did not abolish child labor, any state that tried to abolish it would suffer, because of the unfair competition from child-labor states. In order to protect the public good, therefore, the Keating-Owen Act was necessary.

A majority of the Court did not agree. In the majority opinion, written by Justice Day, the Court held that the power to regulate commerce is the power "to control the means by which commerce is carried on," not the "right to forbid commerce from moving."

It was true that the federal government had prevented some types of interstate commerce. For example, lottery tickets, impure food, and people who had been kidnapped, could not be transported across state lines. But in these cases, Day argued, "the use of interstate transportation was necessary to the accomplishment of harmful results." In the case of the child labor dealt with in the Keating-Owen Act, "the goods shipped are of themselves harmless."

Day admitted that states who did not allow child labor would be at a disadvantage relative to those who did. However, "this fact does not give Congress the power to deny transportation in interstate commerce." Under the Tenth Amendment, states had to be free to make their own decisions.

Objections from "The Great Dissenter"

Justice Holmes was known as "the great dissenter" because he so often disagreed with the majority opinion of the Court. A liberal at a time when the Court was quite conservative, he often wrote the minority opinion, as he did in this case. "It does not matter whether the supposed evil precedes or follows the transportation," Holmes wrote. "It is enough that in the opinion of Congress that transportation encourages the evil."

Despite Holmes's eloquent objections, the vote was 5-4 in favor of Dagenhart, and America's first child-labor legislation was overturned. The public was outraged. The *New York Evening Mail,* for example, called it a "victory of sordidness over our little ones." Senator Owen announced plans to introduce an amended version of his bill that would include language forbidding any court to declare it unconstitutional.

More realistically, members of Congress opposed to child labor turned away from the federal government's

John William Davis, U.S. Solicitor General, in 1924. © *AP/Wide World Photos.*

power to regulate commerce and toward its power to tax. On 24 February 1919, Congress passed a revenue act that levied a stiff tax against products made by child labor. But that law was struck down by the courts in the *Child Labor Tax Case* of 1922.

A Young Worker's Response

Finally, in 1941, the Supreme Court overturned *Hammer v. Dagenhart* in a case called *United States v. Darby,* Meanwhile, in 1923, Reuben Dagenhart had been interviewed about his experience with the case. Then aged 20, Dagenhart expressed great regret that he had never had the chance to go to school:

> I don't see that I got any benefit. I guess I'd have been a lot better off if they hadn't won it. Look at me! A hundred and five pounds, a grown man and no education. I may be mistaken, but I think the years I've put in the cotton mills have stunted my growth. They kept me from getting any schooling. I had to stop school after the third grade and now I need the education I didn't get . . . It would have been a good thing in this state if that law they passed had been kept.

Related Cases

Champion v. Ames, 188 U.S. 321 (1903).
Hipolite Egg Co. v. United States, 220 U.S. 45 (1911).
Hoke v. United States, 227 U.S. 308 (1913).
United States v. Darby, 312 U.S. 100 (1941).

Bibliography and Further Reading

Bickel, Alexander M., and Benno C. Schmidt, Jr. *History of the Supreme Court of the United States,* Vol. 9: *The Judiciary and Responsible Government.* New York: Macmillan, 1984.

Johnson, John W., ed. *Historic U.S. Court Cases, 1690–1990: An Encyclopedia.* New York: Garland Publishing, 1992.

Witt, Elder. *Congressional Quarterly's Guide to the U.S. Supreme Court,* 2nd ed. Washington, DC: Congressional Quarterly, 1990.

ADKINS V. CHILDREN'S HOSPITAL

Legal Citation: 261 U.S. 525 (1923)

Appellants
Jesse C. Adkins, et al.; Minimum Wage Board of District of Columbia

Appellee
Children's Hospital of the District of Columbia

Appellants' Claim
That the U.S. Congress has the right to establish minimum wages for women and children.

Chief Lawyer for Appellants
Felix Frankfurter

Chief Lawyer for Appellee
Wade H. Ellis

Justices for the Court
Pierce Butler, Joseph McKenna, James Clark McReynolds, George Sutherland (writing for the Court), Willis Van Devanter

Justices Dissenting
Oliver Wendell Holmes, Edward Terry Sanford, William Howard Taft (Louis D. Brandeis did not participate)

Place
Washington, D.C.

Date of Decision
9 April 1923

Decision
Minimum wage laws for women are unconstitutional because they interfere with the liberty of contract guaranteed by the Fifth and Fourteenth Amendments.

Significance
The Supreme Court ruled that Congress does not have the power to set minimum wages for women as a special group, slowing down the Consumers' League drive to show that a ceiling on wages without a floor left women vulnerable. It also stopped efforts to equalize pay between men and women, a discrepancy that remained until the Equal Pay Act of 1963.

Willie Lyons, a 21-year-old elevator operator, desperately wanted to keep her job. Lyons worked at the Congress Hall Hotel in Washington, D.C. where many members of Congress and their families lived. She felt that the work was easy, the hours short, and the surroundings clean and pleasant. She had been happy at work and with her pay—$35 a month, plus two meals a day.

Then the District of Columbia Minimum Wage Board set $16.50 a week as the base pay for all female hotel workers. The Congress Hall Hotel had to fire her, or face legal penalties. Lyons knew she could not find a better job elsewhere for the same salary. So she petitioned the court for an injunction to keep the board—under Jesse Adkins—from enforcing its orders on the Congress Hall Hotel.

On 19 September 1918, Congress passed a law establishing the District of Columbia Minimum Wage Board. This statute set the minimum wage paid to any woman or child working in the nation's capital. For example, the board had fixed a weekly salary of $16.50 for women employed where food was served, $15.50 for those who worked in printing, and $15 for laundry workers, with beginning laundresses earning $9. Lyons feared her skills could not realistically command these wages in the competitive marketplace, and that her current wages were the best she could earn. If the Congress Hall Hotel fired her, Lyons knew she would not find work elsewhere.

At the same time that Lyons was trying to obtain an injunction against the board's decision, the Children's Hospital of the District of Columbia was having its own problems with the Minimum Wage Board. The hospital employed a large number of women in a variety of different jobs. A few of them earned less than $16.50 a week. Like Lyons, the hospital sued to restrain the board from enforcing its minimum wage ruling on the ground that it violated the Fifth Amendment's Due Process Clause.

However, in both cases the Supreme Court of the District of Columbia affirmed the constitutionality of the law. On appeal, the Court of Appeals of the District of Columbia affirmed the lower court's decision.

History of the Minimum Wage

Federal law under the Fair Labor Standards Act of 1938 requires and controls a minimum hourly wage that governs all employers doing interstate business. In addition, most states have similar minimum wage statutes. The fight for a minimum wage began in the nineteenth century and grew out of state-level outrage over the rise of sweatshops, which forced workers—especially women, children, and immigrants—to work over 10 hours a day for low wages often in hazardous conditions. Minimum wage supporters argued that all workers deserved living wages. In 1912, Massachusetts became the first state to enact a minimum wage law. In the 1920s and 1930s, other states followed Massachusetts' example, some motivated by the Great Depression. However, state supreme courts and the U.S. Supreme Court struck down minimum wage legislation as unconstitutionally violating the freedom-to-contract rights of employers.

President Franklin Roosevelt worked with Congress to pass the National Industrial Recovery Act of 1933, which gave the president the authority to create a minimum wage as part of the federal government's power to regulate interstate business. However, the Supreme Court disagreed and again declared minimum wages unconstitutional. President Roosevelt tried once more in 1937 to have minimum wage legislation enacted with the Fair Labor Standard Act. Finally, the Supreme Court upheld the constitutionality of the act in 1941. Beginning at 25 cents an hour and rising to $5.15 an hour in 1997, the minimum wage increases only by congressional approval.

Source(s): *West's Encyclopedia of American Law,* vol. 7 Minneapolis, MN: West Publishing, 1998.

Yet after a rehearing, the court reversed its judgment, and a divided bench declared the law unconstitutional. Further appeals carried the two cases, *Adkins v. Children's Hospital* and *Adkins v. Lyons,* to the Supreme Court of the United States.

The legal questions the Court faced were whether Congress had the power to prescribe a minimum wage for women in the District of Columbia, or if such wage-fixing by restricting an individual's "liberty of contract" (protected by Due Process Clauses of the Fifth and Fourteenth Amendments) was an unconstitutional use of the state's police power. Further, it was questionable whether the law was discriminatory, because it protected only women.

Legal and political controversy swirled about these questions. In *Lochner v. New York* (1905) the Supreme Court held that it was unconstitutional for New York to limit the number of hours male bakers could work to ten per day. However, in *Bunting v. Oregon* (1917), the justices upheld a law setting ten hours as the maximum hours per day that people could work in mills, factories, or manufacturing.

Protective Legislation v. Equality

The First Wave women's movement was also hopelessly divided over the issue of special rights versus equal rights for women, as it had been since 1908, when the Supreme Court upheld Oregon's hours law for women in *Muller v. Oregon.* Alice Paul and supporters Anne Henrietta Martin and Burbita Shelton Matthews wanted all inequalities between women and men in the law eradicated from jury service, property, custody, guardian-

ship, marriage, divorce, and work. They recognized immediately the sexism implied in legislation to protect only women workers. Paul's slogan "Equality not Protection" repudiated these statutes.

However, Paul's former colleagues in the suffrage movement—Florence Kelley, Jane Addams, Julia Lathrop, and Margaret Dreir Robbins—championed the new wages and hours laws. Their views were shared by groups such as the League for Women Voters and the National Consumers' League, whose stated goals included social welfare legislation for women and children. They were joined by the National Federation of Business and Professional Women, women in the labor movement, and bureaucrats in the Women's Bureau (part of the Department of Labor) created in 1920. In their minds, support for the Equal Rights Amendment (ERA) would set back the protective legislation for women that had been winning support in the states.

But Are they Constitutional?

After the arguments, Justice Sutherland, delivered the opinion of a divided Court. With reasoning that is reminiscent of modern jurists such as Ruth Bader Ginsburg, he said:

> We cannot accept the doctrine that women of a mature age . . . may be subjected to restrictions upon their liberty of contract which could not lawfully be imposed in the case of men under similar circumstances.

In arguing that it was unfair to apply minimum wage laws to women but not to men, Sutherland went on:

It is simply and exclusively a price-fixing law, confined to adult women . . . who are legally as capable of contracting for themselves as men.

And,

If women require a minimum wage to preserve their morals men require it to preserve their honesty.

Sutherland also highlighted the inconsistencies of the board's orders, pointing out that if a woman employed to serve food required a minimum wage of $16.50, he questioned the fairness of a beginning laundresses earning only $9 a week.

Finally, Sutherland concluded:

It may be said, that if in the interest of public welfare the police power may be invoked to justify the fixing of a minimum wage, it may, when the public welfare is thought to require it, be invoked to justify a maximum wage . . . If in the face of the guarantee of the Fifth Amendment this form of legislation shall be legally justified, the field for the operation of the police power will have been widened to a great and dangerous degree.

Justices Taft and Sanford disagreed, arguing:

Legislatures in limiting freedom of contract between employee and employer . . . proceed on the assumption that employees, in the class receiving less pay, are not upon a full level of equality of choice with their employers and . . . are prone to accept pretty much anything that is offered. They are peculiarly subject to the overreaching of the harsh and greedy employer. The evils of the sweating system and long hours and low wages which are characteristic of it are well known.

While Sutherland had said that the wages paid to an employee were the "heart of the contract," Taft felt that this opinion exaggerated the importance of one part of the contract—wages—over other terms, such as hours.

Justice Holmes believed that Congress did have the right to establish minimum rates of pay for women:

The end, to remove conditions leading to ill health, immorality, and the deterioration of the race, no one would deny to be within the scope of constitutional legislation.

Justice Brandeis, whose daughter, Elizabeth, was the secretary of the District's minimum wage board, took no part in the decision. This split the Court 5-3, with the majority voting to overrule the minimum wage law for women. In 1936, *Morehead v. New York ex rel. Tipaldo* reaffirmed the *Adkins* decision.

After *Adkins,* union leaders such as Samuel Gompers railed against the Court, fuming, "The Court ranges itself on the side of property and against humanity." He insisted that women "not only are . . . less than able to defend themselves on the economic fields, but they are absolutely without means of defense in the political field."

The minimum-wage boards in the states believed that their laws should be enforced as if the Court had not overruled Congress. Congressmen vowed to curb the Court. Senators, such as Simeon Fess, proposed that two-thirds vote of the Supreme Court be henceforth required for decisions. U.S. Senator William E. Borah wanted agreement among at least seven of the nine judges for future Court decisions. Senator Robert LaFollette suggested giving Congress the power to overrule the Supreme Court by reposing a law after an adverse decision. These reformers saw the Court as overstepping its boundaries and trying to legislate for Congress.

With the Great Depression of the 1930s, Americans came to agree with them. They swept President Franklin D. Roosevelt into the White House in 1932 on the promise of a New Deal. In 1936, Roosevelt sent Congress his "court-packing" plan, which would have added six judges to the Supreme Court, all appointed by him. The progressives, in the long run, were victorious.

Today, historians are somewhat more sympathetic to the Adkins Court. In 1978, legal scholar Lawrence H. Tribe wrote in *American Constitutional Law*:

While the Court justified the limitation of women's working hours by reference to the perceived social and biological need to limit the participation of women in the labor force [in *Radice v. New York,* which upheld a law prohibiting the employment of women in restaurants between 10:00 p.m. and 6:00 a.m. because of their "peculiar and natural functions"], the Court initially [in *Adkins v. Children's Hospital*] struck down women's minimum wage laws, which could not so easily be assimilated to sexist assumptions about the nature and role of women.

One thing is certain: *Adkins v. Children's Hospital* and *Adkins v. Lyons* would further the disintegration of the women's movement in the 1920s over the issue of equal versus special rights for women. Three years after the passage of the Nineteenth Amendment (1920), and the same year that the Supreme Court ruled in *Adkins v. Children's Hospital* and *Adkins v. Lyons* (1923), Alice Paul and her militant National Woman's Party introduced the Equal Rights Amendment into Congress. Section 1 read: "Equality of rights under the law shall not be abridged by the United States or by any state on account of sex." Then, in 1937 the Supreme Court overturned its ruling in *Adkins* with *West Coast Hotel v. Parrish.* However, in

1980, presidential candidate Ronald Reagan forced the Republicans to break from tradition by dropping the ERA plank from its platform, and in 1982, the ERA failed to win the endorsement of the necessary number of the states. This left open many of the issues dividing the women's movement in 1923, issues that have not disappeared and which continue to be debated to this day.

Related Cases

West Coast Hotel Co. v. Parrish, 300 U.S. 379 (1937).
Planned Parenthood of Southeastern Pennsylvania v. Casey, 505 U.S. 833 (1992).

Bibliography and Further Reading

Goldstein, Leslie Friedman. *The Constitutional Rights of Women,* rev. ed. Madison: University of Wisconsin Press, 1989.

Hoff, Joan. *Law, Gender, and Injustice: A Legal History of U.S. Women.* New York: New York University Press, 1991.

Tribe, Lawrence H. *American Constitutional Law.* Mineola, New York: The Foundation Press, 1988.

MOREHEAD V. NEW YORK

Legal Citation: 298 U.S. 587 (1936)

Petitioner
Warden Morehead

Respondent
People of State of New York

Petitioner's Claim
That the minimum wage law that allowed the New York State Industrial Commission to fix wages based upon the class of services provided by female employees denies the employer the right to enter into contracts as provided under the Fourteenth Amendment of the Constitution of the United States.

Chief Lawyer for Petitioner
Henry Epstein

Chief Lawyers for Respondent
Nathan L. Miller, Arthur Levitt

Justices for the Court
Pierce Butler (writing for the Court), James Clark McReynolds, Owen Josephus Roberts, George Sutherland, Willis Van Devanter

Justices Dissenting
Louis D. Brandeis, Benjamin N. Cardozo, Charles Evans Hughes, Harlan Fiske Stone

Place
Washington, D.C.

Date of Decision
1 June 1936

Decision
The New York act was found unconstitutional due to its violation of the right of due process of the law between the employer and the employee.

Significance
Morehead v. New York challenged the establishment of a minimum wage for women and minors based upon "the value of the service or class of service rendered." This case denied the states' rights in regulating wages and fair labor laws for women and minors. The Supreme Court declared the New York Labor Act unconstitutional, stating that it violated the right of due process to enter into contracts granted by the Fourteenth Amendment of the Constitution of the United States. The judgment in this case upheld the employer's right to negotiate wages with female employees even though those wages were below the standard established by the state industrial commissioner.

Morehead, a manager of a laundry, was jailed by the state industrial commissioner of New York for not adhering to the mandatory minimum wage set for women. Morehead appealed his case in the Supreme Court of New York, where the New York Labor Act was found to be in violation of both New York State and U.S. Constitutions. Because of the federal implications of Morehead's case, the U.S. Supreme Court granted a writ of *certiorari* (a written order commanding that the lower court forward the proceedings of a case to a higher court for review) and acted upon the case. The U.S. Supreme Court ruled that the New York act violated the U.S. Constitution and upheld the lower appellate court's decision that Morehead had the right to negotiate contracts with employees, thereby releasing him from illegal imprisonment.

In 1936, the conservative justices of the Supreme Court had a narrow view of a minimum wage. They believed that by establishing minimum wages and standards boards to control wages, the states were enacting laws that opposed the rights and freedoms established by the Fifth Amendment and upheld by the Fourteenth Amendment of the U.S. Constitution. Justice Butler, writing for the majority, stated

> The right to make contracts about one's affairs is a part of the liberty protected by the due process clause. Within this liberty are provisions of contracts between employer and employee fixing the wages to be paid. In making contracts of employment, generally speaking, the parties have equal right to obtain from each other the best terms they can by private bargaining.

These regulatory boards were seen as an extension of police power for the states.

Ruling in favor of Morehead prevented state legislature from overseeing and protecting employees who found it difficult to act in their own behalf, especially women and minors. This decision also gave employers an unfair advantage to contract wages that were substandard and based on perceived value of the service, rather than being adequate to meet the cost of living needs of women in sole support of dependents.

The justices used a similar case from 1923, *Adkins v. Children's Hospital,* as the guiding principles for deciding this case. In 1918, Congress enacted a law in the District of Columbia that guaranteed a minimum wage to women and children that met their needs to "maintain decent standards of living." This case was challenged in 1923 before the Supreme Court of the United States, and was ruled unconstitutional. The District of Columbia Act, as it became known, was seen as an extension of police power for the state, which interfered with the ability of an employer and employee to enter into private contracts. The Supreme Court ruled that this act prohibited due process of the law as granted by the Fifth Amendment.

A Dissenting Opinion

Four of the justices, including Chief Justice Hughes, disagreed with the majority opinion. Hughes, writing the dissenting opinion, cited several points. He stated "I can find nothing in the Federal Constitution which denies to the state the power to protect women from being exploited by overreaching employers through the refusal of a fair wage as defined in the New York statute and ascertained in a reasonable manner by competent authority." He first noted that the petitioner, Warden Morehead, did not challenge the fairness of the wage being prescribed by the state industrial commissioner and that the investigation into the wages Morehead was contracting was "careful and deliberate." The justices had to assume that the procedures had been followed as established by the New York act.

Hughes also found that the definition of a fair wage was more restrictive in the *Adkins* case, and therefore should not be applied to the case before the Court in 1936. The New York act provided not only for a fair wage for women based upon the standard of an adequate living wage, but also upon a standard of reasonable value of the services provided. The District of Columbia's act prescribed a wage that provided an adequate standard for the cost of living. This additional element as stated by Justice Hughes was meant to improve the standard "by requiring a fair equivalence of wage and service."

One of the most crucial points of dissension for the justices was the limitations placed upon the liberty of contract. The overriding question was whether or not the Fifth and the Fourteenth Amendments of the U.S. Constitution interfered with the state's power to protect special groups of citizens. Hughes, Brandeis, Stone, and Cardozo took into consideration whether groups of employees who had no organizing body such as a trade union and weak collective bargaining power were being protected by the state act by establishing a minimum wage and commission to oversee its enactment. In previous decisions, the U.S. Supreme Court agreed that the "liberty of contract" was a qualified right in which limitations could be used to protect exploited groups and to serve the public interest, and in such a light, the act was appropriate according to the dissenting justices.

Resolution and Reversal

In 1937, less than one year later, the *Morehead* decision and the *Adkins v. Children's Hospital* verdicts were reversed. There was a public outcry at both national party conventions, denouncing the decision. When *West Coast Hotel v. Parrish* was brought before the U.S. Supreme Court in December of 1936, the justices decided in a 5-4 decision "that the establishment of minimum wages for women was constitutionally legitimate." It was noted "that the Constitution did not speak of the freedom of contract, and that liberty was subject to the restraints of due process." States were empowered to set the standards of public welfare and control labor relations.

Impact

By ruling in favor of Morehead, and declaring the New York Labor Act unconstitutional, the Supreme Court gave employers the power to control wages for women and minors. The states no longer had jurisdiction over the employment contractual process, and special groups were no longer protected from unscrupulous or overreaching employers who sought to gain higher profits by offering lower wages. Employee groups with weak bargaining power and little organization, and who had to accept whatever wages were offered in order to subsist, were left with little recourse to seek payment for the services provided to employers.

The Court's narrow view of minimum wage legislation so outraged the voting public that this decision was denounced at the national conventions for both political parties and was later reversed, conferring the right of states to establish minimum wage protection. In 1938, the Fair Labor Standards Act went into effect providing a national minimum wage of no less than 80 cents and the establishment of regulatory boards to oversee wage and hours standards.

Minimum wage legislation is still a hotly debated topic 50 years after the first provisions of the Fair Labor Standards Act were enacted. Today, approximately 80 percent of the workers in the United States are protected by this act and are guaranteed a minimum wage. Similar to the New York Labor Act of 1936, minimum wage legislation today guarantees an income above poverty level that will enable all workers to fulfill the basic needs of food, clothing and housing for themselves, their families, and dependents.

Related Cases

Lochner v. New York, 198 U.S. 45 (1905).
Bunting v. State of Oregon, 243 U.S. 426 (1917).
Adkins v. Children's Hospital, 261 U.S. 525 (1923).

Meyer v. Nebraska, 262 U.S. 390 (1923).
West Coast Hotel v. Parrish, 300 U.S. 379 (1937).

Bibliography and Further Reading

Ayers, Mary Ellen. "The Quest for a Living Wage: The History of the Federal Minimum Wage Program." *Monthly Labor Review,* Vol. 120, no. 12, December 1997, p. 40.

Britannica Online. "Adkins v. Children's Hospital." http://www.eb.com:180/cgi-bin/g?DocF=micro/5/59.html

U.S. Department of Labor. "The Women's Bureau: An Overview 1920–1997." http://www.dol.gov/dol/wb/public/info_about_wb/interwb.htm

WEST COAST HOTEL V. PARRISH

Legal Citation: 300 U.S. 379 (1937)

Appellant
West Coast Hotel Company

Appellee
Elsie Parrish

Appellant's Claim
That Parrish was not due back pay to bring her up to the level she would have received under Washington's 1913 minimum wage law.

Chief Lawyers for Appellant
John W. Roberts, E. L. Skeel

Chief Lawyers for Appellee
C. B. Conner, Sam M. Driver

Justices for the Court
Louis D. Brandeis, Benjamin N. Cardozo, Charles Evans Hughes (writing for the Court), Owen Josephus Roberts, Harlan Fiske Stone

Justices Dissenting
Pierce Butler, James Clark McReynolds, George Sutherland, Willis Van Devanter

Place
Washington, D.C.

Date of Decision
29 March 1937

Decision
The public interest in setting a minimum wage for women and children is more important than freedom of contract.

Significance
In one of the rare instances in which the Supreme Court overruled one of its own precedents, *West Coast Hotel v. Parrish* set the stage for the passage of the Fair Labor Standards Act of 1938.

In the late nineteenth century, many Americans believed women were a separate class from men—physically, economically, and socially. Wisconsin, presuming females were "handicapped for motherhood" by working long hours, passed the first "hour law" for women in 1867. The statute limited the workday of women to ten hours. By 1907, 20 states had passed similar laws. Five years later, Massachusetts passed the nation's first minimum wage law, and over the next two years 14 states did the same.

Protective legislation regulating hours and wages clashed with the nineteenth century understanding of liberty, specifically the right to contract one's labor, called "liberty of contract." Many felt the Constitution guaranteed this right in Article I, Section 10 and in the Fifth and Fourteenth Amendments. The two ideas clashed dramatically in 1905, with *Lochner v. New York,* and in 1908, with *Muller v. Oregon.*

Most employers and male workers fought change. Lawyers battled in the courtrooms over whether or not "liberty of contract" meant starvation wages for women and children. In both 1923's *Adkins v. Children's Hospital* and 1936's *Morehead v. New York ex rel. Tipaldo,* the Supreme Court had upheld "freedom of contract." In *Morehead,* which invalidated New York's minimum wage law for women and children, the Court had ruled that *any* minimum wage law denied due process.

A Test Case

The Great Depression of the 1930s heated up the debate. Reformers fixed their hopes on Elsie Parrish—a grandmother. In 1933, she had gone to work as a chambermaid at the Cascadian Hotel in Wenatchee, Washington. When her job ended, the hotel offered her $17 for the balance of her services. Parrish and her husband knew that the state's minimum wage law for women (1913) had set wages at a minimum of $14.50 a week—adequate "for the decent maintenance of women" and "not detrimental to health and morals." Women could work no more than 48 hours a week.

The couple sued the hotel for $216.19 back pay due under the new scale. Parrish lost in county court, but the Washington Supreme Court upheld the minimum

James Clark McReynolds

James Clark McReynolds (1862—1946), an associate justice on the U.S. Supreme Court from 1914 until 1941, grew up in an area of Kentucky characterized by frontier based individualism. McReynolds' strictly religious parents gave him a sharply defined sense of right and wrong. Later at the University of Virginia, a law professor reinforced this ethic by teaching the law as a permanent, inflexible entity.

McReynolds practiced corporate law in Nashville from 1884 to 1903, when the city enjoyed great economic expansion. There he developed a legal philosophy that favored the rights of business individuals.

McReynolds worked as assistant U.S. attorney general, and later U.S. attorney general, before President Woodrow Wilson appointed him to the Supreme Court. In his judicial opinions, McReynolds supported individual contractual and business rights, opposed monopolies, and strictly limited the federal government to the powers enumerated in the U.S. Constitution. In a noteworthy dissent in the Gold Clause cases in 1935, which marked the end of the gold standard for American currency, McReynolds remarked that the Constitution as he knew it was "gone."

McReynolds, however, had unkind words for female lawyers, Jews, and African Americans, who curiously did not receive protection as individuals in his judicial opinions.

Source(s): Cushman, Clare, ed. *The Supreme Court Justices: Illustrated Biographies, 1789–1993.* Washington, DC: Congressional Quarterly Inc., 1993.

Friedman, Leon, and Fred L. Israel, eds. *The Justices of the U.S. Supreme Court 1789-1969: Their Lives and Major Opinions.* New York: Chelsea House Publishers, 1969.

---

wage law and ordered payment. The West Coast Hotel Company appealed to the Supreme Court, basing its arguments on *Adkins v. Children's Hospital.* The appeal raised a dilemma for the Court: Whether in the middle of the depression the justices should reverse their decision in *Adkins* and protect working people.

E. L. Skeel, representing West Coast Hotel, went to the heart of the matter: The state could not deprive citizens of their right to contract their labor by passing wage or hour laws. He mocked the idea that lawmakers could get away with this by using the police power of the state. Parrish's side countered this assertion by claiming that the act was a valid and reasonable exercise of the state's police power. Citing *Radice v. New York* (1924), attorneys C. B. Conner and Sam M. Driver claimed the legislature had the right to decide what conditions were of public concern and how best to remedy them.

In delivering the opinion of the majority, Chief Justice Hughes reviewed the minimum wage law of the state of Washington.

> Women and minors [must] be protected from conditions of labor which have a pernicious effect on their health and morals . . . Inadequate wages and unsanitary conditions of labor exert such pernicious effect.

> It shall be unlawful to employ women or minors in any industry or occupation . . . under conditions . . . detrimental to their health or morals; . . . to employ women workers in any industry . . . at wages which are not adequate for their maintenance.

> There is hereby created a commission to be known as the "industrial Welfare Commission" . . . to establish such standards of wages and conditions of labor for women and minors . . .

Hughes then turned his attention to whether the Washington law violated a person's freedom of contract. He denied that the Constitution protected freedom of contract. "It speaks of liberty and prohibits the deprivation of liberty without due process of law. But the liberty safeguarded requires the protection of law against the evils which menace the health, safety, morals and welfare of the people." With these few words he rejected an absolute right of freedom of contract where a strong public interest could be shown.

> What can be closer to the public interest than the health of women and their protection from unscrupulous and overreaching employers? And if the protection of women is a legitimate end . . . payment of a minimum wage fairly fixed . . . is not admissible to that end? The legislature was clearly entitled to consider the situation of women in employment, the fact that they are in a class receiving the least pay, that their bargaining power is relatively weak, and that they are the ready victims of those who would take advantage of their necessitous circumstances. The legislature was entitled to

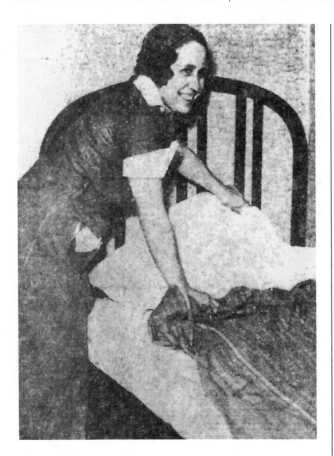

Elsie Parrish makes a bed at Omak Hotel, 1937. © North Central Washington Museum, Wenatchee, Washington.

adopt measures to reduce the evils of the "sweating system," the exploiting of workers at wages so low as to be insufficient to meet the bare cost of living, thus making their very helplessness the occasion of a most injurious competition.

Finally, Hughes said that when women endured exploitation their health suffered, which "casts a direct burden for their support upon the community. What these workers lose in wages the taxpayers are called upon to pay. The bare cost of living must be met."

Justice Sutherland wrote the dissent. In a curiously modern voice foreshadowing modern feminist arguments, he asked,

> Does the legislation here involved . . . create an arbitrary discrimination? We think it does. Difference of sex affords no reasonable ground for making a restriction applicable to the wage contracts of all working women from which like contracts of all working men are left free. Certainly the suggestion that the bargaining ability of the average woman is not equal to that of the average man would lack substance. The ability to make a fair bargain, as everyone knows, does not depend on sex.

A Close Vote

On 29 March 1937, by a 5-4 vote the Supreme Court upheld the minimum wage law in Washington, ordering the West Coast Hotels Company to pay Parrish the money owed plus court costs. She declared, "I'm not sure I understand all the things but I'm glad its all over."

Two months after *West Coast Hotel v. Parrish*, 16 states added minimum wage laws to their books. The decision was the beginning of the end of strict judicial adherence to "freedom of contract," which had given employers an advantage probably needed earlier. It also paved the way for the passage of the Fair Labor Standards Act, which one year later extended a minimum wage to workers regardless of gender.

The Fair Labor Standards Act, also called the Wages and Hours Law, established a federal minimum wage of 40 cents per hour and a maximum work week of 40 hours. It extended to men the benefits women had already won. The act prohibited employing children under the age of 16 and the hiring of 16- to 18-year-olds in hazardous occupations. The law applied only to enterprises that engaged in or affected interstate commerce, specifically exempting many other occupations, such as domestic, seasonal, agricultural, and professional jobs.

West Coast Hotel v. Parrish has been called "the switch in time that saved nine" because had the Court not overruled itself, President Franklin D. Roosevelt—angry that the Court had voided much of his New Deal legislation—would have "packed" it. Six of his own appointees would then have joined the other nine members in a blatant attempt to manipulate the Court's decisions.

Related Cases

Lochner v. New York, 198 U.S. 45 (1905).
Muller v. Oregon, 208 U.S. 412 (1918).
Adkins v. Children's Hospital, 261 U.S. 525 (1923).
Morehead v. New York ex rel. Tipaldo, 298 U.S. 587 (1936).
United States v. Darby, 312 U.S. 100 (1941).

Bibliography and Further Reading

Cushman, Robert E. *Leading Constitutional Decisions.* New York: Appleton-Century-Crofts, 1958.

Hoff, Joan. *Law, Gender, and Injustice: A Legal History of U.S. Women.* New York: New York University Press, 1991.

Johnson, John W., ed. *Historic U.S. Court Cases, 1690–1990: An Encyclopedia.* New York: Garland Publishing, 1992.

Kanowitz, Leo. *Women and the Law: The Unfinished Revolution.* Albuquerque: University of New Mexico Press, 1969.

Otten, Laura A. *Women's Rights and the Law.* Westport, CT: Praeger, 1993.

Tribe, Lawrence H. *American Constitutional Law,* 2d ed. Mineola, NY: The Foundation Press, 1992.

MULFORD V. SMITH

Legal Citation: 307 U.S. 38 (1939)

Appellant
James H. Mulford

Appellee
Nat Smith

Appellant's Claim
That penalties under the Agricultural Adjustment Act of 1938 for overproduction are unconstitutional.

Chief Lawyers for Appellant
A. J. Little, L. E. Heath

Chief Lawyer for Appellee
Omer W. Franklin

Justices for the Court
Hugo Lafayette Black, Felix Frankfurter, Charles Evans Hughes, Stanley Forman Reed, Owen Josephus Roberts (writing for the Court), Harlan Fiske Stone

Justices Dissenting
Pierce Butler, James Clark McReynolds (Louis D. Brandeis did not participate)

Place
Washington, D.C.

Date of Decision
17 April 1939

Decision
The Supreme Court upheld the Agricultural Adjustment Act of 1938.

Significance
Justice Roberts, who had written the opinion striking down the first Agricultural Adjustment Act, *United States v. Butler* (1936), also wrote the opinion here. His change in attitude is a vivid illustration of the important role he played as a swing vote on the Court.

James H. Mulford was a tobacco producer who had been fined under the terms of the Agricultural Adjustment Act of 1938, a piece of legislation that was part of President Franklin Roosevelt's New Deal agenda for combatting the Great Depression. Under the terms of the act, the federal government set a production quota for each tobacco grower. If a grower exceeded this amount, the tobacco auction warehouseman—in this case, Nat Smith—was obliged to penalize the grower. The purpose of this scheme was to prevent tobacco growers from "dumping" their product and disordering the market, thus adding to the economic chaos that held sway throughout the country.

Mulford sued in the District Court for the Middle District of Georgia, challenging the federal act. After the district court upheld the penalty levied against him, Mulford took his case to the U.S. Supreme Court.

Justice Roberts Reverses Himself

Owen J. Roberts had often been a swing vote on the Court during the early years of the New Deal. From 1933 to 1937, the Court was dominated by justices who were holdovers from earlier, highly conservative Courts that believed, above all things, in the *laissez faire* approach to economic matters. That is, they believed that the federal government should not interfere in the marketplace. With the onset of the Great Depression in 1929, however, this became a dangerous attitude— at least in the eyes of Roosevelt and other New Dealers. For the first five years he was in office, Roosevelt found the Supreme Court opposed to nearly every major piece of legislation he proposed.

One of these rejected statutes was the Agricultural Adjustment Act of 1933, which the Court struck down by a vote of 6-3 in *United States v. Butler,* for which Justice Roberts wrote the majority opinion. The next year, the standoff between Roosevelt and the Courts reached a climax when the president proposed a plan to "pack" the Court with justices who would pass his New deal legislation. In 1937—perhaps partly in response to this threat—Roberts softened his attitude towards the New Deal, and in *West Coast Hotel v. Parrish* (1937), he joined the 5-member majority to become the deciding vote

---

Swing Vote

A swing vote refers to a minority interest or neutral segment of the voters that combines its voting power with that of other minority interests or that of majority interests, creating a controlling interest. The swing vote comes into play in the state and federal supreme courts when justices vote whether to uphold or strike down the rulings of lower courts. Justices considered swing voters often make the difference in close and controversial decisions. These justices sometimes hold views that fall in the middle of the political spectrum, that is, in between liberal and conservative or in between Democratic and Republican views. Since the U.S. Supreme Court includes nine justices and rulings are made based on majority votes, the swing voter makes the difference in 5-4 votes. Many legal scholars characterized Justice Byron R. White (1962-1993), for example, as a swing voter.

Source(s): Lance Liebman "Swing Man on the Supreme Court." *The New York Times*, 8 October 1972.

---

upholding a state minimum wage law modeled on New Deal principles. Thus he performed what has come to be known as the "switch in time that saved nine"—nine justices, that is.

Thereafter, Roberts—and the Court—consistently voted to uphold major New Deal legislation. No more vivid illustration of his reorientation exists than *Mulford,* in which Roberts, again writing for the Court, now upheld the second Agricultural Adjustment Act as an appropriate exercise of Congress's commerce power:

> Any rule, such as that embodied in the Act, which is intended to foster, protect, and conserve . . . commerce, or to prevent the flow of commerce from working harm to the people of the nation, is within the competence of Congress . . . The motive of Congress in exerting the power is irrelevant to the validity of the legislation . . . The provisions of the Act under review constitute a regulation of interstate and foreign commerce within the competency of Congress under the power delegated to it by the Constitution.

Roberts, and a majority of the members of the Hughes Court, now admitted that they were confronting an economic emergency that was national in scope and required national legislative remedies. Their weapon of choice in combatting the Depression would remain Congress's power to regulate interstate commerce. Holdouts remained on the Court—James C. McReynolds had the dubious distinction of never voting to uphold New Deal legislation—but Roberts was not among them.

Related Cases
United States v. Butler, 297 U.S. 1 (1936).
West Coast Hotel v. Parrish, 300 U.S. 379 (1937).

Bibliography and Further Reading
Badger, Anthony J. *Prosperity Road: The New Deal, Tobacco, and North Carolina.* Chapel Hill: University of North Carolina Press, 1980.

Maidment, R. A. *The Judicial Response to the New Deal: The U.S. Supreme Court and Economic Regulation, 1934–1936.* New York, NY: Manchester University Press, 1991.

Saloutos, Theodore. *The American Farmer and the New Deal.* Ames: University of Iowa Press, 1982.

HAGUE V. COMMITTEE FOR INDUSTRIAL ORGANIZATION

Legal Citation: 307 U.S. 496 (1939)

Petitioner
Frank Hague

Respondent
Committee for Industrial Organization

Petitioner's Claim
That city officials' use of ordinances requiring permits for public meetings and public distribution of literature intentionally and unconstitutionally interfered with union activities.

Chief Lawyers for Petitioner
Charles Hershenstein, Edward J. O'Mara, James A. Hamill

Chief Lawyers for Respondent
Morris L. Earnst, Spaulding Frazer

Justices for the Court
Hugo Lafayette Black, Charles Evans Hughes, Stanley Forman Reed, Owen Josephus Roberts (writing for the Court), Harlan Fiske Stone

Justices Dissenting
Pierce Butler, James Clark McReynolds (Felix Frankfurter and William O. Douglas did not participate)

Place
Washington, D.C.

Date of Decision
5 June 1939

Decision
By a vote of 5-2, the Supreme Court struck down the ordinances as violative of the rights of free speech and peaceable assembly.

Significance
Hague marked the first time that the First Amendment was used to prevent government suppression of expressive activity. It served to open public areas like parks and streets to free discussion.

In the 1930s, Jersey City, New Jersey, passed a city ordinance requiring groups advocating civil disobedience or overthrow of the government to obtain a permit from the chief of police before they could publicly meet or distribute literature in public places. In 1937, when representatives from the Congress of Industrial Organizations (the CIO) arrived in Jersey City to urge workers to exercise their right to organize—newly granted by the National Labor Relations Act (1935)—the ordinance was used as an excuse to arrest the labor leaders and run them out of town. Various groups representing organized labor were also repeatedly denied permits to hold meetings or hand out printed information on grounds that their members were Communists.

Then, with the aid of the American Civil Liberties Union (ACLU), these groups, collectively called the Committee for Industrial Organization, sued Mayor Frank Hague and other Jersey City officials in federal district court. Alleging that their First Amendment rights of free speech and free assembly had been violated, the groups won an injunction preventing enforcement of the ordinances. After the injunction was upheld by the U.S. Third Circuit Court of Appeals, Hague and other Jersey City executives petitioned the U.S. Supreme Court for review of this finding.

Justices Uphold a Right of Access to Public Places

The seven justices who participated in deciding *Hague* agreed that the ordinance was unconstitutional and the injunction should be upheld, although they disagreed about the reasons for doing so. After Justice Butler announced the decision of the Court, Justices Roberts and Stone delivered the two main concurring opinions. Justice Roberts saw the public areas where the committee members wished to gather as public forums protected by the First Amendment. The right to assemble there and freely discuss whatever they wished was, he reasoned, among the privileges extended to citizens by the Privileges and Immunities Clause of the Fourteenth Amendment:

> Although it has been held that the Fourteenth Amendment created no rights in citizens of

Frank Hague. © The Library of Congress.

the United States, but merely secured existing rights against state abridgment, it is clear that the right to peaceably assemble and discuss these topics, and to communicate respecting them, whether orally or in writing, is a privilege inherent in citizenship of the United States which the Amendment protects.

Justice Stone, while agreeing that the ordinance violated constitutional guarantees of freedom of speech and association, located those guarantees elsewhere in the Fourteenth Amendment:

> It has been explicitly and repeatedly affirmed by this Court, without a dissenting voice, that freedom of speech and of assembly for any lawful purpose are rights of personal liberty secured to all persons, without regard to citizenship, by the due process clause of the Fourteenth Amendment.

Justice Stone's broader view of freedom of speech and assembly as extending to all, regardless of citizenship status, would later be adopted by the Court as a whole. *Hague* also had the effect of providing organized labor with constitutional protection for the first time. It served as a deterrent to public officials accustomed to exercising their power arbitrarily or in a deliberately discriminatory fashion. Perhaps most importantly, this decision marked the first time that the First Amendment was used to prevent government suppression of expressive activity rather than merely to prevent criminal prosecution for such activity after the fact. In the aftermath of the decision, public areas such as streets and parks were universally recognized as arenas for the free exchange of ideas, regardless of the political content of those ideas.

Related Cases
United States v. Cruikshank, 92 U.S. 542 (1875).
Cox v. New Hampshire, 312 U.S. 569 (1941).

Bibliography and Further Reading
Abernathy, M. Glenn. *The Right of Assembly and Association,* 2nd ed. Columbia: University of South Carolina Press, 1981.

Forbath, William E. *Law and the Shaping of the American Labor Movement.* Cambridge, MA: Harvard University Press, 1991.

Tomlins, Christopher L. *The State and the Unions: Labor Relations, Law, and the Organized Labor Movement in America, 1880–1960.* New York, NY: Cambridge University Press, 1985.

POLLOCK V. WILLIAMS

Legal Citation: 322 U.S. 4 (1944)

The Thirteenth Amendment officially abolished slavery and any form of involuntary servitude. The amendment also gave Congress the power to enact laws to enforce those provisions. To address involuntary servitude, Congress passed the Peonage Abolition Act of 1867. Congress defined peonage as forcing someone to work in order to extract payments for a debt. In the twentieth century, the Supreme Court heard a number of cases, all originating in the South, that defined peonage more broadly, and struck at the heart of any system of forced labor (other than in prisons).

After Reconstruction, many southern states tried to limit employment opportunities for African Americans. Without special licenses, African Americans were often limited to farm work, and to get those jobs they had to sign labor contracts. Some laws made it a crime for workers to break their contracts, or forced them to pay off debts to their employers by working off what they owed. In *Bailey v. Alabama* (1911), the Court said states could not make it a crime for a worker to break a labor contract. At that time, Florida had a similar statute, and it passed a revised version in 1919.

The Florida law said contract workers who received money from an employer and then did not honor their contract were committing fraud and would be charged with a misdemeanor. If someone arrested under the law refused to pay back the money or honor the contract, that was *prima facie,* or implied, proof of fraudulent intent. Since African Americans and migrant workers were typically forced to sign labor contracts and often received advances on their wages, the law was implicitly directed at them.

Emanuel Pollock's $5 Debt

In October of 1942, Emanuel Pollock, a resident of Brevard County, Florida, agreed to work for J. V. O'Albora. Pollock, an illiterate African American laborer, received a $5 advance from O'Albora. Three months later, Pollock was charged and convicted for breaking the 1919 Florida statute. Pollock did not have a lawyer during the trial and said he did not understand the charges against him; nevertheless, he pleaded guilty, admitting he had quit his job without repaying the $5 and had no money to pay it back. The trial judge ordered Pol-

Appellant
Emanuel Pollock

Appellee
H. T. Williams

Appellant's Claim
That a Florida law regarding the failure to perform labor after receiving an advance was unconstitutional, under the Thirteenth Amendment.

Chief Lawyer for Appellant
Raymer R. Maguire

Chief Lawyer for Appellee
John C. Wynn

Justices for the Court
Hugo Lafayette Black, William O. Douglas, Felix Frankfurter, Robert H. Jackson (writing for the Court), Frank Murphy, Owen Josephus Roberts, Wiley Blount Rutledge

Justices Dissenting
Stanley Forman Reed, Harlan Fiske Stone

Place
Washington, D.C.

Date of Decision
10 April 1944

Decision
Upheld appellant's claim.

Significance
The Court, drawing on its reasoning in previous "peonage" cases, ruled that the Florida law had a coercive effect. Under the law, a person who failed to honor a work contract could be arrested for fraud, even if the accused had no intent to commit fraud. The ruling offered further legal protection to rural, southern African Americans, who were the target of the peonage laws.

lock to serve 60 days in jail, since he could not pay a $100 fine. Pollock was placed in the custody of H. T. Williams, sheriff of Brevard County.

On 11 January 1943, the county circuit court ordered Williams to release Pollock, ruling that the Florida statute was unconstitutional. The state supreme court, however, reversed the lower court's order, and *Pollock v. Williams* went to the Supreme Court.

On a 7-2 vote, the Court struck down the Florida law, saying that the Florida Supreme Court had misread the precedents on the matter. In his opinion, Justice Jackson traced the history of federal attempts to end peonage, starting with the Thirteenth Amendment. He also pointed out the attempt by various states to circumvent the intent of the Antipeonage Act. "The present Act," he wrote, "is the latest of a lineage, in which its antecedents were obviously associated with the practice of peonage."

A key point in the Florida Supreme Court's decision had been the *prime facie* section of the 1919 law. The court ruled that since Pollock pleaded guilty, the implied guilt defined by that part of the statute was not relevant. Jackson, however, disagreed. According to the facts of the case, Jackson said, "the crime cannot be gleaned from the record." The law, under its *prima facie* provision, "purported to supply the element of intent." By pleading guilty, Pollock only went along with what the law already seemed to dictate. The presumption of Pollock's intent to defraud was written in the law, and this presumption "had a coercive effect in producing the plea of guilty."

Jackson seemed to show some impatience with the Florida legislature's use of the *prima facie* tacit as a way to pin criminal guilt on someone who broke a labor contract:

> As we have seen, Florida persisted in putting upon its statute books a provision creating a presumption of fraud from the mere non-performance of a contract for labor service three times after the courts ruled that such a provision violates the prohibition against peonage . . . The undoubted aim of the Thirteenth Amendment as implemented by the Antipeonage Act was not merely to end slavery but to maintain a system of completely free and voluntary labor throughout the United States . . . Congress has put it beyond debate that no indebtedness warrants a suspense of the right to be free from compulsory service. This congressional policy means that no state can make the quitting of work any component of a crime . . .

Chief Justice Stone and Justice Reed dissented. Reed, in his dissent, argued that the Court had placed too much emphasis on the *prima facie* portion of the law, using its supposed unconstitutionality to strike down the entire law. Reed wrote that the first part of the law was valid: states have a right to criminally punish fraud in a labor contract, just as they might with other types of fraud. The Court however, has not wavered since *Pollock* from its attacks on any form of peonage.

Related Cases

Bailey v. Alabama, 219 U.S. 219 (1911).
Whitney v. California, 274 U.S. 357 (1927).

Bibliography and Further Reading

Biskupic, Joan, and Elder Witt, eds. *Guide to the U.S. Supreme Court.* Washington, DC: Congressional Quarterly, Inc., 1997.

Elliott, Stephen P., ed. *A Reference Guide to the U.S. Supreme Court.* New York: Facts on File Publications, 1986.

Hall, Kermit L., ed. *The Oxford Companion to the Supreme Court of the United States.* New York: Oxford Press, 1992.

New York Times, April 11, 1944.

GLIDDEN COMPANY V. ZDANOK, ET AL.

Legal Citation: 370 U.S. 530 (1962)

Petitioner
Durkee Famous Foods Division of the Glidden Company

Respondent
Zdanok, et al.

Petitioner's Claim
That the original ruling against Durkee was improperly constituted because a U.S. Court of Claims judge, rather than a Circuit Court judge, had sat on the court when it heard the case.

Chief Lawyer for Petitioner
Chester Bordeau

Chief Lawyer for Respondent
Morris Shapiro

Justices for the Court
William J. Brennan, Jr., Tom C. Clark, Arthur Goldberg, John Marshall Harlan II (writing for the Court), Potter Stewart, Earl Warren, Byron R. White

Justices Dissenting
Hugo Lafayette Black, William O. Douglas

Place
Washington, D.C.

Date of Decision
25 June 1962

Decision
That the U.S. Court of Claims judge had been entitled to sit on the circuit court case; the Court refused to consider any other aspect of the case, letting stand the circuit court judgment that workers from a closed-down plant did indeed have seniority rights at the next new plant that the company opened.

Significance
The circuit court case established that workers have seniority rights at other plants in addition to the one where they originally worked. The Supreme Court decision established that U.S. Court of Claims judges were entitled to sit on the circuit court.

Glidden Company v. Zdanok, et al. is one of those cases in which the procedures of the courts are just as important as the actual subject of the case. The history of the *Glidden* case began in 1957 when the Durkee Famous Foods Division of the Glidden Company closed a plant in Elmhurst, Queens (one of the five boroughs of New York City). Soon after, Durkee opened a new plant in Bethlehem, Pennsylvania.

The Durkee plant in Elmhurst had been unionized, and workers there had established seniority rights. Seniority means that decisions about who to lay off are based not on the preference of the manager, but on the length of time someone had been working at the plant. The workers who have been at the plant the longest are the last to be laid off and the first to be rehired.

Management Rights vs. Seniority

The workers at the Durkee plant claimed that their seniority rights applied to the new plant that Durkee opened when they closed the one in Elmhurst. From the management's point of view, this was an infringement of their rights, forcing them to hire workers and then to give them seniority rights at the new company. (Seniority rights often apply to other issues besides layoffs, such as choice of vacation dates, choice of shifts, right to have holidays off, etc. . . . .)

Workers and managers from the Durkee Food Division fought about this issue in the Second Circuit Court of Appeals in New York. That court eventually ruled that the workers did indeed have seniority rights at Durkee's new factory in Bethlehem. However, there was something unusual about the second circuit court at the time. On the bench sat Judge Joseph W. Madden, who was not actually a federal circuit court judge but one from the U.S. Court of Claims.

Ruling on the Judge

The Durkee company's parent corporation, Glidden Company, objected to the fact that Judge Madden had sat in on the case. They claimed that his participation made the circuit court's ruling invalid, and they asked the Supreme Court to consider their case on that basis.

The Court did agree to hear the case, but only the part that concerned Judge Madden. From the outset, they refused to rule on the seniority issue. If they found that Judge Madden should not have been involved, the case would go back for another hearing to the circuit court. If they found that Judge Madden's participation had been constitutional, the circuit court decision would stand.

Article I and Article III

The Glidden Company's objection to Judge Madden's participation was based on the distinction the Constitution makes between the judicial and the legislative branches of government. The judicial branch—the Supreme Court plus the federal court system—is established in Article III of the Constitution. The legislative branch—Congress—is established in Article I.

Federal judges are appointed by the president and subject to the approval of the Senate. Under these circumstances, however, there is the question of what guarantees the independence of the judiciary. If judges are constantly worried about being fired, they may be more concerned about pleasing their employers than about rendering justice. Likewise, if judges are worried about their salaries, their decisions may be based on the wish to please rather than on their best understanding of the law.

Therefore, Article III of the U.S. Constitution builds in two important protections for federal judges:

> The judges, both of the Supreme and inferior courts, shall hold their offices during good behavior, and shall at stated times, receive for their services, a compensation, which shall not be diminished during their continuance in office.

In other words, unless a judge is guilty of "bad behavior"—judicial misconduct such as taking bribes or showing bias—that judge's job is guaranteed for life. Also, as long as that judge stays in office, his or her salary cannot be reduced. No disgruntled president or senator can threaten a federal judge with being fired or even with getting a cut in pay.

The U.S. Court of Claims is a very different type of court, and its judges work under a different system. The Court of Claims was set up in 1855 to relieve Congress from having to hear about private citizens' claims on the federal government. For example, if a widow of a veteran thought she should receive the veteran's pension, she might bring a claim against the federal government. In 1854, Congress would have had to consider that claim. In 1855, the Court of Claims could render a decision.

Congress is established by Article I of the Constitution. For that reason, the Court of Claims is considered an "Article I" court, while the Supreme Court and the federal circuit court system are considered "Article III" courts.

The Glidden Company argued that Judge Madden did not have constitutional Article III protections. Therefore, the possibility existed that he might not render as impartial a decision as an Article III judge. Theoretically, he could be threatened with the loss of his job or a cut in his pay.

In their suit, the Glidden Company never suggested that Judge Madden had not done a good job. Rather, they said that they had the right to an Article III judge. Because they had not gotten one, they considered their case invalid.

What Protection Does a Judge Need?

As a matter of fact, Congress has passed laws guaranteeing that Article I judges have their jobs for life. Therefore, a majority of the Supreme Court ruled that Judge Madden's participation on the circuit court was perfectly acceptable. The Court cited the high regard in which they held the court of claims, as well as the fact that claims court judges' jobs are protected.

Justice Douglas and Black dissented. In their opinion, Article III and Article I courts should never be confused. True, Article I judges held their jobs for life, but this was only because Congress had passed a bill saying so. There was nothing stopping Congress from repealing this legislation if it chose. Moreover, the dissenters said, Article I judges did not have protection for their salaries. Only a constitutional amendment, guaranteeing both their jobs and their salaries, would make them as independent as Article III judges, and would therefore empower them to hear cases in federal circuit court.

The dissenters also suggested that Article I judges had different qualifications from Article III judges. As Justice Douglas wrote in his decision, "Men [sic] of highest quality chosen as Article I judges might never pass muster for Article III courts when tested by their record of tolerance for minorities and for their respect of the Bill of Rights . . ."

Despite these arguments, a majority of the Court chose to affirm Judge Madden's participation on the circuit court. Thus, the *Glidden* decision had two important results: it established workers' seniority rights in more than one plant operated by their companies, and it affirmed the right of Article I judges to make circuit court decisions.

Related Cases

Martin v. Hunter's Lessee, 14 U.S. 304 (1816).
Colegrove v. Green, 328 U.S. 549 (1946).
Baker v. Carr, 369 U.S. 186 (1962).
Stone v. Powell, 428 U.S. 465 (1976).

Michigan v. Long, 463 U.S. 1032 (1987).

Felker v. Turpin, 518 U.S. 1051 (1996).

Bibliography and Further Reading

"Agency Shop Ban Is Left Standing." *New York Times,* October 10, 1961, p. 85.

Biskupic, Joan, and Elder Witt, eds. *Congressional Quarterly's Guide to the U.S. Supreme Court,* 3rd ed. Washington, DC: Congressional Quarterly, Inc., 1996.

"High Court Bars Review of Case on Job Seniority." *New York Times,* October 9, 1962, p. 30.

MARYLAND V. WIRTZ

Legal Citation: 392 U.S. 183 (1968)

Appellants
The states of Maryland, Texas, Alabama, Arizona, Arkansas, Colorado, Delaware, Florida, Hawaii, Illinois, Iowa, Kansas, Maine, Massachusetts, Mississippi, Missouri, Nebraska, New Mexico, North Carolina, North Dakota, Ohio, Oklahoma, South Carolina, South Dakota, Vermont, Virginia, Wyoming; and the Fort Worth [Texas] Independent School District

Appellee
W. Willard Wirtz, U.S. Secretary of Labor, et al.

Appellants' Claim
That the Court should enjoin [prevent] enforcement of the Fair Labor Standards Act as amended in 1966, which required states to meet federal standards for paying minimum wage and overtime in their schools and hospitals.

Chief Lawyers for Appellants
Alan M. Wilner, Assistant Attorney General of Maryland; Charles Alan Wright

Chief Lawyer for Appellee
Erwin N. Griswold, U.S. Solicitor General

Justices for the Court
Hugo Lafayette Black, William J. Brennan, Jr., Abe Fortas, John Marshall Harlan II (writing for the Court), Earl Warren, Byron R. White (Thurgood Marshall did not participate)

Justices Dissenting
William O. Douglas, Potter Stewart

Place
Washington, D.C.

Date of Decision
10 June 1968

Decision
That the Fair Labor Standards Act as amended did indeed apply to state schools and hospitals, and that states should obey the amended provisions and pay minimum wage and overtime.

Significance
Maryland v. Wirtz was an important step in the battle over the nature of federalism—the balance of power between the states and the federal government. This decision clearly established the sovereignty of the federal government, even if a federal ruling could be shown to have harmful effects on the states' ability "to provide for the welfare or necessities of their inhabitants."

When the U.S. Constitution was first submitted to the 13 colonies for ratification, the colonies were concerned about maintaining the autonomy they had enjoyed before the Revolution. For this and other reasons, the states refused to ratify the Constitution until the Bill of Rights was added. The Tenth Amendment to the Constitution specifically addresses the question of states' rights:

> The powers not delegated to the United States by the Constitution, nor prohibited by it to the States, are reserved to the States respectively, or to the people.

One of the most important rights that was delegated to the United States was the right to regulate interstate commerce. The so-called "Commerce Clause," Article I, Section 8 of the Constitution specifies that, "The congress shall have power . . . to regulate commerce . . . among the several States . . ." The tension between the states' rights to govern themselves and the federal government's right to regulate interstate commerce was at the heart of the conflict in *Maryland v. Wirtz*.

Minimum Wage and Overtime

To understand *Maryland v. Wirtz*, it is necessary to go back to 1938, when Congress first passed the Fair Labor Standards Act (FLSA). In its capacity as regulator of interstate commerce, Congress was able to pass some of the first national labor legislation, specifying that any employee "engaged in commerce of in the production of goods for commerce" should receive a minimum wage and overtime pay.

In 1961, Congress widened the coverage of the FLSA. Now it concerned not only those employees directly engaged in interstate commerce, but all employees who worked at enterprises engaged in interstate commerce. In other words, if any part of the company you worked for had to do with interstate commerce, you were entitled to federally set minimum wages and overtime pay, even if you personally had nothing to do with commerce between the states.

In 1966, Congress broadened the FLSA once again. Now it included hospitals, institutions, and schools, which were considered to be involved in interstate commerce by virtue of the fact that they bought, used, and sometimes sold goods made in other states. Moreover, even if these hospitals, institutions, and schools were run by state governments, they were still covered by the FLSA.

Interstate Commerce and Labor Peace

The state of Maryland, soon joined by 27 other states and a school district, challenged this latest expansion of the national labor legislation. It claimed that state-run organizations were beyond Congress' power under the Commerce Clause of the Constitution. They also claimed that the law ran counter to the Eleventh Amendment, which forbade the federal court system to rule on suits between the citizens of two different states. Finally, it argued that even if the Constitution did allow the expanded legislation, schools and hospitals were not engaged in interstate commerce and so should not be included in the act.

The Court ruled 6-2 in favor of Congress' right to pass the FLSA. It offered three major arguments:

(1) The Commerce Clause did indeed enable Congress to regulate the hours and wages of employees working for companies engaged in interstate business. First, it was clear that businesses with lower wages and no overtime enjoyed a competitive advantage over businesses with better wages and working conditions. Without federal legislation, interstate commerce would tend to flow in the direction of those states that paid the least. Therefore, if Congress evened out wages across the states, it was legitimately acting to regulate interstate commerce.

(2) Furthermore, said the Court, Congress had found that "labor peace"—an absence of strikes and other labor disputes—could be better achieved by mandating certain basic standards for workers, such as minimum wages and overtime pay. Labor peace meant that interstate commerce would flow freely, without interruptions caused by strikes or other disturbances. Therefore, Congress could pass minimum-wage legislation and overtime requirements as part of its efforts to regulate interstate commerce.

(3) Although federal and state interests might sometimes conflict, "the State may be forced to conform its activities to federal regulation" when engaging in "economic activities that are validly regulated by the Federal government."

The majority opinion in *Maryland v. Wirtz* caused great dismay among state governments, who claimed that they could not afford to pay the higher wages demanded by the new legislation. On the other hand, the decision was supported by the AFL-CIO and by the American Federation of State, County, and Municipal Employees (AFSCME), the public employees' union, both of whom had joined the federal government with "friend of the court" briefs.

Disrupting the Fiscal Policy of the States

The decision in *Maryland v. Wirtz* also provoked sharp dissent from two Supreme Court justices, Douglas and Stewart. In his minority opinion, Justice Douglas raised the spectre of the federal government disrupting:

> . . . the fiscal policy of the States . . . If constitutional principles of federalism raise no limits to the commerce power where regulation of state activities are concerned . . . could Congress compel the States to build super-highways crisscrossing their territory in order to accommodate interstate vehicles, to provide inns and eating places for interstate travelers, to quadruple their police forces in order to prevent commerce-crippling riots, etc.? Could the Congress virtually draw up each State's budget to avoid disruptive effect[s] . . . on commercial intercourse?

Federal Regulation vs. States' Rights

The decision in *Maryland v. Wirtz* was overturned after only eight years, in a decision called *National League of Cities v. Usery* (1976). The majority in *National League* seemed to agree with the minority in *Wirtz*, finding that a state was not just another entity in the economy

W. Willard Wirtz, U.S. Secretary of Labor. © Archive Photos.

but was a special, independent element that had been given a unique place in the Constitution. Thus in *National League,* the Court held that when federal and state interests collided, federal interests frequently had to give way.

But this decision was overruled again in *Garcia v. San Antonio Metropolitan Transit Authority* (1986). In *Garcia,* the Court appeared to go back to its original finding in *Wirtz:* that with rare exceptions, the Constitution had not given any kind of sacred power to the states.

Garcia built upon *Wirtz,* taking that decision one step further. In *Garcia,* the Court held that states' power lay not in any constitutional guarantees, but in the political process itself. The people of each state could elect men and women to Congress. These representatives would presumably refrain from taking any actions that might hurt the states who had elected them. This is the definition of federalism that still stands, despite critics' fears of a federal policy that might cause economic or other hardships to the states.

Related Cases

National League of Cities v. Usery, 426 U.S. 833 (1976).
Garcia v. San Antonio Metropolitan Transit Authority, 469 U.S. 528 (1985).

Bibliography and Further Reading

Biskupic, Joan, and Elder Witt, eds. *Congressional Quarterly's Guide to the U.S. Supreme Court,* 3rd ed. Washington, DC: Congressional Quarterly, Inc., 1996.

DelMonte, Rosemarie E. "And the States Stand Alone."*Creighton Law Review,* Vol. 19, no. 1, fall 1986, pp. 105–131.

GOLDBERG V. KELLY

Legal Citation: 397 U.S. 254 (1970)

Appellants
John Kelly, et al.

Appellee
Jack R. Goldberg, Commissioner of Social Services of the city of New York

Appellants' Claim
State and city welfare officials were terminating financial aid without prior notice and hearing, violating due process.

Chief Lawyer for Appellants
Lee A. Albert

Chief Lawyer for Appellee
John J. Loflin, Jr.

Justices for the Court
William J. Brennan, Jr. (writing for the Court), John Marshall Harlan II, William O. Douglas, Thurgood Marshall, Harry A. Blackmun, Byron R. White

Justices Dissenting
Hugo Lafayette Black, Warren E. Burger, Potter Stewart

Place
Washington, D.C.

Date of Decision
23 March 1970

Decision
Since New York's public assistance termination procedure did not allow the payment recipients to be heard before the cancellation, it violated the procedural due process.

Significance
Goldberg v. Kelly changed the constitutional opinion regarding traditional distinction between rights and privileges in relation to the Fourteenth Amendment's Due Process Clause.

The Principles Involved

Before *Goldberg v. Kelly*, the Due Process Clause of the Fourteenth Amendment protected U.S. residents in certain situations defined as their legal rights through common law.

Common law refers to governmental principles and courses of action which owe their authority to older bodies of law. In relation to the U.S. Constitution, common law usually refers to governmental procedures handed down from England and the American colonies before the American Revolution. The statutes and case laws subsumed by common law usually apply to those rules and principles having to do with a person's security and the security of property. Common law is in contrast to laws enacted by the legislature. In other words, the Due Process Clause of the Fourteenth Amendment guaranteed some sort of governmental hearing if a person's rights were compromised.

Traditionally, courts, through common law, have interpreted the basic rights of an individual as life, liberty, and property. This was in contrast to a person's privileges or benefits received from the government. If the government denied a "benefit" like public employment, welfare or the like, the Due Process Clause was invalid. No hearing was required. The legal interpretation had been that if the government was providing something it did not have to provide, it could impose any conditions it wanted.

In contrast, there was also an "unconstitutional conditions" doctrine that said even though the government could deny benefits for any given reason, it could not deny these benefits if a person's constitutionally protected interests were violated. That was before *Goldberg v. Kelly*.

During the 1960s especially, it was already becoming apparent that the government had become more of a partner with U.S. residents than previously—to the point where a person's life and security were entangled closely with governmental "privileges," such as licenses of all sorts, social security benefits, employment and welfare.

At least one legal scholar pointed out the necessity of creating a new order of property so that in modern

Procedural Due Process

Procedural due process covers the act of arresting and trying people for crimes as well as other government steps to restrict the life, liberty, and property of people. Procedural due process places limits on the power of state and federal governments, requiring them to follow to specific procedures for arrests and trials. For procedural due process violation claims, courts must ascertain whether the plaintiffs suffered deprivation of life, liberty, and property and to which procedural safeguards they were entitled.

The Bill of Rights outlines these basic procedural protections, which entitle the accused to freedom from being tried for the same crime more than once, freedom from providing self-incriminating evidence and testimony, freedom from cruel and unusual punishment, and freedom from unreasonable searches and seizures. These protections also include the right to be informed of the crime being charged, the right to a fair and speedy public trial by an impartial jury, the right to representation by an attorney, and the right to cross-examine witnesses.

society, these new relationships with the government which had been thought of previously as merely "privileges" or "benefits" would be protected by the safeguards included in the Due Process Clause. In short, the difference between rights and privileges had begun to blur. As this distinction between rights and privileges diminished, another grew to take its place. This would be known as the principle of "entitlement" which became the basis for the Supreme Court to establish a shield of procedural protections to keep the government from erroneously or capriciously depriving a person of something it had given, at its discretion.

With *Goldberg v. Kelly*, the meaning of property—as used in the Due Process Clause—expanded to include welfare benefits, previously thought of as a privilege or benefit.

What Happened

In New York City, a number of residents had been receiving financial aid from the federally-assisted Aid to Families with Dependent Children (ADC) or from New York State's general Home Relief program. With no prior notice, these residents alleged, state and city welfare workers were about to terminate, or had terminated financial aid. Since there had been no prior notice or public hearing, these actions violated the Due Process Clause of the Fourteenth Amendment. The group of New York residents took their case to the U.S. District Court for the Southern District of New York.

When these cases began, no requirement of prior notice or pre-termination hearing existed. After Kelly, et al. began their court actions, the state and city welfare authorities decided to change their procedures. In essence, the authorities (caseworkers) now had to have an informal discussion with a recipient if there were doubts about the recipient's eligibility. Then the welfare recipient received a letter with the reasons for ter-

mination at least seven days before the effective date of termination.

Furthermore, the recipient now had the right to present a written statement to be reviewed by the superior of the administrator who originally approved the termination or suspension. If the superior agreed with the original decision, the benefits would stop immediately. Only then could recipients have the right to a public hearing where they could appear in person, offer oral evidence, confront and cross-examine witnesses, and have public records of the hearing.

Not good enough, said the appellants, who challenged whether these procedures met constitutional guidelines. The district court agreed, saying that a post-termination hearing was constitutionally insufficient. Only a pre-termination hearing would satisfy the Due Process Clause.

State and city officials argued that the informal pre-termination combined with the post-termination hearing dispensed with any due process issues. Of all the defendants, only the Commissioner of Social Services of the City of New York appealed.

In a 5-4 decision, the Supreme Court affirmed the district court's decision. Justice Brennan's opinion held that under the Fourteenth Amendment, procedural due process requirements could only be fulfilled by a pre-termination hearing. Also, the possibility that a truly needy recipient might lose benefits accidentally far outweighed the state's concern about its fiscal and administrative resources.

Finally, according to Brennan's opinion, while the pre-termination hearing did not have to resemble a trial, it needed to meet the minimum procedural requirements of allowing the recipient the opportunity to confront and cross-examine welfare department witnesses, to retain an attorney if so desired, and to be able to present oral evidence to someone impartial, who would make a decision based only on the legalities involved and the evidence produced at the hearing.

Related Cases
Goss v. Lopez, 419 U.S. 565 (1975).
Mathews v. Eldredge, 424 U.S. 319 (1976).

Lockett v. Ohio, 438 U.S. 586 (1978).
Honday v. Oberg, 114 S. Ct. 2331 (1994).

Bibliography and Further Reading
Seidman, Louis M., Gerald R. Stone, Cass R. Sunstein, and Mark V. Tushnet. *Constitutional Law.* Little, Brown and Company, 1986.

NATIONAL LEAGUE OF CITIES v. USERY

Legal Citation: 426 U.S. 833 (1976)

Appellant
National League of Cities, et al.

Appellee
W. J. Usery Jr., U.S. Secretary of Labor

Appellant's Claim
That 1974 congressional amendments to the Fair Labor Standards Act, placing state governments under the authority of minimum wage and maximum hour provisions in the act, constituted a violation of the Tenth Amendment.

Chief Lawyer for Appellant
Charles S. Rhyne

Chief Lawyer for Appellee
Robert Bork, U.S. Solicitor General

Justices for the Court
Harry A. Blackmun, Warren E. Burger, Lewis F. Powell, Jr., William H. Rehnquist (writing for the Court), Potter Stewart

Justices Dissenting
William J. Brennan, Jr., Thurgood Marshall, John Paul Stevens, Byron R. White

Place
Washington, D.C.

Date of Decision
24 June 1976

Decision
That congressional use of the Fair Labor Standards Act to regulate the states' employment policy was unconstitutional because it violated the Tenth Amendment, which reserves for the states all power not delegated to the federal government.

Significance
Although numerous Supreme Court decisions have spawned new interpretations of well-known constitutional amendments such as the First, Fifth, or Fourteenth, *National League of Cities v. Usery* was one of the Court's few cases dealing with the Tenth Amendment. The Court's decision in *Usery* seemed a harbinger of increased authority for state legislatures against the powers of the federal government. *Usery* was also the first decision in some 40 years to restrict the power of the federal government over interstate commerce, a power which had increased significantly under the "New Deal" of President Franklin D. Roosevelt in the 1930s.

A Violation of the Tenth Amendment

In 1938, during a tidal wave of legislative action associated with President Franklin D. Roosevelt's New Deal, Congress passed the Fair Labor Standards Act (FLSA). The FLSA established minimum-wage provisions, requiring employers to pay their workers a certain hourly figure. Likewise, it set the wage scale for overtime, which it defined as anything over 40 hours per week, as one and a half times the regular hourly rate. The Court would later identify the purpose behind the latter provision: to provide a disincentive for employers to keep any one employee on the job more than 40 hours a week. Like much of the legislation arising from those years, the FLSA expanded the power of the federal government over business and industry; as for state, county, and municipal governments, however, the act explicitly excluded these entities from its purview.

Starting in 1961, Congress began to amend the act, extending its provisions to include employees in the public as well as the private sector. In 1966, employees of state hospitals, institutions, and schools were placed under the act, and the Supreme Court recognized the constitutionality of these and the 1961 provisions in its 1968 *Maryland v. Wirtz* ruling. Then in 1974, Congress further amended the act, defining "employer" in such a way that the term would include "a public agency," a designation identified as "the Government of the United States, the government of a State or political subdivision thereof . . ." Thus the wage and hour provisions of the FLSA were extended to include virtually all employees working for states or their political subdivisions.

To state and local governments, and to organizations such as the National League of Cities, the amendment to the FLSA seemed to be a violation of the Tenth Amendment. The latter, the last of the Bill of Rights passed in 1791, states simply that "the powers not delegated to the United States by the Constitution, nor prohibited to it by the States, are reserved to the States respectively, or to the people." Together with the National Governor's Conference and various city and state governments, the National League brought a legal action in the District Court for the District of Columbia. The named respondent was President Gerald R.

Ford's Secretary of Labor, W. J. Usery, Jr., who would later enjoy recognition as the chief negotiator between the owners and the players' union in the 1994 Major League Baseball strike.

In their suit, the appellants asked for declaratory and injunctive relief against the application of the amendments to them. But a three-judge panel ruled in favor of the secretary of labor, and granted his motion to dismiss the complaint due to the appellants' inability to state a claim on which relief might be granted. The district court in its ruling did, however, state that it was "troubled" by the appellants' claims that the amended FLSA would impede their ability to carry on essential government functions, a subject that would later catch the attention of Justice Rehnquist for the Supreme Court. The district court judged these contentions "substantial," and observed that "it may well be that the Supreme Court will feel it appropriate to draw back from the far-reaching implications" of its ruling in *Maryland v. Wirtz*. "But that is a decision," the lower court held, "that only the Supreme Court can make . . ."

So the case came before the Court, designated as *California v. Usery*. The case was argued twice, first on 16 April 1975, and nearly a year later, on 2 March 1976. The appellants on the briefs in the original argument were officials representing the states of Arizona (Bruce Babbitt, future U.S. Senator and later Secretary of the Interior under the Clinton administration), Delaware, Indiana, Iowa, Maryland, Massachusetts, Mississippi, Missouri, Montana, Nebraska, Nevada, New Hampshire (future U.S. Senator Warren Rudman), Oklahoma, Oregon, South Carolina, South Dakota, Texas, Utah, and Wyoming. On behalf of the appellants, the states of Virginia and New York filed briefs of *amici curiae* urging reversal, as did the National Association of Counties, the National Institute of Municipal Law Officers, and the Public Service Research Council. On the other side, briefs urging affirmance were filed by officials representing the states of Alabama, Colorado, Michigan, and Minnesota, as well as the American Federation of Labor and Congress of Industrial Organizations (AFL/CIO), the Coalition of American Public Employees, the International Conference of Police Associations, and the Florida Police Benevolent Association.

The Court Affirms

The Court ruled 5-4 for the appellants. Writing for the majority, Justice Burger held that "insofar as the 1974 amendments operate directly to displace the States' abilities to structure employer-employee relationships in areas of traditional government functions . . . they are not within the authority granted Congress by the Commerce Clause." Quoting from *Fry v. United States* (1975), Rehnquist went on to say that ". . . Congress has sought to wield power in a fashion that would impair the States' 'ability to function effectively in a

federal system'." Therefore, "Congress may not exercise its power to regulate commerce so as to force directly upon the States its choices as to how essential decisions regarding the conduct of integral governmental functions are to be made."

Thus, in upholding *Fry*, the Court overruled *Wirtz*. To explain the steps whereby the Court had reached this decision, Rehnquist began by elucidating the commerce powers granted to Congress under Article I of the Constitution, which he called "a grant of plenary authority." Quoting Chief Justice John Marshall in *Gibbons v. Ogden* (1824), Rehnquist referred to Congress's authority as "the power to regulate; that is, to prescribe the rule by which commerce is to be governed." In *Fry*, the Court had made it clear that "wholly private" activity could be governed: "[e]ven activity that is purely intrastate in character may be regulated by Congress, where the activity . . . affects commerce among the States or with foreign nations." Thus the commerce powers of Congress were unquestionably broad, a fact which the appellants did not dispute. "Their contention, on the contrary," the Court stated, "is that when Congress seeks to regulate directly the activities of States as public employers, it transgresses an affirmative limitation on the exercise of its power akin to other commerce power affirmative limitations contained in the Constitution."

The Court, Rehnquist wrote, "has never doubted that there are limits upon the power of Congress to override state sovereignty." Likewise the appellees had "agreed that our federal system of government imposes definite limits on the authority of Congress to regulate the activities of the States." Indeed, as Rehnquist went on to show, there was a venerable tradition of respect for the bounds of congressional commerce power over the states, and in this vein the Court cited Justice Harlan Fiske Stone's plurality ruling in *New York v. United States,*, wherein the Court held that Congress could not impose taxes on the states.

At the close of its examination of congressional commerce power as compared with that of the states, the Court noted the appellee's argument that "the cases in which this Court has upheld sweeping exercises of authority by Congress . . . have already curtailed the sovereignty of the States quite as much as the 1974 amendments to the Fair Labor Standards Act." The Court did not agree with this contention: "it is one thing to recognize the authority of Congress to enact laws regulating individual businesses," but "it is quite another to uphold a similar exercise of congressional authority directed, not to private citizens, but to the States as States." There was a line which Congress could not cross, "not because Congress may lack an affirmative grant of legislative authority" in a given matter, "but because the Constitution prohibits it from exercising the authority in that manner."

The Court next addressed the issue of the increased costs the states would undergo in complying with the provisions of the amendments. These issues, as the Court indicated, were "not critical to our decision of the case." Nonetheless, it was noted that a number of governments feared the consequences of their inability—due to the drain on their finances imposed by the new wage requirements—to deliver "traditional services" such as fire and police protection. Likewise, affirmative-action programs were threatened by the heightened demands on state and local treasuries. The Court referred to fire and police protection, sanitation, public health, and parks and recreation as "functions . . . which governments are created to provide." Thus, if Congress could impair such functions, "we think there would be little left of the States' 'separate and independent existence.'"

Finally, the Court addressed the appellee's contention that a ruling in favor of the appellants would be inconsistent with *Fry*, in which the Court had upheld the use of the Economic Stabilization Act of 1970 to impose a temporary freeze on the wages of state and local government employees. The difference, the Court indicated, was that *Fry* involved emergency measures, and "the limits imposed upon the commerce power when Congress seeks to apply it to the States are not so inflexible as to preclude temporary enactments tailored to combat a national emergency." As for *Wirtz*, which "relied heavily" on a broad definition of commerce powers in *United States v. California* (1936), the Court overruled its earlier judgment.

Dissent: The Tenth as a "Truism"

Justice Blackmun concurred with the Court, though he expressed reservations: "I am not untroubled," he wrote, "by certain possible implications of the Court's opinion . . . but it seems to me that it adopts a balancing approach, and does not outlaw federal power in areas such as environmental protection, where the federal interest is demonstrably greater" than that of the states. He did not, he wrote, "read the opinion so despairingly as does my Brother Brennan."

The latter offered a sharp dissent, in which Justices Marshall and White joined. Using much of the same material that the Court had cited in its ruling, Brennan found quite a different interpretation. He cited Justice John Marshall, including the latter's opinion in *Gibbons*, as opposing attempts to curtail Congress's commerce power. Just as the Court had found a lengthy tradition of respect for state authority, Brennan found the same history of honor for the power of Congress.

To Brennan, the meaning of the Tenth Amendment with regard to state commerce power was much less profound than it was to the rest of the Court. "My Brethren do not successfully obscure today's patent usurpation of the role reserved for the political process," he wrote, "by their purported discovery in the Constitution of a restraint derived from sovereignty of the States on Congress' exercise of the commerce power." He cited the Court's observation in *United States v. Darby* that "the amendment states but a truism that all is retained which has not been surrendered." In this view, the amendment was not saying anything of great import. Rather, it was simply indicating, to make an analogy, that the portion of the glass that is not full is empty—all powers not delegated are reserved.

Brennan concluded by disagreeing with the Court's holding on nearly every item cited, including *Fry*, *Wirtz*, and the financial burdens imposed on the states under the FLSA. Given the fact that the 1977 budget recommended the disbursement of $60.5 billion in federal assistance to the states, the largest estimate of cost submitted by the appellants—$1 billion—"pales in comparison." In conclusion, Brennan wrote that "We are left with a catastrophic judicial body blow at Congress' power under the Commerce Clause." There was in this, he held, "an ominous portent of disruption of our constitutional structure."

Justice Stevens also offered a dissenting opinion, though his disagreement was much less dramatic. He thought it was wrong to say that "the Federal Government may not interfere with a sovereign State's inherent right to pay a substandard wage to the janitor at the state capitol" when it could impose all manner of other requirements on the state and the janitor, including "[forbidding] him from burning too much soft coal in the capitol furnace, from dumping untreated refuse in an adjacent waterway . . . or from driving either [his] truck or the Governor's limousine over 55 miles an hour." This did not mean he disagreed with the basic viewpoint of the appellants, he indicated, but "my disagreement with the wisdom of this legislation may not . . . affect my judgment with respect to its validity."

Impact

At the time, *National League of Cities v. Usery* seemed a harbinger of a new era of federalism on the part of the Court. There may have been a rising tide of sentiment in favor of state governments, but the decision itself only stood for nine years. In 1985, the Court heard the case of *Garcia v. San Antonio Metropolitan Transit Authority*, which again involved the commerce power of Congress to impose a minimum wage law on a city. The Court upheld the commerce power, thus overturning its ruling in *Usery*. This time Brennan was in the majority, along with fellow *Usery* dissenters Marshall, Stevens, and White. Blackmun, who had earlier indicated reservations about the *Usery* decision, proved to be the swing vote. The dissenting minority was composed of the remaining members of the *Usery* majority, along with Justice Sandra Day O'Connor, who had replaced Justice Stewart. But the final decision had not yet been made with regard to the Tenth Amendment: in *New York v. United States* (1992), the Court again ruled in favor of a state against Congress, finding that a federal mandate involving hazardous waste disposal constituted a violation of congressional power. In the case, O'Connor cited *Wirtz, Usery* and other rulings as indication of the Court's "unsteady path" with regard to Tenth Amendment issues.

Related Cases

Gibbons v. Ogden, 22 U.S. 1 (1824).
United States v. California, 297 U.S. 175 (1936).
United States v. Darby, 312 U.S. 100, 124 (1941).
Maryland v. Wirtz, 392 U.S. 183 (1968).
Fry v. United States, 421 U.S. 542 547 (1975).
Reeves, Inc. v. Stake, 447 U.S. 429 (1980).
Garcia v. San Antonio Metropolitan Transit Authority, 469 U.S. 528 (1985).
New York v. United States, 505 U.S. 144 (1992).

Bibliography and Further Reading

Biskupic, Joan, and Elder Witt. *Guide to the U.S. Supreme Court,* third edition. Washington, DC: Congressional Quarterly Inc., 1997.

Goldstein, Joseph. *The Intelligible Constitution: The Supreme Court's Obligation to Maintain the Constitution as Something We the People Can Understand.* New York: Oxford University Press, 1992.

Gordon, Susan L. " *New York v. United States*: On the Road Back to *National League of Cities* and Substantive Limits on Congress's Commerce Clause Power." *Journal of Energy, Natural Resources & Environmental Law,* Vol. 14, 1994, pp. 83-111.

Hall, Kermit L., ed. *The Oxford Companion to the Supreme Court of the United States.* New York: Oxford University Press, 1992

Kurland, Philip B., ed. *The Supreme Court Review.* Chicago: University of Chicago Press, 1977.

Levy, Leonard W., ed. *Encyclopedia of the American Constitution.* New York: Macmillan, 1986.

Tushnet, Mark V. "Why the Supreme Court Overruled *National League of Cities.*" *Vanderbilt Law Review,* Vol. 47, October 1994, pp. 1623–55.

Witt, Elder. *Congressional Quarterly's Guide to the Supreme Court,* second edition. Washington, DC: Congressional Quarterly Inc., 1990.

Witt, Elder, advisory editor. *The Supreme Court A to Z. CQ's Encyclopedia of American Government,* revised edition. Washington, DC: Congressional Quarterly, Inc., 1994.

GARCIA V. SAN ANTONIO METROPOLITAN TRANSIT AUTHORITY

Legal Citation: 469 U.S. 528 (1985)

Appellant
Joe G. Garcia

Appellee
San Antonio Metropolitan Transit Authority, et al.

Appellant's Claim
That the San Antonio Metropolitan Transit Authority (SAMTA) owed their employees overtime pay according to the Fair Labor Standards Act (FLSA).

Chief Lawyer for Appellant
Laurence Gold

Chief Lawyer for Appellee
William T. Coleman, Jr.

Justices for the Court
Harry A. Blackmun (writing for the Court), William J. Brennan, Jr., Thurgood Marshall, John Paul Stevens, Byron R. White

Justices Dissenting
Warren E. Burger, Sandra Day O'Connor, Lewis F. Powell, Jr., William H. Rehnquist

Place
Washington, D.C.

Date of Decision
19 February 1985

Decision
SAMTA was not immune from overtime and minimum wage requirements set forth in the FLSA and must pay appellant his overtime wages.

Significance
The Court voted in favor of the federal labor standards requiring overtime pay, weakening state and Tenth Amendment rights. In the process the Court reversed a precedent first set by *National League of Cities v. Usery*.

Background to Dispute

When the federal government first designed minimum wage and overtime requirements in 1938, transportation and government employees were exempt. In 1974 Congress enacted amendments to the Federal Labor Standards Act (FLSA) which nullified those exemptions. The San Antonio Transit System, later known as the San Antonio Metropolitan Transit Authority (SAMTA), complied with the requirements until the landmark case *National League of Cities v. Usery* in 1976. In that decision, the Supreme Court ruled that federal attempts to define minimum wage and overtime requirements in "areas of traditional governmental functions . . . are not within the authority granted Congress by the Commerce Clause." As the primary public transportation provider in greater San Antonio, SAMTA abandoned the requirements according to *National League of Cities*. In 1979, the Wage and Hour Administration of the Department of Labor decided SAMTA was not performing a "traditional governmental function" and therefore was beholden to the wage requirements set forth in the FLSA Amendments of 1974. On 21 November 1979, SAMTA filed a suit against the secretary of labor claiming that it should be exempt from the requirements. On the same day, Joe G. Garcia and other SAMTA employees seeking overtime pay filed a civil action suit against SAMTA. The decision of the employees' civil action case was postponed until the Court could ascertain whether SAMTA was exempt from the federal requirements.

SAMTA's case came before the Federal District Court for the Western District of Texas. The issue before the court was whether administering a city transportation system constituted a "traditional governmental function" as stated in *National League of Cities*. Although that case set forth examples of "traditional government function[s]," it did not definitively categorize services that could be considered as such. As a result, there have been several cases before federal and state courts that have turned on the interpretation of a "traditional governmental function." The district court decided that SAMTA did provide a service considered a "traditional governmental function" and was thus immune from federal wage and overtime requirements. In at least three other cases dealing with the same issue, federal courts of appeals held that municipal transportation was not a "traditional governmental function." The district court case was appealed by the secretary of labor, with Joe Garcia appearing on the appellant's behalf. A decision was entered for SAMTA again; the secretary of labor and Joe Garcia entered another appeal.

Case Goes to the U.S. Supreme Court

In considering *Garcia v. San Antonio Metropolitan Transit Authority,* the Supreme Court weighed the viability of the decision first reached in *National League of Cities.* In that case the Court outlined four questions regarding Tenth Amendment and states' rights that should be answered before enforcing wage requirements. These questions addressed violations of state interests and sovereignty. Equally important, according to *National League of Cities,* was whether the service provided could be considered a "traditional governmental function." The Supreme Court threw out this qualification, arguing that any definition of a "traditional governmental function" would be arbitrary and static. Indeed, the framers of the Constitution could not have anticipated many functions performed by state governments in the modern age. The operation of a municipal airport was one example given by the Court. In overturning the *National League of Cities* Justice Blackmun wrote in the majority opinion that any:

> attempt to draw the boundaries of state regulatory immunity in terms of "traditional governmental function" is not only unworkable but is also inconsistent with established principles of federalism.

In essence, the Court refused to judge what could be considered a state's domain in regard to commerce when delivering a public service. The Court acknowledged the volatility of state's rights in light of this decision. Justifying this opinion, the Court explained that there are limits to federal encroachment outlined in the Constitution and they should be sufficient in protecting a state's sovereignty. In this case, the majority concluded, state autonomy is not threatened by the federal overtime requirements and must be honored by SAMTA.

Four Justices Dissent

In the dissenting opinion written by Justice Powell, grave reservations were voiced about the consequences of overturning *National League of Cities.* Most important, the four dissenting justices did not feel that the case presented in *Garcia v. San Antonio Metropolitan Transit Authority* was strong enough to overturn all of the prior decisions based on *National League of Cities.* This argument was bolstered by the fact that the five justices forming the majority opinion in *Garcia* voted

to affirm *National League of Cities* in 1976. In the minority opinion, by refusing to define what constitutes a "traditional governmental function" the Court abdicated its responsibility. The dissenting opinion pointed out that nebulous definitions come before the Court all the time and its express purpose is to strike a balance that would allow the definition to be applied in the future. Furthermore, if the Court does not define traditional state functions, the interpretation will be left up to Congress—exactly what the overturning of *National League of Cities* permits. This clearly contradicts the Tenth Amendment, which was written into the Constitution at the behest of anti-Federalists to protect states' rights. Forcing SAMTA to respect regulations set forth in the FLSA according to the Commerce Clause disabled checks and balances designed by the framers to protect state sovereignty. Citing one of the most famous cases in history, Blackmun stated:

> At least since *Marbury v. Madison,* it has been the province of the federal judiciary "to say what the law is" with respect to the constitutionality of Acts of Congress.

The dissenting justices had additional concers about the effect of overturning *National League of Cities.* With the Commerce Department dictating wage requirements to the states, the latter might base future policy decisions on those federal requirements. State policies that could be affected included municipal budgets, city planning, and tax assessment. However, both Justices O'Connor and Rehnquist predicted in their dissent that the Supreme Court had not heard the last of the *National League of Cities* and Tenth Amendment States' rights issue. In their opinion, the decision reached in *Garcia v. San Antonio Metropolitan Transit Authority.* would eventually be reversed.

Related Cases

Marbury v. Madison, 5 U.S. 137 (1803).
National League of Cities v. Usery, 426 U.S. 833 (1976).

Bibliography and Further Reading

Biskupic, Joan, and Elder Witt, eds. *Congressional Quarterly's Guide to the U.S. Supreme Court,* 3rd ed. Washington, DC: Congressional Quarterly, Inc., 1996.

Cushman, Robert F. *Cases in Constitutional Law,* 7th ed. Englewood Cliffs, NJ: Prentice-Hall, Inc., 1989.

Epstein, Lee, and Thomas G. Walker. *Constitutional Law for a Changing America: Institutional Powers and Constraints,* 3rd ed. Washington DC: Congressional Quarterly, 1998.

Farber, Daniel A. "The Constitution's Forgotten Cover Letter: An Essay on the New Federalism and the Original Understanding." *Michigan Law Review,* December 1995, p. 615.

Hall, Kermit L., ed. *The Oxford Companion to the Supreme Court of the United States.* New York: Oxford University Press, 1992.

Kincaid, John. "Constitutional Federalism: Labor's Role in Displacing Places to Benefit Persons." *PS: Political Science & Politics,* June 1993, p. 172.

Markoe, Jeannine C. "Fair Labor Standards Act: Public Sector Liability." *Government Finance Review,* June 1995, p. 48.

McClay, Wilfred M. "A More Perfect Union? Toward a New Federalism." *Commentary,* September 1995, p. 28.

Mikhail, Sheila A. "Reversing the Tide Under the Commerce Clause." *Journal of Criminal Law and Criminology,* summer 1996, p. 1493.

Orren, Karen. "The Primacy of Labor in American Constitutional Development." *American Political Science Review,* June 1995, p. 377.

Rivkin, David B., Jr., and Lee A. Casey. "Federalism." *Commentary,* December 1996, p. 47.

Wilson, Jerome L. "States Need a Simple Guarantee of Rights." *The National Law Journal,* February 13, 1995, p. A21

LECHMERE, INC. V. NLRB

Legal Citation: 502 U.S. 527 (1992)

Petitioner
Lechmere, Inc.

Respondent
National Labor Relations Board

Petitioner's Claim
That prohibiting distribution of organizational literature and evicting non-employees for trespassing on private parking property was justifiable.

Chief Lawyer for Petitioner
Robert P. Joy

Chief Lawyer for Respondent
Michael R. Dreeben

Justices for the Court
Anthony M. Kennedy, Sandra Day O'Connor, William H. Rehnquist, Antonin Scalia, David H. Souter, Clarence Thomas (writing for the Court)

Justices Dissenting
Harry A. Blackmun, John Paul Stevens, Byron R. White

Place
Washington, D.C.

Date of Decision
27 January 1992

Decision
Lechmere, Inc. did not violate the National Labor Party Act by forbidding communication between non-employee union organizers and (Lechmere) employees on private parking property.

Significance
The main issue confronted in this case was whether rights of employees under provision seven of the National Labor Relations Act superseded the property rights of their employer. The U.S. Supreme Court held that the method of trespass (in this case using the petitioner's parking lot to communicate with their employees by placing hand bills on car windshields) as well as any other alternative, was inappropriate and unlawful. The Court ruled that no "unfair labor practice" occurred when the petitioners barred non-employee union organizers because private property rights were inviolate.

In an effort to organize about 200 employees working in the shopping plaza owned and operated by Lechmere, Inc., the United Food and Commercial Workers Union initiated recruitment operations in the petitioner's parking lot. The union placed leaflets on windshields of cars in a parking zone which they assumed was used by employees. (Prior to this action, advertisements in a local newspaper did not give results; union organizers had found a leaflet strategy practical.) However, Lechmere banned this kind of solicitation on his property, and organizers were asked to leave plaza property. Lechmere removed all the handbills.

Because Lechmere Inc. occupied and operated their shopping plaza in a large metropolitan area, the parking property was separated from an adjacent highway by a 4-foot grassy strip. From that public location, union organizers started to pass out handbills to passing motorists. For one month, the union practiced this mode of informing employees (early in the morning and late in the evening, assuming that passing drivers were primarily store employees) and they picketed Lechmere. However, union efforts were to no avail. Even mailing and phone contact (with approximately 20 percent of Lechmere employees) did not result in more than one signature on a union authorization card.

Unfair Labor Practices Charged

In view of the petitioner's ban on members of non-employee unions from organizing their activities on private corporate property, the firm was sued by the union. The union's suit charged Lechmere with "unfair labor practice" and maintained its ban violated provisions of the National Labor Relations Act. Consequently, the National Labor Relations Board joined the union as a co-respondent. The suit was initially presented to an Administrative Law Judge (ALJ) who held that the petitioner should not ban union organizers from the parking zone. The ALJ also ruled Lechmere should make a public proclamation that representatives of the union would be permitted to distribute their literature to employees and that they would not be limited to access to parking areas. The National Labor Relations Board (NLRB) accepted and approved the recommended order of the ALJ. Lechmere appealed to the U.S. Court of Appeals for the First Circuit, which affirmed the board's ruling. Again, the petitioner appealed to the higher, U.S. Supreme Court and was granted a hearing on *certiorari*.

Section 7 of the National Labor Relations Act (NLRA) stipulates that "employees shall have right to self-organization, to form, join, or assist labor organizations." Further, section 8 recognizes the illegality of an employer engaging in "unfair labor practice . . . to interfere with, restraint, or coerce employees in the exercise of rights guaranteed in (section) 7." These two sections of the NLRA were the legal statutes on which the respondent (the National Labor Relations Board) presented arguments against the petitioner when the case came before the Supreme Court.

Property Rights Upheld

The U.S. Supreme Court majority opinion held that barring non-employee union organizers from access and occupation of corporate property did not represent an "unfair labor practice." The majority decision relied, in part, on *NLRB v. Babcock* (1956), in which a litigant successfully challenged a company ban on a non-employee union from recruiting in a company parking lot. Although that decision recognized the legitimate attempts of unions to organize employees, the Court recognized that the "right to distribute (union literature) is not absolute, but must be accommodated to the circumstances." They explained that circumstances might warrant permission to trespass on private property whenever distribution of "organizational literature" was especially difficult. In *Babcock,* such circumstances were present. Thus the company was ordered to permit organizers access to private company property in order to distribute materials. But, the Court rejected the endorsement of the National Labor Relations Board which directed Lechmere to permit unimpeded access of union organizers to employees on corporate property because "an employer cannot be compelled to allow distribution of union literature by non-employee organizers on his property." The justices felt that the only exception which could mandate requiring an employer to permit access to employees on company property was if employees were "beyond the reach" of information about their right to organize. The Court further cited precedence set in *Central Hardware Co. v. NLRB* (1972) and in *Hudgens v. National Labor Relations Board* (1976) wherein similar sets of circumstances existed (as in the *Lechmere* case). The need to provide "accommodation" of employees rights according to section 7 of the NLRA only superseded an employer's property rights when access to employees was not feasible. Compromise did not have to be discussed when access to employees was otherwise feasible.

Citing the *Babcock* case, the majority justices concluded that the NLRA did not extend protection to non-employee union organizers but rather, applied to exceptional circumstances where "the inaccessibility of employees makes ineffective the reasonable attempts by non-employees to communicate with them through the usual channels." As long as non-employee union organizers had alternative access to employees, the right for employees to self-organize without interference by an employer (according to sections 7 and 8 of the NLRA) was not violated. Moreover, according to *Babcock,* the Court opined that "an employer may validly post his property against non-employee distribution of union literature." Accordingly, the Supreme Court cited two additional reasons why the National Labor Relations Board improperly endorsed lower court rulings. The union had other avenues available for "nontrespassory access" to employees and (according to *Babcock*) there existed no clear evidence that the petitioner's denial of union access to its private property automatically created a circumstance wherein it became unrealistic for the union to reach employees and communicate with them in any other way. Prohibiting trespass on the petitioner's private parking lot did not place employees "beyond the reach," of union organizers since other means of communication were available (mailings, phone calls, home visits, and advertising). Furthermore, since union non-employee organizers had been able to picket at the entrance of the shopping center for a period of time, the Court found the respondent's argument was flawed.

Minority Opinion

Three justices joined in a dissenting opinion which faulted the Court for its ready recognition of the necessity to allow union communication with employees to inform them of the advantages of self-organization despite the fact that non-employee organizers were unable to gain access to private property in order to accomplish that goal. The minority justices felt that the Court's findings were inconsistent and misunderstood the narrow parameters of the *NLRB v. Babcock* decision in 1956. Inaccessibility to employees could not be the only justifiable basis under which labor organizers could demand access to private property. Although the Court felt that picketing and signs on an adjacent and public grassy strip were sufficient, the dissenting justices reasoned that union organizers did not have appropriate access to employees. Rather, balancing the rights of employees against private property rights according to the right of access criteria (established by the National Labor Relations Board) had to be considered regardless of whether alternatives existed which provided a means of communicating with employees. Specifically, the decision to order compliance with the NLRA also depended on determining which effect was most damaging, "the degree of impairment" sustained by employees if access to them was denied a labor organization or "the degree of impairment" sustained by the private property owner if trespass was ordered.

The minority justices reasoned it was inappropriate, according to section 7 of the NLRA, to regard its provisions as applicable only to employees and not to non-employee union organizers. They recognized that the purpose of communicating with employees directly, to appropriately advise and augment self-organization, could not be limited because employees were isolated in the workplace. For that purpose, alternative methods of approach were marginally effective. The dissenting justices also felt that rules pertaining to the right of self-organization and labor organizations made no distinction between employees and non-employees. Finally, they reasoned that strict holdings in *Babcock* were inharmonious with later judgments of the U.S. Supreme Court.

Impact

In rendering its decision in *Lechmere, Inc. v. NLRB* the U.S. Supreme Court held that private property rights could not be superseded even when non-employee organizers engaged in trespassing on private company property to solicit employee involvement in union-sponsored, self-organization. Stressing that the National Labor Relations Act (NLRA) conferred rights only to employees (not to non-employee organizers), the Court produced a ruling which reset boundaries in which organized labor could operate. Lechmere, Inc. (and,

therefore, all employers) could bar union organizers from its property, whenever there existed alternative methods of communication with employees in order to inform them about their rights to organize. Accommodation of efforts by labor unions did not always entail unequivocal access to employer-owned property. The Court explained that "non-employee organizational trespassing had generally been prohibited except where unique obstacles prevented nontrespassory methods of communication." Justices thus held that provisions of the National Labor Relations Act were enforceable only if employees were "beyond the reach of reasonable union efforts to communicate with them." Private property rights otherwise superseded the right of unions efforts to enable self-organization by employees.

Related Cases

NLRB v. Babcock & Wilcox Co., 351 U.S. 105 (1956).
Central Hardware Co. v. NLRB, 407 U.S. 539 (1972).
Hudgens v. National Labor Relations Board, 424 U.S. 507 (1976).

Bibliography and Further Reading

Hall, Kermit L., ed. *Oxford Companion to the Supreme Court of the United States.* New York: Oxford University Press, 1992.

CHAMBER OF COMMERCE OF THE UNITED STATES V. REICH

Legal Citation: 74 F.3d 1322 D.C. Cir. (1996)

Appellants
Chamber of Commerce of the United States, et al.

Appellee
Robert B. Reich, U.S. Secretary of Labor

Appellants' Claim
That Executive Order No. 12,954, which prevents the U.S. government from contracting with employers who hire permanent replacement workers during a lawful strike, violates the National Labor Relations Act (NRLA) and the Procurement Act, and is unconstitutional.

Chief Lawyer for Appellants
Timothy B. Dyk

Chief Lawyer for the Appellee
John A. Rogovin

Justices for the Court
A. Raymond Randolph, David Bryan Sentelle, Laurence H. Silberman (writing for the Court)

Justices Dissenting
None

Place
Washington, D.C.

Date of Decision
2 February 1996

Decision
That the Executive Order is regulatory in nature and is preempted by the NLRA.

Significance
The decision confirmed the circumstances under which the judiciary can properly review Executive Orders and rule on their validity. The decision determined that the Procurement Act does not give the president broad discretionary power to set labor policy. The decision also clarified the preemption doctrine, which establishes that federal law preempts any state or local law, and that a narrowly specific law preempts a more general one.

One of the president's concerns as the country's chief executive is the economical and efficient management of government. This includes setting the budget for purchasing goods and services from private contractors-an amount that totaled $437 billion in 1994. The Federal Property and Administrative Services Act (the Procurement Act) gives the president broad authority to set the conditions for federal contracts with private sector providers. The law's stated intent is "to provide for the Government an economical and efficient system for . . . procurement and supply . . ." On 8 March 1995, President Clinton issued Executive Order No. 12,954, 60 Fed. Reg 13,023, which stated that "to ensure the economical and efficient administration and completion of Federal Government contracts, contracting agencies shall not contract with employers that permanently replace lawfully striking employees." The president's rationale was that replacement workers would be less efficient than permanent workers, and thus would raise the cost of the products and goods being produced. Secretary of Labor Robert Reich was charged with developing the specific regulations to implement this order, and on 25 March, Secretary Reich issued the final implementing regulations.

On 15 March, the Chamber of Commerce, American Trucking Associations, Inc., Labor Policy Association, National Association of Manufacturers, Bridgestone/Firestone, Inc., and Mosler Inc. filed suit for declaratory and injunctive relief against the enforcement of the order. They argued that the order conflicted with the National Labor Relations Act (NLRA), the Procurement Act, and the Constitution. The district court found that the appellants' claims were not yet appropriate because Secretary Reich had not finalized the regulations asked for in the Executive Order. That decision was reversed on appeal, and on remand, the district court again found in favor of the government. The district court ruled that the appellants' claim was not reviewable by the courts because of the broad discretionary authority given the president under the Procurement Act. This decision was then appealed to the U.S. Court of Appeals for the District of Columbia.

Authority to Review Executive Orders

The Court first grappled with the issue of judicial authority to review executive orders. The judiciary has always been extremely cautious in reviewing the actions of the other branches of the government because the Constitution created separation of powers for the executive, legislative, and judicial branches. In addition, the United States inherited from English law the principle of sovereign immunity, which protects the chief executive from lawsuits. The landmark *Marbury v. Madison* (1803) case, however—which Jethro K. Keiberman called "the most celebrated case in American history"—established that sovereign immunity is not absolute, and that the Supreme Court may review the executive branch to determine whether its actions are constitutional.

The Administrative Procedures Act was formulated to help define the circumstances under which executive actions could be subject to judicial review. The appellee in *Chamber of Commerce,* (in this case, the government) argued that the appellants did not have the statutory cause of action necessary under the Administrative Procedures Act (APA) to waive sovereign immunity. Sovereign immunity had been upheld in *Dalton v. Specter* (1994), when the Supreme Court refused to review a claim challenging an Executive Order by President Bush, and the government claimed that this precedent should be applied to its case here. But the court of appeals rejected the government's sovereign immunity claim, ruling that the action was being brought against the secretary of labor, not the president. Since the secretary's powers were limited by the terms of the NLRA, his regulations for the enforcement of the Executive Order—which conflicted with the statute—were considered individual rather than sovereign actions. Furthermore, the court of appeals noted that while the *Dalton* case upheld sovereign immunity, it did raise some doubt on non-statutory judicial review of presidential action, because that decision stated "we may assume for the sake of argument that some claims that the President has violated a statutory mandate are judicially reviewable outside the framework of the APA."

Finding no apparent available statutory cause of action on which to base judicial review in this case, the appeals court considered whether appellants were entitled to bring a non-statutory cause of action challenging the legality of the Executive Order. The Court noted that until the beginning of the 1900s, it was unclear whether the courts could consider non-statutory review of executive action, but in a 1902 case, *American School of Magnetic Healing v. McAnnulty,* the Supreme Court ruled that "acts of all [a government department's] officers must be justified by some law, and in case an official violates the law to the injury of an individual the courts generally have jurisdiction to grant relief . . ."

Former U.S. Secretary of Labor Robert Reich, 1997. © AP/Wide World Photos.

This reasoning was affirmed in several subsequent cases, establishing that courts have the authority to review executive orders when their legality is in question.

Preemption Doctrine

The courts have relied on the doctrine of preemption to determine which law should prevail when statutes are in conflict. The preemption doctrine specifies that a federal law preempts any state or local law, and that unless Congress clearly states otherwise, a specific law will preempt a more general one. The appellants' chief argument was that the Executive Order conflicted with the NLRA, which gives employers the right to hire permanent replacement workers during a strike. The government, however, countered that the Procurement Act, passed in 1949 several years after the original NLRA was passed, gives the president broad discretion to set federal procurement policy and should therefore preempt the NLRA. The government argued that previous executive orders employing broad discretion—to ensure equal employment opportunities and to limit the size of wage increases—were upheld by appeals courts when they were challenged on the grounds that they were beyond the president's authority. But the court of appeals rejected this reasoning. The court noted that because "[t]he Procurement Act was designed to address broad concerns quite different from the more focused question of the appropriate balance of power between management and labor in collective bargaining," there was a conflict between the Executive Order and the NLRA.

In a series of cases through which it determined that Congress intended the NLRA to balance the rights of employer and worker, and to avoid a multitude of conflicting interpretations of labor policy, the Supreme Court worked out two types of NLRA preemption. The first prohibits state and local regulation of activities that are protected under section 7 of the NLRA or that are defined as unfair labor practices under the section 8. The other forbids regulation of labor relations that Congress has intended to be unregulated and left to free market forces. The appeals court noted that "When the government acts as a purchases of goods and services NLRA preemption is still relevant." Finding that the Executive Order "surely goes to the heart of United States labor relations policy," the Court ruled that the Executive Order was regulatory in nature and therefore preempted by the NLRA.

Impact

Chamber of Commerce of the United States v. Reich upheld the ruling in *Marbury v. Madison* that actions of the executive branch can be subject to judicial review. It further clarified the principles by which the courts could determine which law should prevail when different statutes are in conflict. The decision stated that the Procurement Act cannot be interpreted to give the president authority to set procurement policy in such a way that it, in effect, regulates national labor policy.

The issues in *Chamber of Commerce* show how the constitutional system of checks and balances works. The decision clarifies that the broad powers invested in the president by acts of Congress must be used in ways that are constitutional and that also conform to the express intent of the legislature.

Related Cases

Marbury v. Madison, 5 U.S. 137 (1803).
American School of Magnetic Healing v. McAnnulty, 187 U.S. 94 (1902).
Dalton v. Specter, 511 U.S. 462 (1994).

Bibliography and Further Reading

Leiberman, Jethro K. *The Enduring Constitution: An Exploration of the First 200 Years.* New York, Harper & Row, 1986.

LEGISLATIVE POWERS

Governmental Structure

During the short period of governance under the Articles of Confederation the United States learned a valuable lesson. In order for a democratic government to function there must be a central governing body and that body must be granted a minimum amount of authority. After the Revolutionary War there was justifiable concern regarding the structure of government and, in particular, how much power would be allocated to the central government. Under the Articles the founders satisfied their fear of tyrannical government by denying the central government rudimentary authorities such as the power to raise or collect taxes, the power to coin money, and the power to provide for the common peace and defense of the nation. The weakness of the federal government became manifest in Shay's Rebellion in which the federal government proved incapable of quelling a small uprising of farmers seeking compensation for war debts.

Congressional Powers

One of the intentions of the founders in designing a new constitution was to ensure that the federal government had sufficient power to run the country. The delicate task they faced was that of striking a compromise between federal power and individual and states' rights. One of the strategies the founders employed to maintain this balance was to use ambiguous wording in the various provisions of the document. They realized that they could not possibly anticipate every conflict that would arise over the issue of power. The founders therefore structured government in such a way that competing forces would work against each other to resolve conflicts over power. Although the founders realized that many of the specific conflicts over power would be resolved as they arose, they were forced to define the basic powers of government. The Constitution enumerates, or explicitly defines, the legislative powers granted to the legislative branch in Article I, Section 8. Here Congress is granted the power to tax, regulate commerce, provide a common currency, and raise and support an army and navy. The Constitution also grants Congress the power to enact laws "necessary and proper" to execute its constitutional authority. This is known as the "elastic" or "necessary and proper" clause. It is perhaps the most controversial of the enumerated powers granted to Congress as it renders a subjective range to legislative power.

Apart from the Constitution, the powers of the legislative branch have been defined, in large part, by the Supreme Court. Though it is often presumed that the Constitution granted the Supreme Court the power to review legislative statutes for their constitutionality, the power of "judicial review" was in fact claimed by the Court in *Marbury v. Madison* (1803). It was here that Chief Justice John Marshall held that it is the power of the Supreme Court to determine whether acts passed by Congress and the president were consistent with the Constitution. The issues that the Supreme Court has been called upon to resolve concerning the parameters of legislative power center around the relationship between Congress and the states, and the relationship between Congress and the president.

Legislative Powers and the States

The landmark case which essentially determined whether Congress would have constitutional authority to govern the various states of the union was *McCulloch v. Maryland* (1819). On the surface the Court was to determine whether Maryland had the power to tax a national bank. However, Chief Justice Marshall, who is to the Supreme Court what George Washington is to the presidency, chose to address the broader issue of legislative versus state power in his historic opinion. Marshall's opinion would set the precedent for defining the range of the "necessary and proper" clause of Article I, Section 8 of the Constitution. In effect, Marshall ruled that when state and federal laws conflicted, states must defer to the federal statute. "The government of the United States, though limited in its powers, is supreme; and its laws, when made in pursuance of the Constitution, form the supreme law of the land" (McCulloch). This ruling served to clarify what had been presumed to be the implied range of legislative power vis-a-vis the states outlined in the Constitution.

The Court has elsewhere upheld congressional rule over state law in *South Carolina v. Katzenbach* (1966). Here Southern states headed by South Carolina challenged the power of Congress to enforce provisions of the Voting Rights Act of 1965 which was designed to eliminate discrimination against black voters. In the Civil War, amendments to the Constitution authorized Congress to enforce the amendments "by appropriate legislation." In this case the Voting Rights Act was an "appropriate" means of enforcing the prohibition of discrimination against voting qualifications on the basis of race provided by the Fifteenth Amendment. South Carolina requested that Nicholas Katzenbach, the United States Attorney General at the time, be prohibited from enforcing sections of the Voting Rights Act on the grounds that it violated the Tenth Amendment. The Tenth Amendment states that the powers not delegated to the federal government "are reserved to the states." South Carolina claimed that Congress had legislated in an area, election laws, that had been reserved to the states. The Supreme Court ruled that the Voting Rights Act was an "appropriate" means of enforcing the provisions of the Fifteenth Amendment. This decision made it clear that the legislature's power to enforce Constitutional Amendments would take precedent over state's rights.

The balance of power between the federal and state governments has also been affected by policies made "outside" the Constitution. The arrangements that Congress makes with other countries through treaties can significantly impose upon state power. The question of whether this is constitutionally justified has been a subject of legal controversy. Congressional authority over arrangements made with foreign nations through treaties with regards to state authority was addressed by the Court in *Missouri v. Holland* (1920). In 1916 the United States had entered into a treaty with Great Britain designed to save certain species of birds from extinction. The subsequent Migratory Bird Treaty of 1918 authorized the regulation of killing, capturing, and selling of birds specified in the treaty. The state of Missouri challenged the act on the ground that it violated its Tenth Amendment rights. Justice Oliver Wendell Holmes wrote the opinion of the Court which held that the treaty did not violate the constitutional balance of power between the federal and state governments. However, the states had justifiable fears that the United States was granted the jurisdiction by this case to enter into treaties that would violate states' rights. To calm these fears a Constitutional Amendment was proposed by Senator John Bricker (the Bricker Amendment) the basic design of which was to protect states' rights against policies made by treaties with foreign nations. Although a revised version of the amendment failed by only one vote in the Senate, the concerns of the states were clearly acknowledged by Congress.

Recently the states have attempted to reclaim some of the power they have lost to Congress by imposing term limits on members of Congress. There seemed to be a legitimate opportunity for the states to succeed given that the members of the 104th Congress had campaigned in favor of term limits in their "Contract With America." However, Congress failed to pass a constitutional amendment enforcing term limits on its members, which forced states to take the initiative. Arkansas passed a state statute limiting the terms of members of the United States House of Representatives to six years and the terms of United States Senators to 12 years. In *U.S. Term Limits v. Thornton* (1995) the Court ruled that Arkansas did not have the authority to determine the qualifications for service in the United States Congress. Justice John Paul Stevens explained that the Constitution already provides the qualifications for service in Article I, Sections 2, 4, and 6 and any attempt by the states to alter these qualifications was unconstitutional. Justice Stevens held that the Arkansas petitioners' attempt to limit the terms of members of Congress "must fall because it is an indirect attempt to evade the Qualifications Clauses' requirements and trivializes the basic democratic principles underlying those Clauses" (Thornton).

Legislative Powers and the President

In *Immigration and Naturalization Service v. Chadha* (1983) the range of legislative power in relation to that of the executive came under review. The case called into question the power of Congress to include legislation provisions that would enable the legislature to negate the president's or others' enforcement of legislation should the executive deviate from what Congress considered to be the design of the law. This practice, know as the "legislative veto," was declared unconstitutional in *Chadha* on the ground that it overstepped the boundaries of congressional authority in the realm of law making. The Immigration and Naturalization Act had granted the Attorney General the authority to make decisions concerning whether deportable aliens could be permitted to remain in the country. However, the act also included a provision that enabled Congress to override the decisions made by the Attorney General. In this case the Attorney General had permitted Chadha to remain in the country while Congress elected to deport him. The Court ruled that Congress did not have the authority to veto enforcement decisions after legislation had been passed. Despite the efforts by the Court to curtail the use of the legislative veto it is still commonly practiced by Congress today.

The relationship of power between the president and Congress has also been defined by the ability of Congress to delegate power to the executive. Delegation power pertains to the activities of which Congress authorized the president and agencies to engage in to meet the objectives of a given piece of legislation. In the Tariff Act of 1922 Congress had delegated to the president the discretion to raise or lower tariffs in accordance with U.S. foreign trade interests. J. W. Hampton Jr., and Company, a victim of a tariff increase, challenged the constitutionality of this act on the basis that it authorized too much power to the president. In *J. W. Hampton Jr., and Co. v. United States* (1928) the Court found no constitutional indiscretion with Congress delegating authority to the president to fix tariff rates.

Although the justification for congressional delegation of power to the president was apparent in this case the Court would later place limits on this power. In *Panama Refining Co. v. Ryan* (1935) the Court held that specific parameters must be laid down in the delegation of power to the president to enforce legislative statutes. In this case the president was given the discretion to set ceilings on crude oil production in order to equalize supply and demand fluctuations between states. Because of the Great Depression Congress seemed justified in granting such broad latitude to the president to regulate interstate oil transactions. The Court, however, did not see it this way finding that Congress must set specific parameters on the delegation of power to the president and agencies to enforce laws.

The delegation power of Congress recently came under the scrutiny of the Court in a case involving the constitutionality of the line-item veto. The Line Item Veto Act, which granted the power to the president to alter legislation after passage, was challenged by Senator Robert Byrd in *Raines v. Byrd* (1997). Although the act only granted the president authority to strike certain sections of appropriations bills, those who voted against the measure feared an overextension of executive power over the legislature. Senator Byrd and others argued that the act violated their Article I voting power in that laws that they had approved could be subsequently nullified by the president under the act. The senators claimed that the act put them in "a position of unanticipated and unwelcome subservience to the president" (Byrd). Although the Court agreed with the reasoning of the petitioners, it could not nullify the statute because the members of Congress who objected to the line-item veto and filed suit did not provide sufficient evidence of injury. In other words, there had yet to be a line-item veto to which they were constitutionally entitled to object. However in *Clinton v. City of New York* (1998) the Court ruled that the power delegated to the president in the Line Item Veto Act was unconstitutional.

Although the majority of the legal debates involving legislative powers can be divided into the general categories of legislative power versus state power and legislative power versus presidential power, the Court has also resolved constitutional matters regarding legislative investigative powers. During the peak of the Cold War there was a growing concern that members of the Communist party in the United States were undermining American democracy. In the minds of many Americans the efforts by members of Congress and, in particular the often unjustified allegations of Senator Joseph McCarthy, to expose Communist party activity constituted a violation of civil rights. Congress therefore held a number of investigative hearings in an effort to incriminate "un-American" activities. In *Watkins v. United States* (1957) Chief Justice Earl Warren ruled that although Congress has the authority to conduct hearings as part of the legislative process it does not have the authority to probe into the private affairs of individuals. "There is no general authority to expose the private affairs of individuals without justification in terms of the functions of the Congress" (Watkins).

See also: **Federal Powers and the Separation of Powers, Federalism and State Powers, Judicial Powers, Judicial Review**

Bibliography and Further Reading

Cornell University Web Site: "Supreme Court Cases" ("www.supct.law.cornell.edu"), 1998.

Davidson, Roger H., and Walter Oleszek. *Congress and Its Members.* Washington, DC: Congressional Quarterly Press, 1981.

DiClerico, Robert E. *The American President.* Englewood Cliffs, NJ: Prentice Hall, 1990.

Ducat, Craig. *Constitutional Interpretation.* St. Paul, MN: West Publishing Company, 1996.

Jewel, Malcolm, and Samuel Patterson. *The Legislative Process in the United States.* New York: Random House, 1977.

Hinckley, Barbara. *Stability and Change in Congress.* New York: Harper & Row, Publishers, 1988.

Keefe, William J., and Morris S. Ogul. *The American Legislative Process.* Englewood Cliffs, NJ: Prentice Hall, 1989.

Wilson, Woodrow. *Congressional Government: A Study in American Politics.* Baltimore: Johns Hopkins University Press, 1956 (originally published in 1885).

GIBBONS V. OGDEN

Legal Citation: 22 U.S. 1 (1824)

Appellant
Thomas Gibbons

Appellee
Aaron Ogden

Appellant's Claim
That the exclusive right granted by the state of New York to Aaron Ogden to operate steamships within state waters was in conflict with the steamship license issued under an act of Congress to Thomas Gibbons.

Chief Lawyers for Appellant
Thomas A. Emmet, Thomas J. Oakley

Chief Lawyers for Appellee
William Wirt, Daniel Webster, David B. Ogden

Justices for the Court
Gabriel Duvall, William Johnson, John Marshall (writing for the Court), Joseph Story, Thomas Todd, Bushrod Washington

Justices Dissenting
None (Smith Thompson did not participate)

Place
Washington, D.C.

Date of Decision
2 March 1824

Decision
That a state cannot grant exclusive rights to navigate in its waters, because this is a breach of Congress' right to regulate interstate commerce, as guaranteed by the Constitution.

Significance
This was the first case ever to go to the Supreme Court under the Commerce Clause of the U.S. Constitution.

The case of *Gibbons v. Ogden* has been called "the emancipation proclamation of American commerce." The ruling in this case established the importance of commerce between the states, and of any technological advance that might enable commerce between the states.

Steamships: Navigating for the Future

The first chapter in the *Gibbons v. Ogden* story began in 1807, when Robert Fulton and Robert R. Livingston won the exclusive right to operate steamboats in New York waters. Soon after, they won another exclusive grant to operate steamships in the state of Louisiana, thus obtaining control over some of the major commercial water routes in the United States.

Soon, other people began to get into the steamboat business. They too won monopolies to operate steamboats in the waters of various states. Meanwhile, the United States was expanding westward, and steamboats were becoming increasingly important in connecting the various parts of the growing nation. But since many different companies had carved up the rights to different state waterways among themselves, it was difficult for any single company to carry goods from state to state.

Citizens of New York state began to complain about the way monopolies dominated the steamboat business. The New Jersey legislature also took action: they passed a law authorizing its officials to seize and confiscate any steamboats operating under the New York monopoly. Clearly, the situation did not bode well for interstate commerce.

A Fight Between Two Partners

Enter Thomas Gibbons and Aaron Ogden. These two men had once been partners in a steamship business. But soon, they had a falling out and began a complicated series of legal battles. One of these became the landmark case of *Gibbons v. Ogden*.

When the case began, Aaron Ogden was operating a steamship line between New York and Elizabethtown, New Jersey. Ogden had bought a license from Livingston, granting him access to Livingston's exclusive rights to New York steamboat traffic.

The steamboat, which revolutionized commerce, began operating consistently on the Delaware River out of Philadelphia in 1787. © Lithograph by J. F. Reigart and L. N. Rosenthal. The Library of Congress/Corbis.

Gibbons resented the monopolistic power of his former partner. He began running his own boats between New York and New Jersey. Ogden, in turn, tried to get an injunction against Gibbons from the Chancellor of New York State.

According to Ogden, New York State law protected his monopoly. Gibbons, on the other hand, pointed out that he had a license to engaged in the "coasting" trade, a license issued under an Act of Congress. Ogden claimed that state law took precedence here. Gibbons argued that federal law overrode the laws of a single state.

The first round of the fight went to Ogden. New York State courts found that the state did have the right to issue exclusive licenses, because navigation, not commerce, was involved. Of course, said the New York courts, if Congress actually passed a law that concerned navigation, state law might be overruled. But since no such law had been passed, New York was within its rights.

Commerce or Navigation?

However, the U.S. Supreme Court saw things differently. In the decision written by Chief Justice Marshall, the Court began by referring to the so-called "Commerce" clause of the U.S. Constitution: "Congress shall have the power . . . to regulate commerce with foreign nations, and among the several States, and with the Indian tribes . . ."

The Court also cited a provision of the Constitution that gave Congress the power to "promote the progress of science and useful arts . . ."

Basically, the Court ruling acknowledged the importance of steamship traffic to U.S. interstate commerce. Since steamships helped to facilitate commerce, the Court found that they came under Congress' power to regulate commerce. Therefore, any state attempts to regulate steamship activity between states—such as Gibbons' ships, which traveled between New York and New Jersey—was a breach of the Constitution.

The Court ruling established three major principles:

(1) "Commerce" as defined by the Constitution is not limited simply to buying and selling, but also includes navigation;

(2) The operation of steamships is an aspect of commerce, and therefore protected under the U.S. Constitution;

(3) States could not make any laws that would in any way result in the restriction of interstate commerce, which, again, was protected under the U.S. Constitution.

Implications for the Future

The immediate impact of *Gibbons v. Ogden* was to open up the field for a wide range of steamship companies, and, consequently, to promote nationwide steamship travel and commerce in the United States. However, the ruling had even more far-reaching implications. For example, when railroads, telegraphs, telephones, oil and gas pipelines, and airplanes were developed, they relied upon the protection of *Gibbons v. Ogden* to operate across state borders. Even today, when questions of interstate commerce come before the Court, the case of *Gibbons v. Ogden* helps to shape the Court's decisions.

Related Cases

Shreveport Rate Cases, 234 U.S. 342 (1914).
Mulford v. Smith, 307 U.S. 38 (1939).
National League of Cities v. Usery, 426 U.S. 833 (1976).

Bibliography and Further Reading

Dangerfield, George. *Quarrels That Have Shaped the Constitution,* rev. and expanded edition, ed. John A. Garraty. New York: Harper & Row, 1987.

Epstein, Lee, and Thomas G. Walker. *Constitutional Law for a Changing America: Institutional Powers and Constraints,* 3rd ed. Washington DC: Congressional Quarterly, 1998.

Johnson, John W. *Historic U.S. Court Cases, 1690-1990: An Encyclopedia.* New York: Garland Publishing, 1992.

Kauper, Paul G. *Constitutional Law: Cases and Materials.* Boston: Little, Brown, 1972.

Pollak, Louis H., ed. *The Constitution and the Supreme Court: A Documentary History,* Vol. I, Cleveland, World Publishing Co., 1966.

Saye, Albert B. *American Constitutional Law.* St. Paul: West, 1979.

KENDALL V. UNITED STATES

Legal Citation: 37 U.S. 524 (1838)

Appellant
Amos Kendall, U.S. Postmaster General

Appellee
United States

Appellant's Claim
That Kendall should not have to order the Post Office Department to pay certain funds to a firm that did business with them, even though a federal court had ordered him to, if he himself, in his official capacity, did not believe the funds should be awarded.

Chief Lawyers for Appellant
Francis Scott Key; Benjamin F. Butler, U.S. Attorney General

Chief Lawyers for Appellee
Richard S. Coxe, Reverdy Johnson

Justices for the Court
Henry Baldwin, Philip Pendleton Barbour, John Catron, John McKinley, John McLean, Joseph Story, Roger Brooke Taney, Smith Thompson (writing for the Court), James Moore Wayne

Justices Dissenting
None

Place
Washington, D.C.

Date of Decision
12 March 1838

Decision
That the act Kendall objected to was merely "ministerial" and did not require judgment or discretion on his part; therefore, he was obligated to follow the directive of the federal court.

Significance
The decision in *Kendall v. United States* was a major step in the definition of the powers of the three different branches of government: executive, legislative, and judicial. The Court found that although the president "was beyond the reach of any other department" (except if he or she were being impeached), other members of the executive branch were subject to the rulings of federal court in many instances.

The story of Kendall's fight with the government begins as a story of government corruption. Under President Andrew Jackson, the Post Office Department was known for the large amounts of money that frequently changed hands between the department and the big contractors who were hired to transport the mail. Washington became filled with stories of scandals concerning large contractors who kept their lucrative contracts by unfairly fighting off competition and regarding vague contracts that no one could interpret precisely.

Finally, in 1835, Jackson removed the head of the department (the man was appointed to a post overseas) and replaced him with Amos Kendall. Kendall was a major supporter of Jackson and something of a crusader. He did his best to clean up the department, but he ran into trouble concerning an alleged debt to the firm of Stockton and Stokes, a firm that carried the mail between Washington, Baltimore, and Philadelphia, and between Washington and Wheeling, Virginia (today West Virginia).

A Carriage and a Pair of Horses

Stockton and Stokes claimed that the department owed them money. Kendall found no evidence of any legitimate debt. Stockton and Stokes made the mistake of offering Kendall's wife a carriage and a pair of horses if he allowed the claim. Kendall was incensed. Stockton and Stokes then appealed to Congress. Here the trouble began.

Congress, which is responsible for the appropriation of funds, might have ruled on the claim, but they did not. Instead, they passed an act directing the solicitor of the treasury to decide the matter. The treasury, of course, was an entirely different department from the post office. Moreover, Kendall was head of his department, whereas the solicitor of the treasury was only a junior official in the treasury. Kendall was insulted once again.

Kendall also did not like the fact that the solicitor, Virgil Maxcy, was a good friend of the firm in question. Without even asking Kendall, Maxcy not only allowed the original claim, he called for Kendall's department to pay another $40,000. Kendall made his

Amos Kendall, U.S. Postmaster General. © The Library of Congress.

objections known, but he did pay the original claim. He refused, however, to pay the $40,000.

The President Fails to Intervene

Frustrated in their efforts to get money that they regarded as legitimately theirs, Stockton and Stokes went to President Jackson himself. Jackson, however, refused to act. Instead, he referred them back to Congress. The House of Representatives did nothing in response, but the Senate reiterated that Maxcy's recommendation should be followed. In other words, Kendall was supposed to pay the $40,000.

Kendall was stubborn, and he believed he was in the right. He refused to pay. So Stockton and Stokes went to the U.S. Circuit Court of the District of Columbia. They asked for a *writ of mandamus,* an order forcing Kendall to act.

Because the president had failed to take any decisive action in the matter to this point, and because Kendall, as part of the Cabinet, represented the president, Kendall began to feel concerned. He felt that Jackson's lack of action had shown the executive branch in a bad light. In circuit court he filed an opinion of the president's official lawyer, Attorney General Benjamin F.

Butler, arguing that a U.S. circuit court had no power to force a member of the executive branch to do anything related to his job.

Stockton and Stokes refused to back down from their claim. The case went to court. Meanwhile, both Kendall and Maxcy turned to the press to argue their points. The case became an 1838 version of a "media circus."

The Separation of Powers

The controversy stemmed from an argument about the separation of powers. The U.S. Constitution clearly establishes three branches of government: a legislative branch, led by Congress, to make the laws, an executive branch, led by the president, to execute the laws, and a judicial branch, led by the Supreme Court, to interpret the laws. That way, in theory, no one branch would become too powerful.

Kendall's lawyers argued that if a federal court could force a member of the executive branch to take a particular action as part of his governmental duties, the court was usurping the power of executive authority. If so, the separation of powers called for in the Constitution would be violated.

Opposing lawyers, hired by Stockton and Stokes, likewise appealed to the separation of powers. But in their opinion, Kendall was the one who was violating the separation. Richard S. Coxe, for example, accused Kendall of wanting to break down the judicial branch of government, take over the legislative branch of government, destroy the safeguards set up by the Constitution, and make the executive branch all-powerful.

The arguments also covered the issue of whether the action of paying the $40,000 was merely "ministerial" (routine) or if it was an action that required judgment and discretion. Kendall's lawyers agreed that if the act were ministerial, then the courts could order Kendall to perform it. However, they argued, the act was actually far more than ministerial; it required judgment and discretion. In that sense, Kendall was representing the president. And no court should be able to force the president to take a particular governmental action.

Kendall Loses—and Wins

Unfortunately for Kendall, the Supreme Court did not agree with him at all. They found unanimously that the circuit court did indeed have the power to order him to pay the debt. True, the president himself was "beyond the reach of any other department"—unless Congress should decide to impeach him—but only the president had that kind of power.

The Court found that other members of the executive branch might have their duties divided into two parts. One part, true, required judgment and discretion and might be seen as representing the chief executive. But the other part was "subject to the control of the law, and not to the direction of the president." This part of an official's duties was indeed subject to a court's ruling. Therefore, Kendall should pay the money that he had been ordered to pay.

The Court's decision caused a great deal of controversy. Some segments of the public and the press applauded the "spirit of independence" shown by the Court. Others held that the Supreme Court had "no right to assume authority over the executive."

The Kendall story has a fascinating postscript. Although Kendall did go ahead and pay the money as ordered, Stockton and Stokes were still not satisfied. They sued Kendall for the money they had lost by his long delay. By this time, Kendall had left public office and become the campaign manager of Martin Van Buren, who would become America's next President. Van Buren was a Democrat running against an opponent from the Whig party. A jury of one Democrat and eleven Whigs found against Kendall and ordered him to pay $11,000 in damages.

Kendall was burdened by many debts and refused to pay this one. He said he would rather go to jail than cheat his legitimate creditors by paying anything to Stockton and Stokes. Finally, former President Jackson intervened. He helped pass a law abolishing imprisonment for debt in the District of Columbia—if the debtor was appealing his debt to a higher court. Then, in 1845, the Supreme Court found in Kendall's favor. They ruled that he did not have to pay damages to Stockton and Stokes because he had not been acting in his private capacity, but rather as a government official. Kendall went on to ask Congress to pay his lawyer's fees and other costs for the damages suit. Congress agreed. Kendall was a victor at last.

Related Cases

Marbury v. Madison, 5 U.S. 137 (1803).
Martin v. Hunter's Lessee, 1 Wheat. 304 (1816).

Francis Scott Key. © *The Library of Congress/Corbis.*

Bibliography and Further Reading

Biskupic, Joan, and Elder Witt, eds. *Congressional Quarterly's Guide to the U.S. Supreme Court,* 3rd ed. Washington, DC: Congressional Quarterly, Inc., 1996.

Hall, Kermit L., ed. *The Oxford Companion to the Supreme Court of the United States.* New York: Oxford University Press, 1992.

Swisher, Carl B. *The History of the Supreme Court of the United States: The Taney Period, 1836–64,* Vol. V. New York: Macmillan, 1974.

COOLEY V. BOARD OF WARDENS

Legal Citation: 53 U.S. 299 (1852)

Appellant
Aaron B. Cooley

Appellee
Board of Wardens of the Port of Philadelphia

Appellant's Claim
Ship master Aaron B. Cooley protested a port regulation making him pay half the normal fee for a pilot although he did not use one. The regulation, Cooley claimed, was an invasion of the exclusive authority of Congress over foreign and interstate commerce.

Chief Lawyers for Appellant
Campbell, Dallas

Chief Lawyers for Appellee
Morris, Tyson

Justices for the Court
John Catron, Benjamin Curtis (writing for the Court), Peter Vivian Daniel, Robert Cooper Grier, Samuel Nelson, Roger Brooke Taney

Justices Dissenting
John McLean, James Moore Wayne (John McKinley did not participate)

Place
Washington, D.C.

Date of Decision
2 March 1852

Decision
The Court divided interstate and foreign commerce into two categories for which separate national and local rules could apply. Federal rules would apply to business of a "character to require uniformity of treatment" while "local peculiarities of ports" could be appropriately left to the "legislative discretion of the several states."

Significance
The 6-2 decision allowing authority over commerce to be split between federal and state governments was easy to declare but has proven difficult to apply. Local and state laws under the precedent set by *Cooley* have, however, been consistently upheld in the absence of any action by Congress to provide more specific guidance.

The decision in *Cooley v. Board of Wardens* concerned the running battle among the justices during the first 50 years of the Supreme Court over the proper roles of the federal and state governments. Delivering an opinion that allowed states to exercise power over commerce, Justice Curtis took some pleasure from the offense that the decision gave the Federalist Party. The Federalists favored national power over state power and were therefore concerned about the decision. Curtis wrote a friend before the decision was announced:

> [I]t is adverse to the exclusive authority of Congress and not in accordance with the opinions of [Justices] McLean and Wayne, who are the most high-toned Federalists on the bench. But it rests on grounds perfectly satisfactory to myself, and it has received the assent of five judges [Justice McKinley abstained] out of eight.

The case arose out of an 1803 Pennsylvania law requiring masters of ships who refused the services of pilots to nevertheless pay half the regular pilot fee. The money was allocated for "the relief of distressed and decayed pilots, their widows and children." Aaron Cooley, who sued the port's Board of Wardens for the return of fees he had been forced to pay, believed that the fees had been unconstitutionally levied.

Somewhat similar Massachusetts and New York taxes for the relief of destitute immigrants had been declared unconstitutional by a 5-4 vote in the earlier *Passenger Cases* decision. The Philadelphia pilot fee, however, was levied on the operations of ships in the Philadelphia harbor, not imposed on passengers or commodities like the Massachusetts and New York taxes. Moreover, counsel for the pilots could also point to specific congressional authorization in a 1789 act which stated that pilots "shall continue to be regulated in conformity to the existing laws of states . . . until further provision shall be made be Congress."

Consequently, Curtis reasoned, the mere fact that Congress had the power to make such "further provision" did not "imply a prohibition on the States to exercise the same power." Judge McLean, writing for himself and Judge Wayne, thought such a state law had to be affirmed by Congress to be valid. According to Chief Justice William H. Rehnquist in *The Supreme Court: How It Was, How It Is,* Justice Daniel was "one hundred and eighty degrees on the other side of the question . . . He thought such a state law was valid whether Congress approved it or disapproved it." Daniel, in fact, concurred with Curtis on the question; he differed only on the reasoning.

Chief Justice Taney, a states' rights advocate, was "elated at the victory," according to the constitutional scholar, Alexander M. Bickel of Yale, primarily because of the defeat of McLean and Wayne.

Curtis would himself quietly split with Taney after the Chief Justice handed down his most famous—or infamous—decision, *Scott v. Sandford* (1857), upholding the Fugitive Slave Act. The ostensible reason given by Curtis, a Massachusetts resident, was that the salary paid to justices was too low. Jere S. Williams, however, reported in *The Supreme Court Speaks:*

> [I]t is now known he left because he felt the *Dred Scott* decision descended to a purely political level and that the Court had thereby become so debased it could no longer play its rightful role as an independent, co-ordinate branch of the federal government.

Related Cases
The Passenger Cases, 7 How. 283 (1849).
Bibb v. Navajo Freight Lines, 359 U.S. 520 (1959).

Bibliography and Further Reading
Bickel, Alexander M., and Benno C. Schmidt. *History of the Supreme Court of the United States.* New York: Macmillan, 1984.

Epstein, Lee, and Thomas G. Walker. *Constitutional Law for a Changing America: Institutional Powers and Constraints,* 3rd ed. Washington DC: Congressional Quarterly, 1998.

Rehnquist, William H. *The Supreme Court: How It Was, How It Is.* New York: William Morrow & Co., Inc, 1987.

Williams, Jere S. *The Supreme Court Speaks.* Austin: University of Texas Press, 1946.

Benjamin Curtis. © Archive Photos.

WYNEHAMER V. THE PEOPLE

Legal Citation: 13 N.Y. 378 (1856)

Appellant
James Wynehamer

Appellee
People of the State of New York

Appellant's Claim
That the law prohibiting the sale of alcohol under which Wynehamer was indicted was unconstitutional, because it abridged his constitutional right to dispose of his own property as he saw fit.

Chief Lawyer for Appellant
A. J. Parker

Chief Lawyer for Appellee
A. Sawin

Justices for the Court
Chief Justice Denio, Justices Comstock (writing for the court), Hubbard, Johnson, Johnson, Mitchell, Selden, Wright

Justices Dissenting
None

Place
Albany, New York

Date of Decision
March 1856

Decision
That the prohibitionary law violated the portion of the state constitution declaring that no citizen be deprived of life, liberty, or property without due process of law.

Significance
The case struck down an early prohibition statute with higher-law doctrine, and set the stage for national prohibition to be proposed as a constitutional amendment.

The Temperance Movement

Wynehamer v. the People of the State of New York was an important early prohibition case. The case pitted an early prohibition statute against the rights of due process. The court of appeals ruled that the statute banning the sale of alcohol was unconstitutional, because it deprived a citizen of his rightful property without due process. In doing so, it supported the era's general movement towards "higher-law" doctrine—the idea that certain natural laws prevailed even if they were not stated explicitly in the Constitution.

The mid-nineteenth century saw the emergence of a fervent anti-alcohol movement. Consumption of liquor was cited as the cause of many social ills, including poverty, insanity, gambling, and all sorts of immorality. The "temperance" movement, which advocated drinking only in moderation, tried to convince people to set a strong moral example for the weak-willed. Slowly, this attitude gave way to a more forceful approach that advocated the complete prohibition of alcohol. Twelve states during the antebellum period attempted to pass laws banning the sale of alcohol. On 9 April 1855, the State of New York passed a statute entitled "An Act for the Prevention of Intemperance, Pauperism and Crime."

Prohibition and Property

The *Wynehamer* case was straight-forward. In July of 1855, James Wynehamer, a Buffalo bar owner, was arrested and indicted for selling intoxicating liquors in violation of the new statute. Although the accused protested that he was being denied his constitutional right to be tried by a jury of his peers, the trial took place in the court of special sessions, with a six-person jury. Wynehamer pleaded not guilty. His counsel argued that the statute under which he had been indicted was unconstitutional. Since Wynehamer had legally purchased his liquors before the enactment of the statute, he was being denied his right to dispose of his property as he saw fit. The court of special sessions disagreed and found the defendant guilty. He was fined fifty dollars and forced to remain interred until the fine was paid. Wynehamer appealed the judgment, which was then upheld by the Supreme Court of the Eighth

This woodcut shows the afflictions caused by overindulging in alcohol, c. 1820. © Corbis-Bettmann.

District. The case was then reviewed by the court of appeals.

The court of appeals reversed the judgments of the two lower courts with a vote of five to three, determining that the prohibition act violated "the provision of the state constitution which declares that no person shall be deprived of life, liberty or property, without due process of law." In order to do so, the court first had to establish that intoxicating liquors were indeed property, a principle which Justice George M. Comstock deemed uncontroversial in his groundbreaking opinion. Although it was true, Comstock admitted, that "intoxicating drinks are a species of property which performs no beneficent part in the political, moral, or social economy of the world," that fact did not diminish their status as property. If arguments about its moral value were allowed to subvert the idea of property, he asserted, "then there is no private right entirely safe," and "the guarantees of the constitution are a mere waste of words."

The court's final decision was tantamount to a declaration that a natural or higher law protected private property. Comstock referred to a passage in William Blackstone's *Commentaries* in which the author declares

that the importance accorded the rights of property outweighs even the public good. Theories of the public good may be supported by large numbers of people, declared Comstock, but "there are some absolute private rights beyond their reach." Without taking on the issue of whether temperance idealists were right or wrong about the pernicious effects of alcohol, Comstock dismissed their attempt at prohibition as unconstitutional.

Dissenting judges argued that the legislature had the right to regulate, restrict, or even prohibit traffic in property for the sake of preventing injury and protecting the community. If the right of traffic or transmission of property was considered an inalienable right, wrote Judge T. A. Johnson, then "the right to property and its transmission would be held superior to the right to life and liberty." Two other judges joined Johnson in dissenting, but the majority was not convinced.

In striking down a prohibition statute with higher-law principles, the New York Court of Appeals contributed to the growing practice of higher-law jurisprudence in the nineteenth century. It also established the legal environment in which a successful enactment

The Temperance Movement

The temperance movement, which sought to greatly reduce or eliminate the sale and consumption of alcohol, first emerged in the early 1800s as part of a religious evangelical revival that swept the United States. During the nineteenth century, the per capita consumption of alcohol in America continued to grow and so did the temperance movement. Maine in 1846 became the first "dry" state, and a dozen others soon followed. Difficulties in enforcement led most states to abandon their liquor laws within a quarter-century, and the temperance movement abated. The rise of political groups such as the Women's Christian Temperance Union (WCTU) signalled a resurgence of the temperance movement. The upheaval of World War I, along with a shortage of grain caused by the war, gave temperance activists an opportunity to move prohibition legislation forward.

In 1919 Congress ratified the Eighteenth Amendment, which prohibited the manufacture, sale, and consumption of alcohol in the United States. Prohibition, however, was repealed by the Twenty-first Amendment in 1933. By then, the temperance movement had ceased to be a viable force in American political life.

Source(s): *West's Encyclopedia of American Law.* St. Paul, MN: West Group, 1998.

of prohibition could occur by constitutional amendment. The New York court was in keeping with the nation's focus on property rights in the antebellum era, a focus that would take on very political overtones in the years leading up to the Civil War. It also foreshadowed the U.S. Supreme Court's struggle with issues of due process, a process that began in the 1850s and continued until the final decades of the nineteenth century.

Bibliography and Further Reading

Cushman, Robert F. *Leading Constitutional Decisions.* Englewood Cliffs, NJ: Prentice-Hall, Inc., 1982.

Johnson, John W., ed. *Historic U.S. Court Cases, 1690–1990: An Encyclopedia.* New York: Garland Publishing, 1992.

Wiecek, William M. "Prohibition and the Due Process Clause." John W. Johnson, ed. *Historic U.S. Court Cases: an Encyclopedia.* New York: Garland, 1992.

SCOTT V. SANDFORD

Legal Citation: 60 U.S. 393 (1857)

Plaintiff
Dred Scott

Defendant
John F. A. Sanford

Plaintiff's Claim
That Scott, who was a slave, had become a free man when his owner had taken him to a state designated as "free" under the 1820 Missouri Compromise.

Chief Lawyers for Plaintiff
Samuel M. Bay, Montgomery Blair, George Ticknor Curtis, Alexander P. Field, Roswell M. Field, David N. Hall

Chief Defense Lawyers
Hugh A. Garland, H. S. Geyer, George W. Goode, Reverdy Johnson, Lyman D. Norris

Justices for the Court
John Archibald Campbell, John Catron, Peter Vivian Daniel, Robert Cooper Grier, Samuel Nelson, Roger Brooke Taney (writing for the Court), James Moore Wayne

Justices Dissenting
Benjamin Curtis, John McLean

Place
Washington, D.C.

Date of Decision
6 March 1857

Decision
That Dred Scott was still a slave, regardless of where his owner took him.

Significance
The Dred Scott decision effectively ended the Missouri Compromise, hardening the political rivalry between North and South and paving the way for Civil War.

Dred Scott was born in Virginia sometime in the late 1790s, although historical records concerning the exact time and place are incomplete. Because Scott was black and born into slavery, no one at the time would have taken much interest in such details.

Scott's owner was Peter Blow, who owned a reasonably successful plantation. In 1819, Blow took his family and several slaves, including Scott, to Alabama to start a new plantation. Blow grew tired of farming, and in 1830 moved to St. Louis, Missouri. St. Louis was then a booming frontier town, and Blow opened a hotel. Both Blow and his wife became seriously ill and died.

Scott's travels westward in a sense mirrored the expansion of the United States during this time period. From the original 13 states on the Atlantic Seaboard, American colonists had pushed to the Mississippi River and beyond. This expansion gave rise to serious political problems. Southern states wanted to bring slavery and the plantation lifestyle into the new territories, whereas the Northern states wanted to keep the territories free. Both sides were afraid that, when portions of the territories were eventually admitted as states, the other side would gain political supremacy in Congress owing to the new states' senators and representatives. In 1820, the North and the South struck a deal called the Missouri Compromise. Missouri was admitted to the union as a slave state and Maine was admitted as a free state, preserving the political balance in Congress. Further, slavery was forbidden in any territory north of, but permitted in any territory south of, Missouri's northern border at approximately 36 degrees latitude north.

After the Blows' deaths, their estate sold Scott to an army doctor named John Emerson. Emerson took Scott with him during tours of duty in Illinois and in that part of the Wisconsin and Iowa Territories which would become Minnesota. Both Illinois and Minnesota were within the free territory of the Missouri Compromise. Emerson returned to St. Louis and died 29 December 1843. He left everything, including Scott, to his wife and appointed as executor his wife's brother, John F. A. Sanford.

Dred Scott. © The Library of Congress.

Scott Sues for Freedom

Tired of a lifetime of slavery, Scott tried to buy his freedom from the widow Emerson, without success. Scott had acquired more education than most slaves and realized that his travels into a free territory might give him a claim to freedom. Represented by former Missouri Attorney General Samuel M. Bay, on 6 April 1846, Scott sued for his freedom in the Missouri Circuit Court for the City of St. Louis. Sanford and the widow Emerson were represented by George W. Goode. Because Sanford was the estate executor for Scott's former master, the official reports bear his name as the primary defendant, misspelled to read "Scott v. Sandford."

Legally, Scott's suit was for assault and false imprisonment. A slave could be punished and kept as property, but a free person could not, so the legal charges were in fact window dressing for the issue of Scott's freedom. On 30 June 1847, the case came to trial before Judge Alexander Hamilton. Bay committed a technical error in presenting the plaintiff's evidence, and the jury returned a verdict that same day in Emerson and Sanford's favor. Hamilton granted Bay's motion for a new trial, which was held on 12 January 1850, again before Judge Hamilton. This time, Scott's lawyers were Alexander P. Field and David N. Hall. Sanford had by this time

completely taken over the widow Emerson's affairs and retained Hugh A. Garland and Lyman D. Norris for the defense.

At the second trial, the jury held that Scott was a free man, based on certain Missouri state court precedents that held that even though Missouri was a slave state, residence in a free state or territory resulted in a slave's emancipation. Scott's freedom was short-lived, however.

Sanford appealed to the Missouri Supreme Court. After more than two years, Judge William Scott announced that court's decision on 22 March 1852. Scott reversed the jury verdict of the second trial, stating that Dred Scott was still a slave. Although Judge Scott's decision was couched in legal terms concerning states' rights and the legality of slavery within Missouri's borders, in fact the real basis for the decision was the rise to power of pro-slavery Democrats on the court. Judge Scott justified the court's decision to reverse those legal precedents that supported Dred Scott's freedom by stating that blacks were destined to be slaves:

> We are almost persuaded that the introduction of slavery amongst [Americans] was, in the providence of God, who makes the evil passions of men subservient to His own glory, a means of placing that unhappy race within the pale of civilized nations.

Scott Tries Federal Courts

Following the Missouri Supreme Court's decision, the case was sent back to Judge Hamilton in St. Louis, who was supposed to issue the final order dismissing the case and returning Scott to slavery. Hamilton procrastinated, however, which gave Scott time to hire a new lawyer and get his case into the federal courts. Scott replaced Field and Hall. His new lawyer was Roswell M. Field, who was unrelated to the previous Field. The new Field realized that Sanford had moved to New York City, and was no longer a resident of Missouri. Therefore, Field initiated new proceedings on 2 November 1853, in federal court, under legal provisions that give federal courts jurisdiction over cases between citizens of different states. This principle is called "diversity jurisdiction," and is still valid today. Diversity jurisdiction enabled Scott, as a citizen of Missouri, to sue Sanford, as a citizen of New York, in federal court. The issue of Scott's freedom was now before Judge Robert W. Wells of the U.S. Court for the District of Missouri, located in St. Louis.

At the circuit court's 1854 April Term, Wells held that Scott was a Missouri "citizen" for diversity jurisdiction purposes, despite the fact of Scott's slavery. The case then went to trial, which was held on 15 May 1854. In this, Scott's third freedom trial, the jury ruled in San-

An illustration of the Fugitive Slave Law, 1851.

ford's favor and held that Scott was still a slave. This was despite the fact that Wells, who was a Southerner, was sympathetic to Scott's cause. Field promptly appealed to the U.S. Supreme Court in Washington, D.C. He convinced the distinguished lawyer Montgomery Blair to represent Scott before the Supreme Court, although Scott was virtually penniless.

Blair, who also was originally from Missouri, had successfully pursued political and legal ambitions in Washington. His residence was the now-famous Blair House on Pennsylvania Avenue. Blair was assisted by George Ticknor Curtis. With the assistance of Southern proslavery interests, who recognized the potential importance of the Scott case, Sanford also retained some very eminent lawyers. Sanford was represented before the Supreme Court by former Senator Henry S. Geyer, who like Blair had come from Missouri and made a name for himself as a Washington lawyer. Geyer was assisted by former Senator and U.S. Attorney General Reverdy Johnson, who was a personal friend of Chief Justice Roger B. Taney.

Victory for Slavery, Defeat for Scott

The *Scott* case was filed with the Supreme Court on 30 December 1854, and set for oral argument on the Court's February 1856 Term. The political makeup of the Court weighed heavily in its eventual decision. Southern and pro-slavery justices had a clear majority.

Test Cases

The Supreme Court frowns on test cases, or "friendly" suits. Chief Justice Roger B. Taney once described "friendly" suits as an example of "contempt of the court, and highly reprehensible." Justice David J. Brewer wrote, "It never was the thought that, by means of a friendly suit, a party beaten in the Legislature could transfer to the courts an inquiry as to constitutionality of the legislative Act."

Clearly there has been no justification in the court's eyes, as Brewer noted, for any attempt to reverse the constitutional vote of a legislature by means of a test case. There was another practical reason behind his statement: the justices are only human and can review only so many cases per session.

A famous example of a test case was *Roe v. Wade* (1973), which legalized abortion. By the time the case came before the court, "Roe" (Norma McCorvey) had long since given birth to her baby; nonetheless, she agreed to participate in a case to test an 1859 Texas abortion statute.

Source(s): Biskupic, Joan and Witt, Elder. *Guide to the U.S. Supreme Court,* third edition Washington, DC: Congressional Quarterly, 1997.

The Missouri Compromise

When Missouri applied for admittance to the Union in 1819, the United States was equally divided between free and slave states, with 11 of each. Since slavery already existed in Missouri Territory, it sought admission as a slave state, which infuriated New England abolitionists and other opponents of slavery. Southerners were equally incensed when a ban on the importation of slaves was suggested as a precondition for Missouri's statehood.

Henry Clay of Kentucky offered a compromise: since Maine had also requested admission to the Union, he proposed that Missouri enter as a slave state and Maine be admitted as a free state. The existing parity between free and slave states would remain. Moreover, according to the proposal which became the Missouri Compromise, an imaginary line would be drawn at the 36 degrees, 30 minutes north parallel—the southern boundary of Missouri. No territory above that line could be admitted as a slave state, and no territory below it could enter as a free state.

The Missouri Compromise was repealed by the Kansas-Nebraska Act in 1854, which introduced popular sovereignty over the slavery issue.

Source(s): Hurwitz, Howard L. *An Encyclopedic Dictionary of American History* New York: Washington Square Press, 1974.

Campbell was from Alabama. Catron was from Tennessee. Curtis was from Massachusetts, but was sympathetic to the South. Daniel was from Virginia. Grier was from Pennsylvania, but he was a conservative states' rights advocate. McLean, from Ohio, was the only openly anti-slavery justice on the Court. Nelson was from New York, but like Grier he was a defender of states' rights and lukewarm to the anti-slavery cause. Taney, the chief justice, was from Maryland and the leader of the Court's Southern majority. Finally, Wayne was from Georgia. The justices also were conscious of the fact that 1856 was an election year, and that the *Scott* decision would have important political consequences.

During the 1856 February Term, the justices listened to the parties' arguments for three days. Scott's attorneys presented the "free soil" argument, one favored by Northern abolitionists: once a slave stepped into a free state or territory, he or she was emancipated, or else the power to prohibit slavery was meaningless. Sanford's attorneys presented the states' rights argument, which favored the institution of slavery: Scott had been a slave in Missouri, he had returned to Missouri, and had subjected himself to the jurisdiction of Missouri law and Missouri courts. Therefore, Missouri was entitled to declare Scott a slave, and ignore the fact that Scott would not be a slave elsewhere.

Not surprisingly, most of the justices were in favor of rejecting Scott's freedom plea. However, they could not agree on the proper legal grounds. Some justices wanted to hold that a slave could not sue in federal court, other justices wanted to discuss congressional power to prohibit slavery in the territories and the constitutionality of the Missouri Compromise. The justices decided to postpone their decision until after the presidential election and ordered Scott's and Sanford's lawyers to re-argue the case during the Court's 1856 December Term.

In November of 1856, Democrat James Buchanan was elected president. Buchanan, indifferent to the slavery issue, would sit idly by over the next four years while the country was split into North and South and headed toward the Civil War. After the second round of oral argument in December, during which the parties reiterated the same basic positions, Chief Justice Taney announced the majority of the Court. Taney and six other justices voted to hold that Scott was still a slave. Taney refused to recognize any rights for blacks as citizens under the U.S. Constitution:

> We think they are not, and that they are not included, and were not intended to be included, under the word "citizens" in the Constitution, and can therefore claim none of the rights and privileges which that instrument provides for and secures to the citizens of the United States. On the contrary, they were at that time considered as a subordinate and inferior class of beings, who had been subjugated by the dominant race, and, whether emancipated or not, yet remained subject to their authority and had no rights or privileges but such as those who held the power and the Government might choose to grant them.

From this holding, Taney went on to state that Scott was a slave wherever he went, and could be reclaimed at any time by his lawful owner under that provision of the Constitution that forbids Congress from depriving Americans of life, liberty, and property without due process of law. Taney held that Scott was "property" and therefore the Missouri Compromise was unconstitutional:

An Act of Congress which deprives a citizen of the United States of his property, merely because he came himself or brought his property into a particular Territory of the United States, and who had committed no offense against the laws, could hardly be dignified with the name of due process of law.

Scott was a slave once again, and the South had won an important victory. The Missouri Compromise, which had preserved the political status quo for nearly 40 years, was swept away. The North would eventually prevail and abolish slavery, but it would do so only after many battles of a much different and bloodier nature during the Civil War.

Related Cases
Stader v. Graham, 10 How. 82 (1851).
Ableman v. Booth, 21 How. 506 (1859).
Commonwealth v. Aves, 18 Pickering 193 (1936).

Bibliography and Further Reading
Ehrlich, Walter. *They Have No Rights: Dred Scott's Struggle for Freedom.* Westport, CT: Greenwood Press, 1979.

Fehrenbacher, Don Edward. *Slavery, Law, and Politics: The Dred Scott Case in Historical Perspective.* New York: Oxford University Press, 1981.

Johnson, John W. *Historic U.S. Court Cases, 1690-1990: An Encyclopedia.* New York: Garland Publishing, 1992.

Kutler, Stanley I. *The Dred Scott Decision: Law or Politics?* Boston: Houghton Mifflin, 1967.

McGinty, Brian. "Dred Scott's Fight for Freedom Brought Him a Heap O' Trouble." *American History Illustrated,* May 1981, pp. 34-39.

Sudo, Phil. "Five Little People Who Changed U.S. History."*Scholastic Update,* 26 January 1990, pp. 8-10.

CHAMPION V. AMES

Legal Citation: 188 U.S. 321 (1903)

Appellant
Charles F. Champion

Appellee
John C. Ames

Appellant's Claim
That a federal statute prohibiting the carrying of lottery tickets across state lines was unconstitutional.

Chief Lawyer for Appellant
Moritz Rosenthal

Chief Lawyer for Appellee
Beck, Assistant Attorney General

Justices for the Court
Henry Billings Brown, John Marshall Harlan I (writing for the Court), Oliver Wendell Holmes, Joseph McKenna, Edward Douglass White

Justices Dissenting
David Josiah Brewer, Melville Weston Fuller, Rufus Wheeler Peckham, George Shiras, Jr.

Place
Washington, D.C.

Date of Decision
23 February 1903

Decision
Lottery tickets were traffic and carrying them from one state to another was interstate commerce. Under its power to regulate commerce among the states, Congress could prohibit the carrying of lottery tickets from state to state.

Significance
Champion v. Ames was the first recognition of a federal police power. In this case, the Court defined the commerce power of Congress in broad terms, recognizing Congress' power to prohibit the transportation of certain items. Because of this de facto federal police power, national protective legislation grew quickly, leading to the Pure Food and Drug Act and the Mann Act.

Charles F. Champion was accused of violating an Act of Congress of 2 March 1895 entitled An Act for the Suppression of Lottery Traffic through National and Interstate Commerce and the Postal Service. The case before the Supreme Court involved the constitutionality of the first section of the act, which forbade the carrying from one state to another of lottery tickets. Champion was indicted in the U.S. District Court for the Northern District of Texas for conspiracy involving lottery tickets. The indictment charged that on or about 1 February 1899, in Dallas County, Texas, Champion and Charles B. Park conspired to carry lottery tickets from one state to another. Champion and Park had sent a box containing, among other things, two lottery tickets by way of the Wells-Fargo Express Company from Texas to Fresno, California. Champion was arrested in Chicago. Champion filed a writ of *habeas corpus,* which was dismissed by the Circuit Court of the United States for the Northern District of Illinois. The writ of *habeas corpus* complained that Champion was restrained of his liberty by the Marshal of the United States and that the act of 1895 was void under the Constitution of the United States.

An Element Confessedly Injurious to the Public Morals

Champion argued that the carrying of lottery tickets from one state to another state by an express company engaged in carrying freight and packages from state to state, although the tickets may be contained in a box, did not constitute commerce among the states within the meaning of the Constitution. Article 1, section 8, clause 3 of the Constitution gives Congress the power "to regulate commerce with foreign nations, and among the several states, and with the Indian tribes."

The government argued that express companies, when in the business of transportation from one state to another, are instrumentalities of commerce among the states. The government also argued that carrying lottery tickets from one state to another is commerce which Congress may regulate and that Congress may make such an activity an offense.

Justice Harlan I, writing for the majority, defined commerce as "commercial intercourse between nations and parts of nations in all its branches." The word "among" in the Commerce Clause referred to those internal concerns that affect the states generally, but not to those which are completely within a particular state. The Court defined "power" as the power to regulate or to prescribe the rule by which commerce is to be governed. In *Hanley v. Kansas City Southern R. Co.* (1903) the Court said that transportation for others, as an independent business, is commerce, whether or not the goods are sold after delivery. Prior cases showed that commerce among the states embraced navigation, intercourse, communication, traffic, the transit of persons, and the transmission of messages by telegraph. The prior cases also showed that the power of Congress to regulate commerce was plenary, complete in itself, and could be exerted by Congress to its utmost extent, subject only to the limits the Constitution places on it. "In determining the character of the regulations to be adopted, Congress has a large discretion which is not to be controlled by the courts, simply because, in their opinion, such regulations may not be the best or most effective that could be employed."

It was argued that lottery tickets were not of any real value in themselves and therefore are not subjects of commerce. But the tickets had a monetary value in the market among those who chose to sell or buy lottery tickets. Therefore, because lottery tickets were subject to traffic, they were subjects of commerce. The regulation of the carriage of such tickets from state to state, at least by independent carriers, was a regulation of commerce among the several states.

Champion's counsel argued that the act did not in fact regulate the carrying of lottery tickets from state to state, but in effect prohibited such carrying, and Congress was given the authority to regulate, not to prohibit. The Court responded that the Constitution did not define a legitimate regulation of interstate commerce, but left to the discretion of Congress the means employed in executing that power. As long as the end was legitimate and within the scope of the Constitution, the means used were constitutional.

The Court noted that in determining whether regulation could sometimes take the form of prohibition, the nature of the interstate traffic could not be overlooked. In *Phalen v. Virginia* (1850) after observing that the suppression of nuisances injurious to public health or morality was among the most important duties of government, the Court said,

> Experience has shown that the common forms of gambling are comparatively innocuous when placed in contrast with the widespread pestilence of lotteries . . . The latter infests the whole community; it enters every dwelling; it reaches every class; it preys upon the hard earnings of the poor; it plunders the ignorant and simple.

If a state considering suppressing lotteries could take into view the evils of lotteries, Congress, having the power to regulate commerce among the states, should be able to provide that such commerce is not polluted by the carrying of lottery tickets from one state to another. The only part of the Constitution that a person wanting to send lottery tickets from one state to another might invoke is that no person shall be deprived of liberty without due process of law. "But surely it will not be said to be a part of anyone's liberty . . . that he shall be allowed to introduce into commerce among the states an element that will be confessedly injurious to the public morals."

The Court noted that Congress, in passing the act, was only supplementing the action of states which, for the protection of the public morals, prohibit lotteries. The act said, in effect, that it would not permit the declared policy of the states, which sought to protect their people against the mischiefs of the lottery business, to be overthrown or disregarded by the agency of interstate commerce. "We should hesitate long before adjudging that an evil of such appalling character, carried on through interstate commerce, cannot be met and crushed by the only power competent to that end."

The Court stated that regulation may sometimes appropriately assume the form of prohibition. This had been illustrated by regulations regarding the transportation from one state to another of diseased cattle and liquor, and by the Sherman Anti-Trust Act, which prohibited unlawful restraints and monopolies. In *Addyston Pipe & Steel Co. v. United States* (1899), the Court said,

> Under this grant of power to Congress that body . . . may enact such legislation as shall declare void and prohibit the performance of any contract between individuals or corporations where the natural and direct effect of such a contract will be . . . to directly . . . regulate to any substantial extent interstate commerce.

The Court did not agree that the constitutional guarantee of liberty to the individual to enter into private contracts limited the power of Congress and prevented it from legislating on the subject of such contracts. In fact, the Court felt the opposite was true, that the provision regarding the liberty of the citizen was to some extent limited by the Commerce Clause of the Constitution and that the power of Congress to regulate interstate commerce allowed Congress to prohibit citizens from entering into private contracts which regulate commerce among the states.

Suppression of Lotteries is a Power of the States

Chief Justice Fuller, writing the dissent, noted that the power to impose restraints on persons and property to conserve and promote public health, good order, and prosperity was a power that has always belonged to the states. The suppression of lotteries as a harmful business fell within this police power.

> To hold that Congress has general police power would be to hold that it may accomplish objects not entrusted to the general government, and to defeat the operation of the 10th Amendment, declaring that the powers not delegated to the United States by the Constitution, nor prohibited by it to the states, are reserved to the states respectively, or to the people.

Impact

Congress had no constitutional mandate to protect public health, welfare or morals, which traditionally were the responsibilities of the states through their police powers. But in the late nineteenth century Congress began to develop a federal police power to deal with social problems of national scope. To justify this, Congress used its authority over interstate commerce. In *Champion v. Ames,* known as the Lottery Case, the Court sanctioned the new federal police power, noting that the act did not interfere with the sale of lottery tickets within states and thus did not infringe on states' rights. The Court justified the ban on carrying lottery tickets over state lines as Congress' power to suppress "an evil of such appalling character," thus propounding the noxious products doctrine.

In 1904, the Court enlarged on the *Champion v. Ames* ruling, upholding a police use of the federal tax power to hinder the marketing of colored oleomargarine. The Court cited the Lottery Case as a precedent when upholding the Pure Food and Drug Act and the Mann Act, which prohibited transporting women across state lines for immoral purposes.

Issues of the extent of Congress' power over interstate commerce and the existence of a federal police power were central to the Progressive Party's attempts at rescuing the poor through strengthening the state. The importance of the harmfulness of a product in justifying a federal police power, stressed in the Lottery Case, gave flexibility that allowed the Court to step back from this position as progressivism declined.

Related Cases

Addyston Pipe & Steel Co. v. United States, 175 U.S. 211 (1899).
Hanley v. Kansas City S. R. Co., 187 U.S. 617 (1903).

Bibliography and Further Reading

Hall, Kermit L., ed. *The Oxford Companion to the Supreme Court of the United States.* New York: Oxford University Press, 1992.

Johnson, John W. *Historic U.S. Court Cases, 1690–1990: An Encyclopedia.* New York: Garland Publishing, 1992.

Levy, Leonard W., ed. *Encyclopedia of the American Constitution,* Vol. 4. New York: Macmillan, 1986.

Witt, Elder, ed. *Congressional Quarterly's Guide to the U.S. Supreme Court.* Washington, DC: Congressional Quarterly, Inc., 1979.

MCGRAIN V. DAUGHERTY

Legal Citation: 273 U.S. 135 (1927)

Appellant
John J. McGrain

Appellee
Mally S. Daugherty

Appellant's Claim
That the U.S. Senate had not exceeded its authority in compelling a witness to testify before a committee investigating the Teapot Dome scandal.

Chief Lawyer for Appellant
George W. Wickersham

Chief Lawyers for Appellee
Arthur I. Vorys, John P. Phillips

Justices for the Court
Louis D. Brandeis, Pierce Butler, Oliver Wendell Holmes, James Clark McReynolds, Edward Terry Sanford, George Sutherland, William Howard Taft, Willis Van Devanter (writing for the Court)

Justices Dissenting
None (Harlan Fiske Stone did not participate)

Place
Washington, D.C.

Date of Decision
17 January 1927

Decision
The Senate had not exceeded its authority because congressional investigations are presumed to serve some legislative purpose.

Significance
The Supreme Court's decision in *McGrain v. Daugherty* dramatically expanded Congress's ability to investigate the lives and activities of citizens.

Teapot Dome

The case of *McGrain v. Daugherty* dealt with Congress's power to investigate. In this instance, the legislative body was investigating into a far-reaching scandal that came to be known as Teapot Dome. Since 1909, the U.S. government had set aside three tracts of oil-bearing land—Elk Hills and Buena Vista in California and Teapot Dome in Wyoming—for use by the U.S. Navy in case of an emergency oil shortage. When President Warren G. Harding took office in 1920, he transferred the reserves from the custody of the U.S. Navy to his close friend and newly appointed Secretary of the Interior, Albert B. Fall. Within two years, and without congressional approval, Fall leased the Teapot Dome Reserve to a private oil company without competitive bidding. These activities were later brought to light by the press.

In October of 1923, an investigation revealed that Fall had received cash and cattle in exchange for the lease on Teapot Dome and other oil reserves. Fall was tried and initially acquitted for conspiracy to defraud the government. In 1929, he was convicted of bribery, fined $100,000, and sentenced to a year in jail. For a time, Fall had enjoyed the protection of powerful friends in the government, including Attorney General Harry M. Daugherty. However, widespread distrust of the Department of Justice and of Daugherty (who resigned in 1924), as well as the pressures brought to bear by extensive press coverage of the scandal, caused Congress to initiate an investigation of Daugherty's failure to prosecute the malefactors in the scandal.

Daugherty's Brother Is Called to Testify

Called before the Senate's investigating committee was Mally S. Daugherty, brother of the former attorney general. Daugherty refused to appear and was promptly placed under arrest by John J. McGrain, the sergeant-at-arms of the Senate. Daugherty successfully gained his release by demanding a writ of *habeas corpus*. In his petition, he argued that the Senate had exceeded its powers under the Constitution by compelling him to testify on a non-legislative matter. A lower court agreed, saying: "What the Senate is engaged in doing is not investigating the Attorney

Harry N. Daugherty
(left) sits with Thomas
Dixon, 1931.
© AP/Wide World
Photos.

General's office; it is investigating the former Attorney General. What it has done is to put him on trial before it. In so doing it is exercising the judicial function. This it has no power to do." McGrain then appealed this decision to the U.S. Supreme Court. The Court had to address the question of whether, since there is no express provision in the Constitution for congressional investigations, this power is implied as part of its legislative function.

McGrain Prevails in High Court

On 17 January 1927, the Supreme Court issued its decision. In an 8-0 ruling, the Court upheld Congress' contempt conviction against Daugherty. In doing so, it embraced a broad interpretation of Congress' power to investigate the lives and activities of private citizens. Calling the power to compel testimony an "attribute of the power to legislate," the justices found the first function indispensable to the second.

Teapot Dome Scandal

The Teapot Dome scandal of the 1920s became a permanent symbol of corruption in the U.S. government. It marked the first time in U.S. history that an officer in a president's cabinet was convicted of a felony and served a prison sentence.

The scandal involved an area in Wyoming, called Teapot Dome, that had been set aside in 1909 by President William Howard Taft for naval petroleum reserves in the event of war. In 1920, Congress gave the secretary of the Navy broad powers to lease naval reserves, sell oil, or exchange it for naval supplies or construction. When Albert Bacon Fall became secretary of the interior under President Warren G. Harding, he revised an executive order giving the Navy control over the reserves so that leasing would not require the approval of the secretary of the Navy. Fall recommended the Navy take royalties on oil sold from leased reserves not

in cash, but in oil certificates that would pay for naval construction.

The illegal moneys Fall received from leasing to oil barons allowed him to pay eight years worth of back taxes on his ranch, buy a racehorse and cattle, purchase a neighboring ranch, and build a hydroelectric plant.

The Teapot Dome scandal led to nine separate trials. Each individual involved was investigated for charges of conspiracy to defraud the U.S. government, contempt of the U.S. Senate, contempt of court for jury shadowing, perjury, accepting a bribe, and giving a bribe.

Source(s): Knappman, Edward W., ed. *Great American Trials.* Detroit, MI: Visible Ink Press, 1994.

In rendering its decision, the unanimous majority addressed two principal questions. The first was whether a congressional committee can compel a private individual to appear before it to give testimony, despite the fact that, in the Court's determination, there is no provision for this power in the Constitution. Citing examples from both British parliamentary history and the annals of the U.S. Congress, Justice Van Devanter concluded that "the power of inquiry—with process to enforce it—is an essential and appropriate auxiliary to the legislative function." "A legislative body cannot legislate wisely or effectively in the absence of information respecting the conditions which the legislation is intended to affect or change." Van Devanter added, "and where the legislative body does not itself possess the requisite information—which not infrequently is true—recourse must be had to others who do possess it."

The second question the Court had to address was whether Daugherty's testimony was requested in order to obtain information in aid of the legislative function. In rejecting the lower court's determination that the Senate had attempted to perform a judicial function, the Court concluded that the information obtained from Daugherty's testimony could be used as an aid in drafting future laws. As Van Devanter opined: "The only legitimate object the Senate could have in ordering the investigation was to aid it in legislating, and we think the subject matter was such that the pre-sumption should be indulged that this was the real object. An express avowal of the object would have been better; but in view of the particular subject matter was not indispensable."

Impact

The impact of the Supreme Court's decision in *McGrain v. Daugherty* was felt most acutely by the subjects of congressional investigations in the 1950s, when suspected Communists were compelled to testify before House and Senate committees. The Supreme Court often relied upon the presumption of legislative purpose outlined in this case to justify those investigations.

Related Cases

Reed v. County Commissioners of Delaware County, 277 U.S. 376 (1928).
Leonard v. Earle, 279 U.S. 392 (1929).
Adams v. Maryland, 347 U.S. 179 (1954).
Costello v. United States, 350 U.S. 359 (1956).

Bibliography and Further Reading

Chandler, Ralph C. *The Constitutional Law Dictionary.* Santa Barbara, CA: ABC-Clio, Inc., 1987.

Cushman, Robert Fairchild with Susan P. Koniak. *Leading Constitutional Decisions.* Englewood Cliffs, NJ: Prentice-Hall, Inc., 1992.

Menez, Joseph Francis. *Summaries of Leading Cases of the Constitution.* Savage, MD: Littlefield, Adams, 1990.

BALDWIN V. G. A. F. SEELIG, INC.

Legal Citation: 294 U.S. 511 (1935)

Appellant
Baldwin, for the state of New York

Appellee
G. A. F. Seelig, Inc.

Appellant's Claim
That G. A. F. Seelig, Inc., a milk distributor, had no right under the New York Milk Control Act to sell milk in New York state, milk that had been purchased outside the state at a price lower than the minimum established by the act.

Justices for the Court
Louis D. Brandeis, Pierce Butler, Benjamin N. Cardozo (writing for the Court), Charles Evans Hughes, James Clark McReynolds, Owen Josephus Roberts, Harlan Fiske Stone, George Sutherland, Willis Van Devanter

Justices Dissenting
None

Place
Washington, D.C.

Date of Decision
4 March 1935

Decision
The New York Milk Control Act violated the commerce clause of the U.S. Constitution.

Significance
Baldwin v. G. A. F. Seelig, Inc. reinforced federal control over interstate commerce, making it difficult for states to use alleged health concerns as a pretext for keeping out products from other states in order to protect their own industries.

G. A. F. Seelig, Inc. was a milk distributor that bought its milk from a creamery in Fair Haven, Vermont and sold it in its home state of New York. Every day, the company purchased some 200 cans of milk and 20 cans of cream, a "can" being equal to 40 gallons. Seelig sold 90 percent in the original cans to hotels, restaurants, and other large facilities. The remaining 10 percent was repackaged in individual bottles and sold directly to consumers.

Under the New York Milk Control Act, dealers such as G. A. F. Seelig had to pay producers (such as the creamery in Vermont) a certain price for milk. If they paid less, the state commissioner of farms and markets would refuse to license the sale of the milk in the state of New York. The price G. A. F. Seelig paid was below the minimum, and therefore the commissioner denied the company a license to sell its milk within the state. Seelig filed suit against the state, in the person of Baldwin and other officials, and the case went to the District Court of the United States for the Southern District of New York. The court issued a split decree: with regard to the milk sold in the "original packages" or cans, Seelig indeed had a right to resell it in New York. However, the court ruled for Baldwin and the state with regard to the repackaged, consumer-sized bottles.

The Cross-Appeal

New York took its case to the Supreme Court on a cross-appeal, which meant that Baldwin was now the appellant, and G. A. F. Seelig the appellee. As noted by Justice Cardozo, who would give the Court's opinion, New York did not attempt to assert that it had authority to regulate the price paid for milk in Vermont; nor did it claim power to prevent anyone from bringing in milk from Vermont (assuming there was no health issue involved), regardless of the price paid. The only area in which New York claimed authority was in prohibiting the sale of such milk once it had entered the state or, as Cardozo put it, "The importer . . . may keep his milk or drink it, but sell it, he may not."

The "Metropolitan Milk District," which consisted of New York City and surrounding areas, bought some 70 percent of its milk from within the state. As for the other 30 percent, according to Cardozo, the price provision of the Milk Control Act helped "keep the system unencumbered by competition from afar." Whereas milk prices would tend to be relatively uniform within the state, in Vermont they might be lower. The act removed the economic incentive for buying milk from outside New York. To some, it appeared that the act simply served to protect the jobs of New York milk producers. But the state, in its case, asserted that the Milk Control Act had been put in place ultimately to protect the health of its citizens. By ensuring that New York milk producers earned a good profit and thus stayed in business, the act maintained a strong milk industry within the state. This, in turn, meant a milk industry was under state health control, control which would presumably be forfeited to other states if New York producers were consistently undersold and forced out of business.

Violation of the Commerce Clause

Justice Cardozo gave the Court's opinion, the only opinion on record for the case. He began by clarifying the issue, stating that New York was only trying to limit the *sale* of milk purchased from another state, not the purchase itself. But even so, Cardozo noted, the act violated the Constitution and presented a barrier to interstate traffic every bit as effective as the tariff by which independent nations often restrict trade. Article I, Section 8, Clause 3, the "commerce clause," gives power over interstate commerce to Congress, not the states. Therefore, "it is the established doctrine of this court that a state may not, in any form or under any guise, directly burden the prosecution of interstate business."

With regard to the argument that New York milk producers should be kept in business in order to maintain state control over the milk industry for the sake of its citizens' health, Cardozo saw this only as a smokescreen for protection of local industry. Furthermore, if one state is able to make an exception to the commerce clause, he suggested, this paves the way for each state to make its own laws regarding trade. In other words to behave as though it were a nation rather than a state that is subject to the federal government. To allow this, Cardozo remarked ominously, "would be to invite a speedy end of our national solidarity." As for any possible argument that underpaid farmers in New York would seek to relax sanitary controls in order to cut

costs, Cardozo again dismissed the idea. Such actions on the part of a farmer, he said, would have to be dealt with by more direct methods designed specifically to prevent the sale of milk that does not meet health standards. Presumably, such laws were already in place.

Keeping Trade Open between the States

Cardozo did not deny states the right to prevent the sale of products which fail to meet their health standards. However, he opposed the use of such standards as a means of protecting local industry. Thus the Court struck down Baldwin's cross-appeal on the issue of selling the milk to individual consumers. There is no evidence that the opinion of the Court was less than unanimous.

Baldwin was not the first case involving one state's attempt to regulate commerce with another state. The case of *Gibbons v. Ogden*, for instance, was heard in 1824 and concerned a steamboat franchise with questionable restrictive clauses. Fourteen years after *Baldwin*, in *Hood v. DuMond*, the Court ruled that a state had no authority to refuse a license to a company processing milk for sale outside the state. In the years since *Baldwin*, the Court has generally upheld the maintenance of free trade between states except in instances involving health questions. Even in such situations, as in the case of *Dean Milk Company v. Madison*, the Court has placed the burden of proof on the state, to show that it is genuinely protecting the health of its citizens and not the health of its industry.

Related Cases

Gibbons v. Ogden, 8 Wheat. 1 (1824).
Hood v. DuMond, 336 U.S. 525 (1949).
Dean Milk Company v. Madison, 340 U.S. 349 (1951).

Bibliography and Further Reading

Bartholomew, Paul C., and Joseph F. Menez. *Summaries of Leading Cases on the U.S. Constitution*, 13th ed. Savage, MD: Rowman & Littlefield Publishers, Inc., 1990.

Chandler, Ralph C., et al. *The Constitutional Law Dictionary*, Vol. 2. Santa Barbara, CA: ABC-Clio, 1987.

Hall, Kermit L., ed. *The Oxford Companion to the Supreme Court of the United States*. New York: Oxford University Press, 1992.

A.L.A. SCHECHTER POULTRY CORPORATION V. UNITED STATES

Legal Citation: 295 U.S. 495 (1935)

Petitioner
A.L.A. Schechter Poultry Corporation

Respondent
United States

Petitioner's Claim
That the code of fair business practice established under the National Industrial Recovery Act of 1933 could not affect its business because the code did not have the force of law.

Chief Lawyer for Petitioner
Joseph Heller

Chief Lawyer for Respondent
Donald P. Richberg

Justices for the Court
Louis D. Brandeis, Pierce Butler, Benjamin N. Cardozo, Charles Evans Hughes (writing for the Court), James Clark McReynolds, Owen Josephus Roberts, Harlan Fiske Stone, George Sutherland, Willis Van Devanter

Justices Dissenting
None

Place
Washington, D.C.

Date of Decision
27 May 1935

Decision
That the federal legislation establishing the National Recovery Administration was unconstitutional in that it delegated too much law-making power to non-governmental individuals.

Significance
The decision overturned the major effort of the first administration of Franklin Roosevelt (1933-1937) to regulate and control the economy during the Great Depression.

The New Deal on Trial

During the "first 100 days" of the administration of Franklin D. Roosevelt, a number of bills were passed by Congress to deal with the Great Depression. Although separate bills dealt with different aspects of unemployment, banking, agriculture, and other problems, the central piece of legislation dealing with the economy as a whole was the National Industrial Recovery Act. Under that act, the government created the National Recovery Administration, whose function was to regulate the economy to ensure that prices were not cut and that businesses operated at prices that would keep them going. In order to do this, businesses would select, through their business associations, delegates to code authorities for each type of business. Labor unions and the consuming public would also be represented on these code authorities. The authorities would write specific regulations governing each business, setting prices, wages, and specific conditions for each type of business. The concept was that business could determine a fair code of competition, and at these prices, individual companies would not undercut the rest.

At first, the only sanction against companies not obeying the codes was that they would be denied the right to display a "Blue Eagle," a symbol of the National Recovery Administration. However, the codes would have the force of law and the federal government could extend other punishments to firms not following the codes.

The principles involved seemed to violate several long-standing views of the American economic system. In particular, the legislation allowed private business associations, in agreement with their unions, to create standards that would restrain trade, an apparent violation of the Sherman Anti-Trust Act. Furthermore, the codes would have the force of law, even though they had been prepared by the non-legislative groups collected in the code authorities.

Arguing for the federal government, attorneys working under Donald R. Richberg suggested that extraordinary times required extraordinary measures. In effect, Richberg and his associates were taking the doctrine of implied powers that had been established in *McCulloch v. Maryland* in 1819 and extending it greatly to cover the economic crisis of the 1930s.

The Schechter brothers.
© UPI/Corbis-Bettmann.

The Schechter case arose when a particular chicken packing firm on Long Island, New York, violated the code for its industry in several regards. Among the many violations cited were some related to health conditions. However, the firm claimed that it did not need to obey the codes established by the code authority because the codes did not have the force of law.

The Court agreed with the attorneys for the Schechter firm, spelling out a number of objections to the law and finding it unconstitutional. While extra-

---

The National Industrial Recovery Act of 1933

In June of 1933, Congress passed the National Industrial Recovery Act (NIRA), one of the central policy initiatives of President Roosevelt's New Deal. The act established the National Recovery Administration (NRA), which would operate as a coordinating committee for business and labor. Through the NRA, industrial leaders could create regulatory codes which would be exempt from prosecution on antitrust grounds. These codes would set guidelines in competitive practices, hours, and wages in various industries.

In addition, the NIRA pumped more than $3 billion into the Public Works Administration (PWA). The PWA and NRA proved popular with the public: the former put

men to work in public works and the latter helped ensure fair treatment of labor.

Administered by Hugh Johnson, the NRA and its Blue Eagle symbol were a fixture of public life for over a year. By 1934, the NRA hit troubled times due to concerns expressed by senators that the agency's codes amounted to price-fixing. In May of 1935, the Supreme Court struck down the NIRA in *A.L.A. Schechter Poultry Corp. v. United States.*

Source(s): Bacon, Donald C., et al., eds. *The Encyclopedia of the United States Congress.* New York: Simon & Schuster, 1995.

---

ordinary crises called for extraordinary remedies, that did not justify the creation or the enlargement of constitutional powers. Congress could not abdicate or transfer to others its power to legislate. Congress could delegate rule-making, but it must lay down policies and standards and not turn over the creation of policies and standards to others. The "Codes of Competition" were meant, in fact, to be codes of law, and they were designed not merely to ensure competition, but to bring about the rehabilitation of the economy. No court rulings had ever justified the delegation of legislative power to the president (who appointed the boards), nor had the courts ever justified turning legislative power over to associations of companies or individuals. The code making authority was therefore unconstitutional. For good measure, the Court also ruled that the Schechter Company was not truly an interstate business, as it marketed its product entirely within New York.

With the striking down of the National Recovery Administration, the Roosevelt administration and Congress turned to more specific pieces of legislation designed to stimulate the economy, to increase employment, and to provide relief and security for employees. In effect, the Court had prevented the federal government from establishing a system of business regulation designed by businesses themselves, and preserving some aspects of a free market.

Related Cases

McCulloch v. Maryland, 17 U.S. 316 (1819).

National Labor Relations Board v. Jones & Laughlin Steel, 301 U.S. 1 (1937).

Bibliography and Further Reading

Johnson, Hugh. *Blue Eagle, From Egg to Earth.* New York: Greenwood Press, 1968 (1935).

Ohl, John K. *Hugh S. Johnson and the New Deal.* DeKalb, IL: Northern Illinois University Press, 1985.

Richberg, D. R. *The Rainbow, after the Sunshine of Prosperity, the Deluge of the Depression.* Garden City, NY: Doubleday, 1936

CARTER V. CARTER COAL CO.

Legal Citation: 298 U.S. 238 (1936)

Petitioner
James Walter Carter

Respondent
Carter Coal Co.

Petitioner's Claim
That the Bituminous Coal Conservation Act of 1935, part of President Franklin Roosevelt's New Deal, was an unconstitutional intrusion of the federal government into rights reserved for the states under the Tenth Amendment.

Chief Lawyers for Petitioner
Frederick H. Wood, William D. Whitney, Richard H. Wilmer

Chief Lawyer for Respondent
Karl J. Hardy

Justices for the Court
Pierce Butler, Charles Evans Hughes, James Clark McReynolds, Owen Josephus Roberts, George Sutherland (writing for the Court), Willis Van Devanter

Justices Dissenting
Louis D. Brandeis, Benjamin N. Cardozo, Harlan Fiske Stone

Place
Washington, D.C.

Date of Decision
18 March 1936

Decision
By a vote of 6-3, the Court struck down the act, holding that the Commerce Clause of Article II of the Constitution does not grant Congress the right to regulate commercial activities and labor relations.

Significance
Carter marked the last time the Supreme Court would use the Tenth Amendment to override the Commerce Clause.

In the midst of the Great Depression, President Franklin Roosevelt developed plans for the New Deal, a series of programs designed to curb the disastrous effects of the economic depression that enveloped the country. As a part of the New Deal, Congress passed the Bituminous Coal Conservation Act of 1935, and it was legislation meant to control overproduction and self-defeating competition between coal mining companies. The philosophical heart of the act—as of the entire New Deal plan—was the belief that the Commerce Clause of Article II of the Constitution empowered Congress with the authority to regulate most aspects of American industry.

James Walter Carter, a shareholder in the Carter Coal Company, filed suit in the Supreme Court of the District of Columbia seeking an injunction to prevent the company from complying with the coal act. After James Carter's suit was dismissed, he filed an appeal with the U.S. Court for the District of Columbia. While that appeal was still pending, he also petitioned the U.S. Supreme Court for review of the trial court's dismissal. In the U.S. Supreme Court, his suit was combined with several others challenging the coal act.

Citing States' Rights, Court Stymies New Deal Legislation

Justice Sutherland wrote the opinion of the Court, which paid scant attention to the dire conditions then extant in the coal mining business. Instead, it concentrated on an argument that had dogged the nation since its foundation: the competition between states' rights and federal power.

> The ruling and firmly established principle is that the powers which general government may exercise are only those specifically enumerated in the Constitution, and such implied powers as are necessary and proper to carry into effect the enumerated powers. Whether the end sought to be attained by an act of Congress is legitimate is wholly a matter of constitutional power and not at all of legislative discretion.

According to the Court, the commerce power, which the president and Congress saw as the constitutional

The Bituminous Coal Conservation Act

Bituminous coal, or soft coal, has a lower carbon content than anthracite, or hard coal. The latter, the highest grade of coal, is used for domestic heating; bituminous coal is good only for industrial heating and for coke.

The Bituminous Coal Conservation Act of 1935 was designed to achieve a variety of purposes that included the stabilizing of the coal-mining industry; the promotion of interstate commerce in coal; the marketing of bituminous coal by cooperative enterprises; the tax guidelines on the sale of such coal; the identification of the production, sale, and use of bituminous coal with a national public interest; and the conservation of bituminous coal.

These justifications were enumerated in section 1 of the act. Section 2 established a National Bituminous Coal Commission within the Department of the Interior; section 3 presented the conditions governing the coal tax; and section 4 established guidelines for a nationwide "Bituminous Coal Code" and made a number of labor provisions. Under the Coal Code, prices could be fixed at certain minimums, and all coal mines throughout the United States would be required to abide by these prices.

---

rationale for the coal act, did not apply. As it had done many times before, the Court distinguished direct effects on interstate commerce, which Congress could control, from indirect ones, which it could not. Here, the effects were deemed indirect because coal mining was "manufacturing" which took place in a set location, not commerce or trade which crossed state lines. If there was to be regulation of coal mining, therefore, the Constitution mandated that it take place at the state level. The coal act was struck down.

Since 1933, when Roosevelt took office, the Supreme Court had developed a record of opposing most New Deal legislation that came before it. In frustration, Roosevelt developed a plan for "packing" the Court with justices who would be more amenable to his economic plan for rescuing the country. The plan ultimately failed, but the composition of the Court began to change nonetheless. In 1937, one of the ultra-conservative "Four Horsemen" (named for the Biblical Four Horsemen of the Apocalypse that brought destruction to the land), holdovers from the preceding Taft Court, Justice Van Devanter, announced his retirement, opening up the first of seven vacancies Roosevelt was to fill

over the next few years. And in the spring of 1937, Justice Roberts switched his voting posture toward the New Deal. Starting with *National Labor Relations Board v. Jones & Laughlin Steel Corp.* (1937), the Court abandoned its embrace of states' rights and the Tenth Amendment, and took up the Commerce Clause and the New Deal agenda.

Related Cases

Schechter Poultry Corp. v. United States, 295 U.S. 495 (1935).

National Labor Relations Board v. Jones & Laughlin Steel Corp., 301 U.S. 1 (1937).

Bibliography and Further Reading

Benson, Paul Revere. *The Supreme Court and the Commerce Clause, 1937-1970.* New York: Dunellen, 1970.

Leuchtenburg, William Edward. *The FDR Years: On Roosevelt and His Legacy.* New York: Columbia University Press, 1995.

Redish, Martin H. *The Constitution as Political Structure.* New York: Oxford University Press, 1995.

UNITED STATES V. CAROLENE PRODUCTS COMPANY

Legal Citation: 304 U.S. 144 (1938)

Petitioner
United States

Respondent
Carolene Products Company

Petitioner's Claim
That congressional legislation outlawing the shipment of adulterated milk was a constitutionally permissible regulation of interstate commerce.

Chief Lawyers for Petitioner
Homer S. Cummings, Brien McMahon

Chief Lawyer for Respondent
George N. Murdock

Justices for the Court
Hugo Lafayette Black, Louis D. Brandeis, Pierce Butler, Charles Evans Hughes, Owen Josephus Roberts, Harlan Fiske Stone (writing for the Court)

Justices Dissenting
James Clark McReynolds (Benjamin N. Cardozo and Stanley Forman Reed did not participate)

Place
Washington, D.C.

Date of Decision
25 April 1938

Decision
Congressional regulation of "filled milk" was held to be constitutionally permissible.

Significance
The Supreme Court's decision in *United States v. Carolene Products Company* marked a significant change in its thinking about when and in what type of cases it would review the constitutionality of federal legislation. What began as a spat over filled, or adulterated milk became the occasion for a substantial rethinking of judicial review. Justice Harlan Stone's famous footnote in this case has sparked voluminous legal debate over the ensuing decades.

A Dispute over Filled Milk

In 1923, Congress passed the "Filled Milk Act," a law which banned the shipment of "skimmed milk compounded with any fat or oil other than milk fat, so as to resemble milk or cream." It acted under its constitutional authority to regulate interstate commerce, in hopes of preventing the distribution of what it called an "adulterated article of food, injurious to the public health." The Carolene Products Company of Illinois was indicted under the law after it attempted to market a product called "Milnut," a flavorful combination of condensed skimmed milk and coconut oil designed to seem like condensed milk or cream. The company protested the indictment, arguing that the Filled Milk Act exceeded Congress' authority to regulate interstate commerce and deprived the company of its property without due process. The District Court for Southern Illinois ruled in favor of the Carolene Products Company, prompting the United States to appeal the case to the U.S. Supreme Court.

High Court Rules

On 25 April 1938, the Supreme Court issued its decision. By a vote of 6-1, with two justices not participating, the Court overturned the lower court decision and ruled in favor of the United States. Justice Stone delivered the opinion of the majority, with Justice James McReynolds the lone dissenter.

In presenting his argument, Justice Stone first outlined the parameters of Congress' ability to regulate interstate commerce. Quoting an earlier case, Stone determined that that power is "complete in itself, may be exercised to its utmost extent, and acknowledges no limitations, other than are prescribed in the Constitution." With regard to the specifics of the case at hand, he concluded: "The prohibition of the shipment of filled milk in interstate commerce is a permissible regulation of commerce"—provided, in his view, that Fifth Amendment due process protections were observed.

Stone and his fellow justices found no violations of due process in the Congress' actions. In fact, Stone concluded, the prerogatives of due process had been scrupulously followed:

Justice Harlan Fiske Stone. © Photograph by Harris and Ewing. Collection of the Supreme Court of the United States.

The Filled Milk Act was adopted by Congress after committee hearings, in the course of which eminent scientists and health experts testified. An extensive investigation was made of the commerce in milk compounds in which vegetable oils have been substituted for natural milk fat, and of the effect upon the public health of the use of such compounds as a food substitute for milk.

Stone then turned his attention to a consideration of when and how the Court ought to review congressional laws like the one it had been asked to rule on here. In doing so, he acknowledged Congress' attempt to "red flag" the issue of filled milk by defining it in the statute as a threat to public health. But he declared that the Court would have been inclined to find in its favor "even in the absence of such aids" because

> the existence of facts supporting the legislative judgment is to be presumed, for regulatory legislation affecting ordinary commercial transactions is not to be pronounced unconstitutional unless in the light of the facts made known or generally assumed it is of such a character as to preclude the assumption that it rests upon some rational basis within the knowledge and experience of the legislators.

This doctrine gave Congress wide latitude to regulate in commerce cases like the one at issue here.

Stone expanded on these ideas in a footnote to his opinion that has become one of the hallmarks of modern American jurisprudence. In the famous "footnote four," Stone suggested that there may be circumstances in which the Court must exercise a more rigorous form of judicial review, known in legal circles as "strict scrutiny." He named three specific types of cases in which this narrower presumption of constitutionality should prevail. First, he urged special judicial review in cases where "legislation appears on its face to be within a specific prohibition of the Constitution, such as those of the first ten Amendments." Second, he cited cases of "legislation which restricts those political processes which can ordinarily be expected to bring about repeal of undesirable legislation," such as voting rights and freedom of assembly cases. Finally, and most importantly for the course of American law, he called for heightened review of cases where "prejudice against discrete and insular minorities" may tend "to curtail the operation of those political processes ordinarily to be relied upon to protect minorities." In essence, Stone was creating a hierarchy of cases, each with its own standard of judicial review. Commercial regulation cases would be viewed with the least amount of scrutiny, because it was to be assumed that the legislators were acting with good reason unless there was clear evidence to the contrary. Cases involving the curtailment of political liberties or discrimination against religious or ethnic groups, values at the heart of a democratic society, were accorded the most intense scrutiny the Court could provide.

Debate and Dissent

Stone's doctrine came to be known as the "preferred freedoms" doctrine and sparked much legal debate. Even among the justices there was disagreement on both sides. Justice McReynolds dissented from the opinion entirely, while Justice Black refused to concur in the provisions of footnote four. He would have gone further than Stone in presuming the constitutionality of all laws passed by Congress. Later scholars debated the meaning of the phrase "discrete and insular minorities" and argued over whether whites, gays, and other groups claiming discrimination could demand strict scrutiny under this doctrine.

Impact

The impact of the Supreme Court's decision in *United States v. Carolene Products Company* went well beyond the regulation of an obscure milk product. Stone's "preferred freedoms" doctrine established new parameters for judicial review of federal legislation. The Court continues to struggle with the question of when and with what level of scrutiny to intervene in cases involving the lawmaking power.

Related Cases

United States v. Lowden, 308 U.S. 225 (1939).
Katzenbach v. McClung, 379 U.S. 294 (1964).
United States v. Bass, 404 U.S. 336 (1972).
Sugarman v. Dougall, 413 U.S. 634 (1973).

Bibliography and Further Reading

Chandler, Ralph C. *The Constitutional Law Dictionary*. Santa Barbara, CA: ABC-Clio, Inc., 1987.

Cushman, Robert Fairchild with Susan P. Koniak. *Leading Constitutional Decisions*. Englewood Cliffs, NJ: Prentice-Hall, Inc., 1992.

Menez, Joseph Francis. *Summaries of Leading Cases of the Constitution*. Savage, MD: Littlefield, Adams, 1990.

UNITED STATES V. DARBY

Legal Citation: 312 U.S. 100 (1941)

Appellant
United States

Appellee
Fred W. Darby

Appellant's Claim
That the Constitution grants Congress power under the Commerce Clause to regulate workers' hours and wages.

Chief Lawyers for Appellant
Robert H. Jackson, U.S. Attorney General; Francis Biddle, U.S. Solicitor General

Chief Lawyer for Appellee
Archibald B. Lovett

Justices for the Court
Hugo Lafayette Black, William O. Douglas, Felix Frankfurter, Charles Evans Hughes, Frank Murphy, Stanley Forman Reed, Owen Josephus Roberts, Harlan Fiske Stone (writing for the Court)

Justices Dissenting
None (James Clark McReynolds did not participate)

Place
Washington, D.C.

Date of Decision
3 February 1941

Decision
The Supreme Court upheld the Fair Labor Standards Act of 1938 regulating wages and hours.

Significance
Darby was part of a running Court debate that began in 1903, when it upheld legislation forbidding interstate transportation of lottery tickets. The twentieth century has seen other attempts—including the act under consideration here—to make the Commerce Clause a means of promoting the public welfare on a national scale.

In 1938, Congress passed the last major piece of New Deal legislation, the Fair Labor Standards Act. It was based on the Commerce Clause of Article I, section 8 of the Constitution, which provides that: "The Congress shall have Power . . . To Regulate Commerce . . . among the several States." It set maximum hours and minimum wages for workers employed in industries whose products were shipped across state lines. The act was the final piece of President Franklin Roosevelt's economic and social welfare package, which embodied his administration's plan to lift the country out of the Great Depression.

Fred W. Darby was a Georgia industrialist whose firm finished lumber, which was then shipped out of state. The federal government indicted Darby under the Fair Labor Standards Act for paying his workers less than the prescribed minimum wage and requiring them to work longer than the prescribed maximum work week. In federal district court, Darby challenged the act on Fifth and Tenth Amendment grounds, claiming that Congress was attempting to assume a power that the Constitution reserved for the individual states, rather than the federal government. The district court agreed, saying that the act was an attempt to regulate manufacturing, which was not interstate commerce. The federal government then appealed this judgment directly to the U.S. Supreme Court.

Supreme Court Unanimously Upholds Fair Labor Standards Act

Writing for a unanimous Court, Justice Stone upheld the act as an appropriate exercise of Congress's power to regulate interstate commerce. First, however, he had to address a Supreme Court precedent that pointed the other way. In *Hammer v. Dagenhart* (1918), the Court struck down federal legislation aimed at controlling child labor. Based on the Commerce Clause, the Child Labor Act was found to be an infringement on the powers reserved to the states in the Tenth Amendment. A bare majority of the justices had voted against the law, with Oliver Wendell Holmes writing an important dissenting opinion in which he stated that the commerce power allowed Congress to regulate not just products shipped through interstate commerce, but their effects. It was the Holmes dissent that Stone alluded to now:

> In that case . . . the powerful and now classic dissent of Mr. Justice Holmes [set] forth the fundamental issues involved, that Congress was without power to exclude the products of child labor from interstate commerce. The reasoning and conclusion of the Court's opinion there cannot be reconciled with the conclusion which we have reached, that the power of Congress is plenary to exclude any article from interstate commerce subject only to the specific prohibitions of the Constitution . . . The conclusion is inescapable that *Hammer v. Dagenhart,* was a departure from the principles which have prevailed in the interpretation of the commerce clause both before and since the decision and that such vitality, as a precedent, as it then had has long since been exhausted. It should be and now is overruled.

The decision did not put an end to the controversy. While *Darby* established the constitutionality of the Fair Labor Act, there still remained some confusion about whether it covered employees who engaged who engaged "in commerce" or "in the production of goods for commerce." In *Maryland v. Wirtz* (1968), the Court ruled that the act also covered state employees. Eight years later, however, in *National League of Cities v. Usery* (1976), the Court overturned *Wirtz* and revived the rule of *Hammer v. Dagenhart* to say that state and municipal employees were not covered by the Fair Labor Act. Then in 1985, the Court revisited the issue in *Garcia v. San Antonio Metropolitan Transit Authority* (1985), overruling *Usery.*

Related Cases
Hammer v Dagenhart, 247 U.S. 251 (1918).
Maryland v. Wirtz, 392 U.S. 183 (1968).
National League of Cities v. Usery, 426 U.S. 833 (1976).
Garcia v. San Antonio Metropolitan Transit Authority, 469 U.S. 528 (1985).

Robert H. Jackson, U.S. Attorney General. © The Library of Congress.

Bibliography and Further Reading

Moss, David A. *Socializing Security: Progressive-Era Economists and the Origins of American Social Policy.* Cambridge, MA: Harvard University Press, 1996.

Orren, Karen. *Belated Feudalism: Labor, the Law, and Liberal Development in the United States.* New York, NY: Cambridge University Press, 1991.

Tomlins, Christopher L., and Andrew J. King, eds. *Labor Law in America: Historical and Critical Essays.* Baltimore, MD: Johns Hopkins Press, 1992.

WOODS V. CLOYD W. MILLER CO.

Legal Citation: 333 U.S. 138 (1948)

Appellant
Tighe E. Woods, Housing Expediter, Office of the Housing Expediter

Appellee
Cloyd W. Miller Co., et al.

Appellant's Claim
That the authority of Congress to regulate rents by virtue of the War Power Act had terminated.

Chief Lawyer for Appellant
Philip B. Perlman, Solicitor General of Washington, D.C.

Chief Lawyer for Appellee
Paul S. Knight

Justices for the Court
Hugo Lafayette Black, Harold Burton, William O. Douglas (writing for the Court), Felix Frankfurter, Robert H. Jackson, Frank Murphy, Stanley Forman Reed, Wiley Blount Rutledge, Fred Moore Vinson

Justices Dissenting
None

Place
Washington, D.C.

Date of Decision
16 February 1948

Decision
The continuation of rent control by Housing and Rent Act of 1947, enacted after the termination of hostilities, was unanimously held to be a valid exercise of the war power.

Significance
The war power, a vague power that enables Congress to establish special rules and regulations during times of war, extends beyond the time frame of actual declaration of war into the time after hostilities cease that is still heavily affected by the cost of the war. This extends into the regulation of housing rental control that had been enacted during World War II to offset the necessary slowing and halting of commercial construction of housing to free materials for the war effort.

The Housing and Rent Act became effective 1 July 1947, and the following day Tighe Woods demanded of his tenants increases of 40 percent and 60 percent for rental accommodations in the Cleveland Defense-Rental Area, an admitted violation of the act.

The district court, in *Woods v. Cloyd W. Miller Co.* was of the view that the authority of Congress to regulate rents by virtue of the war power ended with the Presidential Proclamation terminating hostilities on 31 December 1946. It also concluded that even if the war power continues, Congress did not act under it because it did not say so, and only if Congress says so, or enacts provisions so implying, can it be held that Congress intended to exercise such power. The district court expressed the further view that rent control is not within the war power because "the emergency created by housing shortage came into existence before the war." It also concluded that the act in effect provides "low rentals for certain groups without taking the property or compensating the owner in any way."

Woods sued to enjoin violations of Title II of the Housing and Rent Act of 1947. The district court denied a permanent injunction on the grounds that the act was unconstitutional. The decision was then appealed to the Supreme Court.

The Supreme Court concluded, in the first place, that the war power sustained the legislation. The war power includes the power "to remedy the evils which have arisen from its rise and progress" and continues for the duration of that emergency. Whatever may be the consequences when war is officially terminated, the war power does not necessarily end with the cessation of hostilities.

The constitutional validity of the legislation followed *a fortiori* from past cases. The legislative history of the act made abundantly clear that the deficit in housing which in considerable measure was caused by heavy demobilization of veterans and by the cessation or reduction in residential construction during the period of hostilities due to allocation of building materials to military projects had not yet been eliminated. Since the war effort contributed heavily to that deficit, Congress has power even after cessation of hostilities

Solicitor General

The solicitor general is an officer of the U.S. Department of Justice who represents the U.S. government in cases before the U.S. Supreme Court. This means that the solicitor and the solicitor's staff are the chief courtroom lawyers for the government, preparing legal briefs and making oral arguments in the Court. The solicitor general also decides which cases the United States should appeal from adverse lower-court decisions.

Congress established the office of solicitor general in 1870 as part of the legislation creating the Department of Justice. Although early solicitors occasionally handled federal trials, for the most part the solicitor general has concentrated on appeals to the Supreme Court. In this role the solicitor has come to serve the interest of both the executive branch and the Court.

The solicitor general occasionally files *amicus curiae* briefs in cases where the U.S. government is not a party but important government interests are at stake. Sometimes the Court itself will request that the solicitor file a brief where the government is not a party.

Four former solicitors general later served on the Supreme Court: William Howard Taft, Stanley Forman Reed, Robert H. Jackson, and Thurgood Marshall.

Source(s): *West's Encyclopedia of American Law,* Vol. 9. St. Paul/Minneapolis, MN: The West Group, 1998.

to act to control the forces that a short supply of the needed article created.

The Court also recognized that the force of the effects of war under modern conditions may be felt in the economy for years and years, and that if the war power can be used in days of peace to treat all the wounds which war inflicts on society, it may not only swallow up all other powers of Congress but largely obliterate the Ninth and Tenth Amendments as well. But the Court felt that there were no such implications in this decision. The Court was dealing only with the consequences of a housing deficit greatly intensified during the period of hostilities by the war effort.

The Court found that under the act, the Housing Expediter was authorized to remove the rent controls in any defense-rental area if in their judgment the need no longer exists by reason of new construction or satisfaction of demand in other ways. The Court rejected the argument that the act, by its exemption of certain classes of housing accommodations, violated the Fifth Amendment. Congress did not need to control all rents or none. It can select those areas or those classes of property where the need seems the greatest.

Justice Jackson concurred in the opinion, but uttered misgivings about the concept of war power. He stated the belief that the government asserts no constitutional basis for the legislation other than the vague, undefined, and undefinable "war power." It is the most dangerous power to free government, usually invoked in haste and excitement when calm legislative consideration of constitutional limitation is difficult. The constitutional basis of such a power should be scrutinized with care, particularly when the war power is invoked to do things to the liberties of people, or to their property or economy that only indirectly affect conduct of the war and do not relate to the management of the war itself.

Related Cases
Block v. Hirsh, 256 U.S. 135 (1921).

Bibliography and Further Reading
Biskupic, Joan, and Elder Witt, eds. *Congressional Quarterly's Guide to the U.S. Supreme Court,* 3rd ed. Washington, DC: Congressional Quarterly, Inc., 1996.

Hall, Kermit L., ed. *Oxford Companion to the Supreme Court.* New York: Oxford University Press, p. 909.

BERMAN V. PARKER

Legal Citation: 348 U.S. 26 (1954)

Appellants
Berman and other owners of a department store in Washington, D.C.

Appellees
The National Capital Planning Commission, the Commissioners of the District of Columbia, the District of Columbia Redevelopment Land Agency

Appellants' Claim
The government's taking of their store was unconstitutional because it was contrary to the guarantees of the Fifth Amendment.

Chief Lawyers for Appellants
James C. Toomey, Joseph H. Schneider, Albert Ginsberg

Chief Lawyer for Appellees
Simon Sobeloff, Solicitor General

Justices for the Court
Hugo Lafayette Black, Harold Burton, Tom C. Clark, William O. Douglas (writing for the Court), Felix Frankfurter, Sherman Minton, Stanley Forman Reed, Earl Warren

Justices Dissenting
None (John Marshall Harlan II not yet appointed)

Place
Washington, D.C.

Date of Decision
22 November 1954

Decision
Congress and its agencies (which functioned as the District's local government) may take appellants' department store and the land as long as they pay compensation to the owners.

Significance
The decision determined that state legislatures may exercise wide latitude in determining what serves a "public purpose." And they also have broad leeway in choosing the means to achieve these "public ends." As long as they pay compensation, legislatures may lawfully take property from a private owner and give it to another private owner for his private use.

The Fifth Amendment limits the federal government's power (known as "eminent domain") to seize private property: "nor shall private property be taken for public use, without just compensation." The courts have held that the Fifth Amendment limits also apply to the states under the Fourteenth Amendment's "due process" clause. In addition, the constitution of virtually every state requires payment when property is taken.

Under a 1945 Redevelopment Act for the District of Columbia, Congress created the National Capital Planning Commission. The commission was authorized to design comprehensive plans providing for housing, business, and public buildings. To achieve these plans, the commission could condemn land and lease or sell it to private parties for clearance and redevelopment.

Rebuilding the Nation's Capital

In 1950, the Planning Commission proposed to begin redevelopment in the District's southwestern area. In that section lived some 5,000 persons, 98 percent of whom were considered to be African American. Surveys prepared for the commission suggested that residential dwellings in the area were run down. According to these surveys, some 58 percent had only outdoor toilets. More than 80 percent had no central heating, and 29 percent had no electricity. The commission estimated that two out of three dwellings were beyond repair.

The Planning Commission's scheme for this blighted area was approved by the District Commission, which served as Washington's local government. Upon its approval, the plan was certified to the Redevelopment Land Agency. This agency had the task of actually acquiring the property in the area. Once it assembled the land, the agency would transfer to public agencies property to be used for public purposes, such as streets, parks, and schools. It would then lease or sell the remaining land to one or more private companies or individuals.

Included in the property to be condemned under the 1950 redevelopment plan was a department store in reasonably good condition. The store's owners brought suit to prevent the government from seizing their property. Since their store posed no threat to public order, health, or safety, the owners argued its confiscation would not to serve any legitimate public purpose.

Moreover, they argued their property was not being taken for "public use" as specified in the Fifth Amendment. The Redevelopment Agency planned to transfer their land to a private owner, who would develop it for his own private use. When the District Court upheld the Redevelopment Act's constitutionality and dismissed their claim, the store's owners appealed to the Supreme Court.

Writing the opinion for a unanimous court, Justice Douglas affirmed the District Court's decision. Simply by the act of paying compensation, the government demonstrated that an act had a "public" purpose. The people's agreement to payment was sufficient to prove that the public somehow benefits whenever property is transferred from one private owner to another private owner.

Within the District of Columbia, Douglas noted, Congress has "all the legislative powers which a state may exercise over its affairs." Since each case was different, no exact definition of these "police powers" was possible. In economic matters, a legislature could do pretty much anything it wanted to do. Certainly it was up to the legislature to decide that "the public needs to be served by social legislation." Douglas also noted that even in cases of eminent domain, when the government seizes people's homes and property, "the role of the judiciary . . . is an extremely narrow one."

There Are No Limits on the Public's Needs

Douglas went on to argue that a legislature's police powers are total and unlimited. (His statement to this effect subsequently was much quoted.)

> Public safety, public health, morality, peace and quiet, law and order—these are some of the more conspicuous examples of the traditional application of the police power to municipal affairs. Yet they merely illustrate the scope of the power and do not delimit it . . . The concept of the public welfare is broad and inclusive . . . The values it represents are spiritual as well as physical, aesthetic as well as monetary. It is within the power of the legislature to determine that the community should be beautiful as well as healthy, spacious as well as clean, well-balanced as well as carefully patrolled. In the present case, the Congress . . . [has] made determinations that take into account a wide variety of values. It is not for us to reappraise them. If those who govern the District of Columbia decide that the Nation's Capital should be beautiful as well as sanitary, there is nothing in the Fifth Amendment that stands in the way.

Once Congress had decided that a certain act serves a public purpose, then it could use any means to achieve that goal. "Once the object is within the authority of Congress, the means by which it will be attained is also for Congress to determine." Eminent domain is among the methods Congress may legitimately use. And it may seize land as well as buildings. "If the agency considers it necessary . . . to take full title to the real property involved, it may do so. It is not for the courts to determine . . ."

Earlier, Douglas had declared that in eminent domain or takings cases "the role of the judiciary . . . is an extremely narrow one." That role, he concluded, was solely to inquire whether "just compensation" has been paid. The legislature has unlimited discretion in deciding what constitutes a "public" purpose, and it may use any means to achieve that purpose. "The rights of these property owners are satisfied when they receive that just compensation which the Fifth Amendment exacts as the price of the taking."

Related Cases

Penn Central Transportation Co. v. New York City, 438 U.S. 104 (1978).
Hawaii Housing Authority v. Midkiff, 467 U.S. 229 (1984).

Bibliography and Further Reading

Ball, Howard, and Philip Cooper. *Of Power and Right: Hugo Black, William O. Douglas, and America's Constitutional Revolution.* New York: Oxford University Press, 1992.

Duram, James C. *Justice William O. Douglas.* Boston: Twayne, 1981.

Simon, James. *Independent Journey: The Life of William O. Douglas.* New York: Harper & Row, 1980.

BARENBLATT V. UNITED STATES

Legal Citation: 360 U.S. 109 (1959)

Petitioner
Lloyd Barenblatt

Respondent
United States

Petitioner's Claim
That compelled testimony before Congress about Communist affiliations violates First Amendment rights.

Chief Lawyer for Petitioner
Edward J. Ennis

Chief Lawyer for Respondent
Philip R. Monahan

Justices for the Court
Tom C. Clark, Felix Frankfurter, John Marshall Harlan II (writing for the Court), Potter Stewart, Charles Evans Whittaker

Justices Dissenting
Hugo Lafayette Black, William J. Brennan, Jr., William O. Douglas, Earl Warren

Place
Washington, D.C.

Date of Decision
8 June 1958

Decision
By a vote of 5-4, the Supreme Court narrowly upheld Lloyd Barenblatt's conviction for contempt of Congress for refusing to answer questions about his alleged past affiliation with the Communist Party.

Significance
Barenblatt marked a retreat from the Court's prior ruling that freedom of speech and association limited Congress' ability to inquire into political beliefs and affiliations.

In 1954, when he was called to testify before a subcommittee of the House Un-American Activities Committee (HUAC), Lloyd Barenblatt had recently left his job as a psychology professor at Vassar College. The committee, which had been organized in the midst of the Cold War to investigate Communist infiltration of various elements of American society, was then engaged in an inquiry into the field of education, and it was interested in Barenblatt's membership in a Communist club at the University of Michigan, where he had been a graduate student from 1947 to 1950. Although the only evidence the subcommittee had about the club indicated that it was merely a forum for intellectual debates about political issues, HUAC considered its inquiry to be vital to national security. When Barenblatt, citing his Fifth Amendment right not be forced to incriminate himself, refused to answer the subcommittee's questions about his club activities and associations at the University of Michigan, he was convicted of contempt of Congress in the U.S. District Court for the District of Columbia. After his conviction was upheld in the U.S. Court of Appeals for the District of Columbia, Barenblatt petitioned the U.S. Supreme Court for *certiorari,* or review, of the decision against him.

Just two years earlier, in *Watkins v. United States* (1957), the Supreme Court had placed limits on Congress's authority to question citizens about their political beliefs and associations. Congress and its committees, the Court said, were obliged to limit their inquiries to those that were pertinent to legislative functions. In that case, the subject of the inquiry had been convicted of contempt of Congress because he refused to answer HUAC's questions about others who might have had Community affiliations—to "name names," as the procedure was known at the time. Such questions, the Court found, were unrelated to the committee's legitimate function, and John T. Watkins's conviction was overturned.

Congress responded to *Watkins* with attempts to counteract the Court's own authority, and a majority of the justices apparently saw fit to retreat from the hard line they had previously taken toward HUAC. This time, when almost the same questions were asked of

The Hollywood Ten

The Hollywood Ten trials stand as a landmark in the history of the abuse of civil liberties. Ten screenwriters and directors—Alvah Bessie, Herbert Biberman, Lester Cole, Edward Dmytryk, Ring Lardner, Jr., John Howard Lawson, Albert Maltz, Samuel Ornitz, Adrian Scott, and Dalton Trumbo—were subpoenaed before the House Un-American Activities Committee to answer questions regarding affiliation with the Communist party. Each of them refused to answer the questions on the grounds that such questions violated their First Amendment right to privacy or a right to remain silent, regarding their political beliefs or affiliations. The courts rejected the argument, found the ten guilty of contempt of Congress, and gave them prison sen-

tences lasting from six months to one year and a monetary fine.

The trials created a precedent for making political belief a test of employment, blacklisting individuals accused of being Communist sympathizers by motion picture companies, radio and television broadcasters, and other firms in the industry occurred. As respected author E. B. White commented, "Ten men have been convicted, not of wrong-doing but of wrong thinking; that is news in this country and if I have not misread my history, it is bad news."

Source(s): Knappman, Edward W., ed. *Great American Trials* Detroit, MI: Visible Ink Press, 1994.

Lloyd Barenblatt as had been asked of John Watkins, five of the nine justices agreed that these questions were pertinent to the subcommittee's authorization to investigate Communist influences in education.

Government Interest in Self-Preservation Found to Outweigh First Amendment Concerns

Whereas before HUAC, Barenblatt had relied on his Fifth Amendment privilege against self-incrimination, his petition for judicial review of his contempt conviction cited his First Amendment right to freedom of speech and association. Justice Harlan, in his opinion for the Court, now had no trouble dismissing such concerns—as well as the Court's own recent precedent.

Undeniably, the First Amendment in some circumstances protects an individual from being compelled to disclose his associational relationships. However, protections of the First Amendment, unlike a proper claim of the privilege against self-incrimination under the Fifth Amendment, do not afford a witness the right to resist inquiry in all circumstances. Where First Amendment rights are asserted to bar governmental interrogation, resolution of the issue always involves a balancing by the courts of the competing private and public interests at stake in the particular circumstances shown. These principles were recognized in the Watkins Case, where, in speaking of the First

Amendment in relation to congressional inquiries, we said . . . : "It is manifest that despite the adverse effects which follow upon compelled disclosure of private matters, not all such inquiries are barred . . ."

Barenblatt has never been formally overturned. However, as the heat of public sentiment against the supposed Red Menace cooled and the power of HUAC waned, the Supreme Court once again began to reverse the convictions of witnesses who proved unwilling to cooperate with sometimes intrusive congressional investigations.

Related Cases
Watkins v. United States, 354 U.S. 178 (1957).
United States v. Shelton, 148 F.Supp. 926 (1957).
Russell v. United States, 369 U.S. 749 (1962).

Bibliography and Further Reading
Alfange, Dean, Jr. "Congressional Investigations and the Fickle Court." *University of Cincinnati Law Review,* Vol. 30, spring, 1961, pp. 113-171.

Fried, Richard M. *Nightmare in Red: The McCarthy Era in Perspective.* New York: Oxford University Press, 1991.

Johnson, John W. *Historic U.S. Court Cases, 1690-1990: An Encyclopedia.* New York: Garland Publishing, 1992.

O'Reilly, Kenneth. *Hoover and the Un-Americans: The FBI, HUAC, and the Red Menace.* Philadelphia: Temple University Press, 1983.

REYNOLDS V. SIMS

Legal Citation: 377 U.S. 533 (1964)

Appellant
R. A. Reynolds

Appellee
M. O. Sims

Appellant's Claim
That representation in both houses of state legislatures must be based on population.

Chief Lawyer for Appellant
W. McLean Pitts

Chief Lawyer for Appellee
Charles Morgan, Jr.

Justices for the Court
Hugo Lafayette Black, William J. Brennan, Jr., Tom C. Clark, William O. Douglas, Arthur Goldberg, Potter Stewart, Earl Warren (writing for the Court), Byron R. White

Justices Dissenting
John Marshall Harlan I

Place
Washington, D.C.

Date of Decision
15 June 1964

Decision
The Supreme Court held that the equal representation guarantee of the Fourteenth Amendment requires that the configuration of districts be based on population distribution.

Significance
Reynolds v. Sims rendered at least one house of most legislatures unconstitutional. Within two years, the boundaries of legislative districts had been redrawn all across the nation.

The Supreme Court began what came to be known as the reapportionment revolution with its opinion in the 1962 case, *Baker v. Carr*. *Baker v. Carr* held that federal courts are able to rule on the constitutionality of the relative size of legislative districts. The next year, in *Gray v. Sanders* (1963), the Court declared Georgia's county unit system of electoral districts unconstitutional. Since the Georgia electoral system was based on geography, rather than population, winners of the popular vote often lost elections. *Gray v. Sanders* gave rise to the phrase "one person, one vote," which became the motto of the reapportionment revolution. The Court's decision in *Wesberry v. Sanders* (1964), which invalidated Georgia's unequal congressional districts, articulated the principle of equal representation for equal numbers of people.

The decision in *Wesberry*, which concerned federal election districts, was based on Article I of the Constitution, which governs the federal legislative branch. In the landmark case of *Reynolds v. Sims*, which concerned representation in state legislatures, the outcome was based on the Fourteenth Amendment requirement that, "Representatives shall be apportioned among the several states according to their respective numbers." That is, equal protection under the Fourteenth Amendment—which only applies to the states—guarantees that each citizen shall have equal weight in determining the outcome of state elections.

Reynolds was just one of 15 reapportionment cases the Court decided in June of 1964. All of these cases questioned the constitutionality of state redistricting legislation mandated by *Baker v. Carr*. The Court decided each case individually, but it announced the controlling philosophy behind the decisions in *Reynolds v. Sims*.

Reynolds originated in Alabama, a state which had especially lopsided districts and which produced the first judicially mandated redistricting plan in the nation. M.O. Sims, for whom the case is named, was one of the resident taxpaying voters of Jefferson County, Alabama, who filed suit in federal court in 1961, challenging the apportionment of the Alabama legislature. At that time the state legislature consisted of a senate with 35 members and a house of represen-

The Census

Every ten years since 1790, the United States has conducted a census as authorized by the Constitution. This is far more than a simple headcount; census data provides a detailed national portrait which assists the federal, state, and local governments (and private entities, who also access the information) in demographic-based planning. The Census Bureau distributes detailed questionnaires to households, and the cumulative answers help to determine not only population, which governs the apportionment of representatives at the state and federal levels, but other trends that will influence policy in areas that range from education to the building of interstate highways.

Determining apportionment remains the primary constitutional purpose of the census, and Congress has oversight as to the form and method of the count. Federal marshals were the first census takers, but by 1880 it became necessary for the Census Bureau to hire legions of employees. Since 1970, the census has been by mail. By 1990, critics charged that the mail-based census might not be effective enough, given the existence of a homeless population largely outside its reach.

Source(s): Bacon, Donald C., et al., eds. *The Encyclopedia of the United States Congress.* New York: Simon & Schuster, 1995.

tatives with 106 members. The plaintiffs in the original suit alleged that state legislative districts had not been redrawn since the 1900 federal census, when the majority of the state's residents lived in rural areas. Since population growth in the state over the next 60 years was uneven, the plaintiffs alleged that residents of Jefferson County were seriously underrepresented at the state level.

Shortly after the Supreme Court handed down its decision in *Baker v. Carr* in March of 1962, under pressure from the federal district court that was still considering Sims's case, the Alabama legislature adopted two reapportionment plans, one for each house. These plans were to take effect in time for the 1966 elections. In July of 1962, the district court declared that the existing representation in the Alabama legislature violated the Fourteenth Amendment's Equal Protection Clause. The district court further declared that the redistricting plans recently adopted by the legislature were unconstitutional. After specifying a temporary reapportionment plan, the district court stated that the 1962 election of state legislators could only be conducted according to its plan. The 1962 Alabama general election was conducted on the basis of the court-ordered plan, which was immediately appealed to the U.S. Supreme Court.

"Legislators Represent People, Not Trees"

Chief Justice Warren began his opinion for the Court by noting that because there appeared to be no political remedy to malapportionment in Alabama, the federal courts were obliged to make a ruling. The Equal Protection Clause of the Fourteenth Amendment guarantees that each citizen's vote will have equal weight in determining the outcome of state elections. In order to insure that this happened, the federal courts had to devise and enforce redistricting plans that would result in each state representative being elected by and

responsive to roughly the same number of voters. As Warren put it:

> Legislators represent people, not trees or acres. Legislators are elected by voters, not farms or cities or economic interests. As long as ours is a representative form of government, and our legislatures are those instruments of government elected directly by and directly representative of the people, the right to elect legislators in a free and unimpaired fashion is a bedrock of our political system.

For the Court, the effect of substantial disparities in population from one district to the next was to deprive some voters of the franchise, while granting others more than one vote.

The Court did recognize some practical limitations on the ideal represented by the principle of "one person, one vote." It was not possible to come up with exact mathematical ratios of how the electorate was to be divided in a given state. And there had to be some acknowledgment of traditional political subdivisions and differing community interests. However, the Court specifically ruled out the use of the federal model in state legislatures. That is, while in the U.S. Congress the number of representatives is based on state population, regardless of its size each state sends two representatives to the Senate. In *Reynolds* the Court found that there was convincing evidence that three-fourths of the original state constitutions envisioned that the number of representatives sent to both houses of their state legislatures would be determined by population.

With one stroke, at least one house of most state legislatures was rendered unconstitutional. Over the next two years, the political map of virtually the entire country was redrawn. Yet problems remained. The lone dissenter in *Reynolds* was Justice Harlan, who argued, as he had in *Baker v. Carr,* that the Court was interfering with the political process and with the principle of federalism that bound individual states to the union by recognizing their autonomy. Indeed, because the Court could arrive at no precise formula for redistricting, partisan gerrymandering, or manipulation of election boundaries, resulted in more and more litigation. Mathematical models ultimately failed, and new, clearly nonsensical election boundaries began themselves to threaten fair representation.

Justice Harlan declared in his dissent that, "The Constitution is not a panacea for every blot upon the public welfare, nor should this Court, ordained as a judicial body, be thought of as a general haven for reform movements." But where the political process cannot itself cure partisan advantages born of gerrymandering, the Court has continued to intervene, mandating reapportionment to insure fair and effective representation.

Related Cases

Baker v. Carr, 369 U.S. 186 (1962).

Gray v. Sanders, 372 U.S. 368 (1963).

Wesberry v. Sanders, 376 U.S. 1 (1964).

Bibliography and Further Reading

Balinski, M. L. *Fair Representation: Meeting the Ideal of One Man, One Vote*. New Haven, CT: Yale University Press, 1982.

Cortner, Ricard C. *The Reapportionment Cases*. Knoxville: University of Tennessee Press, 1970.

Grofman, Bernard. *Voting Rights, Voting Wrongs: The Legacy of Baker v. Carr*. New York, NY: Priority Press, 1990.

Johnson, John W., ed. *Historic U.S. Court Cases, 1690-1990: An Encyclopedia*. New York: Garland Publishing, 1992.

POWELL V. MCCORMACK

Legal Citation: 395 U.S. 486 (1969)

Petitioner
Adam Clayton Powell, Jr.

Respondent
John McCormack

Petitioner's Claim
That the House of Representatives had no constitutional right to exclude Powell, a member who met all constitutional requirements for office.

Chief Lawyers for Petitioner
Arthur Kinoy, Herbert O. Reid

Chief Lawyer for Respondent
Bruce Bromley

Justices for the Court
Hugo Lafayette Black, William J. Brennan, Jr., William O. Douglas, Abe Fortas, John Marshall Harlan II, Thurgood Marshall, Earl Warren (writing for the Court), Byron R. White

Justices Dissenting
Potter Stewart

Place
Washington, D.C.

Date of Decision
16 June 1969

Decision
Powell could not be excluded from the House by majority vote, because he met the qualifications of age, citizenship, and residence set down in the Constitution.

Significance
Powell v. McCormack settled many long-standing questions about the constitutional status of membership in Congress.

Article I, Section 1 of the U.S. Constitution sets out the qualifications for a member of Congress. It states that a House member must be at least 25 years old, a U.S. citizen for at least seven years, and a resident of a district from which he or she was elected. The House can, however, expel a member for conduct "inconsistent with the trust and duty of a member," on a two-thirds vote. This case hinges on an attempt by the House to exclude, rather than expel, a duly elected member.

Adam Clayton Powell, an African American congressman from New York, had been duly elected to serve in the 90th Congress. However, he was denied his seat when a majority of the House of Representatives voted to exclude him. The House's action followed charges that Powell had misappropriated public funds and abused the process of the New York courts. Powell and a group of his constituents filed suit in the district court against Speaker of the House John McCormack and other House officials, alleging that the resolution to exclude him violated his constitutional right to serve so long as he met the specified age, citizenship, and residence requirements. Powell, who was subsequently re-elected to his seat in a special election, sought back pay along with recompense for other damages.

The Court Rulings

The district court dismissed Powell's complaint on the grounds that it had no jurisdiction to rule on the matter. The court of appeals affirmed this decision. It cited lack of jurisdiction as well, adding that the case was moot because the 90th congressional session had come and gone. It also affirmed the right of Congress to expel its members. Despite rulings by two lower courts in McCormack's favor, the Supreme Court agreed to review the case. On 16 June 1969 the Supreme Court issued its decision. By a vote of 8-1, it ruled in Powell's favor. In doing so, the Court had to address several thorny issues.

Moot Point

Disagreeing with the court of appeals ruling, the Supreme Court decided that Powell's case was not moot because Powell's back pay was still at issue:

John W. McCormack. © Archive Photos.

Simply stated, a case is moot when the issues presented are no longer "live" or the parties lack a legally cognizable interest in the outcome . . . Petitioner Powell has not been paid his salary by virtue of an allegedly unconstitutional House resolution. That claim is still unresolved and hotly contested by clearly adverse parties.

Next, the Court had to address the issue of whether it had the right to intervene in what seemed to be an internal House of Representatives issue. The Court resolved this potential violation of the separation of powers by holding that, while Congress has the sole authority to judge the qualifications of its members, it may not add to the qualifications of age, citizenship, and residency spelled out in the Constitution:

> Our examination of the relevant historical materials leads us to the conclusion that petitioners are correct and that the Constitution leaves the House without authority to exclude any person, duly elected by his constituents, who meets all the requirements for membership expressly prescribed in the Constitution.

Making a Distinction

The Court also addressed the distinction between exclusion—which the House voted on in this case—and expulsion, which the House can only put into effect by a two thirds vote. The Court concluded that, while the House did in fact vote to exclude Powell by more than a two-thirds margin, this may not have been the result had the House members been voting to expel. The majority opinion dismissed the respondent's attempt to equate the two terms:

> Although respondents repeatedly urge this Court not to speculate as to the reasons for Powell's exclusion, their attempt to equate exclusion with expulsion would require a similar speculation that the House would have voted to expel Powell had it been faced with that question . . . [T]he proceedings which culminated in Powell's exclusion cast considerable doubt upon respondents' assumption that the two-thirds vote necessary to expel would have been mustered.

Powell v. McCormack was about more than Adam Clayton Powell's right to occupy a congressional seat or receive his back pay. It was also about when the Supreme

---

The Right to Run for Public Office

Strictly speaking, there is no constitutionally guaranteed right to run for public office. The Constitution sets guidelines for presidential and congressional candidates concerning age, citizenship, and residency. It would be hard to make a case for the idea that the Constitution forbids that right to any duly qualified citizen, particularly inasmuch as the Tenth Amendment reserves all unenumerated rights for the states or the people. States and local districts may set their own qualifications, but unless these are closely aligned with those in the Constitution governing candidacies for high national office, such laws would be ripe for a Fourteenth Amendment challenge. The right to run for public office is common to constitutional democracies such as the United States and Britain. The two fundamental features of free elections are a secret ballot and the right of individuals to run for public office.

Source(s): Scruton, Roger. *A Dictionary of Political Thought*, second edition. London: Macmillan, 1996.

Adam Clayton Powell swaps a black power salute with an admirer, 1969. © AP/Wide World Photos.

Court possesses the right to rule on issues of congressional qualification, and it gave the Court the opportunity to establish guidelines on what is a "political question" that federal courts cannot rule on because of separation of power grounds. It was one of the last decisions written by the legendary Chief Justice Warren.

Related Cases
Kilbourn v. Thompson, 103 U.S. 168 (1881).
Baker v. Carr, 369 U.S. 186 (1962).
Bond v. Floyd, 385 U.S. 116 (1966).

Bibliography and Further Reading
Barrett, Edward L., William Cohen, and Jonathan D. Varat. *Constitutional Law: Cases and Materials.* Westbury, NY: The Foundation Press, Inc., 1989.

Chandler, Ralph C. *The Constitutional Law Dictionary.* Santa Barbara, CA: ABC-Clio, Inc., 1987.

Goldman, Sheldon. *Constitutional Law: Cases and Essays.* New York, NY: Harper and Row, 1987.

Johnson, John W., ed. *Historic U.S. Court Cases, 1690-1990: An Encyclopedia.* New York: Garland Publishing, 1992.

Karst, Kenneth L., ed. *Encyclopedia of the American Constitution.* New York, NY: Macmillan Publishing Company, 1986.

Kay, Richard S. and Stephen P. Elliot, eds. *A Reference Guide to the U.S. Supreme Court.* New York, NY: Sachem Publishing Associates, Inc., 1986.

NORTHERN PIPELINE CO. V. MARATHON PIPE LINE CO.

Legal Citation: 458 U.S. 50 (1982)

Petitioner
Northern Pipeline Co.

Respondent
Marathon Pipe Line Co.

Petitioner's Claim
That an appellate court ruling that non-Article III bankruptcy courts are unconstitutional should be dismissed.

Chief Lawyer for Petitioner
John L. Devney

Chief Lawyer for Respondent
Melvin I. Orenstein

Justices for the Court
Harry A. Blackmun, William J. Brennan, Jr. (writing for the Court), Thurgood Marshall, Sandra Day O'Connor, William H. Rehnquist, John Paul Stevens

Justices Dissenting
Warren E. Burger, Lewis F. Powell, Jr., Byron R. White

Place
Washington, D.C.

Date of Decision
28 June 1982

Decision
That Article 1 federal bankruptcy courts were unconstitutional.

Significance
Forced Congress to abandon its relatively new method of adjudicating bankruptcy matters and reemphasized the Article III principles of an independent federal judiciary, but a greatly divided opinion by the Court failed to significantly clear up what was already a muddy issue considering jurisdiction between Article I and Article III courts.

The *Northern Pipeline Co. v. Marathon Pipe Line Co* case settled an issue in which the two interested parties had only a minor role in the debate itself. The case was a spin-off of a fairly routine corporate bankruptcy case, in which Northern Pipeline Co. had filed for reorganization in Minnesota. As part of the proceeding that company filed a suit for breach of contract against the Marathon Pipe Line Co. Marathon asked for dismissal of that suit on the grounds that the system of bankruptcy courts which Congress had created in 1978 was unconstitutional because its judges lacked the protections in Article III of the U.S. Constitution, which guaranteed a judiciary free from congressional or public meddling. Judges were supposed to be appointed for life and guaranteed that their salaries could not be lowered.

When the framers of the Constitution put together their vision of how the U.S. government would work, they felt that separation of powers between the executive, legislative and judicial branches, as well as a system of checks and balances among the three, was necessary to avoid a possible slip into tyranny. One of the factors which led to the Revolutionary War was that the King of Great Britain held control over the colonial judges' tenure and salary, and could cut their pay or recall them if he was not satisfied with their performance, effectively negating the judges' autonomy. One of the principles set forth under Article III of the Constitution was that federal judges would serve for life, if they so chose, and their salaries could not be diminished during their tenure. This was designed to insulate judges against unfavorable reactions to their rulings from Congress or the electorate, thus guaranteeing their independence. The Constitution did permit Congress, however, to create courts of lower order, as it saw the need, and previous court decisions had decided that non-Article III courts could exist for certain circumstances.

In 1978, Congress revamped the federal method of hearing bankruptcy cases. Since 1938, bankruptcy cases had been heard either by a federal district judge or a referee, and bankruptcy referees had been in existence even earlier than that. Under the Bankruptcy Act of 1978, a special category of bankruptcy courts and judges was created, whose judges would serve 14-year

Bankruptcy

Bankruptcy is a process whereby an individual or corporation deeply in debt gains relief from that debt, in exchange for a marred credit record that will take years to correct. Under the most common form of bankruptcy as applied to individuals, the debtor, under orders from a judge, liquidates (sells off) all but a few exempt assets such as a car and house; then a court-appointed trustee repays creditors. Repayment may be only a percentage of the debt. For instance, the debtor may offer a creditor 64 cents in repayment for every dollar owed. This type of bankruptcy proceeding, called liquidation, is governed by chapter 7 of the U.S. bankruptcy code. Under another common type, rehabilitative bankruptcy, the debtor is allowed to keep assets in addition to the exempt assets, and a judge establishes a reorganization plan for repayment of debt. Rehabilitation, under chapter 11 of the code, is typically applied to persons with income great enough to facilitate repayment.

Source(s): *West's Encyclopedia of American Law* St. Paul, MN: West Group, 1998.

terms and whose salaries would be subject to adjustment under the Federal Salary Act. Those judges also had slightly expanded powers compared to the old referees concerning what aspects of bankruptcy proceedings they would be permitted to oversee. The regular Article III district courts did have oversight powers over the bankruptcy courts, and appeals from bankruptcy court decisions could be heard by district courts or appeals courts.

The bankruptcy court rejected Marathon's appeal to dismiss the case, but the district court overturned that decision, holding that bankruptcy matters must be heard by a proper Article III court. The Supreme Court upheld the appeals court verdict, but by a plurality rather than a majority, meaning there was some limited dissent even within that portion of the Court that agreed on the decision. The official decision of the Court was that Northern's suit against Marathon could not be heard by a non-Article III court, that Article I bankruptcy courts were not constitutionally acceptable, and that Article I courts were only acceptable in certain circumstances. A dissent within the plurality, however, held that the only part of the decision which was proper was that the suit in question could not be heard by an Article I court, and that the Court decided more than it needed to by decreeing that the bankruptcy court system was unconstitutional. Two separate dissents further confused the situation.

Three Acceptable Categories

The plurality opinion, written by Justice Brennan, decided that the only acceptable uses of Article I, also called legislative, courts were those which had already been approved of by the Court. These fell into three categories. The first was courts in territories of the United States not within the country itself. The second exception was military court martials. The third exception, and the only one which needed to be considered for the case at hand, was public rights cases, or cases in which the government and an individual or private interest were interested parties. The plurality held that while Congress did have an interest in regulating bankruptcy matters, it was not an interested party in proceedings between two private interests, and therefore those proceedings must be heard by an Article III judge. The decision killed the 1978 bankruptcy reform plan, but the Court made its judgment non-retroactive, ruling that to overturn previous decisions rendered by the bankruptcy courts would impose unjust hardship on parties affected by those decisions. Justices Rehnquist and O'Connor concurred in the decision, but felt it was too broad. They felt the constitutionality of the courts themselves was not at issue in the case, only the appropriateness of them hearing the case in question.

Justice White wrote a dissent, joined by Chief Justice Burger and Justice Powell, which said it was not necessary to assume the three examples of legislative courts cited by the plurality were the only ones which could be allowed merely because they were the only ones which had been thus far explicitly approved. Indeed, the dissent claimed that close examination showed that there was no distinction between jurisdiction of Article III and Article I courts, that both varieties heard all types of cases on a regular basis throughout the country. It also claimed that the oversight Article III courts held over the bankruptcy courts made those courts acceptable under Article III. Justice White wrote that Article III need not be taken as an absolute ban on legislative courts for any category of cases, but should be viewed as a principle to be weighed in the acceptability of such courts, along with other pragmatic concerns such as seeing that specialized cases were heard by specialized judges, expediting the legal process, and allowing Congress to maintain some flexibility in its maintenance of the court system.

While the decision was viewed at the time as an attempt to clear up what the dissent admitted "has been characterized as one of the most confusing and controversial areas of constitutional law," it was generally regarded as a failure in that respect. As Maryellen Fullerton, assistant professor of law at Brooklyn Law School, wrote in the *Brooklyn Law Review:*

> Unfortunately, Marathon did little to resolve this confusion. The Supreme Court produced four separate opinions . . . so contradictory that no one can safely predict the Court's ruling on future cases involving Article I federal courts.

Related Cases

Ex parte Bakelite Corp., 279 U.S. 438 (1929).
Toth v. Quarles, 350 U.S. 11 (1955).

Baker v. Carr, 369 U.S. 186 (1962).
Glidden Co. v. Zdanok, 370 U.S. 530 (1962).
Buckley v. Valeo, 42 U.S. 1 (1976).
Fullilove v. Klutznick, 448 U.S. 448 (1980).

Bibliography and Further Reading

American Bar Association Journal, September 1982.

Brooklyn Law Review, winter 1983, p. 207.

Harvard Law Review, November 1982, p. 257.

Land and Water Review, Vol. 18, p. 313.

SOUTH DAKOTA V. DOLE

Legal Citation: 483 U.S. 203 (1987)

Petitioner
State of South Dakota

Respondent
Elizabeth Dole, U.S. Secretary of Transportation

Petitioner's Claim
That a law withholding federal highway funds from states which did not adopt a minimum drinking age of 21 years was in violation of the Twenty-first Amendment to the Constitution, and of constitutional limits on the spending power of Congress.

Chief Lawyer for Petitioner
Roger A. Tellinghuisen, Attorney General of South Dakota

Chief Lawyer for Respondent
Cohen, U.S. Deputy Solicitor General

Justices for the Court
Harry A. Blackmun, Thurgood Marshall, Lewis F. Powell, Jr., William H. Rehnquist (writing for the Court), Antonin Scalia, John Paul Stevens, Byron R. White

Justices Dissenting
William J. Brennan, Jr., Sandra Day O'Connor

Place
Washington, D.C.

Date of Decision
23 June 1987

Decision
That Title 23 U.S.C. 158, passed by Congress in 1984, did not violate the spending-power clause; rather, in view of a four-part test regarding aspects such as its "pursuit of 'the general welfare,'" the Court found that 158 was a noncoercive effort to benefit all.

Significance
Although the Twenty-first Amendment has not often been challenged in the Supreme Court, *South Dakota v. Dole* addressed other, perennial issues such as spending power, the relative authority of the federal government and that of the states, and the line between inducement and encouragement. Perhaps most significant was the last point, because it related to questions of how or whether Congress may financially reward behavior it deemed beneficial, or withhold such rewards in the face of behavior it wanted to discourage.

Legal Drinking Age

In 1984, Congress passed into law 23 U.S. 158, which ordered the U.S. secretary of transportation to deny a certain percentage of federal highway funds to states which allowed persons under 21 years of age to drink alcoholic beverages. South Dakota had a law which allowed anyone 19 years of age or older to purchase beer containing up to 3.2 percent alcohol. (Presumably—though the Supreme Court did not specifically address this issue in *South Dakota v. Dole*—the state did not allow citizens to drink beverages with higher alcohol content until they reached the age of 21.)

South Carolina took the federal government to court over 158, naming Secretary of Transportation Elizabeth Dole (wife of Senator Bob Dole, and future director of the U.S. Red Cross) as the respondent. The suit in district court sought a declaratory judgement that 158 violated Article I, section 8, clause 1 of the Constitution, which limits congressional spending power, as well as section 2 of the Twenty-first Amendment, which South Dakota interpreted as a limitation on federal authority over states' liquor distribution systems—including age limits.

The district court rejected South Dakota's claims, and the Court of Appeals for the Eighth Circuit affirmed. When the case came before the Supreme Court, a number of entities filed briefs of *amici curiae* on either side. Those urging reversal of the lower courts' rulings included the states of Colorado, Hawaii, Kansas, Louisiana, Montana, New Mexico, Ohio, South Carolina, Tennessee, Vermont, and Wyoming; as well as the Mountain States Legal Foundation, the National Conference of State Legislatures, and the National Beer Wholesalers' Association. Those urging affirmance included the Insurance Institute for Highway Safety, the National Council on Alcoholism, the National Safety Council, and United States Senator Frank R. Lautenberg.

A Four-Part Test

The Court voted 7-2 to affirm the rulings of the lower courts. Chief Justice Rehnquist, writing for the majority, held that "the bounds of" the Twenty-first Amendment had "escaped precise definition." In any case, the

Elizabeth Dole, U.S. Secretary of Transportation. © The Library of Congress.

Court did not need to look at the present legal action in light of the Amendment, or at South Dakota's claim that Congress was trying to directly legislate a national minimum drinking age. Instead, the proper arena in which to address the case was from the standpoint of the spending powers clause, and to evaluate the constitutionality of the measures by which "Congress has acted indirectly under its spending power to encourage uniformity in the states' drinking ages."

In *United States v. Butler* (1936), *Steward Machine Co. v. Davis* (1937), and other cases, the Court had addressed issues relating to the spending powers of Congress. Through such cases, it had developed a four-part test to limit the exercise of such power. First, such exercise "must be in pursuit of the general welfare," the latter a phrase directly from the Constitution; and in making this determination, Rehnquist wrote, "courts should defer substantially to the judgment of Congress." Second, if Congress wants to put conditions on the states' receipt of federal funds, it should do so in an unambiguous way that makes the states fully aware of their choices and the consequences. Third, these conditions should be related "to the federal interest in particular national projects or programs." And fourth, of course, the spending regulations could not violate the Constitution.

The only serious challenge, either from South Dakota or from the dissenters on the Court, came in the area of the fourth stipulation. Here the Court turned not to the Twenty-first Amendment, as the petitioners urged, but to *Butler,* which established that Congress had greater power to indirectly regulate the states by withholding funds than it did to directly regulate. In other words, while it might be difficult under the Constitution for Congress to tell a state what its minimum drinking age should be, there was less limitation on Congress's power to withhold federal highway funds from a state which refused to comply with what Congress viewed as appropriate drinking-age regulations. Rehnquist's point in this area was further reinforced by *Oklahoma v. Civil Service Commission* (1947), in which the Court found that "the United States is not concerned with, and has no power to regulate, local political activities"—yet it did "have power to fix the terms upon which its money allotments to states could be disbursed."

Finally, the Court noted that the "punishment" imposed on South Dakota was minor, and hardly coercive. If it refused to raise its drinking age, the state would lose five percent of its federal highway funds. As he concluded, Chief Justice Rehnquist quoted the Court's opinion in *Steward Machine Co.*: "[E]very rebate from a tax when conditioned upon conduct is in some measure a temptation. But to hold that motive or temptation is equivalent to coercion is to plunge the law in endless difficulties." In the end, the Court had held—and the present Court reaffirmed the concept—that freedom of will, not coercion, determined results.

Dissent: 158 Attempts to Regulate

Justices Brennan and O'Connor dissented, both holding that 158 did indeed abridge states' rights to regulate issues involving liquor sale and consumption. Justice Brennan issued a short opinion in which he voiced his disagreement with the majority and his agreement with Justice O'Connor, who wrote at greater length on the thesis that "158 is not a condition on spending reasonably related to the expenditure of federal funds . . . Rather, it is an attempt to regulate the sale of liquor, an attempt that lies outside Congress' power to regulate commerce . . ."

In O'Connor's view, section 158 failed two of the Court's four tests: not only was it unconstitutional, but "establishment of a minimum drinking age of 21 is not sufficiently related to interstate highway construction to justify so conditioning funds appropriated for that purpose." The National Conference of State Legislatures, O'Connor wrote, had properly drawn the line between "permissible and impermissible conditions on federal grants" when, in its brief to the Court, it posited that "the difference turns on whether the requirement specifies in some way how the money should be spent,

---

The Twenty-first Amendment

Two facts set the Twenty-first Amendment: it was the only amendment passed to repeal a previous amendment, and it was the only one ratified (albeit indirectly) by the electorate through a vote for delegates.

The Eighteenth Amendment (1919) prohibited the manufacture, sale, and distribution of alcohol. The Volstead Act (1919) authorized the creation of a Prohibition Bureau to enforce the law. In spite of this and the Supreme Court's tacit approval for broadened government police powers, as evidenced by decisions such as *Olmstead v. United States* (1928), the new law-enforcement mechanism proved ineffective.

The opposition to Prohibition spread to the Democratic Party, which in its 1932 presidential platform called for repeal of the Eighteenth Amendment. The Senate passed an amendment resolution, and on 20 February 1933, the House endorsed it as well. The new amendment, in addition to repealing the Eighteenth, contained a prohibition against transporting alcohol in violation of state law.

During the months between April and November, citizens of 38 states voted for delegates, and with 73 percent of the votes in favor of repeal, the actual ratification conventions were mere formalities.

Source(s): Bacon, Donald C., et al., eds. *The Encyclopedia of the United States Congress.* New York: Simon & Schuster, 1995.

---

so that Congress' intent in making the grant will be effectuated." If it specified the ways to use funds—such as building highways—and left it at that, then a law was constitutional; any further commentary wandered into the area of regulation: "A requirement that is not such a specification is not a condition, but a regulation, which is valid only if it falls within one of Congress' delegated regulatory powers." O'Connor found the present case different from those addressed in *Butler* and *Oklahoma*, nor did the regulations in 158 fit with Congress's powers under the Commerce Clause of the Constitution. Therefore, Justice O'Connor concluded, "Because . . . 158 . . . cannot be justified as an exercise of any power delegated to the Congress, it is not authorized by the Constitution. The Court errs in holding it to be the law of the land, and I respectfully dissent."

Impact

The issue which originally brought about the legal action in *South Dakota v. Dole* would become a moot one. By 1998, the National Highway Traffic Safety Administration, an agency of the federal government, reported at its Website that "Age 21 'drinking laws' remain in all states and continue to save lives (an estimated 846 in 1996 alone)." The larger concerns, however, have not gone away. *South Dakota v. Dole* was mentioned several times in testimony before Congress in the mid- to late 1990s as the executive branch considered guidelines for federal policy with regard to tobacco—specifically, a "tobacco settlement" in which the federal government would receive vast sums of money as a payoff from cigarette manufacturers for the health problems caused by tobacco. Also under consideration before Congress at the close of the century were a variety of proposals regarding changes to tax laws. Among the benefits suggested for a flat tax or a national sales tax were limits on spending coercion. Much of the present tax law, advocates of such proposals suggested, were made to encourage certain behaviors and discourage others. A simple tax, they indicated, would prevent governmental attempts at behavior modification.

Related Cases

United States v. Butler, 297 U.S. 1 (1936).
Steward Machine Co. v. Davis, 301 U.S. 548 (1937).
South Carolina v. Baker, 485 U.S. 505 (1988).
New York v. United States, 505 U.S. 144 (1992).
Printz, Sheriff/Coroner, Ravalli County, Montana v. United States, 521 U.S. 98 (1996).
Seminole Nation of Florida v. Florida, 517 U.S. 44 (1996).

Bibliography and Further Reading

Biskupic, Joan, and Elder Witt. *Guide to the U.S. Supreme Court,* 3rd ed. Washington, DC: Congressional Quarterly Inc., 1997.

"Constitutional Law—*South Dakota v. Dole*: Federal Conditional Spending Is Subjected to a Multi-Pronged Analysis." *Memphis State University Law Review,* Vol. 18, summer 1988, pp. 741-59.

Erickson, Patricia, and Scott C. Peterson. *South Dakota v. Dole: The Drinking Age Issue.* Pierre, SD: South Dakota Legislative Research Council, 1987.

Hall, Kermit L., ed. *The Oxford Companion to the Supreme Court of the United States.* New York: Oxford University Press, 1992.

The Highway Safety Desk Book http://www.nhtsa.dot
.gov.

Levy, Leonard W., ed. *Encyclopedia of the American Constitution, Supplement I.* New York: Macmillan, 1986.

"*South Dakota v. Dole*: A Study in Conditional Spending and Missed Opportunity." *Hastings Constitutional Law Quarterly,* Vol. 15, summer 1988, pp. 649-668.

MISTRETTA V. UNITED STATES

Legal Citation: 488 U.S. 361 (1989)

Petitioner
John Mistretta

Respondent
United States

Petitioner's Claim
That the Sentencing Reform Act of 1984 violated the constitutional separation-of-powers doctrine by establishing a Sentencing Commission of judges with "excessive legislative powers."

Chief Lawyer for Petitioner
Alan B. Morrison

Chief Lawyer for Respondent
Charles Fried, U.S. Solicitor General

Justices for the Court
Harry A. Blackmun (writing for the Court), William J. Brennan, Jr., Anthony M. Kennedy, Thurgood Marshall, Sandra Day O'Connor, William H. Rehnquist, John Paul Stevens, Byron R. White

Justices Dissenting
Antonin Scalia

Place
Washington, D.C.

Date of Decision
18 January 1989

Decision
The Constitution does not prevent Congress from appointing a body of experts within the judicial branch to develop guidelines for matters unique to their area of knowledge, making the Sentencing Reform Act valid.

Significance
Mistretta v. United States dealt with the separation-of-powers doctrine in the Constitution. In most of its cases involving separation of powers prior to *Mistretta*, the Court had tended to rule in favor of those who challenged statutes that threatened the principle of separation. This had been the case seven years before in 1982 when *Northern Pipeline Co. v. Marathon Pipe Line Co.* was decided and the trend was reversed. Previously the Court had struck down a 1978 law that had established a group of judges with wide-ranging authority in bankruptcy cases.

The Sentencing Reform Act Comes Under Challenge

"For almost a century," Justice Blackmun wrote for the Supreme Court in *Mistretta v. United States*, "the Federal Government employed in criminal cases a system of indeterminate sentencing." There were statutes addressing specific crimes, of course, but judges had considerable latitude in establishing sentences. Hand in hand with this system of indeterminate sentencing went another system: that of parole boards, who decided when a prisoner should be released from incarceration and placed under the supervision of a parole officer.

The idea behind this arrangement was an optimistic one—that the prison system could rehabilitate criminals and make them useful members of society. The system required that judges and parole officers work closely together, and each had broad discretionary powers within their realms. Under the Constitution, Congress had the power to establish sentences for federal crimes, but the legislative branch tended to defer to the judicial branch in the area of sentencing, as it assumed that judges knew more about a given case than did Congressmen in Washington.

Soon, however, problems began to arise from this arrangement. Indeterminate sentencing resulted in great disparities—relatively heavy sentences for lesser crimes, or the reverse, all depending upon the judge who reviewed the case. A further problem came from the fact that the prison and parole systems were not rehabilitating criminals, but were recycling the same people again and again through a chain from crime to trial to prison to parole. As a result, in 1958 Congress called for the creation of judicial councils to establish sentencing guidelines. Fifteen years later, in 1973, the United States Parole Board adopted a set of guidelines for the length of time a prisoner should be confined, and in 1976 Congress passed the Parole Commission and Reorganization Act. Much greater reforms followed in 1984, with the passage of the legislation that would be challenged in *Mistretta*.

A Senate Report on the 1984 legislation cited two problems with the "outmoded rehabilitation model": disparity in sentencing, and prison terms whose length was made uncertain because parole boards too often

Checks and Balances

The Constitution provides for the separation of powers and a system of checks and balances to prevent the rise of a single branch of government over the other two. Each branch—executive, legislative, and judicial—acts as a check on and balances the power of the other two. The powers of the branches are mixed in such a way that no one branch is completely separable from the others. The framers of the Constitution designed a lock-and-alarm mechanism to prevent any faction or individual from "stealing" the government. Control of the executive branch, for instance, does not mean control of all executive functions, because the Senate must approve all presidential appointments of Cabinet officers, judges, and ambassadors. Congress does not hold all legislative power; the president, through the exercise of the veto, can override the vote of the legislature in certain cases. Both the executive and the legislative branches can be overridden by a decision of the judiciary, whose members are appointed by the executive branch and approved by the legislative.

Source(s): Bacon, Donald C., et al., eds. *The Encyclopedia of the United States Congress.* New York: Simon & Schuster, 1995.

intervened and shortened them. Therefore Congress passed the Sentencing Reform Act of 1984. The act rejected the rehabilitation model; it consolidated the sentencing functions of judges and parole boards by creating the United States Sentencing Commission; it established sentences of fixed length that could be shortened only by a prisoner's good behavior; it made the Sentencing Commission's guidelines binding on the courts, although it did give judges some discretion with regard to mitigating factors in a given offense; and it authorized limited appellate review of sentences. The act established further the Sentencing Commission as an independent entity operating within the judicial branch of government. The commission would consist of seven voting members, three of them federal judges chosen from a list of six recommended to the president by the Judicial Conference of the United States. No more than four members of the commission could belong to the same political party, and the attorney general (or his or her designee) would serve as an eighth, non-voting member of the commission. The commission was charged with developing sentencing guidelines, periodically reviewing and revising the guidelines it established, and reporting to Congress any amendments it made.

On 10 December 1987, John M. Mistretta was indicted, along with another defendant, in the U.S. District Court for the Western District of Missouri on three counts relating to a cocaine deal. Mistretta moved to have the Sentencing Commission's guidelines ruled unconstitutional, his claim being that the Sentencing Commission violated the separation of powers doctrine. Mistretta held that by creating the commission, Congress had established a judicial body with legislative powers. The district court disagreed, ruling that the commission was in effect an executive agency, and that its guidelines were similar in structure to rules established by comparable entities. Nor was the act invalid because it required judges, whose powers are granted

in Article III of the Constitution, to serve on the commission. Nonetheless, the court stated that its ruling does not imply a lack of "serious doubts about some parts of the Sentencing Guidelines and the legality of their anticipated operation."

Mistretta having plead guilty to the first of his three indictment counts, conspiracy and agreement to distribute cocaine, the federal prosecutor moved to dismiss the other two counts. The motion was granted, and in accordance with commission guidelines, Mistretta was sentenced to 18 months in prison to be followed by three years of supervised release, along with a $1,000 fine and a $50 special assessment. He filed a notice of appeal in the Eighth Circuit, but both sides—Mistretta and the attorneys representing the United States—petitioned the Supreme Court to review the case before the circuit court gave its judgment. Rule 18 of the Court allowed petitioners to take such an extraordinary step if the issue to be decided was of "imperative public importance." The Court held that this was one of the situations, and agreed to review the case, along with an ancillary legal action, *United States v. Mistretta.* The Sentencing Commission filed an *amicus curiae* brief urging affirmance, as did an attorney representing Joseph E. DiNova. Lawyers representing the United States Senate and the National Association of Criminal Defense Lawyers also filed briefs.

"An Unusual Hybrid"

By an 8-1 vote, the Court upheld the Sentencing Guidelines. Congress had neither delegated "excessive legislative power" to the commission, nor had it violated the separation-of-powers principle by establishing the commission within the judicial branch, by requiring federal judges to serve on the commission and share authority with non-judges, or by giving the president power to appoint and remove commission members. Nothing in the Constitution, the Court held, prohibited Congress from delegating to an expert body within the Judicial Branch the intricate task of formulating sentencing guidelines consistent with such significant statutory discretion as is present here, nor from calling upon the accumulated wisdom and experience of the Judicial Branch in creating policy on a matter uniquely within the ken of judges.

A judge, the Court's ruling suggested, would best know the business of judges, and Congress was simply calling on the knowledge and experience of the commission members.

Justice Blackmun, writing for the majority, first addressed the delegation-of-powers issue, which Mistretta had raised with his charge that Congress had given the Committee excessive legislative authority. In this context, Blackmun quoted Chief Justice William Howard Taft, who wrote in the Court's opinion on *Field v. Clark* (1892): "In determining what [Congress] may do in seeking assistance from another branch, the extent and character of that assistance must be fixed according to common sense and the inherent necessities of the government co-ordination." Common sense in the present situation, the Court indicated, would dictate some delegation of power, particularly in "our increasingly complex society, replete with ever changing and more technical problems." Congress itself had established "the specific tool" that the commission was to use, the guidelines system, and while the Court could not "dispute [the] petitioner's contention that the Commission enjoys significant discretion in formulating guidelines," there was no basis in the Court's past rulings to say that a delegation could not "exercise judgment in matters of policy." In fact, the highly technical and complex nature of the commission's task was one that especially lent itself to delegation: since members of Congress were not likely to be authorities on sentencing laws, it was wise for them to work with people who were.

Justice Blackmun turned next to the separation of powers issue. President James Madison, often called "the master builder of the Constitution" for his central role in framing the document, had written that

> the greatest security against a gradual concentration of the several powers in the same department, consists in giving to those who administer each department, the necessary constitutional means, and personal motives, to resist encroachments of others.

Without these "means and motives," the United States could be in danger of becoming a dictatorship, and the Court had consistently upheld the separation doctrine. In cases specifically related to the judicial branch, the Court had been wary of attempts to assign to judges tasks that other branches could more prop-

erly accomplish, and of laws that "threaten[ed] the institutional integrity of the Judicial Branch." In the present case, Mistretta held that Congress had on the one hand given too much authority to the judicial branch, by delegating to the commission legislative authority, and on the other hand had removed power from the judiciary by authorizing a member of the executive branch—the president—to appoint and dismiss commission members. With regard to these claims, the Court considered the commission from three standpoints: its "location" in the judicial branch, its composition, and the power of the president over it.

The commission was "located in the judicial branch, but it was not a court, nor did it hold judicial power." It was, as Justice Blackmun observed, "a peculiar institution within the framework of our Government." Although Article III of the Constitution limited the work of the judiciary to "Cases" and "Controversies," exceptions were possible, as in a situation involving a commission delegated to establish guidelines specifically relevant to the judicial branch. Nor did the existence of the commission within the judicial branch in any way threaten the power or integrity of the judiciary; given its lack of judicial power, there was no way that it could. As for its composition and Mistretta's challenge to its requirements that three federal judges serve on the commission and share their authority with non-judges, the Court admitted that "We find Congress' requirement of judicial service somewhat troublesome . . ." But "troublesome" did not equal "unconstitutional." Whereas the Constitution specifically prohibits legislators from serving in any other office during their term of service, it contained no such provisions for judges. Similarly, with regard to the president's power to appoint and remove members, it did not follow from this mere fact that the president therefore controlled the commission. Under the Constitution, the president has power to appoint many judges—including those on the Supreme Court—but history has shown that judges by no means necessarily do the bidding of the executive who appointed them.

Thus, the Court held that, although the commission was "an unusual hybrid," it was constitutional. "Nor does our system of checked and balanced authority," concluded the Court, "prohibit Congress from calling upon the accumulated wisdom and experience of the Judicial Branch in creating policy on a matter uniquely within the ken of judges."

Dissent: "A Sort of Junior-Varsity Congress"

Justice Scalia dissented, writing, "because I can find no place within our constitutional system for an agency created by Congress to exercise no governmental power other than the making of laws." The problem with the commission, he held, was precisely its lack of judicial or executive powers. He was concerned that responsibility for making laws could be delegated to "experts" in a given field— people with no official accountability. "How tempting," he wrote,

> to create an expert Medical Commission (mostly M.D.'s, with perhaps a few Ph.D.'s in moral philosophy) to dispose of such thorny, 'no-win' political issues as the withholding of life-support systems in federally funded hospitals, or the use of fetal tissue for research.

The commission, in Scalia's view, was an unelected body with the powers of an elective legislature.

Scalia particularly took issue with the Court's holding on the commission's location. The fact that Congress chose to locate the commission within the judicial branch, he suggested, was merely a trick of language, but it did not change the facts. In accordance with its ruling in *Humphrey's Executor v. United States* (1935), the Court should ask which of the three branches controlled the commission, as the answer would solve the question of its location. Citing his dissent in *Morrison v. Olson* (1988), which upheld a statute providing for an independent counsel to investigate members of the executive branch, Scalia held that the Court's present decision made its earlier ruling seem logical by comparison. The Court had already— wrongly, in his opinion— authorized the creation of offices within the executive branch that were not subject to ordinary standards of accountability; now, by extending that principle to the judicial branch, it had made a mistake "we will live to regret . . ." Ignoring the Constitution's strict guidelines regarding separation of powers, Scalia concluded, the Court had in effect created "a new Branch altogether, a sort of junior-varsity Congress."

Impact

Although few would question the need for a system of sentencing guidelines, some observers were disturbed by the Court's rejection, in its *Mistretta* ruling, of strict separation-of-powers doctrine. Others, however, viewed the ruling as an example of flexibility on the part of the Court—a common-sense decision, as the Court itself had suggested. With *Metropolitan Washington Airports Authority v. Citizens for the Abatement of Aircraft Noise* (1991), the Court struck down the creation of a congressional review board with veto power over an interstate airport authority, holding that the statute in question violated the doctrine of separation.

Related Cases

Humphrey's Executor v. United States, 295 U.S. 602 (1935).
Nixon v. Administrator of General Services, 433 U.S. 425 (1977).
Northern Pipeline Co. v. Marathon Pipe Line Co., 458 U.S. 50 (1982).
Morrison v. Olson, 487 U.S. 654 (1988).
Metropolitan Washington Airports Authority v. Citizens for the Abatement of Aircraft Noise, 501 U.S. 252 (1991).
Nixon v. United States, 506 U.S. 224 (1993).
Clinton v. Jones, 520 U.S. 681 (1997).

Bibliography and Further Reading

Auld, L. Patrick. "Justice Byron White and Separation of Powers." *Political Studies Quarterly,* spring 1998, p. 337.

Covey, Russell Dean. "Adventures in the Zone of Twilight: Separation of Powers and National Economic Security in the Mexican Bailout." *Yale Law Journal,* March 1996, p. 1311.

Hall, Kermit L., ed. *The Oxford Companion to the Supreme Court of the United States.* New York: Oxford University Press, 1992.

Witt, Elder. *Congressional Quarterly's Guide to the Supreme Court,* 2nd ed. Washington, DC: Congressional Quarterly Inc., 1990.

Witt, Elder, ed. *The Supreme Court A to Z. CQ's Encyclopedia of American Government,* revised ed. Washington, DC: Congressional Quarterly, Inc., 1994.

U.S. TERM LIMITS V. THORNTON

Legal Citation: 514 U.S. 779 (1995)

Petitioner
U.S. Term Limits, Inc.

Respondents
Ray Thornton, Winston Bryant, Bobbie Hill

Petitioner's Claim
That Amendment 73 to the Arkansas Constitution, which limited the terms of officials elected to office in the legislative branch of the federal government, does not violate the Qualifications Clause or any other part of the U.S. Constitution.

Chief Lawyers for Petitioner
George O. Jernigan, Jr., Richard F. Hatfield, Winston Bryant

Chief Lawyers for Respondents
Doyle L. Webb, Stephen Engstrom, Elizabeth J. Robben, Sherry P. Bartley

Justices for the Court
Stephen Breyer, Ruth Bader Ginsburg, Anthony M. Kennedy, David H. Souter, John Paul Stevens (writing for the Court)

Justices Dissenting
Sandra Day O'Connor, William H. Rehnquist, Antonin Scalia, Clarence Thomas

Place
Washington, D.C.

Date of Decision
22 May 1995

Decision
That the "Term Limits Amendment" would erode the structure designed by the framers to form a 'more perfect Union"; accordingly, the amendment was judged unconstitutional.

Significance
During the 1980s and 1990s, sentiment in favor of term limitations grew throughout the nation. Career politicians, according to the grass-roots organizers who were attempting to sway public opinion, had a way of becoming complacent and unresponsive to their constituents; yet with the advantages given by the electoral system to incumbents, they were more likely to be reelected than their challengers. The solution, it seemed, was to put a limit on the number of terms a senator or representative could serve. Short of a nationwide movement for a constitutional amendment, this aim could be achieved through state action.

Arkansas Rejects Career Politicians

The 1980s and 1990s saw a surge of enthusiasm for term limits. Around the country, citizens became aware of the fact that certain senators and representatives seemed to have become permanent fixtures Washington, D.C. With each year of "serving" their states or districts, these politicians gained more power and more influence, enjoyed greater advantages, and drifted further from the needs of their constituents. The nature of the American political process was such that incumbents tended to win elections; therefore, the answer was to "throw the bums out"—the "bums" being the incumbents. This, at least, was the view of term-limits advocates, who urged that a cap be placed on the number of terms an official elected to fill a position in the federal government could serve. According to the *New Republic,* U.S. Term Limits, a citizen's group, sent out a "huge red, white and blue envelope" containing a letter that began,

> Fellow American, most members of Congress view their job as guaranteed for life. The average rate [of reelection] for incumbent congressmen over the last decade has been almost 98 percent. Why? Because it is almost impossible for a challenger to come anywhere near matching an incumbent's war chest! [i.e., their election budget] . . . term limits is the greatest movement of the twentieth century!

By the time the U.S. Supreme Court heard the case of *U.S. Term Limits v. Thornton,* some 23 states had term-limitation statutes in place. Most of these, like the Arkansas provision challenged in *Thornton,* addressed that sector of public life in which term-limits advocates held that the most change was needed: Congress. In the general elections of 3 November 1992—when, incidentally, the nation voted in Arkansas's Governor Bill Clinton as its president by a 43 percent plurality—Arkansas voters had an opportunity to decide on a proposed amendment to limit terms of senators and representatives. The preamble of Amendment 73 said in part, "The people of Arkansas find and declare that elected officials who remain in office too long became preoccupied with reelection and ignore their duties as representatives of the people."

Ray Thornton (left) sits with M. Caldwell Butler on the set of Face the Nation. © AP/Wide World Photos.

Amendment 73 had term-limit provisions for the state's executive and legislative branches. Section 3, the portion challenged in *Thornton* was the provision for Congress. Specifically, section 3(a) limited representatives to no more than three terms, or six years; and 3(b) established the maximum length for senatorial service as two terms, or 12 years. The "self-executing" amendment would apply to all persons seeking election after 1 January, 1993.

Ten days after Arkansas voters approved Amendment 73, Bobbie Hill filed a complaint in the Circuit Court for Pulaski County, Arkansas. The suit named herself, the League of Women Voters, and other Arkansas "citizens, residents, taxpayers and registered voters" as plaintiffs. The suit named the governor (which was still Bill Clinton, now on his way to the White House), other state officials, and the Republican and Democratic parties of Arkansas as defendants. State Attorney General Winston Bryant intervened as a defendant in support of the amendment, along with U.S. Term Limits, Inc.

The circuit court ruled that Amendment 73 violated Article I of the U.S. Constitution. Contained in Article I is the Qualifications Clause, which the court held should constitute the entirety of the qualifications imposed on candidates for the Senate or the House. Article I, section 2, clause 2 states that "No Person shall be a Representative who shall not have attained to the age of twenty-five years, and been seven Years a Citizen of the United States, and who shall not, when elected, be an inhabitant of that State in which he shall be chosen." In other words, as long as one was 25 years old or older, had been a citizen for seven years or more,

and was a legal resident in the state where one chose to run for the House, one was eligible. The qualifications for the Senate in section 3, clause 3, imposed the same set of criteria—age, term of citizenship, and residence—though in different amounts. Section 3 states that "No Person shall be a Senator who shall not have attained to the Age of thirty Years, and been nine Years a Citizen of the United States, and who shall not, when elected, be an Inhabitant of that State for which he shall be chosen." Beyond those three criteria, there were no constitutional restrictions on who could be a member of Congress.

The Arkansas Supreme Court affirmed the ruling of the lower court by a 5-2 vote. Writing for a plurality of three justices, Justice Robert L. Brown held that the amendment was unconstitutional because the states had no power to "change, add to, or diminish" the requirements in the Qualifications Clause. "The uniformity in qualifications mandated in Article I," he wrote, "provides the tenor and the fabric for representation in the Congress. Piecemeal restrictions by State would fly in the face of that order." Amendment 73 was not, as the respondents claimed, "merely a ballot access amendment." This was a claim they had tried to make based on its language, which stated than anyone who had served more than the maximum number of terms "shall not be eligible to have his/her name placed on the ballot . . ." "Its intent and effect," the state's high court held, was "to disqualify congressional incumbents from further service." Two other justices on the Arkansas Supreme Court, however, questioned this ruling, with one of them pointing out that the Constitution nowhere *prevents* states from imposing additional qualifications for congressional service.

The Qualifications Clause and Other Prohibitions

The U.S. Supreme Court agreed to consolidate several related cases. Upon review it voted 5-4 to affirm the ruling of the lower court. Justice Stevens, for the majority, wrote that section 3 of Amendment 73, the part pertaining to senators and representatives, did indeed violate the Constitution. Though Article I, section 5, clause 1 gave each House of Congress power to judge the "Qualifications of its own Members," it did not grant them authority to alter or add to the qualifications already established in the Constitution. The Court had established this in *Powell v. McCormack* (1969), which had sprung from attempts by the House to bar Representative Adam Clayton Powell, Jr., from his seat following allegations of wrongdoing on his part in 1966. A review of its *Powell* decision convinced the Court in the present case that the constitutional qualifications for elective service could not be supplemented by Congress.

The Constitution similarly prohibits states from adding congressional qualifications, the Court ruled. The petitioners had argued that states had this authority under the Tenth Amendment, which reserves for them all powers not granted to the federal government, but the Court rejected this for two reasons. First, since the power to add qualifications did not exist in the Constitution prior to the writing of the Tenth Amendment, it could not be considered a power "reserved" for the states. Second, it seemed fairly clear that the framers of the Constitution intended for that document, and not the states, to be the exclusive source of qualifications for prospective members of Congress. Other parts of the Constitution demonstrate this, as does the historical record and commentary by various judges and justices. Further, to quote the *Powell* decision, the "fundamental principle of our representative democracy . . . [is] that the people should choose whom they please to govern them." If the states were given free reign to add restrictions, this would result in a "patchwork . . . inconsistent with the framers' vision of a uniform National Legislature representing the people of the United States."

Thus, Justice Stevens wrote, a state term-limits measure was unconstitutional "when it has the likely effect of handicapping a class of candidates and has the sole purpose of creating additional qualifications indirectly." With regard to the petitioners' claim that it was a mere "ballot access amendment," the Court indicated that it hardly mattered what they called it: the amendment was "an indirect attempt to evade . . . the Qualifications Clauses' requirements and trivialize[d] the basic democratic principles underlying those Clauses." Nor did the Court go along with the claim that Amendment 73 was a measure granted to the state by the Elections Clause in Article I, section 4, clause 1, which gives states the power to regulate "Times, Places and Manner of holding Elections." This Clause, the Court held, was put in place "to protect the integrity and regularity of the election process . . . not to provide [states] with license to impose substantive qualifications that would exclude classes of candidates from federal office."

The Court addressed the question of how citizens could hope to impose term limits if Amendment 73 was unconstitutional in the conclusion of its ruling, when it held that "State imposition of term limits for congressional service would effect such a fundamental change in the constitutional framework that it must come through a constitutional amendment properly passed under the procedures set forth in Article V [of the Constitution]." Without such an amendment, which would apply to the nation as a whole, the use of term limits by one state on its own "would erode the structure designed by the framers to form a 'more perfect Union'."

Justice Kennedy issued a concurring opinion, in which he addressed objections raised by the dissent and "explain[ed] why [their] course of argumentation runs counter to fundamental principles of federalism." The importance of the federalist system had been presented in several parts of the *The Federalist,* he wrote, and the necessity of protecting that system's power from encroachment by the states had been recognized even before the passage of the Fourteenth Amendment. Then, following the passage of the Fourteenth Amendment and its subsequent challenge in the *Slaughterhouse* Cases (1873), the Court had reinforced the holding that "rights stem from sources other than the States."

Dissent: An Ironic Ruling

Justice Thomas, in an opinion joined by Chief Justice Rehnquist, Justice O'Connor, and Justice Scalia, dissented. "It is ironic," he began, "that the Court bases today's decision on the right of the people 'to choose whom they please to govern them'" when its ruling indicated that neither the people of Arkansas nor their legislature had a right to make such a choice. "Nothing in the Constitution," Justice Thomas wrote,

> deprives the people of each State of the power to prescribe eligibility requirements for candidates who seek to represent them in Congress. The Constitution is simply silent on this question. And where the Constitution is silent, it raises no bar to action by the States or the people.

Beginning an opinion which stretched to more than 87 pages without footnotes—slightly longer than that of the majority opinion and Kennedy's concurrence—Justice Thomas addressed "first principles" since "the majority fundamentally misunderstands the notion of 'reserved' powers." Because the Constitution is based on the principle that all powers stem from the people, Justice Thomas held, it was incumbent on the Court to point to a place in that document which would have expressly forbidden the people of Arkansas from voting to enact Amendment 73. Justice Thomas then took apart the majority's Tenth Amendment argument, which it had made by reference to cases as widely separated in time as *McCulloch v. Maryland* (1819) and *Garcia v. San Antonio Metropolitan Transit Authority* (1985). "Despite the majority's citation of *Garcia* and *McCulloch*," Justice Thomas wrote, "the only true support for its view of the Tenth Amendment comes from Joseph Story's 1833 treatise on constitutional law." As valuable as Story's insights were in *Commentaries on the Constitution of the United States,* Justice Thomas wrote, Story had not been one of the framers.

Having addressed the Tenth Amendment argument from a number of perspectives, Justice Thomas wrote of Amendment 73, "Whatever one might think of the wisdom of this arrangement, we may not override the decision of the people of Arkansas unless something in the Federal Constitution deprives them of the power to enact such measures." The Qualifications Clause, he held, was not that "something," and he addressed this topic in a lengthy argument. He then turned to the historical record, finding that "[t]o the extent that the records from the Philadelphia [constitutional] Convention itself shed light on this case, they tend to hurt the majority's position." As for the majority's claim that the absence of discussion of term limits during the ratification period proves the framers' intention, Thomas wrote that this argument ". . . cuts both ways. The recorded ratification debates also contain no affirmative statement that the states cannot supplement the constitutional qualifications." Justice Thomas then addressed various other historical items and assessed the logical implications of the Court's ruling. Drawing to a conclusion, he returned to his starting-point: the absurdity of a law that prevented the people from having electoral choice on the basis that they must have electoral choice. "Either the majority's holding is wrong," Justice Thomas wrote, "and Amendment 73 does not violate the Qualifications Clauses, or . . . the electoral system that exists without Amendment 73 is no less unconstitutional than the electoral system that exists with Amendment 73."

Impact

Just as the Court's decision in *Thornton* was split more or less between the liberals who opposed term limits and the conservatives who supported them, the reac-

tion in political journals was on similar lines. Jeffrey Rosen in the liberal *New Republic,* writing before the Court reviewed the case, suggested that "The justices will be on solid ground if they strike down term limits on the theory that no temporary majority—in a federal or state legislature or state plebiscite—should be able to add qualifications for office that thwart the will of the voters in each district." As it turned out, this was close to what the majority decided. The conservative *National Review,* in a review of the case after the decision, praised Justice Thomas's "long, dispassionate, lucid, and thoroughly persuasive" dissenting opinion. Thomas' dissent, wrote Lino A. Graglia was "a call to revolution: for the Court not to invalidate policy choices on which the Constitution is silent would be for the Court hardly to invalidate any policy choices at all and to permit policy-making on basic social issues to revert to the control of the people." Even the radical Lenora Fulani, perennial candidate for the presidency, decried the *Thornton* ruling, calling it an "indicat[ion] to many Americans that the time has come to impose term limits on the Supreme Court, too." Yet the Republican Revolution of the 1994 elections, which brought about Republican majorities in both Houses of Congress for the first time since 1954, proved that sweeping change was possible without term limits. On 29 March 1995, the new House of Representatives voted on a term limits amendment. The initiative lost by a vote of 227 to 204.

Related Cases

McCulloch v. Maryland, 4 Wheat. 316 (1819).

Powell v. McCormack, 395 U.S. 486 (1969).

Bullock v. Carter, 405 U.S. 134 (1972).

FERC v. Mississippi, 456 U.S. 742 (1982).

Garcia v. San Antonio Metropolitan Transit Authority, 469 U.S. 528 (1985).

United States v. Lopez, 514 U.S. 549 (1995).

Bibliography and Further Reading

Cutler, Lloyd. "Now Is the Time for All Good Men . . ." *William & Mary Law Review,* Vol. 30, no. 387, 1989, p. 395.

Fulani, Lenora. "Black Empowerment: No Matter What the Court Says, Term Limits Will Reign Supreme." *New Pittsburgh Courier,* July 1, 1995.

Graglio, Lino A. "Does Constitutional Law Exist?" *National Review,* June 26, 1995, pp. 31-34.

Rosen, Jeffrey. "Coming to Terms." *The New Republic,* December 12, 1994, pp. 18-19.

PRINTZ V. UNITED STATES

Legal Citation: 521 U.S. 98 (1997)

Petitioner
Jay Printz, Sheriff/Coroner, Ravalli County, Montana

Respondent
United States

Petitioner's Claim
That Congress's use of the Brady Act to require "chief law enforcement officers" (CLEOs) in a local jurisdiction to conduct background checks of handgun purchasers, and to perform other duties, is unconstitutional.

Chief Lawyer for Petitioner
Stephen P. Halbrook

Chief Lawyer for Respondent
Walter Dellinger, Acting Solicitor General

Justices for the Court
Anthony M. Kennedy, Sandra Day O'Connor, William H. Rehnquist, Antonin Scalia (writing for the Court), Clarence Thomas

Justices Dissenting
Stephen Breyer, Ruth Bader Ginsburg, David H. Souter, John Paul Stevens

Place
Washington, D.C.

Date of Decision
27 June 1997

Decision
That the "Necessary and Proper" Clause in Article I of the Constitution did not give Congress authority to override state legislatures and require local CLEOs to perform background checks.

Significance
Inasmuch as *Printz v. United States* was about gun control, it would prove to be a setback for those who wanted to limit citizens' rights to own guns under the Second Amendment. However, *Printz* was more concerned with freedom from federal interference in local affairs, and as such it represented a small step back from the Court's pro-federal government stance in preceding years. Sheriff Jay Printz himself, having won an earlier round in the battle that took his case before the Supreme Court, told *USA Today* in 1994 that the Brady Bill was part of ". . . a trend toward federalization. This is just the tip of the iceberg." As for further attempts to strengthen the Brady Act with the proposed "Brady Bill II," he stated, "They're trying to disarm the American public."

John Hinckley Helps Write the Brady Bill

On 30 March 1981, a young man named John Hinckley—who later claimed he was inspired by the movie *Taxi Driver* and a desire to impress its young star, actress Jodie Foster—fired shots at President Ronald Reagan. Wounded in the shooting were the president, a secret service agent, and White House Press Secretary James Brady. President Reagan, who had been in office only two months, would recover from his wounds; Brady, on the other hand, would be paralyzed for life. The next month, a Turkish youth fired on the Pope, but did not kill him; but the soldiers who shot Egyptian President and Nobel laureate Anwar Sadat in October succeeded in their mission. Around the world, it seemed that a new age of assassination had come about, rivaling the spate of shootings in the 1960s that killed President John F. Kennedy and his brother Bobby, as well as civil rights leader Martin Luther King and his colleague Malcolm X.

Many in the United States believed that domestic violence could be curtailed through revisions to the Second Amendment, which grants citizens the right to keep and bear arms. Out of that earlier era of assassinations had come the Gun Control Act (GCA) of 1968, which among other things forbid arms sales to anyone under the age of 21 and prevented the transfer of a firearm to a convicted felon or a fugitive from justice. While most of these provisions seemed reasonable, conservatives feared that the true aim of anti-gun foes was a revocation of Second-Amendment rights, and the polity divided into two hostile camps on the gun control issue. In James Brady and his wife Sarah, whose lives had been forever altered for the worse by a handgun, gun-control advocates gained a valuable ally: a former aide to a conservative president who happened to be an advocate of gun control. Hence when in 1993 Congress passed a bill amending the GCA, it was called the Brady Act.

The Brady Act contained numerous provisions, but most significant for the purposes of *Printz v. United States* were those relating to background checks. The act authorized the attorney general of the United States to put in place a computerized instant background check system by 30 November 1998; and in the mean-

James Brady, White House Press Secretary, with President Reagan. © Archives Photos.

time, it established certain interim provisions. Under these provisions, firearm dealers desiring to sell a handgun must first receive from the person buying it a statement called the Brady Form. The Brady Form contains the transferee's name, address, date of birth, and a sworn statement that the transferee is not among the class of prohibited purchasers such as felons and fugitives. Second, the dealer must verify the identity of the buyer by examining an identification document. Third, he must provide the CLEO of the prospective buyer's home jurisdiction with a copy of the completed Brady Form. Unless the CLEO earlier notifies the dealer that he has no reason to believe the transaction is illegal, the dealer has to wait five business days before concluding the sale. The law thus made it incumbent on CLEOs to "make a reasonable effort to ascertain within 5 business days whether receipt or possession would be in violation of the law, including research in whatever State and local record keeping systems are available and in a national system designated by the Attorney General." The interim provisions contained other stipulations, including an order that a CLEO should be able to present a rejected gun-buyer with written reasons for the denial and an order that the CLEO destroy Brady Forms after a certain period of time.

Sheriffs Jay Printz of Ravalli County, Montana, and Richard Mack of Graham County, Arizona, filed separate actions challenging the constitutionality of these interim provisions, the fulfillment of which would place an enormous extra burden on their schedules. In both cases, the district court ruled that the Brady Act's interim provision requiring CLEOs to perform background checks was unconstitutional, but held that this could be separated from the rest of the act, leaving a system of voluntarily conducted background checks in place. The Court of Appeals for the Ninth Circuit reversed by a divided vote, finding that none of the Brady Act's interim provisions were unconstitutional.

The Majority Takes Its Cue from History

The U.S. Supreme Court reversed by a 5-4 vote. Because there was no text in the Constitution which addressed the specific question of whether Congress could legally compel state officers to execute federal law, wrote Justice Scalia, the Court looked for its answers in "historical understanding and practice, in the Constitution's structure, and in this Court's jurisprudence." Though he warned that by itself an observation of constitutional practice was inconclusive, Justice Scalia noted that such an observation "tends to negate the existence of the congressional power asserted here." The early enactments of Congress showed that the federal government considered it within its power to require state judges to enforce federal law in the judicial branch, but there was less evidence to justify such congressional influence in the state executive realm. Even though *The Federalist* contained portions suggesting that the federal government could impose responsibilities on state officers, there was nothing therein to suggest that these responsibilities could be forced on the states without consent. The assumption instead seemed to be that the states would consent, as Justice O'Connor had observed in *FERC v. Mississippi* (1982). The historical record simply did not bear out the existence of "executive commandeering federal statutes," except perhaps in very recent years.

The Brady Bill—Does It Really Fight Crime?

The Brady Handgun Control Act provides gun-control measures such as the establishment of a five-day waiting period for purchase of a firearm. The law's passage in 1993 highlighted the continuing controversy over gun control. In 1996, President Bill Clinton called for measures to tighten Brady Bill restrictions with regard to persons convicted of misdemeanors in domestic abuse cases. According to Bob Walker of Handgun Control Inc., Clinton's new measures would "close a real loophole in the law" and keep a "significant number of defendants who plea-bargain felonies down to misdemeanors" from easily purchasing guns. Tanya Metaksa of the National Rifle Association (NRA) criticized the new restrictions as "feel-good legislation that won't work." Metaksa suggested that punishing abusers by preventing them from buying guns would not curb violence, since domestic abuse most often does not involve firearms. A headline in *US News* noted that at least both sides agree on one thing: the law will not prevent most criminals from obtaining handguns.

Source(s): "A New Round for and Against the Brady Bill." *US News & World Report,* September 9, 1996, p. 8.

Turning to the Constitution itself, one saw at work a system of "dual sovereignty," whereby states surrendered some of their powers and gained others. "The Framers," Justice Scalia wrote, "rejected the concept of a central government that would act upon and through the States, and instead designed a system in which the State and Federal Governments would exercise concurrent authority over the people." To simply "impress into its service . . . at no cost to itself . . . the police officers of the 50 States" would be an unlawful way of augmenting the federal government's power. If the federal government exerted too much control over the states, this could also have an ill effect on the separation of powers into three branches. The Brady Act, Justice Scalia wrote, "effectively transfers the President's responsibility to administer the laws enacted by Congress . . . thousands of CLEOs in the 50 States . . ."

The dissent asserted that the Brady Bill was valid by the "Necessary and Proper" Clause in Article I, section 8, which grants Congress power "To make all Laws which shall be necessary and proper for carrying into execution" the powers granted to Congress—in this case the Commerce Clause grant of power to regulate handgun sales. Justice Scalia held that the Brady Bill's constitutionality could not be sustained on this basis alone, not when it violated the principle of state sovereignty. Citing *New York v. United States* (1992), Justice Scalia held that it was unlawful for the federal government to directly compel a state to enact or enforce a federal regulatory program. The whole object of the Brady Act's provisions in this situation was to compel the state executive toward certain actions, Justice Scalia wrote; hence it was pointless to attempt, as the dissent did, a type of "balancing analysis."

Given that it had eliminated CLEOs' responsibility to conduct background checks, the Court had no need to review the petitioners' concerns about the provisions requiring them to destroy Brady Forms after a certain amount of time. As for the more significant severability question—whether the interim provisions could be pulled out of the Brady Act without invalidating the entire act—the Court declined to address this issue. Removal of CLEOs' requirements would leave open the question of whether firearms dealers could be required to comply, and since no such dealers were before the Court as petitioners, the question was left unanswered.

Justice O'Connor issued a short concurring statement, as did Justice Thomas. The former noted that precedent, both in the form of earlier Court rulings, and of past practice, supported the Court's ruling. The Brady Bill, she wrote, further violated the Tenth Amendment's reservation of powers to the states. Justice Thomas, too, cited Tenth Amendment backing for the Court's decision, and wrote separately to further emphasize the enumeration—and therefore limitation—of federal powers over the states.

The Dissent Offers a Different Reading of History

Of the four dissenters, several wrote opinions questioning the majority's reading of history, particularly of the ruling in *New York*. Justice Stevens, in an opinion joined by the other three—Justices Breyer, Ginsburg, and Souter—held that Congress was fully authorized by the Constitution to impose affirmative obligations (i.e., "You must do this . . .") on citizens. "This conclusion," he wrote, "is firmly supported by the text of the Constitution, the early history of the Nation, decisions of this Court, and a correct understanding of the basic structure of the Federal Government." The present case did not require a study of the more complex issues raised in *New York*, he wrote, nor was it necessary to consider questions such as whether local or federal officials could better carry out a federal program. "The question," as Justice Stevens put it, "is whether Congress, acting on behalf of the people of the entire Nation, may require local law enforcement officers to perform certain duties during the interim needed for the development of a federal gun control program."

The measures suggested in the Brady Act's interim provisions were appropriate in a national emergency, such as that posed by the rash of handgun-related crimes. In its ruling, the Court was going beyond upholding the powers of the states under the Tenth Amendment, Justice Stevens suggested, and instead limiting the authority of Congress. "There is not a clause, sentence, or paragraph in the entire text of the Constitution of the United States," he wrote, "that supports the proposition that a local police officer can ignore a command contained in a statute enacted by Congress pursuant to an express delegation of power enumerated in Article I" of the Constitution. Justice Stevens went on to question the Court's review of the historical record in *New York* and elsewhere. He concluded by observing that the provision before the Court's review was comparable to a statute requiring local law-enforcement officers to report the identities of missing children to the Crime Control Center of the Justice Department, rather than "an offensive federal command to a sovereign state."

Justice Souter, too, dissented; his principal difference with Justice Stevens being that his primary objections came from *The Federalist*. Justice Breyer, joined by Justice Stevens, issued an opinion in which he added to the latter's dissent by noting the uniquely American difficulty of reconciling the power of the national government with that of local government. Looking at the past experience of federal program implementation, he noted, it was not necessary to read the Brady Act as overwhelming a state government's powers. As for the majority's view that measures such as those provided in the act were unconstitutional, Justice Breyer sided with Justice Stevens that "the Constitution is itself silent on the matter."

Impact

Like many Supreme Court cases, *Printz* was not really about the issue it supposedly addressed—in this case, gun control. Instead, it was about the relative power of the federal and state governments, an issue raised in numerous parts of the Constitution, including the Tenth Amendment. Jerome L. Wilson pointed out the difference between the practical and the constitutional issues in the title of his August of 1997 *New Jersey Law Journal* article, "It Wasn't About Handguns at All." Yet as in many cases, to those involved, the practical issue was the important question. At an earlier stage in the history of the case, Sarah Brady told *USA Today* that "In light of the success of the Brady law in stopping the cash-and-carry sale of handguns to felons . . . any sheriff who doesn't use the five days to do a background check should be ashamed." Many viewed the verdict in *Printz* as a judgment on handgun control itself, not on federalism; certainly it was the first major challenge to the Brady Act, just three months after the latter had been passed by Congress. But a writer in *News Media & the Law* perhaps best glimpsed the constitutional implications by noting that the U.S. District Court in South Carolina could use the Supreme Court's *Printz* ruling to strike down the South Carolina Driver's Privacy Protection Act. The latter, which the writer said limits public access to Department of Motor Vehicles records and places an undue burden on the states, could be challenged on the basis of a Tenth-Amendment violation.

Related Cases
National League of Cities v. Usery, 426 U.S. 833 (1976).
FERC v. Mississippi, 456 U.S. 742 (1982).
INS v. Chadha, 462 U.S. 919 (1983).
Garcia v. San Antonio Metropolitan Transit Authority, 469 U.S. 528 (1985).
Bowsher v. Synar, 478 U.S. 714 (1986).
South Carolina v. Baker, 485 U.S. 505 (1988).
Gregory v. Ashcroft, 501 U.S. 452 (1991).
New York v. United States, 505 U.S. 144 (1992).

Bibliography and Further Reading
"Congress Should Steer Clear of State Drivers' Records." *News Media & the Law,* summer 1997, p. 2.

Davis, Robert. "Judge Shoots Down Brady Law's Background Checks." *USA Today,* 18 May 1994, p. 3.

Podgers, James. "Gun Law Under Fire: Court Challenges to Brady Bill Produce Conflicting Results." *ABA Journal,* August 1994, pp. 83-84.

Wilson, Jerome L. "It Wasn't About Handguns at All." *New Jersey Law Journal,* 18 August 1997, p. S-3.

MILITARY ISSUES

Military Society

The term "military" refers to the society within the armed forces and the individual lives of professional soldiers. The professional armies of early Europe grew to be societies separate from civilian societies with special laws addressing unique needs. While civilian criminal law seeks to maintain peace and tranquility, military justice promotes order, high morale, and discipline. This difference is recognized in the U.S. Constitution. Through its constitutional powers, Congress established a military justice system with its own laws, procedures, and courts, including the court-martial, a military court that tries members of the armed services for crimes described in the Uniform Code of Military Justice. This system, one of the largest judicial systems in the United States, largely parallels state and federal civilian systems.

Origins of Modern Military Justice

Like civilian law, military law derived from Roman law dating back to the first century B.C. Roman society was a military society and a single justice system served both civilian and military needs. Following introduction of the Roman legal system in England in the eleventh century by William the Conqueror, the desire for separate legal systems grew. Courts-martial involving trials conducted within the military appeared in France and Germany around the sixteenth century. In the early seventeenth century, Gustavus Adolphus, the influential King of Sweden, adopted a body of military law separate from English common law to discipline his army. Courts-martial procedures were soon introduced within the English military and England created a national military legal system by 1649. Parliament became involved in military justice with the passage of the Mutiny Act in 1689 thus setting the English precedent of legislative control over military issues.

Weeks after the epic confrontation between colonial militia and British troops at Lexington and Concord, Massachusetts in April of 1775, the Second Continental Congress formed an American army. The colonial leaders who orchestrated political rebellion against Britain suddenly had to decide how to insure discipline and control in the new armed forces. Of less interest at the time were individual "rights" of the soldiers. The 1775 Articles of War established the basis for American military justice. Influenced by the British legal system, the colonists adopted a system in which the main national legislative body was responsible for enacting military law. The colonists, essentially copying the British body of law, believed that a system developed from the successes of two empires, Roman and Britain, would be difficult to improve upon under such urgency. The founders observed that the "prosperity" of nations in history corresponded with the level of military discipline in their armies.

The Constitution in 1788 further defined military authority by designating the president as commander-in-chief in Article II and giving Congress power in Article I "to declare War . . . to raise and support Armies . . . to provide and maintain a Navy; To make Rules for the Government and Regulations of the land and naval Forces . . ." Civilian control over the military was firmly established. The Court in *Dynes v. Hoover* (1857) reaffirmed that Congressional power to regulate servicemembers was clearly separate from Article III of the Constitution, which established civilian judicial authority. The federal government exercised its constitutional authority by conducting the first draft of men into the army during the Civil War.

Over the next century, Congress passed legislation on several occasions revising the Articles of the Constitution. Commanding officers held powers for court-martial as a key tool to maintain order and discipline. The officer could convene a court, select the members from officers in his command, and serve as the reviewing authority with power to disapprove a sentence and return it to the court. The Articles of War did not originally include common law felonies, such as murder, assault, rape, and larceny. In 1863 the role of commander expanded to include court-martial jurisdiction over such crimes, but only in time of war or rebellion. For the first time soldiers could be tried by military authorities for common law offenses. The Court in *Ex parte Milligan* (1866) held that this new court-martial jurisdiction did not extend to civilians.

In World War I Congress passed the Selective Service Act of 1917. On charges that the draft violated the

Thirteenth Amendment prohibition of servitude, the Supreme Court upheld the law in a series of cases known as the *Selective Draft Law Cases* (1918). The Court unanimously ruled that the authority to draft came from the war powers and the Necessary and Proper Clause. The Thirteenth Amendment was not intended to prohibit duties individuals owed their nation, such as military service and jury duty.

The basic Articles of War, first written in 1775, remained largely unchanged through World War II. Critics charged that the military justice system was essentially "un-American" with commanding officers holding almost unrestricted power over judicial proceedings. They attempted at times to push major revisions through Congress, but achieved only limited success.

Following World War II, returning veterans expressed substantial dissatisfaction with the harshness and arbitrariness of the military justice system. An investigative board established in 1946 found that commanding officers held too much control in the courts-martial process, often leading to excessive punishments and unfairness in the treatment of officers and enlisted men. In response, Congress created the Uniform Code of Military Justice in 1951 placing divergent laws of the varied services into one law composed of 140 articles. Under the code's authority, the president established evidence rules and courts-martial procedures in a Manual for Courts-Martial. The Manual, which followed civilian federal court procedures and punishments as much as feasible, became the basic source of military justice authority along with the Constitution, the Code, various service regulations, and the U.S. Court of Military Appeals. The Court of Military Appeals, created by Congress, is the highest court in the military judicial system, and is composed of three civilian judges appointed by the president for 15 year terms.

Reflecting the special needs for order, efficiency, and discipline, three levels of courts-martial were established: summary, special, and general. The summary court-martial is the most limited in scope, applying only to enlisted personnel charged with minor offenses and serves to resolve cases quickly. This form varies significantly from civilian criminal processes, as certain rights do not apply. The intermediate level, special courts-martial, can address all cases except capital offenses. Composed of three-judge panels, it is limited in the types of punishment it can apply. General courts-martial, the most powerful trial court in the military judicial system, can address any violations of the Code and may impose death penalties. The proceedings must include a military judge and no fewer than five panel members. The Military Judicial System procedural safeguards protecting the rights of servicemembers become more extensive as the severity of the alleged crimes increase. The courts-martial trials primarily apply to servicemembers committing crimes on military posts or

while wearing a uniform. When someone violates both military and state criminal codes, they may be tried in either system. Jurisdiction over servicemembers ends when they leave the military. Regarding actual court proceedings, few differences exist between civilian and military trials. However, though the Code extend almost all procedural constitutional protections to the military courtroom, the commanding officer still retains considerable power. In 1968 Congress passed the Military Justice Act granting more power to military judges over court proceedings and limiting the commanders' powers.

Shortly after the creation of the Code, cases addressing the distinction between military and civil criminal systems began to reach the Court. In *Orloff v. Willoughby* (1953) the Court held that the civilian courts "are not given the task of running the Army." Through the separation of powers doctrine, the Court in *Parisi v. Davidson* (1972) further recognized the autonomy of the judicial military system. The U.S. Supreme Court holds no authority to review military cases using writs of *certiorari* powers. It can accept *habeas corpus* petitions, however, alleging constitutional rights violations for those being detained and cases challenging military jurisdiction. For example, the Court in *Middendorf v. Henry* (1976) ruled that summary courts-martial proceedings do not constitute criminal prosecutions and are therefore not held to the same standard of due process. The courts have also refused involvement in a range of national security issues by invoking the "political question" doctrine. The doctrine defers resolution to the two political branches of government.

The Code describes certain punishable offenses very similar to civilian crimes, though it does not distinguish between felonies and misdemeanors. Such crimes include homicide, sex offenses, property and theft offenses, and alcohol and drug-related offenses. Sex offenses include rape, adultery, and indecent assault.

Many other offenses in the Code do not appear in the U.S. justice system. Other offenses treated severely in the military are relatively minor in civilian law. Obedience to authority is an essential and unique part of military society. Being "absent without leave," or AWOL, is the most common offense in the military. Violations of general orders, disrespect or contempt for officials, and insubordination are other forms of disobedience crimes. Mutiny, which involves efforts to override military authority and the failure to report mutiny, are capital offenses. Desertion, the intent to avoid hazardous duty or important service, is also one of the more serious offenses a servicemember can commit. The Persian Gulf War led to substantial challenges by members of the all-volunteer military. In *United States v. Thun* (1993) a serviceman was convicted of desertion for avoiding a Persian Gulf assignment.

Yet other crimes unique to the military are not so precisely defined in the Code. These crimes are addressed as "conduct unbecoming an officer" under "General Articles." Such offenses give commanders a great deal of flexibility in maintaining order and discipline, but critics claim they are unconstitutionally vague. The Supreme Court ruled in *Parker v. Levy* (1974) that they were neither vague nor overbroad, but rather served a specific function unique to the military in maintaining obedience and discipline. As the Court noted, the military was "a society apart from civilian society." Conduct Unbecoming applies only to commissioned officers while the General Articles applies to both officers and enlisted personnel. Both address a wide range of conduct that could "bring discredit upon the services." A General Article charge may accompany any other Code violation. Conduct Unbecoming includes making false official statements, uttering defamatory statements about another officer, public drunkenness, disorderly conduct, and adultery. The Court of Military Appeals in *United States v. Frazier* (1992) upheld a soldier's conviction for maintaining an intimate relationship with another soldier's wife.

All civilian crimes are addressed through judicial processes. However, as the military has some unique offenses, it also has unique procedures to maintain discipline and morale without holding courts-martial. These means include "nonpunitive measures" and "nonjudicial punishment." Because the military regulates such a broad range of behavior and to ensure efficiency of command, a commanding officer has authority to apply "nonpunitive measures" for minor Code violations. Relevant behavior includes neglect and inattention, shoplifting, intoxication, fighting, writing bad checks, and driving under the influence. Such measures could involve withholding privileges, counseling, reductions in rank, reassignment of duties, and revocation of security clearances. Complaint procedures allow for review of the commander's actions.

"Nonjudicial punishment" provides actions commanding officers could take for minor offenses to maintain discipline and morale without holding a court-martial. Such action is appropriate when "nonpunitive measures" are inadequate. Punishments are limited and the accused can consult with legal counsel but has no Sixth Amendment right to representation of an attorney. The accused could demand trial by court-martial and has a right to appeal results of the informal hearing. Despite the fact that a court-martial lacks procedural protections and judicial review, the Court in *Middendorf v. Henry* (1976) ruled that the process did not violate the Constitution's Due Process Clause since the accused had the option of a court-martial trial where representation by counsel would be available. Procedural safeguards enjoyed by American civilian citizens were largely extended to military personnel by the Court in *United States v. Jacoby* (1960). The Court held "that the protections in the Bill of Rights, except those which are expressly or by necessary implication inapplicable, are available to members of our armed forces." The Court in *United States v. Davis* (1994) further reaffirmed the application of certain constitutional rights to servicemembers. Regarding the Sixth Amendment's right to a speedy trial, servicemembers are actually entitled through military code to a speedier trial than that provided by federal or state courts. A 1977 military court ruled that the Sixth Amendment right to a public trial applied to special and general courts-martial, even in cases involving security concerns. An accused can also request a trial rather than be subjected to nonjudicial punishment. The Sixth Amendment right to counsel also applies to military personnel in specific and general courts-martial, but not summary courts-martial. The Fifth Amendment provides safeguards from self-incrimination, connecting oneself with a crime. The Code conforms to this protection and even expands on it. In addition, the Manual requires full Miranda warnings advising military personnel of their rights at the time of their arrest. The Fourth Amendment's prohibition against unreasonable search and seizure also applies to servicemembers, including application of probable cause standards. The exclusionary rule barring use of illegally obtained evidence also applies to courts-martial. Civilian-like search warrants are obtained through commanding officers. Some types of search and seizure are exempt, including border searches for national security purposes, persons reporting to military confinement, and entry or exit from military installations.

The civil rights of servicemembers have limitations as Congress attempted to balance the demands of military society with constitutional freedoms. Limitations include the right to a grand jury indictment before trial for a capital offense in the time of war or public danger, and freedom of speech and assembly. Another difference is that juries are not selected randomly as in civilian judicial system. Jurors are selected by the commanding officer and are normally officers. However, an enlisted defendant can request that one-third of the jurors be enlisted servicemembers, but they are still selected by the commanding officer.

The Universal Military Training and Service Act of 1948 which, in establishing a peacetime draft, exempted persons opposed to any form of war due to religious training or belief, but not for personal moral codes. The Court, later loosening this standard, ruled in *Welsh v. United States* (1970) that any attempt to distinguish between theistic religious beliefs and nontheistic beliefs based more on ethics violated the Establishment Clause. Servicemembers could qualify for a discharge from the armed forces under conscientious objector status if they opposed war in any form and the opposition was based on deeply held beliefs. The 1991 Persian Gulf War led to many conscientious objector applications.

Because of the conscientious objector provisions and reliance on an all-volunteer army, the issue of religious freedom in military did not frequently arise in the latter twentieth century. Military demands outweigh individual religious freedom under certain circumstances such as refusal to obey orders, inoculation against disease, and adherence to uniform standards, the latter decided in *Goldman v. Weinberger* (1986). Congress passed a law allowing the wearing of religious apparel or other symbols while in uniform if they did not interfere with the performance of military duties and if they were "neat and conservative." In some instances religious freedom protections prevailed. A district court in 1972 ruled that compulsory chapel attendance violated the Establishment Clause. In *Abington School District v. Schempp* (1963) the Court ruled that Congress can provide for religious needs in some ways without violating the Establishment Clause, such as by employing a chaplain corps.

Freedom of speech, including symbolic speech, is substantially more limited for military personnel than civilians because they are barred from criticizing the government, including the president, commanding officers, Congress, and others, and participation in parades and demonstrations. An example of these restrictions was provided in 1993 when an Air Force general was reprimanded and forced to retire after making comments about newly elected President Bill Clinton in 1993. Similarly, political participation is restricted due to the subordination of the military to civilian control under the Constitution. The military is not to interfere with the functioning of the democratic society. In contrast, servicemembers can be required to participate in parades supporting political views not embraced by the individual military personnel. Military personnel may publish newspapers and other materials while off-duty, but are subject to a censorship process when writing on military matters or foreign policy. In *Near v. Minnesota* (1931) the Court recognized the seriousness of jeopardizing national security through publication of certain information.

Sex, Gender, and Gay Rights in the 1990s

The first official restriction of homosexuality in the military came in the Articles of War of 1916 when homosexual conduct was classified a felony offense. Homosexuality was thereafter considered incompatible with military society by being detrimental to morale. The military even retained a right to regulate homosexual activity of military personnel when occurring away from military facilities. Homosexual conduct and even knowledge of one's sexual orientation was the basis for

criminal charges and discharge. Over 15,000 homosexuals were discharged from the military in the 1980s with a federal court in 1989 holding that constitutional protections were different in the military. However, another federal court later ruled in 1993 that distinctions based on sexual orientation had no rational basis.

The issue of gay rights in the military became hotly contested in 1993 when President Clinton attempted to end discrimination based on sexual orientation. In the face of substantial political opposition, a compromise policy known as "don't ask, don't tell" was enacted in the National Defense Authorization Act of 1994. The policy allowed gays to serve as long as they kept their sexual orientation to themselves and did not engage in homosexual acts. Servicemembers could not be asked about their sexual orientation. Several servicemembers who faced dismissal after publicly claiming their homosexuality filed suits in 1994 challenging the policy. The bases for challenge were freedom of speech under the First Amendment and equal protection under the Due Process Clause of the Fifth Amendment. In 1998 a federal appeals court ruled that the policy did not violate the constitutional right to due process by subjecting homosexuals to a separate set of regulations from others. The judge indicated he could not second-guess military decisions bearing on military capability or readiness.

In 1948 Congress institutionalized gender discrimination when it passed the Women's Armed Services Integration Act excluding women from combat roles. Similarly, women were denied entrance to the military academies primarily for the reason that the academies were to produce future combat officers, and women were not eligible for combat duty. Gender discrimination was extensive. As an example, a military policy granted greater benefits to spouses of male servicemembers than spouses of female servicemembers. The Court in *Frontiero v. Richardson* (1973) ruled that the differential treatment violated equal protection of the law. On the other hand, a federal law granted women naval officers longer periods of commissioned service than men because of the combat exclusion policies. When the law was challenged by male officers on the ground of discrimination, the Court ruled in *Schlesinger v. Ballard* (1975) that it did not violate equal protection rights under the Constitution. Similarly, the Court in *Goldberg v. Rostker* (1981) upheld women's ineligibility for draft registration because of the combat exclusion laws. With the end of the military draft in the mid-seventies, women began to be more fully integrated into the all-volunteer military, especially due to the decreasing population of available men at the time. Military "fraternization" policies became more common forbidding "unduly familiar relationships" between officers and enlisted personnel, and officers of different rank.

The military academy restriction ended in 1991 through judicial and Congressional action. Equivalent standards were maintained with minimal physical requirement adjustments at the academies. But even with the fallout of the highly publicized Tailhook Convention sex scandal in 1991, sexual harassment in the academies became rampant. Female cadets were persistently accused of lowering academy standards and causing the end of popular masculine traditions. President Clinton opened combat roles to women in the Air Force in 1993 and the Navy in 1994. Only Army and Marine units engaged in direct ground combat remained closed. Though policies were changing by the late 1990s, acceptance was not. Issues of menstruation, pregnancy, motherhood, and lesser physical strength persisted. Critics claimed that equal opportunity, political correctness and a feminist social agenda were adversely affecting military readiness and social fabric, and, in turn, national security. As the century comes to a close, constitutional questions regarding women in combat continue, but are considered more a political question to be resolved by Congress or the executive branch rather than by the courts.

Bibliography and Further Reading

Byrne, Edward M. *Military Law,* Second Edition. Annapolis, MD: Naval Institute Press, 1976.

Francke, Linda Bird. *Ground Zero: The Gender Wars in the Military.* New York: Simon & Schuster, 1997.

Herbert, Melissa S. *Camouflage Isn't Only for Combat: Gender, Sexuality and Women in the Military.* New York: New York University Press, 1998.

Kohn, Richard H. *The United States Military under the Constitution of the United States, 1789-1989.* New York: New York University Press, 1991.

Lurie, Jonathan. *Arming Military Justice: Volume 1, The Origins of the United States Court of Military Appeals, 1775-1950.* Princeton, NJ: Princeton University Press, 1992.

Shanor, Charles A., and L. Lynn Hogue. *Military Law in a Nutshell,* 2nd Edition. St. Paul, MN: West Publishing Co., 1996.

Wolinsky, Marc, and Kenneth Sherrill, editors. *Gays and the Military: Joseph Steffan Versus the United States.* Princeton, NJ: Princeton University Press, 1993.

LUTHER V. BORDEN

Legal Citation: 48 U.S. 1 (1849)

Appellant
Martin Luther

Appellee
Luther M. Borden

Appellant's Claim
Luther M. Borden, acting under the martial law that had been declared by the state of Rhode Island, had invaded and searched Martin Luther's home. Martin Luther claimed that the government, under which Borden had acted, was not the legitimate government of Rhode Island. Therefore, Borden was guilty of trespass.

Chief Lawyers for Appellant
Benjamin F. Hallett; Nathan Clifford, U.S. Attorney General

Chief Lawyers for Appellee
John Whipple, Daniel Webster

Justices for the Court
Robert Cooper Grier, John McLean, Samuel Nelson, Roger Brooke Taney (writing for the Court), James Moore Wayne

Justices Dissenting
Levi Woodbury (John Catron, Peter Vivian Daniel, and John McKinley did not participate)

Place
Washington, D.C.

Date of Decision
3 January 1849

Decision
That the Court did not have the power to decide that a state government was not legitimate.

Significance
Since its inception, the Supreme Court has had to distinguish between interpreting the law—which is its duty—and creating law or policy—which are the duties of the legislative and executive branches. *Luther v. Borden* was an important step in the Court's defining "political questions," about which it could have no opinion.

The story of *Luther v. Borden* goes back to a tumultuous period in Rhode Island history, the time of the so-called Dorr Wars. Unlike the other original states, Rhode Island did not adopt a new constitution when the colonies separated from Great Britain. Instead, it treated as its constitution the charter granted by King Charles II in 1663. This charter limited the right to vote to "freeholders"—men who owned property. Men who did not own property wanted to see their state adopt a new constitution, or at least to change the laws that concerned voting.

Large landowners and other powerful people in Rhode Island fought to keep the old charter and its voting laws in place. As late as the legislative sessions in January and June of 1841, suffrage reform was defeated. So a new reform organization was created, under the leadership of Thomas W. Dorr.

Dorr and his colleagues called a convention for 6 October 1841, at which they drafted a new constitution. Although this convention was completely outside the boundaries of Rhode Island law, it was approved by a referendum held that December. Many people without property, who would not have been allowed to vote under existing Rhode Island law, did vote in the referendum. The following year, on 18 April of 1842, a new group of state officers, with Dorr as governor, was elected under the new constitution. The old charter government continued to operate, however, and its legislature passed severe penalties against anyone who voted in any election under the Dorr government.

Insurrection in Providence

Dorr decided to take more decisive action. On 14 May 1842, he and his party tried to seize the arsenal in Providence, the state capital. The insurrection failed and Dorr fled from the state. Although there had been no actual violence during the insurrection, rumors flew that Dorr was going to invade the state. Fearful of invasion, the charter government declared martial law on 24 June 1842.

Dorr's movement soon collapsed, but not before it had helped to discredit the charter government. Finally, the old government called a constitutional convention,

Martial Law

Martial law is implemented when constitutional law is suspended, and civil authority is replaced by military government. Usually this occurs in times of natural disaster, war, or other forms of unrest. During the twentieth century, nationwide martial law has been declared, and sustained for long periods of time, in countries ranging from the Philippines to Poland.

Martial law has been imposed in the United States during the enforcement of civil rights or during urban rioting. One of the most notable uses of martial law occurred in Little Rock, Arkansas, in 1957, when President Eisenhower sent in federal troops to enforce inte-gration of public schools. The California National Guard was activated in 1992 to deal with rioting in Los Angeles following the handing down of a "not guilty" verdict for four white police officers charged with beating black motorist Rodney King. Martial law was also proclaimed twice during the Civil War, when President Abraham Lincoln suspended the writ of *habeas corpus,* and in Hawaii following the bombing of Pearl Harbor by the Japanese on 7 December 1941.

Source(s): Bradley, David and Fishkin, Shelley Fisher, eds. *The Encyclopedia of Civil Rights in America* Armonk, NY: Sharpe, 1998.

at which suffrage was broadened to some extent, though not to the extent that the Dorr forces had wanted. Meanwhile, across the nation, Dorr's own standing became a source of controversy. People questioned whether he was a patriot who wanted to expand democracy or a traitor who had threatened the lives, liberty, and property of his fellow citizens.

Eventually, Dorr was convicted of treason against the state of Rhode Island and sentenced to life imprisonment at hard labor. Another pro-Dorr movement petitioned the Supreme Court to free Dorr, claiming that he had only been acting as the lawful governor of Rhode Island. The Supreme Court denied the petition, but Dorr was finally freed on 27 June 1845, under amnesty granted by the Rhode Island legislature.

Which Was the Rightful Government?

Meanwhile, Martin Luther, a Dorr supporter from the town of Warren, decided to sue Luther M. Borden and others for trespass. During the period of martial law, Borden had entered and searched Luther's home without a warrant. Luther's mother, Rachel Luther, also brought an action against Borden for his allegedly high-handed procedures during the search.

Luther's case started out in circuit court, under Supreme Court Justice Story and District Judge John Pitman. Luther's argument was simple: since the people had a right to change their government, and since they had changed from the charter government to Dorr's regime, Borden had represented an illegitimate government. As a private citizen, he had had no right to enter Luther's home.

Borden's counter-argument was equally simple. He contended that the charter government, which he represented, was the legitimate government of Rhode Island at the time he had entered Luther's home. Therefore, he had had the right to carry out the official business of that government, just as any police officer might do.

Political vs. Natural Rights

The circuit court jury found in Borden's favor, and the case went on to the Supreme Court. For various reasons, however, the case was not argued for several more years.

Meanwhile, in 1843, the state of Rhode Island adopted a new constitution, and the government that operated under it was widely recognized as the state's

Nathan Clifford. © The Library of Congress/Corbis.

Rodney King and the LAPD

In the early hours of 3 March 1991, motorist Rodney King was stopped by Los Angeles, California, police officers following a three-mile, high-speed chase. According to arrest reports filed later, King refused orders to exit the car, then put up such a struggle that officers had to use batons and stun-guns to subdue him. Unbeknownst to the officers, the entire incident had been captured on video by a nearby resident, and the resulting 81-second tape told a different story. In it, King seemed to offer little resistance to the officers who kicked and beat him to the ground while others watched.

The highly publicized first trial of Theodore J. Briseno, Stacey C. Koon, Laurence M. Powell, and Timothy E. Wind for assault, excessive force by a police officer, and filing a false report resulted in not guilty verdicts, with a deadlocked jury on one charge against Powell. Within hours of the verdict on 29 April 1992, rioting erupted in LA, leaving 58 people dead and causing $1 billion in damages.

The landmark second trial for violations of civil rights was significant due to the jury not only having to deal with a question of guilt or innocence, but also dealing with how best to assuage outraged civic sensibilities. On 4 August 1993, Koon and Powell were found guilty and sentenced to 30 months imprisonment. Briseno and Wind were acquitted.

Source(s): Knappman, Edward W., ed. *Great American Trials.* Detroit, MI: Visible Ink Press, 1994.

legitimate government. Martin Luther was fined $500 and had to serve six months in jail for having helped the Dorr government. Justice Story died and was succeeded by Justice Woodbury, who had not taken part in the earlier court battles. By 1849, when the Supreme Court handed down its decision in *Luther v. Borden,* the whole question of which Rhode Island government was legitimate seemed rather like ancient history.

Nevertheless, the lawyers for each side argued over the political principles involved. Luther's lawyers contended that the people of Rhode Island, faced with an exclusionary, minority government, had had the right to adopt their own constitution and establish their own government.

Borden's lawyers countered that the right to vote was not a "natural right," but rather a political one; that is, that men were not born with the right to vote, but rather were granted that right on the basis of the rules their government made. (Life, liberty, property, and the pursuit of happiness, by contrast, were all considered natural rights with which no government could legitimately interfere.) After all, said Borden's lawyers, even the Dorr government had refused the right to vote to men under the age of 21 and to men who had not lived in Rhode Island for more than a year. The question remained as to why then limiting suffrage to property holders made the charter government illegitimate.

Where Does the Court Get Its Power?

In effect, the Supreme Court decided not to decide. It argued that it had no jurisdiction in this matter, because to decide would be to decide which Rhode Island government was the legitimate one. But, said the Court, the very nature of a court's power derives from the power of the government that sets it up. If courts could then turn around and invalidate the very governments that empowered them, the whole nature of political power would be in question.

An engraving of Justice Roger Brooke Taney. © Corbis-Bettmann

Chief Justice Taney, writing the Court's majority opinion, explained that no court should take up what he called "political questions"—questions about who should be in power or what laws should be made. Rather, the Supreme Court and all other courts should take a narrower role, merely interpreting the laws made by the legislature and evaluating in that light the actions taken by the executive.

Taney's ruling was not particularly crucial in deciding the affairs of Luther, Dorr, or Rhode Island, which, as we have seen, were already settled by the time his decision was handed down. However, issues of the legitimacy of government were to become extremely important in the period that followed the Civil War. During Reconstruction, Congress passed many laws restricting who might vote or hold office in the former Confederate states—laws that were bitterly opposed by many people in those states. Because of the precedent set in *Luther v. Borden,* the Court was able to stay out of those conflicts.

Related Cases

Marbury v. Madison, 5 U.S. 137 (1803).
Martin v. Hunter's Lessee, 1 Wheat. 316 (1819).
Cohens v. Virginia, 6 Wheat. 264 (1821).
Foster v. Neilson, 2 Pet. 253 (1829).
United States v. Texas, 143 U.S. 621 (1892).

Bibliography and Further Reading

Johnson, John W., ed. *Historic U.S. Court Cases, 1690–1990: An Encyclopedia.* New York: Garland Publishing, 1992.

Rosenblum, Victor G., and A. Didrick Castberg. *Cases in Constitutional Law, Political Roles of the Supreme Court.* Homewood, IL: The Dorsey Press, 1973.

Swisher, Carl B. *The History of the Supreme Court of the United States: The Taney Period, 1836-64,* Vol. 5. New York: Macmillan, 1974.

EX PARTE MILLIGAN

Legal Citation: 71 U.S. 2 (1866)

Petitioner
Lambdin P. Milligan

Respondent
United States

Petitioner's Claim
A military commission was not a competent tribunal for the trial of the petitioner, a military commission may not try nor convict him, and the petitioner should be released.

Chief Lawyers for Petitioner
J. S. Black, J. E. McDonald, J. A. Garfield, David Dudley Field, A. L. Roache, John R. Coffuth

Chief Lawyers for Respondent
James Speed; Henry Stanbery, U.S. Attorney General; Benjamin F. Butler

Justices for the Court
Salmon Portland Chase, Nathan Clifford, David Davis (writing for the Court), Stephen Johnson Field, Robert Cooper Grier, Samuel Freeman Miller, Samuel Nelson, Noah Haynes Swayne, James Moore Wayne

Justices Dissenting
None

Place
Washington, D.C.

Date of Decision
3 April 1866

Decision
The trial of Milligan on charges of treason and conspiracy, was found to be illegal because it was conducted by a military court.

Significance
A military court may not try an ordinary citizen unconnected with the military or an area of the country directly involved in war. The jurisdiction to try this citizen falls to the civil and federal courts. The right to a trial by jury is preserved, and regardless of whether the citizen is guilty of the crimes tried by the military court, the court may not pass judgment nor sentence the individual.

During the Civil War, Lambdin Milligan was charged by a military commission of conspiring against the federal government. Some of the charges included giving aid and comfort to the rebels and inciting an insurrection. He was also charged with disloyal practices and violations of the laws of war.

The military commission charged that he, with others, conspired to seize the U.S. state arsenal, and to release the prisoners of war confined in the military prison. Then, the commission charged, Milligan planned to arm these prisoners, and join the forces of the South who planned to invade the states of Kentucky, Indiana, and Illinois. Milligan was convicted and sentenced to hang. He appealed his case to the Supreme Court.

Justice Davis, delivering the opinion of the Court, said the U.S. circuit court had authority to certify questions in a proceeding for a writ of *habeas corpus* to inquire into a sentence of a military commission, and that the Supreme Court has jurisdiction to hear and determine them. The act of Congress "relating to *habeas corpus*" approved 3 March 1863, conferred jurisdiction on the circuit court of Indiana to hear such a case.

Davis said that a military commission had no jurisdiction to try and sentence someone who was not a resident of one of the rebellious states, nor a prisoner of war. Davis believed that Congress can grant no such power. The right of trial by jury is preserved to everyone accused of crime, who is not attached to the military in actual service.

Martial law, Justice Davis wrote, cannot arise from a threatened invasion. The invasion must be real, such as one that closes the courts and deposes the civil administration. Military rule can never exist where the courts are open, and in the proper and unobstructed exercise of their jurisdiction. Davis also wrote that the suspension of the privilege of the writ of *habeas corpus* does not suspend the writ itself. The writ issues as a matter of course; and on the return made to it the court decides whether the party applying is denied the right of proceeding any further with it.

If the military trial of Milligan was contrary to law, then he was entitled, on the facts stated in his petition, to be discharged from custody by the terms of the act of Congress of 3 March 1863. He could not be treated as a prisoner of war, when he had lived in Indiana for over 20 years and was arrested there.

Justice Chase delivered a concurring order but a different opinion. He was joined by Justices Wayne, Swayne, and Miller. He stated that though the crimes with which Milligan was charged were of the gravest character, it is more important to the country and to every citizen that he should not be punished under an illegal sentence, sanctioned by the Supreme Court, than that he should be punished at all. The laws which protect the liberties of the whole people must not be violated or set aside in order to inflict, even upon the guilty, unauthorized though merited justice.

Related Cases

Marbury v. Madison, 5 U.S. 137 (1803).

Ex parte Quirin, 317 U.S. 1 (1942).

Bibliography and Further Reading

Biskupic, Joan, and Elder Witt, eds. *Congressional Quarterly's Guide to the U.S. Supreme Court,* 3rd ed. Washington, DC: Congressional Quarterly, Inc., 1996.

Cushman, Robert F. *Cases in Constitutional Law,* 7th ed. Englewood Cliffs, NJ: Prentice-Hall, Inc., 1989.

Epstein, Lee, and Thomas G. Walker. *Constitutional Law for a Changing America: Institutional Powers and Constraints,* 3rd ed. Washington DC: Congressional Quarterly, 1998.

Johnson, John W. *Historic U.S. Court Cases, 1690-1990: An Encyclopedia.* New York: Garland Publishing, 1992.

EX PARTE QUIRIN

Legal Citation: 317 U.S. 1 (1942)

Petitioners
Richard Quirin, et al.

Respondent
Albert Cox, Brigadier General, Provost Marshal of the Military District of Washington

Petitioners' Claim
That the president lacks the power to set up special military tribunals to try war crimes, and that civil courts have the right to review decisions made by these special military courts.

Chief Lawyer for Petitioners
Kenneth C. Royall

Chief Lawyer for Respondent
Francis Biddle, U.S. Attorney General

Justices for the Court
Hugo Lafayette Black, James Francis Byrnes, William O. Douglas, Felix Frankfurter, Robert H. Jackson, Stanley Forman Reed, Owen Josephus Roberts, Harlan Fiske Stone (writing for the Court)

Justices Dissenting
None (Frank Murphy did not participate)

Place
Washington, D.C.

Date of Decision
31 July 1942

Decision
The Supreme Court held that the president has the power to set up military courts in time of war, but that the decisions of these tribunals can be reviewed by civil courts.

Significance
Ex Parte Quirin established the principle that, in times of war, enemy agents can be tried by military courts. Such defendants do not have the right to a civil jury trial, although the decisions of the courts martial are subject to review by civilian courts.

Richard Quirin was one of eight German saboteurs captured just after the United States entered World War II. The eight were accused of violating the unformalized international law of war and the Articles of War enacted by the U.S. Congress. The petitioners had been detained for trial on charges of attempting to undermine the American war effort. Their trials were to be held before a military commission set up for that purpose by President Franklin D. Roosevelt.

The eight saboteurs applied to the District Court of the District of Columbia for permission to file petitions for *habeas corpus*, challenging their confinement, in the U.S. Supreme Court. When the district court turned them down, they applied directly to the Supreme Court. In their petitions, they challenged the authority of the president to set up the military tribunal and asserted their right under the Fifth and Sixth Amendments to trial by jury, a procedure with more safeguards than are observed in military courts.

Supreme Court Holds Special Session as Saboteurs Face Death Penalty

The military trial went forward, even while the Supreme Court considered their petitions. By 27 July 1942, all the evidence had been submitted at the military trial. The case was closed except for the arguments of prosecutors and defense lawyers. On 28 July 1942, the Supreme Court met in special session to consider the saboteurs' petitions. (This was an ex parte proceeding because the petitioners were not present, having been confined in military prisons.) The Court rejected all eight. Six of the prisoners were executed a little more than a week later.

The Court did not consider the guilt or innocence of the alleged saboteurs. The only issue in the case was the authority of the military tribunal. In an opinion finally released 29 October 1942, Chief Justice Stone, writing for a unanimous Court, cited the president's powers as commander-in-chief to uphold the creation of a military tribunal in times of war. The legitimacy of the tribunal was also supported by congressional legislation authorizing military trials for those accused of violating the law of war. Although they did not have a right to ordinary civilian procedures such as a grand jury hearing or trial by jury, defendants such as the eight German saboteurs do have the right to have the judicial denial of petitions for writs of *habeas corpus* reviewed by federal appellate courts, including the Supreme Court.

In 1866, in *Ex parte Milligan,* a case resulting from restrictions on civil liberties during the Civil War, the Supreme Court ruled that military courts have no jurisdiction over civilians in time of war in areas where civil courts remain open. Lambdin P. Milligan was a northerner with Confederate sympathies who attempted to seize arms from federal arsenals and to liberate Confederate soldiers from northern prisons. Now, in *Quirin,* the Court distinguished its earlier ruling by declaring that the German saboteurs, unlike Milligan, were "enemy belligerents":

> The spy who secretly and without uniform passes the military lines of a belligerent in time of war, seeking to gather military information and communicate it to the enemy, or an enemy combatant who without uniform comes secretly through the lines for the purpose of waging war by destruction of life or property, are examples of belligerents who are . . . offenders against the law of war subject to trial and punishment by military tribunals.

Related Cases

Ex parte Milligan, 71 U.S. 2 (1866).
In re Debs, 158 U.S. 564 (1895).
United States v. Curtiss-Wright Corp., 299 U.S. 304 (1936).

Bibliography and Further Reading

Belknap, Michael R. "The Supreme Court Goes to War: The Meaning and Implications of the Nazi Saboteur Case." *Military Law Review,* Vol. 89, 1980, pp. 59-95.

Fellman, David. *The Defendant's Rights Today.* Madison: University of Wisconsin Press, 1976.

Frances Biddle, U.S. Attorney General. © The Library of Congress.

UNITED STATES V. CAUSBY

Legal Citation: 328 U.S. 256 (1946)

Petitioner
United States

Respondent
Causby, et ux.

Petitioner's Claim
That overflights by military airplanes above a private farm do not constitute an appropriation of property.

Chief Lawyer for Petitioner
Walter J. Cummings, Jr.

Chief Lawyer for Respondent
William E. Comer

Justices for the Court
William O. Douglas (writing for the Court), Felix Frankfurter, Frank Murphy, Stanley Forman Reed, Wiley Blount Rutledge

Justices Dissenting
Hugo Lafayette Black, Harold Burton (Robert H. Jackson did not participate, Fred Moore Vinson not yet appointed)

Place
Washington, D.C.

Date of Decision
27 May 1946

Decision
The overflights by military planes were held to render the farm worthless and hence constitute a taking of property warranting compensation by the U.S. government.

Significance
The Supreme Court's decision in *United States v. Causby* expanded the protections afforded to property owners for government "taking" of their property. Whereas previous courts had interpreted the takings clause to consist of only the direct seizure of property, the Court in this decision expanded that interpretation to include taking by indirect means. Subsequent decisions would further modify this reinterpretation.

Legal Background

The case of *United States v. Causby* revolved around the controversial "takings clause" of the U.S. Constitution. The Fifth Amendment of the Constitution prohibits the taking of private property "for public use, without just compensation." For many years, the courts interpreted the term "public use" quite liberally, rarely finding that a taking was not for public use. For instance, courts allowed local governments to take property from landowners for use by privately-owned utility concerns, such as water companies. As long as a project involved some public benefit and did not merely enrich a private company or government agency, a taking of property could be justified.

In most cases, there is no room for disputing whether or not a piece of property has been taken by the government. However, in rare instances, the government does not in fact appropriate the property but acts in such a way as to so reduce the value of the property that the owner feels it has been taken away from him or her. Inevitably the government argues that it has not in fact taken the property and is not obligated to provide compensation. *United States v. Causby* is a paradigmatic case in this regard.

The Case at Hand

The respondent, Causby, owned 2.8 acres of farmland near an airport outside of Greensboro, North Carolina. During World War II, the U.S. government began using the airport for military purposes. Heavy bombers and fighter planes began to fly over Causby's property with increasing frequency at all hours. Often the fighters would fly so low as to blow the leaves off the tops of Causby's trees. This created a roar so deafening that Causby's chickens would panic, running into walls and killing themselves. About 150 of the fowl were killed in this manner, prompting Causby to give up his chicken farming business entirely. He brought suit against the government, claiming that his property had been rendered worthless for commercial purposes and thus had, in effect, been "taken" from him. A lower court ruled in Causby's favor and the United States appealed before the U.S. Supreme Court.

High Court Affirms

On 27 May 1946, the Supreme Court ruled on the case. It agreed with Causby that the use of his farmland was a taking in effect, and that Causby was entitled to his just compensation under the Fifth Amendment. Justice Douglas wrote the opinion for the majority, with Justice Black, joined by Justice Burton, dissenting.

Declaring the air "a public highway," Douglas rejected Causby's claim that his airspace had been taken from him. "To recognize such private claims to the airspace would clog these highways," Douglas opined, "seriously interfere with their control and development in the public interest, and transfer into private ownership that to which only the public has a just claim." However, he did concede "that if the landowner is to have full enjoyment of the land, he must have exclusive control of the immediate reaches of the enveloping atmosphere." Thus the low altitude overflights constituted an invasion of Causby's space "in the same category as invasions of the surface."

From there, it was no great leap for Douglas to conclude that the government had in effect appropriated Causby's property. He wrote:

> Flights over private land are not a taking, unless they are so low and so frequent as to be a direct and immediate interference with the enjoyment and use of the land. We need not speculate on that phase of the present case. For the findings of the Court of Claims plainly establish that there was a diminution in value of the property and that the frequent, low-level flights were the direct and immediate cause.

Black Dissents

Dissenting in this case was Justice Black, joined by Justice Burton. "The concept of taking property as used in the Constitution has heretofore never been given so sweeping a meaning," Black groused. He anticipated a future in which air traffic would play an increasingly intrusive role in the everyday lives of citizens. "[T]he solution of the problems precipitated by these technological advances and new ways of living cannot come about through the application of rigid constitutional restraints formulated and enforced by the courts," Black wrote. Only legislative bodies, he argued, possessed the wisdom and the flexibility to devise solutions to these problems.

Impact

The Supreme Court's decision in *United States v. Causby* expanded the definition of a taking to include physical intrusion upon property by the government. In subsequent cases, the Court would limit that definition to the near total loss of property and not the mere reduction of property value. This was a definitive case.

Related Cases

United States v. Kansas City Insurance Co., 339 U.S. 799 (1950).
Armstrong v. United States, 364 U.S. 40 (1960).
Griggs v. Allegheny County, 369 U.S. 84 (1962).
Chongris v. Corrigan, 409 U.S. 919 (1972).

Bibliography and Further Reading

Chandler, Ralph C. *The Constitutional Law Dictionary.* Santa Barbara, CA: ABC-Clio, Inc., 1987.

Cushman, Robert Fairchild with Susan P. Koniak. *Leading Constitutional Decisions.* Englewood Cliffs, NJ: Prentice-Hall, Inc., 1992.

Menez, Joseph Francis. *Summaries of Leading Cases of the Constitution.* Savage, MD: Littlefield, Adams, 1990.

TOTH V. QUARLES

Legal Citation: 350 U.S. 11 (1955)

Appellant
Audrey M. Toth

Appellee
Donald A. Quarles, Secretary of the U.S. Air Force

Appellant's Claim
That the U.S. District Court of Appeals erred in holding Robert Toth liable to prosecution under Article 3(a) of the Uniform Code of Military Justice.

Chief Lawyer for Appellant
William A. Kehoe, Jr.

Chief Lawyers for Appellee
Simon E. Sobeloff, Solicitor General; Lt. Col. Chester W. Wilson

Justices for the Court
Hugo Lafayette Black (writing for the Court), Tom C. Clark, William O. Douglas, Felix Frankfurter, John Marshall Harlan II, Earl Warren

Justices Dissenting
Harold Burton, Sherman Minton, Stanley Forman Reed

Place
Washington, D.C.

Date of Decision
7 November 1955

Decision
The appeals court decision was reversed, allowing Toth to avoid prosecution.

Significance
The decision declared the 1950 Uniform Code of Military Justice to be unconstitutional, thus barring trials of civilians for crimes committed while in the armed forces.

A Death In Korea

Robert Toth was a civilian when military police arrived at the Pittsburgh steel plant where he worked, to arrest him. Five months had passed since he had been honorably discharged from the United States Air Force. Still, Toth was charged with murder, a crime of sufficient seriousness to allow the former sergeant's prosecution under the Uniform Code of Military Justice.

Toth and another airman, Thomas Kinder, had been on guard duty at an airbase in South Korea on 27 September 1952, when they discovered a civilian, Bang Soon Kil, who appeared to be drunk. Bang Soon was taken into custody. While being driven to the base headquarters, he grabbed at Toth's sidearm. Toth allegedly stopped the jeep and pistol-whipped the prisoner. When the two airmen arrived at headquarters, their commanding officer, Lieutenant George Schreiber, ordered them to take Bang Soon away and shoot him.

By the time military authorities discovered the murder, Toth had been honorably discharged, but his two colleagues were still in the air force. Both were court-martialed. Schreiber was sentenced to life imprisonment, but the punishment was reduced to five years, forfeiture of pay, and a dishonorable discharge. Kinder was also sentenced to life imprisonment, but the term was reduced to two years and a dishonorable discharge. Toth had returned to civilian life, but military prosecutors indicted him under the Article 3(a) of the 1950 Uniform Code of Military Justice. According to the code, anyone who had left the service remained liable to prosecution if the penalty for their alleged offense exceeded five years and the case could not be tried by a civilian court. Because Toth's case fit the guidelines, he was arrested on 13 May 1953 and returned to South Korea to stand trial by court martial.

Toth's sister Audrey immediately filed for a writ of *habeas corpus*. A district court order stalled the proceedings against Toth on the ground that the military had no power to apprehend a civilian and hold him for trial. Toth was returned to the United States and released on bail. Although Toth fought the indictment on the ground that he was a civilian and could not be tried by a military court, the U.S. Court of Appeals ruled on 25 March 1954 that he was still liable to be tried for murder. The court ruled that Toth's honorable discharge did not excuse him from charges for crimes that might have occurred while he was still in the service. Naming Air Force Secretary Donald A. Quarles as the government's representative in the suit, Toth appealed the decision, attempting to reinstate the original district court ruling placing him beyond the reach of military authorities. As a jurisdictional dispute between different branches of government, the case was now a constitutional issue and eligible for appeal before the U.S. Supreme Court.

A Gap In Jurisdiction

When it was argued on 8 and 9 February 1955, only eight members of the Court heard the Toth case because of Justice Robert Jackson's death. The case was re-argued on 13 October after Justice Harlan was sworn in as Jackson's replacement. With three dissents, the Court ruled in Toth's favor on 7 November.

The Court concerned itself with Bang Soon Kil's murder only as a matter of fact and its chronology relative to the date of Toth's discharge. The Court was more concerned with the manner in which the military justice code assumed powers normally reserved, in civilian life, for the judiciary branch of government, not Congress, which had signed the military rules into law.

The Court found that Toth's relationship with the military was completely over at the time of his arrest. The majority could find nothing in the Constitution giving the military jurisdiction over civilians, despite the government's contention that Article 1 gave the military the right to regulate itself. The Court determined that such rules only applied to persons still actually in military service.

In his opinion, written for the majority, Justice Black noted that traditional constitutional safeguards like the right to trial by jury and independent appellate judges did not exist in the military justice system. Because Toth, as a civilian, was entitled to such protections, he could not be properly tried by the military. Justice Black

also noted that this situation was not confined to the Toth case. To allow this prosecution to go forward would place millions of other veterans within the reach of military courts after their return to civilian life. The Court was, however, amenable to the idea that Congress could give federal courts the power to pursue criminal accusations against ex-service personnel who had returned to civilian life.

Justices Reed, Burton, and Minton disagreed with the majority position. In an opinion written by Justice Reed, the dissenters felt that military courts were capable of holding fair trials, despite differences from the civilian justice system. Making disciplinary rules was entirely within Congress's power to regulate the armed forces, agreed the dissenters, who felt that the Court should not interfere. Justice Minton added that he did not consider Toth to be a full-fledged civilian at the time of his arrest, since Congress, through the military code, retained jurisdiction over Toth for a crime committed while he was still on active duty.

No one was ever seriously punished for the murder of Bang Soon Kil. Air Force Secretary Harold E. Talbott reduced the sentences of the two men convicted of the crime. George Schreiber, who had ordered the killing, was dismissed from the service after serving 20 months of his five-year sentence. Thomas Kinder, who had pulled the trigger, was allowed to return to active Air Force duty after Secretary Talbot suspended his dishonorable discharge. Robert Toth, who insisted he had not been present when the killing took place, was not tried, as a result of the Supreme Court's decision.

Bibliography and Further Reading

Bishop, Joseph W., Jr. *Justice Under Fire: A Study of Military Law.* New York: Charterhouse, 1974.

"Crucial Case of Murder." *Time,* 31 August 1953, p. 10.

Huston, Luther A. "Military Trial of Civilians Upheld For Major Crimes During Service." *New York Times,* 26 March 1954, p. 1.

———. *New York Times,* 7 November 1955, p. 1.

UNITED STATES V. SEEGER

Legal Citation: 380 U.S. 163 (1965)

Petitioner
United States

Respondent
Daniel Andrew Seeger

Petitioner's Claim
That only conscientious objection due to organized beliefs allowed exemption to service.

Chief Lawyer for Petitioner
Archibald Cox, U.S. Solicitor General

Chief Lawyer for Respondent
Kenneth W. Greenwalt

Justices for the Court
Hugo Lafayette Black, William J. Brennan, Jr., Tom C. Clark (writing for the Court), William O. Douglas, Arthur J. Goldberg, John Marshall Harlan II, Potter Stewart, Earl Warren, Byron R. White

Justices Dissenting
None

Place
Washington, D.C.

Date of Decision
8 March 1965

Decision
Upheld the appellate court's reversal of respondent's conviction of having refused to submit to military induction.

Significance
The ruling determined that conscientious objectors, who oppose participation in war on religious grounds, are entitled by law to seek exemption from compulsory military service if they hold unorthodox spiritual beliefs that are fundamentally equivalent to a traditional belief in God.

Since Congress first instituted compulsory military service during World War I with the Draft Act of 1917, the issue of religious objection to conscription has caused controversy. Though the First Amendment protects the free exercise of religious belief, the Supreme Court has consistently maintained that there is no constitutional right to exemption from draft registration or military service. Congress, however, has allowed such an exemption by statute. The law requires that a person seeking exemption prove both that his religious beliefs prohibit him from participating in war, and that these religious beliefs are sincere.

Defining Religious Belief

Central to the issue of conscientious objector exemption has been the definition of religious belief. The 1917 Draft Law provided exemption only to those who were members of a "well-recognized religious sect or organization . . . whose existing creed or principles [forbid] its members to participate in war in any form." This, in effect, meant only organized religions in the traditional Judeo-Christian sense. In *United States v. MacIntosh* (1931), though, Chief Justice Charles Evans Hughes's opinion slightly expanded the definition. He wrote that the "essence of religion is belief in a relation to God involving duties superior to those arising from any human relation." This definition became the basis for that adopted by Congress when it revised draft laws in the 1940s.

The Selective Training and Service Act of 1940 reflected growing tolerance of religious diversity. It allowed conscientious objector status to persons conscientiously opposed to "war in any form" because of "religious training and belief," even if that belief was not contained in the dogma of an established church. In 1948, Congress changed the law to specify that religious training and belief should require belief "in relation to a Supreme Being involving duties superior to those arising from any human relation but [not including] essentially political, sociological, or philosophical views or a merely personal moral code."

Daniel Andrew Seeger, an agnostic, was convicted in the District Court for the Southern District of New York

Conscientious Objectors

A conscientious objector is someone who refuses to submit to conscription for military service on the basis of a moral prohibition against participation in war. It is customary for governments to require proof of commitment to a religious faith which proscribes military involvement. Examples of groups with deeply pacifist belief systems include Anabaptists, Mennonites, Amish, and Quakers. Thanks to effective lobbying in 1940, several of these groups secured the right of participation in Civilian Public Service (CPS) camps.

One may ask if it is unfair for such groups to enjoy the right of conscientious objection, since it would seem to violate the First Amendment separation of church and state. However, failure to respect their beliefs would violate these citizens' freedom of religion. Some pacifists have called for conscientious-objector provisions not related to religion, but again, it would be difficult to establish guidelines for such.

Source(s): Bradley, David and Shelley Fisher Fishkin, eds. *The Encyclopedia of Civil Rights in America.* Armonk, NY: Sharpe, 1998.

for refusing induction into military service. Seeger had filed for exemption in 1957, after his student draft classification had expired and he was reclassified 1-A. In his exemption claim, he declared that he was conscientiously opposed to war in any form because of his religious belief, but neither acknowledged nor denied a belief in a Supreme Being. He used the writings of philosophers Plato, Aristotle, and Spinoza to support his ethical belief in moral integrity "without belief in God, except in the remotest sense." Though his belief was determined to be sincere and based upon individual training and belief, Seeger was denied exemption because his claim was not based on "belief in relation to a Supreme Being" as specified in the draft statute. The trial court convicted Seeger, who appealed. The court of appeals reversed the trial court's decision, ruling that the Supreme Being requirement in the draft law distinguished "between internally derived and externally compelled beliefs" and thus was an "impermissible classification" under the Fifth Amendment's Due Process Clause. The Supreme Court, which considered Seeger's case along with the related cases of two other defendants, Arno Sascha Jakobson and Forest Britt Peter, unanimously affirmed the appellate court's judgment.

Since the lower court had found Seeger's belief to be sincerely held, the issue in question was the definition of religious belief. This question, said the Court, was a narrow one—whether the phrase "Supreme Being" as used in the statute meant only the orthodox concept of God, or a "broader concept of a power or being, or a faith, 'to which all else is subordinate or upon which all else is ultimately dependent.'" Examining the development of draft laws since 1917, the Court found no evidence that Congress wanted the act to apply only to those holding traditional theocratic beliefs, and noted the "well-established congressional policy of equal treatment for those whose opposition to service is grounded in their religious tenets." In his opinion

for the unanimous court, Justice Clark wrote that the draft law's terminology was meant to include all religions, and further emphasized that exempting some religions but not others would be unconstitutional. Under this interpretation, the Court found, the proper test of religious belief should be "whether a given belief that is sincere and meaningful occupies a place in the life of its possessor parallel to that filled by the orthodox beliefs in God of one who clearly qualifies for the [conscientious objector] exemption."

Justice Clark noted that this construction appropriately acknowledged "the ever-broadening understanding of the modern religious community." He cited the work of theologians Paul Tillich and John A. T. Robinson, Bishop of Woolwich, and the analysis of ethicist David Saville Muzzey, as well as the findings of the Second Vatican Council, as examples of this more tolerant understanding. And he emphasized that it is not the role of government to judge the truth of any person's religious beliefs. "As Mr. Justice Douglas stated in *United States v. Ballard* (1944) . . . ," Clark wrote, "Men may believe what they cannot prove. They may not be put to the proof of their religious doctrines or beliefs. Religious experiences which are as real as life to some may be incomprehensible to others."

But, Clark emphasized, Congress clearly stated that the conscientious objector exemption should exclude persons whose beliefs are based on a "merely personal moral code." The Court determined that Congress intended this part of the law to exclude those whose moral code was not related to religious belief. Since the Court had already determined that Seeger's claim met the standard for religious belief, it could not therefore be considered a merely personal moral code. "We think it clear," Clark wrote, "that the beliefs that prompted [Seeger's] objection occupy the same place in his life as the belief in a traditional deity holds in the lives of his friends, the Quakers." The Court upheld the circuit court's reversal of Seeger's conviction.

In a separate concurring opinion, Justice Douglas reiterated the importance of equal protection in religious matters. If Congress were to distinguish between religions, he wrote, this would violate both the free exercise of the First Amendment and the Due Process Clause of the Fifth Amendment. Douglas also added that "The words 'a Supreme Being' have no narrow technical meaning in the field of religion." He cited Hinduism and Buddhism, neither of which is based on the concept of a Supreme Being, as beliefs that "illustrat[e] the fluidity and evanescent scope of the concept." Douglas wrote that he was confident that Congress's tolerance and sophistication would acknowledge this broad construction of religious belief.

Vietnam Era Ferment

The *Seeger* decision came at a time when American military involvement in Vietnam was increasing. As casualties mounted after the mid-1960s, more and more young men were drafted and sent to fight an officially undeclared war on foreign soil. Many Americans felt the reasons for U.S. involvement were not clear, and increasing numbers questioned and then protested the war. The draft became a central issue. Many challenged the government by defying the draft law; they burned draft cards and refused induction. Though the Supreme Court found that the federal statute criminalizing draft card burning did not violate the First Amendment, the Court did protect dissent in rulings that Kermit L. Hall in *The Oxford Companion to the Supreme Court of the United States* claimed "reflected the mood of an American public growing increasingly disaffected with the Vietnam conflict." *Seeger*, Hall suggested, "made it easier for young men who did not wish to participate in the war to gain exemption from military service as conscientious objectors." Hall believed that the Court interpreted religious belief very broadly because a literal reading of the draft law-requiring a belief in a Supreme Being—would violate the First Amendment's prohibition against the establishment of religion. The *Seeger* ruling, Hall concluded, "blatantly distorted the intent of Congress" and "increased the numbers of men who could avoid serving in an increasingly unpopular war." It is important to note, however, that the Court, in *Gillette v. United States* (1971), did not grant conscien-

tious objector status to persons who opposed only what they considered to be unjust conflicts.

In 1967, Congress revised the draft laws again. The Military Selective Service Act of 1967 reflected the *Seeger* decision, and took out the requirement in the exemption clause that specified belief in a Supreme Being:

> [Nothing] contained in this Act shall be construed to require any person to be subject to combatant training and service in the land or naval forces of the United States who, by reason of religious training and belief, is conscientiously opposed to participation in war in any form. As used in this subsection, the term religious training and belief does not include essentially political, sociological, or philosophical views, or a merely personal code.

And in 1970, the Court construed the conscientious exemption provision to include persons who object to war on moral or ethical grounds based on beliefs "held with the strength of traditional religious convictions" (*Welsh v. United States*).

The draft ended in 1973, when the United States converted to an all-volunteer military. By April of 1975, men were no longer required to register with their draft boards. But registration was reimposed by President Carter in 1980 after the invasion of Afghanistan by the Soviet Union, and continues as a precaution against underestimating the number of military personnel needed in a future crisis.

Related Cases
United States v. MacIntosh, 283 U.S. 605 (1931).
United States v. Ballard, 322 U.S. 78 (1944).
Welsh v. United States, 389 U.S. 333 (1970).
Gillette v. United States, 401 U.S. 437 (1971).

Bibliography and Further Reading
Hall, Kermit L. ed. *The Oxford Companion to the Supreme Court of the United States.* New York: Oxford University Press, 1992.

Johnson, John W., ed. *Historic U.S. Court Cases, 1690-1990: An Encyclopedia.* New York: Garland Publishing, 1992.

Witt, Elder, *Congressional Quarterly's Guide to the U.S. Supreme Court,* 2nd ed. Washington, DC: Congressional Quarterly Inc., 1979.

MONOPOLIES AND ANTITRUST LAW

In the free market, competition is often ruthless. Antitrust law regulates this competition in order to prevent unfairness in the conduct of business. The term antitrust refers to the industrial giants of the nineteenth century, corporations which organized themselves into jointly managed units known as trusts. Through size and strength, the trusts single-handedly controlled the nation's most important markets, crushing all competitors, dictating prices, and erratically supplying goods and services to consumers. This led to the condition of overall dominance known as monopoly. Derived from the Greek for "right of exclusive sale," monopoly control over a market is illegal under antitrust law. The law also forbids several forms of anticompetitive behavior. Steep criminal and civil penalties, backed by federal and state enforcement, help to promote its underlying premise of fair competition. Open markets, it is believed, provide fertile ground for a healthy economy by encouraging new investment, job creation, stable prices, and a reliable marketplace.

Historical Background

Monopolies have existed in civilizations throughout history. English law, for instance, granted the right of monopoly to the nation's guilds through parliamentary or royal decree during the middle ages. This practice diminished in the seventeenth century, and tentative judicial action against unfair trade had begun by the early eighteenth century. It was the Industrial Revolution, beginning in the 1870s, with its expansion of commerce and new markets, that brought greater demand for action from the courts. Yet the English common law only gave American law a contradictory legacy. This was the notion that hindering competition was more or less bad, but that courts generally should only take limited roles in evaluating contracts for fairness. Some short-term restraints were considered "reasonable," other more general restraints "unreasonable". And there were always exceptions.

Inheriting this so-called "rule of reason," late nineteenth century America was thus unable to address its problems. With only a smattering of market-interference laws in twelve states, approaches varied widely. At best, courts sometimes refused to enforce business contracts because they prevented competitors from entering a market. Federal law was silent.

This lack of legal controls helped give rise to the trusts. Following the Civil War, an industrial boom had begun transforming the nation's economic base from agriculture to industry. This fundamental change brought headaches for industries, which were producing more goods than consumers needed. Initially, their incorporation into trusts was self-protective. Resources could be pooled and risks reduced through their merger into oil trusts, steel trusts, mining trusts, sugar trusts, and so on. Monopoly power also meant strength, and by the end of the century, the trusts were flexing their muscles arrogantly. Companies such as Standard Oil and industry captains such as steel magnate J. P. Morgan fixed prices to suit themselves and to eliminate competitors. If rivals tried to enter a market, the monopolists would sell their goods at a loss until the competitors were destroyed, after which prices shot back up. Consumers were powerless, as were businesses whose livelihoods the trusts imperiled. Farmers, for instance, could not count upon the nation's railroad system to transport their goods affordably to market, since the railroads gave preferential treatment in the form of heavy discounts to larger-volume customers. Public outrage in the 1880s led to demand for reform to reign in the "fat cats" and "robber barons".

Federal Law

Feeling the push of populist pressure, Congress passed two landmark pieces of federal legislation. Utilizing its constitutional power to regulate interstate business, it first put in effect the Interstate Commerce Act of 1887, which required the railroads to maintain fair rates and to cease discrimination. Three years later came the passage of the Sherman Anti-Trust Act of 1890, a sweeping assault on the trusts that remains the basis of federal antitrust law today. The Sherman Anti-Trust Act forbade the formation of trusts, monopolies, and, generally, the restraint of free trade. Allowing both criminal and civil prosecution of offenders, the law placed special emphasis on civil lawsuits by authorizing the award of triple the amount of damages suffered. Today, each criminal violation of the Sherman Anti-Trust Act is a felony carrying a maximum $350,000 fine and imprisonment of up to three years.

Although seeming to usher in a new era in business regulation, antitrust law was sluggishly enforced and quickly hit judicial roadblocks. In fact, the Supreme Court dealt a blow to the Sherman Anti-Trust Act in its first consideration of the law, *United States v. E. C. Knight* (1895), where the majority ruled that manufacturing was not a form of interstate business. The Court therefore held that the law did not apply to a trust which refined over 98 percent of the nation's sugar. Only in the late 1890s did the Court uphold prosecutions, first against the railroads. Two major trusts were toppled in 1911, when the Supreme Court ordered the dissolution of the Standard Oil Company and the American Tobacco Company. Yet even in *Standard Oil Co. of New Jersey v. United States* (1911), the Court championed the Sherman Anti-Trust Act, holding that it did not ban all restraints upon trade, but only ones found to be anticompetitive. Moreover, lower courts were still free to interpret cases subjectively according to the "rule of reason".

Antitrust Enforcements

Impatience with these rulings and the slow pace of enforcement led to further reforms in 1914. Congress clarified the law with an explicit new statute, the Clayton Act, which spelled out four illegal anticompetitive practices. It prohibited discriminating by selling the same product or service at different prices to similar buyers, forcing buyers to enter exclusive contracts, dominating markets through corporate mergers, and sharing common board members between competing companies. Yet even the Clayton Act still left much uncertain, emphasizing that its forbidden practices were only illegal if the effect "may be substantially to lessen competition" or "tend to create a monopoly." Additionally, in 1914, Congress created the Federal Trade Commission (FTC), the federal agency charged with enforcing antitrust law. The Federal Trade Commission Act also showed the unwillingness of Congress to be too specific about antitrust, aiming broadly at "unfair methods of competition."

Legislative changes peaked toward the middle of the twentieth century as Congress strengthened and refined aspects of the Clayton Act. In 1936, the Robinson-Patman Act tightened the earlier law's ban on price discrimination. The last major piece of federal legislation was the Celler-Kefauver Antimerger Act of 1950, which closed loopholes in the Clayton Act's restriction on mergers, preventing anticompetitive purchases of rival businesses' assets and deceitful transfers of stock purchases.

Throughout the twentieth century, Congress has done less to influence antitrust law than have the executive and the judicial branches. Federal enforcement, which belongs to the FTC and the Justice Department,

depends entirely on the political mood of a given presidential administration. President Theodore Roosevelt, a self-declared "trustbuster," made vigorous enforcement a priority at the turn of the century, as did his successor, William Howard Taft. The pendulum swung in the 1920s under the noninterventionist policies of President Calvin Coolidge, and then back again in the 1930s when President Franklin D. Roosevelt hotly pursued monopolies. Even in recent decades, politics have governed enforcement. The deregulatory Reagan era had little taste for antitrust cases, but the Clinton years have shown a renewed appetite. At all times, the Supreme Court has had the most definitive influence. This reflects a kind of legislative design, as Congress intentionally crafted the outline rather than the details of antitrust law. Through a vast body of federal cases, the Court has filled in the blanks with a complex set of rules, exceptions and doctrines. And yet its approach has been in nearly constant flux.

Monopoly Cases

For monopoly cases, the Court has used vastly different yardsticks. Early on, the majority in *United States v. U.S. Steel Corp.* (1920) wrote "[T]he law does not make mere size an offense, or the existence of unexerted power an offense." Only abusive practices by a dominant business, the Court found, were evidence of illegal monopolization. This outlook changed in *United States v. Aluminum Co. of America* (2d Cir. 1945), where a federal appeals court shifted the focus of consideration from abuses to market share, holding that "immunity from competition is a narcotic." Justice Learned Hand's opinion led to the creation of a standard two-part test. Companies acted illegally when they possessed monopoly power in a relevant market, and when they excluded competitors to gain or protect that power. Still in use, the test has yielded somewhat in recent decades as lower courts have given dominant businesses more room to legally increase their market share.

The legality of mergers, too, has varied from one period to another. Corporations merge for economic gain, and this is not always harmful to competition. Yet in the antitrust heyday of the late 1960s, the Court regarded with alarm a merger between two companies that had only a combined five percent output in their market, ruling in *Brown Shoe Co. v. United States* (1967) that such a merger violated the Celler-Kefauver Act. Little over a decade later, the popularity of deregulation and the Court's own relaxed views led to an explosion of corporate mergers that has continued through the late 1990s. Not all mergers are evaluated in the same way, however, since special circumstances pertain to certain industries. The federal Bank Merger Act and Bank Holding Company Act, for instance, provide for close scrutiny of mergers between banks.

Much antitrust case law emerges from the Sherman Anti-Trust Act's ban on "[e]very contract, combination . . . or conspiracy in restraint of trade . . ." Restraint of trade cases concern business contracts and agreements. Some of the century's most aggressive antitrust law evolved in this area, led by the Warren Court in the 1960s. By defining certain practices as illegal in all circumstances, the Court struck widely at cooperative business deals that limited productive output, restrictions placed by manufacturers upon dealers, and "tying" arrangements in which purchase of a given product was required in order to purchase another product. In the 1970s and 1980s, the Court, altering its stance under the influence of academic arguments, embraced the so-called doctrine of economic efficiency. Holding that some restraint of trade actually was beneficial to the economy, its rulings set higher standards for antitrust litigation and made winning more difficult for those prosecuting antitrust cases. In *Brunswick Corp. v. Pueblo Bowl-O-Mat* (1977), the Court retreated from its long-held stand that the failure of individual companies was bad for competition, accepting instead that reduced competition would be offset by reduced costs and increased output on the part of successful firms. By the 1990s, the efficiency doctrine showed signs of waning.

While some anticompetitive practices are judged harshly, others receive more tolerance. Courts generally condemn price-fixing, for instance. But another questionable practice, the refusal of one business to deal with another, is evaluated according to a variety of factors. Antitrust law acknowledges that sellers may select their own customers. Thus some individual refusals to deal are legal. However, a refusal may be illegal if the seller has monopoly power, intends to monopolize, or uses the refusal as part of an otherwise illegal restraint of trade. Group boycotts are unlawful. Also sometimes illegal are agreements requiring a customer to deal exclusively with a seller, particularly if they harm the chances of competitors in the market.

Several exceptions exist throughout all levels of antitrust law. Unions have been exempt from antitrust law since passage of the Clayton Act, which disregarded human labor as a commodity. Uniquely among pro-

fessional sports, major league baseball also enjoys an exemption. The Supreme Court ruled early on that baseball is a sport and not a business in *Federal Baseball Club of Baltimore v. National League of Professional Baseball Clubs* (1922). The Newspaper Preservation Act of 1970, passed amid economic pressures which threatened the existence of multiple newspapers in communities, allows mergers and joint operation by publishers that otherwise would be illegal under antitrust law.

States have closely modeled their antitrust statutes on federal law. They prosecuted antitrust cases extensively before World War I, but were largely inactive in antitrust litigation until the 1970s. A period of resurgence saw the passage of new state laws and the Supreme Court's recognition that states, under a doctrine called parens patriae, had the right to bring certain antitrust lawsuits under federal law, too. In response, state attorneys general pursued antitrust cases on a wide variety of fronts, notably banking. This reinvigoration was also evident in the most controversial antitrust action of the 1990s, when, in 1998, 20 states joined the federal government in its long-running case against computer software giant Microsoft.

See also: Business and Corporate Law

Bibliography and Further Reading

Hall, Kermit L. *The Magic Mirror: Law in American History.* New York: Oxford Univ. Press, 1989

Horn, Gell, and William Kovacic, eds. *West's Antitrust in a Nutshell,* 4th ed. no copyright date.

Roach, Robert F. "Bank Mergers and the Antitrust Laws: The Case for Dual State and Federal Enforcement." *William and Mary Law Review,* October 1994

Walbolt, Sylvia H. "Antitrust Compliance Manual." *Practicing Law Institute Corporate Law and Practice Course Handbook Series,* April-July 1998

Wegener, Richard J. "Terminations and Refusal to Deal." *American Law Institute—American Bar Association Continuing Legal Education,* March 19, 1998

West's Encyclopedia of American Law. St. Paul: West Group, 1998

SLAUGHTERHOUSE CASES

Legal Citation: 16 Wallace 36 (1873)

Appellants
Butchers' Benevolent Association of New Orleans; The Livestock Dealers' and Butchers' Association of New Orleans

Appellees
The Crescent City Live Stock Landing and Slaughter House Company; State of Louisiana

Appellants' Claim
That the state's establishment of a monopoly in stock slaughtering violated the Thirteenth and Fourteenth Amendments.

Chief Lawyers for Appellants
John Campbell, J. Q. A. Fellows

Chief Lawyer for Appellees
T. J. Durant

Justices for the Court
Salmon Portland Chase, Nathan Clifford, David Davis, Ward Hunt, Samuel Freeman Miller (writing for the Court), William Strong

Justices Dissenting
Joseph P. Bradley, Stephen Johnson Field, Noah Haynes Swayne

Place
Washington, D.C.

Date of Decision
14 April 1873

Decision
The state of Louisiana was within its regular police powers to protect public health to establish a monopoly slaughterhouse down river from New Orleans.

Significance
Although the court ruled that the state-established slaughterhouse monopoly was legal, it ruled that the Fourteenth Amendment, originally intended to protect the civil rights of freed slaves, also protected other citizens against hostile action by state governments. However, the decision favored the state's own interpretation of when such rights would be violated.

The Slaughterhouse Monopoly

On 8 March 1869, the state of Louisiana created a 25-year monopoly on livestock slaughtering in the area of New Orleans, including three parishes of the state. The slaughterhouse was to be established down-river from New Orleans, and butchers who wished to slaughter animals would be required to rent space for that purpose at the facility built by the Crescent City Live Stock Landing and Slaughter House Company. The purpose of the law was to prevent butchers and others from landing stock throughout the city of New Orleans, driving the animals through the streets, and slaughtering them on various premises scattered throughout residential neighborhoods. The movement of the stock, holding them in pens through the city, slaughtering them and leaving animal waste and blood in different districts of the city constituted a major threat to public health and safety.

By confining all slaughtering operations to one locale—distant, and down-river from the city—the stench and waste from the slaughterhouse would not pollute the city. However, butchers complained about being forced by the state to pay rent to the established monopoly company for the space to slaughter their own animals. The state, they claimed, had interfered with their business.

In arguing against the state monopoly, the attorneys for the butchers' associations brought a new line of argument that would have far-reaching implications. While there were traditional common-law arguments to be made against a state monopoly, the attorneys added a new line of thinking by pointing out that the Thirteenth and Fourteenth Amendments to the Constitution prohibited servitude and the taking of rights without due process of law. Even though these amendments had been introduced to protect the former slaves, the attorneys argued, the Constitution could not specifically offer special protections to former slaves without also offering those protections to all citizens.

Monopoly as "Servitude"

After discussing the history of servitude and slavery, the attorneys for the appellants pointed out that slavery had taken many forms in the past, one of which was

---

Equal Protection

Equal protection is the constitutional right of all people and all classes of people in the United States to share in the rights and privileges enjoyed by other people and classes of people in similar conditions and circumstances. The Fourteenth Amendment of the Constitution serves as the foundation of the equal protection guarantee and requires that the states treat individuals and groups or classes of individuals the same given the circumstances.

Equal protection cases do not question the validity of laws in most cases, but rather the application of laws; for example, when laws are applied to only certain members of the population. While no hard and fast rules exist for determining the constitutionality of state classifications, the Supreme Court relies on different tests for making this determination, such as whether a classification serves a legitimate purpose or whether it is being used to discriminate on the basis of a classification such as being a Native American or an immigrant. Landmark equal protection cases and laws of the nineteenth and twentieth centuries have addressed the rights of various ethnic groups, homosexuals, the disabled, and the poor.

Source(s): *West's Encyclopedia of American Law* Minneapolis, Minnesota: West Publishing, 1998.

---

to subject individuals in specific areas to special restrictions on their rights, by "enthralling" the land. The attorneys claimed that the act of establishing the state monopoly in slaughtering made three parishes of the state "enthralled ground," by eliminating a specific right to conduct business in those three parishes. They further pointed out that the Fourteenth Amendment, for the first time, established citizenship in the United States and made it unconstitutional for any state to deny the rights of citizens to anyone within their state. One right of citizenship was the right to conduct business, and the state had taken that right away, thus violating the Fourteenth Amendment.

Justice Miller, writing the opinion of the Court, argued that butchers could still exercise their right to conduct their business, it just had to be done in the state-established slaughterhouse. As long as the rate charged by the monopoly was fair and did not discriminate, the butchers could not claim that their rights had been invaded. He further pointed out that the intent of the Fourteenth Amendment had been to specifically overturn the *Dred Scott* decision of 1857. That decision had ruled that slaves and former slaves were not citizens and that they could not bring suit in federal court. Without the Fourteenth Amendment, former slaves would have been governed in court proceedings by the pre-Civil War *Dred Scott* ruling. However, by defining citizenship in the United States, and by stating that the previous condition of servitude did not diminish citizenship, the amendment made it possible for former slaves to exercise all of their rights as citizens, including court actions. Hence, Miller generally limited the effect of the Thirteenth and Fourteenth Amendment to former slaves.

In their dissents, Justices Field, Bradley, and Swayne showed that the logic of applying the Thirteenth and Fourteenth Amendments to all citizens and the rights to conduct business was a telling argument. Bradley argued that a citizen was not a free man unless he could follow his own trade. However, Bradley believed the state could force butchers, under police power, to slaughter in certain districts, but could not force them

Justice Stephen Johnson Field. © The Library of Congress.

Justice Samuel Freeman Miller. © Archive Photos.

to do so in a state-established monopoly slaughterhouse. Field and Swayne believed that the Thirteenth and Fourteenth Amendments should apply very broadly, beyond former slaves.

The decision showed that the Thirteenth and Fourteenth Amendments to the Constitution, although originally intended to deal with the civil rights of former slaves, could be much more broadly applied. The amendments would later prove very useful in preventing states from interfering in business expansion, and would become essential legal tools in the growth of American business in the last decades of the nineteenth century. However, the ruling favored the state of Louisiana, and showed that the Court would not interpret the Fourteenth Amendment as protecting any rights of citizens against action by states unless the rights were specifically Federal rights guaranteed by the

Constitution, the Bill of Rights, or by existing federal statute.

In 1884, the issue once again came before the Supreme Court. Surprisingly, in *Butchers' Union Co. v. Crescent City Co.,* the state of Louisiana had decided to break the monopoly and to allow butchers to operate their own slaughterhouses. The monopoly company, Crescent City, sued to regain sole rights to the business, arguing that the state had issued a binding monopoly contract to the company. The legislature and the constitution of Louisiana permitted the state to break the monopoly, but a circuit court ruled in favor of the monopoly. The Supreme Court overturned the circuit court, and affirmed the right of the state to break its own contract in this case. While appearing to side in 1873 with Crescent City Live Stock Company, and then appearing in 1884 to side against it, the Court's actions seem to be inconsistent. In fact, the Court in both cases decided in favor of the state's ability to control its own behavior in this area of rights.

Related Cases

Butcher's Union Co. v. Crescent City Co., 111 U.S. 746 (1884).

Hawaii Housing Authority v. Midkiff, 467 U.S. 229 (1984).

Bibliography and Further Reading

Biskupic, Joan, and Elder Witt. *Congressional Quarterly's Guide to the U.S. Supreme Court,* 3rd ed. Washington, DC: Congressional Quarterly, Inc., 1996.

Cushman, Robert F. *Leading Constitutional Decisions.* Englewood Cliffs, NJ: Prentice-Hall, Inc., 1982.

Epstein, Lee, and Thomas G. Walker. *Constitutional Law for a Changing America: Institutional Powers and Constraints,* 3rd ed. Washington DC: Congressional Quarterly, 1998.

Hall, Kermit L., ed. *The Oxford Companion to the Supreme Court of the United States.* New York: Oxford University Press, 1992.

Johnson, John W., ed. *Historic U.S. Court Cases, 1690–1990: An Encyclopedia.* New York: Garland Publishing, 1992.

Warren, Charles. *The Supreme Court in U.S. History,* Vol. 2. Littleton, CO: Rothman, 1987.

UNITED STATES V. E. C. KNIGHT

Legal Citation: 156 U.S. 1 (1895)

Appellant
United States

Appellees
E. C. Knight Company, American Sugar Refining Company, Franklin Sugar Company, Spreckels Sugar Refining Company, Delaware Sugar House

Appellant's Claim
That lower courts erred in finding that the named sugar refining companies had not violated the Sherman Anti-Trust Act of 1890.

Chief Lawyers for Appellant
Lawrence Maxwell Jr., U.S. Solicitor General; Richard Olney, U.S. Attorney General

Chief Lawyers for Appellees
John E. Parsons, John G. Johnson

Justices for the Court
Henry Billings Brown, David Josiah Brewer, Stephen Johnson Field, Melville Weston Fuller (writing for the Court), Horace Gray, George Shiras, Jr., Edward Douglass White

Justices Dissenting
John Marshall Harlan I (Howell Edmunds did not participate)

Place
Washington, D.C.

Date of Decision
21 January 1895

Decision
The Court upheld the Sherman Anti-Trust Act, but found that it did not apply to manufacturing.

Significance
The decision severely weakened the Sherman Anti-Trust Act of 1890, the federal government's first attempt to limit the power of industrial monopolies.

The Age of Monopolies

Throughout the late 1800s, scores of industrial and agricultural tycoons formed trusts, whose combined wealth allowed them to squeeze smaller competitors out of business. With so much power settling into the hands of monopolies, the potential for abuse by those willing to manipulate the national economy to enrich private fortunes was enormous. Public concern was sufficient for Congress to act, in spite of the federal government's reluctance to interfere with corporate interests. On 2 July 1890, Congress passed the Sherman Anti-Trust Act, making illegal, "every contract, combination in the form of trust or otherwise, or conspiracy, in restraint of trade." On the surface, the act seemed to empower the federal government to protect free competition in business from monopolies. The vague wording of the bill and the lack of a governmental agency to enforce its terms ensured that any action brought against corporations under the bill would wind up in the courts.

One such consolidation occurred in 1892 when four Philadelphia-area sugar refineries—the E. C. Knight Company, Franklin Sugar Company, Spreckels Sugar Refining Company, and Delaware Sugar House—agreed to sell out to the American Sugar Refining Company in exchange for American Company stock. By combining these plants, 90 percent of all sugar sold in the U.S. would suddenly be refined by a single company. The U.S. government immediately filed suit against E. C. Knight and the other companies of the "Sugar Trust," attempting to cancel the stock transfer on grounds that it violated the Sherman Anti-Trust Act. The government action argued that ultimate aim of the stock transfer was to completely control the price of sugar throughout the country.

Both the government suit and a subsequent appeal were dismissed by the Circuit Court for the Eastern District of Pennsylvania. As far as the Pennsylvania court was concerned, the American Sugar Company merger had taken place within state lines and had no bearing on the Sherman Act's rules regarding interstate commerce. U.S. Attorney General, Richard Olney, continued the suit by appealing to the U.S. Supreme Court on 24 October 1894. Again, the "Sugar Trust" was victorious.

Robber Barons

A handful of mid- to late nineteenth century railroad owners and executives became known as the "robber barons" because of the illegal and monopolistic practices they used to control the U.S. railroads. Without laws and regulations, the robber barons largely did what they wanted, amassing wealth and power through their railroad monopolies.

Jay Gould, perhaps the most notorious of the robber barons, took over the Erie Railroad by bribing politicians, issuing fraudulent stock, launching price wars, influencing the gold market, and deceiving business associates. Other key robber barons included Edward Henry Harriman and James J. Hill who competed with each other for control of the Northwest railroads. Harriman's Union Pacific eventually seized the Pacific Coast,

while Hill's Great Northern Railway connected the North and West. The two briefly formed the monopoly Northern Securities Company, which the U.S. Supreme Court broke up in 1904.

Around the turn of the century, the robber barons' dominance began to wane because of growing public anger over ticket price fluctuations and stock market dips stemming from the railroads. During this period, the federal government dealt a series of blows to the robber barons in the form of laws, regulations, and court orders, which led to policies that curbed the formation of monopolies.

Source(s): *West's Encyclopedia of American Law* Minneapolis, Minnesota: West Publishing, 1998.

Manufacturing And Transportation

On 21 January 1895 the Court upheld the ruling against the government. Chief Justice Fuller wrote that the terms of the Sherman Act were not written to directly prohibit monopolies, but were instead aimed at preventing corporations from monopolizing commerce. The Court echoed the Pennsylvania court's separation of manufacturing and transportation as two distinct processes. The refining of sugar was a manufacturing process and not in itself an act connected to the product's transportation across state lines. Because all of the companies named in the Knight case were located in one state, Pennsylvania, the Sherman Act's prohibitions against restraint of interstate trade did not apply. The government, wrote Fuller, had not proven that there was any conspiracy by the refineries to interfere with interstate commerce.

Only Justice Harlan dissented. Harlan believed that the government was the only body powerful enough to protect the American people against corporations gaining control of aspects of everyday life, such as the price of basic foods. Unlike his colleagues, he believed that the "Sugar Trust" did constitute an unlawful combination in restraint of free trade. The American Sugar Refining Company admitted it was in the business of selling its product throughout the United States, not just in Pennsylvania. Harlan believed the company should therefore be subject to national, not just state, regulations.

Harlan noted that the majority opinion had not found the Sherman Act to be unconstitutional, but he felt that the decision defeated the main reason the law had been passed. His analysis would accurately reflect the fate of other labor cases passed before the Court in the coming years. The *Knight* decision's narrow interpretation of the Sherman Act rendered the law toothless until decisions in the *Addyston Pipe & Steel Co. v. United States* (1899) and *Northern Securities Co. v. United States* (1904) cases resurrected the act as an effective instrument of federal regulation.

Richard Olney. © Archive Photos.

Samuel Insull Trial

During the business boom of the early 1900s, Samuel Insull forged a corporate empire of utility companies. At the height of his utility reign, his companies operated in 39 of the 48 states. To make the empire work, one of his electric companies would sell properties to another Insull company at a profit, with the second company then selling to a third.

On 2 October 1934, Insull and 15 others were charged through Utility Securities Company with fraudulently scheming to induce investors nationwide to buy the common stock of Corporation Securities Company at inflated prices. The Insull-controlled companies were also charged with maintaining a fictitious market for the common stock, thus misleading prospective investors as to its value. To carry out the scheme, the defendants had used the mail to send circulars to those they intended to defraud. On 24 November 1934, Insull and the others were found not guilty.

The revelations of the trial produced immediate legislation, such as the Federal Securities and Exchange Act, to regulate the issuance of securities, control stock exchanges, and protect the unwary from holding companies. The trial provides insight into a time when a stock manipulator could build a pyramid of commercial wealth, making as much as a million dollars a week, at the expense of thousands of small investors doomed innocently to ruin.

Source(s): Knappman, Edward W., ed. *Great American Trials.* Detroit, MI: Visible Ink Press, 1994.

Related Cases

Addyston Pipe & Steel Co. v. United States, 175 U.S. 211 (1899).
Northern Securities Co. v. United States, 193 U.S. 197 (1904).

Bibliography and Further Reading

"A Sugar Trust Victory." *New York Times,* 22 January 1895, p. 1.

Eichner, Alfred S. *The Emergence of Oligopoly: Sugar Refining As A Case Study.* Baltimore: Johns Hopkins Press, 1969.

Fiss, Owen M. *History of the Supreme Court of the United States: Troubled Beginnings of the Modern State 1888-1910.* New York: Macmillan, 1993.

Johnson, John W., ed. *Historic U.S. Court Cases, 1690–1990: An Encyclopedia.* New York: Garland Publishing, 1992.

Josephson, Matthew. *The Robber Barons.* New York: Harcourt, Brace, 1934.

Keller, Morton. *Affairs of State: Public Life In Nineteenth Century America.* Cambridge: Belknap Press, 1977.

Thorelli, Hans. *The Federal Antitrust Policy.* Baltimore: Johns Hopkins Press, 1955.

Chief Justice Melville Weston Fuller. © The Library of Congress/Corbis.

NORTHERN SECURITIES CO. V. UNITED STATES

Legal Citation: 193 U.S. 197 (1904)

Appellant
Northern Securities Company

Appellee
United States

Appellant's Claim
That the Northern Securities holding company did not represent a conspiracy in restraint of trade under the Sherman Anti-Trust Act.

Chief Lawyers for Appellant
John W. Griggs, George B. Young, John G. Johnson

Chief Lawyers for Appellee
Philander Chase Knox, U.S. Attorney General; William A. Day

Justices for the Court
David Josiah Brewer, Henry Billings Brown, William Rufus Day, John Marshall Harlan I (writing for the Court), Joseph McKenna

Justices Dissenting
Melville Weston Fuller, Oliver Wendell Holmes, Rufus Wheeler Peckham, Edward Douglass White

Place
Washington, D.C.

Date of Decision
14 March 1904

Decision
That the Northern Securities Company was a trust in the meaning of the law, and that it was a combination in restraint of trade, and that the Sherman Anti-Trust law did apply.

Significance
By upholding the ruling of the Circuit Court of Minnesota, which had held that the Northern Securities Company was an illegal combination in restraint of trade, the Supreme Court put a stop to further combination in railroad companies. Furthermore, the court ruled that the Sherman Act could be used to break up companies already formed, paving the way for more vigorous antitrust litigation. However, the dissents in the case paved the way for "reasonable" monopolies.

Northern Securities—Legitimate Business or Monopoly?

In 1896, the Supreme Court had prevented a merger planned by J. P. Morgan, who controlled the Northern Pacific Railroad, with the Great Northern Railroad, controlled by J. J. Hill. In this early plan, Morgan would simply exchange control of the Great Northern by obtaining stock in Northern Pacific. Foiled in this plan, the railroad investors planned another means to achieve the same end. On 13 November 1901, they formed Northern Securities Company in New Jersey. This company would acquire stock from both railroad companies and give, in exchange, stock in Northern Securities. At the time of the plan, Northern Pacific had 5,500 miles of railroad, while Great Northern had 4,128 miles. Both railroads operated from the upper Midwest to the Northwest of the United States.

The railroad executives argued that their plan would put their operations on a stronger footing, and would assist in expanding international trade. Northern Securities had purchased interests in the Burlington lines, operating from Iowa toward the south and east. Railroad cars used to carry goods from the Midwest to Seattle for export to Asia would return with cargoes destined not only for the upper Midwest, but with cargoes for the south and east, through the Burlington connection. Attorneys for the railroad argued that the companies' intent had not been to monopolize or to restrain trade. Their aim was the opposite—to help in national development through more efficient linkages of suppliers and markets.

However, on 9 April 1903, the circuit court in Minnesota ruled that the Northern Securities company formed a combination in restraint of trade, thereby violating the Sherman Anti-Trust Act of 1890. Justice Harlan wrote the opinion of the court, ruling that the Sherman Act did apply, and that it applied to all restraints of trade, whether reasonable or unreasonable. Congress had the power to pass the act. Combinations that extinguished competition among railroads were illegal under the act. Furthermore, the act suggested that any combination that tended to restrict trade or create a monopoly was illegal, and it was clear that Northern Securities had that tendency. Corporations created by the various states were subject to the law of the land.

The other judges on the Court offered important and interesting views on this case. Justice Brewer, although concurring in the decision, dissented on one point. He brought up the "rule of reason," suggesting that only unreasonable restraints of trade were outlawed under the Sherman Act, and that the combination proposed by the railroads should have been outlawed on the grounds that it was unreasonable, not simply that it tended to restrain trade. Justice White pointed out that all the Northern Securities Company would do was own stock—the Sherman Act had never made it illegal for one firm to own stock in another. He also pointed out that all railroads had grown larger by combinations, and that all of those combinations had "tended" to create some degree of restraint of trade. By the majority opinion, White argued, all growth of railroad companies would be prevented. Justice Holmes took this argument further. He pointed out that Congress could never have intended through the Sherman Act to prevent all combination. All combinations of businesses of any kind could be said to have the tendency to reduce competition. If taken to an extreme, the Sherman Act could lead to the universal disintegration of society into individuals. Furthermore, the combination set up by Northern Securities was not intended to exclude others from the field, but only to make more efficient the operations and marketing of the two firms and their connecting lines. Holmes, Fuller, White, and Peckham dissented from the decision written by Harlan. The close 5-4 decision, with the partial dissent by Brewer, and the arguments of the other dissenters suggested that in the future, a rule of reason might be applied. If companies could argue that their intent was only to be more efficient and to meet reasonable goals, they might be able to build on the logic suggested by Brewer and Holmes and the other dissenters, to create larger combinations.

Related Cases

Munn v. Illinois, 94 U.S. 113 (1876).
In re Debs, 158 U.S. 564 (1895).
United States v. E. C. Knight, 156 U.S. 1 (1895).
Allegeyer v. Louisiana, 165 U.S. 578 (1897).
Holden v. Hardy, 169 U.S. 366 (1898).

Philander Chase Knox, U.S. Secretary of State. © Archive Photos.

Bibliography and Further Reading

Biskupic, Joan, and Elder Witt. *Congressional Quarterly's Guide to the U.S. Supreme Court,* 3rd ed. Washington, DC: Congressional Quarterly, Inc., 1996.

Bringhurst, Bruce. *Antitrust and the Oil Monopoly: The Standard Oil Cases, 1890-1911.* Westport, CT: Greenwood Press, 1979.

Cushman, Robert F. *Leading Constitutional Decisions.* Englewood Cliffs, NJ: Prentice-Hall, Inc., 1982.

Hall, Kermit L., ed. *The Oxford Companion to the Supreme Court of the United States.* New York: Oxford University Press, 1992.

Meyer, B. H. *A History of the Northern Securities Case.* New York: Da Capo Press, 1972.

SWIFT AND CO. V. UNITED STATES

Legal Citation: 196 U.S. 375 (1905)

Appellant
Swift and Company

Appellee
United States

Appellant's Claim
That the meat packing operations of Swift and Company were entirely conducted within a state, and thus could not fall under the jurisdiction of the Interstate Commerce Clause of the Constitution, and could not be judged to be a violation of the Sherman Anti-Trust Act, which was only intended to regulate interstate trade. Further, that the provisions of the Sherman Act were so general and vague that they could not be applied in a particular instance.

Chief Lawyers for Appellant
John S. Miler, Merritt Starr

Chief Lawyers for Appellee
William H. Moody, U.S. Attorney General; William A. Day

Justices for the Court
David Josiah Brewer, Henry Billings Brown, William Rufus Day, Melville Weston Fuller, John Marshall Harlan 1, Oliver Wendell Holmes (writing for the Court), Joseph McKenna, Rufus Wheeler Peckham, Edward Douglass White

Justices Dissenting
None

Place
Washington, D.C.

Date of Decision
30 January 1905

Decision
That the operations of Swift, although conducted locally, were national and interstate in scope, and subject to the Sherman Act.

Significance
This decision broke new ground in showing that the Sherman Anti-Trust Act would apply to businesses which, even when conducted on a local basis, were involved in selling a product which went into interstate trade. Holmes showed that the distinction between intrastate trade and interstate trade was often blurred, and that a major business such as the Swift meat-packing industry, which operated in several states, was an interstate business.

When is a business interstate?

The Swift meat-packers operated in a number of states, near stockyards in Chicago, East St. Louis, Omaha, St. Paul, Kansas City, and at other major railway terminal points. The company would purchase livestock at the stockyards, slaughter the stock in its own facilities, and then sell the meat to others at its own plants. The purchasers would then ship the fresh meat by rail, often out of state to wholesalers in many cities. Because Swift conducted each of its operations entirely within a particular state, it could argue its operations were local in each case. It purchased, processed, and sold locally. Even if the stock had been shipped a thousand miles through several states before purchasing it, and then the meat was shipped a thousand miles by others, Swift could logically point out that its own businesses, in each case, did not extend beyond a few miles between the stockyard and its own slaughterhouses and meat-packing plants. Attorney General Moody and William A. Day, for the government, pointed out that while a business may be intrastate in operation, it could be interstate in overall effect. Swift company was such an operation.

As Justice Holmes further noted in his opinion, Swift and its affiliate companies had come to control about 60 percent of the national market in fresh meat. Many of the practices of the company were designed to manipulate the interstate price of the stock purchased. For example, several buyers would appear at stock auctions and artificially bid to give the appearance of competitive bidding, keeping the price low. However, on occasion, the buyers would temporarily bid up a price to ensure that the press would report particularly high prices for stock in a particular town. At that point, many stock shippers would send livestock to that town in order to get higher prices, flooding the market. Then the Swift buyers would return to their practice of offering low prices. In this way, by controlling the bidding, the company could get artificially low prices for its supplies, while at the same time charging its regular full price for its meat products. It was practices such as these that caused the government to bring its case under the Sherman Anti-Trust Act for conspiracy or combination in restraint of trade.

Packing house workers in Chicago, Illinois, 1906. © The Library of Congress/Corbis.

Regarding the question of interstate trade, the company's attorneys pointed out that all purchases and sales of the company were made locally. Thus, the operations of the company could not be considered interstate trade and fell beyond the scope of the federal government. Regarding the question of manipulation of market by bidding, the attorneys pointed out that in a competitive bidding situation, buyers were always able to accept any insincerely offered bid.

Holmes rejected both lines of thought, arguing that the company's intent was to monopolize the industry. The company knew that its products were being sold interstate, and in fact, it could not have operated unless its products were intended for the interstate market. It also knew that the livestock it purchased were shipped interstate. Therefore, its manipulation of the market had interstate effects, and the company sought and obtained rebates from railroad companies. Furthermore, the issue of "insincere bidding" did not simply mean that higher bids were offered as bluffs, as suggested by the attorneys for the firm. Rather, the bidding was set up in such a way as to cause the market to rise, then fall. By manipulating the bidding, Swift could purchase livestock at well below what would have been a free market price.

Justice Holmes did agree that the language of the Sherman Act was vague and that the company could only learn what was prohibited by the Court's ruling that certain actions were regarded as restraint of trade. Thus, one of the purposes of the ruling in this case was to establish what sorts of practices would be illegal, and the only modifications to the lower court decision were made to clarify what was legal and illegal.

Related Cases
United States v. E. C. Knight and Co., 156 U.S. 1 (1895).
Northern Securities Co. v. United States, 193 U.S. 197 (1904).

Bibliography and Further Reading
Biskupic, Joan, and Elder Witt, eds. *Congressional Quarterly's Guide to the U.S. Supreme Court,* 3rd ed. Washington, DC: Congressional Quarterly, Inc., 1996.

Clemen, R. A. *American Livestock Industry.* New York: 1923.

Hall, Kermit L., ed. *The Oxford Companion to the Supreme Court of the United States.* New York: Oxford University Press, 1992.

UNITED STATES V. STANDARD OIL

Legal Citation: 221 U.S. 1 (1911)

Plaintiff
U.S. Justice Department

Defendant
Standard Oil of New Jersey

Plaintiff's Claim
That Standard Oil was a monopoly and engaged in a conspiracy of restraint of trade.

Chief Lawyer for Plaintiff
Frank B. Kellogg

Chief Defense Lawyer
John G. Milburn

Justices for the Court
William Rufus Day, John Marshall Harlan I, Oliver Wendell Holmes, Charles Evans Hughes, Joseph Rucker Lamar, Horace Harmon Lurton, Joseph McKenna, Willis Van Devanter, Edward Douglass White

Justices Dissenting
None

Place
Washington, D.C.

Date of Decision
15 May 1911

Decision
Sustained the circuit court dissolution order.

Significance
Although the Court sustained the order to dissolve Standard Oil by introducing the "rule of reason," the Court opened the door to future collaboration in restraint of trade among the component companies.

A Challenge to Monopolies

Since the passage of the Sherman Anti-Trust Act in 1890, complaints had mounted that Standard Oil of New Jersey violated the letter and spirit of the law by unfair practices. By 1906, federal authorities estimated that Standard Oil controlled over 80 percent of the oil production in the United States. By charging excessive prices for products for which there was no competition, such as kerosene, and by undercutting its competition in other areas, the company had driven many smaller firms out of business. Furthermore, the company offered rebates to oil producing companies if they would ship oil through Standard Oil pipelines, rather than those of competitors. Majority ownership of the firm was held by a small group, led by John D. Rockefeller. Monopolistic practices had allowed the firm to reap excessive profits. From an original investment of about $70 million, stockholders had earned profits over a fifteen year period of more than $700 million.

Despite evidence uncovered by journalists and executives of oil companies destroyed by Standard Oil, attorneys general during the Cleveland, Harrison, McKinley, and Roosevelt administrations refused to act against the corporation. Theodore Roosevelt's second administration, faced with mounting public outrage over the company's practices, finally ordered an investigation and prosecution of Standard Oil. The case was continued by Roosevelt's successor, William Howard Taft, who had made a promise to vigorously prosecute the *Standard Oil* case during his presidential campaign in 1908.

On 20 November 1909, after eight months of argument, the St. Louis Federal Circuit Court handed down its opinion. Judge Walter Henry Sanborn, representing a unanimous court, ruled that many of the companies controlled by Jersey Standard were potentially competitive, yet the holding company gave the corporation the absolute power to prevent competition. The effect of the stock transfers from the component companies to Standard Oil of New Jersey was a direct and substantial restriction of interstate commerce.

The court also ruled that Standard Oil of New Jersey had tried to monopolize the petroleum industry. The judge ruled that "the combination and conspiracy in restraint of trade and its continued execution which have been found to exist, constitute illegal means by which the conspiring defendants combined, and still combine and conspire to monopolize a part of interstate and international commerce." However, in directing how the corporation should be dissolved, the court ruled that holdings in the subsidiary companies could be distributed to shareholders in Standard Oil in proportion to their holdings in that company. As a result, the small group which controlled Standard Oil would, in turn, become owners of the companies into which the larger firm was dissolved. That arrangement would almost guarantee little competition among the resulting companies. An alternative plan proposed dividing the ownership of the subsidiary firms among the major owners thus fostering competition among the successor firms. However, such an arrangement was not seriously considered.

Standard Oil of New Jersey appealed the decision to the Supreme Court. The federal case brought by Frank Kellogg was assisted by President William Howard Taft's attorney general, George Wickersham, who presented the government's arguments. However, neither Kellogg nor Wickersham challenged the stock transfer provision of the circuit court ruling. In the decision of this case, Justice Day introduced the "rule of reason" which

John D. Rockefeller, c. 1911. © AP/Wide World Photos.

stated effectively that if a restraint of trade was ancillary to a legitimate business transaction, and reasonable in the eyes of the contracting parties and the general public, then such restraints of trade were not illegal. In effect, the rule of reason allowed the courts to judge certain monopolies reasonable. Justice White argued that to strictly enforce the Sherman Act against all agreements in restraint of trade would bring the economy to a halt, by attacking all sorts of contracts which were the essence of trade.

The resulting companies which emerged from the dissolution of Standard Oil of New Jersey included major gasoline suppliers such as Exxon, Amoco, Mobil, Chevron, Standard of California, others. The decision in *United States v. Standard Oil,* while hailed as a victory for anti-trust prosecution, in effect stood as a judicial endorsement of the movement toward extremely large corporate monopolies. These monopolies could then dominate a whole sector of the economy through restraining agreements and common ownership.

Related Cases

Puerto Rico v. Shell Co., 302 U.S. 253 (1937).
United States v. E. I. du Pont de Nemours & Co., 351 U.S. 377 (1956).

Frank B. Kellogg. © The Library of Congress.

Berkey Photo, Inc. v. Eastman Kodak Co., 603 F.2d 263 (2nd Cir. 1979).

Bibliography and Further Reading
Bringhurst, Bruce. *Antitrust and the Oil Monopoly, The Standard Oil Cases, 1890-1911.* Westport, CT: Greenwood Press, 1979.

Miller, Arthur S. *The Supreme Court and American Capitalism.* New York: Free Press, 1968.

Nash, Gerald P. *United States Oil Policy, 1890-1914.* Pittsburgh: University of Pittsburgh Press, 1968.

STAFFORD V. WALLACE

Legal Citation: 258 U.S. 495 (1922)

Petitioner
Stafford and Company, a firm engaged in the buying and selling of livestock

Respondent
Henry C. Wallace, U.S. Secretary of Agriculture

Petitioner's Claim
That the operation of stockyards did not constitute interstate commerce, and therefore Congress did not have authority under the commerce clause of the U.S. Constitution to enforce the Packers and Stockyards Act of 1921.

Chief Lawyer for Petitioner
E. Godman

Chief Lawyer for Respondent
James Montgomery Beck, U.S. Solicitor General

Justices for the Court
Louis D. Brandeis, John Hessin Clarke, Oliver Wendell Holmes, Joseph McKenna, Mahlon Pitney, William Howard Taft (writing for the Court), Willis Van Devanter

Justices Dissenting
James Clark McReynolds (William Rufus Day did not participate)

Place
Washington, D.C.

Date of Decision
1 May 1922

Decision
Upheld the authority of Congress to enforce the act over stockyards, which the Court ruled were not "places of rest or a final destination," but rather "a throat through which the current of commerce flows."

Significance
Stafford v. Wallace marked a milestone in the Court's interpretation of the powers granted to Congress under Article I, Section 8 of the U.S. Constitution. Specifically, *Stafford* expanded the "stream of commerce" doctrine introduced by Justice Holmes in *Swift and Co. v. United States* (1905). With *Stafford*, the Court determined that Congress had the further power to curb monopolistic business practices in intrastate industries that belonged to a stream of interstate commerce. As such, the case helped signal the Court's trend in the first half of the twentieth century toward an interpretation of interstate commerce favorable to the powers of the government.

Stockyards in the Stream of Commerce

In the early 1900s, the stockyards of Chicago, along with the steel mills of Pittsburgh and the financial markets of New York City, seemed to be a symbol of American economic power. Not surprisingly, perhaps, writer Upton Sinclair had set his controversial novel *The Jungle* (1906), which exposed corruption and brutality in business, in the stockyards of Chicago. Through the facilities of companies such as the Union Stockyards & Transit Company, which was incorporated under Illinois law in 1865, passed some 15 million cattle, calves, hogs, and sheep in 1920. This made the stockyards of Chicago the largest in the world. And as the Supreme Court was to discover, some five companies held virtual control over the operations of the Union and other stockyards in the great Chicago livestock center.

When *Stafford v. Wallace* went before the Supreme Court, Chief Justice Taft went to great lengths in order to establish the extent to which the Chicago stockyards constituted a single point, by no means a terminal one, along a vast stream of interstate commerce. From their point of origin in diverse livestock-raising locales, cattle from Wyoming, sheep from Montana, and hogs from Kansas (to use a few likely examples) would be shipped by farmers to a commission merchant at the Chicago stockyards, with whom the farmer had an agreement to sell the livestock on consignment. Thus the commission merchant did not pay for the livestock; he simply arranged their sale and would take a portion of the profits. Upon receiving the live animals, he would have them driven from the cars to assigned pens, where they would be watered and fed.

In the bill submitted by Stafford's lawyer, E. Godman, to the Supreme Court in *Stafford v. Wallace,* the petitioner would attempt to establish that this constituted the completion of the transportation of the livestock. Through Godman, Stafford would further assert that livestock consigned to commission merchants were sold by them for a commission, and not "on their own account" as owners; that sales took place only at the stockyard and nowhere else; that such commissions were fixed at a certain price per head; and that the commission merchants simply passed the payment along to the original owners and shippers, minus their own commissions and other expenses. Stafford's counsel presented a number of other claims, all of them intending to show that shipment through the stockyards did not constitute a continuous flow of commercial activity, but rather that there was a series of transactions starting and stopping, from farmer to shipper to commission broker to dealer to purchaser. The purpose of all of this was to establish that the traffic in livestock at the yards constituted a sort of closed circuit, and not a mere series of points on a long line.

Naturally, this was not a question of purely academic concern. If Stafford's counsel could show that the activities of the stockyards were not part of interstate commerce, but were purely intrastate in nature, it would place those activities beyond the purview of Congress and its Packers and Stockyards Act of 1921. If, on the other hand, the stockyards fell under the authority of the legislative branch, the latter could enforce antitrust laws. For some two decades prior to the 1922 case, as Justice Taft stated in his opinion for the majority, the meat-packing industry had been dominated by five companies: Swift, Armour, Cudahy, Wilson, and Morris. These "Big Five," it appeared to the federal government, were engaged in a conspiracy to control the costs of livestock, and in 1903, the government had filed a bill in equity to force them to desist from the alleged conspiracy.

Taking on the Monopolies

Swift appealed an injunction under the bill, and the case went before the Supreme Court in 1905 as *Swift v. United States*. The Court sustained the injunction, with a unanimous opinion written by Justice Holmes: "Although the combination alleged embraces restraint and monopoly of trade within a single state," Holmes wrote, "its effect upon commerce among the States is not accidental, secondary, remote, or merely probable." He then went on to deign the "stream of commerce" doctrine thus:

> When cattle are sent for sale from a place in one state, with the expectation that they will end their transit, after purchase, in another, and when in effect they do so, with only the interruption necessary to find a purchaser at the stock yards, and when this is a typical constantly recurring course, the current thus existing is a current of commerce among the states, and the purchase of the cattle is a part and incident of such commerce.

Seven years later, in 1912, Swift was again indicted for violation of anti-trust laws, and acquitted. A 1917 Federal Trade Commission (FTC) investigation found that the packers of the "Big Five" did indeed have a conspiracy in operation, whereby they controlled all aspects of the facilities through which livestock were sold. A bill in equity filed in 1920 with the Supreme

Court of the District of Columbia illustrated the effects of this control through tactics such as "wiring on." Under the latter scheme, an unsuspecting shipper might take his stock to one yard and, not being pleased with the price offered, might take it to another yard—not knowing that the two yards were in collusion. Once he got to the second yard, he would find the price offered was the same as at the first, with his profit further reduced by the loss incurred in his shipping of the livestock to the second yard. Such factors influenced the passing of the Packers and Stockyards Act of 1921, a law aimed at preventing such unfair practices. With *Stafford v. Wallace,* and the associated case of *Burton v. Clyne,* the act came under challenge.

Writing for a 7-1 majority (Justice Day took no part in the proceedings), Chief Justice Taft began by clarifying the issue in question. The case had come to the Court's attention not so that it could decide who was right—Stafford and Company on the one hand, the FTC and Congress on the other—about specific violations of antitrust law; but rather to determine whether Congress had authority to pass, and the government to enforce, the Packers and Stockyards Act of 1921. Under the latter, stockyards were defined, as were stockyard owners, commission people, and dealers, and the dealers were required to register with the state. The secretary of agriculture (who at that time was Henry C. Wallace) had power to make rules, prescribe the means by which the different entities had to keep their accounts, and to fix rates. All of this was established, Taft indicated, for the purpose of ensuring a steady "stream of commerce":

> The object to be secured by the act is the free and unburdened flow of live stock from the ranges and farms of the West and the Southwest through the great stockyards and slaughtering centers on the borders of that region, and thence in the form of meat products to the consuming cities of the country in the Middle West and East, or, still, as live stock, to the feeding places and fattening farms in the Middle West or East for further preparation in the market.

"The chief evil" whose fear instigated the passage of the bill, Taft wrote, was the collusion of packers, commission people, and dealers who in some combination could affect prices to their benefit—and to the harm of the people who raised the cattle, not to mention the consumer. Given the monopolies at work in the stockyard, there was a situation "full of opportunity and temptation, to the prejudice of the absent shipper and owner."

Defining and Expanding the Concept

The stockyards, Taft stated, "are not a place of rest or final destination" in interstate commerce; rather, they are "but a throat through which the current flows, and the transactions which occur there are only incident to this current from the West to the East, and from one state to another." The sale of stock within a yard could not therefore be

> merely local transactions. They create a local change of title, it is true, but they do not stop the flow; they merely change the private interests in the subject of the current, not interfering with, but, on the contrary, being indispensable to, its continuity.

The stockyards act, therefore, treated the yards as "great national public utilities to promote the flow of commerce from the ranges and farms of the West to the consumers in the East." As to whether the yards should be under federal jurisdiction, that question had been decided in *Munn v. Illinois* (1877). Similarly, *United States v. Union Stock Yards Co.* (1912) established the yards as an agency of interstate commerce inasmuch as they received livestock by rail. At issue in *Stafford,* then, was the highly focused question of "whether the business done in the stockyards, between the receipt of the live stock in the yards and the shipment of them therefrom, is a part of interstate commerce." To make that determination required a closer look at the 1905 *Swift* case.

After reviewing the bill in equity brought in 1905 "against substantially the same packing firms as those against whom this legislation is directed," the Court upheld the bill. Justice Holmes wrote for the majority, "the scheme as a whole seems to us to be within reach of the law." As for the monopoly allegedly engaged in by Swift, it was surely interstate in character: "Although the combination alleged embraces restraint and monopoly of trade within a single state, its effect upon commerce among the states is not accidental, secondary, remote, or merely probable." In the final analysis, "commerce among the states is not a technical legal conception, but a practical one, drawn from the course of business." Given this solid practical understanding, Taft wrote, the Court refused to involve itself in an "inquiry into the noninterstate character of . . . incidents and facilities" that constituted part of an interstate transaction, and which "when considered alone and without reference" to other elements could appear to be outside interstate commerce.

The next year, in 1923, Taft reiterated his admiration for the *Swift* ruling with a decision in which he said that the earlier case "was a milestone in the interpretation of the commerce clause of the Constitution." Meanwhile, in *Stafford* he wrote that "the principles of the Swift Case have become a fixed rule of this Court in the construction and application of the commerce clause." As an example he cited the Court's ruling in *Lemke v. Farmer's Grain Co.* earlier in 1922, a challenge involving the sale of wheat from North Dakota granaries to Minnesota merchants.

Taft devoted the remainder of his opinion to closing up any further areas of contention on the part of *Stafford.* Hence, he noted that the ruling in question was not a bill in equity, as it had been in *Swift,* or a conspiracy indictment, but a *law* passed by Congress, and Taft stated that "this Court [would] certainly not substitute its judgment for that of Congress in such a matter unless the relation of the subject to interstate commerce and its effect upon it [were] clearly nonexistent." He made special note of *Hopkins v. United States* and *Anderson v. United States,* two related 1898 cases involving commission merchants and stockyards, as well as several others which might have seemed to bear on *Stafford,* but did not. Therefore, he affirmed the orders of the district court, an opinion to which Justice McReynolds dissented without filing a written opinion.

Impact

Coming as it did after years during which the Court had often supported the powers of the states and corporations against that of the federal government, *Stafford* marked a growing emphasis on federal authority in commerce. This trend continued in the 1930s under President Franklin D. Roosevelt, in spite of two rulings that struck down his National Industrial Recovery Act (NIRA) and Agricultural Adjustment Act (AAA). In the 1960s, with *Heart of Atlanta Motel v. United States* (1964), the federal government would use control over interstate commerce to enforce civil rights law, by ruling that Congress could use is commerce power to prevent interstate commerce by companies that discriminate on the basis of race. *United States v. Lopez* (1995), on the other hand, would show that congressional commerce power had its limits, when it was determined that a ban on handguns in public schools could not be justified under the commerce clause.

Related Cases

Munn v. Illinois, 94 U.S. 113 (1877).
Anderson v. United States, 171 U.S. 604 (1898).
Hopkins v. United States, 171 U.S. 604 (1898).
Swift and Co. v. United States, 196 U.S. 375 (1905).
United States v. Union Stock Yards, 226 U.S. 286 (1912).
Lemke v. Farmers' Grain Co., 258 U.S. 50 (1922).
Heart of Atlanta Motel v. United States, 379 U.S. 421 (1964).
United States v. Lopez, 514 U.S. 549 (1995).

Bibliography and Further Reading

Bartholomew, Paul C., and Joseph F. Menez. *Summaries of Leading Cases on the Constitution,* 13th ed. Totowa, NJ: Littlefield Adams, 1990.

Biskupic, Joan, and Elder Witt. *Guide to the U.S. Supreme Court,* 3rd ed. Washington, DC: Congressional Quarterly Inc., 1997.

Hall, Kermit L., ed. *The Oxford Companion to the Supreme Court of the United States.* New York: Oxford University Press, 1992.

Levy, Leonard W., ed. *Encyclopedia of the American Constitution.* New York: Macmillan, 1986.

Witt, Elder. *Congressional Quarterly's Guide to the Supreme Court,* 2nd ed. Washington, DC: Congressional Quarterly Inc., 1990.

NATIONAL SECURITY

Of Highest Concern

Every nation defends itself. Most governments, in fact, regard national security as their highest concern. From military readiness to foreign policy and domestic laws, governments devote vast resources to protecting their nations in many ways. This fundamental responsibility never changes, but how it is defined by a government and its people can vary dramatically over time. Political, cultural and social forces, occurring within a nation itself and on the world stage, all work to shape the definition of what makes it secure. Constitutional law tells governments broadly what they can and cannot do in the name of security. Whether in peacetime or in war, the Constitution imposes stability and limits upon official power.

Responsibility

The U.S. Constitution divides responsibility for national security among the three branches of federal government. This system, known as the separation of powers, reflects the intent of the Constitution's framers that no single branch become too powerful. Thus each branch oversees the other through checks and balances with specific powers being neatly drawn. The president makes foreign policy through treaties with other nations, appoints ambassadors, and serves as the commander in chief of the armed forces. These executive branch powers are limited by those of the legislative branch. Congress imposes taxes to provide for defense, and the Senate ratifies the president's treaties and appointment of ambassadors before either can go forward. Although the president commands the armed forces, Congress alone may declare war. Overseeing these two branches is the judiciary. The courts' role is to see that they each exercise their own constitutional powers legally, without encroaching upon one another, while also safeguarding the civil liberties of citizens when they are threatened.

History, however, has blurred these neat lines. In the twentieth century, presidents have increasingly asserted control over national security in ways that have reduced the power of the legislative branch. Lawmakers have resisted this encroachment, yet with little success. The judiciary, for its part, has shown reluctance to intervene either to stop this trend or to uphold civil liberties that become captive to new definitions of the national interest. The practical conduct of national security thus has posed a hard question: who is in charge?

Congress and the president shared power comfortably until the Civil War. In 1861, President Abraham Lincoln took unprecedented action by ordering the blockade and capture of ships bound for Confederate ports, an action that brought a legal challenge by ship owners. They argued that he had exceeded his authority because Congress had not declared war. By a narrow 5-4 majority, the Supreme Court upheld the president's blockade in *The Prize Cases* (1862), named after an area of maritime law called prize law. The Court acknowledged that, even without a formal declaration by Congress, a state of war existed. Even though no branch of the government had the right to make war on one of its own states, laws passed in 1795 and 1807 gave the president the statutory right to suppress an insurrection. Decisions in this regard, the Court determined, belonged to the president, who could legally defend the nation without the need of action by Congress.

Presidential Power

Over the next 80 years, lawmakers and presidents jostled over national security. Immediately following the Civil War, Congress reasserted itself by refusing to ratify treaties. World War I saw President Woodrow Wilson claim broad presidential powers to regulate food and fuel prices, which, though highly controversial, became law in 1917. Wilson's agenda during the crisis also led Congress to prohibit alcohol, while conferring on the president sweeping authority over industry, national transportation, and exports. In the name of national security, civil liberties were sharply curtailed, as the Wilson administration pushed through passage of the Espionage Act of 1917. The administration then used this law, along with the much older Alien and Sedition Act of 1798, to prosecute over two thousand cases against war protesters and dissenters. But presidential power did not outlast this period. After the war, a resurgent Congress rejected many of the president's national security proposals.

The government clampdown on civil liberties was met with approval by federal courts. No cases reached the Supreme Court until shortly after the war, but then it refrained from interfering. One case, *Schenck v. United States* (1919), held that government limits on freedom of speech could be acceptable during wartime, and thus rejected the appeal of a man convicted for distributing pamphlets attacking the military draft. Justice Oliver Wendell Holmes set forth the so-called test for "clear and present danger," defining the suppression of free speech as permissible when words "will bring about the substantive evils that Congress has a right to prevent." The Court upheld other convictions for publishing articles criticizing the war, hindering military enlistment, calling for labor strikes, and other offenses deemed unpatriotic. Not for several decades would this judicial outlook change.

Greater assertions of presidential power came about in the World War II. Even before the formal declaration of war in December of 1941, President Franklin D. Roosevelt exercised emergency powers. He began a naval war against Germany, seized defense factories, and created the Office of Price Administration (OPA), an administrative body for setting consumer prices that Congress only subsequently empowered with legislation in 1942. During the war, the president mobilized virtually every aspect of the national economy, utilizing industries for defense production and rationing fuel to consumers.

National Security during War

As before, the executive branch also sacrificed civil liberties to the war effort. In February of 1942, an official War Department memo expressed alarm that "112,000 potential enemies of Japanese extraction are at large today," and reasoned that the absence of any sabotage to date "is a disturbing and confirming indication that such action will be taken." Within two months, the Roosevelt administration declared the entire West Coast a military area, evacuated and detained 112,000 Japanese Americans, and held them in "relocation centers" for the duration of the war. About 70,000 of the detainees were U.S. citizens. A legal challenge against the internment in *Korematsu v. United States* (1943) failed. Extreme measures by the government, the Court held, were justified in wartime by the compelling interest in maintaining national security.

During the Cold War era, presidential power grew. Presidents Harry Truman and Lyndon Johnson sent U.S. troops to Korea and Vietnam without a congressional declaration of war. Known euphemistically as police actions, these deployments, at least initially, brought no objection from Congress. Politicians of the era commonly accepted the premise that the national defense depended upon stopping Communist expansion around the globe. Leaving this up to the president,

Congress concerned itself with fighting "the Red menace" at home, investigating alleged Communist infiltration of the government, army, and entertainment industries. Besides asserting the power to wage war, the executive branch issued sweeping orders. The Constitution does not define the extent of the power to issue a so-called "executive order," which is remarkably similar to legislation. In 1952, however, it was tested when President Truman seized the nation's private steel mills in order to prevent an imminent labor strike from harming the Korean War effort. The steel industry succeeded in stopping this takeover in *Youngstown Sheet & Tube Co. v. Sawyer* (1952), which the Supreme Court, in one of its few intrusions into the national security area, held unconstitutional. Finding that the president had usurped lawmakers' role, Justice Hugo Black's opinion insisted that the executive branch must observe the separation of powers.

The Vietnam War eventually produced a backlash against presidential power. Despite promises by President Richard Nixon to end the unpopular war, hostilities continued, casualties increased in number, and the United States expanded fighting into Cambodia. At home, social upheaval accompanied legal challenges to the president's war effort. Some lawsuits claimed that the war was unconstitutional because Congress had not declared it. The Supreme Court rejected these arguments. *DaCosta v. Laird* (1973) upheld military conscription, and in *Holtzman v. Schlesinger* (1973), a suit brought by members of Congress, the Court rejected their challenge to the president's right to wage undeclared war by noting a long history of the very practice and concluding that Congress had the legislative power to resist presidential actions.

But the justices ruled differently in a major civil liberties case. The lawsuit in *New York Times Company v. United States* (1971) began when the White House tried to stop publication of government war documents by the *Times* and the *Washington Post*. This was a 7,000-page classified study on the Vietnam War through 1968, popularly called the "Pentagon Papers". The newspapers claimed the government's censorship violated the First Amendment. Claiming national security interests, the Nixon administration said publication would hurt the nation militarily and prolong the war. The Supreme Court rejected this argument and allowed publication, but only in a sharply divided manner that included nine separate opinions. While varying in their reasons, the majority would not permit the government to curtail speech rights before material was even published, an unconstitutional abridgment known as prior restraint. The decision marked an historical watershed in limiting the government's power to put its definition of national security above the First Amendment.

A Need for Balance

Lawmakers frustrated with presidential war-making passed the War Powers Act of 1973. An attempt to enforce the Constitution's balance of power, the law curtails the president's ability to send troops into foreign areas in the absence of a declaration of war. It requires presidents to report to Congress first, and, within 60 days of deployment, to begin a troop recall that lasts no longer than thirty days. Congress may at any time force a recall of troops. No president has liked nor been terribly held back by the War Powers Act. While the nation has not engaged in a protracted war since the Vietnam era, the law stopped no president from sending U.S. forces into conflict, whether President Ronald Reagan in Lebanon and Grenada or President George Bush in the Persian Gulf and Panama. The federal courts have rejected lawsuits demanding enforcement of the law, notably in *Crockett v. Reagan* (1982), which held that Congress' lawmaking power was sufficient to address any problems.

The National Security Council (NSC) has played a pivotal role since the late twentieth century. Established in 1947 and placed under executive branch control two years later, the NSC originally was a small advisory group. Gradually, it assumed policy functions that formerly belonged to the State Department. Thus from 1968 to 1972, National Security Advisor Henry Kissinger took the primary role in shaping President Nixon's foreign policies on Vietnam and the Middle East, eclipsing the role of Nixon's own secretary of state. By the mid-1980s, having attained its highest influence to date under President Reagan, the council became enmeshed in the Iran-Contra scandal. This grew out of the Reagan administration's backing of anti-Communist rebels, the Contras, in their war against the Nicaraguan government. The administration's position failed to win congressional support. After Congress banned U.S. military aid to the rebels, the NSC violated the ban by secretly selling weapons to the government of Iran, and then giving proceeds from those sales to the Contra rebels.

An investigation of the scandal lasted over six years, led to numerous prosecutions, and resulted in a few convictions that were overturned on appeal or reversed by presidential pardon.

In the 1980s and 1990s, broader definitions of national security emerged. The collapse of the Soviet Union effectively ended the Cold War, which had been the fundamental paradigm in national security for over four decades. Now, the rise of international terrorism, new economic challenges, and even the illegal drug trade were all characterized as national security issues. The National Security Council became the coordinating point for all government agencies on national security matters as its expanding mission involved the heads of the military and the Central Intelligence Agency (CIA), and even on occasion such cabinet members as the secretary of the treasury and the director of the Office of National Drug Control Policy. Official views on what endangered the nation, and what protected it, once again were seen to change almost as quickly as the world.

Bibliography and Further Reading

Dorsen, Norman. "Civil Liberties, National Security and Human Rights Treaties: A Snapshot in Context." *U.C. Davis Journal of International Law and Policy,* Spring 1997

Hall, Kermit L., ed. *The Oxford Companion to the Supreme Court of the United States.* New York: Oxford University Press, 1992

Peterson, Todd D. "The Law and Politics of Shared National Security Power—A Review of the National Security Constitution". *George Washington Law Review,* March 1991

Schwartz, Bernard. *A History of the Supreme Court.* New York: Oxford University Press, 1993

West's Encyclopedia of American Law. St. Paul: West Group, 1998

AARON BURR TRIAL

Legal Citation: 25 Fed. Cas. 187 (No. 14,694) (1807)

Prosecution
United States

Defendant
Former Vice-President Aaron Burr

Crime Charged
"Treason" within the meaning of Article III, section 3 of the Constitution

Chief Prosecutors
George Hay, William Wirt, Gordon MacRae

Chief Defense Lawyers
Edmund Randolph, John Wickham, Luther Martin, Benjamin Botts

Judges
Chief Justice John Marshall, District Judge Cyrus Griffin

Place
Richmond, Virginia

Date of Decision
1 September 1807

Decision
Burr was declared not guilty.

Significance
The Burr treason trial was the only time in American history that a court tried such a high-level official of the United States for treason. Although Burr was acquitted, his political career was destroyed.

With the exception of scholars of American history, most people are oblivious as to how unstable the political situation in the United States was in the early decades of the 1800s. In the years immediately following the Revolutionary War, the country suffered under the disastrous Articles of Confederation of 1781 until the Constitution was ratified in 1788. However, even after the Constitutional Convention, there were serious differences amongst the political elite. The two main political camps were the Federalists and the Democratic-Republicans and they had fundamentally different notions over what direction the new United States should take in its foreign policy.

The Federalists believed that, since the United States had been shaped by the cultural and economic influence of Great Britain, the Revolutionary War should not prevent the re-establishment of ties with the "Mother Country." The Democratic-Republicans believed that the United States should ally itself with France instead. Not only had France provided critical assistance to the colonies during the Revolutionary War, but the French Revolution had installed a government in France that professed belief in democratic ideals.

Further, an alliance with France, a European great power, represented the only viable opportunity for the fledgling United States to oppose the might of the British Empire. Aaron Burr's political career put him squarely in the center of this schism.

Aaron Burr's Roller-Coaster Career

Burr's impeccable credentials as an American patriot made him an unlikely candidate for the treason with which he was to be charged. Born in Newark, New Jersey, and educated at what became Princeton University, he was commissioned as an officer in the American army during the Revolutionary War. Burr distinguished himself in combat, and by the end of the war had risen to the rank of lieutenant colonel. After the war, Burr turned his energies to the legal profession. He did not graduate from a law school but instead studied law under an attorney's supervision, a practice which today is permitted by only one state (Virginia) but was then common. Burr was successful in his studies, and in 1782 he was admitted to the New York state bar.

Burr capitalized on his successful career and entered into politics. He joined the pro-French Democratic-Republicans and became their candidate for vice-president in the elections of 1800. At the time, members of the Electoral College cast two votes each for the presidency: one for the presidential candidate and one for the vice-presidential candidate. Each Democratic-Republican elector had cast a vote for Burr and a vote for the party's presidential candidate, Thomas Jefferson. The result was a tie, and it fell to the House of Representatives to decide the outcome of the election. After a bitter battle and 36 ballots, the House voted for Jefferson, and Burr became vice-president. Understandably, Jefferson suspected Burr of disloyalty and in 1804 managed to arrange his rejection by the Democratic-Republicans for a second vice-presidential nomination.

Burr and Alexander Hamilton, one of the principal Federalists, became intense adversaries and quarrelled at every opportunity. In 1804, with Burr seeking the governorship of New York, Hamilton publicly denounced him and expressed his opinion that Burr was unfit for public office. Furious, Burr challenged Hamilton to a duel.

Hamilton accepted. On 11 July 1804, at Weehawken, New Jersey, Burr shot Hamilton in the chest. Hamilton died soon thereafter.

Although he won the duel, Burr lost in the ensuing political uproar. State authorities in both New York and New Jersey sought to prosecute Burr for Hamilton's death, and Hamilton's supporters made Burr a political outcast in Washington.

For reasons that remain unclear to this day, in March of 1805 Burr left the increasingly hostile capitol for the frontier lands of the recently acquired Louisiana Purchase. Burr abandoned his allegiance to the Democratic-Republicans, and concocted a grandiose plan to lead a revolt with British assistance in these western lands. Burr hoped to establish a "Western Empire" with himself as ruler.

Burr's imperial ambitions were supported by Anthony Merry, the British envoy to the United States. Burr also had other powerful allies for his scheme. Senator Jonathan Dayton of New Jersey and a wealthy Ohioan named Harman Blennerhassett joined Burr and extended financial support for the planned revolt. Finally, Burr had the support of General-in-Chief of the Army James Wilkinson, who was also one of the joint commissioners for the Territory of Louisiana.

The conspirators' procrastination, however, proved to be their undoing. By the fall of 1806, still they had not moved. Great Britain's new foreign minister, Charles James Fox, recalled Anthony Merry and termi-

Vice President Aaron Burr. © AP/Wide World Photos.

nated British support for Burr's plan. Wilkinson grew nervous, and went to President Jefferson with the details of Burr's conspiracy. When Burr finally decided to act in November 1806, he used Blennerhassett's Ohio estates and private island as the base of operations for the revolt. Jefferson arranged for Ohio Governor Edward Tiffin to send in the local militia and the conspiracy was crushed. Burr went into hiding but was arrested within a few months.

Burr Tried Before Chief Justice Marshall

On 26 March 1807, Burr was taken by his captors to Richmond, Virginia, for trial before the federal court. Normally, Judge Cyrus Griffin of the District of Virginia would have presided over the trial. At the time, however, Supreme Court Chief Justice John Marshall was present in Richmond to hear appeals from the "circuit"

President Thomas Jefferson. © The Library of Congress.

that encompassed Virginia. Griffin soon found himself playing second fiddle to the eminent Marshall, who took control over the widely publicized trial.

The principal charge against Burr was treason against the United States. The prosecutors also made a related charge of "high misdemeanors" against Burr. George Hay, William Wirt, and Gordon MacRae formed the team of prosecutors for the government. Hay was a prominent attorney, thanks largely to his political connections as James Monroe's son-in-law. Wirt, a tall blond man, had a reputation for having an excellent courtroom presence. MacRae was primarily a politician and, in addition to being a prosecutor, was also Virginia's Lieutenant Governor.

Burr's defense attorneys were Edmund Randolph, John Wickham, Luther Martin, and Benjamin Botts. The distinguished Randolph was not only a former attorney general, but had served as George Washington's secretary of state and as governor of Virginia as well. Wickham, Martin and Botts were also widely respected and prominent attorneys.

Their task was also much easier than that of the prosecution, due to the particular requirements of Article III, Section 3 of the Constitution. Article III, Section 3 states that:

Treason against the United States, shall consist only in levying War against them, or in adhering to their Enemies, giving them Aid and Comfort. No Person shall be convicted of Treason unless on the Testimony of two Witnesses to the same overt Act, or on Confession in open Court.

Thus, the prosecution not only had to produce two witnesses, but those witnesses had to have seen some overt act by Burr in "levying war" or leading the planned revolt against the United States. Luckily for Burr, he had not been present in Ohio when Governor Tiffin's militia stormed Blennerhassett's island compound. As Burr himself stated, Jefferson's prompt action based on General Wilkinson's confession led to the destruction of the plot before the procrastinating Burr had taken much action: "Mr. Wilkinson alarmed the President and the President alarmed the people of Ohio."

Marshall's concern over whether the prosecution could bear the heavy burden of proof demanded by the Constitution caused the trial to be delayed until 3 August 1807. In the interim, the prosecution presented a series of witnesses, including General Wilkinson. These witnesses testified as to treasonous statements made by Burr and on the military preparations made on Blennerhassett's island. The evidence presented convinced a grand jury that Burr should be tried on the charges filed against him, and Marshall finally opened the trial.

The prosecution, led by Wirt, argued that Burr's involvement in the conspiracy made him "constructively present" on the island and thus involved in an overt act. Referring to the mercenaries arrested during the Blennerhassett raid, Wirt said:

What must be the guilt of [Burr], to that of the poor ignorant man who was enlisted into his services with some prospect of benefiting himself and family?

Definition of an Overt Act Debated

Burr's defense counsel countered Wirt's impressive oratory by keeping the focus of attention on the prosecution's strained interpretation on what constituted an "overt act." After all, the only act of the revolt remotely "overt" had been the preparations at Blennerhassett's island during which Burr had not been present.

Therefore, Botts retorted:

Acts on the island were not acts of war; no war could be found in Mississippi or Kentucky. There was no bloody battle. There was no bloody war. The energy of . . . [the] government prevented that tragical consequence.

On 31 August, Marshall made a lengthy ruling on the arguments presented by both sides, later turning the tide in favor of Burr. Marshall held that if the prosecution had proven with two witnesses that Burr had "procured" or caused the men and material to assemble on the island to launch a revolt, then the necessary overt act could be established. The prosecution had not done this, however. All they had presented at trial was testimony that would "confirm" or "corroborate" such eyewitnesses, but not any eyewitnesses themselves. Therefore, the prosecution's evidence was inadmissible and the jury had to ignore it.

Faced with Marshall's ruling, the jury had no choice. On 1 September, the jury acquitted Burr when it gave its somewhat backhanded verdict that "We of the jury say that Aaron Burr is not proved to be guilty under this indictment by any evidence submitted to us."

Although he was acquitted, the press and public still considered Burr a traitor and his political career was ruined. Burr went to Europe for several years, staying one step ahead of moneylenders who financed his lifestyle, and finally returned to the United States in 1812. He lived out the rest of his life in obscurity, dying a broken man in 1836.

Bibliography and Further Reading

Burr, Aaron. *Reports of the Trials of Colonel Aaron Burr.* New York: Da Capo, 1969 (repr. of 1808 ed.).

Lomask, Milton. *Aaron Burr.* New York: Farrar, Straus & Giroux, 1982.

Nolan, Charles J., Jr. *Aaron Burr and the American Literary Imagination.* Westport: Greenwood, 1980.

Parmet, Herbert S. and Marie B. Hecht. *Aaron Burr: Portrait of an Ambitious Man.* New York: Macmillan, 1967.

Wilson, R. J. "The Founding Father." *New Republic,* June 1983, pp. 25-31.

IN RE NEAGLE

Legal Citation: 135 U.S. 1 (1890)

Plaintiff
Thomas Cunningham, Sheriff of the County of San Joaquin, California

Defendant
David Neagle

Plaintiff's Claim
That in killing Judge David S. Terry, Neagle was merely acting in his capacity as U.S. Marshall, charged with protecting the life of Supreme Court Justice Stephen J. Field, and that Neagle should therefore not be charged with murder.

Chief Lawyers for Plaintiff
California Attorney General G. A. Johnson, Z. Montgomery

Chief Defense Lawyers
Joseph H. Choate; William Henry Harrison Miller, U.S. Attorney General

Justices for the Court
Samuel Blatchford, Joseph P. Bradley, David Josiah Brewer, Horace Gray, John Marshall Harlan I, Samuel Freeman Miller

Justices Dissenting
Melville Weston Fuller, Lucius Quintus C. Lamar (Stephen Johnson Field did not participate)

Place
Washington, D.C.

Date of Decision
1890

Decision
That Neagle was indeed acting in his capacity as U.S. Marshall and was therefore not to be indicted for murder.

Significance
The decision to view Neagle as acting in his capacity as federal marshall, rather than as a candidate for indictment for murder by a state grand jury, was an affirmation of the power of both the federal government and of its executive branch, in whose name Neagle was acting.

At first glance, the story of *In re Neagle* reads like a crime thriller. It has everything: romance, murderous revenge, and a heroic federal marshall who risks his own life to protect a Supreme Court justice. Significantly, however, the case established the power of the federal government to supersede a state's criminal court system and to grant immunity to government officials acting in service of their country.

The first chapter of the story is set in California in 1883. William Sharon, a wealthy citizen of Nevada, sued in federal court in California to nullify his marriage to Sarah Althea Hill. According to Sharon, the marriage contract in Hill's possession was a forgery, and he wanted it back.

Sharon died before the suit was over, but a decision in his favor was handed down after his death. Meanwhile, Hill had fallen in love with David S. Terry, a distinguished lawyer who had once been chief justice of the California Supreme Court.

The Seeds of Vengeance

Sharon's heir still wanted the new Mrs. Terry to give back her marriage contract to Sharon. In 1888 he brought suit to that effect, also in federal court in California. Two local federal judges sat on this court, along with Supreme Court Justice Stephen J. Field. As was the custom in those days, Supreme Court justices also served part of the year as federal court judges.

Field had formerly been an associate justice on the California Supreme Court under Chief Justice Terry. When Terry had left the post of chief justice, Field had succeeded to it. Yet Terry was now to become Field's bitter enemy.

When the three-judge panel, headed by Field, called Mrs. Terry and her husband as a party to the suit, both she and her husband denied that Sharon's heir had any rights. Soon afterward, on 14 August 1888, one of the other judges on the panel found himself on a train leaving Fresno, California, the home of the Terrys. The Terrys "grossly insulted" the judge, according to the account of the case written up by Justice Miller in the Supreme Court decision. Reportedly, Mrs. Terry actually pulled the judge's hair, while Mr. Terry said, "The best thing to do with him would be to take him out into the bay and drown him."

Cartoon showing California judge David S. Terry stabbing S. A. Hopkins. © The Library of Congress/Corbis.

On 3 September 1888, the three-judge panel ruled against Mrs. Terry once again. She shouted at the judge, causing Justice Field to ask the marshall to remove her from the courtroom.

> [Mr. Terry] . . . struck the marshall a blow in his face so violent as to knock out a tooth. He then unbuttoned his coat, thrust his hand under his vest, apparently for the purpose of drawing a bowie-knife, when he was seized by persons present and forced down on his back.

Mr. Terry did eventually draw a bowie knife, so that others had to wrestle it away from him. "The most prominent person engaged in wresting the knife from Terry," wrote Justice Miller, "was Neagle . . ." Meanwhile, Mrs. Terry was trying to open a small satchel that she had with her. When the satchel was taken from her, it was found to contain a revolver.

Murder or Duty?

Both Mr. and Mrs. Terry were sentenced to imprisonment for contempt. From then on, they were frequently heard to make open threats against Justice Field. The threats seemed so genuine that when Field was planning to return to California to resume his duties as Circuit Court Judge, David Neagle was appointed a deputy marshall for the Northern District of California and was assigned to protect Justice Field.

One early morning, while Field's train had stopped at Fresno, the Terrys boarded the train. Although Neagle suggested to Justice Field that he have breakfast in his own sleeping car, Field insisted on going to eat in the regular breakfast car. When the Terrys entered the car, Mrs. Terry saw Field and ran quickly out of the room. Terry, on the contrary, took his seat. Soon, however, he came to stand behind Field and began to beat him on both sides of his face. As Miller described it:

> He also had his arm drawn back and his fist doubled up, apparently to strike a third blow, when Neagle, who had been observing him all this time, arose from his seat with his revolver in his hand, and in a very loud voice shouted out: "Stop! Stop! I am an officer!" Upon this Terry turned his attention to Neagle, and, as Neagle testifies, seemed to recognize him, and immediately turned his hand to thrust it in his bosom, as Neagle felt sure, with the purpose of drawing a bowie-knife. At this instant Neagle fired two shots from his revolver into the body of Terry, who immediately sank down and died in a few minutes.

Immediately afterwards, Mrs. Terry rushed in, her satchel in her hand. She threw herself on Terry's body—some say, to remove his bowie knife, for when Terry was later examined, he was found to be unarmed.

The "Peace of the United States"

Neagle was jailed for murder and feared what might happen to him in a community dominated by the Terrys' friends. He was able to obtain a writ of *habeas corpus*—perhaps because the judge who issued it, Lorenzo Sawyer, was the same judge who had been harassed and threatened by the Terrys in an earlier incident on a train.

With the writ, Neagle was freed, but he still faced the possibility of a murder trial. The sheriff in the jurisdiction where he had killed Terry appealed to the Supreme Court for the return of the prisoner. The question was whether Neagle was liable for murder—however justified—under the laws of the state of California, or if was he acting in his capacity as federal marshall, and therefore subject only to federal law. (Laws about murder are always state laws.)

The Supreme Court ruled in favor of the man who had evidently saved the life of one of its members. Miller explained:

> It would be a great reproach to the system of government of the United States, declared to be within its sphere sovereign and supreme, if there is to be found within the domain of its powers no means of protecting the judges, in the conscientious and faithful discharge of their duties, from the malice and hatred of those upon whom their judgments may operate unfavorably . . .

Miller went on to compare Deputy Marshal Neagle with a sheriff. Just as a sheriff is charged with keeping the peace of a state, he wrote, so must a marshall keep the peace of the nation. In protecting a federal judge, Neagle had fulfilled his responsibilities as a U.S. marshall.

Two justices did dissent from this opinion. They objected to the intrusion of federal power into the hitherto sacred domain of state criminal law. However, even these dissenters praised Neagle for his courage and quick thinking, and expressed their belief that even if he had been tried, a jury surely would have acquitted him.

Related Cases

Ex Parte Grossman, 267 U.S. 87 (1925).

Schick v. Reed, 419 U.S. 256 (1974).

Bibliography and Further Reading

Epstein, Lee, and Thomas G. Walker. *Constitutional Law for a Changing America: Institutional Powers and Constraints,* 3rd ed. Washington DC: Congressional Quarterly, 1998.

Fairman, Charles. *History of the Supreme Court of the United States, Vol. VII, Reconstruction and Reunion, 1864-1888.* New York: Macmillan, 1987.

Hall, Kermit L., ed. *Oxford Companion to the Supreme Court of the United States.* New York: Oxford University Press, 1992.

Williams, Jerre S. *The Supreme Court Speaks.* Freeport, NY: Books for Libraries Press, 1956, 1970.

ZEMEL V. RUSK

Legal Citation: 228 F. Supp 65 (D.C.D. Conn 1964)

Plaintiff
Louis Zemel

Defendants
Dean Rusk, U.S. Secretary of State; Robert F. Kennedy, U.S. Attorney General

Plaintiff's Claim
That it is unconstitutional for the secretary of state and attorney general to limit the location of travel of a citizen of the United States.

Chief Lawyer for Plaintiff
Leonard B. Boudin

Chief Defense Lawyer
Benjamin C. Flannagan

Judges
J. Joseph Smith, Circuit Judge; District Judge Claire; District Judge Blumenfeld

Place
U.S. District Court, District of Connecticut

Date of Decision
20 February 1964

Decision
That restrictions to travel, if made in a nondiscriminatory fashion, were valid in the interests of national security.

Significance
The district court upheld, and the Supreme Court later declined to rehear, a lower court order that declared it is within the jurisdiction of the secretary of state and the attorney general to impose restrictions on travel that are declared by the president of the United States. The Passport Act of 1926 and Immigration and Nationality Act of 1952 were upheld as constitutional.

The plaintiff, a citizen of the United States residing within the judicial district of Connecticut, brought action against U.S. Secretary of State Dean Rusk and U.S. Attorney General Robert F. Kennedy for a declaratory judgment to enjoin the enforcement and execution of two acts of Congress, namely, the Passport Act of 1926 and the Immigration and Nationality Act of 1952, both of which the plaintiff claimed were repugnant to the Constitution. Jurisdiction of the Court was invoked and a three-judge court was convened to hear the constitutional questions in issue.

On 31 March 1962, while the plaintiff was the holder of a valid U.S. passport of standard form and duration, he applied by letter to the director of the Passport Office at Washington, D.C. for permission to have his passport validated for travel to Cuba as a tourist. The Passport Office denied him the permission requested, with the explanation that only persons whose travel might be in the best interests of the United States, such as newsreporters and businesspeople with previously established interests, could be eligible; and specifically that tourist travel was excluded. Thereafter, on 1 May 1962, the petitioner requested a hearing on his application without reciting any new reason, except that he felt justified in wanting to make the trip. He was sent a copy of the current administrative procedures of the Passport Office and was advised that in those instances where foreign travel was restricted and generally applicable to everyone, no administrative procedures for review or appeal were provided. Repeated attempts by the petitioner and his attorney failed to secure him permission to travel to Cuba.

It was the plaintiff's contention that the Passport Act of 1926 did not authorize the action taken, and that the acts were unconstitutional, because they interfered with the rights of a citizen: the right to travel under the Fifth, Ninth and Tenth Amendments, the right to the freedom of speech, belief and association under the First Amendment. Moreover, it was an arbitrary and unreasonable denial of due process under the Fifth Amendment. The plaintiff also argued that it was an invalid delegation of legislative power because it did not contain adequate standards and safeguards.

The plaintiff asked for a declaratory judgment and an injunction decreeing that the Immigration and Nationality Act of 1953 and the Passport Act of 1926 were unconstitutional, and that the secretary of state's regulations restricting travel to Cuba were thus without any authority in law.

The court maintained that this was truly a substantial constitutional challenge to the sovereignty of the nation. The plaintiff's effort to enjoin the secretary of state from enforcing the statutory law and its attendant regulations was not merely the simple and seemingly harmless application of a lone tourist. It was in fact a pilot case precedent which, if sustained, would open up an immediate thoroughfare for unrestricted travel between the United States and Cuba. Such an act of judicial audacity would not only defeat the clear intention of Congress as established by law, but also strike down the declared foreign policy of the executive branch of the national government.

The issue in this case was whether or not geographical passport restrictions imposed by the secretary of state with respect to travel to Cuba were authorized by congressional act and if so, whether those statutes which purport to grant such authority were repugnant to constitutional limitations. It was the court's finding that Congress had granted adequate authority to the executive department to make these regulations, that their application in this instance did not violate due process, and that the statutes which authorized the regulations were valid and constitutional.

Passport control was not designed solely to protect internal security. So many phases of internal security are intertwined with foreign affairs in the administration of passport control that the two become inseparable. It is one where Congress legislates broad laneways of authority to the executive, within which he or she must exercise his or her discretion in effectively administering that authority in a fast changing climate of world affairs. Congress established, by law, the president's right to regulate and control passport visas within broad bounds of executive discretion. There has been no claim of arbitrariness in the administration of these regulations. No passport holder has claimed to have been denied because of personal beliefs, writings, character, race, religion or the like. It does in fact bar the travel of all Americans to a specific geographical area.

In both times of war and upon the declaration by the president of a national emergency, these restrictions on travel departure and entry may be imposed. The time or term of their application is limited until the president or Congress shall otherwise order. All of the conditions established by law for the exercise of the power were therefore fulfilled.

Related Cases
Kent v. Dulles, 357 U.S. 116 (1958).
Aptheker v. Secretary of State, 378 U.S. 500 (1964).

Bibliography and Further Reading
Biskupic, Joan and Elder Witt. *Congressional Quarterly's Guide to the U.S. Supreme Court,* 3rd ed. Washington, DC: Congressional Quarterly, Inc., 1996.

Hall, Kermit, ed. *The Oxford Companion to the Supreme Court.* New York: Oxford University Press, p. 43.

NATIVE AMERICANS

Tribal Governance

Contemporary federal court decisions, statutes, and presidential statements often provide strong support for tribal self-government. According to U.S. judicial doctrine, for example, tribal legal regimes survive as manifestations of indigenous sovereign powers, rather than as creations of federal law. In keeping with this notion, the Bill of Rights of the Constitution does not apply to actions of tribal governments because the first ten amendments to the Constitution bind only the federal government and its agencies, not independent sovereigns such as Indian nations. Furthermore, a criminal defendant can be convicted for the same crime in federal and tribal court without being placed in double jeopardy, because the protection against double jeopardy in the U.S. Constitution does not apply to situations where a person is convicted for the same crime by two separate sovereigns.

If Native American tribes are not federal agencies, however, neither are they mere voluntary associations, like private clubs, whose powers are limited to admitting and excluding members. Instead, they are governing bodies with the power to direct and coerce individuals engaged in activities within their territory, more like cities and states. The U.S. Supreme Court has affirmed, for example, that tribes may impose taxes on activities by Native Americans and non-Native Americans alike in Indian Country.

The Supreme Court has also tried to place some limits on tribes' sovereign powers, particularly where non-Native Americans or Native Americans who are members of other tribes are involved. Finding that the incorporation of tribes into the United States necessarily reduced the scope of tribal powers, the Supreme Court has held that tribal sovereignty does not include the power to engage in foreign relations, to wage war, to alienate (transfer an ownership interest in) tribal land, or to impose criminal punishments on non-members of the tribe. The Court has also restricted the power of tribes to regulate the activities of non-members on land that is owned by non-members but is located within the reservation, at least if those activities have no substantial bearing on the health or well-being of tribal members. These determinations by the Supreme Court are judge-made law, drawing on the history and practices of federal Native American law, but not directly tied to language of the U.S. Constitution or specific federal statutes. Consequently, the Court ordinarily acknowledges in its decisions limiting tribal powers that Congress can restore those powers by enacting legislation that offers a contrary interpretation of the history and practice.

Monitoring Government Interference

In order to make tribal sovereignty more meaningful, the U.S. Supreme Court has had to reject efforts by states and local governments to regulate activities in Indian Country. Like any other government, a tribe must be free to make choices about matters such as environmental quality, family life, and economic organization without outside interference. The Supreme Court has been emphatic that states lack authority over Native Americans on reservations, but it has been less clear about state authority over non-Native Americans. Particularly in situations where non-Native Americans engage in activity on non-Native American owned land, the federal government has not shown a preference for tribal authority; where the tribe has not attempted to regulate the activity at issue, where tribal interests will not be seriously compromised, and where the activity jeopardized off-reservation interests, the Supreme Court has shown some inclination to permit state power over non-Native Americans on reservations. For example, the Court has upheld state sales taxes on non-Native American purchasers of cigarettes that are sold by tribal smokeshops on reservations, even though tribal members who purchase the same cigarettes cannot be taxed by the state. The Court has also affirmed state power to zone parts of reservations that are owned by non-Native Americans and that have been opened to the public. The Court has not, however, allowed states to regulate certain gambling on Native American lands, at least where the revenue from gambling funds important tribal functions, and where the state does not totally prohibit that type of gambling off the reservation.

By making the issue of tribal versus state authority on reservations turn, in part, on questions of who owns the land and who is being regulated, the Supreme Court has made it difficult to govern Indian Country. Many tribes complain that unless they have complete control over the territory of their reservations, they cannot effectively regulate air and water pollution, raise revenue through taxes, guide economic development, or provide for child welfare. Furthermore, uncertainty concerning which government has jurisdiction has led to costly litigation. Increasingly, states and tribes have found it in their mutual interest to negotiate and agree about the allocation of power to regulate reservation activities. Furthermore, because Congress has the power to override Supreme Court decisions determining state and tribal authority over Native Americans or non-Native Americans in Indian Country, states and tribes sometimes appeal to Congress to make an allocation. Congress took such action in 1988, when it enacted the Indian Gaming Regulatory Act. This statute established a complex scheme of tribal and state jurisdiction over different types of gambling on reservations.

Support for Tribal Sovereignty

In recent decades, Congress, like the Supreme Court, has often recognized and supported tribal sovereignty. Since the 1960s self-determination for Native American tribes has been the official federal policy, as is reflected in numerous pieces of congressional legislation. In 1975, for example, Congress enacted the Indian Self-Determination and Education Assistance Act. This statute authorizes federal agencies providing services to Native Americans to contract with tribes so that the tribes can deliver the services themselves. The purpose of this statute was to liberate Native American tribes from some of the bureaucratic control exercised by the Bureau of Indian Affairs. Another congressional affirmation of tribal sovereignty is the Indian Child Welfare Act of 1978. This statute requires that cases involving foster care and adoptive placement of Native American children be heard in tribal rather than state courts when the children are living or have their permanent home on the reservation. Even in some cases where the Native American children live off-reservation, the Indian Child Welfare Act requires that the cases be transferred from state to tribal court. This act affirms both the value of tribal courts and the importance to Native American tribes of controlling the fate of their children when those children must be separated from their parents. Support for tribal sovereignty is also apparent in various federal environmental laws, such as the Clean Air Act and the Clean Water Act, that accord tribes the same status as states in implementing their regulatory schemes. Finally, Congress reinforced tribal sovereignty in 1991 when it adopted a statute affirming tribal criminal jurisdiction over non-member Native Americans, overriding an earlier ruling to the contrary by the United States Supreme Court.

Statements of the president of the United States, especially since the 1970s, have declared support for tribal sovereignty as well. The most memorable phrase from these presidential statements recognizes a "government-to-government" relationship between the United States and the Native American tribes. This language cautions the other branches of government that Native American tribes should be treated with the respect due other governmental entities.

Treaty-making before 1871

From 1776 to 1871, the United States made more than 400 treaties with Native American tribes, and nearly all of them were ratified by the Senate in the same manner as treaties with foreign nations. American expansion encountered varying levels of resistance, from guerrilla warfare in the swamps of Florida to great cavalry battles on the plains in the 1860s. In some instances, the government simply used treaties to create the appearance of legality for what was actually a confiscation of land at gunpoint. In other parts of the country, treaties were part of a long process of diplomacy, accommodation, and confrontation that lasted for decades. Some treaties were very strong, others weak, and each must be understood in the context of the time and circumstances in which it was made.

Until the 1820s, the United States was preoccupied with securing its borders with Native American tribes. This was not motivated by Christian morality as much as by the need to legitimize the new American state in the eyes of European powers; to establish superior American claims to the Great Lakes, the Mississippi valley, and Florida, which were also claimed by Britain, France, and Spain; and to create peaceful conditions for the development of its existing settlements still east of the Appalachian Mountains.

During the Revolutionary War itself, the new American government negotiated treaties of alliance with the Wabanaki confederacy and with the tribes of the Ohio River valley. Once peace had been restored by the Treaty of Paris in 1783, American diplomats entered into alliances with the Haudenosaunee and with the southern confederacy of Cherokee, Creek, Choctaw, and Chicksaw, hoping to secure a safe, pro-American frontier. In the treaties of this period, tribes simply accepted U.S. "protection" and U.S. authority to regulate Native American trade. In other words, they agreed to be included in a new American sphere of influence. Apart from trade issues, however, they gave up none of their right to self-government, as the U.S. Supreme Court concluded in its famous 1832 decision, *Worcester v. Georgia*.

The Haudenosaunee and Ohio valley nations also continued to renew their treaties with Britain, however. As far as they were concerned, everything west of the Appalachians was still Indian Country; the U.S.-

Canadian border did not extend into that region. American settlements west of the Appalachians led to a great uprising under Tecumseh, which coincided with the War of 1812. Once again, tribes fought on both sides, and their future was a major issue at the peace negotiations. The Treaty of Ghent (1814) made it clear that the U.S.-Canadian border did indeed divide Indian Country, and that only the U.S. could make treaties with the tribes south of that line.

The Treaty of Ghent secured the northern border of the States, while the U.S. purchase of Florida and Louisiana eliminated competition for tribal alliances with France and Spain as far west as the Mississippi. American diplomacy shifted from securing peace to acquiring lands for settlement, chiefly from tribes already under U.S. protection, between the Appalachian crest and the Mississippi. At first, tribes attempted to keep some of their main villages and farmland, selling only small parcels on the fringes of their territories. Beginning in the 1830s, however, the U.S. aimed for their complete "removal." To acquire lands for the relocation of eastern nations such as the Cherokee and Delaware, the U.S. made treaties with tribes west of the Mississippi, such as the Osage and Comanche. Treaties with the eastern tribes worked out the details of their move, which included the sale of their homelands to help pay for expenses, and for the development of new schools, farms, and roads in the west. Needless to say, many eastern tribes resisted, and those who left their homes did so only to avoid war.

American leaders still believed that the plains were economically worthless, and did not hesitate to promise the removed tribes that they would enjoy security and self-government in their new western homes forever. The U.S. even pledged that this western "Indian Territory" would remain exclusively Native American and would never be included within any state. At the same time, these removal treaties involved the U.S. more directly in internal tribal affairs than ever before. After arranging for the sale of the tribes' homelands, federal officials spent the proceeds on education, health, and social programs, as specified by each treaty. The federal government became a banker for removed tribes under these treaties. In legal terms, it became a trustee, managing tribal funds and property.

By the 1840s, American settlements had begun on the Pacific coast and on the edges of the Great Plains. Mexico had won its independence from Spain, and was viewed as the main obstacle to American expansion. In the Mexican War, the U.S. seized all Mexican territory north of the Rio Grande, and quickly made treaties with the largest nomadic Native American tribes of the Southwest—the Navajo, Apache, and Ute—to secure the new international border. In the ten years following the Mexican War, the U.S. made treaties for the first time with the tribes of the West Coast, from California to Washington, although the Senate never ratified Cal-

ifornia treaties and some Oregon treaties. The Puget Sound (Washington State) treaties were particularly important for U.S. policy, because they helped settle the western border between the U.S. and British North America (Canada), a border so hotly disputed that it almost led to a third British-American war in 1854. Small and chiefly dependent on fishing, West Coast tribes generally agreed to cede most of their lands in exchange for the protection of their fishing rights.

Native American treaties made after the Mexican War contained some crucial new provisions, reflecting the growing military power and expansionism of Euro-Americans. Instead of merely accepting U.S. "protection," the Southwest and West Coast tribes agreed to "submit" to federal laws or regulations concerning Native Americans. Never before had the U.S. tried to extend its legislative power to Native Americans inside Native American territory. In a growing number of treaties in the 1850s, moreover, tribes agreed that the president could take land for roads and railroads, and divide the remaining Native American land into individual family farms ("allotments"). Any land left over was to be sold to pay for farming equipment, schools, and hospitals, which would be managed by the Office of Indian Affairs. Some tribal leaders believed that individualizing land ownership would give Native Americans stronger legal rights to keep their lands. Others simply felt they had no choice but to accept these new conditions. Allotment was carried out chiefly in Iowa, Kansas, Nebraska, and other valuable farming areas on the fringes of the Great Plains, where settlers created the greatest pressure. Most tribes of the desert and West Coast were not allotted, although their treaties authorized allotment. These tribes had little good farmland, and settlers in their regions were more interested in mining, logging and fishing.

By 1860, then, the U.S. employed treaties to establish total social programs under federal administration, which were aimed at "civilizing" Native Americans and assimilating them into the general population. Tribal territories became "reservations," and tribal laws were subject to federal laws. But these treaty provisions did not apply everywhere. An exception to this trend was the Indian Territory (Oklahoma), where removal treaties expressly guaranteed the right of tribes to complete self-government. These tribes observed the changes surrounding them—particularly the growing tide of settlers in Texas, Colorado and New Mexico—with alarm. When the first shots of the Civil War were fired at Fort Sumter, most tribes in the Indian Territory shifted their allegiances to the South. Treaties with the Confederate States of America, concluded in 1861, guaranteed the permanent independence of the Native American nations, were the South to win the war. As in the Revolutionary War and the War of 1812, then, Native American tribes fought on both sides to fulfill their treaty obligations.

As a result of the Union's victory in 1865, Oklahoma tribes, like the South itself, were forced to sign surrenders and to undergo the federally supervised "reconstruction" of their economies and political systems. Former slaves became tribal members under many of these treaties, and had the right to take shares of tribal lands and funds. On the whole, the U.S. renewed its old treaty commitments to tribal self-government in the Indian Territory, but subjected the tribal councils to special federal "governors" or Native American agents, or to a federal veto over their laws. This made tribes such as the Cherokee and Chickasaw more like present-day Puerto Rico or the Virgin Islands: partly self-governing, but still within the U.S. political system.

The Sioux of Minnesota and Dakota, together with allied tribes as far south as Colorado, also launched an offensive against encroaching settlements from 1864 to 1865. Although the Minnesota Sioux fared badly, and their leaders were hanged by President Lincoln, the plains war continued until 1868. Anxious to acquire additional lands on the plains for the resettlement of Civil War veterans and the post-war flood of European immigrants, the U.S. made more treaties and purchased more Native American land in the period between 1865 and 1868 than it previously had during any comparable period. At the same time, U.S. negotiators were forced to give the main plains tribes stronger assurances of the finality and permanence of their new reservation borders. In particular, the U.S. agreed that no more Native American land could be sold or opened for settlement, except with the approval of three-fourths of the adult men of the tribe. Tribal leaders hoped this would prevent the U.S. from trying to make future "treaties" with a handful of friendly individuals who did not represent the whole tribe.

Congressional Control after 1871

At the end of the treaty era, Native American tribes still controlled one-tenth of the contiguous 48 states, or about one-fourth of the land between the Mississippi and the Rocky Mountains. Immigration from Europe accelerated, however, reaching its peak in the 1880s. The Indian Territory, and the large plains reservations, posed barriers to further settlement, but were protected by strong treaties, under which the U.S. had promised to provide the tribes with substantial financial aid for their development. Further allotment was impossible under the final round of plains treaties, and tribes were unwilling to part with any more of their reservations. Concerned by the increasing costs and difficulties of negotiating for more Native American land, Congress ordered the president to stop making Native American treaties in 1871.

This did not stop the president from making "agreements" with the tribes for their land, usually at the request of Congress. Agreements made after 1871 were essentially the same as treaties, except they did not imply that Native American tribes were independent nations. Often, they were made with tribal leaders chosen by the U.S., in violation of the tribes' own political processes, or in violation of the tribes' earlier treaties. The 1874 agreement for the purchase of the gold-rich Black Hills of South Dakota was typical. The 1874 agreement was negotiated with a few individual Sioux, although the 1868 Sioux treaty required the approval of three-fourths of the men of the tribe. Congress then passed a law ruling that the agreement overrode the treaty. The Sioux went to war over this – the war in which Custer fell – but the U.S. had the military power to wear down Sioux resistance and hold onto the Black Hills.

At the same time, the U.S. began to build railways through tribal lands in violation of treaties, and to establish federally controlled Native American courts and police on the reservations in order to enforce federal laws. Many of these laws were designed to destroy Native American culture rather than to protect Native Americans from settlers; one such example is a provision prohibiting any kind of traditional religious ceremonies, or "medicine men." In 1887, Congress passed the Dawes Severalty Act (General Allotment Act), which authorized allotments and the sale of "surplus" lands on those reservations where the tribes had not already agreed to this by treaty. A separate law, the Curtis Act, provided for the allotment of the Indian Territory as well. The Oklahoma tribes vigorously opposed this as a violation of their treaties, and they brought their objections to the U.S. Supreme Court. In two crucial decisions, *Cherokee Nation v. Hitchcock* (1902) and *Lone Wolf v. Hitchcock* (1903), the Supreme Court held that Congress has the power to modify or terminate Native American treaties without the Native Americans' consent.

This opened the way for Congress to treat all Native Americans the same, regardless of the treaties they have signed. Throughout the nineteenth century, Congress appropriated funds for Native American schools, hospitals, and other programs treaty-by-treaty. Treaties determined how much federal aid each tribe received, and how it was used. In 1921, the Snyder Act abolished this practice. All services and programs were combined into a single annual appropriation, broken down by objects (such as "health care") rather than by treaties. As a result, Native American tribes with weak treaties got more than they had bargained for, and tribes with strong treaties got less. More importantly, tribes could no longer use their treaties to demand any services at all. The Snyder Act and subsequent federal laws left Native American social programs to the discretion of Congress. After purchasing most of the country by treaty, the U.S. was no longer willing to pay the agreed price.

In the final days of World War II, in fact, Congress decided that it was time to "wind up" the Native American business. Many believed that Native Americans stayed on reservations only because they expected to be repaid someday for all of their broken treaties. This led Congress to establish the Indian Claims Commission in 1946. Although the commission was supposed to complete its work in ten years, it was still not finished when Congress decided to reassign its cases to the U.S. Court of Claims in 1978. The commission was not given the power to enforce Native American treaties, only to decide how much compensation each tribe should receive for broken promises. The Commission adopted a general rule of taking the value of the land or money promised to tribes a century ago, and adding interest. For example, if the U.S. had promised to set aside a reservation in 1868, and the land could have been sold for $1,000 in 1868, the tribe was awarded $1,000 plus interest from 1868. Land values were artificially low in the nineteenth century, however, since Native American tribes were being forced to give up so much of it, creating a temporary market surplus. Thus tracts worth billions today, like the Black Hills, were valued at 1 percent of their current price; with interest, this figure increased to about 10 percent. If tribal land had been taken without a treaty, moreover, the commission did not add the interest.

In House Concurrent Resolution 108 (1953), Congress declared its goal of terminating federal responsibilities for Native Americans as quickly as possible, and of making Native Americans ordinary citizens of the states. This "termination" program was very selective, targeted at tribes who were relatively prosperous and well-educated, such as the Menominee of Wisconsin and Klamath of Oregon. Congress assumed that "termination" not only ended tribes' eligibility for special Native American social programs, but also abolished (or "abrogated") their treaties. A 1968 Supreme Court decision involving the Menominee disagreed. Native American treaties continue in effect unless expressly abrogated by Congress, the Court explained. Since Congress had not specifically mentioned the Menominee treaty in its legislation "terminating" the tribe, Menominee treaty rights, such as hunting and fishing rights, could still be exercised by the members of the tribe. This decision paved the way for federal court decisions in the 1970s, reaffirming Native American treaty rights that both Congress and the States had believed to be extinct.

The decade from 1968 to 1978 was critical for the development of Native American treaty law. President Nixon declared an end to the termination policy of House Concurrent Resolution 108, and made a clear commitment to restoring and strengthening tribal self-government. Federal courts in Oregon and Washington handed Northwest tribes stunning victories in treaty fishing-rights disputes. Despite years of violence and efforts to overturn these decisions legislatively, both the Supreme Court and Congress eventually upheld them. On the other hand, Congress imposed a land-claims settlement on Alaska in 1971, which was intended to end tribal self-government in that state. In 1978, furthermore, the Bureau of Indian Affairs adopted rules for deciding which tribes are "recognized as eligible to receive federal services," and treaties were not mentioned as having any role in these decisions. The decade ended, as it began, with a surprise decision by the Supreme Court. In *Oliphant v. Suquamish Indian Tribe* (1978), the Court held that tribal rights may be lost by "implication," even rights that were never given up by treaty or taken away by Congress.

As the 1970s ended, then, there were signs of greater respect for Native American treaty rights, although Congress, the president, and the courts reserved their power to disregard treaties. The fishing-rights cases had demonstrated that at least some provisions in treaties could still have considerable economic significance. At the same time, the major Native American policy issues of the 1970s and 1980s—education, health, better resource management, and stronger tribal governments—were being addressed through a growing number of federal aid programs, rather than through the enforcement of treaties.

Indian Reorganization Act as a Springboard

Despite the often undermining influence of federal law, derivations of the earliest encountered Native American legal systems continue to function today in land set aside under federal protection for the residence of tribal Native Americans and in other areas collectively described in federal law as "Indian Country." Native American legal regimes have been transformed after years of contact with non-Native American law and culture, so that the formal institutions more closely resemble U.S. courts, legislative bodies, and regulatory apparatus; the formal rules of everyday conduct, too, codified in ordinances, more closely parallel U.S. norms. On some reservations, for example, there are tribal environmental protection agencies that regulate pollution, and tribal taxing authorities that levy and collect taxes.

Much of this transformation of tribal governments has occurred as a result of the Indian Reorganization Act of 1934, a federal statute that offered tribes some freedom from federal bureaucratic control if they would organize themselves under constitutions modeled after the U.S. Constitution. The Indian Reorganization Act provided that tribal members could take a vote on whether to accept its terms, and about three-fourths of the tribes that held referenda agreed to develop tribal constitutions under the act. The federal rules setting forth who could vote and how many votes were needed to accept the act did not always produce results that reflected the general wishes of tribal communities. Nonetheless, constitutions stimulated by the Indian Reorganization Act continue to prevail on many reservations. Some Native American nations, like the Navajo, preferred to develop their governing systems independent of the act; nothing in the act prevented them from doing so.

The protections of individual rights found in amendments to the U.S. Constitution do not apply to modern tribal governments, because those constitutional provisions control only activities of the federal government and of the states. However, a federal statute enacted in 1968, known as the Indian Civil Rights Act, limits the punishments that tribal courts may impose, and requires that tribal legal institutions comply with some, but not all, of the provisions of the Bill of Rights in the U.S. Constitution. For example, the federal constitutional prohibition against the establishment of religion and the federal requirement that criminal defendants be provided with free counsel do not apply to Native American tribes through the Indian Civil Rights Act. The reason for these and other exceptions was Congress' desire to preserve distinctive features of tribal cultures and to protect tribes against financially burdensome requirements that they could not reasonably fulfill. Furthermore, even when the Indian Civil Rights Act does incorporate provisions of the Bill of Rights, those requirements are interpreted, wherever possible, to accommodate the special features of tribal cultures. Thus, for example, the requirement of equal protection of the laws in the Indian Civil Rights Act uses the same language as a comparable Constitution. Equality, however, does not necessarily mean the same thing for the tribes as it does for the federal or state governments; one such example is when the issue is whether an Native American tribe may exclude non-Native Americans from juries or from voting in tribal elections.

Out of respect for tribal sovereignty, Congress generally provided that when an individual wants to challenge tribal actions as contrary to the terms of the Indian Civil Rights Act, she or he must do so in tribal court. There is no recourse to a federal court to enforce the Indian Civil Rights Act unless the individual is in a position to bring a petition for a writ of *habeas corpus* (a claim that she or he is being held in custody in violation of law). Normally this writ is only available to criminal defendants who have been convicted in tribal courts and who claim that their convictions were obtained without adherence to the Indian Civil Rights Act (for example, if evidence was improperly seized or if the criminal statute used as the basis for conviction violated the right to free speech).

Some tribes have protection for individual rights built into their own constitutions and fundamental laws. The Navajo, for example, have their own require-

ment that individuals be afforded due process of law if the government is acting to deprive them of life, liberty, or property. Thus, an individual who is unhappy with the actions of the tribal government can appeal to tribal law as well as to the Indian Civil Rights Act for redress. The Indian Civil Rights Act has been controversial among Native American people because it can be used to erode distinctive tribal cultures and legal systems, especially when those systems reflect values favoring informality, communal belonging and responsibility, and decision-making by consensus (universal agreement) rather than majority rule. As tribal governments have become more like the non-Native American U.S. government, however, it is possible that a corresponding need for the protection of individual rights has arisen.

Federal measures such as the Indian Reorganization Act and the Indian Civil Rights Act have put great pressure on tribal governments to conform to U.S. institutions. Nonetheless, tribal legal systems still have some distinctive features. First, informal traditional institutions and norms persist amidst the more formal legal systems. In some tribes, for example, religious leaders oversee dispute resolution despite the existence of tribal courts, and clan-based local groups control policy-making despite the existence of a centralized tribal council. Second, the values and procedures that are reflected in even formal tribal law sometimes differ from those embodied in U.S. law. Navajo inheritance law, for example, recognizes oral wills and prefers individuals who have cared for the deceased in his or her final years; American law does not. Also, many tribal legal systems reject the separation of powers and judicial review that are so fundamental to U.S. law. Some distinctive qualities of Native American justice, such as the emphasis on restitution to victims in criminal cases and special sensitivity to the interests of grandparents in child custody disputes, are finding a receptive audience among non-Native Americans today.

Thus, despite European and American claims to conquest and dominion over Native American lands and peoples, Native American law and government have not been extinguished. Tribal legal institutions perform important functions of defining tribal membership and office-holding requirements, regulating the use of tribal resources, establishing rules for everyday conduct, and resolving disputes. However, because of their different traditions and values, lack of resources, and the need to reconcile American and Native American forms, tribal governments need not and do not always behave like their non-Native American counterparts.

Jurisdiction of U.S. Government

The U.S. Congress asserts the right to define and limit, indeed to abolish, tribal law and government. It rests this power on Article I of the Constitution, which authorizes Congress to regulate commerce "with the Native American tribes," to enter into treaties, to make war, and to exercise power over federal lands. Congress and the Supreme Court sometimes justify federal power by invoking the existence of a federal guardianship toward the Native Americans, which resulted from the weakening of tribal governments by historic U.S. policy. Many Native American groups and modern legal scholars do not accept the federal government's understanding of the scope of congressional power over Native American affairs. Adopting a narrow interpretation of the Indian Commerce Clause, they would limit that federal power to the regulation of trade and commerce between Native Americans and non-Native Americans, excluding all internal tribal matters. Whatever the source and scope of Congress' power, however, all agree that it excludes overlapping state authority in Indian Country. The Supreme Court has acknowledged state authority over Native American affairs only in isolated instances involving non-Native Americans and where the exercise of state power would not thwart tribal self-government.

Exercising its powers, Congress has enacted criminal laws that apply to Native American/non-Native American crimes and specified "major" crimes in Indian Country, has made certain state laws applicable in Indian Country in some states, has restricted the sale or lease of tribally-owned lands, has regulated trading and the sale of liquor in Indian Country, has required that tribal governments afford individuals some of the civil rights enumerated in the Bill of Rights, and has even terminated the legal status of some tribes. Most of Congress' laws affecting Native Americans can be found in Title 25 of the United States Code, which compiles all Congressional enactments relating to Native Americans. These statutes indicate the range of Native American groups to which they apply by the way they define the term "tribe." Some definitions—such as in the portion of the Non-Intercourse Act prohibiting transfers of Native American land without federal permission—are quite broad. Others are narrower, limiting the application of federal law to tribes that have been officially recognized by the Department of the Interior as generally entitled to federal benefits.

Because of its power of judicial review, the U.S. Supreme Court can set limits on Congressional power respecting tribal law and government. It has largely declined to do so. In the nineteenth century, the Court described congressional power as all-encompassing, or

"plenary," and dismissed challenges to particular federal actions as entailing "political questions" unsuitable for judicial resolution. On these bases, the Court rejected Native American suits protesting the forcible break-up of communal tribal lands in violation of specific treaty promises.

Modern Supreme Court doctrine acknowledges more room for judicial intervention. First, any federal action that might impair Native American rights must be interpreted in the manner most favorable to the Native Americans. This rule of statutory interpretation prevents Congress from diminishing Native American self-government or treaty rights unless it is quite explicit about its intent to do so. Thus, for example, certain federal criminal laws that prohibit the killing of wildlife are not applied to Native Americans with treaty rights to hunt those particular animals or to use them for ritual purposes, because the laws do not contain language that denies the Native Americans' rights. Second, federal law that operates to deny Native Americans their property must be accompanied by the payment of "just compensation" in accordance with the Fifth Amendment to the Constitution, at least if that property has been recognized by the federal government through treaty or by statute. Third, congressional action regarding Native Americans and tribes can be challenged under the Due Process Clause of the Fifth Amendment if it does not rationally further the federal government's fiduciary relationship (a relationship founded in trust) toward the Native Americans. Although the Supreme Court has never actually used this language to reject an act of Congress, it has invoked the same principle to invalidate actions by federal administrative agencies that adversely affect Native American interests. If, for example, the federal agencies that must approve leases of Native American lands and minerals do not carefully oversee compliance with the lease provisions by the lessees, or the federal agencies responsible for investing Native American trust funds do not invest the funds prudently, Native American tribes may sue the federal government for breach of trust.

Bibliography and Further Reading

Malinowski, Sharon, and Anna Sheets, eds. *The Gale Encyclopedia of Native American Tribes.* Detroit: Gale Research, Inc., 1998.

Thornton, Russell. *American Indian Holocaust and Survival: A Population History Since 1492.* Norman, OK: University of Oklahoma Press, 1990.

JOHNSON V. MCINTOSH

Legal Citation: 21 U.S. 543 (1823)

Appellants
Johnson, Graham

Appellee
William McIntosh

Appellants' Claim
That title to land purchased by private individuals directly from Indian tribes is entitled to recognition by the United States.

Chief Lawyers for Appellants
Harper, Webster

Chief Lawyers for Appellee
Winder, Murray

Justices for the Court
Gabriel Duvall, William Johnson, John Marshall (writing for the Court), Joseph Story, Smith Thompson, Thomas Todd, Bushrod Washington

Justices Dissenting
None

Place
Washington, D.C.

Date of Decision
February term, 1823

Decision
The Court upheld McIntosh's claim and affirmed the lower court's decision denying U.S. recognition of land title purchased from Indian tribes by individuals.

Significance
The landmark ruling reaffirmed the legal basis by which the United States established its land base. In this decision and two companion cases, Chief Justice Marshall reconciled European concepts of "discovery," U.S. independence, tribal dependence on U.S. control, and Indian human rights. A relationship with tribes based on dependence and trust evolved. The U.S. government held plenary (absolute) power over Indian affairs, yet had legal responsibilities for protection and fair treatment. Tribes retained a limited right to occupy lands not acquired by the United States through treaty or conquest, but were restricted with respect to how they could sell those lands.

When European colonists arrived in North America, they found Indian societies with established governments, laws, and customs. As early as 1532, Spain specifically addressed the question of Indian land ownership and concluded that Indians held a certain right to the land that Spain could not acquire simply by "discovery." This right could only be acquired by treaty or "just war." European adoption of the treaty process meant accepting three assumptions: (1) Tribes had sovereign powers enabling them to enter into an agreement free of other parties. ("Sovereignty" means the power of a government to regulate its own internal business free of outside control.) (2) Indians held some form of title to the land that they could give to someone else. (3) The transfer of land was a matter between governments, not individuals.

Such land ownership issues were a central concern of the future founders of the United States in the eighteenth century. With Indian nations holding military supremacy over the colonists for many years, the early colonists negotiated with Indian governments as between two sovereign powers. Indian tribes remained free and independent nations within their own territories, governed by their own laws and customs rather than by the rules of U.S. common law. It was in this setting, just prior to the Revolutionary War, that Mr. Johnson and Mr. Graham, acting on their own behalf, purchased land northwest of the Ohio River outside the colonies from the Illinois and Piankeshaw Indian tribes in 1773 and 1775.

Upon conclusion of the Revolutionary War in 1776, numerous hostilities erupted between various tribes and the United States and its citizens. In 1779, in an effort to claim control over new land won from the British, the state of Virginia passed an act proclaiming exclusive right to the territory containing the two parcels purchased by Johnson and Graham for the "commonwealth." The Indians retained a right to continue living in the region until the lands could be purchased by the state. The act negated all previous transactions made by Indians to individuals for their private use.

The newly formed federal government immediately began to define a national policy for treating the tribes, acquiring Indian lands, and restoring order to its frontiers, where conflicts had been marked with arrogance and ruthlessness. The government expressed clear recognition of tribal "ownership" in the Northwest Ordinance of 1787, an ordinance guiding how to govern newly acquired lands from the British not previously in colonies. The historic document stated that Indian "lands and property shall never be taken from them without their consent." The 1789 U.S. Constitution further recognized tribal political presence as one of three kinds of sovereign governments within the United States borders. The two others were the federal government and states. Article I of the Constitution gave Congress authority to "regulate commerce with foreign Nations and with the Indian Tribes." Article VI of the Constitution recognized treaties as having the same weight as laws passed by Congress. Questions persisted however as to whether tribes actually "owned" the land, and, if so, what kind of title they had and how it could be transferred. To address these tough issues facing the nation, the newly formed U.S. Congress passed the Indian Trade and Intercourse Act of 1790 as one of its first actions. Among other things, the act established restrictions on tribes' rights to sell lands to parties other than the U.S. government.

With the U.S. government assuming the exclusive role in land purchases from tribes and sales of those lands to its citizens, William McIntosh acquired lands from the U.S. government including the parcels purchased by Johnson and Graham some four decades earlier. Johnson and Graham filed suit challenging McIntosh's acquisition by claiming they held legal title to the land through their earlier direct purchase from the tribes. The District Court for Illinois ruled in favor of McIntosh. Johnson and Graham next took their case to the U.S. Supreme Court.

The Discovery Doctrine

Chief Justice Marshall, writing on behalf of the Court in 1823 with no dissenting opinions, carefully constructed new fundamental rules of land acquisition "supported by reason." Summarizing earlier European concepts of "discovery," Marshall wrote "that discovery gave title to the government by whose subjects it was made, against all other European governments [which] necessarily gave to the nation making the discovery the sole right of acquiring the soil from the natives." The tribes

> were admitted to be the rightful occupants of the soil, with a legal as well as just claim to retain possession of it, and to use it according to their own discretion; but their rights to complete sovereignty, as independent nations, were necessarily diminished, and their power to dispose of the soil at their own will, to whomever they pleased, was denied by the

original fundamental principle, that discovery gave exclusive title to those who made it [the discovery].

By briefly reviewing the history of early North American settlement by European nations, Marshall acknowledged "the universal recognition of these principles." Title to discovery went to governments, not individuals. The two land parcels in question actually lay in territory claimed by France but transferred to British jurisdiction by the 1763 Treaty of Paris. Next, title of the two parcels "was forfeited by the laws of war" from Great Britain to the United States as a result of the Revolution. Marshall wrote, "It is not for the courts of this country to question the validity of this title, or to sustain one which is incompatible with it." Meanwhile, the Intercourse Act served to reaffirm the exclusive right of the federal government to acquire land from Indians. In sum, Marshall wrote, the "absolute ultimate title has been considered as acquired by discovery, subject only to the Indian title of occupancy, which title the discoverers [United States] possessed the exclusive right of acquiring."

In respect to what happened to the Indian peoples following "discovery" of their lands, Marshall wrote, "Humanity acting on public opinion, has established that the conquered shall not be wantonly oppressed" since the "new and old members of the society mingle with each other; the distinction between them is gradually lost, and they make one people." Marshall asserted "the new subjects should be governed as equitably as the old."

The Court held that tribes retained a right to occupy the land and that "title of occupancy" could only be passed from government to government, tribal to federal. This transfer had not occurred prior to the time of purchase by Johnson and Graham. Therefore, the land title they purchased only had legal status within tribal law and "cannot be recognized in the courts of the United States." McIntosh was declared the rightful owner.

Impact

Together with the Intercourse Act, the Court and Congress attempted to establish a foundation for the recognition and orderly disposition of Indian property interests. The decision held that tribes did not own absolute title to their lands, but a lesser interest described as a right of occupancy. The tribal right to sell their land to non-Indians was restricted, with any transfer of land being illegal unless approved by the federal government. The United States held exclusive right to obtain Indian land title either "by purchase or conquest." In what constituted a compromise, Marshall accepted neither that discovery ended all Indian title claims nor that Indians maintained absolute title unaffected by European claims of discovery. The Court's decision represented an effort to fit Indian land title claims into the European system of land ownership and minimize the effects on the previous acquisition of millions of acres by the United States and its European predecessors. Many of the original eastern states had negotiated directly with Indian tribes for their lands and those transfers were never approved by Congress.

The *Johnson* decision thus held that tribes did not retain full national sovereignty. Congress obtained its power to restrict Indian rights through the "discovery doctrine." The *Johnson* decision was the first of three Supreme Court decisions over nine years, known as the Marshall Trilogy, that established the foundation for U.S. Indian law and defined the nature and extent of the doctrine of inherent tribal sovereignty. In 1831, in *Cherokee Nation v. Georgia* Justice Marshall found that although the Cherokee, and other tribes, were distinct societies and separate politically, they were still under the control of the United States. Tribes were not foreign nations but "domestic dependent nations." In *Worcester v. Georgia* in 1832, the third opinion of the trilogy, Marshall established that tribes were not within state jurisdictions. Georgia could not enforce state laws on tribal lands. The tribes could regulate their own activities limited only by treaties or acts of Congress, thus recognizing Congress' plenary (total) powers over tribal rights.

The Court had to resolve other aspects of Indian land disposal at times. In 1955 in *Tee-Hit-Ton Indians v. United States,* the Court ruled that compensation required by the Fifth Amendment for lands taken, such as through condemnation, by the United States did not apply to Indian lands unless their property rights had been previously recognized in some formal manner, such as treaty.

In the 1970s, tribes began to challenge the early land transactions that had not been approved by the federal government as required by the Intercourse Act and the *Johnson* decision. In 21 lawsuits in the seven eastern states and Louisiana, tribes claimed that their right of possession as recognized by Marshall was never legally surrendered. In 1972, several tribes filed suit seeking 7.5 million acres and $150 million in damages for alleged illegal land transfers in Maine and Massachusetts. In *Passamaquoddy Tribe v. Morton,* a U.S. district court in 1975 ruled that the tribes had legal standing to pursue the claim in courts. The claim was settled in 1980 before proceeding to the Supreme Court. Through the resulting Maine Indian Claims Settlement Act of 1986, the tribes received $81.5 million, much of which was used to purchase 300,000 acres of timbered land. In a 1985 decision in *County of Oneida v. Oneida Indian Nation,* the Court ruled that a 1795 agreement between the tribe and the state of New York transferring 100,000 acres was invalid because of federal approval was not given. These cases highlight the complex historical relationships between tribes and the eastern states.

Related Cases
Cherokee Nation v. Georgia, 30 U.S. 1 (1831).
Worcester v. Georgia, 31 U.S. 515 (1832).
Tee-Hit-Ton Indians v. United States, 348 U.S. 272 (1955).
Passamaquoddy Tribe v. Morton, 528 F.2nd 370 (1975).
County of Oneida v. Oneida Indian Nation, 430 U.S. 226 (1985).

Bibliography and Further Reading
National Congress of American Indians. http://www.ncai.org.

Wilkinson, Charles F. *American Indians, Time, and the Law.* New Haven, CT: Yale University Press, 1987.

Wunder, John R., ed. *Native American Law and Colonialism, Before 1776 to 1903.* New York: Garland Publishing, Inc., 1996.

CHEROKEE NATION V. GEORGIA

Legal Citation: 30 U.S. 1 (1831)

Plaintiff
Cherokee Indian Nation

Defendant
State of Georgia

Plaintiff's Claim
That under the Supreme Court's power to resolve disputes between states and foreign nations, the Court could forbid Georgia from unlawfully attempting to move the Cherokees from their lands.

Chief Lawyer for Plaintiff
William Wirt

Chief Defense Lawyer
None

Justices for the Court
Henry Baldwin, William Johnson, John Marshall (writing for the Court), John McLean

Justices Dissenting
Smith Thompson, Joseph Story (Gabriel Duvall did not participate)

Place
Washington, D.C.

Date of Decision
5 March 1831

Decision
That the Court had no power to hear the dispute, because Indian tribes are not foreign nations.

Significance
By refusing to help the Cherokees, the Court left the Indians at the mercy of land-hungry settlers. The Cherokees ultimately were forced to move to Oklahoma along the famous "Trail of Tears."

The Cherokee Indians originally inhabited much of America's southeastern seaboard. In the seventeenth and eighteenth centuries, European settlers pushed the Cherokees from many of their lands. Unlike most Indians, however, the Cherokees were able to resist white encroachment by adapting to white ways. After the American Revolution, the Cherokees copied white farming methods and other aspects of the white economy. The Cherokees sent some of their children to American schools, and permitted mixed marriages. Further, they signed a series of treaties with the federal government that seemed to protect what remained of their lands.

The Cherokee presence was particularly strong in Georgia, where they prospered under the new ways. Cherokee plantations even had slaves. However, in 1828 prospectors discovered gold in Cherokee territory. Georgia wanted to give the land to whites, and enacted laws to force the Cherokees to leave. The Cherokees fought back, hiring white lawyers to represent them.

The Cherokees' chief lawyer was William Wirt. He went directly to the Supreme Court and asked for an injunction forbidding Georgia from removing the Cherokees. Because Article III, Section 2 of the U.S. Constitution gives the Court original jurisdiction in cases to which a state is a party, Wirt did not have to go through the Georgia state courts and could not go through the lower federal courts. Unfortunately, Article III, Section 2 generally limits the Court's jurisdiction to cases involving American citizens, and Indians were not yet recognized as citizens. The only arguable basis for jurisdiction was the Court's power to hear disputes "between a State, or the Citizens thereof, and foreign States, Citizens or Subjects."

Therefore, Wirt had to convince the Court that the Cherokees were a foreign nation, or the Court would refuse to act. Georgia was an ardent supporter of states' rights, and since the state denied that the federal courts had jurisdiction, Georgia refused to send anyone to represent the state.

Wirt reminded the Court that the Cherokees had uncontestable rights to the lands in Georgia:

A political cartoon showing injustice and cruelty against the Cherokee Nation, c. 1850. © Corbis-Bettmann.

The boundaries were fixed by treaty, and what was within them was acknowledged to be the land of the Cherokees. This was the scope of all the treaties.

Next, Wirt begged the Court to prevent what was about to happen to the Cherokees:

> The legislation of Georgia proposes to annihilate them, as its very end and aim . . . If those laws be fully executed, there will be no Cherokee boundary, no Cherokee nation, no Cherokee lands, no Cherokee treaties . . . They will all be swept out of existence together, leaving nothing but the monuments in our history of the enormous injustice that has been practised towards a friendly nation.

That same day, the Supreme Court denied Wirt's petition, holding that the Cherokees and other Indian tribes were only "domestic dependent nations," not foreign nations, and thus the Court had no authority to help them. A year later, in the 1832 case of *Worcester v. Georgia*, the Court freed some missionaries who were sympathetic to the Cherokee cause and had been arrested by Georgia authorities, but only because the missionaries were white citizens. Powerless to resist, the Cherokees were stripped of all their lands by 1838. In that year, over 7,000 soldiers forced the Cherokees to

The "Trail of Tears"

Of the many injustices visited by the United States on Indian tribes, the removal of the Cherokee nation from their Georgia homeland to Oklahoma in the winter of 1838–39 was one of the most inexcusable. Over the course of their journey, on a route called the "Trail of Tears," one-quarter of the Cherokee people died.

The Cherokee had been almost unique among Indians in their establishment of a European-style government. Hoping in vain to preserve their lands in northwest Georgia against the spread of white settlement, in the early 1800s they adopted many of the features that they hoped would qualify them as "civilized" in the eyes of the federal government. Not only did they become

the only Native American group with a written language, thanks to the efforts of the linguist Sequoyah, they also established a parliamentary and constitutional form of government with a capital at New Echota. In addition, they took up cattle-raising and farming, a departure from the traditional Native American hunter-gatherer economy.

But these efforts proved futile. In 1828, Georgia declared void all Cherokee laws, and claimed their lands for the state.

Source(s): Garraty, John A. *A Short History of the American Nation.* New York: Harper, 1981.

leave what was left of their territory for relocation in Oklahoma. Over 4,000 Cherokees died during the journey of thousands of miles to the west, which became known as the Trail of Tears.

Related Cases

Fletcher v. Peck, 10 U.S. 87 (1810).
Johnson v. McIntosh, 21 U.S. 523 (1823).
Worcester v. Georgia, 6 U.S. 515 (1832).

Bibliography and Further Reading

Guttmann, Allen. *States' Rights and Indian Removal: the Cherokee Nation v. the State of Georgia.* Boston: D.C. Heath, 1965

Johnson, John W. *Historic U.S. Court Cases, 1690–1990: An Encyclopedia.* New York: Garland Publishing, 1992.

Lumpkin, Wilson. *The Removal of the Cherokee Indians from Georgia.* New York: Arno Press, 1969.

Peck, Ira. "Worcester v. Georgia: the Campaign to Move the Cherokee Nation." *Senior Scholastic,* November 1982, pp. 17-20.

Warren, Mary Bondurant. *Whites Among the Cherokees.* Danielsville: Heritage Papers, 1987.

Wilkins, Thurman. *Cherokee Tragedy.* Norman: University of Oklahoma Press, 1986.

WORCESTER V. GEORGIA

Legal Citation: 31 U.S. 515 (1832)

Appellant
Samuel A. Worcester

Appellee
State of Georgia

Appellant's Claim
That the state of Georgia had no right to prosecute Worcester for illegally living on Cherokee land because the state of Georgia had no right of sovereignty over Cherokee land.

Justices for the Court
Gabriel Duvall, William Johnson, John Marshall (writing for the Court), John McLean, Joseph Story, Smith Thompson

Justices Dissenting
Henry Baldwin

Place
Washington, D.C.

Date of Decision
3 March 1832

Decision
Samuel Worcester, tried, convicted, and sentenced by the state of Georgia for illegally living in the lands of the Cherokee Nation encompassed by the state of Georgia, was found by the Supreme Court to have legally lived in Cherokee Nation, by virtue of the facts that the Cherokee Nation is a nation within itself, and that the state of Georgia had no authority to mandate laws within the territory confined by the Cherokee Nation. The acts established by the state of Georgia that affected the lands of the Cherokee Nation were deemed unconstitutional and void.

Significance
This case reestablished the sovereignty of the Cherokee Nation, and other Native American Nations, as nations separate from the United States and exempt from the laws of the States of the Union that may surround their territory.

Samuel Worcester was indicted in a superior court in Georgia "for residing on the 15th of July, 1831, in that part of the Cherokee Nation attached by the laws of the State of Georgia, without license or permit, and without having taken the oath to support and defend the constitution and laws of the State of Georgia, etc." To this indictment he pleaded that, on that date, in the Cherokee Nation, he was a citizen of Vermont and entered the Cherokee Nation as a missionary under the authority of the president of the United States and with permission of the Cherokee Nation was engaged in preaching the gospel. He added that Georgia should not maintain the prosecution, as several treaties between the Cherokee Nation and the United States recognized the Cherokee Nation as a sovereign nation, and that the laws under which he was indicted were repugnant to the treaties, were unconstitutional and void, and were repugnant to the 1802 act of Congress entitled "An Act to regulate trade and intercourse with the Indian tribes." The superior court overruled the plea, and the plaintiff in error was tried, convicted, and sentenced to four years of hard labor.

President Andrew Jackson and the United States cited and admonished the state of Georgia and commanded the state to appear before the Supreme Court, pursuant to a writ of error. Chief Justice Marshall delivered the opinion of the Court.

Marshall felt that the indictment and plea in the case brought up two questions. The first dealt with the validity of the treaties made by the United States with the Cherokee Nation, and the second question was the validity of a statute of the state of Georgia entitled "An Act to prevent the exercise of assumed and arbitrary power by all persons, under pretext of authority from the Cherokee Indians," etc., that stated that all white people residing within the Cherokee Nation must conform to the rules of Georgia, including license or permit from a state official of Georgia to live in the Cherokee Nation, taking an oath to the state of Georgia, and, failing to do so, being sentenced to a minimum of four years hard labor. The extraterritorial power to each legislature being limited in the action of its own citizens, Marshall wrote that the very passage of the act was an assertion of jurisdiction over the Cherokee Nation.

John Ross

John Ross (1790–1866) grew up in the ways of Anglo-Saxons, but later embraced his Cherokee heritage. Born in present-day Alabama, Ross was seven-eighths European (mostly Scottish). As a young man, he operated as a merchant near present-day Chattanooga and in northwest Georgia, site of the independent Cherokee Nation. He became involved in Cherokee political affairs during the 1810s and, in 1828, gained election as principal chief of the Cherokee. Faced with federal government demands that the Cherokee vacate their lands, Ross favored resistance. But a minority clique under Major Ridge signed a treaty with President Andrew Jackson in 1835, and in mid-1838 the Cherokee embarked on the Trail of Tears, a trek that killed almost one-quarter of the tribe.

After a period of unrest after the move, the Cherokee entered a period of peace in the 1850s. This ended with the Civil War. Ross supported the Confederacy, but there is evidence to suggest that he was coerced. After the war, in part as a result of his negotiation, the federal government agreed to an 1866 treaty which preserved the Cherokee Nation intact.

Source(s): Coleman, Kenneth, and Charles Stephen Gurr, eds. *Dictionary of Georgia Biography.* Athens: University of Georgia Press, 1983.

John Ross. © The Library of Congress.

The treaty between the United States and the Cherokee Nation was based on the previous treaties between the Native American Nations and Great Britain. Accordingly, the United States received the Cherokee Nation into their favor and protection. The Cherokee acknowledged themselves to be under the protection of the United States and no other power. Protection did not imply the destruction of the protected. The manner in which this stipulation was understood by the American government was explained by the language and acts of the first president. The sixth and seventh articles stipulated for the punishment of the citizens of either country who may commit offenses on or against the citizens of the other. The only inference to be drawn from this was that the United States considered the Cherokees as a nation. Marshall wrote that multiple treaties between the United States and the Cherokee Nation again and again affirmed the Cherokee Nation's right to self-government and recognized it as a distinct community, occupying its own territory, over which the state of Georgia had no right.

Based on these arguments, Marshall wrote that the act of the state of Georgia under which the plaintiff was prosecuted was void. Marshall further wrote that the act of the state of Georgia interfered with the relations established between the United States and the

Cherokee Nation and was in direct hostility with treaties repeated in a succession of years. Furthermore, according to Justice Marshall, the forcible seizure and abduction of Worcester, who was residing in the Cherokee nation, with its permission, and by authority of the President of the United States, was also a violation.

Related Cases

McCullough v. Massachusetts, 17 U.S. 316 (1819).
Cohens v. Virginia, 19 U.S. 264 (1821).
Gibbons v. Ogden, 22 U.S. 1 (1924).

Bibliography and Further Reading

Biskupic, Joan, and Elder Witt. *Congressional Quarterly's Guide to the U.S. Supreme Court,* 3rd ed. Washington, DC: Congressional Quarterly, Inc., 1996.

Cushman, Robert F. *Leading Constitutional Decisions.* Englewood Cliffs, NJ: Prentice-Hall, Inc., 1982.

Hall, Kermit L., ed. *The Oxford Companion to the Supreme Court of the United States.* New York: Oxford University Press, 1992.

Johnson, John W., ed. *Historic U.S. Court Cases, 1690–1990: An Encyclopedia.* New York: Garland Publishing, 1992.

UNITED STATES EX REL. STANDING BEAR V. CROOK

Legal Citation: 25 F.Cas. 695 (1879)

Petitioners
Standing Bear and other Ponca Indians

Respondent
George Crook, U.S. Army General

Petitioners' Claim
That confinement of American Indians by the U.S. Army violated the Due Process Clause of the Fourteenth Amendment.

Chief Lawyers for Petitioners
John L. Webster, Andrew J. Poppleton

Chief Lawyer for Respondent
Genio M. Lambertson

Justice for the Court
Elmer S. Dundy

Place
Lincoln, Nebraska

Date of Decision
12 May 1879

Decision
The Court upheld Standing Bear's claim and ordered the Poncas released from U.S. custody.

Significance
The ruling established that Indians are "persons" under U.S. law and those who are not members of tribes have rights to challenge U.S. actions. Issues surrounding Standing Bear's vulnerability to the whim of U.S. officials led reformers to lobby for major changes in U.S. Indian policy. As a result, the 1887 Dawes Act converted communally-controlled reservation lands into individually-owned land parcels. Though passed with good intentions, the act proved disastrous to Indian social and economic well-being; its harmful effects were still felt by the close of the twentieth century. In the 1990s Congress similarly sought to limit the rights of immigrants and foreign terrorist suspects to challenge their detentions.

Before European "discovery" of North America, the Ponca Indians were originally part of a larger Siouan language group in eastern North America. The Siouan group gradually migrated westward, settling in various places. The Ponca and Omaha segments worked their way up the Mississippi and Missouri Rivers before eventually splitting apart. In the thirteenth century, the Ponca settled in future Dakota territory, near the mouth of the Niobara River where it joins the Missouri. With increasing numbers of whites entering the area by the mid-nineteenth century, food sources including wild game significantly declined and foreign diseases such as smallpox spread rapidly. This resulted in the death of a majority of native peoples in the region. Through this trauma, the Ponca remained a small peaceful tribe.

In 1858, the Ponca ceded over 2,000,000 acres of land to the United States in a treaty, keeping less than 100,000 acres for a reservation. The Ponca soon moved onto the reservation and began a transition to an agricultural economy. The United States's delay in providing assistance promised in the treaty led to increased hardships. In addition, the more aggressive Sioux Indians and whites raided the Ponca for their food, possessions, and horses. By 1865, the Ponca signed another treaty, moving their reservation for better protection. However, the following year a treaty between the United States and the mighty Sioux nation inadvertently placed most of the new Ponca reservation in a Sioux reservation. Hostilities renewed, with the Sioux destroying Ponca crops, stealing livestock, and killing tribe members. By the 1870s the Ponca, facing food shortages and continued Sioux raids, were increasingly desperate. The United States, in an effort to appease the Sioux and protect the Ponca, decided to remove the Ponca against their will to the recently established Indian Territory in the future state of Oklahoma.

Meanwhile, in the wake of the Civil War, Congress in 1868 ratified the Fourteenth Amendment to the Constitution guaranteeing that "all persons" have due process and equal protection of the laws. However, throughout much of the nineteenth century, the legal rights of Indian individuals were not a major concern of the federal government and or the courts. U.S.-Indian relations were largely directed by treaties rather

---

The Dawes Severalty Act

The Dawes Severalty Act, named after Senator Henry L. Dawes of Massachusetts, is sometimes called the General Allotment Act. Passed in February of 1887, it established federal Indian policy for the next half-century, until its effective repeal by the passage of the Indian Reorganization Act of 1934.

Under the Dawes Severalty Act, the president was authorized to order a survey of Indian reservations and, from the results, to allot homesteads to members of tribes. The act provided for each head of household to receive 160 acres, single adults 80 acres, and unmarried children 40 acres. These lands would be exempt from local property taxes for 25 years, but the owners were also prohibited from selling their allotments during that period. The land remaining would be sold to non-Indians. The allotment provisions proved disastrous to the Indians. The allotments chopped up land previously belonging to Indians and allowed much of it to be transferred to non-Indians. It forced Indians to adopt an agrarian lifestyle by expecting them to live off of their homesteads rather than hunting and gathering over a vast territory.

Source(s): Bacon, Donald C., et al., eds. *The Encyclopedia of the United States Congress.* New York: Simon & Schuster, 1995.

---

than common law until Congress ended the treaty making period in 1871. Dealings with individual Indians were essentially avoided. In addition, the Bureau of Indian Affairs (BIA) had established an extensive system for policing and punishment that essentially operated beyond the reach of the courts. Indian agents with ready access to the military had broad authority. It is likely that within this system thousands of individuals were detained for a wide range of alleged actions through the years. However, by the 1870s Indian issues rose in the national eye as the West became increasingly settled and reformers shifted attention from the slavery issue. A demand for major reforms in the treatment of Indians gathered momentum.

Indians Are "Persons"

Having received funding and direction from the federal government, Indian agents from the BIA began seeking land in 1877. Among a group of Ponca that traveled to Indian Territory with the agents to find land was a respected tribal leader named Standing Bear. Greatly discouraged by what they saw, the group abruptly returned to the Ponca reservation. However, by the end of April a large group of Poncas were convinced to move and left for their new home. Fearing that Standing Bear and his brother were serving as a disruptive force with the remaining Ponca, the Indian agent directed the military to arrest and confine them. With Ponca resistance somewhat defused, the last group, including Standing Bear, began their journey southward in May. Conditions along the journey were harsh and Standing Bear's daughter died on the trip. In their new home, the Ponca found that no reservation had yet been established apart from other tribal lands. Through 1878, with the lack of housing and little government support for cultivation, many died, including a son of Standing Bear. Distressed, he and over 20 others left in January of 1879 to return home. Upon arrival at the Omaha Reserva-

tion en route to their homeland, they were arrested in a strictly military operation and taken to Fort Omaha, Nebraska, with the intent of being sent back to Indian Territory.

Lawyers for Standing Bear filed for a writ of *habeas corpus,* a request that a person being detained be brought before a court to review the legality of the imprisonment, with the U.S. Circuit Court of the District of Nebraska. Standing Bear argued before Judge Elmer Dundy that, having committed no crime and not being informed why he was arrested, he should be released. He also claimed to no longer be a member of the Ponca, having left the tribe in Indian Territory so as to adopt "the general habits of the whites" and become self-sufficient. General George Crook, on behalf of the United States, responded that the Ponca prisoners were still members of the tribe and had disobeyed Indian agent orders to settle in Indian Territory and pursue "the habits and vocations of civilized life." Crook, using the 1857 *Dred Scott* slavery case findings, argued that Indians, like blacks, did not possess rights to sue in federal courts as part the Fourteenth Amendment's Due Process Clause. He contended only U.S. citizens could request writs.

With an Indian suing a U.S. Army general for the first time in the federal courts, the trial received national attention. Judge Dundy ruled on several key points. First, Dundy found that U.S. *habeas corpus* law applied "to all mankind" without requirement of citizenship, and that "even an Indian" is a person under the *Webster Dictionary* definition. Dundy wrote that when "a person is charged we do not inquire upon the trial in what country the accused was born nor to what race he belongs." Therefore, Dundy continued, "it would, indeed, be a sad commentary on . . . our laws, to hold that Indians . . . cannot test the validity of an alleged illegal imprisonment." Therefore, Standing Bear could bring the lawsuit. Second, Dundy found that all persons in the United States had the "natural and inherent right . . . to . . . life, liberty, and pursuit of happiness." Therefore, Standing Bear had the legal right to withdraw from tribal membership. Third, Dundy assessed whether the United States had legal power to dictate to Indians who were not members of tribes where to live. He could not find any law or treaty that gave the United States that power.

Dundy concluded that the United States could use military force to remove a person from a reservation, but law required the person be turned over to civilian custody after removal, which had not happened with Standing Bear. The army had no broad authority to detain Indians without full civilian due process protections. Dundy wrote, "In time of peace no authority, civil or military, exists for transporting Indians from one section of the country to another, without the consent of the Indians, nor to confine them to any particular reservation against their will." Dundy ordered Standing Bear and the other Poncas "discharged from custody." Crook filed an appeal, but the United States decided to drop the case.

Impact

Standing Bear was the first case to challenge the U.S. government's extensive use of military authority over Indians and to question the legal authority of the United States to confine Indians on reservations against their will. The decision was the first recognition that Indians were persons under the Fourteenth Amendment. However, Indians still did not have citizenship status, and their precise legal standing remained poorly defined. The Indian Citizenship Act of 1924 later provided some clarification.

Freed, Standing Bear, and the others promptly returned to the Niobara River area but were without a country, living on an island overlooked in the Sioux treaty. Standing Bear filed suit to reclaim reservation lands given to the Sioux, eventually winning judgment in December of 1880 with Judge Dundy again presiding. However, a presidential commission including General Crook was created to study the Ponca situation. Based on the commission's findings, President Rutherford B. Hayes recommended to Congress in January of 1881 that each Ponca be provided 160 acres of land, either in Indian Territory or on the Niobara, whichever the individuals wished. The allotment would be nontaxable for 30 years and funding for agricultural supplies would be provided. Congress passed an act adopting the recommendations, but another nine years passed before the Niobara Ponca received their lands. Meanwhile, Standing Bear became a spokesman for Indian rights touring the eastern states before his death in 1908.

The court held in *Standing Bear* that any person not a citizen of the United States and in custody of U.S. authorities has the right to challenge the custody's legality through the writ of *habeas corpus*. That Indians on reservations had writ powers posed a significant new threat to the previously unchallenged powers of BIA Indian agents. Indians now had much the same rights as foreign nationals. However, the *Standing Bear* decision was largely ignored as court precedent in this regard. Few legal challenges to the authority of Indian agents followed. Many continued to argue that Indians should be subjected to military authority due to their "conquered" status.

Importantly, *Standing Bear* contributed toward a major change in U.S.-Native American policy with substantial implications across the nation. The earlier policy of isolating Indians on reservations dramatically changed in the 1880s to a policy of forcing Indians to blend into the dominant white culture. In 1887, Congress passed the General Allotment Act, also known as the Dawes Act. The act applied the basic concepts of the Hayes commission report to Indians throughout the nation. The act authorized the BIA to divide communally-owned tribal land, such as reservations, among tribal members in small sections, called allotments. Supporters of Standing Bear's cause believed this act would free Indians from arbitrary relocation by U.S. authorities by making them private property owners. Actually, the Indian controlled land base in the United States substantially eroded from 138 million acres in 1887 to only 52 million acres in 1934. "Surplus" lands, often the more agriculturally productive, were made available to whites. Towns grew within reservation boundaries. Congress, upon seeing the devastation to Indian society that allotments had wrought, ended the allotment era in 1934.

The issue of individuals' status under the Due Process Clause rose again in the 1990s, spurred by an increasingly anti-immigrant mood in the United States. Congress fundamentally changed U.S. immigration laws with passage of the Illegal Immigration Reform and Immigrant Responsibility Act of 1996. The law substantially reduced the legal rights of alien immigrants who were subject to either expulsion or criminal prosecution for attempting to reenter the United States. Immigrants could be deported without a trial or hearing before a judge. As with the BIA in the *Ponca* case, the Immigration and Naturalization Service (INS) was given broad powers in an expedited removal process that stripped federal courts of their authority to review INS decisions. Similarly, Congress passed the Anti-Terrorism and Effective Death Penalty Act of 1996 which allowed detention of noncitizens in U.S. jails outside the rules of due process by prohibiting the filing of *habeas corpus* petitions.

Related Cases

Dred Scott v. Sandford, 60 U.S. 393 (1857).
Lone Wolf v. Hitchcock, 187 U.S. 553 (1903).

United States v. Omaha Tribe of Indians, 253 U.S. 275 (1920).

United States v. Sioux Nation of Indians, 448 U.S. 371 (1980).

Bibliography and Further Reading

Grable, David M. "Personhood Under the Due Process Clause: A Constitutional Analysis of the Illegal Immigration Reform and Immigrant Responsibility Act of 1996." *Cornell Law Review,* Vol. 83, 1998, pp. 820-65.

Lake, James A., Sr. "Standing Bear! Who?" *Nebraska Law Review,* Vol. 60, 1981, pp. 451-D503.

McLaughlin, Michael R. "The Dawes Act, or Indian General Allotment Act of 1887: The Continuing Burden of Allotment: A Selective Annotated Bibliography." *American Indian Culture and Research Journal,* Vol. 20, 1996, pp. 59-D105.

Native American Rights Fund. http://www.narf.org.

Tibbles, Thomas H. *Standing Bear & the Ponca Chiefs.* Lincoln: University of Nebraska Press, 1995.

Ex Parte Crow Dog

Legal Citation: 190 U.S. 556 (1883)

Petitioner
Crow Dog of the Sioux Indian Nation

Respondent
United States

Petitioner's Claim
That the U.S. court system does not have jurisdiction over crimes committed within the boundaries of an Indian reservation by one tribal member against another.

Chief Lawyer for Petitioner
A. J. Plowman

Chief Lawyer for Respondent
Samuel F. Phillips, U.S. Solicitor General

Justices for the Court
Samuel Blatchford, Joseph P. Bradley, Stephen Johnson Field, Horace Gray, John Marshall Harlan I, Stanley Matthews (writing for the Court), Samuel Freeman Miller, Morrison Remick Waite, William Burnham Woods

Justices Dissenting
None

Place
Washington, D.C.

Date of Decision
17 December 1883

Decision
Upheld Crow Dog's claim and overturned the lower court's decision sentencing him to death for a murder.

Significance
The ruling established that U.S. courts did not have criminal jurisdiction in cases where one Native American murders another on reservation lands. The Court ruled that tribes held exclusive jurisdiction over their own internal affairs, including murder cases. The decision, however, prompted a swift congressional reaction. Since 1885 Congress has exercised absolute (plenary) power over tribal jurisdiction by excluding certain crimes from that jurisdiction. Through the 1990s many tribes expanded their justice systems. However, because of the wide diversity in the tribal court systems, neither Congress nor the U.S. courts created a consistent set of rules guiding allocation of specific cases to state, federal, or tribal courts.

Because Indian issues were so prominent in early U.S. history, the first U.S. Congress passed the Indian Trade and Intercourse Act in 1790, followed by a series of amendments until settling on a final version in 1834. The act, while regulating trade with Indians and tribal legal jurisdiction, served to recognize tribal sovereignty. "Sovereignty" means the power of a government to establish its own structure, define who its citizens may be, assess taxes, and administer justice, among other things. But the Intercourse Act also limited the scope of tribal sovereignty by maintaining that Congress had the last word in limiting and affirming tribal rights and powers. Congress' absolute authority is called "plenary power." Initially, the Intercourse Act primarily addressed crimes by non-Indians against Indians on Indian-owned lands. The act explicitly excluded crimes by Indians against Indians from U.S. jurisdiction. However, an 1817 amendment to the act broadened U.S. criminal jurisdiction by including crimes Indians committed against non-Indians on Indian lands.

In a series of three landmark rulings between 1823 and 1832 the Supreme Court established the concept of semi-independent tribal governments existing within the United States. In *Worcester v. Georgia* (1832) case, Chief Justice John Marshall wrote that tribes were "domestic dependent nations" whose right to occupy their lands and exercise their inherent powers was essentially free of state controls and subject only to the ultimate authority of the federal government. The Court legitimized congressional exercise of control over tribal affairs through the Intercourse acts by defining the nature of tribal limited sovereignty.

Based on the 1817 Intercourse Act amendment, Congress passed the 1854 General Crimes Act, also known as Indian Country Crimes Act, giving federal courts criminal jurisdiction over various offenses committed on Indian lands. Though seemingly broad in scope, federal jurisdiction was actually fairly limited. Two key exclusions from the Crimes Act were crimes between Indians and situations where offenders were punished under tribal law. The law was primarily aimed at crimes between Indians and non-Indians. Consistent with the Intercourse Act and prior court findings, the 1854 act reflected a broad respect for tribal sovereignty.

The Indian Civil Rights Act

The Indian Civil Rights Act of 1968 was enacted at a time when Native American groups were involved in bringing about a resurgence in Native American cultures and demanding that their civil rights be recognized. North Carolina Senator Sam Ervin, Jr., received authorization from the Senate Judiciary Committee in 1961 to conduct hearings on the state of constitutional rights among Native Americans. Ervin introduced in 1965 nine bills designed to "provide our Indian citizens with the rights and protections conferred upon all other American citizens." The Senate debated these sporadically for the next three years until it passed them into law as the Indian Civil Rights Act. Among the act's measures were constitutional exemptions for tribal leadership to allow a greater measure of Indian self-government.

Meanwhile, Senator Robert Kennedy in 1967 conducted an investigation regarding the state of education among Native Americans and made proposals recommending that Indians run their own schools. Kennedy's panel, chaired by Edward Kennedy after his brother's assassination in 1968, issued its final report in 1969 and called for a number of self-governance measures consistent with those in the Indian Civil Rights Act.

Source(s): Bacon, Donald C., et al., eds. *The Encyclopedia of the United States Congress.* New York: Simon & Schuster, 1995.

Since signing a treaty with the Delaware Indians in 1778, the United States negotiated approximately 400 treaties with tribes across the nation based on the notion of tribal sovereignty. In 1868 the United States signed a treaty with the Sioux of the Dakotas. Among other issues, the treaty recognized U.S. responsibility for ensuring the Sioux had "an orderly government" and noted that "they shall be subject to the laws of the United States, and each individual shall be protected in his rights of property, person, and life." Soon Congress' Indian policy begin to shift, however. Treaty-making abruptly came to a close in 1871 when Congress, in taking away the president's powers to negotiate treaties with Indians, began to exert greater influence over internal Indian affairs on reservations.

An Orderly Government

Crow Dog, whose Indian name was Kan-gi-Shun-ca, and Spotted Tail, also known as Sin-ta-ge-le-Scka, were members of the Brule Sioux Band of the Sioux Nation. Crow Dog, at odds with Spotted Tail over several personal and public matters, shot and killed him in August of 1881. Through application of traditional Sioux law, the families settled the matter by Crow Dog's family paying restitution to the victim's relatives in the form of $600 cash, eight horses, and a blanket. Believing the Sioux punishment too light for murder, federal agents arrested Crow Dog and charged him with murder. The Dakota territorial court found him guilty of the charge and sentenced Crow Dog to be executed. Crow Dog appealed, claiming federal courts had no jurisdiction over crimes committed by one Indian against another. The U.S. Supreme Court then granted *certiorari* requesting the lower court to forward case proceedings for Court review.

U.S. Solicitor General Samuel E. Phillips argued before the Court that U.S. courts had jurisdiction in the

Crow Dog case based upon specific language in the Sioux treaty. Justice Matthews, writing on behalf of the Court in an era before justice vote counts and dissenting opinions were given, disagreed with this argument. The Court held that the most important aspect of "an orderly government," as referenced in the treaty, is its ability to self-govern. This autonomy included "the regulation by themselves of their own domestic affairs, the maintenance of order and peace among their own members by the administration of their own laws and customs." Given the sovereignty status of tribes as recognized in *Worcester,* tribal members were subject to U.S. laws not as individuals but as members of "a dependent community" that hopefully would "become a self-supporting and self-governed society." Matthews concluded that assumptions about what rights a tribe may have simply from the reading of a treaty were not enough to decrease tribal sovereignty and impose the laws of one nation "over the members of a community separated by race . . . [and] by tradition." For the United States to have jurisdiction over a particular kind of crime, Congress must clearly state so. The resolution worked out between Crow Dog's and Spotted Tail's families was ruled sufficient justice.

Impact

The *Crow Dog* decision represented to many an extreme application of the doctrine of tribal sovereignty and self-government. Stunned by the Court's finding, two years later Congress passed the Major Crimes Act of 1885. The law essentially overturned the *Crow Dog* decision by identifying seven crimes on Indian lands over which federal courts would assume jurisdiction, including murder. The act was immediately challenged, leading to a Supreme Court decision in 1886 in *United States v. Kagama* (1886). The Court upheld Congress' power to interject the United States in internal tribal disputes and the validity of the Major Crimes Act. The decision reaffirmed the "plenary power" of Congress over tribal jurisdiction, meaning Congress could alter tribal rights at will. The list of crimes addressed by the act expanded during the century to include 16 by 1993.

In seeming contradiction to the anti-sovereignty decision in *Kagama,* ten years later in 1896 the Court followed the *Worcester* and *Crow Dog* line of reasoning in the *Talton v. Mayes* (1896) case by recognizing that tribal powers pre-existed the Constitution. The Court ruled tribes need not conduct grand jury hearings as normally required by the Fifth Amendment. The *Crow Dog* and *Talton* decisions essentially recognized that tribes were largely independent nations free from constitutional constraints and general federal laws. To limit specific tribal powers, Congress must explicitly act through its plenary powers. The first modern opinion by the Court regarding the principle of exclusive tribal court jurisdiction occurred in *Williams v. Lee* (1959). The Court, basing its ruling on *Worcester,* stressed the importance of tribal courts in maintaining tribal sovereignty and proclaimed that state jurisdiction did not extend into Indian country.

However, constraints over tribal criminal jurisdiction emerged with decisions in *Oliphant v. Suquamish Indian Tribe* (1978) and *Duro v. Reina* (1990). In the landmark *Oliphant* case, the Court held that tribes did not hold criminal jurisdiction over non-Indians accused of crimes on Indian lands. In *Duro,* the Court held that tribes did not have jurisdiction over Indians who were not members of the particular tribe in whose lands a crime occurred. The nonmember Indians were treated the same as non-Indians. Importantly, the Court stated that the powers of tribal sovereignty only applied to individuals freely consenting to be members of that tribe. The *Duro* decision thus established the doctrine of "consent-based" sovereignty. This shift in perspective sharply contrasted with the prior traditional "territory-based" perspective by which tribes held sovereign rights over lands they controlled.

The *Crow Dog* decision clearly demonstrated the spirit of respect and sympathy the courts frequently paid to the doctrine of tribal sovereignty as they would to the laws of any sovereign nation. However, by triggering a quick congressional response, *Crow Dog* marked a major transition in the application of federal criminal jurisdiction within Native American society. The Court decision reflected prevailing legal concepts in the United States to that time, that general federal laws did not apply to reservations unless Congress had explicitly stated that a particular law did actually apply. Since 1885, the assumption significantly changed to the perspective that general federal laws did apply unless a particular Native American right or U.S. policy was clearly violated. The Supreme Court consis-

tently opposed efforts of lower courts and government officials to infringe on tribal sovereignty without explicit legal justification.

The tribal courts were not an important concern of the federal government until the 1880s when a system began to emerge on reservation lands. A century later, jurisdiction of tribal courts was a key issue as tribes gained increasing economic and political power. However, a major factor in the 1990s prohibiting establishment of uniform rules guiding tribal court jurisdiction was the diversity of tribal courts. In the 1934 Indian Reorganization Act (IRA), Congress formalized recognition of the tribal court system. By 1997, a total of 150 tribal courts were organized under the IRA. Over 20 courts persisted under the earlier system, and some tribes, like the Navajo, refused to organize under the IRA retaining their traditional court system. Among these almost 200 courts, some established wide-ranging jurisdiction codes while others were very restricted and perhaps staffed by individuals with no legal training. Some tribes had no court system at all. The Court consequently followed a narrow path between recognizing a defined field of exclusive tribal court jurisdiction and operating within the reality of the variation and limitation of tribal courts.

Tribal courts also chronically suffered from a shortage of funding. Congress attempted to remedy that problem with passage of the 1994 Tribal Justice Act. The act declared a commitment to enhance funding support for the tribal justice system, though little actually appeared during the next several years. Still, tribal courts were increasingly shaping their own destinies throughout the 1990s, including establishment of intertribal appeals courts. However, lacking further clarity from the Supreme Court, tribal courts continued to operate within the shadows of the more developed federal court system.

Related Cases

Worcester v. Georgia, 6 Pet. (31 U.S.) 515 (1832).
United States v. Kagama, 118 U.S. 375 (1886).
Talton v. Mayes, 163 U.S. 376 (1896).
Williams v. Lee, 358 U.S. 217 (1959).
Oliphant v. Suquamish Indian Tribe, 435 U.S. 191 (1978).
Duro v. Reina, 495 U.S. 676 (1990).

Bibliography and Further Reading

Harring, Sidney L. *Crow Dog's Case: American Indian Sovereignty, Tribal Law, and United States Law in the Nineteenth Century.* Cambridge, MA: Cambridge University Press, 1994.

Native American Rights Fund. http://www.narf.org.

Wilkins, David E. *American Indian Sovereignty and the U.S. Supreme Court: The Masking of Justice.* Austin: University of Texas Press, 1997.

UNITED STATES V. WINANS

Legal Citation: 198 U.S. 371 (1906)

Appellant
United States

Appellee
A commercial fishing company

Appellant's Claim
That the fishing company, by putting in place a device known as a fishing wheel and by other forceful means, had deprived the Yakima Indian tribe of its rights to fish in its traditional spot on the Columbia River as per a treaty signed with the United States government during the nineteenth century.

Chief Lawyer for Appellant
Henry M. Hoyt, U.S. Solicitor General

Chief Lawyer for Appellee
Charles H. Carey

Justices for the Court
David Josiah Brewer, Henry Billings Brown, William Rufus Day, Melville Weston Fuller, John Marshall Harlan I, Oliver Wendell Holmes, Joseph McKenna (writing for the Court), Rufus Wheeler Peckham

Justices Dissenting
Edward Douglass White

Place
Washington, D.C.

Date of Decision
15 May 1906

Decision
That the treaty takes precedent over state law, that the fishing wheel did displace the Native Americans from their rightful fishing spot. Remanded to the circuit court to determine the method of reconciling Native Americans' rights to fish in the area in question with the respondents' state-granted right to operate a fishing wheel.

Significance
Determined that private ownership of land did not preclude Native Americans from gaining access to waters which were adjacent to that land. Also, affirmed the notion that states reserve the right to regulate off-reservation fishing rights.

In the long history of American jurisprudence, few disputes have found themselves in the courts more often than the fishing rights of the Yakima Indians, and Native American fishing rights in the state of Washington in general. The continuing dispute has led to numerous court battles, as well as hard feelings and even violent confrontations since a series of treaties were signed in the middle of the nineteenth century. Landmark decisions concerning these controversies have been rare, but rather the various decisions over the years have served more as links in a chain, coming together to sort out the confusion which marks the fight over Native American rights, treaty interpretation, private interests and state jurisdiction. One such case is *United States v. Winans.*

Around 1859, Isaac Stevens, the first governor of the Washington Territory, signed treaties with 17,000 Native Americans in the territory. Because Washington was still a territory at that time, Stevens was an officer of the federal government and not of the state of Washington, which did not as yet exist. The treaties called for the Native Americans, including the Yakimas, to give up claim to their lands and remove themselves to reservations and granted Native Americans the right to continue to fish unmolested in their "usual and accustomed places." For the Yakimas, this included a particular spot on the Columbia River.

When the Western states came into existence, they often were reluctant to recognize the treaty rights which had been vested in the Native Americans by the federal government. Native Americans were often forced to turn to the courts for relief, and the courts could not always be counted on to apply the treaty rights. Rulings were sometimes handed down that state laws superseded treaties made by the federal government, or that such treaties became defunct once states came into being. This was despite the fact that when the treaties were made, the understanding was that they were treaties between two sovereign powers, no different than a treaty made between the United States and a country such as France or Bolivia.

Very early in the twentieth century a private commercial fishing company held title to the land adjacent to the Yakimas' "usual and accustomed place" for fishing on the Columbia River. The company did not want the Yakimas to traverse its land en route to the river, which the Native Americans had no choice but to do. The company also received a license from the state to put up a fishing wheel, a large device which captures large numbers of fish. The device was located as such that it prevented the Yakimas from using their historical spot. They tried to gain relief from the circuit court in Washington, but their request was thrown out. That court essentially found that the Yakimas' treaty with the federal government guaranteed them little if anything in off-reservation fishing rights and said that the company was within its rights to keep the Native Americans off its lands and install the fishing wheel, and the Yakimas were entitled to no protection.

When the case found its way to the Supreme Court in 1905, Henry Hoyt, the solicitor general for the United States, took up the Native Americans' cause in an attempt to enforce its treaty and pleaded before the Court:

> The Indian claim is not merely meritorious and equitable; it is an immemorial right, like a ripened prescription . . . A decree for appellants must consider the reasonable rights of both parties; restricting the fish wheels if they can be maintained at all, as to their number, method and daily hours of operation. Nor can the Indians claim an exclusive right, and it may be just to restrict them in reasonable ways as to times and modes of access to the property and their hours of fishing. But by some proper route, following the old trails, and at proper hours, with due protection for the defendants' buildings, stock and crops, free ingress to and egress from the fishing grounds should be open to the Indians, and be kept open.

The defendants countered by arguing that their ownership of the land was valid in every way and should not be compromised by the treaty. They said that the fishing wheel was merely a more modern and effective method of doing what the Native Americans had always done by more primitive methods, and claimed use of modern technology should not be held against them.

Court Sides with the Yakimas

The Supreme Court sided with the Native Americans on all the major points. As to the question of what the treaty entitled the Native Americans to in regards to off-reservation fishing rights, the Court soundly rebuked the opinion of the lower court:

> It was decided that the Indians acquired no rights but what any inhabitant of the territory or state would have. Indeed, acquired no rights but such as they would have without the treaty. This is certainly an impotent outcome to negotiations and a convention, which

seemed to promise more and give the word of the Nation for more.

The Court also ruled that the Native Americans had a right to traverse the land—even if privately owned—which needed to be crossed to reach their fishing spot:

> The contingency of the future ownership of the lands, therefore, was foreseen and provided for—in other words, the Indians were given a right in the land—the right of crossing it to the river—the right to occupy it for the extent and for the purpose mentioned. No other conclusion would give effect to the treaty. And the right was intended to be continuing against the United States and its grantees as well as against the state and its grantees.

The Court also decided that the use of fishing wheels under the existing circumstances deprived the Native Americans from exercising their treaty right. It did not, however, ban the use of the devices entirely, but remanded the issue to the circuit court for further consideration. Justice McKenna wrote:

> The respondents urge an argument based on the different capacities of white men and Indians to devise and make use of instrumentalities to enjoy the common right . . . But the result does not follow that the Indians may be absolutely excluded . . . In the actual taking of fish white men may not be confined to a spear or crude net, but it does not follow that they may construct and use a device which gives them exclusive possession of the fishing places, as it is admitted a fish wheel does.

One passage in the opinion, however, was later used to construct arguments opposed to off-reservation fishing rights. Near the end of the opinion, Justice McKenna wrote: "It was within the competency of the nation to secure to the Indians such a remnant of the great rights they possessed as 'taking fish at all usual and accustomed places.' Nor does it restrain the state unreasonably, if at all, in the regulation of the right." This was later used as a precedent to demonstrate that state regulation of off-reservation fishing rights was justifiable. Typically in the long dispute over the issue, the *United States v. Winans* decision had something for both sides to take both solace and defeat in.

Related Cases

Menominee Indian Tribe of Wisconsin v. Thompson, WL 797196 (7th Cir. [Wis.] 1998).

Bibliography and Further Reading

Moquin, Wayne, with Charles Van Doren. *Great Documents in American Indian History.* Praeger Publishers, 1973.

Washington Law Review, November 1975, p. 61.

WINTERS V. UNITED STATES

Legal Citation: 207 U.S. 564 (1908)

Appellants
Henry Winters, John W. Acker, Chris Cruse, Agnes Downs and the Empire Cattle Company

Appellee
United States

Appellants' Claim
That appropriated water rights to the Milk River of Montana were valid and had priority over those of the Fort Belknap Native Americans and the United States.

Chief Lawyer for Appellants
Edward C. Day

Chief Lawyer for Appellee
Sanford, Assistant Attorney General

Justices for the Court
William Rufus Day, Melville Weston Fuller, John Marshall Harlan I, Joseph McKenna (writing for the Court), Oliver Wendell Holmes, William Henry Moody, Rufus Wheeler Peckham, Edward Douglass White

Justices Dissenting
David Josiah Brewer

Place
Washington, D.C.

Date of Decision
6 January 1908

Decision
Found in favor of the United States affirming two lower court decisions that the tribes held implied water rights through their agreement with the United States that took priority over latter nearby settlers.

Significance
This landmark ruling set U.S. policy regarding Native American water rights in the western United States. Agreements and treaties establishing Indian Reservations, though not explicitly claiming water rights, contained an implied reserved right to the amount of river water necessary to effectively pursue the purposes of the reservations. The decision created the Winters doctrine, defining a form of water right unique to Native American tribes.

After acquiring rights to the western lands from other European countries, the federal government still had to negotiate actual possession through treaties and agreements with the numerous Native American tribes. The newly gained property rights of the federal government included the power to dispose of the public lands and water in the West.

Two major systems of water rights are found in the United States. The water abundant states in the East established the *riparian* system. The more arid West applied an *appropriative* system. Under the riparian system, an owner of land that borders a stream has the right to make reasonable use of the water. The right is attached to the land and cannot be terminated even if not used. The owners are also entitled to continuation of the stream flow from the upstream source. The appropriative system operates quite differently. Water rights are not linked to the land, rather they belong to the first person who makes beneficial use of the water. An appropriator maintains the right to continue using the water without interference by later appropriators. However, the right is retained only as long as the water is used for benefit. The popular phrase "use it or lose it" was often connected to the appropriative water system.

During early western settlement, Congress permitted the states to control, distribute, and manage water on the public lands. The public could appropriate the water in accordance with state law. Through the second half of the nineteenth century, settlement and development of public lands occurred under various federal land laws, such as the Homestead Act of 1862 which opened the public lands to settlement. In 1877, the Desert Land Act opened all previously unappropriated, "surplus," water on the public lands for "use of the public for irrigation, mining and manufacturing purposes subject to existing rights." The act designated the states to regulate this appropriation of surplus water, but left the door open for the federal government to later assert water rights. Later, the federal government began to take a more active role with inception of land reclamation and flood control projects, assertion of Native American rights, and development of interstate agreements.

Reservation Populations

According to the U.S. Census Bureau, 808,163 people live on the largest Indian reservations—those with 10,000 people or more, which constitute a large portion of the nation's Native American population of 1,878,285. Just over half of the population of the largest reservations is Native American, a group which includes American Indians and Alaskan Natives. Thus out of more than 808,000 people, 437,431 (54 percent) are Native Americans. This figure, less than a quarter of the nation's total Native American population, suggests a large degree of movement to non-reservation locales.

The largest tribal area is the Navajo and Trust Lands territory in Arizona, New Mexico, and Utah, which holds 148,451 people, 96 percent of whom are Native American. The next-largest reservation, the Pine Ridge and Trust Lands of Nebraska and South Dakota, is much smaller, with just 12,215 people, of whom 91.5 percent are Native American. The reservation at East Cherokee, North Carolina, has 5,388 Native Americans. Other substantial reservations include Fort Apache (11,182 Native Americans), Gila River (9,825), and Papago (8,480), all in Arizona.

Source(s): *Statistical Abstract of the United States 1997.* Washington, DC: U.S. Government, 1997.

Water for the Pursuit of "Civilization"

In 1874, the U.S. government withdrew from settlement a large area of the future state of Montana for the exclusive use of the Gros Ventre, Piegan, Blood, Blackfeet, and River Crow Indians. However, as the U.S. population continued to push westward, the United States negotiated an agreement in 1888 with the tribes to transfer much of the land back to the United States to promote settlement of the area. As part of the agreement, Congress retained a small part of the formerly withdrawn lands specifically for the Gros Ventre and Assiniboing tribes, called the Fort Belknap Native Reservation. The lands relinquished by the tribes returned to the public domain and became available to settlers through the various land laws.

Much of the new reservation was suitable to pasture, feed and graze large numbers of cattle and horses and other portions were suitable for farming and cultivation. But large quantities of water were needed for irrigation to make them productive. In 1889 the United States constructed houses and buildings on the reservation for its officers in charge and appropriated a small amount of water from the Milk River which formed the reservation's northern boundary. The water was used for domestic use and irrigation to raise crops including grain, grass, and vegetables.

Almost a decade later in 1898, the Fort Belknap Natives diverted a much larger flow to water about 30,000 acres of land to raise crops. The Native Americans needed the waters to stabilize their rural economy and continue their pursuit of "civilization" under federal guidance.

Meanwhile, Henry Winters and the stockholders of the Matheson Ditch Company and Cook's Irrigation Company acquired lands upstream from the reservation under the Homestead and Desert Land Acts. The Empire Cattle Company soon purchased the lands. Shortly before the Belknap Indians began diverting Milk River waters, the settlers posted various signs along the river and its tributaries at the points of intended diversion containing notices of appropriation, describing the proposed means of diversion, and where the water was to be used. Forty days after posting the notices, Winters and the others built numerous dams, reservoirs, and ditches upstream from the reservation to divert Milk River waters from the river channel for their use.

The United States filed suit in federal district court to restrain Winters and the cattle company from diverting water out of Milk River above the reservation. Winters claimed their rights to the Milk River waters and its tributaries were established prior to the river use by the United States and the Natives. Winters also asserted that the Native Americans and the United States could obtain sufficient water from a large number of springs and several streams on the reservation. Winters argued the river waters were indispensable. If use of the waters was blocked, their land's productivity would be ruined. The loss would compel the settlers to abandon their homes and a substantial and irreparable damage would have been inflicted. Though the amount of damages could not be estimated, Winters asserted it would greatly exceed $100,000.

The district court ruled in favor of the United States, and an appeals court affirmed the decision. Winters then appealed to the U.S. Supreme Court.

A Special Right

By a 8-1 decision, the Court found in favor of the U.S. government. Justice Joseph McKenna, writing for the majority, found that the key factor was the 1888 agreement creating the Fort Belknap Indian Reservation.

McKenna found it unnecessary to determine the validity of Winter's water right claim because when the Fort Belknap land was reserved in 1888, water rights for the Native Americans were reserved as well by implication.

McKenna wrote that the reservation was originally part of a much larger traditional territory the Native Americans rightly occupied. The expansive region was adequate to meet the needs of a nomadic people. However, government policy dictated the Native Americans become a pastoral and westernized people and the Native Americans agreed to change their lifestyle. Consequently, the original territory became larger than necessary but a smaller tract would be inadequate without changing its condition. The arid lands without irrigation were not favorable to more permanent settlement.

McKenna acknowledged the difficulty of interpreting implicit elements of agreements. But, a standard established in *United States v. Winans* (1905) required that interpretation of ambiguities in agreements and treaties between the United States and the Native Americans must be made in favor of the Natives. McKenna found that the Court was faced with two questions. First, did Congress, in creating the Fort Belknap Indian Reservation by agreement, imply a guaranteed reasonable quantity of water to the Native Americans. Secondly, did Congress terminate this reservation of water when it admitted Montana to the Union one year later "upon an equal footing with the original States."

In answering the first question, McKenna emphasized that the reservation was created to change the Native Americans' "nomadic and uncivilized" habits, making them into "a pastoral and civilized people." Without water to irrigate the lands, however, the reservation would be "practically valueless" and "civilized communities could not be established thereon." The fundamental purpose of the reservation would be "impaired or defeated."

Regarding the second question, McKenna wrote,

> it would be extreme to believe that within a year Congress destroyed the reservation and took from the Indians the consideration of their grant, leaving them a barren waste—took from them the means of continuing their old habits, yet did not leave them the power to change to new ones.

McKenna, ruling in favor of the United States, found it unreasonable to assume that Native Americans would settle on reservation lands to begin farming and grazing without having the water to successfully pursue those activities. Justice Brewer dissented alone without stating his objections.

Impact

The Court's decision created the "Winters doctrine" which guided the future management of Native

reserved water rights. Oddly, for decades after *Winters,* the issue of Native American water rights was largely ignored. The Winters doctrine was eventually affirmed in *Arizona v. California* (1963) concerning Lower Colorado River water. The Court went a step further than *Winters* by actually identifying how to determine the quantity of water desirable for tribal use. The Court ruled the quantity should not be based on the size of the existing reservation population, but on the amount of reservation acreage potentially productive with irrigation.

Some key characteristics of the doctrine included: (1) establishment of an Indian reservation by treaty, statute or executive order included an implied reservation of rights to water sources within and bordering the reservation; (2) the water rights were reserved at the date the reservation was created; (3) the quantity of water reserved for Native American use was the amount sufficient to irrigate all the practical reservation acreage; and, (4) the water rights can not be lost by non-use. Also, those who held water rights prior to creation of a reservation could retain those rights. As a result of *Winters,* Native American rights blended aspects of appropriative and riparian rights. While the rights became established at the time a reservation was established and the rights of existing users were recognized, rights to water from streams within or bordering reservations were tied to the land and could not be lost because of non-use.

The Winters doctrine also served as a model broader non-Native application. Any time the federal government reserved land for a public purpose, water rights were also provided in sufficient quantity and quality so that the purpose for which the land was designated could be satisfied.

A lingering difficulty with such implied reserved rights was that normally the actual volume of water reserved was not known. For example, concerns were that designation of lands for wilderness purposes would carry some unspecified quantity of water. The manner in which water allocations were recognized enormously affected continued development in the West. Many worried that unresolved reserved water rights could limit the efficient use of limited water resources. Furthermore, uncertainty persisted even when rights were awarded since the conditions of ownership were still not well defined. Could the rights could be bought, sold, or traded for other water rights? To avoid expensive and lengthy legal battles, many states and tribes pursued complex negotiations in the late twentieth century to specifically establish water allocations for the various users.

Related Cases

United States v. Winans, 198 U.S. 371 (1905).
Arizona v. California, 373 U.S. 546 (1963).
Cappaert v. United States, 426 U.S. 128 (1976).

Bibliography and Further Reading

Ellison, Brian A. "The Advocacy Coalition Framework and Implementation of the Endangered Species Act." *Policy Studies Journal,* spring 1998.

Fowler, Loretta. *Shared Symbols, Contested Meanings: Gros Ventre Culture and History, 1778–1984.* Ithaca: Cornell University Press, 1987.

McGuire, Thomas R., William B. Lord, and Mary G. Wallace, eds. *Indian Water in the New West.* Tucson: University of Arizona Press, 1993.

Parman, Donald L. *Indians and the American West in the Twentieth Century.* Bloomington: Indiana University Press, 1994.

Pisani, Donald J. *Water, Land, and Law in the West: The Limits of Public Policy, 1850–1920.* Lawrence: University Press of Kansas, 1996.

WILLIAMS V. LEE

Legal Citation: 358 U.S. 217 (1958)

Petitioners
Paul Williams, Lorena Williams

Respondent
Hugh Lee

Petitioners' Claim
That the Supreme Court of Arizona had erred in claiming jurisdiction in a civil suit occurring on Navajo Indian reservation land.

Chief Lawyer for Petitioners
William W. Stevenson

Chief Lawyer for Respondent
Norman M. Littell

Justices for the Court
Hugo Lafayette Black (writing for the Court), William J. Brennan, Jr., Tom C. Clark, William O. Douglas, Felix Frankfurter, John Marshall Harlan II, Potter Stewart, Earl Warren, Charles Evans Whittaker

Justices Dissenting
None

Place
Washington, D.C.

Date of Decision
12 January 1958

Decision
In favor of the appellants, reversing the Supreme Court of Arizona decision.

Significance
The decision affirmed the jurisdiction of Indian tribal courts.

A Question of Jurisdiction

If Hugh Lee's collection suit against Paul and Lorena Williams had taken place nearly anywhere else in the United States, the dispute might have gone no further than a local claims court. Instead the *Williams v. Lee* case ended up in the U.S. Supreme Court, where its outcome hinged on precedents set over a century earlier.

Lee was the proprietor of the Ganado Trading Post, a general store located on the Navajo Indian Reservation in Arizona. After trying unsuccessfully to collect money for goods he had sold on credit to Paul and Lorena Williams, Lee decided to sue in the Arizona courts. The Williams, both of whom were members of the Navajo tribe, responded by stating that the disputed transaction took place on Navajo land and therefore should be decided by a Navajo tribal court. They asked the state courts to dismiss the case.

The two sides soon found themselves arguing before the Arizona Supreme Court, not about Lee's bill, but over who had jurisdiction in the case. The state court decided in favor of Lee. Although Lee was a non-Indian operating a business on Navajo property under a valid Federal Bureau of Indian Affairs license, the Arizona court noted that no act of Congress prevented state courts from settling civil suits between Indians and non-Indians on reservation lands.

The U.S. Supreme Court agreed to hear the Williams' appeal of the Arizona Supreme Court decision on 20 November 1958 because the case concerned the important question of state power over Indian affairs. On 12 January 1959, the Court unanimously reversed the Arizona court's ruling, deciding that jurisdiction in the matter belonged to the Navajo tribal court.

The Court looked to an 1832 case as an important precedent regarding the interference of states in internal Indian affairs. In 1828 the state of Georgia had passed statutes forbidding the Cherokee to enact laws on their own reservation or to testify against white men in non-Indian courts. Later state laws made it a crime for any white man to set foot on Cherokee land after 1 March 1831 without taking an oath of allegiance to the state and without a permit from Georgia's governor. Far from being a measure to protect the Cherokee, the latter laws intended to remove whites already living on the reservation with Cherokee permission, particularly missionaries aiding in Indian efforts to resist the encroachments of white settlers and their state government.

The law was tested when a Christian missionary named Samuel A. Worcester was arrested by the state of Georgia for refusing to leave the Cherokee Reservation. Although Worcester was licensed by the federal government to practice as a missionary on Cherokee land, he was in violation of Georgia law and found himself sentenced to four years in a state penitentiary. Worcester's appeal reached the Supreme Court, which overturned his conviction in a politically controversial 1832 decision. Writing for the 1958 Court in the *Williams v. Lee* decision, Justice Black quoted Chief Justice John Marshall's opinion a century and a quarter earlier:

> The Cherokee nation . . . is a distinct community, occupying its own territory . . . in which the laws of Georgia can have no force, and which the citizens of Georgia have no right to enter, but with the assent of Cherokees themselves or in conformity with treaties, and with the acts of Congress. The whole intercourse between the United States and this nation is, by our constitution and laws, vested in the government of the United States.

The Supreme Court's *Worcester v. Georgia* decision implicitly recognized all Indian tribes as self-governing "nations" within the borders of the United States. The ruling also allowed the federal government to assume all power in dealing with the tribes, invalidating state pretensions to such power. The state of Georgia ignored the U.S. Supreme Court decision regarding Samuel Worcester, who was forced to ask for a state pardon to obtain his freedom. The Court's ruling that state powers were invalid on Indian land nevertheless became an accepted principle of American law in the century after his release.

The Treaty of 1868

The Supreme Court found general proof of the Navajo right to self-government in the *Worcester* decision. More specific proof was found in a treaty signed on 1 June 1868 by the Navajo tribe and General William Tecumseh Sherman, who was acting on behalf of a U.S. government peace commission. According to the Treaty of 1868, state courts were to have jurisdiction in suits by reservation Indians against non-Indians. Trials involving crimes by non-Indians against other non-Indians on reservation land were similarly to be decided in state courtrooms. Jurisdiction over crimes committed by or against Indians, however, was to remain exclusively in the hands of Navajo tribal courts. Then, in 1871, Congress declared that no Indian tribe should be considered an independent nation with which the U.S. government could execute a treaty, reversing the implications of the *Worcester* decision. The 1871 law was not retroactive, however, so the terms of the Treaty of 1868 and its rules governing legal jurisdiction survived. Justice Black and his colleagues found no reason to declare the rules invalid 90 years later.

The Court did not examine the matter of the money Paul and Lorena Williams allegedly owed Hugh Lee. By unanimously affirming the right of Navajo self-government, the Court ensured that any such legal claims were to be decided by a tribal court.

Related Cases

Worcester v. Georgia, 6 Pet. 515 (1832).
A-1 Contractors v. Strate, 76 F.3d 930 (1996).

Bibliography and Further Reading

Prucha, Francis P. *The Great Father: The United States Government and the American Indians.* Lincoln: University of Nebraska Press, 1984.

Starkey, Marion L. *The Cherokee Nation.* North Dighton: JG Press, 1995.

WHITE MOUNTAIN APACHE TRIBE V. BRACKER

Legal Citation: 448 U.S. 136 (1980)

Petitioner
White Mountain Apache Tribe

Respondent
State of Arizona

Petitioner's Claim
That the state of Arizona could not impose taxes on a non-Indian logging company doing business with the White Mountain Apache Tribe on Fort Apache Reservation.

Chief Lawyer for Petitioner
Neil Vincent Wake, Michael J. Brown

Chief Lawyer for Respondent
Ian A. Macpherson

Justices for the Court
Harry A. Blackmun, William J. Brennan, Jr., Warren E. Burger, Thurgood Marshall (writing for the Court), Lewis F. Powell, Jr., Byron R. White

Justices Dissenting
William H. Rehnquist, John Paul Stevens, Potter Stewart

Place
Washington, D.C.

Date of Decision
27 June 1980

Decision
That the state taxes failed the federal preemption test regulating jurisdiction on Indian reservations among federal, state and tribal governments. The taxes therefore were invalid.

Significance
The decision thwarted the state's attempt to extend its authority over economic transactions on the reservation. It also upheld the Supreme Court's long-standing tradition of limiting state jurisdiction over Indian tribes, as well as its more recent pattern of protecting tribal self-government and economic development.

Throughout most of the history of federal Native American policy, the United States government has consistently restricted the states' jurisdiction over Native American tribes and reservations located within their borders. Though state governments have repeatedly attempted to regulate tribal activities, the federal government generally has preferred to leave the management of reservations and their resources largely in the hands of Congress.

This situation has frequently created tension between the 27 states containing reservations within their borders and the nearly 300 federally recognized tribes that reside there. As Stephen Pevar wrote in *The Rights of Indians and Tribes*, "states resent the fact that reservation Indians are not normally subject to state taxation and regulation, and Indians resent the states' constant attempts to tax and regulate them." The economic implications of this power struggle have become even more prominent over the past several decades. As noted in the 1988 publication, *Indian Tribes as Sovereign Governments*, "the steady increase of economic activity in Indian Country has given states added incentive to enforce their tax laws there." The federal courts, therefore, frequently have played a decisive role in regulating the jurisdictional balance among tribal, state, and federal governments.

The Supreme Court's position on the tribal-state relationship has moved over time from a strict exclusion of any state regulation to a more modified—though still restrictive—stance. In 1832, *Worcester v. Georgia* held that the Cherokee tribe had complete sovereignty on its reservation, subject only to federal regulation and exempt from any state jurisdiction. This position gradually softened, as the Court handed down a series of decisions that granted states limited authority on reservations, in areas such as criminal cases involving only non-Indians (*New York ex rel. Ray v. Martin,* 1945) and taxation of non-Indians at reservation stores (*Moe v. Salish & Kootenai Tribes,* 1976, and *Washington v. Confederated Tribes of the Colville Indian Reservation,* 1980). Generally speaking, the only state laws applicable on reservations are those with express federal authorization. States continue, however, to try to regulate tribes in areas not already approved by Congress. In order to be valid, these state laws must pass two tests—the federal preemption test and the infringement test—a hurdle which few such laws have cleared.

The 1980 Supreme Court case of *White Mountain Apache Tribe v. Bracker* involved the state of Arizona's attempt to extend its jurisdiction over a Native American reservation through taxation. Arizona had imposed taxes on Pinetop Logging Company, a combination of two non-Indian enterprises that had contracted with the tribally-organized Fort Apache Timber Company to conduct logging operations on the Fort Apache Reservation. The taxes included both a fuel tax and a motor carrier license tax intended to compensate the state for use of its roads.

With the Apache tribe intervening as the plaintiff, Pinetop challenged the taxes in state court, declaring them preempted by federal law. When that decision, and that of the Arizona Court of Appeals in 1978, went against the plaintiff, the case went to the Supreme Court. The Court ruled in a 6-3 decision that the taxes were indeed preempted by federal law and therefore were invalid. Justice Marshall wrote the majority opinion, joined by Chief Justice Burger and Justices Brennan, Blackmun, Powell, and White. The dissenting opinion, written by Justice Stevens, included Justices Rehnquist and Stewart.

Broadly speaking, the federal preemption test used by the Court asked if the state law in question regulates an area already sufficiently covered by federal law; if so, the federal law would preempt it. The test also asked if the state law threatened tribal sovereignty and economic viability. An extensive interpretation of the preemption test comes from the 1965 Supreme Court decision in *Warren Trading Post v. Arizona Tax Commission*. The Apache Court relied heavily on this case in rendering its decision.

In the *Apache* decision, the Court emphasized several factors. It found first of all that the timber operation and the revenues it generated on the Fort Apache reservation already came under extensive federal regulation. Therefore, no room remained for additional state regulation. The Court also found that as the state had no purpose for the tax other than raising general revenue, it would provide no services with the money generated that justified the tax on tribal activities. The fact that the case involved tribal natural resources which the federal government had placed under a sustained yield harvesting program also dissuaded the Court from allowing the state to interfere in any way. Finally, the decision found that the taxes' burden ultimately would fall on the tribe, and that the timber industry proved crucial to the economic viability of

many of the tribe's governmental programs. The state taxes thus hindered tribal sovereignty and economic development on the reservation.

The *Apache* ruling, along with a similar decision in *Central Machinery v. Arizona Tax Commission* in the same year, thus prevented state taxation of an economic transaction occurring on a Native American reservation, even when a non-Indian business was involved. It therefore upheld the Supreme Court's longstanding history of restricting state jurisdiction over tribal governments and resources. The decision also specifically protected tribal sovereignty and economic growth, a goal that has characterized federal Indian policy since the late 1960s. By limiting state regulation and taxation, such rulings may also encourage other non-Indian companies to do business with tribes on reservations.

In the decade following the *Apache* decision, it became unclear whether the Court's pattern of supporting tribal rather than state interests would hold. In 1983, *Rice v. Rehner* validated state liquor laws imposed on a non-Indian business on the reservation, while in *Cotton Petroleum Corporation v. New Mexico* in 1989, the Court allowed a state tax on oil and gas produced on tribal land by a non-Indian company. The latter decision, according to Stephen Pevar, "represents a retreat from the broad principles of the preemption doctrine," principles which the earlier *Apache* ruling firmly upheld.

Related Cases

Blaze Construction Company, Inc. v. Taxation and Revenue Department of State of New Mexico, 884 P2d 803 (1994).
Loveness v. State ex rel. Arizona Department of Revenue, 963 P.2d 303 (1998).

Bibliography and Further Reading

Indian Tribes as Sovereign Governments: A Sourcebook on Federal-Tribal History, Law, and Policy. Oakland: AIRI Press, 1988.

Kreshick, Kyra. "Supreme Court Decisions in Taxation: 1979 Term." *Tax Lawyer*, Vol. 34, no. 2, winter 1981, pp. 462-472.

Pevar, Stephen L. *The Rights of Indians and Tribes: The Basic ACLU Guide to Indian and Tribal Rights*. Carbondale, IL: Southern Illinois University Press, 1992.

Trail, Mary Jean. "Federal Preemption in Indian Law: An Analysis of *White Mountain Apache Tribe v. Bracker* and *Central Machinery v. Arizona State Tax Commission*." *Arizona Law Review*. Vol. 24, no. 1, winter 1982, 194-209.

LYNG V. NORTHWEST INDIAN CEMETERY PROTECTION ASSOCIATION

Legal Citation: 485 U.S. 439 (1988)

Petitioner
Richard E. Lyng, U.S. Secretary of Agriculture

Respondent
Northwest Indian Cemetery Protection Association, et al.

Petitioner's Claim
Construction of a road and harvesting of timber through areas held sacred by Native American was in violation of their rights under the Free Exercise Clause of the First Amendment and also in violation of various federal statutes.

Chief Defense for Petitioner
Andrew J. Pincus

Chief Lawyer for Respondent
Marilyn B. Miles

Justices for the Court
Sandra Day O'Connor (writing for the Court), William H. Rehnquist, Antonin Scalia, John Paul Stevens, Byron R. White

Justices Dissenting
Harry A. Blackmun, William J. Brennan, Jr., Thurgood Marshall (Anthony M. Kennedy did not participate)

Place
Washington, D.C.

Date of Decision
19 April 1988

Decision
Construction of the proposed road does not violate the First Amendment regardless of its effect on the religious practices of respondents because it compels no behavior contrary to their belief.

Significance
Strengthened federal government's right to make land-use and other decisions in spite of the objections of religious minorities.

In the 1970s the U.S. Forest Service planned to build a road through the Chimney Rock section of the Six Rivers National Forest to link the California towns of Gasquet and Orleans. The section through which the road was planned was held sacred by Native American tribes resident in the area and was used by them as a site for various religious rites. In response to comments on a draft statement of its environmental impact report, in 1977 the Forest Service commissioned a study of these sites and the possible impact of the proposed road. The study was finished in 1979, and it found the entire area to be "significant as an integral and indispensable part of Indian religious practice" and that construction of the road "would cause serious and irreparable damage to the sacred areas which are an integral and necessary part of the belief systems and lifeway of Northwest California Indian peoples." Thus the study recommended that the road not be built.

The Forest Service rejected the recommendation of the study and in 1982 issued a final environmental impact statement regarding the proposed road. It planned to build the road despite the recommendation of the study, but consideration was given to the points raised, and construction plans were adjusted accordingly. Although alternative routes completely away from the area were rejected because private land would have to be acquired and some of the areas had soil stability problems, the Forest Service selected a route for the road that was as far removed as possible from various sites where specific rituals took place. The Forest Service also adopted a plan to allow timber harvesting in the area, with a half-mile buffer zone around all significant sites identified by the 1979 study.

A group of interested parties, among them the state of California, individual members of Native American tribes, a Native American association, and conservation groups, filed suit in district court claiming that road construction or harvesting of timber in the area would violate several federal statutes and violate the rights of Native Americans who used the various sites in the area for religious purposes under the Free Exercise Clause of the First Amendment. The district court found for the group on both statutory and constitutional claims, the latter because both plans would "seriously damage the salient visual, aural, and environmental qualities" of the area. It further found that the road and timber-harvesting plans would violate government trust responsibility regarding water and fishing rights of residents of the Hoopa Valley Indian Reservation. The district court issued a permanent injunction barring implementation of both plans.

The court of appeals affirmed the injunction on statutory grounds but rejected part that had been rendered moot by passage of congressional legislation that designated most of the property as wilderness area, under which timber harvesting and other commercial activities are prohibited; it also rejected the district court's finding regarding a breach of government trust responsibility regarding the Hoopa Valley Indian Reservation. A majority upheld the district court's constitutional ruling, finding that the government had not proven a compelling interest for the construction of the road. The government petitioned for *certiorari* on the constitutional issue

The Majority Opinion

The Court ruled 5-3 (Justice Kennedy abstained) in favor of the petitioner on constitutional grounds and remanded the case for further proceedings on the statutory issues, which the government claimed it could resolve. The majority found that both lower courts had not proceeded according to the principle of judicial economy, under which constitutional questions are not addressed unless necessary. Had they acted in accord with judicial economy, they would have determined if a constitutional finding on behalf of the respondents would have granted them more relief than had they prevailed on statutory grounds alone. If the respondents would gain no additional relief on constitutional grounds, then a constitutional decision was "unnecessary and therefore inappropriate."

The injunction consisted of four sections, two of which forbade timber harvesting and road building until compliance with environmental statutes could be proven. The sections dealing with the immediate Chimney Rock area, which was the subject of the First Amendment claim, prohibited the same activities, this time without any qualifying language. The majority found that this part of the injunction must have been supported at least in part on First Amendment grounds, since such broad relief would not be granted on statutory grounds alone.

The majority rejected the respondent group's First Amendment claim, basing their decision on *Bowen v. Roy* (1986), in which two Native American applicants for state welfare benefits objected to the state's use of a Social Security number for their stepdaughter on religious grounds. O'Connor's opinion quoted Roy: "The Free Exercise Clause affords an individual protection from certain forms of governmental compulsion; it

does not afford an individual a right to dictate the conduct of the Government's internal procedures." The land was publicly owned, and the plan did not coerce individuals into actions contrary to their religious beliefs; nor was any person denied "an equal share of the rights, benefits, and privileges enjoyed by other citizens." The majority rejected respondents' attempts to distinguish this case from *Bowen v. Roy* because "the government action is not at some physically removed location where it places no restriction on what a practitioner may do" and the use of a Social Security number "did not interfere" with the practice of religion, simply by refusing to make the comparison:

> Since the Court cannot determine the truth of the underlying religious beliefs that led to the religious objections . . . we cannot say that the one form of incidental interference with an individual's spiritual activities should be subjected to a different constitutional analysis than the other.

The Court continued by rejecting comparisons to various other cases in which challenges to government programs on religious grounds were sustained, in one instance a case involving compulsory school attendance, because in these cases the programs required coercive action. In absence of such coercion, the majority declared that "government simply could not operate" if every program had to be in compliance with the religious beliefs of every American, however sincere and deeply held. Such controversies are inevitable in a diverse society, and any attempts to "reconcile the various competing demands on government" were the function of legislatures, not the Constitution and the Court.

Further discussion noted that the government took many steps to ameliorate the impact of the road on the area, and it rejected the respondents' claim that the injunction was valid under the American Indian Religious Freedom Act, which the Court declared was in fact a policy statement only and did not create any "cause of action or any judicially enforceable rights."

The Dissent

The minority, in an opinion written by Justice Brennan, took a more expansive view of the Free Exercise Clause, declaring that it "is directed against any form of governmental action that frustrates or inhibits religious practice," a claim the majority had flatly rejected by saying, "The Constitution, however, says no such thing," and quoting the First Amendment: "Congress shall make no law . . . prohibiting the free exercise [of religion]." Brennan noted, however, that one definition of the word *prohibit* is "to prevent from doing something."

A good portion of the dissent focused on the nature of Native American religious beliefs, finding a central-ity of land and reverence for nature in contrast to Western views. For many Native Americans, the land is a "sacred, living being," not a "fungible" asset to be managed. The construction of a road through the area would "completely frustrate the practice of their religion" and in effect will destroy it.

The minority did not accept the majority's distinction between government action that required conduct contrary to one's religious belief and action that prevented conduct according to that religious belief: "The harm to the practitioners is the same" in either case. The majority reading of *Bowen v. Roy* as applicable to the case at hand was "altogether remarkable," since the finding in that case emphasized the "internal" nature of the government action at question, whereas government "land-use decisions are like to have substantial external effects . . ." In this case the government action would "virtually destroy" the respondents' religion. Such a substantial harm did raise a constitutional question, and leaving the issue to the legislature was an "abdication" that would result in the government having "the unilateral authority to resolve all conflicts in its favor, " a result that does nothing to balance the interest of the government with that of Native Americans.

Impact

The Court's ruling in *Lyng* has been criticized for its unwillingness to consider the effects of government programs or policies while focusing only on the form the government action takes. In a *Cornell Law Review* article, J. Brett Pritchard stated:

The scope of the constitutional guarantee of free exercise of religion now depends on the Court's tenuous distinction between regulations that coercively impact religious practices and regulations that only make it more difficult for an individual to practice his beliefs.

Related Cases

Sherbert v. Verner, 374 U.S. 398 (1963).

Wisconsin v. Yoder, 406 U.S. 205 (1972).

Thomas v. Review Board, Indiana Employment Security Div., 450 U.S. 707 (1981).

Bowen v. Roy, 476 U.S. 693 (1986).

Bibliography and Further Reading

Brownstein, Alan E. "Constitutional Wish Granting and the Property Rights Genie." *Constitutional Commentary*, spring 1996, pp. 7–54.

McCarthy, Colman. "American Indians Want Religious Freedom Law." *National Catholic Reporter*, 21 January 1994, p. 27.

Pritchard, J. Brett. "Conduct and Belief in the Free Exercise Clause: Developments and Deviations in Lyng v. Northwest Indian Cemetery Protective Association." 76 *Cornell Law Review*, 268, November 1990.

Sitomer, Curtis J. "Religion Loses to Road Building in High Court." *Christian Science Monitor*, 20 April 1988.

Tapahae, Luralene. "After the Religious Freedom Restoration Act: Still No Equal Protection for First American Worshipers." 24 *New Mexico. Law Review*, 331, Spring 1994.

EMPLOYMENT DIVISION V. SMITH

Legal Citation: 494 U.S. 872 (1990)

Appellants
Employment Division, Department of Human Resources of the State of Oregon, et al.

Appellees
Alfred L. Smith, Galen W. Black

Appellants' Claim
That members of the Employment Division, under an Oregon statute disqualifying employees discharged for work-connected misconduct, are not eligible for unemployment benefits.

Chief Lawyer for Appellees
Susanne Lovendahl

Chief Lawyer for Appellants
William F. Gary

Justices for the Court
Sandra Day O'Connor, William H. Rehnquist, Antonin Scalia (writing for the Court), John Paul Stevens, Byron R. White (Anthony M. Kennedy did not participate)

Justices Dissenting
Harry A. Blackmun, William J. Brennan, Jr., Thurgood Marshall

Place
Washington, D.C.

Date of Decision
17 April 1990

Decision
The Court felt that it was necessary for lower court decisions to reflect whether the drug usage was acceptable before a ruling could be made about the workers' First Amendment rights.

Significance
A state must determine whether religious use of a drug (peyote) is legal. If so, then individuals fired for such use were entitled to benefits; if state law prohibits religious use of drugs and such prohibition is consistent with the U.S. Constitution, then the state is free to withhold unemployment compensation benefits.

Two persons were employed by an Oregon nonprofit corporation as drug and alcohol abuse rehabilitation counselors. As a matter of policy, the corporation required its counselors to abstain from use of non-prescription drugs. Both counselors were members of the Native American Church, a religious organization of American Indians. One of the central practices of the church is peyotism, or the ingestion of small amounts of peyote—a cactus with hallucinogenic properties—for sacramental purposes. After taking part in a church ceremony in which they each ingested a small amount of peyote, both counselors were discharged from their jobs for violating the corporation's drug policy. The counselors applied to the Employment Division of Oregon's Department of Human Resources for unemployment compensation, but the department's Employment Appeals Board ultimately denied their applications on the grounds that the counselors had been discharged for misconduct connected with work. The Oregon Court of Appeals, reversing the board's decisions, held that the denial of benefits to persons who were discharged for engaging in a religious act constituted an unjustified burden on the right of free exercise of religion. The court of appeals also remanded the cases to the board for further findings as to the religious nature of the counselors' acts

The Supreme Court of Oregon, holding that further findings were unnecessary, affirmed both judgments as modified. In its opinion as to the first counselor, the Oregon Supreme Court held that there was no violation of the Oregon State Constitution's freedom of religious provisions, but that the U.S. Supreme Court's decisions in *Sherbert v. Verner* (1963) and *Thomas v. Review Board of the Indiana Employment Security Division* (1981), required a holding that there had been a significant burden on religious rights under the exercise of religion clause of the Constitution's First Amendment. The Oregon Supreme Court also ruled that the state's interest in denying benefits was not greater than in *Sherbert v. Verner* or *Thomas v. Review Board of the Indiana Employment Security Division*, since the board had erroneously relied on the state's interest in proscribing the use of dangerous drugs rather than its interest in the financial integrity of the unemployment com-

Frank Dayish, president of the Native American Church of North America, and members use peyote in religious ceremonies.
© Photograph by Marc F. Henning. AP/Wide World Photos/Daily Times.

pensation fund. The court noted that although the possession of peyote was a crime in Oregon, such possession was lawful in many jurisdictions. In its opinion as to the second counselor, the Oregon Supreme Court noted that other courts had acknowledged the role of peyote in the Native American Church, and quoted at length a description of the practice of peyotism from a California Supreme Court decision which held that the practice was permitted in California.

On *certiorari,* the U.S. Supreme Court vacated and remanded the respect in both cases. In an opinion by Justice Stevens, it was held that a necessary predicate to a court evaluation of the counselor's federal claim was an understanding of the legality of their conduct as a matter of state law. Although the Oregon Supreme Court had made no definitive ruling on the question of whether the practice of peyotism violated state law, its opinions were written in such a way that the possibility could not be disregarded that Oregon's legislation or state constitution might be construed to permit peyotism. But the possibility that the counselors' conduct would be unprotected if it violated state law was nonetheless sufficient to council against affirming the Oregon's Supreme Court's holding. Thus, it was necessary to vacate judgements and remand the cases for further proceedings in order to attain a definitive ruling concerning the status of peyotism as a matter of state law.

The Religious Freedom Restoration Act

In 1993, Congress passed the Religious Freedom Restoration Act (RFRA), which established prohibitions against interference by federal, state, or local governments in citizens' freedom of religion except where a compelling interest can be shown. The enactment of the RFRA resulted in part from a lobbying effort by an array of secular and religious groups, including the United States Catholic Conference, the American Civil Liberties Union, the Baptist Joint Committee, the Anti-Defamation League, and Americans United for Separation of Church and State.

These groups were motivated by the Supreme Court's decision in *Employment Division v. Smith,* which they viewed as an infringement on First Amendment rights. Previously, courts required a compelling reason to burden religious freedom, but that decision, in the eyes of detractors, offered no such compelling reason. "Thus, under the Court's view of the First Amendment," wrote David W. Kinkopf in the *National Catholic Reporter,* "a neutral and generally applicable criminal law that prohibited the consumption of alcohol could be enforced against a Catholic priest and the communicants who drank wine during the Eucharist."

Source(s): Kinkopf, David W. "Court Ponders Broad Religious Freedom Issues," *National Catholic Reporter,* 6 June 1997, p. 9.

Justices Brennan, Marshall, and Blackmun dissented, expressing the view that the Oregon Supreme Court's opinions should have been affirmed, because the Oregon Supreme Court disavowed any interest of the state in enforcing criminal laws through the denial of unemployment benefits, and thus it was unnecessary to determine whether the counselors' conduct was criminal under state law.

Related Cases
Sherbert v. Verner, 374 U.S. 398 (1963).
Thomas v. Review Board of the Indiana Employment Security Division, 450 U.S. 707 (1981).

Bibliography and Further Reading

Campbell, Joan Brown, James M. Dunn, and James A. Rudin. "Religious Liberty Requires Unceasing Vigilance." *USA Today (Magazine),* September 1996, p. 58.

Eastland, Terry. "Religion, Politics & the Clintons." *Commentary,* January 1994, p. 40.

Gaffney, Edward, Jr. "Pass the Peyote: The Religious Freedom Restoration Act." *Commonweal,* January 28, 1994, p. 5.

Greene, Abner S., "The Political Balance of the Religion Clauses." *Yale Law Journal,* May 1993, p. 1611.

Hall, Kermit L., ed. *The Oxford Companion to the Supreme Court.* New York: Oxford University Press, p. 725.

McClay, Wilfred M. "The Worst Decision Since 'Dred Scott'?" *Commentary,* October 1997, p. 52.

Neuman, Gerald L. "The Global Dimension of RFRA." *Constitutional Commentary,* spring 1997, p. 33.

Rosen, Jeffrey. "Anti-antidisestablishmentarianism: Too Much Religious Freedom." *The New Republic,* February 24, 1997, p. 10.

Silverglate, Harvey A. "Paying the Piper Who Protects Our Freedoms." *The National Law Journal,* April 29, 1996, p. A17.

Solove, Daniel J. "Faith Profaned: The Religious Freedom Restoration Act and Religion in the Prisons." *Yale Law Journal,* November 1996, p. 459.

SEMINOLE TRIBE OF FLORIDA V. FLORIDA

Legal Citation: 517 U.S. 44 (1996)

Petitioner
Seminole Tribe of Florida

Respondent
State of Florida

Petitioner's Claim
That the state of Florida violated the Indian Gaming Regulatory Act of 1988 (IGRA) by refusing to negotiate with the Seminoles to establish gambling casinos on the reservation.

Chief Lawyer for Petitioner
Bruce S. Rogow

Chief Lawyer for Respondent
Jonathan A. Glogau

Justices for the Court
Anthony M. Kennedy, Sandra Day O'Connor, Antonin Scalia, William H. Rehnquist (writing for the Court), Clarence Thomas

Justices Dissenting
Stephen Breyer, Ruth Bader Ginsburg, John Paul Stevens, David H. Souter

Place
Washington, D.C.

Date of Decision
27 March 1996

Decision
That IGRA violates the Eleventh Amendment, and therefore Native American tribes cannot sue states in federal court for failure to negotiate a gaming compact in good faith, as provided in the act.

Significance
By removing the primary means of enforcing IGRA, the decision limits its effectiveness, thereby impacting tribal economic viability, federal support for tribal sovereignty, and state-tribal relationships. The decision also marks a conservative turn in the Supreme Court's stance on the balance of power between federal and state governments and may affect state accountability in several legal areas outside of Native American law.

Beginning in the late 1970s, the establishment of tribally-operated bingo houses and gambling casinos on Native American reservations developed into an increasingly controversial issue. Gaming operations had created conflict among tribes, their non-Indian neighbors and state officials, and had caused divisions within tribal communities as well.

In 1988, Congress enacted the Indian Gaming Regulatory Act (IGRA) with several stated objectives: to clarify the regulation of gaming among federal, state, and tribal laws, to prevent the involvement of organized crime in Indian gaming, and to foster tribal sovereignty and encourage economic growth on reservations. The act divided games into three classes, each with its own level of regulation. It stated that in order to operate Class III games—casino-style gambling that typically involves high stakes—tribes must reside in a state that permits such gaming, and must establish a gaming compact with the state. The act also required the state to negotiate in good faith with the tribe; if the state failed to do so, IGRA authorized a tribe to sue the state in federal court.

In 1992, the Seminole tribe of Florida brought the state of Florida and its governor to federal district court for failing to negotiate a gaming compact in good faith. Negotiations had broken down over what type of gaming operation the tribe could run. The defendants argued that state sovereign immunity prevented the Seminoles from suing Florida in a federal court, but the court denied the motion. The Eleventh Circuit Court of Appeals reversed the decision in 1994, arguing that the Eleventh Amendment did protect the defendants from lawsuit. In 1996, the Supreme Court upheld that decision in a 5-4 split. Chief Justice Rehnquist wrote the majority opinion, joined by Justices Kennedy, O'Connor, Scalia, and Thomas, while Justices Stevens and Souter wrote dissenting opinions, the latter joined by Justices Breyer and Ginsburg.

The majority opinion in *Seminole Tribe of Florida v. Florida* held that the Eleventh Amendment prevents private suits against state governments in federal court. In order to override this restriction, a case must meet two requirements. First, Congress must explicitly state in a statute that it intends to abrogate state sovereign

---

Tribal-Sponsored Gambling

In the last decades of the twentieth century, the federal government conferred on Indian tribes the right to sponsor gambling casinos on tribal property. Tribes throughout the nation have been quick to respond, and many groups that were formerly destitute have suddenly become powerful economic players. The same is true among non-Indian groups selected to implement gambling as a means of economic recovery, most notably in Tunica County, Mississippi.

There are numerous arguments against tribal-sponsored gambling, including its interference with traditional Native American cultures. On the other hand, it is hard to justify removal of gambling rights now that they have been conferred.

Source(s): Eadington, William R., ed. *Indian Gaming and the Law.* Reno, NV: Institute for the Study of Gambling and Commercial Gaming, University of Nevada, 1990.

---

immunity and allow a suit against a state in federal court. Secondly, that statute's authority must emanate from Section 5 of the Fourteenth Amendment. In establishing this second provision, the Court overturned the 1989 Supreme Court decision in *Pennsylvania v. Union Gas,* which held that the Interstate Commerce Clause in Article I of the Constitution also allowed Congress to abrogate state sovereign immunity.

In *Seminole Tribe,* the Court ruled that though IGRA met the first requirement to override the Eleventh Amendment, it failed to meet the second. According to the Court, the Indian Commerce Clause, like the Interstate Commerce Clause, granted Congress no authority to abrogate state sovereign immunity. The decision also held that the *Ex Parte Young* doctrine did not apply. *Ex Parte Young* authorizes private suits against state officials in federal court, rather than directly against states, and has traditionally been used to circumvent the Eleventh Amendment and hold states responsible for violations of federal law. In *Seminole Tribe,* the Court ruled that because Congress had already provided a detailed remedial scheme within IGRA, it precluded the application of *Ex Parte Young.* Unfortunately for the Seminoles, the Court had just declared the primary component of that very remedial scheme—suing a recalcitrant state in federal court—unconstitutional.

The Supreme Court's ruling in *Seminole Tribe* had its most immediate impact on IGRA and the parameters of Native American gaming. The decision rendered the primary means of enforcing IGRA illegal, thus leaving tribes with three choices when faced with a state that refuses to negotiate a gaming compact for Class III games: they can file suit in a state court, operate gaming operations without a tribal-state compact, or ask the secretary of the interior to prescribe gaming regulations for them.

These options generally seem less effective than the one struck down by the Supreme Court. State courts usually award plaintiffs smaller damages than federal courts, while leaving federal courts out of the equation limits federal appeals to the Supreme Court, which does not hear all cases. As for operating Class III gambling

without a compact, Anthony J. Marks wrote in the summer 1996 issue of the *Loyola of Los Angeles Entertainment Law Journal* that a tribe that chooses this option "will do so at its own peril," since "this activity could result in criminal punishment or an injunction prohibiting the operation of Class III games."

Given the revenues already generated by Indian gaming, and the degree to which many reservation communities have depended on it for economic rejuvenation, the *Seminole* decision could pose a serious threat to those tribes currently without compacts. According to Mike Williams in an *Atlanta Journal Constitution* article from March 1996, tribal gaming operated in 23 states and brought in $6 billion dollars annually. To many Indian communities, the economic boost that gambling casinos represent offers a remedy for high unemployment, low life expectancy, substandard housing and education, alcoholism, and hopelessness. As a 1995 Minnesota Indian Gaming Association publication noted, "casino gaming has begun generating desperately needed revenues for tribal governments, resulting in a gradual improvement in the quality of life on most Indian reservations. However, the ravages caused by centuries of deprivation, poverty, and neglect cannot be corrected overnight." Unfortunately many non-Native Americans resent casino-generated economic growth on the reservations, thus prompting state governments to oppose Indian gaming.

Beyond the immediate scope of gaming regulation, the *Seminole* decision also holds more general implications for Indian tribes' relationships to state and federal governments. Since its inception, the United States government has passed through several contradictory phases regarding its official policy toward Native Americans, though each phase ultimately removed more land and resources from Indian control. Beginning in the late 1960s, the federal government moved away from its campaign to terminate tribes as political units and began encouraging tribal self-determination and economic development. Throughout this history of shifting federal policy, the United States has consistently given Congress ultimate authority regarding

Indian tribes and strictly limited state jurisdiction. Stephen L. Pevar noted in *The Rights of Indians and Tribes,* published in 1992, how the Supreme Court had consistently ruled that "the state's interest is secondary to the tribe's interest in self-government," particularly on reservations where tribal sovereignty and economic welfare seemed at stake.

What role does the *Seminole* decision play in this complex balance of power between tribal, state, and federal governments? To some, the ruling seems a clear threat to the encouragement of self-determination and economic growth embodied by legislation such as IGRA. *Seminole Tribe*'s impact may not be so clear-cut, however. Some tribal leaders opposed the passage of IGRA itself as an erosion of tribal sovereignty, arguing that requiring a tribal-state compact for Class III gaming expanded states' jurisdiction on reservations. And if tribes, barred from suing states in federal court to force them to negotiate, choose instead to ask the secretary of the interior to establish gaming rules, state governments are left out of the equation altogether. Exactly what kind of regulations a given secretary might impose remains unclear, and is certainly subject to the prevailing political climate.

Finally, *Seminole Tribe*'s significance reaches beyond Native American issues into broader questions of federalism and constitutional interpretation. This decision, combined with other Supreme Court rulings such as *Atascadero State Hospital v. Scanlon* (1985) and *United States v. Lopez* (1995), marks a trend in which the more conservative justices have pushed for greater protection of states' rights over federal regulation. *Seminole Tribe* could affect future decisions in environmental legislation, bankruptcy, copyrights, and labor law. In all of these areas, it could become more difficult for private interests to bring states to federal court for violations of federal laws.

Related Cases

Ex parte Young, 209 U.S. 123 (1909).
Atascadero State Hospital v. Scanlon, 473 U.S. 234 (1985).
Pennsylvania v. Union Gas Co., 491 U.S. 1 (1989).
United States v. Lopez, 514 U.S. 549 (1995).

Bibliography and Further Reading

Chemerinsky, Erwin. "Restricting Federal Court Jurisdiction." *Trial,* July, 1996, pp. 18-19.

Gibson, S. Elizabeth. "Sovereign Immunity in Bankruptcy: The Next Chapter." *American Bankruptcy Law Journal,* Vol. 70, no. 2, spring, 1996, pp. 195-216.

Hovenkamp, Herbert. "Judicial Restraint and Constitutional Federalism: The Supreme Court's *Lopez* and *Seminole Tribe* Decisions." *Columbia Law Review,* Vol. 96, no. 8, December, 1996, pp. 2213-2247.

Marks, Anthony J. "A House of Cards: Has the Federal Government Succeeded in Regulating Indian Gaming?" *Loyola of Los Angeles Entertainment Law Journal,* Vol. 17, no. 1, summer, 1996, pp. 157-199.

Miller, Joseph E. III. "Abrogating Sovereign Immunity Pursuant to its Bankruptcy Clause Power: Congress Went Too Far." *Bankruptcy Developments Journal,* Vol. 13, no. 1, winter, 1996, pp. 197-234.

Pevar, Stephen L. *The Rights of Indians and Tribes: The Basic ACLU Guide to Indian and Tribal Rights.* Carbondale, IL: Southern Illinois University Press, 1992.

Piscitelli, Kathryn S. "*Seminole Tribe of Florida v. Florida*: Can State Employees Still Sue in Federal Court?" *Labor Law Journal,* Vol. 47, no. 4, April, 1996, pp. 211-217.

Williams, Mike. "Indians Lose Court Fight on Casinos." *Atlanta Journal Constitution,* 28 March 1996, sec. A, pp. 1-2.

HORNELL BREWING CO. ET AL. v. SETH BIG CROW

Legal Citation: 133 F.3d 1087 (1998)

Appellant
Hornell Brewing Co. et al.

Appellee
Seth H. Big Crow et al.

Appellant's Claim
The Rosebud Sioux Tribal Court did not have inherent and exclusive jurisdiction over the personal property rights vested in the estate of Crazy Horse.

Justices for the Court
Judge Donald Lay (writing for the Court), Judge Pasco M. Bowman, Judge Diane E. Murphy.

Justices Dissenting
None

Place
Minneapolis, Minnesota

Date of Decision
14 January 1998

Decision
Found in favor of Hornell and reversed the Rosebud Sioux Supreme Court ruling by finding that the tribal courts lacked legal authority over disputes originating outside reservation boundaries.

Significance
The decision added further clarification of tribal court jurisdiction issues nationwide. The marketing activities of Hornell outside the Rosebud Sioux Reservation did not fall within the tribe's inherent sovereign authority. In the 1990s, a series of court decisions narrowed the jurisdiction of tribal courts with respect to non-Indians.

The unique legal relationship between the U.S. government and the several hundred federally-recognized Indian tribes is complex. Tribes were self-governing independent nations before the arrival of Europeans to North America's eastern coast. From the beginning of settlement, the American colonies recognized and honored this inherent sovereignty, the long-standing right to govern themselves. This formal recognition was later reflected in treaties, early federal laws, and Supreme Court cases after the founding of the United States. Despite recognition of tribal sovereignty, the United States retained plenary (absolute) power over tribes to determine and revise the limits of their sovereignty. Perhaps, no aspect of the U.S.-tribal relationship is more complex than the determination of legal jurisdiction between tribal, state, and federal court systems.

Regarding subject matter jurisdiction of tribal courts, two factors must be considered: were either of the parties involved Native Americans, and did the action take place on tribal lands. In criminal jurisdiction matters, the Court in *Oliphant v. Suquamish Indian Tribe* (1978) greatly limited tribal jurisdiction over non-Native Americans. However, in civil jurisdiction tribes held considerably more authority. That authority faced greater limitations, however, as federal court decisions were issued. In 1981, the Supreme Court in *Montana v. United States* established a general rule that Native American tribes lack legal civil authority over the conduct of nonmembers on non-Native American land within a reservation, subject to two exceptions. One exception was if the nonmembers had entered consensual relationships with the tribe or its members. The second exception concerned activity directly affecting the tribe's political integrity, economic security, health, or welfare.

Lakota Pride

Crazy Horse, whose name in Lakota was Tasunke Witko, helped lead Sioux and Cheyenne Indians against General George A. Custer's cavalry at the 1876 Battle of Little Big Horn. After the battle, Crazy Horse went to live with his mother's relatives. He was soon killed at Fort Robinson, Nebraska, in 1877. Crazy Horse was a famous and highly respected leader of the Oglala

Sioux, recognized as a spiritual and political leader. In 1982, the U.S. Postal Service issued a stamp honoring Crazy Horse, and a national Crazy Horse Monument was being constructed in South Dakota in the late twentieth century. The Rosebud Sioux Reservation, where descendants of Crazy Horse lived, was also located in South Dakota.

In 1992, Hornell Brewing Co. of Brooklyn, New York introduced an alcoholic beverage labeled "The Original Crazy Horse Malt Liquor" sold in 40-ounce containers in most states. Owned and marketed by Hornell, the beer was actually brewed by the G. Heileman Brewing Co. Inc. of LaCrosse, Wisconsin, the nation's fifth largest brewery, and several other breweries. In response to immediate Native American protests, a federal law was passed later that year prohibiting federal approval of such labels. However, in 1993 a federal judge struck down the law as a violation of free speech.

Seth H. Big Crow, Sr. was a descendant of Crazy Horse and an administrator of Crazy Horse's estate. With the demise of the federal law in court and Hornell's continued marketing of the beverage, Big Crow filed suit in the Rosebud Sioux Tribal Court against Hornell and its associated breweries in 1994. The suit challenged Hornell's right to use the Crazy Horse name in the manufacture, sale, and distribution of the alcoholic beverage. Crazy Horse had in fact opposed the use of alcohol by his people. Big Crow claimed defamation, violation of the estate's right of publicity, and negligent and intentional infliction of emotional distress. He also alleged violations of the Lanham Act and the Indian Arts and Crafts Act, seeking injunctive and declaratory relief, as well as damages.

The trial court found *Montana* irrelevant to this case since it applied only to questions of tribal regulatory and legislative issues, not tribal adjudicatory authority. Even if *Montana* was applicable, the court concluded the breweries' conduct likely satisfied both of *Montana's* exceptions. Big Crow appealed to the Rosebud Sioux Supreme Court.

In considering the subject matter jurisdiction issue, the Rosebud Sioux Supreme Court held that the trial court inappropriately applied the *Montana* precedence. In May of 1996, the supreme court ruled the breweries had sufficient contact with the Rosebud Sioux Reservation to establish tribal jurisdiction and the estate had established subject-matter jurisdiction. The tribal supreme court also held that the tribal court improperly dismissed Big Crow's Lanham Act claim, but acknowledged Big Crow did not have legal standing to sue under the Indian Arts and Crafts Act. The Rosebud Sioux Supreme Court remanded the case back to the tribal court for a "prompt trial on the merits."

In response to the tribal court's ruling, Hornell filed suit in July of 1996 in the U.S. District Court for the District of South Dakota against Big Crow, the Rosebud

Sioux Tribal Court, and the tribal court judge, seeking declaratory and injunctive relief. Hornell argued that the tribal courts had neither personal jurisdiction over the breweries nor subject matter jurisdiction over Big Crow's claims. In finding in favor of Hornell, the federal district court issued an order prohibiting the Rosebud Sioux Tribal Court from conducting any further proceedings on the case. The district court disagreed with the rationale applied by the Rosebud Sioux Supreme Court to establish subject matter jurisdiction over the estate's claims.

The federal district court disagreed with the tribal supreme court by finding the *Montana* case directly applied, but neither *Montana* exception were satisfied. The tribal courts, therefore, had no subject matter jurisdiction over Big Crow's claims. The court issued an injunction order against the tribal supreme court's previous decision that the case should be resolved on its merits by the tribal trial court. However, the federal court believed the tribal courts needed to examine some other issues further. Therefore, the district court remanded the case to the tribal court to conduct an evidentiary hearing on the issues of personal and subject matter jurisdiction, but to not proceed on the merits. Still claiming no tribal jurisdiction existed for this case, Hornell appealed the decision to remand the case back to the tribal court to the U.S. Court of Appeals for the Eighth Circuit. The tribal court, tribal judge, and Big Crow also appealed the preliminary injunction to the federal appeals court.

The Limits of Tribal Jurisdiction

Hornell, of course, argued against recognizing tribal court jurisdiction since none of their activity occurred on the reservation. The issues in Big Crow's claim were the breweries' manufacture, sale, and distribution of Crazy Horse Malt Liquor. Big Crow claimed Hornell seized control of tribal property, the image of Crazy Horse, without actually stepping on the reservation.

By unanimous decision, the three-judge panel appeals court found that the conduct of Hornell outside the Rosebud Sioux Reservation was not within the tribe's jurisdiction. Judge Lay, writing for the court, used a Supreme Court decision in *Strate v. A-1 Contractors* (1997) issued while *Hornell* was proceeding through the court system. *Strate* addressed legal issues related to non-Native American use of private lands located within reservation boundaries. A non-Native American driver of a truck owned by a non-Native American company collided with an automobile driven by a non-Native American widow of a deceased tribal member on the Fort Berthold Indian Reservation. The collision occurred on a state highway crossing through reservation land. The widow filed a personal injury suit in tribal court, and the tribal court concluded it had jurisdiction to settle her claim. Upon appeal, a federal dis-

trict court concluded the tribal court had civil jurisdiction. The Eighth Circuit Court of Appeals then
reversed the district court's judgment, concluding that
under *Montana,* the tribal court lacked subject matter
jurisdiction over the dispute. The U. S. Supreme Court
affirmed the decision equating the state highway with
private non-Native American land. The Court concluded that the *Montana* rule and its two exceptions
governed the jurisdiction.

Lay, in considering subject matter jurisdiction, noted
that unless specifically provided in federal law or treaty,
tribal jurisdiction over the activities of nonmembers
applied only in limited circumstances, primarily civil
jurisdiction over non-Native Americans for actions on
their reservations. Lay emphasized that "on their reservations" was the key factor. The precedent established
in *Montana* was that Native American tribes do not have
civil jurisdiction over the actions of non-Native Americans outside their reservations. Therefore, the key issue
was that the breweries did not actually conduct their
activities on the Rosebud reservation or even within
South Dakota. Tribes lacked any legal authority to
determine external relations.

Big Crow countered that Hornell engaged in the sale
of other beverages, including some alcoholic beverages,
on the reservation. The Rosebud Sioux Supreme Court
had also asserted subject matter jurisdiction because the
breweries' product affected the health and welfare of the
tribe. The tribe, they contended, should be able to
resolve the harm suffered by its members on the reservation. Lay found these arguments irrelevant. In fact,
the district court rejected this reasoning, too, by stating,

> If providing a forum for its members would be
> a sufficient reason to confer subject matter
> jurisdiction upon the tribal courts when a
> tribal member is a party to a lawsuit, it follows
> that the tribal courts would always have civil
> subject matter jurisdiction over non-Indians.
> There would have been no reason for the dis-
> cussion in *Montana* regarding the broad gen-
> eral rule of no civil jurisdiction over non-
> Indians and the two narrow exceptions to that
> general rule. Therefore, this Court does not
> agree that the second *Montana* exception pro-
> vides tribal civil subject matter jurisdiction
> over the brewing companies in this case, under
> the present record.

Lay strongly agreed with this conclusion. The tribal
court had even argued that although Crazy Horse Malt
Liquor was not sold on the Rosebud Sioux Reservation,
it was advertised on the Internet and was available to
tribal members on the reservation. Therefore, a direct

effect on tribal members existed, they argued. However,
Lay found that advertising outside the reservation and
on the Internet did not directly affect the health and
welfare of the tribe. The Internet was similar to use of
airwaves for national broadcasts. The tribe held no proprietary interest.

Lay found that the breweries' conduct outside the
Rosebud Sioux Reservation did not violate tribal sovereignty since the tribe had no adjudicatory authority.
Lay canceled the district court's order of remand and
the preliminary injunction. Lay concluded the Rosebud Sioux Tribal Court lacked adjudicatory authority
over Hornell's actions outside the Rosebud Sioux
Reservation.

Impact

The *Hornell* decision further defined the limits of tribal
court jurisdiction over non-Native Americans in the
United States. Regarding the social issues, Native Americans and others argued that such products as Hornell's
malt liquor still treats Native Americans as mascots.
Inclusion of an image of an eagle feather bonnet and
medicine wheel, both of spiritual importance to Native
American traditions, would be the same as placing
the crucifix on a beer bottle or placing the image of a
rabbi on pork rind packages. Native American, religious
groups, and groups representing ethnic minorities
challenged corporations to responsibly respect the various cultural traditions composing contemporary American society.

Related Cases

Oliphant v. Suquamish Indian Tribe, 435 U.S. 191 (1978).
Montana v. United States, 450 U.S. 544 (1981).
Strate v. A-1 Contractors, 117 S.Ct. 1404 (1997).

Bibliography and Further Reading

"Battle Continues over Crazy Horse Malt Liquor on
Appeal." *Modern Brewery Age,* 1 July 1996.

"Hornell Brewing Co. Wants Crazy Horse Case out of
Tribal Court System." *Modern Brewery Age,* 24 November 1997.

Metz, Sharon and Michael Thee. "Brewers Intoxicated
with Racist Imagery." *Business and Society Review,* spring
1994.

Wilkins, David E. *American Indian Sovereignty and the
U.S. Supreme Court: The Masking of Justice.* Austin: University of Texas Press, 1997.

Wilkinson, Charles F. *American Indians, Time, and the
Law: Native Societies in Modern Constitutional Law.* New
Haven, CN: Yale University Press, 1987.

TAXATION

History

Although several countries in Europe, including France and Great Britain, had begun a personal income taxation system in the 1700s, the United States did not adopt an income tax until 1862, during the Civil War. A few years later, however, this wartime measure was repealed.

In 1894 Congress tried again by initiating a two percent tax on individual and corporate income. But in 1895 the Supreme Court declared the levy unconstitutional. Article 1 of the U.S. Constitution states that "direct taxes shall be apportioned among the several states." Direct taxes are those which are levied on the property, business, or income of the individual who pays the tax. The Court ruled that the U.S. Constitution prohibited the federal government from enacting an income tax because revenue derived from the tax would not be distributed in direct proportion to the nation's population.

It would take the ratification of the Sixteenth Amendment in February of 1913 to pave the way for creation of a national income tax. The amendment provided Congress with the power to levy "taxes on income, from whatever source derived, without apportionment among the several States." The Tariff Act of 1913 included a provision for a tax on individual and corporate incomes. Before a national income tax was adopted, the U.S. government relied primarily on income generated from tariffs. Today, that has shifted and income taxes are a major budget revenue.

The IRS

The Internal Revenue Service (IRS) enforces the Internal Revenue Code, which includes federal laws regarding the payment and collection of taxes, such as income, employment, and estate. The individual income tax is determined using a progressive tax rate. This means that tax rates are allocated to income brackets and as income rises, so does the tax rate percentage. In theory, this structure shifts a greater tax burden to those who have higher incomes and thus have a greater ability to pay. In the late 1990s, the tax rates started at 15 percent in the lowest income bracket and gradually increased to an upper limit of approximately 40 per-

cent in the highest income bracket. Corporate taxation has a less progressive structure and is based on a company's net profits.

To determine taxable net income, taxpayers are allowed to subtract certain types of deductions from their gross income. Many of these deductions are intended to stimulate specific types of savings or spending that benefit our society, such as a deduction for charitable contributions. The mortgage deduction is designed to encourage home ownership. A taxpayer is allowed to subtract interest paid on a loan that has been assured of payment by the pledging of a home. The home may be a house, cooperative apartment, condominium, house trailer, or houseboat. In a mortgage loan, property is temporarily transferred to the creditor until the borrower has paid the loan in full. To qualify for the mortgage deduction, the loan may be a mortgage to purchase a home, a second mortgage, a line of credit, or a home equity loan. The points, or fees, paid by a borrower to obtain a home mortgage loan can also be deducted.

Capital gains and losses are taxed at a different rate than ordinary income. Capital gains or losses are created by the sale or trade of a capital asset. Property held for personal use is considered a capital asset. Examples of capital assets include stocks or bonds, a house, a car, furnishings, land, a coin or stamp collection, jewelry or gems, or precious metals.

The sale of noncapital assets is treated as ordinary gain or loss and taxed accordingly. Noncapital assets are often used in the course of a trade or business and include depreciable property (items whose value can be written off on taxes over multiple years), property held for future sale to customers, real property, and accounts or notes receivable. Creative endeavors are also considered noncapital assets and include a copyright on a literary, musical, or artistic composition.

Capital assets are classified as either short term or long term. Long-term capital assets are generally items held for more than one year. Net capital gain is net long-term capital gains less net short-term capital losses. The resulting net capital gain is taxed at a more favorable rate than ordinary income. As an example, during most of the 1990s, ordinary income was subject to a top rate of almost 40 percent while the highest tax rate for net capital gains was 28 percent.

There are additional deductions or credits that taxpayers can subtract from gross income but they are subject to limitations as set forth by the Internal Revenue Code. These deductions include medical and dental expenses, contributions to individual retirement accounts (IRAs), casualty and theft losses, and employee business expenses.

Social Security and Medicare

In 1935, Congress enacted the Social Security Act to provide old-age benefits. The plan created the Old-Age, Survivors, and Disability Insurance (OASDI) to assist workers and their families and Medicare, a health insurance plan for people over 65. These benefits, in addition to other programs to aid those in need, were to be financed through a payroll tax. Employers make automatic deductions, or withholdings, from an employee's wages for Social Security and Medicare taxes. However, the withholdings account for only one-half of the taxes due and employers are required to match the employee's contribution. The employer is responsible for making the payment of Social Security and Medicare taxes to the U.S. Treasury. While there is a maximum amount of wages that are subject to Social Security taxes, all wages are subject to Medicare tax. The amount of the taxes and the benefits for Social Security and Medicare are adjusted frequently to keep pace with inflation. In addition to Social Security and Medicare withholdings, employers may also be responsible for making automatic payroll deductions for federal, state, and municipal taxes.

Sole proprietors, or people who work for themselves, are subject to a self-employment tax, which is composed of a Social Security tax and a Medicare tax. The self-employment tax is separate from the federal income tax and is based on net earnings from business operations. The tax is calculated by subtracting business-related expenses from gross income. Allowable deductions include expenditures such as rent, insurance, depreciation of property, and business and travel entertainment. However, many of these expenses are deductible subject to certain limitations. A self-employed individual may also have to make estimated quarterly tax payments for both federal and state taxes.

Levies, Tariffs and Duties

The federal government also imposes taxes on the manufacture, purchase, sale, or consumption of certain commodities. These levies, called excise taxes, are assessed on items such as alcohol, tobacco, and firearms. There is an excise tax imposed on gasoline and diesel fuel and the revenue derived from this motor-fuel tax is earmarked for highway construction, improvement, and maintenance. There also is a luxury tax, which has been repealed on all items except automobiles. The tax is assessed on the amount that the vehicle's price exceeds the base sticker amount. This tax will be phased out by the year 2002.

Import duties are also considered excise taxes. Import duties are taxes, or tariffs, on merchandise imported into the United States from other countries. The purpose of the tariffs is to protect the interests of U.S. manufacturers against foreign competitors. The duty is meant to level the playing field with countries, such as Japan, who have imposed strict import limits on U.S. goods into their country. Additionally, U.S. residents may have to pay a duty to the U.S. Customs Service on items they have purchased in other countries and are bringing into the United States.

State and local governments also assess a variety of revenue-generating taxes. Most states and some cities levy individual income taxes with the lower rates than federal tax rates. Alaska, Florida, Nevada, South Dakota, Texas, Washington, and Wyoming do not impose state income taxes. Sales taxes, especially at the retail level, are a major source of income for many local governments. The sales tax is considered a regressive tax because both the poor and the rich pay the same amount. Thus the tax consumes a larger portion of income of the low-income taxpayers. To correct this problem, some goods, which are considered essentials, are exempt from a sales tax altogether or taxed at a lower rate. Examples of essential goods include food, clothing, and drugs.

State taxes are also imposed on real and personal property. Real property is permanent and nonmovable and includes land and buildings. By its nature, real property can only be taxed by the state where it is located. The process of determining and listing the value of real property for taxation purposes is called an assessment. A tax is then levied based on a certain percentage of the assessed value. Additions or improvements to real estate will cause the assessed value of a property to increase. If a taxpayer fails to pay property taxes, a tax lien will be imposed against the owner and the property will not be able to be sold until the back taxes are paid.

Personal property is movable and classified as either tangible or intangible. Tangible property is physical property that has value in and of itself, such as automobiles or equipment. The value of intangible property does not come from the property itself but from the rights it assigns. Examples of intangible property include accounts receivable, stocks, and bonds. Tangible personal property that is in a permanent location can only be taxed by one state. Intangible personal property, however, may be subject to taxation by several states.

Corporations or manufacturers are often assessed special business-related taxes. Sales taxes may be levied on goods at various stages throughout the production and distribution of a product. Because these taxes are often assessed on gross receipts that have not had expenses deducted, it is possible that the taxable value of the product at a given stage includes the taxes already paid at an earlier stage. To avoid this situation from happening, a value-added tax method is often used. The value-added tax is determined using net receipts calculated by subtracting expenses from total sales. Corporations are also liable to pay corporate franchise taxes. These taxes are measured by income and considered a cost of the privilege of doing business in a state. Franchise, in this case, is a privilege conferred by a government grant to a company; for instance, a franchise to operate a train system.

Employers must pay taxes to their state for unemployment compensation, an insurance program for employees who lose their jobs through no fault of their own. A person who is fired for good cause, such as misconduct, does not qualify for unemployment insurance. The program was instituted by the federal government through the Social Security Act of 1935 but it is administered by individual states. Unemployment compensation provides unemployed individuals a certain amount of money each week for a specified time.

There are also state and federal estate and inheritance taxes. The estate tax is a levy for the privilege of transferring property when someone dies and is assessed on the entire estate before its distribution to heirs. The inheritance tax is the tax imposed to each heir for the privilege of transferring the descendent's property to them.

Bibliography and Further Reading

Duarte, Joseph S. *The Income Tax Is Obsolete*. New Rochelle, NY: Arlington House Publisher, 1974.

Internet Revenue Service Web site. Available at: http://www.irs.ustreas.gov

Reader's Digest Family Legal Guide. Pleasantville, NY: Reader's Digest Association, Inc., 1981.

Bernstein, Peter W. (ed.)*The Ernest & Young Tax Guide 1997*. New York: John Wiley & Sons, Inc., 1997.

HYLTON V. UNITED STATES

Legal Citation: 3 U.S. 171 (1796)

Petitioner
Daniel Hylton

Respondent
United States

Petitioner's Claim
That a federal tax imposed upon private carriages violated the Constitution's requirement that direct taxes be imposed in proportion to the populations of each state.

Chief Lawyer for Petitioner
Ingersoll, Attorney General of Pennsylvania

Chief Lawyer for Respondent
Alexander Hamilton, U.S. Secretary of the Treasury

Justices for the Court
Samuel Chase, James Iredell, William Paterson, James Wilson

Justices Dissenting
None (William Cushing and Oliver Ellsworth did not participate)

Place
Washington, D.C.

Date of Decision
8 March 1796

Decision
That the tax imposed on private carriages was a duty, rather than a direct tax, and thus needed only to be uniform across the United States, rather than proportional to the population of each state.

Significance
This case involved the first challenge to the power of the newly formed federal government to impose taxes under the Constitution. In upholding the carriage tax, the Supreme Court recognized the broad power of Congress in the area of taxation, a power that has continually been recognized since the *Hylton* decision. More importantly, however, the decision was one of a number of events in the early and middle 1790s which established the supremacy of the federal government over the states.

In 1791, only two years had passed since the ratification of the U.S. Constitution and the establishment of the federal government. Alexander Hamilton, one of the principal proponents of the Constitution and the first secretary of the treasury, secured the imposition of taxes on distilled spirits and carriages in that same year. Passed more as a social measure than as a means of raising revenue, both the alcohol tax and the carriage tax would lead to separate events solidifying the central role of the federal government in the newly formed republic.

The tax on distilled spirits led to the Whiskey Rebellion of 1794, when a group of farmers protested the imposition of the liquor tax. The rebellion was suppressed by the federal militia, thereby establishing the authority of the federal government to enforce federal revenue laws. Albeit more peaceful, the Court's upholding of the carriage tax signified as important an event as the government's suppression of the Whiskey Rebellion in establishing the authority of the federal government to impose taxes under the Constitution.

The congressional act of 1791 at issue in *Hylton* provided for the "laying of duties upon carriages for the conveyance of persons." It was undisputed that Daniel Hylton owned 125 carriages, and that he failed to pay the taxes imposed by the act. The United States brought an action in the Circuit Court for the District of Virginia, seeking to enforce the tax. Hylton defended the action claiming that the tax violated Article I, section 9 of the Constitution, which provides that "[n]o Capitation, or other direct Tax, shall be laid, unless in Proportion to the Census . . ." The circuit court held in favor of the government, and Hylton appealed to the U.S. Supreme Court.

On appeal, the question was whether the tax on carriages constituted a direct tax which was required to be apportioned among the states. At the time of the case, and indeed until the Sixteenth Amendment was ratified in 1913, the Constitution contained two provisions relating to the power of Congress to impose taxes. Article I, section 8 of the Constitution gives Congress a broad power to "lay and collect Taxes, Duties, Imposts and Excises . . ." That section also provides, however, that "all Duties, Imposts and Excises shall be uniform throughout the United States." The second provision, as discussed above, is found in Article I, section 9, and requires any direct tax to be laid in proportion to the population of each state.

Two brief examples illustrate how these requirements function. Suppose that the carriage tax was a duty, and thus under Article I, section 8 required to be uniform throughout the United States. In this case, the amount of tax on each carriage would have to be the same for each citizen subject to the tax. Thus, a Virginia citizen having 10 carriages would have to pay the same amount as a New York citizen having 10 carriages. On the other hand, if the tax was a direct tax required to be apportioned among the states, then the total amount collected from the citizens of any one state would have to be in proportion to their population. For example, say that the government collected a total of $100,000 in revenue from the carriage tax, and say that New York accounted for 25 percent of the total population of the United States. Under the apportionment provision, New York would have to account for $25,000 of the revenue collected, regardless of the number of carriages owned in the state.

Court Recognizes Congress's Broad Authority to Tax

Considering the carriage tax in light of these two provisions, all four justices who heard the case found that the tax was not a direct tax required to be apportioned among the states, and thus was within Congress's broad power to lay taxes. Each justice wrote a separate opinion stating his views. Justice Chase concluded that the tax was in the nature of a duty. He reasoned that a tax on expenses is an indirect tax, and "an annual tax on a carriage for the conveyance of persons, is of that kind." Thus, Justice Chase concluded that the tax was not a direct tax, and was within Congress's taxing power. Justice Chase also suggested that, as used in the Constitution, there are only two direct taxes: poll taxes and taxes on land.

Justice Paterson likewise concluded that the carriage tax was not a direct tax. Justice Paterson agreed with Justice Chase that the carriage tax was in the nature of a tax on expenses or consumption, and thus in the nature of a duty rather than a direct tax. He also reasoned that the tax was not a direct tax because it would be impossible to apportion a tax on carriages among the states in any fair manner. Likewise, Justice Iredell went to length, using specific examples, to show that it would be impossible to apportion the carriage tax fairly among the populations of the states. Thus, he concluded, "since it cannot be apportioned, it must be uniform." Justice Iredell also agreed with Justice Chase's conclusion that only poll taxes and taxes on land are direct taxes. Justice Iredell stated, "Perhaps a direct tax

Justice William Paterson. © The Library of Congress.

in the sense of the Constitution, can mean nothing but a tax on something inseparably annexed to the soil: Something capable of apportionment under all such circumstances. A land or a poll tax may be considered of this description."

Impact

In some respects the Court's decision was a highly technical discussion of the differences between direct and indirect taxes. This aspect of the case is of little long term significance, particularly in light of the Sixteenth Amendment to the Constitution. Ratified in 1913, the Sixteenth Amendment grants Congress the power to collect taxes on income, and explicitly provides that this tax need not be apportioned among the states. As the federal government derives the bulk of its revenues from the income tax, the *Hylton* decision is of little import today. However, placed in historical context, the decision was extremely significant. It, along with the suppression of the Whiskey Rebellion, established the federal government's clear authority to enact revenue laws and to enforce those laws. And, in a more general sense, the decision was one of a number of events, beginning with the ratification of the Constitution and culminating in the federal government's victory in the Civil War, which established the supremacy of the federal government over the state governments in the American republic.

Related Cases

Pacific Insurance Co. v. Soule, 74 U.S. 433 (1868).
Veazie v. Fenno, 75 U.S. 533 (1869).
Eisner v. Macomber, 252 U.S. 189 (1920).

Bibliography and Further Reading

Hall, Kermit L., ed. *The Oxford Companion to the Supreme Court of the United States.* New York: Oxford University Press, 1992.

Morrison, Samuel E., ed. *Oxford History of the United States, 1783-1917.* London: Oxford University Press, 1927.

Ratner, Sidney. *Taxation and Democracy in America.* New York: Octagon Books, 1980.

HEAD MONEY CASES: CUNARD STEAMSHIP COMPANY V. SAME; SAME V. SAME

Legal Citation: 112 U.S. 580 (1884)

Appellants
Edye & Another, Cunard Steamship Company

Appellee
W. H. Robertson

Appellants' Claim
That the tax levied by Congress in the Immigration Act of 1882, which required shippers to pay 50 cents for each foreign passenger brought into the United States, was unconstitutional.

Chief Lawyers for Appellants
Edwards Pierrepoint, Philip J. Joachimsen, George DeForest Lord

Chief Lawyer for Appellee
Samuel Field Phillips, U.S. Solicitor General

Justices for the Court
Samuel Blatchford, Joseph P. Bradley, Stephen Johnson Field, Horace Gray, John Marshall Harlan I, Stanley Matthews, Samuel Freeman Miller (writing for the Court), Morrison Remick Waite, William Burnham Woods

Justices Dissenting
None

Place
Washington, D.C.

Date of Decision
8 December 1884

Decision
That Congress had the right to levy a tax on immigrants, not as part of its general powers of taxation, but as an aspect of its power to regulate commerce; and that even if there had been a treaty concerning immigration, it and any other U.S. treaty would be subject to modification or repeal by Congress.

Significance
The *Head Money Cases* helped to consolidate federal control over immigration, as well as to expand congressional power to levy taxes as it exercised its constitutional duties.

On 2 October 1882, the Dutch ship *Leerdam* steamed into New York Harbor. The *Leerdam* had come from the port of Rotterdam, in Holland, bearing 382 immigrants who wished to settle in the United States. Some 20 of these immigrants were babies less than a year old, another 59 were children between the ages of one and eight.

Just two months before, on 3 August 1882, Congress had passed the Immigration Act, specifying that the owners of any ships bringing immigrants into the United States should pay a tax of fifty cents per person. As the Supreme Court later explained, this money was intended

> to raise a fund for the sick, the poor, and the helpless immigrants . . . to mitigate the evils inherent in the business of bringing foreigners to this country, as those evils affect both the immigrant and the people among whom he [sic] is suddenly brought and left to his own resources.

So the firm of Funch, Edye & Co., who were responsible for the *Leerdam* in the United States owed $191 in "head money" for the immigrants they had transported. The company paid the money—but under protest. Then they brought suit against the man who had collected the money. This suit, along with two others very similar to it, was brought before the Supreme Court under the title of the *Head Money Cases*.

Illegal Taxes and Broken Treaties

The appellants had three arguments. First, they claimed that Congress did not have the power to tax immigrants' entry into the United States, for according to the Constitution, Congress could levy taxes only for the common defense or the general welfare of the country. True, Congress had claimed that it was levying this tax as part of its power to regulate trade. But, Edye's lawyers argued, "Emigration is not a 'business' to be regulated by federal law." The appellants also argued that the tax was not applied uniformly throughout the United States, but only at ports where immigrants entered the country. As all taxes levied by Con-

Immigration Regulation Today

As of 1998, immigration regulation is governed by the Immigration Act of 1990, also known as IMMACT. IMMACT established an annual limit of 675,000 immigrant admissions to the United States. This limit does not include refugee, asylum, or other humanitarian admissions. There also are no limits for immigrants who are spouses, minor children, or parents of U.S. citizens.

Under IMMACT, 140,000 of the total annual admissions may be for employment-based reasons. The act favors the admission of professionals and investors, and places an annual limit of 10,000 on admission of lesser-skilled persons.

IMMACT also has a diversity component that reserves 55,000 annual admissions for immigrants from coun-

tries that traditionally do not have strong family or job ties to the United States. Each diversity-based immigrant must have a high school degree or its equivalent, or two years of experience in an occupation requiring two years of training.

Immigrants who enter the United States by commercial aircraft or vessel pay a six dollar fee when their ticket for travel is issued. The U.S. Immigration and Naturalization Service enforces the immigration laws and manages the various admissions.

Source(s): U.S. Commission on Immigration Reform. *Becoming an American: Immigration and Immigrant Policy.* (1997).

---

gress should be uniform, they felt this particular tax was unfair. Finally, the appellants argued that the Immigration Act that levied the tax was void because it conflicted with the treaties made between the United States and other friendly nations. Since such treaties permitted immigration, the appellants said, Congress had no right to override those treaties by then taxing immigration.

The Right to Tax

In a unanimous decision, the Supreme Court found against the appellants, coming out in strong support of Congress' right to have passed the Immigration Act. They took up each of the appellants' arguments in turn.

First, they said emphatically that Congress did indeed have the right to regulate the entry of immigrants into the United States. Previous Court decisions had held that individual states did not have this right, but if the states did not have that right, surely Congress must have it, for it was inconceivable that:

> . . . the framers of the Constitution have so worded that remarkable instrument, that the ships of all nations, including our own, can, without restraint or regulation, deposit here, if they find it to their interest to do so, the entire European population of criminals, paupers, and diseased persons, without making any provision to preserve them from starvation, and its concomitant sufferings, even for the first few days after they had left the vessel.

Indeed, said the Court, immigration certainly was a business—and quite a profitable business—for the owners of those steamships and sailing ships that brought

over hundreds of immigrants. Surely it was only fair to expect those who profited from immigration to make some payment into a fund designed to help poor immigrants and their children. Surely, too, it was necessary to protect the states and cities where those immigrants landed from having to shoulder the entire burden of immigration by themselves.

Second, the Court said that the "head money" tax was uniform, in the sense that it operated "with the same effect in all places where the subject of it . . . [was] found . . ." The question was not whether ships bringing immigrants into New York were taxed more than, say, ships bringing tourists into Boston. The question was whether all ships bringing immigrants into a city were taxed in the same way.

Finally, the Court pointed out that no foreign nation had complained about any treaty violations. "We are not satisfied that this act of Congress violates any [treaty]," wrote Justice Miller. However, he went on to say, even if the Immigration Act were in conflict with a treaty, Congress had the right to modify or repeal treaties as it chose, just as it had the right to modify or repeal the laws it made.

As an example, Miller cited a Court decision made concerning the extension of a tax on tobacco to "the Cherokee tribe." Once, the Cherokee had been considered a nation, and the United States had entered into a treaty with them. Later, Congress passed a law that seemed to override that treaty. In the Court's opinion, Congress had that power.

A Legacy for Immigrants

To the contemporary reader, the *Head Money Cases* show two sides of America's views towards its immigrants. On the one hand, there is the image of immigrants as "criminals, paupers, and diseased persons," who must be regulated and somehow kept within bounds by the federal government. On the other hand, there is the image of immigrants as "helpless" and needing "humane . . . protection" against starvation and other hardships of arriving alone and friendless in a new country.

In addition, there is a third image: the notion of immigrants as the product of commerce: "that branch of foreign commerce which is involved in immigration." Such an image reminds us of how much the United States depended upon immigrants as a source of labor and population growth in the rapid economic development of the 1880s and 1890s.

Related Cases

Brown v. Maryland, 12 Wheat. 419 (1827).
Woodruff v. Parham, 8 Wall. 123 (1869).
Low v. Ausitn, 13 Wall. 29 (1872).
Complete Auto Transit Inc. v. Brady, 430 U.S. 274 (1977).
Bacchus Imports Ltd. v. Dias, 468 U.S. 263 (1984).

Bibliography and Further Reading

Bartholomew, Paul C. *Summaries of Leading Cases on the Constitution.* Totowa, NJ: Littlefield, Adams & Co., 1976.

Biskupic, Joan, and Elder Witt. *Congressional Quarterly's Guide to the U.S. Supreme Court,* 3rd ed. Washington, DC: Congressional Quarterly, Inc., 1996.

Hall, Kermit L., ed. *The Oxford Companion to the Supreme Court of the United States.* New York: Oxford University Press, 1992.

POLLOCK V. FARMERS' LOAN & TRUST COMPANY

Legal Citation: 157 U.S. 429 (1895)

Appellant
Charles Pollock

Appellee
Farmers' Loan & Trust Company

Appellant's Claim
That the Wilson-Gorman Tariff Act of 1894 violated Article 1, sections 2, 8, and 9 of the Constitution.

Chief Lawyers for Appellant
William D. Guthrie, Clarence A. Seward, Joseph H. Choate

Chief Lawyer for Appellee
Herbert B. Turner, James C. Carter

Justices for the Court
David Josiah Brewer, Henry Billings Brown, Stephen Johnson Field, Melville Weston Fuller (writing for the Court)

Justices Dissenting
Horace Gray, John Marshall Harlan I, George Shiras, Jr., Edward Douglass White (Howell Edmunds Jackson did not participate)

Place
Washington, D.C.

Date of Decision
8 April 1895

Decision
Tax bonds and real estate was found to be untaxable.

Significance
A majority of the Court seemed to agree that the income tax was unconstitutional; however, one justice was missing during the deliberations, leading to a deadlock on the key issue of whether the income tax was uniformly applied. Not wanting to invalidate the law without clearly determining that and other points, the Court voted to rehear the general income tax issue.

Pollock v. Farmers' Loan & Trust Company was one of the most controversial and closely watched cases of its day. It featured an appellant and appellee who were actually on the same side, two Supreme Court rulings just weeks apart, and arguments that sometimes relied more on emotion than logic and legal precedent.

The case dealt with the constitutionality of a federal income tax. During the 1890s, a political reform movement called Populism arose in America. The Populists were political descendants of the agrarian reformers of the 1870s and 1880s, who tried to defend the economic interests of farmers from perceived threats by big business. The Populists expanded their platform to include workers and small entrepreneurs—anyone who suffered from the economic policies fostered by the country's monied interests. To finance greater reform and make the wealthy pay more in taxes, the Populists advocated an income tax.

An economic crisis in 1893 reduced government revenues and hastened the drive for an income tax. The next year, Congress passed a two percent tax on incomes over $4,000. Only about two percent of wage earners made enough to pay the tax. It was the first time Congress had passed an income tax during peacetime; the only other income tax had come during the Civil War and lasted until 1872. The new tax was understandably unpopular with wealthy Americans, and Charles Pollock, a Massachusetts investor, devised a plan to challenge the law in court.

Pollock's Suit

Pollock owned shares in the Farmers' Loan & Trust Company, an investment bank that bought stocks and bonds. Under the new tax law, the company had to pay income tax on its profits from stocks and bonds (just as Pollock owed on his individual investment). Acting on behalf of the other stockholders—and with the full cooperation of Farmers' Loan—Pollock sued to prevent the bank from paying the tax. He claimed the law violated Article I, sections 2, 8, and 9, of the Constitution, which spells out certain limits on Congress's power to tax.

A New York circuit court denied Pollock's request but allowed the case to pass directly to the Supreme

Court. The Court, realizing the importance of the issue, made two exceptions to its usual procedures: it took a case in which both parties agreed to the suit, and it let the U.S. attorney general argue a case in which the government was not a party.

Arguments began on 7 March 1895. The country's major papers followed the case, and the Court's gallery was jammed with spectators. By the last day, dozens of people had to be turned away. Pollock's attorneys, led by Joseph Choate, broke their case into three parts. First, the income tax applied to money made from state and municipal bonds, and such a tax infringed on the sovereignty of the states and limited their ability to raise revenue. Second, the tax on income from land was the same as a tax on the land itself, making it a direct tax. (The Court had already defined a land tax as a direct tax). According to the Constitution, direct taxes are legal only if they are applied equally to each state, based on its population. The income tax, if it were direct, was not apportioned equally, and so was unconstitutional. Finally, Choate and his team argued that even if the income tax were an indirect tax, it was not uniformly applied, as demanded by Article I, Section 8 of the Constitution.

Legal scholars have since questioned the strength of these last two points. Choate, however, flavored his arguments with impassioned pleas to strike down a law that he claimed was unfair and a threat to American values. Some of the justices seemed sympathetic to this line of attack.

Choate Carries the Day

Choate was a familiar figure in front of the Supreme Court. During the 1880s and 1890s he argued many cases before that tribunal. A cultured man, Choate helped found the Metropolitan Museum of Art and was a reformer within the Republican Party. He later served as ambassador to England. In *Pollock* he cemented his legal reputation with a fiery attack on the income tax.

The trial had clearly become an issue of haves versus have-nots, of trying to redistribute wealth by taxing America's rich. To Choate, the tax was ". . . communistic in its purposes and tendencies, and is defended here upon principles as communistic, socialistic—what I should call them—populistic as ever have been addressed to any political assembly in the world." Later, Choate lamented that the Court was at "a parting of the ways" with American tradition if it allowed separate taxation for the rich and the poor.

Choate's oratory carried some weight—but not enough to clinch a clear victory. On the first point, infringing on the states by taxing income from state bonds, the Court agreed with Pollock, 8-0. On the second point, a 6-2 majority found that the tax on income

Joseph Hodges Choate was the most famous legal orator and trial lawyer of his time. © Painting by Oscar White. Corbis Corporation.

from land was the same as a tax on the land itself, so it was direct. On the uniformity issue, the Court split 4-4. It also split on whether or not a tax on income from personal property was also direct, even though it had a clear precedent to follow. In *Springer v. United States* (1881), the Court had ruled that the Civil War income tax was indirect.

The Court deadlocked because its ninth justice, Howell E. Jackson, was sick with tuberculosis and missed the case. Chief Justice Fuller, who wrote the decision, was reluctant to strike down the income tax without a clear vote from the Court. The official decision: "Reversed in part and affirmed in part by a divided court."

Realizing it could not leave the income tax in legal limbo, the Court readily agreed to rehear the case with all nine members present. The second *Pollock v. Farmers' Loan & Trust Company* began less than a month later.

Related Cases

The Head Money Cases, 112 U.S. 580 (1884).
Pollock v. Farmers' Loan & Trust Company (rehearing), 158 U.S. 601 (1895).

Bibliography and Further Reading

Biskupic, Joan, and Elder Witt. *Guide to the U.S. Supreme Court.* Washington, DC: Congressional Quarterly, Inc., 1997.

Cushman, Robert F. *Leading Constitutional Decisions.* Englewood Cliffs, NJ: Prentice-Hall, Inc., 1982.

Foner, Eric, and John Garrity, eds. *The Reader's Companion to American History.* Boston: Houghton Mifflin, 1991.

Hall, Kermit L., ed. *The Oxford Companion to the Supreme Court of the United States.* New York: Oxford University Press, 1992.

Johnson, John W., ed. *Historic U.S. Court Cases, 1690–1990: An Encyclopedia.* New York: Garland Publishing, 1992.

The New York Times, 14 March 1895.

Shnayerson, Robert. *The Illustrated History of the Supreme Court of the United States.* New York: Harry A. Abrams, Inc., 1986.

Witt, Elder, ed. *The Supreme Court A to Z.* CQ's Encyclopedia of American Government. Washington, DC: Congressional Quarterly, Inc., 1993.

POLLOCK V. FARMERS' LOAN & TRUST COMPANY (REHEARING)

Legal Citation: 158 U.S. 601 (1895)

Appellant
Charles Pollock

Appellee
Farmers' Loan & Trust Company

Appellant's Claim
That the Wilson-Gorman Tariff Act of 1894 violated Article 1, sections 2, 8, and 9 of the Constitution.

Chief Lawyers for Appellant
William D. Guthrie, Clarence A. Seward, Joseph H. Choate

Chief Lawyer for Appellee
Herbert B. Turner, James C. Carter

Justices for the Court
David Josiah Brewer, Stephen Johnson Field, Melville Weston Fuller (writing for the Court), Horace Gray, George Shiras, Jr.

Justices Dissenting
Henry Billings Brown, John Marshall Harlan I, Howell Edmunds Jackson, Edward Douglass White

Place
Washington, D.C.

Date of Decision
20 May 1895

Decision
Found the general income tax provision of the act unconstitutional.

Significance
Just weeks after failing to reach a definitive decision on the constitutionality of the income tax, the Court reheard. *Pollock* and struck down the law. The income tax issue, however, did not subside, as Populists and others called for an amendment to the Constitution giving Congress power to levy such a tax.

In its first hearing of *Pollock v. Farmers' Loan & Trust Company,* a divided Supreme Court failed to reach a definitive ruling on all the points raised in the case. The Court decided 8-0 that taxing income from state bonds was a federal infringement on the states. A clear majority also supported Pollock's claim that the tax on income from land was the same as a tax on the land itself, so it was a direct tax. The Constitution gave Congress the power to levy a direct tax only if it were apportioned equally among the states, based on their population. By that definition, the income tax was not direct. On the last key points, the Court deadlocked 4-4, unable to decide if the tax was uniform—another constitutional requirement for a tax—and whether or not a tax on personal property was also direct. Not wanting to invalidate the income tax law without reaching a clear decision on all the major points, the Court agreed to rehear *Pollock.*

The Court would have avoided the second hearing if all nine members had been present the first time. But Justice Jackson missed the first case, suffering from tuberculosis. This time, the seriously ill Jackson struggled to Washington to hear what he knew was an important case. Arguments began on 6 May 1895 and the Court delivered its decision two weeks later.

Emotions Run High

The income tax and the first *Pollock* hearing stirred passions across the country. The Populists and other reformers who backed the tax saw it as a just way for the wealthiest Americans to pay their fair share toward running the government. Business interests decried the law as communistic. Justice Fields seemed to share the conservative viewpoint; in his concurring decision from the first case, he wrote, "the present assault upon capital is but the beginning . . . till our political contests will become a war of the poor against the rich." Justice Harlan, who favored the tax, wrote in his private papers that Fields acted like a "madman" throughout the *Pollock* ordeal. The outcome of the second hearing was clearer, but no less emotional, than the first.

This time, the Court ruled 5-4 to strike down the law. A majority agreed that a tax on income from both

The U.S. Supreme Court, 1894. © Photograph by C. M. Bell. The Library of Congress/Corbis.

land and personal property was direct, and thus unconstitutional. Having finally reached a clear decision on those major points, the Court struck down the entire law, since most of the anticipated revenue was supposed to come from the tax on income from land and personal property. Chief Justice Fuller again wrote the decision, and he explained that the Court felt compelled to strike down the entire law. If it did not, the decision "would leave the burden of the tax to be borne by professions, trades, employment, or vocations; and in that way what was intended as a tax on capital would remain in substance a tax on occupations and labor."

As in the first case, the Court ignored its own precedents on tax law. A 1796 case, *Hylton v. United States*, held that the only direct taxes were poll taxes and taxes on land. Fuller dismissed that case, saying it did not have the weight of law. He also found that an earlier case upholding the Civil War income tax did not apply in *Pollock*.

The four dissenting justices, including Jackson, wrote separate opinions. Since the Court split 4-4 the first time, Jackson's vote to uphold the law should have carried the day for the tax. Instead, one justice switched his vote the second time, voting against the tax. Most observers felt that Justice Shiras was the one who changed his vote, dooming the law.

The harshest dissent came from Justice Harlan. A *New York Times* reporter described Harlan as he read his dissent, saying the justice gestured wildly at Chief Justice Fuller and flashed "thinly disguised sneers." Harlan used "a caustic tone, almost of sarcasm," that upset

many of the lawyers in the courtroom. One observer said that Harlan harbored presidential ambitions, and the dissent was more a campaign speech than a legal opinion.

In his closing, Harlan said the ruling put the majority of Americans at a disadvantage with the wealthy:

> Thus, undue and disproportioned burdens are placed upon the many, while the few, safely entrenched behind the rule of apportionment among the states on the basis of numbers, are permitted to evade their share of the responsibility for the support of government ordained for the protection of the rights of all. I cannot assent to an interpretation of the Constitution that impairs and cripples the just powers of the national government in the essential matter of taxation, and at the same time discriminates against the greater part of the people of our country.

The Income Tax Refuses to Die

The Court's ruling in *Pollock* was not popular. Even a fairly conservative law journal, the *American Law Review*, found fault with the Court's reasoning. The income tax remained a controversial political issue. The year after *Pollock*, William Jennings Bryan attacked the decision while campaigning for president. During his famous "Cross of Gold" speech at the Democratic Convention, Bryan said, "The income tax was not unconstitutional when it was passed; it was not unconstitutional when it went before the Supreme Court for the first time, it did not become unconstitutional until one of the judges changed his mind, and we cannot be expected to know when a judge will change his mind. The income tax is just."

The Democrats began a drive to amend the Constitution to allow an income tax. In 1909, both houses of Congress, by overwhelming majorities, approved the Sixteenth Amendment, giving Congress the power to levy the tax. The amendment was ratified in 1913, and the first income tax was collected in 1916. This was only the third time that a constitutional amendment was passed in response to a Supreme Court decision. The Eleventh Amendment followed a decision that allowed a citizen of another state or a foreign citizen to sue a state in federal court. And the Fourteenth Amendment was partly a response to the Dred Scott case, which ruled African Americans could not be U.S. citizens.

Related Cases

The Head Money Cases, 112 U.S. 580 (1884).
Pollock v. Farmers' Loan & Trust Co., 157 U.S. 429 (1895).

Bibliography and Further Reading

Biskupic, Joan, and Elder Witt. *Guide to the U.S. Supreme Court.* Washington, DC: Congressional Quarterly, Inc., 1997.

Cushman, Robert F. *Cases in Constitutional Law,* 7th ed. Englewood Cliffs, NJ: Prentice-Hall, Inc., 1989.

Hall, Kermit L., ed. *The Oxford Companion to the Supreme Court of the United States.* New York: Oxford University Press, 1992.

Hofstadter, Richard, ed. *Great Issues in American History From Reconstruction to the Present Day.* New York: Vintage Press, 1969.

New York Times. 21 May 1895; 22 May 1895.

Shnayerson, Robert. *The Illustrated History of the Supreme Court of the United States.* New York: Harry A. Abrams, Inc., 1986.

Witt, Elder, ed. *The Supreme Court A to Z.* Washington, DC: Congressional Quarterly, Inc., 1993.

STEARNS V. MINNESOTA

Legal Citation: 179 U.S. 223 (1900)

Appellant
Fred Stearns, Aitkin County Auditor

Appellee
State of Minnesota

Appellant's Claim
That a Supreme Court of Minnesota decision sustaining a state statute making railroad property subject to taxation was in conflict with earlier contracts making railroads exempt from property tax.

Chief Lawyer for Appellant
C. W. Bunn

Chief Lawyers for Appellee
H. W. Childs, W. B. Douglas, A. W. Merrill

Justices for the Court
David Josiah Brewer (writing for the Court), Henry Billings Brown, Melville Weston Fuller, Horace Gray, John Marshall Harlan I, Joseph McKenna, Rufus Wheeler Peckham, George Shiras, Jr., Edward Douglass White

Justices Dissenting
None

Place
Washington, D.C.

Date of Decision
3 December 1900

Decision
The Supreme Court of Minnesota decision was reversed.

Significance
The Court found that contractual obligations of federal trusteeship outweighed the right of states to levy property taxes.

Old Railroads and New Taxes

In the *Stearns v. Minnesota* case, a state's obligation to impose its tax laws uniformly collided with an agreement made before the territory's undeveloped lands were incorporated into the Union. The land, which would become the state of Minnesota, was claimed as the property of the United States government in 1803 as part of the Louisiana Purchase. In the interest of expanding transportation into the area, Congress entered into agreements with railroad companies interested in building lines into the area. On 28 September 1850, Congress gave the railroads the swampy land upon which the lines would be built with the understanding that the railroad companies would be taxed on the property only in the event that the land was sold. As tracks were laid and commerce intensified, the railroad companies were not entirely without obligation. After Minnesota became a state on 12 May 1858, the railroads paid the state three percent of their gross earnings in lieu of taxes.

This financial deal, which was a common arrangement between territorial legislatures and businesses during the development of the North American continent, was not destined to last without controversy. As was the case in other states, the constitution of the new state of Minnesota provided that all property would be equally and uniformly taxed on its actual cash value. Exempted properties included schools, hospitals, and churches. For a time, the railroads remained untouched by these ordinary state taxes. The first sign of change came in 1871, when the state constitution was amended to require that if any changes were to be made in the tax relationship between Minnesota and the railroads, the new tax law would have to be passed by public referendum.

It is not clear if the railroads saw this as a warning, but 15 years passed before the voters of Minnesota took action. In November of 1896, the Minnesota legislature signed an act repealing all previous tax exemption laws. The railroads suddenly found themselves faced with property assessment and taxation for the first time.

The railroads challenged the new law in Minnesota's Supreme Court, accusing the state of reneging on earlier agreements. The court disagreed, ruling that the state constitution was unequivocal on the point of uniform taxation for all. Even if the gross earnings payments amounted to equal taxation, the court ruled, the legislature had no power to make special deals outside of the uniform rules. The decision found that the railroads were subject to ordinary property taxes.

Obligations of A Trustee

This collision between the railroads and the state's new tax legislation brought both sides before the U.S. Supreme Court. Reflected in Justice Brewer's written opinion, the case centered on two issues. First, the Court decided that an agreement by the railroads to pay the state a gross earnings percentage did exist. Furthermore, the agreement constituted a valid contract. As an example, Justice Brewer cited the case of the St. Paul and Duluth Company, which had been given land by the state in return for building a railroad. "If both parties were competent to enter into such an agreement, a contract was made," the Court concluded. The Northern Pacific Railroad was operating under a similar agreement.

The Court noted that the contract which Minnesota had so recently ruled invalid had been in effect for 30 years without complaint. "Whether the revenues of the State were benefited or injured by this method of taxation, we are not advised, but it appears that neither party challenged it," wrote Justice Brewer. "Both the railroads and the State accepted and acted under it for nearly a third of a century." The Court found no grounds allowing Minnesota to change the terms of the original contract.

The second point upon which the case hinged was the ownership of the lands in question at the time that the railroad contracts were made. The Court pointed out that the lands had been conveyed to the state government by the U.S. Congress as a trust, not as an outright gift. Control over public lands, like the water-logged geography upon which the railroads had built their lines, was ultimately under the control of the U.S. government. If the federal government wished to grant such land to private enterprise, while withholding legal title and exempting a company from state taxes unless that state reimbursed the company the cost of building the railroad, it was within Congress's power to do so. If the state agreed to accept the land as trustee and promote the use for which Congress had given it to private enterprise in the first place, the Court found no reason why the state should weaken that trust by taxing it.

The Court recognized that Minnesota's legislature was trying to fulfill its obligation to enforce fair and uniform taxes. Minnesota's obligation as trustee of the land granted by the federal government, however, overrode this concern in the eyes of the Court. Justice White filed a separate opinion in agreement with the majority. Justice White felt that enforcing Minnesota's 1896 tax amendment would deny the railroads equal protection under the law. Without the benefit of due process, the railroads would be forced to both comply with the original contract and obey the new tax laws, which were incompatible with the old agreement.

Related Cases

Duluth and I.R.R. Co. v. St. Louis County, 179 U.S. 302 (1900).
City of Parkersburg v. Baltimore and O.R. Co., 296 F. 74 (1923).

Bibliography and Further Reading

Biskupic, Joan, and Elder Witt, eds. *Congressional Quarterly's Guide to the U.S. Supreme Court,* 3rd ed. Washington, DC: Congressional Quarterly, Inc., 1996.

McCray v. United States

Legal Citation: 195 U.S. 27 (1904)

Appellant
Leo W. McCray

Appellee
United States

Appellant's Claim
That a federal excise tax on artificially colored oleomargarine was unconstitutional under the Fifth and Tenth Amendments.

Chief Lawyers for Appellant
William Guthrie, Miller Outcalt

Chief Lawyer for Appellee
Solicitor General Henry Hoyt

Justices for the Court
David Josiah Brewer, William Rufus Day, John Marshall Harlan I, Oliver Wendell Holmes, Joseph McKenna, Edward Douglass White (writing for the Court)

Justices Dissenting
Henry Billings Brown, Melville Weston Fuller, Rufus Wheeler Peckham

Place
Washington, D.C.

Date of Decision
31 May 1904

Decision
The Court denied the appellant's claim and let stand a fine of $50 against the appellant.

Significance
The Court refused to examine the motives behind Congress's reason for passing this tax, saying it was beyond the Court's jurisdiction. Congress had the right to use a tax to achieve broader social or economic aims, as well as to raise revenue.

Benjamin Franklin once asserted, "In this world, nothing can be said to be certain, except death and taxes." That certainty never stopped Americans from trying to avoid taxes when they could, even on something as mundane as margarine.

Article 1, Section 8 of the Constitution explicitly gives Congress the power to collect taxes and duties. In 1886, Congress passed a law placing an excise tax of ten cents per pound on oleomargarine that was artificially colored yellow. Oleo that was not colored was taxed at only a quarter-cent per pound.

The Oleomargarine Act of 1886, and an amended version in 1902, resulted from lobbying pressure by butter manufacturers. The butter makers faced competition from the producers of oleomargarine, a cheaper butter substitute made from combined animal and vegetable fats. Since consumers preferred butter's yellow color, the oleo manufacturers added yellow artificial coloring to their product. The ten-cent excise tax ended oleo's price advantage over butter.

One way to avoid the higher tax was to sell the uncolored oleo, but few people wanted to buy it. Another way was to sell margarine that was colored yellow, but was taxed at the lower rate. That's what Leo McCray tried to do.

Colored Butter and Constitutional Rights

Leo McCray was a licensed retailer of oleomargarine. He bought a fifty-pound block of colored oleo that had been taxed at only one-quarter cent per pound. The federal government learned of this and fined him $50, claiming McCray bought the oleo knowing it was colored and knowing that it had been mistakenly taxed at the lower rate.

McCray challenged the fine on two counts. First, he tried to make a distinction between adding artificial coloring ingredients directly to the oleo and adding a natural ingredient that might happen to have an artificial color in it. McCray's oleo included butter that had been colored with "Wells-Richardson's improved butter color." Apparently, even natural butter sometimes had to be colored to give it the deep yellow hue consumers preferred. Under the meaning of the statute,

Special Interest Groups

Special interest groups, also known as lobbyists, seek to advance the interests of corporations and industry in federal and state government. In contrast, public interest groups lobby on behalf of groups of citizens committed to a particular interest, such as the environment, consumer protection, or family values. Lobbying by interest groups is protected by the First Amendment to the U.S. Constitution, which provides that "Congress shall make no law . . . abridging . . . the right of the people to assemble, and to petition the Government for a redress of grievances."

Special interest groups act in all three branches of the federal government. In the legislative branch, they form relationships with legislators through campaign assistance during elections and then enjoy private audiences with legislators who are in office. Special interest groups seek to influence the executive branch through reports to presidential task forces and agency heads. In the judicial branch, special interest groups file test cases to advance particular goals and write briefs to provide input in cases in which they are not parties.

Special interest groups are as diverse as the American Butter Institute, the Tobacco Institute, and the National Frozen Pizza Institute.

Source(s): Herrnson, Paul S., Ronald G. Shaiko, and Clyde Wilcox, eds. *The Interest Group Connection: Electioneering, Lobbying, and Policymaking in Washington.* Chatham: Chatham House Publishers, Inc., 1998.

McCray argued, this coloring was not a direct ingredient in the oleo, so the margarine was not subject to the ten-cent tax.

McCray also raised larger constitutional issues in his defense. The ten-cent tax, if it did apply, would deny him his right to property without due process, which was prohibited under the Fifth Amendment. Also, by passing a tax designed to hamper the oleo industry, Congress had interfered with the police powers reserved for the states, as described in the Tenth Amendment. With that intent, McCray's complaint charged, Congress had violated "those fundamental principles of equality and justice which are inherent in the Constitution of the United States."

The Ohio federal district court that heard the case rejected McCray's claims and ordered him to pay the $50 fine. Then, because of the constitutional issues raised, the case went to the Supreme Court.

Balancing the Powers of the Judicial and Legislative Branches

In a 6-3 decision, the Court affirmed the lower court's decision. Writing for the majority, Justice White quickly dismissed McCray's first point. Artificially colored butter added to the oleo did make the oleo itself artificially colored, and thus subject to the higher tax.

McCray's second point, White summarized, rested on examining Congress' motive for imposing the tax in the first place. The tax raised revenue, as Congress was allowed to do under the Constitution. What could not be thoroughly determined was whether or not the tax was also designed to destroy the country's oleomargarine manufacturers. And if this were the case, whether or not this action was just. White and the other concurring justices did not say, and observed:

> . . . no instance is afforded from the foundation of the government where an act which was within a power conferred, was declared to be repugnant to the Constitution, because it appeared to the judicial mind that the particular exertion of the constitutional power was either unwise or unjust. To announce such a principle would amount to declaring that in our constitutional system, the judiciary was not only charged with the duty of upholding the Constitution, but also with the responsibility of correcting every possible abuse arising from the exercise by the other departments of their conceded authority. So to hold would be . . . a mere act of judicial usurpation.

White's notion of ignoring the larger intent of a tax law went unchallenged until 1922. That year, in *Bailey v. Drexel Furniture Co.*, the Court said it could examine why Congress passed a tax, and nullify the law if its intent fell beyond Congress' constitutional powers. In *Bailey*, the Court struck down a tax that was primarily designed to stop child-labor abuses in the furniture industry. In that case, the Court said Congress was infringing on the states' police power to regulate industry.

Related Cases

Bailey v. Drexel Furniture Co., 259 U.S. 20 (1922).
Davis v. Boston & M. R. Co., 89 F.2d 368 (C.C.A. 1937).
United States v. Falk, 479 F.2d 616 (7th Cir. 1973).

Bibliography and Further Reading

Biskupic, Joan, and Elder Witt. *Guide to the U.S. Supreme Court,* 3rd ed. Washington, DC: Congressional Quarterly, Inc., 1997.

Cushman, Robert F. *Cases in Constitutional Law,* 5th ed. Englewood Cliffs, NJ: Prentice Hall, 1984.

Hall, Kermit L., ed. *The Oxford Companion to the Supreme Court of the United States.* New York: Oxford Press, 1992.

Johnson, John W., ed. *Historic U.S. Court Cases, 1690-1990: An Encyclopedia.* New York: Garland Publishing, 1992.

Levy, Leonard, ed. *Encyclopedia of the American Constitution.* New York: Macmillan, 1986.

BAILEY V. DREXEL FURNITURE CO.

Legal Citation: 259 U.S. 20 (1922)

Appellant
J. W. Bailey, individually and as Collector of Internal Revenue for the District of North Carolina

Appellee
Drexel Furniture Company

Appellant's Claim
That the use of the taxing power of by federal government to regulate child labor does not violate a state's control of its internal affairs.

Chief Lawyer for Appellant
James M. Beck, U.S. Solicitor General

Chief Lawyer for Appellee
William P. Bynum

Justices for the Court
Louis D. Brandeis, William Rufus Day, Oliver Wendell Holmes, Joseph McKenna, James Clark McReynolds, Mahlon Pitney, William Howard Taft (writing for the Court), Willis Van Devanter

Justices Dissenting
John Hessin Clarke

Place
Washington, D.C.

Date of Decision
15 May 1922

Decision
Reasoning that the Constitution sanctions only federal tax regulation that has incidental, rather than penalizing effects, the Court by a vote of 8-1 stuck down the child labor law.

Significance
This case marked the second time the U.S. Supreme Court declared a child labor law unconstitutional—and signalled perhaps a highwater mark of a *laissez-faire* approach to jurisprudence.

Even as the Progressive movement led to passage of social welfare legislation, the Supreme Court remained a bastion of conservatism. The Court struck down the first federal child labor law in 1918. The 1916 Keating-Owen Act employed Congress's power to regulate commerce by barring products manufactured with child labor. But in *Hammer v. Dagenhart* (1918) the Court declared the law unconstitutional because the Commerce Clause governed only interstate transportation of goods, not their manufacture.

Congress tried again to combat abuses of child labor with the Child Labor Tax, enacted in 1919. This legislation imposed a ten percent tax on the net profits of companies that employed underage workers. Once again, the Court found that Congress had exceeded its authority, using the federal taxing power to invade the sovereignty of the states. Chief Justice Taft, exercising his formidable talent for "massing" the Court, managed to convince seven of his fellow justices to vote with him. Writing for the majority, he declared:

> Grant the validity of this law, and all that Congress would need to do, hereafter, in seeking to take over to its control any one of the great number of subjects of public interest, jurisdiction of which the states have never parted with, and which are reserved to them by the Tenth Amendment, would be to enact a detailed measure of complete regulation of the subject and enforce it by a so-called tax upon departures from it. To give such magic to the word "tax" would be to break down all constitutional limitation of the powers of Congress and completely wipe out the sovereignty of the states.

Although in *McCray v. United States* (1904) the Court had found that Congress's taxing power could be used for just such regulatory purposes, Taft sought to distinguish that case from the one before the Court. He did so by declaring that this tax, unlike the earlier one, was unconstitutionally punitive:

> The difference between a tax and a penalty is sometimes difficult to define, and yet the con-

---

Laissez-Faire

The idea of *laissez-faire* (pronounced "less-say-FAIR") is said to have originated from a comment by a tradesman when questioned by Louis XIV's finance minister as to the best economic system: "*Laissez faire, laissez passer*"—in essence, "Let people do what they do." *Laissez-faire,* literally "to let do," became the slogan of French Physiocrats, who were distinguished by their opposition to government interference in economic policies.

Central to *laissez-faire* philosophy was the idea that economic systems run efficiently on their own. Even when dramatic rises or falls in prices occur, the market will correct itself without government intervention.

In Britain during the late eighteenth century, the idea of *laissez-faire* was taken up by economist Adam Smith and social philosophers Jeremy Bentham and John Stuart Mill. It became a popular approach to economics in the United States during the nineteenth century. By the beginning of the twentieth century, *laissez-faire* became perceived as contributing to monopolies.

The 1929 stock market crash and the New Deal led to the end of *laissez-faire* as a dominant system. Later, some of its principles were adopted by thinkers such as F. A. Hayek and Michael Oakeshott and politicians such as Ronald Reagan and Margaret Thatcher.

Source(s): Scruton, Roger. *A Dictionary of Political Thought,* second edition. London: Macmillan, 1996.

---

sequences of the distinction in the required method of their collection often are important. Where the sovereign enacting the law has power to impose both tax and penalty, the difference between revenue production and mere regulation may be immaterial, but not so when one sovereign can impose a tax only, and the power of regulation rests in another.

Reverting to the Commerce Clause, Congress did finally manage to outlaw child labor with the Fair Labor Standards Act of 1938, New Deal legislation that regulated wages and hours. This statute was upheld by the Supreme Court in *United States v. Darby* (1941), which explicitly overturned *Hammer v. Dagenhart.*

Related Cases

McCray v. United States, 195 U.S. 27 (1904).
Hammer v. Dagenhart, 247 U.S. 251 (1918).
United States v. Darby, 312 U.S. 100 (1941).

Bibliography and Further Reading

Mnookin, Robert H. *In the Interest of Children: Advocacy, Law Reform, and Public Policy.* New York: W. H. Freeman, 1985.

Rubin, Eva R. *The Supreme Court and the American Family: Ideology and Issues.* New York: Greenwood Press, 1986.

Wood, Stephen B. *Constitutional Politics in the Progressive Era: Child Labor and the Law.* Chicago: University of Chicago Press, 1968.

NASHVILLE, CHATTANOOGA, & ST. LOUIS RAILWAY V. WALLACE

Legal Citation: 288 U.S. 249 (1933)

Appellants
Nashville, Chattanooga, & St. Louis Railway

Appellee
Roy Wallace, comptroller of the Treasury of the State of Tennessee

Appellants' Claim
That a Tennessee tax on gasoline stored in the state, but used for interstate commerce, was unconstitutional.

Chief Lawyersfor Appellants
Will R. King, Martin L. Pipes

Chief Lawyers for Appellee
W. F Berry Jr., Edwin F. Hunt

Justices for the Court
Louis D. Brandeis, Pierce Butler, Benjamin N. Cardozo, Charles Evans Hughes, James Clark McReynolds, Owen Josephus Roberts, Harlan Fiske Stone (writing for the Court), George Sutherland, Willis Van Devanter

Justices Dissenting
None

Place
Washington, D.C.

Date of Decision
6 February 1933

Decision
Plaintiff's claim denied.

Significance
The ruling on the constitutionality of the Tennessee tax was almost secondary to the decision's impact on "declaratory judgments." Previously, the Court had denied that it had the jurisdiction to make declaratory judgments. In *Nashville*, however, the Court said that it would review declaratory judgment cases if, in substance, they were similar to the kinds of issues normally subject to Supreme Court review.

In some legal cases, a plaintiff does not want a court to take a definitive action, such as issuing an injunction or overturning a ruling. Instead, the plaintiff seeks a clarification of a legal point before an action takes place, a clarification that will be binding. Someone entering a contract, for example, might want to know before she signs if a certain act will breach the agreement. This type of judicial decision is called a declaratory judgment.

Courts had been reluctant to make these judgments, but starting in the early twentieth century, some states gave their courts the right to hear such cases, and the issue of declaratory judgments came up before the Supreme Court. Article III of the Constitution says that the Court's jurisdiction covers "cases" or "controversies." In *Willing v. Chicago Auditorium Association* (1928), the Court said that the Constitution barred it from making declaratory judgments. But five years later, in *Nashville, Chattanooga, & St. Louis Railway v. Wallace*, the Court found occasions where it would review cases involving declaratory judgments.

Tennessee was one of the states which allowed its courts to make these judgments. In *Nashville*, the railway company wanted a declaratory judgment against an excise tax before the state actually collected it. The tax, two cents per gallon, applied to any gas sold or stored in Tennessee. The railway company bought its gas out of state and stored it in Tennessee, then used it to fuel its trains on out-of-state railways. The company asserted that the gas was used strictly in interstate commerce, so Tennessee had no right to tax it, since the Commerce Clause of the Constitution gave Congress control over interstate commerce. Both the county court and Tennessee Supreme Court refused to make a declaratory judgment against the tax, and the railway appealed to the U.S. Supreme Court.

The Court Examines "Substance" over "Form"

When it decided to hear *Nashville*, the Supreme Court asked the attorneys to address whether the Court even had jurisdiction in the matter; that is, whether it involved a case or controversy. That issue was also the first one addressed by Justice Stone in his decision for the unanimous Court. Whether the case before the Court was called declaratory or anything else did not matter as much as whether this was a case of enough import that the Court was charged with deciding it. Stone argued *that Nashville* was such a case.

Even though the railway company was not seeking an injunction against the tax, the legal issues the company raised were the same as if it had. Thus, Stone wrote:

> The question lends itself to judicial determination and is of the kind which this Court traditionally decides . . . Obviously the appellant, whose duty to pay the tax will be determined by the decision of this case, is not attempting to secure an abstract determination by the Court of the validity of a statute . . . or a decision advising what the law would be in an uncertain or hypothetical state of facts.

Stone went on to say that states might change the form of their judicial procedures, such as allowing declaratory judgments, but the Supreme Court's role remained the same: to protect the constitutional rights of Americans.

Having established that the Court did have jurisdiction in this matter, Stone quickly dismissed the railway's arguments. Once the company unloaded and stored the gas in Tennessee, it "ceased to be a subject of transportation in interstate commerce and lost its immunity as such from state taxation."

Congress Codifies Declaratory Judgments

The year after *Nashville,* Congress passed the Federal Declaratory Judgment Act. The new law gave the Supreme Court and other federal courts the power to make declaratory judgments when cases involved "actual controversy." In 1937, the Supreme Court upheld the law in *Aetna Life Insurance Co. v. Haworth.* According to Chief Justice Hughes, said the courts could make declaratory judgments regarding legal controversies, but he implied that they were not obligated to do so.

Since then, the Court has noted the difficulty in determining when a declaratory judgment should be made. In the decision for *Maryland Casualty v. Pacific Coal & Oil* (1941), Justice Frank Murphy wrote:

> The difference between an abstract question and a "controversy" contemplated by the Declaratory Judgment Act is one of degree . . . Basically, the question in each case is whether the facts alleged, under all the circumstances, show that there is a substantial controversy between parties having adverse legal interests, of sufficient immediacy and reality to warrant the issuance of a declaratory judgment.

Related Cases
Village of Euclid v. Ambler Realty Co., 272 U.S. 365 (1926).
Willing v. Chicago Auditorium Association, 277 U.S. 274 (1928).
Aetna Life Insurance Co., v. Haworth, 300 U.S. 227 (1937).
Maryland Casualty v. Pacific Coal and Oil, 312 U.S. 270 (1941).

Bibliography and Further Reading
Biskupic, Joan, and Elder Witt. *Guide to the U.S. Supreme Court.* Washington, DC: Congressional Quarterly, Inc., 1997.

Elliott, Stephen P., ed. *A Reference Guide to the U.S. Supreme Court.* New York: Facts on File Publications, 1986.

Hall, Kermit L., ed. *The Oxford Companion to the Supreme Court of the United States.* New York: Oxford Press, 1992.

UNITED STATES V. BUTLER

Legal Citation: 297 U.S. 1 (1936)

Petitioner
United States

Respondent
William H. Butler

Petitioner's Claim
That the Agricultural Adjustment Act of 1933, which provided for payments to farmers for reduced production from taxes imposed on commodities producers, was a valid exercise of Congress's taxing and spending powers.

Chief Lawyers for Petitioner
Homer S. Cummings, U.S. Attorney General; Stanley F. Reed, U.S. Solicitor General

Chief Lawyers for Respondent
Edward R. Hale, Bennett Sanderson

Justices for the Court
Pierce Butler, Charles Evans Hughes, James Clark McReynolds, Owen Josephus Roberts (writing for the Court), George Sutherland, Willis Van Devanter

Justices Dissenting
Louis D. Brandeis, Benjamin N. Cardozo, Harlan Fiske Stone

Place
Washington, D.C.

Date of Decision
6 January 1936

Decision
The Supreme Court struck down the Agricultural Adjustment Act, finding that it overstepped the powers reserved for the states in the Tenth Amendment.

Significance
Although *Butler* was the first Supreme Court case to test Congress's power to spend money in support of the public welfare, today the case is remembered most for Justice Stone's dissenting opinion chastising the majority for a lack of judicial restraint in striking down yet another piece of New Deal legislation.

As part of his attempt to alleviate, if not eliminate the dire effects of the Great Depression, President Franklin Roosevelt proposed a package of reforms collectively known as the New Deal. One the major initiatives of the New Deal was an effort to prop up farm prices by paying farmers to reduce their production. This initiative, called the Agricultural Adjustment Act (AAA), was passed by Congress in 1933. It proposed to fund these farm payments by levying taxes on commodities producers.

Pursuant to this legislation, the federal government presented William H. Butler, acting as a representative for a cotton processing plant, with a claim for taxes on the plant. Butler recommended that the company not pay the taxes, and the government took him to court, where it was awarded with a decree ordering Butler to pay. Butler appealed this judgment to Second Circuit Court of Appeals and won. The U.S. government than asked the Supreme Court to review this decision.

Court Strikes Down AAA as a Violation of the Tenth Amendment

The government based its case on the taxing and spending power specifically provided for in Article I, section 8 of the Constitution, which provides: "The Congress shall have Power to lay and collect Taxes . . . to . . . provide for the . . . general Welfare of the United States." Writing for the Court, Justice Roberts agreed that the taxes levied under the AAA were constitutionally permissible because they were intended to serve the "national" welfare, rather than some local interest. However, he immediately went on to declare that the taxes were nonetheless prohibited by the Tenth Amendment, which reserved to the states all powers that the Constitution did not specifically assign to the federal government. Regulation of agriculture, declared Roberts, was a state matter.

Justice Stone wrote a caustic dissent, which was joined by Brandeis and Cardozo. Stone criticized Roberts's methods of constitutional interpretation. More pointedly, he criticized the majority for attempting to create law, not just interpret the legislation passed by elected representatives of the American people. In assuming an activist role, Stone warned, the

Spending Power Provision of Article One

The U.S. Constitution gives Congress the exclusive power to spend money from the U.S. Treasury. This spending power appears in the limitations on federal powers in section nine of article one of the Constitution: "No money shall be drawn from the Treasury, but in consequence of appropriations made by law."

Congress spends money by passing appropriations bills, which are the end result of the annual federal budget process. It begins when the federal departments, agencies, and bureaus estimate their financial needs for the upcoming fiscal year and report them to the president. The president and the Office of Management and Budget then prepare a budget proposal for Congress.

Next the House of Representatives holds hearings in various subcommittees of the House Appropriations Committee, which makes recommendations to the entire House. The House then debates, amends, and passes an appropriations bill. After the Senate engages in a similar process and passes its own bill, a House-Senate committee adjusts differences in the two bills, and both houses approve a final bill. If the president does not veto it, it becomes law and determines how much money the government has to operate with during the upcoming fiscal year.

Source(s): Sanford, William R., Ph.D., and Green, Carl R., Ph.D. *Basic Principles of American Government.* New York: Amsco School Publications, Inc., 1983.

Court posed a particular danger. The doctrine of judicial review, which lent the judicial branch its power, made the Supreme Court the ultimate arbiter of the law. The majority should be mindful of the responsibility that goes along with the power to say what the law is:

> The power of courts to declare a statute unconstitutional is subject to two guiding principles of decision which ought never to be absent from judicial consciousness. One is that courts are concerned only with the power to enact statutes, not with their wisdom. The other is that while unconstitutional exercise of power by the executive and legislative branches of the government is subject to judicial restraint, the only check upon our own exercise of power is our own sense of self-restraint.

The Supreme Court struck down the AAA, as it had other New Deal proposals. This opposition, however, was short lived. In 1937, Roosevelt precipitated a crisis when he proposed a plan to "pack" the Court with justices of his own choosing who would approve his legislative agenda. The plan failed, but in the meanwhile, the Court changed its orientation as some formerly conservative justices began voting for progressive New Deal reforms and others resigned from the Court altogether. Congress's power to tax and spend in support of the general welfare was upheld in *Steward Machine Co. v.*

Davis (1937), which affirmed the constitutionality of another New deal program, Social Security. And in *Mulford v. Smith* (1939) and *Wickard v. Filburn* (1942), the Court upheld the Second Agricultural Adjustment Act (1938) in an opinion written, once again, by Justice Roberts.

Related Cases
A.L.A. Schechter Poultry v. United States, 295 U.S. 495 (1935).
Ashwander v. Tennessee Valley Authority, 297 U.S. 288 (1936).
National Labor Relations Board v. Jones and Laughlin Steel Corp., 301 U.S. 1 (1937).
Steward Machine Co. v. Davis, 301 U.S. 548 (1937).
Helvering v. Davis, 301 U.S. 619 (1937).
Mulford v. Smith, 307 U.S. 38 (1939).
Wickard v. Filburn, 317 U.S. 111 (1942).

Bibliography and Further Reading
Forte, David, ed. *The Supreme Court in American Politics: Judicial Activism vs. Judicial Restraint.* Lexington, MA: Heath, 1972.

Hamilton, David E. *From New Day to New Deal: American Farm Policy From Hoover to Roosevelt, 1928-1933.* Chapel Hill: University of North Carolina Press, 1991.

Sharkansky, Ira. *The Politics of Taxing and Spending.* Indianapolis, IN: Bobbs-Merrill, 1969.

STEWARD MACHINE CO. V. DAVIS

Legal Citation: 301 U.S. 548 (1937)

Petitioner
Charles C. Steward Machine Co.

Respondent
Harwell G. Davis, Collector of Internal Revenue for the District of Alabama

Petitioner's Claim
That the payroll tax used to fund unemployment compensation under the Social Security Act of 1935 was an abuse of Congress' power to tax and spend.

Chief Lawyers for Petitioner
William Logan Martin, Neil P. Sterne, Walter Bouldin

Chief Lawyers for Respondent
Homer S. Cummings, U.S. Attorney General; Charles E. Wyzanski, Jr., Special Assistant Attorney General; Robert H. Jackson, Assistant Attorney General

Justices for the Court
Louis D. Brandeis, Benjamin N. Cardozo (writing for the Court), Charles Evans Hughes, James Clark McReynolds, Owen Josephus Roberts, Harlan Fiske Stone, George Sutherland, Willis Van Devanter

Justices Dissenting
Pierce Butler

Place
Washington, D.C.

Date of Decision
24 May 1937

Decision
The Supreme Court upheld the unemployment feature of the Social Security tax.

Significance
Together with a companion case, *Helvering v. Davis* (1937), which upheld the old-age benefits of Social Security and which was decided the same day, *Steward Machine* endorsed the use of taxation to achieve social change.

The Social Security Act of 1935 was the crowning achievement in President Franklin Roosevelt's experiment in social engineering. Part of the so-called Second New Deal, it fulfilled the last of three goals Roosevelt set for this program. With the Works Progress Administration (WPA), Roosevelt sought to bring public relief to the unemployed, who numbered in the millions during the Great Depression. With the National Labor Relations Act (NLRA), the federal government aligned itself with organized labor in an effort to reform unfair labor practices and promote industrial efficiency. With Social Security, Roosevelt sought to assist the economically disadvantaged through unemployment insurance, old age pensions, survivors' insurance, and grants to the states to aid helpless individuals such as those who were blind and impoverished. Social Security proved to be Roosevelt's most lasting legacy to the nation. At the outset, however, it was not clear whether employers—who were obliged to withhold the taxes to pay for the program—would comply.

Steward Machine Company was an Alabama Corporation that paid its social security taxes in compliance with the federal legislation, then filed a claim for a refund with the commissioner of internal revenue. The company also sued in federal district court to recover the amount of its contribution, claiming that the statute authorizing collection of the Social Security tax was in conflict with the U.S. Constitution. After the district court ruled against Steward Machine, and the federal court of appeals upheld this judgment, the company took its suit to the U.S. Supreme Court.

Steward Machine's primary complaint was that the unemployment feature of the Social Security Act was in conflict with the Tenth Amendment, which provides: "The powers not delegated to the United States by the Constitution, nor prohibited by it to the States, are reserved to the States respectively, or to the people." Before Social Security, public welfare had largely been considered a state matter, and in fact various states themselves imposed unemployment taxes on employers. In imposing federal unemployment taxes, Congress was, Steward Machine declared, abusing its constitutional power to tax and spend.

Court Upholds Unemployment Feature of Social Security

Writing for the Court, Justice Cardozo observed, first, that the Social Security Act authorized those employers who already contributed to a state unemployment fund to credit 90 percent of such payments against their federal tax. Secondly, and more importantly, he declared that there is no conflict between the Tenth Amendment and Article I, Section 8, of the Constitution, which grants Congress the power "to lay and collect taxes . . . to . . . provide . . . for the General Welfare of the United States":

> The [Social Security] statute does not call for a surrender by the states of powers essential to their quasi sovereign existence . . . A credit to taxpayers for payments made to a state under a state unemployment law will be manifestly futile in the absence of some assurance that the law leading to the credit is in truth what it professes to be. An unemployment law framed in such a way that the unemployed who look to it will be deprived of reasonable protection is one in name and nothing more . . . A wide range of judgment is given to the several states as to the particular type of statute to be spread upon their books . . . What they may not do, if they would earn the credit, is to depart from those standards which in the judgment of Congress are to be ranked as fundamental.

Steward Machine is in marked contrast to a decision handed down just a year earlier. In *United States v. Butler* (1936), the Court struck down another piece of New Deal legislation on grounds that the Tenth Amendment limited Congress's ability to tax and spend. The opinion for the majority in *Butler* was written by Justice Roberts, who had been voting with the Court's conservative bloc. In the interim, Roosevelt, who had grown weary of the Court repeatedly blocking his legislative agenda, announced a proposal to "pack" the Court with justices of his own choosing. The proposal failed, but—perhaps not coincidentally—Roberts began voting with the Court's more liberal justices. The change in orientation became known as "the switch in time that saved nine"—justices, that is. Whatever his motives, Roberts did help salvage the New Deal and preserve Social Security for future generations.

Related Cases

Helvering v. Davis, 301 U.S. 619 (1937).
State of Nevado v. Skinner, 884 F.2d 445 (1989).

Bibliography and Further Reading

Brock, William R. *Welfare, Democracy, and the New Deal.* New York, NY: Cambridge University Press, 1988.

Landy, Marc K., and Martin A. Levin, eds. *The New Politics of Public Policy.* Baltimore, MD: Johns Hopkins University Press, 1995.

Schick, Allen. *Congress and Money: Budgeting, Spending, and Taxing.* Washington, DC: Urban Institute, 1980.

HELVERING V. DAVIS

Legal Citation: 301 U.S. 619 (1937)

Petitioner
Guy T. Helvering, Commissioner of Internal Revenue

Respondent
George P. Davis

Petitioner's Claim
That the Social Security Act of 1935, authorizing payroll taxes on employers to fund old-age benefits, was a constitutional expansion of Congress's taxing and spending power.

Chief Lawyer for Petitioner
Homer S. Cummings, U.S. Attorney General

Chief Lawyer for Respondent
Edward F. McClennan

Justices for the Court
Louis D. Brandeis, Benjamin N. Cardozo (writing for the Court), Charles Evans Hughes, Owen Josephus Roberts, Harlan Fiske Stone, George Sutherland, Willis Van Devanter

Justices Dissenting
Pierce Butler, James Clark McReynolds

Place
Washington, D.C.

Date of Decision
24 May 1937

Decision
The Supreme Court upheld the old-age benefit provisions of the Social Security Act.

Significance
In upholding the constitutionality of the Social Security Act in *Helvering* and a companion case, *Steward Machine Co. v. Davis* (1937), the Supreme Court signaled a major shift towards support of President Franklin D. Roosevelt's New Deal agenda.

Franklin D. Roosevelt was first elected president in 1932 as the nation was sinking ever deeper into the Great Depression. In an effort to combat America's economic woes, Roosevelt set about instituting an ambitious program of social and economic reform that came to be known as the New Deal. The first New Deal lasted from 1932 to 1934 and had little effect. Part of the problem with the program was that much of the legislation designed to implement it was declared unconstitutional. At the time, a majority of the seats on the Supreme Court were held by conservative justices who objected to Roosevelt's progressive reforms.

In January of 1935, Roosevelt outlined a plan for long-term reform that came to be known as the second New Deal. It consisted of three principle priorities: public relief, labor reform, and social security. But Roosevelt still faced the problem of an uncompromising High Court. After he won the 1936 presidential election by a landslide, he began to put into motion a plan to "pack" the Court with additional justices who shared his legislative agenda. In February of 1937, he submitted a scheme for reorganizing the federal judiciary to Congress. Among other reforms, Roosevelt proposed adding one justice to the Supreme Court for every sitting justice over the age of 70, up to a maximum number of 15, if those over 70 declined to retire.

Roosevelt's court-packing plan achieved its goal—even though it was ultimately defeated in Congress. It managed to exert enough pressure on the Court that in May of 1937, just days before the Court handed down its decision in *Helvering,* Willis Van Devanter, one of the ultra-conservative justices known as the "Four Horsemen" (after the Four Horsemen of the Apocalypse, the biblical scourges who wrecked havoc on the land), announced his retirement, thus permitting Roosevelt to appoint a replacement of his own choosing. At the same time, Justice Roberts, often a swing vote on the Court, changed his stance towards New Deal legislation. After having been hostile towards Roosevelt's plans, his vote in favor of the Social Security Act in *Helvering* marked the beginning of a series of votes in which he sided with the Court majority to uphold major New Deal programs.

President Franklin D. Roosevelt signs a bill in the company of his cabinet. U.S. Attorney General Homer Cummings stands at the far left, 1934. © AP/Wide World Photos.

In *Helvering,* George P. Davis, a shareholder, sued the Edison Electric Illuminating Company of Boston, to prevent the company from deducting money from his wages in order to fund benefits paid to retired workers in conformity with the new Social Security Act. The district court permitted the Internal Revenue Service, in the person of Commissioner Guy T. Helvering, to intervene in the lawsuit, essentially taking the place of the defendant electric company. After the district court dismissed Davis' case, he appealed to the United States First Circuit Court of Appeals, which reversed this decision. The IRS then asked the U.S. Supreme Court to review this decision.

Supreme Court Upholds the Centerpiece of New Deal Social Reforms

Davis argued that the Social Security Act represented an expansion of Congress' taxing and spending power, granted in Article I, section 8 of the Constitution. Such an expansion, he claimed, violated the Tenth Amendment, which reserved to the states those powers not specifically enumerated in the Constitution. Welfare, like that represented by social security, he said, was properly the province of state governments.

Justice Cardozo, writing for a majority of the justices, countered that money spent for the general welfare was properly the subject of federal, not state legislation. Furthermore, what was at stake was not a local problem, but a "nationwide calamity" requiring a concerted national effort:

Spreading from state to state, unemployment is an ill not particular but general, which may be checked, if Congress so determines, by the resources of the nation. If this can have been doubtful until now, our ruling today in the case of the Steward Machine Co . . . has set the doubt at rest. But the ill is all one or at least not greatly different whether men are thrown out of work because there is no longer work to do or because the disabilities of age make them incapable of doing it.

Together, *Helvering,* which upheld old-age benefits, and *Steward Machine Co.,* which upheld unemployment benefits, validated the Social Security Act. Roosevelt would regard it as the finest achievement of the New Deal.

The Four Horsemen of the Hughes Court

President Franklin Delano Roosevelt's New Deal in the 1930s was a legislative effort to pull the United States out of the Great Depression. The legislation sought to exercise federal powers to effect social welfare, hour and wage regulation, and tax subsidies for disadvantaged persons.

Two groups of Supreme Court justices under Chief Justice Charles Evans Hughes formed around the New Deal legislation. Supporters included famous liberal justices such as Benjamin Cardozo and Louis D. Brandeis. The opposition included conservative justices Pierce Butler, James Clark McReynolds, George Sutherland, and Willis Van Devanter. In an allusion to the Apocalypse and to Notre Dame's football defense, these justices became known as the Four Horsemen. Despite the severity of the Great Depression, they saw a greater danger in governmental power unconstrained by the plain language of the U.S. Constitution.

In 1937, President Roosevelt proposed legislation to allow him to appoint an extra justice every time one over seventy did not retire. The law would have allowed him to appoint a majority to defeat the Four Horsemen. The law failed to pass, however, just as the Four Horsemen began to retire and thus to lose influence in the Supreme Court.

Source(s): Cushman, Clare, ed. *The Supreme Court justices: illustrated biographies, 1789-1993.* Washington, DC: Congressional Quarterly Inc., 1993.

White, G. Edward. *American Judicial Tradition: Profiles of Leading American Judges.* New York: Oxford University Press, 1988.

Related Cases

Head Money Cases, 112 U.S. 580 (1884).
United States v. Butler, 297 U.S. 1 (1936).
Steward Machine Co. v. Davis, 301 U.S. 548 (1937).

Bibliography and Further Reading

Epstein, Richard Allen. *Bargaining with the State.* Princeton, NJ: Princeton University Press, 1993.

Lee, A. Alton. *A History of Regulatory Taxation.* Lexington: University of Kentucky Press, 1973.

Leuchtenberg, William E. *The Supreme Court: The Constitutional Revolution in the Age of Roosevelt.* New York: Oxford University Press, 1995.

NEW YORK V. UNITED STATES

Legal Citation: 326 U.S. 572 (1946)

Petitioner
State of New York

Respondent
United States

Petitioner's Claim
That sales of mineral water by the state of New York were exempt from federal taxation.

Chief Lawyer for Petitioner
Orrin G. Judd

Chief Lawyer for Respondent
Paul A. Freund

Justices for the Court
Harold Burton, Felix Frankfurter (writing for the Court), Frank Murphy, Stanley Forman Reed, Wiley Blount Rutledge, Harlan Fiske Stone

Justices Dissenting
Hugo Lafayette Black, William O. Douglas (Robert H. Jackson did not participate)

Place
Washington, D.C.

Date of Decision
14 January 1946

Decision
The federal tax was held to be valid.

Significance
The Supreme Court's decision in *New York v. United States* substantially curtailed the immunity of state economic activity from federal taxation.

Mineral Water at Issue

The case of *New York v. United States* revolved around the unlikeliest of subjects: mineral water. The state of New York had set up the Saratoga Springs Authority, a publicly-owned company to bottle and sell natural spring water. The federal government, in a 1932 revenue act, imposed a tax on mineral water. The Saratoga Springs Authority refused to pay the tax, on the grounds that as a state agency it was immune from federal taxation. The United States then sued to recover the tax revenue. A district court sided with the United States, and the Circuit Court of Appeals for the Second Circuit affirmed this judgment. The state of New York, joined by 45 other states seeking clarification on the issue of immunity, then appealed this decision to the U.S. Supreme Court.

High Court Rules

On 14 January 1946, the Supreme Court issued its decision. A majority of 6-2 sided with the federal government and affirmed the lower court rulings. The Saratoga Springs Authority was held not to possess immunity from federal taxation and ordered to pay the levy. Justice Frankfurter delivered the opinion of the Court, while several members of the majority filed concurring opinions.

In reaching his conclusion, Frankfurter relied heavily on an earlier case, *State of South Carolina v. United States,* in which a state was denied immunity from federal taxes on its liquor business. "We certainly see no reason for putting soft drinks in a different constitutional category from hard drinks," Frankfurter reasoned. He then turned his attention to the extent of the federal taxing power, which he defined extensively as encompassing "every subject" other than exports explicitly exempted from taxation under Article I, Section 9. While it had long been assumed that the federal and state governments enjoyed reciprocal immunity from the taxing power of the other, Frankfurter dismissed the absolute nature of this proposition. "The federal government is the government of all the States," he wrote "and all the States share in the legislative process by which a tax of general applicability is laid."

Frankfurter addressed the state of New York's contention that its activity represented essential governmental function exempt from federal taxation. But the majority found it impossible to use this standard. Frankfurter wrote:

> New York urges that in the use it is making of Saratoga Springs it is engaged in the disposition of its natural resources. And so it is. But in doing so it is engaged in an enterprise in which the State sells mineral waters in competition with private waters, the sale of which Congress has found necessary to tap as a source of revenue for carrying on the National Government. To say that the States cannot be taxed for enterprises generally pursued, like the sale of mineral water, because it is somewhat connected with a State's conservation policy, is to invoke an irrelevance to the federal taxing power.

On the question of when to impose a tax, Frankfurter favored allowing Congress to make that determination on a case-by-case basis. In rendering this decision, Frankfurter explicitly acknowledged that the judgment signaled "a shift in emphasis to that of limitation upon immunity."

Dissenting Voices

Justice Douglas penned a ringing dissent, on which he was joined by Justice Black. Douglas argued that the determination of what constituted essential state activity was best left up to the states themselves. "The notion that the sovereign position of the States must find its protection in the will of a transient majority of Congress is foreign to and a negation of our constitutional system," Douglas wrote. To him, the dismissal of tax immunity contained in the majority opinion was a violation of the sovereignty provisions implicit in the Tenth Amendment. More importantly, in his view,

this approach would not have the desired effect. As he wrote:

> There is no showing whatsoever that an expanding field of state activity even faintly promises to cripple the federal government in its search for needed revenues. If the truth were known, I suspect it would show that the activity of the States in the fields of housing, public power and the like have increased the level of income of the people and have raised the standards of marginal or sub-marginal groups. Such conditions affect favorably, not adversely, the tax potential of the federal government.

Impact

The Supreme Court's decision in *New York v. United States* limited the power of states to challenge the federal government's taxing authority. The doctrine of nonequivalence, in which the federal and state governments were believed to be free of each other's taxing authority, was largely struck down by this decision.

Related Cases

Hulbert v. Twin Falls County, Idaho, 327 U.S. 103 (1946).
Maryland v. Wirtz, 392 U.S. 183 (1968).
Frye v. United States, 421 U.S. 542 (1975).
National League of Cities v. Usery, 426 U.S. 833 (1976).

Bibliography and Further Reading

Chandler, Ralph C. *The Constitutional Law Dictionary.* Santa Barbara, CA: ABC-Clio, Inc., 1987.

Cushman, Robert Fairchild, with Susan P. Koniak. *Leading Constitutional Decisions.* Englewood Cliffs, NJ: Prentice-Hall, Inc., 1992.

Menez, Joseph Francis. *Summaries of Leading Cases of the Constitution.* Savage, MD: Littlefield, Adams, 1990.

SOUTH CAROLINA V. BAKER

Legal Citation: 485 U.S. 505 (1988)

Plaintiff
State of South Carolina

Defendant
James A. Baker III, U.S. Secretary of the Treasury

Plaintiff's Claim
That section 310(b)(1) of the Tax Equity and Fiscal Responsibility Act (TEFRA) of 1982, which removed federal income tax exemption from non-registered state bonds, violated the Tenth Amendment and the doctrine of intergovernmental tax immunity.

Chief Lawyer for Plaintiff
John P. Linton

Chief Defense Lawyer
Charles Fried, U.S. Solicitor General

Justices for the Court
Harry A. Blackmun, William J. Brennan, Jr. (writing for the Court), Thurgood Marshall, William H. Rehnquist, Antonin Scalia, John Paul Stevens, Byron R. White

Justices Dissenting
Sandra Day O'Connor (Anthony M. Kennedy did not participate)

Place
Washington, D.C.

Date of Decision
20 April 1988

Decision
That section 310(b)(1) of TEFRA did not violate either the Tenth Amendment's reservation of power to the states or the principle of intergovernmental tax immunity, whereby states were not liable to federal taxes and vice versa.

Significance
By invalidating the judgment in *Pollock*, *South Carolina v. Baker* effectively destroyed the concept of state immunity from federal taxation. In the years leading up to the Civil War, the most significant cases involving intergovernmental tax immunity had concerned attempts by the states to levy taxes directly or indirectly against the federal government. With the question of whether the federal or state governments had greater sovereignty decided, however, Washington began to exercise larger financial powers over the states. By 1988, bonds were the only remaining area of state immunity from federal taxes, and *Baker* dealt with that final question.

South Carolina Takes on TEFRA

Up to the time of *South Carolina v. Baker,* states issued bonds in two forms, registered and bearer bonds. The difference between these lay in the manner of transferring ownership. When someone bought a registered bond, it was recorded on a central list, and if they sold or gave it away, the conditions of ownership required that this transaction be registered with the state. A bearer bond, by contrast, functioned more like ordinary money: ownership was a matter of possession, transferred by physically handing it over to someone else.

In 1982, Congress passed the Tax Equity and Fiscal Responsibility Act, or TEFRA, which dealt with a variety of tax issues. One of these was the problem of tax evasion. According to the Internal Revenue Service (IRS), as much as $97 billion in income had gone unreported in 1981. There were a number of explanations for this, including simple tax evasion, as well as the vast amounts of money gained every year in criminal transactions. Congress saw one easy way to close off an area of tax evasion: by requiring that all bonds be registered. Otherwise, as assistant secretary of the treasury for Tax Policy, Chapoton, testified before the House Ways and Means Committee, people could use bearer bonds for financial transactions without reporting their gains. The Senate Finance Committee duly noted that "registration will reduce the ability of noncompliant taxpayers to conceal income and property from the reach of the income, estate, and gift taxes"; therefore Congress included provisions in TEFRA to address this situation.

Section 310 of TEFRA, as Justice Brennan later noted in his majority opinion for the Supreme Court, "was designed to meet these concerns by providing powerful incentives to issue bonds in registered form." Accordingly, the statute imposed tax penalties on corporations who issued non-registered bonds, thus providing them with a strong reason not to do so. Since it could not do the same with states, the federal government took a different approach to unregistered state bonds, addressed in section 310(b)(1). The latter statute denied federal tax exemption for interest earned on non-registered state bonds.

One of the reasons individuals purchase bonds is for the tax exemptions on interest, which in the past have made them a popular way of saving for retirement, or for a child's college education. With the new law in place, buyers would have a strong compulsion to purchase only registered bonds. The state of South Carolina, however, viewed this as federal interference, and charged that Washington had violated the Tenth Amendment and the doctrine of intergovernmental tax immunity.

Since it was a state, South Carolina was able to take its case directly to the Supreme Court as a petitioner. The Court appointed Samuel J. Roberts as special master to investigate the situation, and the National Governor's Association (NGA) intervened on South Carolina's side. Special Master Roberts concluded after hearings that 310(b)(1) was constitutional, whereupon South Carolina and the NGA filed exceptions to several of his findings. In the subsequent case, briefs of *amici curiae* were filed by the states of Alaska, Arizona, Florida, Hawaii, Indiana, Iowa, Louisiana, Maryland, Mississippi, Missouri, Montana, New Hampshire, New Jersey, North Carolina, North Dakota, Ohio, Oklahoma, Pennsylvania, Vermont, Virginia, West Virginia, Wisconsin, and Wyoming. The Government Finance Officers Association and the Public Securities Association filed briefs as well.

The End of State Immunity

The Court overruled the exceptions to the Special Master's Report, and ruled in favor of the respondent, by a 7-1 vote. Justice Brennan, writing for the Court, first addressed the Tenth Amendment question. Section 310(b)(1), he held, did not violate the amendment, or other constitutional principles of federalism, by its provision "effectively compelling States to issue bonds in registered form."

The limits placed by the Tenth Amendment on congressional authority to regulate state activities, the Court held, are "structural, not substantive." What this meant was that if South Carolina wanted a change in national policy, it had to do so through its senators and its representatives in Congress, not through the Court. The state had not claimed that the congressional provision had in any way deprived it of its rights to participate in the political process of the nation, or that it had been somehow isolated from the other states by the policies of Congress. As for the charges it had made, which Brennan characterized as a complaint that "Congress was uninformed and chose an ineffective remedy," these "do not amount to an allegation that the political process operated in a defective manner."

Still addressing the Tenth Amendment issue, the Court next turned to the NGA's contention that section 310 (in Brennan's words) "commandeers the state legislative and administrative process by coercing States

James Baker, U.S. Secretary of Treasury. © AP/Wide World Photos.

into enacting legislation authorizing bond registration and into administering the registration scheme." Brennan compared this claim with the one addressed by the Court in *FERC v. Mississippi* (1982). That case questioned whether a statute represented an attempt "to control or influence the manner in which States regulate private parties." In the present situation, however, Congress was only requiring "[t]hat a state wishing to engage in a certain activity must take administrative and sometimes legislative action to comply with federal standards regulating that activity." This, the Court held, was hardly the same thing.

Turning to the doctrine of intergovernmental tax immunity, the Court again found 310(b)(1) valid—even though to do so was inconsistent with the Court's ruling in *Pollock* that interest from state bonds was immune from a "nondiscriminatory" federal tax. Subsequent decisions had already undermined *Pollock,* a judgment which occurred at a time when the federal government had no authority to tax individual income gained directly under contract with a state government, or vice versa. This prevention of taxes "on" another government had been eliminated by later rulings. Furthermore, the Constitution provided no immunity from taxation for owners of state bonds, nor did states have the right to issue bonds offering lower interest rates than other issuers. Section 310 applied taxes to individuals, not states, and any administrative costs the states incurred in implementing the changeover to registered bonds did not constitute a "tax" in any meaningful sense of the word. Finally, 310 was directed not only at states, but at local governments, the federal government, and private corporations, in each case with the aim of assuring that all long-term bonds were issued in registered form.

Concurring Opinions and a Lone Dissent— "The Tyranny of Small Decisions"

A number of justices issued concurring opinions. Justice Stevens pointed out that although the Court supported its case by reference to *Garcia v. San Antonio Metropolitan Transit Authority* (1985), "the outcome of [the present] case was equally clear," in *South Carolina v. Regan* (1984) "well before [*Garcia*] was decided." He cautioned that "neither the Court's decision today, nor what I have written in the past, expressed any opinion about the wisdom of taxing the interest on bonds issued by state or local governments." Justice Scalia concurred in part and concurred in the judgment, taking exception with aspects of the Court's ruling on that part of the case dealing with the Tenth Amendment. He did not agree with the Court's contention "that the 'national political process' is the state's only constitutional protection." Whereas the Court had used the *Garcia* ruling to support this, Scalia held that the latter ruling "explicitly disclaim[s] . . . the proposition attributed to it in today's opinion . . ." Chief Justice Rehnquist, also concurring, observed that, "While I agree that the principles of intergovernmental tax immunity are not threatened in this case, in my view the Court unnecessarily casts doubt on the protective scope of the Tenth Amendment in the course of upholding 310(b)(1)."

Justice O'Connor, in a dissenting opinion, questioned the Court's decision to overrule *Pollock*. Furthermore, she interpreted the Tenth Amendment as protecting the states from any tax, or threat of a tax, on state and municipal bonds, and supported this contention by reference to the Guarantee Clause in Article IV, section 4 of the Constitution. As for the Court's characterization of intergovernmental tax immunity as a thing of the past, she wrote that, "constitutional principles do not depend on the rise or fall of particular legal doctrines." The provisions in section 310 would have adverse effects on states, and would ultimately cost them money, a consequence that the Court had not properly taken into account. In the eyes of the Court, section 310 seemed a small measure designed to circumvent tax evasion—a small step. O'Connor, however, quoting Laurence Tribe in his book *American Constitutional Law* warned against "the tyranny of small decisions . . . the prospect that Congress will nibble away at state sovereignty, bit by bit, until someday essentially nothing is left but a gutted shell."

Impact

As Justice Brennan had indicated, the principle of intergovernmental tax immunity—and indeed intergovernmental sovereignty—was, if not a dead issue, a dying one when it came before the Court in *Baker*. The ruling also ended hopes cherished by states invigorated by the earlier decision in *National League of Cities v. Usery* (1976), which had appeared to promise a new era of Tenth-Amendment challenges to federal authority. Federal-state cooperation, or—to use a term coined under President Franklin D. Roosevelt's New Deal— "cooperative federalism" would increasingly be viewed as a situation in which the national government controlled the purse strings, while states administered federally mandated programs.

Related Cases

McCulloch v. Maryland, 4. Wheat. 316 (1819).
Pollock v. Farmers' Loan & Trust Co., 157 U.S. 429 (1895).
National League of Cities v. Usery, 426 U.S. 833 (1976).
South Carolina v. Regan, 465 U.S. 367 (1984).
Garcia v. San Antonio Metropolitan Transit Authority, 469 U.S. 528 (1985).
New York v. United States, 505 U.S. 144 (1992).
Printz v. United States, 521 U.S. 98 (1996).

Bibliography and Further Reading

Hall, Kermit L., ed. *The Oxford Companion to the Supreme Court of the United States.* New York: Oxford University Press, 1992.

Witt, Elder. *Congressional Quarterly's Guide to the Supreme Court,* 2nd ed. Washington, DC: Congressional Quarterly Inc., 1990.

Witt, Elder, ed. *The Supreme Court A to Z. CQ's Encyclopedia of American Government,* rev. ed. Washington, DC: Congressional Quarterly, Inc., 1994.

MISSOURI V. JENKINS

Legal Citation: 495 U.S. 33 (1990)

Appellant
State of Missouri

Appellee
Kalima Jenkins

Appellant's Claim
That a federal court order requiring an increase in a school district's property taxes, in violation of state tax limits, violates intergovernmental tax immunities.

Chief Lawyer for Appellant
H. Barrow Farr III

Chief Lawyer for Appellee
Allen R. Snyder

Justices for the Court
Harry A. Blackmun, William J. Brennan, Jr., Anthony M. Kennedy, Thurgood Marshall, Sandra Day O'Connor, William H. Rehnquist, Antonin Scalia, John Paul Stevens, Byron R. White (writing for the Court)

Justices Dissenting
None

Place
Washington, D.C.

Date of Decision
18 April 1990

Decision
The Supreme Court approved an indirect method of raising school district property taxes necessary to implement a court ordered desegregation program.

Significance
Jenkins vividly illustrates the difficulties of attempting to implement complicated school desegregation orders without violating the autonomy of local government.

In 1983, the U.S. District Court for the Western District of Missouri ruled that the Kansas City, Missouri, School District (KCMSD) and the state of Missouri had operated a racially segregated school system. To remedy this situation, a costly "magnet school" plan was proposed to attract students from the mostly-white suburbs into the mostly-black KCMSD. The court ordered the state to pay seventy-five percent of the cost of this program and the school district to pay twenty-five percent. This order posed a problem, for the portion assigned to the district exceeded tax limits set by the state. The district court, after determining that KCMSD had exhausted all other means of raising revenue, ordered the district tax levy to be increased through the 1991-1992 fiscal year.

The state appealed, arguing that a federal court lacks the power to order an increase in local taxes. The federal court of appeals, however, affirmed the district court's orders, modifying them only by indicating that in the future the court should not set the tax rate, but should authorize the district to do so. To make this scheme work, the district court would be required to prevent the state laws from operating so as to prevent a KCMSD tax increase. Clearly this new order violated the principle of intergovernmental immunities, which dictates that the state and the federal governments are not subject to one another's taxes. The state of Missouri, mindful of its autonomy, appealed both orders to the U.S. Supreme Court.

Court Sidesteps Issue of Tax Immunities

By a unanimous vote, the Supreme Court struck down the order directly raising the school district's property tax. The alternative proposed by the appellate court, however, was another matter. Writing for the Court, Justice White declared that this indirect method of setting aside state tax limits was the best solution to an stubborn problem:

> The District Court believed that it had no alternative to imposing a tax increase. But there was an alternative, the very one outlined by the Court of Appeals . . . The difference between the two approaches is far more than a matter of form. Authorizing and directing

local government institutions to devise and implement remedies not only protects the function of those institutions but, to the extent possible, also places the responsibility for solutions to the problems of segregation upon those who have themselves created the problems.

In a concurring opinion, Justice Kennedy declared this to be a distinction without a difference. For him—and for the three justices who joined his opinion—the federal government could not impose a state tax, either directly or indirectly. His belief was based on the principle of intergovernmental immunities, which in turn found its justification in the Tenth Amendment.

The Tenth Amendment declares that all the rights not expressly assigned to the federal government in the Constitution are reserved to the individual states. It was made part of the Bill of Rights at the insistence of the anti-federalists who, enduring the early years of the republic, were concerned that state sovereignty would disappear in the face of an all powerful central governmental authority. Serious erosion of the strength of the Tenth Amendment began early in the twentieth century with the growth of federal regulatory agencies.

The highwater mark of this erosion was President Franklin Roosevelt's New Deal agenda, with its multitude of federal agencies designed to combat the Great Depression in the 1930s. At around the same time, the Supreme Court began to reshape the doctrine of intergovernmental tax immunities to grant the federal government a greater share. As the demand for federal services grew, the federal government began making inroads into state tax structures. The argument for federalism was once again implicitly made by the majority in *Jenkins* in its attempts to address what it saw as an urgent national problem.

Related Cases

Brown v. Board of Education of Topeka, 347 U.S. 483 (1954).
Milliken v. Bradley, 433 U.S. 267 (1974).

Bibliography and Further Reading

Armor, David J. *Forced Justice: School Desegregation and the Law.* New York, NY: Oxford University Press, 1995.

Canan, Martha M. "High Court Ruling Limits Federal Role in Desegregation." *The Bond Buyer,* June 13, 1995, p. 3.

Carmody, Cris. "Missouri Reduces Fiscal 1996 Desegregation Payment to District." *The Bond Buyer,* July 11, 1995, p. 5.

Chemerinsky, Erwin. "Race and the Supreme Court." *Trial,* October 1995, p. 86.

"Courting Trouble." *National Review,* July 10, 1995, p. 16.

Coyle, Marcia. "The Court's New View: Colorblind? Rulings Put Heavy Burden on Racial Classifications." *The National Law Journal,* July 10, 1995, p. A1.

England, Robert E., and David R. Morgan. *Desegregating the Schools: Strategies, Outcomes, and Impacts.* Millwood, NY: Associated Faculty Press, 1986.

"Lost Right?" *National Review,* July 10, 1995, p. 14.

Kunen, James S. "The End of Integration." *Time,* April 29, 1996, p. 38.

Persons, Georgia A. "Is Racial Separation Inevitable and Legal?" *Society,* March-April 1996, p. 19.

Rosen, Jeffrey. "The Color-Blind Court." *The New Republic,* July 31, 1995, p. 19.

Thomas, Andrew Peyton. "Equal Time." *National Review,* September 14, 1998, p. 26.

Wolters, Raymond. *The Burden of Brown: Thirty Years of School Desegregation.* Knoxville: University of Tennessee Press. 1984.

NORDLINGER V. HAHN

Legal Citation: 505 U.S. 1 (1992)

Petitioner
Stephanie Nordlinger, et al.

Respondent
Kenneth Hahn, Tax Assessor, Los Angeles County

Petitioner's Claim
Proposition 13 of the California State Constitution violated the Equal Protection Clause of the U.S. Constitution. Petitioner also claimed that her 'right to travel' was violated because the higher property assessment forced her to remain in a particular locale in order to limit taxation.

Chief Lawyer for Petitioner
Carlyle W. Hall, Jr.

Chief Lawyer for Respondent
Rex E. Lee

Justices for the Court
Harry A. Blackmun (writing for the Court), Anthony M. Kennedy, Sandra Day O'Connor, William H. Rehnquist, Antonin Scalia, David H. Souter, Clarence Thomas, Byron R. White

Justices Dissenting
John Paul Stevens

Place
Washington, D.C.

Date of Decision
18 June 1992

Decision
The Supreme Court upheld the lower courts' decision that Proposition 13 did not violate the Fourteenth Amendment. They found that the proposition supported legitimate state interests as required by the Equal Protection Clause. The justices also held that Nordlinger's right to travel was not infringed. A homebuyer was informed up front about the tax liability of the property; she could choose to not buy if the tax burden would be too great. The state did not prevent her from relocating, particularly as Nordlinger had been a resident of Los Angeles County prior to purchasing a home.

Significance
In *Nordlinger v. Hahn* the Supreme Court affirmed the state's right to enact a tax assessment structure which established the amount of taxes due based upon the purchase price, or "acquisition value" of the property. Prior cases established a precedent for allowing states a great deal of latitude in creating classifications which were reasonable systems of taxation.

Historical Property Values and New Owners

From 1967 through 1977 the state of California experienced a period of rapidly rising property taxes along with a boom in the real estate market, which also increased property tax valuations. Homeowners saw significant increases in their tax levies, as much as doubling or tripling at times. State legislators sought a variety of tax relief measures to control the spiraling increases. In 1978, California tax payers voted Article XIIIA (also known as Proposition 13) into effect as an amendment to their state constitution. This proposition encompassed an "acquisition value" tax assessment for property, which assessed taxes based upon the purchase price of the property rather than the real value of the property. Provided the home did not change ownership or have new construction or property improvement, property was assessed up to the current appraised value for fiscal year 1975-76. Exemptions from the reassessment included adults over the age of 55 who changed their principle residences to ones of equal- or lesser-value, or transfers of property between spouses or between parents and children. Over time long-term property owners paid significantly lower taxes than new owners did on similar pieces of property based upon the historic value of the home. The tax restructuring also included a 1 percent tax rate ceiling cap and a limit of a 2 percent assessment valuation increase annually for all property owners.

Stephanie Nordlinger purchased a home in Los Angeles County, California, in November of 1988. In the early months of 1989, Nordlinger received a tax reassessment of her newly purchased home with a resulting tax increase of 36 percent from the previous year. Upon further investigation she discovered that her tax liabilities were as much as five times more than some of her neighbors who had owned similar lots since 1975. Nordlinger brought suit against the County of Los Angeles and the county tax assessor in Los Angeles County Superior Court, where she requested a tax refund for unfair assessment. Her complaint was dismissed, and she appealed to the California Court of Appeals, who affirmed the lower court's dismissal. The court noted that a previous challenge to Article XIIIA had already been rejected by the California Supreme Court.

In 1992, the constitutionality of Proposition 13 was tested in the U.S. Supreme Court. On a writ of *certiorari,* the case was remanded to the Supreme Court for review and a decision on the constitutionality of Proposition 13. Nordlinger claimed that her rights of equal protection had been infringed, and in particular her right to travel. Her case alleged that the exemptions to Proposition 13 (transfer of homes by owners over the age of 55, and the transfer of property ownership between parents and children) were directly classified by California residency. Because she did not fall into either of these classes and had rented an apartment prior to her home purchase, she held that she was denied the same tax relief provided to propertied residents of the state.

An 8-1 Decision

In an 8-1 decision, the Supreme Court upheld the decision of the lower courts. Entering the opinion for the Court, Justice Blackmun first stated that Nordlinger had not identified any obstacle that prevented her from moving within the state of California nor had she identified any obstacle that prevented others from settling in or traveling to California. Her claim of violation of right to travel was dismissed.

The Court then turned to the other issues of constitutionality. They held that Proposition 13 furthered legitimate state concerns. First, the state had a rational interest in the preservation and stability of local communities. The proposition discouraged rapid turnover of property ownership and inhibited the displacement of lower income families by those with higher income. It also prevented chain operations from forcing established sole proprietor businesses to close or move.

It was the opinion of the Court that the state could legitimately determine that new property owners did not have the same "reliance interest" as established property owners did. A new property owner has complete information about tax liability and assessment when they initiate the purchase. If the new owner calculates that the tax liability will be greater in the future than he can reasonably pay, he can choose to not purchase the property. The Court contrasted this to an established owner who does not have the same option of deciding not to buy his home if the tax liability is too great; he already carries that burden. In order to meet his tax obligations, he may be forced to sell the property or to use income meant for other necessities to pay the taxes levied against him. The justices concluded that "will of the people of California," who used democratic process to approve Article XIIIA, must stand and denied Nordlinger's request to overturn the proposition.

Impact

Nordlinger v. Hahn along with several other cases provided states with a significant latitude in establishing tax structure without violating the Equal Protection Clause of the U.S. Constitution. States can establish taxation which, while causing a significant disparity between property owners, would protect the vested interest of long-term taxpayers and maintain the stability of the tax base within the state or local community. The voting tax payers of California agreed to the tax structure, therefore the "will of the people" ruled through a democratic process.

Related Cases

Village of Euclid v. Ambler Realty Co., 272 U.S. 365 (1926).
Penn Central Transportation Co. v. New York, 438 U.S. 104 (1978).
Heckler v. Mathews, 465 U.S. 728 (1984).
Cleburne v. Cleburne Living Center, Inc., 473 U.S. 432 (1985).

Bibliography and Further Reading

California Taxpayers' Association. "Proposition 13: Love It or Hate It, Its Roots Go Deep." *Cal-Tax Research,* November, 1993. http://www.caltax.org/research/prop13/prop13.html.

FindLaw, Inc. *An Internet Legal Resource.* http://www.findlaw.com

"Excerpts of Proposition 13 Oral Arguments: Hall for Petitioner: No 'Legitimate Objective' to California System." *The Recorder,* 19 June 1992.

Mauro, Tony. "Proposition 13 Secure after Nordlinger Argument," *New Jersey Law Journal,* 9 March 1992.

Morris, John E. "Weak Case, Strong Appeal," *The Recorder,* 18 February 1992.

Northwestern University. *Oyez, oyez, oyez: A Supreme Court Database.* http://court.it-services.nwu.edu/oyez/cases.

GLOSSARY

A

Abandonment The surrender, relinquishment, disclaimer, or cession of property or of rights. Voluntary relinquishment of all right, title, claim, and possession, with no intention of reclamation.

The giving up of a thing absolutely, without reference to any particular person or purpose, such as vacating property with no intention of returning it, so that it may be appropriated by the next comer or finder. The voluntary relinquishment of possession of a thing by the owner with intention of terminating ownership, but without vesting it in any other person. The relinquishing of all title, possession, or claim, or a virtual, intentional throwing away of property.

Accessory Aiding or contributing in a secondary way or assisting in or contributing to as a subordinate.

In criminal law, contributing to or aiding in the commission of a crime. One who, without being present at the commission of an offense, becomes guilty of such offense, not as a chief actor, but as a participant, as by command, advice, instigation, or concealment; either before or after the fact of commission.

One who aids, abets, commands, or counsels another in the commission of a crime.

Accessory after the fact One who commits a crime by giving comfort or assistance to a felon, knowing that the felon has committed a crime, or is sought by authorities in connection with a serious crime.

Accomplice One who knowingly, voluntarily, and with common intent unites with the principal offender in the commission of a crime. One who is in some way involved with commission of a crime; partaker of guilt; one who aids or assists, or is an accessory. One who is guilty of complicity in a crime charged, either by being present and aiding or abetting in it, or having advised and encouraged it, though absent from place when it was committed. However, the mere presence, acquiescence, or silence, in the absence of a duty to act, is not enough, no matter how reprehensible it may be, to constitute one an accomplice. One is liable as an accomplice to the crime of another if he or she gave assistance or encouragement or failed to perform a legal duty to prevent it with the intent thereby to promote or facilitate commission of the crime.

Accord An agreement that settles a dispute, generally requiring a compromise or satisfaction with something less than what was originally demanded.

Acquittal The legal and formal certification of the innocence of a person who has been charged with a crime.

Action Conduct; behavior; something done; a series of acts.

A case or a lawsuit; a legal and formal demand for the enforcement of one's rights against another party asserted in a court of justice.

Actual authority The legal power, expressed or implied, that an agent possesses to represent and to bind into agreement the principal with a third party.

Actual damages Compensation awarded for the loss or the injury suffered by an individual.

Adjudication The legal process of resolving a dispute. The formal giving or pronouncing of a judgment or decree in a court proceeding; also the judgment or decision given. The entry of a decree by a court in respect to the parties in a case. It implies a hearing by a court, after notice, of legal evidence on the factual issue(s) involved. The equivalent of a determination. It indicates that the claims of all of the parties thereto have been considered and set at rest.

Administrative agency An official governmental body empowered with the authority to direct and supervise the implementation of particular legislative acts. In addition to *agency,* such governmental bodies may be called commissions, corporations (i.e., FDIC), boards, departments, or divisions.

Administrative law The body of law that allows for the creation of public regulatory agencies and contains all of the statutes, judicial decisions, and regulations that govern them. It is the body of law created by administrative agencies to implement their powers and duties in the form of rules, regulations, orders, and decisions.

Administrator A person appointed by the court to manage and take charge of the assets and liabilities of a decedent who has died without making a valid will.

Admissible A term used to describe information that is relevant to a determination of issues in any judicial proceeding so that such information can be properly considered by a judge or jury in making a decision.

Adultery Voluntary sexual relations between an individual who is married and someone who is not the individual's spouse.

Adversary system The scheme of American jurisprudence wherein a judge renders a decision in a controversy between parties who assert contradictory positions during a judicial examination, such as a trial or hearing.

Affidavit A written statement of facts voluntarily made by an affiant under an oath or affirmation administered by a person who is authorized to do so by law.

Affirmative action Employment programs required by federal statutes and regulations designed to remedy discriminatory practices in hiring minority group members; i.e., positive steps designed to eliminate existing and continuing discrimination, to remedy lingering effects of past discrimination, and to create systems and procedures to prevent future discrimination; commonly based on population percentages of minority groups in a particular area. Factors considered are race, color, sex, creed, and age.

Agent One who agrees and is authorized to act on behalf of another, a principal, to legally bind an individual in particular business transactions with third parties pursuant to an agency relationship.

Age of consent The age at which a person may marry without parental approval. The age at which a female is legally capable of agreeing to sexual intercourse, so that a male who engages in sex with her cannot be prosecuted for statutory rape.

Age of majority The age at which a person, formerly a minor or an infant, is recognized by law to be an adult, capable of managing his or her own affairs and responsible for any legal obligations created by his or her actions.

Aggravated assault A person is guilty of aggravated assault if he or she attempts to cause serious bodily injury to another or causes such injury purposely, knowingly, or recklessly under circumstances manifesting extreme indifference to the value of human life; or attempts to cause or purposely or knowingly causes bodily injury to another with a deadly weapon. In all jurisdictions, statutes punish such aggravated assaults as assault with intent to murder (or rob or kill or rape) and assault with a dangerous (or deadly) weapon more severely than "simple" assaults.

Alien Foreign-born person who has not been naturalized to become a U.S. citizen under federal law and the Constitution.

Alimony Payment a family court may order one person in a couple to make to the other when the couple separates or divorces.

Alimony pendente lite Temporary alimony awarded while separation and divorce proceedings are taking place. The award may cover the preparation for the suit, as well as general support.

Alternative dispute resolution Procedures for settling disputes by means other than litigation; i.e., by arbitration, mediation, or minitrials. Such procedures, which are usually less costly and more expeditious than litigation, are increasingly being used in commercial and labor disputes, divorce actions, in resolving motor vehicle and medical malpractice tort claims, and in other disputes that otherwise would likely involve court litigation.

Amendment The modification of materials by the addition of supplemental information; the deletion of unnecessary, undesirable, or outdated information; or the correction of errors existing in the text.

Amicus curiae [*Latin, Friend of the court.*] A person with strong interest in or views on the subject matter of an action, but not a party to the action, may petition the court for permission to file a brief, ostensibly on behalf of a party but actually to suggest a rationale consistent with his or her own views. Such amicus curiae briefs are commonly filed in appeals concerning matters of a broad public interest; i.e., civil rights cases. They may be filed by private persons or by the government. In appeals to the U.S. courts of appeals, an amicus brief may be filed only if accompanied by written consent of all parties, or by leave of court granted on motion or at the request of the court, except that consent or leave shall not be required when the brief is presented by the United States or an officer or agency thereof.

Amnesty The action of a government by which all persons or certain groups of persons who have committed a criminal offense—usually of a political nature that threatens the sovereignty of the government (such as sedition or treason)—are granted immunity from prosecution.

Annulment A judgment by a court that retroactively invalidates a marriage to the date of its formation.

Answer The first responsive pleading filed by the defendant in a civil action; a formal written statement that admits or denies the allegations in the complaint and sets forth any available affirmative defenses.

Apparent authority The amount of legal power a principal knowingly or negligently bestows onto an agent for representation with a third party, and which the third party reasonably believes the agent possesses.

Appeal Timely resort by an unsuccessful party in a lawsuit or administrative proceeding to an appropriate superior court empowered to review a final decision on the ground that it was based upon an erroneous application of law.

Appeals court *See* Appellate court or Court of appeal.

Appellate court A court having jurisdiction to review decisions of a trial-level or other lower court.

Appellate jurisdiction The power of a superior court or other tribunal to review the judicial actions of lower courts, particularly for legal errors, and to revise their judgments accordingly.

Apportionment The process by which legislative seats are distributed among units entitled to representation. Determination of the number of representatives that a state, county, or other subdivision may send to a legislative body. The U.S. Constitution provides for a census every ten years, on the basis of which Congress apportions representatives according to population. However, each state must have at least one representative. *Districting* is the establishment of the precise geographical boundaries of each such unit or constituency. Apportionment by state statute that denies the rule of one-person, one-vote is violative of equal protection laws.

Arbitration The submission of a dispute to an unbiased third person designated by the parties to the controversy, who agree in advance to comply with the award—a decision to be issued after a hearing at which both parties have an opportunity to be heard.

Arraignment The formal proceeding whereby the defendant is brought before the trial court to hear the charges against him or her and to enter a plea of guilty, not guilty, or no contest.

Arrest The detention and taking into custody of an individual for the purpose of answering the charges against him or her. An arrest involves the legal power of the individual to arrest, the intent to exercise that power, and the actual subjection to the control and will of the arresting authority.

Arrest warrant A written order issued by an authority of the state and commanding the seizure of the person named.

Arson At common law, the malicious burning or exploding of the dwelling house of another, or the burning of a building within the curtilage, the immediate surrounding space, of the dwelling of another.

Assault At common law, an intentional act by one person that creates an apprehension in another of an imminent harmful or offensive contact.

Assumption of risk A defense, facts offered by a party against whom proceedings have been instituted to diminish a plaintiff's cause of action or defeat recovery to an action in negligence, which entails proving that the plaintiff knew of a dangerous condition and voluntarily exposed himself or herself to it.

Attachment The legal process of seizing property to ensure satisfaction of a judgment.

Attempt An undertaking to do an act that entails more than mere preparation but does not result in the successful completion of the act.

Attractive nuisance doctrine The duty of an individual to take necessary precautions around equipment or conditions on his or her property that could attract and potentially injury children unable to perceive the risk of danger, such as an unguarded swimming pool or a trampoline.

Avoidance An escape from the consequences of a specific course of action through the use of legally acceptable means. Cancellation; the act of rendering something useless or legally ineffective.

B

Bail The system that governs the status of individuals charged with committing crimes from the time of their arrest to the time of their trial, and pending appeal, with the major purpose of ensuring their presence at trial.

Bait and switch A deceptive sales technique that involves advertising a low-priced item to attract customers to a store, then persuading them to buy more expensive goods by failing to have a sufficient supply of the advertised item on hand or by disparaging its quality.

Balancing A process sometimes used by the Supreme Court in deciding between the competing interests represented in a case.

Bankruptcy A federally authorized procedure by which a debtor—an individual, corporation, or municipality—is relieved of total liability for its debts by making court-approved arrangements for their partial repayment.

Battery At common law, an intentional unpermitted act causing harmful or offensive contact with the person of another.

Beneficiary An organization or a person for whom a trust is created and who thereby receives the benefits of the trust. One who inherits under a will. A person entitled to a beneficial interest or a right to profits, benefit, or advantage from a contract.

Bigamy The offense of willfully and knowingly entering into a second marriage while validly married to another individual.

Bilateral contract An agreement formed by an exchange of promises in which the promise of one party supports the promise of the other party.

Bill A declaration in writing. A document listing separate items. An itemized account of charges or costs. In equity practice, the first pleading in the action, that is, the paper in which the plaintiff sets out his or her case and demands relief from the defendant.

Bill of attainder A special legislative enactment that imposes a death sentence without a judicial trial upon a particular person or class of persons suspected of committing serious offenses, such as treason or a felony.

Bill of rights The first ten amendments to the U.S. Constitution, ratified in 1791, which set forth and guarantee certain fundamental rights and privileges of individuals, including freedom of religion, speech, press, and assembly; guarantee of a speedy jury trial in criminal cases; and protection against excessive bail and cruel and unusual punishment.

A list of fundamental rights included in each state constitution.

A declaration of individual rights and freedoms, usually issued by a national government.

Bill of sale In the law of contracts, a written agreement, previously required to be under seal, by which one person transfers to another a right to, or interest in, personal property and goods, a legal instrument that conveys title in property from seller to purchaser.

Black codes Laws, statutes, or rules that governed slavery and segregation of public places in the South prior to 1865.

Bona fide [*Latin, In good faith.*] Honest; genuine; actual; authentic; acting without the intention of defrauding.

Bona fide occupational qualification An essential requirement for performing a given job. The requirement may even be a physical condition beyond an individual's control, such as perfect vision, if it is absolutely necessary for performing a job.

Bonds Written documents by which a government, corporation, or individual—the obligator—promises to per-

form a certain act, usually the payment of a definite sum of money, to another—the obligee—on a certain date.

Booking The procedure by which law enforcement officials record facts about the arrest of and charges against a suspect, such as the crime for which the arrest was made, together with information concerning the identification of the suspect and other pertinent facts.

Breach of contract The breaking of a legal agreement that had been sealed by the signing of a written, legal contractual document.

Bribery The offering, giving, receiving, or soliciting of something of value for the purpose of influencing the action of an official in the discharge of his or her public or legal duties.

Brief A summary of the important points of a longer document. An abstract of a published judicial opinion prepared by a law student as part of an assignment in the case method study of law. A written document drawn up by an attorney for a party in a lawsuit or by a party appearing pro se that concisely states the (1) issues of a lawsuit; (2) facts that bring the parties to court; (3) relevant laws that can affect the subject of the dispute; and (4) arguments that explain how the law applies to the particular facts so that the case will be decided in the party's favor.

Broker An individual or firm employed by others to plan and organize sales or negotiate contracts for a commission.

Burden of proof The duty of a party to prove an asserted fact. The party is subject to the burden of persuasion—convincing a judge or jury—and the burden of going forward—proving wrong any evidence that damages the position of the party. In criminal cases the persuasion burden must include proof beyond a reasonable doubt.

Burglary The criminal offense of breaking and entering a building illegally for the purpose of committing a crime therein.

Bylaws The rules and regulations enacted by an association or a corporation to provide a framework for its operation and management.

C

Capacity The ability, capability, or fitness to do something; a legal right, power, or competency to perform some act. An ability to comprehend both the nature and consequences of one's acts.

Capital punishment The lawful infliction of death as a punishment; the death penalty.

Case law Legal principles enunciated and embodied in judicial decisions that are derived from the application of particular areas of law to the facts of individual cases.

Cause Each separate antecedent of an event. Something that precedes and brings about an effect or a result. A reason for an action or condition. A ground of a legal action. An agent that brings something about. That which in some manner is accountable for a condition that brings about an effect or that produces a cause for the resultant action or state.

A suit, litigation, or action. Any question, civil or criminal, litigated or contested before a court of justice.

Cause in fact The direct cause of an event. Commonly referred to as the "but for" rule, by which an event could not have happened but for the specified cause.

Cause of action The fact or combination of facts that gives a person the right to seek judicial redress or relief against another. Also, the legal theory forming the basis of a lawsuit.

Caveat emptor [*Latin, Let the buyer beware.*] A warning that notifies a buyer that the goods he or she is buying are "as is," subject to all defects.

Cease and desist order An order issued by an administrative agency or a court proscribing a person or a business entity from continuing a particular course of conduct.

Censorship The suppression or proscription of speech or writing that is deemed obscene, indecent, or unduly controversial.

Certiorari [*Latin, To be informed of.*] At common law, an original writ or order issued by the Chancery or King's Bench, commanding officers of inferior courts to submit the record of a cause pending before them to give the party more certain and speedy justice.

A writ that a superior appellate court issues on its discretion to an inferior court, ordering it to produce a certified record of a particular case it has tried, in order to determine whether any irregularities or errors occurred that justify review of the case.

A device by which the Supreme Court of the United States exercises its discretion in selecting the cases it will review.

Challenge for cause Request from a party that a prospective juror be disqualified for given causes or reasons.

Change of venue The removal of a lawsuit from one county or district to another for trial, often permitted in criminal cases where the court finds that the defendant would not receive a fair trial in the first location because of adverse publicity.

Charter A grant from the government of ownership rights in land to a person, a group of people, or an organization, such as a corporation.

A basic document of law of a municipal corporation granted by the state, defining its rights, liabilities, and responsibilities of self-government.

A document embodying a grant of authority from the legislature or the authority itself, such as a corporate charter.

The leasing of a mode of transportation, such as a bus, ship, or plane. A *charter-party* is a contract formed to lease a ship to a merchant in order to facilitate the conveyance of goods.

Chattel An item of personal property that is movable; it may be animate or inanimate.

Circumstantial evidence Information and testimony presented by a party in a civil or criminal action that permit conclusions that indirectly establish the existence or nonexistence of a fact or event that the party seeks to prove.

Citation A paper commonly used in various courts—such as a probate, matrimonial, or traffic court—that is served upon an individual to notify him or her that he or she is required to appear at a specific time and place.

Reference to a legal authority—such as a case, constitution, or treatise—where particular information may be found.

Citizens Those who, under the Constitution and laws of the United States, or of a particular community or of a foreign country, owe allegiance and are entitled to the enjoyment of all civil rights that accrue to those who qualify for that status.

Civil action A lawsuit brought to enforce, redress, or protect rights of private litigants (the plaintiffs and the defendants); not a criminal proceeding.

Civil death The forfeiture of rights and privileges of an individual who has been convicted of a serious crime.

Civil law Legal system derived from the Roman *Corpus Juris Civilis* of Emperor Justinian I; differs from a common-law system, which relies on prior decisions to determine the outcome of a lawsuit. Most European and South American countries have a civil law system. England and most of the countries it dominated or colonized, including Canada and the United States, have a common-law system. However, within these countries, Louisiana, Quebec, and Puerto Rico exhibit the influence of French and Spanish settlers in their use of civil law systems.

A body of rules that delineate private rights and remedies and govern disputes between individuals in such areas as contracts, property, and family law; distinct from criminal or public law.

Civil liberties Freedom of speech, freedom of press, freedom from discrimination, and other natural rights guaranteed and protected by the Constitution, which were intended to place limits on government.

Civil rights Personal liberties that belong to an individual owing to his or her status as a citizen or resident of a particular country or community.

Class action A lawsuit that allows a large number of people with a common interest in a matter to sue or be sued as a group.

Clause A section, phrase, paragraph, or segment of a legal document, such as a contract, deed, will, or constitution, that relates to a particular point.

Closing The final transaction between a buyer and seller of real property.

Closing argument The final factual and legal argument made by each attorney on all sides of a case in a trial prior to a verdict or judgment.

Code A systematic and comprehensive compilation of laws, rules, or regulations that are consolidated and classified according to subject matter.

Coercion The intimidation of a victim to compel the individual to do some act against his or her will by the use of psychological pressure, physical force, or threats. The crime of intentionally and unlawfully restraining another's freedom by threatening to commit a crime, accusing the victim of a crime, disclosing any secret that would seriously impair the victim's reputation in the community, or by performing or refusing to perform an official action lawfully requested by the victim, or by causing an official to do so.

A defense asserted in a criminal prosecution that a person who committed a crime did not do so of his or her own free will, but only because the individual was compelled by another through the use of physical force or threat of immediate serious bodily injury or death.

Cohabitation A living arrangement in which an unmarried couple live together in a long-term relationship that resembles a marriage.

Cohabitation agreement The contract concerning property and financial agreements between two individuals who intend to live together and to have sexual relations out of wedlock.

Collateral Related; indirect; not bearing immediately upon an issue. The property pledged or given as a security interest, or a guarantee for payment of a debt, that will be taken or kept by the creditor in case of a default on the original debt.

Collective bargaining agreement The contractual agreement between an employer and a labor union that governs wages, hours, and working conditions for employees which can be enforced against both the employer and the union for failure to comply with its terms.

Comity Courtesy; respect; a disposition to perform some official act out of goodwill and tradition rather than obligation or law. The acceptance or adoption of decisions or laws by a court of another jurisdiction, either foreign or domestic, based on public policy rather than legal mandate.

Commerce Clause The provision of the U.S. Constitution that gives Congress exclusive power over trade activities between the states and with foreign countries and Native American tribes.

Commercial paper A written instrument or document such as a check, draft, promissory note, or a certificate of deposit, that manifests the pledge or duty of one individual to pay money to another.

Commercial speech Advertising speech by commercial companies and service providers. Commercial speech is protected under the First Amendment as long as it is not false or misleading.

Common law The ancient law of England based upon societal customs and recognized and enforced by the judgments and decrees of the courts. The general body of statutes and case law that governed England and the American colonies prior to the American Revolution.

The principles and rules of action, embodied in case law rather than legislative enactments, applicable to the government and protection of persons and property that derive their authority from the community customs and traditions that evolved over the centuries as interpreted by judicial tribunals.

A designation used to denote the opposite of statutory, equitable, or civil; for example, a common-law action.

Common-law marriage A union of two people not formalized in the customary manner as prescribed by law but created by an agreement to marry followed by cohabitation.

Community property The holdings and resources owned in common by a husband and wife.

Commutation Modification, exchange, or substitution.

Comparable worth The idea that men and women should receive equal pay when they perform work that involves comparable skills and responsibility or that is of comparable worth to the employer; also known as pay equity.

Comparative negligence The measurement of fault in percentages by both parties to a negligence action, so that the award of damages is reduced proportionately to the amount of negligence attributed to the victim. In order to recover, the negligence of the victim must be less than that of the defendant.

Compelling state interest A basis of upholding a state statute, against constitutional challenges grounded on the First and Fourteenth Amendments, due to the important or "compelling" need for such state regulations. Often state laws implemented under a state's police power are deemed to have satisfied a compelling state interest and therefore will survive judicial scrutiny.

Compensatory damages A sum of money awarded in a civil action by a court to indemnify a person for the particular loss, detriment, or injury suffered as a result of the unlawful conduct of another.

Complaint The pleading that initiates a civil action; in criminal law, the document that sets forth the basis upon which a person is to be charged with an offense.

Conclusive presumption The presumption that a fact is true upon proof of another fact. Evidence to the contrary cannot refute the presumed fact. Proof of a basic fact creates the existence of the presumed fact, and that presumed fact becomes irrebuttable.

Concurrent jurisdiction The authority of several different courts, each of which is authorized to entertain and decide cases dealing with the same subject matter.

Concurrent powers The ability of Congress and state legislatures to independently make laws on the same subject matter.

Concurrent resolution An action of Congress passed in the form of an enactment of one house, with the other house in agreement, which expresses the ideas of Congress on a particular subject.

Concurring opinion An opinion by one or more judges that provides separate reasoning for reaching the same decision as the majority of the court.

Conditional Subject to change; dependent upon or granted based on the occurrence of a future, uncertain event.

Conditional acceptance A counter offer. Acceptance of an offer that differs in some respects from the original contract.

Condition precedent A stipulation in an agreement that must be performed before the contract can go into effect and become binding on the parties. In terms of estates, the condition must be performed before the estates can vest or be enlarged.

Condition subsequent A stipulation in a contract that discharges one party of any further liability or performance under an existing contract if the other party fails to satisfy the stipulation.

Confession A statement made by an individual that acknowledges his or her guilt in the commission of a crime.

Conflict of interest A term used to describe the situation in which a public official or fiduciary who, contrary to the obligation and absolute duty to act for the benefit of the public or a designated individual, exploits the relationship for personal benefit, typically pecuniary.

Consent Voluntary acquiescence to the proposal of another; the act or result of reaching an accord; a concurrence of minds; actual willingness that an act or an infringement of an interest shall occur.

Consent decree An agreement by the defendant to cease activities, alleged by the government to be unlawful, in exchange for the dismissal of the case. The court must approve the agreement before it issues the consent decree.

Consideration Something of value given by both parties to a contract that induces them to enter into the agreement to exchange mutual performances.

Consolidation The process of combining two or more parts together to make a whole.

Consolidation of corporations The formation of a new corporate entity through the dissolution of two or more existing corporations. The new entity takes over the assets and assumes the liabilities of the dissolved corporations.

Conspiracy An agreement between two or more persons to engage jointly in an unlawful or criminal act, or an act that is innocent in itself but becomes unlawful when done by the combination of actors.

Constituent An individual, a principal, who appoints another to act in his or her behalf, an agent, such as an attorney in a court of law or an elected official in government.

Constitution of the United States A written document executed by representatives of the people of the United States as the absolute rule of action and decision for all branches and officers of the government, and with which all subsequent laws and ordinances must be in accordance unless it has been changed by a constitutional amendment by the authority that created it.

Consumer An individual who purchases and uses products and services in contradistinction to manufacturers who produce the goods or services and wholesalers or retailers who distribute and sell them. A member of the general category of persons who are protected by state and federal laws regulating price policies, financing practices, quality of goods and services, credit reporting, debt collection, and other trade practices of U.S. commerce. A purchaser of a product or service who has a legal right to enforce any implied or express warranties pertaining to the item against the manufacturer who has introduced the goods or services into the marketplace or the seller who has made them a term of the sale.

Contempt An act of deliberate disobedience or disregard for the laws, regulations, or decorum of a public authority, such as a court or legislative body.

Content neutral The principle that the government may not show favoritism between differing points of view on a particular subject.

Contingent fee Payment to an attorney for legal services that depends, or is contingent, upon there being some recovery or award in the case. The payment is then a percentage of the amount recovered—such as 25 percent if the matter is settled, 30 percent if it proceeds to trial.

Continuance The adjournment or postponement of an action pending in a court to a later date of the same or another session of the court, granted by a court in response to a motion made by a party to a lawsuit. The entry into the trial record of the adjournment of a case for the purpose of formally evidencing it.

Contraband Any property that is illegal to produce or possess. Smuggled goods that are imported into or exported from a country in violation of its laws.

Contract implied in fact *See* Implied contract.

Contracts Agreements between two or more persons that create an obligation to do, or refrain from doing, a particular thing.

Contributing to delinquency A criminal offense arising from an act or omission that leads to juvenile delinquency.

Contributory negligence Negligence on the part of the plaintiff for failure to exercise reasonable care for his or her own safety, and which contributes to the negligence of the defendant as the actual cause of the plaintiff's injury.

Conversion Any unauthorized act that deprives an owner of personal property without his or her consent.

Copyright An intangible right granted by statute to the author or originator of certain literary or artistic productions, whereby, for a limited period, the exclusive privilege is given to the person to make copies of the same for publication and sale.

Corporations Artificial entities that are created by state statute, and that are treated much like individuals under the law, having legally enforceable rights, the ability to acquire debt and pay out profits, the ability to hold and transfer property, the ability to enter into contracts, the requirement to pay taxes, and the ability to sue and be sued.

Cosigner An obligor—a person who becomes obligated, under a commercial paper, such as a promissory note or check—by signing the instrument in conjunction with the original obligor, thereby promising to pay it in full.

Counsel An attorney or lawyer. The rendition of advice and guidance concerning a legal matter, contemplated form of argument, claim, or action.

Counterclaim A claim by a defendant opposing the claim of the plaintiff and seeking some relief from the plaintiff for the defendant.

Counteroffer In contract law, a proposal made in response to an original offer modifying its terms, but which has the legal effect of rejecting it.

Court below The court from which a case was removed for review by an appellate court.

Court of appeal An intermediate federal judicial tribunal of review that is found in thirteen judicial districts, called circuits, in the United States.

A state judicial tribunal that reviews a decision rendered by an inferior tribunal to determine whether it made errors that warrant the reversal of its judgment.

Court of claims A state judicial tribunal established as the forum in which to bring certain types of lawsuits against the state or its political subdivisions, such as a county. The former designation given to a federal tribunal created in 1855 by Congress with original jurisdiction—initial authority—to decide an action brought against the United States that is based upon the Constitution, federal law, any regulation of the executive department, or any express or implied contracts with the federal government.

Court of equity A court that presides over equity suits, suits of fairness and justness, both in its administration and proceedings. Courts of equity no longer exist due to the consolidation of law and equity actions in federal and state courts.

Court of general jurisdiction A superior court, which by its constitution, can review and exercise a final judgment in a case under its authority. No further judicial inspection is conducted, except by an appellate power.

Covenant An agreement, contract, or written promise between two individuals that frequently constitutes a pledge to do or refrain from doing something.

Credit A term used in accounting to describe either an entry on the right-hand side of an account or the process of making such an entry. A credit records the increases in liabilities, owner's equity, and revenues as well as the decreases in assets and expenses.

A sum in taxation that is subtracted from the computed tax, as opposed to a deduction that is ordinarily subtracted from gross income to determine adjusted gross income or taxable income. Claim for a particular sum of money.

The ability of an individual or a company to borrow money or procure goods on time, as a result of a positive opinion by the particular lender concerning such borrower's solvency and reliability. The right granted by a creditor to a debtor to delay satisfaction of a debt, or to incur a debt and defer the payment thereof.

Creditor An individual to whom an obligation is owed because he or she has given something of value in exchange. One who may legally demand and receive money, either through the fulfillment of a contract or due to injury sustained as a result of another's negligence or intentionally wrongful act. The term *creditor* is also used to describe an individual who is engaged in the business of lending money or selling items for which immediate payment is not demanded but an obligation of repayment exists as of a future date.

Criminal law A body of rules and statutes that defines conduct prohibited by the government because it threatens and harms public safety and welfare and that establishes punishment to be imposed for the commission of such acts.

Cross-examination The questioning of a witness or party during a trial, hearing, or deposition by the party opposing the one who asked the person to testify in order to evaluate the truth of that person's testimony, to develop the testimony further, or to accomplish any other objective. The interrogation of a witness or party by the party opposed to the one who called the witness or party, upon a subject raised during direct examination—the initial questioning of a witness or party—on the merits of that testimony.

Cruel and unusual punishment Such punishment as would amount to torture or barbarity, any cruel and degrading punishment not known to the common law, or any fine, penalty, confinement, or treatment so dispro-portionate to the offense as to shock the moral sense of the community.

Custodial parent The parent to whom the guardianship of the children in a divorced or estranged relationship has been granted by the court.

D

Damages Monetary compensation that is awarded by a court in a civil action to an individual who has been injured through the wrongful conduct of another party.

Death penalty *See* Capital punishment.

Debtor One who owes a debt or the performance of an obligation to another, who is called the creditor; one who may be compelled to pay a claim or demand; anyone liable in a claim, whether due or to become due.

In bankruptcy law, a person who files a voluntary petition or person against whom an involuntary petition is filed. A person or municipality concerning which a bankruptcy case has been commenced.

Declaration of rights *See* Bill of rights.

Decree A judgment of a court that announces the legal consequences of the facts found in a case and orders that the court's decision be carried out. A decree in equity is a sentence or order of the court, pronounced on hearing and understanding all the points in issue, and determining the rights of all the parties to the suit, according to equity and good conscience. It is a declaration of the court announcing the legal consequences of the facts found. With the procedural merger of law and equity in the federal and most state courts under the Rules of Civil Procedure, the term *judgment* has generally replaced *decree*.

Decriminalization The passing of legislation that changes criminal acts or omissions into noncriminal ones without punitive sanctions.

Deed A written instrument, which has been signed and delivered, by which one individual, the grantor, conveys title to real property to another individual, the grantee; a conveyance of land, tenements, or hereditaments, from one individual to another.

De facto [*Latin*, In fact.] In fact; in deed; actually.

Defamation Any intentional false communication, either written or spoken, that harms a person's reputation; decreases the respect, regard, or confidence in which a person is held; or induces disparaging, hostile, or disagreeable opinions or feelings against a person.

Defendant The person defending or denying; the party against whom relief or recovery is sought in an action or suit, or the accused in a criminal case.

Defense The forcible repulsion of an unlawful and violent attack, such as the defense of one's person, property, or country in time of war.

The totality of the facts, law, and contentions presented by the party against whom a civil action or criminal prosecution is instituted in order to defeat or diminish the plaintiff's cause of action or the prosecutor's case. A reply to the claims of the other party, which asserts reasons why the claims should be disallowed. The defense may involve an absolute denial of the other party's factual allegations or may entail an affirmative defense, which sets forth completely new factual allegations. Pursuant to the rules of federal civil procedure, numerous defenses may be asserted by motion as well as by answer, while other defenses must be pleaded affirmatively.

De jure [*Latin,* In law.] Legitimate; lawful, as a matter of law. Having complied with all the requirements imposed by law.

Delegation of powers Transfer of authority by one branch of government in which such authority is vested to some other branch or administrative agency.

Deliberate Willful; purposeful; determined after thoughtful evaluation of all relevant factors; dispassionate. To act with a particular intent, which is derived from a careful consideration of factors that influence the choice to be made.

Delinquent An individual who fails to fulfill an obligation, or otherwise is guilty of a crime or offense.

Domestic partnership laws Legislation and regulations related to the legal recognition of non-marital relationships between persons who are romantically involved with each other, have set up a joint residence, and have registered with cities recognizing said relationships.

Demurrer An assertion by the defendant that although the facts alleged by the plaintiff in the complaint may be true, they do not entitle the plaintiff to prevail in the lawsuit.

Denaturalization The deprivation of an individual's rights as a citizen.

Deportation Banishment to a foreign country, attended with confiscation of property and deprivation of civil rights.

The transfer of an alien, by exclusion or expulsion, from the United States to a foreign country. The removal or sending back of an alien to the country from which he or she came because his or her presence is deemed inconsistent with the public welfare, and without any punishment being imposed or contemplated. The grounds for deportation are set forth at 8 U.S.C.A., sec. 1251, and the procedures are provided for in secs. 1252–1254.

Deposition The testimony of a party or witness in a civil or criminal proceeding taken before trial, usually in an attorney's office.

Desegregation Judicial mandate making illegal the practice of segregation.

Desertion The act by which a person abandons and forsakes, without justification, a condition of public, social, or family life, renouncing its responsibilities and evading its duties. A willful abandonment of an employment or duty in violation of a legal or moral obligation.

Criminal desertion is a husband's or wife's abandonment or willful failure without just cause to provide for the care, protection, or support of a spouse who is in ill health or impoverished circumstances.

Detention hearing A proceeding to determine the restraint to be imposed upon an individual awaiting trial, such as bail or, in the case of a juvenile, placement in a shelter.

Deterrent Anything that discourages or obstructs a person from committing an act, such as punishment for criminal acts.

Detriment Any loss or harm to a person or property; relinquishment of a legal right, benefit, or something of value.

Diplomatic immunity A principle of international law that provides foreign diplomats with protection from legal action in the country in which they work.

Directed verdict A procedural device whereby the decision in a case is taken out of the hands of the jury by the judge.

Direct examination The primary questioning of a witness during a trial that is conducted by the side for which that person is acting as a witness.

Direct tax A charge levied by the government upon property, which is determined by its financial worth.

Disaffirm Repudiate; revoke consent; refuse to support former acts or agreements.

Disbar To revoke an attorney's license to practice law.

Discharge To liberate or free; to terminate or extinguish. A discharge is the act or instrument by which a contract or agreement is ended. A mortgage is discharged if it has been carried out to the full extent originally contemplated or terminated prior to total execution.

Discharge also means to release, as from legal confinement in prison or the military service, or from some legal obligation such as jury duty, or the payment of debts by a person who is bankrupt. The document that indicates that an individual has been legally released from the military service is called a discharge.

Disclaimer The denial, refusal, or rejection of a right, power, or responsibility.

Discovery A category of procedural devices employed by a party to a civil or criminal action, prior to trial, to require the adverse party to disclose information that is essential for the preparation of the requesting party's case and that the other party alone knows or possesses.

Discretion Independent use of judgment to choose between right and wrong, to make a decision, or to act cautiously under the circumstances.

Discretion in decision making Discretion is the power or right to make official decisions using reason and judgment to choose from among acceptable alternatives.

Discrimination In constitutional law, the grant by statute of particular privileges to a class arbitrarily designated from a sizable number of persons, where no reasonable distinction exists between the favored and disfavored classes. Federal laws, supplemented by court decisions, prohibit discrimination in such areas as employment, housing, voting rights, education, and access to public facilities. They also proscribe discrimination on the basis of race, age, sex, nationality, disability, or religion. In addition, state and local laws can prohibit discrimination in these areas and in others not covered by federal laws.

Dishonor To refuse to accept or pay a draft or to pay a promissory note when duly presented. An instrument is dishonored when a necessary or optional presentment is made and due acceptance or payment is refused, or cannot be obtained within the prescribed time, or in case of bank collections, the instrument is seasonably returned by the midnight deadline; or presentment is excused and the instrument is not duly accepted or paid. Includes the insurer of a letter of credit refusing to pay or accept a draft or demand for payment.

As respects the flag, to deface or defile, imputing a lively sense of shaming or an equivalent acquiescent callousness.

Disinherit To cut off from an inheritance. To deprive someone, who would otherwise be an heir to property or another right, of his or her right to inherit.

Dismissal A discharge of an individual or corporation from employment. The disposition of a civil or criminal proceeding or a claim or charge made therein by a court order without a trial or prior to its completion which, in effect, is a denial of the relief sought by the commencement of the action.

Disposition Act of disposing; transferring to the care or possession of another. The parting with, alienation of, or giving up of property. The final settlement of a matter and, with reference to decisions announced by a court, a judge's ruling is commonly referred to as disposition, regardless of level of resolution. In criminal procedure, the sentencing or other final settlement of a criminal case. With respect to a mental state, denotes an attitude, prevailing tendency, or inclination.

Disposition hearing The judicial proceeding for passing sentence upon a defendant who was found guilty of the charge(s) against him or her.

Dispossession The wrongful, nonconsensual ouster or removal of a person from his or her property by trick, compulsion, or misuse of the law, whereby the violator obtains actual occupation of the land.

Dissent An explicit disagreement by one or more judges with the decision of the majority on a case before them.

Dissolution Act or process of dissolving; termination; winding up. In this sense it is frequently used in the phrase *dissolution of a partnership.*

Division of powers *See* Separation of powers.

Divorce A court decree that terminates a marriage; also known as marital dissolution.

Domicile The legal residence of a person, which determines jurisdiction for taxation and voting, as well as other legal rights and privileges. Considered to be the permanent residence of an individual, or the place where one intends to return after an absence, such as in the case of the president who physically lives in the White House, but has a domicile in his or her home state.

Double indemnity A term of an insurance policy by which the insurance company promises to pay the insured or the beneficiary twice the amount of coverage if loss occurs due to a particular cause or set of circumstances.

Double jeopardy A second prosecution for the same offense after acquittal or conviction or multiple punishments for the same offense. The evil sought to be avoided by prohibiting double jeopardy is double trial and double conviction, not necessarily double punishment.

Draft A written order by the first party, called the drawer, instructing a second party, called the drawee (such as a bank), to pay money to a third party, called the payee. An order to pay a certain sum in money, signed by a drawer, payable on demand or at a definite time, to order or bearer.

A tentative, provisional, or preparatory writing out of any document (as a will, contract, lease, and so on) for purposes of discussion and correction, which is afterward to be prepared in its final form.

Compulsory conscription of persons into military service.

A small arbitrary deduction or allowance made to a merchant or importer, in the case of goods sold by weight or taxable by weight, to cover possible loss of weight in handling or from differences in scales.

Due process of law A fundamental, constitutional guarantee that all legal proceedings will be fair and that one will be given notice of the proceedings and an opportunity to be heard before the government acts to take away one's life, liberty, or property. Also, a constitutional guarantee that a law shall not be unreasonable, arbitrary, or capricious.

Duress Unlawful pressure exerted upon a person to coerce that person to perform an act that he or she ordinarily would not perform.

Duty A legal obligation that entails mandatory conduct or performance. With respect to the laws relating to customs duties, a tax owed to the government for the import or export of goods.

E

Easement A right of use over the property of another. Traditionally the permitted kinds of uses were limited, the most important being rights of way and rights concerning flowing waters. The easement was normally for the benefit of adjoining lands, no matter who the owner was (an easement appurtenant), rather than for the benefit of a specific individual (easement in gross).

Emancipation The act or process by which a person is liberated from the authority and control of another person.

Embezzlement The fraudulent appropriation of another's property by a person who is in a position of trust, such as an agent or employee.

Eminent domain The power to take private property for public use by a state, municipality, or private person or corporation authorized to exercise functions of public character, following the payment of just compensation to the owner of that property.

Employment at will A common-law rule that an employment contract of indefinite duration can be terminated by either the employer or the employee at any time, for any reason; also known as terminable at will.

Encumbrance A burden, obstruction, or impediment on property that lessens its value or makes it less marketable. An encumbrance (also spelled incumbrance) is any right or interest that exists in someone other than the owner of an estate and that restricts or impairs the transfer of the estate or lowers its value. This might include an easement, a lien, a mortgage, a mechanic's lien, or accrued and unpaid taxes.

Entitlement An individual's right to receive a value or benefit provided by law.

Entrapment The act of government agents or officials that induces a person to commit a crime he or she is not previously disposed to commit.

Enumerated powers Authority specifically granted to a body of the national government under the U.S. Constitution, such as the powers granted to Congress in Article I, Section 8.

Equal Pay Act Federal law which mandates the same pay for all persons who do the same work without regard to sex, age, race or ability. For work to be "equal" within meaning of the act, it is not necessary that the jobs be identical, but only that they be substantially equal.

Equal protection The constitutional guarantee that no person or class of persons shall be denied the same protection of the laws that is enjoyed by other persons or other classes in like circumstances in their lives, liberty, property, and pursuit of happiness.

Equitable Just; that which is fair and proper according to the principles of justice and right.

Equitable action A cause of action that seeks an equitable remedy, such as relief sought with an injunction.

Equity The pursuit of fairness. In the U.S. legal system, a body of laws that seeks to achieve fairness on an individual basis. In terms of property, the money value of property in excess of claims, liens, or mortgages on the property.

Error A mistake in a court proceeding concerning a matter of law or fact which might provide a ground for a review of the judgment rendered in the proceeding.

Escrow Something of value, such as a deed, stock, money, or written instrument, that is put into the custody of a third person by its owner, a grantor, an obligor, or a promisor, to be retained until the occurrence of a contingency or performance of a condition.

Espionage The act of securing information of a military or political nature that a competing nation holds secret. It can involve the analysis of diplomatic reports, publications, statistics, and broadcasts, as well as spying, a clandestine activity carried out by an individual or individuals working under a secret identity for the benefit of a nation's information gathering techniques. In the United States, the organization that heads most activities dedicated to espionage is the Central Intelligence Agency.

Establishment Clause The provision in the First Amendment which provides that there will be no laws created respecting the establishment of a religion, inhibiting the practice of a religion, or giving preference to any or all religions. It has been interpreted to also denounce the discouragement of any or all religions.

Estate The degree, quantity, nature, and extent of interest that a person has in real and personal property. An estate in lands, tenements, and hereditaments signifies such interest as the tenant has therein. *Estate* is commonly used in conveyances in connection with the words *right, title,* and *interest,* and is, to a great degree, synonymous with all of them.

When used in connection with probate proceedings, the term encompasses the total property of whatever kind that is owned by a decedent prior to the distribution of that property in accordance with the terms of a will, or when there is no will, by the laws of inheritance in the state of domicile of the decedent. It means, ordinarily, the whole of the property owned by anyone, the realty as well as the personalty.

In its broadest sense, the social, civic, or political condition or standing of a person; or a class of persons considered as grouped for social, civic, or political purposes.

Estate tax The tax levied upon the entire estate of the decedent before any part of the estate can be transferred to an heir. An estate tax is applied to the right of the deceased person to transfer property at death. An "inheritance tax" is imposed upon an heir's right to receive the property.

Estoppel A legal principle that precludes a party from denying or alleging a certain fact owing to that party's previous conduct, allegation, or denial.

Euthanasia The merciful act or practice of terminating the life of an individual or individuals inflicted with incurable and distressing diseases in a relatively painless manner.

Eviction The removal of a tenant from possession of premises in which he or she resides or has a property interest, done by a landlord either by reentry upon the premises or through a court action.

Excise tax A tax imposed on the performance of an act, the engaging in an occupation, or the enjoyment of a privilege. A tax on the manufacture, sale, or use of goods or on the carrying on of an occupation activity, or a tax on the transfer of property. In current usage the term has been extended to include various license fees and practically every internal revenue tax except the income tax (i.e., federal alcohol and tobacco excise taxes).

Exclusionary rule The principle based on federal constitutional law that evidence illegally seized by law enforcement officers in violation of a suspect's right to be free from unreasonable searches and seizures cannot be used against the suspect in a criminal prosecution.

Exclusive jurisdiction The legal authority of a court or other tribunal to preside over a suit, an action, or a person to the exclusion of any other court.

Exclusive power The authority held solely by one individual, such as the President, or one group, such as a regulatory committee.

Exclusive right The privilege that only a grantee can exercise, prohibiting others from partaking in the same.

Executive agreement An agreement made between the head of a foreign country and the President of the United States. This agreement does not have to be submitted to the Senate for consent, and it supersedes any contradicting state law.

Executive orders Presidential policy directives that implement or interpret a federal statute, a constitutional provision, or a treaty.

Executor The individual named by a decedent to administer the provisions of the decedent's will.

Ex parte [*Latin, On one side only.*] Done by, for, or on the application of one party alone.

Expatriation The voluntary act of abandoning or renouncing one's country and becoming the citizen or subject of another.

Expert witness A witness, such as a psychological statistician or ballistics expert, who possesses special or superior knowledge concerning the subject of his or her testimony.

Ex post facto laws [*Latin, "After-the-fact" laws.*] Laws that provide for the infliction of punishment upon a person for some prior act that, at the time it was committed, was not illegal.

Express Clear; definite; explicit; plain; direct; unmistakable; not dubious or ambiguous. Declared in terms; set forth in words. Directly and distinctly stated. Made known distinctly and explicitly, and not left to inference. Manifested by direct and appropriate language, as distinguished from that which is inferred from conduct. The word is usually contrasted with *implied*.

Express contract An oral or written contract where the terms of the agreement are explicitly stated.

Expressed power *See* Enumerated powers.

Express warranty An additional written or oral guarantee to the underlying sales agreement made to the consumer as to the quality, description, or performance of a good.

Extortion The obtaining of property from another induced by wrongful use of actual or threatened force, violence, or fear, or under color of official right.

Extradition The transfer of an accused from one state or country to another state or country that seeks to place the accused on trial.

F

Family court A court that presides over cases involving: (1) child abuse and neglect; (2) support; (3) paternity; (4) termination of custody due to constant neglect; (5) juvenile delinquency; and (6) family offenses.

Federal circuit courts The 12 circuit courts making up the U.S. Federal Circuit Court System. The twelfth circuit presides over the District of Columbia. Decisions made by the federal district courts can be reviewed by the court of appeals in each circuit.

Federal district courts The first of three levels of the federal court system, which includes the U.S. Court of Appeals and the U.S. Supreme Court. If a participating party disagrees with the ruling of a federal district court in its case, it may petition for the case to be moved to the next level in the federal court system.

Felon An individual who commits a crime of a serious nature, such as burglary or murder. A person who commits a felony.

Felony A serious crime, characterized under federal law and many state statutes as any offense punishable by death or imprisonment in excess of one year.

Fiduciary An individual in whom another has placed the utmost trust and confidence to manage and protect property or money. The relationship wherein one person has an obligation to act for another's benefit.

First degree murder Murder committed with deliberately premeditated thought and malice, or with extreme atrocity or cruelty. The difference between first and second degree murder is the presence of the specific intention to kill.

Forbearance Refraining from doing something that one has a legal right to do. Giving of further time for repayment of an obligation or agreement; not to enforce a claim at its due date. A delay in enforcing a legal right. Act by which a creditor waits for payment of debt due by a debtor after it becomes due.

Within usury law, the contractual obligation of a lender or creditor to refrain, during a given period of time, from requiring the borrower or debtor to repay the loan or debt that is then due and payable.

Foreclosure A procedure by which the holder of a mortgage—an interest in land providing security for the performance of a duty or the payment of a debt—sells the property upon the failure of the debtor to pay the mortgage debt and, thereby, terminates his or her rights in the property.

Forgery The creation of a false written document or alteration of a genuine one, with the intent to defraud.

Formal contract An agreement between two or more individuals in which all the terms are in writing.

Franchise A special privilege to do certain things that is conferred by government on an individual or a corporation and which does not belong to citizens generally of common right (i.e., a right granted to offer cable television service).

A privilege granted or sold, such as to use a name or to sell products or services. In its simplest terms, a franchise is a license from the owner of a trademark or trade name permitting another to sell a product or service under that name or mark. More broadly stated, a franchise has evolved into an elaborate agreement under which the franchisee undertakes to conduct a business or sell a product or service in accordance with methods and procedures prescribed by the franchisor, and the franchisor undertakes to assist the franchisee through advertising, promotion, and other advisory services.

The right of suffrage; the right or privilege of voting in public elections. Such a right is guaranteed by the Fifteenth, Nineteenth, and Twenty-fourth Amendments to the U.S. Constitution.

As granted by a professional sports association, franchise is a privilege to field a team in a given geographic area under the auspices of the league that issues it. It is merely an incorporeal right.

Fraud A false representation of a matter of fact—whether by words or by conduct, by false or misleading allegations, or by concealment of what should have been disclosed—that deceives and is intended to deceive another so that the individual will act upon it to her or his legal injury.

Freedom of assembly *See* Freedom of association.

Freedom of association The right to associate with others for the purpose of engaging in constitutionally protected activities, such as to peacefully assemble.

Freedom of religion The First Amendment right to individually believe and to practice or exercise one's belief.

Freedom of speech The right, guaranteed by the First Amendment to the U.S. Constitution, to express beliefs and ideas without unwarranted government restriction.

Freedom of the press The right, guaranteed by the First Amendment to the U.S. Constitution, to gather, publish, and distribute information and ideas without government restriction; this right encompasses freedom from prior restraints on publication and freedom from censorship.

Full Faith and Credit Clause The clause of the U.S. Constitution that provides that the various states must recognize legislative acts, public records, and judicial decisions of the other states within the United States.

Full warranty The guarantee on the workmanship and materials of a product. If the product is defective in any way, then the consumer is entitled to corrective action from the manufacturer, at no cost to the consumer, and within a reasonable amount of time.

Fundamental rights Rights which derive, or are implied, from the terms of the U.S. Constitution, such as the Bill of Rights, the first ten amendments to the Constitution.

G

Gag rule A rule, regulation, or law that prohibits debate or discussion of a particular issue.

Garnishment A legal procedure by which a creditor can collect what a debtor owes by reaching the debtor's property when it is in the hands of someone other than the debtor.

General partnership A business relationship with more than one owner where all parties manage the business and equally share any profits or losses.

Gerrymander The process of dividing a particular state or territory into election districts in such a manner as to accomplish an unlawful purpose, such as to give one party a greater advantage.

Good faith Honesty; a sincere intention to deal fairly with others.

Grandfather clause A portion of a statute that provides that the law is not applicable in certain circumstances due to preexisting facts.

Grand jury A panel of citizens that is convened by a court to decide whether it is appropriate for the government to indict (proceed with a prosecution against) someone suspected of a crime.

Grand larceny A category of larceny—the offense of illegally taking the property of another—in which the value of the property taken is greater than that set for petit larceny.

Grounds The basis or foundation; reasons sufficient in law to justify relief.

Guarantee One to whom a guaranty is made. This word is also used, as a noun, to denote the contract of guaranty or the obligation of a guarantor, and, as a verb, to denote the action of assuming the responsibilities of a guarantor.

Guaranty As a verb, to agree to be responsible for the payment of another's debt or the performance of another's duty, liability, or obligation if that person does not perform as he or she is legally obligated to do; to assume the responsibility of a guarantor; to warrant.

As a noun, an undertaking or promise that is collateral to the primary or principal obligation and that binds the guarantor to performance in the event of nonperformance by the principal obligor.

Guardian A person lawfully invested with the power, and charged with the obligation, of taking care of and managing the property and rights of a person who, because of age, understanding, or self-control, is considered incapable of administering his or her own affairs.

Guardian ad litem A guardian appointed by the court to represent the interests of infants, the unborn, or incompetent persons in legal actions.

H

Habeas corpus [*Latin, You have the body.*] A writ (court order) that commands an individual or a government official who has restrained another to produce the prisoner at a designated time and place so that the court can determine the legality of custody and decide whether to order the prisoner's release.

Hate crime A crime motivated by race, religion, gender, sexual orientation, or other prejudice.

Hearing A legal proceeding where issues of law or fact are tried and evidence is presented to help determine the issue.

Hearsay A statement made out of court that is offered in court as evidence to prove the truth of the matter asserted.

Heir An individual who receives an interest in, or ownership of, land, tenements, or hereditaments from an ancestor who had died intestate, through the laws of descent and distribution. At common law, an heir was the individual appointed by law to succeed to the estate of an ancestor who died without a will. It is commonly used today in reference to any individual who succeeds to property, either by will or law.

Homicide The killing of one human being by another human being.

Hung jury A trial jury duly selected to make a decision in a criminal case regarding a defendant's guilt or innocence, but who are unable to reach a verdict due to a complete division in opinion.

I

Immunity Exemption from performing duties that the law generally requires other citizens to perform, or from a penalty or burden that the law generally places on other citizens.

Impeachment A process used to charge, try, and remove public officials for misconduct while in office.

Implied consent Consent that is inferred from signs, actions, or facts, or by inaction or silence.

Implied contract A contract created not by express agreement, but inferred by law, based on the conduct of the parties and the events surrounding the parties' dealings.

Implied power Authority that exists so that an expressly granted power can be carried into effect.

Implied warranty A promise, arising by operation of law, that something that is sold will be merchantable and fit for the purpose for which it is sold.

Imprimatur [*Latin, Let it be printed.*] A licence or allowance, granted by the constituted authorities, giving permission to print and publish a book. This allowance was formerly necessary in England before any book could lawfully be printed, and in some other countries is still required.

Inalienable Not subject to sale or transfer; inseparable.

Inalienable rights Rights (i.e., life, liberty, and the pursuit of happiness) which cannot be ceded or transferred without permission from the individual who possesses them.

Incapacity The absence of legal ability, competence, or qualifications.

Income tax A charge imposed by government on the annual gains of a person, corporation, or other taxable unit derived through work, business pursuits, investments, property dealings, and other sources determined in accordance with the Internal Revenue Code or state law.

Incorporate To formally create a corporation pursuant to the requirements prescribed by state statute; to confer a corporate franchise upon certain individuals.

Indemnity Recompense for loss, damage, or injuries; restitution or reimbursement.

Indeterminate That which is uncertain or not particularly designated.

Indictment A written accusation charging that an individual named therein has committed an act or admitted to doing something that is punishable by law.

Indirect tax A tax upon some right, privilege, or corporate franchise.

Individual rights Rights and privileges constitutionally guaranteed to the people, as set forth by the Bill of Rights, the ability of a person to pursue life, liberty, and property.

Infants Persons who are under the age of the legal majority—at common law, 21 years, now generally 18 years. According to the sense in which this term is used, it may denote the age of the person, the contractual disabilities that nonage entails, or his or her status with regard to other powers or relations.

Information The formal accusation of a criminal offense made by a public official; the sworn, written accusation of a crime.

Inherent Derived from the essential nature of, and inseparable from, the object itself.

Inherent powers Implicit control, which by nature cannot be derived from another.

Inherent rights Rights held within a person because he or she exists. *See also* inalienable rights.

Inheritance Property received from a decedent, either by will or through state laws of intestate succession, where the decedent has failed to execute a valid will.

Inheritance tax A tax imposed upon the right of an individual to receive property left to him or her by a decedent.

Injunction A court order by which an individual is required to perform or is restrained from performing a particular act. A writ framed according to the circumstances of the individual case.

In loco parentis [*Latin, In the place of a parent.*] The legal doctrine under which an individual assumes parental rights, duties, and obligations without going through the formalities of legal adoption.

Inquisitorial system A method of legal practice in which the judge endeavors to discover facts while simultaneously representing the interests of the state in a trial.

Insanity defense A defense asserted by an accused in a criminal prosecution to avoid liability for the commission of a crime because, at the time of the crime, the person did not appreciate the nature or quality or wrongfulness of the act.

Insider In the context of federal regulation of the purchase and sale of securities, anyone who has knowledge of facts not available to the general public.

Insider trading The trading of stocks and bonds based on information gained from special private, privileged information affecting the value of the stocks and bonds.

Insurance A contract whereby, for a specified consideration, one party undertakes to compensate the other for a loss relating to a particular subject as a result of the occurrence of designated hazards.

Intangibles Property that is a "right," such as a patent, copyright, trademark, etc., or one that is lacking physical existence, like good will. A nonphysical, noncurrent asset that exists only in connection with something else, such as the good will of a business.

Intent A determination to perform a particular act or to act in a particular manner for a specific reason; an aim or design; a resolution to use a certain means to reach an end.

Intermediate courts Courts with general ability or authority to hear a case (trial, appellate, or both), but are not the court of last resort within the jurisdiction.

Intestate The description of a person who dies without making a valid will or the reference made to this condition.

Involuntary manslaughter The act of unlawfully killing another human being unintentionally.

Irrevocable Unable to cancel or recall; that which is unalterable or irreversible.

Item veto *See* Line item veto.

J

Joint committee Members of two houses of a state or federal legislature that work together as one group.

Joint resolution A type of measure that Congress may consider and act upon; the other types of measures being bills, concurrent resolutions, and simple resolutions, in addition to treaties in the Senate.

Judicial discretion Sound judgment exercised by a judge in determining what is right and equitable under the law.

Judicial review A court's authority to examine an executive or legislative act and to invalidate that act if it is contrary to constitutional principles.

Jurisdiction The geographic area over which authority extends; legal authority; the authority to hear and determine causes of action.

Jurisprudence From the Latin term *juris prudentia*, which means "the study, knowledge, or science of law;" in the United States, more broadly associated with the philosophy of law.

Jury In trials, a group of people selected and sworn to inquire into matters of fact and to reach a verdict on the basis of evidence presented to it.

Jury nullification The ability of a jury to acquit the defendant despite the amount of evidence against him or her in a criminal case.

Jus sanguinis The determination of a person's citizenship based upon the citizenship of the individual's parents.

Jus soli The determination of a person's citizenship based upon the individual's place of birth.

Just cause A reasonable and lawful ground for action.

Justifiable homicide The killing of another in self-defense or in the lawful defense of one's property; killing of another when the law demands it, such as in execution for a capital crime.

Juvenile A young individual who has not reached the age whereby he or she would be treated as an adult in the area of criminal law. The age at which the young person attains the status of being a legal majority varies from state to state—as low as 14 years old, as high as 18 years old; however, the Juvenile Delinquency Act determines that a youthful person under the age of eighteen is a "juvenile" in cases involving federal jurisdiction.

Juvenile court The court presiding over cases in which young persons under a certain age, depending on the area of jurisdiction, are accused of criminal acts.

Juvenile delinquency The participation of a youthful individual, one who falls under the age at which he or she could be tried as an adult, in illegal behavior. *See also* Delinquent child.

L

Landlord A lessor of real property; the owner or possessor of an estate in land or a rental property, who, in an exchange for rent, leases it to another individual known as the tenant.

Lapse The termination or failure of a right or privilege because of a neglect to exercise that right or to perform some duty within a time limit, or because a specified contingency did not occur. The expiration of coverage under an insurance policy because of the insured's failure to pay the premium.

The common-law principle that a gift in a will does not take effect but passes into the estate remaining after the payment of debts and particular gifts, if the beneficiary is alive when the will is executed but subsequently predeceases the testator.

Larceny The unauthorized taking and removal of the personal property of another by a person who intends to permanently deprive the owner of it; a crime against the right of possession.

Lease A contractual agreement by which one party conveys an estate in property to another party, for a limited period, subject to various conditions, in exchange for something of value, but still retains ownership.

Legal defense A complete and acceptable response as to why the claims of the plaintiff should not be granted in a point of law.

Legal tender All U.S. coins and currencies—regardless of when coined or issued—including (in terms of the Federal Reserve System) Federal Reserve notes and circulating notes of Federal Reserve banks and national banking associations that are used for all debts, public and private, public charges, taxes, duties, and dues.

Legation The persons commissioned by one government to exercise diplomatic functions at the court of another, including the ministers, secretaries, attachés, and interpreters, are collectively called the *legation* of their government. The word also denotes the official residence of a foreign minister.

Legislation Lawmaking; the preparation and enactment of laws by a legislative body.

Legislative intent The history of events leading to the enactment of a law that a court refers to when interpreting an ambiguous or inconsistent statute.

Liability A comprehensive legal term that describes the condition of being actually or potentially subject to a legal obligation.

Libel and slander Two torts that involve the communication of false information about a person, a group, or an entity, such as a corporation. Libel is any defama-

tion that can be seen, such a writing, printing, effigy, movie, or statue. Slander is any defamation that is spoken and heard.

Lien A right given to another by the owner of property to secure a debt, or one created by law in favor of certain creditors.

Limited liability partnership A form of general partnership that provides an individual partner protection against personal liability for certain partnership obligations.

Limited warranty A written performance guarantee that only covers workmanship or materials for a specified period of time.

Line item veto The power that governors in some states have to strike individual items from appropriation bills without affecting any other provisions.

Litigation An action brought in court to enforce a particular right. The act or process of bringing a lawsuit in and of itself; a judicial contest; any dispute.

Living will A written document that allows a patient to give explicit instructions about medical treatment to be administered when the patient is terminally ill or permanently unconscious; also called an advance directive.

Loan shark A person who lends money in exchange for its repayment at an interest rate that exceeds the percentage approved by law and who uses intimidating methods or threats of force in order to obtain repayment.

Lobbying The process of influencing public and government policy at all levels: federal, state, and local.

Lower court The court where a suit was first heard. *See also* Court below.

M

Magistrate Any individual who has the power of a public civil officer or inferior judicial officer, such as a justice of the peace.

Majority Full age; legal age; age at which a person is no longer a minor. The age at which, by law, a person is capable of being legally responsible for all of his or her acts (i.e., contractual obligations), and is entitled to the management of his or her own affairs and to the enjoyment of civic rights (i.e., right to vote). The opposite of minority. Also the *status* of a person who is a major in age.

The greater number. The number greater than half of any total.

Malfeasance The commission of an act that is unequivocally illegal or completely wrongful.

Malice The intentional commission of a wrongful act, absent justification, with the intent to cause harm to others; conscious violation of the law that injures another individual; a mental state indicating a disposition in disregard of social duty and a tendency toward malfeasance.

Malice aforethought A predetermination to commit an act without legal justification or excuse. A malicious design to injure. An intent, at the time of a killing, willfully to take the life of a human being, or an intent willfully to act in callous and wanton disregard of the consequences to human life; but *malice aforethought* does not necessarily imply any ill will, spite, or hatred towards the individual killed.

Malpractice The breach by a member of a profession of either a standard of care or a standard of conduct.

Mandate A judicial command, order, or precept, written or oral, from a court; a direction that a court has the authority to give and an individual is bound to obey.

Manslaughter The unjustifiable, inexcusable, and intentional killing of a human being without deliberation, premeditation, and malice. The unlawful killing of a human being without any deliberation, which may be involuntary, in the commission of a lawful act without due caution and circumspection.

Material Important; affecting the merits of a case; causing a particular course of action; significant; substantial. A description of the quality of evidence that possesses such substantial probative value as to establish the truth or falsity of a point in issue in a lawsuit.

Material fact A fact that is necessary in determining a case, without which there would be no defense. Disclosure of the fact is necessary for the reasonable person to make a prudent decision.

Mediation A settlement of a dispute or controversy by setting up an independent person between two contending parties in order to aid them in the settlement of their disagreement.

Mens rea [*Latin, Guilty mind.*] As an element of criminal responsibility, a guilty mind; a guilty or wrongful purpose; a criminal intent. Guilty knowledge and willfulness.

Merger The combination or fusion of one thing or right into another thing or right of greater or larger importance so that the lesser thing or right loses its individuality and becomes identified with the greater whole.

Minor An infant or person who is under the age of legal competence. A term derived from the civil law, which described a person under a certain age as *less than* so many years. In most states, a person is no longer a minor after reaching the age of 18 (though state laws might still prohibit certain acts until reaching a greater age; i.e., purchase of liquor). Also, less; of less consideration; lower; a person of inferior condition.

Misdemeanor Offenses lower than felonies and generally those punishable by fine, penalty, forfeiture, or imprisonment other than in a penitentiary. Under federal law, and most state laws, any offense other than a felony is classified as a misdemeanor. Certain states also have various classes of misdemeanors (i.e., Class A, B, etc.).

Mistrial A courtroom trial that has been terminated prior to its normal conclusion. A mistrial has no legal effect and is considered an invalid or nugatory trial. It differs from a "new trial," which recognizes that a trial was completed but was set aside so that the issues could be tried again.

Mitigating circumstances Circumstances that may be considered by a court in determining culpability of a defendant or the extent of damages to be awarded to a plaintiff. Mitigating circumstances do not justify or excuse an offense but may reduce the severity of the charge. Similarly, a recognition of mitigating circumstances to reduce a damage award does not imply that the damages were not suffered but that they have been partially ameliorated.

Mitigation of damages The use of reasonable care and diligence in an effort to minimize or avoid injury.

Monopoly An economic advantage held by one or more persons or companies deriving from the exclusive power to carry on a particular business or trade or to manufacture and sell a particular item, thereby suppressing competition and allowing such persons or companies to raise the price of a product or service substantially above the price that would be established by a free market.

Moratorium A suspension of activity or an authorized period of delay or waiting. A moratorium is sometimes agreed upon by the interested parties, or it may be authorized or imposed by operation of law. The term also is used to denote a period of time during which the law authorizes a delay in payment of debts or performance of some other legal obligation. This type of moratorium is most often invoked during times of distress, such as war or natural disaster.

Mortgage A legal document by which the owner (buyer) transfers to the lender an interest in real estate to secure the repayment of a debt, evidenced by a mortgage note. When the debt is repaid, the mortgage is discharged, and a satisfaction of mortgage is recorded with the register or recorder of deeds in the county where the mortgage was recorded. Because most people cannot afford to buy real estate with cash, nearly every real estate transaction involves a mortgage.

Motion A written or oral application made to a court or judge to obtain a ruling or order directing that some act be done in favor of the applicant. The applicant is known as the moving party, or the movant.

Motive An idea, belief, or emotion that impels a person to act in accordance with that state of mind.

Murder The unlawful killing of another human being without justification or excuse.

N

National origin The country in which a person was born or from which his or her ancestors came. It is typically calculated by employers to provide equal employment opportunity statistics in accordance with the provisions of the Civil Rights Act.

Naturalization A process by which a person gains nationality and becomes entitled to the privileges of citizenship. While groups of individuals have been naturalized in history by treaties or laws of Congress, such as in the case of Hawaii, typically naturalization occurs on the individual level upon the completion of the following steps: (1) an individual of majority age, who has been a lawful resident of the United States for five years, petitions for naturalization; (2) the Immigration and Naturalization Service conducts an investigation to establish whether the petitioner can speak English and write English, has a general knowledge of American government and history, especially in regards to the principles of the Constitution, and is in good moral standing; (3) a hearing is held before a U.S. district court, or, when applicable, a state court of record; and (4) a second hearing is held after a period of at least thirty days when the oath of allegiance is administered.

Natural law The unwritten body of universal moral principles that underlie the ethical and legal norms by which human conduct is sometimes evaluated and governed. Natural law is often contrasted with positive law, which consists of the written rules and regulations enacted by government. The term *natural law* is derived from the Roman term *jus naturale*. Adherents to natural law philosophy are known as naturalists.

Necessary and Proper Clause The statement contained in Article I, Section 8, Clause 18 of the U.S. Constitution that gives Congress the power to pass any laws that are "necessary and proper" to carrying out its specifically granted powers.

Necessity A defense asserted by a criminal or civil defendant that he or she had no choice but to break the law.

Negligence Conduct that falls below the standards of behavior established by law for the protection of others against unreasonable risk of harm. A person has acted negligently if he or she has departed from the conduct expected of a reasonably prudent person acting under similar circumstances.

Negligence is also the name of a cause of action in the law of torts. To establish negligence, a plaintiff must prove that the defendant had a duty to the plaintiff, the defendant breached that duty by failing to conform to the required standard of conduct, the defendant's negligent conduct was the cause of the harm to the plaintiff, and the plaintiff was, in fact, harmed or damaged.

No-fault divorce Common name for the type of divorce where "irreconcilable" differences are cited as the reason for the termination of the marriage. Fault by either party does not have to be proven.

Nolo contendere [*Latin, I will not contest it.*] A plea in a criminal case by which the defendant answers the charges made in the indictment by declining to dispute or admit the fact of his or her guilt.

Nominal damages Minimal money damages awarded to an individual in an action where the person has not suffered any substantial injury or loss for which he or she must be compensated.

Nonprofit A corporation or an association that conducts business for the benefit of the general public without shareholders and without a profit motive.

Notary public A public official whose main powers include administering oaths and attesting to signatures, both important and effective ways to minimize fraud in legal documents.

Notice Information; knowledge of certain facts or of a particular state of affairs. The formal receipt of papers that provide specific information.

Nuisance A legal action to redress harm arising from the use of one's property.

Null Of no legal validity, force, or effect; nothing. The phrase "null and void" is used in the invalidation of contracts or statutes.

O

Obscenity The character or quality of being obscene; an act, utterance, or item tending to corrupt public morals by its indecency or lewdness.

Option A privilege, for which a person had paid money, that grants that person the right to purchase or sell certain commodities or certain specified securities at any time within an agreed period for a fixed price.

A right, which operates as a continuing offer, given in exchange for consideration—something of value—to purchase or lease property at an agreed price and terms within a specified time.

Ordinance A law, statute, or regulation enacted by a municipal corporation.

Original jurisdiction The authority of a tribunal to entertain a lawsuit, try it, and set forth a judgment on the law and facts.

Overbreadth doctrine A principle of judicial review that holds that a law is invalid if it punishes constitutionally protected speech or conduct along with speech or conduct that the government may limit to further a compelling government interest.

P

Palimony The settlement awarded at the termination of a non-marital relationship, where the couple lived together for a long period of time and where there was an agreement that one partner would support the other in return for the second making a home and performing domestic duties.

Pardon The action of an executive official of the government that mitigates or sets aside the punishment for a crime.

Parens patriae ["Parent of the country."] The principle that the state should provide for and protect the interests of those who cannot take care of themselves, such as juveniles or the insane. The term also refers to the state's authority to bring legal suits on behalf of its residents, such as antitrust actions.

Parental liability A statute, enacted in some states, that makes parents liable for damages caused by their children, if it is found that the damages resulted from the parents' lack of control over the acts of the child.

Parent corporation An enterprise, which is also known as a parent company, that owns more than 50 percent of the voting shares of its subsidiary.

Parole The conditional release of a person convicted of a crime prior to the expiration of that person's term of imprisonment, subject to both the supervision of the correctional authorities during the remainder of the term and a resumption of the imprisonment upon violation of the conditions imposed.

Parol evidence *Parol* refers to verbal expressions or words. Verbal evidence, such as the testimony of a witness at trial.

Parol evidence rule The principle that a finalized, written contract cannot be altered by evidence of contempo-

raneous oral agreements to change, explain, or contradict the original contract.

Partnership An association of two or more persons engaged in a business enterprise in which the profits and losses are shared proportionally. The legal definition of a partnership is generally stated as "an association of two or more persons to carry on as co-owners of a business for profit" (Revised Uniform Partnership Act sec. 101 [1994]).

Patent Open; manifest; evident.

Patents Rights, granted to inventors by the federal government, pursuant to its power under Article I, Section 8, Clause 8, of the U.S. Constitution, that permit them to exclude others from making, using, or selling an invention for a definite, or restricted, period of time.

Pawnbroker A person who engages in the business of lending money, usually in small sums, in exchange for personal property deposited with him or her that can be kept or sold if the borrower fails or refuses to repay the loan.

Payee The person who is to receive the stated amount of money on a check, bill, or note.

Peremptory challenge The right to challenge a juror without assigning, or being required to assign, a reason for the challenge.

Perjury A crime that occurs when an individual willfully makes a false statement during a judicial proceeding, after he or she has taken an oath to speak the truth.

Personal property Everything that is the subject of ownership that does not come under the denomination of real property; any right or interest that an individual has in movable things.

Personal recognizance *See* Release on own recognizance.

Petition A written application from a person or persons to some governing body or public official asking that some authority be exercised to grant relief, favors, or privileges.

A formal application made to a court in writing that requests action on a certain matter.

Petit jury The ordinary panel of twelve persons called to issue a verdict in a civil action or a criminal prosecution.

Petit larceny A form of larceny—the stealing of another's personal property—in which the value of the property that is taken is generally less than $50.

Plaintiff The party who sues in a civil action; a complainant; the prosecution—that is, a state or the United States representing the people—in a criminal case.

Plain view doctrine In the context of searches and seizures, the principle that provides that objects perceptible by an officer who is rightfully in a position to observe them can be seized without a search warrant and are admissible as evidence.

Plea A formal response by the defendant to the affirmative assertions of the plaintiff in a civil case or to the charges of the prosecutor in a criminal case.

Plea bargaining The process whereby a criminal defendant and prosecutor reach a mutually satisfactory disposition of a criminal case, subject to court approval.

Pleading Asking a court to grant relief. The formal presentation of claims and defenses by parties to a lawsuit. The specific papers by which the allegations of the parties to a lawsuit are presented in proper form; specifically, the complaint of a plaintiff and the answer of a defendant, plus any additional responses to those papers that are authorized by law.

Plurality The opinion of an appellate court in which more justices join than in any concurring opinion.

The excess of votes cast for one candidate over those votes cast for any other candidate.

Pocket veto A method of indirectly vetoing a bill due to a loophole in the Constitution. The loophole allows a bill that is left unsigned by the president or by the governor of a state at the end of a legislative session to be vetoed by default.

Police power The authority conferred upon the states by the Tenth Amendment to the U.S. Constitution which the states delegate to their political subdivisions to enact measures to preserve and protect the safety, health, welfare, and morals of the community.

Poll tax A specified sum of money levied upon each person who votes.

Polygamy The offense of having more than one wife or husband at the same time.

Power of attorney A written document in which one person (the principal) appoints another person to act as an agent on his or her behalf, thus conferring authority on the agent to perform certain acts or functions on behalf of the principal.

Precedent A court decision that is cited as an example or analogy to resolve similar questions of law in later cases.

Precinct A constable's or police district. A small geographical unit of government. An election district created for convenient localization of polling places. A county or municipal subdivision for casting and counting votes in elections.

Preferential treatment Consideration for an individual which is prioritized based on whether the person meets a certain requirement, such as residency. In employment, this type of consideration has been found to be a violation of fair employment practices.

Preliminary hearing A proceeding before a judicial officer in which the officer must decide whether a crime was committed, whether the crime occurred within the territorial jurisdiction of the court, and whether there is probable cause to believe that the defendant committed the crime.

Premarital agreement *See* Prenuptial agreement.

Premeditate To think of an act beforehand; to contrive and design; to plot or lay plans for the execution of a purpose.

Prenuptial agreement An agreement, made prior to marriage, between individuals contemplating marriage, to establish and secure property and other financial rights for one or both of the spouses and their children.

Preponderance of evidence A standard of proof that must be met by a plaintiff if he or she is to win a civil action.

Pre-sentence hearing A hearing commenced after the criminal trial judge examines the pre-sentence report and other relevant materials before passing sentence on the defendant.

Pre-sentence investigation Research that is conducted by court services or a probation officer relating to the prior criminal record, education, employment, and other information about a person convicted of a crime, for the purpose of assisting the court in passing sentence.

Pre-sentence report The written report of the pre-sentence investigation for the judge to evaluate before passing sentence on the defendant. Typically the report covers the following: description of the background, employment history, residency and medical history; information on the environment to which the defendant will return and the resources that will be available to him or her; the probation officer's view of the defendant; full description of the defendant's criminal record; and recommendations on sentencing.

Presentment A grand jury statement that a crime was committed; a written notice, initiated by a grand jury, that states that a crime occurred and that an indictment should be drawn.

In relation to commercial paper, presentment is a demand for the payment or acceptance of a negotiable instrument, such as a check. The holder of a negotiable instrument generally makes a presentment to the maker, acceptor, drawer, or drawee.

Pretrial motion A written or oral request made to the court before the trial to obtain a ruling in favor of the movant, such as a motion to dismiss or a motion to suppress evidence.

Preventive detention The confinement in a secure facility of a person who has not been found guilty of a crime.

Prima facie [*Latin*, On the first appearance.] A fact presumed to be true unless it is disproved.

Prima facie case A case that, because it is supported by the requisite minimum of evidence and is free of obvious defects, can go to the jury; thus the defendant is required to proceed with its case rather than move for dismissal or a directed verdict.

Primary liability In commercial law, the liability of a contract signer.

Principal A source of authority; a sum of a debt or obligation producing interest; the head of a school. In an agency relationship, the principal is the person who gives authority to another, called an agent, to act on his or her behalf. In criminal law, the principal is the chief actor or perpetrator of a crime; those who aid, abet, counsel, command, or induce the commission of a crime may also be principals. In investments and banking, the principal refers to the person for whom a broker executes an order; it may also mean the capital invested or the face amount of a loan.

Prior restraint Government prohibition of speech in advance of publication.

Privacy In constitutional law, the right of people to make personal decisions regarding intimate matters; under the common law, the right of people to lead their lives in a manner that is reasonably secluded from public scrutiny, whether such scrutiny comes from a neighbor's prying eyes, an investigator's eavesdropping ears, or a news photographer's intrusive camera; and in statutory law, the right of people to be free from unwarranted drug testing and electronic surveillance.

Private That which affects, characterizes, or belongs to an individual person, as opposed to the general public.

Private nuisance Anything that creates an unreasonable interference with the use and enjoyment of the property of an individual or small group.

Private property Property that belongs exclusively to an individual for his or her use. This tangible property can be possessed or transferred to another, such as a house or land.

Privilege An advantage, benefit, or exemption possessed by an individual, company, or class beyond those held by others.

Privileges and immunities Concepts contained in the U.S. Constitution that place the citizens of each state on an equal basis with citizens of other states with respect to advantages resulting from citizenship in those states and citizenship in the United States.

Probable cause Apparent facts discovered through logical inquiry that would lead a reasonably intelligent and prudent person to believe that an accused person has committed a crime, thereby warranting his or her prosecution, or that a cause of action has accrued, justifying a civil lawsuit.

Probate The court process by which a will is proved valid or invalid. The legal process wherein the estate of a decedent is administered.

Probate court Called Surrogate or Orphan's Court in some states, the probate court presides over the probate of wills, the administration of estates, and, in some states, the appointment of guardians or approval of the adoption of minors.

Probation A sentence whereby a convict is released from confinement but is still under court supervision; a testing or a trial period. It can be given in lieu of a prison term or can suspend a prison sentence if the convict has consistently demonstrated good behavior.

The status of a convicted person who is given some freedom on the condition that for a specified period he or she acts in a manner approved by a special officer to whom he or she must report.

An initial period of employment during which a new, transferred, or promoted employee must show the ability to perform the required duties.

Procedural due process The constitutional guarantee that one's liberty and property rights may not be affected unless reasonable notice and an opportunity to be heard in order to present a claim or defense are provided.

Product liability The responsibility of a manufacturer or vendor of goods to compensate for injury caused by a defective good that it has provided for sale.

Promissory note A written, signed, unconditional promise to pay a certain amount of money on demand at a specified time. A written promise to pay money that is often used as a means to borrow funds or take out a loan.

Property A thing or things owned either by government—public property—or owned by private individuals, groups, or companies—private property.

Property right A generic term that refers to any type of right to specific property whether it is personal or real property, tangible or intangible; i.e., a professional athlete has a valuable property right in his or her name, photograph, and image, and such right may be saleable by the athlete.

Pro se For one's own behalf; in person. Appearing for oneself, as in the case of one who does not retain a lawyer and appears for himself or herself in court.

Prosecute To follow through; to commence and continue an action or judicial proceeding to its ultimate conclusion. To proceed against a defendant by charging that person with a crime and bringing him or her to trial.

Prosecuting attorney An appointed or elected official in each judicial district, circuit, or county, that carries out criminal prosecutions on behalf of the State or people. Federal crimes are prosecuted by U.S. Attorneys.

Prosecution The proceedings carried out before a competent tribunal to determine the guilt or innocence of a defendant. The term also refers to the government attorney charging and trying a criminal case.

Protective order A court order, direction, decree, or command to protect a person from further harassment, service of process, or discovery.

Provision Anticipated accommodation(s) that may need to be made to fulfill an obligation in the event that something happens.

Proximate cause An act from which an injury results as a natural, direct, uninterrupted consequence and without which the injury would not have occurred.

Proximate consequence or result A consequence or result that naturally follows from one's negligence and is reasonably foreseeable and probable.

Proxy A representative; an agent; a document appointing a representative.

Public forum An open-discussion meeting that takes place in an area which is accessible to or shared by all members of a community.

Public hearing The due process of an individual before a tribunal to hear evidence and testimony in determination of the defendant's guilt or innocence.

Punitive damages Monetary compensation awarded to an injured party that goes beyond that which is necessary to compensate the individual for losses and that is intended to punish the wrongdoer.

Purchase To buy; the transfer of property from one person to another by an agreement, which sets forth the price and terms of the sale. Under the Uniform Commercial Code (UCC), taking by sale, discount, negotiation, mortgage, pledge, lien, issue, reissue, gift, or any voluntary transaction.

Q

Quiet enjoyment A covenant that promises that the grantee or tenant of an estate in real property will be able to possess the premises in peace, without disturbance by hostile claimants.

Quitclaim deed An instrument of conveyance of real property that passes any title, claim, or interest, that the grantor has in the premises but does not make any representations as to the validity of such title.

Quorum A majority of an entire body; i.e., a quorum of a legislative assembly.

Quota A quantitative boundary set for a class of things or people.

R

Rape A criminal offense defined in most states as forcible sexual relations with a person against that person's will.

Ratification The confirmation or adoption of an act that has already been performed.

Reapportionment The realignment in legislative districts brought about by changes in population and mandated in the constitutional requirement of one person, one vote.

Reasonable care The degree of caution that a rational and competent individual would exercise in a given circumstance. It is an subjective test used to determine negligence.

Reasonable person A phrase frequently used in tort and criminal law to denote a hypothetical person in society who exercises average care, skill, and judgment in conduct and who serves as a comparative standard for determining liability.

Rebut To defeat, dispute, or remove the effect of the other side's facts or arguments in a particular case or controversy.

Rebuttable presumption A conclusion as to the existence or nonexistence of a fact that a judge or jury must draw when evidence has been introduced and admitted as true in a lawsuit but that can be contradicted by evidence to the contrary.

Recall The right or procedure by which a public official may be removed from a position by a vote of the people prior to the end of the term of office.

Recognizance A recorded obligation, entered into before a tribunal, in which an individual pledges to perform a specific act or to subscribe to a certain course of conduct.

Redlining A discriminatory practice whereby lending institutions refuse to make mortgage loans, regardless of an applicant's credit history, on properties in particular areas in which conditions are allegedly deteriorating.

Redress Compensation for injuries sustained; recovery or restitution for harm or injury; damages or equitable relief. Access to the courts to gain reparation for a wrong.

Redress of grievances The right to request relief from the government for an injustice or wrong it has committed, as guaranteed by the First Amendment.

Referendum The right reserved to the people to approve or reject an act of the legislature, or the right of the people to approve or reject legislation that has been referred to them by the legislature.

Refugees Individuals who leave their native country for social, political, or religious reasons, or who are forced to leave as a result of any type of disaster, including war, political upheaval, and famine.

Regulation A rule of order having the force of law, prescribed by a superior or competent authority, relating to the actions of those under the authority's control.

Regulatory agency *See* Administrative agency.

Rehabilitation The restoration of former rights, authority, or abilities.

Release A contractual agreement by which one individual assents to relinquish a claim or right under the law to another individual against whom such a claim or right is enforceable.

Release on own recognizance The release of an individual who is awaiting trial without a bail bond. It is used in place of bail when the judge is satisfied that the defendant will appear for trial, given the defendant's past history, his or her roots in the community, his or her regular employment, the recommendation of the prosecutor, the type of crime, and the improbability that the defendant will commit another crime while awaiting trial.

Remand To send back.

Remedy The manner in which a right is enforced or satisfied by a court when some harm or injury, recognized by society as a wrongful act, is inflicted upon an individual.

Removal The transfer of a person or thing from one place to another. The transfer of a case from one court to another. In this sense, removal generally refers to a transfer from a court in one jurisdiction to a court in another, whereas a change of venue may be granted simply to move a case to another location within the same jurisdiction.

Rent Control The system by which the federal, state, and local governments regulate rent rates by placing ceilings on the amount that private individuals can be charged for rent.

Replevin A legal action to recover the possession of items of personal property.

Replevy In regards to replevin, the return of goods to the original owner pending the outcome of the case. Also, the release of an individual on bail.

Repossession The taking back of an item that has been sold on credit and delivered to the purchaser because the payments have not been made on it.

Reprieve The suspension of the execution of the death penalty for a period of time.

Rescind To declare a contract void—of no legal force or binding effect—from its inception and thereby restore the parties to the positions they would have occupied had no contract ever been made.

Rescission The cancellation of a prison inmate's tentative parole date. The abrogation of a contract, effective from its inception, thereby restoring the parties to the positions they would have occupied if no contract had ever been formed.

Reservation A clause in a deed of real property whereby the grantor, one who transfers property, creates and retains for the grantor some right or interest in the estate granted, such as rent or an easement, a right of use over the land of another. A large tract of land that is withdrawn by public authority from sale or settlement and appropriated to specific public uses, such as parks or military posts. A tract of land under the control of the Bureau of Indian Affairs to which a Native American tribe retains its original title of ownership, or that has been set aside from the public domain for use by a tribe.

Reserve Funds set aside to cover future expenses, losses, or claims. To retain; to keep in store for future or special use; to postpone to a future time.

Residence Personal presence at some place of abode.

Resolution The official expression of the opinion or will of a legislative body.

Restraining order A command of the court issued upon the filing of an application for an injunction, prohibiting the defendant from performing a threatened act until a hearing on the application can be held.

Restrictive covenant A provision in a deed limiting the use of the property and prohibiting certain uses. A clause in contracts of partnership and employment prohibiting a contracting party from engaging in similar employment for a specified period of time within a certain geographical area.

Retainer A contract between attorney and client specifying the nature of the services to be rendered and the cost of the services.

Retribution Punishment or reward for an act. In criminal law, punishment is based upon the theory that every crime demands payment.

Reverse discrimination Discrimination against a group of people that is alleged to have resulted from the affirmation action guidelines applied for a different group of people who were historically discriminated against by the former group.

Revocation The recall of some power or authority that has been granted.

Rider A schedule or writing annexed to a document such as a legislative bill or insurance policy.

Right of legation *See* Legation.

Right-to-work laws State laws permitted by section 14(b) of the Taft-Hartley Act that provide in general that employees are not required to join a union as a condition of getting or retaining a job.

Robbery The taking of money or goods in the possession of another, from his or her person or immediate presence, by force or intimidation.

Rule of law Rule according to law; rule under law; or rule according to a higher law.

S

Sabotage The willful destruction or impairment of, or defective production of, war material or national defense material, or harm to war premises or war utilities. During a labor dispute, the willful and malicious destruction of an employer's property or interference with his or her normal operations.

Sales agreement A present or future covenant that transfers ownership of goods or real estate from the seller to the buyer at an agreed upon price and terms.

Search warrant A court order authorizing the examination of a place for the purpose of discovering contraband, stolen property, or evidence of guilt to be used in the prosecution of a criminal action.

Second degree murder The unlawful taking of human life with malice, but without premeditated thought.

Secured transactions Business dealings that grant a creditor a right in property owned or held by a debtor to assure the payment of a debt or the performance of some obligation.

Security Protection; assurance; indemnification.

Security deposit Money aside from the payment of rent that a landlord requires a tenant to pay to be kept separately in a fund for use should the tenant cause damage to the premises or otherwise violate terms of the lease.

Sedition A revolt or an incitement to revolt against established authority, usually in the form of treason or defamation against government.

Seditious libel A written communication intended to incite the overthrow of the government by force or violence.

Segregation The act or process of separating a race, class, or ethnic group from a society's general population.

Self-defense The protection of one's person or property against some injury attempted by another.

Self-incrimination Giving testimony in a trial or other legal proceeding that could subject one to criminal prosecution.

Sentencing The post-conviction stage of a criminal justice process, in which the defendant is brought before the court for the imposition of a penalty.

Separate but equal The doctrine first enunciated by the U.S. Supreme Court in *Plessy v. Ferguson*, 163 U.S. 537, 16 S. Ct. 1138, 41 L. Ed. 256 (1896), establishing that different facilities for blacks and whites was valid under the Equal Protection Clause of the Fourteenth Amendment as along as they were equal.

Separation of church and state The separation of religious and government interest to ensure that religion does not become corrupt by government and that government does not become corrupt by religious conflict. The principle prevents the government from supporting the practices of one religion over another. It also enables the government to do what is necessary to prevent one religious group from violating the rights of others.

Separation of powers The division of state and federal government into three independent branches.

Settlement The act of adjusting or determining the dealings or disputes between persons without pursuing the matter through a trial.

Sexual harassment Unwelcome sexual advances, requests for sexual favors, and other verbal or physical conduct of a sexual nature that tends to create a hostile or offensive work environment.

Share A portion or part of something that may be divided into components, such as a sum of money. A unit of stock that represents ownership in a corporation.

Shield laws Statutes affording a privilege to journalists not to disclose in legal proceedings confidential information or sources of information obtained in their professional capacities.

Statutes that restrict or prohibit the use of certain evidence in sexual offense cases, such as evidence regarding the lack of chastity of the victim.

Shoplifting Theft of merchandise from a store or business establishment.

Silent partner An investment partner in a business who has no involvement in the management of the business.

Slander *See* Libel and slander.

Small claims court A special court, sometimes called conciliation court, that provides expeditious, informal, and inexpensive adjudication of small claims.

Sole proprietorship A form of business in which one person owns all the assets of the business, in contrast to a partnership or a corporation.

Solicitation Urgent request, plea or entreaty; enticing, asking. The criminal offense of urging someone to commit an unlawful act.

Sovereignty The supreme, absolute, and uncontrollable power by which an independent state is governed and from which all specific political powers are derived; the intentional independence of a state, combined with the right and power of regulating its internal affairs without foreign interference.

Specific performance An extraordinary equitable remedy that compels a party to execute a contract according to the precise terms agreed upon or to execute it substantially so that, under the circumstances, justice will be done between the parties.

Standing committee A group of legislators, who are ranked by seniority, that deliberate on bills, resolutions, and other items of business within its particular jurisdiction.

Stare decisis [*Latin, Let the decision stand.*] The policy of courts to abide by or adhere to principles established by decisions in earlier cases.

State courts Judicial tribunals established by each of the fifty states.

Status offense A type of crime that is not based upon prohibited action or inaction but rests on the fact that the offender has a certain personal condition or is of a specified character.

Statute An act of a legislature that declares, proscribes, or commands something; a specific law, expressed in writing.

Statute of frauds A type of state law, modeled after an old English law, that requires certain types of contracts to be in writing.

Statute of limitations A type of federal or state law that restricts the time within which legal proceedings may be brought.

Statutory Created, defined, or relating to a statute; required by statute; conforming to a statute.

Statutory law A law which is created by an act of the legislature.

Statutory rape Sexual intercourse by an adult with a person below a statutorily designated age.

Steering The process whereby builders, brokers, and rental property managers induce purchasers or lessees of real property to buy land or rent premises in neighborhoods composed of persons of the same race.

Stock A security issued by a corporation that represents an ownership right in the assets of the corporation and a right to a proportionate share of profits after payment of corporate liabilities and obligations.

Strict liability Absolute legal responsibility for an injury that can be imposed on the wrongdoer without proof of carelessness or fault.

Subcontractor One who takes a portion of a contract from the principal contractor or from another subcontractor.

Sublease The leasing of part or all of the property held by a tenant, as opposed to a landlord, during a portion of his or her unexpired balance of the term of occupancy.

Subpoena [*Latin, Under penalty.*] A formal document that orders a named individual to appear before a duly authorized body at a fixed time to give testimony.

Subsidiary Auxiliary; aiding or supporting in an inferior capacity or position. In the law of corporations, a corporation or company owned by another corporation that controls at least a majority of the shares.

Substantive due process The substantive limitations placed on the content or subject matter of state and federal laws by the Due Process Clauses of the Fifth and Fourteenth Amendments to the U.S. Constitution.

Substantive law The part of the law that creates, defines, and regulates rights, including, for example, the law of contracts, torts, wills, and real property; the essential substance of rights under law.

Suffrage The right to vote at public elections.

Summons The paper that tells a defendant that he or she is being sued and asserts the power of the court to hear and determine the case. A form of legal process that commands the defendant to appear before the court on a specific day and to answer the complaint made by the plaintiff.

Suppression or exclusion of evidence The dismissal of evidence put forth by the prosecution by a judge; often due to the unconstitutionality of the method of seizure of said evidence.

Supremacy clause The clause of Article VI of the U.S. Constitution that declares that all laws and treaties made by the federal government shall be the "supreme law of the land."

Supreme court An appellate tribunal with high powers and broad authority within its jurisdiction.

Surrogate mother A woman who agrees under contract to bear a child for an infertile couple. The woman is paid to have a donated fertilized egg or the fertilized egg of the female partner in the couple (usually fertilized by the male partner of the couple) artificially inseminated into her uterus.

Suspended sentence A sentence given after the formal conviction of a crime that the convicted person is not required to serve.

Syllabus A headnote; a short note preceding the text of a reported case that briefly summarizes the rulings of the court on the points decided in the case.

Symbolic speech Nonverbal gestures and actions that are meant to communicate a message.

T

Tenant An individual who occupies or possesses land or premises by way of a grant of an estate of some type, such as in fee, for life, for years, or at will. A person who has the right to temporary use and possession of a particular real property, which has been conveyed to that person by the landlord.

Testator One who makes or has made a will; one who dies leaving a will.

Testify To provide evidence as a witness, subject to an oath or affirmation, in order to establish a particular fact or set of facts.

Testimony Oral evidence offered by a competent witness under oath, which is used to establish some fact or set of facts.

Title In property law, a comprehensive term referring to the legal basis of the ownership of property, encompassing real and personal property and intangible and tangible interests therein; also a document serving as evidence of ownership of property, such as the certificate of title to a motor vehicle.

In regard to legislation, the heading or preliminary part of a particular statute that designates the name by which that act is known.

In the law of trademarks, the name of an item that may be used exclusively by an individual for identification purposes to indicate the quality and origin of the item.

Tortfeasor A wrongdoer; an individual who commits a wrongful act that injures another and for which the law provides a legal right to seek relief; a defendant in a civil tort action.

Tortious Wrongful; conduct of such character as to subject the actor to civil liability under tort law.

Tort law A body of rights, obligations, and remedies that is applied by the courts in civil proceedings to provide relief for persons who have suffered harm from the wrongful acts of others. The person who sustains injury or suffers pecuniary damage as the result of tortious conduct is known as the plaintiff, and the person who is responsible for inflicting the injury and incurs liability for the damage is known as the defendant or tortfeasor.

Trade secret Any valuable commercial information that provides a business with an advantage over competitors who do not have that information.

Trade union An organization of workers in the same skilled occupation or related skilled occupations who act together to secure for all members favorable wages, hours, and other working conditions.

Transfer To remove or convey from one place to another. The removal of a case from one court to another court within the same system where it might have been instituted. An act of the parties, or of the law, by which the title to property is conveyed from one person to another.

Treason The betrayal of one's own country by waging war against it or by consciously or purposely acting to aid its enemies.

Treaty A compact made between two or more independent nations with a view to the public welfare.

Trespass An unlawful intrusion that interferes with one's person or property.

Trial A judicial examination and determination of facts and legal issues arising between parties to a civil or criminal action.

Trial court The court where civil actions or criminal proceedings are first heard.

Truancy The willful and unjustified failure to attend school by one required to do so.

Trust A relationship created at the direction of an individual, in which one or more persons hold the individual's property subject to certain duties to use and protect it for the benefit of others.

Trustee An individual or corporation named by an individual, who sets aside property to be used for the benefit of another person, to manage the property as provided by the terms of the document that created the arrangement.

U

Unenumerated rights Rights that are not expressly mentioned in the written text of a constitution but instead are inferred from the language, history, and structure of the constitution, or cases interpreting it.

Unconstitutional That which is not in agreement with the ideas and regulations of the Constitution.

Uniform commercial code A general and inclusive group of laws adopted, at least partially, by all of the states to further uniformity and fair dealing in business and commercial transactions.

U.S. Constitution *See* Constitution of the United States.

U.S. Court of Appeals *See* Court of appeals.

U.S. Supreme Court *See* Supreme court.

Usury The crime of charging higher interest on a loan than the law permits.

V

Valid Binding; possessing legal force or strength; legally sufficient.

Vandalism The intentional and malicious destruction of or damage to the property of another.

Venue A place, such as the territory, from which residents are selected to serve as jurors.

   A proper place, such as the correct court to hear a case because it has authority over events that have occurred within a certain geographical area.

Verdict The formal decision or finding made by a jury concerning the questions submitted to it during a trial. The jury reports the verdict to the court, which generally accepts it.

Veto The refusal of an executive officer to assent to a bill that has been created and approved by the legislature, thereby depriving the bill of any legally binding effect.

Void That which is null and completely without legal force or binding effect.

Voidable That which is not absolutely void, but may be avoided.

Voir dire [*Old French, To speak the truth.*] The preliminary examination of prospective jurors to determine their qualifications and suitability to serve on a jury, in order to ensure the selection of a fair and impartial jury.

Voluntary manslaughter The unlawful killing of a person falling short of malice, premeditation or deliberate intent but too near to these standards to be classified as justifiable homicide.

W

Waive To intentionally or voluntarily relinquish a known right or engage in conduct warranting an inference that a right has been surrendered.

Waiver The voluntary surrender of a known right; conduct supporting an inference that a particular right has been relinquished.

Ward A person, especially an infant or someone judged to be incompetent, placed by the court in the care of a guardian.

Warrant A written order issued by a judicial officer or other authorized person commanding a law enforcement officer to perform some act incident to the administration of justice.

Warranty deed An instrument that transfers real property from one person to another and in which the grantor promises that title is good and clear of any claims.

White collar crime Term for nonviolent crimes that were committed in the course of the offender's occupation, such as commercial fraud or insider trading on the stock market.

Will A document in which a person specifies the method to be applied in the management and distribution of his or her estate after his or her death.

Workers' compensation A system whereby an employer must pay, or provide insurance to pay, the lost wages and medical expenses of an employee who is injured on the job.

Work release program A sentencing alternative designed to permit an inmate to continue regular employment during the daytime but to return to prison at night for lockup.

Writ An order issued by a court requiring that something be done or giving authority to do a specified act.

Writ of assistance A court order issued to enforce an existing judgment.

Writ of certiorari *See* Certiorari.

Writ of habeas corpus *See* Habeas corpus.

Z

Zoning The separation or division of a municipality into districts, the regulation of buildings and structures in such districts in accordance with their construction and the nature and extent of their use, and the dedication of such districts to particular uses designed to serve the general welfare.

ALPHABETICAL LIST OF COURT CASES

Volume IV

The following list includes the name of each case covered in this volume of *Great American Court Cases* and the page number on which coverage of the case begins. The case names are arranged in alphabetical order. Names not found here might be located within the cumulative index in the back of this volume.

Chronological List of Court Cases

Volume IV

The following list includes the name of each case covered in this volume of *Great American Court Cases* and the page number on which coverage of the case begins. The case names are arranged in alphabetical order under the year in which the corresponding case took place. Names not found here might be located within the cumulative index in the back of this volume.

CUMULATIVE INDEX

This index cites cases, people, events, and subjects in all four volumes of Great American Court Cases. Roman numerals refer to volumes.

A

A.L.A. Schechter Poultry Corporation v. United States, **I**: 579; **IV**: 283, 376-378 (main)

Aaron Burr trial, **IV**: 460-463 (main)

abandonment, **III**: 282

Abate v. Mundt, **III**: 641

Abington School District v. Schempp, **I**: 89-91 (main), 98, 103, 118, 132, 146, 153; **IV**: 420

Ableman v. Booth, **IV**: 119, 232-235 (main)

abolition, **II**: 85; **III**: 71-73, 78; **IV**: 366 (box)

Abood v. Detroit Board of Education, **I**: 3, 166, 342

abortion, **I**: 235-236, 506, 552-557; **II**: 369; **III**: 387, 391-393, 406-408, 412-424, 431-436, 445-449, 461-467

government funding, **III**: 425-430, 441-444

parental consent, **III**: 284, 437-440, 458-460

right to privacy, **III**: 47, 409-411

right to travel, **III**: 117

spousal consent, **I**: 552; **III**: 421-424

state powers, **III**: 454-457

Abortion Control Act, **I**: 552

Abrams v. Johnson, **III**: 659-660 (main)

Abrams v. United States, **I**: 171, 172-175 (main), 221

abstention doctrine, **I**: 216-218; **IV**: 270-272

abuse

child, **I**: 494; **II**: 219, 275-276, 290; **III**: 260, 278-280, 382-383

spousal, **III**: 260, 265-267, 272 (box)

academic freedom, **I**: 289-291, 512 (box)

accidents (automobile), **IV**: 511

actual malice, **I**: 232-234, 250, 358, 386, 405, 411-412, 440, 446-460

Adair v. United States, **IV**: 45-46 (main), 301

Adams v. New York, **II**: 355

Adams v. Williams, **II**: 397-399 (main)

Adams, John, **IV**: 104

Adamson v. California, **II**: 294, 301-302 (main), 305, 311

Adarand Constructors, Inc. v. Pena, **III**: 3, 27-29 (main), 69

Adderley v. Florida, **I**: 1, 41-42 (main), 213

Addyston Pipe & Steel Co. v. United States, **IV**: 369, 444

Adickes v. Kress, **III**: 83

Adkins v. Children's Hospital, **IV**: 293, 299, 311-314 (main), 316, 318

Adkins v. Lyons, **IV**: 312

Adler et al. v. Board of Education of the City of New York, **I**: 16-18 (main)

Administrative Procedure Act, **III**: 490-493

adoption, **III**: 187 (box), 237, 243, 282, 284-287, 449-453, 472

adult entertainment. *See also* pornography. **I**: 350-352, 482-485, 490-492, 594-595; **II**: 207

adultery, **I**: 385, 523; **III**: 262

advertising, **I**: 235-236, 242-244, 262-264, 267-268, 275-276, 314-316, 323-325, 329 (box), 341-343, 377-378; **III**: 102; **IV**: 510-512

abortion, **III**: 387

cigarette, **II**: 156 (box)

truth in, **I**: 328-331; **IV**: 18

Aetna Life Insurance Co. v. Haworth, **IV**: 536

affirmative action programs, **I**: 291; **III**: 1-37, 69, 170-173, 191-196, 247, 314-317, 335, 510; **IV**: 14

Afghanistan

Soviet invasion of, **III**: 328

Africa v. Pennsylvania, **I**: 65

African Americans, **I**: 26-29, 34-36, 38, 187, 200-201, 205-208, 212-213, 306-307, 525-527, 559; **II**: 7-8, 17, 46-47, 112, 188-189, 194-196, 211-212, 240-242, 295-298, 507, 516, 539; **III**: 2-3, 67, 81-83, 108-109, 115-117, 205-207, 212-214, 219-222, 580-582; **IV**: 118, 260, 363-367

admission to universities, **III**: 34, 183, 551-553

affirmative action programs, **III**: 15-16, 23-24, 170-173

Amistad revolt, **III**: 71-73

busing, **III**: 541-542

child custody, **III**: 186-187

club membership, **III**: 137-138

employment discrimination, **IV**: 270, 325; **III**: 146-147, 192, 202-204

housing discrimination, **III**: 123-124, 131-132, 151-153, 514-515, 520-522

protection from lynching, **III**: 78-80

segregation, **III**: 84-85, 106-107, 110-114, 183, 188-190, 511-513, 516-519, 523-540, 543-545, 551-553

voting rights, **III**: 583, 585-590, 593-596, 603-609, 620, 630-631, 634-635, 637, 645-647, 656

Afroyim v. Rusk, **II**: 337; **III**: 359, 362, 363-364 (main)

age discrimination, **III**: 148-150, 208-211, 247

Age Discrimination in Employment Act, **III**: 149 (box), 208, 247, 575

age of majority, **II**: 219; **III**: 285 (box), 318-321, 423; **IV**: 401-404

Agins v. Tiburon, **II**: 153

Agnello v. United States, **II**: 395

Agostini v. Felton, **I**: 99

Agricultural Adjustment Act, **IV**: 8-10, 321-322, 537-538

agricultural industry, **I**: 341-343; **IV**: 8-10, 321-322, 537

Agricultural Marketing Agreement Act, **I**: 341-343

Aguilar test, **II**: 452

Aguilar v. Felton, **I**: 112, 135

Aguilar v. Texas, **II**: 356, 452

Aid to Families with Dependent Children programs, **III**: 121-122, 126 (box), 129-130

AIDS, **III**: 473

Aikins v. Kingsbury, **IV**: 59

Air Force, U.S., **I**: 124-126; **III**: 307-308; **IV**: 243-245, 432-433

Air Pollution Control Act, **IV**: 78 (box)

airline industry, **II**: 165-168, 387, 455-458, 504; **III**: 60

Airport Commissioners v. Jews for Jesus, Inc., **I**: 280-282 (main)

banks, **IV:** 110-111
Barclay v. Florida, **I:** 307
Barenblatt v. United States, **IV:** 390-391 (main)
Barnes v. Costle, **III:** 572
Barnes v. Glen Theatre, Inc., **I:** 351, 594-595 (main)
Barnes-O'Brien test, **I:** 351
Barron v. Baltimore, **IV:** 114-116 (main)
Bartkus v. Illinois, **II:** 94-95 (main)
Bas v. Tingy, **IV:** 105 (box)
Baskerville v. Culligan Int'l Co, **III:** 573
Bates v. Little Rock, **I:** 2, 203
Bates v. State Bar of Arizona, **I:** 242-244 (main), 323
Batson v. Kentucky, **II:** 186, 211-212 (main); **III:** 215
battery (crime), **II:** 75, 115, 197; **III:** 391
Bayard v. Singleton, **IV:** 105 (box)
Beal v. Doe, **II:** 70; **III:** 387, 425-427 (main), 442
Bean v. Southwestern Waste Management Corp., **III:** 174-176 (main)
Beauharnais v. Illinois, **I:** 439, 493
Beck v. Ohio, **I:** 529
Beer v. United States, **III:** 628
Bell v. Burson, **IV:** 62
Bell v. Ohio, **II:** 27, 35-36 (main)
Bell v. U-32 Board of Education, **I:** 273-274 (main)
Bell v. Wolfish, **III:** 165-167 (main), 377
Bellotti v. Baird, **III:** 388, 437-440 (main)
Bendectin
  as a cause of birth defects, **II:** 160
benefits
  employment, **III:** 337-342 ; **IV:** 63-65
  for survivors, **III:** 326-327
  unemployment, **IV:** 504-506, 539-540, 542
Bennis v. Michigan, **II:** 171, 180, 532-534 (main)
Benton v. Maryland, **II:** 93-94, 96-97 (main)
Berkemer v. McCarty, **II:** 106-107 (main)
Berkowitz, David, **I:** 295
Berman v. Parker, **II:** 460 (box); **IV:** 388-389 (main)
Bethel School District No. 403 v. Fraser, **I:** 277-279 (main)
Better Business Bureau, **IV:** 18
Betts v. Brady, **II:** 251, 272, 289
beyond all reasonable doubt standard, **II:** 289
Bibb v. Navajo Freight Lines, **IV:** 6, 11-12 (main)
Bible reading in public school, **I:** 90 (box)
Bigelow v. Virginia, **I:** 235-236 (main); **III:** 387
Bill of Rights, **I:** 505; **II:** 92-93, 95; **III:** 533; **IV:** 114-116
bills of attainder, **II:** 68-71, 233

birth defects, **II:** 160
Bituminous Coal Conservation Act, **IV:** 379-380
Black & White Taxicab & Transfer Co. v. Brown & Yellow Taxicab & Transfer Co., **II:** 135
Black Panthers, **I:** 375
Black, Hugo Lafayette, **I:** 17, 78, 87, 183, 188, 213, 523; **II:** 300-301, 307; **III:** 107, 599, 613, 616; **IV:** 59, 208, 498
Blackledge v. Perry, **II:** 104
Blackmun, Harry A., **I:** 163, 236; **II:** 159, 346; **III:** 145, 319, 346, 415, 447; **IV:** 341
blacks. *See* African Americans
Block v. Hirsh, **IV:** 50-52 (main)
blockades, **III:** 120-122
Bloom v. Illinois, **II:** 89
Blue Chip Stamps v. Manor Drug Stores, **III:** 426
blue laws, **I:** 64, 84-85
BMW of North America, Inc. v. Gore, **II:** 159, 163-164 (main)
Board of County Commissioners v. Seber, **III:** 5
Board of County Commissioners, Wabaunsee County, Kansas v. Umbehr, **I:** 332-334 (main)
Board of Directors, Rotary International v. Rotary Club of Duarte, **III:** 343-344 (main)
Board of Education of Kiryas Joel v. Grumet, **I:** 132, 135-137 (main)
Board of Education of Picataway v. Sharon Taxman, **III:** 30
Board of Education v. Allen, **I:** 98
Board of Education v. Mergens, **I:** 83
Board of Education v. Pico, **I:** 265, 345
Bob Jones University v. United States, **III:** 183-185 (main)
Bob Jones University, **III:** 183-185
Boerne v. Flores, **I:** 65, 141-143 (main), 282
Bolger v. Youngs Drug Products Corp., **I:** 267-268 (main), 417
Bolling v. Sharpe, **III:** 68, 532-533 (main)
bona fide occupational qualification, **III:** 149 (box), 304-306, 325, 346
Bond v. Floyd, **IV:** 273-275 (main)
bonds
  registration of, **IV:** 546
book banning
  in public schools, **I:** 265-266, 466 (box)
Boos v. Barry, **I:** 55-57 (main)
Booth v. Maryland, **II:** 215-217 (main)
bootlegging, **I:** 516
Bordenkircher v. Hayes, **II:** 103-105 (main)
Bork, Robert, **III:** 492
Bowe v. Colgate-Palmolive, **III:** 304-306 (main)
Bowen v. Roy, **IV:** 502
Bowers v. Hardwick, **I:** 506; **III:** 473, 475-477 (main), 481

Bowman v. Railway Co., **II:** 359
Bowsher v. Synar, **IV:** 165-167 (main)
Boy Scouts of America, **III:** 494-496
boycotts, **I:** 361-363; **II:** 87; **IV:** 294-296
Boyd v. United States, **II:** 234, 259, 355, 361, 372, 413, 425
Boykin v. Alabama, **II:** 270
Boynton v. Virginia, **III:** 106-107 (main)
Boynton, Bruce, **III:** 106
Bradfield v. Roberts, **I:** 158
Bradwell v. Illinois, **III:** 67, 295-297 (main), 306
Brady Handgun Control Act (Brady Bill), **I:** 563, 565 (box); **IV:** 413-416
Brady, James, **I:** 565 (box); **IV:** 413
Brady, Sarah, **I:** 565 (box)
Bragdon v. Abbott, **III:** 248, 497
brain death, **III:** 42-45
Bram v. United States, **II:** 234
Branch v. Texas, **II:** 17, 22, 26
Brandeis, Louis D., **I:** 7, 505; **IV:** 57 (box), 543 (box)
Brandenburg v. Ohio, **I:** 8, 166, 221-223 (main)
Branti v. Finkel, **I:** 59, 336
Branzburg v. Hayes, **I:** 252, 358, 375-376 (main), 393
Braunfeld v. Brown, **I:** 64, 84-85 (main), 92
breach of contract. *See* contract law
breach of the peace, **I:** 2, 179, 185-186, 200-201, 205-208, 212-213, 226-228, 555-557, 587; **II:** 98, 453
breaking and entering, **II:** 16, 222, 379, 411
Breard v. Alexandria, **I:** 184
Breedlove v. Suttles, **III:** 581, 601
Breithaupt v. Abram, **II:** 259
Brennan, William J., Jr., **I:** 44, 49, 53, 93, 122, 400, 462, 481 (box), 524, 574; **II:** 73, 76, 305, 312, 490; **III:** 125, 138, 195, 251, 308, 316, 411, 429, 540, 621; **IV:** 68
Brewer v. Williams, **II:** 463
Brewer, David Josiah, **IV:** 299
Breyer, Stephen, **I:** 570; **IV:** 184
bribery, **II:** 297; **III:** 633; **IV:** 32, 171, 371
Brinegar v. United States, **II:** 173, 355
broadcasting industry, **I:** 245-247, 250-252, 355-360, 381-384, 389-395, 397, 404, 544-546; **II:** 325; **III:** 25-26
  cable television, **I:** 338-340; **IV:** 26-28
  fairness doctrine, **I:** 219-220, 246 (box), 377-378
  government regulation of, **I:** 502
Broadrick v. Oklahoma, **I:** 45-47 (main), 281
Broin, et al. v. Philip Morris Incorporated, et al., **II:** 165-168 (main)
Brotherhood of Railroad Trainmen v. Virginia State Bar, **I:** 36

Contract with America, **II:** 129 (box); **IV:** 350

contributions, political. *See* campaigns

Contributors to the Pennsylvania Hospital v. City of Philadelphia, **IV:** 59

Controlled Substance Act, **II:** 171

Cook, Fred J., **I:** 219

Cooley v. Board of Wardens, **IV:** 81, 358-359 (main)

Coolidge v. New Hampshire, **II:** 393-396 (main), 438, 486, 500, 522 (box)

Coolidge, Calvin, **IV:** 134 (box)

Copelon, Rhonda, **III:** 442

Coppage v. Kansas, **IV:** 300-302 (main)

copyright law, **I:** 419, 435 (box)

corporal punishment, **III:** 154-156

corporate law. *See also* employment law; labor law. **III:** 102, 104; **IV:** 2-4, 92-95, 147-149

corporations, **III:** 104; **IV:** 2, 37-38, 42-44, 450-452, 514

government, **I:** 314-316

corruption, **IV:** 263

Cotton Petroleum Corporation v. New Mexico, **IV:** 500

Counselman v. Hitchcock, **II:** 315

County of Allegheny v. ACLU, **I:** 116, 129-130 (main), 160, 326

County of Oneida v. Oneida Indian Nation, **III:** 6; **IV:** 478

County of Riverside v. McLaughlin, **II:** 508-510 (main)

County of Sacramento v. Lewis, **III:** 64-66 (main)

court martial, **IV:** 417, 432

court of claims, **IV:** 228, 327-329

court packing, **I:** 14; **IV:** 8, 56, 104, 138, 141, 145, 313, 321, 380, 538, 541

courts

organization of circuit, **II:** 310 (box); **IV:** 227

organization of federal appellate, **II:** 300 (box); **IV:** 227, 251

organization of federal district, **II:** 327 (box); **IV:** 227

Cox Broadcasting Corp. v. Cohn, **I:** 358, 381-384 (main)

Cox v. Louisiana, **I:** 1, 42, 166, 205-208 (main), 212

Cox v. New Hampshire, **I:** 1, 11-13 (main), 166

Coy v. Iowa, **II:** 290; **III:** 383

Coyle v. Oklahoma, **IV:** 194

Coyle v. Smith, **IV:** 194-195 (main)

Craig v. Boren, **III:** 69, 317, 321, 322-323 (main), 350

Craig v. Harney, **I:** 382

Crawford v. Board of Education of Los Angeles, **III:** 550

Crawford-El v. Britton, **I:** 347-349 (main)

Crazy Horse, **IV:** 510-512

Creationism Act, **I:** 127-128

Creationism theory, **I:** 67-71

creches

display of, **I:** 129-130, 159-161

Creedon v. Cloyd W. Miller Co, **IV:** 386

Crime Act of 1994, **I:** 563

Crime Victims Protection Act, **I:** 384

crimes. *See* specific crimes

Criminal Appeals Act, **III:** 116

criminal law, **II:** 61-80; **IV:** 253-254

criminal procedure, **II:** 81-129

distinction from civil procedure, **II:** 181 (box)

criminal syndicalism, **IV:** 241-242

Criminal Syndicalism Act of California, **I:** 7 (box)

Crockett v. Reagan, **IV:** 459

Crooker v. California, **II:** 254 (box)

cross-examinations, **I:** 532-534; **III:** 382-383

right to, **II:** 307-308

crosses

display of, **I:** 326-327

Crow Dog, Ex Parte, **IV:** 488-490 (main)

cruel and unusual punishment, **I:** 392; **II:** 2, 9-11, 15-23, 31-45, 48-55, 175-177, 333, 336-347; **III:** 154-156, 160-162, 223-225, 265-267, 421, 476

Cruzan v. Director, Missouri Department of Health, **I:** 97; **III:** 39, 46-48 (main), 50

Cubby, Inc. v. CompuServe, Inc., **I:** 421-423 (main), 431

Culombe v. Connecticut, **II:** 110

Cummings v. Missouri, **II:** 68

curfews, **III:** 93-96, 377 (box)

Curran v. Mount Diablo Council of the Boy Scouts of America, **III:** 494-496 (main)

curriculum laws, **I:** 511-513

Curtis Act, **IV:** 472

Curtis, Benjamin, **IV:** 358

Curtis Publishing Co. v. Butts, **I:** 232, 250, 440, 451-453 (main)

Customs Service, U.S., **I:** 465, 549-551

Cyber Promotions, Inc. v. America Online, Inc., **I:** 424-426 (main)

D

DaCosta v. Laird, **IV:** 458

dairy industry, **IV:** 137-139, 374-375, 381-383

Dallas v. Stanglin, **I:** 13

Dalton v. Specter, **IV:** 347

damages, **II:** 131-168; **III:** 33, 55

civil, **II:** 149-151

compensatory, **I:** 413, 443, 451; **II:** 131, 158, 163-164, 167; **IV:** 31

for wrongful death, **III:** 118-120

liquidated, **II:** 131

nominal, **II:** 131

punitive, **I:** 413, 444, 451; **II:** 131, 158-159, 163-164; **III:** 56; **IV:** 31

Dames & Moore v. Regan, **IV:** 151

Dandridge v. Williams, **III:** 129-130 (main)

Danforth v. Planned Parenthood of Central Missouri, **III:** 422

Daniels v. Williams , **III:** 65

Darrow, Clarence, **I:** 67; **II:** 296

Dartmouth College v. Woodward, **IV:** 37

Darwinism, **I:** 67-71

date rape, **III:** 332 (box)

Daubert v. Merrell Dow Pharmaceuticals, Inc., **II:** 91, 160-162 (main)

Davis v. Alaska, **I:** 532-534 (main)

Davis v. Bandemer, **III:** 642-644 (main)

Davis v. Beason, **I:** 64

Davis v. Davis, **III:** 468

Davis v. Massachusetts, **I:** 369

Davis v. N.J. Zinc Co., **III:** 59

Dawes Severalty Act (General Allotment Act), **IV:** 472, 484-487

Day, William Rufus, **II:** 360

De Jonge v. Oregon, **I:** 1, 9-10 (main)

de novo review, **II:** 536

Dean Milk Company v. Madison, **IV:** 375

Dean v. District of Columbia, **III:** 487

death, **III:** 42-54, 64-66

Debs, Eugene V., **IV:** 285-288

Debs, In Re, **IV:** 285-288 (main)

Debs v. United States, **I:** 172; **IV:** 275

debt adjustment, **IV:** 208-209

debts, **IV:** 47-49, 60-62

Decent Interval, **I:** 257

decisions (judicial)

retrospective application of, **II:** 379-381

declaratory relief

definition of, **II:** 131

defamation. *See also* libel. **I:** 385-386, 405, 407, 411-412, 418, 439-441, 535-538, 541-543; **IV:** 510-512

Defense of Marriage Act, **III:** 472

DeFunis v. Odegaard, **III:** 2

Delaware v. Prouse, **II:** 356, 418-421 (main), 530

Delaware v. Van Arsdall, **I:** 534

delinquency, **II:** 219

Dellums v. Bush, **IV:** 168-170 (main)

Democratic National Committee, **I:** 270

Democratic-Republicans, **IV:** 460

demonstrations

against race discrimination, **I:** 224-228

against segregation, **I:** 41-42, 200-201, 205-208, 212-213

at abortion clinics, **I:** 555

at embassies, **I:** 55

nonviolent, **I:** 227 (box), 363, 581, 584-586, 589, 592; **II:** 88; **III:** 509

picketing, **I:** 579-580, 585 (box)

violent, **I:** 389; **IV:** 45, 127

denaturalization, **II:** 336

Dennis v. Sparks, **I:** 230

Dennis v. United States, **I:** 8, 32, 166, 189-191 (main), 195, 198, 222

Dennison, William, **II:** 84-86

Denver Area Educational Consortium v. Federal Communications Commission, **IV:** 26-28 (main)

Department of Agriculture, U.S., **III:** 62

McCulloch v. Maryland, **I:** 316; **IV:** 110-111 (main), 349, 376, 412

McDonald v. Santa Fe Trail Transp. Co., **III:** 172

McDonald v. Standard Oil Co., **III:** 59

McDonald v. United States, **II:** 410

McGowan v. Maryland, **I:** 84, 128

McGrain v. Daugherty, **IV:** 371-373 (main)

McGuire v. McGuire, **III:** 259

McHenry, G. Stewart, **I:** 323

McIntyre v. Ohio Elections Commission, **I:** 317-319 (main)

McIver v. Krischer, **III:** 40

McKeiver v. Pennsylvania, **II:** 221, 223, 229-231 (main); **III:** 377

McLaurin v. Oklahoma State Regents for Higher Education, **III:** 509, 517, 523-525 (main), 527

McNabb v. United States, **II:** 249

McNabb-Mallory rule, **II:** 249-250

McNeese v. Board of Education, **I:** 217

McReynolds, James Clark, **II:** 364; **IV:** 319 (box), 543 (box)

McVeigh v. Cohen, **III:** 490-493 (main)

McWilliams v. Fairfax County Board of Supervisors, **III:** 573

meat-packing industry, **IV:** 448-449

media
coverage of prison conditions, **I:** 392-395

Medicaid, **III:** 425-430, 441-444; **IV:** 183

medical benefits, **III:** 143-145

medical testing, **I:** 558-560

medical treatment
refusal of, **III:** 52
right to refuse, **I:** 95-97; **III:** 40, 42-48, 50

medicine. *See* health-care industry; health-care law

Medlock test, **I:** 403

Megan's Law, **I:** 536 (box)

membership lists, **I:** 16, 202-204

Memoirs of a Woman of Pleasure, **I:** 475-477

Memoirs v. Massachusetts, **I:** 471, 475-477 (main), 481 (box)

Memorandum on Religious Expression in the Public Schools of 1995, **I:** 105

Mendenhall-Royer test, **II:** 505

Mennonites, **I:** 101 (box)

menorahs
display of, **I:** 129-130, 326

mental capacity
during the commission of a crime, **II:** 236-239
to confess, **II:** 109-111
to plead guilty, **II:** 269-270
to receive the death penalty, **II:** 43-45, 51-53
to stand trial, **II:** 15, 223, 269-270

mental health, **II:** 2, 269; **III:** 292-294, 367, 374-375, 397-400, 499-502; **IV:** 160

mental retardation, **III:** 503-504, 506 (box)

mere evidence rule, **II:** 383

Meredith, James, **I:** 452

Meritor Savings Bank v. Vinson, **III:** 69, 556, 561-563 (main), 568

Metro Broadcasting, Inc. v. Federal Communications Commission, **III:** 25-26 (main), 28

Metropolitan Edison v. People Against Nuclear Energy, **IV:** 85

Metropolitan Washington Airports Authority v. Citizens for the Abatement of Aircraft Noise, **IV:** 408

Meyer v. Grant, **I:** 294

Meyer v. Nebraska, **I:** 101, 511-513 (main), 514; **III:** 90

Miami Herald Publishing Company v. Tornillo, **I:** 220, 318, 379-380 (main)

Michael M. v. Superior Court of Sonoma County, **III:** 328, 332-333 (main)

Michigan Campaign Finance Act, **I:** 292-294

Michigan Department of State Police v. Sitz, et al., **II:** 502-504 (main)

Michigan v. Long, **II:** 178-179 (main)

Michigan v. Summers, **II:** 431-433 (main)

Michigan v. Tucker, **II:** 102

Michigan v. Tyler, **II:** 386

Middendorf v. Henry, **IV:** 418

Migratory Bird Act, **IV:** 198-200

Migratory Bird Hunting Stamp Act, **IV:** 199 (box)

Migratory Bird Treaty, **IV:** 199 (box), 350

Miike, Lawrence H., **III:** 485

military, the, **I:** 65, 237-239, 506; **II:** 329-331; **III:** 290, 307-308, 314-317, 329-331, 358, 472, 478-480, 490-493, 557, 611, 621; **IV:** 243-245, 417-436, 457

military courts, **IV:** 418-421, 426-429
polygraph tests, **II:** 329-331

Military Issues, **IV:** 417-421

Military Justice Act, **IV:** 418

military law, **III:** 307-308, 490-493; **IV:** 152-153, 418-421, 428-429, 432-433

military orders, **III:** 97-99

Military Selective Service Act, **II:** 68-71; **IV:** 436

Milk Control Act, New York, **IV:** 137-139, 374-375

Miller test, **I:** 417, 462, 471, 480-481, 486, 491, 494, 498, 500, 503

Miller v. California, **I:** 245, 417, 462-463, 471, 480-481 (main), 486, 491, 494, 498, 500, 503

Miller v. Johnson, **III:** 647-649 (main), 655, 659

Miller v. Texas, **I:** 562

Miller v. United States, **II:** 528

Miller, Samuel Freeman, **IV:** 264, 465

Milligan, Ex parte, **IV:** 426-427 (main)

Milliken v. Bradley, **III:** 542, 544, 546-548 (main), 550

Mills v. Alabama, **III:** 633

Mills v. Hableutzel, **III:** 234

Milton, John, **I:** 369

Mincey v. Arizona, **II:** 416-417 (main), 486

Mine Workers v. Illinois Bar Association, **I:** 51

Minersville School District v. Gobitis, **I:** 74-75 (main), 76

minimal scrutiny doctrine, **III:** 335

minimum wage, **IV:** 283, 297-299, 303-304, 311-320, 330-332, 336-342

mining industry, **IV:** 289-290, 379-380

Minneapolis Eastern Railway Co. v. the State of Minnesota, **IV:** 268

Minneapolis Star v. Minnesota Commissioner of Revenue, **I:** 358, 402-404 (main)

Minnesota Mortgage Moratorium Law, **IV:** 53-55

Minnesota Private Pension Benefits Protection Act, **IV:** 63

Minnesota v. Dickerson, **II:** 524-526 (main)

Minnesota v. Olson, **II:** 118-120 (main)

Minor v. Happersett, **III:** 77, 298-301 (main), 579

Minton, Sherman, **I:** 17

Miracle, The, **I:** 192

Miranda rights, **II:** 75-77, 82, 100-102, 109-111, 115-117, 121-123, 253-258, 262-266, 273-274, 277-282, 439; **IV:** 419
during traffic stops, **II:** 106-107

Miranda v. Arizona, **II:** 75, 82, 100, 106, 116, 122, 234, 240, 250 (box), 252 (box), 254, 255-258 (main), 262, 278, 300, 318, 378, 401, 437

miscegenation laws, **I:** 525-527

misdemeanors
distinction from felonies, **II:** 61, 198 (box)

Mishkin v. New York, **I:** 475

missionaries, **IV:** 482, 498

Mississippi Burning, **I:** 306

Mississippi University for Women v. Hogan, **III:** 306, 321, 334-336 (main), 348, 568

Mississippi v. Johnson, **IV:** 260-262 (main)

Missouri Compromise, **IV:** 363-367

Missouri ex rel. Gaines v. Canada, **III:** 68, 516-517 (main)

Missouri v. Holland, **IV:** 198-200 (main), 350

Missouri v. Jenkins, **IV:** 549-550 (main)

Mistretta v. United States, **IV:** 405-408 (main)

Mitchell v. Laird, **IV:** 168

mitigating circumstances, **II:** 2, 31-34, 66 (box)

Mobile v. Bolden, **III:** 630-631 (main), 646

Model Business Corporation Act, **IV:** 1

Moe v. Salish & Kootenai Tribes, **IV:** 499

Monell v. Department of Social Services, **III:** 108

pre-emption doctrine, **IV:** 346-348, 500

pregnancy. *See also* abortion; discrimination against pregnant women. **III:** 143-145, 331, 345-347

    reports in school newspapers, **I:** 408

Pregnancy Discrimination Act, **III:** 145, 311, 345-347

prenuptial agreement, **III:** 263 (box)

prescriptions, **I:** 240-241

Presentment Clause, **IV:** 163, 183

Presidential Election Campaign Fund Act, **I:** 269-272

presidential powers, **II:** 138-140; **IV:** 98, 150-151, 156-159, 260-262, 346-348

    to conduct air strikes, **IV:** 243-245

    to declare war, **IV:** 168-170

    to forbid arms sales, **IV:** 142-143

    to issue executive orders, **IV:** 147-149

    to pardon, **I:** 4-5; **IV:** 129-130, 159-161

    to remove people from office, **II:** 149-151; **IV:** 131-133, 140-141

    to set up military tribunals, **IV:** 428-429

    to veto, **IV:** 134-136, 182-185

presidential succession, **IV:** 157 (box)

Press-Enterprise Co. v. Superior Court of California, **I:** 359; **II:** 323

Presser v. Illinois, **I:** 562

Preston v. United States, **II:** 260, 391

Prigg v. Pennsylvania, **IV:** 117-119 (main)

primaries, **III:** 588-590, 593-594, 623-624

Primus, In re, **I:** 50-51 (main)

Prince v. Massachusetts, **III:** 184, 310

Prince v. Prince, **III:** 262-264 (main)

Printz v. United States, **I:** 563, 569; **IV:** 413-416 (main)

prior restraint, **I:** 165, 209-211, 256-258, 358, 364-370, 396, 490; **III:** 163-164

Prison Litigation Reform Act, **I:** 349; **III:** 538 (box)

prisoners' rights, **I:** 347-349, 392; **II:** 9-11, 43-45, 75-77, 334, 341-347, 411-413, 453-454, 465-467; **III:** 90-92, 160-162, 165-167, 537-538; **IV:** 224, 405

prisons, **III:** 324-325

    overcrowding, **III:** 165-167

    conditions, **I:** 348 (box), 392

Privacy Protection Act, **I:** 390 (box), 507

privacy rights. *See* right to privacy

private clubs. *See* club membership

private enterprise, **IV:** 138 (box)

private persons, **I:** 405, 407

private property, **I:** 260 (box)

privateering, **IV:** 255

Privileges and Immunities Clause, **I:** 290; **II:** 190; **III:** 13-14, 180,

199, 200 (box), 201, 300, 418-420, 579; **IV:** 222-223, 323

Prize cases, **IV:** 120-122 (main)

probable cause, **I:** 390, 550; **II:** 118, 363-368, 376, 386, 398, 406, 418, 423, 431, 445-447, 452, 455-458, 470, 486-488, 495-497, 505, 508-510, 535-539, 543-545, 551; **III:** 565

probate law, **IV:** 253-254

probation, **II:** 333

Procurement Act, **IV:** 346-348

Proffitt v. Florida, **II:** 24, 41

Progressive movement, **III:** 163; **IV:** 196, 215, 298

Progressive, The, **III:** 163-164

prohibition, **I:** 516; **II:** 170, 358-359, 363, 366-368, 532; **IV:** 129 (box), 360-362

promissory estoppel, **I:** 414

property rights. *See also* Takings Clause. **II:** 382-384, 459-461, 518-523; **III:** 223-225, 259, 520-522; **IV:** 32

    due process guarantee, **IV:** 60-62, 360-362

    eminent domain power, **IV:** 50-52, 114-116, 388-389, 430-431

    ex post facto laws, **IV:** 253

    forfeiture, **II:** 180-183

    freedom of contract, **III:** 123; **IV:** 21, 58-59

    historic preservation law, **IV:** 212-214

    housing discrimination, **III:** 514-515

    Native Americans, **IV:** 134 (box), 476-481, 484-487

    real estate covenants, **III:** 521 (box)

    state actions, **IV:** 66-69, 192, 230-231

    zoning, **IV:** 75-76

property taxes, **IV:** 513, 528-529, 551-552

property values, **III:** 151-153

Proposition 187, **III:** 354, 366

Proprietors of the Charles River Bridge v. the Proprietors of the Warren Bridge, **IV:** 37-38 (main)

prostitution, **II:** 296, 532

proximate cause, **II:** 136-137

Pruneyard Shopping Center v. Robins, **I:** 259-261 (main); **IV:** 68

public employees. *See* firefighters; government officials; police officers

public enterprise, **IV:** 138 (box)

public figures, **I:** 232-234, 385-386, 411-412, 447 (box), 451-453

public forum doctrine, **I:** 259, 301

public function concept, **III:** 589 (box)

public health, **I:** 508; **II:** 386; **III:** 160-162, 174-176, 205; **IV:** 78, 289, 292, 298, 305-306, 319, 374-375, 377, 382, 440

Public Health Cigarette Smoking Act, **III:** 59

Public Health Service Act, **III:** 461

public information, **I:** 381-384

public lands, **IV:** 501-503

Public Use Clause, **II:** 460

Public Utilities Commission v. Pollak, **I:** 505

Public Works Employment Act, **III:** 2, 11 (box)

publishing industry, **I:** 366-367, 402-404, 437, 465-469, 475-477

publishing law, **I:** 232-234, 357-360, 364-365, 371-376, 379-380, 385-391, 396-401, 411-415, 421-423, 431-433, 442-448, 451-453; **III:** 163-164

Puerto Rico Games of Chance Act, **I:** 275

Puerto Rico v. Branstad, **II:** 84, 112-114 (main)

Pulley v. Harris, **II:** 40-42 (main)

punitive damages, **I:** 413, 444, 451; **II:** 131, 158-159, 163-164; **III:** 56; **IV:** 31

Pure Food and Drug Act, **IV:** 370

Q

Qualifications Clause, **IV:** 274 (box), 395, 409-412

quid pro quo harassment, **III:** 555, 562 (box), 572

Quilici v. Village of Morton Grove, **I:** 562

Quinlan, Karen Ann, **III:** 39, 42-45

Quirin, Ex Parte, **IV:** 428-429 (main)

quotas

    race, **III:** 34 (box)

R

R.A.V. v. City of St. Paul, **I:** 167, 298-299 (main), 306

R.I.S.E., Inc. v. Kay, **III:** 212-214 (main)

race discrimination. *See* discrimination

Racial Integrity Act, **I:** 525

racial quotas, **III:** 191-193

racism. *See also* discrimination. **I:** 298-299, 306-307; **II:** 194-196, 295-298; **III:** 78-80, 84-89, 93-101, 106-107, 110-112, 115-117, 151-153, 174-176

Racketeer Influenced and Corrupt Organizations Act (RICO), **II:** 284 (box), 323; **III:** 464-467

racketeering, **III:** 464-467

Radice v. New York, **IV:** 313, 319

radio, **I:** 219-220, 377-378, 393 (box); **III:** 25

Rail Passenger Service Act, **I:** 315

Railroad Commission of Texas v. Pullman Company, **I:** 217; **IV:** 270-272 (main)

railroads, **II:** 136-137, 492-494; **III:** 511-513; **IV:** 45, 201-205, 266-272, 285-288, 303-304, 446-447, 528-529

Raines v. Byrd, **IV:** 178-181 (main), 183, 351

THE CONSTITUTION
OF THE UNITED STATES

On 21 February 1787, Congress adopted the resolution that a convention of delegates should meet to revise the Articles of Confederation. The Constitution was signed and submitted to Congress on 17 September of that year. Congress then sent it to the states for ratification; the last state to sign, Rhode Island, did so 29 May 1790.

Preamble

We The People of the United States, in Order to form a more perfect Union, establish Justice, insure domestic Tranquility, provide for the common defence, promote the general Welfare, and secure the Blessings of Liberty to ourselves and our Posterity, do ordain and establish this Constitution for the United States of America.

Art. I

Sec. 1. All legislative Powers herein granted shall be vested in a Congress of the United States, which shall consist of a Senate and House of Representatives.

Sec. 2. The House of Representatives shall be composed of Members chosen every second Year by the People of the several States, and the Electors in each State shall have the Qualifications requisite for Electors of the most numerous Branch of the State Legislature.

No Person shall be a Representative who shall not have attained to the Age of twenty five Years, and been seven Years a Citizen of the United States, and who shall not, when elected, be an Inhabitant of that State in which he shall be chosen.

Representatives and direct Taxes shall be apportioned among the several States which may be included within this Union, according to their respective Numbers, which shall be determined by adding to the whole Number of free Persons, including those bound to Service for a Term of Years, and excluding Indians not taxed, three fifths of all other Persons. The actual Enumeration shall be made within three Years after the first Meeting of the Congress of the United States, and within every subsequent Term of ten Years, in such Manner as they shall by Law direct. The Number of Representatives shall not exceed one for every thirty Thousand, but each State shall have at Least one Representative; and until such enumeration shall be made, the State of New Hampshire shall be entitled to chuse three, Massachusetts eight, Rhode-Island and Providence Plantations one, Connecticut five, New-York six, New Jersey four, Pennsylvania eight, Delaware one, Maryland six, Virginia ten, North Carolina five, South Carolina five, and Georgia three.

When vacancies happen in the Representation from any State, the Executive Authority thereof shall issue Writs of Election to fill such Vacancies.

The House of Representatives shall chuse their Speaker and other Officers; and shall have the sole Power of Impeachment.

Sec. 3. The Senate of the United States shall be composed of two Senators from each State, chosen by the Legislature thereof, for six Years; and each Senator shall have one Vote.

Immediately after they shall be assembled in Consequence of the first Election, they shall be divided as equally as may be into three Classes. The Seats of the Senators of the first Class shall be vacated at the Expiration of the second Year, of the second Class at the Expiration of the fourth Year, and of the third Class at the Expiration of the sixth Year, so that one third may be chosen every second Year; and if Vacancies happen by Resignation, or otherwise, during the Recess of the Legislature of any State, the Executive thereof may make temporary Appointments until the next Meeting of the Legislature, which shall then fill such Vacancies.

No Person shall be a Senator who shall not have attained to the Age of thirty Years, and been nine Years a Citizen of the United States, and who shall not, when elected, be an Inhabitant of that State for which he shall be chosen.

The Vice President of the United States shall be President of the Senate, but shall have no Vote, unless they be equally divided.

The Senate shall chuse their other Officers, and also a President pro tempore, in the Absence of the Vice President, or when he shall exercise the Office of President of the United States.

The Senate shall have the sole Power to try all Impeachments. When sitting for that Purpose, they shall be on Oath or Affirmation. When the President of the United States is tried, the Chief Justice shall preside: And no Person shall be convicted without the Concurrence of two thirds of the Members present.

Judgment in Cases of Impeachment shall not extend further than to removal from Office, and disqualification to hold and enjoy any Office of honor, Trust or Profit under the United States: but the Party convicted shall nevertheless be liable and subject to Indictment, Trial, Judgment and Punishment, according to Law.

Sec. 4. The Times, Places and Manner of holding Elections for Senators and Representatives, shall be prescribed in each State by the Legislature thereof; but the Congress may at any time by Law make or alter such Regulations, except as to the Places of chusing Senators.

The Congress shall assemble at least once in every Year, and such Meeting shall be on the first Monday in December, unless they shall by Law appoint a different Day.

Sec. 5. Each House shall be the Judge of the Elections, Returns and Qualifications of its own Members, and a Majority of each shall constitute a Quorum to do Business; but a smaller Number may adjourn from day to day, and may be authorized to compel the Attendance of absent Members, in such Manner, and under such Penalties as each House may provide.

Each House may determine the Rules of its Proceedings, punish its Members for disorderly Behaviour, and, with the Concurrence of two thirds, expel a Member.

Each House shall keep a Journal of its Proceedings, and from time to time publish the same, excepting such Parts as may in their Judgment require Secrecy; and the Yeas and Nays of the Members of either House on any question shall, at the Desire of one fifth of those Present, be entered on the Journal.

Neither House, during the Session of Congress, shall, without the Consent of the other, adjourn for more than three days, nor to any other Place than that in which the two Houses shall be sitting.

Sec. 6. The Senators and Representatives shall receive a Compensation for their Services, to be ascertained by Law, and paid out of the Treasury of the United States. They shall in all Cases, except Treason, Felony and Breach of the Peace, be privileged from Arrest during their Attendance at the Session of their respective Houses, and in going to and returning from the same; and for any Speech or Debate in either House, they shall not be questioned in any other Place.

No Senator or Representative shall, during the Time for which he was elected, be appointed to any civil Office under the Authority of the United States which shall have been created, or the Emoluments whereof shall have been encreased during such time; and no Person holding any Office under the United States, shall be a Member of either House during his Continuance in Office.

Sec. 7. All Bills for raising Revenue shall originate in the House of Representatives; but the Senate may propose or concur with Amendments as on other Bills.

Every Bill which shall have passed the House of Representatives and the Senate, shall, before it become a Law, be presented to the President of the United States; If he approve he shall sign it, but if not he shall return it, with his Objections to that House in which it shall have originated, who shall enter the Objections at large on their Journal, and proceed to reconsider it. If after such Reconsideration two thirds of that House shall agree to pass the Bill, it shall be sent, together with the Objections, to the other House, by which it shall likewise be reconsidered, and if approved by two thirds of that House, it shall become a Law. But in all such Cases the Votes of both Houses shall be determined by yeas and Nays, and the Names of the Persons voting for and against the Bill shall be entered on the Journal of each House respectively. If any Bill shall not be returned by the President within ten Days (Sundays excepted) after it shall have been presented to him, the Same shall be a Law, in like Manner as if he had signed it, unless the Congress by their Adjournment prevent its Return, in which Case it shall not be a Law.

Every Order, Resolution, or Vote to which the Concurrence of the Senate and House of Representatives may be necessary (except on a question of Adjournment) shall be presented to the President of the United States; and before the Same shall take Effect, shall be approved by him, or being disapproved by him, shall be repassed by two thirds of the Senate and House of Representatives, according to the Rules and Limitations prescribed in the Case of a Bill.

Sec. 8. The Congress shall have Power To lay and collect Taxes, Duties, Imposts and Excises, to pay the Debts and provide for the common Defence and general Welfare of the United States; but all Duties, Imposts and Excises shall be uniform throughout the United States;

To borrow Money on the credit of the United States;

To regulate Commerce with foreign Nations, and among the several States, and with the Indian Tribes;

To establish an uniform Rule of Naturalization, and uniform Laws on the subject of Bankruptcies throughout the United States;

To coin Money, regulate the Value thereof, and of foreign Coin, and fix the Standard of Weights and Measures;

To provide for the Punishment of counterfeiting the Securities and current Coin of the United States;

To establish Post Offices and post Roads;

To promote the Progress of Science and useful Arts, by securing for limited Times to Authors and Inventors the exclusive Right to their respective Writings and Discoveries;

To constitute Tribunals inferior to the supreme Court;

To define and punish Piracies and Felonies committed on the high Seas, and Offences against the Law of Nations;

To declare War, grant Letters of Marque and Reprisal, and make Rules concerning Captures on Land and Water;

To raise and support Armies, but no Appropriation of Money to that Use shall be for a longer Term than two Years;

To provide and maintain a Navy;

To make Rules for the Government and Regulation of the land and naval Forces;

To provide for calling forth the Militia to execute the Laws of the Union, suppress Insurrections and repel Invasions;

To provide for organizing, arming, and disciplining, the Militia, and for governing such Part of them as may be employed in the Service of the United States, reserving to the States respectively, the Appointment of the Officers, and the Authority of training the Militia according to the discipline prescribed by Congress;

To exercise exclusive Legislation in all Cases whatsoever, over such District (not exceeding ten Miles square) as may, by Cession of particular States, and the Acceptance of Congress, become the Seat of the Government of the United States, and to exercise like Authority over all Places purchased by the Consent of the Legislature of the State in which the Same shall be, for the Erection of Forts, Magazines, Arsenals, dock-Yards, and other needful Buildings; —And

To make all Laws which shall be necessary and proper for carrying into Execution the foregoing Powers, and all other Powers vested by this Constitution in the Government of the United States, or in any Department or Officer thereof.

Sec. 9. The Migration or Importation of such Persons as any of the States now existing shall think proper to admit, shall not be prohibited by the Congress prior to the Year one thousand eight hundred and eight, but a Tax or duty may be imposed on such Importation, not exceeding ten dollars for each Person.

The Privilege of the Writ of Habeas Corpus shall not be suspended, unless when in Cases of Rebellion or Invasion the public Safety may require it.

No Bill of Attainder or ex post facto Law shall be passed.

No Capitation, or other direct, Tax shall be laid, unless in Proportion to the Census or Enumeration herein before directed to be taken.

No Tax or Duty shall be laid on Articles exported from any State.

No Preference shall be given by any Regulation of Commerce or Revenue to the Ports of one State over those of another: nor shall Vessels bound to, or from, one State, be obliged to enter, clear, or pay Duties in another.

No Money shall be drawn from the Treasury, but in Consequence of Appropriations made by Law; and a regular Statement and Account of the Receipts and Expenditures of all public Money shall be published from time to time.

No Title of Nobility shall be granted by the United States: And no Person holding any Office of Profit or Trust under them, shall, without the Consent of the Congress, accept of any present, Emolument, Office, or Title, of any kind whatever, from any King, Prince or foreign State.

Sec. 10. No State shall enter into any Treaty, Alliance, or Confederation; grant Letters of Marque and Reprisal; coin Money; emit Bills of Credit; make any Thing but gold and silver Coin a Tender in Payment of Debts; pass any Bill of Attainder, ex post facto Law, or Law impairing the Obligation of Contracts, or grant any Title of Nobility.

No State shall, without the Consent of the Congress, lay any Imposts or Duties on Imports or Exports, except what may be absolutely necessary for executing it's inspection Laws: and the net Produce of all Duties and Imposts, laid by any State on Imports or Exports, shall be for the Use of the Treasury of the United States; and all such Laws shall be subject to the Revision and Controul of the Congress.

No State shall, without the Consent of Congress, lay any Duty of Tonnage, keep Troops, or Ships of War in time of Peace, enter into any Agreement or Compact with another State, or with a foreign Power, or engage in War, unless actually invaded, or in such imminent Danger as will not admit of delay.

Art. II

Sec. 1. The executive Power shall be vested in a President of the United States of America. He shall hold his Office during the Term of four Years, and, together with the Vice President, chosen for the same Term, be elected, as follows.

Each State shall appoint, in such Manner as the Legislature thereof may direct, a Number of Electors, equal to the whole Number of Senators and Representatives to which the State may be entitled in the Congress: but no Senator or Representative, or Person holding an Office of Trust or Profit under the United States, shall be appointed an Elector.

The Electors shall meet in their respective States, and vote by Ballot for two Persons, of whom one at least shall not be an Inhabitant of the same State with themselves. And they shall make a List of all the Persons voted for, and of the Number of Votes for each; which List they shall sign and certify, and transmit sealed to the Seat of the Government of the United States, directed to the President of the Senate. The President of the Senate shall, in the Presence of the Senate and House of Representatives, open all the Certificates, and the Votes shall then be counted. The Person having the greatest Number of Votes shall be the President, if such Number be a Majority of the whole Number of Electors appointed; and if there be more than one who have such Majority, and have an equal Number of Votes, then the House of Representatives shall immediately chuse by Ballot one of them for President; and if no person have a Majority, then from the five highest on the List the said House shall in like Manner chuse the President. But in chusing the President, the Votes shall be taken by States, the Representation from each State having one Vote; A quorum for this Purpose shall consist of a Member or Members from two thirds of the States, and a Majority of all the States shall be necessary to a Choice. In every Case, after the Choice of the President, the Person having the greatest Number of Votes of the Electors shall be the Vice President. But if there should remain two or more who have equal Votes, the Senate shall chuse from them by Ballot the Vice President.

The Congress may determine the Time of chusing the Electors, and the Day on which they shall give their Votes; which Day shall be the same throughout the United States.

No Person except a natural born Citizen, or a Citizen of the United States, at the time of the Adoption of this Constitution, shall be eligible to the Office of President; neither shall any Person be eligible to that Office who shall not have attained to the Age of thirty five Years, and been fourteen Years a Resident within the United States.

In Case of the Removal of the President from Office, or of his Death, Resignation, or Inability to discharge the Powers and Duties of the said Office, the Same shall devolve on the Vice President, and the Congress may by Law provide for the Case of Removal, Death, Resignation or Inability, both of the President and Vice President, declaring what Officer shall then act as President, and such Officer shall act accordingly, until the Disability be removed, or a President shall be elected.

The President shall, at stated Times, receive for his Services, a Compensation, which shall neither be encreased nor diminished during the Period for which he shall have been elected, and he shall not receive within that Period any other Emolument from the United States, or any of them.

Before he enter on the Execution of his Office, he shall take the following Oath or Affirmation:—"I do solemnly swear (or affirm) that I will faithfully execute the Office of President of the United States, and will to the best of my Ability, preserve, protect and defend the Constitution of the United States."

Sec. 2. The President shall be Commander in Chief of the Army and Navy of the United States, and of the Militia of the several States, when called into the actual Service of the United States; he may require the Opinion, in writing, of the principal Officer in each of the executive Departments, upon any Subject relating to the Duties of their respective Offices, and he shall have Power to grant Reprieves and Pardons for Offences against the United States, except in Cases of Impeachment.

He shall have Power, by and with the Advice and Consent of the Senate, to make Treaties, provided two thirds of the Senators present concur; and he shall nominate, and by and with the Advice and Consent of the Senate, shall appoint Ambassadors, other public Ministers and Consuls, Judges of the supreme Court, and all other Officers of the United States, whose Appointments are not herein otherwise provided for, and which shall be established by Law: but the Congress may by Law vest the Appointment of such inferior Officers, as they think proper, in the President alone, in the Courts of Law, or in the Heads of Departments.

The President shall have Power to fill up all Vacancies that may happen during the Recess of the Senate, by granting Commissions which shall expire at the End of their next Session.

Sec. 3. He shall from time to time give to the Congress Information of the State of the Union, and recommend to their Consideration such Measures as he shall judge necessary and expedient; he may, on extraordinary Occasions, convene both Houses, or either of them, and in Case of Disagreement between them, with Respect to the Time of Adjournment, he may adjourn them to such Time as he shall think proper; he shall receive Ambassadors and other public Ministers; he shall take Care that the Laws be faithfully executed, and shall Commission all the Officers of the United States.

Sec. 4. The President, Vice President and all civil Officers of the United States, shall be removed from Office on Impeachment for, and Conviction of, Treason, Bribery, or other high Crimes and Misdemeanors.

Art. III

Sec. 1. The judicial Power of the United States, shall be vested in one supreme Court, and in such inferior

Courts as the Congress may from time to time ordain and establish. The Judges, both of the supreme and inferior Courts, shall hold their Offices during good Behaviour, and shall, at stated Times, receive for their Services, a Compensation, which shall not be diminished during their Continuance in Office.

Sec. 2. The judicial Power shall extend to all Cases, in Law and Equity, arising under this Constitution, the Laws of the United States, and Treaties made, or which shall be made, under their Authority; —to all Cases affecting Ambassadors, other public Ministers and Consuls; —to all Cases of admiralty and maritime Jurisdiction; —to Controversies to which the United States shall be a Party; —to Controversies between two or more States; —between a State and Citizens of another State; —between Citizens of different States, —between Citizens of the same State claiming Lands under Grants of different States, and between a State, or the Citizens thereof, and foreign States, Citizens or Subjects.

In all Cases affecting Ambassadors, other public Ministers and Consuls, and those in which a State shall be Party, the supreme Court shall have original Jurisdiction. In all the other Cases before mentioned, the supreme Court shall have appellate Jurisdiction, both as to Law and Fact, with such Exceptions, and under such Regulations as the Congress shall make.

The Trial of all Crimes, except in Cases of Impeachment, shall be by Jury; and such Trial shall be held in the State where the said Crimes shall have been committed; but when not committed within any State, the Trial shall be at such Place or Places as the Congress may by Law have directed.

Sec. 3. Treason against the United States, shall consist only in levying War against them, or in adhering to their Enemies, giving them Aid and Comfort. No Person shall be convicted of Treason unless on the Testimony of two Witnesses to the same overt Act, or on Confession in open Court.

The Congress shall have Power to declare the Punishment of Treason, but no Attainder of Treason shall work Corruption of Blood, or Forfeiture except during the Life of the Person attainted.

Art. IV

Sec. 1. Full Faith and Credit shall be given in each State to the Public Acts, Records, and judicial Proceedings of every other State. And the Congress may by general Laws prescribe the Manner in which such Acts, Records and Proceedings shall be proved, and the Effect thereof.

Sec. 2. The Citizens of each State shall be entitled to all Privileges and Immunities of Citizens in the several States.

A Person charged in any State with Treason, Felony, or other Crime, who shall flee from Justice, and be found in another State, shall on Demand of the executive Authority of the State from which he fled, be delivered up, to be removed to the State having Jurisdiction of the Crime.

No Person held to Service or Labour in one State, under the Laws thereof, escaping into another, shall, in Consequence of any Law or Regulation therein, be discharged from such Service or Labour, but shall be delivered up on Claim of the Party to whom such Service or Labour may be due.

Sec. 3. New States may be admitted by the Congress into this Union; but no new States shall be formed or erected within the Jurisdiction of any other State; nor any State be formed by the Junction of two or more States, or Parts of States, without the Consent of the Legislatures of the States concerned as well as of the Congress.

The Congress shall have Power to dispose of and make all needful Rules and Regulations respecting the Territory or other Property belonging to the United States; and nothing in this Constitution shall be so construed as to Prejudice any Claims of the United States, or of any particular State.

Sec. 4. The United States shall guarantee to every State in this Union a Republican Form of Government, and shall protect each of them against Invasion; and on Application of the Legislature, or of the Executive (when the Legislature cannot be convened) against domestic Violence.

Art. V

The Congress, whenever two thirds of both Houses shall deem it necessary, shall propose Amendments to this Constitution, or, on the Application of the Legislatures of two thirds of the several States, shall call a Convention for proposing Amendments, which, in either Case, shall be valid to all Intents and Purposes, as Part of this Constitution, when ratified by the Legislatures of three fourths of the several States, or by Conventions in three fourths thereof, as the one or the other Mode of Ratification may be proposed by the Congress; Provided that no Amendment which may be made prior to the Year One thousand eight hundred and eight shall in any Manner affect the first and fourth Clauses in the Ninth Section of the first Article; and that no State, without its Consent, shall be deprived of it's equal Suffrage in the Senate.

Art. VI

All Debts contracted and Engagements entered into, before the Adoption of this Constitution, shall be as valid against the United States under this Constitution, as under the Confederation.

This Constitution, and the Laws of the United States which shall be made in Pursuance thereof; and all Treaties made, or which shall be made, under the Authority of the United States, shall be the supreme Law of the Land; and the Judges in every State shall be bound thereby, any Thing in the Constitution or Laws of any State to the Contrary notwithstanding.

The Senators and Representatives before mentioned, and the Members of the several State Legislatures, and all executive and judicial Officers, both of the United States and of the several States, shall be bound by Oath or Affirmation, to support this Constitution; but no religious Test shall ever be required as a Qualification to any Office or public Trust under the United States.

Art. VII

The Ratification of the Conventions of nine States, shall be sufficient for the Establishment of this Constitution between the States so ratifying the Same.

The Word, "the," being interlined between the seventh and eighth Lines of the first Page, the Word "Thirty" being partly written on an Erazure in the fifteenth Line of the first Page, The Words "is tried" being interlined between the thirty second and thirty third Lines of the first Page and the Word "the" being interlined between the forty third and forty fourth Lines of the second Page.

Attest William Jackson Secretary

Done in Convention by the Unanimous Consent of the States present the Seventeenth Day of September in the Year of our Lord one thousand seven hundred and Eighty seven and of the Independence of the United States of America the Twelfth. In witness whereof We have hereunto subscribed our Names,

G° WASHINGTON—Presid[t] and deputy from Virginia

New Hampshire: John Langdon, Nicholas Gilman

Massachusetts: Nathaniel Gorham, Rufus King

Connecticut: W[M] Sam[L] Johnson, Roger Sherman

New York: Alexander Hamilton

New Jersey: Wil: Livingston, David Brearley, W[M] Paterson, Jona: Dayton

Pennsylvania: B Franklin, Thomas Mifflin, Rob[T] Morris, Geo. Clymer, Tho[S] Fitzsimons, Jared Ingersoll, James Wilson, Gouv Morris

Delaware: Geo: Read, Gunning Bedford jun, John Dickinson, Richard Bassett, Jaco: Broom

Maryland: James M[C]Henry, Dan of S[T] Tho[S] Jenifer, Dan[L] Carroll

Virginia: John Blair—, James Madison, Jr.

North Carolina: W[M] Blount, Rich[D] Dobbs Spaight, Hu Williamson

South Carolina: J. Rutledge, Charles Cotesworth Pinckney, Pierce Butler

Georgia: William Few, Abr Baldwin

Articles in addition to, and Amendment of the Constitution of the United States of America, proposed by Congress, and ratified by the Legislatures of the several States, pursuant to the fifth Article of the original Constitution.

[The first ten amendments went into effect November 3, 1791.]

Art. I

Congress shall make no law respecting an establishment of religion, or prohibiting the free exercise thereof; or abridging the freedom of speech, or of the press; or the right of the people peaceably to assemble, and to petition the government for a redress of grievances.

Art. II

A well regulated Militia, being necessary to the security of a free State, the right of the people to keep and bear Arms, shall not be infringed.

Art. III

No Soldier shall, in time of peace be quartered in any house, without the consent of the Owner, nor in time of war, but in a manner to be prescribed by law.

Art. IV

The right of the people to be secure in their persons, houses, papers, and effects, against unreasonable searches and seizures, shall not be violated, and no Warrants shall issue, but upon probable cause, supported by Oath or affirmation, and particularly describing the place to be searched, and the persons or things to be seized.

Art. V

No person shall be held to answer for a capital, or otherwise infamous crime, unless on a presentment or indictment of a Grand Jury, except in cases arising in the land or naval forces, or in the Militia, when in actual service in time of War or public danger; nor shall any person be subject for the same offence to be twice put in jeopardy of life or limb; nor shall be compelled in any criminal case to be a witness against himself, nor be deprived of life, liberty, or property, without due process of law; nor shall private property be taken for public use, without just compensation.

Art. VI

In all criminal prosecutions, the accused shall enjoy the right to a speedy and public trial, by an impartial jury of the State and district wherein the crime shall have been committed, which district shall have been previously ascertained by law, and to be informed of the nature and cause of the accusation; to be confronted with the witnesses against him; to have compulsory process for obtaining witnesses in his favor, and to have the Assistance of Counsel for his defence.

Art. VII

In Suits at common law, where the value in controversy shall exceed twenty dollars, the right of trial by jury shall be preserved, and no fact tried by a jury, shall be otherwise re-examined in any Court of the United States, than according to the rules of the common law.

Art. VIII

Excessive bail shall not be required, nor excessive fines imposed, nor cruel and unusual punishments inflicted.

Art. IX

The enumeration in the Constitution, of certain rights, shall not be construed to deny or disparage others retained by the people.

Art. X

The powers not delegated to the United States by the Constitution, nor prohibited by it to the States, are reserved to the States respectively, or to the people.

Art. XI

Jan. 8, 1798

The Judicial power of the United States shall not be construed to extend to any suit in law or equity, commenced or prosecuted against one of the United States by Citizens of another State, or by Citizens or Subjects of any Foreign State.

Art. XII

Sept. 25, 1804

The Electors shall meet in their respective states, and vote by ballot for President and Vice-President, one of whom, at least, shall not be an inhabitant of the same state with themselves; they shall name in their ballots the person voted for as President, and in distinct ballots the person voted for as Vice-President, and they shall make distinct lists of all persons voted for as President, and of all persons voted for as Vice-President, and of the number of votes for each, which lists they shall sign and certify, and transmit sealed to the seat of the government of the United States, directed to the President of the Senate; —The President of the Senate shall, in the presence of the Senate and House of Representatives, open all the certificates and the votes shall then be counted; —The person having the greatest number of votes for President, shall be the President, if such number be a majority of the whole number of Electors appointed; and if no person have such major-

ity, then from the persons having the highest numbers not exceeding three on the list of those voted for as President, the House of Representatives shall choose immediately, by ballot, the President. But in choosing the President, the votes shall be taken by states, the representation from each state having one vote; a quorum for this purpose shall consist of a member or members from two-thirds of the states, and a majority of all the states shall be necessary to a choice. And if the House of Representatives shall not choose a President whenever the right of choice shall devolve upon them, before the fourth day of March next following, then the Vice-President shall act as President, as in the case of the death or other constitutional disability of the President. —The person having the greatest number of votes as Vice-President, shall be the Vice-President, if such number be a majority of the whole number of Electors appointed, and if no person have a majority, then from the two highest numbers on the list, the Senate shall choose the Vice-President; a quorum for the purpose shall consist of two-thirds of the whole number of Senators, and a majority of the whole number shall be necessary to a choice. But no person constitutionally ineligible to the office of President shall be eligible to that of Vice-President of the United States.

Art. XIII

Dec. 18, 1865

Sec. 1. Neither slavery nor involuntary servitude, except as a punishment for crime whereof the party shall have been duly convicted, shall exist within the United States, or any place subject to their jurisdiction.

Sec. 2. Congress shall have power to enforce this article by appropriate legislation.

Art. XIV

July 28, 1868

Sec. 1. All persons born or naturalized in the United States, and subject to the jurisdiction thereof, are citizens of the United States and of the State wherein they reside. No State shall make or enforce any law which shall abridge the privileges or immunities of citizens of the United States; nor shall any State deprive any person of life, liberty, or property, without due process of law; nor deny to any person within its jurisdiction the equal protection of the laws.

Sec. 2. Representatives shall be apportioned among the several States according to their respective numbers, counting the whole number of persons in each State, excluding Indians not taxed. But when the right to vote at any election for the choice of electors for President and Vice President of the United States, Representatives in Congress, the Executive and Judicial officers of a State, or the members of the Legislature thereof, is denied to any of the male inhabitants of such State, being twenty-one years of age, and citizens of the United States, or in any way abridged, except for participation in rebellion, or other crime, the basis of representation therein shall be reduced in the proportion which the number of such male citizens shall bear to the whole number of male citizens twenty-one years of age in such State.

Sec. 3. No person shall be a Senator or Representative in Congress, or elector of President and Vice President, or hold any office, civil or military, under the United States, or under any State, who, having previously taken an oath, as a member of Congress, or as an officer of the United States, or as a member of any State legislature, or as an executive or judicial officer of any State, to support the Constitution of the United States, shall have engaged in insurrection or rebellion against the same, or given aid or comfort to the enemies thereof. But Congress may by a vote of two-thirds of each House, remove such disability.

Sec. 4. The validity of the public debt of the United States, authorized by law, including debts incurred for payment of pensions and bounties for services in suppressing insurrection or rebellion, shall not be questioned. But neither the United States nor any State shall assume or pay any debt or obligation incurred in aid of insurrection or rebellion against the United States, or any claim for the loss or emancipation of any slave; but all such debts, obligations and claims shall be held illegal and void.

Sec. 5. The Congress shall have power to enforce, by appropriate legislation, the provisions of this article.

Art. XV

March 30, 1870

Sec. 1. The right of citizens of the United States to vote shall not be denied or abridged by the United States or by any State on account of race, color, or previous condition of servitude—

Sec. 2. The Congress shall have power to enforce this article by appropriate legislation—

Art. XVI

February 25, 1913

The Congress shall have power to lay and collect taxes on incomes, from whatever source derived, without apportionment among the several States and without regard to any census or enumeration.

Art. XVII

May 31, 1913

The Senate of the United States shall be composed of two senators from each State, elected by the people thereof, for six years; and each Senator shall have one vote. The electors in each State shall have the qualifications requisite for electors of the most numerous branch of the State legislature.

When vacancies happen in the representation of any State in the Senate, the executive authority of such State shall issue writs of election to fill such vacancies: *Provided*, That the legislature of any State may empower the executive thereof to make temporary appointments until the people fill the vacancies by election as the legislature may direct.

This amendment shall not be so construed as to affect the election or term of any senator chosen before it becomes valid as part of the Constitution.

Art. XVIII

January 29, 1919

After one year from the ratification of this article, the manufacture, sale, or transportation of intoxicating liquors within, the importation thereof into, or the exportation thereof from the United States and all territory subject to the jurisdiction thereof for beverage purposes is hereby prohibited.

The Congress and the several States shall have concurrent power to enforce this article by appropriate legislation.

This article shall be inoperative unless it shall have been ratified as an amendment to the Constitution by the legislatures of the several States, as provided in the Constitution, within seven years from the date of the submission hereof to the States by Congress.

Art. XIX

August 26, 1920

The right of citizens of the United States to vote shall not be denied or abridged by the United States or by any States on account of sex.

The Congress shall have power by appropriate legislation to enforce the provisions of this article.

Art. XX

February 6, 1933

Sec. 1. The terms of the President and Vice-President shall end at noon on the twentieth day of January, and the terms of Senators and Representatives at noon on the third day of January, of the years in which such terms would have ended if this article had not been ratified; and the terms of their successors shall then begin.

Sec. 2. The Congress shall assemble at least once in every year, and such meeting shall begin at noon on the third day of January, unless they shall by law appoint a different day.

Sec. 3. If, at the time fixed for the beginning of the term of the President, the President-elect shall have died, the Vice-President-elect shall become President. If a President shall not have been chosen before the time fixed for the beginning of his term, or if the President-elect shall have failed to qualify, then the Vice-President-elect shall act as President until a President shall have qualified; and the Congress may by law provide for the case wherein neither a President-elect nor a Vice-President-elect shall have qualified, declaring who shall then act as President, or the manner in which one who is to act shall be selected, and such person shall act accordingly until a President or Vice-President shall have qualified.

Sec. 4. The Congress may by law provide for the case of the death of any of the persons from whom the House of Representatives may choose a President whenever the right of choice shall have devolved upon them, and for the case of the death of any of the persons from whom the Senate may choose a Vice-President whenever the right of choice shall have devolved upon them.

Sec. 5. Sections 1 and 2 shall take effect on the 15th day of October following the ratification of this article.

Sec. 6. This article shall be inoperative unless it shall have been ratified as an amendment to the Constitution by the legislatures of three-fourths of the several States within seven years from the date of its submission.

Art. XXI

December 5, 1933

Sec. 1. The eighteenth article of amendment to the Constitution of the United States is hereby repealed. . . .

Art. XXII

February 26, 1951

Sec. 1. No person shall be elected to the office of the President more than twice, and no person who has held the office of President, or acted as President for more than two years of a term to which some other person was elected President shall be elected to the office of the President more than once. But this Article shall not apply to any person holding the office of President when this Article was proposed by the Congress, and shall not prevent any person who may be holding the office of President, or acting as President, during the term within which this Article becomes operative from holding the office of President or acting as President during the remainder of such term.

Article XXIII

March 29, 1961

Sec. 1. The District constituting the seat of Government of the United States shall appoint in such manner as the Congress may direct:

A number of electors of President and Vice-President equal to the whole number of Senators and Representatives in Congress to which the District would be entitled if it were a State, but in no event more than the least populous state; they shall be in addition to those appointed by the states, but they shall be considered, for the purposes of the election of President and Vice-President, to be electors appointed by a state; and they shall meet in the District and perform such duties as provided by the twelfth article of amendment.

Sec. 2. The Congress shall have power to enforce this article by appropriate legislation.

Article XXIV

January 24, 1964

Sec. 1. The right of citizens of the United States to vote in any primary or other election for President or Vice-President, for electors for President or Vice-President, or for Senator or Representative in Congress, shall not be denied or abridged by the United States or any state by reason of failure to pay any poll tax or other tax.

Sec. 2. The Congress shall have power to enforce this article by appropriate legislation.

Article XXV

February 23, 1967

Sec. 1. In case of the removal of the President from office or his death or resignation, the Vice-President shall become President.

Sec. 2. Whenever there is a vacancy in the office of the Vice-President, the President shall nominate a Vice-President who shall take the office upon confirmation by a majority vote of both houses of Congress.

Sec. 3. Whenever the President transmits to the President pro tempore of the Senate and the Speaker of the House of Representatives his written declaration that he is unable to discharge the powers and duties of his office, and until he transmits to them a written declaration to the contrary, such powers and duties shall be discharged by the Vice-President as Acting President.

Sec. 4. Whenever the Vice-President and a majority of either the principal officers of the executive departments, or of such other body as Congress may by law provide, transmit to the President pro tempore of the Senate and the Speaker of the House of Representatives their written declaration that the President is unable to discharge the powers and duties of his office, the Vice-President shall immediately assume the powers and duties of the office as Acting President.

Thereafter, when the President transmits to the President pro tempore of the Senate and the Speaker of the House of Representatives his written declaration that no inability exists, he shall resume the powers and duties of his office unless the Vice-President and a majority of either the principal officers of the executive department, or of such other body as Congress may by law provide, transmit within four days to the President pro tempore of the Senate and the Speaker of the House of Representatives their written declaration that the President is unable to discharge the powers and duties of his office. Thereupon Congress shall decide the issue, assembling within 48 hours for that purpose if not in session. If the Congress, within 21 days after receipt of the latter written declaration, or, if Congress is not in session, within 21 days after Congress is required to assemble, determines by two-thirds vote of both houses that the President is unable to discharge the powers and duties of his office, the Vice-President shall continue to discharge the same as Acting President; otherwise, the President shall resume the powers and duties of his office.

Article XXVI

July 7, 1971

Sec. 1. The right of citizens of the United States, who are eighteen years of age or older, to vote shall not be denied or abridged by the United States or by any State on account of age.

Sec. 2. The Congress shall have power to enforce this article by appropriate legislation.

CHRONOLOGY OF U.S. SUPREME COURT JUSTICES

Justice	Appointing President	Years Served
John Jay	George Washington	Chief: 1789-1795
John Rutledge	George Washington	Associate: 1790-1791, Chief: 1795-1795
William Cushing	George Washington	Associate: 1790-1810
James Wilson	George Washington	Associate: 1789-1798
John Blair	George Washington	Associate: 1790-1795
James Iredell	George Washington	Associate: 1790-1799
Thomas Johnson	George Washington	Associate: 1790-1799
William Paterson	George Washington	Associate: 1793-1806
Samuel Chase	George Washington	Associate: 1796-1811
Oliver Ellsworth	George Washington	Chief: 1796-1800
Bushrod Washington	John Adams	Associate: 1799-1829
Alfred Moore	John Adams	Associate: 1800-1804
John Marshall	John Adams	Chief: 1801-1835
William Johnson	Thomas Jefferson	Associate: 1804-1834
Henry Brockholst Livingston	Thomas Jefferson	Associate: 1807-1823
Thomas Todd	Thomas Jefferson	Associate: 1807-1826
Gabriel Duvall	James Madison	Associate: 1811-1835
Joseph Story	James Madison	Associate: 1812-1845
Smith Thompson	James Monroe	Associate: 1823-1843
Robert Trimble	John Quincy Adams	Associate: 1826-1828
John McLean	Andrew Jackson	Associate: 1830-1861
Henry Baldwin	Andrew Jackson	Associate: 1830-1844
James Moore Wayne	Andrew Jackson	Associate: 1835-1867
Roger Brooke Taney	Andrew Jackson	Chief: 1836-1864

Justice	Appointing President	Years Served
Philip Pendleton Barbour	Andrew Jackson	Associate: 1836-1841
John Catron	Andrew Jackson	Associate: 1837-1865
John McKinley	Martin Van Buren	Associate: 1838-1852
Peter Vivian Daniel	Martin Van Buren	Associate: 1842-1860
Samuel Nelson	John Tyler	Associate: 1845-1872
Levi Woodbury	James Polk	Associate: 1845-1851
Robert Cooper Grier	James Polk	Associate: 1846-1870
Benjamin Curtis	Millard Fillmore	Associate: 1851-1857
John Archibald Campbell	Franklin Pierce	Associate: 1853-1861
Nathan Clifford	James Buchanan	Associate: 1858-1881
Noah Haynes Swayne	Abraham Lincoln	Associate: 1862-1881
Samuel Freeman Miller	Abraham Lincoln	Associate: 1862-1890
David Davis	Abraham Lincoln	Associate: 1862-1877
Stephen Johnson Field	Abraham Lincoln	Associate: 1863-1897
Salmon Portland Chase	Abraham Lincoln	Chief: 1864-1873
William Strong	Ulysses S. Grant	Associate: 1870-1880
Joseph P. Bradley	Ulysses S. Grant	Associate: 1870-1892
Ward Hunt	Ulysses S. Grant	Associate: 1873-1882
Morrison Remick Waite	Ulysses S. Grant	Chief: 1874-1888
John Marshall Harlan I	Rutherford B. Hayes	Associate: 1877-1911
William Burnham Woods	Rutherford B. Hayes	Associate: 1881-1887
Stanley Matthews	James A. Garfield	Associate: 1881-1889
Horace Gray	Chester A. Arthur	Associate: 1882-1902
Samuel Blatchford	Chester A. Arthur	Associate: 1882-1893
Lucius Quintus C. Lamar	Grover Cleveland	Associate: 1888-1893
Melville Weston Fuller	Grover Cleveland	Chief: 1888-1910
David Josiah Brewer	Benjamin Harrison	Associate: 1890-1910
Henry Billings Brown	Benjamin Harrison	Associate: 1891-1906
George Shiras, Jr.	Benjamin Harrison	Associate: 1892-1903
Howell Edmunds Jackson	Benjamin Harrison	Associate: 1893-1895
Edward Douglass White	Grover Cleveland	Associate: 1894-1910, Chief: 1910-1921
Rufus Wheeler Peckham	Grover Cleveland	Associate: 1896-1909

Justice	Appointing President	Years Served
Joseph McKenna	William McKinley	Associate: 1898-1925
Oliver Wendell Holmes	Theodore Roosevelt	Associate: 1902-1932
William Rufus Day	Theodore Roosevelt	Associate: 1903-1922
William Henry Moody	Theodore Roosevelt	Associate: 1906-1910
Horace Harmon Lurton	William Howard Taft	Associate: 1910-1914
Charles Evans Hughes	William Howard Taft	Associate: 1910-1916, Chief: 1930-1941
Willis Van Devanter	William Howard Taft	Associate: 1911-1937
Joseph Rucker Lamar	William Howard Taft	Associate: 1911-1916
Mahlon Pitney	William Howard Taft	Associate: 1912-1922
James Clark McReynolds	Woodrow Wilson	Associate: 1914-1941
Louis D. Brandeis	Woodrow Wilson	Associate: 1916-1939
John Hessin Clarke	Woodrow Wilson	Associate: 1916-1922
William Howard Taft	Warren G. Harding	Chief: 1921-1930
George Sutherland	Warren G. Harding	Associate: 1922-1938
Pierce Butler	Warren G. Harding	Associate: 1923-1939
Edward Terry Sanford	Warren G. Harding	Associate: 1923-1930
Harlan Fiske Stone	Calvin Coolidge	Associate: 1925-1941, Chief: 1941-1946
Owen Josephus Roberts	Herbert Hoover	Associate: 1930-1945
Benjamin N. Cardozo	Herbert Hoover	Associate: 1932-1938
Hugo Lafayette Black	Franklin D. Roosevelt	Associate: 1937-1971
Stanley Forman Reed	Franklin D. Roosevelt	Associate: 1938-1957
Felix Frankfurter	Franklin D. Roosevelt	Associate: 1939-1962
William O. Douglas	Franklin D. Roosevelt	Associate: 1939-1975
Frank Murphy	Franklin D. Roosevelt	Associate: 1940-1949
James Francis Byrnes	Franklin D. Roosevelt	Associate: 1941-1942
Robert H. Jackson	Franklin D. Roosevelt	Associate: 1941-1954
Wiley Blount Rutledge	Franklin D. Roosevelt	Associate: 1943-1949
Harold Burton	Harry S. Truman	Associate: 1945-1958
Fred Moore Vinson	Harry S. Truman	Chief: 1946-1953
Tom C. Clark	Harry S. Truman	Associate: 1949-1967
Sherman Minton	Harry S. Truman	Associate: 1949-1956

Justice	Appointing President	Years Served
Earl Warren	Dwight D. Eisenhower	Chief: 1953-1969
John Marshall Harlan II	Dwight D. Eisenhower	Associate: 1955-1971
William J. Brennan, Jr.	Dwight D. Eisenhower	Associate: 1956-1990
Charles Evans Whittaker	Dwight D. Eisenhower	Associate: 1957-1962
Potter Stewart	Dwight D. Eisenhower	Associate: 1959-1981
Byron R. White	John F. Kennedy	Associate: 1962-1965
Arthur Goldberg	John F. Kennedy	Associate: 1962-1965
Abe Fortas	Lyndon B. Johnson	Associate: 1965-1969
Thurgood Marshall	Lyndon B. Johnson	Associate: 1967-1991
Warren E. Burger	Richard Nixon	Chief: 1969-1986
Harry A. Blackmun	Richard Nixon	Associate: 1970-1994
Lewis F. Powell, Jr.	Richard Nixon	Associate: 1972-1987
William H. Rehnquist	Richard Nixon	Associate: 1972-1986, Chief: 1986-
John Paul Stevens	Gerald R. Ford	Associate: 1975-
Sandra Day O'Connor	Ronald Reagan	Associate: 1981-
Antonin Scalia	Ronald Reagan	Associate: 1986-
Anthony M. Kennedy	Ronald Reagan	Associate: 1988-
David H. Souter	George Bush	Associate: 1990-
Clarence Thomas	George Bush	Associate: 1991-
Ruth Bader Ginsburg	Bill Clinton	Associate: 1993-
Stephen Breyer	Bill Clinton	Associate: 1994-